EXPLORING PUBLIC RELATIONS

Visit the *Exploring Public Relations* Companion Website at
www.pearsoned.co.uk/tench to find valuable **student** learning
material including:

- Extra case studies
- Links to relevant sites on the web
- An online glossary to explain key terms

We work with leading authors to develop the strongest educational materials in public relations, bringing cutting-edge thinking and best learning practice to a global market.

Under a range of well-known imprints, including Financial Times Prentice Hall, we craft high quality print and electronic publications which help readers to understand and apply their content, whether studying or at work.

To find out more about the complete range of our publishing, please visit us on the World Wide Web at: www.pearsoned.co.uk

Exploring
Public Relations

Ralph Tench

Principal Lecturer and Public Relations Subject Group Leader
Leeds Metropolitan University

and

Liz Yeomans

Principal Lecturer
Leeds Metropolitan University

FT Prentice Hall
FINANCIAL TIMES

An imprint of **Pearson Education**

Harlow, England • London • New York • Boston • San Francisco • Toronto • Sydney • Singapore • Hong Kong
Tokyo • Seoul • Taipei • New Delhi • Cape Town • Madrid • Mexico City • Amsterdam • Munich • Paris • Milan

Pearson Education Limited
Edinburgh Gate
Harlow
Essex CM20 2JE
England

and Associated Companies throughout the world

Visit us on the World Wide Web at:
www.pearsoned.co.uk

First published 2006

ISBN-13: 978-0-273-68889-1
ISBN-10: 0-273-68889-8

British Library Cataloguing-in-Publication Data
A catalogue record for this book is available from the British Library

Library of Congress Cataloging-in-Publication Data
A catalog record for this book is available from the Library of Congress

10 9 8 7 6 5 4 3 2 1
10 09 08 07 06

Typeset in 9/12 *Stone Serif* 59
Printed and Bound by Mateu-Cromo Artes Graficas, Spain

The publisher's policy is to use paper manufactured from sustainable forests.

Contents

Part 3   Public relations specialisms   309

Supporting resources

Visit **www.pearsoned.co.uk/tench** to find valuable online resources

Companion Website for students
- Extra case studies
- Links to relevant sites on the web
- An online glossary to explain key terms

For instructors
- Complete, downloadable Instructor's Manual
- PowerPoint slides that can be downloaded and used as OHTs

For more information please contact your local Pearson Education sales representative or visit **www.pearsoned.co.uk/tench**

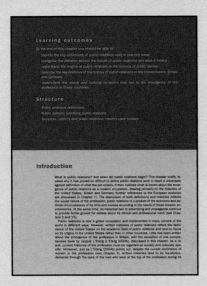

Learning outcomes enable you to focus on what you should have achieved by the end of the chapter.

The **Introduction** provides a concise overview of the themes and issues explored within the chapter.

The **Think about . . .** boxes encourage the reader to reflect upon specific examples and issues involved in public relations.

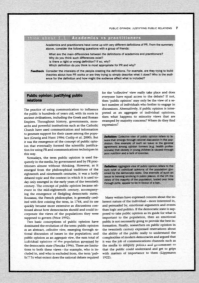

Definition boxes explain key words and concepts where they first appear.

Case studies provide a range of exciting material for seminar or private study.

Mini case studies illustrate issues and concepts with specific reference to real life scenarios.

Boxes deliver a wealth of information about the public relations industry.

Each chapter also has a number of **Activities** that provide an opportunity to put what is being learnt in to practice.

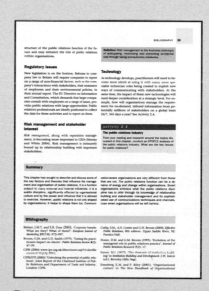

Each chapter ends with a **Summary** that draws together all the outcomes of the chapter in a concise overview.

About the authors

Dr Ralph Tench is the subject leader for public relations at Leeds Metropolitan University. The public relations subject group includes 16 academic staff and a portfolio of 10 undergraduate, postgraduate and professional courses. As principal lecturer he teaches on undergraduate and postgraduate programmes as well as supervising MA and PhD research. Since joining the university he has been instrumental in helping develop the public relations portfolio to include: diplomas for the PRCA and the CIPR; MBA and MA programmes. A member of the CIPR he has presented his research around the world and taught at several European universities specialising in public relations. Ralph previously worked as a news and sports reporter before moving into consultancy, latterly with Manchester's Communique (Burson-Marsteller). His client portfolio included FTSE100 companies as well as public sector clients. Ralph has a dual psychology degree from the University of Sheffield and a doctorate from Leeds Metropolitan University. As an active researcher he manages internal and external research teams and focuses on corporate relations, corporate social responsibility and public relations education. Recent externally funded projects have included an annual contract into freelancing in the communication and creative sectors since 2000; a major research project for the CIPR to benchmark public relations education in the UK; and a media perception study of corporate social responsibility. He is widely published in books and academic journals ranging from management to education journals. Ralph has sat as a panel member and chair for programme validations for the CIPR's course approvals. He has worked as a consultant to UK universities setting up undergraduate programmes in public relations. He currently holds external examinerships for Kingston and Southampton universities.

Liz Yeomans is principal lecturer in public relations at Leeds Metropolitan University where she holds departmental responsibility for the coordination of postgraduate programmes. Since joining the university, Liz has helped establish a centre of excellence in public relations education and training. As well as contributing to the BA (Hons) Public Relations, Liz has developed and taught new courses for working professionals – including the nationally recognised Chartered Institute of Public Relations Diploma. She has also developed communication modules for general masters programmes, including the MBA, and led the development of masters routes in public relations and a short course in public affairs. As a CIPR member, she has contributed book reviews to the Institute's *Profile* magazine; is a member of the judging panel for the CIPR's Local Government Group's Excellence awards; and has sat as a panel member for CIPR course approvals. Liz has been external validator for several public relations and communications programmes in the UK and currently holds external examinerships for London Metropolitan and Manchester Metropolitan universities. Liz previously worked for EMAP, one of the UK's leading magazine publishers, before joining the Government Information Service where she worked on civil service recruitment, teacher recruitment, employment and education campaigns. Liz was latterly principal public relations officer at Hampshire County Council where she led change communications within the education service. She has a degree in english and media studies from the University of Southampton, and an MSc in public relations from the University of Stirling. In the field of teaching, learning and assessment, Liz was highly commended (jointly with Anne Gregory) in Leeds Metropolitan University's Chancellor's Awards, and has published joint papers on peer assessment. She has presented papers at international conferences and has had articles published in the *Journal of Communication Management* and *Journal of Public Affairs*.

The contributors

Richard Bailey is senior lecturer in public relations at Leeds Metropolitan University. He has over 15 years' experience in business journalism, consultancy and in-house public relations management. He specialised in public relations professional training before joining the university in 2003, where he teaches on undergraduate, postgraduate and professional courses. His weblog devoted to public relations can be found at www.prstudies.com.

Shirley Beresford is senior lecturer in public relations and marketing at Leeds Metropolitan University, where she teaches on undergraduate, postgraduate and professional courses. She has been an active member of the Chartered Institute of Marketing for 15 years and works as an examiner for their postgraduate courses. Prior to joining Leeds Metropolitan in 1999, Shirley had a 15-year career in arts, leisure, tourism and public sector PR and marketing management. Shirley's research interests lie in the development of arts marketing and PR.

Ryan Bowd is senior lecturer at Leeds Metropolitan University and an award-winning PR practitioner and Associate Director of UK-based Connectpoint PR with a client portfolio of experience including global petroleum companies, sports drinks brands, sporting events and eyewear manufacturers to niche luxury brands. Ryan mixes a professional life of communications practice and academic teaching and learning. Research interests include the fields of reputation, corporate social responsibility (CSR) and communications. Ryan is currently undertaking PhD research on the subject of corporate social responsibility communications at Manchester Metropolitan University.

Gerard Choo is senior lecturer in public relations at Leeds Metropolitan University, where he is course leader of the MAs in public relations and public relations management. He is studying the foundations of public relations theory and the implications of these foundations on the planning and practice of PR for his PhD at the University of Warwick. He previously worked in PR and marketing at the Media Corporation of Singapore and its associated and predecessor companies.

Lee Edwards is lecturer in public relations at Leeds Metropolitan University, where she teaches on undergraduate, postgraduate and professional courses. She holds an MPhil in cross-cultural management from the University of Auckland and is pursuing a PhD focusing on the nature of power in public relations. Prior to joining the

University in 2004, Lee specialised in technology public relations and worked with some of the largest global technology brands during her professional career, including Microsoft, Dell and Siemens.

Johanna Fawkes was principal lecturer at Leeds Metropolitan University until 2004. She led the BA in public relations and taught across the portfolio, specialising in mass communications and persuasive psychology. She also taught at the London College of Printing and the University of Central Lancashire, after 15 years in public sector PR. She holds an MA in creative writing from Lancaster University and has written papers for a variety of journals, conferences and PR books. She is now a freelance writer and researcher on public relations issues. Johanna is chief examiner for the CIPR courses.

Professor Anne Gregory is the UK's only full-time professor of public relations and director of the Centre for Public Relations Studies at Leeds Metropolitan University. Before moving into academic life, Anne spent 12 years in practice, holding senior appointments both in-house and in consultancy. Anne is still actively involved in consultancy and training work. She was President of the UK Institute of Public Relations in 2004 and edits the Institute's Public Relations in Practice series. She is research coordinator for the Global Alliance, has published in several journals and is joint editor of the *Journal of Communication Management*.

Paul Gillions is an independent consultant and has advised companies and organisations in Europe, North America, Australia and Asia on a broad range of public policy initiatives and impacts. He is a specialist in issue, crisis and risk management, and regularly leads sessions on scenario planning and coalition building. Paul is a Fellow of the Royal Society of Arts, a member of the Institute of Directors and the Chartered Institute of Public Relations, and was first selected for entry in Debrett's *Distinguished People of Today* in 1988.

Dr Sierk Horn is lecturer in Japanese Studies at the University of Leeds and Adj. Professor at Freie Universität Berlin, Germany. He holds a PhD and is a qualified lecturer in Japanese studies. His main fields of research are cross-cultural marketing and management concepts, Japanese business and consuming behaviour in east Asia. He has published widely in, amongst other areas, intercultural competence in accessing Japanese markets.

Graham Hughes is a principal lecturer in marketing at Leeds Metropolitan University. He is the marketing subject group leader and teaches marketing communications on a range of undergraduate, postgraduate and professional courses. He holds an MA in marketing from

Lancaster University and has held senior marketing management positions in a range of organisations including BL, the Weir Group and MCB University Press. He is currently senior examiner for the integrated marketing communications module on the CIM diploma and co-authors the Butterworth Heinemann coursebook for the new CIM marketing communications module with Chris Fill from the University of Portsmouth.

Dennis Kelly is a director of the Centre for Public Relations Studies at Leeds Metropolitan University and a Fellow of the Chartered Institute of Public Relations. Dennis is an experienced communications practitioner and was the founder and managing director of a major UK public relations consultancy. He also spent 12 years in a senior capacity with BT and his experience encompasses all aspects of internal and external communications in both the public and private sectors. He has been responsible for numerous award-winning campaigns and has been recognised with IPR 'Swords of Excellence'. Areas of special interest include strategic campaign planning, integrated communications, internal communications and professional development in public relations.

Martin Langford is an international authority on crisis communications and a recipient of the 'Public Relations Professional of the Year' award from *PR Week* for his work in this discipline. Dubbed the 'Master of Disaster' by the UK's *Daily Telegraph*, Martin has led clients through over 350 crisis assignments. Martin is co-founder of issues and communications consultancy Kissmann Langford. He previously spent 32 years at the international public relations consultancy Burson-Marsteller where he led the London operation for the company and was subsequently based in Singapore, managing their ASEAN offices.

Dr Robert Leach retired from full-time teaching in 2004 as a principal lecturer at Leeds Metropolitan University, where he is now a visiting research fellow. He holds degrees from Oxford and London universities and a PhD from Leeds Metropolitan. He has published numerous journal articles as well as several books on government and politics, including *Local Governance in Britain* and *Political Ideology in Britain*. He is currently working on a new version of a best-selling textbook on British politics.

Daniel Löwensberg is lecturer at the Hull University Business School. He has experience at Leeds Metropolitan University as a leader of postgraduate courses in public relations and in teaching public relations in the UK and in France. His research interests cover the areas of corporate identity, PR teaching, international PR, and PR research tactics. Before joining academia, Daniel was a PR and marketing communications professional in the airline and tourism industries, and a committee member of the Airline Public Relations Organisation (APRO) in London for many years.

Karl Milner is senior lecturer at Leeds Metropolitan University. He is also a Consulting Partner of Finsbury Ltd, the City of London-based financial PR firm where he works within the political and regulatory practice advising blue-chip clients on their interactions with government in the UK and Brussels. Prior to moving to Finsbury in 2000, Karl worked for the lobbying firm GJW Government Relations. Karl came to lobbying from politics, where he worked in various roles from constituency agent to parliamentary researcher for a number of prominent Labour politicians culminating in working for Rt Hon Gordon Brown MP for four years in the run up to the 1997 general election.

Dr Kevin Moloney is principal lecturer at Bournemouth University where he teaches public relations and corporate communications to undergraduate and postgraduate students. He researches into how these persuasive communications influence and are influenced by the political economy and civil society. He is the author of *Lobbyists For Hire* (1996) and *Rethinking PR: The spin and the substance* (2000). Before teaching, he worked in PR and marketing for 20 years.

Jo Powell is senior lecturer in public relations at Leeds Metropolitan University. She is deputy course leader for the BA in public relations and teaches on undergraduate and professional programmes. Before joining Leeds Metropolitan, Jo accumulated more than 15 years' management experience in corporate communication for organisations including the BBC, Abbey National and Yorkshire Bank.

Meriel Pritchard is senior lecturer in communication studies at the University of Chester. Prior to this she taught at Leeds Metropolitan University, after a career in public relations, marketing, advertising and corporate communications, both as a consultant and in-house. She is a past chief external examiner for the CIPR diploma and foundation and her research interest is the interface between higher education and employment.

György Szondi is senior lecturer in public relations at Leeds Metropolitan University. His PhD at the University of Salzburg, Austria, involves researching the concepts of public relations and public diplomacy for the European Union. György set up and chaired the public relations programme at Concordia International University in Estonia and has been a regular speaker and trainer at conferences and workshops throughout eastern Europe. His interests and publications include organisational communication, public relations for the European Union, EU referendum, public diplomacy, risk and crises communication. György worked for Hill and Knowlton in Budapest and in its international headquarters in London. He holds a bachelor degree in economics, an MSc in public relations from the University of Stirling and an MSc in physics.

Rüdiger Theilmann is senior lecturer in public relations at Leeds Metropolitan University. He holds an MA in communications from the University of Munich. Following his MA Rüdiger worked for a number of consultancies mainly in the consumer sector focusing on German and Italian SMEs. After that he lectured at University of Stuttgart-Hohenheim and University of Applied Sciences Schwäbisch Gmünd University of Design in Germany. Before joining Leeds Metropolitan he was senior lecturer at International University Concordia Audentes in Tallinn (Estonia) where he was the leader of the MA communication management course. His academic interests are mainly in corporate identity and image, PR research and evaluation and PR theories.

Dr Neil Washbourne is senior lecturer in media studies at Leeds Metropolitan University, where he teaches on the undergraduate degree in media and popular culture. He holds a doctorate from the University of Surrey concerning uses of new technology in the global environmental movement and has had articles published in *International Studies in Management and Organisation* and *Journal of International Sociology*. He is writing a book entitled a *Mediating Politics: newspapers, radio, television and internet* for Open University Press, which develops his research interests in the differences between mediated politics across institutional and technological sites of media.

Paul Willis is strategy and planning director at Ptarmigan, a multiple award-winning public relations agency and former *PR Week* 'Consultancy of the Year'. He has been a member of the board since 1998. He has worked as a consumer PR consultant for BT, BMW MINI, Britannia Building Society, Green Flag, npower, Reebok, Wm Morrison and Yorkshire Bank. Paul has lectured on public relations to audiences as diverse as corporate communications professionals, civil servants and students. Before crossing into the agency world, Paul began his career running a media and research unit for a group of MPs at Westminster. Paul is chair of the Practitioner Advisory Panel at Leeds Metropolitan University.

Sue Wolstenholme runs Ashley Public Relations. Clients have included Amnesty International (relaunching the *Secret Policeman's Ball*) the Mayor of Athens and the Post Office. Sue led MA and BA courses in public relations, awarded by the University of Exeter and the postgraduate foundation and diploma for the Institute of Public Relations. She is the director of communication for the Royal Cornwall Hospitals NHS Trust and the president of the EUPRERA jury to find the best thesis on public relations in Europe. Sue is a former external examiner at Leeds Metropolitan University.

Emma Wood is senior lecturer at Queen Margaret University College in Edinburgh. She is co-editor of the *Journal of Communication Management* and has published chapters on corporate communication and corporate identity in *The Public Relations Handbook* (2002 and 2004). Before joining academia Emma worked in industry, latterly as assistant director of the Confederation of British Industry (CBI) Scotland where she was responsible for public relations. Emma is a former external examiner at Leeds Metropolitan University.

Foreword

What a good meeting place! This is the metaphor that first came to my mind when looking at the manuscript of *Exploring Public Relations.* Many things have been brought together, among others: societal and organisational contexts *and* theories *and* programme areas *and* sectors of application; general systems of knowledge *and* pedagogical specifics; theoretical basing *and* practical (managerial) application; a sense of Leeds Metropolitan University identity and focus *and* an international orientation.

To find all these aspects (and many more) integrated into a single introductory text is a rewarding experience for any teacher of public relations. This certainly holds true for me in my external perspective. Having taught public relations in Austria for over 20 years, I have contantly oscillated between textbooks that emphasise one or several of the above aspects at the expense of others and vice versa. Another challenge has been to expose my students to a sensible mix of truly international research and practice traditions. This book addresses this issue well and I can therefore envisage students and practitioners from outside the UK gaining great benefits from reading and studying alongside *Exploring Public Relations.*

As a meeting place, the book brings together not only different areas of content but also accumulated experiences of the researchers, academics and practitioners in the field of public relations who have contributed to the book. I shall certainly encourage my Salzburg students to participate in this intellectual and international experience. *Exploring Public Relations* will bring home to them the greater European and international world of public relations, but it carries also the very specific flavour of a dynamic university teaching team with whom we have had a successful Erasmus exchange programme in public relations for the past decade.

Professor Benno Signitzer
Salzburg University
Department of Communication
Area of Public Relations & Corporate Communication
Salzburg, Austria

Background

This book started with the idea that a textbook should put the student at the centre of the learning experience. This meant that we wanted students to learn better by involving them in a personal journey that brought the subject to life on the page and spurred them on to find out more. While it is true that textbooks in general are becoming more student centred for subjects as varied as biology, law, media and psychology, this has not been the case in public relations. Also, while there was a growing range of excellent theoretical texts and a continuing supply of books offering practical tips for would-be public relations practitioners, few attempted to bridge the divide between theory and practice that made sense to an undergraduate student. Added to this, we observed that in the UK some of the most popular and comprehensive textbooks in public relations were largely from the United States but these did not adequately reflect the development of public relations theory and practice in the UK, Europe or elsewhere. A gap for a comprehensive, mainly European textbook was waiting to be filled.

So who to write such a comprehensive text? For this we looked to our colleagues – people who are part of the Public Relations Subject Group at Leeds Metropolitan University who teach on our well-established undergraduate programmes. We also looked to our wider network – senior practitioners who have contributed to our subject area and undergraduate programme, former colleagues who have moved on to careers elsewhere and past external examiners. The common thread among these contributors is their experience of public relations teaching and learning at Leeds Metropolitan University, which is now in its 16th year. During this period more than 1000 full-time students have graduated in public relations and moved on to successful careers in public relations consultancy or in-house for public and private sector organisations. Other, part-time students are practitioners in mid-career and have attended our short courses to further their professional development. Some of these alumni have contributed case studies to this book.

Target audience

This book is written primarily for second-year undergraduates and above who are studying public relations as a single subject (i.e. a bachelors in public relations), jointly with another subject, or as a single module or unit within a wider programme.

Book structure

The book is divided into four parts. Part 1 provides important background knowledge to help you understand the broad business and societal context in which public relations plays a role. Included here, for example, are chapters on democracy and on the international (or multicultural) context of public relations. In Part 2 there is a chapter on the related, but often ignored topic of persuasion and propaganda to help you arrive at your own definitions; while Part 3 includes emerging specialisms such as technology PR, financial PR and public affairs. Part 4 comprises chapters that are not conventionally included within a public relations textbook. In this section, for example, the chapter on campaigning organisations and pressure groups is written largely from the perspective of the campaigning organisation, rather than from a business perspective. The final chapter provides some themes and questions that we hope student readers will take up as topics for investigation and research. Public relations is an evolving discipline and its growth requires continual questioning to challenge its boundaries and establish its terrain. As students, teachers, researchers and practitioners we are all responsible for achieving this aim.

Pedagogy

This is an educational textbook for public relations and therefore includes a number of devices that we hope will help both students and tutors to get the most out of the material. First, each chapter begins with a list of the *Learning outcomes* which students should achieve after engaging with the material. We have structured the book to have a range of consistent pedagogy which support the reader in understanding the chapter subject. For example, there are regular *Activities,* which give instructions on where to look for further information or how to engage further with topics. *Think abouts* are included to encourage reflection and for the reader to pause and think a little more deeply about the issues and ideas that are being presented and discussed. We have attempted to define as many terms or phrases that may not be universally understood or which form part of the specialist language related to that topic or area of study with *Definition* boxes. Finally we have included many cases studies (*Case studies* and *Mini case studies*) which aim to exemplify and apply the principles under discussion.

We hope you find the material included in the chapters stimulating and refreshing in helping you with your studies. Most important, just enjoy reading the book!

Acknowledgements

In addition to the invaluable contributors already mentioned, we would like to acknowledge other academic colleagues who have superbly supported this project:

Jeremy Baker – London Metropolitan University
Sue Carpendale – University of Suffolk
Richard Dolphin – University of Northampton
Bertil Flodin – Con Brio Communications AB
Dennis Foy – Wolverhampton University
Anne Geerdink – Hogeskolen Van Amsterdam
Axel Gryspeerdt – Catholic University, Louvain
Magne Hauge – Norwegian School of Management
John Hitchins – College of St Mark and St John
Maria Hopwood – Teeside University
Oyvind Ihlen – University of Oslo
Julia Jahansoozi – University of Central Lancashire
Jacquie L'Etang – University of Stirling
Mohammed Mizra – Huddersfield University
Rachel O'Dowd – Waterford Institute of Technology
Oddgeir Tveiten – Adger University College
Caroline Wilson – University of Central England

We would particularly like to extend warm thanks to our friend and former colleague Jo Fawkes for her generous support and critical eye in helping to prepare the final manuscript. Thanks also to Thomas Sigel (Senior Acquisitions Editor), Andy Peart (Development Editor), Peter Hooper (Editorial Assistant/Development Editor), Anita Atkinson (Desk Editor), Jo Barber (Marketing Manager), Oli Adams (Marketing Executive), Helen Baxter (copy editor), Helen Woodcock (proofreader), Hilary Luckcock (picture researcher), Nikki Bannister and Lynette Miller (permissions editors) at Pearson for their encouragement and helping us see through the project to completion.

Finally, but not least, we would like to thank our families. For Ralph, this dedication goes to the 'family that never sleeps' – Catherine, Anna and William – for being themselves, agreeing to postpone a few trips and providing the best possible distraction as the project grew. For Liz these thoughts and thanks go to John, Daniel and Hannah Faulkner for their patience, tolerance, humour and endless supplies of tea and coffee when deadlines loomed.

Publisher's Acknowledgements

We are grateful to the following for permission to reproduce copyright material:

Figures 2.2 and 2.3 redrawn from *Managing Public Relations, 1st Edition*, pub Holt, Rinehart and Winston, reprinted by permission of James E. Grunig (Grunig, J. E. and Hunt, T. 1984); Figures 2.5, 8.3, 10.1, 10.2 and 11.4 redrawn from *Effective Public Relations, 8th Edition*, reprinted by permission of Pearson Education, Inc. (Cutlip, S. M. *et al.* 2000); Table 3.1 from What is public relations? in *Handbook of Public Relations, 2nd Edition*, edited by A. Theaker, pub Routledge, reprinted by permission of Taylor & Francis Group (Fawkes, J. 2004); Table 3.2 from *Public Relations Education in the UK. A research report for the Chartered Institute of Public Relations*, reprinted by permission of the Chartered Institute of Public Relations (Fawkes, J. and Tench, R. 2004); Table 3.3 from National Commission on Public Relations Education, *A Port of Entry – public relations education for the 21st century*, Copyright 1999. Reprinted with permission by The Public Relations Society of America (www.prsa.org) (Port of Entry 1999); Figure 6.1 redrawn from *Effective Corporate Relations: Applying Public Relations in Business and Industry* edited by N. Hart, pub McGraw-Hill, reprinted by permission of Mrs. I. B. Hart (Peach, L. 1987); Table 6.1, Figures 6.3 and 6.4 reprinted from *Business Horizons*, Vol. 34, Issue 4, A. B. Carroll, The pyramid of corporate social responsibility: Toward the moral management of organizational stakeholders, pp. 39–48, Copyright 1991 with permission from Elsevier (Carroll, A. B. 1991); Table 6.3 adapted from Management learning perspectives on business ethics in *Management Learning* edited by J. Burgoyne and M. Reynolds, Copyright © Robin Snell, 1997, reprinted by permission of Sage Publications Ltd., (Snell, R. 1997); Figure 7.1 adapted from Sixth Annual Edelman Trust Barometer 2005, © Daniel J. Edelman, Inc., reprinted by permission of Daniel J. Edelman, Inc.; Table 7.1 from European Business Readership Survey 2004: Ipsos Media, reprinted by permission of Ipsos UK; Table 7.2 reprinted from *Public Relations Review*, Vol. 27, R. S. Zaharna, 'In-awareness' approach to international public relations, pp. 135–48, Copyright 2001, with permission from Elsevier (Zaharna, R. S. 2001); Figure 7.3 redrawn from J. Watson, *Media Communication. An Introduction to Theory and Process, 2nd Edition*, pub 2003, Palgrave Macmillan, reproduced with permission of Palgrave Macmillan (Watson, J. 2003); Table 7.3 from http://www.wuv.de/daten/unternehmen/charts/092003/779/ reprinted by permission of Endmark International Namefinding AG; Figure 7.7 reprinted by permission of Future Foundation 2004; Tables 8.1, 12.1 and 16.1 adapted from *Managing Public Relations, 1st Edition*, pub Holt, Rinehart and Winston, reprinted by permission of James E. Grunig (Grunig, J. E. and Hunt, T. 1984); Figure 8.2 redrawn from *Manager's Guide to Excellence in Public Relations and Communication Management*, reprinted by permission of Lawrence Erlbaum Associates, Inc. (Dozier, D. M. *et al.* 1995); Table 8.2 from *Excellent Public Relations and Effective Organizations*, reprinted by permission of Lawrence Erlbaum Associates, Inc. (Grunig, L. A. *et al.* 2002); Figure 8.4 redrawn from Evolution of the manager role in public relations practice in *Journal of Public Relations Research*, 7(1), reprinted by permission of Lawrence Erlbaum Associates, Inc. (Dozier, D. M. and Broom, G. M. 1995); Figures 10.4 and 10.5 taken from *Planning and Managing Public Relations Campaigns, 2nd Edition* by A. Gregory, published by Kogan Page 2000, reprinted by permission of Kogan Page (Gregory, A. 2000); Figure 10.7 produced by Kirsty Innes MCIPR on behalf of the Sea Fish Industry Authority (Sea Fish); Figure 11.2 redrawn from http://www.echoresearch.com, reprinted by permission of Echo Research Ltd.; Table 11.2 adapted from Guardian Unlimited, 1 March 2005, Copyright Guardian Newspapers Limited 2005, data reprinted by permission of Audit Bureau of Circulations; Table 11.3

adapted from *Markt- und Werbepsychologie Bd. 2: Praxis, 2nd Edition*, pub Fachverlag Wirtschaftspsychologie, reprinted by permission of the author (Neumann, P. 2003); Figure 11.5 first published in Evaluation of public relations: the achilles heel of the profession in *International Public Relations Review*, 15(4), updated and reprinted by permission of the author (Macnamara, J. R. 1992); Table 11.5 adapted from Medienresonazanalyse. Paper presented at Redaktion und wissenschaftlicher Beirat der Pressesprecher, Berlin, 7 May, reprinted by permission of K. Merten (Merten, K. and Wienand, E. 2004); Figure 12.1 redrawn from Shareholding versus stakeholding: a critical review of corporate governance in *Corporate Governance: An International Review*, 12(3), reprinted by permission of Blackwell Publishing (Letza, S. et al. 2004); Figures 13.2 and 13.3 reprinted by permission of Daniel Löwensberg; Figure 15.1 redrawn from *Managing Business Ethics, 3rd Edition*, reprinted by permission of John Wiley & Sons, Inc. (Trevino, L. K. and Nelson, K. A. 2004); Figure 15.3 adapted from *Public Relations Ethics, 1st Edition*, reprinted by permission of Wadsworth, a division of Thomson Learning (Seib, P. and Fitzpatrick, K. 1995); Table 17.2 adapted from *Engaging People at Work to Drive Strategy and Change*, reprinted by permission of McKinsey & Company and the author, John Smythe, Partner in Engage for Change. Research produced whilst acting as Organisational Fellow with McKinsey (Smythe, J. 2004); Figure 17.3 redrawn from *Making the Connections: using internal communication to turn strategy into action*, pub Gower, reprinted by permission of Ashgate Publishing Ltd. (Quirke, B. 2000); Table 17.3 adapted from *Transforming Internal Communication: how to align communication strategy with corporate goals*, reprinted by permission of Optima Publishing Ltd., www.business-intelligence.co.uk (Kernaghan, S. et al. 2001); Figure 17.4 from Effective employee communication in *Effective Corporate Relations: Applying Public Relations in Business and Industry* edited by N. Hart, pub McGraw-Hill, reprinted by permission of Mrs. I. B. Hart (Arnott, M. 1987); Figure 18.2 adapted from Annual Report, www.bitc.org.uk, accessed 18 February 2005, reprinted by permission of Business in the Community (BITC 2005); Picture 18.2 © KCCW 2005, reprinted by permission of Andrex Marketing, Kimberly-Clark Limited; Figure 18.3 redrawn from Co-operative Bank Ethical Policy, Co-operative Bank internal publication, reprinted by permission of The Co-operative Bank; Picture 18.3 used with permission of Justin McKeown, Harrison Cowley; Table 20.1 adapted from *Crisis Communications: A Casebook Approach, 2nd Edition*, reprinted by permission of Lawrence Erlbaum Associates, Inc. (Fearn-Banks, K. 2002); Figure 26.1 adapted from Marketing communications activities in *Marketing Communications: Principles and Practice* by P. Kitchen, pub Thomson Business Press, reprinted by permission of Thomson Learning (EMEA) Ltd. (Hughes, G. 1998); Table 26.1 adapted from

You talkin' to me? Marketing Communications in the Age of Consent, www.shapetheagenda.com, reprinted by permission of The Chartered Institute of Marketing (Chartered Institute of Marketing 2004); Figure 26.2 redrawn from *Marketing Communication: Contexts, Strategies and Applications, 3rd Edition*, reprinted by permission of Pearson Education Ltd. (Fill, C. 2002); Table 26.2 adapted from *Marketing Communication: Contexts, Strategies and Applications, 3rd Edition*, reprinted by permission of Pearson Education Ltd. (Fill, C. 2002); Table 27.1 from *IEG Sponsorship Report – Outline*, reprinted by permission of IEG, Inc. (IEG 2003); Figure 27.4 redrawn from *Sponsorship 2002*, reprinted by permission of Mintel International (Mintel 2002); Figure 27.5 redrawn from Pilot Group: Sponsor Visions 2004 in *Werben und Verkaufen*, www.wuv.de, reprinted by permission of pilot checkpoint GmbH (Pilot Group 2004); Figure 27.6 redrawn from Sponsorship comes of age in *insidedge sensor*, pub Mediaedge:cia, reprinted by permission of MEC UK Ltd. (Mediaedge:cia Anon 2004); Tables 28.1 and 28.2 from *CCI Corporate Communication Practices and Trends Study 2003: Final Report*, March 2004, www.corporate. comm.org/pdf/report2003pdf, reprinted by permission of Dr. Michael B. Goodman, Director, Corporate Communication Institute at Fairleigh Dickinson University (CCI 2004); Figure 28.3 redrawn from P. Kitchen and D. Schultz (eds), *Raising the Corporate Umbrella: Corporate Communication in the 21st Century*, pub 2001, Macmillan Press, reproduced with permission of Palgrave Macmillan (Kitchen, P. and Schultz, D. 2001); Table 28.3 from C. G. Cheney and L. T. Christiansen, Organizational identity: Linkages between internal and external communication in *The New Handbook of Organizational Communication* edited by F. M. Jablin and L. L. Putnam, p. 238, copyright 2001 by Sage Publications, Inc., reprinted by permission of Sage Publications, Inc. (Cheney C. G. and Christiansen L. T. 2001); Table 28.4 adapted from *Excellence in Public Relations and Communication Management*, reprinted by permission of Lawrence Erlbaum Associates, Inc. (Grunig, J. E. ed. 1992); Figure 28.7 redrawn from *Exploring Corporate Strategy, 5th Edition*, reprinted by permission of Pearson Education Ltd. (Johnson, G. and Scholes, K. 1999); Figure 29.2 redrawn from *Using Research in Public Relations: Applications to Program Management, 1st Edition*, reprinted by permission of Pearson Education, Inc. (Broom, G. M. and Dozier, D. M. 1990); Figure 30.1 redrawn from *Mass Communication Theory: An Introduction, 2nd Edition*, Copyright © Denis McQuail, 1987, reprinted by permission of Sage Publications Ltd. (McQuail, D. 1987); Table 30.1 from *Public Communication Campaign Evaluation: An environmental scan of challenges, criticisms, practice, and opportunities*, www.gse.harvard.edu/hfrp/pubs/onlinepubs/pcce, reprinted by permission of Harvard Family Research Project (Coffman, J. 2002); Figure 31.1 redrawn from *Standing Room Only: Strategies for Marketing the Performing*

Arts, reprinted by permission of Harvard Business School Press (Kotler, P. and Scheff, J. 1997).

Picture 1.1: David Dyson/Camera Press; Picture 1.2: Jon Arnold Images/Alamy; Picture 2.1: Syed Jan Sabawoon/European Pressphoto Agency: Picture 2.2: ©Reuters/Corbis; Picture 3.1: Getty Images; Picture 4.1: ©Reuters/Corbis; Picture 4.2: Kieron McCarron/ BBC; Picture 4.3: ©Maher Attar/Corbis Sygma; Picture 5.1: Jeremy Nicholl/Alamy; Picture 5.2: Image Courtesy of Advertising Archives; Picture 6.1: ©Reuters/Corbis; Picture 6.2: AFP/Getty Images; Picture 7.1: European Community Audio Visual Library; Picture 8.1: ©Peter Turnley/Corbis; Picture 8.2: ©Urban Thierry/Corbis Sygma; Picture 9.1: Methodos SPA, Italy; Picture 9.2: ©Richard Klune/Corbis; Picture 10.1: Johnny Green/ PA/Empics; Picture 11.1: Jack Sullivan/Alamy; Picture 11.2: Alisdair Macdonald/Rex; Picture 12.1: ©Gideon Mendel/Corbis; Picture 12.2: Impact Photos; Figure 13.1: ©Pepsico. Used with permission; ©3 Com. Used with permission; Unnumbered picture p. 259 Courtesy of Advertising Archives; Picture 14.2: HMSO; Picture 14.3: Mary McCartney/PETA; Picture 15.1: AFP/Getty Images; Picture 15.2: ©William Gottlieb/Corbis; Picture 16.1 courtesy of Connectpoint PR www.connectpoint.co.uk; Picture 16.2 used with kind permission of the Manchester Evening News; Picture 16.3: ©Darrell Gulin/Corbis; Unnumbered picture on p. 367 used with permission of Everton Football Club; Picture 17.1: Getty Images Sport; Picture 19.1: Nick Cobbing/Rex; Picture 19.2: EPA/Empics; Picture 20.1: ©Reuters/Corbis; Picture 20.2: Rex; Picture 22.1 photograph reprinted by permission of Timothy Soar; Unnumbered picture on p. 435 and material used in mini case study "How trade publications are used" reprinted by permission of Carey Jones Architects; Picture 23.1: Sipa Press/Rex; Picture 23.2: Tony Kyracou/Rex; Picture 24.1: Eddie Mulholland/Rex; Picture 24.2: Ryan Bowd; Picture 25.1: PhotoDisc; Picture 25.2: ©Simon Marcus/Corbis; Picture 26.1: ©Jason Szenes/Corbis; Picture 27.1: BYB/Rex; Picture 27.2: Crispin Thruston/Rex; Picture 28.1 adapted from CBI offices location map from http://www.cbi.org.uk/ndbs/staticpages.nsf/staticpages/atwork/offices.html?OpenDocument, reprinted by permission of CBI; Picture 29.1: Stuart Franklin/Magnum Photos; Picture 29.2: Andrew Testa/Panos Pictures; Picture 29.3: Nick Cobbing/Panos Pictures; Picture 30.1: Anti-Social Behaviour Unit, The Home Office; Picture 30.2: ©James Leynse/Corbis; Picture 31.2: ©L A Daily/Corbis Sygma.

The Chartered Institute of Public Relations for the material 'Key Facts About PR in the UK', 'Key Facts about the UK's Chartered Institute of Public Relations (CIPR)', 'European Public Relations Associations', 'Chartered Institute of Public Relations Code of Conduct' and the press release 'Charter Status for the UK Institute of Public Relations' February 2005 all taken from their website www.cipr.co.uk; Melanie Gerlis for permission to use diary extracts and photograph; Business in the Community for an extract from '2004 PerCent Standard Results', taken from their website www.bitc.org.uk, and extracts from the case studies 'GlaxoSmithKline – Barretstown – Therapeutic recreation for children with serious illnesses', 'Scottish Nappy Company Limited – Environmental Award' and 'Everton Football in the Community – Disability Football Development Programme' taken from the Business in the Community's Awards for Excellence 2004 on their website www.bitc.org.uk; Unilever Plc for an extract from the Unilever Ethical Guidelines and Code of Business Principles taken from their website www.unilever.com; The Foreign Policy Centre for an extract from *Trading Identities – Why Countries and Companies are Taking On Each Other's Roles* by Wally Olins; Lawrence Erlbaum Associates Inc for an extract from 'Explicating Relationship Management as a General Theory of Public Relations' by John A. Ledingham, published in *Journal of Public Relations Research* Volume 6 Number 3, 2003, and an extract from *The Dynamics of Persuasion* by Richard M. Perloff; Portfolio Communications for the case study 'Mummy: The Inside Story' taken from their website www.portfoliocomms.com; Westminster City Council Communications Team for the case study 'Bin There Done That'; Kogan Page for an extract from *Planning and Managing Public Relations Campaigns* 2nd Edition by Anne Gregory published by Kogan Page 2000; Taylor and Francis Group for an extract from *Revealing the Corporation: Perspectives on Identity, Image, Reputation, Corporate Branding and Corporate Level Marketing* by John M. T. Balmer and Stephen A. Grayser published by Routledge 2003; Bayer AG for an extract from the Bayer Mission Statement, from their website www.bayer.com; Nestlé S. A. for an extract from Nestlé's Business Principles and the Nestlé strap-line, from their website www.nestle.com; Sage Publications Limited for extracts from *Using Communication Theory: An Introduction to Planned Communications* by Sven Windahl, Benno Signitzer and Jean Olsen © Sven Windahl, Benno Signitzer and Jean Olsen 1991, and *Organizational Culture and Identity* by Michael Parker © Michael Parker 2000; The Society of European Affairs Professionals for an extract from their Code of Conduct, taken from their website www.seap.eu.org; The Global Alliance for Public Relations and Communications Management for an extract from the case study 'PR World, Inc' and an extract from 'Global Protocol on Public Relations Protocol – Summer 2002', both from the Global Alliance website www.globalpr.org; Ryan Bowd for the case study 'The evolution of the exclusive: media relations by media partnership' The Chartered Institute of Personnel and Development, London, for an extract from the CIPD Factsheet *Managing the Psychological Contract* December 2004; Sally-Anne Watts, Head of Corporate Affairs and Communications, Northampton General Hospital NHS Trust, for the case study 'A Hospital Communicates'; BT and BITC for material in the case study 'BT Community Partnership Programme'; BT, Justin McKeown at Harrison Cowley PR and Beth Courtier for the material and photograph in case study 'BT "Am I listening?" campaign'; Russell Grossman, Head of Internal Communications, BBC, for the case study 'BBC and Hutton – The Internal Communication Role in a Crisis' and the accompanying photograph; Kimberley-Clark and Guide Dogs for the Blind for the case study and photograph in 'Guide Dogs for the Blind and Andrex'; Simon Williams, Director of Corporate Affairs, Co-operative Financial Services, for the case studies 'The Co-operative Bank: Customers Who Care, Safer Chemicals Campaign', 'The Co-operative Bank' and 'Co-operative Bank', from the Co-operative Bank website www.co-operativebank.org.uk; and the Department of Treasury and Finance, State Government of Victoria, for an extract from a Government Press Briefing used in the case study 'Melbourne Gas crisis'; Paul Willis, Ptarmigan Consultants, for the case studies and accompanying photographs 'Media relations driving sales – a fishy story', 'Connecting with Customers – Quality Street hits the road' and 'Communicating a brand personality – Mini Roof Gardens', and for the case study 'Nationwide Giant Shirt' from the Ptarmigan website www.ptarmiganpr.co.uk; Carey Jones Architects for material in the case study 'How trade publications are used'; Ash Communications for the case study 'Smartlite' taken from their website www.ashcommunications.com, telephone: 0044 (0)207 734 566, email: sue@ashcommunications.com; Richard Casofsky for an extract from 'The Practitioner Diary of Richard Casofsky'; F. P. Vickers for the case study 'A 'David and Goliath' Public Affairs Battle on the English Channel' by F. P. Vickers and K. Moloney; The Financial Services Authority for an extract from a FSA Press release FSA/PN/037/2002 12th April 2002 from their website www.fsa.gov.uk; Jo Powell and Pace Micro Technology plc for an extract from the case study 'Pace Micro Technology'; Julius Duncan, Lawton Public Relations, for an extract from 'A Practitioners Guide to the IPO'; Fox Parrack Hirsch Communications for the case study 'Avanti-Fujitsu Consulting' from their website www.foxps.com; Diageo Plc for an extract from the 'Diageo Code of Marketing Practice for Alcoholic Beverages' from their website www.diageo.com; Institute of Practitioners in Advertising for the case study 'It Only Works If It All Works: O2', adapted from the IPA Effectiveness Awards paper by Andrew Cox, Alex Harris, Sophie Maunder, Louise Cook and Joanna Bamford from the website www.warc.com; Elsevier for extracts from 'Reputation Management: The New Face of Corporate Public Relations' by James G. Hutton, Michael B. Goodman, Jill B. Alexander and Christina M. Genest, published in *Public Relations Review* Volume 27, 2001 © Elsevier 2001; Emerald Group Publishing Limited for an extract from 'On Considering the Meaning of Managed Communication: Or Why Employees Resist Excellent Communication' by Christine Daymon published in *Journal of Communication Management* Volume 4 Number 3, 2000 © Emerald Group Publishing Limited; Mortimer Chadwick Gray for the case study 'Charles Yorke'; Haymarket Business Publications Limited for extracts from 'Vodafone UK and Corporate Donations' published in *PR Week* 24th September 2004, 'The English Tea Experience' published in *PR Week* 21st January 2005, 'Frieze art fair 2004' published in *PR Week* 14th January 2005, and 'BAFTA Awards' published in *PR Week* January 2005, © Haymarket Business Publications Limited; Financial Dynamics for the case study 'CPP Group'; Crawley Borough Council Communications Division for the case study 'Vote and Post Campaign'; Chris Hines for the case study 'Surfers Against Sewage' based on material from the Surfers Against Sewage website www.sas.org.uk and an interview with Chris Hines; Cambridge University Hospitals NHS Foundation Trust for the case study 'Public Involvement – Addenbrooke's Hospital, Cambridge University Hospitals NHS Foundation Trust'; Mezei Márk, Sawyer Miller Group, for the case study 'Overcoming Public Opposition and Mobilising Support for the Waste Management Site of Sventgal, Hungary'; Arts Council England for an extract from 'Spend by Art Form' from their website www.artscouncil.org.uk; Harvard Business School Press for an extract from *Standing Room Only: Strategies for Marketing and Performing Arts* by Philip Kotler and Joanne Scheff; Leeds Grand Theatre for the case study 'Leeds Grand Theatre'; Shirley Beresford for the case study 'Endemol UK' and an extract from an unpublished research interview with Steve Donoughue; Tim Hincks, Chief Creative Officer, Endemol UK, for the case study 'Endemol UK'; Steve Donoughue for his participation in the research interview conducted by Shirley Beresford; The European Commission for an extract from their website http://www.europa.eu.int/comm/dgs/press_communication/guide/index2_en.htm © European Communities 1995– 2005.

We are grateful to the Financial Times Limited for permission to reprint the following material:

Fig 3.2 Where do SMEs and start-ups find their information and advice on marketing, from FT Creative Business, © Financial Times, 13 July 2004; Gregory spins into IPR big chair, © Financial Times, 19 January 2004; Mini-case 7.6 The difference a name makes, © Financial Times, 6 May 2004; NGOs win greater trust than media and big businesses, © Financial Times, 24 January 2005.

In some instances we have been unable to trace the owners of copyright material, and we would appreciate any information that would enable us to do so.

PART 1

The context of public relations

This first part of the book provides you with the background knowledge you will require to understand the role and purpose of public relations (PR) set against the broader business and societal contexts within which it operates. Chapter 1 discusses how public relations is defined in different ways and how it has evolved as a contemporary practice in both the United States and Britain. Chapter 2 discusses how public relations is organised as a management function inside organisations and how it relates to other functions such as marketing. We then turn to the role of the public relations practitioner in Chapter 3 to focus on what public relations practitioners do. In acknowledging PR's special relationship with journalism, we discuss the contemporary media environment in Chapter 4. Arguably, public relations is essential to modern democratic societies. In Chapter 5 we discuss the nature of democracy and how public relations plays a part in it. Examining the societal context of public relations from the organisation's perspective, Chapter 6 highlights corporate social responsibility. Finally, in Chapter 7, the emerging international context of public relations is introduced.

CHAPTER 1
Public relations origins:
definitions and history

Introduction

What is public relations? And when did public relations begin? This chapter briefly reviews why it has proved so difficult to define public relations work or reach a universally agreed definition of what the job entails. It then outlines what is known about the emergence of public relations as a modern occupation, drawing primarily on the histories of the United States, Britain and Germany (further references to the European evolution are discussed in Chapter 7). The discussion of both definitions and histories reflects the social nature of the profession; public relations is a product of the economic and political circumstances of its time and evolves according to the needs of these broader environments. At the same time, its historical ties to advertising and propaganda continue to provide fertile ground for debate about its ethical and professional merit (see Chapters 3 and 15).

Public relations is now a global occupation and implemented in many corners of the world in different ways. However, written histories of public relations reflect the dominance of the United States on the academic field of public relations and tend to focus on its origins in the United States rather than in other countries. Little has been written about the emergence of the profession in Britain, with the exception of one comprehensive book by Jacquie L'Etang (L'Etang 2004b), discussed in this chapter. As a result, current histories of the profession must be regarded as socially and culturally specific. Moreover, and as L'Etang (2004b) points out, despite the current dominance of women in the profession (see Chapter 3), written histories tend to be his-stories, delivered through the eyes of the men who were at the top of the profession during its emergence. Women who worked in public relations in its early years, even if they were few, would in all probability have taken a different view of developments. These issues should be taken into account when reading this chapter. There is much still to be said and understood about the emergence of this modern-day discipline.

Public relations definitions

Public relations (PR) is used in a huge range of industries and in each one slightly different skills and competencies have emerged among practitioners. As a result, there is no one universally agreed definition of PR (Grunig 1992; L'Etang 1996; White and Mazur 1996; Moloney 2000). The likelihood is that if you ask three practitioners and three academics to define PR, all six answers will be different in some way. In part, this is because the profession is still young. It certainly gives lots of scope for debate, as described in the following section, which outlines some of the most common views of PR among academics and practitioners (Cutlip et al. 2000). See Activity 1.1.

PICTURE 1.1 This chapter will consider the historical evolution of public relations and its practice. Debates continue as to whether this should include press agents such as the UK's well-known publicist Max Clifford. (*Source*: David Dyson/Camera Press.)

activity 1.1

Defining public relations

With a group of friends, write down your definition of PR. Now think about how you arrived at that definition:

- Is it based on your experience of PR and what you observe PR practitioners doing?
- Is it based on what you read about PR in the newspapers?
- Is it based on what your tutors have told you about PR?

Now compare your definitions:

- How different are they?
- What do they have in common?
- What are the differences and why do you think they exist?

Each of you will have different thoughts about what should and should not be included in the definition. See if you can agree on a common set of ideas, then test them on other friends and see how far they agree or disagree.

Academic definitions of public relations

Harlow (1976) found 472 different definitions of PR coined between 1900 and 1976. He built his own definition from these findings, offering:

> *Public relations is a distinctive management function which helps establish and maintain mutual lines of communication, understanding, acceptance and cooperation between an organisation and its publics; involves the management of problems or issues; helps management to keep informed on and responsive to public opinions; defines and emphasises the responsibility of management to serve the public interest; helps management keep abreast of and effectively utilise change; serving as an early warning system to help anticipate trends; and uses research and ethical communication techniques as its principal tools. (Harlow 1976: 36)*

This definition contains overall goals, processes and tasks of PR and positions the profession firmly within the organisation, as a management role. It covers most aspects of PR, but is somewhat long winded and other researchers have tried to simplify things by separating tasks from strategy.

Grunig and Hunt (1984: 6), for example, went to the opposite extreme from Harlow and defined PR in one sentence as 'the management of communication between an organisation and its publics'. Grunig (1992) argues that this definition allows for differences in practice between practitioners in different contexts, but still includes important elements, such as the management of communication and the focus on external relationships. Kitchen (1997) is even briefer with his definition, suggesting that PR can be defined as 'communication with various publics', although he does add to this by arguing that PR is an important management function and has a strategic role to play.

Other definitions focus on 'ideal' communications practices: two-way communications and building positive relationships between organisations and their publics. Some include its strategic importance to organisations and recognise its influence on reputation (Hutton 1999; Grunig and Grunig 2000). Cutlip et al. (2000: 6) combine these aspects and suggest: 'Public relations is the management function that establishes and maintains mutually beneficial relationships between an organization and the publics on whom its success or failure depends.'

White and Mazur (1996: 11) offer a definition based on the goals of PR: 'To influence the behaviour of groups of people in relation to each other. Influence should be exerted through dialogue – not monologue – with all the different corporate audiences, with public relations becoming a respected function in its own right, acting as a strategic resource and helping to implement corporate strategy.'

term PR is often a synonym for deception and that everyday understanding of PR is usually determined by the visible results of PR activity (e.g. media coverage). However, the idea of *persuasion* has been left out of academic definitions, despite recognition of its importance in the profession's history, as we will see later in this chapter (see also Chapter 14 for further explorations of persuasion). Some academics point this out and argue that we should explicitly recognise the fact that PR is biased in favour of commercial interests. They define PR in terms of its social effects. L'Etang (1996), for example, suggests that the narrow focus of traditional definitions, which begin and end with the interests of the organisation, blinds practitioners and academics to the social and political costs and benefits of PR.

Moloney (2000: 6) agrees with L'Etang that PR is too multifaceted to be incorporated into a single definition, but that its effect on society demands extensive investigation regardless. His view is that PR is about power and 'manipulation against democracy' (p.65) because it is so often used to support government and commercial interests at the expense of other interests. Insofar as he uses definitions, he suggests that PR can be defined differently as a 'concept' ('communications management by an organisation with its publics'), as a practice ('mostly dealing with the media') and in terms of its effects on society ('a category of persuasive communications done through the mass media or through private lobbying by groups to advance their material or ideological interests'). See Activity 1.2.

Key debates on definitions

All these definitions highlight the fact that PR is about managing communication in order to build good relationships and mutual understanding between an organisation and its most important audiences (Gordon 1997). However, it is important to recognise that they do incorporate underlying assumptions that presume its main function is to promote the organisation's interests and some writers have objected to this. Botan and Hazelton (1989), for example, argue that such definitions tend to present a view of PR as a neutral communications channel and only partially reflect actual practice, in which the main job of a PR officer is to manipulate public opinion for the benefit of organisations.

If we look at the views of PR held by the general public, most people think of PR as a means by which people are persuaded to think or behave in a particular way (Kitchen 1997; Cutlip et al. 2000). Botan and Hazelton (1989), Kitchen (1997) and Cutlip et al. (2000) all emphasise that popular usage of the

---

activity 1.2

Key debates

Why do you think academics disagree about definitions of PR? Is it because they don't understand PR or because they have different views about its contribution to society? Summarise, in your own words, the key debates between different PR definitions. How would you explain these definitions to your friends and family?

Practitioner definitions of public relations

Practitioner definitions of PR tend to be more based in the reality of the day-to-day job, often use the term 'public relations' interchangeably with other terms such as organisational communication or corporate communication (Grunig 1992; Hutton 1999) and often include concepts of persuasion and

PICTURE 1.2   The 1978 'Mexican Statement' has defined public relations as 'the art and social science of analyzing trends, predicting their consequences, counselling organizational leaders, and implementing planned programs of action which will serve both the organization and the public interest'. (*Source:* Jon Arnold Images/Alamy.)

influence. You could argue that this kind of flexibility means simply that practitioners have difficulty explaining exactly what their job entails – and indeed, this seems to be the case.

In 1978, the First World Assembly of Public Relations Associations in Mexico defined PR as 'the art and social science of analyzing trends, predicting their consequences, counselling organizational leaders, and implementing planned programs of action which will serve both the organization and the public interest (Newsom et al. 2000: 2). The definition offered by the Public Relations Society of America, coined in 1988, is similarly broad: 'Public relations helps an organization and its publics adapt mutually to each other' (Public Relations Society of America 2004).

More recent definitions have been more detailed. In a recent survey by the Department of Trade and Industry (DTI) and the UK Chartered Institute of Public Relations (CIPR), PR was defined as 'influencing behaviour to achieve objectives through the effective management of relationships and communications' (Department of Trade and Industry and Institute of Public Relations 2003: 10). This definition is an attempt to combine the idea of managed communications with exercising influence on relationships and achieving mutual understanding, to incorporate as broad a range of activity as possible.

The CIPR defines PR as: 'About reputation – the result of what you do, what you say and what others say about you. Public relations is the discipline which looks after reputation, with the aim of earning understanding and support and influencing opinion and behaviour. It is the planned and sustained effort to establish and maintain goodwill and mutual understanding between an organisation and its publics' (Institute of Public Relations 2004).

Some practitioners disagree with this definition because it leads with the concept of reputation and they do not believe this is the primary focus for PR programmes. However, the Public Relations Consultants Association (PRCA) in the UK has also adopted the CIPR definition for use by its members (Public Relations Consultants Association 2004) and it is included in some UK-based text and practitioner books on PR (e.g. Gregory 1996; Harrison 2000; Genasi 2002). Given this consistency, we can assume that this formal definition is the one most regularly referred to by practitioners in this country (see Think about 1.1).

Academics and practitioners have come up with very different definitions of PR. From the summary above, consider the following questions with a group of friends:

- What are the main differences between the definitions of academics and practitioners?
- Why do you think such differences exist?
- Is there a right or wrong definition? If so, why?
- Which definition do you think is most appropriate for PR and why?

Feedback   Consider the interests of the people creating the definitions. For example, are they trying to build theories about how PR works or are they trying to simply describe what it does? Who is the audience for the definition and how might the audience affect what is included?

Public opinion: justifying public relations

The practice of using communication to influence the public is hundreds of years old, with its roots in ancient civilisations, including the Greek and Roman Empires. Throughout history, governments, monarchs and powerful institutions such as the Catholic Church have used communication and information to generate support for their cause among the populace (Grunig and Hunt 1984; Cutlip et al. 2000). But it was the emergence of the concept of public opinion that eventually formed the scientific justification for using PR and communications techniques in this way.

Nowadays, the term public opinion is used frequently in the media, by government and by PR practitioners almost without thinking. However, as it emerged from the philosophical traditions of the eighteenth and nineteenth centuries, it was a hotly debated topic and the context in which it is used today only emerged in the early years of the twentieth century. The concept of public opinion became relevant in the mid-eighteenth century, accompanying the emergence of fledgling democratic states. Rousseau, the French philosopher, is generally credited with first coining the term, in 1744, and its use quickly became more extensive as discussions continued about how democracies should and could incorporate the views of the populations they were supposed to govern (Price 1992).

Two basic conceptions of public opinion have dominated the evolution of the term: public opinion as an abstract, *collective view*, emerging through rational discussion of issues in the population; and public opinion as an *aggregate view*, the sum total of individual opinions of the population governed by the democratic state (Pieczka 1996). There are limitations to both these views – for example, who is included in, and who is excluded from, the term 'public'? To what extent does the rational debate required for the 'collective' view really take place and does everyone have equal access to the debate? If not, then 'public opinion' may only be the view of a select number of individuals who bother to engage in discussions. Alternatively, if public opinion is interpreted as an aggregate of individual opinions, then what happens to minority views that are swamped by majority concerns? Where do they find expression?

> **Definition:** *Collective view* of public opinion refers to issues that emerge through rational discussion in the population. One example of such an issue is the general agreement among opinion formers (e.g. health professionals) that obesity in young children is caused through poor nutrition and a lack of exercise.

> **Definition:** *Aggregate view* of public opinion refers to the sum total of individual opinions of the population governed by the democratic state. One example of such an issue is banning smoking in public places. In the UK the views of the majority of the population, tested over time through polls, appear to be in favour of a ban.

Many writers have expressed concern about the inherent nature of the individual – more interested in, and persuaded by, emotional arguments and events than logic and politics. If the democratic state is supposed to take public opinion as its guide for what is important to the population, then an emotional public is not necessarily going to provide the best information. Finally, researchers on public opinion in the twentieth century expressed reservations about the ability of the public really to understand the complexities of modern democracies and argued that it was the job of communications channels such as the media to simplify politics and government so that the public could understand and get to grips with matters of importance to them (Lippmann 1922).

The end of the nineteenth and turn of the twentieth century saw a rise in interest in the social and behavioural characteristics driving publics and public opinion, while the philosophical debates took a back seat. Particularly important in this development was the emergence of social research techniques – and in particular survey research – that enabled 'public opinion' on particular issues to be defined and quantified. This also resulted in the gradual dominance of the aggregate view of public opinion over the collective view (researching an abstract concept on the basis of concrete individual opinions made no scientific sense and so the approach had to be rejected). As a result, public opinion nowadays is interpreted most frequently as the view of the majority and we often see survey statistics in the media that suggest we all think in a particular way about a particular matter (see Activity 1.3).

As literacy levels and the media industry have expanded in modern states, the ability to quantify public opinion through research has also opened up new routes for it to be influenced. While the idea of influencing the public to cater to the interests of governments and elites is not new, the challenge to do so became more urgent in the twentieth century as a result of concerns about the public's ability to develop understanding of complex issues on the back of their own independent research (Price 1992).

---

activity 1.3

Surveys and public opinion

PR practitioners often use surveys as a means of making a particular topic newsworthy. For example, you might see an article announcing the latest findings on levels of debt incurred by students taking a degree or the amount of alcohol drunk each week by men and women in their early twenties. Take a look at the newspapers for the past two weeks and find an example of a survey that has created some 'news' about a particular topic and consider the following questions:

Q To what extent do the views expressed in the survey findings correspond to your own views?

Q How do your views differ and why do you think that might be?

Q Would you support governments or organisations taking action based on these survey findings (for example, making new laws to limit alcohol consumption or reducing student fees)? Why/Why not?

Q Has the news story changed your view of the issue being discussed? Why/Why not?

Feedback

Consider the motivations of the organisations carrying out the survey (they are usually mentioned in the news article). What motivations might they have for being associated with a particular issue? What kind of influence are they hoping to have on general views of the matter being researched?

Mass communication methods, and particularly the media, offered ready-made channels to communicate messages about such issues in a manageable format to an increasingly literate population. Public opinion became inseparable from communication and, as we will see from the case studies outlined below, PR practitioners in business and government were not slow to understand this logic and take advantage of the rapidly growing media industries to put their views across in logical and emotional forms that could influence individuals who were fundamentally open to persuasion (Ewen 1996).

Business, politics and public relations: country case studies

Wherever PR is practised, its history is tied to its social, political and economic context. This chapter outlines the history of PR in only three countries: the United States, Britain and Germany. PR practices elsewhere are shaped and constrained by the forces that caused them to emerge in the first place. Therefore, the accounts in this chapter should not be treated as a definitive history of the profession, but as case studies of countries where PR has reached a recognised level of sophistication and professionalism. Accounts of public relations in other countries have been given elsewhere and students should refer to *The Global Public Relations Handbook* (Sriramesh and Verčić 2003) for an excellent starting point. For further discussion on the international aspects of PR practice, see Chapter 7.

The United States: private interests in public opinion

Many PR textbooks written by US scholars include a brief overview of public relations history in that country (Grunig and Hunt 1984; Wilcox et al. 1992; Cutlip et al. 2000). For the most part, they focus on the role of key companies and figures including Ivy Lee, P.T. Barnum and Edward Bernays in defining the practice and techniques of PR (Cutlip 1994). In addition to these texts, Ewen (1996) provides a useful overview of the broad social context for understanding the emergence of PR in the United States.

The first widespread use of PR in the United States was in the service of politics. Cutlip et al. (2000) chart the use by American Revolutionaries during the War for Independence (1775–1782), of techniques commonly used today, including symbols, slogans, events, agenda setting (promoting certain topics

mini case study 1.1

Early US public relations in practice

During the early nineteenth century, presidential campaigns included a press secretary for the first time and there was general recognition of the need for public support of candidates if they were to be successful. In the commercial world, banks were the first to use PR to influence their publics, while later in the century large conglomerates such as Westinghouse electric corporation set up their own PR departments.

to influence the themes covered by the media) and long-term campaign development (see Mini case study 1.1).

In the late nineteenth century, recognition of the social impact of poor business practices on the working populace in the United States led to the emergence of 'progressive publicists' – individuals and groups arguing through the media for social reform in order to counter the negative effects of enterprise. Perhaps the first to recognise the need for formal publicity in order to support a cause, they couched their arguments in rational terms with the intent to appeal to public opinion and generate support for their cause. The resulting '*reform journalism*', pressing for social change, gained momentum and became a real thorn in the side of businesses.

The benefits of the reform movement depended on your perspective; business leaders regarded reform journalism as '*muckraking*', overstating the case against business and ignoring much of the social good it provided. The fear was that too much reform journalism might incite social disorder. As a result, from these very early days, businesses used communication to try and counter this tendency and establish social control by proposing and communicating ideas through the media that would unite the public and stabilise opinions (Ewen 1996). Increasing levels of literacy, combined with the advent of mass communication channels in the form of a rapidly expanding newspaper industry and new technologies such as the telegraph and wireless, meant that media relations quickly became established as a major tool for both sides of the debate.

Definition: *Reform journalism* refers to journalists who opposed the exploitation of workers for the sake of profit and pressed for social change to curb the negative effects of enterprise.

Definition: *Muckraking* is unearthing and publicising misconduct by well-known or high-ranking people or organisations.

By the turn of the century a number of individual PR consultancies had set up, catering mainly to private sector interests trying to defend themselves against the muckrakers. Clients included railroad companies, telecommunications companies, Standard Oil and companies interested in lobbying state and federal governments (Cutlip et al. 2000). Communications, largely media based, tended to be practised by organisations in crisis rather than on an ongoing basis and most businesses hired journalists to combat media on their own terms. As a result, the PR practised was predominantly press agentry (see Chapter 8), using the media to influence public opinion (Grunig and Hunt 1984).

It was in this environment that Ivy Lee emerged as the first formal and widely recognised PR practitioner. Making his mark as a publicity agent for the Pennsylvania Railroad, he argued that businesses had to build bridges to a sceptical public if they were to establish understanding and buy-in to their practices. If they did not, their legitimacy would be called into question and their operations constrained more by public opinion than by good business principles. He put this into practice by opening up communications for the Railroad and being the first to issue press releases to keep journalists up to date with events (Ewen 1996; Cutlip et al. 2000).

Lee embraced the principles of accuracy, authority and fact in communications, formalising this in his Declaration of Principles in 1906. He suggested that these principles would generate the best arguments for convincing public audiences. However, corporations were slow to adopt this level of transparency and while their communications may have been accurate in principle, their practices were still shrouded in secrecy. Indeed, Lee's definition of 'fact' was frequently interpreted by him and his employees as information that could *become* fact in the public's mind as a result of a persuasive argument. As a result, 'muckraking' and the debate over reform continued (Ewen 1996).

The importance of communication was given two additional sources of credibility at the turn of the century, both of which eventually contributed to the wider take-up of PR as a business function. First, increases in disposable income and disposable goods created a new category of public – the consumer. Consumers had a new and very personal interest in the successful functioning of business and organisations were quick to exploit the potential for uniting their consumer base through advertising and PR.

Second, social psychology emerged and gained credibility as the science of persuasion. It provided a scientific basis for the arguments in favour of using PR to create a general public 'will' by shaping press coverage of a particular issue. The underlying objective, echoing the original motives behind reform journalism, was to rationalise irrational public opinion through the power of ideas and argument.

Edward Bernays, nephew of Sigmund Freud and regarded by many as the father of modern PR, was heavily influenced by social psychology and reflected this in his two books: *Crystallizing Public Opinion* (1923) and *Propaganda* (1928). Originally an arts journalist who used his PR career as a publicist for the arts, Bernays wrote books that were practitioner focused, case study based, backed up by insights from the social sciences into how the public mind could be controlled through persuasive techniques (see Chapter 14, p. 271 on persuasion). This combination of practical tactics substantiated by scientific argument was extremely powerful and an increasing number of practitioners, many of whom had gained expertise in propaganda during the war years and subsequently joined the PR profession, were heavily influenced by his ideas (Ewen 1996).

Bernays and Lee were not the only influential practitioners at this time: Theodore Roosevelt's sophisticated use of the press during his presidential campaigns left a significant legacy for subsequent political PR practice, while Henry Ford, Samuel Insull and Theodore Vail all implemented impressive public relations strategies for the motor, electricity and telecommunications industries (Cutlip et al. 2000).

By the 1930s, commercial, non-commercial entities and government routinely implemented PR strategies, and their popularity was enhanced by the multiplication of outlets as the newspaper industry expanded and commercial radio started broadcasting. Techniques became more sophisticated as social research, which neatly divided populations into manageable groups with predictable characteristics, enabled specific targeting of communications. Increasingly, images were combined with words to increase the emotional pull of rational arguments, an important aspect of communication that continues today (Ewen 1996).

However, the advent of the Depression in the 1930s, when millions of Americans lost their jobs and savings, again called into question the ethics of business and the degree of social good it provided. The myth of a prosperous America full of happy consumers belied the reality experienced by hundreds of thousands of normal American families forced onto the breadline. Perhaps not surprisingly, businesses communicated much less vigorously during this period – but it was not the end of PR. Under the leadership of President Franklin D. Roosevelt, the federal government used communications to promote recovery strategies including social enterprise. Roosevelt focused strongly on personal communication, integrating strategic messages with the power of charismatic and credible leadership – a highly persuasive technique.

The result was a shift in public opinion towards an ethos of social good – a movement that businesses quickly realised they had to align themselves with to remain credible in light of such economic hardship. For the first time, companies joined together in industry associations and societies, in order to generate stronger and more unified messages promoting social progress as a result of free enterprise. Business, it was argued, was inherently in the public interest. Perhaps the most obvious demonstration of this was at the World Fair in 1939, which included representatives from all types of businesses, symbolised democracy and forged an idealistic link between business and the greater public good. The advent of the Second World War helped the business sector to recover further from the Depression and reinforce its positive image (Ewen 1996).

During the Second World War, PR was used widely by the armed forces and emerged as the discipline that could promote American interests and identity overseas. Wartime PR also made extensive use of advertising to generate popular support for the conflict, a combination still used today in marketing and communications strategies.

In the immediate aftermath of war, the overall theme of commercial PR remained welfare capitalism, rather than unfettered free enterprise. However, the origins of PR as an essentially manipulative discipline were never far away, despite this apparent nod to public interest. In 1955, Bernays published *The Engineering of Consent*, underpinning PR as a discipline that could shape and mould public opinion, rather than engage and have a dialogue with individual groups. Television, the ultimate visual medium with a correspondingly large capacity to influence viewers on an emotional level, increased the level of commercial interest in mass media and the manipulation of opinion once more dominated the PR industry.

In subsequent years, the PR industry was characterised by an increasing number of associations

TABLE 1.1   Key publications in the early years of American public relations

Author	Title	Year
Ivy Lee	*Declaration of Principles*	1906
Edward Bernays	*Crystallizing Public Opinion*	1923
Edward Bernays	*Propaganda*	1928
Rex Harlow	*Public Relations Journal*	1944
Edward Bernays	*The Engineering of Consent*	1955

promoting sector-based interests, the consolidation of the consultancy industry, increasing amounts of literature, including the first *Public Relations Journal*, established in 1944 by PR baron Rex Harlow, and academic training for the profession. Harlow was also a key figure in the establishment of the Public Relations Society of America in 1947. Table 1.1 shows key historical publications in American PR.

Britain: public interest in private opinions

While commercial interests adopted and drove the development of PR in the United States, it was the public sector, and local government in particular, that was the driving force behind the early use of PR in Britain (see Chapter 30). As noted in the introduction, little has been written about the history of PR in Britain, with the exception of Jacquie L'Etang's (2004b) professional history. Her book forms the basis for much of the discussion that follows.

In the same way as the business sector in the United States began to use public relations as a means of protecting itself against attacks from the reformists, local governments in Britain found themselves looking to PR techniques to reinforce the importance of their role in the face of potential central government cutbacks during the 1920s and 1930s. Local communities and businesses did not understand what the role of local government was and regarded it as a bureaucratic irritant rather than a valuable service. As a result, the focus of much early PR in Britain was on the presentation of facts to persuade the public – genuine truths about what local government contributed to the public good. It was assumed that the power of truth would persuade both the public and central government to be more supportive of local officials and policies. As early as 1922, the local government trade union, the National Association of Local Government Officials (NALGO), recommended that all local councils include a press or publicity division in their makeup (L'Etang 2004b).

While central government did not make so much use of communications strategies in peacetime, the development of PR was also closely linked to the use of propaganda during the two world wars. Truth, here, was not so critical but its sacrifice

---

box 1.1   Documentary film in UK public relations

Documentary film was one of the most popular forms of both internal and external communication in both the public sector and corporations between the 1930s and the late 1970s. Under the influence of Stephen Tallents, state-sponsored film units were attached to the Empire Marketing Board, the Post Office (GPO), the Ministry of Information during the Second World War and, following the war, the Central Office of Information. One of the most famous documentaries of this early period was *Night Mail* (1936) made for the GPO, scripted by the poet W.H. Auden and with music composed by Benjamin Britten. The nationalisation of key industries after the war led to other public sector film units being set up for internal training and external promotion. Examples of these are British Transport Films (BTF) and the National Coal Board Film Unit.

Corporate film units were connected to Dunlop and ICI, but it is the Shell Oil Film Unit that is regarded as one of the most celebrated of the Documentary Movement. The films were often released into cinemas and while many were indirectly related to the company's activities (Shell's first film was *Airport* (1934)), the themes were more general, thus exerting a subtle influence on the public. Another group of films made by the Shell Oil Film Unit were educational and unrelated to oil. These films covered topics such as traditional rural crafts, the evolution of paint and the environment. When film was replaced by video in the 1980s, Shell continued as one of the key players in the audio-visual communications industry.

Source: adapted from www.screenonline.org.uk/film/id/964488/index.html (British Film Institute)

mini case study 1.2

Basil Clarke – Britain's first public relations consultant?

Basil Clarke was a former *Daily Mail* journalist who founded his own consultancy, Editorial Services, in 1926, following a career in several government ministries where he directed public information. Editorial Services was founded jointly with two practising consultants, R.J. Sykes of London Press Exchange (LPE) and James Walker of Winter Thomas. Basil Clarke is credited by some as the 'father' of PR in Britain, partly because of his government track record and partly because he drafted the Institute of Public Relations' first code of practice.

Source: L'Etang 2004a

was justified in light of the need to win at all costs. The need to unite a population under one cause did create opportunities to persuade using other messages and means. One of these was the British Documentary Film Movement, inspired by John Grierson, who focused on using film to educate the public on matters of public interest. Visual communications were thus used to present 'truth', in the form of a rational argument, in a compelling fashion (L'Etang 2004b). See also Box 1.1 (p.11).

The propaganda industry during both world wars spawned many post-war practitioners, individuals seeking a new profession in a world where propaganda was no longer required. In addition, many wartime journalists were left jobless once peace broke out and frequently went into PR. In the years following the Second World War, the commercial sector in Britain woke up to the possibilities of communication and the industry started to expand more rapidly. Almost 50 years after the first US consultancies, the first UK consultancies were established and in-house practitioners in commercial organisations became much more common (L'Etang 2004b). See Mini case study 1.2.

Perhaps because of the early influence of public sector bureaucracy, PR practitioners were quick to organise themselves as a group in Britain, first under the auspices of the Institute of Public Administration and subsequently as an independent Institute of Public Relations (IPR). The IPR was established in 1948 under the leadership of Sir Stephen Tallents – a career civil servant and a keen supporter of publicity and propaganda from his tenure as Secretary of the Empire Marketing Board in the 1920s and 1930s, where he used communications to promote the reputation of the British Empire and its products among its trading partners. As the first Public Relations Officer in Britain, he joined the Post Office in 1933 and then moved to the BBC in 1935. Throughout his professional life, he used the widest range of tools at his disposal to promote the interests of his employer to the public, including radio, telegraph, film and, of course, newspapers. He was also a strong advocate for recognition of the publicity role

as a profession in itself, with a specific and unique skills base. This was reflected in the Institute's immediate role as a lobbying body to encourage recognition of PR as a separate profession (L'Etang 2004b).

The IPR also served as a body through which practitioners could share their expertise and establish standards for their rapidly expanding number. The vast majority of its founding members came from the public sector and subsequently set up the first interest group within the Institute, focusing in particular on the need to recognise PR as an important role in local government (L'Etang 2004b).

This early institutionalisation of the profession means that, in many ways, the presentation of PR in Britain has been heavily influenced by the efforts of the IPR as the industry body. Key themes emerging from early years of PR practice have permeated the approach taken by the Institute, including: the importance of truth as the 'ideal' PR tool; the conception of PR as a public service; and the potential for PR to be used as a means for promoting freedom, democracy and, in particular, the British way of life – this last being particularly influenced by institutions such as the British Council using PR in this way. In addition, the IPR conceptualised PR very broadly, specifically extending the definition of communications beyond pure media relations (L'Etang 2004b).

The emergence of PR consultancies in the 1950s, often based on editorial services and media liaison, confirmed the existence of PR as a distinct profession, separate from its cousins marketing and propaganda – although these boundaries were often blurred. Indeed, although the IPR was intent on maintaining a broad conception of communications in its definition of the profession, the reality was that the ex-journalists entering the profession could provide a unique, easily identifiable service on the back of their media expertise that did not overlap with advertising or other marketing disciplines and therefore served the profession well.

The IPR, dominated by in-house and public sector practitioners, had difficulty catering to the specific interests of independent consultancies. One particular concern included the maintenance of professional standards and reputation across a wide range of small organisations. In light of this, a specific consultancy association, the Society of Independent Public Relations Consultants (SIPRC), was created in 1960 and worked closely with the IPR. However, the SIPRC itself was poorly defined and eventually folded. Subsequently, in 1969, the Public Relations Consultants Association was set up and still exists alongside the IPR today (L'Etang 2004b).

By the 1970s, then, the British PR industry had established itself as an identifiable body with a national institute and increasing numbers of practitioners. Standards of practice, areas of competence and the range of services provided were all discussed and developed. With this institutional basis in place, the next phase of development was driven by commercial interests. A rapid expansion, particularly in the consultancy sector, took place in the 1980s and continued in the 1990s. It was initially driven by deregulation and privatisation programmes for state-owned companies under the Conservative government during the 1980s.

Deregulation opened up opportunities for private sector operators in two ways: first, as consultants to lucrative public sector accounts such as the NHS and, second, as professional lobbyists on behalf of the bidding companies (Miller and Dinan 2000). Privatisation during the 1980s and early 1990s of national utilities, including oil, gas, water and telecommunications, prompted extensive use of public relations consultants by government departments. Persuading the public to buy shares in the new companies required more than standard Government Information Service briefings to standard media. Sophisticated techniques were needed to create sound marketing strategies, build public perceptions of the value of the opportunity and then persuade them actually to buy shares in the new companies (Miller and Dinan 2000; Pitcher 2003).

These programmes were highly successful: by the early 1990s and the completion of the privatisation programmes, 12 million members of the British public owned shares (Pitcher 2003). Media headlines were generally positive and company reputations began on a high. The newly privatised companies were the first to recognise the value of PR and continued the use of consultancies after their initial flotation (Miller and Dinan 2000).

The knock-on effects of this for the financial sector were considerable. From now on, listed companies had to communicate with the general public as well as with the privileged few who had previously made up their target audience. Communications had to be simpler and reach a wider range of people. In-house practitioners – if there were any – turned to consultants for support and the new specialism of investor relations was born (Miller and Dinan 2000; Pitcher 2003).

Deregulation of professions such as law and accounting, as well as the financial services industry, also created new opportunities for the PR industry by prompting the companies concerned to market themselves and communicate directly with their customers. For most, the concept of talking to the 'man in the street' was unknown and the newly expert PR consultancies were able to provide valuable support and advice (Miller and Dinan 2000). Increasing numbers of mergers and acquisitions in these new markets have underpinned the growth of PR during the last two decades, with communications strategies often the deciding factor between success or failure (Davis 2000; Miller and Dinan 2000).

The growth in PR that these processes prompted eased off in the early 1990s, but the social and economic environment continued to encourage PR activity. The 1980s had seen the (right of centre) Conservative government consistently emphasise the virtue of individual rights over community responsibilities – home ownership rather than council tenancy, share ownership rather than taxes. By the end of the decade, this mentality had become embedded in Britain; private interests were automatically regarded as superior to social concerns. In this environment, PR was used by groups and individuals to justify their decisions by making their voices heard above the general cacophony of the market (Moloney 2000).

The key characteristics of this evolution are reflected in the nature of PR in Britain today, particularly in the debates around PR's use of truth, the ethics and morality of the profession, the justification for using PR in terms of mutual benefit rather than one-sided advantage and the ongoing blurring of boundaries between marketing, propaganda and PR. Moreover, the fluidity of movement between journalism and PR has also given rise to the ongoing relationship between the two professions – there is plenty of antagonism despite the symbiotic relationship. Also of interest are the contrasts with the United States, where commercial interests drove an early and clear focus on the principles of free enterprise, situating private sector PR clearly in the capitalist arena. Federal government use of communications during the Depression and two world wars also helped establish the legitimacy of PR and, combined, these factors resulted in much faster development of the formality, size and sophistication of the profession than was the case in Britain.

Germany: industrialists, politics and critique

As with most countries outside the United States, information on the development of the PR industry in Germany is not widely available. Baerns (2000) and Nessmann (2000) offer the most comprehensive overviews so far. PR-type activities in Germany emerged considerably earlier than in the United States or Britain and was accompanied by critical analysis from social commentators suspicious of its potential to dominate public communication. The dynamics that led to its emergence were similar to those elsewhere: industrialisation; new forms of technology; increasing democracy and literacy; urbanisation; and the emergence of the mass media (Nessmann 2000).

Nessmann (2000) argues that PR as an activity first emerged in Germany in the early eighteenth century, although it was not formally termed PR until the mid-twentieth century. Practical applications of media relations can be seen with the systematic news office of Frederick the Great (1712–1886), Napoleon's mobile printing press that he used to circulate favourable stories about his military campaigns and his practice of monitoring foreign news coverage to check how his image was developing abroad. State media relations can be traced back to 1807, while in the mid-nineteenth century German industrialists were already recognising the importance of the views of the general public as well as of their own employees as sources of social legitimacy in the rapidly industrialising economy (see Mini case study 1.3).

The German state also cottoned on relatively early to the value of PR, with a press department set up in the Foreign Ministry in 1871, the Navy commissioning its own press officers in 1894 and the first municipal press office set up in Magdeburg in 1906 (Nessmann 2000).

From an academic perspective, this early development of PR practice was accompanied from the mid-nineteenth century by an increasingly critical view of PR among academics, as an exploitative medium used primarily by political and commercial groups, even as the need for it as a source of legitimacy for such organisations was also acknowledged. At around the same time, a debate emerged in relation to the German media, about the separation of clearly labelled advertising materials from unbiased editorial contributions (Baerns 2000). This debate revolved around the need for the press to retain its credibility by separating advertising from journalism, so that its legitimacy as an information-carrying channel for the general public could be sustained. In fact, the debate continues today and Baerns (2000: 245) points out that as recently as the 1990s, the German press council issued guidelines that stated: 'The credibility of the press as a source of information demands particular care in dealing with public relations texts.' While Baerns points out that these statements have not necessarily led to a black and white distinction between advertising, PR materials and 'pure' journalism in the modern media, the existence of the debate does highlight the cultural dynamics that frame PR practice in Germany.

As in the United States and Britain, the First World War brought with it new opportunities for press relations and propaganda by the state and this growth in the practice and understanding of the discipline led to a corresponding flourishing of the profession in the post-war years. During the Third Reich, however, the sophistication of new PR techniques was relegated to the back seat while Adolf Hitler promoted the use of propaganda techniques and press censorship to cement his regime.

The term PR finally came into general use in the 1950s, when the influence of the American occupation in West Germany resulted in both linguistic and practical adoption of the term and its modern practice. Germany's professional PR associations were founded in this post-war period and the industry once again expanded rapidly in the newly democratic state.

mini case study 1.3

The first public relations stunt

In 1851, German steelmaker Krupp executed what was perhaps the first PR 'stunt' when it transported a two-ton block of steel to the Great Exhibition in London, an effort that generated significant publicity and recognition for the company across the world. Krupp remained at the forefront of communicative efforts among German industrialists, along with other conglomerates including Siemens, Henkel, Bahlsen and AEG. Each recognised the value of media relations, circulating reports about their activities to the media on a regular basis, while Krupp established the first formal press office in a German company in 1893.

Summary

The histories presented here highlight the social nature of PR. It is a profession that applies the value of communication to situations where it is required. In the United States, the private sector has been the most active force driving the development of the profession, while in Britain, first the public then the private sector have resulted in the industry we see today. In other countries such as Germany, different cultural and social dynamics affect the practice, popularity and implementation of communications and will shape the PR industry in different ways.

Perhaps because communications techniques can be so widely applied, definitions of PR are various. While the general principles of using relationship management and dialogue in order to exert influence on target audiences are evident in most definitions, controversy exists about other aspects of the profession – such as reputation management – and whether they are core to its practice. These debates are unlikely to disappear in the near future. Whether they relate to the relative youth of the profession, the fast changing world in which it operates and the correspondingly rapid changes in the demands made on it, or simply the complexity of the practice itself, the reality is that the social nature of PR will always mean that it differs from one context to the next. Practitioners need to establish the principles that are most appropriate in their personal and professional situation and operate accordingly. The chapters in this book outline some of the issues that they will need to consider: personal and professional ethics, the sector in which they operate, the specialism they choose and the audiences they target.

Bibliography

Baerns, B. (2000). 'Public relations and the development of the principle of separation of advertising and journalistic media programmes in Germany' in *Perspectives on Public Relations Research*. D. Moss, D. Verčić and G. Warnaby. London: Routledge.

Bernays, E. (1923). *Crystallizing Public Opinion*. New York: Boni and Livenight.

Bernays, E. (1928). *Propaganda*. New York: H. Liveright.

Bernays, E. (1955). *The Engineering of Consent*. Norman, OK: University of Oklahoma Press.

Botan, C.H. and V. Hazelton (1989). *Public Relations Theory*. Hillsdale, NJ: Lawrence Erlbaum Associates.

Cutlip, S.M. (1994). *Public Relations: The unseen power. A history*. Hillsdale, NJ: Lawrence Erlbaum Associates.

Cutlip, S.M., A.H. Center and G.M. Broom (2000). *Effective Public Relations;* 8th edition. Upper Saddle River, NJ: Prentice Hall.

Davis, A. (2000). 'Public relations, business news and the reproduction of corporate power'. *Journalism* **1**(3): 282–304.

Department of Trade and Industry and Institute of Public Relations (2003). *Unlocking the Potential of Public Relations: Developing good practice*. London: European Centre for Business Excellence.

Ewen, S. (1996). *PR! A Social History of Spin*. New York: Basic Books.

Genasi, C. (2002). *Winning Reputations: How to be your own spin doctor*. Basingstoke: Palgrave.

Gordon, J.C. (1997). 'Interpreting definitions of public relations: Self assessment and a symbolic interactionism-based alternative'. *Public Relations Review* **23**(1): 57–66.

Gregory, A. (1996). *Public Relations in Practice*. London: Kogan Page.

Grunig, J.E. (1992). *Excellence in Public Relations and Communication Management*. Hillsdale, NJ: Lawrence Erlbaum Associates.

Grunig, J.E. and L.A. Grunig (2000). 'Public relations in strategic management and strategic management of public relations: theory and evidence from the IABC excellence project'. *Journalism Studies* **1**(2): 303–321.

Grunig, J.E. and T. Hunt (1984). *Managing Public Relations*. New York: Holt, Rinehart & Winston.

Harlow, R.F. (1976). 'Building a definition of public relations'. *Public Relations Review* **2**(4).

Harrison, S. (2000). *Public Relations: An introduction*. London: Thomson Learning.

Hutton, J.G. (1999). 'The definition, dimensions and domain of public relations'. *Public Relations Review* **25**(2): 199–214.

Institute of Public Relations (2004). *What is Public Relations?* London: Institute of Public Relations.

Kitchen, P.J. (1997). *Public Relations: Principles and practice*. London: International Thomson Business Press.

L'Etang, J. (1996). 'Public relations as diplomacy' in *Critical Perspectives in Public Relations*. J. L'Etang and M. Piezcka. London: International Thomson Business Press.

L'Etang, J. (2004a). 'Public relations and democracy' in *Handbook of Corporate Communication and Public Relations: Pure and applied*. S.M. Oliver. London: Routledge.

L'Etang, J. (2004b). *Public Relations in Britain: A history of professional practice in the 20th century*. Mahwah, NJ: Lawrence Erlbaum Associates.

Lippmann, W. (1922). *Public Opinion*. New York: Harcourt Brace Jovanovich.

Miller, D. and W. Dinan (2000). 'The rise of the PR industry in Britain 1979–98'. *European Journal of Communication* **15**(1): 5–35.

Moloney, K. (2000). *Rethinking Public Relations: The spin and the substance*. London: Routledge.

Nessmann, K. (2000). 'The origins and development of public relations in Germany and Austria' in *Perspectives on Public Relations Research*. D. Moss, D. Verćić and G. Warnaby. London: Routledge.

Newsom, D., J.V. Turk and A. Scott (2000). *This is PR*. Belmont, CA: Wadsworth.

Pieczka, M. (1996). 'Public opinion and public relations' in *Critical Perspectives in Public Relations*. J. L'Etang and M. Pieczka. London: International Thomson Business Press.

Pitcher, G. (2003). *The Death of Spin*. Chichester: John Wiley & Sons.

Price, V. (1992). *Public Opinion*. Newbury Park, CA: Sage.

Public Relations Consultants Association (2004). 'What is PR?' London: Public Relations Consultants Association.

Public Relations Society of America (2004). *About Public Relations*. New York: Public Relations Society of America.

Sriramesh, K. and D. Verćić (2003). *The Global Public Relations Handbook*. Mahwah, NJ: Lawrence Erlbaum Associates.

White, J. and L. Mazur (1996). *Strategic Communications Management: Making public relations work*. Harlow: Addison-Wesley.

Wilcox, D.L., P.H. Ault and W.K. Agee (1992). *Public Relations: Strategies and tactics*. New York: Harper-Collins.

CHAPTER 2
Management and organisation of public relations

Introduction

The way each organisation manages, structures and undertakes its public relations activity is unique; that is because every organisation is unique. A single-issue pressure group has a focused purpose and its range of target publics is often very specific. A large government department, such as the UK's Department of Health, touches the lives of every citizen in a variety of ways, from prenatal ultrasound scanning to childhood and adult illnesses, through to terminal care. Some business enterprises operate in tiny niche markets in one country while others operate in numerous markets on a global scale.

Public relations is used by some organisations in a very narrow way, typically to support sales and marketing activity. An example is a small business promoting its menus, prices and opening hours to students through the local media. Other organisations use public relations in a whole host of ways, for example, a large retailer such as Wal-Mart will develop relationship programmes with financial analysts, government officials and politicians, the local community, employees, consumers and suppliers.

Sometimes public relations is a stand-alone function; sometimes it is located within marketing or human resources. A number of large enterprises now have their senior public relations person on the board with all other communication disciplines, including marketing reporting to them.

Public relations also operates under a number of guises: corporate communication, corporate affairs, public affairs, communication management, public relations, reputation management ... the list seems to expand almost every year.

This chapter examines the range of factors that influence the way public relations is managed and organised in different types of organisation. It also points to some current societal and regulatory developments which will affect the way public relations is conducted in the future – a future that is full of opportunity and growth.

Importance of context

Organisations do not exist in isolation. Business history is littered with companies that did not spot changing industry trends quickly enough and adapt – Olivetti used to make superb typewriters, but where is it now? Other companies such as Nike and McDonald's have been held to account by activist groups over their production activities in the developing world; activism is now a part of modern life in developed societies.

Public relations means what the words imply. It is about the relationships organisations have with various publics, both internal and external. Those publics comprise people who are, in turn, affected by developments and trends in society. The environment in which organisations operate is dynamic. Society is changing: new issues and trends arise, some of them very quickly. For example, corporate social responsibility was not such a well-recognised issue for many large organisations even 10 years ago (see Chapters 6 and 18).

Similarly, organisations themselves are changing. The workforce is different – for example, there are more women and part-time workers – and attitudes are different. Because people are empowered in their lives outside work, for example, in having more choices about where they live and the lifestyles they lead, they are no longer willing to remain disempowered at work (Smythe 2004). Furthermore, organisations are much more accountable to external publics who want to know what they stand for, how they conduct themselves and the impact they have on society and the environment.

Given the critical role that public relations has in 'establish(ing) and maintain(ing) goodwill and mutual understanding between an organisation and its publics' (CIPR 2004), it is clear that careful consideration has to be given to both the external and internal contexts in which it operates. This will, of course, vary between different organisations, depending on the nature of their business, their size, their sphere of operation and their culture.

External environment

The external environment is vitally important for organisations because it determines the future. Smart organisations constantly scan the external environment to identify emerging issues. Having spotted these issues early, precious time is bought for the organisation to adjust itself to those issues, to engage with them and to influence their development.

The external environment can be divided into two main areas: the 'macro' and the 'task' environment.

Macro environment

This environment might be described as containing the 'big picture' issues over which the organisation has no control. These are the issues that emerge from the actions of governments, economic and societal trends and from scientific and technological developments. Sometimes called the 'remote' or 'societal' environment, the macro environment originates beyond, and

PICTURE 2.1 Public relations activity ranges from consumer and business to business sales support to government communications during times of conflict such as war. The 'allied forces' commander at a press conference in Kabul, Afghanistan. (*Source:* Syed Jan Sabawoon/EPA Photos.)

Political	Economic
Employment legislation Trade legislation Change of government Political alliances between nations	Interest rates Levels of employment Value of the currency Energy costs
Social	**Technological**
Lifestyle changes Social attitudes Demographic changes Purchasing habits	New technologies Access to technology Cost of research and development Impact of new technologies on work practices

FIGURE 2.1   Example of a PEST analysis

usually irrespective of, any single organisation's operating situation (Steyn and Puth 2000).

To make sense of this, environmental analysts examine the macro environment under a series of headings. The most well-known analytical tool is PEST, which segments the overall environment into four topic areas – **P**olitical, **E**conomic, **S**ocial and **T**echnological. Figure 2.1 presents some examples of subjects that could come under each of these areas. What is important about these subjects is the impact they might have on existing relationships or what they reveal about the need to develop a relationship. The identification of these subjects could present public relations issues for an organisation (see Chapter 19 for further discussion).

Increasingly, the limitations of PEST fail to do justice to the complex modern environment. An extension of PEST is EPISTLE, which includes the four existing elements of PEST, but also gives consideration to **I**nformation, **L**egal and the green **E**nvironment. The 'information' heading invites special consideration for its ability to empower people via new technologies, although it must be remembered that people who are deprived of relevant information will become disenfranchised and unable to engage in debate effectively. The legal environment is becoming increasingly complex. Organisations need to be aware not only of national regulations, but also of transnational legislation such as EU law. Furthermore, non-binding but moral undertakings carried out by nations such as the Kyoto Agreement often lead to national protocols. The green environment is the cause of increasing concern and no analysis of the macro environment would be complete without reference to environmental concerns.

Clearly, different organisations will be impacted in different ways by these macro issues. An arms manufacturer will be very susceptible to political shifts (e.g. arms export bans to particular countries) and a clothes manufacturer needs to be acutely aware of social trends (e.g. consumer preferences based on changing lifestyles). However, a careful eye needs to be kept on all areas because they will affect the longer term issues that organisations, and therefore public relations, will need to address.

It is important to understand trends emerging from the political, economic, technological and social environments and how these various trends interact with each other. While there are literally hundreds of issues and trends in the wider environment, it is worth picking out a few for special mention. The themes of globalisation, information, pluralism and consumerism/individualism and, of course, the news media, are selected here because of their relevance to public relations.

Globalisation

Public relations people who work for global organisations will understand the need to communicate across timelines, cultures, languages and different communication delivery systems. But even if the organisation is local, what it does may have global impacts and attract global attention. A local clothes store may buy stock from an intermediary who is supplied by a manufacturer who damages the environment in a developing country.

Organisations also need to be sensitive about what they put on their website for national audiences, as websites may be accessed by people from other cultures who may take great offence at what is said – for example, encouragement to drink alcohol may offend cultures where alcohol is frowned on.

Information and information technology

This is connected to the theme of globalisation. The fact that information can be sent and accessed immediately across time and geographical boundaries brings great opportunities, but also can provide threats for the professional communicator. Activists can organise quickly and misinformation can spread worldwide at the click of a mouse. Contrariwise, organisations can engage with stakeholders in innovative ways. They can provide information instantly and research topics thoroughly without relying on physical information resources such as reference libraries. All this bring pressures for organisations and communicators that need to be geared for action 24/7 (24 hours a day, seven days a week). See Mini case study 2.1, overleaf.

It also needs to be remembered that there are still many communities that do not have access to these technologies, which also need to be catered for (see Chapter 25 and, in particular, the debate surrounding the 'digital divide').

mini case study 2.1

Asian tsunami disaster

The tsunami in the Indian Ocean struck on 26 December 2004, the day after Christmas Day in Christian countries and traditionally a national holiday. When news emerged in the early morning of 26 December, the public relations staff in the US headquarters of a number of hotel chains were still in bed. They had to react quickly with few support mechanisms available. Technology meant that they could communicate relatively quickly with concerned families via websites, semi-automated helplines and email.

Pluralism

It is thought that a plural (diverse) society offers the most favourable conditions for democracy and protection against totalitarianism (Kornhauser 1960). Within a highly industrialised and urbanised society such as in Britain, for example, the merging of values and ideals, together with understanding and accepting different cultures and alternative views, are taken as a sign of advancing civilisation. But at the same time it increases uncertainty and insecurity as people question religious beliefs and authority norms. Counter to this, the rise of nationalism, fundamentalism and activism can pose a threat to these liberalising forces (Herriot and Scott-Jackson 2002). Stepping among and around the tensions involved is a great challenge for professional communicators. They have to assert or defend a particular position without offending anyone. They have to consider their role in conflict resolution and dialogue, especially if one party refuses to accept any compromise. For example, reconciling pro- and anti-abortion lobbyists can be seen as a major challenge.

> **Definition:** *Pluralism* is the idea that society comprises a diverse range of groups with different cultures and that all these groups have political and economic rights.

Consumerism and individualism

In consumer societies, people know their rights. Expectations are rising all the time and many organisations feel beleaguered by the demands placed on them. Similarly, some would say that in an attempt to replace the old certainties, people in developed societies are becoming ever more consumerist and very individualistic (Ritzer 2004). In place of church and community, they are seeking to associate with like-minded others in pursuance of their own tastes and values. The number of pressure groups, non-governmental organisations (NGOs), special interest associations and clubs of all kinds, many supported by the new technologies that facilitate global affiliations, is burgeoning.

Professional communicators have to deal with knowledgeable, assertive individuals and groups. For example, in Britain, the parents' lobby for healthier school dinners (given prominence by the celebrity chef Jamie Oliver) encouraged Prime Minister Tony Blair to make election promises to improve food quality in schools ('Blair acts on Jamie's plan for schools', *The Observer* 20 March 2005, Gaby Hinsliff and Amelia Hill). This promise, in turn, will affect the food industry – particularly those companies associated with pre-packaged 'fast' food. Companies that are actively monitoring the consumer environment will be prepared for widespread change in public opinion against fast food.

News media

The news media, comprising newspapers and broadcast channels, have been revolutionised over the last few years (see also Chapter 4). Global news businesses owned by powerful groups and individuals, often with their own political agendas, are setting the political backdrop and leading public opinion in a way that simply was not the case in the last century (Hargreaves 2003). Furthermore, the demand for 24/7 news, along with the increasing amounts of space that journalists have to cover without a matching increase in personnel, means that the media are becoming increasingly dependent on sources with their own biases – often public relations professionals. An environment where 'PRisation of the media' (Moloney 2000) is becoming more prevalent could be regarded as advantageous for the public relations industry. But is that good for the public interest? Some would say (e.g. Gregory 2003) that the press should be free to challenge vested interests and that there should be a distance between public relations people and journalists. For example, it is suggested that in the financial area the relationships between financial public relations specialists and journalists are too cosy and the media have not been as challenging of some corporate activities as they should be because they are dependent on key public relations sources for their information (Rampton and Stauber 1995). See Think about 2.1.

What other macro or global trends do you think are important? What might be the implications for public relations professionals? How might you communicate with rural communities in developing countries that do not have access to the internet or mobile phones?

Feedback For further details of global trends read J. Naisbitt and P. Aburdene (1991) *Megatrends 2000*, London: Pan with Sidgwick and Jackson. Also '*think-tanks*' such as Demos and research companies, for instance MORI, undertake futures research in a range of subjects.

Definition: A '*think-tank*' is an organisation made up of experts who undertake research and provide advice to governments.

Task environment

Apart from the links to the macro external environment, organisations are also affected by things closer to home, termed the 'task environment'. These factors are more within their control and usually relate to groups of individuals (publics) who have quite definable characteristics, such as customers or shareholders.

Esman (1972) has divided those publics into four categories that are characterised by their relationship with an organisation (see Figure 2.2).

The following may help to explain how these linkages work:

■ *Enabling* linkages connect the organisation to those who have the power and resources to allow it to exist.
■ *Functional* linkages either provide some kind of input to the organisation or consume its outputs.
■ *Normative* linkages are to peer organisations.
■ *Diffused* linkages are to those who have no formal relationship with the organisation, but may take an interest in it.

Chapter 12 gives more detail on the nature of publics, but it is worth making the point here that there has been a shift away from the idea of the organisation as an autonomous monolith accountable to no-one but its shareholders (as espoused by

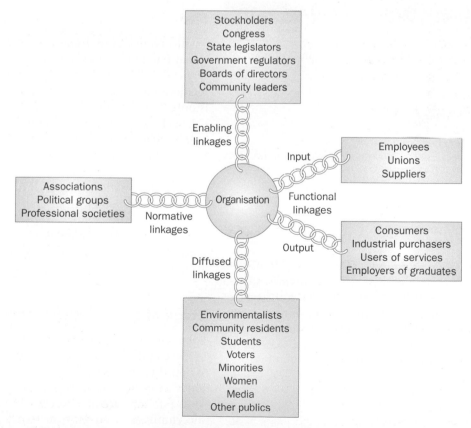

FIGURE 2.2   Esman's organisational relationship linkages (*source:* Grunig and Hunt 1984: 141)

Friedman 1970) towards the notion of organisations as stakeholding communities. Freeman (1984) first articulated this in a systematic way, arguing that organisations were defined by the relationship they had with their stakeholders. Stakeholders are not just those groups that management believe to have a legitimate interest in the organisation, but those groups who decide for themselves that they will take a stake in the organisation. The actions of activist groups have made this a living reality for many organisations. For example, in Britain, Huntingdon Life Sciences is a firm that breeds animals for experiments. The premises have been lobbied by activist groups for many years, to the point where special security measures have had to be taken, both for the property and for employees, some of whom have been seriously threatened with violence and had their own cars and homes damaged.

Stakeholding theory has itself progressed. In the 1990s the idea of the corporate community emerged and in the new century, Halal (2000) encouraged organisations to recognise that stakeholders can collaborate with them in problem solving. The role of the organisation is to pull together the economic resources, political support and special knowledge of all stakeholding groups (see Activity 2.1).

---

activity 2.1

Stakeholding

Who are the stakeholders for a university? How would you describe the linkages between a university and its:

- students
- lecturers
- administrators
- governors
- local communities
- local and central government education departments?

Internal environment

As well as being profoundly affected by external factors, the way communication is organised is shaped by the nature of the enterprise itself and the type of operation it undertakes. The kind of enterprise will determine the balance of public relations activities and their relative priority. Here are just some of the factors that should be considered.

Sector

If the organisation is located in a stable, well-established industry sector such as furniture manufacturing, it is likely that pre-planned and sustained public relations

activity can be maintained. Fast growing and turbulent sectors such as IT will require quick, *reactive*, as well as proactive, programmes. That is not to say that activity should not be planned, but an inbuilt capability to react to the fast moving market is a key requirement.

> **Definition:** *Reactive* denotes the need sometimes for a quick response to an issue or crisis. It can also describe public relations activity that is driven by the demands of others rather than the plans of the communicators.
> Proactive allows for a more planned approach, where there is time available.

Different sectors require different types of programme. The emphasis in the confectionary sector is likely to be in marketing communication, whereas local authority work is more likely to focus on community involvement. Furthermore, work for a government department, indeed any work for the public or not-for-profit sector, requires communication professionals to be aware of the need for accountability to the public who pay taxes. Work in the private sector means that shareholders and the profit motive are significant and this creates different priorities for communication.

Size

Small organisations usually have small, multifunctional public relations departments. Public relations services could even be totally outsourced to a public relations consultancy. It may be, that public relations is only part of the responsibilities of a single individual, such as a sales, marketing or general office manager. Such individuals may be part of the management team and their activities will be seen as critical to the success of the organisation.

Large organisations may well have large public relations departments with several public relations specialists taking on a whole raft of activities. They may or may not work in standalone public relations departments and they may or may not be part of management.

Stage of organisational development

Public relations activity is often dictated by the stage of development that the organisation has reached. When the organisation is at *startup* stage, most suppliers, customers and employees will be well known. Thus public relations effort is often face to face and the emphasis is on growth. Hence marketing communications, which is aimed at supporting the sales of goods and services (see 'Public relations tasks' section later, p.29) will be very important.

When companies reach maturity, it is probable that they will undertake the full range of public relations activity. Offering public shares in the company may be under consideration, which will require financial public relations. The organisation may want to influence government regulation affecting its sector or processes, in which case it may engage a public affairs consultancy (see Chapter 23). It will probably want a strong corporate identity and may have a well-developed corporate social responsibility (CSR) programme including active community relations (see Chapters 6 and 18 for more on CSR and community relations activities). See Table 2.1 (overleaf) for public relations activity structure at various points in an organisation's lifecycle.

Culture

One of the most significant influences in determining how the public relations function is organised is the culture of an organisation. There are many definitions of *organisational culture* but a commonly articulated view is that it is 'the set of conscious and unconscious beliefs and values, and the patterns of behaviour (including language and symbol use) that provide identity and form a framework of meaning for a group of people' (McCollom 1994, cited in Eisenberg and Riley 2001, pp. 306–7). Culture, in other words, is a shorthand term for ways in which people think and behave within an organisation. Leaders of organisations, too, can make a difference, in that they can attempt to define and shape *corporate culture* – how they want people to think and behave. Leaders, in turn, will be affected by their *national cultures*, which will have specific characteristics – for example, strong individualism has been identified as a characteristic of American culture (Hofstede 1991). (Chapter 17, which focuses on internal communication, goes into culture in more detail, but it is also important to mention it here.)

As a broad generalisation, most successful private sector organisations tend to be *entrepreneurial,* whereas many public sector organisations are *systematised* (Grunig and Grunig 1992). No value judgements are being made here – the culture is driven by the nature of the organisation and the job of work that needs to be done. Business enterprises have to make money in a competitive environment. Their public relations functions will tend to be proactive, seeking to exploit competitive advantage and supporting the profit-making activities in the firm.

Public sector organisations are characterised by a service mission. They are usually social enterprises concerned with supporting the lives of citizens. Making money is not their priority, although they need to demonstrate that they spend it wisely in the service of the community. They react to the requirements of their publics and act in predictable, dependable ways. Their public relations departments are often concerned with providing information or engaging their publics in dialogue, therefore a systematised and interactive mode of operation is appropriate (see Chapter 30).

However, it would be a mistake to think that public bodies are never entrepreneurial in character, whatever their mission. There is some highly creative and proactive work in the public sector as evidenced by the numerous awards they win (see www.cipr.uk/ lgg/index.htm). Equally it would be a mistake to assume that all successful private sector organisations are unbureaucratic: the banking industry is a good example of bureaucratic organisation.

From all the foregoing it can be seen that both external and internal influences are critical to the way public relations is organised. Yet, it can be observed that there is often little systematic review of these factors. Public relations structures are often placed in a particular location in the organisation at a point in time and remain there until there is a major, normally externally driven, incident, such as a crisis, that prompts a radical review of public relations' worth and position (Gregory and Edwards 2004). See Activity 2.2.

---

activity 2.2

Different organisations

Research two organisations within the same sector that appear to you to have different characters. Why are they so different? Sectors that provide useful organisational comparisons are:

- the motor industry, e.g. Volvo and BMW
- clothes retailing, e.g. TopShop and Marks & Spencer
- supermarkets, e.g. Carrefour and Aldi or Tesco and Morrison
- furniture, e.g. IKEA and MFI;
- airlines, e.g. Cathay Pacific and Virgin.

Go to company websites and look at media stories about the companies to help with your comparisons.

Feedback

Points of difference may include country of origin, leadership style, price/target market, age of organisation and product design. Manifestations of cultural difference may be evident in kinds of advertising, colours used, attitudes of staff, layout of stores, company initiatives and after-sales service.

Definition: An *entrepreneur* is someone who looks for opportunities to start new projects, reach new markets, lead in a creative way.

Entrepreneurial organisations are often led by a charismatic leader, tend to be authoritarian and proactive, take the initiative and are prepared to take risks.

TABLE 2.1   Example of how public relations activity may be structured at various stages of the organisational lifecycle

	Startup	Growth	Maturity	Decline
Public relations orientation	Marketing communication	Marketing communication Internal communication	Marketing communication Community relations Internal communication Financial public relations Public affairs	Marketing communication Investor relations Internal communication
Examples of public relations activity	Face-to-face • meetings • presentations • social events Printed literature • product/service brochures • corporate brochure • business cards Website Media relations • news releases • press conferences	Merchandise Joint promotions Media relations • news releases • press conferences • facility visits • features • exclusives Internal communication • briefings • noticeboards • emails	Corporate social responsibility programme • educational support • charity giving • employee volunteering • community projects Investor relations • city analysts briefings • shareholder liaison • financial press Issues management • government lobbying Internal communication • intranet • employee conferences • newsletters • project groups	Crisis management Mergers and acquisitions Internal communication • working with HR to handle layoffs and redundancies or new working arrangements Marketing communication • customer retention • supplier relations • retention
Staffing	Public relations undertaken as part of marketing duties	Public relations specialist or consultancy	Public relations department and consultancy if required	Specialist public relations staff and specialist consultancies

Note: This chart is progressive: all the activities undertaken at an earlier stage in the lifecycle will also be undertaken at a later stage.

Systems theory

It is clear that organisations are not free-floating bodies unaffected by what is around them. They are affected by and in turn affect the environment in which they operate. One of the theories used by public relations academics (Grunig and Hunt 1984; Cutlip et al. 2000) to explain this is systems theory (a detailed overview and critique of systems theory and public relations is given in Chapter 8). *Systems* theory describes organisations as a set of subsystems that affect each other and jointly interact with the external environment. Organisations have to adjust and adapt as they change from within and as the environment changes. They form part of a social system that consists of individuals or groups (publics) such as suppliers, local communities, employees, customers and governments who all interact with it. Public relations is there to develop and maintain good relationships with these publics, to help the organisation achieve its objectives.

So which subsystem does public relations fit into? When considering this question Grunig and Hunt (1984) have turned to the work of organisational theorists who describe organisations as having typically five subsystems (see Figure 2.3).

The following may help explain Figure 2.3:

■ *Production* subsystems produce the products or services of an organisation.
■ *Maintenance* subsystems work throughout the organisation encouraging employees to work together – human resources, for example.
■ *Disposal* subsystems encompass the marketing and distribution of products and services.
■ *Adaptive* subsystems help the organisation adjust to its changing environment, such as the strategic planning role.
■ *Management* subsystems control and direct all the other subsystems and manage any conflicting demands that they might have. They also negotiate between the requirements of the environment (for example, demand for a particular product) and the survival needs of the organisation (supply of that product). Usually the board and senior management of the organisation undertake this responsibility.

Taking a systems perspective, it can be seen that public relations professionals have a *boundary-spanning* role. They work at the boundaries within organisations, working with all the internal subsystems by helping them to communicate internally. They also help these subsystems with their external communication by both providing expert advice on what and how to communicate and by helping them with

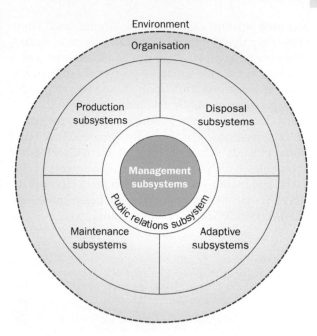

FIGURE 2.3   Organisational subsystems (*source:* Grunig and Hunt 1984: 9)

implementation. For example, public relations may work closely with marketing (disposal subsystem) on product support and with senior management (management subsystem) on investor relations.

> **Definition:** *Systems* refers to the theory that describes how organisations work in terms of interlocking and interdependent systems of communication, production, etc. It embraces both the internal and external environments.
>
> **Definition:** *Systematised* organisations tend to be authoritarian, highly structured and reactive in nature.

Location of public relations in organisations

Apart from all the external and internal considerations just discussed, the location of public relations within an organisation depends on a variety of other factors: the position of the most senior practitioner; the tasks allocated to the function; and how it is situated in relation to other functions.

Position of the senior practitioner

The position of the *senior public relations practitioner* provides a good indication of how the function is regarded within organisations. Grunig and Hunt (1984) say that public relations can be seen as valued when the function is within the 'dominant coalition' – in other words, the group of people who determine 'what the organisation's goals should be'. Certainly, an aspiration of public relations professionals over many decades has been to obtain a place on the board of organisations. Undoubtedly progress has been made towards this goal. Now all the UK's FTSE100 companies have public relations departments (CIPR 2004) and there are indications that more senior practitioners are being appointed to board positions (CIPR/DTI 2003; Gregory and Edwards 2004).

> **Definition:** *Senior practitioners* are people who occupy a formal senior management position in their organisations or people who hold a skilled role that requires several years of experience to gain the competence necessary to do the job.

Work done by Moss et al. (2000) and Moss and Green (2001) in Britain and Toth et al. (1998) in the United States has identified an alternative senior role: that of *senior adviser*. The senior adviser is not actually on the board, but reports directly to the CEO or chair of the board and holds a special position of power and influence. A good (if controversial) example of this is Alistair Campbell, Communications Director to the UK Prime Minister Tony Blair until 2003. Campbell did not occupy a Cabinet position, but he was clearly a powerful figure constantly alert to the communication issues surrounding government policy and decision making and advising the Prime Minister directly. Another, less well-known, example of a senior adviser is Will Whitehorn who supported Richard Branson during Virgin's period of expansion during the 1990s.

Board level and senior advisor communicators will usually take a research-based approach to public relations. They will know their public's views and be well informed of all the issues likely to affect the organisation. Their role will be to counsel and advise senior managers. They will also know the business intimately and be good at business as well as at communication (Gregory and Edwards 2004). See Think about 2.2.

PICTURE 2.2   Alistair Campbell was the UK Prime Minister's Communications Director until 2003 and although he did not occupy a Cabinet position, he was a powerful figure constantly alert to the communication issues surrounding government policy and decision making. (*Source:* © Reuters/Corbis.)

think about 2.2   **Top public relations practitioners**

Why do you think more public relations practitioners are achieving senior positions within organisations? Has education played a part in this development? Or is it the ever-changing communication demands of the modern world?

Public relations roles

Research undertaken by US researchers Broom and Smith (1979) and Dozier and Broom (1995) identifies two dominant public relations roles:

- The *communication manager*, who plans and manages public relations programmes, advises management, makes communication policy decisions and oversees their implementation.
- The *communication technician*, who is not involved in organisational decision making, but who implements public relations programmes such as writing press releases, organising events, producing web content. Technicians usually do not get too involved in research or evaluation: they are the 'doers'.

The communication manager role itself divides into three identifiable types:

- The *expert prescriber*, who researches and defines public relations problems, develops programmes to tackle these problems and then implements them, sometimes with the assistance of others.
- The *communication facilitator*, who acts as communication broker, maintaining two-way communication between an organisation and its publics, liaising, interpreting and mediating.
- The *problem-solving process facilitator*, who helps others solve their communication problems, acts as a counsellor/adviser on the planning and implementation of programmes. This role can be fulfilled by specialist consultancies as well as the in-house person.

Two other roles, sitting between the manager and technician are also noted:

- *Media relations* role, a highly skilled job requiring profound knowledge and understanding of the media. This is not just about the dissemination of messages, but a crucial function where the needs of the media are met in a sophisticated way. This is a role often fulfilled by a senior journalist who has made the crossover to public relations.
- *Communication and liaison role*, meaning the individual who represents the organisation at events and meetings and creates opportunities for management to communicate with internal and external publics.

The classification into manager and technician roles does not mean that lines are fixed. Most public relations professionals perform a mix of manager and technician work, but the point is that one role will tend to predominate. Entry-level practitioners are normally entrusted with technical tasks at the initial stages of their career. As practitioners become more experienced they may move on to the manager role. (A fuller discussion of these roles can be found in Chapters 3 and 8.)

Of course, there is enormous variety within these roles. A technician employed for their writing skills may be involved in a range of work, such as writing press releases, speech writing, writing for the web, or may be involved in just one job, for example producing the house journal.

The communication manager may be responsible for the full public relations programme or, if they work for a large corporate organisation, they may be responsible for one specialist area such as government or investor relations.

Public relations tasks

Van Riel (1995) divides corporate communication, as he labels it, into three areas:

- *Management communication* is communication by management aimed at developing a shared vision, establishing and maintaining trust in the leadership, managing change and empowering and motivating employees. Van Riel regards management communication as the responsibility of all managers. They may have a communication expert to help them with developing effective communication, but he warns against the danger of thinking that hiring an expert absolves management of its overall responsibility.
- *Marketing communication* is aimed at supporting the sale of goods and/or services. This will include advertising, sales promotion, direct mail, personal selling and market-oriented public relations – or publicity, as he calls it. Typically this includes media relations and events. Since Van Riel wrote his book, new media marketing has emerged as a major force and public relations professionals are often involved in this.
- *Organisational communication* is a host of communication activities usually at a corporate level, not

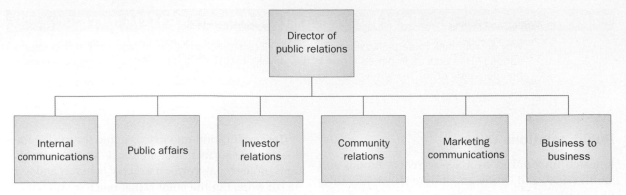

FIGURE 2.4   Public relations department structured in functions

all of which will be necessarily located in the public relations department, which include public affairs, environmental communication, investor relations, labour market communication, corporate advertising, internal communication and public relations.

Such a division along *functional* lines is often reflected in the structure of public relations departments. Figure 2.4 shows a typical functional structure. In such a structure an individual or group will look after all the activities falling within the area, whether these are media relations, sponsorship, events or individual relationships.

Cutlip et al. (2000) choose to categorise public relations work along *task* lines. They list 10 elements (see Figure 2.5) that summarise what public relations practitioners do at work.

Figure 2.6 is an example of a public relations department structured on task lines.

An obvious danger of both these approaches is that the specialist individuals or teams become function or task oriented and lose the overall picture of organisational priorities. The job of the manager is to ensure this does not happen. One way in which this is approached in consultancies is to put together project teams for accounts as they are won. These comprise functional and task experts drawn from across the consultancy who work on other cross-functional/task accounts concurrently.

Many in-house teams use a mixture of functional and task teams. For example, it is not unusual to have a press office that serves all the functional teams simply because this is a particular type of expertise and it would be inefficient to have a press specialist based in each team. It could also be dangerous since different functional teams could give out different messages reflecting their own priorities, rather than the overall and coordinated view of the corporate organisation.

Because they are part of the support function of an organisation, public relations departments and people will operate with all other departments, offering support and advice as required. This is part of the boundary-spanning role described earlier and fits in very well with the systems theory approach. However, organisations are complex and some areas of responsibility do not always fit neatly into functional departments. For example, internal communication is sometimes based in public relations, sometimes in marketing and sometimes in human resources. Again, some departments seem to have less well-defined boundaries than others and public relations is a good example of this.

There are two main departments where there is potential for both close cooperation and 'turf' or territorial disputes – marketing and human resources. The legal department is a third area that requires special attention.

Marketing

The relationship between public relations and marketing can be a fractious one (for more on this debate see Chapter 28). For decades there have been non-productive arguments about whether public relations is a part of marketing or vice versa. There are misconceptions on both sides.

For many marketing people public relations is all about getting free 'publicity' in the media to support the promotion of products and services to consumers. However, public relations, as this book amply demonstrates, is much more than that: it is about building relationships with numerous stakeholders, using a whole range of channels and techniques. As the idea of organisations as networks of stakeholding communities gains credence in the business world (Freeman 1984; Halal 2000), there is growing recognition that public relations, with its particular skills

Writing and editing

Print and broadcast news releases, feature stories, newsletters, correspondence, website/online media, shareholder/annual reports, speeches, brochures, AV scripts, advertisements, product and technical materials

Media relations and placement

Contacting news media, magazines, supplements, trade publications and freelancers to get them to publish material about the organisation. Responding to media requests

Research

Gathering information about public opinion trends, issues, political climate, legislation, media coverage, special interest groups and other concerns relating to stakeholders. Online searches. Designing research, surveys and hiring research firms

Management and administration

Programming and planning with other managers, determining needs, prioritising, defining publics, setting goals, and objectives, developing strategy and tactics, administering personal budgets and managing programmes

Special events

Arranging and managing news conferences, conventions, openings, ceremonies, anniversaries, fund-raising events, visiting dignitaries, contests, awards, facility visits

Speaking

Gaining speaking platforms, coaching others, speaking to groups

Production

Of multimedia, artwork, typography, photography, layout, DTP, AV, either personally or by other specialists

Training

Media training and public appearance, preparation for others, coaching others in writing and communication skills. Helping introduce change in culture, policy, structure and process

Contact

Liaising with media, community, internal and external groups. Listening, negotiating, managing conflict, mediating, meeting and entertaining guests and visitors

Counselling

Advising management on social, political and regulatory environments, crisis avoidance and management, working with others on issues management

FIGURE 2.5   Cutlip and colleagues' categorisation of public relations work (*source:* Cutlip, Scott, M., Center, Allen H., Broom, Glen M., *Effective Public Relations*, 8th Edition, © 2000, pp. 36–37. Adapted by permission of Pearson Education, Inc., Upper Saddle River, NJ.)

in relationship building, has a role far beyond marketing communication.

This is a sentiment that is not missed by marketers either. Marketing is broadening its remit to include the internal 'customer' and other (non-profit) relationships, bringing to bear its considerable knowledge base and expertise in managing consumer relationships to other stakeholders. For

example, the 'corporate branding' debate in marketing circles recognises that organisations have many stakeholders and that if a whole organisation is to gain support, then all stakeholders, not just customers, will need to be addressed (Balmer and Gray 2003).

However, marketing has some way to go in adjusting its basic philosophy. Marketing assumes that

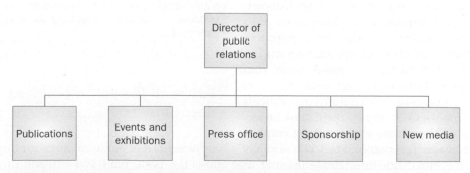

FIGURE 2.6   Public relations department structured by tasks

Why do you think there is tension between the marketing and public relations disciplines? Have you been aware of this tension on work experience or placements? Is it reflected in the attitudes of tutors for these subjects?

Feedback Marketing sees public relations as only marketing communications and as a 'cheap option'. It does not appreciate that placing material in the media is more difficult than paying for advertising. Further, it does not appreciate the skill involved in media relations. Neither does it recognise the range of stakeholding relationships that public relations practitioners need to manage and maintain.

Public relations sees marketing as being powerful because of the size of budgets. It does not think that customer focus is all important, as marketing people do. It considers encroachment on public relations territory as a threat. (For more information, read Hutton 2001.)

there is a 'profit' in any exchange relationship – the organisation comes out as the net beneficiary. The notion of relationships being of value in themselves is one of the key tenets of public relations and is a point of major difference between the disciplines.

However, as the two functions develop it is inevitable that the distinction between them will blur. Indeed, many organisations now have a single communication function integrating all aspects of the organisation's communication, often headed by a board-level director who can be either a marketing or a public relations professional – sometimes both.

Human resources or personnel

As the section earlier indicated, Van Riel regards organisational communication and internal communication as part of the overall corporate communication remit. It is evident that the public relations and human resources/personnel functions should and must work in a collaborative way to communicate with employees. For example, where there is a reorganisation, a merger, an acquisition or layoffs, human resources must play the lead role in renegotiating employees' contracts, terms and conditions and location. However, public relations is vital to communicating these kinds of change in an appropriate and timely way and in helping to maintain morale.

Human resources is sometimes the host department for internal communication. Irrespective of its physical location, public relations' involvement in strategic communication objectives, together with its knowledge of communication techniques and content, are good reasons for close collaboration.

Human resources and public relations departments both regard employees as one of their most important stakeholders. Recruiting and retaining employees is being increasingly recognised by CEOs as vitally important (Hill and Knowlton 2003) because as 'knowledge' becomes the differentiator adding value

to organisations, the collective 'knowledge' of its workforce becomes increasingly precious (see also Chapter 17).

Legal

Organisations in crisis or under threat turn to their legal departments for advice. Lawyers are naturally cautious and their instinct is to keep quiet and say nothing that might incriminate an individual or make the organisation liable in any way. However, today's organisation is held to account for what it does not say and do as well as for what it actually says and does. Stakeholders value transparency and honesty. It is imperative therefore that lawyers and public relations professionals work closely together, each contributing their particular knowledge and skills to manage issues, crises and risks.

Battles for ascendancy among specialist functions are essentially futile. What matters is that the interests of the organisation and its publics are well served. That is best done by fellow professionals working together to fulfil that common aim (see Think about 2.3 and Activity 2.3).

Future of the public relations department

New directions in public relations are discussed at the end of this book, but it is worth pointing out a number of developments that are likely to impact on the structure of the public relations function of the future and may enhance the role of public relations within organisations.

Regulatory issues

New legislation is on the horizon. Reforms to company law in Britain will require companies to report on a range of non-financial factors, such as the company's interactions with stakeholders, their treatment of employees and their environmental policies, in their annual report. The EU Directive on Information and Consultation, which demands that larger companies consult with employees on a range of issues, provides public relations with large opportunities. Public relations professionals are ideally positioned to collect the data for these activities and to report on them.

Risk management and stakeholder interest

Risk management, along with reputation management, is becoming more important to CEOs (Murray and White 2004). Risk management is intimately bound up in relationship building with important stakeholders.

> **Definition:** Risk management is the business technique of anticipating, minimising and preventing accidental loss through taking precautionary measures.

Technology

As technology develops, practitioners will need to become more adroit at using it with many more specialist technician roles being created to exploit new ways of communicating with stakeholders. At the same time, the impact of these new technologies will need deeper consideration at a strategic level. For example, how will organisations manage the requirement for on-demand, tailored information from potentially millions of stakeholders on a global basis 24/7, 365 days a year? See Activity 2.4.

activity 2.4

The public relations industry

From your reading and research around the topics discussed in this chapter, conduct an EPISTLE analysis of the public relations industry. What are the key issues for public relations?

Summary

This chapter has sought to describe and discuss some of the key factors and theories that influence the management and organisation of public relations. It is a function subject to many external and internal influences. It is a subtle discipline, significantly affected by organisational culture and by the power and influence that it is allowed to exercise. However, public relations is not only shaped by organisations; it helps to shape them too. Communication-aware organisations are very different from those that are not. The public relations function can be a dynamo of energy and change within organisations. Smart organisations embrace what the public relations discipline has to offer through its knowledge of relationship building and stakeholder management and its sophisticated use of communications techniques and channels. Less smart organisations will be left behind.

Bibliography

Balmer, J.M.T. and E.R. Gray (2003). 'Corporate brands: What are they? What of them?'. *European Journal of Marketing* **37**(7/8): 972–997.

Broom, G.M. and G.D. Smith (1979). 'Testing the practitioners impact on clients'. *Public Relations Review* **5**(2): 47–59.

CIPR (2004) www.ipr.org.uk/direct/news.asp?v1=tactfile accessed 10 July 2004.

CIPR/DTI (2003) 'Unlocking the potential of public relations'. Joint Report of the Chartered Institute of Public Relations and Department of Trade and Industry. London: CIPR.

Cutlip, S.M., A.H. Center and G.M. Broom (2000). *Effective Public Relations*, 8th edition. Upper Saddle River, NJ: Prentice Hall.

Dozier, D.M. and G.M. Broom (1995). 'Evolution of the managerial role in public relations practice'. *Journal of Public Relations Research* **7**(2): 17.

Esman, M.J. (1972). 'The elements of institution building' in *Institution Building and Development*. J.W. Eaton (ed.). Beverley Hills: Sage.

Eisenberg, E.M. and P. Riley (2001). 'Organizational culture' in *The New Handbook of Organizational*

Communication: Advances in theory, research and methods. F.M. Jablin and L.L. Puttnam (eds). Thousand Oaks, CA: Sage.

Freeman, R.E. (1984). *Strategic Management: A stakeholder approach.* Boston, MA: Pitman.

Friedman, M. (1970). 'The social responsibility of business is to increase its profits'. *The New York Times Magazine*, 13 September.

Gregory, A. (2003). 'Public relations and the age of spin'. Inaugural lecture at Leeds Metropolitan University, 26 March.

Gregory A. and L. Edwards (2004). 'Patterns of PR: Public relations management among Britain's "most admired" companies'. Report for Eloqui Public Relations. Leeds: Leeds Metropolitan University.

Grunig, J.E. and L.A. Grunig (1992). 'Models of public relations and communication' in *Excellence in Public Relations.* J.E. Grunig (ed). Mahwah, NJ: Lawrence Erlbaum Associates.

Grunig, J.E. and T. Hunt (1984). *Managing Public Relations.* New York: Holt, Rinehart & Winston.

Halal, W.E. (2000). 'Corporate community: A theory of the firm uniting profitability and responsibility'. *Strategic Leadership*, **28**(2): 10–16.

Hargreaves, I. (2003). *Journalism, Truth or Dare?* Oxford: Oxford University Press.

Herriot, P. and W. Scott-Jackson (2002). 'Globalisation, social identities and employment'. *British Journal of Management* **13**: 249–257.

Hill and Knowlton (2003). *Corporate Reputation Watch.* London: Hill and Knowlton PR Ltd.

Hofstede, G.H. (1991). *Cultures and Organizations.* New York: McGraw-Hill.

Hutton, J.G. (2001). 'Defining the relationship between public relations and marketing: Public relations' most

important challenge' in *The Handbook of Public Relations.* R.L. Heath (ed.). Thousand Oaks, CA: Sage.

Kornhauser, W. (1960). *The Politics of Mass Society.* London: Routledge.

McCollom, M. (1994). 'The cultures of work organizations'. *Academy of Management Review* **19**: 836–839.

Moloney, K. (2000). *Rethinking Public Relations.* London: Routledge.

Moss, D.A. and R. Green (2001). 'Re-examining the manager's role in public relations: What management and public relations research teaches us'. *Journal of Communication Management* **6**(2): 18–132.

Moss, D.A., G. Wamaby and A. Newman (2000). 'Public relations practitioner role enactment at the senior management level within UK companies'. *Journal of Public Relations Research* **12**(4): 227–308.

Murray, K. and J. White (2004). 'CEO views on reputation management: A report on the value of public relations. as perceived by organisational leaders'. London: Chime PLC.

Rampton, S. and J. Stauber (1995). *Toxic Sludge is Good for You.* Monroe, ME: Common Courage Press.

Ritzer, G. (2004). *The Globalisation of Nothing.* Thousand Oaks, CA: Pine Forge Press.

Smythe, J. (2004). *Engaging People at Work to Drive Strategy and Change.* London: McKinsey and Company.

Steyn, B. and G. Puth (2000). *Corporate Communication Strategy.* Sandown: Heinemann Publishers (Pty).

Toth, E.L., S.A. Serini, D.K. Wright and A.G. Emig (1998). 'Trends in public relations roles: 1990–1995'. *Public Relations Review* **24**(2): 53–175.

Van Riel, C.B.M. (1995). *Principles of Corporate Communication.* London: Prentice Hall.

Role of the public relations practitioner

Introduction

Everyone thinks they know what public relations practitioners do. They either hang out with celebrities and sell kiss 'n' tell stories to the Sunday newspapers or they whisper in politicians' ears and 'spin' the entire national media. Don't they?

A glance at the contents page of this book will suggest otherwise. Each chapter addresses a particular area of public relations theory or practice and while there are chapters on media relations and public affairs, the reality does not match the image (which may be disappointing for some).

This chapter aims to show where people work in public relations and what they do in the jobs. It explores the problems caused by difficulties in defining the field, but also the opportunities for individual and professional development. Public relations practice is linked to public relations theory and the need for individuals to undertake lifelong learning is stressed. The role of education and the question of professionalism are also discussed, along with the role of professional bodies.

Traditionally, books about public relations have tended to be either too academic to shed much light on the practice or 'how to' lists by retired practitioners who only describe what they did in their heyday. This chapter aims to bridge that divide by setting practice clearly in a theoretical context and including examples of practice from different countries. It also reflects a range of experiences, through case studies and diaries, of being a practitioner at the start of the twenty-first century. Throughout the chapter you will be able to read mini case histories and diaries of public relations practitioners who are working in different types of settings to help you appreciate the diversity of the practice and hopefully gain an insight into what people actually do.

activity 3.1

What is public relations all about?

Ask your friends and family what they think PR is all about and/or which PR practitioners they have heard of.

Feedback

Chances are that the responses will not be flattering and that the individuals named may be high profile themselves or certainly represent activities or individuals with a significant media interest (sport, music, politics).

You may also find that media relations is the function or activity most closely associated with these individuals. Take a quick look at the contents list of this book and the breadth and range of subject matter covered under PR. Are these activities reflected in most people's understanding of the practice? Probably not.

activity 3.2

Comparing public relations in two countries

Look at the information in Boxes 3.1 and 3.2. What are the key differences? How does each country's PR association define PR? Look at each of their websites (the Spanish site has an English translation).

Feedback

Check out other websites – how do their ideas and statistics vary? How many have English translations? Does the UK site have other languages available? If not, why not? (See also Chapter 7.)

Who does what: the bigger picture

Definitions of field

Chapter 1 has already explored the historical evolution of PR and discussed the various definitions that are provided from a range of sources including academics, practitioners, national and international professional bodies.

This lack of an agreed definition is, however, still a problem for the practice. Deciding what it is and what people do has evidently caused much distraction and expenditure of individual and collective energies. Some of the long-winded definitions still do not easily convey what the discipline stands for and

Who are the public relations practitioners?

There is a lot of confusion about who does what in public relations (PR) – see Activity 3.1. It may be helpful to look at some facts about the industry in Britain and in Spain (see Boxes 3.1 and 3.2 and then complete Activity 3.2).

---

box 3.1 Key facts about public relations in Britain

According to the UK's Chartered Institute of Public Relations (CIPR):

- On a global scale, the UK PR market is second only to that of the United States.
- Private and public sector organisations in Britain will spend about £6bn on PR services this year.
- A *Guardian* poll shows that more than 30% of UK media companies will increase spending on less expensive media over the next few months, including PR, direct marketing and email marketing (Source: *The Guardian* 20 August 2003).
- PR is one of the top three career choices for graduates (Source: The UK Graduate Careers Survey 2003).
- A survey of 300 marketing professionals by the Marketing Society showed that nine out of every 10 believed that PR will become more important (over the next five years) than TV/radio advertising, sponsorship, email marketing and events/exhibitions (Source: *Financial Times*, Creative Business 21 October 2003).
- There are approximately 2800 PR consultancies in Britain.
- The combined turnover of the top 20 PR consultancies in 2004 was more than £366m (Source: *PR Week*).
- All listed FTSE100 companies have a PR department communicating on their behalf.

Source: www.cipr.co.uk (CIPR)

box 3.2	**Key facts about public relations in Spain**

- PR is defined as: 'Strategies for generating trust between the company and its audiences, thus developing a favourable predisposition.'
- Turnover: €192.3m.
- Growth on previous year: 22%.
- 71% of companies consider their relation with their PR agency is very good and that 78% of agencies have a very high level of commitment.
- Agencies have an average of 21 employees.
- The average agency is 10 years old.
- 100% of agencies demand proficiency in at least two languages.
- Postgraduates make up 82% of agency employees.

Source: *El Estudio de la Comunicación y las Relaciones Públicas en España* (The Study of Communications and Public Relations in Spain), compiled in 2002 (using data from 2000) by ADECEC, IESE and PricewaterhouseCoopers

ADECEC (Asociación de Empresas Consultoras en Relaciones Públicas y Comunicación), is the Spanish association of businesses dedicated to PR and communications consultancy. It is a non-profit-making organisation founded in January 1991 by a group of professionals from Spain's main PR consultancies.

ADECEC's member companies employ more than 1000 people and are active in the field of PR and communication, not only in Spain but also abroad. ADECEC, as a sector representative, holds as its mission to dignify the profession for the people working in it and to contribute to growth in the practice of PR in Spain.

Source: www.adecec.com

what people do. Fawkes (2004) argues that the synthesised UK CIPR definition of PR below is one that at least simplifies the discussion and helps students and practitioners understand what it is they do or should be doing: 'Public relations is about reputation – the result of what you do, what you say and what others say about you' (CIPR 2005).

However, modern ideas about PR are moving away from reputation as the key concept, to relationship building, so the CIPR definition may be revised or fade from use. Note also the rather different description by the Spanish PR association (Box 3.2). In fact, it is worth pointing out that the problem with definitions extends to problems with language. As Verčić et al. (2001) point out, the term 'public relations' is founded wholly on US references and does not translate across the Atlantic. Their own three-year research programme on PR in Europe (European Body of Knowledge (EBOK)) showed that all except English speakers had problems with the term 'public relations'. For example, the German *Offentlich keitsarbeit* carries associations with the public sphere and public opinion, perhaps rooted in the origins of European PR through public bodies, such as central and local government, rather than the corporate work of early PR in the United States.

So, shall we abandon the search for a decent description? It could be said that they encourage ring-fencing and competition and work against integrated communication approaches to problem solving. Other disciplines have similar problems, after all.

However, Hutton (2001) says that PR has lost the battle for supremacy with marketing and is terminally threatened by its failure 'to define itself and to develop sophisticated and progressive theory' or develop its central tenet or core concept. He comments that 'there remains a critical need for public relations to define its intellectual and practical domain . . . to regain control of its own destiny' (2001: 205). See Activity 3.3 (overleaf).

The debate will continue to unfold in journals and textbooks and at conferences for years to come. In the meantime, students and practitioners still need to be able to describe their jobs in terms meaningful to their friends and family. This chapter aims to provide information and insight to assist in that goal.

Of course, the answers to many of the questions raised by Activity 3.3 will depend on the type of role, its level and whether it is in-house or consultancy. The next section looks at how organisations see the role of the PR practitioner, before going on to look at what individuals do on a daily basis.

activity 3.3

Job descriptions

One way of gathering information about what PR practitioners do is to look at the job ads. Find a publication or look online at *PR Week* or *The Guardian* for PR jobs. Read the adverts and make a note of what the employers are looking for. What job titles are advertised? What skills do they mention? How many ask for relevant qualifications? What specific knowledge (e.g. IT)? What personal qualities?

Feedback

Some of the job titles will vary from corporate communications to head of media. The duties described may not vary so much. The differences and similarities in these ads offer real insight into what people do in PR.

PICTURE 3.1   Does Samantha from *Sex in the City* represent what public relations is and what practitioners do? (*Source:* Getty Images.)

Role of the communicator

In Chapter 2 we discussed the division between managers and technicians in PR practice. However, the dichotomy is not always clear-cut. Most PR practitioners are involved in both manager and technician work, but it is generally accepted that one role may dominate. On entry into the practice and at the start of their career, most recruits are given technical tasks. Through experience and after time this generally means they move on to fulfilling the more managerial role (see mini case studies on practitioner roles and responsibilities and Figure 3.1).

The emphasis on these roles of the communicator has also had an effect on the advancement of women in PR, as is explored more fully in Chapter 9, which also discusses the disappointing absence of research into the status of black and ethnic minority PR personnel. Another issue about the roles of communicators is that so many of the texts are US based.

The 2001 research report by Verčić et al. showed that for European respondents the key concepts for PR were 'communications' and 'relationships' (the respondents refused to choose between these two, on the grounds they were too interrelated to separate).

Four dimensions emerged as key roles for PR:

1   managerial
2   operational
3   reflective
4   educational.

The first two overlap with the familiar managerial/technician debate to some extent but the last two are not covered and are worth expanding:

- Reflective PR is described as the role of analysing 'changing social values to adjust organisations, standards and values of social responsibility' and is aimed at influencing the dominant coalition.
- Educational PR aims to increase the communication competence of employees.

Reflective PR emerged as the core role for PR in the eyes of European scholars and practitioners, with the aim of evolving a PR perspective on the organisation, parallel to the financial or legal perspectives taken by those elements of an organisation.

In many ways, the struggle to define the role of the communicator has an edge to it: this is not just an academic debate. PR practitioners need to demonstrate their value to the employing organisations – whether it is reputation management or relationship building that they are offering. Neither is the comparison with financial or legal aspects of an organisation misplaced. As Hutton (2001: 214) points out, the failure to have a clear rationale for PR has led to erosion of its base:

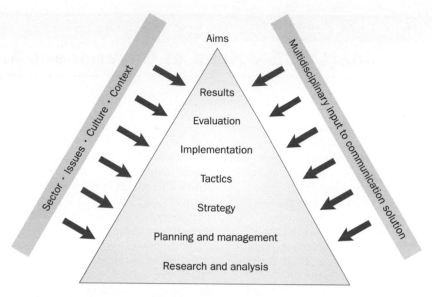

FIGURE 3.1   The public relations practitioner as 'communicator'

Many corporate public relations departments have lost responsibility for crisis communications to management consulting firms and marketing departments, some have lost responsibility for corporate identity programmes to marketing departments, some have lost government relations to legal departments, and some have lost internal/employee communications to human resources departments.

The drive to get on the board of directors is also connected to the desire to be taken seriously. There is some success in this area: as Box 3.1 shows, all the top 100 companies in Britain have PR departments. The question is: how much authority do they have within those companies? A survey by Watson Helsby Consultancy of PR directors at 28 of Britain's top companies, including BP, Vodafone and HSBC, found that while most reported directly to the chief executive, many failed to get the attention of the board. The survey found that only 30% of PR people sat on their company executive committees and none on the board (*Financial Times* 22 October 2003).

Other evidence suggests a flourishing time ahead for PR. For example, PR was considered the best return on investment by entrepreneurs in a survey for the *Financial Times* in 2004, as shown in Figure 3.2.

Mini case study 3.1 (overleaf) illustrates the kind of career available in PR and the richness (and challenge) of the PR role at a senior level. The communicator is often expected to play a wide range of roles.

The PR practitioner must be adaptable, energetic, versatile, diplomatic and resilient to get along with a mixed group of clients and stakeholder groups. Pieczka refers to the existence of 'an expertise which is distinctive yet flexible enough to be applicable across a wide

field' and suggests that public relations expertise is a complex interactive structure organised through past experience and current exigencies (demands), which modifies itself through action (Pieczka 2002: 321–322).

This perspective would suggest that there is no one paradigm or template for the role but that it is a dynamic process created through the interface of our

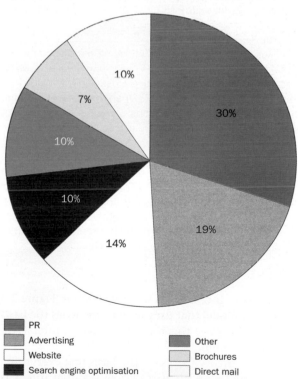

PR
Advertising
Website
Search engine optimisation

Other
Brochures
Direct mail

FIGURE 3.2   What type of marketing activity gives the best return on investment for startup SMEs?
(*Source: FT Creative Business* 13 July 2004 based on research by new2marketing accessed www.ipr.org.uk, July 20)

mini case study 3.1

Katherine Bennett OBE – Head of Government Affairs, Airbus UK

Role at Airbus

Katherine joined Airbus UK as Head of Government Affairs in 2004. Her role encompasses managing relationships between Airbus and national, regional and local government. She takes the lead on all public policy issues affecting the company and ensures that key government and interested stakeholders are kept informed and aware of company developments. Her time is split between Bristol, where Airbus UK's HQ is based and an office in Westminster, London. The Government Affairs Department has a direct reporting function to the managing director in the UK.

In the public affairs industry, the managing director's direct involvement is a prerequisite for the function. Government affairs needs to be integral in company strategy and direction. This integration can take a number of forms, whether in considerations over avoidance of risk, ensuring there is a supportive legislative background for the company's forward plans and product development or indeed issues surrounding sustainability and CSR.

Airbus's Communications Team is a sister department to Government Affairs and the two functions are closely aligned, which allows joint allocation of resources when required and the necessary coordination of messages to Airbus's key audiences.

Issue management

Airbus is the market leader in aircraft manufacturing and sales, employing over 50,000 people worldwide, of which 13,000 are in the UK and represent highly skilled research and development (R&D) and manufacturing jobs. The UK business is the Airbus 'Centre of Excellence' for wing design and manufacture and also heads up the integration of landing gear and fuel systems for Airbus aircraft.

One of Katherine's first challenges was to ensure the UK business was fully represented and involved in the unveiling of the new A380 aircraft. With the capacity of seating 555 passengers, this is the largest civil airliner ever launched and brought a completely new dimension to the aircraft market in terms of customer offering and innovative systems technology.

The unveiling ceremony took place in Toulouse, France, in front of over 5000 assembled media, government representatives and customer representatives. Katherine undertook the coordination of the logistics, media activity and protocol surrounding the participation of UK Prime Minister Tony Blair. The key part of this activity was to ensure the smooth running of a two-way satellite link between Blair and Airbus employees back in the UK.

The event was probably one of the largest product unveilings ever seen and the media coverage reflected this. Over 500 media representatives with 60 film crews attended the ceremony. In the UK, the event attracted 650 separate items of media coverage, including BBC/ITV main TV news slots of more than two minutes. The Airbus website had live coverage, and received 3,419,398 hits that day.

Background

Katherine is a member of the Chartered Institute of Public Relations and graduated in history and politics from Leicester University. She has a postgraduate diploma in marketing from the Chartered Institute of Marketing. Katherine's previous employment was with Vauxhall/GM UK where for nearly nine years she also headed up their government affairs function. Her time at Vauxhall involved managing numerous public policy lobbying campaigns and issues management such as major industrial restructuring programmes and CSR. Her time with GM included several months based in the USA. Before joining Vauxhall, Katherine was an account manager in the Public Affairs Department of Hill and Knowlton (an international PR company) working on behalf of energy, charity and automotive clients. While at Hill and Knowlton she undertook several in-house training courses. Katherine was awarded the Order of the British Empire in June 2004 for services to the motor industry and charity.

Source: based on interview with author and information supplied by Katherine Bennett.

past and our interactions with the present. Figure 3.3 presents a model that uses systems theory as the basis for the concept of this role as a dynamic, interactive and open system.

Systems theory works on the basis that everything in the social world is part of a system that interacts with other systems in that the whole equals more than the sum of its parts (von Bertalanffy 1969). Building on the work of Katz and Kahn (1978), PR scholars (e.g. Cutlip et al. 2000) use systems theory to explain the interactions between organisations and their environments, interactions between organisations and interactions within organisations. (Systems theory is fully explained in Chapter 8.)

This model assumes that the PR practitioner is part of an open system interacting with other systems, and therefore the nature of the role will not be fixed but depend on the influences both in and out of the system, from early experiences and education through to ongoing *continuing professional development (CPD)*. Key to this model is that the system does not exist in isolation, but only exists insofar as it relates to

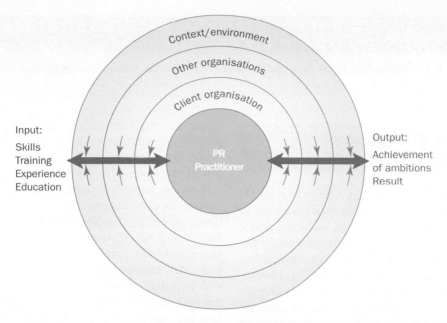

FIGURE 3.3   Public relations practitioner role within systems theory

other systems. This model also reaffirms that the PR practitioner as counsel must be aware of the context of their own role, and the context of the organisation or client they are representing. That requires an interest in, and understanding of, the wider community, whether it is political, economic, sociological, and any number of other ways to frame the narrative of the twenty-first century.

> **Definition:** CPD (continuing professional development) acknowledges in all professions (law, medicine, accountancy, PR, etc.) the role of continued learning and updating throughout the career.

There is an increasing body of research, with enormous potential for further development, looking at the role of the practitioner and using a number of methodologies to explain and measure the role. Moss et al. (2004) have identified a number of common themes in both the UK and USA among senior practitioners, such as their part in the dominant coalition and their contribution to strategic decision making.

Wilkin (2001) provides an interesting and controversial perspective on the implications of global communication; Allan (2000) on the social divisions and hierarchies reproduced by the news media. Research among employers' needs in graduates tends to highlight the requirement for employees who can manage change and understand the context the organisation is functioning in and can evidence the more abstract cognitive powers.

The argument supports the idea that the role of the PR practitioner is a very wide-ranging one, far wider than many PR exponents might feel happy with, but worth considering if we want to move PR onto a higher plane. Those with a background in corporate communications will already recognise the role. It is often with the introduction of a corporate communicator and the playing out of territorial and functional wars that the true potential of a role, which both oversees and connects, is appreciated, not only by senior management but also by the organisation as a whole. This is a role which, with the right training and development, can become synonymous with the PR role (see Figure 3.4). (See also Chapters 2 and 10 on the management and planning of PR activities.) See Think about 3.1 (overleaf).

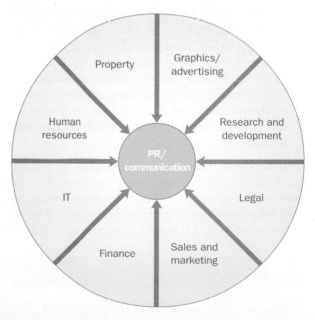

FIGURE 3.4   Public relations/communication role within an organisation

think about 3.1 | **Public relations and its influence within organisations**

Is there anywhere in the organisation where public relations does not have a role to play?

What public relations people do: individual practitioners

Lots of people work in PR and in a range of roles. As Activity 3.3 showed, there is a huge variety of job titles in trade or national newspapers, including public relations/corporate communications *consultant, executive, manager, director, officer, advisor, counsellor*, etc. To help us understand in more detail what these individuals are actually doing it is necessary to simplify and classify the locations in which they are working. So, there are three simple categories of where people work in public relations:

1 In-house (employed by an organisation, whether a public or private company or a public body, charity or non-governmental organisation, NGO).
2 Consultancy (agency where practitioners work for one or more different clients for a fee).
3 Freelance practitioner (where an individual works for himself and is employed by in-house departments or consultancies on a short-term contract basis either for a specific project or to fill in during peaks in demand or because staff absence requires additional resource).

While much of the work is the same across these categories, there are key differences:

- In-house: get to know one organisation in depth, work across wide range of PR activities, from writing/editing house journal to arranging visits by or to MPs/opinion formers, etc., get to know a sector or industry well, e.g. music, motoring.
- Consultancy: work across many accounts, variety of clients, changing environment, may work in specialist area such as technology, finance or public affairs.

Fawkes (2004) argues that understanding the practice is helped by analysing how people engage in different activities. She does this by describing the common PR areas with examples of what practitioners will do in each area (see Table 3.1, Box 3.3 (p 46) and Activity 3.4.).

Skills for the ideal practitioner

So what skills are needed to work in PR? It would probably be quicker to identify those which are not required, although that is not easy either. Because there are so many kinds of work and so many kinds of employer, there is room in PR for everyone from the extrovert party person to the researcher glued to the PC.

However, some indication of what employers are looking for can be gleaned by their responses to questions posed by Fawkes and Tench (2004b) (see Table 3.2–p 48). This research shows that there was agreement from employers that literacy was the primary skill required by PR graduates. Both in-house and consultancy employers also ranked teamwork as the next most important attribute, followed by problem solving, analytical thinking, research skills, IT skills and numeracy. There were some variations between the employer groups, with in-house employers giving greater weighting to IT skills over research skills – the opposite of consultants' priorities.

Another insight into skills required by PR practitioners can be found in the results of the major research-based investigation into PR education in the United States, presented in the Public Relations Society of America (PRSA) *Port of Entry* report (1999) (see Table 3.3–p 48). This surveyed employers and debated with other academics before concluding that the range of knowledge and skills listed in Table 3.3 were desirable in PR practitioners.

While the DTI/IPR report (2003) is not about education, but practice and the future of the sector, it is notable that the practitioner requirements shown in Table 3.4 are very much more limited than those suggested by practitioners and educators in the United States.

activity 3.4

In-house and consultancy jobs

Look at the job ads you gathered in Activity 3.3. How many of them are for in-house, how many for consultancy jobs? What differences are there in the skills, qualifications and interests they require?

Feedback

It may be easier to find in-house jobs, especially for public sector jobs, as they are more likely to advertise in national newspapers. Consultancies often advertise in *PR Week* in the UK or recruit informally through word of mouth and 'headhunting' (asking an individual to change agencies). You can find out about some of these jobs by looking at the PR agency's website.

TABLE 3.1 Examples of what public relations people do (*source*: Fawkes 2004)

Public relations activity	Explanation	Examples
Internal communication	Communicating with employees	In-house newsletter, suggestion boxes
Corporate PR	Communicating on behalf of whole organisation, not goods or services	Annual reports, conferences, ethical statements, visual identity, images
Media relations	Communicating with journalists, specialists, editors from local, national, international and trade media, including newspapers, magazines, radio, TV and web-based communication	Press releases, photocalls, video news releases, off-the-record briefings, press events
Business to business	Communicating with other organisations, e.g. suppliers, retailers	Exhibitions, trade events, newsletters
Public affairs	Communicating with opinion formers, e.g. local/national politicians, monitoring political environment	Presentations, briefings, private meetings, public speeches
Community relations/ corporate social responsibility	Communicating with local community, elected representatives, headteachers, etc.	Exhibitions, presentations, letters, meetings, sports activities and other sponsorship
Investor relations	Communicating with financial organisations/individuals	Newsletters, briefings, events
Strategic communication	Identification and analysis of situation, problem and solutions to further organisational goals	Researching, planning and executing a campaign to improve ethical reputation of organisation
Issues management	Monitoring political, social, economic and technological environment	Considering effect of US economy and presidential campaign on UK organisation
Crisis management	Communicating clear messages in fast changing situation or emergency	Dealing with media after major rail crash on behalf of police, hospital or local authority
Copywriting	Writing for different audiences to high standards of literacy	Press releases, newsletters, web pages, annual reports
Publications management	Overseeing print/media processes, often using new technology	Leaflets, internal magazines, websites
Events management, exhibitions	Organisation of complex events, exhibitions	Annual conference, press launch, trade shows

Before turning to the academic debates about skills, it is worth looking at mini case study 3.2 (p 49), which lists the kind of skills required by one particular sector, financial and investor relations (IR). (See also Chapter 24.)

The skills debate

What skills do PR practitioners need in order effectively to deliver results and how do they acquire these skills? The wider UK contextual framework for education and training puts skills centre stage. In some ways this has worked in favour of PR education and training. No one will argue the need for 'skills' in one form or another. The debate over skills has been muddied by the different terminologies employed and by the fact that whereas some skills may be transferable and portable, others are very subject specific. The UK Qualifications and Curriculum Authority (QCA), the Dearing Report (1997), Coopers and Lybrand and many others have come up with a variety of skills categories. Specifying skills as learning outcomes is now driving the educational agenda. This may be a useful discipline, but can exclude other equally important agendas. The discourse of skills can take on a life of its own, even to the exclusion of some skills we might think should be taken for granted but, in fact, cannot be. Undergraduates may lack basic literacy skills, for example, something we might (and practitioners do, according to Fawkes and Tench 2004a) see as essential for the PR role.

Practitioner diary 11–14 November

Two weeks in the life of financial public relations consultant, Melanie Gerlis, associate partner for Finsbury financial public relations consultants

Thursday 11 November

Client reported results today so I was in at 6.45am – only advantage is that we can get a taxi and there is no traffic! Results themselves are not very exciting and today has proved a busy day in the markets, so we don't expect a huge amount of coverage. There is a rumour going round the market that my client is going to be bought by a German competitor (this rumour has been doing the rounds for three years!) so the unwilling management all wore their Armistice poppies in order to present a united front . . . They did a presentation to sell-side analysts this morning which went smoothly. As ever, the Q&A session is always more worrying than the presentation but all questions asked had been prepared for which made a pleasant change.

Another client (an Italian retail bank) has sent a letter complaining about our services over the last two years. We are more than certain that this is not a fair reflection of the work we have done (which has included a glowing profile in the *Financial Times* and *The Banker*) and I am having to write a response that makes sure they know that this is the case without explicitly saying 'you are wrong'. It is a difficult balance to strike.

OK coverage coming in on the newswires/*Evening Standard* on the client that reported results, although as suspected mostly about the possible German approach (the *Daily Mail* – unsurprisingly – is calling it 'Operation Sealion', the codename given to the abortive invasion of Britain by Hitler in 1940).

Just got a call from a client who we worked for five months ago – his deal collapsed but we did a good few weeks of hard work and had put in an abort fee. I have been chasing him for ages and he has finally agreed to pay us – will believe it when I see it but good to know he agrees in principle!

The Sunday Times is writing a feature on pension fund trustees (who have shown themselves to be very powerful in bid situations such as the proposed private equity bid for WH Smith which they eventually blocked) – as we look after three private equity companies (including Permira, the largest in Europe) we have been trying all day to find someone to be quoted in this feature and I have finally pinned someone down.

Very busy day today – difficult to describe but the 170 emails in my inbox are some indication. And a potential client dinner tonight . . .

Friday 12 November

I had to get in early again today in order to look through all this morning's press coverage of yesterday's client results and be in a position to summarise them to one of the partners here (who had gone up to Manchester on business) before he then spoke to the client. This is both a moment of damage limitation and self-promotion: if the press coverage had been dreadful, we would need to acknowledge where we went wrong/could do better before the client gets too exercised about its FPR firm; if the press coverage had been fantastic, we would want to claim credit before any other advisor (banks, in-house PR, investor relations)!

Press coverage of results was not particularly strong, but at the same time there wasn't too much about the client needing to do a transaction with its German competitor, so on the whole the client was relieved. This is clearly something that won't go away, though, so we had to give our thoughts on the strategy going forward: namely, to demonstrate – as much as possible – how well the client is doing as an independent

box 3.3 (continued)

firm. I think this will be more difficult than it seems as most of the new initiatives will take a relatively long period of investment before they turn to profit/competitive advantages, but it is certainly worth trying.

At about 11am we heard that my team – that looks after the financial services sector – had won a very competitive pitch for a high-profile UK mortgage bank. We had beaten several of our major competitors, including both those who have been in the industry for several years and those who had recently launched as a challenge to our business. Our pitch had taken place on Thursday and it has been unusual in recent years to get a positive response so quickly. Most UK companies now see changing FPR advisor as a very big change but at the same time tend to leave the decision making at the bottom of their 'to do' lists. The guy in my team who was part of the winning pitch has only been at the firm for about a month and this was particularly endorsing for him – both personally and in the eyes of the company. So a few of us went out to lunch to celebrate (curry and champagne – very glamorous!). We then carried on celebrating for most of the afternoon, doing most of our work in a pub from our mobile phones and Blackberries. Not the usual way of spending an afternoon, but it was a great celebratory moment and also a Friday at the end of a particularly hard-working week.

Weekend 13/14 November

No surprising news/press calls relating to my clients. *The Mail on Sunday* wrote about the client that reported results last week: 'The market is now reaching fever pitch, with some predicting a bid at any moment'; *The Independent* wrote: 'It is already less profitable than its two main European competitors . . . It is a prime takeover candidate' – as I say, this isn't going away . . .

I got a few calls on my mobile on the back of a *Sunday Telegraph* report on a transaction that another team is doing. Most journalists have my mobile number because of a very contentious and ever-moving transaction that I worked on through several weekends last year and tend to call me in desperation when they can't get hold of my colleagues! I was able to get hold of the right person to return these calls, so annoyingly journalists have the right strategy . . .

One of my friends works in the same industry as me, also in charge of financial services, and I met her for lunch on Saturday. She had been one of the losing teams in the pitch we had won on Friday (from a newer firm) and she was almost too upset to talk about it. They had put in three weeks of very hard work and it reminded me just how much resource winning new business can demand from an agency. I was surprised, however, how seriously she took this and spent a lot of time telling her about times when we had been in the same situation in order to make her feel better!

(See Box 3.6 (pp 57–8) for the next diary entry.)
(*This is a diary of the day-to-day experiences of a financial PR manager. See Chapter 24 for more details.* Source: *Melanie Gerlis.*)

Definition: The *Dearing Report* was a report by Sir Ron Dearing in the UK into the whole of UK higher education (HE), which came up with specific recommendations for the sector as it moved towards the millennium. Many of his proposals were applauded and adopted by HE institutions.

What is clear is that skills have become an integral component of benchmarking (setting achievement and quality levels), and are therefore now part of the curriculum. There has been a trend in the last decade towards generic skills and towards the involvement of employers and educationalists in defining those skills. This has led to new concepts such as 'employability' and 'externality'. These have translated in the UK into the requirement for all students to have a personal progress file, which records and reflects on their individual achievements, and which follows on from school-based records of achievement. This sits well with the portfolio-based work of many PR-related HE courses.

This at least provides us with a potential paradigm for the PR practitioner where they become a lifelong learner and are able to reflect on their own learning and development throughout their career (and beyond). Education and training does not end with the last day of term or the last exam. From school, through education and training where learning logs or portfolios are used to evidence and assess certain skills, including reflection, through to CPD responsibility for our own learning, we never stop learning (see Mini case study 3.3–p 49).

Hargie (2000) suggests that competence in a profession involves three sets of skills:

1. cognitive (the knowledge base)
2. technical or manipulative skills inherent in a profession
3. social or communication skills.

TABLE 3.2   Key graduate skills (*source*: Fawkes and Tench 2004b)

Employers – combined evaluation of skills	Not important	%	Fairly important	%	Very important	%
Numeracy	7	7	65	63	28	27
Literacy	0	0	0	0	101	98
IT skills	2	2	49	47.5	49	47.5
Problem solving	1	1	21	20	77	75
Analytical thinking	0	0	26	25	73	70
Teamwork	0	0	11	10	87	84
Research skills	0	0	56	54	45	44

TABLE 3.3   *Port of Entry* recommendations on knowledge and skills (*source:* PRSA 1999)

Necessary knowledge includes	Necessary skills include
Communication and public relations theories	Research methods and analysis
Societal trends	Management of information
Legal requirements and issues	Problem solving and negotiation
Public relations history	Management of communication
Multicultural and global issues	Strategic planning
Participation in the professional PR community	Issues management
Working with a current issue	Audience segmentation
Applying cross-cultural and cross-gender sensitivity	Informative and persuasive writing
Communication and persuasion concepts and strategies strategies	Community relations, consumer relations, employee relations, other practice areas
Relationships and relationship building	Technological and visual literacy
Ethical issues	Managing people, programmes and resources
Marketing and finance	Sensitive interpersonal communication
Use of research and forecasting	Fluency in a foreign language
Organisational change and development	Ethical decision making
Message production	
Public speaking and presentation	

TABLE 3.4   DTI/IPR recommendations on knowledge and skills (*source:* based on DTI/IPR 2003)

Necessary knowledge includes	Necessary skills include
Understanding of business	Written and verbal communication
Corporate strategy	Creativity
Finance and corporate governance	Media relations
Data analysis	Crisis management
Audience research	Issues management
Management of resources and people	Interpersonal skills
	Credibility and integrity
	Flexibility

---

mini case study 3.2

Financial investor relations skills

- Understand in-depth how the markets work
- Count top opinion formers among contacts
- Able to talk to top broadsheet financial journalists
- Have the ear of the board members, if not on the board
- Understand the financial calendar and rules/regulations of the Stock Exchange

- Overview of all communication activity related to financial and investor relations
- Oversee production of annual report, etc.
- Effective proof-reading skills/on-press checking
- Manage media events
- Train senior management in media interviews
- Produce media and other stakeholder information

He points out that education and training have usually focused on the first at the expense of interpersonal skills. For the PR practitioner, interpersonal skills must surely be as important as any other and perhaps even a given.

This is a confusing situation, but the graduate in disciplines related to PR has the advantage that the sector already encompasses skills and employability as a key component, even intrinsic to the subject matter. Therefore, a portfolio that may evidence skills the student has mastered, illustrated in outcomes such as strategic campaign planning, press release writing or event management, may also be valuable for taking around to interviews to show employers what they can actually do and have done.

The Hargie approach to the skills debate, outlined above, mirrors the earlier suggestion that PR practitioners must have a wide range of skills to move up

---

mini case study 3.3

A student placement with MINI (Emma Knight)

I realised my interest in the PR profession as the UK government's 'spin doctors' were frantically 'burying bad news' in the wake of September 11th. I wondered who dealt with crisis management, image preservation and damage limitation.

Having worked for two years, I decided my first step was to get a good educational foundation. Navigating a diagonal career path from my current position (sales) to where I wanted to be (PR), seemed like the slow-track approach.

I opted for a university degree to give me the fundamental underpinning theory and practice required to kick start my career. University also offered support from practising lecturers who encouraged me to take my industrial year placement.

This was how I came to work as a PR year-placement student for MINI in 2004 – an international brand, part of an international organisation, the BMW Group.

The environment in which I worked was fast paced and continually changing. MINI was and still is one of the most exciting and fun brands in the motor industry, which provided lots of scope for PR. As a student, I was fortunate to be involved in projects at the strategic planning stages as well as implementation.

A typical day? There wasn't one. But that is the beauty of most PR roles, I think. Obviously there were some routine tasks such as preparing press kits and collating daily press coverage, but the majority of my role was spent working on projects to support the brand. I would arrange logistics for events, book flights and hotels for journalists, compile itineraries for press trips and host journalists at events.

In order to get the information I required for a press release, make an event work or obtain permission for a certain activity, occasionally my 'typical day' would be spent on the phone or writing emails to nobody other than MINI and BMW Group employees.

I believe building internal relations is among the most challenging issues that an in-house PR practitioner must deal with. Cynical though it may seem, everyone needs a favour once in a while. If you haven't any favours to cash in on, a potentially simple job can become quite time consuming.

PR as an industry is not always given the credibility it warrants. Fortunately PR for MINI is considered a fundamental part of the brand's presentation. As a sector I believe practitioners will continue to face the ongoing challenge of being taken seriously. It is the responsibility of each practitioner to promote PR as an indispensable function that adds value to an organisation. Do it, if not for the sector, for the sake of your budget!

Source: Emma Knight

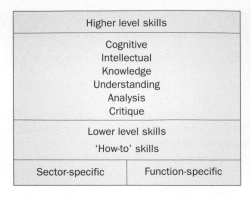

Higher level skills	
Cognitive Intellectual Knowledge Understanding Analysis Critique	
Lower level skills	
'How-to' skills	
Sector-specific	Function-specific

FIGURE 3.5   Skills range

the continuum. The UK-based perspective is supported by evidence from the United States. The PRSA study (1999) provides a wide perspective on addressing the 'next PR crisis', which is ensuring appropriate education and training. The emphasis here is on the complementary approach of knowledge that graduates are expected to have and skills specific to the profession (see Figure 3.5).

The model of the PR practitioner is now someone who encompasses both higher level and 'how to' skills, and is still (and always will be) learning. This provides a continuum with, at one end, someone ready to learn and, at the other, no end point as there is always room

---

box 3.4   Public relations competency factors

a) Strategy and action

1 Takes a strategic/long-term view
- plans ahead, remains focused on organisational objectives
- thinks beyond immediate issues and links to business
- has a vision of objectives and reviews them regularly

2 Investigates and analyses
- gathers, probes, tests information; analytical, gets to heart of issue
- uses a wide variety of sources, grasps key facts quickly
- analyses potential outcomes of situation

3 Makes decisions and acts
- willing to make tough, unpopular decisions based on information
- suggests various solutions, decides on course of action quickly
- makes things happen and acts with confidence

b) People skills

4 Understands others
- open minded when considering others, interested, empathic
- looks for win–win and mutual benefit
- shows respect, works to understand motivation of others

5 Leads and supports
- provides direction, advice and coaching
- fosters openness and information sharing, acknowledges contributions
- elevates insights to the board

c) Personal communication

6 Networks
- talks easily at all levels internally and externally
- builds strong, extended infrastructure across functions
- builds relationships with gatekeepers and is visible

7 Communicates
- verbally and in writing, clearly, consistently and convincingly
- supports arguments with facts and figures
- confronts senior people with difficult issues

d) Personal characteristics

8 Takes responsibility for high standards
- consistent with clear personal values aligned with organisation
- sets high goals and standards, accepts responsibility for them
- handles criticism well and learns from it

9 Maintains a positive outlook
- responds well to changes or setbacks, manages pressure well
- aware of difference between setback and failure, uses humour
- deals with ambiguity well, grasping the opportunity

10 Prepares thoroughly
- spends time understanding tasks and objectives, scenario plans
- involves team in planning
- constantly aware of arising issues

Source: Gregory 2005

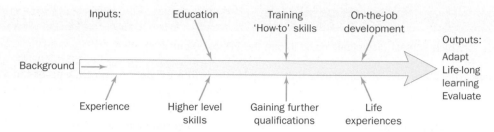

FIGURE 3.6   Public relations practitioner lifecycle

to learn more. What point they are at on that continuum will depend on background and experiences and the context in which they function. The school leaver who joins an agency on a trial period will be at one end of the continuum. If the employer provides in-house training, supports them through further education and training and the student wants to learn and develop, then they are as likely to get to the boardroom position in due course as someone who has come up a different route. They will be moving up the continuum. Their ability to succeed will be a combination of their own abilities and experiences and the expectations and input of others around them. This links well with the model of the practitioner as a system.

Gregory (2005) conducted research for the UK Communication Directors' Forum with board-level practitioners to draw up competency characteristics for the PR community. The research involved depth interviews with seven senior practitioners and identified 10 competency factors organised under four themes (see Box 3.4 and Figure 3.6).

Role of theory in practice

The value of theory as underpinning practice is up for discussion. Some practitioners will have managed very well for many years without theory, or rather they will have relied on their own version of common sense theory. Others have taken postgraduate courses, like a masters degree or the CIPR Diploma and been exposed to theory through education. Increasingly, public relations graduates who have studied theoretical modules in their degree courses are joining the profession and shaping the expectations of the next generation. The theory that practitioners have been exposed to will inform the role they play.

Relevant to this discussion is research conducted by Tench and Fawkes (2005) into PR education in Britain. Research was conducted with employers of PR students who were asked about different aspects of the curriculum and its value. Related to theory the practitioners were asked about the dissertation and how important it was as a core part of a public relations curriculum. The research found there was more enthusiasm for dissertations among in-house employers than consultancies, with over three-quarters (78%) of the former supporting dissertations, as against 56% of consultancies (see Figure 3.7, overleaf). Qualitative comments help explain these responses. Support for the dissertation was expressed as: '[proves] the student's understanding and application of theory and practice, assuming that the topic of the dissertation is relevant'; 'closest thing to thinking through a situation

---

A public sector practitioner's view

Working in the complex communication environment of local government, one seasoned PR practitioner, Michael McGivern from Chester City Council, has a particular view on the role of the PR practitioner. He suggests that they fulfil the textbook definition of 'communication technicians', but that in many cases that is all they are seen as. However, 'once your reputation is established, you will be called on as problem-solving facilitators'. He concludes that they operate under a communications management system in theory only, and that, in practice, senior management and other decision-makers see practitioners as advisors and facilitators rather than as one of them, the final decision-makers. 'This in turn means our role as organisational positioners is essentially theoretical.'

Which subject disciplines could inform the PR role (apart from PR)?

Feedback There are lots of disciplines that are relevant to the education and training of the PR practitioner:

- business and management/human resource management
- communication subject areas: marketing/marketing communication/advertising
- psychology
- cultural studies
- politics/sociology/social psychology
- media
- human geography.

The list is, in fact, endless. Are there any that are not in some way relevant?

from start to finish which is what is required to handle PR campaigns for clients'; 'a dissertation shows an ability to think and analyse, takes planning and writing skills and hopefully places demands on a student'. It should be noted that a minority of employers were extremely dismissive of all theory, and dissertations in particular: 'PR is concise; dissertations are long', said one.

Tench and Fawkes argue that the supporters seem to appreciate what a dissertation involves, unlike the detractors who clearly place no value at all on abstract thought. They argue that there are serious implications 'for the intellectual health of the industry. There is also evidence of a "shopping list" approach to education, with [a number of] employers mentioning the lack of benefit to them of a dissertation.'

The range of theory relevant to PR is explored fully in Chapters 8 and 9, but it is worth pointing out here that the majority of employers do value the role of theory in educating practitioners, albeit not so much as they value actual practical experience. Moreover, it is not only the views of employers that count in this

debate. See Think about 3.2, as Cheney and Christensen (2001: 167) point out:

Still, it is important that a discipline's theoretical agenda not simply be beholden to trends already present or incipient in the larger society. Otherwise, a discipline can fail to exercise its own capacity for leadership on both practical and moral grounds.

Professionalism

The issue of defining PR to protect its jurisdiction (or borders), discussed at the beginning of the chapter, has an impact not only on practice, as described earlier, but also on issues concerning the professionalisation of PR (Pieczka and L'Etang 2001).

There are a number of different approaches (called 'trait' and 'process') to what defines a profession and some controversy over whether PR qualifies for the term. For example, practitioners are not licensed, as doctors or lawyers are – indeed, even the UK CIPR's 8000 membership represent perhaps one-third, maybe less, of all eligible practitioners.

The 2000 Global Alliance of PR associations, however, declared its guiding principles of professionalism to be characterised by:

- mastery of a particular intellectual skill through education and training
- acceptance of duties to a broader society than merely one's clients or employers
- objectivity and high standards of conduct and performance (Theaker 2004).

The problematic nature of some of these concepts, such as defining or measuring 'objectivity' or the

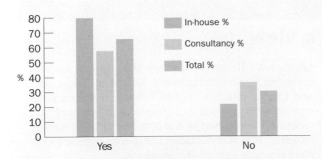

FIGURE 3.7   Should public relations degrees include a dissertation? (*Source:* Tench and Fawkes 2005)

difficulties in controlling members' standards of behaviour, is not examined.

However, everyone agrees with the first point: that education plays a key part in establishing any profession. L'Etang (2002) called education the 'crucial plank in PR's quest for professional status' and this view is shared by the PRSA *Port of Entry* (1999), which quotes Kerr (1995) as saying 'a profession gains its identity by making the university the port of entry'.

The development of PR education is discussed in more detail below. However, to set the context, there has always been a tension between education as training for the profession and as an end in itself. Research (Chan 2000, cited in Rawel 2002) continues to show that practitioners want PR education to be primarily of service to the industry. The focus for many academics, including Neff and Grunig, is also employability and the perspective of the profession: 'Research must address problems faced by working professionals and be directed toward improvement of the profession' (Grunig and Grunig 2000: 36).

L'Etang and Pieczka (1996: 11), on the other hand, argue that 'public relations practitioners must be generalists and . . . [develop] a habit of flexibility and a sensitivity to different ways of seeing the world'. Like Grunig, these authors stress the importance of education to the professionalisation of PR, but they assert that the professional status of the practitioner will be enhanced by intellectual reflexivity, following a multidisciplinary approach, rather than relying on one particular model of PR as the foundation for its education (see Think about 3.3).

Professional bodies

Another requirement for a profession is the existence of a body that represents and, in some cases – although not for PR – licenses its members to practise. The UK's professional body is the Chartered Institute of Public Relations (CIPR).

Key facts about the UK's Chartered Institute of Public Relations (CIPR)

■ The CIPR was founded in 1948 and awarded charter status in 2005.
■ The Institute has over 8000 members, with a turnover of £3m.

■ The CIPR is the largest professional body for PR practitioners in Europe.
■ The CIPR is a founding member of the Global Alliance for Public Relations and Communication Management.
■ CIPR membership has more than doubled in the last 10 years.
■ Approximately 60% of its members are female – this has grown from only 20% in 1987.
■ 45% of its members work in PR consultancy and 55% work in-house.
■ Two-thirds of CIPR members are based outside London.
■ The CIPR has a strict code of conduct that all members must abide by.
■ Membership grades (of the total CIPR membership):
  – Members: 56%
  – Fellows: 4%
  – Associates: 19%
  – Affiliates: 10%
  – Students: 10%
  – Global Affiliates: 1%.

The Institute represents and serves the interests of people working in PR, offering access to information, advice and support and providing networking and training opportunities through a wide variety of events, conferences and workshops.

The six grades of membership (Member, Fellow, Associate, Affiliate, Student and Global Affiliate) span the different levels of experience and qualifications in PR. Membership assessment is rigorous and is based on educational qualifications and multidisciplinary experience, ensuring standards are high.

The CIPR is represented throughout the UK by 13 regional groups and has 13 sectoral groups, these being:

■ arts, sports and tourism
■ construction and property
■ corporate and financial
■ education and skills
■ fifth estate – not-for-profit sector
■ government affairs
■ health and medical
■ internal communication alliance
■ international PR
■ local government
■ marketing communications

European public relations associations

PRVA – Public Relations Verband (Austria)
BPRCA – Belgian Public Relations Consultants Association
APRA – Czech Association of Public Relations Agencies
DKF – Dansk Kommunikationsfrening (Denmark)
STiL – Finnish Association of Communicators
Information, Presse & Communication (France)
DPRG – Deutsche Public Relations Gesellschaft EV (Germany)
HPRCA – Hellenic Public Relations Consultancies Association (Greece)
PRII – Public Relations Institute of Ireland
FERPI – Federazione Relazioni Pubbliche Italiana
Beroepsvereniging voor Communicatie (Netherlands)
Kommunikasjonsfreningen (Norway)
NIR – Norwegian Public Relations Consultants Association
APECOM – Association of Public Relations Consultancies in Portugal
PACO – Russian Public Relations Association
APRSR – Public Relations Association of the Slovak Republic
PRSS – Public Relations Society of Slovenia
ADECEC – Assoc de Empresas Consultoras en Relaciones Publicas (Spain)
SPRA – Swedish Public Relations Association
BPRA – Bund der Public Relations Agenturen der Schweiz (Switzerland)
PRCI – Public Relations Consultancies Inc. of Turkey
PRCA – Public Relations Consultants Association (UK)

Source: www.cipr.co.uk (CIPR)

- science, technology and engineering
- women in PR

The aims of the CIPR are:

- To provide a professional structure for the practice of public relations
- To enhance the ability and status of our members as professional practitioners
- To represent and serve the professional interests of our members
- To provide opportunities for members to meet and exchange views and ideas
- To raise standards within the profession through the promotion of best practice – including the production of best practice guides, case studies, training events and a continuous professional development scheme, Developing Excellence.

Source: www.cipr.co.uk (CIPR)

The following statements and comments are from the press release (February 2005) from the CIPR to announce the Charter status approval for the Institute:

This marks the 'coming of age' of the PR profession and is official recognition of the important and influential role that public relations plays in business, government and democratic society.

The award of a Charter by the Privy Council is affirmation of the role the Institute plays in the public relations industry – providing leadership, developing policy, raising standards through training and education, and making members accountable through the Code of Conduct.

Chris Genasi, 2005 President of the Chartered Institute of Public Relations, said:

This is a milestone for the Institute and the PR industry. The CIPR can now implement its strategy to further improve and support the industry with the formal stamp of approval from Government.

The IPR has been acknowledged as the official body to strengthen and lead the profession. The Government has recognised the PR industry as a leading player in public and corporate life and PR practitioners as professionals with specialist skills, knowledge and qualifications.

Colin Farrington, Director General of the CIPR, said:

Chartered status will make it easier for employers, clients and the general public to distinguish between PR practitioners who are prepared to commit to the industry code of conduct and to be accountable, and those who aren't. Membership of the Institute has always been about professionalism, commitment and standards and now Chartered status gives CIPR members external, third party approval and endorsement. Membership of CIPR is a clear demonstration of professionalism.

Source: www.cipr.co.uk (CIPR)

Box 3.5 details other European associations. All their websites contain much relevant information for further investigation (see Activity 3.5).

---

activity 3.5

Join an institute

Find the web address of the national institute where you are studying or working. Search the website for details about the national association. How many people are members? What benefits does membership bring? Could you be an associate or student member? Talk to a friend or colleague about the benefits of membership. If it is possible for you to be a member, why not think about joining?

Education and research

The first UK undergraduate degree in PR was launched at Bournemouth in 1989, followed by Leeds Metropolitan University and the College of St Mark and St John, Plymouth in 1990. The pioneer postgraduate courses were launched at Stirling University in 1989 and Manchester Metropolitan University shortly after. Research conducted in 2003 found 22 PR or similar undergraduate degrees in Britain, of which 13 were then approved by the CIPR. With the addition of non- or recently approved CIPR courses, it is estimated that approximately 500 PR undergraduates enrolled on UK PR courses in 2004 (Tench and Fawkes 2005).

PR education continues to evolve (Fawkes and Tench 2004a) and while most PR educators have practitioner backgrounds, many in Britain now have over a decade of teaching and research experience (L'Etang 1999). Teaching academics in the UK institutions are also increasingly acquiring doctorates and other research qualifications. New ideas, drawing on critical theory and other cultural and political approaches (see below) are being developed and taught as academics seek to expand the theoretical frameworks with which to critique PR and its role in society.

There has been a worldwide growth in courses at higher education (HE) level that aim to feed the profession, including general degrees covering PR as one part of a wider remit and specialist PR degrees (the UK CIPR approves a number) that focus on PR and its related context, with a commensurate growth in academics and academic publishing. According to Fawkes and Tench (2004b) even here the emphases in the programmes differ, from PR as a management discipline with an emphasis on strategy (in the business schools) to PR as an aspect of media activity with an emphasis on communication (media schools).

For many years the United States was the main repository of PR research; now Britain and Europe have developed an impressive research base. The term 'public relations' may not be familiar in other European countries, but the roles are similar. Van Ruler and Verčić (2004) highlight both the common underlying themes, such as professionalisation and the influence of communication technologies, set against the 'similar yet idiosyncratic' national backdrops, where differences are more obvious, from a study of PR within national contexts.

In addition, there are many other academic and functional disciplines, such as the social sciences, business and management, cultural studies, linguistics, media studies and psychology that also input into the research underpinning for the sector. This interdisciplinary approach is a strength; it provides a wide range of methodological options, such as a cultural studies approach to deconstruct PR case studies (Mickey 2003) rather than sticking to the traditional PR methodologies. This is known as theoretical pluralism (Cobley 1996).

Drawing on a wide range of references such as those outlined in Chapters 8 and 9 should increase the credibility in terms of knowledge and expertise of the practitioner who is pursuing a PR qualification.

Another backdrop to the role are the national initiatives within Britain at secondary and HE levels to encourage more vocational and skills-based programmes as a complement to the traditional academic route. This trend, which also attracts funding, means that a discipline such as PR, which successfully links academic, skills and employability, is well positioned for growth. So PR can be taught as a new-style foundation degree in the way that other subjects might not, given the inherent employer input prerequisite. Again, this may prove to be both a strength and a weakness: a strength because this offers a way forward where funding in more traditional programmes has been curtailed; a weakness because PR may lose academic credibility and become just another vocational training ground (see Mini case study 3.5). See also Boxes 3.6 and 3.7 – pp 56–9.

mini case study 3.5

Corporate communications for a university

David Marshall, Director of Corporate Communications at the University of Chester, emphasises the role of the PR practitioner as educator. He suggests that there are three stakeholder groups, all part of a continuum.

A key part of the role will be to advise the senior management team, taking them 'on a journey about changing the behaviour of the organisation'. At this boardroom level of education, the PR practitioner will need to speak their language and gain credibility through the appropriate use of theory and models. This is what he terms *strategic education*.

Then there is the *technician education* which is understanding and communicating the 'how to' but always within the strategic overview. You cannot divorce the theory from the practice and it is no good knowing lots about theory but less about the applied. The PR practitioner therefore must have the 'how to' confidence, which may span a number of different areas, such as media training, briefing design consultancy; and working with corporate video teams.

The final tranche in the educational triangle is *educating staff to represent the organisation*, the traditional ambassadors and advocates, both through strategic education (they need to see the bigger picture) and through technical training. This perspective suggests that the PR practitioner needs to know about education and training others and the best means of communicating sometimes difficult messages. It may be a foregone conclusion that because the PR practitioner knows about communication, they themselves will be effective communicators.

We know from the teaching profession that having the knowledge is not the same as being able to impart it.

David believes that the corporate communications role will often kick start this three-level process. The arrival of the corporate communications role will spark the discussion. The organisation will realise that it needs the corporate communications function. 'What surprises me is how many organisations struggle along without one for so long. All organisations need to be able to have an overview.'

---

box 3.6   Practitioner diary 15–18 November

More from the practitioner diary of Melanie Gerlis, associate partner for Finsbury financial public relations consultants

Monday 15 November

The son of one of my clients is in here on work experience this week. He is a recent graduate (2:1 in politics and philosophy from Leeds University) who is considering a career in PR and wants to learn more about it. I think it is a good idea to get work experience/internships before making decisions and admire people who have the energy to sort this out (even if it means using their parents' contacts . . .). However, I was struck by how difficult it is to explain exactly what we do. I talked to him for about an hour and realised that I hadn't explained: when the company was founded; its mission; our client list; and what we actually do all day! Instead, I had talked quite broadly about: how different the FPR industry is today compared to eight years ago (when I started); how financial reporting in the press has become much more sensationalist; and why it is difficult to expand our FPR model outside the UK – on reflection I don't think that any of this can have genuinely interested him at all. I have left him in the capable hands of one of the account executives who will hopefully be a bit more specific and will actually give him some work to do. Until people actually get stuck in I think it's very difficult to explain and understand.

Monday is 'conference call day' – most clients who have internal PR teams like to have weekly updates on Mondays. We talk about anything of relevance in the Sunday press (which can often set the agenda for the week ahead) and any other business that will relate to our ongoing work for the week. I regularly have a call with one client at 11.30am and a Europe-wide call with another client at 3pm. Depending on the workload, there is another client who likes a call at 4pm and another one that we talk to monthly on a Monday at 1pm – there are Mondays when I really don't move from my desk/headset! However, we do insist on regular contact – sometimes the client doesn't realise that they are doing something newsworthy that we can use for good coverage, and sometimes the client is so busy that they forget to tell us something of enormous significance that we then could get caught out on later in the week. The discipline of a regular call ensures that the communicators are communicating.

box 3.6 (continued)

Extra conference call put in at 5pm today – we are advising a hedge fund that is being bought by a US-based investment bank and have been expecting this transaction since July (i.e. for nearly four months). Eventually seems like we are getting somewhere but just tried to call in (to conference call) and the number we were given doesn't work. Given that the call combines people in New York, Paris and London, we could end up working late getting everyone on the same phone line even before we work out what work needs to be done. Very frustrating.

Tuesday 16 November

Difficult journey in today – tube shut; no cash for a cab; cash machine broken, etc. Amazingly I was only half an hour late.

The timing is still moving for this hedge fund sale – the latest is now 'hopefully by Thanksgiving' (Thursday week). The client, ideally, would like no press coverage of the transaction at all as they are worried about making public the very large amounts of money they will make and we are having to manage their expectations considerably as the UK press is particularly focused on wealth.

Lots of journalists chasing other stories today – LK Bennett, Phase 8 and Toys Я Us are all apparently up for sale and as a few of my clients are private equity companies (who have recently been buying out the high street) I got a lot of calls on the back of it – the *Financial Times* and *Sunday Times* are particularly keen to follow retail stories (although this is generally the most popular sector for most journalists). Frustratingly, I haven't yet been able to glean much more information from either bankers or clients.

We are organising a couple of events which involve some dull administration – one is a press conference in Paris at the end of this month for which our (French private equity) client is paying for journalists' travel and accommodation and people are being surprisingly picky about which Eurostar train they want to take/how long they want to stay in Paris/where they'd like to stay, etc. On reflection, I think we should have simply not given them the choice – it would be far easier to have dictated the train times we were prepared to pay for and let them make their own arrangements if they had specific requests. We are also organising our own Christmas drinks party for about 30 journalists in our sector and given that we have only just come up with the idea and format it is difficult to find anywhere in December that isn't already booked. And this is before we've even invited anyone.

Wednesday 17 November

I had a 10am meeting near home this morning so was afforded an extra bit of sleep which was great! The meeting wasn't particularly productive as it was with a client who likes to see us very regularly, even if there isn't anything specific to discuss. But it shows willing to turn up at their offices, rather than doing everything over the telephone/by email.

One of my insurance clients had an EGM (extraordinary general meeting) today to approve a rights issue it announced earlier this month, which extended its number of shares by an additional 50%. All shareholders are invited to vote to ensure that any change to the company's structure/policy/etc. is approved by its ultimate owners. The meeting was one of the smallest I've ever been to – three people from the company (who were the only shareholders present) and its advisors! Most votes had come in by proxy instead and there was an overwhelming majority so I guess corporate democracy was still in evidence. The client also agreed to pay us an extra fee for the work involved in the rights issue so we felt very satisfied with the outcome!

Work continued into the evening as my company celebrated its 10th anniversary with a drinks party at Christie's in St James's. All our clients were invited, together with luminaries from various banks, newspapers, Westminster and Whitehall. There was a very good turnout and I spent most of the time between 6.30 and 9.30 talking to contacts and clients, introducing them to each other and trying to steer clear of drinking too much champagne. There were quite a few people that I hadn't seen since our annual party last year so it was good to catch up, but on the whole I found it more like work than pleasure. We did then move on to a nearby wine bar and club to continue the celebrations more informally, but only once the very important people had left! I finally got home at 3am in a less than sober state, but by no means worse than some of my colleagues and the lingering journalists . . .

Thursday 18 November

Woke up worse for wear and went straight to a background meeting between my insurance client and a newswire journalist. As this was a client meeting, I got a taxi into the City and dutifully contacted a few colleagues to make sure that they would make it into the office (they all did!) and catch up on any

▶

box 3.6 (continued)

gossip that I missed out on. Five minutes before my meeting was due to happen, the journalist cancelled (very rude, very annoying, but sadly not that unusual).

I had several emails/messages from people who had been at the party (for various stages), all of whom had enjoyed the evening. Our boss sent an email later in the day summarising the goodwill generated:

> We had four national newspaper editors, seven city editors, four No 10 special advisors, a Cabinet minister, an EU trade commissioner and just over 30 chairmen and chief executives as well as many other interesting people from different walks of life. We have had a huge number of complimentary emails from clients, advisors and journalists.

A PR man to the core!

(See Box 3.7 for the next diary entry.)

(This is a diary of the day-to-day experiences of a financial PR manager. See Chapter 24 for more details. Source: *Melanie Gerlis.)*

---

box 3.7 **Practitioner diary 19–25 November**

More from the practitioner diary of Melanie Gerlis, associate partner for Finsbury financial public relations consultants

Friday 19 November

Very quiet day today as we had cleared the decks in anticipation of this investment bank/hedge fund transaction today, which didn't happen – again. We are now being told this will happen before Thanksgiving (next Thursday) but I have ceased to believe in it.

Sunday journalists still chasing for information on LK Bennett sale – all I could glean is that the price being touted in the press is higher than most people think will be the reality but this isn't something that people want to write about at this stage as they would be contradicting themselves.

Weekend 20/21 November

Business pages rather thin on the ground in terms of financial services stories so didn't get any press calls this weekend. Most of my boss's email re our party appeared in the business section of the *Observer*, which I'm sure he'll be delighted with!

Monday 22 November

Good interview with the finance director of my insurance client appeared in the weekly publication, *Financial News*, today. As it is a relatively small client, this is pretty good coverage and I am pleased because we had to twist the client's arm to get him to be a bit more proactive with the media. He is described as 'rapid speaking and focused but with an easy laugh', which is a relief as sometimes he can come across as a bit dry and uninteresting if he is uncomfortable.

The graduate who was here last week on work experience has proved extremely useful and has been asked to stay another fortnight. It has been interesting to watch someone go from complete ignorance to writing press storyboards for a major M&A (merger and acquisition) transaction. Proves the point that until you actually sit down and do the work it is difficult to understand.

We had drinks this evening to celebrate my insurance client's successful rights issue – a room in a bank full of advisors (mostly men) in grey suits. But some nice thank you speeches to make us all feel worthy.

Tuesday 23 November

Hedge fund client rang this morning to let me know that his sale will not be happening this week (so much for 'before Thanksgiving').

In the meantime, we are still trying to get journalists to commit to train times to and from Paris for a press conference next Tuesday. So far two out of four have actually agreed (different) times to travel, both of which are different to mine – secretary not happy. We also spent most of the day writing background

box 3.7 (continued)

information of all the journalists going on the trip and the publications that they work for in order to prepare the client prior to the press conference. I am getting concerned that we still haven't seen any evidence of what the client intends to say at this conference.

We are trying to persuade the *Financial Times* to write a big 'corporate restructuring' feature based on our Italian banking client whose CEO has totally reshaped the business after the last two years. We have managed to convince the comment editor, which is a very good start, but now have to ask the people who actually do the work (the journalists) to commit their time – ideally this side of Christmas. I suspect the workload will fall to the Milan correspondent, whom, unfortunately, I don't know – since (irritatingly) he has yet to return any of my calls on this.

Wednesday 24 November

The Business Life editor of the *Financial Times* has been persuaded to commission a corporate restructuring story on our Italian banking client, which is great news – it took a lot of convincing on my part and we are still at the mercy of our client pulling their finger out and not being unreasonable (unfortunately, they usually are . . .), but we can hopefully end the year on a better footing.

All seems in place for the press conference in Paris, I just need to organise myself for three days out of the office next week, which is more difficult than it should be. Luckily, I am well connected with my telephone and Blackberry and will hopefully be able to enjoy being away from the daily grind.

One of my other clients (another investment bank) has asked us to send them a broad strategy paper for their press activity next year. I have decided to do this on the back of telephone conversations with journalists so that I can back up my (very macro) suggestions with facts. I spoke to the banking editors at the *Wall Street Journal Europe* and *Financial Times* today and both conversations were extremely useful – both journalists have emphasised the need for the client to have a more visible European figurehead which will really please the new head of European banking who would like to have a higher profile.

Thursday 25 November

I had breakfast with a potential client this morning (another investment bank – isn't life exciting!). Actually a very useful breakfast – they don't use any external PR at the moment and are rumoured to be planning for an IPO (initial purchase offer) early next year so it is good to have an early 'in' with their head of PR.

Spent most of today writing up the journalist feedback on my existing investment banking client and turning it into a useful document. Took much longer than I expected to turn a few quotes into a strategy paper.

Yet another conference call about another transaction (private equity company buying a very small German car parts maker) – postponed throughout the day. We were finally meant to have this call at 5.30pm and it was postponed until tomorrow. I look forward to going through the same process again.

Pay day so all worth it . . .

(This is a diary of the day-to-day experiences of a financial PR manager. See Chapter 24 for more details. Source: *Melanie Gerlis.)*

Summary

This chapter has demonstrated the range of skills demanded of PR practitioners and, it is hoped, dispelled the false images of celebrity or spin presented in the introduction. It has shown the different ways in which PR is organised and delivered in Britain and in other countries and examined the issue of professionalism, as well as highlighting information about professional bodies in Britain and elsewhere. Finally, it addressed the evolving role of education in shaping the future of PR by providing the PR practitioner of the future.

This 'ideal' will be able to manage the complex, dynamic context and functions of their organisation as they will possess the cognitive, technical, social and communication skills to gain the confidence of colleagues from other sectors and functions. They will facilitate communication within their organisation, as well as with external publics; they will be able to advise senior management using their higher level skills as well as oversee more detailed hands-on activity (not least because they will have a clear understanding of relevant theories and their value to practice); they will be committed to lifelong learning and continual professional development, as well as being active in the professional body; and they will also educate others about the value of PR and in this way help reinforce the position of PR as a profession.

Is this too much to ask? Perhaps, but it is not impossible that practitioners of the future, who will achieve these kinds of standard are, even now, reading this chapter.

Bibliography

Allan, S. (2000). *News Culture*. Milton Keynes: Open University Press.

Bernstein, D. (1986). *Company Image and Reality*. Cassell.

Brody, E.W. (1992). 'We must act now to redeem PR's reputation'. *Public Relations Quarterly* **37**(3) in F. Cropp and J.D. Pincus (2001). 'The mystery of public relations' in *Handbook of Public Relations*. R.L. Heath (ed.). Thousand Oaks, CA: Sage.

Chan, G. (2000). 'Priorities old and new, for the research of public relations practice in the UK and their implications for academic debate'. Internal paper cited in 'How far do professional associations influence the direction of public relations education?'. A. Rawel. *Journal of Communication Management* **7**(1): 71–78.

Chartered Institute of Public Relations (2005). *www.cipr.co.uk*.

Cheney, G. and L.T. Christensen (2001). 'Public relations as contested terrain' in *Handbook of Public Relations*. R.L. Heath (ed.). Thousand Oaks, CA: Sage.

Cobley, P. (ed.) (1996). *The Communication Theory Reader*. London: Routledge.

Cutlip, S.M., A.H. Center and G.M. Broom (2000). *Effective Public Relations*, 8th edition. Upper Saddle River, NJ: Prentice Hall.

Dearing Report (1997). Higher education in the learning society: Report of the National Committee. The National Committee of Inquiry into Higher Education. London: HMSO.

DTI/IPR (Department of Trade and Industry/Institute of Public Relations) (2003). Unlocking the Potential of Public Relations: Developing Best Practice. London: DTI/IPR.

DeSanto, B. and D. Moss (2004). Defining and refining the core elements in public relations/corporate communications context: What do communication managers do? Paper presented at the 11th International Public Relations Symposium, Lake Bled, Slovenia.

Dowling, G. (2001). *Creating Corporate Reputations*. Oxford: Oxford University Press.

DTI/IPR (2003). 'Unlocking the potential of public relations. London: IPR.

Fawkes, J. (2004). 'What is public relations?' in *Handbook of Public Relations*. A. Theaker (ed.). London: Routledge.

Fawkes, J. and R. Tench (2004a). Does practitioner resistance to theory jeopardise the future of public relations in the UK? Paper presented at the 11th International Public Relations Research Symposium, Lake Bled, Slovenia.

Fawkes, J. and R. Tench (2004b). Public relations education in the UK. A research report for the Chartered Institute of Public Relations.

Garnham, N. (2000). 'Information society as theory or ideology'. *Information, Communication and Society* **3**:139–152.

Green, L. (2002). *Communication Technology and Society*. Thousand Oaks, CA: Sage.

Gregory, A. (2005). Research into competency characteristics of senior communicators for the UK Communications Directors' Forum. Research seminar presented at Leeds Metropolitan University, February.

Grunig, J.E. and L.A. Grunig, (2000). 'Implications of the IABC excellence study for PR education'. *Journal of Communication Management* **7**(1): 34–42.

Hague, P. (1998). *Questionnaire Design*, 3rd edition. London: Kogan Page.

Hargie, O. (2000). *The Handbook of Communication Skills*, 2nd edition. London: Routledge.

Heath, R.L. (2001). 'Shifting foundations: Public relations as relationship building' in *Handbook of Public Relations*. R.L. Heath (ed.). Thousand Oaks, CA: Sage.

Holtzhausen, D. (2002). 'Towards a post-modern research agenda for public relations'. *Public Relations Review* **28**(3): 251–264.

Hutton, J.G. (1999). 'The definition, dimensions and domain of public relations'. *Public Relations Review* **25** (2): 199–214.

Hutton, J.G. (2001). 'Defining the relationship between public relations and marketing' in *Handbook of Public Relations*. R.L. Heath (ed.). Thousand Oaks, CA: Sage.

Institute of Public Relations (2004). *Profile* **42**, April: 7.

Katz, D. and R.L. Kahn (1978). *The Social Psychology of Organizations*, 2nd edition. New York: John Wiley & Sons.

Kerr, C. (1995). *The Use of the University*, 4th edition. Cambridge, MA and London: Harvard University Press.

L'Etang, J. (1999). 'Public relations education in Britain: An historical review in the context of professionalisation'. *Public Relations Review* **25**(3): 261–289.

L'Etang, J. (2002). 'Public relations education in Britain: A review at the outset of the millennium and thoughts for a different research agenda'. *Journal of Communication Management* **7**(1): 43–53.

L'Etang, J. and M. Pieczka (eds) (1996). *Critical Perspectives in Public Relations*. London: ITBP.

McQuail, D. (2002). *Mass Communication Theory*. London: Sage.

Mickey, T. (2003). *Deconstructing Public Relations*. Hillsdale, NJ: Lawrence Erlbaum Associates.

Miles, S. (2001). *Social Theory in the Real World*. London: Sage.

Moss, D., A. Newman and B. DeSanto (2004). Defining and redefining the core elements of management in public relations/corporate communications context: What do communication managers do? Paper presented at the 11th International Public Relations Research Symposium, Lake Bled, Slovenia.

Neff, B.D., G. Walker, M.F. Smith and P.J. Creedon (1999). 'Outcomes desired by practitioners and academics'. *Public Relations Review* **25**(1): 29–44.

Pieczka, M. (2002). 'Public relations expertise deconstructed'. *Media Culture and Society* **24**(3): 301–323.

Pieczka, M. and J. L'Etang (2001). 'Public relations and the question of professionalism' in *Handbook of Public Relations*. R.L. Heath (ed.). Thousand Oaks, CA: Sage.

PRSA (Public Relations Society of America) (1999). (National Commission on Public Relations Education) *A Port of Entry – public relations education for the 21st century*. New York: PRSA.

Rawel, A. (2002). 'How far do professional associations influence the direction of public relations education?' *Journal of Communication Management* **7**(1): 71–78.

Schirato, T. and S. Yell (2000). *Communication and Culture*. London: Sage.

Tench, R. (2003). 'Stakeholder influences on the writing skills debate: A reflective evaluation in the context of vocational business education'. *Journal of Further and Higher Education* **27**(4), November .

Tench, R. and J. Fawkes (2005). Mind the gap – exploring attitudes to PR education between academics and employers. Paper presented at the Alan Rawel CIPR Academic Conference, University of Lincoln, March.

Theaker, A. (2004). 'Professionalism and regulation' in *Handbook of Public Relations*. A. Theaker (ed.). London: Routledge.

Turk, J.V., C. Botan and S.P. Morreale (1999). 'Meeting education challenges in the information age'. *Public Relations Review* **25**(1): 1–4.

Varey, R. (1997). 'Public relations in a new context: a corporate community of co-operation'. Paper presented at the 3rd Annual Conference of the Public Relations Educators' Forum.

Verćić, D., B. van Ruler, G. Butzchi and B. Flodin (2001). 'On the definition of public relations: A European view'. *Public Relations Review* **27**(4): 373–387.

van Ruler, B. and D. Verćić (eds) (2004). *Public Relations and Communication Management in Europe*. Berlin: de Gruter.

von Bertalanffy, L. (1969). *General Systems Theory: Foundations, development, applications*, 2nd edition. New York: Braziller.

Wilcox, D.L., P.H. Ault and W.K. Agee (2003). *Public Relations: Strategies and tactics*, 5th edition. New York: Addison–Wesley.

Wilkin, P. (2001). *The Political Economy of Global Communication: An introduction*. London: Pluto Press.

Windahl, S., B. Signitzer and J. Olson (1992). *Using Communication Theory*. London: Sage.

CHAPTER 4

Media context of contemporary public relations and journalism

Learning outcomes

By the end of this chapter you should be able to

■ identify the dynamic structures of radio, television and the press and their implications for the day-to-day practices of journalism

■ recognise the changing structures of concentrated ownership in the UK media industry and use media theories to make sense of them

■ discuss the implications of contemporary regulation of the media for the public interest

■ evaluate arguments for the distinctiveness and importance of the idea of 'the public interest' and explore how 'public interest' is created

■ discuss the globalisation of media ownership, new technology and media audiences that affect the UK media context

■ consider the ways in which the contemporary media context causes problems for the ethical behaviour of journalists and public relations practitioners.

Structure

■ Contemporary media context: the UK media industry

■ Theories of media

■ Regulating the media: from public interest to the market

■ 'Public interest'

■ Issues for public relations arising from the global media environment

■ Ethics of journalism and public relations

Introduction

At 6.07am on the morning of Monday 27 May 2003, Andrew Gilligan, a BBC journalist and defence correspondent, reported live on air on BBC Radio 4's flagship morning news programme, *Today*, that:

> the central claim in his [Prime Minister, Tony Blair's] dossier which he published in September [2002, was wrong] . . . [he] knew that the forty five minute figure was wrong *even before it [the government] decided to put it in* . . . Downing Street . . . *ordered a week before publication* . . . *it to be* sexed up, *to be made more exciting and ordered more facts to be* . . . *discovered.* (Coates 2004: our emphasis)

This news report then includes an extremely serious allegation. The allegation was that the serving prime minister and his 'spin doctors' pressured the intelligence services to report selectively the information they had and subsequently carefully edited it in order to justify the political goal of military engagement to topple the Iraqi regime. This news report was repeated in a toned-down form later on the same day on Radio 4, Radio 5 Live and in the BBC1 *10 O'Clock News*. It became the object of broader radio, television and newspaper coverage concerning the Labour government's case for a 'war on Iraq' and its attempt to convince public opinion of the 'serious and current' threat posed to the UK's interests by Saddam Hussein's regime. It subsequently became a key concern of the

Hutton Inquiry set up to investigate the circumstances surrounding the death of Dr David Kelly, a senior 'weapons of mass destruction' scientific expert, who was found to have been the key source of Andrew Gilligan's story.

Although the government was exonerated by the Inquiry, there is no doubt that public trust in the prime minister was shaken by these events. Furthermore, the BBC director general and chairman were pressured to resign (see also the BBC Case study in Chapter 17) after having been found to have been irresponsible in checking the editorial procedures that had allowed Gilligan to make his claim. This may have additional repercussions when the operating conditions of the BBC are considered under the 2006 Charter review.

What is highlighted by this news story and the subsequent media and political debate are the dynamic *political*, *economic* and *social conditions* under which contemporary journalism is carried out and the ethical considerations to which they give rise. Some have argued that in combination these factors have produced a *culture of spin* in which truth is secondary to attempts to influence the public for the benefit of private interests (Pitcher 2003).

Newspapers, which are subject to little regulation, have received the most blame for encouraging this culture of spin, although, as our example shows, other media are also implicated. This is the *media context* in which journalists and public relations practitioners engage in cooperative and conflictual relationships and which structures the news that citizens/readers/listeners rely on in order to make sense of the world.

Contemporary media context: the UK media industry

The communication media discussed in this chapter are the national newspapers, and radio and television stations that are available to the majority of the population of the United Kingdom. The UK has privately owned media in which corporations control large sections of the press, radio stations and television. This is known as *concentrated media ownership* and

these features of concentrated ownership are broadly similar to other European countries (Kelly et al. 2004). Some larger and more diversified media corporations own newspaper chains, magazine chains, radio and television. This is known as *cross-media (concentrated) ownership*. The broad outlines of media ownership in the fast changing sector of each medium in the UK today are represented in the next section.

> **Definition:** *Concentrated media ownership* refers to sections of the press, radio and television that are concentrated into a few companies or corporations.

Communication media

Newspapers

There are 1000 newspapers in the UK, including hundreds of local papers, 12 national dailies and 14 national Sunday papers. In 1997, 87% of sales were of newspapers owned by the top four newspaper groups, with Rupert Murdoch's News International accounting for 33% of all national daily press sold (Stokes and Reading 1999). National newspapers employ 2500 journalists, down from 3500 in the early 1970s, while the number of pages in daily newspapers increased between 63% and 125% between the mid-1980s and mid-1990s (Davis 2000). This has led to the increasing reliance of journalists on information from public relations practitioners who provide them with press releases and a decrease in the likelihood of investigative reporting.

PICTURE 4.1 The 'Iraq dossier' was produced by the UK government to argue its case for the war in Iraq. Its publication and subsequent media reporting had major political and media repercussions. (*Source:* © Reuters/ Corbis.)

Despite an increasing population, daily national newspaper sales declined by 6% between 1992 and 2002 and the sale of Sunday nationals declined by 13% in the same period (McNair 2003). This has led not only to a more concentrated and massively competitive market, in particular between *tabloids*, but also to attempts by the *broadsheets* to change in order to maintain market share.

Definition: *Tabloids* are small-format newspapers, sometimes referred to as the 'popular press', often written in a sensationalist style and containing a large number of photographs.

Definition: *Broadsheets* are large-format newspapers, sometimes referred to as 'serious' or 'quality' newspapers.

Beginning with *The Independent*, for example, some broadsheets changed to a 'compact' format that looks more like a tabloid newspaper. In order to maintain readership, papers have engaged in *'exclusives'*, *'tabloidisation'* and a variety of price-cutting strategies. These changes in the press have lent dynamism to the culture of spin since it has not been obliged by law to meet requirements of objectivity or impartiality.

Definition: *Exclusives* are stories that are made available to one newspaper about issues and people (for example, an interview with Princess Diana's former butler). 'Exclusives' are often supplied by public relations consultancies on behalf of their clients.

Definition: *Tabloidisation* occurs when a 'quality' broadsheet attempts to broaden its appeal to popular interests – for example, through a greater focus on 'human interest' stories and celebrity gossip.

Television

There are five national *terrestrial* UK TV channels: BBC1 and BBC2, ITV, Channel4 and Channel5. The last two started broadcasting in 1982 and 1997 respectively. There are 14 ITV licences, which have been amalgamating since the early 1990s and which are now owned by three companies: Granada Media, Carlton Communications and Scottish Media Group (Doyle 2002b). Since the mid-1980s, satellite television has emerged as an important TV provider in the UK, with BSkyB as the leading company, although it has taken until 2001 to become highly profitable (Doyle 2002a). Satellite TV has led to increased access to multi-channel television, including important new news providers such as Sky News and CNN.

Definition: *Terrestrial channels* are television channels that broadcast from the soil of the UK and not via satellite. Terrestrial channels are subject to greater regulation.

The government White Paper on Communications (DCMS-DTI 2000) showed the importance of these developments: in December 1980, UK viewers had access to 400 hours of television per week; by 2000 this had increased 100 fold to 40,000 hours. This has led to increased competition and a fall in audience share for all terrestrial channels. For those dependent on advertising for income (ITV, Channel4, Channel 5) this has led to potential falls in total income – held at bay, for now, by the massive expansion of TV broadcasting to 24 hours a day for these broadcasters.

Radio

There are five BBC national FM/LW radio stations (1, 2, 3, 4 and 5 Live) and three national commercial

---

box 4.1 **Impact of media commercialisation in the UK: implications for public relations**

The key effects of the dynamic commercialisation of media for public relations have been:

- the extension of the media cycle to 24 hours puts pressure on journalists actively to seek stories across the whole day and opportunities for public relations practitioners to place them
- the competitive 'chasing' of opportunities to be in contact with particular audiences (publics) means organisations of all kinds must think carefully about how they can use specific media to access niche audiences
- the expansion of the size and economic weight of media corporations in comparison with national media gives them greater market control
- greater emphasis on profitability and the economic benefits of media market control
- an increased role for independent producers and small media companies providing services to larger ones and therefore also of cultural intermediaries who design media products for fragmented audiences
- the expansion of freelance positions in journalism and public relations and a consequent increase in personal and professional competition for secure employment in these professions
- greater opportunities for, and difficulties in, media management for corporations and governments.

activity 4.1

Evaluating media content and context

Review the media available to you where you live. Check what choice of newspapers, radio stations and terrestrial news you have access to. Can you find examples of the transformation of media context discussed in this section – for example, the 24-hour media cycle, concentrated media ownership, a greater role for freelance employees and the targeting of niche audiences?

stations (Classic FM, Talksport and Virgin AM). The BBC also runs 38 local radio stations and there are about 200 local commercial stations. Commercial radio in the UK started late, in 1973, when independent local radio (ILR) was set up. ILR station owners have benefited from the capacity to merge and have 'become national operators by stealth' (Barnard 2000: 55). They include Capital and GWR, who owned all or substantial shares in 14 and 28 stations respectively in 2000. Since the early 2000s, digital (DAB) stations have been developed both by the BBC (BBC 7, BBC 6 Music, BBC Asian) and the commercial sector (Core, Life, Oneword) as well as DAB access to existing FM stations (Radio 4, BBC World Service, Classic FM) (Bobbett 2002). The expansion of radio stations in the 1990s led to a growth of 184% in radio's share of the national advertising market (Barnard 2000) and a multiplication of chances to access *niche audiences* for advertisers on the commercial stations (see Box 4.1 – earlier – and Activity 4.1).

Definition: Niche audiences are groups with shared interests who are traditionally hard to reach. Radio programmes that target Asian youths, retired people or jazz fans, for example, allow advertisers to reach a better defined audience than mainstream broadcasters.

Theories of media

The above 'facts' in themselves tell us little about why changes are occurring and what they mean for the role of the media in society. They need to be analysed within theories of media. In detailing different theories that interpret these changes in different ways we necessarily enter into controversies.

Liberal pluralism

This is a key theory in media studies and also the main 'common sense' assumption of media commentators. As such, this theory is rarely explained clearly. It is assumed that the mass media play predominantly informative roles in our society: that

they give citizens access to a variety of facts and opinions that enable us to make up our minds on the key issues of the day. This approach is not concerned about *media concentration* in itself. Rather it focuses attention on whether media concentration makes a difference to the *variety of information and ideas* we have access to. It is assumed that, as long as a very basic variety of media with different views is available, then the actual details of ownership are irrelevant.

Pluralism (diversity) of sources of information is the key issue for liberal pluralists, who assume that market-based media typically produce competition between different media owners and therefore the required variety of sources of information. From this perspective the concentration of media only rarely becomes so great as to close down sources of alternative ideas.

Liberal pluralist theories additionally construct the journalist as *autonomous* within these plural media worlds – not overly affected by anything other than the news values of timeliness, newness, etc. that guide journalistic practice (van Zoonen 1998; Campbell 2004). Other media theorists are less optimistic on this point (Davis 2002). Liberal pluralism only appears at all plausible in societies where media are relatively free from state control. Many societies do not benefit from this (limited) good fortune.

Political economy of media

Political economy theories view the question of diversity of media in quite a different way. They tend to be suspicious about liberal pluralist claims that we experience diversity or plurality in media. Rather they argue that a superficial multiplicity of coverage in our newspapers and in radio and TV hides a more general lack of *diversity* of opinion expressed in them precisely because of the concentration of media ownership (Mosco 1996).

In discussing the consequences of the concentration of mono-media and cross-media ownership, political economy approaches focus on the *power relations* that control the production, distribution and consumption of media (Mosco 1996). The state and corporations are considered to be the most powerful media actors. The implication of this power is that certain people get to decide what ideas and views people will and *will not* have access to and further will influence the perspectives that are used to discuss those views (Herman and Chomsky 1988; Mosco 1996; Philo, 1999). In this model, contrary to the liberal pluralist focus on the autonomy of journalism, journalists and the editorial practices of media are seen as responsible for the lack of diversity of coverage since they are the authors of the media stories.

Institutional/contextual analysis of media

Institutional (or contextual) theories of media have arisen in relation to the other two dominant theories. Barnett and Gaber (2001) argue that for both liberal pluralists and political economy approaches '*the identity* of the media owners is irrelevant' (our italics). Political economy approaches, they assert, assume that media coverage 'will by definition uphold the basic nostrums of *capitalism*' (2001: 58.) and, as we have already seen, liberal pluralism assumes that if ownership is widespread enough then media will 'ensure that a proper plurality of views . . . will be available' (ibid.).

Definition: *Capitalism* is an economic system based on privately owned businesses producing and distributing goods, the key features of which are a free, competitive market and making a profit from the sale of goods and services.

In contrast, Barnett and Gaber do consider the activities of *particular* media owners and investigate the subtle and particular influences that are brought to bear on journalists through owners' enforcement of particular practices of editorial control and, for example, the appointment of editors with views consistent with their own.

Above all, however, Barnett and Gaber suggest focusing more attention on the journalistic environment in which influence comes not so much from the particular actions of owners as from *everyday operational and journalistic practices* (p.59). To fill strict deadlines on a regular basis, it is simply much easier to sit at a desk, phone regular sources and rely on the provision of press releases by public relations practitioners in the local and national governments, corporations, trade unions and pressure groups (Davis 2000; Campbell 2004). In this context, some sources – government and corporations – have more resources and influence than others. It is this context of journalism as the brokering of perspectives and views of sources in its dynamic and disputed context that is a more appropriate framework for understanding contemporary media. Like the political economy approach, the contextual approach recognises that *power relations* are crucial, but considers that *power is diffused* throughout the day-to-day activity of media rather than concentrated in the hands of elites in the state and corporate world (see Think about 4.1).

Regulating the media: from public interest to the market

Recognition of the power of media has led to regulation. Regulation of broadcasting has depended on making clear the distinction between public and private interests and the idea that it is appropriate for broadcast media to have to serve the 'public interest'. As a result, broadcast media have been subject to law and policy since the 1920s in the UK and across Europe, to encourage some diversity of expression that supports this aim. The balance between public and state interest has varied across European countries in the twentieth century (Humphreys 1996). Regulation has involved:

- requiring the provision of certain kinds of content necessary to the public (news, current affairs, science, educational and religious programming), ensuring impartiality of media coverage and universal accessibility of media provision
- disallowing monopolisation of mono- and cross-media ownership.

Broadcast media

Currently, broadcast media in the UK are regulated by a new combined regulator, the Office for Communications (OFCOM), which took over the roles of five previous regulatory bodies in the sphere of broadcasting and telecommunications, and the conditions of the BBC Royal Charter, at the end of 2003. The need for a combined regulator was argued by the Labour government to encourage the dynamism of the media market in the UK and recognise convergences between technologies that were blurring the

---

think about 4.1   Media power and the limits of liberal pluralism

With the analysis of media context and content you carried out in Activity 4.1 you can also raise questions about the limits of liberal pluralism in making sense of media content.

- Does the variety of information and type of ideas we have access to depend on control over media by powerful owners or the state? (What stories are emphasised and what neglected in a five-minute radio news bulletin? How are they covered and how does that encourage you to think of the people or institution which is the object of the broadcast story?)
- What constrains the so-called autonomy of the journalist that liberal theory insists on?
- Which everyday journalistic practices define the form and contents of journalists' stories?

box 4.2	**Aims of the broadcast media laws**

- To encourage media to deliver economic performance for itself and to benefit the UK economy. This market philosophy has increasingly affected the BBC since audiences have become an important measure of accountability and a major factor in arguments for increasing or maintaining the level of the licence fee.
- To allow for greater levels of concentrated mono- and cross-media ownership (even breaking with some of the controls over non-UK nationals' ownership of UK media).
- To de-emphasise some elements of the previously accepted public service philosophy and incorporate a new focus on consumers.

boundaries between broadcasting and telecommunications. Similar debates have been occurring in most other European countries (Kelly et al. 2004).

Public policy concerning broadcasting ownership has regularly been related to concerns over *genuine pluralism of the media* (as discussed above) and the fear that privately owned media could not, on their own, provide all of the required media needs of the public (Doyle 2002a). Since the 1980s, government policy concerning media has encouraged the role of media as economic actors that benefit their owners and the broader population. Previously it had always

been thought that the *free market* and *public service* philosophies were incompatible. Conservative governments led the way in market-oriented media policy (Goodwin 1999) through the Broadcasting Act of 1996 and, following the election of a Labour government in 1997, the OFCOM Act of 2002 and the Communications Act 2003 which took it further. These laws are summarised in Box 4.2.

The mission statement of OFCOM (which can be found on the home page of its website) is evidence of these shifts. Its stated role is in 'serving citizen-*consumers* in the digital age' (our italics). The shift to

PICTURE 4.2   Ratings wars: *Strictly Come Dancing*, shown on BBC on Saturday evenings, delivered an estimated peak audience of 11.2m compared to ITV's 9.9m viewers of *The X Factor* (*The Guardian*, 13 December 2004) – evidence of the BBC's efforts to appeal to consumer interests. (*Source:* Kieron McCarron/BBC.)

a market-based policy puts in doubt some of the historic regulation of media for the public interest by giving greater power to the private interests of corporations at the expense of a still greater commitment to media pluralism.

> **Definition:** *Free market* means the idea that businesses – in this case media organisations – operate competitively without government interference to provide a service that the market wants.

> **Definition:** *Public service* represents the idea that broadcast media have a responsibility to provide a service to inform, educate and entertain the public. Implicit in this idea is that minority interests are catered for.

The press

In contrast to broadcast media, and in common with most of Europe, the press in the UK has been self-regulated. Since the 1990s, the industry has regulated itself through the Press Complaints Commission (PCC), but as an organisation it has only advisory powers and a voluntary code of practice. It works by means of speedy judgements made over complaints about particular media stories (often involving privacy issues), rather than through the much slower systems whereby complainants go through the courts. It does not operate according to an ideal of public service but more like the 'complaints department of a commercial organization' (Petley 1999: 155).

The lack of effective demand for the press to meet public service requirements similar to those of broadcast media is indicative of the power of organised press interests in resisting any attempts to impose constraints on the industry. To find out more about the PCC and its role, go to www.pcc.org.uk/students/faqsanswered.htm (see Activity 4.2).

'Public interest'

Although, as we have seen, regulation of broadcasting in the UK has been based on the distinction between *public and private interests*, this distinction is, in

activity 4.2

Questioning broadcasting regulation

In the UK, OFCOM regulates to encourage both media diversity and a competitive UK media industry. What tensions arise in achieving these different outcomes? Are the interests and needs of citizens and consumers always the same? How does OFCOM balance them? (Take a look at OFCOM's website at www.ofcom.gov.uk)

fact, greatly contested. There are philosophical difficulties in defining interests at all since they seem to require distinguishing consumer wants and desires from what might be termed 'real' interests (Lewin 1991). This opens up the potential for *paternalistic* administration of peoples' 'real' interests that are known by experts, but not by people themselves.

> **Definition:** *Paternalism* is when an elite group of people, often experts, make decisions on behalf of the general public, about what is 'good' or appropriate.

We need to explore the concept of the public interest since it has been of enormous importance in the history of *representative democracy* and in the way media have been perceived as a public resource.

> **Definition:** *Representative democracy* is a system of democracy whereby people are allowed to vote for somebody to represent them in government. In the UK, this happens at local level in council elections and at national level in the House of Commons.

One of the first distinctions to be made is between public interest and private interest. It may be in a sports fan's private interest – or to their advantage – if television covers sports extensively, even to the exclusion of, say, news and current affairs programming. It would not be in the public interest, however, since news programming is necessary for the public in general to become and remain informed about important issues affecting public life. The latter programming would benefit all whereas the former organisation of sports television would benefit only a minority.

The second important distinction is between public interest as *shared private interests* and a more radical conception of the public interest as 'the interests of the public as a collective body' (Heywood 1999: 243). For the former a good example would be the provision of security against external aggression: this is a private interest that all members of the community have in common. What distinguishes the more radical conception of public interest is that we do not conceive of it as the collective interests of individuals but as *them as a collective body*.

This radical public interest is difficult to measure. This is the case, in part, because politicians regularly use such collective concepts in a very loose way ('the common good', 'the national interest') and as a result they become devalued. In addition, the public is 'included' as a reference point in politicians' speeches and also the media programmes. For example, the use of opinion polls, vox pop interviews ('voice of the people') and phone-ins constantly elicits and manufactures the opinions of some members of the public as one measure of where the public interest lies. Because of this the public interest as an idea has been subject to growing criticism. It is also difficult to measure because scholars and politicians have used ideas for talking about the public that assume that people are primarily, or entirely, motivated by selfish interests. This discussion has arisen, to a degree, in line with the increased focus on market-oriented media.

It is convenient for media providers to believe that people are self-interested and that the 'public interest' is an incoherent conception. In that way they do not have to serve the public and perhaps will avoid the language of the public altogether. Alternatively, they can use it inappropriately as in the case when a large minority of the population chooses, individually, to consume the same media programme (soap opera audiences of 17 million in the UK, for example) and this is taken as a measure of the public interest (common interest) when, at best, it measures only what some members of the public have *shown an interest in*.

In addition to this distinction between the public interest as a shared interest in common between all and something that has interested a large minority of the population, there is an important distinction to be made with regard to narrower publics. Imagine any interest group organising to effect changes in their local radio station – for example, in broadcasting more 'local' issues. In order to organise they need to discuss and debate, set policy and organise the practical circumstances of any action they take. Such a group is organising the collective interest of the group they gather together. As such they are one example of an emergent public (one of many such 'publics' – see Chapter 12). Imagine likewise, a small audience of a local cable television programme. They are interested in the programme but do not necessarily, as an audience, further interact with each other or influence each others' thinking or action. As such they are merely an *aggregate 'public'*, one of many 'publics'.

> **Definition:** An *aggregate public* is a group of individuals who make up an audience for a television programme but who do not necessarily interact and influence each other.

The relation between the different concepts of public/publics can be seen in Figure 4.1.

What is generally termed the public interest (B) relates to interests people have collectively, whether or not they are aware of them. It is an emergent phenomenon arising in relation to the needs (rather than merely wants) of 'the public' as a collective entity. 'Emergent' refers to the creation or recognition of in-

	Aggregate	Emergent
The public	**A** What people are (happen to be) interested in	**B** The public interest
Publics	**C** What a group or stakeholders are interested in	**D** The collective interests of a group or stakeholders

FIGURE 4.1 Aggregate and emergent concepts of the 'public interest'

terests arising out of the interaction of people. This view holds that the discussion, debate and cooperation of views are crucial in order to articulate the public interest rather than merely adding together (aggregating) the views of individuals. There can be similar emergent interests for small subgroups of society or 'publics' (D).

The *aggregate* versions of the public or 'publics' (A and C) are measured not by needs recognised in debate but rather the desires, wishes or proclaimed preferences of individuals. Further these are merely added together (aggregated) rather than being themselves a product of debate and discussion. Aggregate conceptions of public or publics are often used by commercial companies to argue that what people buy or watch en masse is (simply) the interest of that public or those publics. The concept of the public interest, on the other hand, allows (and requires) a critical assessment of these preferences.

Heywood (1999) has cogently argued that the emergent conception of the public interest (since it can be used to deny people's expressed preferences in order to fulfil their 'needs' or 'interests') is a device often used manipulatively to give 'the public' something that those in authority desire them to have. Fortunately, the public interest can be shown to exist even if the clear identification of that public interest can always be contested, for the following reasons: first, an unrestrained pursuit of self-interest is self-defeating (therefore something other than mere self-interest must exist); and, second, and most importantly, in the existence of *public goods*.

> **Definition:** *Public goods* are required by everybody but no one, individually, has an incentive to produce. Examples of these are energy conservation and the problems of pollution.

Public goods also exist in the media sphere where neither individuals nor market forces will produce them. They have been described as: 'general education,

think about 4.2 **The public interest**

Why might we want to distinguish between the public interest defined as the aggregation of individual decisions (like 16 million people deciding to watch a football match) and the debate and discussion, through media, whereby a sense of the public interest might emerge? (For example, should we be shown terrorists' videos of real executions?)

If we use this distinction, does it make a difference to how we understand the roles of broadcasters?

objective information, universally accessible media of communication, public libraries . . . markets provide these things at best *unequally, if at all*' (Leys 2001: 220, our italics).

These goods, Leys suggests, would not be provided by the private or market sector because the level of profits attainable from their provision is simply too low. If this is the case then we have a powerful reason for recognising the public interest and then regulating media on that basis (see Think about 4.2).

Public interest and the problem of paternalism

The difficulty in clearly articulating where the public interest lies opens the concept to paternalistic roles for experts. This makes provision for the public interest inherently problematic (Scruton 1983). There might, for example, be a variety of ways of providing for the public interest in media. Vasquez and Taylor, for instance, argue that 'public interest is partly created and sustained through a process of communication' (2001: 149). Two important consequences follow from this:

1 'Public interest', although important in its requirements and consequences, does not have any *simple and easily identifiable existence* outside public debate about what it might be: to fully exist, 'public interest' needs to be articulated and identified in wide-ranging and inclusive discussions.
2 The fact that public interest does not exist independently of discussion means that media have a crucial role to play in *providing the resources and the environment* through which conceptions of the public interest can be articulated and debated.

Traditionally, as we have seen, national broadcasting has been charged with providing the context in which 'public interest' can be debated. However, there are several reasons why the communicative creation and maintenance of the public interest places the BBC and terrestrial channels, which in the UK also have public service duties, in difficulties.

First, the BBC has never been independent enough of government – which selects the director general

(DG), and through the DG the board of governors, and sets the level of the licence fee – to articulate a public interest philosophy in a coherent and consistent manner free from government control.

Second, even when the BBC has been able to act more independently than at present, it was not able to act in a self-evident public interest – which, as we have seen, must be created in debate. What it did was *interpret* a public service philosophy of what was *good* for the audience without giving the audience the resources to articulate alternatives. The BBC has acted, for the most part, as if *serving the public* were unproblematic. The relatively low level and indirectness of the accountability of the BBC to its audiences means that there has been little check on how adequately it has actually done so.

Third, it is not perfectly clear how well and fully the BBC has served the public interest in providing *pluralism of media content*.

> **Definition:** Media pluralism means 'the presence of a number of *different and independent voices*, and of *different political opinions and representations of culture* within the media' (Doyle 2002b: 11, our italics).

But to what extent have the BBC and the terrestrial channels carried this out? The BBC's definition of impartiality in its news, politics, and current affairs programming has been interpreted in terms of the presentation of the views of the governing political party (currently Labour), the opposition (in this case, the Conservatives) and, to an extent, the Liberal Democrats. Although inclusive in one way it also excludes a variety of other minority political parties or viewpoints (different and independent) from debate and discussion.

The BBC has been very slow in allowing groups to represent themselves, preferring to allow expert makers to produce programming (representations of culture). How often do minority groups get to make programmes themselves, especially for mainstream, rather than specifically minority, audiences?

Although there is genuine disagreement on precisely how much pluralism has been delivered by public service broadcasting, there has been enough

activity 4.3

Paternalism and the public interest

Find examples of media defining what is good for people to read, watch or listen to. How have they used their editorial power to close down debates? How do they represent (if at all) the variety of views, cultures, lifestyles and attitudes in your country or region today?

disquiet on this point to encourage the development of normative approaches that emphasise radical reform of the media system in order to fulfil the demands of pluralism for the public interest. Curran (2000) suggests the supplementation of the existing public service and the private enterprise sectors to empower people precisely by 'enabling them to explore where their interest lies' through access to a thoroughly pluralistic media. He suggests the development of new media sectors to supplement the existing commercial and public service ones. This is in line with Vasquez and Taylor's (2001) emphasis on the communicative creation of the public interest. The difficulty is that these concerns seem both necessary and also quite idealistic in a context where media policy has made a long move towards market philosophies. This move is occurring within European countries (Kelly et al. 2004) and across the world (Doyle 2002b) (see Activity 4.3).

Issues for public relations arising from the global media environment

The shift of media regulation from a public to a more market-based philosophy also marks a broader globalisation of media and of the media environment that affects the practice of public relations and journalism. The contexts that have changed are:

- globalisation of media ownership (whereby media moguls from one part of the world own newspapers, radio and TV stations all over the world and link them in global economic strategies)
- development of new media formats, frameworks and platforms
- important technological developments
- changes in audiences' loyalties.

Globalisation of media ownership

The concentration of mono- and cross-media ownership, already examined with regard to the UK, also has a worldwide dimension. From the 1960s, alongside the increase in general transnational and global companies (TNCs), we have seen the rise of global media companies.

For example, Rupert Murdoch's News Corporation owns newspapers, publishing companies, and TV and radio stations across the UK, the USA, Australia and the Far East. This enables control over media markets, the deployment of economies of scale, and cross-media subsidisation on a global scale. Increasingly, media corporations have become part of global conglomerates with more tightly organised relationships to making profits in a context where serving *which* public interest becomes a fundamental, and very complex, question.

New formats, frameworks and platforms

New, smaller scale, global media organisations have been created around new products and media formats. CNN is a key example since its global reach is not only economic, but relates also to cultural globalisation through the provision of new media outlets that create a sense of the news 'worldwide' (Volkmer 1999). Established media providers such as the BBC, through its World Service radio and TV broadcasting and its planned Arabic-language TV service, has expanded into this new global news market, as have providers from the Arab/Muslim world such as Al-Jazeera TV (El-Nawawy and Iskander 2002), (in)famous for playing videotapes of Osama Bin-Laden's speeches. Al-Jazeera has itself diversified further during 2006 with the setting up of an English language version, employing established western journalists. Satellite has provided a new media platform for the delivery of media services, often by new methods of payment such as the subscription model most famously employed with success by BSkyB, whose income now exceeds that of the BBC. Once such a new platform is widespread, it encourages the dynamic commercial provision of alliances between media companies for establishing the distribution of new channels and services. Concerns over *convergent* technologies have, as we have already seen, been taken up into UK media regulation policy.

> *Definition:* Convergence refers to the process of technologies coming together from different directions. The mobile telephone is the product of the convergence between telecommunications (sending/receiving messages) and computers (processing information). Once in existence, the phone can also be used to combine (converge) further technologies – taking photographs using the phone for example.

Technological developments

The availability of inexpensive new technology is also being used to change the roles of public relations personnel and journalists – the ethical dilemmas of

PICTURE 4.3   Al-Jazeera TV is (in)famous for playing videotapes of Osama Bin-Laden's speeches which have subsequently been broadcast worldwide through western media channels. (*Source:* © Maher Attar/Corbis Sygma.)

which we shall explore later in this chapter. The technological developments of light digital cameras, highly portable sound equipment, mobile global communications and the internet have led, according to Bennett and Entman (2001), to a paradoxical outcome: 'flattening media and political power hierarchies as concentration of media ownership and co-operation grows' (pp.478–479).

A tension has been created between TNCs motivated by control over existing markets and small, but sometimes worldwide, media companies aiming to create markets for new media products. These media products are designed for technological tools and communication devices that allow space and time, and thereby lives, to be reconfigured. The mobile telephone is the most dynamic recent example of myriad 'time-shifting' technologies developed for domestic and personal use since the video recorder in the late 1970s. These technologies open up new possibilities for small companies but also encourage the further intensification of 24-hour media culture. This leads to the customisation of media production and consumption. For example, the contemporary digital mobile phone allows companies to commercialise ring tones and news services. Individual mobile phone users access what services they like, although often they are only making 'choices' from menus set by TNCs.

The customisability of media production and consumption via new technology is thus a double-edged sword. It can lead to challenges to the powerful media elites but also the erosion of conceptions of 'the public interest' as media users make *individualised* choices and thereby consume a very different array of images, sounds and symbols from their neighbours.

While some welcome the world wide web as aiding the dissemination of genuine news, others argue that it will lead to an extension and intensification of the 'culture of spin' (Pitcher 2003).

Changes in loyalty

The contemporary media environment challenges the older one. As media outlets increase in number, the potential is always present for the erosion of previously settled audience loyalty. The share of the TV market for BBC1, for example, has reduced in line with the expansion in audience access to a wider range of terrestrial and non-terrestrial TV channels. With regard to news, for example, this means that BBC1 early evening news which had 8.2 million viewers in 1989 now gets 5.9 million viewers (McNair 2003) in spite of an increased UK population. The media environment is now that of the *fragmentation of audiences* and there is deep concern that it is no longer possible to talk about such communicatively constructed entities as 'the public'. These shifts in the attention of audiences are likely to continue and some have feared it will lead to the end of 'the public' altogether (Boggs 2000; Franklin 2004). These changes raise questions about new options for public relations personnel and the creation of new potential employers.

The new global media environment, as a product of economic globalisation and concentration of media ownership and the fragmenting effects of new formats, new technology and changed loyalties of audiences, leads to a world of exciting possibilities but it is also one of increased insecurity and risk and greater ethical dilemmas. These changes also raise difficulties in espousing and fulfilling public interest aspects of professional codes of conduct, as the next section seeks to explore.

Ethics of journalism and public relations

The transformation of the global media context raises both new and, in a more insistent manner, older ethical questions for those working in journalism and public relations. As we have seen, the competitive and dynamic nature of the industry discourages the public interest role of journalists whose work is tending to become more an adjunct to the private profit functions of media corporations. It also works with the dominant culture of journalism, which emphasises technical skills rather than the reflective and ethical approaches the globalisation of the media requires. New ethical dilemmas raised in this context include whether it is possible to restrict ethical consideration

box 4.3	**Professional codes of ethics**

Codes of ethics produced by professional bodies perform a variety of roles (Banks 2004). They can be:

- rhetorical devices: to establish or legitimate the role of the profession
- aspirational: establishing values which cannot now be practised with any regularity but are 'an ideal to strive for'
- educational: offering a standard and way of approaching ethical concerns rather than detailed guidance to individual cases.

Source: Banks 2004: 117–121

to one country alone (Keeble 2001) and how the intercultural complexity brought to firms and countries through globalisation can be appropriately served (Day et al. 2001). The working lives of journalists and public relations practitioners occur in a variety of settings. The division of complex working lives across different employers, work practices, technical skills and work groups discourages broader thinking about ethical concerns and makes it difficult to establish the links needed to create responsibility for issues more general than 'getting the job done' and to resist the agenda-setting activity of more powerful actors. Further, their roles, as we discussed earlier, are interdependent, and this has led to sometimes bitter jurisdictional or power struggles between journalism and public relations (Pieczka and L'Etang 2001).

It is instructive to understand both occupations as involved in strategies of professionalisation (Collins 1990; Macdonald 1995; Friedson 2001). Such strategies have the joint aims of producing monopolies in the market for their services based on claims to expertise and to lead to fuller recognition within the social order (Macdonald 1995). Many occupations have tried to professionalise in this way in order to 'evade the control of others' (Collins 1990) in the work situations of contemporary society. In order to do so, as Friedson (2001: 214) argues: 'They must persuade others that the discipline is of special value either to the public at large or to an important interest of the state or an influential elite'.

We can see this process in the way both the UK's National Union of Journalists (NUJ) and the Chartered Institute of Public Relations (CIPR) have updated their professional codes since the mid-1980s to take on board changes in society and media. Neither occupation has been very successful in claiming special knowledge nor does either seem to have incorporated the overwhelming majority of potential practitioners into their respective occupational bodies. Of

late they have put more effort into trying to show that their work is of special value to the public, while not imposing too powerful constraints on practitioners who might be reluctant to join if membership would damage their occupational chances. Both therefore have changed professional codes in ways that *decrease* the sanctioning power of the organisation over practitioners who fall foul of them. In this respect, they are aspirational and rhetorical documents (see below) rather than codes that really restrict and sanction inadequate or unethical performance.

Both the NUJ and the CIPR highlight the role of 'the public interest' in their codes of practice in seeking to persuade others of their integrity. The NUJ Code of Conduct forbids intrusion into people's private lives unless there are 'overriding considerations of public interest' (section 6).[1] The section of the CIPR's Code of Conduct on 'principles of good practice' suggests that an important part of their integrity as a profession lies in 'honest and responsible regard for the public interest', which might override the responsibility towards client confidentiality if 'the public interest is at stake'.[2] Both codes can be found at, respectively, www.nuj.org.uk and www.cipr.org.uk

Since professions, in part, define themselves in terms of the special knowledge and practices in which they engage, codes of ethics embody arguments or claims for professional autonomy: for the right to set one's own goals and standards (see Box 4.3). The CIPR has recently obtained its own charter and in achieving this has had to demonstrate the reputation of an established profession (Pieczka and L'Etang 2001; Morgan 2004). Involvement of the CIPR can be seen in the

---

[1] Find at www.nuj.org.uk/inner.php?docid=59&PHPSESSID =dcdc9f4e22a758f1b28b8953o2989cc5

[2] Find at www.cipr.co.uk/Membership/membership.htm

light of the debate concerning 'spin' arising in relation to the findings of the Hutton Inquiry, in particular the roles of journalists and public relations practitioners in the attempts to convince public opinion of the potential challenge to the UK's national interest posed by the Iraqi regime. In the UK, both professional bodies have been rethinking their relationship to the culture of spin in the light of the reports on government communications (Phillis, Hutton and Butler) and, in the aftermath of the Hutton Report, the BBC's Neil Report into journalistic and editorial roles. Is it possible that the culture of spin is an artefact of a particular configuration of circumstances: of competitive media, slack and inappropriate regulation of the press and a particular culture of journalism and public relations that could be significantly changed by efforts in the commitments of the professions and the division of tasks in the media? Such is Pitcher's (2003) argument and the hope of journalists and public relations practitioners who have recently been discussing what might be done. The 2004 President of the CIPR, Professor Anne Gregory, who has been very active in these debates and the attempt to make public relations more trustworthy, thinks so too, as she speculates that 'genuine public relations is ethical and a force for good' (Urquhart 2004). Such a role cannot, however, be merely wished into existence. As John Street argues in relation to journalism, these roles concern power and require changes to 'the allocation of resources and the organisation of practices' (Street 2001: 160). Both journalists and public relations practitioners have, perhaps rightly, often been seen as 'the lapdogs of partial interests, not the watchdogs of the public interest' (p.146.).

However, if the culture of spin is the product of a linking of circumstances, it might be amenable to change. Such change would need to face the tough challenge of the professional codes of the NUJ and CIPR, meeting in practice their aspirational and rhetorical functions. In its newly acquired chartered status, the CIPR will need to demonstrate both a sharpening of its code and also evidence that it is properly monitored and enforced (cf. Friedson 2001). Such a demonstration of trustworthiness will involve real change, requiring public relations practitioners

---

activity 4.4

Impacts of the global media environment

Look for examples of any one of the issues discussed here:

- globalisation of media ownership
- new formats, frameworks and platforms
- technological developments
- changes in audience loyalty.

What difference do they make to individuals' consumption of media? What difference do they make to the role of the journalist? What difference do they make to the role of the public relations practitioner?

---

activity 4.5

Public interest and the ethics of public relations

Does public relations contribute to the 'culture of spin'? Find some 'best case' examples where public relations as a profession lives up to Professor Anne Gregory's exacting requirements to be ethical and promote 'the public interest'.

---

to recognise conflicts of interest between truth telling and 'trying to keep clients happy' (Morgan 2004; Ryle 2004). Professor Gregory sees the need to face these difficulties since 'making consistent ethical decisions in a diverse world where cultures and values clash is not easy' (Ryle 2004). The benefits of chartered status might, however, be so great as to be worth the effort to demonstrate trustworthiness. Practising in a media context in which quick fixes, fast decisions and the exploration of ethically dubious opportunities are quite routine will prove exacting, if worthwhile. If success in the charter process does lead to 'work in *the public interest* to promote the highest standards of ethical public relations' (YEP 2004, our italics) then we shall all benefit. The critical attitude implicit in the analysis of the power of occupational roles will require tough questions to be asked of any claims that the charter process has produced such an outcome (see Activities 4.4 and 4.5).

Summary

This chapter has discussed the UK media context of contemporary public relations and journalism, highlighting the central role of media ownership, together with changing media regulation, practices and technologies in today's global environment. The changing nature of media audiences from mass consumers to personal users of media was identified. Key theories for understanding the media context were discussed and, in particular, the issue of 'the public interest' that underpins many assumptions about the role of media in society. Our discussion led to questions of ethics for both the public relations practitioner and journalist raised by public concern around 'the culture of spin' and of whether the aspirations of professionalism for both occupations can help solve the problems inherent in a public sphere where vested commercial interests are at stake.

Bibliography

Banks, S. (2004). *Ethics, Accountability and the Social Professions*. Basingstoke and New York: Palgrave Macmillan.

Barnard, S. (2000). *Studying Radio*. London: Arnold.

Barnett, S. and I. Gaber (2001). *Westminster Tales: The twenty-first-century crisis in political journalism*. London: Continuum.

Bennett, W.L. and R.M. Entman (2001). 'Communication and the future of democracy' in *Mediated Politics: Communication in the future of democracy*. W.L. Bennett and R.M. Entman. (eds). Cambridge: Cambridge University Press.

Bobbett, D. (ed.) (2002). *World Radio TV Handbook: The directory of international broadcasting*. Milton Keynes: WRTH Publications.

Boggs, C. (2000). *The End of Politics: Corporate power and the decline of the public sphere*. New York and London: Guilford Press.

Bourdieu, P. (2000). *On Television and Journalism*. London: Polity.

Campbell, V. (2004). *Information Age Journalism: Journalism in an international context*. London: Arnold.

Coates, T. (ed.) (2004). *The Hutton Inquiry*. London and New York: Tim Coates.

Collins, R. (1990). 'Market closure and the conflict theory of the professions' in *Professions in Theory and History: Rethinking the study of the professions*. M. Burrage and R. Tortstendahl (eds). London: Sage.

Curran, J. (2000). 'Media and democracy' in *Mass Media and Society*, 3rd edition. J. Curran and M. Gurevitch (eds). London: Arnold.

DCMS-DTI (2000). *A New Future for Communications*, London: DCMS-DTI, Government White Paper, Department of Culture, Media and Sport, 12 December.

Davis, A. (2000). *Public Relations Democracy*. Manchester: Manchester University Press.

Davis, A. (2002). *Public Relations Democracy*. London: Polity.

Day, K.D., Q. Dong and C. Robins (2001). 'Public relations ethics: An overview and discussion of issues for the 21st century' in *Handbook of Public Relations*. R.L. Heath (ed.). Thousand Oaks, CA and London: Sage.

Doyle, G. (2002a). *Understanding Media Economics*. London: Sage.

Doyle, G. (2002b). *Media Ownership*. London: Sage.

El-Nawawy, M. and A. Iskander (2002). *Al-Jazeera: How the free Arab news network scooped the world and changed the Middle East*. Cambridge, MA: Westview Press.

Franklin, B. (2004). *Packaging Politics: Political communications in Britain's media democracy*, 2nd edition. London: Arnold.

Friedson, E. (2001). *Professionalisation: The third logic*. Cambridge: Polity.

Gamble, A. (2000). *Politics and Fate*. London: Polity.

Goodwin, P. (1999). 'The role of the state' in *The Media in Britain: Current debates and developments*. J. Stokes and A. Reading (eds). Basingstoke: Macmillan.

Gregory, A. (2001). 'Professionalism and regulation' in *The Public Relations Handbook*. A. Theaker (ed.). London and New York: Routledge.

Herman, E.S. and N. Chomsky ([1988] 1994). *Manufacturing Consent: The political economy of the mass media*. London: Vintage.

Heywood, A. (1999). *Political Theory: An introduction*, 2nd edition. Basingstoke: Palgrave.

Humphreys, P.J. (1996). *Mass Media and Media Policy in Western Europe*. Manchester: Manchester University Press.

Keeble, R. (2001). *Ethics for Journalists*. London: Routledge.

Kelly, M., G. Mazzoleni and D. McQuail (eds) (2004). *The Media in Europe: The Euromedia handbook*. London: Sage.

Lewin, L. (1991). *Self-interest and Public Interest in Western Politics*. Oxford: Oxford University Press.

Leys, C. (2001). *Market-driven Politics: Neoliberal democracy and the public interest*. London: Verso.

Macdonald, K.M. (1995). *The Sociology of the Professions*. London: Sage.

McNair, B. (2003). *News and Journalism in the UK*, 4th edition. London: Routledge.

Morgan, J. (2004). 'PR has more to offer than media coverage'. *Financial Times*, 26 February: 13.

Mosco, V. (1996). *The Political Economy of Communication*. London: Sage.

Petley, J. (1999). 'The regulation of media content' in *The Media in Britain: Current debates and developments*. J. Stokes and A. Reading (eds). Basingstoke: Macmillan.

Philo, G. (ed.) (1999). *Message Received: Glasgow Media Group research 1993–1998*. Harlow: Longman.

Pieczka, M. and J. L'Etang (2001). 'Public relations and the question of professionalism' in *Handbook of Public Relations*. R.L. Heath (ed.). Thousand Oaks, CA and London: Sage.

Pitcher, G. (2003). *The Death of Spin*. London: John Wiley & Sons.

Ryle, S. (2004). '"To PR or not to PR": Ethics in PR'. *The Observer*, 20 June: 22.

Scruton, R. (ed.) (1983). *A Dictionary of Political Thought*. London: Pan/Macmillan.

Stokes, J. and A. Reading (eds) (1999). *The Media in Britain: Current debates and developments*. Basingstoke: Macmillan.

Street, J. (2001). *Mass Media, Politics and Democracy*. Basingstoke and New York: Palgrave.

Urquhart, L. (2004). 'Gregory spins into IPR big chair'. *Financial Times*, 19 January: 22.

Van Zoonen, L. (1998). 'One of the girls? The changing gender of journalism' in *News, Gender and Power*. C. Carter, G. Branston and S. Allan (eds). London: Routledge.

Vasquez, G. and M. Taylor (2001). 'Research perspectives on "the public"' in *Handbook of Public Relations*. R.L. Heath (ed.). Thousand Oaks, CA: Sage.

Volkmer, I. (1999). *News in the Global Sphere: A study of CNN and its impact on global communication*. Luton: University of Luton Press.

YEP (anon) (2004). 'PR Institute seek Royal Charter'. *Yorkshire Evening Post*, 2 July.

CHAPTER 5
Public relations and democracy

Introduction

'Government of the people, by the people, for the people' was US President Abraham Lincoln's definition of democracy. Democracy is now taken for granted over much of the modern world, although for nearly all states it is relatively recent, fragile and imperfect. Throughout recorded history, a single ruler (monarchy or dictatorship) or rule by a privileged few has been far more common. The growth of public relations has been linked to the growth of democracy, as the need arose to communicate persuasively with voters. Today, political communications is an important aspect of public relations work, some of which is described in Chapter 23. Public relations activity is often particularly scrutinised during election campaigns, providing many useful insights into the links between public relations and democracy.

Democracy emerged gradually in some countries (e.g. Sweden, the UK and the USA), more suddenly and dramatically in others. It was only the fall of the Berlin Wall in 1989 that enabled the peoples of eastern Europe behind the 'iron curtain' to throw off communist dictatorship and establish (or re-establish) democracy. It was only in 1990 that Nelson Mandela was released from his long imprisonment and South Africa began the transition from white minority rule and the racist system of apartheid to a democracy representing all its peoples.

Most states today claim to be democratic, sometimes in their official titles, more commonly in written constitutions. Yet the extent of real democracy in the modern world is contentious. There are different interpretations of democracy (Held 1996) and different views over the extent of real power and influence that ordinary people have over the decisions that affect them. The word democracy comes from ancient Greek, and means literally 'rule of the people'. A form of democracy was practised in the fifth and fourth centuries BC in Athens, where the citizens assembled together to decide on major public issues, including peace and war. This 'direct democracy' was feasible in relatively small city-states, but hardly practical in the more extensive empires or nation-states of later periods. How could the people rule themselves in such circumstances? The answer to this question was apparently provided with the development of representative democracy over the last two centuries. Rather than govern themselves, the people at periodic intervals elect representatives to govern for them. As governments are subject to re-election, they have (in theory) to pursue the interests of the majority rather than their own interests. Yet the majority can only exercise that power effectively if they have some knowledge of government and public affairs. Democracy, more than any other political system, presumes an effective two-way flow of communication between governors and governed, between those entrusted with immediate responsibility for key decisions and for the delivery of public services, and the wider public who supposedly wield ultimate power. Good public relations can make an important contribution to this process.

This chapter will explore the theoretical and practical implications of varieties of democracy for political communication and public relations. It will seek to identify key democratic institutions and processes within modern multilevel systems of governance. It will examine the opportunities of citizens to influence and actively participate in decision making and the role of good public relations in assisting the democratic process, promoting effective communication between governors and governed. It will also highlight some of the conflicts of loyalty, interests and responsibility that can arise for the professional communicator.

Conditions for representative democracy

There are some essential conditions that any representative democracy worthy of the name must meet. These include:

- regular elections
- a universal franchise – all adults have a right to vote
- secret ballot – to ensure voting is free from intimidation and bribery
- an effective choice of candidates, parties and potential alternative governments, competing on a fair and equal basis
- fair elections – each vote should, as far as possible, count equally
- freedom of speech and expression through free and diverse media to enable voters to make an effective choice based on knowledge of the issues and arguments.

Most of these conditions are largely met in well-established modern representative democracies. Virtually all adults have the right to vote regularly and in secret. They normally have a choice of candidates and parties, although that choice may be relatively limited. Elections are fair in the sense that they are generally free from the grosser forms of ballot rigging and fraud. However, some electoral systems, such as the 'first-past-the-post' system used in the USA and the UK, may be considered unfair as they do not offer each party a proportion of elected representatives roughly equivalent to their share of the vote. Most countries now use other electoral systems, involving more proportional representation (Denver 2002), and such systems have recently been introduced in the UK, but not for elections to Westminster to form the national government (Curtis 2003; Leach 2004) (see Box 5.1).

While the right to free speech is formally guaranteed in modern democratic states this does not ensure a full and well-informed public debate. Ownership and control of the mass media is highly concentrated and the range of views expressed is relatively limited and often highly partisan (as noted in the last chapter). A much wider range of political information and views is now available on the internet, but this has had only a relatively limited impact on the political attitudes and behaviour of the masses so far, although it has proved very useful to minority interests and causes and some extremist groups. (For discussion on political e-communication, see pp. 84 below.) Faced with an unreliable mass media, politicians, parties and those responsible for delivering public services have always sought to get their own message across, but this raises some legal and ethical issues (see

box 5.1	**Voting systems: key terms**

First past-the-post (simple plurality)

Under this electoral system, individual representatives are elected by winning more votes than any other candidate in each electoral area (or constituency) but do not need a majority of the total vote. The system is simple, helps establish good links between elected members and their constituencies and generally delivers strong governments with clear parliamentary majorities. Yet such majorities may be won with a minority of the total vote and the system penalises smaller parties, particularly those whose support is dispersed over the country as a whole rather than concentrated in certain areas. Thus some argue it is unfair.

Proportional representation

An electoral system that gives political parties a share of seats closely proportional to their share of the total vote. Such systems include regional party list systems (e.g. as used in elections for the European Parliament), the single transferable vote (as used in Ireland) and the additional member system (as used in Germany, the Scottish Parliament and the Welsh Assembly). Proportional representation is often linked with a multiparty system and coalition government.

below). Moreover, attempts by politicians and their advisers to put their own selective interpretation (or 'spin') on news stories has sometimes proved counterproductive, leading to some public cynicism and distrust of government, discussed later in this chapter.

Criticisms of modern democracy

There are other, more fundamental, criticisms of modern democracy. Most of the formal conditions outlined above relate to elections, implying that this is the essence of democracy. Some argue that placing a cross on a piece of paper every four or five years does not amount to real democracy, which should enable people to participate more directly and fully in the political process and to influence decisions that affect them (Pateman 1970).

In many countries there is some scope for more direct citizen participation. Several countries, such as Australia, Denmark, France and Switzerland make regular use of referendum on particular issues, particularly constitutional reform or moral issues, such as abortion. In the USA, some states (e.g. California) allow voters by their own initiative to put issues (such as taxation or the legalisation of cannabis) on ballot papers (Hague and Harrop 2001; Game 2004). Many countries have sought to extend citizen or consumer participation in the delivery of public services (see Lowndes et al. 1998, 2001, for initiatives in UK local government). It can prove difficult to persuade people to become involved, perhaps because of the costs in time and energy or perhaps, as some critics

complain, the participation offered is little more than token. However, direct citizen involvement may also contribute to the erosion of representative democracy by giving too much influence to active minorities, self-appointed spokespersons and unelected organisations at the expense of the elected representatives chosen by the majority (Skelcher 1998; Weir and Beetham 1999) (see Activity 5.1).

Democracy implies political equality; each person's voice should count equally. It also assumes that the view of the majority will prevail. Not everyone agrees that this is the case in practice. While *pluralists* suggest that power and influence is relatively widely dispersed,

activity 5.1

Encouraging participation

You are a public relations officer advising on a campaign to encourage parents of pupils to become more involved in the affairs of their school, or patients to participate in decision making on local health services.

What would you propose? What do you think might be the obstacles to the success of such a campaign to encourage more participation? Is there any risk that some voices may not be heard?

Feedback

The starting point is research. This is needed to find out what might enable people to become more involved and what currently prevents their doing so. Possible obstacles to the success of a campaign will be perceptions: that only the voices of the 'powerful' will count; that minority opinions will make no difference; and that public meetings will be held at times when only people with time to spare, and the means to get there, can attend.

elitists argue that it is in fact highly concentrated even in supposedly democratic states.

> **Definition:** *Pluralists* suggest that power and influence are widely dispersed in modern democracies, not just by the right to vote and checks and balances in the political system, but more particularly through the activities and effective influence of countless freely competing pressure groups.

> **Definition:** *Elitists* argue that real political power is effectively concentrated in the hands of an elite few (perhaps an ethnic group or educated minority or big business), who dominate the decision-making process.

There is a long-running debate about the relationship between democracy, on the one hand, and capitalism and free markets on the other. While *Marxists* have long argued that real democracy is impossible in a capitalist system where income and wealth are concentrated in the hands of a dominant class, others (sometimes called *neoliberals*) argue by contrast that democracy and free markets go hand in hand (Downs 1957). To them the real threat to democracy comes from politicians and public officials ('bureaucrats') who seek to increase state intervention, public spending and taxation, thus restricting the free choice of individual consumers and producers (Niskanen 1971, 1973). Indeed, it is often alleged (fairly or otherwise) that effective power is in the hands of 'bureaucrats' (civil servants, local government officers or other appointed officials; or '*quangos*' – such as arts or cultural bodies – rather than the elected representatives of the people) (see Think about 5.1).

> **Definition:** *Marxists* accept the analysis of Karl Marx (1818–1883) that political power reflects economic power. Thus the masses cannot have real power when income and wealth are highly concentrated in the hands of the few (e.g. in capitalist economies).

> **Definition:** *Neoliberals* believe democracy and free market capitalism are mutually dependent and that both are threatened by the growth of state intervention and bureaucracy (the rule of public officials in their own interests).

> **Definition:** *Quango* is an acronym standing for quasi-autonomous non-governmental organisation. In practice quangos are appointed (rather than elected) public bodies. Examples in the UK include the Health and Safety Commission, Learning and Skills Councils, Primary Care Trusts.

Majority rule, even if it is a reality, can present problems for minorities. Democracy assumes that conflicts can be resolved by debate and compromise and that minorities can become majorities if their arguments are sufficiently persuasive. Yet where communities are deeply divided on ethnic, linguistic or religious grounds, there may be permanent minorities who are effectively second-class citizens, excluded from many of the benefits enjoyed by the majority. In such circumstances, minority groups may opt out of democratic politics, using other methods (sometimes including violence) to promote their interests (see Activity 5.2).

It does no service to democracy to ignore some of its serious shortcomings in practice. Political realities fall short of the democratic ideal. Power and influence are unevenly distributed. Public servants may not always serve the public interest. The public itself may be ignorant and apathetic. Minorities can face discrimination. Yet, as the British Prime Minister Winston Churchill once observed: 'Democracy is the worst form of government, except for all those other forms of government that have been tried from time to time' (speech, *Hansard* 11 November, 1947, col. 206). Whatever the deficiencies of democracy, the alternatives, as Churchill noted, are worse. Good public relations may help this 'least bad' form of government to conform more closely to democratic ideals, particularly by improving the quantity and quality of two-way communication between the people and their elected governors.

think about 5.1   Influencing political decision making

Is modern representative democracy really government 'of the people, by the people for the people'? How much influence do ordinary people have over decisions that affect them? Is political power largely concentrated in the hands of the few or relatively widely dispersed, as pluralists suggest? What evidence might be cited in support of either view?

Feedback Look at election turnout figures. In the Iraqi national elections of 2005, 60% of the population voted. Just fewer than 60% voted in the UK national elections of 2001. In the UK, a large number of people do not vote – especially young people and black minorities. During local elections in the UK, turnout is sometimes lower than 30% (see also Table 5.1 on European elections). By way of contrast, people can make their voices heard in other ways, such as a group of mothers campaigning to introduce traffic-calming measures around their local school.

activity 5.2

Minority groups and politics

Can you think of any examples of minorities opting out of democratic politics? Why do they act in this way?

Feedback

Young people and black and minority ethnic (BME) groups are examples in the UK. There might be similar trends in your own country. Being registered to vote is essential in exercising the *right* to vote but there may be many reasons why some people's names are not on the electoral register – including ignorance, inefficiency (having moved house), alienation from the political system or fears about how the register will be used. Not voting may be due to a number of reasons: disillusion ('it makes no difference who wins'); lack of interest in politics; a lack of knowledge about politics; and a view that voting is too time consuming (Electoral Commission 2002a; 2002b).

What would you do to encourage these groups to participate in the democratic process?

Elections and voting

While democracy is not just about elections, they remain crucial to modern representative democracy. The Ukrainian elections in 2004 saw the national elections rerun after mass demonstrations challenged the validity of the incumbent president's re-election. Amid accusations that elections had been rigged and that the opposition party leader had been poisoned (together with visible evidence that he had quickly developed a serious skin condition) the outcome was the majority election of the opposition party.

Elections can matter a great deal. They can change governments, with significant implications for policies. Thus the unexpected socialist victory in the Spanish elections of 2004 led to the withdrawal of Spanish soldiers from the Iraq War. Some elections mark a watershed in a country's history. The result of American presidential elections can have massive implications for the wider world.

But there is a threat to modern representative democracy from public apathy and alienation. Democracy demands involvement in public affairs (see also Chapter 23). In many modern democracies there is a pattern of declining interest and involvement in politics, even in the most simple and limited form of political participation – voting. It was not always so. In most countries the right to vote for whole categories of the population was only conceded after a long struggle. It was therefore highly prized (see Box 5.2, overleaf).

To Mkhondo, the vote involved 'a voice' in his country's affairs, membership of the 'congregation'

PICTURE 5.1   Supporters of Ukraine President Viktor Yushchenko. (*Source:* Jeremy Nicholl/Alamy.)

box 5.2	**Eye witness account of the first post-apartheid election in South Africa in 1994**

Voting in my township began with whistles by the men, ululations by women, and a three quarter hour wait to end apartheid and usher in democracy. As a thirty-eight-year-old black South African, I had never until today had any voice in the affairs of my country. I awoke at 5 a.m. to be in the front seat of history. It was like getting ready for baptism as a new congregation member. Hours later, tense and excited while inscribing a long denied 'X' on the ballot paper, it was like a heady first romance. It ended what once seemed an impossible journey . . . my dignity and self-worth had finally been restored.

Source: Rich Mkhondo, quoted in Marr 1996: 22

and full citizenship, 'dignity and self-worth'. The suffragettes who campaigned for votes for women in the UK and other countries felt similarly. Yet the 'heady first romance' with the ballot box has worn off. Austria, France, Japan, New Zealand, Switzerland and the UK are among countries that have suffered a decline in turnout of over 10% in national elections over the last half century, with most of the fall occurring recently (Hague and Harrop 2001). Less than half of the American electorate have bothered to vote in some recent presidential elections, although turnout rose to 60% in the close contest of 2004.

Turnout in elections for other levels of government such as local councils can be much lower. In the elections for the European Parliament in 2004, turnout levels were abysmally low, both among some established EU states, such as France, Germany and the UK, but also among some countries that had only recently enthusiastically endorsed EU membership (see Table 5.1). The only countries with a high turnout were those where voting was compulsory (e.g. Belgium).

Turnout levels may be improved by using modern communication techniques, including better publicity for elections (see Chapter 7). A generation familiar with text messaging, interactive television and online shopping may find marking a cross with a pencil on paper in some remote hall or schoolroom used as a polling station both old-fashioned and inconvenient. Some countries, such as the USA, have long used voting machines, although these can create problems as the 2000 presidential election demonstrated, particularly in the state of Florida, where many votes were not recorded, leading to the result being challenged in the US Supreme Court. In the UK, there have been experiments with other methods of recording votes, using the telephone or internet, although to date 'e-voting' has made less difference than extending postal voting (see Activity 5.3).

activity 5.3

E-voting

Can you think of any groups that would benefit from e-voting? Try making a list of different groups and the effects e-voting may have on them.

Feedback
The disabled are one group who might benefit from e-voting. However, accessibility to websites for some disabled people is a barrier and postal voting is the preferred choice for this group (Scope 2002).

TABLE 5.1   Turnout for selected countries for the European Parliament elections, 2004

Country	Turnout level	Notes
Belgium	90.8%	Compulsory voting
France	43.1%	
Germany	43.0%	
United Kingdom	38.2%	Improvement on 23% in 1999
Sweden	37.2%	
Estonia	26.9%	New EU member state
Poland	20.4%	New EU member state
Slovakia	16.7%	Lowest turnout in EU for this new member

think about 5.2　Personal voting

Did you vote in the most recent elections in which you were entitled to vote? If not, why not? If you did, how did you feel about it? How might higher turnout be encouraged? Is there a role for public relations in improving electoral participation and, if so, how?

It is sometimes argued that the introduction of proportional representation (see above) would encourage higher turnout, as voters would be more confident that their vote could make a real difference. Yet although proportional representation may make the system fairer, there is little evidence that it boosts turnout (e.g. in elections in the UK for the European Parliament, Scottish Parliament, Welsh Assembly). Indeed, some systems make voting more complicated and confusing and may discourage participation. New systems require effective communication to explain the reasons for change and provide clear guidance to voters over how to register their preferences. Here there is a clear role for public relations in providing information on voting options to the electorate (see Think about 5.2).

Democracy is, or should be, about more than just voting, which is the easiest and most basic form of political participation open to the ordinary citizen. Only a small minority who are actively involved in local community organisations or campaigning groups belong to political parties. Such public apathy not only reduces the legitimacy of governments but also undermines the vitality of democracy itself.

Elections and political parties

If electoral choice is central to our modern conception of democracy, political parties lie at the heart of electoral choice. For some, parties involve everything they find distasteful in politics. They appear divisive,

magnifying differences, sometimes seeming to oppose each other for the sake of it. Politicians infuriate by sticking to the party line, refusing to admit their own side has ever done anything wrong or their opponents anything right. Indeed, it is often suggested that particular issues should be 'taken out of politics', meaning party politics. Perhaps we could manage without parties. Why cannot voters just choose the best men and women for the job and the best policies, regardless of party labels?

Yet political parties have developed in just about every modern representative democracy, which suggests we cannot do without them. Indeed, competition between parties has become almost a defining condition of modern democracy (see Box 5.3).

Today, not all these functions are fully met. Thus, the choice offered by parties can be quite narrow, particularly in those countries such as the USA and the UK which still use the first-past-the-post electoral system (see above). This has tended to create and maintain a two-party duopoly of Republicans and Democrats in the USA, Conservative and Labour in the UK (although here other parties have more recently made headway). In other countries, a number of parties may be represented in the national parliament or assembly, but often the effective choice of a government is between two broad coalitions. Thus in Germany since the Second World War, choice has generally been between the Christian Democrats and the Social Democrats, although both these parties have generally needed support from smaller parties such as the Free Democrats or Greens to form a government.

box 5.3　Functions of parties in modern democracies

- *Political choice* – parties are the main means by which voters are given an effective choice between different teams of leaders and between different policy programmes and principles.
- *Political recruitment* – parties recruit, select and train people for political office.
- *Political participation* – parties provide a chance for ordinary citizens to participate in the political process; members choose candidates and may influence party policy.
- *Reconciling interests* – a successful party must represent a range of interests, classes and communities, and seek a balance between conflicting interests.
- *Communication* – parties provide a two-way channel of communication between political leaders and people.
- *Accountability and control* – because successful parties take responsibility for exercising power (at various levels) it is chiefly through parties that governments are held to account by the public.

Some of the other functions of parties are effectively weakened by a widespread decline in active party membership from a peak in the mid-twentieth century. Thus, parties no longer offer a significant channel for political participation for most people. However, party leaders cannot afford to ignore their dwindling active membership, if only for fear of losing the valuable support that members provide, particularly at elections. Yet if they listen to their members they may risk alienating the broad mass of voters, as party activists are often untypical of ordinary voters, both in their social background and in their political views. The UK Conservative Party has recently suffered from the policy preferences of its elderly members who do not resemble the electorate. Similarly, in the USA both major parties have sometimes chosen candidates and policies which delighted their own activists but alarmed voters.

Parties need to put themselves and their message across effectively if they are to be successful and many seek professional advice from advertising agencies and public relations consultants.

Although voter choice has been extensively studied, there are still hotly contested theories of electoral behaviour. Some argue that voters choose at the ballot box in much the same way as consumers choose in the marketplace; indeed there is an economic theory of democracy based on that assumption (Downs 1957). Political marketing may, therefore, have much in common with the marketing of goods and services. Many voters remain loyal to particular parties, just as many consumers stick with familiar brands of goods, with relatively few changing their allegiance between elections. Often a marked correlation can be observed between party support and various social indicators (such as occupational class, region or age in the UK, religion, language or ethnicity in some other countries). More recently the electorate in many countries has become more volatile, with more 'swing' voters influenced by issues, particularly economic performance. Winning elections may involve first identifying and then persuading these potential swing voters. In the UK, the 'grey vote' or over-55s, whose concerns include pensions, the health service and the economy, are more likely to vote than younger people (Age Concern 2005), but their decision on which party to vote for might be delayed until election day itself. Some of the same considerations apply to the promotion of parties as with marketing any good or service, as one pioneering study recognised a century ago:

Nothing is more generally useful than the party colour ... A party tune is equally automatic in its action ... Only less than automatic than those of colour and tune come the emotional associations called up by the first and simplest meaning of the word or words used for the party name ... From the beginning of the existence and activity of a party, new associations are, however, being created which tend to take the place, in association, of the original meaning of the name. No-one in America, when he uses the terms Republican and Democrat thinks of their dictionary meanings ... Long and precise names which make definite assertions as to party policy are therefore soon shortened into meaningless syllables with new associations derived from the actual history of the party. (Wallas 1908)

Much of this analysis applies today. Name and colour remain crucial in establishing the image of modern parties and in maintaining the loyalty of supporters. Party tunes can still stir emotions, but party emblems, symbols or logos seem more significant in modern political marketing. Some parties are associated with animals, birds or flowers, others with more abstract symbols (see Mini case study 5.1 and Activity 5.4).

Good public relations could, in theory, enable all parties to communicate more effectively with voters, thus improving the quality of political debate, assisting voters in making their choices and enhancing the democratic process. However, this ideal seems far removed from the promotion of parties today. Much party advertising, unlike commercial advertising, is unashamedly negative. It is commonly less concerned to communicate the values and polices of a party than to vilify and ridicule the opposition. Parties have long relied on such negative advertising, largely because it is believed to be effective, exploiting the fear factor – the dire consequences to personal and national prosperity should the other side 'get in'. It also offers fewer 'hostages to fortune' arising from party promises that prove difficult to deliver. Examples of negative campaigning include the UK Conservative Party poster of the Labour Party leader with 'devil's eyes' and, in the run up to the 2005 UK election, Labour Party posters showing the Conservative Party leader and shadow chancellor as flying pigs. This was seen as anti-Semitic, as both men are Jewish, although the Labour Party insisted it was only anti-Conservative (see Picture 5.2).

activity 5.4

Communicating political parties

Consider the names, colours and logos of UK political parties or of any other parties around the world with which you are familiar.

Feedback

How effective do you consider these to be in conveying the values of the party concerned?

mini case study 5.1

Party political communication in action

The professional marketing of political parties has a long history, although not everyone approves of this activity. When the UK Conservatives employed the advertising agency Saatchi and Saatchi with notable success in the 1979 election campaign, their Labour opponents (who then distrusted advertising and marketing people) accused the Conservatives of selling politics like cornflakes or soap powder (Butler 1980; Worcester and Harrop 1982).

Yet Labour then was simply failing to get its message across, a lesson it subsequently learned, perhaps almost too well. Following further defeats, the party introduced a new red rose logo (in imitation of the French socialists) under the leadership of Neil Kinnock in the 1980s. Then, under Tony Blair, the party dropped its formal commitment to nationalisation in 1995 and was rebranded as 'New Labour' (but without a formal name change), which paid handsome electoral dividends in

1997 (Butler and Kavanagh 1997). Some old Labour stalwarts complained that New Labour was all marketing, with little substance.

A more striking example of party rebranding is provided by the Italian communists. Following the fall of the Berlin Wall in 1989, which heralded a general collapse of communism, the old Italian Communist Party (PCI) became the Democratic Party of the Left (PDS), with an oak tree symbol. Subsequently, it moved further away from its communist roots, abandoning the hammer and sickle and combining with other centre-left parties in the Olive Tree Alliance. Yet, as with the Labour Party in the UK, some old party members objected to the transformation, and broke away to establish the *Rifondanzione Communista* or 'Refounded Communists'.

Source: Hellman (2000) in Kesselman and Krieger 2002: 484–486.

Yet if negative advertising works at one level, it may have a corrosive effect on faith in politicians, governments and even democracy itself. The pervasive negative message is that politicians are 'all the same' – incompetent, untrustworthy and 'sleazy'. Perhaps this is one reason for the apparent growth of political apathy and alienation. If those who advise parties cannot agree on some voluntary code of practice in their own promotional work (be it advertising or public relations) there may be a case for *watchdog* bodies (such as the Electoral Commission in the UK) to take a more proactive role in drawing up rules of acceptable party campaigning.

PICTURE 5.2   This poster, from the 1979 Conservative election campaign, is one of the most celebrated examples of effective negative political advertising. The image of a 'dole' (unemployment pay) queue reminds voters of rising unemployment under the then Labour Government. The brief slogan involves a double message. 'Labour (or the workers) are not working' and 'The Labour Government isn't working'. The positive message 'Vote Conservative' is relegated to a small-print sub-text. (*Source*: Advertising Archives.)

Definition: *Watchdog* is a term used to describe a body that monitors behaviour and activities in different sections of society to protect the consumer or citizen.

Pressure groups and democracy

If the role of parties in modern democracy has become more problematic, the contribution of *pressure groups* is now generally viewed positively. It was not always so. Such groups have sometimes been seen as sinister 'hidden persuaders', insidiously pushing the interests of unrepresentative and self-interested minorities and subverting the democratic processes of elections and representative assemblies. There is something in the criticism. Some political cultures (the French, for example) remain suspicious of the role of such groups in frustrating the will of the people. Americans, however, have tended to emphasise the crucial contribution of countless freely competing groups to the democratic process.

Definition: A *pressure group* may be any organised group that seeks to exert influence on government (at any level) to influence particular policies or decisions.

There is extensive literature on types of groups, tactics and behaviour (e.g. Grant 2000; Coxall 2001). This is explored later, in Chapter 29. Here we will concentrate on the contribution of pressure groups to democracy and the more general implications for public relations.

The role of pressure groups may be distinguished from political parties in the democratic process in that they do not normally contest elections, although it is a tactic occasionally employed. They seek influence rather than formal positions of power. Unlike parties, they do not aspire to form the government. Yet they can offer more extensive opportunities for public participation in the political process than elections or parties. Today, many more people are actively involved with groups than parties. Compared with the broad, blunt and occasional electoral process, group influence is often very specific, relating to particular causes, interests and decisions, and continuous rather than sporadic. The information, arguments and supporting evidence supplied by groups helps educate politicians and people. On many issues, groups representing opposed views and interests are in competition. All this can be said to contribute to the democratic process and improves the quality of decision making. In the USA, in particular, a

pluralist theory of democracy built substantially around pressure group activity has developed to supplement the formal representative institutions process (Dahl 1961).

Critics suggest that while some interests, particularly business interests, are well resourced and influential, other interests including the poor, the sick, and consumer interests are relatively neglected. Some sections of the community are more actively involved than others. Pressure group bargaining favours better resourced and more easily organised interests. In practice, it is often group spokespersons, permanent staff and a small minority of dedicated activists who exert effective influence rather than the mass of members. Spokespersons are rarely elected and sometimes virtually self-appointed and may not speak for ordinary supporters to whom they are not fully accountable. In larger pressure groups, however, there may be an executive committee that oversees communication and campaigning. In most, communication is a central part of the pressure group's activities, whether that be running websites, organising media events such as scaling buildings or working behind the scenes to establish contact with decision makers. Whether they employ professional public relations staff or simply attract activists with good communication skills, how a pressure group presents itself to the wider public will be a critical aspect of its strategy. For example, some claim to speak for the 'silent majority', although that claim is difficult to validate as long as the majority remains silent!

More seriously, governments are rarely neutral arbiters. They ignore or reject some groups but listen to others, granting recognition and privileged 'insider' status. The most effective influence may be exerted in the 'corridors of power' out of public scrutiny. Indeed there may often be an inverse correlation between influence and noise – the more noise the less influence. Big public demonstrations may sometimes have less effect on policy than a quiet word in the right ear behind the scenes (see also Chapter 23 on the tactics employed by business and pressure groups in influencing or 'lobbying' governments).

All this is not to deny the immense value of pressure groups to democracy. Yet pressure groups are an important supplement to, rather than a substitute for, the formal democratic machinery of elections and representation. Elections can sometimes enable the wider public interest or the will of the majority to triumph over well-financed and well-organised minorities.

As groups are in the business of influencing decision makers, the media and the masses, public relations has much to contribute. Larger groups employ sympathetic and suitably qualified public relations staff. Such work can be hugely rewarding although it can raise ethical issues. Groups are inevitably partisan, concerned with their own specific cause or interest, but some can be so narrowly committed that they become fanatical and intolerant of other interests or views. They may be prepared to ignore, suppress or distort evidence that does not suit their case. Such attitudes clearly present ethical problems for anyone professionally committed to a two-way symmetrical view of public relations (for further discussion on pressure group tactics, see Chapter 29) and even those following the advocate model, which is more appropriate for campaigning, still need to be conscious of ethical considerations.

Democracy and multilevel governance

Most modern democratic states are large and complex, spending two-fifths or more of total national income and employing directly or indirectly a similar proportion of the workforce. While the study of politics tends to focus on central government, national parliaments and ministers responsible for the direction of national policy, this is only a tiny part of the vast apparatus of government in the modern democratic state. Although some of the most important decisions affecting us are still taken by national governments, the process of modern governance involves many other levels (see Table 5.2). These include supranational bodies, such as the United Nations, the North Atlantic Treaty Organisation (NATO) and the European Union, and, at the sub-national level, regional, local and community government. Some of these levels may involve effective democratic control and accountability (e.g. elected regional assemblies and local councils), while others (e.g. most supranational institutions) may involve at best a measure of indirect democratic accountability or none at all (Rhodes 1997; Pierre and Peters 2000).

> **Definition:** *Multilevel governance* is a term that captures the complexity of modern government, which involves many layers or levels. 'Governance' emphasises the process of governing rather than the institutions of government. The term includes all those who contribute to public policy and the delivery of public services.

Although key parts of government are headed by elected politicians, these are heavily outnumbered by appointed public officials who both advise on policy and are largely responsible for implementing it. Thus there can be doubts over elected politicians' real con-

TABLE 5.2 Multilevel governance

Level	Examples
Global	World Trade Organisation, International Monetary Fund, United Nations
Continental	European Union, North American Free Trade Area, North Atlantic Treaty Organisation
Nation-state	France, Germany, Spain, United Kingdom
National/regional	German Länder (e.g. Bavaria), Scottish Parliament and executive, autonomous communities in Spain (e.g. Catalonia)
Local/community	Elected local councils (sometimes involving more than one level – e.g. counties, districts and parishes in parts of England)
Institutional/service	Governing bodies of schools, universities, hospitals (often appointed, but may have elected element)

trol over decision making. Which is really stronger, democracy or bureaucracy?

Furthermore, parts of government are not controlled directly by elected politicians or accountable to voters through the ballot box but involve appointed bodies (commonly termed 'quangos' in the UK – see the earlier definition in this chapter on p. 82). While there are sometimes good reasons for removing particular functions from the control of partisan politicians, the growth of the 'quango state' has aroused considerable criticism from across the political spectrum (Skelcher 1998).

It is not even always clear what exactly is government and what is not, as the public sector today often engages in partnerships with the private sector and works closely with the voluntary sector in a complex network of organisations. This complexity poses further problems for democratic accountability.

The larger, more complex and multi-layered government becomes, the more difficult it is to ensure real democratic accountability at the appropriate level. The delivery of public services requires an extensive local machinery of administration and many crucial decisions may be taken at institutional level, by appointed staff within individual schools and hospitals, for example, with little effective local democratic accountability. While partnerships and networks enable many more people to participate actively in governance, they may blur lines of responsibility, so it is not clear who is really in charge. The sheer complexity of modern multilevel governance provides considerable problems of coordination. Unsurprisingly, there may appear to be a 'democratic deficit' in key institutions and processes.

For example, an academic report commissioned by a quango that criticised the way Scottish Water (a private utility company) communicates with its customers was itself 'suppressed', according to *The Scotsman* (16 August 2004, see http://thescotsman.scotsman.com/opinion.cfm?id=946522004).

The European Union is one very important supranational organisation which is sometimes accused of having a 'democratic deficit', not altogether fairly. The EU is a complex hybrid institution with both indirect accountability, through the governments of member states in the Council of Ministers, and more direct accountability through the elected European Parliament. It used to be argued that this Parliament had little influence over European laws and no effective control over the European Commission, the EU executive whose members are nominated by national governments. However, the European Parliament now has a greater say on legislation, while in October 2004 a substantial majority of Parliament refused to accept the proposed new European Commission and forced changes (see the EU website, www.europa.eu.int). The EU also conducts pan-European communication campaigns on issues such as health, workers' rights and giving up smoking (see Chapter 7 for details). For insight into the range of campaigns, look at the youth portal, www.europa.eu.int/youth/index_en.html

Public relations and modern democracy

Complex modern multilevel governance requires good communication, not least within and between the range of departments, organisations and agencies involved. And as Cutlip et al. (2000) suggest, effective democracy requires effective communication between citizens and government at all levels:

> In a very real sense, the purpose of democracy itself closely matches the purpose of public relations. Successful democratic government maintains responsive relationships with constituents, based on mutual understanding and two-way communication. (Cutlip et al. 2000: 448)

Citizens need full and accurate information on which to base their daily lives and ultimately assess a government's record. However, the presentation of government information and statistics (e.g. on taxation, crime, education and health) is often contentious. Government claims do not always match the public's own experience. Sections of the media and opposition parties frequently complain the figures are misleading and fail to give the true picture. Democracy is or should be a two-way process, giving multiple opportunities for members of the public to communicate their own interests and concerns to government at all levels, to influence and sometimes transform public policy.

Thus democracy requires open government and freedom of information, which provides massive opportunities but creates some problems for those engaged in public relations. The opportunities should be obvious: better communication between all parts of government and the publics they serve and better communication both within the public sector and between the public, private and voluntary sectors. Indeed an increasing number of public relations practitioners find themselves working directly for public sector organisations, for government departments, local councils or hospitals, while others employed by the private and voluntary sectors will have extensive dealings with the public sector at one level or another.

But there are inevitably some conflicts of loyalty and interest, particularly for those employed within the public sector (see Chapter 30). Although democracy implies that the ultimate loyalty should be the wider public interest, there are various stakeholders to consider – the public as voters and citizens, the public as taxpayers and funders of services, the public as service users. Although these categories clearly overlap, they are not identical. The interests of taxpayers (in lower taxes) and service users (in improved, better funded public services) may clearly conflict. (Meeting the communication needs of different stakeholders is explored more fully in Chapter 30.)

Furthermore, public relations staff are employed and paid by particular departments, agencies and services and this can lead to difficult ethical choices. The image and reputation of the employing organisation, such as a hospital, university or police force, may in practice loom larger than the wider public's 'right to know'. Crises may be managed in the interests of institutional damage limitation rather than what may be seen as the public interest.

Within organisations headed by elected politicians there may be further conflicts of loyalty. Many government departments and agencies devote escalating budgets and staffing to make the public aware of new initiatives, laws and benefits that affect them. Yet this necessary publicity for policies can sometimes become inextricably linked with the promotion of the

Government communication: information or propaganda? Events leading to the Phillis Report (2004) in Britain

When Labour entered government in 1997 it brought in a team of special advisors headed by Press Secretary Alastair Campbell to direct their communication strategy. This led to some friction with the civil service, a more antagonistic relationship with the media and increased public distrust for government communication, which became associated in the public mind with 'spin', involving a partisan or distorted interpretation of news. Labour did not invent spin. It was practised, sometimes very effectively, by the previous Conservative government. Indeed, the activity (but not the term, which is a recent US import), is as old as politics. Media criticism of government 'spin' ignores the obvious point that the media also 'spin' news stories through their own selection, emphasis and interpretation. Yet criticism of Labour's news management understandably intensified after the publication of a leaked email from special advisor Jo Moore, suggesting that 9/11 was 'a good day to bury bad news'.

The ensuing scandal ultimately led to the resignation of Moore herself and the minister, Stephen Byers, who had unwisely stood by her. Yet it also raised wider questions about government information and communication that led to the appointment of an independent review, chaired by Bob Phillis. While the review was in progress, a massive political row over the government's use of intelligence information to justify the war with Iraq further dramatised some of the issues surrounding government communication and relations with the media.

The Phillis Report, published in January 2004, described low and diminishing public trust in both politicians and the media (particularly the press), with damaging consequences for public participation in the democratic process. Yet the report, while critical of government 'spin', substantially endorsed some of Labour's dissatisfaction with the traditional approach to communication in the civil service. There was 'a narrow view of communication . . . often limited to media handling'. Communication was 'not seen as a core function of the mainstream civil service'. The Government Information and Communication Service did not cover all those in communication, lacked resources and status and was defective in recruitment and training. There was poor coordination of communication across government departments and agencies. Despite the passing of the Freedom of Information Act 2000 (effective in 2005), there was still a pervasive

culture of secrecy that should be replaced by a culture of openness. There was a need for more direct two-way communication between government and the public. On the specific issue that had led to the review, the role of special advisors, the report acknowledged that they performed a useful role in modern government and were here to stay, but their relationship with the civil service required new guidelines which protected the principle of civil service impartiality.

Specific recommendations included:

- A redefinition of the role and scope of government communications, involving a 'continuous dialogue with all interested parties' and a 'broader range of skills', with the general public being the focus of attention (R1, p. 3).
- A strong central communications structure, headed by a new permanent secretary, Government Communications, to be head of profession, and provide strategic leadership for communications across government (this recommendation accepted following publication of an interim report in 2003) (R2, p. 3).
- Replacement of the Government Information and Communication Service by a new network including all those involved in communication activity, led by the new permanent secretary (R4, p. 3).
- Recruitment and training to raise professional standards and maintain civil service impartiality (R6, p. 4).
- New rules governing the conduct of special advisors and their relationship with civil servants (R7, p. 4).
- Effective implementation of the Freedom of Information Act 2000, to end the culture of secrecy. 'The overriding presumption should be to disclose' (R8, p. 4).
- Clearer rules for the release of statistical information, which 'should be automatically, routinely and systematically made available'. There should be a new statute to control the publication of official statistics to restore public trust (R9, p. 4).
- More direct communication with the public, including televising daily briefings from the prime minister's office, with ministers and press officers answering questions (R10, p. 4) and better customer-driven online communication, involving a redesign of the central government website (R11, p. 5).

politicians and parties responsible for their introduction. Politicians in government naturally want their achievements to be projected in a positive light and may consider that the overriding allegiance of communications staff is to themselves, as the people's elected representatives. Sometimes politicians bring in their own party experts on temporary contracts to take charge of communication and this can lead to serious friction with permanent staff committed to a less partisan approach to publicity. One example is the news management associated with Britain's Labour government from 1997 onwards (see Case study 5.1 earlier).

The Phillis Report thus raises issues not just for the UK's Labour government but for government news management and media coverage of politics in all democracies. While democracy may depend on effective communication, not all communication is in the interests of government. Inevitably, there are stories and figures that a government would prefer to hide or play down, while there are successes that it would wish to emphasise. Opposition parties and interests and sections of the media just as naturally prefer to highlight government problems or failures and discount apparent successes. Even public servants, who may claim to serve the public interest impartially, are inevitably influenced by organisational, professional and personal interests that may not always coincide with the public interest. In addition, there are often fierce differences within public sector organisations, rather than a single impartial public service view. While the wider public want less partial sources of information, including statistics they can trust, information overload can prevent important messages getting through. Likewise, selection and simplification can lead to accusations of omission and distortion. While the Phillis Report is right to emphasise the crucial role of communication in modern democracy, and there is much good sense in its specific recommendations, there are few easy answers to some of the broader questions on which the report touches. These are the issues with which professional communicators will continue to wrestle.

Summary

This chapter has defined and discussed the broad context of democracy in which public relations operates. It has discussed systems of democracy, the role of elections, political parties and the different institutions of governance. It has identified, in particular, the problems facing modern democracies where people are not voting in large numbers and how effective public relations might encourage more people to take part in political decision making. Throughout we have raised issues for the public relations practitioner in both supporting the relationship between public institutions and voters, as well as interacting with these institutions from the vantage point of campaigning organisations. Finally, we have identified, through the case study of the Phillis Report, the issues of personal, professional and organisational allegiances that may conflict with serving the public interest in modern democracies.

Bibliography

Age Concern (2005). 'Government risks losing crucial swing voters' at www.ageconcern.org.uk/Age Concern/News4428.htm, accessed on 13 February 2005.

Butler, D. and D. Kavanagh (1980). *The British General Election of 1979*. Basingstoke: Macmillan.

Butler, D. and D. Kavanagh (1997). *The British General Election of 1997*. Basingstoke: Macmillan.

Coxall, B. (2001). *Pressure Groups in British Politics*. London: Pearson.

Curtis, J. (2003). 'Changing voting systems' in *Developments in British Politics 7*. P. Dunleavy, A. Gamble, R. Heffernan, and G. Peele. Basingstoke: Palgrave Macmillan.

Cutlip, S., A. Center, and G. Broom (2000). *Effective Public Relations*, 8th edition. Upper Saddle River, NJ: Prentice Hall.

Dahl, R. (1961). *Who Governs?* New Haven, NJ: Yale University Press.

Denver, D. (2002). *Elections and Voters in Britain*. Basingstoke: Palgrave Macmillan.

Downs, A. (1957). *An Economic Theory of Democracy*. New York: Harper & Row.

Electoral Commission (2002a). 'Voter engagement among black and minority ethnic communities' at www.electoralcommission.org.uk, accessed on 13 February 2005.

Electoral Commission (2002b). 'Voter engagement and young people' at www.electoralcommission.org.uk, accessed on 13 February 2005.

Game, C. (2004). 'Direct democracy in 2003: Referendums, initiatives and recall' in *Developments in Politics Vol. 15*. S. Lancaster (ed.). Ormskirk: Causeway Press.

Grant, W. (2000). *Pressure Groups and British Politics*. Basingstoke: Palgrave.

Hague, R, and M. Harrop, (2001). *Comparative Government and Politics*. Basingstoke, Palgrave.

Held, D. (1996). *Models of Democracy*. Cambridge: Polity.

Hellman, D. (2002). 'Italy' in *European Politics in Transition*, 4th edition. M. Kesselman and J. Krieger. Boston, MA: Houghton-Mifflin.

Kesselman, M. and J. Krieger (2002). *European Politics in Transition*, 4th edition. Boston; MA: Houghton-Mifflin.

Leach, R. (2004). 'Democracy and elections' in *Developments in Politics, Vol. 15*. S. Lancaster, (ed.). Ormskirk: Causeway Press.

Lowndes, V., G. Stoker, L. Pratchett, D.Wilson and S. Leach (1998). 'Enhancing public participation in local government'. London: DETR.

Lowndes, V., L. Pratchett and G. Stoker (2001). 'Trends in public participation: Part 1 – local government perspectives'. *Public Administration* **79** (1).

Marr, A. (1996). *Ruling Britannia: The failure and future of British democracy*. Harmondsworth: Penguin.

Niskanen, W.A. (1971). *Bureaucracy and Representative Government*. Chicago: Aldine-Atherton.

Niskanen, W.A. (1973). *Bureaucracy: Servant or master?* London: Institute of Economic Affairs.

Pateman, C. (1970). *Participation and Democratic Theory*. Cambridge: Cambridge University Press.

Phillis, R. (Chair) (2004). An independent review of government communication, Cabinet Office at www.gcreview.gov.uk, accessed on 13 February 2005.

Pierre, J. and Peters, B. (2000). *Governance, Politics and the State*. Basingstoke: Macmillan.

Rhodes, R.A.W. (1997). *Understanding Governance: Policy networks, governance, reflexivity and accountability*. Milton Keynes and Philadelphia: Open University Press.

Scope (2002). 'Polls apart: A future for accessible democracy' at www.electoralcommission.org.uk, accessed on 13 February 2005.

Skelcher, C. (1998). *The Appointed State*. Buckingham: Open University Press.

Wallas, G. (1908). *Human Nature in Politics*. London: Constable.

Weir, S. and D. Beetham, (1999). *Political Power and Democratic Control in Britain: The democratic audit of Great Britain*. London: Routledge.

Worcester, R.M. and M. Harrop (1982). *Political Communications: The general election campaign of 1979*. London: Allen & Unwin.

Websites

Age Concern: www.ageconcern.org.uk

Electoral Commission: www.electoralcommission.org.uk

European Parliament: www.europarl.eu.int

European Parliament (UK office): www.europarl.org.uk

European Union: www.europa.eu.int

Times Online: www.timesonline.co.uk

CHAPTER 6

Community and society: corporate social responsibility (CSR)

Learning outcomes

By the end of this chapter you should be able to:

- critically evaluate the role of organisations in their society(ies)
- define the concept of corporate social responsibility in the context of relevant regulatory frameworks
- define and critically evaluate the role of ethics in business policy and practice
- diagnose ethical problems and identify strategies for making ethical decisions in organisational/cultural contexts
- appreciate the environmental complexities that influence organisational communication and public relations strategies.

Structure

- Sustainable business: corporate social responsibility (CSR)
- Business case for corporate social responsibility: why be socially responsible?
- Organisational responsibilities to stakeholders
- Organisational responsibilities to society
- Regulatory frameworks
- Ethics and business practice

Introduction

Enron, Shell UK, Union Carbide and Exxon Corporation are just a few of the major international corporations that have been under the worldwide media spotlight for their corporate actions and activities. Executives from these companies have at varying times over the past 20 years been vilified by the media, attacked by shareholders and customers and in some instances imprisoned. Why? Because the organisations they represent have had a major impact on the social and physical environments in which they operate (e.g. oil and chemical leaks). This chapter will explore the role of organisations in society and how, irrespective of the profit or not-for-profit imperatives, many are taking a critical view of their roles and responsibilities. In many instances (including some of the companies above), this has involved a radical repositioning of the organisation's *vision and values* that are impacting on the operational as well as the public relations (communication) strategies they employ.

Concern for the environment in which a business operates is not a new phenomenon but its prevalence in Anglo-American business policy is growing and, due to the internationalisation of markets and business practice, this is influencing corporate strategy for large PLCs and small to medium-sized enterprises (SMEs) throughout the world. These corporate policy changes are encouraging organisations to increase their awareness and concern for the society(ies) in which they operate. An additional development is in the more sophisticated business use of the societal relationship as part of the corporate strategy and as a marketing tool. This has been demonstrated through the expansion of sponsorship programmes (see Chapter 27) and more recently with the development of

Definition: 'Vision and values' relates to the business practice of identifying an organisation's corporate vision – where it wants to go and how it wants to be perceived through its core values. (Go to the internet and look up value and mission statements for corporations.)

cause-related marketing (CRM) – associating companies or brands with charitable causes (see Chapter 18). This chapter will describe in detail the relationships between an organisation and the community within which it operates. It will explore the complex issue of business ethics with guidelines on how to promote ethical decision making in practice. There are links from this chapter to Chapter 18, which explores how public relations is responding to an increasingly CSR-conscious business environment through the development of communications programmes (see Case study 6.1).

Sustainable business: corporate social responsibility (CSR)

Individual members and groups in the community in which an organisation operates are increasingly being recognised as important *stakeholders* in the long-term security and success of large and small enterprises. Building relationships with these community groups is, therefore, an important issue in corporate and communications strategy. In order to understand how this can be achieved it is essential to understand in more detail the complexities of the relationships between a business and its community(ies).

case study 6.1

BBC World Service Trust – international impact

The aim of the BBC's World Service Trust is to help developing countries and countries in transition to build media expertise for the benefit of the population.

Following 25 years of conflict in Afghanistan, the country is now looking to the future and the Afghan media have a major role to play in uniting the nation, rebuilding its culture and changing the population's mindset from one of war to peace.

The BBC's role has been to help develop the media infrastucture. The work of the BBC World Service Trust has been focused on helping the Afghanistan media to rebuild themselves and ensure they have the necessary broadcasting skills and principles.

The BBC World Service Trust has helped set up a new public service broadcasting body, a strong and independent media network that may reassure the Afghan people that action is being taken to recreate a democratic society. The BBC World Service Trust claims the programme has gone far beyond its remit to rebuild Afghanistan's media infrastructure.

According to the BBC World Service Trust, the impact is as follows:

- increased audience – now estimated at 85% of the population and improved profile for the BBC as a social broadcaster
- staff development opportunities and enhanced motivation for staff from different BBC divisions – including developing skills for BBC journalists working on news gathering
- increased trust – as a result of the BBC's long-term commitment to Afghanistan and production of education programmes, covering human rights, civil society, voter education, women's rights and minority rights
- establishment of an independent media – with a robust infrastructure that allows the reconstruction process to be communicated to even the most isolated communities
- training for Afghan journalists – of whom 20% are women (who were denied employment and education under the Taliban regime)
- media resources and training to use radio and studio equipment.

This example demonstrates how an organisation can get involved with a section of society and make real improvements. In this example, the BBC is using its experience as a broadcaster to help improve the media landscape in a specific country. The engagement with the issues is, however, more than just a practical one; other outputs relate to the communications impact in Afganistan, staff development, perceptions of the BBC and an ability to meet the corporate objectives/mission of the BBC.

Source: www.bbc.co.uk/www.bitc.org.uk

PICTURE 6.1   Being corporately responsible should mean taking steps to avoid having a negative impact on the society in which an organisation operates. (*Source:* © Reuters/Corbis.)

It is also important to define some of the business terminology that is frequently used when analysing businesses in their societal contexts.

> **Definition:** A *stakeholder* is someone who has an interest (stake) in the organisation, which may be direct or indirect interest as well as active or passive, known or unknown, recognised or unrecognised (see also Chapters 11 and 27).

Corporate social responsibility

A well-used business and management term, corporate social responsibility (CSR), is often associated with the phrase 'enlightened self-interest' – how organisations plan and manage their relationships with key stakeholders. CSR is, therefore, an organisation's defined responsibility to its society(ies) and stakeholders. Although organisations are not a state, country or region, they are part of the infrastructure of society and as such they must consider their impact on it. A simple analogy for the impact organisations have on their community has been presented by Peach (1987; see Figure 6.1, overleaf),

which shows the ripples from a stone thrown into a pond to represent the impact of a business on its environment. There are three levels of impact ranging from the *basic* in which a company adheres to society's rules and regulations to the *societal* where a company makes significant contributions towards improving the society in which it operates. In the middle level, companies are perceived to manage their activities so they adhere to the level and go beyond it. For example, this might be a company obeying legal requirements on employment rights as a foundation and then providing more generous interpretations of these legal rulings. Also the company may seek to reduce the negative impact of the organisation on its society without necessarily taking positive action to make improvements that would take it to level three. (See also Box 6.1, overleaf.)

Companies operating at the highest level, *societal*, do exist: companies are increasingly obtaining public recognition and visibility for their positive corporate actions. For example, in the UK, Business in the Community (BITC) has a PerCent Standard (formerly the Per Cent Club), which is awarded as a voluntary benchmark to companies donating at least 1% of pre-tax profits to community/social benefits.

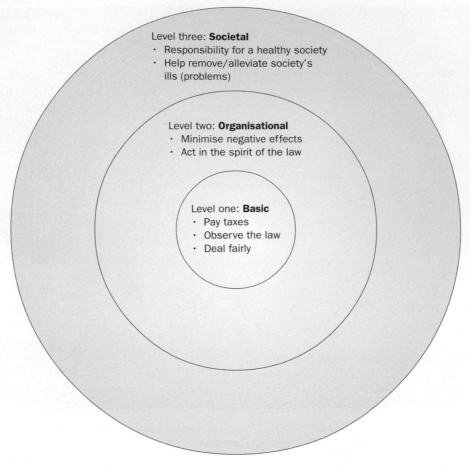

FIGURE 6.1   Impact of a business on its environment (*source:* after Peach 1987: 191–193).

In 2002, 122 companies reporting to the standard invested a total of £854.7m. This demonstrated a significant increase from £303.37m in 1999. Box 6.2 gives the full details from the BITC survey for 2004.

Definition: *Financial regulation* of donations refers to the legal requirement in the UK that any donation over £200 has to be recorded in a company's end of year annual report and accounts (the financial statement to shareholders).

When considering CSR it is important to make a distinction between corporate activities that are intended to contribute to the society and charitable acts or philanthropy (see Activity 6.1).

Philanthropy

One simple definition of *philanthropy* is that 'corporations perform charitable actions'. This is very different from CSR, with philanthropy being a charitable act not necessarily linked to the expectations of society.

box 6.1   Peach model in action

Some clear examples at the *basic* level might be a company in the supermarket retail sector that is profitable, pays its taxes and maintains minimum terms and conditions for its employees. At the highest, *societal*, level you could describe a supermarket retailer that conforms to society's rules and laws but also contributes to its society by funding community initiatives (e.g. holidays for disadvantaged children, investments in school facilities, transport for elderly people, lobbying for improved treatment of waste by local companies in line with its initiatives, contributing to positive legislation change in support of society, surpassing national and international employment rights and conditions, innovation in childcare or part-time mothers' conditions of work, etc.).

| box 6.2 | **PerCent Standard results for 2004** |

In 2004, 152 companies reported their community investment through to the PerCent Standard. Submissions were received from companies in the FTSE250 and Business in the Community's membership. The results found that:

116 companies achieved the 1% Standard
109 companies are members of Business in the Community
 56 companies are members of the FTSE100
 58 are members of the London Benchmarking Group
  6 companies still contributed to their community but made pre-tax losses
 35 companies reported for the first time.

2004 total reported community investment was £934,327,608. This is broken down between:

Cash contribution: £604,509,460 (2003 – £496,623,319; 2001/02 – £381,280,998; 2000 – £244,126,127; 1999 – £200,755,733)

Employee time: £60,618,041 (2003 – £44,819,158; 2001/02 – £38,641,240; 2000 – £28,754,690; 1999 – £25,500,729)

Gifts in kind: £195,848,025 (2003 – £263,204,495; 2001/02 – £101,625,924; 2000 – £41,798,114; 1999 – £35,032,923)

Management costs: £73,351,282 (2003 – £50,086,509; 2001/02 – £42,020,316; 2000 – £28,777,488; 1999 – £22,332,603).

The 2004 top 10 UK givers were:

Allen & Overy – £12,600,000
Vodafone in the UK – £10,514,160
Co-Operative Group – £8,124,661
Procter & Gamble – £6,628,933
Sainsbury's – £6,069,143
Allied Domecq – £5,761,900
BSkyB – £5,054,631
GWR Group – £5,033,145
KPMG – £4,270,234
John Lewis Partnership – £4,166,803

The top 10 in absolute terms were:

GlaxoSmithKline – £144,290,400
Altria – £128,150,272
BP – £50,123,223
Unilever – £45,780,905
Royal Bank of Scotland – £40,100,000
Lloyds TSB – £36,680,000
Barclays – £32,821,803
HBOS – £29,392,310
BHP Billiton – £25,941,192
Anglo-American – £24,158,000

Source: Business in the Community (www.bitc.org.uk)

Philanthropy did occur in large industrial firms in the UK during the nineteenth century (such as Joseph Rowntree, Titus Salt) through the donation of money and amenities such as schools, hospitals or housing for employees and their communities. *Corporate philanthropy* can be perceived as a short-term one-way relationship, which is unpredictable on behalf of the recipient and therefore more difficult to manage and strategically plan for. For example, during the dot-com boom (during the late 1990s when the financial performance and market impact of web-based businesses and technology companies in general were seriously exaggerated), technology company directors commonly gave large sums in charitable donations. The Slate 60 is an annual list of US charitable gifts and pledges that has reported since 1996: in 2002 the total of $4.6bn was down from 2001's high of $12.76bn (see www.slate.msn.com). Depending on the general and sector-specific economic performance, individuals

activity 6.1

Business impact on society

Identify, name and describe a company or organisation that fits into each of the levels in the 'stone in the pond' analogy.

What would those organisations in levels one and two need to do to move towards the third, societal level?

Feedback

You need to consider what changes in ethical business policy or practice would make a difference to society. It is not enough just to make statements of intent.

go on or off the list, reinforcing the unpredictable nature of this type of activity. For example, Bill Gates (the world's richest man and Microsoft's founder) was on the list in 2001 with $2bn in gifts. In 2005 Gates made the largest ever private donation of £400m ($750m) to the child health charity he set up with his wife, Melinda, the Global Alliance for Vaccines and Immunisation (see also Chapter 27). Although gifts can be turned on and off by the donor like a tap, there are some benefactors who donate through trusts, which enable the act to be sustained over longer periods of time (e.g. the Rowntree Foundation or the Wellcome Trust in the UK, the John D. Rockefeller Foundation or the Bill and Melinda Gates Foundation). (See Activity 6.2.)

> **Definition:** *Philanthropy* means 'a love of humankind; practical benevolence especially charity on a large scale' (*Concise Oxford Dictionary* 1995).

> **Definition:** *Corporate philanthropy* is 'a way of giving something back into local communities, improving quality of life for employees, and practicing corporate citizenship' (Cutlip et al. 2000: 470).

In recognition of the interest shown by various stakeholder groups – employees, customers and particularly the financial community and investors – it is now common business practice for large and small to medium-sized enterprises (SMEs) to publish corporate literature and brochures giving details of their community activities and CSR. Non-financial reporting on corporate responsibility in annual reports became prevalent in the mid-1990s. In the UK, for example, BT's annual review and summary financial statement (1996/7), included a section called 'Why we are helping the community: we're all part of the same team'. Within the report BT stated that:

activity 6.2

Identifying CSR and philanthropic actions

List examples of what you might consider to be CSR or philanthropic actions by an organisation/company.

Feedback
Can you make distinctions between the two? Think about each organisation's objectives for the action. What was the intended outcome? What did it hope to achieve? Was it long term? Was it pre-planned or in response to an individual(s) request?

It is increasingly clear that businesses cannot regard themselves as in some way separate from the communities in which they operate. Besides, research has shown that the decision to purchase from one company rather than another is not a decision about price alone.

The practice has evolved to such a degree that companies now produce specific corporate responsibility reports. For example, O2 (formerly part of BT) is a Europe-wide mobile telephone company that launched its first corporate responsibility report in 2003.

Business case for corporate social responsibility: why be socially responsible?

Organisations in developed economies are today influenced by public opinion, shareholders, stakeholders (who can be shareholders, consumers and members of campaign groups) and the political process. Consequently, organisations that ignore their operational environment are susceptible to restrictive legislation and regulation. This is a particular issue in Europe with the increasing power and influence of the European Union, the single currency and the European parliamentary process. Representative bodies for business such as Business in the Community (BITC), CSR Europe, Institute of Business Ethics, Business for Social Responsibility, and the Prince of Wales International Business Leaders Forum (IBLF) have formed to help senior managers deal with the demands of varied stakeholder groups.

Is CSR good business practice? On the one hand, many companies profited from unethical practices in the early part of the twentieth century, as demonstrated by the success of textile and mining industries and more recently with companies manufacturing chemical-based products such as asbestos. Furthermore, Milton Friedman has been the consistent business voice stating that the business of business is simply to increase profits and enhance shareholder value. Friedman (1970) wrote key articles arguing these views in the 1960s and 1970s. Although there are few contemporary academic papers supporting his views, they are frequently cited as the opposing arguments to CSR.

On the other hand, in contrast to Friedman's views, there are the examples of both old and new companies benefiting themselves, their stakeholders and employees through more ethically based practice. Worldwide examples include Cadbury, Lever's, IBM, Co-Operative Bank and Coca-Cola. Even before corporate responsibility became a boardroom agenda item around the turn of the millennium, there is evidence of its commercial value. For example, Johnson & Johnson's chief executive officer, James Burke, demonstrates that companies with a reputation for ethics and social responsibility grew at a rate of 11.3% annually from 1959 to 1990 while the growth rate for similar companies without the same ethical approach was 6.2% (Labich 1992). Furthermore, arguments and evidence are emerging to support CSR's contribution to the financial performance of organisations (Little and Little 2000; Moore 2003).

CSR can contribute to corporate image and reputation (Lewis 2003; Sagar and Singla 2004). The importance of a good reputation can include the following:

- Others are more willing to consider the organisation's point of view.
- It helps to strengthen the organisation's information structure with society and therefore improve resources in all areas.
- It makes it easier for the organisation to motivate and recruit employees – and to promote increased employee morale (Lines 2004).
- It will enhance and add value to the organisation's products and services.

A socially responsible reputation is also a way of differentiating organisations and providing competitive advantage. This is supported by announcements from companies such as McDonald's and BT in the UK that they would be investing more time and resources into socially responsible activities. BT was influenced by a MORI report, which stated that 80% of respondents believed it was important to know about an organisation's socially responsible activities in order to form a positive opinion about them. CEOs worldwide are starting to recognise that CSR is an important agenda item. Research by the India Partnership Forum (2003) shows that nearly 70% of CEOs say that CSR is 'vital' to profitability and that, irrespective of economic climate, it will remain a high priority for 60% of CEOs across the globe.

A company with an acknowledged strategy change on corporate responsibility and environmental engagement is oil firm Royal Dutch/Shell. During 1998, Shell had its first meeting with institutional shareholders (major company investors, e.g. on behalf of pension funds) to explain the company's new policies on environmental and social responsibilities. This initiative came following criticism of the company's action in high-profile environmental issues (e.g. when Shell was challenged by campaign groups over its decision to dismantle the Brent Spar oil platform at sea rather than on land owing to the supposed environmental impact) and human rights cases (execution of human rights activist Ken Sara Wiwo, in Ogoniland, where Shell had a dominant interest).

At the meeting with shareholders, Mark Moody Stuart of Shell Transport and Trading (the company's UK arm) stated that he did not agree with arguments that institutional shareholders were not interested in issues such as social responsibility: 'I don't think there is a fundamental conflict between financial performance and "soft" issues. Many shareholders want outstanding financial returns in a way they can feel proud of or comfortable with.' (See Think abouts 6.1 and 6.2.)

think about 6.1 Shell Europe

During both the Brent Spar and Ogoniland crises, Shell faced a Europe-wide consumer boycott of its fuel products as well as significant media criticism (see above, www.shelluk.co.uk, www. greenpeace.org.uk and Chapter 19). Why do you think Shell took the potentially risky strategy of reopening debate about environmental and societal issues after such high profile vilification by the two important stakeholder groups (consumers of their products and the media)?

Feedback This initiative by Shell clearly demonstrates the company directors' desire to tackle key issues head on but also to make the company more accountable to its publics and specifically to the communities (and therefore stakeholder groups) in which it operates.

think about 6.2 Business effects of CSR

Does CSR stretch an organisation's relationship with, and activities of, its supply chains (companies that supply products and services)? Can you think of suppliers for a company that it should not be associated with?

Feedback Some companies have developed supplier policies that define the requirements for supplier organisations. For example, it would not be socially responsible for a furniture retailer that operates a 'green' purchasing policy to buy its raw materials from suppliers who purchase their wood from unsustainable sources.

PICTURE 6.2 Ken Saro-Wiwa was a human rights activist from the Ogoniland where Shell had a dominant interest. (*Source:* AFP/Getty Images.)

Organisational responsibilities to stakeholders

Stakeholder analysis is a clear way of defining those groups and individuals who have a significant relationship with an organisation (see also Chapter 12). Stakeholders can be described as those with a vested interest in the organisation's operations. Figure 6.2 simply demonstrates the most common stakeholders in for-profit organisations.

These are simplified stakeholder groups which can be expanded and broken down into subgroups. In order for an organisation to act with social responsibility it is necessary to understand the fundamental elements of the organisation's operations and its relationships with stakeholders. To achieve this it can be helpful to ask and analyse the following questions:

1　How is the organisation financed, e.g. shareholders, private ownership, loans, etc.?
2　Who are the customers for the products and services, e.g. agents, distributors, traders, operators, end users, etc.?
3　What are the employee conditions and terms, including status, contracts and hierarchical structures?
4　Are there community interactions at local, regional, national and international levels?

5　Are there governmental, environmental or legislative actions that impact on the organisation?
6　What are the competitor influences on the organisation, e.g. markets, agents, distributors, customers, suppliers?
7　What are the supplier influences on the organisation, e.g. other creditors, financial supporters, competitors?
8　Are there any issues or potential risks that may be affected by local, national or international pressure groups or interests?

CSR from a stakeholder perspective may bring the organisation closer to its stakeholders and importantly improve the two-way flow (Grunig and Hunt 1984) of information and subsequently understanding.

Once stakeholders are identified, you need to define the responsibilities you have towards them and then define and develop strategies to manage these relationships (see Activity 6.3).

---

activity 6.3

Defining organisational stakeholders

(a) Choose an organisation and define its stakeholders.
(b) How would you prioritise these stakeholders in terms of their importance to financial performance for the organisation?

Feedback
Financial performance is important for all organisations but this prioritised list may look different if instead it were arranged according to CSR performance towards stakeholders.

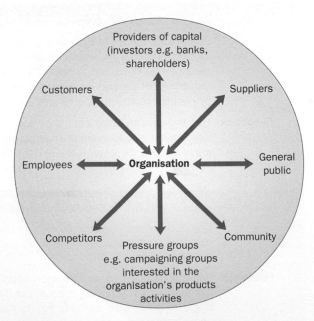

FIGURE 6.2 Typical for-profit organisational stakeholders

Organisational responsibilities to society

Business ethics writer Carroll (1991) argues there are four kinds of social responsibility: economic; legal; ethical; and philanthropic, demonstrated through the CSR pyramid in Figure 6.3.

To aid managers in the evaluation of an organisation's social responsibilities and to help them plan how to fulfil the legal, ethical, economic and philanthropic obligations, Carroll designed a 'stakeholder responsibility matrix' (see Table 6.1, overleaf). Carroll makes the clear distinction that social responsibility does not begin with good intentions but with stakeholder actions.

Carroll's matrix is proposed as an analytical tool or framework to help company managers make sense of their ideas about what the firm should be doing, economically, legally, ethically and philanthropically, with respect to its defined stakeholder groups. In practice, the matrix is effective as it encourages the manager to record both descriptive (qualitative) and statistical data to manage each stakeholder. This information is then useful when identifying priorities in long- and short-term business decision making that involves the multiple stakeholder groups that influence most organisations. It enables these decisions to be made in the context of the company's or organisation's value systems – what it stands for – as well as accommodating economic, social and environmental factors. To express this simply, the manager is able to make decisions in a more informed way with a clear map of the numerous factors that will impact on these decisions. It is a detailed approach to stakeholder management but is one way of providing informed foundations about stakeholders to enable strategies, actions or decisions to be taken that reflect the complex environment in which most organisations operate (see also Figure 6.4, overleaf).

Table 6.1 (overleaf) provides an example of the matrix applied to one stakeholder group and the types of recorded data required. The organisation is a small clothing manufacturing business. The stakeholder group used for the analysis is customers. Each social responsibility cell has been considered in the context of this stakeholder group and data input currently

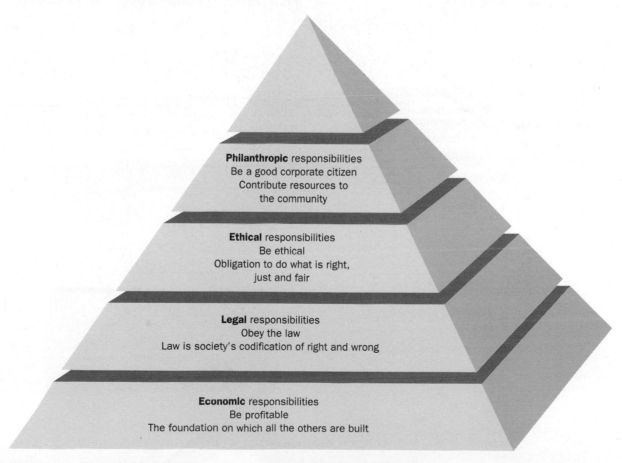

FIGURE 6.3   Corporate social responsibility pyramid (*source:* after Carroll 1991)

TABLE 6.1   Stakeholder responsibility matrix (*source:* after Carroll 1991)

Stakeholders:	Economic	Legal	Ethical	Philanthropic
Providers of capital				
Customers				
Employees				
Community				
Competitors				
Suppliers				
Pressure groups				
General public				

available about the responsibility the firm acknowledges towards this group. Clearly the data included are not exhaustive and further records could be sought or gaps in information identified and subsequently commissioned by the public relations or communications team.

This information will help managers when the organisation is defining corporate strategies for long- and short-term decisions to ensure they accommodate the multiple stakeholder interests.

Regulatory frameworks

As consumers we have product choice – do we go for brand, price or even ethical or corporate responsibility performance? Companies such as Shell, Nike and Nestlé have experienced the threat and financial effects of global boycotts and are realising that greater mobility of stakeholders and globalisation of communication mean that reputation management is increasingly

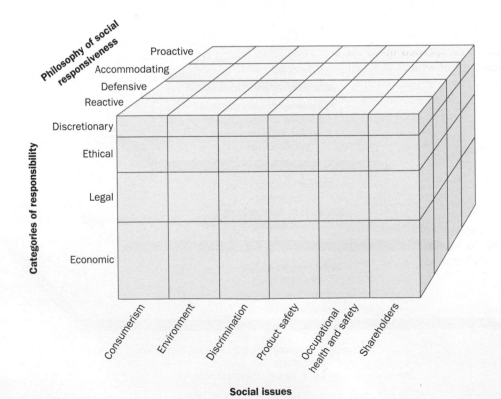

FIGURE 6.4   Carroll's responsibility matrix (*source:* adapted from Carroll 1991)

TABLE 6.2   An application of the stakeholder responsibility matrix to a small clothing manufacturer

Stakeholders	Economic	Legal	Ethical	Philanthropic
Customers	Financially well-managed company Clear financial reporting	Conform to consumer health and safety product guidelines (e.g. quality controls and standards for fire safety of garments, etc.) Correct labelling National and transnational product labelling, e.g. European standards	Fairly priced products Highest quality Products are designed for and fit for purpose (e.g. if for specialist sector such as workwear) Provide best products with the highest standards of care for employers and suppliers Transparent sourcing of materials (no use of child labour or low-paid employees) Do not abuse our suppliers or workers	Give waste products to needy organisations Give unsold products to customers' preferred charities or homeless groups Support other employee and customer initiatives Etc.

important. One manifestation of this is the speed of communication and in particular news distribution globally via new technology, satellite and the emergence of 24-hour news channels. The process of news gathering has been speeded up as has the news production cycle – all of which is crucial for public relations when managing reputation and communication for organisations. Research by the World Economic Forum in 2003 revealed that 48% of people express 'little or no trust' in global companies. Consequently, even large and powerful corporations must adopt more ethical working practices in order to reduce risk and maintain favourable reputation. The growth of organisations such as Business in the Community in the UK and CSR Europe is helping to place CSR in the mainstream of business thinking and encourage more organisations to leverage the opportunities of CSR. This has a number of implications, including the increased need for guidance for companies. Subsequently the past few years have seen the emergence of an increasing number of standards and guidelines in the areas of CSR and sustainable development. These include:

- Dow Jones Sustainability Index
- FTSE 4 Good Index
- Business in the Community's Corporate Responsibility Index

- Global Reporting Initiative's (GRI) Reporting Guidelines.

Public and business attitudes are changing and in 1999 a global poll of 25,000 citizens (MORI 1999) showed that perceptions of companies are more strongly aligned with corporate citizenship (56%) than either brand quality (40%) or the perception of the business management (34%). Further evidence of the public attitude change was reported in the *Financial Times* (2003) which claimed that in the late 1970s the British agreed by two to one that the profits of large companies benefited their customers. In 2003 the public disagreed by two to one. This attitude change is reiterated by Fombrum and Shanley (1990) who found in earlier studies that a business that demonstrates responsiveness to social concerns and gives proportionately more to charity than other firms receives higher reputation ratings by its publics. There is a range of research that demonstrates consumers' willingness to reward socially responsible companies, with far-reaching effects. One such effect is the changing focus of investment decisions. This has resulted in the emergence of 'triple bottom-line' reporting whereby social and environmental performance hold equal importance to financial performance. It can therefore be argued that, in the eyes of consumers, the media, legislators and investors, social

case study 6.2

European campaign – GlaxoSmithKline–Barretstown

Therapeutic recreation for children with serious illness

GlaxoSmithKline (GSK) is one of the world's largest pharmaceutical companies. The company's partnership with Barretstown in Ireland began in 1994 to kick start their European Community Partnership Programme focusing on children's health.

Barretstown was established as the first 'hole in the wall' camp in Europe, building on the success of the first North American camp to enable children with serious illnesses to experience 'summer camp' by providing first-class medical facilities on the site of the camps. Barretstown Castle was donated by the Irish government to provide a similar facility and additional facilities were constructed to adapt to the children's special needs.

Through a programme of activities and adventure in a safe and medically supported environment, children meet and develop friendships with other children. Many paediatricians see their patients' participation in Barretstown as an integral part of clinical treatment. As well as helping children feel better through greater confidence and self-esteem, their experience at Barretstown helps them do more than they ever thought they could. Being involved with the programme helps GSK volunteers learn how to deal sensitively with issues relating to disability.

As Barretstown involves children from countries where GSK has a business operation, it reflects their regional structure and draws different GSK businesses together to work on a shared programme. GSK employees from these countries participate as volunteer carers (helpers) and GSK businesses provide practical support locally, for example funding children's flights to Ireland. GSK's funding has been focused on establishing the 'European Liaison Network' an important interface between Barretstown

and children's hospitals. The network provides a framework across 19 countries for raising awareness about the camp among doctors, parents and children, as well as recruiting children to participate. More than 110 hospitals across Europe nominate children to participate. According to GlaxoSmithKline, the impact is as follows:

- Barretstown provides volunteers with opportunities for personal development, in particular for developing creativity, teamwork and diversity awareness. GSK volunteers learn how to deal sensitively with issues relating to disability, especially the way those children feel about their appearance and body image.
- GSK Barretstown has created a model for other GSK businesses to adapt to local programmes. Several of GSK's businesses have adopted 'therapeutic recreation' as a focus in developing their own community programmes. GSK supports smaller scale programmes with local children's hospitals in Hungary, Portugal and Romania.
- Early data show that the main benefits of the programme are that the children regain self-esteem, develop confidence and have some of their independence restored after what may be long periods of isolation and hospitalisation.
- From serving 124 children in 1994, Barretstown has grown and now supports over 10,000 children drawn from 110 hospitals in 19 European countries.
- The partnership with Barretstown has been key in contributing to building GSK's reputation as a good corporate citizen among internal and external stakeholders.

Source: www.gsk.com/www.bitc.org.uk

and environmental responsibilities are increasingly powerful drivers of reputation. (See Case study 6.2.)

Definition: 'Triple bottom-line' reporting is a phrase increasingly used to describe the economic, environmental and social aspects that are being defined and considered by business. These are sometimes called the three Ps – profit, plant and people!

Ethics and business practice

Before looking in detail at the techniques for operating a business in society (and for implementing CSR programmes, discussed in Chapter 18), we

need to consider the important issue of *ethics* and ethical business practice. *Business ethics* is a substantial issue and an important part of understanding what is called corporate governance. It ranges from high-profile issues about equal opportunities, 'glass ceilings' for women in work, whistleblowing (employees reporting on unethical or illegal activities by their employers), whether large PLCs pay their SME suppliers or contractor on time down to whether it is all right for a director or senior manager to take a ream of paper home for a computer printer, when this is a sackable offence for an office junior!

Business ethics is therefore about us as individual members of society, as part of the community or as part of organisations (whether these are work or

Ethical dilemmas

Ethical dilemmas occur when we are faced with decisions that cause dissonance (conflict) in our loyalty (taken from Festinger's theory of cognitive dissonance, see Chapter 14). Take the example of a cheating colleague who is extracting small amounts of money from the organisation through false expenses claims. If we know about their actions, should we show loyalty to them or to our organisation? We are left with an 'ethical decision'. What do you think you would say or do if it were a director or management colleague in this case? How would you manage the ethical dilemma?

Feedback 'Ethical problems are not caused entirely by "bad apples". They're also the product of organisational systems that either encourage unethical behaviour or, at least, allow it to occur' Trevino and Nelson (1995: 13).

You need to gather all the facts and also consider the impact of your decisions/actions on the organisation as a whole. See the section on ethical decision making.

leisure/interest organisations). For example, we may be an employee of a national supermarket chain and a trustee for a local school or scout group. We make decisions within these environments that have ethical implications and societal impact (see Peach 1987: Figure 6.1). Ethics is an important part of business reality, as managers make decisions that affect a large range of stakeholder groups and communities from the employees of the organisation to the residents who live close to its business sites. (See Think abouts 6.3, 6.4 and 6.5; see also Box 6.3, overleaf.)

Definition: Trevino and Nelson (1995) define *business ethics* as 'the principles, norms and standards of conduct governing an individual or group'.

Definition: Ethics = extension of good management.

Ethical decision making: theory and practice

Business ethics author Snell (1997) argues that there are two approaches to the teaching and understanding of business ethics by practitioners. One of these is termed 'systematic modernism', which is the more explanatory, conservative voice of business leaders and political leaders on societal issues. The explanations are more functional and seek resolutions in the short to medium term, i.e. through legislation, the use of law and order and reliance on individual's social responsibility. In contrast, 'critical modernism' is the current 'underdog' yet this has been influenced more by theoretical ethical debates. It is argued therefore that the critical approach takes business ethics a stage further than just face-value explanations of why something is right or wrong.

Good apples and bad apples

The 'good' and 'bad apple' analogy is frequently used in the context of ethics. Apply this analogy to your own experience and think of an example of unethical conduct. Was it the responsibility of the individual (apple) or the organisation (barrel) or was it a combination of the two?

Feedback Arguably, we are born amoral, not moral or immoral. Psychologists have argued that ethics, as such, are not innate. They are culturally bound and influenced by the social environment we grow up in. We develop and change our personalities throughout our lives – including during our adult life – and research (Rest and Thoma 1986) has found that adults in their 30s who are in moral development programmes develop more than young people.

Individual and corporate ethics

Dissonance or conflict is what causes individual problems with corporate ethics and there are stark examples such as a religious person working for a pharmaceutical company that decides to market an abortion product, or an environmentally conscious employee working for a high-polluting company. What should these individuals do to manage the conflict? What should their management do?

<table>
<tr><td>box
6.3</td><td>**Example of ethical guidelines**</td></tr>
</table>

Unilever has published its ethical guidelines – or ethical principles – as follows: 'Unilever believe that economic growth must go hand in hand with sound environmental management, equal opportunities world-wide and the highest standards of health and safety in factories and offices.'

Its code of business principles covers sensitive issues such as bribery: 'Unilever does not give or receive bribes in order to retain business or financial advantages. Unilever employees are directed that any demand or offer of such a bribe must be immediately rejected.'

Source: www.unilever.com

Table 6.3 (below) highlights how the two schools of thought operate and interpret different ethical issues. (See Activity 6.4.)

Philosophers have studied ethical decision making for centuries and tend to focus on decision making tools that describe what should be done in particular situations (see also Chapter 15). The most well-known philosophical theories are categorised as consequentialist, regarding the consequences of actions, with utilitarianism being the best known and associated with the 'greatest happiness' principle (i.e. the greatest happiness for the greatest number of people). Trevino and Nelson (1995: 67) state that a utilitarian approach to ethical decision making should 'maximise benefits to society and minimise harms. What matters is the net balance of good consequences over bad.'

Generally, utilitarian ethical decision making is therefore focused on what we do and what are the consequences of our actions, i.e. who will be harmed or affected. In a business context, this means which stakeholders will be affected. One method of testing this approach is to ask if everyone acted in the same way, what sort of environment would be created? Just imagine what the impact would be if each of us dropped our lunch wrappers and leftovers onto the floor every day! Extend this out to all businesses draining their waste water/fluids into the nearest river/ocean outlet. This theory does underlie a lot of business writing and thinking and people's approaches to ethical decision making.

A second strand of philosophical thinking is categorised under deontological theories which focus on

TABLE 6.3 Competing modern narratives on business ethics (*source:* adapted from Snell 1997: 185)

Issue	Typical systematic modern narrative	Typical critical modern narrative
Corruption: bribery and extortion	Bad because it dents local or national pride, deters inward investment and is a sign of backwardness	Bad because it is inherently unfair, disadvantaging the politically and economically weak
Protection of the environment	Our sons and daughters will suffer or perish unless we adopt proper controls	Indigenous (native) peoples, rare animal species and future citizens are entitled to a habitable environment
Inflated executive salaries	One should set up systems of corporate governance overseen by non-executive directors to safeguard minority shareholders' interests	One should campaign for wider social justice, including action to help the poor and reduce unemployment
Function of codes of ethics	They are tools for inspiring the confidence of customers and investors, and a means of controlling staff	They are a starting point only. People should be encouraged to develop their own personal moral code
Preferred Kohlberg stages	Conventional reasoning: preserving stability, the rule of law and order and social respectability	Postconventional reasoning: concern for social welfare, justice and universal ethical principles

Ethics in everyday life

Think about how you act in different situations. How would you react if a college friend started telling jokes about people with physical disabilities? Would you smile in an embarrassed way, laugh and hope they wouldn't carry on, confront the speaker and ask them to stop, or what?

Feedback
It is often useful to reflect on our codes of ethics, what we see as right and wrong, and on whether we act on our beliefs or are more interested in how others perceive or see us.

motives and intentions through duties or the action itself rather than the outcome or results. German philosopher Emmanuel Kant wrote about the 'categorical imperative', which asks whether your ethical choice is sound enough to become universally accepted as a law of action that everyone should follow (see Kant 1964). The obvious example is whether telling lies is ever acceptable. Imagine a company context where it was perceived that telling a lie for the good of the company was to its benefit. Kant would argue against this case unless the company is prepared to accept that from that point forward all employees were permitted to lie – a 'categorical imperative'. You need only consider the case of Enron in the USA (see case study in Chapter 20) to appreciate where such an ethical management system will lead with regard to telling mistruths and lies to a range of stakeholders.

Another ethical approach that is popular with business ethics academics and fits into the business context is virtue ethics, which is also founded in traditional philosophical theory. It focuses on the integrity of the actor or individual more than on the act itself. Within this approach it is important to consider the relative importance of communities or stakeholder groups. For example, in a professional context you may be bound by community standards or practical codes of conduct. This can help the individual make ethical decisions because it gives them boundaries to work within.

Changing the culture and changing organisational ethics

Any attempt to change ethical practice within an organisation must be based on a simple assumption that all human beings are essentially good and capable of development and change. Changing ethical practice through changing the culture of an organisation is not a quick fix; it takes time as you have to address the formal and informal organisational subcultures. The culture of an organisation clearly affects what is appropriate or inappropriate behaviour. To understand the culture an audit is necessary and can be car-

ried out through surveys, interviews and observations.

Having completed an audit, the next stage is to write a culture change intervention plan that includes targeting the formal and informal systems.

The formal systems are more transparent and easier to change, as follows:

■ draw up new codes of conduct
■ change structure to encourage individuals to take responsibility for their behaviour
■ design reward systems to punish unethical behaviour
■ encourage *whistleblowers* and provide them with appropriate communications channels and confidentiality
■ change decision-making processes to incorporate attention to ethical issues.

For the informal system, the following may be important:

■ re-mythologise the organisation – revive old myths and stories about foundations, etc. that guide organisational behaviour (revived myths must, however, fit with reality).

See Activity 6.5 and Case study 6.3, overleaf.

Definition: A *whistleblower* is someone who speaks out about an organisation's unethical behaviour or malpractice. Examples are employees who tell the public about financial mismanagement or theft inside an organisation or government employees who leak evidence of wrongdoing such as selling arms to particular regimes or government actions that contravene policy or legal frameworks.

Ethics in practice

To conclude this chapter on business and its role in communities and society, think about the following.

Managers are the key to ethical business practice as they are the potential role models for all employees, customers, suppliers, etc. and also the endorsers of ethical policies. Due to changes in management practice, business process reengineering and the downsizing of western companies, many modern businesses have fewer managers today – yet each manager has more staff to control:

1 How should organisations be ethical? Identify three or four reasons. Divide these reasons into those that are linked to financial gain and those that are societally sympathetic.
2 Are employees attracted to ethical employers? Give reasons why you believe they may or may not be.
3 List those companies you would be proud to work for and those that you would be ashamed to be employed by or represent. What are the key features of each? What are the similarities and differences?

case study 6.3

Co-operative Bank case study

At the Co-operative Bank they have brought it all together extremely well. Established in 1872, it was always a small bank. But in the late 1980s a new managing director asked the bank's few but loyal customers why they were there. From a significant minority, the answer came back that they thought the bank was ethical. The bank then asked 30,000 of them what else they would like. (Most national opinion polls in the UK ask about 2000 people.) The questions were based on the simple premise that a person will only knowingly lend money for something they approve of and as putting money into a bank is indirectly lending it to others it has the same effect. In 1992 this led to the first ethical policy where the bank promised never to invest in areas not approved of by its customers. The results were as follows: 90% only wanted to support governments or businesses supporting human rights; 87% would not fund companies manufacturing or trading in armaments to oppressive regimes; 80% were against animal exploitation; 70% wanted to reduce environmental damage; 66% rejected the fur trade; and 60% did not want to support the production or sale of tobacco products. (See the company website for the current policy.)

The bank also produces reports indicating how well it is doing against the often challenging measures set by its customers, which can also be seen at its website. The policy has worked. During a time of severe economic downturn for most, the bank's profitability almost tripled, from £45.5m in 1996 to £122.5m in 2002.

As the sector grows the research will continue to add to our knowledge or its value. Those expressing values-led decisions are moving up to overtake the profit led – or you could say that people are beginning to ask the true cost of products and services rather than just what is on the price ticket. In a MORI poll for the Co-operative Bank it was found that 25% have actively sought products from companies with a responsible reputation. Interestingly, where they had the facts, 50% have chosen the responsible and 50% have boycotted the irresponsible.

CSR policies have to be well researched and managed as shown here and they have to go deep and for the long term – there are a lot of pressure groups watching very closely and testing claims.

Source: Co-operative Bank (www.co-operativebankcase study.org.uk; www.co-operativebank.co.uk)

Summary

Milton Friedman's perception that the business of business is simply to increase profits and enhance shareholder value has less credibility in the twenty-first century. Also the public is increasingly sophisticated on environmental and ethical issues such as: global warming; worldwide natural disasters such as the Asian tsunami and businesses' responses; animal testing; hunting with dogs in the UK. There is rising power for the consumer in national and international contexts as demonstrated by Shell and Body Shop. The influence of corporate image and reputation on an organisation's business success (Andersen; McDonald's/McLibel) is increasingly recognised, as is the use of business ethics to create competitive advantage (Co-Operative Bank; Body Shop). Enhanced communication (the internet) for and with stakeholders and interest groups, media expansion and global influence (24-hour news) and the mobilisation of

national and international issue and pressure groups (such as Greenpeace or the anti-Iraq War lobby) can all separately and together affect any business today.

This chapter has focused on the role organisations play in their society(ies) and how the understanding of business ethics and CSR may improve business performance and enhance reputation through more effective use of public relations and communication. Chapter 18 will build on these principles to discuss how CSR is being incorporated into many organisations' strategic planning and how public relations is being used to support this.

Discussion in this chapter has focused on:

- stakeholder influences
- ethical decision making
- changing cultural and organisational ethics.

Bibliography

Adams, R., J. Carruthers and S. Hamil, (1991). *Changing Corporate Values*. London: Kogan Page.

Cannon, T. (1992). *Corporate Responsibility*. London, Pitman.

Carroll, A. B. (1991). 'The pyramid of corporate social responsibility: toward the moral management of organizational stakeholders.' *Business Horizons* **34**(4): 39–48.

Clutterbuck, D., D. Dearlove and D. Snow (1992). *Actions Speak Louder: A management guide to corporate social responsibility.* London: Kogan Page.

Concise Oxford English Dictionary, 8th edition (1995). Oxford: Clarendon Press.

Cutlip, S.M., A.H. Center and G.M. Broom (2000). *Effective Public Relations*, 8th edition. Upper Saddle River, NJ: Prentice Hall.

Davies, P.W.F. (ed.) (1997). *Current Issues in Business Ethics.* London: Routledge.

Fombrum, C. and M. Shanley (1990). 'What's in a name? Reputation building and corporate strategy'. *Academy of Management Journal* 33: 233–258.

Friedman, M. (1970). 'The social responsibility of business is to increase its profits'. *New York Times Magazine* 13 September: 32.

Grunig, J. and T. Hunt (1984). *Managing Public Relations.* New York: Holt, Rinehart & Winston.

India Partnership Forum (2003). www.indiapartnershipforum.org, accessed 25 March 2005.

Kant, I. (1964). *Groundwork of the Metaphysic of Morals.* London: Harper & Row.

Klein, N. (2000). *No Logo: Taking aim at the brand bullies.* London: Flamingo.

Labich, K. (1992). 'The new crisis in business ethics'. *Fortune* 20 April: 167–176.

Lewis, S. (2003). 'Reputation and corporate social responsibility'. *Journal of Communication Management* 7(4): 356–364.

Lines, V.L. (2004). 'Corporate reputation in Asia: Looking beyond the bottom line performance'. *Journal of Communication Management* 8(3): 233–245.

Little, P.L. and B.L. Little, (2000). 'Do perceptions of corporate social responsibility contribute to explaining differences in corporate price-earnings ratios? A research note'. *Corporate Reputation Review* 3(2): 137–142.

Moore, G. (2003). 'Hives and horseshoes, Mintzberg or MacIntyre: What future for corporate social responsibility?' *Business Ethics: A European Review* 12(1): 41–53.

MORI (1999). 'Winning with integrity'. London: MORI.

Peach, L. (1987). In *Effective Corporate Relations*. N. Hart (ed.). Maidenhead: McGraw-Hill.

Rest, J.R. and S.J. Thoma (1986). 'Educational programs and interventions' in *Moral Development: Advances in research and theory*. J. Rest (ed.). New York: Praeger.

Sagar, P. and A. Singla (2004). 'Trust and corporate social responsibility: Lessons from India'. *Journal of Communication Management* 8(3): 282–290.

Schwartz, P. and B. Gibb (1999). *When Good Companies Do Bad Things: Responsibility and risk in an age of globalization.* New York: John Wiley & Sons.

Skooglund, C. (1992). 'Ethics in the face of competitive pressures'. *Business Ethics Resource*, Fall: 4.

Snell, R. (1997). 'Management learning perspectives on business ethics' in *Management Learning*. J. Burgoyne and M. Reynolds (eds). London: Sage.

Thomson, S. (2000). *The Social Democratic Dilemma: Ideology, governance and globalization*, London: Macmillan

Trevino, L.K. and K.A. Nelson (1995). *Managing Business Ethics: Straight talk about how to do it right.* New York: Wiley & Sons.

Vandenberg, A. (2000). *Citizenship and Democracy in a Global Era.* London: Macmillan.

Wolstenholme, S. (2004). 'An issues management approach to corporate social responsibility'. Paper presented at the Vilnius Conference, 23 April.

World Economic Forum (2003). www.weforum.com, accessed 26 March 2005.

Websites

BBC: www.bbc.co.uk

British Society of Rheology: www.bsr.org.uk

Business in the Community: www.bitc.org.uk

CadburySchweppes: www.CadburySchweppes.com

Chartered Institute of Public Relations: www.cipr.co.uk

Co-operative Bank: www.co-operativebank.co.uk

CSR Europe: www.csreurope.org

The Gap: www.gap.com

Greenpeace: www.greenpeace.org.uk

GlaxoSmithKline: www.gsk.com

Institute of Business Ethics: www.ibe.org.uk

Nike: www.nike.com

O2: www.mmO2.co.uk

The Shell Group: www.shell.com

Unilever: www.unilver.co.uk

For glossary definitions relevant to this chapter, visit the **selected glossary** feature on the website at: www.pearsoned.co.uk/tench

CHAPTER 7
International context of public relations

Learning outcomes

By the end of this chapter you should be able to:

- define international and global public relations
- identify the driving forces behind the internationalisation of practice and theory
- conceptualise international public relations
- recognise the environmental factors that affect the implementation of an international campaign.

Structure

- Defining international public relations (IPR)
- Factors and driving forces behind internationalisation
- International public relations agency networks
- Global or local approaches to international public relations
- Structures of international public relations
- Special areas of international public relations
- Public relations for a supranational organisation: the European Union
- Critical voices in IPR
- Professionalism on a global level: public relations as a global profession

Introduction

Consultancies with an international network as well as multinational companies' in-house public relations departments often communicate with consumers, media, shareholders or employees who are situated in another country or sometimes even continent. Mergers, acquisitions and outsourcing are taking place on an international scale and result in new organisations, corporate cultures and working practices. International public relations (IPR) practitioners need to identify and understand views, opinions and behaviours of foreign publics in order to communicate effectively with them and to implement public relations campaigns that cross national boundaries.

Several companies with an international interest position themselves as global companies rather than as German, Japanese or British organisations (see Mini case study 7.1 about British Airways). These organisations invest heavily in developing a global image. Many non-governmental organisations (NGOs), such as Greenpeace, Red Cross, Save the Children or Amnesty International, cannot be associated with a particular country either. When they engage in public relations activities to recruit volunteers or raise awareness of a particular issue, they communicate with a variety of peoples and countries all over the globe.

Not only multinational organisations but also countries and their governments frequently engage in international public relations to create a positive reputation and image of the particular country abroad or a receptive environment for achieving foreign or economic policy goals. The Bush administration's fight for the 'hearts and minds' of the Arab people during and after the Iraq War in 2003 and 2004 involved a lot of 'public relations-like' activities both in the Arab countries and in the rest of the world, with the help of several public relations consultants and agencies. A more peaceful example is the Belgian government, which commissioned a public relations agency to restore the country's image and reputation in the European Union (EU) following high-profile child pornography and corruption scandals in 1998. Russian president Vladimir Putin used the services of an international public relations agency in preparation for the presidential elections in 2000. An international media and advocacy campaign was developed to explain policies on the war in Chechnya and his approaches to economic and social reforms to western opinion leaders.

After the fall of the Berlin Wall in 1989, many newly emerged central and eastern European countries relied on public relations to create and communicate a 'sellable' identity to the rest of the world. Examples are Estonia or the Czech Republic, which successfully positioned themselves as independent, democratic and dynamic countries.

Intergovernmental organisations (IGOs), such as the European Union, the International Monetary Fund or the United Nations, also rely on international public relations to communicate with the often unlimited number of publics. Mini case study 7.2 highlights some of the United Nation's 'image problems'.

This chapter examines public relations theory and practice in an international context. It conceptualises international public relations and its main dimensions. We examine how international public relations as a global practice has emerged and its current state. Special attention will be given to the environmental factors that affect the planning and implementation of international campaigns.

mini case study 7.1

British Airways

British Airways (BA) went global in 1996. In June 1997 the airline unveiled a new £60m corporate identity as a part of a three-year £6bn programme that saw the airline investing in new aircraft, services, products and network partners in the build-up to the millennium. British Airways also unveiled a £1m global advertising campaign with the slogan: 'The World is Closer Than You Think.' The new identity was based on 50 'world images', commissioned from ethnic artists around the world and 15 of the designs were presented at a press conference at Heathrow. This involved satellite broadcast linking 150 separate events in 64 different countries and an audience estimated at 30,000 for the 30-minute presentation. The new identity was introduced over the following three years across the company on aircraft, ground vehicles, airport signs and stationary, to establish BA as an 'Airline of the world, for the world'.

BA's plan to fly world images instead of the Union flag backfired, however: the press, UK passengers, staff and even Margaret Thatcher heavily criticised the new identity. Eventually, the airline had to retreat and repaint its planes in 2001, bringing back the Union flag (despite the fact that 60% of non-British passengers liked those world images).

mini case study 7.2

The United Nations (UN)

The UN's reputation and credibility suffered seriously during 2004 and 2005 when a series of scandals shook the organisation and its Secretary General, Kofi Annan. There were accusations that US peacekeepers in Congo had raped women; there were corruption allegations about its 'oil for food' programme in Iraq during Saddam Hussein's reign; Kofi Annan's son was paid by a Swiss firm that held a UN food contract; and in February 2005 a senior officer resigned after sex abuse allegations. An experienced PR and political consultant was appointed as chief of staff to restore the UN's battered reputation and its staff morale, while managing and coordinating the biggest ever tsunami disaster aid operation in Asia.

Defining international public relations (IPR)

As stated in the preface, one of the intentions of this book is to produce a textbook that can be used by students and practitioners in different countries. Until recently, American textbooks have dominated PR literature both in the USA and worldwide, despite the fact that most of them make no or very little reference to other countries or how PR is practised in an international context. For some American writers, international PR is simply about how to overcome barriers that are created by other cultures, including language, laws or cultural issues, which are often identified as 'problems' (Wilcox et. al. 2001), rather than opportunities or the manifestation of diversity.

The first question one might ask is whether *international public relations* exists at all and, if it does, how to define it. Today, very few practitioners would agree with the US PR executive who argued that 'there's no such thing as international public relations' (Angell 1990: 8). Practitioners and scholars alike would rather support Pavlik's view, who as early as the 1980s considered IPR 'one of the most rapidly growing areas of the profession, and one of the least understood' (Pavlik 1987: 64).

IPR is now the new buzzword of the twenty-first century and a rapidly growing area of PR practice. However, PR theory and research has been slow to keep abreast, lagging behind marketing, human resources or management disciplines, which have long developed theories and models of their practices in the international context. It is only recently that PR has 'gone global' and new regions of the world, such as eastern Europe, Asia or Latin America, are being 'discovered' by PR academics. Even in academic literature, the terms IPR and global PR are being used interchangeably and in several contexts. In this chapter, global PR will refer to the *internationalisation of the profession,* which is being practised in more and more countries throughout the globe, while IPR will refer to the planning and implementation of *programmes and campaigns* carried out abroad, involving two or more countries (usually referred to as parent and host countries).

One of the most widely quoted definitions of IPR is that of Wilcox et al. (2001: 283), who defined IPR as 'the planned and organised effort of a company, institution or government to establish mutually beneficial relations with the publics of other nations'.

Definitions of PR emphasise mutual understanding as well as relationship building between an organisation and its publics (see Chapter 1). Relationship building and strengthening are vital factors in building global brands and global reputation. Interestingly enough though, consumers or other publics would hardly define or perceive their connections with a company as relationships. Conceptualising how individuals or certain publics 'understand' an organisation may present some difficulties, especially in an international arena.

Wakefield's (2003: 180) definition also avoids these concepts and is more tangible. IPR is: 'a multinational program that has certain co-ordination between headquarters and various countries where offices and/or publics are located, and that has potential consequences or results in more than one country'.

> **Definition:** *International public relations* is the planned communication activity of a (multinational) organisation, a supra- or international institution or government to create a positive and receptive environment through interactions in the target country which facilitates the organisation (or government) to achieve its policy or business objectives without harming the interests of the host publics.

IPR activities can be *preparative,* with the aim of creating and cultivating a favourable environment, or *situational,* when often a single issue or situation drives communication – like international pressure group activities. Finally, IPR can be simply *promotional,* when product or service promotion is the centre of the programme and PR is supporting the global marketing function, or in an ideal case, integrates and drives communication. IPR is thus the glue of globalisation: it facilitates multinational corporations to reach new publics and markets. (See Box 7.1 and Think about 7.1, overleaf.)

Factors and driving forces behind internationalisation

Globalisation

Globalisation refers to the growth of worldwide networks of interdependence. It has many dimensions, including environmental, military, social and economic globalisation. Globalisation is often equated with Americanisation, especially by its critics. Although it is true that American companies are central to globalisation, the USA itself is affected by this phenomenon. Whether you oppose or support globalisation, it *is* happening, so the main issue is how organisations or countries respond to it.

Environmental issues, health problems, diseases, human rights, migration, organised crime or organised weapons of mass destruction and terrorism are global issues that cannot be resolved and managed by one country without significant (global) public support. An emerging *global public sphere* is where these and many other issues can be articulated and

box
7.1
The main players and their motives in international public relations

The following are groupings or organisations involved with IPR that share similar characteristics:

- *Multinational organisations* (MNOs) with a variety of global business objectives such as increased global sales or creating global brands and raising brand awareness.
- *Nation-states and governments*. Images of nations are important to attract investment, to boost tourism or to achieve foreign policy goals. Reputation is one of the most valuable currencies in international politics and governments often compete for credibility.
- *Intergovernmental organisations* (IGOs) are those whose members are national states. They can be *(inter) regional*, such as the European Union (EU), Association of South East Asian Nations (ASEAN), League of Arab States, the European Space Agency or the North Atlantic Treaty Organisation (NATO) or *global* such as the United Nations (UN), World Trade Organisation (WTO), UNESCO and World Health Organisation (WHO). These organisations make collective decisions to manage particular problems on the global agenda.
- *International non-governmental organisations* (Oxfam, Red Cross, Greenpeace, Amnesty International). NGOs represent every facet of political, social and economic activities and their worldwide number is around 30,000. They claim to be the 'global conscience' and often mount IPR campaigns against large for-profit organisations or governments, 'naming and shaming' them (see also Chapter 29).
- *Public relations consultancies* with an international network (Edelman, Shandwick, Hill and Knowlton, Burson-Marsteller).
- *Virtual communities* that develop on the internet, ignoring the limitations of space and time.

discussed, mostly through the mass media (see also Chapters 9 and 11 for more about the public sphere). Concentration of media ownership, however, may hinder this process since commercial communication can replace public communication. PR and public affairs are often criticised for making public debates and discussions a 'faked version' of a genuine public sphere by displaying power rather than facilitating debates (Thussu 2000).

Many national as well as international surveys confirm the decline in trust in businesses. Citizens and consumers tend to trust non-governmental organisations

(NGOs) rather than global brands and they entitle them to act on their behalf. A study of opinion leaders in eight countries from three continents by Edelman (PR agency) found that in France, Germany and the UK, the four most trusted brands are NGOs: Amnesty International, World Wildlife Fund, Greenpeace and Oxfam (then Microsoft, Bayer and Ford).

The picture is rather different in the USA, where Johnson & Johnson, Coca-Cola and Microsoft are the most trusted brands. Figure 7.1 details the extent to which respondents trust business, government, media and NGOs in western Europe, the USA and China.

think about 7.1 Transparency and accountability

There is increased pressure on the organisations mentioned in Box 7.1 to be transparent and accountable. PR should facilitate both transparency and accountability towards stakeholders. Is this always the case? Could PR be used to hinder transparency and distract attention?

Feedback Unfortunately, PR is sometimes used as 'cosmetic surgery' or as a method of distracting attention or managing perceptions. PR consultancies or practitioners serve and protect the interests and reputations of their clients which may not always be in accordance with the interest of other groups.

The Chinese government, for example, employed an international PR consultancy to improve the country's image in the west after the Tiananmen Square massacre in 1989. In May 2004 a terminal building at Paris' Charles de Gaulle Airport caved in and killed four people. Tony Blair's then spin doctor David Hill saw the tragedy as a chance to undermine the Paris bid for the 2012 Olympics and an opportunity to brief about the failings of the French transport system. It had strong overtones of the Jo Moore scandal in the UK when the government communications advisor sent out email to colleagues on the day of the terrorist attack on the World Trade Center on 11 September 2001 saying that it was 'a good day to bury bad news'.

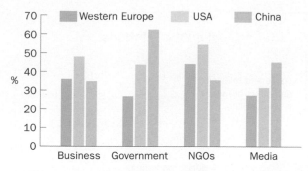

FIGURE 7.1   Trust in business, government, NGOs and media (*source:* adapted from Sixth Annual Edelman Trust Barometer 2005, © Daniel J. Edelman, Inc.)

Mini case study 7.3 is a good example of a global PR campaign launched by Oxfam, which aimed to influence decisions regarding the global coffee market.

Information revolution

Another driving force behind internationalisation is the *information revolution,* which is the result of rapid technological advances in computers, software and communication. It has dramatically changed every aspect of everyday life, resulting in an international information society. The global network society refers to the notion that new communication technologies result in a fundamental shift in social organisation.

Nation-states are no longer in control of power, which is shifting from individual countries to global networks.

The internet has made both interpersonal and mass communication instantaneous. In 1997 the Nobel Peace Prize was awarded to Jodie Williams for helping to create a treaty banning land mines despite the Pentagon's strong opposition. She organised her campaign mostly on the internet. The information evolution has resulted in lower costs of processing and transmitting information. The amount of information that can be stored and transmitted on the net has no limits. In 1993 there were only some 50 websites; by 2000 this number was well over five billion. Command over information has become a major asset in organisations.

A new global culture is emerging parallel to a global consumer society. Interactions between cultures are significantly influenced by the globalising cultural forces, including the international media. The media have also become a multinational corporation with ownership concentration: news that crosses borders gathered and distributed by a few, transnational companies. CNN and the BBC are the two most influential sources of television news, broadcasting 24 hours, seven days a week, although, of course, information does not only flow through the media. Figure 7.2 (overleaf) highlights the most important channels and types of international information flow (see also Think about 7.2).

Oxfam International

In 2002 Oxfam International, a global non-profit organisation, launched the Coffee Rescue Plan, an initiative that encouraged cooperation among governments, large coffee roasters and other stakeholders to help solve the coffee price crisis. To coincide with the launch, Oxfam released a report entitled *Mugged: Poverty in Your Coffee Cup* that described and documented the problems in the global coffee market.

The Coffee Rescue Plan pointed out that the 'Big Four' coffee roasters – Sara Lee, Procter & Gamble, Nestlé and Kraft (owned by Philip Morris) – buy nearly half of the world's coffee crop. They thus dominate the $60b global coffee industry and their healthy profit margins range between an estimated 17% and 26%.

Oxfam contended that the Big Four's business strategy is short-sighted and ultimately self-destructive, as their practices put coffee farmers out of business. Furthermore, the Big Four risk alienating consumers, who are gaining awareness of the social and environmental costs of coffee production. Oxfam pointed to the rise in sales of fair trade coffee, which promotes paying coffee farmers a living wage price, as evidence of growing consumer concern.

The Coffee Rescue Plan calls on large coffee roasters and international governments to increase the market for fair trade coffee. The plan also encourages roasters' governments to bring the current oversupply of coffee back into line with demand and to help ensure that coffee farmers earn a decent living.

Source: http://www.SocialFunds.com

Figure 7.2 was developed before the internet age. How could you complete the wheel in the light of the information revolution?

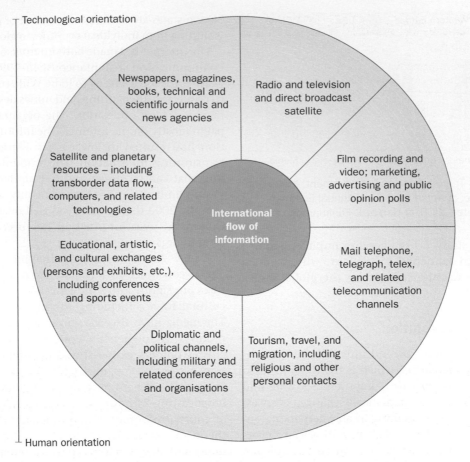

FIGURE 7.2   Channels and types of international information flow (*source:* Mowlana 1986: 2)

The international media outlets (especially TV and news channels) often serve as mediums to reach a global audience in an IPR campaign. Corporations, governments and the media are competing for customers, voters and viewers on a global scale.

Agenda setting

Agenda setting is the process by which the media communicate the relative importance of various issues to the public (Rogers and Dearing 1988). The media agenda is influenced by news values and the media agenda affects the public agenda. The third agenda is the policy agenda influenced and articulated by pressure groups and political actors. Based on the increasing influences of the multinational corporations, Watson (2003) suggested a fourth agenda: the corporate agenda (Figure 7.3). His model of agendas takes into account the dynamic, and often imbalanced, relationship between the public, policy, corporate and media agendas. He places the public agenda in the centre since governments, corporations and the media all try to exert influence on the public. These agendas are related and influenced by

each other as well as by external factors such as PR. PR practitioners constantly influence the media agenda through media relations while the policy agenda can directly be influenced by lobbying. Alongside with PR practitioners, several different groups (including pressure groups) are competing to set and influence these agendas. (See Activity 7.1.)

The internet is changing newspaper readership and TV viewing. As research in 2004 (JupiterResearch,

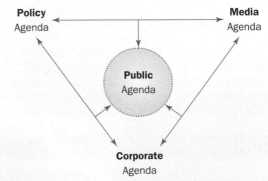

FIGURE 7.3   Tripolar model of agendas: policy, corporate and media (*source:* Watson 2003: 131)

Observing the news

Watch two news programmes on the same day (e.g. national evening news such as the BBC *News at 10* or *ITV News* at 10.30pm in the UK). How many news items were presented during the programme? How many of them dealt with:

- for-profit organisations
- multinational organisations
- overseas (foreign) news
- environmental, corporate or other types of crisis?

Can you identify any differences in the number and nature of news items between the two channels? Do you think that any of these news items could have been the result of PR activities? If yes, why? What kind of overseas stories were included? Did they conform or challenge your view of the country mentioned?

You can repeat the same activity for a national or regional daily newspaper.

http://www.JupiterResearch.com) found, TV is the medium most threatened by the internet, as 27% of European internet users say that they have reduced the time watching TV in favour of the web. These people belong to a young age group, between 15 and 24. Eighteen per cent of internet users across Europe are reducing the time they spend reading print newspapers in favour of the net, an increase of 5% since 2001. This is not only affecting younger generations; the international business community is also changing its readership and viewing habits. A survey of top business executives found that the *Financial Times* lost 12,000 readers during three years. Table 7.1 summarises the average issue readership of international publications in 2004 among 431,000 top European senior executives. (See Mini case study 7.4, overleaf.)

International public relations agency networks

International PR agencies, not surprisingly, play a significant role in the practice of IPR. These networks have offices in many different countries. The local offices' knowledge (including the language and culture), expertise and their relations with the media give more credibility to communication actions as well as strengthening the legitimacy of the campaigns. Hiring PR practitioners means that messages are 'localised' and tailored towards the needs of the publics in the host country. In this sense, multinational

TABLE 7.1   Average international publication issue readership (*source:* European Business Readership Survey 2004, Ipsos Media)

Title	Readership (2004)	Readership (2002)	Reach % (2004)	Reach % (2002)
All international titles	185,854	200,095	43.1	47.3
Dailies				
Financial Times	56,517	68,586	13.1	16.2
Frankfurter Allgemeine Zeitung	46,571	54,994	10.8	13
International Herald Tribune	14,605	11,348	3.4	2.7
Wall Street Journal Europe	11,571	14,204	2.7	3.4
USA Today	6,037	7,615	1.4	4.8
Weeklies				
Business Week	20,072	18,908	4.7	4.5
The Economist	33,200	35,659	7.7	8.4
Newsweek	14,231	18,184	3.3	4.3
Time	20,722	21,826	4.8	5.2
Fortnightlies				
Forbes	23,554	18,193	5.5	4.3
Fortune	16,498	16,579	3.8	3.9
Monthlies				
CFO Europe	13,971	10,671	3.2	2.5
Eurobusiness	4,312	5,922	1.0	1.4
Euromoney	6,815	9,215	1.6	1.8
Harvard Business Review	24,148	24,536	5.6	5.8
Institutional Investor	6,143	7,169	1.4	1.7

mini case study 7.4

Bhopal haunts after 20 years

The speed with which information and news spreads, the fight for exclusivity by the major news corporations and the lack of time for checking the reliability of sources are well demonstrated by this BBC World report about Bhopal on the twentieth anniversary of the catastrophe, in December 2004.

A BBC World reporter was researching the disaster that resulted in the death of 18,000 people after toxic gas leaked in 1984. The reporter consulted a website of Dow Chemical, the company that now owns the infamous Indian factory and was offered an exclusive interview to be broadcast live from Paris on the anniversary. At 9am, the 'spokesman' of the company announced the launch of a $12bn fund 'to finally at long last compensate the victims including the 120,000 who may need medical care'. An hour later the news was the leading bulletin on News 24 and many other BBC, Indian and international news channels. As a result of news of this huge compensation package, Dow Chemical's share price sharply decreased in Frankfurt as well as in New York. The real company was quick to react after hearing the news: at 10am the real Dow spokesperson contacted the BBC and demanded a retraction of the story since it was untrue. It appeared that the BBC reporter was looking for a spokesperson who could be interviewed on the occasion. He ended up on www.Dowethics.com, which is a mimic of the real company's website, set up in 2002 by Yes Men, an anti-corporation pressure group. He contacted a spokesperson, who was none other than one of the main campaigners of Yes Men. The story ended with the BBC apologising for the misinformation.

This case study highlights another tendency, which is a challenge for global companies: pressure groups and anti-corporation activists often set up rogue sites to challenge or damage organisations. These sites can be easily found and can reach vast international audiences.

---

organisations (MNOs) adapt to the culture of the host country through PR and *international* PR becomes *domestic* PR. Through their networks, international PR agencies localise international campaigns and at the same time contribute a great deal to the globalisation of the practice.

Figure 7.4 summarises the different options facing a multinational organisation or a government engaged in IPR. In the parent country, it can commission the local branch of an international PR agency, which has an office in the target country *(1)*, but it can also hire a local PR agency in the host country to work on its behalf *(2)*. If the organisation has an office in the host country, its in-house practitioners can also engage in PR *(3)*. An organisation can directly target the publics of the host country *(4)* (governments tend to use this option, in the form of public diplomacy). Direct targeting is also possible from the parent country through a PR agency commissioned by the MNO *(5)*.

Another cost-effective approach is when some of the 'key publics' of the target countries are brought to the parent country *(6)*. Trentino, a province in Northern Italy, invited journalists from 10 European countries to enjoy the natural beauties and the hospitality of the region. After returning home, these non-travel journalists wrote extensively about the characteristics of the region from different perspectives. Another strategy is to invite international journalists to the corporate headquarter of a multinational organisation.

Only the interactions that take place in the 'international PR space' can be considered truly international

PR practice. This often means that IPR boils down to inter-consultancy or inter-departmental communication *(1, 2, 3)* in the form of:

- programme coordination (with the help of a lead PR agency or the headquarters of the multinational company)
- getting programme elements 'approved' by head office or lead agency
- programme and performance evaluation (effectiveness of the campaign, PR consultants' performance, return on investment)
- financial issues (costs, fees).

A multinational organisation can directly speak to its foreign publics through its website. When we first want to find out information about a foreign organisation or country we are likely to 'Google' that organisation and try to check out its website. This means that the internet is central to any IPR programme. See Activity 7.2.

activity 7.2

Multinational company websites

Select a multinational telecommunications company and check out the company's websites in different countries. You are unlikely to understand the languages of these websites but try to identify their common visual features. Do they have an English version and is it updated? Does the company use the same identity throughout these websites?

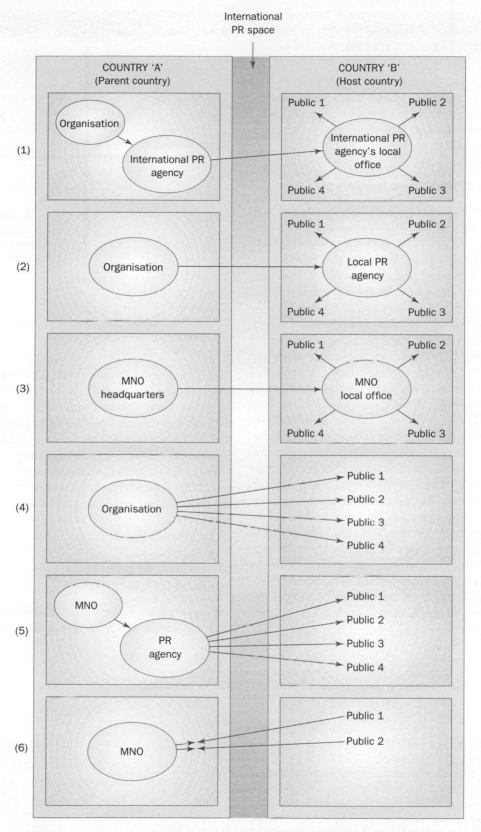

FIGURE 7.4   International public relations 'space' – forms of international public relations

Global or local approaches to international public relations

IPR stretches the boundaries of both practice and theory. The next section examines how universal the principles and concepts of PR theory are and to what extent PR strategies and techniques can be standardised and centralised. See Figure 7.5.

Theory, concepts and models

Practitioners and scholars alike have been interested in whether PR theories and concepts are universal and which factors can influence the practice of PR in an international context. Since the theoretical foundations of PR evolved in the USA and UK, the question is whether these theories are applicable in other parts of the world and if they are, to what extent.

Several studies have focused on the practice of two-way symmetrical communication in a country-specific context, trying to demonstrate the universal use and adaptability of Grunig's models (see Chapters 1, 8 and 9). They test excellence theories and whether US approaches work in other countries. Research conducted in Greece, India and Taiwan identified two additional models: according to the 'personal influence' model, PR practitioners are expected to develop relations with important and influential people while in the 'cultural interpreter model' practitioners interpret local cultures and practices for a multinational organisation. In a study among South African practitioners, Holtzhausen et al. (2003) found no evidence that participants grouped PR practices according to the principles of symmetry and asymmetry. Based on their findings they challenged the application of general principles, based on the excellence project (see Box 7.2), and Grunig's models to international research settings.

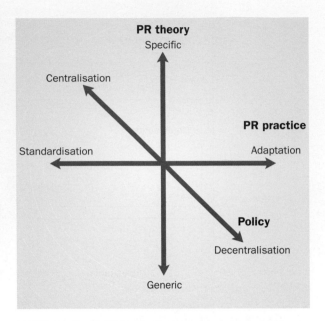

FIGURE 7.5   Multidimensional feature of international public relations theory and practice

The excellence theory has significantly influenced theory and research although the number of its critics is on the increase. Excellence and effectiveness are culture-bound concepts which means that both concepts can be defined in different ways in different cultures. Excellence theory is, however, often used as a benchmark against which the practice of PR is tested in other nations. Importing western theories into other cultures may not always be appropriate.

Structures of international public relations

IPR departments can choose whether they *centralise* communication policy or *decentralise*. Centralisation

---

- Involvement of PR in strategic management
- Empowerment of PR in the dominant coalition or a direct reporting relationship to senior management
- Integrated PR function
- PR as a management function separate from other functions
- Role of the PR practitioner
- Two-way symmetrical model of PR
- A symmetrical system of internal communication
- Knowledge potential for managerial role and symmetrical PR
- Diversity embodied in all roles

Source: Verčić et al. 1996

Planning international programmes – standardisation vs adaptation

	Full standardisation		Full adaptation
Objectives	*		
Messages			*
Channels		*	
Tactics		*	
Evaluation	*		

(or control) means that the parent company's PR team is responsible for planning campaigns and for developing communication policies, procedures and strategies and that the PR departments in the host country are to follow these policies. Timing of events is another example of centralisation. In the case of decentralisation, policy making and planning lie with the organisation's PR departments in the host countries with partial or full autonomy. In reality, centralisation and decentralisation can vary to different degrees and a balance between the two approaches should be maintained. Whether or not an organisation follows a centralised or a decentralised approach, what is crucial is the *coordination* of the communication efforts. This is a point where many multinational companies fall short and only when a crisis hits do they pay more attention to coordination.

Pharmaceutical, IT and telecommunications companies are among the most common clients of international PR agencies. These types of companies often use a combination of centralised and standardised approaches, since their services and products are rather standardised and less culture specific than clothing, food or household products.

According to Jeffrey Lenn (1996), centralisation or decentralisation depends on the following factors:

■ corporate strategy and structure
■ corporate size – smaller MNCs are more likely to centralise their decision making
■ scope of the PR function
■ quality and availability of the PR staff
■ types of programme and issue.

The *standardisation* versus *adaptation* debate is prevalent in many communication disciplines, including the different elements of the marketing mix. Standardisation means a uniform approach in the different countries, while adaptation is a culture-specific approach. The first question to ask is *what* should be standardised in PR throughout the different countries involved or adapted to the local culture. Objectives of

a campaign, messages, channels of communication, tactics and evaluation (see Chapter 10) can be placed on a continuum, full standardisation (the same objective, messages in each country) and full adaptation (the environmental factors determine them) being two extremes (see Box 7.3).

Programme objectives as well as evaluation principles are often standardised but message development and choice of channel are subject to adaptation. According to the level of centralisation and standardisation, Figure 7.6 (overleaf) places the different areas of PR in an international context.

The corporate identity of a multinational company like McDonald's is fully centralised and standardised. The company's corporate social responsibility programme's central policy and concepts could be centralised in the corporate head office but interpretation and implementation may be localised. Media relations are very likely to be fully decentralised and adapted to the specific circumstances in the host country since the ways of 'getting publicity' can vary from country to country. Internal communication is influenced by McDonald's corporate culture (see Chapter 17), which follows the US model, while interpersonal communication is culture bound (i.e. affected by the local norms and values).

Adaptation is determined by environmental factors, which will be discussed in the next section.

A word of caution: centralisation and standardisation should not result in the dominance of the MNO's organisational or societal culture; the diversity of the culture and sensitivity to special features of the host culture must be borne in mind at the very beginning of the planning process. This can be achieved by thorough research into the host culture as well as by involving practitioners or communication experts from the targeted countries at an early stage of planning (this is rarely the case, unfortunately). Thorough and systematic research is the cornerstone of any IPR campaign; its absence can easily result in the failure of the entire campaign.

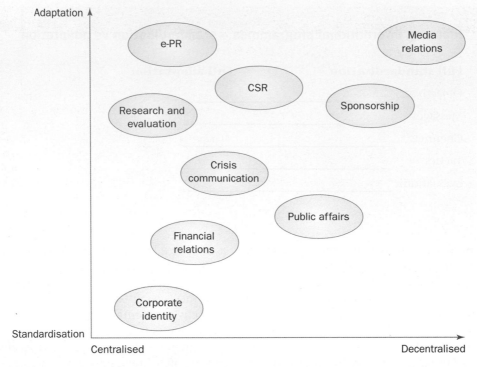

FIGURE 7.6   Dimensions of public relations specialisations in the international context

Mini case study 7.5 highlights an important issue: some US and UK-based multinational companies' PR departments and practitioners tend to believe that they possess specialist PR knowledge that can just be transferred to another country without adaptation. See also Mini case study 7.6.

Culture and environmental factors

Culture influences communication and communication influences culture. If PR is about symmetrical communication between an organisation and its publics with the aim of establishing and maintaining mutual understanding, then culture is central to the practice of PR. For many scholars (Verćić et al.

1996; Banks 2000; Sriramesh 2000; Sriramesh and Verćić 2003), however, culture is important only insofar as programme effectiveness is concerned and culture is often restricted to a simple variable. Effectiveness is always defined with regard to the organisation's perspectives, ignoring the publics' views and interpretation of effectiveness. In this sense the aim of 'understanding' other cultures is simply to direct and control behaviour that is to influence publics' attitudes and behaviours in ways that are advantageous for the organisation. To build trust with a variety of stakeholders and create 'shared understanding of meaning' among different cultures require deeper understanding and appreciation of other cultures by more cooperation and dialogue.

---

mini case study 7.5

A centralised approach

A US corporation specialising in measurement and monitoring, with over 20 offices worldwide, is an example of this approach. The company's headquarters in the USA pushed their 'American ways of thinking and conducting PR' on other global offices located in Beijing, Cologne, London and Tokyo, among others. Design, planning and preparation for the implementa-

tion of PR campaigns were handled in the USA, including the creation of press releases, press presentations and product information documents, giving little chance for contribution from local countries. The head office documentation content was presented to the local regions to perform in the same format but to the different press audiences.

mini case study 7.6

HSBC, The world's local bank

FT

In 2002 a Mexican bank, Bital, was bought by HSBC Bank but nothing happened until January 2004 when Bital's branches were turned into HSBC branches literally overnight. The new identity, including the name and logo, appeared 'out of the blue' on the sides of taxis, buses, plastic bags, airport carts and even on Mexican flower stalls. The new signs said HSBC in bright red, with its hexagonal logo replacing the name of Bital. The initials HSBC are difficult to pronounce in Spanish, so large posters were dropped down the side of tall buildings around Mexico City with nothing but a pronunciation guide: 'Hache, Ese, Bé, Cé'. The company's decision to change the name and not to keep the old name was due to strategic reasons and based on customer research. Customers were more concerned with the convenience aspects of banking rather than about the brand. A more difficult and complex task was the change internally. A new senior management team was installed within two months of the formal takeover with the purpose of 'control and transfer of HSBC's values'.

Source: adapted from 'The difference a day makes', *Financial Times* 6 May 2004, p. 14

To plan and implement international campaigns and to adapt campaign elements to the local culture, the PR practitioner must be familiar with:

- environmental factors that influence the practice of PR
- the cultural profile of the country
- its effects on communication
- the 'public relations culture', including the way PR is practised in the country.

Definition: '*Culture* is the property of a group. It is a group's shared collective meaning system through which the group's collective values, attitudes, beliefs, customs and thoughts are understood. It is an emergent property of the members' social interaction and a determinant of how group members communicate' (Barnett and Lee 2002).

Definition: *Intercultural communication* is communication between people whose cultural perceptions and symbol systems are distinct enough to alter the communication event.

Definition: *Cross-cultural communication* is communication between people from different cultures. Intracultural communication is communication between members of the same culture, including racial, ethnic, and other co-cultures (Samovar et al. 1998).

Definition: *International communication* refers to the cultural, economic, political, social, and technical analysis of communication patterns and effects across and between nation-states. It focuses on global aspects of media and communication systems and technologies (McPhail 2002: 2).

The following discussion refers to *national* cultures but the *organisational* culture of a multinational organisation can also influence the practice of IPR. The third dimension of cultural differences is the *individual* level.

To understand culture's influence on the communication function of PR, American communication scholar, Zaharna (2001) summarises the basic components of IPR based on *intercultural communication*. Using Hall's concepts of 'in-awareness' he identifies culture's influence on the practice of PR. In-awareness refers to the explicit and observable of a culture. The *country profile* and the *cultural profile* help expose the potential cultural and national differences between the parent and the host country. Both profiles identify variables that must be borne in mind when practising PR on an international scale.

Country profile

The country profile includes the host country's political, economic, legal and social structures as well as the level of development of its infrastructure and the structure and characteristics of mass media. Sriramesh (2000) further conceptualised the media environment by proposing a framework that should facilitate effective media relations practice in the host country:

- *Media control* refers to ownership and control of media organisations and control over editorial content.
- *Media outreach* means the ability of the media to diffuse messages, the extent of media saturation. Illiteracy and poverty can hinder outreach of the media to a wider audience.
- *Media access* refers to the extent to which organisations or any segments of society can access the media to disseminate messages.

The country profile can be complemented by level of activism (Sriramesh and Verčić 2003) that would have a bearing on the implementation of a PR campaign. Activism on a global level is on the increase, while PR plays a crucial role in creating activism as well as responding to it (see Chapter 29). (See also Activity 7.3, overleaf.)

activity 7.3

Media consumption in Europe

Figure 7.7 is a result of a study into media consumption in Europe in 2004. Analyse and interpret the findings. How could these results and tendencies influence the planning and implementation of a campaign that targets publics in central and eastern Europe?

Cultural profile

As Zaharna (2001) notes, country profiles outline what may be *feasible* within a particular country; culture profile is about what may be *effective* in that country.

Hall (1976) distinguished between *high-context* and *low-context* cultures, depending on the degree to which meanings come from the settings or from the words being exchanged.

■ In *high-context cultures* such as China, Japan or South Korea, communication relies on the physical context: information is provided through gestures, the use of space and most of the relevant information or meaning is already known by the receiver.

■ In *low-context cultures* such as Germany, Switzerland, Sweden or Canada, more meaning is placed in the language code since the population is less homogeneous. A low-context message therefore requires clear description and unambiguous communication.

These contexts are important with regard to what people pay attention to and what they ignore. Hall proposed that cultures organise time in either a *monochronic* or *polychronic* way. According to the monochronic approach, time is manageable and time commitments, such as deadlines and schedules, are taken seriously and time should not be wasted. Germany, Austria, Switzerland or the USA are examples of this approach while Asian or Latin American cultures represent the polychronic approach. People from these cultures may be engaged in different activities at once and time is less tangible, resulting in a more unstructured and spontaneous lifestyle. These concepts have implications for keeping and observing deadlines or timing events or PR tactics.

Kluckhohn's classification of cultures (cited in Zaharna 2001) includes time and activity orientation and social relationships:

■ *Past-oriented cultures* emphasise history and tradition (e.g. China, Great Britain, eastern European countries).
■ *Present-oriented* cultures value the moment (e.g. Mexico, Latin America).
■ *Future-oriented* cultures emphasis change, innovation and envision the future (e.g. the USA).

Activity orientation is the way culture views activity:

■ *Being orientation* refers to spontaneous, activity, and spiritual rather material values are important (e.g. Asian cultures).
■ *Doing orientation* emphasises achievements, visible accomplishments and thrives on action (e.g. the USA).

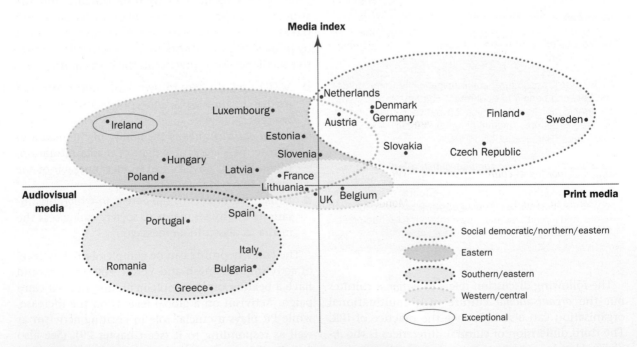

FIGURE 7.7   Media consumption in Europe, 2004 (*source:* courtesy of Future Foundation 2004)

Relational orientation was not mentioned by Zaharna but the concept of relationship is important in PR. Relational orientation is concerned with the ways in which people perceive their relationships with others. Many Arab cultures believe in *authoritarian relationships*, while *collective* cultures (China, Mexico, Latin America) see groups as the most important social entity. *Individualistic relationship* is based on equal rights for all people (USA).

A *linear culture* stresses the beginnings and ends of events, has unitary themes and relies on empirical evidences. A *non-linear* culture would deal with multiple themes and relies on oral communication. These dimensions are important in planning and co-ordinating PR activities.

Hofstede investigated the differences in collective behaviour and found five dimensions of societal culture (see also Chapter 17):

1 *Power distance* is the extent to which inequality and/or unequal distribution of power is tolerated in society. In high power-distance countries (India, Brazil, Greece) people accept power and authority as facts of life. In organisations it means greater centralisation of power. In low power-distance countries (Finland, Norway, the UK) inequality is often minimised.
2 *Individualism* emphasises individual freedom and independence from others, while in a *collective* society people remain attached to tight groups, like family, community or organisation.
3 *Masculinity* is the degree to which dominant values are male oriented while cultures that value *femininity* favours caring and nurturing behaviours.

4 High *uncertainty avoidance* cultures strive to avoid ambiguity, risk and uncertainty, and fear by establishing formal rules and seeking consensus (Greece, Portugal, Japan). For low uncertainty avoidance cultures, risk and uncertainty are inherent in life (Scandinavian countries, the USA).
5 The fifth dimension is about *long-term* versus *short-term orientation*: the time perspective in a society for the gratification of people's needs. Long-term orientation stresses virtuous living in this world, short-term orientation focuses on gratifying needs 'here and now'.

Zaharna's final profile is *communication components*: how cultural differences affect specific, individual PR practices. Verbal and non-verbal communication, visual communication and rhetorical style (the construction of logical arguments and persuasive messages) belong to this profile. The communication matrix consists of the various components of communication and how they relate to each other. Table 7.2 summarises the key dimensions and factors in international programme planning and implementation, based on Zaharna's approach.

It is important to note that research on national cultures has been primarily carried out with western methodologies and biases. The emergence of many new nation-states in eastern Europe as well as in Central Asia, and the opening of China require more research to be carried out with more focus on these countries, including oriental approaches.

While it is true that knowledge about the host country and its culture (including the above mentioned environmental factors) can result in more

TABLE 7.2   An in-awareness approach to international public relations (*source*: adapted from Zaharna 2001: 144)

Country profile	Cultural profile	Communication components
What are the structural features that influence the design and implementation of PR projects?	What are the cultural variations that influence the design and implementation of PR projects?	What are the basic communication components that may be influenced by national or cultural features?
Ways of looking at countries Political structure Economic structure Mass media • control • outreach • access Infrastructure Legal structure Social structure Level of activism	*Ways of looking at cultures* Low/high context Monochronic/polychronic Individualism/collectivism Uncertainty avoidance Masculinity/femininity Power distance Short-term/long-term orientation Activity/being oriented Future/past oriented Linear/non-linear Relationship orientation	*Ways of looking at PR activities* Verbal communication Non-verbal communication Visual communication Rhetorical style Communication matrix Group dynamics Decision-making practices

IPR practitioners need to bridge cultural as well as linguistic gaps. The language of business is English and many organisations throughout Europe or Asia adopt the 'English only' policy. IPR agency network members communicate in English too but the communication between the offices in different countries may be the only intercultural dimension of IPR. Speaking 'the same language' is pivotal in every sense.

English-language slogans are often used in non-English speaking countries. Table 7.3 highlights some well-known multinational companies that also operate in Germany and have used the original slogan without translation, even though only a small number of Germans could actually understand or translate these slogans accurately. Note that even some German companies have used English slogans in Germany.

success, it is also crucial to understand and appreciate the publics' attitudes and opinions in the host country about the parent country in which the MNO is situated or its products are produced.

An often cited aim of PR is *trust* building both nationally and internationally. As we have seen earlier, trust in government, politicians, journalists, media and in businesses varies from country to country. Credibility of these opinion formers and leaders and the institutions they work for may well be different across cultures. The level of trust and credibility may influence the choice of channel being used in the campaign or selecting people to endorse an issue or cause. (See Think about 7.3.)

Public relations culture

Trust in, and credibility of, PR practitioners may differ from country to country, so another factor that can influence PR in an international context is the PR culture of the host country. This is closely related to the practice and state of the art of the profession and is concerned with:

■ the functions of PR in the given country
■ the images of PR and PR practitioners among journalists or the general public
■ the ethical standards of PR and the level of development of the practice
■ the status PR practitioners hold
■ the extent to which PR has become professionalised.

Using some of the aforementioned factors in Table 7.2, three main research sources (Sriramesh and Verčić, 2003; van Ruler and Verčić, 2004; Sriramesh, 2004) provide a country-by-country description of how environmental factors have framed practice: the evolution and current state of the art of the profession.

Some interesting questions emerge at this point that need further research:

■ Can we say that PR is more developed or sophisticated in certain countries than in others?

TABLE 7.3   Understanding corporate slogans (*source:* data from Endmark International Namefinding, August 2003, from www.wuv.de/daten/unternehmen/charts/092003/779/)

Rank	Slogan	Organisation	Fully understood (%)	Believed they had understood (%)
1	Every time a good time	McDonald's	59	65
2	There's no better way to fly	Lufthansa	54	62
3	Come in and find out	Douglas	34	54
4	Powered by emotion	Sat.1	33	49
5	We are drivers too	Esso	31	44
6	Stimulate your senses	Loewe	25	34
7	Share moments, share life	Kodak	24	29
8	Driven by instinct	Audi TT	22	30
9	Where money lives	Citibank	21	34
10	Drive alive	Mitsubishi	18	28
11	Be inspired	Siemens mobile	15	19
12	One group. Multi utilities	RWE	8	15

- Is professionalism a good measure of development?
- Will there be a point in time when PR will reach a point of saturation?

PR practice in different countries is at different stages of 'PR's lifecycles'. Central and eastern European as well as Central Asian countries can provide good opportunities to observe the evolution of PR practice, since in most of these formerly communist countries PR was not practised during the centrally planned communist system and modern PR practice is a recent arrival.

Special areas of international public relations

Countries, regions or even cities, as well as multinational organisations, can engage in IPR. The rivalry between London and Paris in 2005 to host the 2012 Olympics is a good example, as both cities competed to impress and convince the International Olympic Committee – and indeed the world – that their capital is better able to host the games. The 2008 Summer Olympics in Beijing has not only cast the spotlight on China but has also fuelled the growth of the Chinese PR industry. Mega events, such as the Olympics, are often a focus for international PR activities (Harahousou et al. 2004).

These examples (including the ones in Mini case study 7.7) belong to the promotional dimension of IPR and are closely related to *place branding*. Media relations and events management are of crucial importance in these cases.

Depending on the subject of communication, Table 7.4 summarises the several specialisations of IPR for countries.

The media play a crucial role in each of these specialisations but become more active and participatory as we move from destination branding to perception management (see Figure 7.8, overleaf). Countries can engage in these specialisations to different extents and the emphasis may also vary. What is crucial, however, is the strategic approach to, and the coordination of, these specialisations since a variety of actors can be involved (government, ministry of foreign affairs, ministry of culture, national tourist board, embassies, trade associations, etc.). The aggregate of these dimensions (including the media) will result in country reputation and images.

Images of nations

All these specialisations are closely related to images of different countries. Nations throughout the world have always engaged in image cultivation which often relied on propaganda, especially during wartime (see more on this in Chapter 14). One of the major factors that contributed to the 'reinvention' of PR for nation-states in Europe is the end of the Cold War, which resulted in the emergence of new nation-states throughout central and eastern Europe. These countries have quickly realised the importance of creating new, 'Euro-conform' identities and distanced themselves from the old image of 'eastern Europe', a synonym for communism. Latvia, Croatia, Slovakia and Slovenia are among the newly emerged countries that relied heavily on PR to put the country on the map of Europe and to attract foreign investors, boost tourism or prepare the ground for their most important foreign policy goal: to become members of the European Union, which became a reality for eight eastern European countries in 2004. Image making in these countries soon became institutionalised (e.g. the Latvian Institute or the Country Image Centre in Hungary) and these institutions have been important

---

mini case study 7.7

Use of international public relations for towns and regions

According to a nationwide survey in 2004, Luton was considered as the ugliest town in the UK. Its council decided to use PR to persuade locals to love their town as well as to promote it abroad, with special regard to its international airport.

The reputation of Bradford suffered in 2001 when street violence broke out triggered by false rumours of attacks on British Asians. The riot was covered extensively in national as well as international media, the

result of which was investors leaving Bradford, with businesses suffering as well as its university (applications for university places dropped because of the problems).

The Öresund Bridge between Denmark and Sweden was inaugurated in 2000. This region was promoted as a transnational region and PR played a crucial role in the formulation and communication of the region.

Table 7.4 Specialisations of international public relations

Subject	Specialisation	Aim	Examples
Tourism	Destination branding	Attract visitors; boost tourism	Croatia – 'A small country for a great vacation', Latvia – 'The land that sings', New Zealand – '100% Pure New Zealand'
Economic policy	Country (region) branding	To create a 'country brand' that will sell products abroad as well as advance commercial interests abroad; to attract investors; to gain competitive advantage; regeneration of regions; export development; to advance 'country-of-origin' effect	Estonia – 'Positively transforming' Poland – 'Creative tension' Scotland – 'Scotland means business' Tunisia, Cambodia; European Regional Development Funds
Culture (heritage, language, education, sports, films, etc.)	Cultural relations (cultural diplomacy)	Promote culture, language learning; educational exchange; create a favourable opinion about a country; to change negative or false stereotypes	Polish year in Sweden; Erasmus exchange programmes; Olympic Games; Budapest Spring Festival; Cool Britannia; Eurovision Song Contest, BBC World, Deutsche Welle
Foreign policy	Public diplomacy	To create a receptive environment for foreign policy goals; to advance these goals; to get countries to change their policies towards others; treaty negotiations; raising international profile of presidents, politicians, countries	US foreign policy; becoming full members of the EU (e.g. Cyprus; Turkey); Germany's opposition to the war in Iraq; Putin's presidential election in 2000; head-of-state visits
Military policy and operations Anti-democratic regimes' policies	Propaganda, perception management	To exert strategic influence, coercion, justify military actions, 'sell' wars; change regimes; discredit regimes, countries; create crisis situations	US wars in Iraq, Afghanistan; Chinese government's image campaign after the Tiananmen Square massacre in 1989

with regard to national identity and defining how these nations want to be seen by foreign publics. See Box 7.4.

Another driving force behind international governmental PR was the attack on the World Trade Center on 11 September 2001, which made the US government realise that its foreign policy objectives and values are not understood by many nations. 'Why do they hate us?' was a question many Americans asked. America's response was multifaceted. Different task forces and 'think-thanks' were set up to communicate US values, policies, 'images' to the world mostly, however, as a one-way communication. 'Branding US' was one of the responses, which involved the failed advertising efforts in Arab countries. The failure demonstrated that branding in itself is not sufficient, especially if the 'product' itself is problematic. The other reason for failure was the lack of systematic research into Arab cultures at the planning stage. The US government had to realise that it was not engaging in two-way symmetrical communication at all. During and after the attacks on Iraq, PR was involved

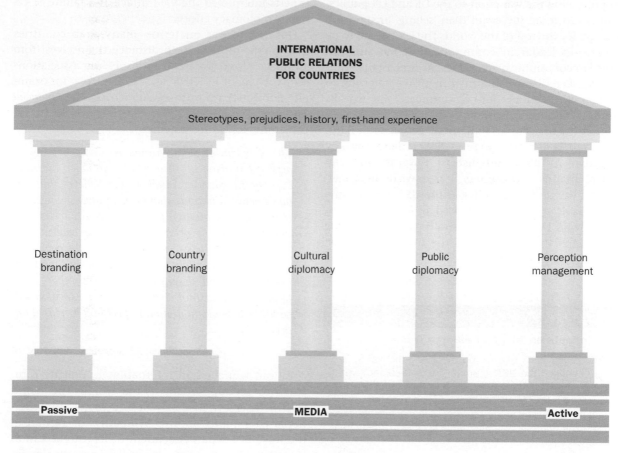

FIGURE 7.8 'Pantheon' of international public relations for countries (*source:* Szondi 2005)

**box
7.4** **How to brand a country**

Wally Olins, a British branding expert, provided the following seven-step plan to brand a country:

1 Set up a working party with representatives of government, industry, the arts, education and the media to start the programme.
2 Find out how the nation is perceived both by its own people and by nations abroad through qualitative and quantitative research.
3 Develop a process of consultation with opinion leaders to look at national strengths and weaknesses, and compare them with the results of the internal and external studies.
4 Create the central idea on which the strategy is based with professional advisors. This needs to be a powerful, simple idea that captures the unique qualities of the nation and can be used as a base from which the entire programme can be developed.
5 Develop ways of articulating the central idea visually, including logos.
6 Look at how the messages required for tourism, inward investment and export can be coordinated and modulated so that they are appropriate for each audience.
7 Create a liaison system through the working party to launch and sustain the programme in government activities and to encourage supportive action from appropriate organisations in commerce, industry, the arts, media and so on.

Source: Olins 1999

in promoting the war effort to the US and UK publics, which was more successful than 'selling' or spinning the war for the rest of the world. The USA is said to be the world leader in communication but still has failed to communicate its values. As Ambassador Holbrook asked: 'How can a man in a cave [referring to Osama Bin Laden] out-communicate the world's leading communication society?'

After the invasion of Iraq, many people from European and Arab nations expressed their disapproval by negative attitudes and distrust towards American global brands. Consumers 'voted with their feet' against the unilateral policy of the USA as their buying behaviour became politicised. In Egypt, for example, several US brands were subjected to boycotting campaigns through leaflets, the internet and text messages. See Activity 7.4.

---

activity 7.4

The effects on image of the Iraq War

How do you think the war on terror and the war in Iraq have changed the USA's/Britain's image abroad? What is the image of the UK in the print media of different countries? Use the web or contacts and try to look at the print media's view of the UK from other country perspectives. *The Guardian* website offers access to media from different countries at www.guardian.co.uk/worldlatest/

Public diplomacy

Foreign policies are indeed common objects of IPR for nation-states and the number of PR practitioners and agencies involved in policy communication is on the increase (for example Ketchum, an international PR agency, offers *public diplomacy* as a service as advertised on its website: www.ketchum. com). Public diplomacy is a term used in many different contexts and often as a positive 'alter ego' of IPR.

Definition: *Public diplomacy* is a government's process of communicating with foreign publics in an attempt to bring about understanding about its nation's ideas and ideals, its institutions and culture, as well as its national goals and current policies (Tuch 1990).

Despite its name, public diplomacy hardly ever addresses the 'general public' of nations but rather the elite, the opinion formers and decision makers of the target country. Ironically, the Arab terrorists who attacked the World Trade Center were educated and trained in the USA and were subject to the US's public diplomacy efforts. Many American foreign policy experts interpreted the 9/11 attack as a failure of US public diplomacy efforts.

During the war on terror, many Arab countries used public diplomacy to distance themselves from an image of terrorists and to dispel any associations or involvement in terrorism. Saudi Arabia, for example, published a position statement in the *Financial Times* in September 2004. The advertisement included the following statements:

> *The Kingdom of Saudi Arabia is utterly opposed to acts of terrorism, all of which is forbidden by Islam . . . The Kingdom of Saudi Arabia believes that disputes between nations should be resolved by negotiation and, if negotiation fails, by reference to international law, not by acts of aggression or violence . . . Saudi Arabia believes that what unites the peoples of the world is ultimately far more important than what divides them and, despite opposition from those eager to promote a clash of civilisations, the Kingdom will continue to work for mutual respect and increased understanding.*

(*Financial Times*, 23 September 2004, p.16)

Taiwan launched an international publicity campaign to get support for its bid to join the World Health Assembly in 2005. Noting that the international community showed sympathy for Taiwan in the wake of China's enactment of its Anti-Secession Law, the government saw it as a good opportunity for Taiwan to translate the world's sympathy into support for its efforts to enhance its international profile. Libya hired a lobbyist to help achieve the country's 'short-term and long-term goals in enhancing US-Libya relations' in 2004. Many other governments have hired American PR agencies to represent them and their countries' interests in the USA. In 1993 Kosovo, threatened by the Serbs, hired Ruder-Finn, an American PR agency to wage an intensive PR campaign in the USA in support of Kosovo and against the 'evil' Serbs.

According to Kunczik, a German scholar who has written extensively about images of nations, one of IPR's main objectives is to establish (or maintain an already existing) positive image of a nation, that is, to appear trustworthy to other actors in the world system by planning and distributing interest-bound information (Kunczik 1997). He distinguishes between *structural IPR* which aims at correcting 'false' images previously created by mass media, and *manipulative IPR*, which tries to create a positive image that in most cases does not reflect reality. This latter approach implies 'perception management', the war on terror and Iraq being recent examples where the US army and government were creating and managing images of the battlefield and minimising 'collateral damage' with the help of Britain's best-known spin doctor, Alistair Campbell.

box 7.5	**UK and Germany: in each other's eyes**

Following the major diplomatic rift between Britain and Germany over the Iraq War, the British Council and the Goethe Institute conducted one of the first opinion surveys of young people in both countries in 2003. The ambiguous relationship between Germany and the UK seems set to continue.

Nearly half of young Germans have a positive or very positive view of Britain, with the English language, the monarchy and the modern, multicultural nature of British society all being especially popular. Eighty-one per cent remember at least one British celebrity, with Robbie Williams, the late Princess of Wales and the Queen being most well known.

Only 11% of Germans have a negative or very negative view of Britain, with political issues being cited as the main reasons for the dislike, particularly the strong British relationship with the USA, a perceived British antipathy to the European Union and issues surrounding the Iraq War being quoted most often. Interestingly, more German youth dislike Germany (17%) than dislike Britain.

Thirty-seven per cent of British youth are positive or very positive about Germany, with German beer, schools and sports coming just ahead of an admiration for the perceived strength of the German economy and the quality of German cars.

Seventeen percent of British youth have a negative or very negative opinion of Germans; a persisting memory of German militarism, perceived right-wing extremism and a lack of German manners or humour are all strong factors. A lack of German trendiness was felt in the UK, with 64% of British respondents unable to name a single German celebrity, although Claudia Schiffer was known to a minority.

Britain features more strongly on the German radar than vice versa, with more than half of German young people having visited the UK. Only one-third of young Britons surveyed have been to Germany. Nearly 100% of young Germans have some knowledge of English, with 25% being fluent English speakers. Less than a quarter of their British counterparts claim to have any knowledge of German.

Source: www.britishcouncil.de

A lack of public diplomacy may well be labelled as a 'PR disaster'. *PR war* is another frequently used term between nation-states, mostly by journalists and in a negative context. It refers to the negotiation process and disagreement between organisations and their publics or between nations.

Cultural diplomacy

Cultural diplomacy is concerned with promoting cultural 'products' such as books, films, TV and radio programmes, art exhibitions, concerts as well as languages abroad. The ultimate goal is to make foreign publics familiar with a nation, its people, culture and language and to create a favourable opinion about the country. The British Council, the Goethe Institute, the Institut Française or the Hungarian Cultural Institute are the leading institutions of cultural promotions for Britain, Germany, France and Hungary respectively. The British Council's main objective is 'to build mutually beneficial relationships between people in the UK and other countries and increase appreciation of the UK's creative ideas and achievements'. These institutions conduct research about the perceptions of their own countries and peoples abroad and aim to improve this 'image', which is often based on prejudices or stereotypes. Read the research in Box 7.5 about how British and German young people perceived each other's country and people. See Think about 7.4.

The findings presented in Box 7.5 and the fact that only 1% of British people go on holiday to Germany are signs of lack of interest in, and knowledge of, Germany. In November 2004 Germany launched an IPR campaign in the UK to counteract the negative image British citizens hold about the Germans and German history and to attract more tourists. This

think about 7.4   **Images of nations**

Are you aware of any study or research that focuses on *your* country's images abroad? Have there been attempts to brand your country abroad? Were they successful?

Compare your image of a country before and after you or a friend visited it. What was your earlier image based on? Did it change? If so, why and how?

may be due to British history teaching, which focuses on the Nazi period. One of the strategies was to invite history teachers from Britain to Germany and 'to educate them about another Germany'. The British media have been accused of perpetuating a 'goose-stepping' image of Germany that was three generations out of date. Prince Harry's appearance as a Nazi officer at a fancy-dress party in January 2005 caused heated debates both in Germany and in the UK.

Germany's case demonstrates that each pillar of the pantheon (presented in Figure 7.8) plays a crucial role. Germany's strongest pillar in the UK is 'country branding': German products are associated with quality, reliability and high performance, the trade mark 'Made in Germany' speaks for itself. Germany as a tourist destination – destination branding pillar – remains the weakest one, while Germany's cultural diplomacy efforts are somewhere in between. In other countries, however, the picture may well be rather different. Germany's position on the war in Iraq (public diplomacy pillar) improved the country's perception in Russia. Research in 2004 confirmed that 62% of Russians surveyed said that their image of Germany improved as a result of its opposition to the war (see http://www.dw-world.de).

IPR campaigns can address only one of the four subjects at a time (for example, tourism or foreign policy) but in order to be successful and coherent the other dimensions must be taken into considerations too. The most important PR activities in IPR campaigns for nation-states are:

- (international) media relations, media monitoring
- events management
- public affairs, lobbying
- public opinion polls, opinion leader research
- image surveys
- advocacy advertisements
- international marketing PR
- (political) crisis management.

See Activity 7.5.

activity 7.5

Developing a country's image

The Hungarian government has approached you and your London-based PR firm to promote Hungary's image in the UK. What are the key issues that must be addressed by a PR campaign? What type of research would you need to conduct? What is the current image of Hungary in the British print media?

Feedback
Apply the pantheon of international public relations for countries (see Figure 7.8).

The number of communication-related professions (diplomacy, PR, advertising, marketing, lobbying) and professionals is increasing, and more and more of them communicate across cultures and with different peoples. These communication professions have started to 'cross-fertilise', testing the boundaries and the validity of each discipline and often encroaching on each other's territory. Public diplomacy is one example of a specialisation in IPR.

Public relations' influence on society

Many scholars maintain that PR is practised only in and by democracies, although there are examples

mini case study 7.8

The 'Latin American school'

The social role of PR is truly reflected in the special characteristics of the Latin American school of thought.

The social and economic imbalance in the countries of Latin America is a major factor in the development of the Latin American PR practice where PR practitioners are active agents of social and political transformation. The Latin American school:

- focuses on the community's interest
- contributes to the well-being of the human, urban and social environments in which organisations operate
- responds to the history and socio-economic reality of the region

- sees PR practitioners as agents of social transformation
- must be embedded in the idea of freedom, justice, harmony and equality
- establishes confidence without manipulation and uses communication to reach accord, consensus and integrated attitudes between an organisation and its publics
- fundamentally views PR as essential for integration and consensus.

Source: Molleda 2000: 520

mini case study 7.9

Evolution of public relations in eastern Europe

PR's evolution in central and eastern Europe has been rather rapid in comparison with western European or American practices. The political and economic changes between 1989 and 1992 enabled PR to gain grounding in the region. Turning centrally planned economies into free market economies in a very short period of time presented great challenges, not only for companies, but for the whole society as well. PR agencies played a significant role in the privatisation of state owned companies as a part of supporting market reforms after the fall of communism.

In many central and eastern European countries the local branches of the international agencies were initially often set up and headed by professionals who had been living and working in the USA or the UK. Another common practice was that American or western European PR practitioners headed the national offices of an international PR network (Szondi 2004a).

Polish PR scholar Ławniczak (2001) characterised the early years of central and eastern European PR practice as *transition public relations*. This has helped organisations to adapt to the change from a centrally planned economy to market economies. The main tasks of transition PR are:

- to build an image of 'capitalism with a human face' in order to secure public acceptance for economic reforms
- to create public awareness of the wide range of possible alternative market economy models
- to facilitate effective functioning of a market economy by promoting entrepreneurship and privatisation, attracting foreign investment and introducing market economy instruments and institutions.

---

when this was not the case (e.g. China's government, see Think about 7.1, earlier). Previously in this chapter, we have seen how PR can be used by governments and nation-states to influence overseas publics.

The effects and influence of PR practices on society at large can be manifold. PR can help to:

- maintain the status quo (western democracies)
- integrate a society (after the collapse of the Soviet Union many Russians remained in the Baltic States and PR has been used to integrate Estonians and Russians)
- transform a society (Latin America, see Mini case study 7.8) or economy (eastern Europe, see Mini case study 7.9)
- build nations (Malaysia, East Timor)
- disintegrate countries, regimes (e.g. Yugoslavia, or Hill and Knowlton's infamous case about using alleged Iraqi atrocities to mobilise public opinion for a war against Iraq in 1991).

Public relations for a supranational organisation: the European Union

PR for and in the European Union (EU) is a massive operation, a very complex and multifaceted process, which presents serious challenges for the PR practitioners involved. The Barroso Commission recognised

the strategic importance of communication and created a new post of 'Institutional Relations and Communication Strategy' in 2004. A Swedish politician, Margot Wallström, became the Commissioner, responsible for: press and institutional relations; Eurobarometer (which monitors EU citizens' opinions on a variety of issues); and representation offices, which represent the EU in different countries. She is often referred to as 'the Commissioner of PR'. In 2004, 10 new member states from central and eastern Europe joined the EU and EU leaders agreed on a European constitution, about which referendums were scheduled for 2005 and 2006.

PICTURE 7.1   Margot Wallström, EU Commissioner (*Source:* European Commission Audio Visual Library.)

'Internal communication' within the EU means the strategic function of communicating with the political elite of 25 member states as well as with their 'general publics'. It is a complex intercultural communication exercise to bring Europe 'closer to the people'. Apathy towards EU affairs is prevalent and manifested in the very low turnout in European elections and referendums (Szondi 2004b; see also Chapter 5 for more on referendums). The EU is seen by many as a gigantic bureaucratic organisation with grey 'eurocrats' who often speak in an unintelligible way, using 'eurospeak'.

The main difficulties lie in the abstract and intangible nature of the EU and its institutions. EU communication has often been labelled as elitist and not directed towards the citizens. The communication deficit is a real challenge to be overcome. European values should be at the heart of EU identity as well as communication strategies. In spite of the fact that the EU's identity is still emerging, the EU has become a brand in itself. Creating and communicating an 'EU identity' is an evolving process that involves the expertise of PR practitioners as well.

The concepts of identity, images and reputation (see Chapter 13) can be applied to the EU, as an organisation as well, although these – and other concepts of PR – are still to be 'discovered' and fully utilised by the EU. Rem Koolhaas, a Dutch architect designed a logo for the EU, which struggles with an 'iconographic deficit': despite the fact that the EU is full of symbols (blue flag with the stars, anthem, passports) it cannot get across a more subtle message about Europe.

The 'EU brand' is not only relevant in an internal but also in an external context: how does the EU 'communicate' with other similar (supranational) organisations or with countries outside the EU? IPR – in the form of public diplomacy – plays a crucial role not only in creating an EU identity but also in communicating it and nurturing the image of the EU outside Europe.

Media relations remains by far the most popular strategy for the EU and its institutions and committees to communicate with citizens (see Box 7.6). A substantial number of journalists are based in Brussels. They attend press conferences, one-to-one briefings,

---

box 7.6	**The European Union's media relations**

The Directorate General Press and Communication (DG Press) works under the authority of the President. Its mission is to:

- inform the media and citizens of the activities of the Commission and to communicate the objectives and goals of its policies and actions
- inform the Commission of the evolution of opinion in the member states.

In order to accomplish its mission, DG Press:
- coordinates the activities of the representations in the member states
- centralises all contacts with the media
- seeks to ensure a coherent approach to communication and information issues within the Commission.

This involves contacts with Directorates General (DGs) and services within the Commission that have information units responsible for sectoral information. The DGs responsible for external relations provide information to citizens of third countries including information for the general public in applicant states.

As regards media activities, the role of the Press and Communication Directorate General is to:

- be available to journalists to explain and inform them on EU policies and the Commission's initiatives
- hold daily press briefings at midday in the Commission's press room
- organise press conferences for the Commissioners as well as technical briefings for high-level officials
- provide and distribute press material (press releases, background notes, etc.) and audiovisual material (photo, sound, video)
- hold interviews and bilateral briefings for journalists
- fix up interviews and briefings with Commissioners or officials
- organise accreditation for journalists, and TV crews and photographers
- inform national and regional media in the member states through the Commission's representations
- coordinate internet activities (Europa website).

Source: adapted from http://www.europa.eu.int/comm/dgs/press_communication/
guide/index2_en.htm.©European Communities 1995–2005

read online press releases and strive for exclusive stories. It is rather difficult to 'spin' stories related to EU affairs; finding an interesting angle of an issue or policy is most crucial as oversimplification often prevails. If there is a success story, the member states are quick to attribute it to themselves while unpopular EU issues are attributed to 'Brussels'.

Politicians usually use the media to get publicity for themselves but in the minds of the viewers or readers they are associated with the EU which can result in diminishing the credibility of EU communication. When journalists report from Brussels they usually show smiling politicians, the buildings of the different institutions or the flying flags of the member states that visually represent the EU because topics themselves can be detailed and lack colour.

Crisis communication and management is one of the most important areas in which the EU needs to develop a common approach. Political and military crises have received more attention but crises in the civil sphere will further challenge the EU. The Chernobyl nuclear disaster, natural catastrophes like floods, fires, heat waves, or health-related crises like the Coca-Cola case in Belgium and the CJD/mad cow disease are good examples of international communication – or PR – crises (see also Chapter 20). Of these cases, the most controversial was the CJD/mad cow disease, which called for more coordination and cooperation among the member states and better communication between the decision makers and the European publics.

The most practised strategy in the EU context is *lobbying* at the decision makers to pursue the interests of corporations. International PR agencies recognised early on the need to set up or move their European headquarters from London to Brussels, where about 15,000 registered lobbying practitioners are based (not counting individual firms, CEOs or law firms). The total number of people somehow involved in lobbying is estimated at 80,000 (see also Chapter 23).

Critical voices in international public relations

IPR – as the war on terror and Iraq demonstrated – could easily be propagandistic in nature or used to 'quick-fix' a tarnished image or justify actions retrospectively. More visibility and transparency will be demanded not only from MNOs but from PR practitioners as well in the future. According to Kunczik (1997), PR is often perceived as 'the art of camouflaging and deceiving and it is assumed that for public relations to be successful, target groups . . . do not notice that they have become the "victims" of public relations efforts'.

Several pressure groups and some scholars view PR in a negative context: it helps multinational organisations maintain their dominance or justify their actions. The 'lobbying machinery' of Brussels, with its lack of transparency has been the subject of many critical voices. These voices accuse PR of 'greenwashing' corporate images to make them appear more environmentally friendly or socially conscious (Balanyá et al. 2003). See Activity 7.6.

---

activity 7.6

Monitoring critical voices

Visit the website of Spinwatch, an organisation that aims 'to foster greater public and political awareness of spin and to campaign against the manipulations of the PR industry in the public interest' (www.spinwatch. server101.com/index.php © 2004 spinwatch). Read some of the articles or case studies that have an international focus. What issues are being raised? What types of challenges are being made against the organisation(s)? Do you agree with them? If you represented the organisation, how would you respond? (See also Chapter 14 for discussion of propaganda.)

Professionalism on a global level: public relations as a global profession

Global PR refers to the *internationalisation of the practice*, namely that PR activities are carried out throughout the globe. This phenomenon is one of the direct consequences of IPR activities. PR is becoming a global profession.

The number of international and *global associations* is on the increase: the International Public Relations Associations (IPRA) promotes the practice of PR on a global scale; the Global Alliance for Public Relations and Communication Management unites national associations worldwide; the International Communications Consultancy Organisation (ICCO) is an umbrella association for more than 850 consultancies, through their trade associations in 24 countries.

IPRA adopted a formal *code of conduct* in 1961, and four years later an international code of ethics, the 'Code of Athens'. ICCO's professional code is called the 'Rome Charter', while Global Alliance developed the Global Protocol of Ethics, which was introduced in Rome in 2003 (see also Chapter 15).

Not only do these associations safeguard professional values through their guidelines, codes of conduct and activities, but they also contribute a great deal towards professionalisation on a global level and aim to enhance the reputation of the PR profession worldwide.

Since American and British practices often serve as models for PR practitioners all over the world, Anglo-American practitioners' responsibility is even bigger. Practitioners worldwide will need to join efforts to fight negative practice and build a better reputation of the profession.

Accreditation and certification of PR practitioners by professional organisations have long been on the agenda, not only at national but at a global level as well. (See Activity 7.7.)

---

activity 7.7

National associations

Go to the website of one or two of the above mentioned associations and browse through them. What are the benefits of joining that particular association? Try to find out what the latest trends in IPR are.

Go to the website of PRIME, which is one of the very few international PR students' associations (www.prime-europe.org). Join the organisation.

As far as the *international body of knowledge* is concerned, theoretical concepts and models are being developed, tested and advanced. Unfortunately, there are only very few books that deal with international or global PR, but this is likely to change in the near future. Separate bodies of knowledge seem to be emerging in a European, South American and Asian context, complementing – or perhaps competing against – Anglo-American theory and practice.

A great deal of effort is made by European PR scholars to identify and clearly distinguish a European body of knowledge, which differs from that of its American counterpart (European Public Relations Body of Knowledge project, EBOK). The Latin American School of Public Relations turned away from the North American approach as early as the 1960s, as an expression of independence and emancipation from imported models (Molleda 2000).

In academic journals, like *Public Relations Review*, the *Journal of Communication Management* or the *Journal of Public Relations Research*, the number of articles with an international focus or relevance is on the increase. Professional and trade journals regularly cover international topics, case studies and practices. One of the latest initiatives has been a truly international PR journal (with a possible launch date in 2007), the *International Journal of Strategic Communication*.

There are international associations that are concerned with *research, education* or academia such as the European Public Relations Education and Research Association (EUPRERA), which unites academics mostly from Europe but from other continents as well. The international body of knowledge is increased by research and is shared and stimulated by international conferences and forums, such as EUPRERA's annual conferences. Another important international conference that brings together educators from all over the world is the International Public Relations Research Symposium, which is held in Bled, Slovenia, every year (papers and details can be found at www.bledcom.com).

During the last couple of years, new courses and modules have been developed in IPR. These include undergraduate and postgraduate university degrees that have an international focus such as the Master in European Public Relations (MARPE), which is delivered in an English-language version jointly by Leeds Metropolitan University and the Dublin Institute in Ireland (see Box 7.7). German, French and Iberian lines are also under development (see MARPE's website: www.master-pr.org). See Activity 7.8.

---

activity 7.8

Dissertation topics

Many of you will have to think about a major research project, dissertation or thesis to write during your studies. Here are a few dissertation topic ideas related to IPR that may help you think about what is possible to research in this area. Your task is to think of more. Where are the gaps? What is not understood? Or what is under-researched?

- Does culture shape the practice of PR or PR efforts affect culture?
- What is the level of professionalisation in your country?
- Explore the public diplomacy activities: of a country; in your country; or what your country does in another one.
- What is the relationship between national culture and corporate culture of a multinational organisation (MNO)?
- To what extent can a company be global without losing its national identity? Does global branding always pay off?
- Using the agenda-setting model, analyse an international campaign, the ways it influenced the different agendas and its impact.
- Select an area of PR (internal communication, crises communication, corporate social responsibility, media relations) and using concepts from this and other chapters, explore its international dimensions (on behalf of a multinational for-profit organisation or NGO).

box 7.7   **An example of an international MA programme, MARPE**

The MARPE curriculum delivered by Leeds Metropolitan University and the Dublin Institute of Technology has a two-semester structure as follows:

Semester 1:

- Theories of Public Relations
- Media and the Public Sphere in the European Union
- Public Affairs and Lobbying in the European Context
- Research Methods.

Semester 2:

- Ethical Communication Management
- Corporate and Specialist Public Relations
- Options (e.g. International Marketing Communication, Brand Management, International Business Environment)
- Dissertation.

Source: www.leedsmet.ac.uk

Summary

This chapter has outlined the main dimensions and elements of IPR, an area still in its infancy. We have identified the main actors in IPR and analysed the different driving forces behind internationalisation and their impact on the practice of PR. PR for countries, regions, cities, as well as for international organisations, is crucial to build a positive reputation abroad. The EU as a supranational as well as a multinational organisation presents a variety of challenges for PR practitioners.

IPR for countries is rather fragmented in the forms of destination and nation branding or public diplomacy; more strategic and coordinated approaches will need to be adopted in the future.

The emergence of new market economies and the ongoing democratisation of Asian countries (facilitated by western PR) will mean that western approaches and theory building will need to incorporate and understand oriental as well as African values, philosophies and practices. PR will become a truly global profession only if and when the world's different philosophies, economies and cultures are reflected and incorporated both in theory and practice.

Bibliography

Angell, R. (1990). '"International PR": a misnomer'. *Public Relations Journal* **46**(10).

Balanyá, B., A. Doherty, O. Hoedeman, A. Ma'anit and E. Wesselins (2003). *Europe Inc. Regional and Global Restructuring and the Rise of Corporate Power*, 2nd edition. London: Pluto Press.

Banks, S. (2000). *Multicultural Public Relations: A social-interpretative approach*, 2nd edition. Ames, IA: Iowa State University Press.

Barnett, G. and M. Lee (2002). 'Issues in intercultural communication research' in *Handbook of International and Intercultural Communication*, 2nd edition. W. Gudykunst and B. Mody (eds). Thousand Oaks, CA: Sage.

Burton, C. and A. Drake (2004). *Hitting the Headlines in Europe: A country-by-country guide to effective media relations*. London and Sterling, VA: Kogan Page.

Culbertson, H.M. and N. Chen (eds) (1996). *International public relations: A comparative analysis*. Mahwah, NJ: Lawrence Erlbaum Associates.

Hall, E.T. (1976). *Beyond Culture*, Garden City. NY: Doubleday.

Harahousou, Y., C. Kabitsis, A. Haviara and N. Theodorakis (2004). 'The Olympic Games: A framework for international public relations' in *Handbook of Corporate Communication and Public Relations*. S. Oliver. London: Routledge.

Holtzhausen, D., B. Petersen and N. Tindall (2003). 'Exploding the myth of the symmetrical/asymmetrical dichotomy: public relations models in the new South Africa'. *Journal of Public Relations Research* **15**(4): 305–341.

Kunczik, M. (1997). *Images of Nations and International Public Relations*. Mahwah, NJ: Lawrence Erlbaum Associates.

Ławniczak, R. (2001). 'Public relations – an instrument for systematic transformation in Central and Eastern Europe' in *Public Relations' Contribution to Transition in Central and Eastern Europe Research and Practice*. R. Ławniczak (ed.). Printer: Poznań.

Lenn, D.J. (1996). 'International public affairs: Managing within the global village' in *Practical Public Affairs in an Era of Change. A Communications Guide for Business, Government, and College*. L. Dennis (ed.). New York: Public Relations Society of America and University Press of America, Inc.

McPhail, T. (2002). *Global Communication. Theories, Stakeholders, and Trends*. Boston, MA: Allyn & Bacon.

Molleda, J.C. (2000). 'International paradigms: The Latin American School of Public Relations'. *Journalism Studies* **2**(4): 513–530.

Morley, M. (2002). *How to Manage Your Global Reputation – A Guide to the Dynamics of International Public Relations*, 2nd edition. London: Palgrave.

Mowlana, H. (1986). *Global Information and World Communication: New frontiers in international relations*. New York: Longman.

Olins, W. (1999). *Trading Identities – Why Countries and Companies are Taking on Each Other's Roles*. London: Foreign Policy Centre.

Pavlik, J.V. (1987). *Public Relations: What research tells us*. Newbury Park, CA: Sage (Communication Text Series, Vol. 16).

Rogers, E.M. and J.W. Dearing (1988). 'Agenda-setting research: Where it has been, where it is going' in *Mass Communication Review Yearbook, Vol.11*. J.A. Anderson (ed.). Newbury Park, CA: Sage.

Samovar, L., R. Porter and L. Stefani (1998). *Communication between Cultures*, 3rd edition. Belmont, CA: Wadsworth.

Sriramesh, K. (2000). 'A framework for understanding, and conducting international public relations'. Paper presented at the International Public Relations Symposium, Lake Bled, Slovenia.

Sriramesh, K. (ed.) (2004). *Public Relations in Asia: An anthology*. Singapore: Thomson Learning.

Sriramesh, K. and D. Verčić (eds) (2003). *The Global Public Relations Handbook. Theory, Research and Practice*. Mahwah, NJ: Lawrence Erlbaum Associates.

Szondi, G. (2004a). 'Hungary' in *Public Relations and Communication Management in Europe. A Nation-by-Nation Introduction to Public Relations Theory and Practice*. B. van Ruler and D. Verčić (eds). Berlin: Mouton de Gruyter.

Szondi, G. (2004b). 'Critical analysis of information campaigns in central and eastern Europe for the referendums to join the European Union'. Paper presented at the Annual Congress of EUPRERA and the DGPuK-Fachgruppe, Leipzig.

Szondi, G. (2005). 'The Pantheon of international public relations for nation states: Country promotion in Central and Eastern Europe' in, *Introducing Market Economy Institutions and Instruments: The Role of Public Relations in Transition Economies* R. Ławniczak (ed.). Poznań: Piar. pl.

Thussu, D.K. (2000). *International Communication. Continuity and Change*. London: Arnold.

Tilson, D.J. and E. Alozie (2004). *Toward the Common Good: Perspectives in international public relations*. Boston, MA: Allyn & Bacon.

Tuch, H. (1990). *Communicating with the World: US public diplomacy overseas*. New York: St. Martin's Press.

Tungate, M. (2005). 'Central Europe – the new frontier in PR'. *PR Week* 18 February.

Tymson, C. and P. Lazar (2002). *The new Australian and New Zealand Public Relations Manual*. Sydney: Tymson Communication.

van Ruler, B. and D. Verčić (eds) (2004). *Public Relations and Communication Management in Europe. A Nation-by-Nation Introduction to Public Relations Theory and Practice*. Berlin: Mouton de Gruyter.

Verčić, D., L. Grunig and J. Grunig (1996). 'Global and specific principles of public relations: Evidence from Slovenia' in *International Public Relations: A Comparative Analysis*. H.M. Culbertson and N. Chen (eds). Mahwah, NJ: Lawrence Erlbaum Associates.

Wakefield, R. (2003). 'Preliminary Delphi research on international public relations programming' in *Perspectives on Public Relations Research*. D. Moss, D. Verčić and G. Warnaby. London: Routledge.

Watson, J. (2003). *Media Communication. An Introduction to Theory and Process*, 2nd edition. London: Palgrave.

Wilcox, D.L., P.H. Ault and W.K. Agee and G.T. Cameron (2001). *Essentials of Public Relations*. New York: Longman.

Zaharna, R.S. (2001). '"In-awareness" approach to international public relations'. *Public Relations Review* **27**:135–148.

PART 2
Public relations theories and concepts

There is no one unifying 'public relations theory'. This part aims to address the conceptual and theoretical frameworks that public relations as an interdisciplinary subject draws upon. This section will demonstrate that public relations is multifaceted and can be interpreted through a number of relevant theoretical perspectives. Where possible, theories are applied to practice through case study examples. Chapters 8 and 9 highlight the key theoretical discussions: they take us from theories that describe how a profession ought to behave (normative theories) through to alternative theoretical approaches drawn from critical theory, the rhetorical perspective, feminism and postmodernism. New research directions for public relations are also highlighted in Chapter 9. Chapter 10 introduces our first 'concept': public relations as planned communication, in which public relations is presented as a process for achieving organisational objectives. Continuing the planning theme, Chapter 11 discusses the role of research and evaluation in the public relations process. Chapter 12 introduces an important concept around which there is an emerging debate: the nature of audiences, publics or stakeholders. There is sometimes confusion around the concepts of image, reputation and identity. Chapter 13 attempts to unpack this confusion as well as firmly identify these concepts as important to understanding public relations within a corporate context. Drawing mainly on theories of social psychology, Chapter 14 aims to demonstrate that the concepts of persuasion and propaganda must be defined and applied in helping us to recognise when public relations is used responsibly and when it is not. Finally, the ethical issues raised by public relations and its role in society inevitably leads to a discussion of ethics and professionalism, which is found in Chapter 15.

CHAPTER 8

Public relations theories – an applied overview: systems theories

Introduction

Public relations theory and practice have traditionally been closely linked. Systems theory, which emerged in the second half of the twentieth century as public relations education was established and was initially the dominant approach to public relations theory, took the view that theory development should improve practice first and foremost. This approach has had a significant influence on the nature of academic thought around public relations, particularly in the United States where many of the earliest university courses in public relations were started. In addition, and because of the wider influence of US-based academic journals, theoretical approaches in the international academic community have often followed this mindset.

This chapter will examine the major approaches to public relations in the systems tradition, the criticism that has led to major revisions in this theory and the evolutions in understanding the operations and concepts surrounding public relations practitioners and the publics they seek to reach. In particular, it will describe the shift of public relations academics' focus from systems theory, with its emphasis on situations, to relationship theory, with its emphasis on communication as the key to relationship management.

Communications theories: laying the foundations

Theories about how PR strategies and tactics work originated in university schools of management and communication, where the first PR courses were taught. Management was one home to PR courses, because PR as a profession is part of the management of organisations. Communications schools were the other, because effective communication forms the basis of good relationship management, a process that lies at the heart of effective PR (Grunig 1992).

Definition: *Theory* comprises a set of propositions or ideas used to explain phenomena, i.e. objects and events we can observe. Familiar theories include the theory of gravity or of evolution.

Definition: *Normative theory* refers to the ideal of how a profession such as PR should be practised.

Early communication theories were relatively simple, focusing on the actual process of one-way persuasive communication and consisting of the following concepts, sometimes abbreviated to SMCRE:

- **S**ender – transmitting the message
- **M**essage – what is being communicated
- **C**hannel – the means by which the message is sent
- **R**eceiver – the target for receiving the message
- **E**ffect – the results, if any, of the communication.

Shannon and Weaver's (1949) theory of communication formed the foundation for modern theories of communication. The only problems arising in this model are:

- *technical*, when the channel malfunctions or alters the message
- *semantic*, when the meaning of the message differs between sender and receiver
- *influence* problems, when the desired persuasive effect does not occur.

Shannon and Weaver, however, leave out two fundamental influences on the communication process: human beings and the environment. To compensate, subsequent models (Harrison 2000) included the following:

PICTURE 8.1   This chapter will look at the evolution of public relations theory and its application in a range of social and political environments. Mass movements (Tiananmen Square protest, the fall of the Berlin Wall and the 2004/5 Ukrainian elections – see Chapter 5) were all influenced by communication techniques. (*Source:* © Peter Turnley/Corbis.)

- *noise* – interference from the external environment that may distort the message
- *feedback* – from the receiver to the sender, which may modify future messages.

Shannon and Weaver's basic model is linear, even when the feedback loop is introduced. This does not necessarily reflect reality, where senders and receivers are capable of playing equal roles in the communications process. Reflecting this parity, Osgood and Schramm proposed a model that reflected a circular communications process, with each participant playing the role of encoding and decoding messages (Mc Quail and Windahl 1993). Finally, and in a theoretical development particularly relevant to PR, Westley and McLean introduced an additional role into the mix – that of the 'gatekeeper', who is positioned between the sender and the receiver of a message and may alter the original message before it reaches its intended recipient (Windahl and Signitzer 1992). Not only does this model allow for the role of PR practitioners as intermediaries between an organisation and its publics, but it also accommodates the role of the mass media, which filters the multitude of messages from organisations and individuals trying to attract the attention of readers, listeners and viewers (see Box 8.1).

Outcomes of communication: the active receiver

Communication theories began by focusing on persuasion as the outcome of communication. However, other outcomes, including informing or instructing individuals, or reinforcing ideas and behaviours, have been taken into account more recently. All outcomes demand an active receiver – that is, someone who actively absorbs and responds to the message, either by allowing themselves to be persuaded (see

Chapter 14, page 271), by accepting and acting on an instruction or by absorbing the information given to them and making an appropriate decision about how to use it.

As many PR practitioners recognise, generating an active reception for a particular message presents perhaps the biggest challenge to the sender. Unfortunately, the sender's control over the reception of the message is limited, for a number of reasons:

- *Source or sender characteristics* may influence the acceptance and value of the message.
- *Receiver personality characteristics* also affect message acceptance and the level of active response.
- *Context* – both the social environment in which the receiver lives (for example, as an employee, an activist or a family group) and the relationship between source and receiver affect the acceptance and interpretation of a message.
- *Message content* is interpreted differently by different people – the original meaning intended by the sender may not be the receiver's interpretation, because of differences in personality, personal background and environment.

The channel may influence the way in which the message is assimilated and the degree to which it is absorbed. Research is fragmented in terms of rules about how media selection might impact effectiveness of communication, but does seem to point to different mechanics of message reception depending on the media used (see Figure 8.1, overleaf).

Despite these difficulties, research has provided guidance on making persuasive communications more effective. If receivers agree with you, for example, presenting arguments supporting their views is likely to have the greatest impact. Presenting both sides of an argument may help if the receiver opposes your message or if the receiver is well-educated. It is also helpful in preventing a change of mind should

---

box 8.1   Theory in practice

Noise and feedback

If your local supermarket is trying to promote a new organic food range to its customers, it might decide to post flyers to the surrounding neighbourhood, highlighting the taste and benefits of the organic food on offer. If that were all you read about the new range, you might feel very enthusiastic about trying a few of the items. However, if, simultaneously, your local paper carries a story about a local scandal where organic farms had been found to be using chemicals, you might regard the claims of the supermarket flyer with a bit more suspicion. This would be an example of environmental 'noise'. Likewise, if the supermarket received complaints from customers saying the products were not as tasty as they'd expected, the supermarket might decide to put more emphasis on the health and environmental benefits of buying organic food, rather than taste, in future promotional activities. This would be an example of 'feedback'.

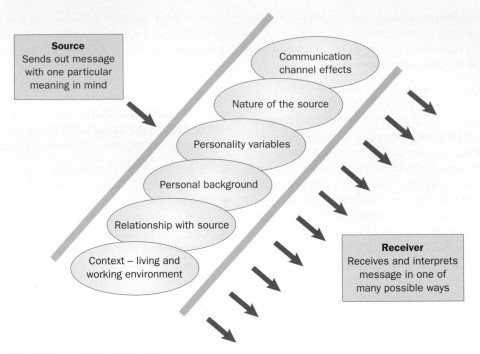

FIGURE 8.1   Influences on the active receiver

the receiver be presented with alternative arguments at a later date (Hovland et al. 1949). When presenting a two-sided argument, your argument should be balanced – obvious omissions on either side may make receivers suspicious (Lumsdaine and Janis 1953).

Communications theories continue to evolve but the principles above provided the underpinning for early theorising in PR. (See Think about 8.1.)

Systems theories: emergence of public relations research

For systems theorists, research begins with the practitioner working for the organisation, the organisation carrying out PR or the situation in which the activity takes place. The main objective of PR is to develop and execute strategies and tactics that will benefit the organisation in a given context.

In 1984, two of the earliest systems theorists, James E. Grunig and Todd Hunt, published *Managing Public Relations*, in which they presented a set of PR *typologies* based on observations of practice in the United States: press agentry/publicist; public information; two-way asymmetric and two-way a symmetric communications (Grunig and Hunt 1984). While these models have been widely referenced since their initial inception by academics from all corners of the globe, it is worth noting that they are culturally specific and may not be relevant to PR practice in other countries (see Table 8.1).

think about 8.1   Communicating

Think of two occasions when you were trying to communicate to a friend or colleague, for example:

1   about your voting intentions, in a student or general election, or for a competition like *Pop Idol*
2   when you wanted them to take a message to another friend, lend you their phone or take notes in a lecture.

Did they understand what you wanted? If not, what were the factors causing confusion? How did you resolve the confusion?

Once they understood, did they comply with what you wanted, by (a) agreeing with your decision or (b) doing what you wanted? If so, why? If not, why not?

Feedback   Think about your relationship with the individual, the differences and similarities in your respective social environments and the perceptions they may have of you. How would these have affected the situation? How does the nature of the request affect the communication and its outcome?

TABLE 8.1   Four models of public relations (*source:* adapted from Grunig and Hunt 1984: 22)

Characteristic	Model			
	Press agentry/ publicity	Public information	Two-way asymmetric	Two-way symmetric
Purpose	Propaganda	Dissemination of information	Scientific persuasion	Mutual understanding
Nature of communication	One-way; complete truth not essential	One-way; truth important	Two-way; imbalanced effects	Two-way; balanced effects
Communication model	Source to receiver	Source to receiver	Source to receiver and feedback	Group to group and feedback
Nature of research	Little; 'counting house'	Little; readability, readership	Formative; evaluative of attitudes	Formative; evaluative of understanding

Definition: *Typology* means identifying the different types of something, usually by working out the key elements that distinguish one kind of PR practitioner or activity, in this case, from another.

The purpose of press agentry is to disseminate a particular point of view through the media and other channels. The communication is one-way: no dialogue with the intended audience is required and the main objective is to put forward one particular view of the world – which may or may not be completely truthful. Wartime communications from governments are a good example of propaganda (see also Chapter 14). Research is almost irrelevant for this type of communication: the nature of the audience is not important; message dissemination to as wide a range of outlets as possible is the main objective.

Public information is related to press agentry, in that one-way information dissemination is the purpose of the activity, but it differs from press agentry in that truth is fundamental. Central and local government departments often create information leaflets and make announcements to explain alterations to policies and processes that affect members of the public – for example, processes for claiming benefits or notifying the department of changes in personal circumstances that might affect their benefit entitlement. The information has to be accurate, true and specific – the main aim is to inform rather than persuade.

Two-way asymmetric communication is more commonly practised today than the first two models. This type of PR is rooted in persuasive communications (see Chapter 14) and aims to generate agreement between the organisation and its audiences by bringing them around to the organisation's way of thinking. Non-governmental organisations (NGOs) such as Oxfam, Greenpeace and the Worldwide Fund for Nature (WWF) practise this type of PR; the information they send out must be beyond reproach in order for them to retain their reputation and credibility and to persuade audiences to their way of thinking. Feedback from audiences is important in this model of communication, but it is used to adapt communications strategies to be more persuasive, not to alter the organisation's position. In line with the objectives of this communication, research here is used to measure attitudes in order to establish the degree of persuasive success achieved.

In two-way symmetric communication the aim is to generate mutual understanding – the two-way communications process should lead to changes in both the audience's *and* the organisation's position on an issue. Research for this type of PR does not just measure attitudes, but also investigates the understanding that has led to those attitudes, therefore establishing the quality of the dialogue taking place.

Searching for excellence

Grunig and his colleagues continued the quest to understand and improve PR with a three-country, long-term study of PR practice, in conjunction with the International Association of Business Communicators (IABC), to establish what might be defined as 'excellence' in PR (Grunig 1992; Grunig et al. 2002). The 10-year study produced a four-level analysis of excellent PR:

- programme level (why, when and how individual communications programmes are implemented)
- departmental level (how the PR department operates and fits in with other departments and the organisation as a whole)

TABLE 8.2   Characteristics of 'excellent' public relations programmes (*source:* Grunig et al. 2002: 9)

I		**Programme level**
	1	Managed strategically
II		**Departmental level**
	2	A single or integrated public relations department
	3	Separate function from marketing
	4	Direct reporting relationship to senior management
	5	Two-way symmetric model
	6	Senior public relations person in the managerial role
	7	Potential for excellent public relations, as indicated by:
		a knowledge of symmetric model
		b knowledge of managerial role
		c academic training in public relations
		d professionalism
	8	Equal opportunity for men and women in public relations
III		**Organisational level**
	9	Worldview for public relations in the organisation reflects the two-way symmetric model
	10	Public relations director has power in or with the dominant coalition
	11	Participative rather than authoritarian organisational culture
	12	Symmetric system of internal communication
	13	Organic rather than mechanical organisational structure
	14	Turbulent, complex environment with pressure from activist groups
IV		**Effects of excellent public relations**
	15	Programmes meet communications objectives
	16	Reduces costs of regulation, pressure and litigation
	17	Job satisfaction is high among employees

■ organisational level (understanding of, and respect given to, communications processes and audience feedback by the organisation and its staff)
■ economic level (the tangible value provided by excellent PR to the organisation, in terms of happy external and internal audiences).

Table 8.2 illustrates the factors that characterise excellent PR practice.

At the heart of the theory is the following proposition from Grunig (1992: 6) about PR effectiveness:

Public relations contributes to organisational effectiveness when it helps reconcile the organisation's goals with the expectations of its strategic constituencies. This contribution has monetary value to the organisation. Public relations contributes to effectiveness by building quality, long-term relationships with strategic constituencies. Public relations is most likely to contribute to effectiveness when the senior public relations manager is a member of the dominant coalition where he or she is able to shape the organisation's goals and to help determine which external publics are most strategic.

According to the study, two-way symmetric communication practices are a keystone for excellent PR, although the authors recognise that in practice, a mix of asymmetric and symmetric approaches is often used. Moreover, the study is based on western principles of PR practice; in other cultural environments different factors are likely to underpin excellence (see Chapter 7).

Critiques of the normative models

The symmetric and asymmetric communication models in particular have stimulated a large body of research into how PR is practised. While evidence suggests that it is associated with ethical and effective communications practices (Grunig 1992), critics have also argued that it is an idealistic model, which misrepresents the communications process in reality, where vested interests dictate the nature of PR practice and rarely encourage a truly balanced communications process (L'Etang 1996).

For example, Cheney and Christensen (2001: 181) argue that Grunig's research is based on self-reports by managers and should therefore be treated with caution. The idea of symmetric communications also obscures the networks of power and influence that shape these practices, as exemplified, for example, by organisations' pre-selection of target publics and topics for dialogue:

Public relations scholars no longer can pretend that dialogue, symmetry and responsiveness are values and practices that concern only the actors involved in the resolution of specific corporate issues. Not only do we need to ask, on an ongoing basis, who is representing whose interests, we also need to look at the broader implications for conflict resolutions between organisations and their stakeholders.

The sentiments of Cheney and Christensen are borne out by many critical scholars, who argue that the social and environmental context of PR can only lead to a profession that is defined by corporate interests. Others, looking either at specific areas of PR activity such as publics or approaches, have adapted the asymmetric and symmetric models in light of what they see as incomplete or inadequate theorisation.

Pieczka (1996) offers an in-depth analysis of the theoretical foundations for systems theories, and Grunig's excellence theory in particular. She points out that the degree of influence that these normative approaches have had should prompt thoughtful investigation into the assumptions that underpin them. Her conclusion is that, while the theory of excellence in itself is well-constructed, it does contain some contradictions. For example, two-way communications advocates openness, dialogue and inclusion – and yet PR practitioners are assumed to be most effective when they are part of an elite, the dominant coalition. She also suggests that the excellence study's research questions, which defined 'effective' PR in terms of organisational benefits, led to a self-fulfilling prophecy that presents two-way communications as most effective and therefore most desirable. For those that do not adopt this view or operate according to its principles, there is an implication of failure. Clearly, this cannot be assumed in, for example, cross-cultural models of PR where cultural influences change the nature of PR practice to suit a particular context.

For Grunig, critiques of his work – and particularly of the idealism inherent in symmetric PR – provided the impetus to reformulate the model, in an effort to improve its relevance to PR practice (Grunig 2001). This new 'mixed motive' model reconceptualises the concepts of asymmetric and symmetric PR, reflecting the dynamics of PR practice and the mixed methods observed in organisations in past research (Dozier et al. 1995). It also attempts to accommodate the range of outcomes of PR practices in light of various contingency factors.

The model builds on concepts from *game theory*, originally developed to study situations of conflict and cooperation. Murphy (1991) argued that game

theory allows us to understand how PR strategies are framed in the light of the interests of various publics balancing the interests of the organisation. In turn, this helps us understand the basic types of outcome of PR activities, in particular how compromise is reached between organisations and their publics – that is, how the two sets of interests are balanced in the communications process.

> **Definition:** *Game theory* is based on observations about negotiation and compromise that demonstrate that many conflicts are based on the zero-sum principle, whereby for someone to win, their opponent has to lose. Win–win outcomes are the result of compromise and mutually satisfactory negotiation.

Practitioners often develop strategies and define goals based on the need to reach a compromise with audiences – for example, persuading 18–30 year olds of the value of an iPod. These are non-zero-sum games, where opportunities exist for all parties to get something out of the negotiations (in this case, the seller gets the money, while the buyer gets a portable music collection). Grunig and his colleagues extended this idea of non-zero-sum situations, where organisations follow their own interests in the light of the interests of other parties, to complete their new model of communications (Figure 8.2).

While Grunig (2001) retains the term 'symmetrical' to describe the model, what is presented is a continuum. At each extreme, asymmetric communications are practised either in the interests only of the organisation or only of the public. In the centre of the continuum, called the win–win zone, mixed motive communications is practised, where the organisation and its publics enter into a dialogue of enlightened self-interest, characterised by negotiation, persuasion and compromise (Figure 8.2, overleaf). This mixed motive communication is equated with symmetric communication by Grunig (2001).

Grunig argues that this continuum of two-way communication more accurately reflects the contingencies that dictate communications practices in an organisation – where, for example, asymmetric communication may be the norm for some issues, but mixed motive models may be practised for those less critical to the organisation's survival. Extending the model, Plowman (1998) further examined the specific strategies that underpinned each approach. He found seven different types of tactic:

1 contending (I win, you lose)
2 collaborating (win–win)
3 compromising (50–50 split)
4 avoiding (lose–lose)

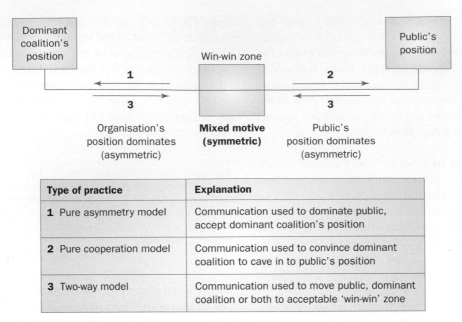

Type of practice	Explanation
1 Pure asymmetry model	Communication used to dominate public, accept dominant coalition's position
2 Pure cooperation model	Communication used to convince dominant coalition to cave in to public's position
3 Two-way model	Communication used to move public, dominant coalition or both to acceptable 'win-win' zone

FIGURE 8.2 New model of symmetry as two-way practices (*source:* Dozier et al. 1995)

5 accommodating (lose–win)
6 unconditionally constructive (strategic reconciliation)
7 win–win or no deal (where either both win or no deal is struck).

Contending and avoiding strategies were used for asymmetric communications in the organisation's interests, while at the other end of the continuum, the strategies used were accommodating and compromising. In the win–win window, strategies included cooperation, being unconditionally constructive, and win–win or no deal. Plowman found not only that these tactics were effective in resolving particular crises, but also that the greater the role of PR in solving organisational problems, the more likely it was to be represented at senior management level and have greater power and influence in the organisation – two of the key factors associated with excellent PR.

Interestingly, while the new model may well represent practice in organisations more effectively in that it avoids prescription of a single model of practice as the 'ideal', Grunig does not attempt to address the critical school's assertion that the PR process is inherently imbalanced. The relative frequency of asymmetric communication in the interests of the public as compared to options that favour the organisation, for example, is not addressed, even though a significant imbalance would cast into question the model's claim to 'provide an ideal combination of a positive and a normative theory' (Grunig 2001: 26). Instead, Grunig leaves deconstruction of PR practice to other authors, whose views are outlined elsewhere in this

chapter and book. (See Think about 8.2 and Mini case study 8.1.)

Publics in public relations

Grunig and Repper (1992) emphasise that, in order for PR to be respected and used effectively by senior managers, it must operate strategically – in a way that delivers real value to the organisation and helps it achieve its business goals. To do this, they argue, practitioners should do research into the characteristics of their target audiences, so that they can better understand how they might relate and respond to the organisation's communications. Based on relevant characteristics, PR practitioners can then segment target audiences and tailor communications activities more effectively.

The basic segmentation proposed by Grunig and Repper is 'active' versus 'passive' publics. Active publics seek out information and respond to organisational initiatives. They are therefore more likely to affect the organisation. Passive publics are those that do not proactively want to engage with the organisation. Some publics may be 'latent', or publics-in-waiting, only becoming active when they are prompted by a particular stimulus. PR practitioners need to know what stimulus will trigger a reaction among these publics so that they can use the right communications at the right time. (This description of what practitioners should and should not do is a good example of normative theory.)

In terms of identifying the types of issue that might trigger a public reaction, Grunig offers a situational

think about 8.2 **Negotiating an evening out**

When you and your friends are discussing where to spend your Friday night, how do you decide?

- Does one person dominate the decision and everyone else has to go along with it?
- Do you try and meet everyone's interests, perhaps by splitting up initially and then meeting up later?
- Does it get too complicated so you give up all trying to go out together and go your separate ways instead?
- Do some people happily give up their ideas and go along with the others?
- Do some people give up their ideas for now and instead do them at a later date?
- Do you either all go out together or not go out at all?

How does the option you chose fit with Plowman's negotiation tactics? Could you negotiate it differently? What stops you doing so?

Is there one person who tends to be the 'peacemaker' and finds a compromise? How much do you all rely on that person? What would happen if they were not there?

mini case study 8.1

Symmetric and asymmetric communication practices on the web

Symmetric communication

Non-governmental organisations have to communicate effectively with their stakeholders and take their views into account if they want to ensure long-term support for their causes. Symmetric, two-way communications are therefore particularly important for them. A good example of this in practice on the web is the Oxfam site, www.oxfam.org.uk. The site is focused on ensuring visitors receive as much information as possible about the organisation and its activities, while offering plenty of opportunity for feedback and contact. It includes:

- aims and objectives of the organisation
- annual reports and evaluations of its activities
- a summary of the different processes used by Oxfam to evaluate its activities in light of these objectives
- frequently asked questions and answers, divided into sections according to areas of most common interest
- updates and headline articles on the most current activities with which Oxfam is involved and progress reports for longer running projects
- press releases and other communications, reports and reviews released by Oxfam
- educational materials relating to Oxfam's aims and objectives
- further opportunities to contact the organisation by post, email or telephone.

Asymmetric communication

Unlike examples of symmetric communications, which are less common, multiple examples of asymmetric communication can be found in all sorts of organisations. For example, Nokia, the global mobile phone manufacturer, is focused on engaging with its community of users, but in a more limited way. The company's Code of Conduct (www.nokia.com/nokia/0,8764,1108,00.html) addresses all major areas of corporate social responsibility: the environment, human rights, ethics and legal limitations, and workplace practices including discrimination and fair trading practices. It also addresses health concerns about mobile phone use, highlighting the fact that it supports research in this area and that findings so far indicate no health risk from mobile phones.

It is clear that the company acknowledges the concerns of its community of stakeholders in the twenty-first century. However, the vast majority of its website is focused on the benefits of its products for its customers, rather than asking users what they think of the company and opening itself up for change in response to their views. The website gives the impression that the image it presents of a responsible company should be sufficient to address whatever concerns people may have.

For those who do have questions to ask the company, there is little opportunity for direct dialogue. While the media can give feedback on the press section of the website using a pre-structured questionnaire, and employees benefit from internal communications, it is not immediately obvious what options other groups have to voice their opinions to the company or ask questions and get direct answers.

theory of publics, which divides up active and passive audiences according to the types of issue that might trigger a response (Grunig 1983). He identified four basic types of public:

1 *All-issue publics* – active on all issues. Often, these types of people are very focused on injustices carried out by or through organisations. They might be equally angered by deforestation, child labour, animal testing and nuclear weapons – and take action against companies involved in any one of these things.

2 *Apathetic publics* – inattentive on all issues. These people are generally not aware of, or are unconcerned by, events in their environment. They are self-focused and they are highly unlikely to take part in any action – from petitions to demonstrations – to make their views heard.

3 *Single-issue publics* – active on one issue in a specific area. These people might have decided to put all their energies into one cause, such as supporting refugees and asylum seekers for example, and to be very active but just in this one area.

4 *Hot-issue publics* – active on one issue that has a high profile and broad societal application (such as domestic violence). Often, these people seize on a theme that is receiving attention in the media (for example, the rights of fathers in cases of family separation and divorce) and will be very active on this one area, but only for a relatively short period of time.

See Think about 8.3.

More recent research on publics argues for a change in how publics are conceived by practitioners and theorists. Leitch and Neilson (2001) criticise the situational theory of publics on a number of levels:

■ It assumes that 'publics' only come into being once the organisation decides to target them.

■ It assumes that publics are equal partners with organisations once the relationship exists.

■ It does not acknowledge the presence of power in the relationship.

This is like saying that your favourite clothing retailer did not believe you existed until you reached the age where you could shop there and that you had exactly the same power as managers to influence how the company operates. If you protested against their working practices in developing countries, for example, you would be given a fair hearing and treated as if your interests were as important as the interests of shareholders and management in making a profit. Clearly, this would be an incorrect assumption.

Other researchers point out that the concept of a 'single-issue' public, with whom the organisation can communicate on a relatively one-dimensional basis, does not equate to reality. Instead, they recognise that individuals relate to organisations on a number of issues and each of those issues may give rise to a different image of the organisation. Moffit's (1994) research revealed that individuals simultaneously hold a range of images of an organisation, some of which may be contradictory, and that they shift between these images almost instantaneously, often within the space of a conversation. Moreover, she also revealed that many of the factors determining these images were not related to the organisation and were out of its control (see also Chapter 13). Cozier and Witmer (2001) argue that the situational theory of publics treats individuals as 'possessions' of the organisation, and does not account for individual motives, rationalities and meaning systems that underpin the way they relate to it. They argue that these processes, as well as the influencing

---

think about 8.3 **Issues**

Consider the following issues:

■ legislation to prevent cruelty to pets
■ abuse of old people cared for in nursing homes
■ new housing developments on a local school playing field
■ child labour practices in developing countries
■ threat to raise student tuition fees.

Take the two issues that you feel most and least strongly about. Why do you feel like this about these issues? What are the factors driving your active or passive response?

Now think about what kinds of communication might prompt you to take action on the issue you feel most strongly about. What kind of support would you be prepared to give to the issue? Why?

Feedback Think about the forms of support that you might offer (e.g. time, money, attendance at a demonstration). Also ask yourself why you choose one form of support over another. What is the limit of your involvement?

mini case study 8.2

Using the web to understand users

One website that recognises the multiple interests of its users and successfully presents an 'electronic meeting place' for them is www.nzgirl.co.nz. The site offers its users a sense of community, the opportunity to participate in multiple publics, and thereby builds multiple relationships with them. Electronic communications are producing a shift towards individual, interactive, relationship-based PR strategies.

Source: Motion 2001

factors that lie outside the organisation's control, are fundamental to understanding the nature and development of publics. This is even more acute in an age of new media, where the internet moderates individual relationships with organisations (see Mini case study 8.2 and Think about 8.4).

Hallahan (2000) argues for a completely different basis for segmentation of publics that he believes better reflects reality. In his view, the situational theory of publics overemphasises active publics at the expense of inactive groups, who may still be important constituents for the organisation. To address this, he proposes a typology of publics based on knowledge and involvement:

- aware publics (high knowledge – low involvement)
- active publics (high knowledge – high involvement)
- aroused publics (low knowledge – high involvement)
- inactive publics (low knowledge – low involvement)
- non-publics (no knowledge – no involvement).

Hallahan's analysis emphasises the role of both knowledge and involvement with an issue or organisation before activism takes place. Individuals may be involved – that is, perceive a particular issue as relevant to them – but unless they have knowledge of the issue they are unlikely to become active. Similarly, if neither knowledge nor involvement is high, then inactive publics are unlikely to move to any of the other categories of public and will remain passive.

Hallahan applies these typologies to strategies for communicating that organisations might adopt. If two-way symmetric communication is the ideal, as systems theory suggests, then active publics are the most likely group to be able to match the organisation's formal communications efforts and structures, simply because they are likely to be organised, have a spokesperson or some kind of leadership and proactively approach the organisation. Aware and aroused publics are less likely to be organised, but individuals within these groups may require the organisation to respond reactively to approaches made by them – or the organisation may need to seek out these groups in order to engage in two-way discussions with them. Finally, inactive publics are unlikely to make any attempts to engage with the organisation, although the organisation itself may want to establish positive relationships with them, since they are often large and long-term groups of constituents. In this case, the onus is on the organisation to develop communications that stand out and engage these inherently passive groups, presenting specific challenges to PR practitioners.

These critiques may leave you thinking that practitioners will have a hard time targeting anyone with any accuracy. It certainly complicates the picture in a number of ways. First, the idea of a single 'public' with a single perception of the organisation is incorrect. Therefore the basis of many communications campaigns may be ineffectual. Hallahan's typology may help improve the effectiveness of different strategies by basing them on the levels of knowledge and involvement that

think about 8.4   Images

To understand Moffitt's findings, consider your own position. If you work part time, what is your image of the company you work for *from the point of view of an employee.* How do you feel about the company *as a customer*? And what do your friends say about the company? Does their opinion affect the way you feel about the company when you are talking to them?

Now think about how your company thinks about its audiences. Does it treat them as one group or does it differentiate between smaller groups or individuals? What criteria does it use to do that? How effective is that differentiation?

Feedback How do you reconcile any contradictions in the way you think about the company? Do you find it straightforward and natural that you might have a different relationship with it once you are 'in the door' as compared to when you are not working?

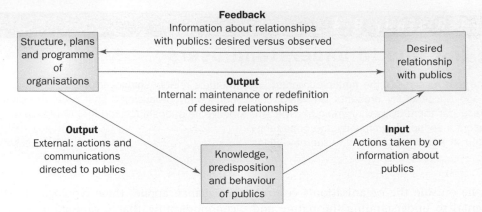

FIGURE 8.3 Open systems model of public relations (*source:* Cutlip, Scott M., Center, Allen H., Broom, Glen M., *Effective Public Relations, 8th Edition*, © 2000, p. 244. Adapted by permission of Pearson Education, Inc., Upper Saddle River, NJ.)

an audience has in relation to a campaign. Second, the impact of a campaign may be watered down due to external factors – practitioners need to account for this in their planning and evaluation. Organisations need to understand and acknowledge the fluidity of relationships for individuals and find a way of relating to them in spite of this 'moving target' dynamic.

Moffitt (1994) suggests that the solution is to address publics in the context of their relationship with the organisation, rather than on an issues basis – for example, as consumers, employees, members of an activist group, or suppliers to the company. Then, within these groups, she suggests organisations research the issues relevant to those people and the range of positions on the issues that they might take. Similarly, Leitch and Neilson (2001) suggest that publics be conceptualised as people who share 'zones of meaning' in relation to an organisation. They may belong to more than one 'zone of meaning' and the combination of these multiple 'zones' will define their relationship with the organisation. For example, a mature university student might also be a parent of a young student and a member of the student council; each of these would be a zone of meaning and the combination of all three produces that individual's relationship with the university. The task for PR practitioners is to establish which zones are relevant and how they might combine to create different relationships with the organisation (Motion and Leitch 1996).

Open systems

Acknowledging the importance of publics and their actions, Cutlip et al. (2000) have proposed an open systems theory of PR.

Open systems are systems that take their environment into account and change their business activities accordingly. Closed systems do not adapt to external

conditions. Cutlip and his colleagues suggest that PR should view itself as part of an open system. It should help the organisation to monitor relevant environmental influences and adapt its activities accordingly, as well as encouraging changes in the external environment that will help the organisation. In this model, two-way symmetric communications and strategic monitoring of the environment are fundamental to good PR practice.

This approach has distinct advantages for practitioners:

- It positions them as strategic advisors to the organisation and therefore gives them access to senior managers and more power to influence organisational activities.
- It limits the potential for crises, since environmental scanning allows the practitioner to anticipate difficulties and take early corrective action.
- It also ensures that PR makes a significant contribution to organisational effectiveness.

Figure 8.3 shows the model of open systems PR. See also Mini case study 8.3.

Extending the systemic view

Beyond North America: cultural issues

As more researchers outside North America entered the field, they tested Grunig and Hunt's typologies and found that country culture has a significant impact on the practice of PR (see Chapter 7). Practitioners use cultural norms and expectations to shape their approach to communication and these play a large part in determining the effectiveness of tactics and strategies. The ability of PR practitioners to

mini case study 8.3

Greenpeace – an open system

For environmental activists, clear communication with the right people at the right time is essential for getting their message across. An organisation like Greenpeace is a classic example of an open-system organisation. Campaign planners have to take into account views from external parties in order to ensure that they develop appropriate and effective communications for the cause they serve. These are just some of the people whose views Greenpeace needs to take into account when deciding which campaigns to execute and how to execute them:

- *biologists and environmental scientists* – to determine which plants, animals or environmental features are in most need of help, as well as to gather useful facts and figures for campaigns
- *its membership* – to determine which causes will generate most support, based on audience interests, as well as which causes would alienate members and therefore need to be avoided
- *public opinion polls* – in order to establish what the public already knows about current or planned Greenpeace campaigns and where more education is required
- *government and policy makers* – to understand what kind of information, in terms of content and presentation, they need to take Greenpeace's position into account when making policy
- *people who are directly affected by Greenpeace campaigns* – for example, whaling communities that might lose their livelihoods if whaling were completely banned. The strongest campaigns need to present alternative options for such people to survive and maintain their living standards.

---

target their audiences effectively is influenced by factors such as:

- extent of technology use, such as the internet, and its availability to individuals at home or work
- preference for face-to-face or electronic communication
- importance of hierarchy and power
- demographics
- split between urban and rural populations.

Sriramesh and Verčič (1995) developed a model for investigating international public relations (IPR) practices, taking into account environmental variables, including:

- infrastructure (political, economic, legal, activism)
- culture (societal and organisational)
- media characteristics (mass media, level of control, media outreach, media access).

Most international studies have taken at least some of these variables into account. Sriramesh (1992) found that the country culture of India, in particular its emphasis on relative power and hierarchy of individuals, resulted in a dominant management culture where managerial decisions were directive rather than consultative. This led to PR departments whose primary function was press agentry – promoting the organisation in a positive light. Two-way communication was not on the agenda. Bardhan (2003) also found the assumptions of western PR models were incongruent with traditional Indian views of relationships and PR. His respondents did not acknowledge the possibility of symmetry in their relationships and

viewed power differentials as normal, rather than a limiting factor. Similarly, Holtzhausen et al. (2003) found that the symmetric/asymmetric dichotomy was not applied by South African PR practitioners and that in fact culture-specific models of practice were based on the requirements of the environment. Rhee (2002) found that the excellence theory of PR did explain South Korean best practice, but that it was also enhanced by collectivist approaches to the work (a recognition of the community role of PR), as well as by elements of Confucianism including a long-term orientation and the importance of status as an organising principle for activity.

Grunig et al. (1995) compared models of PR in Greece, India, Taiwan and the USA and found two models in addition to the original four-way typologies:

- the 'personal influence' model, where the practitioner focuses on developing personal relationships with individuals who are central or highly influential to the success of the organisation
- the 'cultural interpreter' model, which refers to the role carried out by native PR practitioners in multinational companies, who are often consulted about local cultural norms and practices.

The personal influence model has since been recognised in a number of studies. For example, Sriramesh et al. (1999) found that the personal influence model of PR played a large part in determining PR practice in India, South Korea and Japan, and that cultural norms associated with this model were part of the PR mix. Park (2003) found that the personal influence model of PR was significant in South Korea practice, and that old-style, 'publicity' roles for PR were most common. In this context, two-way communications were slow to develop.

In one of few studies on the impact of the social and economic climate on PR practice, Molleda (2000) found that economic, social and political circumstances in Latin America resulted in expectations that organisations would contribute to the development of society; consequently, the PR practitioner has a strong role as both change agent and conscience of the organisation (see Chapter 3 for further discussion).

In an exploratory study, van Ruler et al. (2004) identified four characteristics of European PR:

- managerial
- operational
- reflective
- educational.

Managerial and operational characteristics were closely aligned with the US-derived technical and managerial roles of PR, although they were regarded as equally important in organisations, rather than being designated 'strategic' or 'tactical'. More specific to Europe were the reflective and educational characteristics. Reflective is concerned with 'organisational standards, values and views and aimed at the development of mission and organisational strategies'. This is done through analysing relevant societal values, views and standpoints and discussing their implications with members of the organisation. Educational is concerned with 'the mentality and behaviour of the members of the organisation by facilitating them to communicate, and aimed at internal public groups'. This is done by helping all members of the organisation to communicate with, and respond effectively to, society (van Ruler et al. 2004: 54). See Think about 8.5.

Public relations as relationship management

An important emerging perspective in the systems family of approaches puts the actual relationship of an organisation with its publics at the centre of PR activity. Maintaining and improving that relationship is the objective of PR. This means that strategies and tactics should always be assessed in terms of their effect on the relationship between an organisation and its publics, rather than, for example, the benefits they provide for the organisation.

The focus on relationships broadens the perspectives used to formulate PR strategies and tactics, but also by definition requires greater involvement from organisations. This is not as simple as it sounds – involvement means genuine dialogue, which in itself can be challenging. For example, Kent and Taylor (2002) point out that dialogue in practice frequently fails to meet the expectations of those taking part. The outcomes of dialogue may not be what was desired, and dialogue itself requires disclosure of information that may make the owner of that information vulnerable. Practitioners pressing for greater interaction with publics must recognise, explain and manage these potential risks for organisations as well as for the publics they interact with. See Box 8.2.

Ferguson (1984) was the first to put forward the notion of relationship as a central focus for PR. During the 1990s, the concept of relationships was investigated more fully and the first comprehensive book discussing the area was published in 2000, by Ledingham and Bruning.

Broom et al. (2000) draw on a range of relationship theories, including interpersonal communication, psychotherapy, interpersonal relationships and systems theory. Drawing together the most useful findings, they put forward a tentative framework for

---

think about 8.5 **Cross-cultural communication**

Cultural constraints are important considerations for multinational corporations when implementing global communications programmes. Using the example of an organisation launching a new chocolate bar, what economic, cultural and political factors might need to be considered when putting together a PR campaign for the following countries:

- United Kingdom
- Brazil
- India
- Australia

Feedback Consider factors such as the availability of technology in the campaign, consumers' disposable income, health issues, governmental restrictions, social responsibility considerations. Be specific, don't just list generic headings.

box 8.2	**Theory in practice**

Putting relationships first

The relationship perspective of PR does not require an organisation to give up its interests when deciding how to conduct its PR. But it does mean that wider thinking is required about how those objectives might be achieved. For example, if a computer manufacturer is faced with price increases from its suppliers, ultimately it is going to have to pass on some of those costs to its customers. Without a relationship perspective of communications, the company might decide to increase the cost of its products at short notice, announce it in a press release on the day of the increase and explain little about the conditions that led to the need to raise prices. This could alienate customers, who might feel that their needs and interests are being ignored by the company – after all, they might also be facing a tough economic climate.

A relationship perspective would prompt practitioners to moderate the impact of the price rise on customer opinions by working out what needs to be done to ensure they do not feel aggrieved. The resulting strategy might give six months' notice of the price rise, a full explanation of the reasons behind it, and perhaps offer a senior member of staff for interviews on the topic, rather than just sending out a dry press release that is open to misinterpretation. Customers would then have more complete information and better understand the company's position. They could assess and plan for the change more effectively and would feel that the company has taken their situation into account in its decision.

defining organisational–public relationships (Figure 8.4), based on the following principles:

■ Relationships are characterised by *interdependence*: parties to the relationship adapt in order to pursue a particular function in the relationship.

■ Relationships represent *exchanges or transfers* of information, energy or resources; the attributes of these exchanges represent and define the relationship.

■ Relationships have *antecedents and consequences* that must be taken into account when analysing them; organisation–public relationships therefore have specific antecedents (histories) and consequences (effects or results).

The centrality of communication to the conduct of relationships is unequivocal. Communication is the means by which adaptation is communicated and occurs and movement of resources is operationalised. The communication process should therefore be the starting point for an analysis of organisation–public relationships.

More recently, Ledingham (2003: 190) proposed the following theory of relationship management for PR (see Box 8.3, overleaf):

Effectively managing organisational–public relationships around common interests and shared goals, over time, results in mutual understanding and benefit for interacting organisations and publics.

Because relationships are so complex, a relationship view of PR offers many different perspectives from which to examine the discipline. Factors that affect all

relationships, such as their history, the background of the people or organisations involved and the social context of the relationship, to name just three, can be analysed in a PR context. For example, Ledingham et al. (1999) investigated the effect of time on organisation–public relationships using a survey of 404 residential telephone customers. They found that it was a significant factor in respondents' perceptions of trust, openness, involvement, investment and commitment to the relationship on the part of the organisation and also influenced the propensity of the customer to stay in or leave the relationship.

One problem with early formulations of the relationship perspective is that no single tool existed to measure the health of relationships with specific publics. Recognising this, Huang (2001) developed a cross-cultural scale for measuring public perceptions of organisations based on five dimensions of relationships:

■ control mutuality
■ trust
■ relational satisfaction and relational commitment
■ *renqing* ('favour')
■ *mianzi* ('face').

Definition: *Renqing* (favour) refers to a set of social norms based on the exchange of gifts and support, by which one must abide to get along well with others in Chinese society.

Definition: *Mianzi* (face) refers to face, or face work – the process of impression management, or presenting oneself in an advantageous light, in order to expand or enhance human networks (Huang 2001: 69).

<table>
<tr><td>box
8.3</td><td>**Theory in practice**</td></tr>
</table>

Fourteen conclusions on the organisation–public relationship

Drawing on the literature around PR and relationship management, Ledingham (2003) draws 14 conclusions about the organisation–public relationship:

1   Organisation–public relationships are transactional. *For example, your relationship with your university is based on the fact that you pay fees and they teach you – it is an exchange.*

2   The relationships are dynamic: they change over time. *As you progress through the degree you may do a placement year, which limits your contact with the university for that year and changes the way you view it when you return.*

3   They are goal oriented. *The university wants your fees; you want to successfully complete a degree.*

4   Organisation–public relationships have antecedents and consequences and can be analysed in terms of relationship quality, maintenance strategies, relationship type and actors in the relationship. *You might have had a poor induction week experience, which started you off on the wrong foot with the department you are studying with (antecedent); your tutor is hard to get hold of so you find it difficult to find anyone to discuss your issues with (maintenance strategy); the tutor regards you as a student first and foremost rather than an individual – and vice versa (relationship type); the staff might be great, but you might not get on with the people on your course (actors in the relationship).*

5   They are driven by the perceived needs and wants of interacting organisations and publics. *Your tutors might start out in the relationship assuming that you want to work hard and want to succeed; you might assume that they are there to support you and help you to succeed.*

6   The continuation of organisation–public relationships is dependent on the degree to which expectations are met. *If the subject is not what you expected, you may leave; if you do not submit, or fail, assignments, the university may ask you to leave.*

7   Those expectations are expressed in interactions between organisations and publics. *University prospectuses, websites, letters, course documentation and conversations between tutors and students all set these expectations.*

8   Such relationships involve communication, but communication is not the sole instrument of relationship building. *Your participation in classes, as well as your written work and conversations with other students and staff, all go towards building your image and relationship with tutors and the university.*

9   These relationships are impacted by relational history, the nature of the transaction, the frequency of exchange, and reciprocity. *The more often you visit the students union or local student bars and clubs, the more people you are likely to meet and the closer you may feel to the university and student community.*

10 Organisation–public relationships can be described by type (personal, professional, community, symbolic and behavioural) independent of the perceptions of those relationships. *A student–course relationship might be described as professional (given that it is underpinned by a financial transaction and clear exchange of commitment) or personal (given that it is also underpinned by your own enthusiasm for the subject and your friendships with fellow students).*

11 The proper focus of the domain of PR is relationships, not communication. *Prospectuses that deliver information about courses might get you to enrol in a degree – but you will not feel truly committed until you experience a positive induction week, when events that appeal to your own interests and needs take place, you meet your tutors one to one and you are acknowledged as an individual.*

12 Communication alone cannot sustain long-term relationships in the absence of supportive organisational behaviour. *If your department says it will deliver outstanding teaching but then your tutor is not a good teacher, you will stop going to the tutorials.*

13 Effective management of organisation–public relationships supports mutual understanding and benefit. *If your expectations and those of the course lecturers are the same, then the relationship between you is likely to run extremely smoothly and result in a positive outcome for both parties; if not, one will likely end up feeling dissatisfied and may withdraw from the relationship.*

14 The relationship perspective is applicable throughout the PR process and with regard to all PR techniques.

Source: adapted from Ledingham 2003: 195

Practitioner roles

Practitioner roles have been a major focus for theory development within the systemic perspective. Broom and Smith (1979) proposed five practitioner role models: problem-solving process facilitators; expert prescribers; communication process facilitators; technical services providers and acceptant legitimisers. These were later simplified by Broom and Dozier (1986), who defined two basic roles for the PR practitioner:

■ the communications *technician*, who focuses on tactical matters such as writing, event management and media management
■ the communications *manager*, who has a more strategic communication perspective and will normally create overall strategy, take and analyse client briefings and deal with issues and crises.

These roles have been confirmed in subsequent research. For example, Terry (2001) analysed lobbyists' stories of their jobs and found a clear separation between those who enacted the technician role and those who enacted the manager role. She also found evidence of all five of Broom and Smith's (1979) typologies in the lobbyists' narrations. Kelleher (2001) also found that managers spent significantly more time communicating orally than technicians, and that, with the exception of email, technicians spent significantly more time using traditional written communication.

Dozier and Broom (1995) updated their initial study and showed that gender indirectly affected the role of practitioners (Figure 8.4). Thus, men are more likely to have been longer with the organisation (tenure) and have more professional experience. The longer the tenure: the greater the professional experience; the longer the professional experience, the more likely it is that a practitioner has a managerial rather than a technician role; and the higher the salary.

The excellence study conducted by Grunig and his colleagues argued strongly for PR practitioners to aspire to a managerial role rather than a technician role, since they are able to exert more power and influence among senior management and be more effective for the organisation if they operate from this more senior position (Grunig 1992; Grunig et al. 2002). As a result, a hierarchy has emerged between the two types of role, with managerial roles generally enjoying greater perceived value and status.

Feminists argue that frequently women occupy the communications technician role and if they do carry out the managerial role, they tend to double-task. The technician role has therefore become 'women's work' and been devalued because of social stereotypes associated with professions dominated by women (Creedon 1991). While they do not dispute the influence of managers, feminist researchers have argued that the technician role in itself is of value, is multifaceted and can include decision-making responsibilities (Creedon 1991; Grunig et al. 2001). Dozier and Broom (1995) do not dispute this view of the technician role, but argue that the managerial role will always be better rewarded, because of the strategic value it provides to the organisation. Given that a technician role does not have that inherent strategic content, they suggest it is unrealistic to expect organisations to reward it in the same way.

Lauzen and Dozier (1992) shed further light on the managerial function in their investigation of the manager role as the 'missing link' between environmental challenges and the nature of the PR function within an organisation. In a survey of practitioners, they found that environmental variability in the form of the range and changeability of publics was significantly more likely to result in a managerial type role enactment by the senior PR practitioner and greater organisational power for the PR function. PR practitioners, on the other hard, hand less power the closer they were linked to marketing. In a separate study, they also found that an organisation which thought of itself as an open system, involving

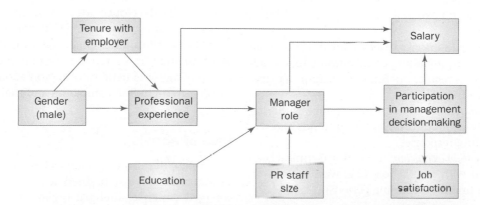

FIGURE 8.4 Interaction between gender, experience, education and managerial role (*source:* Dozier and Broom 1995: 16)

audiences in the development of issues management strategies, also increased the likelihood of managerial role enactment (Lauzen and Dozier 1994). Moss et al. (2000) also found that organisational factors affected the likelihood of a managerial role, including whether the organisation had a strong orientation to its stakeholders and whether PR could demonstrate financial and operational value to the organisation.

For example, if you work for a chemicals company like Monsanto, whose work can be controversial and is a regular target of sometimes violent protests, then your role is highly complex. You need to focus on building long-term reputation among customers and governments, persuading more general audiences that what you are doing will benefit communities around the world, and engage with activists to tackle and survive difficult situations in the short term. If, contrariwise, you work as a communications manager for a regional theatre, your job is likely to focus mainly on short-term promotion of upcoming productions. This is obviously much simpler and more tactical than working for Monsanto! However, if your role involved bidding for Arts Council or local authority grants, working with local communities or fighting closure threats, you would certainly be involved with strategic PR.

Moss et al. (2000), in a study of 10 leading UK companies, found that practitioners were only involved in strategic decision making beyond the communications area if they had a real understanding of business issues other than communications and had good relationships with senior management. PR is not yet seen as a strategic function in its own right and senior PR practitioners need to have a strong understanding of general business principles and practices if they are to be taken seriously by other managers. More recently, Moss et al. (2004) found that senior managers divided up their roles into five main areas:

■ *monitor and evaluator* – organising and tracking PR work
■ *trouble shooting/problem solver* – handling a range of internal and external challenges to the organisation
■ *key policy and strategy advisor* – contributing to top management, including contributions to and advice given in regular briefings and senior management meetings
■ *issues management expert* – intelligence gathering and analysis, monitoring external trends and recommending responses
■ *communication technician* – executing technical tasks associated with the PR role (e.g. writing press releases for financial reporting periods).

While their research was exploratory, it did support findings in earlier studies. The authors suggest that these five roles together reflect a more accurate picture of what it is to be a senior PR practitioner in today's organisations.

Changes abroad: shifts in society and technology

Grunig and Hunt's typologies dominated research throughout most of the 1980s. Towards the end of that decade, other researchers began to identify gaps in knowledge in the field that needed to be addressed in order to advance the academic discipline and the profession. However, the prompt for new research avenues was not solely internally driven. During the last decade of the twentieth century, important changes in society and technology meant that organisations were asked to account for their actions to a greater extent than ever before and this presented significant challenges to PR academics.

Technological advances

In the early 1990s, personal computers grew in number and became a staple element in most organisations' infrastructure. Improvements in usability also meant that people used computers at home for the first time, without needing specialist knowledge to operate them. The gradual spread of such a powerful technology infrastructure set the scene for further technological advances. They came thick and fast: by the mid-1990s, businesses were starting to use technology throughout their operations and connect with audiences in ways they had never dreamed of. The advent of the world wide web, with its global reach and instant communication, meant that business became more transparent; increasingly, organisations were expected to make information about themselves available to publics on the web. The web itself rapidly developed into a hugely popular consumer technology, connecting individuals to unprecedented quantities (and somewhat variable qualities) of information. It is often the first port of call for anyone looking for general information about a particular subject, including companies and their activities.

Rise of activism

Accompanying this technological revolution and the subsequent changes in business, a new type of activism emerged which challenged organisations' claim to legitimacy. While the early and mid-years of the twentieth century had been dominated by trade

PICTURE 8.2   Demonstrators at the Kyoto summit in Japan. (*Source:* Urban Thierry Corbis/Sygma.)

union activism, the 1980s saw an overall decline in the popularity and prevalence of unionism. This was replaced in the 1990s by a new breed of activist demonstrating against global capitalism. They led demonstrations at global governmental summits, national and international boycotts of individual companies and, as shareholders, made new demands for responsible business practices. Organisations choosing to ignore such demands faced the impact of worldwide campaigns against them, often conducted using that borderless, instantaneous communications technology, the web.

During the 1990s, Shell faced extremely damaging customer boycotts in Europe against its planned disposal of the Brent Spar oil platform in the North Sea. It was forced to change the decision and, subsequently, fundamentally changed its communications practices to make them more transparent and to avoid such events in the future. Global clothing brands such as Nike and Gap have also been taken to task by consumers because of the low pay and poor treatment of workers in countries and companies manufacturing their goods (Klein 2000) and have put in place ethical guidelines and minimum standards for suppliers as a result. (See Activity 8.1.)

activity 8.1

Website information

Conduct a web search for information about one of the following companies:

- Gap clothing
- Adidas
- Nokia
- The Body Shop

Apart from their own websites, how much information can you find out about them using the internet? Who writes this information? How wide ranging are the views on the companies?

Now look at their websites. How broad are they? How much information do they hold about the company's principles and values? What about possible objections to their activities? How are they addressed?

Feedback

You may find websites dedicated to attacking the reputation or practices of one of these companies. You may also find examples of good work taking place at a local level. See how much of this is reflected in the official website.

Combine different words with the name of the company to track down different types of information – for example, products, manufacture, ethics or community.

These developments have had a huge impact on the practice of PR. Practitioners now face unprecedented demands for transparency, must respond rapidly to demands for information that may come from anywhere in the world, and need to be agile enough to respond to crises as they occur, in order to contain and control their impact. The change has affected both the practice and content of PR. Ethical, honest communications are now a minimum requirement for organisations. PR practitioners are constantly challenged to act as advocates for audiences who want their views to be heard and taken into account.

In response to these changes, the 1990s also saw a flurry of new perspectives in PR research. As the demands on the profession grew and the number of researchers also increased, different views of PR began to emerge. Researchers, particularly in the UK and Europe, began to question the validity of some of the assumptions of systemic research – for example, that PR's primary role is to help organisations be successful. Critical studies, rhetorical approaches, postmodern perspectives and feminist analyses all made their first strong appearances during this decade.

Summary

This chapter has outlined the main schools of thought contributing to the development of PR theory. Early theories were clearly grounded in systemic views, focused on helping practitioners both understand and execute their responsibilities more effectively. Over the past two decades, theory has since expanded to integrate a much wider range of perspectives.

While systemic views of PR still dominate theory building, the field in the twenty-first century looks much more fragmented than at any time in its history. Some may argue that this does little to help the profession, serving only to confuse practitioners rather than provide the guidance they need in increasingly challenging environments. A different perspective, however, would argue that these developments are vital to the evolution and maturity of the profession. Alternative theoretical developments are discussed in the next chapter.

Bibliography

Bardhan, N. (2003). 'Rupturing public relations metanarratives: the example of India.' *Journal of Public Relations Research* **15**(3): 225–248.

Broom, G.M. and D.M. Dozier (1986). 'Advancement for public relations role models'. *Public Relations Review* **12**(1): 37–56.

Broom, G.M. and G.D. Smith (1979). 'Testing the practitioner's impact on clients'. *Public Relations Review* **5**(3): 47–59.

Broom, G.M., S. Casey and J. Ritchey (2000). 'Concept and theory of organization-public relationships' in *Public Relations as Relationship Management*. L.A. Ledingham and S.D. Bruning. Mahwah, NJ: Lawrence Erlbaum Associates.

Cheney, G. and L.T. Christensen (2001). 'Public relations as contested terrain: A critical response' in *Handbook of Public Relations*. R. Heath (ed.). Thousand Oaks, CA: Sage.

Cozier, Z.R. and D.F. Witmer (2001). 'The development of a structuration analysis of new publics in an electronic environment' in *Handbook of Public Relations*. R. Heath (ed.). Thousand Oaks, CA: Sage.

Creedon, P. (1991). 'Public relations and "women's work": Toward a feminist analysis of public relations roles.' *Public Relations Research Annual* **3**: 67–84.

Cutlip, S.M., A.H. Center and G.M. Broom (2000). *Effective Public Relations*, 8th edition. Upper Saddle River, NJ: Prentice Hall.

Dozier, D.M. and G.M. Broom (1995). 'Evolution of the manager role in public relations practice'. *Journal of Public Relations Research* **7**(1): 3–26.

Dozier, D.M., J.E. Grunig and L.A. Gruning (1995). *Manager's Guide to Excellence in Public Relations and Communication Management*. Mahwah, NJ: Lawrence Erlbaum Associates.

Ferguson, M.A. (1984). *Building Theory in Public Relations: Interorganizational relationships*. Gainesville, Fl: Association for Education in Journalism and Mass Communication.

Grunig, J.E. (1983). 'Communications behaviors and attitudes of environmental publics: two studies'. *Journalism Monographs* **81**.

Grunig, J.E. (1992). *Excellence in Public Relations and Communication Management*. Hillsdale, NJ: Lawrence Erlbaum Associates.

Grunig, J.E. (2001). 'Two-way symmetrical public relations: Past, present and future' in *Handbook of Public Relations*. R. Heath (ed.). Thousand Oaks, CA: Sage.

Grunig, J.E. and T. Hunt (1984). *Managing Public Relations*. New York: Holt, Rinehart & Winston.

Grunig, J.E. and F.C. Repper (1992). 'Strategic management, publics and issues' in *Excellence in Public Relations and Communication Management*. J.E. Grunig. Hillsdale, NJ: Lawrence Erlbaum Associates.

Grunig, J.E., L. Grunig, K. Sriramesh, Y.H. Huang and A. Lyra (1995). 'Models of public relations in an international setting'. *Journal of Public Relations Research* **7**(3): 163–186.

Grunig, L.A., J.E. Grunig and D.M. Dozier (2002). *Excellent Public Relations and Effective Organizations*. Mahwah, NJ: Lawrence Erlbaum Associates.

Grunig, L.A., E.L. Toth and L.C. Hon (2001). *Women in Public Relations*. New York: Guilford Press.

Hallahan, K. (2000). 'Inactive publics: The forgotten publics in public relations'. *Public Relations Review* **26**(4): 499–515.

Harrison, S. (2000). *Public Relations: An introduction*. London: Thomson Learning.

Holtzhausen, D.R., B.K. Petersen and N.J. Tindall (2003). 'Exploding the myth of the symmetrical/asymmetrical dichotomy: public relations models in the new South Africa'. *Journal of Public Relations Research* **15**(4): 305–341.

Hovland, C.I., A.A. Lumsdaine and F.D. Sheffield (1949). 'The effect of presenting "one side" versus "both sides" in changing opinions on a controversial subject' in *Experiments on Mass Communication*. Princeton; NJ: Princeton University Press.

Huang, Y-H. (2001). 'OPRA: A cross-cultural, multiple-item scale for measuring organization-public relationships'. *Journal of Public Relations Research* **13**(1): 61–90.

Kelleher, T. (2001). 'Public relations roles and media choice'. *Journal of Public Relations Research* **13**(4): 303–320.

Kent, M.L. and M. Taylor (2002). 'Toward a dialogic theory of public relations'. *Public Relations Review* **28**: 21–37.

Klein, N. (2000). *No Logo*. London: Flamingo.

Lauzen, M.M. and D.M. Dozier (1992). 'The missing link: The public relations manager role as mediator of organisational environments and power consequences for the function'. *Journal of Public Relations Research* **4**(4): 205–220.

Lauzen, M.M. and D.M. Dozier (1994). 'Issues management mediation of linkages between environmental complexity and management of the public relations function'. *Journal of Public Relations Research* **6**(3): 163–184.

Ledingham, J.A. (2003). 'Explicating relationship management as a general theory of public relations'. *Journal of Public Relations Research* **15**(2): 181–198.

Ledingham, J.A. and S.D. Bruning (2000). *Public Relations as Relationship Management: A relational approach to the study and practice of public relations*. Mahwah, NJ: Lawrence Erlbaum Associates.

Ledingham, J.A., S.D. Bruning and L.J. Wilson (1999). 'Time as an indicator of the perceptions and behavior of members of a key public: Monitoring and predicting organization–public relationships'. *Journal of Public Relations Research* **11**(2): 167–183.

Leitch, S. and D. Neilson (2001). 'Bringing publics into public relations: New theoretical frameworks for practice' in *Handbook of Public Relations*. R. Heath (ed.). Thousand Oaks, CA: Sage.

L'Etang, J. (1996). 'Corporate responsibility and public relations ethics' in *Critical Perspectives in Public Relations*. J. L'Etang and M. Pieczka. London: International Thomson Business Press.

Lumsdaine, A.A. and I.L. Janis (1953). 'Resistance to "counterpropaganda" produced by one-sided and two-sided "propaganda" presentations'. *Public Opinion Quarterly* **17**(3): 311–318.

McQuail, D. and S. Windahl (1993). *Communication Models for the Study of Mass Communication*. London: Longman.

Moffitt, M.A. (1994). 'Collapsing and integrating concepts of public and image into a new theory'. *Public Relations Review* **20**(2): 159–170.

Molleda, J.C. (2000). 'International paradigms: The Latin American school of public relations'. *Journalism Studies* **2**(4): 513–530.

Moss, D., G. Warnaby and A. Newman (2000). 'Public relations practitioner role enactment at the senior management level within UK companies'. *Journal of Public Relations Research* **12**(4): 277–307.

Moss, D., A. Newman and B. DeSanto (2004). 'Defining and redefining the core elements of management in public relations/corporate communications context: What do communication managers do?' Paper presented at the 11th International Public Relations Research Symposium, Lake Bled, Slovenia.

Motion, J. (2001). 'Electronic relationships: Interactivity, internet branding and the public sphere'. *Journal of Communication Management* **5**(3): 217–230.

Motion, J. and S. Leitch (1996). 'A discursive perspective from New Zealand: Another world view'. *Public Relations Review* **22**(3): 297–310.

Murphy, P. (1991). 'The limits of symmetry: A game theory approach to symmetric and asymmetric public relations' in *Public Relations Research Annual*. J.E. Grunig and L.A. Grunig. Hillsdale, NJ: Lawrence Erlbaum Associates.

Park, J. (2003). 'Discrepancy between Korean government and corporate practitioners regarding professional standards in public relations: A co-orientation approach'. *Journal of Public Relations Research* **15**(3): 249–275.

Pieczka, M. (1996). 'Paradigms, systems theory and public relations' in *Critical Perspectives in Public Relations*. J. L'Etang and M. Pieczka. London: International Thomson Business Press.

Plowman, K.D. (1998). 'Power in conflict for public relations'. *Journal of Public Relations Research* **10**(4): 237–261.

Rhee, Y. (2002). 'Global public relations: A cross-cultural study of the excellence theory in South Korea'. *Journal of Public Relations Research* **14**(3): 159–184.

Shannon, C.E. and W. Weaver (1949). *The Mathematical Theory of Communication*. Urbana, IL: University of Illinois Press.

Sriramesh, K. (1992). 'Societal culture and public relations: Ethnographic evidence from India'. *Public Relations Review* **18**(2): 201–211.

Sriramesh, K. and D. Verčić (1995). 'International public relations: A framework for future research'. *Journal of Communication Management* **6**(2): 103–117.

Sriramesh, K., Y. Kim and M. Takasaki (1999). 'Public relations in three Asian cultures: An analysis'. *Journal of Public Relations Research* **11**(4): 271–292.

Terry, V. (2001). 'Lobbyists and their stories: Classic PR practitioner role models as functions of Burkean human motivations'. *Journal of Public Relations Research* **13**(3): 235–264.

van Ruler, B., D. Verčić, G. Butschi and B. Flodin (2004). 'A first look for parameters of public relations in Europe'. *Journal of Public Relations Research* **16**(1): 35–63.

Windahl, S. and B. Signitzer (1992). *Using Communication Theory*. London: Sage.

CHAPTER 9

Public relations theories – an applied overview: alternative approaches

By the end of this chapter you should be able to:

- describe and discuss public relations and social/communication science theories
- compare different approaches to public relations theory, such as critical and rhetorical schools of theory
- evaluate the key debates within public relations research traditions (e.g. management/systems schools versus critical approaches; Anglo-American versus European perspectives).

Structure

- Developing theory: alternative approaches
- Equity in public relations: considering women and minority groups
- New research directions

Introduction

In the last chapter we examined the normative theories – theories that describe how a profession ought to behave – that were developed, particularly from systems theory, to improve the understanding and practice of public relations as a profession. In more recent years, a concern with the social implications and effects of public relations, combined with the emergence of postmodernism, has given rise to different schools of theory development. These new approaches to public relations have cast the profession in a different light and challenged both academics and professionals to think beyond the nature of practice to its impact on audiences, society and the public sphere.

Today we face a more fragmented and challenging academic landscape for public relations than ever. It is more visible in the everyday world and in academic circles. Practitioners have become academics and academics from different disciplines have turned their attention to the field. New insights have been developed and older approaches have been reviewed to include or reflect on public relations. As the chapter suggests, this has led not to consensus about the theoretical nature and content of public relations but, rather, to increasing friction. However, it is precisely these disagreements and conflicts that are generating the most interesting debates about understanding the field of public relations. These debates are explored in this chapter, which examines the major alternative theories of public relations, their evolution and the social impetus that continues to drive theory development.

Developing theory: alternative approaches

Critical theory

Critical theory has its origins in Marxist analysis of society and the economy. In a nutshell, Marx argued that power was determined by ownership of the means of production (capital), which lay in the hands of the bourgeoisie (the owners, or middle classes). The proletariat, or workers, had power inasmuch as they provided the labour to operate the capital, producing surplus value that ultimately created wealth. Marx proposed that this profit was not distributed equally and that, ultimately, the proletariat should overthrow the bourgeoisie in order to seize control of the means of production and redistribute wealth.

Critical theorists take elements of Marxism to analyse phenomena (objects, systems and events) that interest them. When examining PR, critical theorists go beyond the immediate practice of PR, to look at PR in its societal and economic context. For critical theorists, systems theories like those proposed by Grunig and his colleagues are incomplete since they ignore the context of PR in terms of its origin in, and impact on, existing power relations in society.

Generally, critical theorists argue that PR practitioners perpetuate the ability of both corporations and government to maintain a privileged position in society, usually by dominating the news agenda and excluding minority voices from public debate. Miller and Dinan (2000) show how the growth of the PR industry in the UK was a direct result of the shift towards a strong neoliberal agenda favouring privatisation, free markets and individualism during the 1980s and early 1990s. The profession is indebted to commercial and government interests for the size and scope of the industry today and continues to work in their favour.

Critical theorists suggest that PR is inherently tied to corporate interests. For example, Davis (2000) found that the production of business and financial news is in fact the work of a select few parties – specific journalists, analysts, major shareholders and shareholding institutions and corporate PR practitioners. Using the example of a corporate takeover bid, Davis demonstrates that, by excluding non-corporate views from stories (for example, employees or small shareholders), this group of specialists transform business 'news' into messages that reinforce a company's superiority in the marketplace, rather than stories reflecting a more balanced version of events. L'Etang and Pieczka (1996) provide a variety of alternative perspectives of PR as a discipline

weighted in favour of governmental and corporate interests. They argue for a move away from the simplistic view of PR as a management discipline, operating purely within the framework of organisational interests and with apparently few consequences beyond this environment. Similarly, Mickey (2002) analyses a range of case studies using a critical perspective, demonstrating that, even in contexts as diverse as gardening, AIDS prevention and art exhibitions, PR is inextricably linked to the interests it serves and perpetuates the environment in which those interests are most successful. He pinpoints a key argument of the critical school: PR by its very nature is biased and can only work in favour of its corporate masters.

Critical theorists propose two basic arguments that underpin their view of a partisan PR. The 'resource imbalance' perspective proposes that the economic resources available to practitioners and the increasing dearth of funding and staffing in media organisations leads directly to journalists becoming more dependent on PR practitioners for their news stories (Stauber and Rampton 1995; Moloney 2000). In other words, journalists have less time and money than before with which to develop their own stories. At the same time, the number of stories they are required to produce has increased. Organisations, contrariwise, are investing more and more in PR capabilities. As a result, a greater number of more highly skilled PR practitioners can now offer journalists well-written *story leads* that vastly reduce the effort required to write a full story. In a pressured environment, these kinds of lead are invaluable and journalists use them extensively (Pitcher 2003).

> **Definition:** *Story leads* refers to initial ideas for news or feature stories, generated in press releases or directly suggested by PR practitioners, which journalists may or may not follow up.

The 'structural' argument demonstrates that corporate patterns of media ownership result in internal censorship of news stories within media organisations and a news agenda that hesitates to challenge received wisdom, for fear of stepping on owners' and advertisers' toes. (See Think about 9.1.)

The stories that are broadcast or printed are easier for owners and advertisers to digest; they might report new events or product launches, or the latest comings and goings at a senior level. PR sources are popular because they provide stories that 'fit' these corporate requirements and can be widely used (McChesney 1999; Croteau and Hoynes 2001). Some theorists see

think about 9.1   External pressures on journalists

If you were a journalist working for a TV news channel owned by Company A, and one of its main advertisers is Company B, how would you handle a report that criticised Company A's treatment of employees or problems with Company B's new product launch?

Feedback   Critical theorists would argue that you would be under pressure to downplay the story, with some suggesting that self-censorship means the story never even goes to the news editor. (See also Herman and Chomsky's propaganda model in Chapter 14.)

activity 9.1

News analysis

Find a medium-length article in the business section of a newspaper of your choice. After reading the article, ask yourself:

- Who are the main parties discussed in the story?
- Who else might be affected by the events recounted in the story? Why do you think their point of view is not represented?
- How might their views be similar to, or differ from, the views already expressed in the story?
- How would their view change the story if it were included?

Feedback

Put yourself in the position of a company employee. How would the events in the story affect you?

this as a deliberate strategy for supporting the views of capitalists; others suggest that media workers simply absorb a set of values about what can and cannot be said in their medium, creating an agenda of acceptable and unacceptable points of view. (See Activity 9.1.)

Rhetorical perspectives

For the purposes of PR, rhetoric may be defined as 'persuasive strategies and argumentative discourse' (L'Etang 1996b: 106). The concept of rhetoric was originally closely aligned with the development of democracy and early Greek philosophers focused in particular on the ability of rhetoricians to persuade an audience through effective debate and argumentation. Critics such as Plato address the personal ethics of rhetoricians, who may use their skills to their own ends, rather than to further the process of democracy. Aristotle's *The Art of Rhetoric* formally outlined rhetoric as a persuasive science, separating the process from the individual and examining the basic requirements for persuasive success, including research into audiences and the best structure of an argument (L'Etang 1996b).

If we substitute PR for the words 'rhetoric' in the above paragraph, we can clearly see parallels between the discussions centuries ago and those conducted about PR today. However, L'Etang points out the major limitation of the classical view of rhetoric for PR scholars: the problem of *relativism*.

Definition: Relativism is the idea that what is right or wrong, true or false, is not absolute but dependent on the circumstances, situation or culture.

If rhetorical quality is focused on the quality of debate and argument, the substance of that debate – and even the truth of that substance – becomes a secondary, and relative, consideration. For example, one person could have a sophisticated argument that eating people was right another might just have a feeling that it wasn't. The first speaker would win. Extending this further, the ethics associated with communication about a particular issue also become relative, *unless* scholars change their focus to the process of communication, rather than the specific content. Power, influence and access to communication must be considered if the full implications of rhetorical analyses are considered when examining PR practice (L'Etang 1996b).

In fact, rhetorical scholars of PR do adjust their focus, being interested in the nature and ethics of the processes underpinning PR, as well as in the broader impact of the practice on society. As Heath (1992: 19) puts it:

[The] ability to create opinions that influence how people live is the focal aspect of the rhetoric of public relations. In the process of establishing product, service or organizational identity . . . public relations practitioners help establish key terms – especially slogans, axioms and metaphors – by which people think about their society and organizations. These terms shape the way people view themselves as consumers, members of a community, contributors to the arts, and myriad other ways.

Thus, rhetoric is a two-way discussion between parties that has a particular end goal in mind. It takes place, as Heath (1992) puts it, as part of a 'wrangle' of voices and not in isolation. Truth is necessary in order to engender trust in the rhetor (speaker), but individual perspectives must be brought to bear on the discussion in order to generate interpretation and debate. The ultimate outcome is assumed to be agreement between the two parties involved – the process of dialogue resulting in a meeting of minds somewhere in the middle of two extremes.

> **Definition:** An *axiom* is a statement, proposition or idea that people accept as self-evidently true, even though the proposition itself may be unproven.

Heath (2000: 71) argues that PR 'is part of each society's rhetorical processes' enabling organisations and people to strategically manage and negotiate their relationships. Factors influencing its success include:

- the situation in which it takes place
- problems arising from that situation
- audiences
- messages
- message sources
- perceptions of these sources
- channels for communication
- the 'opinion environment'.

Rhetorical analysis of PR includes not just the spoken or written word, but other non-verbal and visual cues used by organisations in the process of persuasion. Thus, the symbolic nature of PR is also incorporated into rhetorical studies.

Cheney and Dionisopoulos (1989) argue that PR is inherently political, rhetorical and symbolic, creating understandings of the world for their organisations and its audiences:

> *Corporate communications specialists are in the business of producing symbols. They, much more than others in the organization, tell various publics "what the organisation is". They shape identity, manage issues, and powerfully locate the organisation in the world of public discourse (1989: 139).*

Given this role, Cheney and Dionisopoulos argue that PR practitioners should be aware of the power they exercise in the interests of their 'bosses', and to the realities and identities that they create. PR practice should be moderated by considerations of ethics, consistency and balance between the interests of the internal audiences, such as employees or management, and external audiences such as customers or shareholders. For those on the receiving end of PR rhetoric, the challenge is to acknowledge those messages while facilitating their own advocacy through participation in relevant groups, engaging with companies where the opportunity arises and ensuring their reading of PR rhetoric is fully informed. (See also Chapter 14 for discussion of symbols and persuasive communication.)

L'Etang (1996b) emphasises the importance of retaining the view of the organisation as a key rhetor in society, rather than reducing analysis to the level of the individual. Only when this analytical viewpoint is incorporated into research can the impact of structural imbalances on the rhetorical process, in the form of power over and access to communications networks, be understood. In light of this understanding, discussions of the ethics of PR can be considered in their full context, rather than simply as an exercise in legitimating (or not) PR activities (see Activity 9.2).

Rhetorical theory can help practitioners become more effective by throwing light on the quality of arguments presented by organisations to justify their decisions. The better the justification, the more effective the PR (Skerlep 2001). It also allows practitioners to work out how the process of understanding develops for audiences. Moffitt (1992), for example, argues that meaning is constructed at the intersection of messages between publics and organisations – that is, in the process of dialogue between the two (see Think about 9.2).

The indispensable role of audiences in creating meaning repositions them at the centre of PR and

---

activity 9.2

What's the *real* story?

Examine a party political press conference or broadcast. (Examples, including videos, from the 2005 UK election can be found at http://news.bbc.co.uk/1/hi/uk_politics/vote_2005/default.stm).

- What message is the speaker communicating about their party's activities and what 'picture' are they presenting of their organisation?
- What symbols are they using to tell the story (e.g. positive use of babies, technology, schoolchildren, nurses or negative stories about devils, wasted resources or other social problems)?
- How do they want me to react to their 'story'?
- What perspectives could have been included in the story but are not mentioned?
- What issues is the person refusing to answer, or avoiding? Why?

Feedback

Consider in your answers what fundamental view of the world the party is presenting – is it one that questions the principles of business or political process, or assumes they are inherently correct? Does it assume we all think the same way? Does it present 'families' or 'immigration' in a different way from other parties?

think about 9.2   **Your university or college**

Do you passively accept what your university says to you about your course? Or does your experience, your opinions, the views of other students and other sources of information all act on their message to create a specific interpretation that is yours alone?

Feedback   Only you can create meaning in light of your own experience. What you tell other people about the university and the course you are on reflects this process of dialogue between what the university says and what you actually experience.

---

mini case study 9.1

Mobil Oil

Crable and Vibbert (1983) studied *advertorial* placements by Mobil Oil. During the 1970s the company published an apparently non-controversial, light-hearted column for Sunday newspapers to generate support for its policies.

Definition: *Advertorial* means paid-for articles that resemble editorial content rather than adverts (see also Chapter 16).

'Observations' included 'cartoons, line art, chatty news items, wide-ranging editorial commentary' and simultaneously put Mobil's point of view across to the popular audience by using metaphor and comparisons with popular themes and issues. The column reached over half a million American homes at its peak (Crable and Vibbert 1983). Analysis of the text showed that the company in fact consistently presented items on six basic issues: regulation, Congress, the media, technology, conservation and appeals to 'common sense'. PR tactics in this case were focused explicitly on promoting business interests, but with no intention of dialogue or discussion – the persuasion element of rhetoric on its own.

---

mini case study 9.2

Three Mile Island nuclear disaster

Dionisopoulos and Crable (1988) illustrate how, in response to a nuclear power accident at Three Mile Island, the nuclear industry attempted to dominate the way issues were defined, including the safety of and need for nuclear power, in order to influence positively public discussion and attitudes towards nuclear power and ensure the survival of the industry.

---

challenges practitioners to keep track of their communications once they are 'released' into the wider environment.

A number of researchers have looked at PR initiatives and explained them in rhetorical terms. (See Mini case studies 9.1 and 9.2.)

Equity in public relations: considering women and minority groups

Taking their lead from organisational studies, some researchers have focused specifically on the actual practitioners of PR and the social distribution of the function among different populations. By far the greatest area of research relates to the role of women in PR and the effects that gender has on their relative power and influence in the profession, both individually and as a group.

Feminist theory

Feminist analyses of PR emerged in the late 1980s, as the number of women in the profession exceeded the number of men for the first time. Today, 70% of PR practitioners are women. Despite the fact that this is a predominantly female profession, studies have repeatedly found gender inequalities in salaries, salary expectations, hiring perceptions and representation at management level (Grunig et al. 2001; Aldoory and Toth 2002).

mini case study 9.3

A female public relations manager

To put these findings into context, take the example of a female PR manager with four staff in her team, managing a budget of £100,000. She might develop and manage PR campaigns primarily linked to marketing and product launches. These can be particularly high pressure and so when the volume of work gets too much for her team she might 'muck in' and help them with the day-to-day tactical jobs like ringing the media or writing press releases. This doubling up of tasks (plus any family commitments) may prevent her from taking part in informal networking activities (such as drinks after work or sporting activities). She therefore has fewer opportunities to influence or impress senior managers and may find it hard to move up the management hierarchy as a result. As a manager, she might be on the management team alongside marketing, HR, finance and other business functions, but if she is the only woman – and working in an area that is seen to be subordinate to marketing – her opinions might not be valued as much as the other managers and decisions are unlikely to reflect her input.

Feminist analyses of the profession have focused in particular on the reasons for this imbalance as well as on feminist interpretations of PR activity. In an analysis of the relationship between organisational structure, influence and gender, O'Neil (2003) summarises the following causes of the persistent inequalities:

1   Female practitioners are predominantly communications technicians; their task orientation prevents them from having greater power and influence on decision making within an organisation.

2   The technician role is generally placed lower in the organisational hierarchy, reducing the opportunity to take part in decisions that affect the future of the organisation.

3   Female practitioners tend to have less employee support than male practitioners; research suggests that this also reduces their power within the organisation and may require them to double up on a technician role, even when they are in a managerial position.

4   As a minority group at the managerial level, women may be regarded as 'tokens' or representatives of other women in the organisation. Research has shown that tokens have less organisational power than dominant groups have and they may have to struggle against negative stereotypes or create a persona that 'fits' with the dominant coalition to avoid threatening the status quo.

5   As well as being excluded from formal power networks such as management, women may be absent from informal power structures such as an 'old boy' network and thereby lose access to organisational resources and support.

6   Female practitioners tend to lack mentors, which may reduce their ability to learn key business skills that might help them progress up the hierarchy.

7   Finally, female PR practitioners may be perceived by senior management to be simply of less value to the organisation than men.

See Mini case study 9.3.

Choi and Hon (2002) tested the effects of gender balance in powerful organisational positions on perceptions of female and male practitioners relative to success. Gender integration at this senior level did improve evaluations of female practitioners and decreased the difference in salary between male and female practitioners. However, female respondents consistently perceived larger gender differences and evaluated men more favourably than male respondents, suggesting that gender-related stereotypes are deep seated, persistent, and perpetuated by women as much as men.

Based on these patterns, several feminist researchers have created the beginnings of feminist theories of PR. Hon (1995) provided a comprehensive feminist view of the field and produced a summary of antecedents (background/history) for, and strategies to, improve women's position in the profession (see Table 9.1).

Hon (1995) critiques liberal feminist approaches arguing for women to take action in order to alter their position, pointing out that such strategies cannot be successful if they rail against institutionalised sexism and organisational stereotypes. Instead, she argues for change at four levels: society, organisation, profession and individual (see Table 9.2).

These echo the findings of a five-year study by Grunig et al. (2001). They found that societal stereotypes of women have led to the devaluation of the

TABLE 9.1 Antecedents of and strategies to address women's position in public relations (*source:* based on Hon 1995: 43–65)

Antecedents	Strategies for change
<ul><li>Marginalisation of the public relations function within the organisation</li><li>Flawed curriculum focusing on technical rather than business skills and thereby degrading the public relations function</li><li>Male-dominated work environment causing:<ul><li>exclusion from men's networks</li><li>reduction in women's self-esteem and self-worth</li><li>few female role models or mentors</li><li>lack of knowledge about or discomfort with male-defined rules for advancement</li><li>outmoded attitudes of senior men</li><li>conflicting messages for women, particularly in relation to personal attributes</li></ul></li><li>Women's balancing act between work and home life</li><li>Gender stereotypes</li><li>Sexual harassment and 'lookism' – a tendency to focus on appearance rather than job performance</li><li>Marketplace factors</li><li>Ageism (working against younger staff)</li></ul>	<ul><li>Buying in and working the system through:<ul><li>*impression management*</li><li>*finding the right place to work*</li><li>*attracting men back into public relations to bolster public relations' status*</li><li>*learning how to fight for salaries*</li><li>*insisting on inclusion in management decision making*</li><li>*denying discrimination exists, to avoid a self-fulfilling prophecy*</li><li>*making choices about work–life balance*</li></ul></li><li>Developing the skills and knowledge needed in public relations</li><li>Demonstrating professionalism</li><li>Self-empowerment through networking</li><li>Radical feminist strategies including:<ul><li>*prescriptions for society, including a fundamental reassessment of societal values and renegotiating gender roles at home and in schools*</li><li>*prescriptions for organisations, including redefining management to acknowledge and incorporate feminine attributes and changing organisational policies*</li><li>*prescriptions for public relations, including educating management about the importance of the profession*</li></ul></li></ul>

TABLE 9.2 Four levels of change to address women's position in public relations (*source:* based on Hon 1995: 65–79)

Societal	Organisational	Professional	Individual
<ul><li>Raise levels of awareness about sexism</li><li>Elect women to high government posts</li><li>Introduce legislation to support working parents</li><li>Outlaw sexual harassment</li><li>Ensure affirmative action is effective</li><li>Ensure equal representation for woman in governmental organisations</li><li>Eradicate sexism in education</li><li>Break down gender stereotypes</li></ul>	<ul><li>Establish family-friendly policies</li><li>Rethink the masculine ethic dominating most organisations</li><li>Value feminine attributes</li><li>Make recruitment, hiring and promotion criteria and processes more objective</li></ul>	<ul><li>Devise specific strategies for overcoming the marginalisation of the function</li><li>Reassess undergraduate education</li><li>Incorporate women's perspectives in the curriculum</li></ul>	<ul><li>Monitor behaviour</li><li>Create a persona of promotability</li><li>Join professional associations</li><li>Help other women</li><li>Become your own boss</li></ul>

profession precisely because it *is* dominated by women. Moreover, long-term changes in women's status could only occur if fundamental patterns of socialisation changed and expectations of women shifted to eliminate stereotypes and recognise the capabilities of women as individuals rather than members of a particular group. They also propose that attracting men back into the profession is essential for long-term professional credibility. Creedon (1991) goes further and argues that, as well as these fundamental changes outside the profession, the profession itself needs to examine its own assumptions and self-perceptions to redress current imbalances in the value attached to different PR roles.

The use in PR of values and attitudes traditionally associated with women have also been examined by researchers. Aldoory (1998) studied leadership styles of 10 female practitioners and educators. They tended to have a personal, interactive approach to their role. They used *transformational* or *interactional* leadership styles, adapting their approach and the language they used according to the situation they were in and aiming to motivate and inspire followers through cooperation and consultation. Grunig et al. (2000) compared feminist values with PR practice and suggested that *inclusivity*, respect, caring, cooperation, equity, self-determination and interconnection could enhance the ethical and effective practice of PR. In practice, educating young practitioners in these values is an important step towards integrating them into future PR practice.

> **Definition:** *Transformational, interactional and inclusive* refer to styles of management and leadership, employing negotiation and adjustment rather than hierarchy or command to make decisions.

It is important to note that while the results of these studies are both consistent and persuasive, some studies do differ in their results. Moss et al. (2004), for example, point out that in their study of senior managers, over half the respondents were women and their patterns of work did not differ significantly from their male counterparts, either in terms of the amount of involvement they had with senior management or the amount of technical tasks executed as a proportion of the overall role. They argue that it is possible that female practitioners in the UK have, at least in part, surmounted the glass ceiling in terms of the responsibilities they take on and are required to fulfil. However, their study did not address other inequities including salary rates, perceived competence or expectations of the managers themselves. These are important areas where research

so far is unanimous in its assessment of the relatively disadvantaged situation for women in PR.

Minority groups

Very little research has been conducted on the position of ethnic minorities within the PR profession, an omission that seems incomprehensible given the increasing diversity within the profession.

Marilyn Kern-Foxworth and her colleagues published an analysis of the managerial roles of black female practitioners in 1994 (Kern-Foxworth et al. 1994). The research was based on self-report questionnaires of black female practitioners, and assessed their roles within the profession. Respondents perceived themselves to be in meaningful roles, frequently managerial, within their organisations, providing strong problem-solving capabilities and valuable advice to management. Respondents' age, education and experience did not differ from previous studies of female practitioners generally, suggesting that affirmative action policies, if implemented, did not reduce the quality of practitioners recruited.

Zerbinos and Clanton (1993) conducted a quantitative survey and found that an interest in communications was the main determinant of career choice for minority PR practitioners. Neither career counsellors nor role models played a part, reflecting the general lack of knowledge about the profession as a whole. The majority of respondents had perceived some discrimination in their roles and almost half had considered leaving the field. However, in contrast, respondents also said that they were reasonably satisfied with the profession and 93% said they would encourage other minority individuals to join the field.

Len-Rios (1998), in a qualitative study of North American minority practitioners' perceptions of their roles, found similar patterns in that, despite progress in terms of opportunities for career advancement and satisfaction with roles, many respondents had experienced covert racial discrimination and felt that barriers to advancement for practitioners of colour still existed. Stereotyping, pigeonholing, positive and negative discrimination on the basis of race or colour, and having a role as 'the minority representative' were all commonly experienced. Len-Rios also emphasised the need to attract more minorities into the profession by increasing the visibility of existing minority practitioners and educating career advisors on PR and the opportunities it offered to minorities.

Kern-Foxworth et al. (1994) emphasised that their study was an initial examination of the roles occupied by black practitioners, and called for more research into the area. Unfortunately, this call has gone largely unheeded, particularly in the UK. As the range

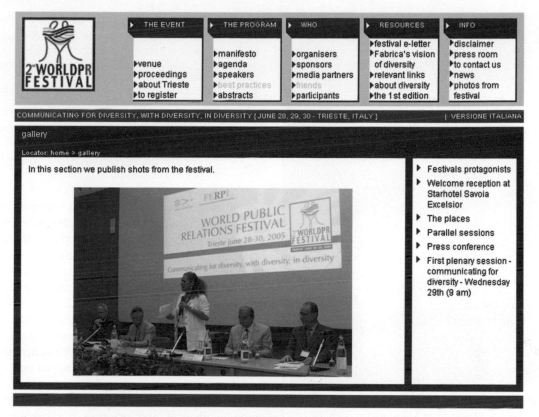

PICTURE 9.1   The World Public Relations Festival in 2005 made diversity its theme. Will public relations become more inclusive? (*Source:* Methodos SPA, Italy)

activity 9.3

Women in public relations

Why do you think so many women work in PR? Ask fellow students and any practitioners:

- What attracted them to the profession?
- What might make them leave?
- Where do they see themselves in 5, 10 and 20 year's time?
- Do they think being female makes a difference to their career opportunities?

of ethnic groups entering the profession increases, greater understanding of their experiences in the profession, as well as a recognition of the new perspectives that they might bring to communication, would enrich the body of knowledge both in this area as well as in the field of PR as a whole (see Think about 9.3 and Activity 9.3.)

Postmodernism

Of all the alternative views of PR, postmodernist views challenge the very foundations of theory building so far. Derina Holtzhausen, in particular, has played a key role in integrating the postmodern approach into PR research and practice (Holtzhausen 2000; 2002) and this summary draws heavily on her work.

PR originates in the modernist paradigm and PR theories, insofar as they seek to present a single explanation or model for PR practice, are wedded to this worldview. Modernist theories and practices

think about 9.3   Connecting with publics

How many students on your course are female? How many from ethnic minorities? What is the situation at PR offices you know from placement or part-time work? What problems do you think there might be in conducting a PR campaign to encourage Asian women to use the public swimming baths if no one in the office understands the cultural factors that might prevent some of them from taking part in mixed events? What about language problems?

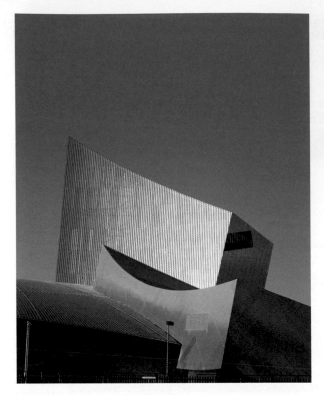

PICTURE 9.2 Like postmodern architecture such as the Imperial War Museum in Manchester, public relations theory is increasingly controversial and debated by both academics and practitioners. Of all the alternative views of public relations, postmodernist views challenge the very foundations of theory building. (*Source:* © Richard Klune/Corbis.)

Definition: *Metanarrative* means an attempt to make sense of the larger picture, or the wider social environment. Critical theorists and postmodernists (see below) suggest organisations and individuals use metanarratives as overarching explanations of the way the world works. They believe reliance on these 'stories' can prevent closer examination of reality.

Definition: *Discourse* here refers to particular ways of making sense of the world, communicated, sustained and justified through language and social institutions

---

A *postmodern* approach to PR can therefore accommodate differences in culture, gender, ethnicity and society in its analyses more effectively than modernist metanarratives. Postmodernists would argue that the overall explanations that characterise normative research, for example, are misguided because they can only ever approximate reality and cannot help practitioners in situations that do not conform to their parameters or expected frameworks. L'Etang (1996c) and Moloney (2000) echo this view when they argue that PR is multifaceted and cannot be defined in a single sentence.

The postmodern acceptance of plurality and diversity among audiences and practices has specific consequences for PR. First, it has implications in terms of the range of types of publics that practitioners affect in their work. Holtzhausen (2002) argues that the profession is facing a future characterised by ever greater fluidity and diversity in its audiences; if practitioners continue to try and present metanarratives to a fragmented world, they will simply fail. Instead, PR practitioners have a duty to act ethically in acknowledging other voices and pointing them out to the organisation when the need arises. As boundary-spanners between an organisation and its publics, practitioners must work reflexively, regularly reviewing how broad the range of perspectives is that they include in their strategies.

This sense of ethical responsibility emerges not least because postmodernists acknowledge the power of PR to create and sustain 'realities' for their audiences, indirectly communicating principles that support the organisations for which they work in a culturally acceptable manner. Postmodernists agree with critical theorists that PR is specifically used to perpetuate the existing system of power relations through, in particular, media relations activity. Extremes of this situation can result in practitioners creating 'hyperrealities' – the practice of representing realities that do not actually exist, through the use of symbols, codes and signs. Mickey (1997) illustrates exactly this process in his analysis of Hill and Knowlton's testimony before Congress on behalf of its client, Citizens for a Free Kuwait, which led to the US decision to go to war with Iraq in 1991. The testimony of a 15-year-old witness to the murder of Kuwaiti babies by Iraqi soldiers was later shown to be unreliable, as she

attempt to create single explanations, or *metanarratives,* that define the social environment. By definition, modernists using metanarratives ignore (or label as 'wrong') variability and phenomena that do not fit with their model. In contrast, postmodernists acknowledge variability and welcome the multiplicity of voices and views of reality that exist in society. Postmodernists do not reject *modernism* but argue that metanarratives have no inherent claim to superiority over other views. Instead, they should be integrated as one of many perspectives available.

Definition: *Modernism*, in PR, means an approach that legitimises the discourse of management and organisations as given and superior. Modernist PR attempts to reduce or eliminate crises, control publics and contribute to organisational effectiveness, usually measured in financial terms.

Definition: *Postmodernism*, in PR, is an approach that understands PR to generate perceived truths among publics through its role as a creator of organisational discourse. Recognition that the language used in PR also generates, sustains and shapes power relations in society.

was related to the Kuwaiti royal family, coached by the PR agency and could not be proved to have been in the country at the time. But the power of her account almost certainly influenced the decision to go to war: hyperrealities can be extremely influential and prompt changes in society to benefit certain groups while excluding others – war being a case in point. This has significant ethical consequences for practitioners and should be explicitly recognised in both theory and practice (Holtzhausen 2002).

In line with critical theorists, postmodernists also argue that balanced, two-way communications is a myth. Members of the dominant coalition (business and government in particular) will always enjoy a more profitable negotiation. Given this, PR practitioners need to accept that their attempts to achieve consensus are equally hypothetical, and instead should be content with outcomes that are recognised to be incomplete for one party. In this way, they do not subsume alternative voices in the process of communication. This may cause some issues for practitioners, but only if the organisation has not recognised the existence of these voices in the first place (Holtzhausen 2000).

Holtzhausen (2000) also reformulates the PR role to one of the organisational activist: someone who brings about fundamental change within the organisation. She presents three types of activism:

1 *Community activist:* this practitioner integrates alternative views from the organisation's publics into communications strategies and makes management aware of their significance. For example, a practitioner developing a corporate social responsibility policy might start by conducting a survey of stakeholder opinions about the company and what kinds of activity they would view positively. She would take the results to senior management and make a recommendation about company policy based on the findings.
2 *Organisational activist:* this practitioner changes the status quo from within. They might work closely with the human resources department in order to generate inclusive internal communications principles and practices that are meaningful to all employees, regardless of gender, ethnicity or sexual orientation.
3 *Public relations activities themselves as a form of activism,* where strategies are designed to instigate change in societal norms or dominant policies. Practitioners developing such policies might work in the non-governmental sector, in environmental charities or organisations supporting particular social issues, such as Fathers for Justice or Mothers Against Drunk Driving.

In sum, PR practitioners face significant challenges from fragmented audiences, greater access to uncontrolled media, a more aggressive media, frequent challenges to government policies and to the principles of capitalism and globalisation, and a greater number of active publics. A postmodern perspective automatically acknowledges this fragmentation and diversity.

New research directions

A number of UK and European researchers, as well as some North American scholars, have integrated other theories into PR perspectives and produced alternative views of the field. A selection follows.

The public sphere and public relations

Perhaps one of the potentially most fruitful new research directions currently emerging in Europe is the integration of Habermas's concept of the public sphere with PR theory. While US researchers conceptualise PR as an organisational function, relating to individual publics as determined by the interests of the organisation, European academics more frequently examine the profession at the societal level, often using the public sphere as a starting point for understanding how both companies and their PR functions contribute to the development of social norms and values through discussion in this arena.

The public sphere was first conceptualised as an ideal by Jürgen Habermas (1989). Habermas argues that the public sphere is a social space that mediates, or provides space for negotiated understanding, between the political sphere and the private sphere. There are two types of public sphere: the *literary public sphere,* where individuals engage with various forms of the arts and culture in order to enhance their self-development and understanding; and the *political public sphere,* which constrains and influences the political sphere through free and open public discussion of government and legislative issues. The views that emerge from the political public sphere are understood to influence the development of the political sphere in democratic societies. Jensen (2001: 135) articulates succinctly some of the characteristics of the public sphere:

Thus, although the public sphere was originally thought of as being an assembly of citizens at a certain location or the population in general, it is not so today; yet it is dependent on freedom of assembly, association and speech. The public sphere is not the media; yet it is dependent on freedom of press and prevention of media monopolisation. The public sphere is not a set of common values, norms or opinions; neither is it the statistical result of opinion polls; yet it can influence institutionalised opinion – and will-formation in society. The public sphere is not the sum or aggregation of individual, private preferences, values and beliefs, although it depends on protection of 'privacy', the integrity of

private life spheres: rights of personality, freedom of be-
lief and of conscience. The public sphere is not *obliged*
or normally able to come to an agreement or a decision;
yet it can influence decisions made by individuals, insti-
tutionalised associations and government.

Habermas's concept of the public sphere has been criticised in particular for representing an ideal that has never existed (Moloney 2000). Habermas would not argue with this view, instead suggesting that the *ideals* of the public sphere – free and open, rational discussion among equals – are desirable and should be a characteristic of modern democracies. However, he says, the commercialisation of the public sphere has distorted communication to the extent that discussions are driven by vested interests rather than being open, rational arguments – to the detriment of democracy (Habermas 1989).

Jensen (2001) has articulated the most comprehensive analytical framework centred on the public sphere, relevant to PR. She proposes a redefinition of the public sphere, recognising the fact that discussions in this arena are presented as being of general public concern, but also accommodating the fact that within the public sphere, multiple different discourses compete simultaneously, mainly through attempting to raise their views in the media and other public fora, or meeting places. She suggests that the public sphere be treated as an 'analytical concept, referring to the discursive processes in a complex network of persons, institutionalised associations and organisations' (2001: 136). Because these various discourses compete, the public sphere is characterised by disagreement rather than agreement. She also suggests an addition to the literary and political public spheres already introduced by Habermas: namely, the public sphere processes of *organisational legitimacy and identity*. It is here that PR is particularly relevant, since it plays a key role in engaging organisations in this part of the public sphere in order to both promote and justify particular organisational identities and 'ways of being'.

Jensen implies that these different elements of the public sphere all influence each other; social expectations change over time as a result of the interaction between discourses in the public sphere. In terms of the development of organisational legitimacy and identity, for example, social expectations of organisational behaviour will influence which discourses are acceptable, while discourses about responsible organisations reduce the discourses present in the political public sphere, which argue for regulation of company activities through purely legislative means. This is most obvious in the areas of corporate social responsibility (see Chapters 6 and 18), where economically successful and legal companies may still be subject to public wrath because they have not taken into account social expectations of corporate responsibility. Economic and legal arguments are of little use when competing against morality.

Integration of the public sphere as an analytical perspective for PR also modifies the concepts of publics traditionally used in normative PR theories. Both Jensen (2001) and Ihlen (2004) argue that traditional conceptions of stakeholder and publics both neglect the interactive, discursive processes that characterise PR activities in the public sphere and fail to explain why particular organisational discourses become a matter for public interest. They therefore omit an important understanding of the operation and effect of PR activities on such groups. Raupp (2004) also argues that PR should recognise that the different publics dealt with by organisations also form part of the public sphere and therefore take part in other, competing discourses – as well as participating in the same discourse on different levels.

Moloney (2000) takes a different view of the utility of the concept of the public sphere. He suggests a redefinition of the public sphere, given the fact that the utopian ideal does not exist, and suggests we now live in a *persuasive* sphere, where citizens must make sense of myriad messages about the merits of a vast range of products, policies and issues. He argues that PR practitioners who set out to persuade should do so in a way that ensures balance between the views that they represent and others who do not have the advantage of membership in the dominant coalition. He also highlights the responsibility of those on the receiving end of persuasive communications, who must actively, not passively 'read' messages and judge them on the basis of their origins and context. This perspective focuses on the groups taking part in the discussions of the public sphere and places responsibility for the quality of those discussions on their readiness to recognise the implications of their position.

For PR, the ethics of practice and content therefore become an important focus. However, ethics and the nature of ethics in PR is itself a widely debated area and the institution of common norms has not been successful in the past (see Chapter 15 for a discussion of ethics). Moreover, the ability and awareness of different members of the public to 'actively read' persuasive messages will differ widely; those who are already socially disadvantaged (for example, by lower levels of education) may be unable or unwilling to engage at this level. While Moloney may well be correct in that we live in a more persuasive than public sphere, the ability to counter this persuasion with greater responsibility from all parties may be easier to achieve in theory than in reality.

Constructivist public relations

Merten (2004) offers a *constructivist* interpretation of PR. The constructivist perspective underpins postmodernism as well as rhetorical theory and argues that PR constructs 'realities' through the promotion of particular dialogues (for example, consumerism or the value of choice). One of the main channels through which this occurs is the media; since journalists are ever more reliant on PR sources for news stories, the power of PR to create reality is increasing.

Merten points out that journalists used to present representations of realities, which were trusted because journalists were usually present at the event being described. However, news outlets and coverage options have widened considerably and journalists can no longer be present for each and every news story. PR acts as an intermediary, providing content to fill the space. However, these third-hand stories are never differentiated. They carry the same kudos as original news stories and are treated as equally real.

From the constructivist perspective then, reality has in fact become a combination of authentic reality (observed first hand) and the representations, or fictions, produced by PR practitioners, among others, which appear in the news. Obviously, the power of PR is significant since it is now in a position to do two things:

1 provide a selection of realities from which journalists can choose to create a story
2 define which events are in the public interest by providing representations and discourses that are only relevant to these events.

A constructivist view of PR has major ethical implications for practitioners. At the very least, they must take seriously the influence they have and understand how their activities can change or sustain inequities in society.

Summary

We live and work in a postmodern world; audiences are fragmented rather than singular and solutions are needed to tackle complex situations. Longino (1996) argues that a successful search for knowledge need not be determined by a final outcome on which all agree. Instead, knowledge may be defined as greater understanding of a particular phenomenon. Furthering knowledge, then, means including new perspectives to generate greater understanding.

PR sits at the intersection of a wide range of both academic and practical disciplines. It is therefore appropriate that we learn more about our own area by integrating other understandings into our body of knowledge. By developing theory in this way, we will offer practitioners not prescriptive solutions, but a range of choices from which they can select options that meet their particular needs. In this way, theory can and will be of genuine help to PR practice.

Bibliography

Aldoory, L. (1998). 'The language of leadership for female public relations professionals'. *Journal of Public Relations Research* **10**(2): 73–101.

Aldoory, L. and E. Toth (2002). 'Gender discrepancies in a gendered profession: A developing theory for public relations'. *Journal of Public Relations Research* **14**(2): 103–126.

Cheney, G. and G.N. Dionisopoulos (1989). 'Public relations? No, relations with publics: A rhetorical-organizational approach to contemporary corporate communications' in *Public Relations Theory*. C.H. Botan and V. Hazelton. Hillsdale, NJ: Lawrence Erlbaum Associates.

Choi, Y. and L.C. Hon (2002). 'The influence of gender composition in powerful positions on public relations practitioners' gender-related perceptions'. *Journal of Public Relations Research* **14**(3): 229–263.

Crable, R.L. and S.L. Vibbert (1983). 'Mobil's epideictic advocacy: "Observations" of Prometheus-bound'. *Communication Monographs* **50**: 380–394.

Creedon, P. (1991). 'Public relations and "women's work": Toward a feminist analysis of public relations roles'. *Public Relations Research Annual* **3**: 67–84.

Croteau, D. and W. Hoynes (2001). *The Business of Media: Corporate media and the public interest*. Thousand Oaks, CA: Pine Forge Press.

Davis, A. (2000). 'Public relations, business news and the reproduction of corporate power'. *Journalism* **1**(3): 282–304.

Dionisopoulos, G.N. and R.E. Crable (1988). 'Definitional hegemony as a public relations strategy: The rhetoric of the nuclear power industry after Three Mile Island'. *Central States Speech Journal* **39**(2): 134–145.

Grunig, L.A., E.L. Toth and L.C. Hon (2000). 'Feminist values in public relations'. *Journal of Public Relations Research* **12**(1): 49–68.

Grunig, L.A., E.L. Toth and L.C. Hon (2001). *Women in Public Relations*. New York: Guilford Press.

Habermas, J. (1989). *The Structural Transformation of the Public Sphere: An inquiry into a category of bourgeois society*. Cambridge: Polity.

Heath, R. (1992). 'The wrangle in the marketplace: A rhetorical perspective of public relations' in *Rhetorical and Critical Approaches to Public Relations*. E. Toth and R. Heath. Hillsdale, NJ: Lawrence Erlbaum Associates.

Heath, R.L. (2000). 'A rhetorical perspective on the values of public relations: Crossroads and pathways toward concurrence'. *Journal of Public Relations Research* **12**(1): 69–91.

Holtzhausen, D.R. (2000). 'Postmodern values in public relations'. *Journal of Public Relations Research* **12**(1): 93–114.

Holtzhausen, D.R. (2002). 'Towards a postmodern research agenda for public relations'. *Public Relations Review* **28**: 251–264.

Hon, L.C. (1995). 'Toward a feminist theory of public relations'. *Journal of Public Relations Research* **7**(1): 27–88.

Ihlen, O. (2004). 'Mapping the environment for corporate social responsibility: Stakeholders, publics and the public sphere'. Paper presented at the EUPRERA International Conference on Public Relations and the Public Sphere: (New) theoretical approaches and empirical studies, Leipzig.

Jensen, I. (2001). 'Public relations and emerging functions of the public sphere: An analytical framework'. *Journal of Communication Management* **6**(2): 133–147.

Kern-Foxworth, M., O. Gandy, B. Hines and D. Miller (1994). 'Assessing the managerial roles of black female public relations practitioners using individual and organizational discriminants'. *Journal of Black Studies* **24**(4): 416–434.

Len-Rios, M. (1998). 'Minority public relations practitioner perceptions'. *Public Relations Review* **24**(4): 535–555.

L'Etang, J. (1996a). 'Corporate responsibility and public relations ethics' in *Critical Perspectives in Public Relations*. J. L'Etang and M. Piezcka. London: International Thomson Business Press.

L'Etang, J. (1996b). 'Public relations and rhetoric' in *Critical Perspectives in Public Relations*. J. L'Etang and M. Pieczka. London: International Thomson Business Press.

L'Etang, J. (1996c). 'Public relations as diplomacy' in *Critical Perspectives in Public Relations*. J. L'Etang and M. Pieczka. London: International Thomson Business Press.

L'Etang, J. and M. Pieczka (1996). *Critical Perspectives in Public Relations*. London: International Thomson Business Press.

Livesey, S.M. (2001). 'Eco-identity as discursive struggle: Royal Dutch/Shell, Brent Spar, and Nigeria'. *Journal of Business Communication* **38**(1): 58–91.

Longino, H. (1996). 'Subjects, power and knowledge: Description and prescription in feminist philosophies of science' in *Feminism and Science*. E. Fox Keller and H. Longino. New York: Oxford University Press.

McChesney, R.W. (1999). *Rich Media, Poor Democracy: Communication politics in dubious times*. Chicago, IL: University of Illinois Press.

Merten, K. (2004). 'A constructivist approach to public relations' in *Public Relations and Communication Management in Europe*. B. van Ruler and D. Verčić. Berlin: Mouton de Gruyter.

Mickey, T.J. (1997). 'A postmodern view of public relations: sign and reality'. *Public Relations Review* **23**: 271–285.

Mickey, T.J. (2002). *Deconstructing Public Relations: Public relations criticism*. Mahwah, NJ: Lawrence Erlbaum Associates.

Miller, D. and W. Dinan (2000). 'The rise of the PR industry in Britain 1979–98'. *European Journal of Communication* **15**(1): 5–35.

Moffitt, M.A. (1992). 'Bringing critical theory and ethical considerations to definitions of a "public"'. *Public Relations Review* **18**(1): 17–29.

Moffitt, M.A. (1994). 'Collapsing and integrating concepts of public and image into a new theory'. *Public Relations Review* **20**(2): 159–170.

Moloney, K. (2000). *Rethinking Public Relations: The spin and the substance*. London: Routledge.

Moss, D., A. Newman and B. DeSanto (2004). 'Defining and redefining the core elements of management in public relations/corporate communications context: What do communication managers do?' Paper presented at the 11th International Public Relations Research Symposium, Lake Bled, Slovenia.

O'Neil, J. (2003). 'An analysis of the relationships among structure, influence and gender: Helping to build a feminist theory of public relations practice'. *Journal of Public Relations Research* **15**(2): 151–179.

Pitcher, G. (2003). *The Death of Spin*. Chichester: John Wiley & Sons.

Raupp, J. (2004). 'Public sphere as a central concept of public relations' in *Public Relations and Communication Management in Europe*. B. van Ruler and D. Verčić. Berlin: Mouton de Gruyter.

Skerlep, A. (2001). 'Re-evaluating the role of rhetoric in public relations theory and in strategies of corporate discourse'. *Journal of Communication Management* **6**(2): 176–187.

Stauber, J. and S. Rampton (1995). *Toxic Sludge is Good for You: Lies, damn lies and the public relations industry*. Monroe, ME: Common Courage.

Zerbinos, E. and G.A. Clanton (1993). 'Minority practitioners: Career influences, job satisfaction, and discrimination'. *Public Relations Review* **19**(1):75–91.

CHAPTER 10
Public relations as planned communication

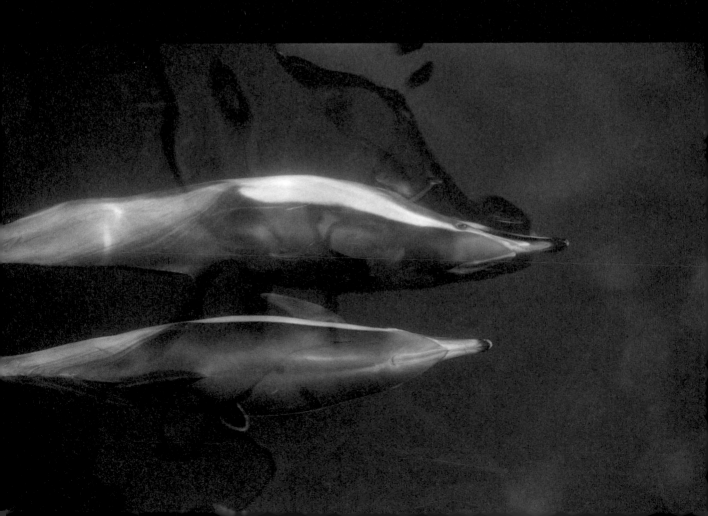

Learning outcomes

By the end of this chapter you should be able to:

- understand why planning is important for public relations programmes
- identify what research is required to underpin sound programmes
- determine appropriate programme objectives
- select and justify chosen strategy and tactics
- determine required timescales and resources
- evaluate the effectiveness of the campaign and review future direction.

Structure

- Why planning is important
- Systems context of planning
- Approaches to the planning process
- Analysis
- Setting objectives
- Identifying publics
- Messages or content
- Strategy and tactics
- Timescales and resources
- Evaluation and review

Introduction

Successful public relations programmes do not just happen. They are the result of sound research, meticulous planning and careful implementation. This does not rule out the impromptu or the reactive, but these are exceptions.

Recent research among Britain's 'most admired companies' (Gregory and Edwards 2004) shows that up to 70% of their communication activity is pre-planned. The majority of the remaining time is spent making the most of unexpected opportunities and reacting to events such as a major media story, and some time is spent in crisis management. But once these incidents are dealt with, the planned approach is resumed.

Planning will not make a poorly conceived programme successful in achieving its objectives, but planning makes it more likely that a programme will be well conceived in the first place. By ensuring that plans are targeted at the right people, use the right channels of communication and say the appropriate things at the right time, all within agreed timescales and budget, the foundations for success are laid.

Planning public relations programmes should not be difficult but time, effort and knowledge of the planning process is required.

This chapter provides an overview of the planning process. It will introduce each of the stages involved in planning public relations programmes and examine some of the theories that underlie the process. Other chapters will discuss some elements of the planning process in more depth (for example, Chapter 11 on research and evaluation). These chapters and further reading will be highlighted throughout this chapter.

Why planning is important

Within the many definitions of public relations that were discussed in Chapter 1, planned or managed communication is frequently mentioned as a defining characteristic of the discipline. Planning for public relations programmes provides a framework that can stimulate thinking; it acts as a prompt for problem solving and it releases creativity while ensuring it is focused and purposeful.

There are a number of very practical reasons for planning public relations activity:

■ Planning focuses effort – by eliminating unnecessary and low-priority work.

■ Planning improves effectiveness – by ensuring the planner works to achieve agreed objectives from the outset.

■ Planning encourages the long-term view – by requiring the planner to look to the organisation's future needs, preparing it for change and helping it manage future risks.

■ Planning assists pro-activity – setting the agenda means planners can be proactive and 'on the front foot'.

■ Planning reconciles conflicts – putting together a comprehensive public relations plan means that potential difficulties and conflicts have to be thought through in the planning stage.

■ Planning minimises mishaps – thinking through potential scenarios means that most eventualities

PICTURE 10.1   Effective public relations planning might help avert media stories like this where shoppers overwhelmed a newly opened London store. (*Source*: Johny Green/PA/Empics.)

Which argument do you find more persuasive: the arguments for planned activity or against? Why? Would these arguments apply to planning a birthday party? Or a study project, such as a dissertation?

can be covered and contingency plans put in place.

■ Planning demonstrates value for money – planners can show they have achieved programme objectives within budget and past achievements also help the planner argue for future resourcing.

So why doesn't everyone plan everything? The following suggests why practitioners are sometimes reluctant to plan, despite the arguments outlined above:

■ Lack of time – planning is time consuming and ongoing work cannot be suspended while it is done.

■ Plans are out of date as soon as they are written – business and particularly communication is conducted in an ever-changing and dynamic environment, so planning has little point.

■ Planning raises unrealistic managerial expectations – too many factors that are outside the planner's control to guarantee results.

■ Plans are too rigid and stifle the impromptu and opportunistic – flexibility of response is a crucial strength of the communication function.

■ Plans are a block to creativity – the approach is formulaic and encourages formulaic activities.

■ Plans always reflect the ideal, not the real – it makes it appear that communication work can be tightly controlled and all ambiguities 'planned out'. The reality of doing public relations work, say some practitioners, is not like that.

See Think about 10.1.

Systems context of planning

Public relations planning is located within the positivist framework and maps across very well to the systems view of organisations (see Chapter 8 for more discussion of systems theory). The 'open system' view of an organisation is an important concept for public relations planning, because an open system assumes that the organisation is an organism or 'living entity with boundaries, inputs, outputs, "through-puts", and enough feedback from both the internal and external environments so that it can make appropriate adjustments in time to keep on living' (McElreath 1997).

Cutlip et al. (2000) present an open systems model of public relations that clearly identifies how all these systems characteristics map on to the planning process (see Figure 10.1). So, for example, 'input'

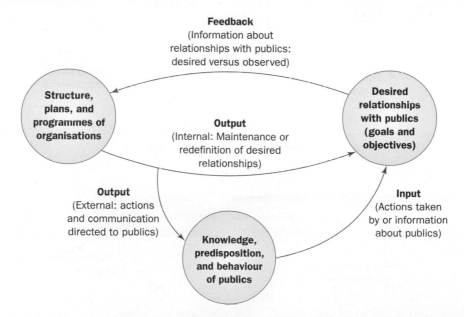

FIGURE 10.1   Open systems model of public relations (*source:* Cutlip, Scott M., Center, Allen H., Broom, Glen M., *Effective Public Relations, 8th Edition,* © 2000, p. 244. Reprinted by permission of Pearson Education, Inc., Upper Saddle River, NJ.)

refers to actions taken by, or information about, publics. These inputs in turn are transformed into goals (aims) and objectives that underpin the desired relationships with publics. By contrast, a 'closed system' approach might neglect to take account of information about publics and thus the planner might formulate aims and objectives in isolation.

Scope of public relations planning

Systematic planning can be applied to public relations activity over a period of several years, such as the Full Stop campaign to prevent child abuse conducted by the UK's National Society for the Prevention of Cruelty to Children, or to short-focused campaigns, such as the launch of a new service, or even to a single activity, such as a press conference.

When discussing the role of the communication planner, Windahl et al. (1992) embrace a wider interpretation of planning programmes or 'campaigns'. Informal communication, which is initiated to begin a dialogue for its own sake, is legitimate and may be 'planned'. It will have a purpose and will involve different publics. For example, key opinion formers may be invited by a university to a hospitality event such as an annual dinner. This occasion may not have a specific planned outcome other than a belief that interpersonal communication is in itself a valuable process which helps people work together in a more cooperative way. This dialogue helps build relationships and a sense of community around the university.

Furthermore, the type of work that planners undertake can be extremely varied. Some planners work for large organisations on large communication projects. For example, government communicators may work on nationwide initiatives such as the one to encourage healthy eating in schools or voting in EU elections, while those working for large corporations may work on global corporate identity initiatives. However, some planners work on quite small projects, for example running an open day for a local charity or volunteering to work with local communities and activists to protest about a local road scheme.

Windahl et al. (1992) also point out that communication initiatives can start at the bottom of an organisation as well as the top. For example, a small department may begin a series of sporting events to build informal communications in the team which eventually widens out into a company-wide and company-supported programme of activities.

This chapter takes the systemic approach to planning, outlined earlier, as its basis. The next step therefore is to examine some of the existing planning approaches.

Approaches to the planning process

The planning process is ordered and enables the public relations planner to structure their approach around certain key aspects (see Figure 10.2). It is helpful to see it as answering six basic questions:

■ What is the problem? (Researching the issue.)
■ What does the plan seek to achieve? (What are the objectives?)
■ Who should be talked to? (With which publics should a relationship be developed?)

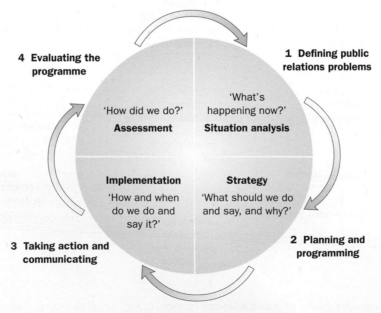

FIGURE 10.2 Cutlip and colleagues' planning model (*source:* Cutlip, Scott M., Center, Allen H., Broom, Glen M., *Effective Public Relations, 8th Edition,* © 2000. Reprinted by permission of Pearson Education, Inc., Upper Saddle River, NJ.)

think about 10.2   **Planning processes**

Look at the public relations planning processes and models described so far. What are the main similarities between them?

- What should be said? (What is the content or message?)
- How should the message be communicated? (What channels should be used for dissemination?)
- How is success to be judged? (How will the work be evaluated against the objectives?)

Marston (1979) provided one of the best known planning formulae for public relations which is encapsulated in the mnemonic RACE – **R**esearch, **A**ction, **C**ommunication and **E**valuation. American academics Cutlip et al. (2000) articulate the public relations planning process as in Figure 10.2.

Gregory (2000) has expanded public relations planning into a sequence of steps that add further detail to the process (see Figure 10.3).

All planning processes follow a basic sequence, whether they are for the strategic management of an organisation or for public relations (see Figure 10.4 and Think about 10.2). The approach advocated here is known as 'management by objectives' (MBO), which means:

- setting objectives and targets
- participation by individual managers in agreeing unit (i.e. department) objectives and criteria of performance

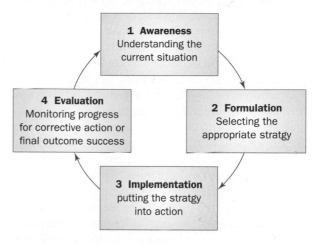

FIGURE 10.4   Basic business planning model

- review and appraisal of results (Mullins 1989: 254).

The MBO system can be integrated into strategic-level corporate planning, at unit level (as in a public relations department) and at the individual level where there is a review of staff performance in a given role (Mullins 1989).

Gregory's planning model in Figure 10.3 provides a sequence of activities and captures the essence of the planning approaches outlined. It will be used to examine the steps of the planning process in detail. However, first it is important to explain the structure of the first part of the diagram.

Although, ideally, the public relations practitioner would undertake analysis of the situation before determining objectives, in practice they are often given objectives by their managers. Such an objective might be to help overturn proposed legislation. In these circumstances it is still vital that the objectives themselves are scrutinised to see if they are appropriate. For example, an organisation may wish to resist the introduction of a stringent piece of environmental legislation because it will be expensive to implement and thereby affect shareholder dividends. However, on investigation, the public relations practitioner may discover that: stakeholders are very much in favour of the legislation; competitor companies will support it; and the company will be out of line if it persists. In this situation the public relations practitioner may recommend that the proposed campaign is abandoned.

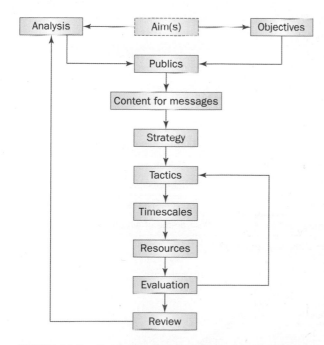

FIGURE 10.3   Gregory's planning model (*source:* Gregory 2000: 44)

The 'aim' element is in a dotted box because sometimes a campaign has a single, simple objective that does not need an overarching aim. If the programme is particularly large, it may be necessary to break down the whole into a series of projects that follow the same basic steps. Each project will have its own specific objectives, publics and content or messages, but this needs to be incorporated into a larger plan which provides a coordinating framework with overall aims, objectives and the message content guidance so that the individual projects do not conflict. (See Figure 10.5.)

Two things need to be borne in mind at this stage. First, the planning template could be seen to encourage a very rigid and undynamic approach. Sometimes practitioners have to move very rapidly in response to unpredictable events. Of course, practitioners must respond to the unplanned. However, even in these circumstances, the template can be used as a checklist to ensure that all the essential elements have been covered. Second, the degree to which any element of the planning process is followed will vary according to the requirements of the task in hand. For example, a full analysis of an organisation's external environment (see also Chapter 2 for an explanation of EPISTLE) will not be required to run an effective open day for families because any key issues will be relatively easy to identify. However, if a major programme is planned, such as the introduction of a new basis for licensing road vehicles, then a full analysis is certainly required, since research about lifestyles, demographics, technological advances and environmental impacts may need to be undertaken to identify and understand the full range of issues which have to be borne in mind by the public relations planner.

The rest of the chapter explores each stage of the planning process in turn.

Analysis

Analysis is the first step of the planning process. The point of analysis, sometimes called 'situation analysis' is to identify the issues or specific problems on which to base the programme. Without identifying the key issues the programme will not have a clear rationale. For example, if the core issue identified for action is that the organisation is seen to be unfriendly towards family carers, there is no point in aiming a recruitment campaign at potential employees such as women without addressing the reasons why the organisation is not an employer of choice for them.

Analysing the environment

This analysis of the external and internal environment is called 'environmental monitoring' by Lerbinger (1972), a phase that is now generally called 'environmental scanning' in the public relations literature (e.g. Grunig et al. 2002).

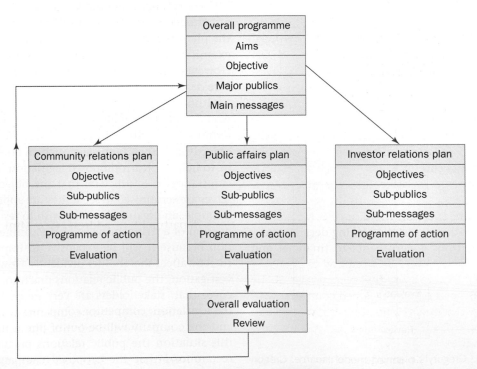

FIGURE 10.5 Framework for multi-project public relations plans (*source:* adapted from Gregory 2000: 46)

This analysis may seem more appropriate to the identification of strategic business issues than communication issues. However, public relations practitioners need to be alert to the wider environmental issues because it is these that will force some sort of action from the organisation. Action always has communication implications. Indeed, one of the major contributions that public relations can make is to maintain an environmental scanning brief on behalf of their organisation. This 'early warning' of issues allows organisations to manage future risks and is a key strategic input at senior management level. In the light of these emerging issues, organisations can make adjustments to their own strategy and actions to align themselves to new realities. (See also Chapter 19.)

Furthermore, issue spotting helps organisations contribute sensibly to public debate at an early stage and hence influence the outcome. Pressure groups, for example, will spot issues early to influence public debate. In one case, the intervention of environmental and human rights activists at a formative stage in the debate led to the stalling of plans to build dams in disputed areas in India.

The main questions to be asked when undertaking this kind of analysis are:

- What are the environmental factors that affect this organisation (identified from the EPISTLE analysis)?
- Which ones are of most importance now?
- Which will become the most important in the next four years?

From this it will be possible to derive a list of the main issues that will affect the organisation. These will differ depending on the country, the industry sector and the particular circumstances the organisation operates in.

It is important to identify whether some of these issues are linked. For example, social and technological changes are often connected: the lifestyle of many people has been transformed by mobile phone technology. As well as current issues, it is vital to identify the long-term forces for change. For example, concerns about obesity in developed economies will have a profound effect on the drinks, confectionary and fast food industries in the coming decade. Many organisations, from governments to financial and leisure companies, will need to respond to changing demographics that will see the average age of the population rising in many developed countries, with profound effects on the nature of health, welfare and educational provision and on the taxation system that supports them.

Having identified the broader environmental issues that affect the organisation and over which it

Strengths	Weaknesses
Good capital reserves Leading-edge products Loyal customer base Good reputation for service delivery Committed employees	Risk averse in investment Limited product line Ageing customer base Bureaucratic Limited skills base
Opportunities	**Threats**
New market opportunities in Russia Potential to acquire competitors Tax breaks if offices relocated	Potential political instability Danger of being overstretched Loss of loyal employee base

FIGURE 10.6   Example of SWOT analysis

has little control, it is then necessary to look at the organisation itself and those things over which it has greater control. A classic way to undertake this internal analysis is to use a technique called SWOT. The first two elements, **s**trengths and **w**eaknesses are particular to the organisation and can usually be changed by it, although all organisations are to a certain extent captive to their own history and culture. However, it is in the organisation's power to address its strengths and weaknesses. The third and fourth, **o**pportunities and **t**hreats, are generally external and can be derived from wider environmental analysis (see Chapter 2), but are usually related to those factors that have a direct impact on it. The four elements of SWOT can be seen as mirror segments in a quadrant. An example of a SWOT analysis is given in Figure 10.6.

Analysing publics

Having analysed the environment and the organisation and identified the key issues, it is then essential to look at the organisation's publics and discover what their attitudes are towards the organisation itself, to the wider issues identified by the EPISTLE (see Chapter 2) and SWOT processes or to the particular issue that management have asked the public relations department to address. (See Mini case study 10.1.)

Cutlip et al. (2000) suggest that research can be informal or formal. Informal or exploratory research methods may involve the use of any of the following:

- Personal contacts – these could be at public meetings (e.g. for shareholders or community) or trade shows.
- Key informants – these can be experts, editors, journalists, politicians.

Sea Fish Industry Authority

Identifying stakeholders

Identifying stakeholders is often a complex business. Figure 10.7 is a stakeholder map of the Sea Fish Industry Authority, a trade body based in Scotland.

The inner circle shows the priority stakeholders with the outer rings showing those with progressively less stake in the organisation.

The Sea Fish Industry Authority (Seafish), established in 1981, works across all sectors of the UK seafood industry to promote quality seafood. Its research and projects are aimed at raising standards, improving efficiency and sustainability and ensuring that the entire industry develops in a viable way.

Seafish is the UK's only cross-industry seafood body working with fishermen, processors, wholesalers, seafood farmers, fish friers, caterers, retailers and the import/export trade. It works closely with some 100 trade bodies across the UK. As an executive non-departmental public body (NDPB), sponsored by the four UK government fisheries departments and funded primarily by a levy on seafood landed, farmed or imported, it is accountable to all these stakeholders, as well as those who provide it with grant assistance for individual project work. Seafish must demonstrate to all these groups that its services offer good value for money.

Mission statement

Seafish works with the seafood industry to satisfy consumers, raise standards, improve efficiency and secure a sustainable future.

- Focus groups – for example, informal discussion groups of employees, groups of consumers or a cross-section of the public. Focus groups can be more structured, however, and use an independent moderator to elicit discussion around key themes.
- Advisory committees, panels or boards – many non-profit organisations have these to gauge responses to ideas.
- Ombudsman/woman – this is someone (usually independent) appointed by an organisation to identify and detect problems.
- Call-in telephone lines (e.g. helplines) – these can be set up with varying degrees of success; however, they do signal that the organisation is 'listening'.
- Mail analysis – this involves examining letters to identify comments and criticisms.
- Online sources – monitoring chatrooms and websites for rumours is an increasingly important source of intelligence.
- Field reports – these are people such as the salesforce who can serve as useful early warning for potentially difficult situations.

Chapter 11, on research and evaluation, goes into detail about how to conduct research, including the range of formal social scientific methods that can be employed, but it is important to mention here that the analysis stage of the planning process makes use of all the available information and intelligence on which public relations programmes are based. This preparation work is vitally important in answering the first basic question, 'What is the problem?'

(For an example of a campaign based on solid research, see Case study 10.1 on BT's 'Am I Listening?' campaign at the end of this chapter.)

If the public relations professional discovers that a key public hold a view different from that of the organisation on an issue, then there are two choices. Either the organisation must change to bring itself into line with what the public expects – for example, it may need to change its transport policy so that the local community is no longer disturbed by rogue parking. Or the organisation may wish to persuade its publics to a particular point of view. For example, it may seek to persuade people living around a chemical plant that the fume emissions genuinely are harmless. If key publics are opposed because they simply do not have relevant or accurate information, that can easily be remedied. If the problem is more complex, for example, the fumes are harmless as long as filtered through specially installed chimney baffles, the safety baffles have to be in place before communication can do its job.

As this last example indicates, sometimes public relations practitioners are asked to solve problems that are not just communication problems. So the planner must analyse the situation to see if they are amenable to communication solutions. Windahl et al. (1992) say that a communication problem can be defined in one of two ways: first, the problem arises from the *lack of* or the *wrong sort of communication*. For example, it may be that a child vaccination is not being taken up because it has been publicised only to doctors, not to parents, and because it has been described by its technical name, not its popular name. Second, the problem is a communication problem if it can be solved by *communication alone*. In this example, if parents are given the required information (*lack of* communication problem solved) and the popular name is used (*wrong sort* of communication

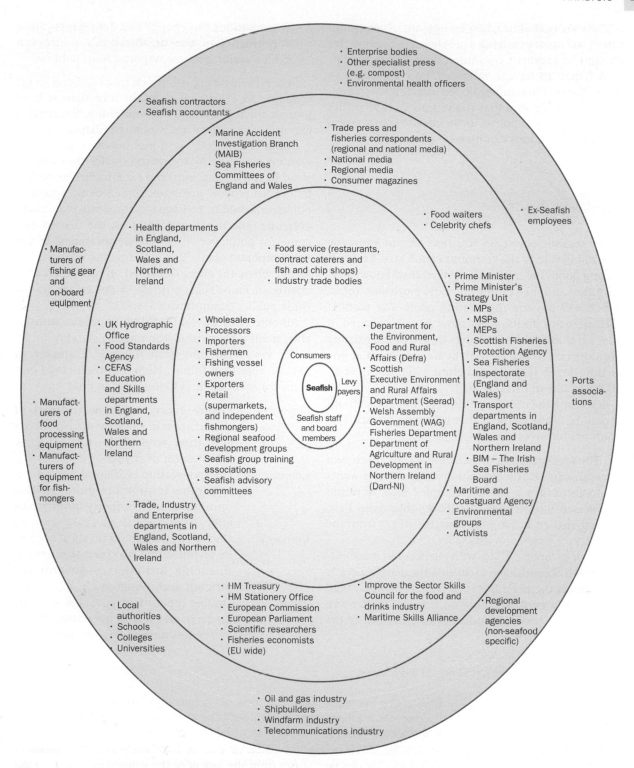

FIGURE 10.7 Stakeholder map of the Sea Fish Industry Authority (Produced by Kirsty Innes MCIPR on behalf of the Sea Fish Industry Authority (Seafish))

problem solved), it is likely that vaccination uptake will increase.

Often what are regarded as 'communication problems' are a mixture of communication and other issues and the public relations practitioner must be able to separate them. For example, if the uptake of child vaccinations were also being affected by suspicion about side-effects, or if they were only available at certain clinics, then there is more than a communication problem. Some other measures such as independent clinical opinion or wider distribution of the vaccine may be needed to stimulate use.

There are occasions when no amount of communication will assist in solving a problem. For example, no amount of excellent communication will make citizens happy to have a rubbish dump sited next to them. The best that can be hoped for is limited protest.

Thus it can be seen that analysis not only identifies the issue, but also points to the precise contribution that public relations can make to its resolution.

Setting objectives

To set realistic objectives it is necessary to know the size and nature of the communication task. Research among publics will have uncovered their knowledge, attitudes and behaviour on any particular topic, which will provide the starting point. The planner then needs to decide what movement is required, if any: a legitimate objective may be to confirm existing attitudes or actions. Objectives are usually set at one of three levels (Grunig and Hunt 1984; Cutlip et al. 2000), as shown in Table 10.1.

According to Grunig and Hunt (1984), three things should be borne in mind that will make the achievement of objectives easier:

1 The level of effect or outcome should be chosen with care. If the communication planner wants to introduce a new or complex idea, it would be sensible to set cognitive objectives first, rather than hoping for conative effects from the start.
2 Choose target publics with advocacy in mind. Research should have identified those who already support the organisational policies or who could be easily enlisted (more on this in Chapter 11). They can then act as advocates on behalf of the organisation.

3 Organisations can change too. Sometimes minor adjustments in the organisation's stance can elicit a major, positive response from publics.

Generally speaking it is much more difficult to get someone to *behave* in a certain way than it is to prompt them to *think* about something, the notable exception being over hot issues (see Chapter 14).

Cutlip et al. (2000) warn that public relations programme objectives all too often describe the tactic instead of the desired outcome for a particular public. In the 'employee' public example below, a tactical objective would be to issue the corporate plan. However, the objective that focuses on the desired outcome for employees is 'to ensure awareness of the new corporate plan'. This is the public relations objective where the effort is focused on confirmation or change in knowledge, attitude or behaviour among those publics communicated with.

All objectives should be SMART: **s**pecific, **m**easurable, **a**chievable (within the planner's ability to deliver) **r**esourced and **t**ime bound. Examples of SMART objectives follow. Note that the desired outcome for each public is highlighted in bold.

Employees: **Ensure every employee is aware** of new corporate plan by 10 November and, three weeks later, can list three priorities for next year.

Community: Use sponsorship of 20 local junior football teams to **promote more positive opinion about company among parents**.

Corporate: Change legislation on taxation of charity giving within two years **through influencing attitudes of government officials and ministers**.

Trade: Double amount of coverage in trade media in one year **to overcome lack of awareness among key suppliers**.

TABLE 10.1 Objectives set at one of three levels

Cognitive (means related to thoughts, reflection, awareness)	Encouraging the target public to *think* about something or to create awareness. For example, local government might want the local community to be aware that it is holding a housing information day. The whole community will not need the service, but part of local government's reason for making them aware is so that they know what a proactive and interested local council they have
Affective (means related to feelings, emotional reaction)	Encouraging the target public to form a particular attitude, opinion or feeling about a subject. For example, a pressure group may want moral support for or against gun ownership
Conative (means related to behaviour, actions or change)	Encouraging the target public to *behave* in a certain way. For example, the local hospital may use television to ask for emergency blood donors following a major incident

Consumer: Increase face-to-face contact with consumers by 20% in 18 months to **counter perception of company being remote.**

Apart from setting SMART objectives, there are four prerequisites for objective setting that will ensure that they are organisationally relevant and deliverable (Gregory 2000):

■ Ally the public relations objectives to *organisational objectives*. If the corporate objective is to grow the company by acquiring other companies, then public relations activity must be focused on that.

■ Ensure the objectives are *public relations* objectives. Employee satisfaction cannot be achieved through communication if the main problem is poor working conditions. The source of the problem must be removed first and this is a management issue.

■ Promise what is *achievable*. It is better to set modest objectives (e.g. cognitive objective) and meet them than to over-promise (e.g. set behavioural objectives) and fail.

■ Work to *priorities*. This way the more important areas of the plan will be achieved. If the planner is then required to work on other things, the least important things can be removed from the plan. Likewise, if there are budget cuts, again the least important activities can be forgone.

As stated earlier, programmes and campaigns can be large or small. Similarly, objectives apply to both large and small programmes and campaigns. They can also be applied in strategic or tactical programmes or campaigns. The examples in Table 10.2 show how. Note how the tactical objectives do not go into detail of the specifics of the tactical approach.

Setting sound objectives is fundamental to public relations planning. They define what the outcomes of the programme should be, they support the strategy, set the agenda for action and are the benchmark

against which the programme will be evaluated. Their importance cannot be overstated. (See Activity 10.1.)

Identifying publics

The section on objectives answered the second basic question in planning programmes, 'What does the plan seek to achieve?' This next section answers the third, 'Who should we talk to?' Chapter 12 is devoted to audiences, publics and stakeholders so this section will be relatively brief.

Research for the proposed programme will have identified the key publics (see section on analysis). Sometimes the key publics are apparent to the planner. If the planned programme is to support a product launch, then existing and potential customers will be a priority. However, groups are often not homogenous. It is incorrect to assume that all-embracing groups such as the *local community* comprise individuals who are similar or who will act in the same way. Within these groups there will be the 'active', 'aware', 'latent' and 'apathetic' publics that Grunig and Repper (1992) discuss. (Explained in Chapter 12.) They will have very different interests and concerns. It is likely that many individuals will belong to more than one stakeholding or public category too. Employees of an organisation may well be partners in a community relations campaign, or consume their organisation's products or services; they may even be shareholders.

TABLE 10.2   Examples of objectives

Issue	Objective for strategic programme	Objective for tactical campaign
Company viewed as environmentally irresponsible	Demonstrate environmental credentials	Promote company recycling scheme in local media
After-sales service perceived as slow and unresponsive	Create awareness of customer service facilities	Publicise guaranteed repair service and 24-hour customer helpline
Proposed legislation will damage environmentally sensitive areas	Change proposed legislation by lobbying government	Galvanise local pressure groups into action

---

<table>
<tr><td>

box 10.1

Ways to segment publics

- By geographics – where they live, work
- By demographics – age, gender, income
- By psychographics – attitudes, opinions
- By group membership – e.g. clubs, societies, parents
- By overt and covert power – e.g. religious leader, information gatekeeper
- By role in decision process – e.g. financial manager, CEO

</td></tr>
</table>

There are many ways in which stakeholders and publics can be segmented and the type of campaign will determine the best way to do that. For example, if a government wants to introduce a new benefit targeted at lower-income families, it makes sense to segment stakeholders by income and where they live. A charity wanting to start up a counselling service for refugees may wish to segment by ethnicity; a leisure company wanting to set up Saturday morning clubs for children will segment by age. (See Box 10.1.)

The practitioner has to decide the most appropriate ways to undertake the segmentation of stakeholders. Then it is important to move from the general to the particular. Broad categories must be divided into discrete groups. This could be done on the basis of the communication effort required for each group or on the basis of their power and influence.

The power/interest matrix (Figure 10.8) is used in strategic planning and can be readily transferred to the communication context. It categorises stakeholders depending on the amount of power they have to influence others and the level of interest they may have in a particular issue. Clearly the more power and interest they have, the more likely their actions are to impact on the organisation, so the support of this group is crucial. Johnson and Scholes (2002) point out that power comes from a number of sources including status in or outside the organisation, the ability to claim resources, (for example, investors money or internal budget) and the symbols of power that individuals have, for example use of titles.

It is possible, even desirable at times, that stakeholders in one segment should move to another. For example, powerful, institutional investors often reside in segment C. It may be in times of crisis that the communicator will want to move them to segment D so that they can use their power and influence with others to support the organisation.

Similarly, just because a stakeholding group appears not to have much interest or power does not mean that it is not important. It may be desirable to stimulate local community groups located in segment B because they in turn are connected to more interested and powerful stakeholders, such as employees, in segment D.

By plotting stakeholders and publics in the power/interest grid it is possible to identify who the key blockers and facilitators of communication are likely to be and to react to this, for example, through more information or dialogue. It is also feasible to identify whether some stakeholders and publics should be repositioned (as above) and who should be maintained in their position.

It is informative to map stakeholders in a number of ways. For example, not only can current position and desired position be mapped, but a useful exercise is to map how stakeholders might move in relation to a developing issue and whether or not this is desirable, preventable or inevitable. Communication strategies can then be devised that accommodate these movements.

Once categorised according to a suitable method, the groups need to be prioritised and the amount of communication effort devoted to them apportioned. Figure 10.9 shows an example of how this might be done for a luxury wallpaper manufacturer.

The number of publics that are communicated with and the depth of that communication is likely to be limited by either a financial or time budget. However, it is important that all the key 'gatekeepers' or leaders of active groups are identified. They may well interpret information for others, act as advocates on the organisation's behalf and catalyse action. Key individuals may belong to more than one group, so public relations activity needs to be coordinated to ensure that there are no conflicting objectives, messages or tactics.

Level of interest

	Low	High
Power Low	A Minimal effort	B Keep informed
High	C Keep satisfied	D Key players

FIGURE 10.8 Power/interest matrix (*source:* adapted from Mendelow 1991, cited in Johnson and Scholes 2002: 208)

Messages or content

The fourth basic question is, 'What should be said?' Traditionally, public relations people have focused on messages. Heath (2000) says this could be explained partly because many practitioners have come from a

Grouping	Percentage of communication effort apportioned
Corporate	**20**
Shareholders (active)	8
Shareholders (latent)	2
Investment analysts	5
Financial press (active)	5
Customers	**30**
Large do-it-yourself retailers	10
Specialist wholesale decorating suppliers	6
Specialist retail outlets	6
Trade press	7
Trade exhibition organisers	1
Consumers	**15**
Consumer press	10
TV and radio specialist programme producers	5
Suppliers	**10**
Raw materials	
Major suppliers	6
Minor suppliers	4
Employees	**15**
Executives	2
Supervisors	2
Shopfloor workers	4
Designers and salesforce	3
Trade union leaders	2
Pensioners	2
Community	**10**
Neighbours	6
Schools	4

FIGURE 10.9 Prioritisation of effort for luxury wallpaper manufacturer

journalistic background, where 'getting the story' out is seen as important. This has led to a focus on 'message design and dissemination to achieve awareness, to inform, to persuade – even manipulate' (Heath 2000: 2).

There are many kinds of campaign where messages are critically important, especially in public information campaigns. So, a country's health department that wants to inform the public about aspects of health care often uses memorable messages. Similarly, road safety messages are encapsulated in slogans such as 'Don't drink and drive'.

Messages are important for four main reasons:

1 Messages assist the awareness and attitude-forming process. Publics who can repeat a message they have seen or heard are demonstrating that it has been received. They are also likely to have a view on it.

2 Messages demonstrate that the communication channels have been appropriate and that the message reached the recipient.

3 Messages are essential in the evaluation process. Messages intended for the media can be evaluated through media content analysis. If the same messages are picked up and repeated by the target public (e.g. through survey research), it demonstrates that the communication has been, at least in part, effective. What publics do with that assimilated message is the other half of the story.

4 Summarising an argument down to its bare essentials in a key message such as 'eat five fruits and vegetables every day' helps focus management minds and imposes discipline on woolly thinking.

However, messages have limitations. They indicate one-way communication: the originator simply checks to see if their communication has been received. If an organisation genuinely wants to enter into a *dialogue* with publics where the outcome will be mutually determined, messaging is not so appropriate. For example, if a new organisation wants to discuss with its employees what its values and goals should be, dialogue is required. Where dialogue is part of the overall purpose of communication, simplistic approaches to messaging are inappropriate. (For more on the different models of communication and their purpose, see Chapter 8.)

How then can programmes that involve dialogue be evaluated if messages are one of the ways to measure communication effectiveness? The obvious answer is: by the quality of the relationship that results from the dialogue. More on this later in the chapter.

Messaging or dialogue initiation is often undervalued or reduced to simple statements, but it is very important. It is the point of contact, providing the meaning between an organisation and its publics. It is 'given' by the organisation, and 'received' by its publics and vice versa. If messages are poorly conceived and the way they are conveyed poorly executed, it can be the end of the communication process. There are four steps in determining messages:

1 Take existing articulated perceptions that encapsulate the issue or problem. For example, it may be that the organisation is regarded as an old-fashioned employer.

2 Define what realistic shifts can be made in those perceptions. If working practices and policies have been completely overhauled, this needs explaining.

3 Identify elements of persuasion. Work on the basis of fact. For example, the organisation may have introduced a crèche and family-friendly work practices. The number of women managers may have increased by 25%; the organisation may have achieved Investors in People status and won a major training award. All these facts demonstrate

that the organisation is not an old-fashioned employer, and should form the platform for programme content. However, facts are rarely enough. People are not just rational beings, so it is important to add human emotion to these facts. People associate more readily with other people and their experiences rather than to purely factual information. For example, providing case studies that people can relate to in a human way and which illustrate how the organisation operates as a social as well as economic unit adds warmth and depth.

4   Ensure that the message or content is deliverable and credible through public relations activity rather than via advertising or direct mail.

See Box 10.2.

The integrity of the message is affected by a range of factors that can determine whether it is taken seriously or not, such as:

■ format – should words or pictures be used?
■ tone – serious or light-hearted?
■ context – is it a day when there is bad news for the business or the country?
■ timing – is it controllable and if so, has the most auspicious time been chosen?
■ repetition – can the message be repeated often enough to be remembered, but not so often as to breed contempt?

Sometimes, circumstances dictate the format of the message and the medium in which it should be conveyed. For example, stock market information has to be provided in a prescribed form and a product recall dictates that advertising is used to get the message out quickly, in the required media and in an unmediated way.

Messages and content are key components of effective communication campaigns. Vague content leads to confusion and wasted effort. Carefully thought-through content is vital to understanding and dialogue – and essential to relationship building. (See Activity 10.2.)

activity 10.2

Message design

Devise an overarching message or slogan for a 'grass roots' or community-led campaign aimed at stopping children dropping litter outside the school premises. What would be a suitable sub-message for children? For parents?

Strategy and tactics

Strategy

The fifth basic question, 'How should the message be communicated?' falls into two parts: strategy and tactics. The temptation for the public relations planner is to move immediately to tactics because in many ways it is easier to think of a raft of ideas than it is to think about the rationale behind them. Implementation – where the tactics are put into action – is often the most exciting part of the planning process, and the most obviously creative. However, an underpinning strategy provides coherence and focus and is a clear driving force. It is the framework that guides the menu of activities. As Windahl et al. (1992: 20) state, communication planning 'should include both systematic and creative elements. Both are essential to information/ communication work'.

There is much discussion on the meaning of 'strategy'. Most books on strategic planning, for example Steyn and Puth (2000), who have applied strategy specifically to communication, provide several definitions and this in itself indicates that there is an issue around precise definitions. Strategy is described as: the 'overall concept, approach or general plan' (Cutlip et al. 2000: 378); the coordinating theme or factor; the guiding principle, or purpose; and 'the big idea', the rationale behind the programme. If an articulated strategy satisfies one or more of these elements it will be broadly satisfactory.

Strategy is dictated by, and springs from, the issues arising from the analysis of the problem and it is the foundation on which tactics are built. Tactics are

---

box 10.2   Typical messages in corporate campaigns

'Company X is the largest manufacturer of widget Y in China, providing 3000 new jobs in two years.'
'Company X has provided shareholder dividends above 5% for seven years.'
'Company X is quoted in *Fortune* magazine as having a strong, forward-thinking board.'
'Company X is committed to corporate social responsibility and has been included in the Dow Jones Sustainability Index since 2001. It sponsored the provision of 200 artificial limbs to victims of land-mines.'

	Example 1	Example 2	Example 3
Objective	Publicise new product	Establish organisation as thought leader	Encourage people to exercise
Strategy	Mount media relations campaign	Position as industry-leading think-tank	Drive home health policy through memorable message
Tactics	Press conference, press releases, exclusives, features, competition	Research reports, speaker platforms, information resource facility, online helpline, sponsorship of awards, etc.	Media campaign, posters, competitions, bus adverts, website, schools programme, etc.

FIGURE 10.10   Different types of strategy

the 'events, media, and methods used to implement the strategy' (Cutlip et al. 2000: 378). In the three examples in Figure 10.10, the first shows how strategy can describe the nature of, and summarise the tactical campaign for, a simple, single objective campaign. The second example is for a conceptual proposition, the third for a slogan-driven campaign encapsulating a key theme. All are equally valid.

Tactics

It is obvious that tactics should be linked to, and flow from, strategy. Indeed, having got the strategy correct, tactics should flow easily and naturally. Strategy should guide brainstorming and be used to reject activities that do not support the strategic intent or the programme objectives. There should be a clear link between objectives, strategy and tactics.

A level of caution is required when planning the tactics of a programme. It is easy for the practitioner to allow creative ideas to take over while ignoring the key aim and objectives. The aim is to get a programme that reaches the right people in sufficient numbers and that has the right level of impact to do the job required, all within acceptable costs and timescales. Sometimes that can be done with a single activity – for example, the international Live Aid concert on 13 July 1985 stimulated global awareness of starvation in Africa overnight.

More usually a raft of complementary tactics over a period of time is required. These will vary depending on the nature of the programme, so the practitioner will need to draw from a palette of tactics as appropriate. For example, if a company wants to launch new and highly visual products such as a range of expensive household accessories, it is important that tactics are selected that will show how these products look and feel. In this case, a range of tactics might include displays at exhibitions, product samples provided to journalists to encourage placement in the consumer media, CDs and websites showing the products in use, in-store demonstrations, brochures and high-quality posters.

In a different situation, for example, if the campaign involves lobbying over some aspect of financial legislation, quite different tactics, such as research reports, seminars, opinion former briefings, one-to-one meetings with members of parliament (MPs), would be more appropriate.

When designing the tactical elements of a campaign, two questions should be asked

1   Is the tactic *appropriate*? Will it reach the target publics? Will it have the right impact? Is it credible and influential? Does it suit the content in terms of creative treatment and compatibility with other techniques used?
2   Is the tactic *deliverable*? Can it be implemented successfully? Is there sufficient budget? Are the timescales correct? Are there the right people and expertise to implement it?

Figure 10.11 (overleaf) is a sample menu of activity that can be used in campaigns. (See also Chapter 3 on the role of the practitioner and Activity 10.3.)

activity 10.3

Public relations tactics

Bearing in mind the content of this section, list the tactics you would use to promote engagement rings. Then list the tactics you would use to encourage the customers of a utility company to pay online.

Feedback

To promote engagement rings, the tactics might include, for example, special shop openings (e.g. after office hours) targeted at couples to enable people to view and try on the rings. This would be the sensory component. Feature articles written for the local press would need to be more factual but would seek to stimulate interest in the shop openings. Photography will be an important part of the media effort. Timing, of course, would be around festive or traditionally romantic occasions such as New Year and St Valentine's day.

Media relations
Press conference
Press release
Articles and features
One-to-one briefings
Interviews
Background briefings/materials
Photography
Video news releases
Website
Email

Advertising (PR led)
Corporate
Product

Direct mail (PR led)
Annual report
Brochures/leaflets
Customer reports
External newsletters
General literature
(also multimedia material)

Exhibitions
Trade and public
Literature
Sampling
Demonstrations
Multimedia

Conferences
Multimedia
Literature
Hospitality

Community relations
Direct involvement
Gifts in kind
Sponsorship
Donations

Special events
AGMs
SGMs
Special occasions

Customer relations
Media relations
Direct mail
Advertising
Internet
Exhibitions
Retail outlets
Sponsorship
Product literature
Newsletter

Internal communication
Videos
Briefings
Newsletters
Quality guides
Compact disk interactive
Email
Intranet

Corporate identity
Design
Implementation

Sponsorship
Sport
Arts
Worthy causes

Lobbying
One-to-one briefings
Background material
Videos
Literature
Group briefings
Hospitality
CDs
Audio cassettes

Research
Organisations
Public relations programmes
Issues monitoring
Results monitoring

Crisis management
Planning
Implementation

Liaison
Internal (including counselling)
External

Financial relations
Annual report
Briefing materials
One-to-one briefing
Media relations
Hospitality
Internet
Extranet

FIGURE 10.11   A selection of public relations activities

Timescales and resources

Time

Time is a finite commodity and the life of a public relations practitioner is notoriously busy. Furthermore, public relations often involves the cooperation of others, and getting them to observe deadlines requires firmness and tact.

Deadlines can be externally imposed or internally driven by the organisation. Internal events may include the announcement of annual results, launching a new service or the appointment of a senior executive. External events may be major calendar dates, such as the Olympic Games, Chinese New Year or Thanksgiving.

To ensure deadlines are met, all the key elements of a project must be broken down into their individual parts and a timeline put against them. Check out Box 10.3, which contains a list of the main elements of a press facility visit.

Each of these elements will need its own action plan and timescale. Thus, preparing the visit areas may include commissioning display boards with photographs and text. That in turn will mean briefing photographers and printers, getting text approved by senior management and so on. It may also involve liaising with, for example, the marketing department for product literature, organising cleaners and arranging for porters to move furniture and erect the displays.

Having split the project down into its individual tasks, it is then useful to use techniques such as critical path analysis (CPA) (see Figure 10.12). There are also software packages available to help with project planning tasks like this (see www.microsoft.com/uk/office/experience). If tasks have to be done to a short timescale, time-saving measures will have to be implemented, such as employing a specialist agency to help or using existing display material.

Once the project is complete, it is vital to undertake a post-event analysis to see how the task could be done more efficiently and effectively another time. Certainly the planner should make a checklist of all the things undertaken so that it can be used for future events.

An annual activity plan allows the peaks and troughs of activity to be identified so that they can be resourced accordingly (see Figure 10.13). The times when activity is less intense can be used for reviewing or implementing other proactive plans.

From this annual planner it is clear that June will be a pressurised month, so extra help may be needed. May, on the other hand, looks fairly quiet, so this may be an ideal time for a team event to review plans and prepare for the future.

box 10.3	**Checklist for a press facility visit**

1 Draw up invitation list
2 Alert relevant departments
3 Select visit hosts
4 Book catering
5 Issue invitations
6 Prepare display materials
7 Write speeches
8 Prepare media packs
9 Brief visit hosts
10 Follow up invitations
11 Prepare visit areas
12 Collate final attendance list
13 Rehearse with visit hosts
14 Facilitate visit
15 Follow up

Resources

There are three areas of resourcing that underpin public relations work; human resources, implementation costs and equipment (Gregory 2000). Having the right staff skills and competencies as well as an adequate budget are critical to success. Skilled investor relations personnel, for example, are rarer and more expensive than general media relations staff (see Chapters 16 and 24 to gain an understanding of the skills involved in these areas). Generally speaking, a single practitioner with a few years experience can handle a broadranging programme of limited depth or a focused in-depth specialism, such as internal communication.

Ideally, the organisation decides its optimum communication programme and resources it accordingly. The reality is usually a compromise between the ideal and the actual budget allocated (Beard 2001). However, it has to be borne in mind that public relations is a relationship-driven activity and therefore people

4 Nov	6 Nov	11 Nov	12 Nov	13 Nov	14 Nov		28 Nov	29 Nov	30 Nov	1 Dec	2 Dec
Draw up invite list	Alert depts Select visit hosts	Book catering Send out invites		Brief visit hosts			Follow up invites	Prepare visit areas	Rehearsals Prepare final guest list	Facility visit	Follow up

FIGURE 10.12 Example of critical path analysis

Activity	January	February	March	April	May	June	July	August	September	October	November	December
One-to-one editor briefings	Trade press × 2	Consumer press × 2	Trade press × 2	Consumer press × 2		Consumer press × 1	Trade press × 1		Consumer press × 2	Trade press × 2		Local press
Advertorials with key journals		The Grocer		Cosmopolitan		Sunday Times Magazine		Woman		Regional Consumer		
News stories (including new products)	News story	Prepared foods	News story	Healthy options	News story	Summer fruits	News story	Barbeque foods	News story	Root veg	News story	Xmas goods
Seasonal themes			Spring promo			Outdoor life			Autumn promo			Winter warmers
Competitions		Trolley dash		Holiday bargains		Picnic hampers		Kids' adventure		Freezer filler		Santa's party
Exhibitions			Ideal Home	Local shows	Local shows	Great Yorkshire Show		Local shows	Local shows			

FIGURE 10.13 Annual media relations plan for a supermarket chain

are more valuable than materials. Media relations work survives without expensive press packs. It cannot survive without people.

When considering the implementation costs of a programme, public relations practitioners have a duty to be effective and efficient. So, for example, if an internal magazine is an appropriate medium, choices have to be made on the number of colours, quality of paper, frequency of publication, and so on. A full-colour, glossy, weekly magazine may be desirable, but would it be effective and efficient? On the other hand, a single-colour publication on cheap paper, issued once a quarter, may fail to make employees feel important or be frequent enough to be meaningful.

There are more difficult decisions to be made requiring knowledge of media (see Chapter 16). Email distribution of press releases is cheap, but of variable effect. Writing and negotiating exclusives with media outlets is time intensive and expensive, but the effects may be more powerful. Deciding on what is the most effective and efficient solution will depend on the public relations problem.

If budgets are restricted, it is important to think creatively about how a similar result can be obtained at a fraction of the cost. Joint ventures with complementary organisations, sponsorship and piggyback mailings (i.e. when one mailing such as an annual statement from a bank is used to include other information) should be considered. See Mini case study 10.2.

Sometimes it can be more effective and efficient to spend slightly more money. Run-ons (i.e. additional copies of a part or all of a publication) of a feature can provide a powerful promotional tool. Holding an employee conference off-site may cost more, but may guarantee their attention. Posting an analyst's briefing to other key shareholders may cost a little extra, but it may retain their support.

While not requiring excessive amounts of equipment to support their work, it is important that practitioners have the right technology to ensure quick and easy access to key stakeholders in a manner that is appropriate (Beard 2001).

Consultancy costs

If a public relations consultancy is hired, it is worth noting that consultancy charges vary. Consultancies

---

mini case study 10.2

3D mummy campaign

Being efficient and effective

Sometimes a little lateral thought and creativity can bring additional efficiency to public relations campaigns. Portfolio Communications looked closely at the needs of an existing client to come up with an imaginative and cost-effective campaign.

The 3D mummy

Bringing a 3000-year-old Egyptian mummy to life was an award winning public relations campaign by Portfolio Communications for supercomputing company SGI Silicon Graphics.

Portfolio's brief was to develop a campaign to popularise SGI's 3D visualisation technology, used by car designers, oil engineers and pharmaceutical companies to study large amounts of data in a visual, 3D format. The campaign needed to appeal to a broad set of media to reach the client's target audiences of ABC1 scientists, engineers and managers.

The campaign began by using a planning tool that contains information on all aspects of consumers' lifestyles. This revealed an excellent match between SGI's target audiences and their tendency to visit museums, with 42% of SGI's AB audience having visited a museum within the last 12 months. It also identified the key publications read by this audience, enabling careful targeting of the right publications for the campaign.

Portfolio approached The British Museum to explore ideas for applying the 3D technology to ancient antiquities. The collaboration saw a mummy recreated in 3D, a virtual unwrapping that was not only a world first, but also resulted in very exciting 3000-year-old discoveries.

The *Financial Times* was identified as a primary target publication read by both museum visitors and SGI customers. Armed with this information, Portfolio approached the *Financial Times* with an advance on the story and the campaign was then rolled out across print, broadcast and online media. The coverage achieved was widespread and included the *Financial Times*, *BBC 6 O'clock News*, BBC News 24, CNN and also key science media/programmes such as *Tomorrow's World*, *New Scientist*, Discovery Channel, *National Geographic* Channel and BBC Radio 4's *Material World*.

Above all, the huge success of the public relations campaign showed The British Museum the potential in bringing the 3D mummy to the general public. The Museum went on to purchase SGI technology as part of a public exhibition called *Mummy: the inside story*, which opened to the public in July 2004.

Source: www.portfoliocomms/mummycase.htm

usually invoice fees, implementation costs and expenses. Fees can be charged in two ways. First, *advisory* fees, which cover advice, attending meetings, preparing reports, etc. Often this is billed at a fixed cost per month based on the amount of time spent – a *retainer*. Sometimes it is billed on a project basis. Second, *implementation* fees are charged to undertake the agreed programme of work and are in addition to advisory fees. There is usually a mark-up fee on bought in services such as print and photography where the consultancy bears the legal responsibility to deliver as contracted. The UK Public Relations Consultancy Association recommends a mark-up of 17.65% to cover things such as indemnity insurance. Value added tax (VAT) or other taxes may also be payable unless the consultancy is below a certain size.

It is important that planners maintain a careful watch on resources. It is a sign of good management if they are efficient and look for value-for-money solutions wherever possible. As an employee or consultant they will be judged on their ability to manage resources as well as being judged on programme effectiveness. Unfortunately, the creative services industry (of which public relations is part) is not well known for its performance in this area (Maconomy Report 2004).

Evaluation and review

Evaluation

Chapter 11 goes into detail about evaluation, but it is important to cover some basic principles here. Public relations is like any other business function. It is vital to know whether the planned programme has done what it set out to do and, if not, why not.

It needs to be stressed that evaluation is an ongoing process and should be considered at the objective-setting stage: it does not just happen at the end of the programme. All the planning approaches emphasise the importance of ongoing monitoring. Throughout its duration, practitioners will be regularly checking to see if the programme is on track. So, for example, media coverage will be evaluated monthly to see if the selected media are using the material supplied (e.g. feature articles or press releases) and to judge how they are using it.

When the programme is complete it will need to be evaluated to discover whether it has met its overall objectives. Sometimes that is relatively easy. For example, if the objective was to achieve a change in legislation and that has happened, then clearly it was successful. Sometimes the situation is rather more complicated. If the plan is to change societal attitudes towards people who have mental health

problems, for example, it will take a long time: different publics will require different amounts and types of communicative effort; as a result the evaluation programme will need to be much more sophisticated and long term, employing formal social scientific research methods (see Chapter 11 for more detail).

Evaluation focuses effort, demonstrates effectiveness and efficiency and encourages good management and accountability. However, a recent survey undertaken by Metrica Research Ltd on behalf of the UK CIPR and the Communications Directors Forum (IPR 2004) found that only 55% of respondents from private organisations undertook systematic evaluation research, although almost all those in the public sector did.

There are a number of principles that can help to make evaluation easier:

- Setting SMART objectives: if objectives are clear and measurable, then judging whether they have been achieved is relatively easy.
- Building in evaluation from the start: if objectives are set with evaluation in mind, the task is simpler.
- Agreeing measurement criteria with whoever will be judging success.
- Evaluating and monitoring as the programme progresses: using ongoing monitoring as a management information tool; examining tactics and channels if things are not developing as the planner intends; revising the strategy if this fails.
- Taking an objective and a scientific approach: the requirement to provide facts and figures about the programme means that the planner may need training in research methods or to employ specialists who are.
- Evaluating processes: the planner needs to make sure they are *managing* the programme well, within budget and to timescales.
- Establishing open and transparent monitoring processes, through, for example, monthly review reports.

Evaluation is contentious among public relations practitioners. Fortunately, the UK Chartered Institute of Public Relations has produced a number of guides or toolkits that can help, but there is still some distance to go in agreeing a common standard. Recent work in America, published by the Institute for Public Relations in Florida, is focusing less on objective setting as the basis for evaluation and more on measuring the quality of relationships. Grunig and Hon's (1999) guide to measuring the quality of relationships indicates that judgements should be made on six key criteria; control, mutuality, trust, satisfaction, commitment, and exchange and commercial relationship. (For more on this, see Chapter 11.)

The value of research: BT's 'Am I Listening?' campaign

BT's award winning 'Am I Listening?' campaign, launched in 2002, illustrates how correctly targeted and implemented research can help to define and evaluate a social marketing campaign.

In 2001, MORI research revealed that BT's CSR reputation had hit a plateau. As a leading CSR practitioner, the group embarked on a research and consultation process to help improve their reputation. The process began with an assessment of CSR perceptions and went on to identify a key social issue that has subsequently underpinned every strand of the campaign.

Key research was initially used to define the campaign:

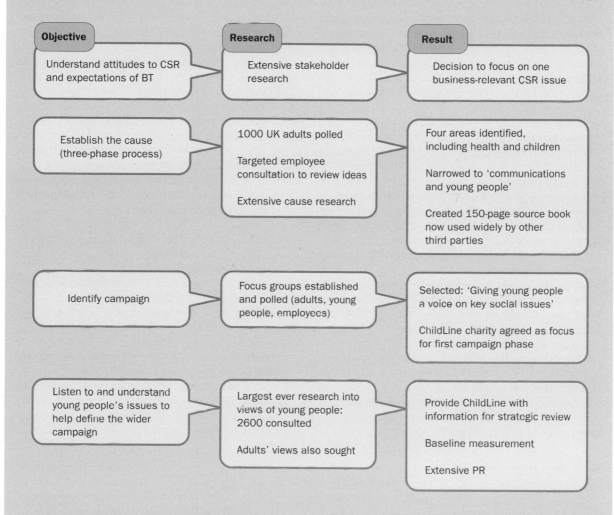

Objective	Research	Result
Understand attitudes to CSR and expectations of BT	Extensive stakeholder research	Decision to focus on one business-relevant CSR issue
Establish the cause (three-phase process)	1000 UK adults polled Targeted employee consultation to review ideas Extensive cause research	Four areas identified, including health and children Narrowed to 'communications and young people' Created 150-page source book now used widely by other third parties
Identify campaign	Focus groups established and polled (adults, young people, employees)	Selected: 'Giving young people a voice on key social issues' ChildLine charity agreed as focus for first campaign phase
Listen to and understand young people's issues to help define the wider campaign	Largest ever research into views of young people: 2600 consulted Adults' views also sought	Provide ChildLine with information for strategic review Baseline measurement Extensive PR

The early consumer research showed that companies should focus on areas where their role would be instantly understood and in line with the business. In the case of BT, this meant focusing on its core business area of communications.

In terms of the issues of concern to BT's own customer base, research revealed a number of issues such as health, homelessness and young people. BT used this information and the previous research, as well as agreed critical success factors, to give a broad theme for a campaign around 'young people' and 'communications'.

BT then embarked on a phase of desktop research to explore possibilities. The source book was created and contains information on over 40 organisations active with young people and communications: existing research on young people's views about this subject, research from organisations about how to include young people in consultation, information on children's rights and other campaigns in the area.

This phase revealed: that there was an increasing but disparate amount of activity in this area; that this issue was high on the government agenda (and indeed international agenda); that there was little corporate activity in this area. BT spoke to a number of key organisations including the UK Youth Parliament in this phase of research and identified a campaign theme of helping give young people a voice.

▶

case study 10.1 (continued)

In developing a strategy for the campaign, it became clear when BT went to consumer and employee groups that the wide concept of the campaign was hard to grasp. The example of ChildLine as a potential charity partner was then used and this had instant recognition and approval by the majority.

BT made a strategic decision that while the campaign's long-term aim was to give young people a voice, they should start where the need is the greatest, with those children who desperately need to be listened to.

This concept tested well among consumer and employee groups. There has long been a link with this charity and it is very much in line with what BT is all about. In addition could easily make the leap from ChildLine to wider issues.

BT commissioned research into the views of young people in order to provide a baseline measure, to provide information to shape the campaign and to provide a platform for raising awareness on the issues. The key findings established that the majority of children and young people in the UK believe that their voices are not being heard and acted on. Adult opinion appears to back this up. Some 83% of adults say that it is very important to listen to children and young people, but only 57% agree that they do listen and act on what they hear. Significantly, the research also highlighted what happens when young people feel they are not listened to and what could happen if adults did listen more. The findings identified some marked differences between the things that young people want to speak out about and the issues that adults think young people are interested in. The research showed that young people would like to be 'active citizens' and speak out on how to run schools, how to improve their local services and how the police should deal with their age group.

The research launch was over-subscribed by important figures active in children's issues. Attendees included three MPs and three peers and selected representatives from health and education bodies, the police and key players in children's issues. Several proactive requests for meetings/shared work with BT were received. Media coverage was extensive, including *BBC Breakfast*, Channel 5 and the *Mirror*, as well as more than 187 regional radio and TV stations, with a circulation of 52 million.

BT have used the contacts made and the issues raised to form an ongoing part of the campaign. For example, BT invited the UK Youth Parliament to be part of the campaign steering group and have established a partnership with them focusing on the wider remit of the campaign; currently a series of round tables is being organised, designed to ensure that young people have their voices heard by opinion formers such as police, doctors and education specialists. BT is now in its second year of research. Case studies are being produced for a publication of examples of how young people are getting their voices heard on issues that are important to them.

The initial research also helped BT to define their campaign strategy and facilitated:

■ Helping ChildLine reach its goal of answering more calls through fundraising and sharing core skills and technical expertise.
■ Developing a programme of listening to young people through research and consultation.
■ Reviewing BT's own policies and procedures for communicating with young people.
■ Raising awareness of the issue and the benefits of listening to children and young people through a series of events/activities and media platforms.
■ Creating projects that will demonstrate the benefits gained when the voices of young people are heard.
■ Ensuring that the campaign becomes a catalyst for coordinated action with organisations that share

| BT customer satisfaction survey (largest in UK corporate history) | Replies encouraged with a £1 contribution to ChildLine for every return | Over 1.3 million responses – a rate of nearly 7% – three times expected (£1.3 million raised for ChildLine)

22% identified ChildLine tie-in as key to them returning the survey

Other BT businesses have used this model to capture research |

| 'Seen and Heard' with the UK Youth Parliament – identifying young people who are making a difference | Young people carried out research to find other young people making a difference | Highly successful publication, with second edition due this year

Potential of creating awards |

▶

case study 10.1 (continued)

BT's goal and working with children and young people to lobby organisations and institutions to listen.

Research continues to be a key campaign tool. Highlights include:

In addition to being used directly as a campaign tool, the research keeps the campaign aligned with the views of young people. It monitors employee awareness and involvement, gauges the impact had by opinion formers and is used to evaluate improvement in BT's CSR reputation.

This multifaceted approach to research has defined BT's award-winning campaign from the outset and continues to guide its ongoing development.

For more information, visit www.bt.com/listening

Review

While evaluation is both an ongoing and end-of-campaign process, a thorough review of all public relations activity should be undertaken regularly, but on a less frequent basis, every 12 months or so. As part of this, the external and internal environment should be surveyed systematically to ensure that all issues have been captured and any new ones accommodated. Campaign strategies should be tested to see if they are still entirely appropriate. Certainly tactics should be reviewed to see if they need refreshing with any new creative input and to ensure that they are addressing the needs of the target publics.

Sometimes new internal or external issues or factors force a major review. For example: new regulations may be introduced by government; the organisation may have merged with another organisation; the chief executive may have retired; a well-organised pressure group may be raising important issues that require changes to the way the organisation operates; or there may be large budget cuts.

Where a major review is required, it is important to take a holistic approach. Programmes always need to be dynamic and flexible enough to embrace opportunities and challenges, but sometime a fundamental reappraisal has to take place. If that is the case, all the stages in the planning process outlined in this chapter need to be taken again. It may be time consuming and demanding, but having done it the planner can be assured that they will have built the foundation for success. (See case study 10.1.)

Summary

This chapter has sought to show that *planning* communication is critical to public relations success. Successful public relations programmes do not just happen. Professional communicators plan. Planning puts them in control. It puts order and purpose into a busy and potentially chaotic and reactive working life. Seeing a planned public relations programme come to life is exciting and rewarding. It also clearly demonstrates to organisational peers and employers that public relations can make a real, measurable difference.

Bibliography

Beard, M. (2001). *Running a Public Relations Department*, 2nd edition. London: Kogan Page.

Cutlip, S.M., A.H. Center and G.M. Broom (2000). *Effective Public Relations*, 8th edition. Upper Saddle River, NJ: Prentice Hall International.

Davis, A. (2004). *Mastering Public Relations*. London: Palgrave.

Freeman, R.E. (1984). *Strategic Management: A stakeholder approach*. Boston: Pitman.

Gregory, A. (2000). *Planning and Managing Public Relations Campaigns*, 2nd edition. London: Kogan Page.

Gregory, A. (2004). 'Scope and structure of public relations: A technology-driven view'. *Public Relations Review* 3(30): 245–254.

Gregory A. and L. Edwards (2004). 'Patterns of PR: Public relations management among Britain's "most admired" companies'. Report for Eloqui Public Relations, Leeds Metropolitan University.

Grunig, J.E. (1994). 'A situational theory of public: Conceptual history, recent challenges and new research'. Paper presented at the International Public Relations Research Symposium, Lake Bled, Slovenia.

Grunig, J.E. and L.C. Hon (1999). 'Guidelines for measuring relationships in public relations'. www.instituteforpr.com/measurement_and_evaluation.pht marticle_id= 1999=1999_guid_measure_relationship, accessed 15 July 2004.

Grunig, G.E. and T. Hunt (1984). *Managing Public Relations*. New York: Holt, Rinehart & Winston.

Grunig, J.E. and F.C. Repper (1992). 'Strategic management, publics and issues' in *Excellence in Public Relations and Communication Management*. J.E. Grunig (ed.). Hillsdale NJ: Lawrence Erlbaum Associates.

Grunig, J.E., L.A. Grunig and D.M. Dozier (2002). *Excellent Public Relations and Effective Organizations*. Mahwah, NJ: Lawrence Erlbaum Associates.

Heath, R.L. (2000). 'Shifting foundations: Public relations as relationship building' in *Handbook of Public Relations*. R.L. Heath (ed.). Thousand Oaks, CA: Sage.

IPR (2004). 'Best practice in the measurement and reporting of PR and ROI. www.ipr.org.uk/direct/news/roi_fullreport.pdf, accessed 15 July 2004.

Johnson, G. and K. Scholes (2002). *Exploring Corporate Strategy*, 6th edition. London: Pearson Education.

Lerbinger, O. (1972). *Designs for Persuasive Communication*. Englewood Cliffs, NJ: Prentice Hall.

Maconomy (2004). Agency Profit Watch Survey. London: Maconomy.

Marston, J.E. (1979). *Modern Public Relations*. New York: McGraw-Hill.

McElreath, M.P. (1997). *Managing Systematic and Ethical Public Relations Campaigns*. 2nd edition. Madison, WI: Brown and Benchmark.

Mendelow, A. (1991) Proceedings of 2nd International Conference on Information Systems. Cambridge, Mass, cited in *Exploring Corporate Strategy*, G. Johnson and K. Scholes, 2002.

MORI (2004). Corporate Social Responsibility Annual Report. London: MORI.

Mullins, L.J. (1989). *Management and Organizational Behaviour*, 2nd edition. London: Pitman.

Steyn, B. and G. Puth (2000). *Corporate Communication Strategy*. Sandown: Heinemann.

Windahl, S. and B. Signitzer (with J.E. Olson) (1992). *Using Communication Theory*. London: Sage.

CHAPTER 11
Public relations research and evaluation

By the end of this chapter you should be able to:

- identify the role of research and evaluation in public relations practice
- define and describe both quantitative and qualitative research approaches
- apply relevant research methods
- understand the different theoretical and practical approaches to evaluation in public relations.

Structure

- Context of research in public relations
- Designing research
- Qualitative vs quantitative research
- Research methods
- Designing research instruments
- Research applications
- Evaluation

Introduction

Research plays a crucial role for many different reasons in public relations. First, it is an integral part of the public relations planning process. Without research it is difficult to set communication objectives, identify publics or develop messages. Second, research is also undertaken to evaluate public relations efforts. Evaluation has been one of the biggest and most talked about issues over many years for the entire public relations industry. Evaluation helps practitioners understand and improve programme effectiveness through systematic measurement and proves the value of public relations efforts to clients, management or other disciplines, such as marketing or integrated communications.

Research and evaluation can also reveal a lot about the current state of public relations practice as well as contribute to the development of the public relations theoretical knowledge base. Research findings have business benefits too and can facilitate attempts to show how public relations can improve the bottom line. This chapter will explore the research process, the most commonly used research methods in public relations and the theory and practice of evaluation. The principles of research approaches and methods would fill a book, therefore in this chapter only the basic principles will be discussed.

Context of research in public relations

Academic research aims to generate theories and models, to describe and analyse trends in public relations. Academic journals, such as the *Journal of Public Relations Research* or *Public Relations Review*, are concerned with theory building and are among the major outlets of academic research. Another important contribution comes from students in the form of undergraduate and postgraduate dissertations and theses as part of a degree. The ability to understand and carry out systematic research highlights the importance of education. Practitioners with a degree in higher education are better equipped in the complex world of research as opposed to those who use only 'seat-of-the-pants' methods.

Research can have different purposes and origins. The primary purpose of research is to contribute to the existing body of knowledge in the field of public relations, even if such research does not deal with the real problems of practice ('basic research'). But the purpose of research is also to answer questions that come out of practice or are imposed by a client ('applied research').

Nevertheless, if we use the term 'research' – either basic or applied – we always mean 'scientific' research, not 'informal, 'quick and dirty' or 'everyday-life research' – as it is often understood by practitioners. For example, Lindenmann (1990) reports results of a survey among public relations professionals in which about 70% of the respondents thought that most research on the subject was informal rather than scientific (Cutlip et al. 2000; Gregory 2000).

In contrast to scientific research, informal research is based on subjective intuition or on the 'authority' of knowledge or 'tenacity', which refers to sticking to a practice because it has always been like that (Kerlinger 1986). It is subjective if information is gathered in an unsystematic way by talking to a couple of people, looking at guidelines ('Five Steps to do World Class Public Relations') or just based on feelings.

Other examples of public relations practice based on informal research are:

- a practice might be considered as best practice because the senior manager of a well-known consultancy declares it to be the latest trend in public relations (based on 'authority')
- an advisory committee, panel or board recommends it (based on 'authority')
- an organisation writes news releases in the same style they have used for the last 10 years ('tenacity' – 'it is the right way because we have always done it like that').

Scientific research is systematic and objective: it follows distinct steps and uses appropriate research design. In doing public relations research we have to guide research by:

- defining the research problem (what to research)
- choosing a general research approach (qualitative or quantitative)
- deciding on research strategy (primary or secondary research)
- selecting the research method (survey, content analysis, focus group, etc.)
- deciding on the research instruments (questions in a questionnaire or categories in a content analysis)
- analysing the data (e.g. Wimmer and Dominick 2003).

See Think about 11.1

Research and evaluation in public relations planning and management

Research is an integrated part of public relations management, which means that it should be included in each step of the public relations planning process. This might sound controversial, since models such as the RACE model – **r**esearch, **a**ction, **co**mmunication and **e**valuation – suggest that research is only undertaken in the first and the last steps: 'research' and 'evaluation'. Nevertheless, this does not mean that research is limited to these steps; it is

think about 11.1 **SWOT and PEST – research or not?**

To identify internal and external environmental factors, SWOT and PEST (or EPISTLE) analyses are often considered to be useful techniques (see Chapter 10). This might be conducted in a meeting in which practitioners of the in-house public relations department gather and do a brainstorming session about the strengths, weaknesses, opportunities and threats of their organisation. But can this be considered as research? SWOT and PEST brainstorms may offer guidelines about what to research but they are not research in themselves. For example, to explore the weaknesses of an organisation, a focus group discussion might be conducted. Only by doing a SWOT or PEST analysis with proper research methods does it become research. Doing a SWOT or PEST analysis by subjective intuition might reveal interesting ideas but is not research.

crucial in each step. The following four points refer to the four stages in the Cutlip et al. (2000) planning process shown in Chapter 10:

- using research to define public relations problems
- using research to assess public relations plans and proposals
- using research during programme implementation
- using research for programme impact.

Using research to define public relations problems

Research findings such as problem definitions or identifying publics are key inputs for programme planning. For example, an organisation might have a bad image in the media and turn to a public relations consultancy to address this problem. The consultancy is very likely to use research to find the reasons for the image problem, before developing a strategy to address it. This process can be defined as *problem definition* and *situation analysis* and should address the following research questions (see Chapter 10 for more detail):

- What are the internal and external environmental factors that affect the organisation?
- Who are the publics?
- What do they know? What do they think about key issues?
- How are public–organisation relationships characterised?
- What media do publics rely on or prefer for information?

Using research to assess public relations plans and proposals

Before implementing a plan, its various elements can be tested through a variety of measures: expert assessment; using checklists as criteria; testing messages in focus group discussions; or in a survey among key publics. Initial identification of publics, messages, strategies or tactics included in the plan might be subject to assessment. The assessment might result in changes in the programme.

Using research during programme implementation

Process research aims at improving programme performance and takes place while the programme is in operation (in process). It is also referred to as *monitoring* or *formative* evaluation. It enables the public relations

practitioner to modify campaign elements, such as messages (too complicated, misunderstood, irrelevant), channels (inappropriate choice for delivering a particular message) or the chosen strategies and tactics. Research during implementation enables the practitioner to make corrections according to circumstances and issues that were not foreseen during the planning process, especially in the case of complex and long-term programmes. It can also document how the programme is being implemented, including the practitioner's own activity, resources allocated or timing of the programme.

Using research for programme impact

Finally, research is done to measure programme impact or effectiveness with respect to goals and objectives. Principles of programme evaluation will be discussed in the second half of the chapter.

Areas of research

Lerbinger (1977) offers a classification that defines areas of public relations research less concerned with the process of programmes. He distinguishes four major categories of public relations research as: environmental monitoring (or scanning); public relations audits; communication audits; and social audits. Table 11.1 identifies these categories of research and defines the scope of each approach.

Designing research

After identifying questions that help assess the initial situation, we have to decide how to research them. This demands a research plan that answers the following questions:

- What types of data are of interest?
- Which research approach should be followed: qualitative or quantitative research?
- Which research methods are appropriate?
- How should the research instruments be designed?

Type of data: primary or secondary research?

Information or data can be gathered in two basic ways: through primary or secondary research. Primary research generates data that are specific for the case under investigation. Primary data are directly retrieved ('in the field') from the research object through empirical research methods – interview,

TABLE 11.1 Categories of research and their scope (*source:* based on Lerbinger 1977: 11–14)

Categories of research	Scope of research
Environmental monitoring (scanning)	Issues and trends in public opinion Issues in mass media Social events which may have significant impact on an organisation Competitor communications analysis
Public relations audit	Assesses an organisation's public relations activities
Communication audits	All forms of internal and external communications are studied to assess their consistency with overall strategy as well as their internal consistency Narrower than a public relations audit
Social audits	Measures an organisation's social performance

focus group, survey, content analysis or observation (Wimmer and Dominick 2003).

Secondary research or 'desk research', in contrast, uses data that have already been gathered, are available through different sources and can be analysed sitting at the desk as opposed to gathering data 'in the field' (Neumann 2001). The term 'secondary' implies that somebody else has already collected this information through primary research and documented the results in various sources. A specific type of secondary research is 'data mining', which is the exploration and analysis of existing data with reference to a new or specific research problem.

Data about size and composition of media audiences such as newspaper readership or television audiences are available to the practitioners and are published regularly. Table 11.2 is an example from *The Guardian*'s media supplement.

Secondary data are available from many different sources like libraries, government records, trade and professional associations, as well as organisational files. The following list includes some of the large UK and European datasets:

- Annual Employment Survey, which covers about 130,000 businesses (www.statistics.gov.uk)
- British Social Attitudes survey (www.natcen.ac.uk)
- Chartered Institute of Public Relations posts useful resources of research on its website (www.cipr.co.uk)
- Eurobarometer, which monitors public opinion in member states on a variety of issues (enlargement, social situation, health, culture, information technology, environment, the euro, defence policy, etc.)
- Eurostat, the Statistical Office of the European Communities

TABLE 11.2 UK national daily newspaper circulation excluding bulks, February 2005 (*source:* adapted from Guardian Unlimited, 1 March 2005, www.media.guardian.co.uk/circulationfigures/tables/0,11554,1437317,00. html Copyright Guardian Newspapers Limited 2005. Data from Audit Bureau of Circulations)

Title	Feb 2005	Feb 2004	% change
Daily Express	887,574	906,738	−2.11
Daily Mail	2,330,665	2,311,849	0.81
Daily Mirror	1,719,743	1,900,250	−9.50
Daily Record	480,417	494,212	−2.79
Daily Star	854,291	909,240	−6.04
Daily Telegraph	855,994	873,380	−1.99
FT	394,892	415,534	−4.97
Guardian	340,499	352,005	−3.27
Independent	227,305	222,799	2.02
Sun	3,273,016	3,397,372	−3.66
Times	638,723	614,610	3.92

activity 11.1

Secondary research

You are commissioned by the Department of Health to design a public relations campaign to raise awareness of obesity in the UK. You are interested in hard facts about this disease. What types of secondary sources would you turn to? Put together a small research report on the topic.

Feedback

Start with the following link: www.official-documents. co.uk.

■ online research services such as LexisNexis (www.lexis-nexis.com)
■ population census, which is held every 10 years (www.census.ac.uk).

Caution must be taken when interpreting and using secondary research findings since they can reflect the views and interests of the sponsoring organisations. (See Activity 11.1)

Starting research

As a first step to start research in Case study 11.1, research questions must be developed. Key questions in the first stage of the planning process are:

1   What do residents know about the service?
2   What do residents think about recycling?
3   Are residents willing to recycle?

A next step is the question of which type of data to use to answer these questions. Primary or secondary

case study 11.1

Research and evaluation: 'Bin There Done That'

The following case study on Westminster City Council's campaign about recycling will be used throughout the rest of the chapter.

Background

The improvement of doorstep recycling formed part of a new Westminster cleansing contract. Recycling was seen as a critical part of the cleansing service. Getting doorstep recycling right was seen as essential for the council to meet government targets by 2010. Large increases to landfill tax and costs of incineration also made the success of the new service vital.

Objectives

■ To change the behaviour of residents to increase take-up of service by one-quarter and thereby recycle a greater proportion of waste – from 30 tonnes per week to 50 tonnes per week
■ To position the authority as the leading recycling authority through raising the City Survey satisfaction rating from 43% to 60% for recycling
■ To increase awareness of recycling service among target audience to drive up usage to help us meet government targets for tonnage of recycled household waste by 2010

Planning and implementation
Audit
Westminster City Council's (WCC) in-house public relations department examined its market extensively before committing to the final campaign. Quantitative research surveying 502 residents in July 2003 found that:

■ 60% of residents did not feel informed about the service
■ 98% said that recycling was important
■ 72% said they would recycle only if the council made it easier first.

To accurately target audience and message, WCC conducted two focus groups of Westminster residents drawn from across the borough in July 2003. One group recycled regularly and one had never recycled.

The focus group research found that there was a shocking lack of knowledge about WCC's recycling service, confusion over what materials could be recycled and an emphatic desire for the process to be made easy.

Two campaigns were market tested to the groups. Both groups unanimously opted for a 'we've made it easy, you make it happen' message.

Strategy
WCC had to vastly improve the information sent to households, providing clear, concise and accurate information about the types of material that could be recycled.

Its communications had to:

Reinforce that the Council had made the service easier (a single bin for all goods) promote two way communications (a helpline and website were introduced) deliver strong messages that were easy to understand.

The Bin There Done That (BTDT) campaign was adopted after trialling a number of alternatives, as it met these criteria. The research had shown that messages must be clear, simple, easy and immediately

▶

case study 11.1 (continued)

recognisable as WCC. The campaign included:

- a two-week teaser campaign (something's coming to your doorstep)
- rollout of service information campaign (ways to recycle)
- advertising campaign (Bin There Done That)
- intensive field marketing follow-up campaign
- follow-through information campaign.

Evaluation and measurement

Evaluation was ongoing. Trained council staff surveyed over 16,000 homes and as a result some new messages were adopted, e.g. how to order replacement bins that neighbours had stolen! Final evaluation compared the council's 2002/3 City Survey conducted by MORI with the 2003/4 MORI City Survey, a specially commissioned populus survey on communication messages and analysis of tonnages and rates of participation.

Results of analysis were then compared against objectives.

- *Objective 1: change behaviour of residents to recycle a greater proportion of their waste – increase from 30 tonnes per week to 50 tonnes per week.* Tonnage for doorstep recycling increased from 30 tonnes per week to 85 tonnes per week.

After seeing the campaign, people were much more likely to recycle: 68% of those aware of the campaign now recycle whereas only 45% who were unaware chose to do so.

Of residents who were aware of the campaign, 73% thought that the council had made recycling easier for them. This is nearly twice as many (40%) as those who had not seen the campaign.

- *Objective 2: position the authority as the leading recycling authority through raising City Survey satisfaction rating from 43% to 60% for recycling.* There was almost a 20% increase in satisfaction rating to 61% for the recycling service (City Survey 2002/3 to 2003/4). The Association of London Government Survey of Londoners 2003 found an increased satisfaction rating for recycling of only 7% across all London boroughs.

The City Survey 2003/4 found that residents felt more strongly about the importance of recycling. Recycling was the fourth most important service. In 2002/3 recycling did not even make an appearance in the list of top 10 services.

Residents also believed that recycling was the second 'elective' (voluntary) service that they most benefited from, behind libraries (53%) – recycling 35%. This shows an increase from 2002/3 of 25% (City Survey 2002/3 to 2003/4).

Of the public that were aware of the campaign, 84% thought it was a good idea to recycle compared with 70% who were unaware of the campaign (December 2003).

- *Objective 3: increase take-up rate of service by one-quarter.* The increase in take-up for the doorstep recycling service has almost trebled – from 4843 participants in May 2003 to 12,572 in December 2003.

Source: www.cipr.co.uk/member_area and Westminster City Council Communication Team

---

research might be conducted. An example of secondary research would be to find and use research data that has been gathered by other city councils in the UK or use data from research in other countries about the acceptance of recycling. Nevertheless, the validity of such data would be questionable since the local situation, awareness and traditions would not have been considered. Therefore it is more appropriate to conduct primary research.

Qualitative vs quantitative research

The question of whether to use qualitative or quantitative research methods is widely discussed in the academic and professional community. However, the answer depends on each research question: *qualitative* approaches are often used to explore areas about which no knowledge exists yet and results are expressed in words ('qualities'); *quantitative* approaches are used to deliver comparable, generalisable results, expressed in numbers ('quantities').

Definition: *Qualitative* research aims to identify and explore in depth phenomena such as reasons, attitudes, etc.

Definition: *Quantitative* research aims to quantify variables such as attitudes or behaviours and points out correlations between them. Results can be generalised which means research that generates findings that can be applied to a wider public or situation.

Qualitative and quantitative research approaches are complementary and should be combined rather than used as alternatives. In research terms this is often

PICTURE 11.1 Research 'in the field': data gathering can take place in a wide range of settings. (*Source:* Jack Sullivan/Alamy.)

council's recycling service, confusion over what materials could be recycled and a huge motivation for the process to be made easy. Especially since the motivation of residents to recycle ('are residents willing to recycle?', 'What might determine their willingness to recycle?') was rather an unexplored issue, it was appropriate to use a qualitative approach. The results of the focus groups could then be used in the survey that gave a representative overview of what Westminster residents know and think.

Research methods

The main research methods used in public relations research and evaluation are:

- qualitative: intensive or in-depth interviews and focus groups
- quantitative: surveys and content analysis.

In the case of the BTDT campaign, focus groups or surveys were used as methods to research knowledge, attitudes and motivation of Westminster residents to behave in a certain way. But it is not always so obvious what the most appropriate method is, as Think about 11.2 (overleaf) demonstrates.

described as the *mixed method* approach (Lindlof and Bryan 2002). Mini case study 11.1 gives an example.

Qualitative and quantitative approaches both have advantages and disadvantages, which are summarised in Table 11.3 (overleaf).

Westminster City Council's BTDT campaign is another good example of how qualitative and quantitative methods can be combined. The focus groups found that there was a lack of knowledge about the

Intensive or in-depth interviews

Intensive interviews are a specific type of personal interview. Unlike surveys, they do not attempt to generalise answers. So when is it appropriate to use intensive interviews? Their main purpose is to explore attitudes and attitude-relevant contexts. The biggest advantage is the wealth of detail that they can provide. On the negative side, they are sensitive to interviewer bias. The answers might easily be influenced by the behaviour of the interviewer, so well-trained

mini case study 11.1

Qualitative or quantitative?

The Inland Revenue (UK tax-gathering authority) is a public sector organisation that wants to research its image among employees, prior to developing a corporate identity programme. Since this is the first time that the internal image has been researched, not a lot of information is available about issues that are relevant in the eyes of the employees. Therefore, the first step might be to hold focus group discussions as a

qualitative approach. The goal is to explore relevant features of the image. The second step would be to analyse the results of these focus groups to develop standardised questionnaires that are then distributed to all employees. The features of the image that were explored in the focus groups are assessed by the employees and provide a general view of the employees of their organisation.

TABLE 11.3 Advantages and disadvantages of quantitative and qualitative research techniques (*source:* adapted from Neumann 2003: 150)

	Potential advantages	Potential disadvantages
Quantitative approaches	Generate comparable results Results can be generalised Can be guided by less experienced researchers (e.g. interviewers) Higher acceptance by clients	Quantitative methods can only find out what is put in through prepared questions or categories Can guide respondents into a rather irrelevant direction Do not allow deeper analysis of reasons
Qualitative approaches	Provide insights into causes and motivations Explore information that is completely unknown or unpredicted	Time consuming and demand financial resources Demand qualified researchers Limited generalisation Results are influenced by researcher

interviewers are needed to minimise the bias. Intensive interviews are characterised by:

- generally *smaller samples* of interviewees
- *open questions* that probe the reasons *why* respondents give specific answers: they elaborate on data concerning respondents' opinions, values, motivations, experiences and feelings
- *customised* – or reactive – to individual respondents in so far as the order and/or wording of questions can be changed, or new questions added, during the interview depending on the answers given
- *non-verbal behaviour* of respondents is recorded and contributes to the results.

Focus groups

Focus group or group interviewing is like an intensive interview, with 6 to 10 respondents who interact with each other. Focus groups generate qualitative data. The interviewer plays the role of a moderator leading the respondents in a relatively free discussion about the topic. The interactions between the group members create a dynamic environment that gives respondents additional motivation to elaborate on their attitudes, experiences and feelings.

Main disadvantages are that groups can become dominated by a self-appointed group leader who monopolises the conversation. Focus groups depend heavily on the skills of the moderator who must know when to intervene to stop respondents from discussing irrelevant topics, probe for further information and ensure all respondents are involved in the discussion.

In the BTDT campaign, focus groups were not only conducted to explore attitudes of the residents; they were also used to test messages for the campaign. The use of focus groups helped the public

---

think about 11.2 **Evaluation of a news release**

After releasing a news story about new online services on behalf of its client, a large telecommunications provider, ABC public relations consultancy discusses how to evaluate the outcome of this activity. Should it:

- measure the media coverage by monitoring media (newspapers, radio, TV, www) and analysing circulation numbers and readership figures using available media data, or
- conduct a representative survey among relevant publics?

Feedback With the first suggestion, it can be very precisely tracked in which media the news has come up. Additionally, the media data provide figures on the number and type of reader (age, gender, education, income, etc.) who might have seen or read the news. But this is already the weak point in the evaluation: it remains unclear whether they have read the news, what they think about the news and whether they can recall the news.

Using a survey, in contrast, gives clear evidence of what people know and think about the online services of the telecommunications provider. But it remains rather vague as to where they have obtained their information. It might be that the information originates from sources other than the media coverage of the news release.

How to conduct a focus group study

There are 12 basic steps in focus group research:

1 Is a focus group study really appropriate?
2 Define the problem.
3 Decide who will moderate.
4 Determine the number of groups necessary.
5 Design a screening questionnaire for selecting a sample.
6 Recruit participants according to screening results.
7 Develop question guideline for the moderator.
8 Brief the moderator.
9 Select and brief focus group observers.
10 Prepare facilities and check catering arrangements.
11 Conduct the session.
12 Analyse the data and report findings.

Source: Broom and Dozier 1990; Wimmer and Dominick 2003

relations department to understand that the main criterion for residents doing recycling is convenience. If a survey were used as the only method, it could have provided misleading results. A survey would have measured positive attitudes of the residents about recycling. But why do only few practise it? The focus groups could explore and explain in-depth the gap between attitudes and behaviour: the inconvenience of recycling.

Box 11.1 gives some rules for conducting a focus group study.

Surveys

The survey among Westminster residents illustrates the kind of decisions that have to be taken when conducting a survey.

Which type of survey should be conducted?

Table 11.4 (overleaf) details the types of survey and their advantages and disadvantages. (See Activities 11.2 and 11.3.)

How many people should be interviewed and how will you select them?

Since most research cannot reach all members of a population (all units of consideration to be researched), a sample has to be drawn. There are various sampling designs that can be used to select the units of research. For example, in our case of the BTDT campaign, the population consists of all residents of Westminster from which a sample is drawn.

The sample consists of 502 residents, which is a sufficient sample size to ensure validity of the results.

What do you want to measure?

Before developing a survey questionnaire, you need to decide what you want to measure. A basic distinction is to research awareness/knowledge/beliefs (cognitions), attitudes, behaviour.

In the BTDT campaign the key research questions cover these aspects:

■ What do residents know about the service (knowledge)?
■ What do residents think about recycling (attitudes)?
■ Are residents willing to recycle or what prevents them from recycling (motivation/behaviour)?

What are you going to ask?

The next step is to develop 'instruments for measurement', that is, framing the right kind of questions. The key research questions in the BTDT campaign indicate

activity 11.2

Types of survey

In the BTDT campaign the sample consisted of 502 residents. But which type of survey would be the most appropriate method to collect data?
Consider and write down:

■ How will respondents be reached?
■ What might be the response rate?
■ Think about cost and time effectiveness, too.

TABLE 11.4 Types of survey

Method	Requirements	Advantages	Disadvantages
Mail survey – self-administered questionnaires (self-explanatory)	Mailing list Reply envelope Cover letter (separate) Incentives Follow-up mailings	Anonymity Specific mailing lists available Low cost, little time to prepare and conduct Respondent convenience	Response rate Slow data collection Only standardised questions Response: only motivated respondents – not representative
Telephone survey	Telephone numbers Interviewers Training and instruction (manner of speaking, what to say . . .)	Interviewers can clarify questions Speed, costs Control, probing complex answers High response rates, completeness of questionnaires	Reach of respondents Limited use of scales, visual materials
Personal interview (face to face)	Interviewers and training	Interviewers can clarify questions Use of scales and visual materials	No anonymity Expensive Interviewer bias
Online surveys	Website Email list	Inexpensive Respondent convenience Anonymity	No control who is contacted Only internet users Not representative Low response rates

'what' is to be measured, but they are not yet the questions that are used in a questionnaire. In general, the objects of research – in this case, knowledge, attitudes, behaviour – can be measured with various types of question and scale. Developing questions means to develop instruments that measure knowledge, attitude, etc. These concepts are *operationalised* through the questions (Wimmer and Dominick 2003).

> **Definition:** *Operationalisation* of a concept (knowledge, attitudes, behaviour) means showing how this concept is to be measured.

Are you going to measure attitudes or images?

Images or attitudes can be measured using a variety of different techniques and instruments. Instruments are the specific questions or scales with which attitudes are measured. The next section gives an idea about the instruments that can be used depending on the object (e.g. attitudes about fast food), the respondents and the situation. The instruments are either quantitative, with standardised scales, or qualitative, going more in depth and providing insights that are not generated by quantitative approaches.

Further instruments can be classified as direct or indirect. Direct instruments clearly reveal the purpose of the questioning, for example, 'Do you intend to recycle?' Indirect instruments are used when there is the danger that respondents might answer in a 'socially acceptable' manner or follow existing stereotypes in their answers, instead of revealing their real attitudes.

An example of the choice of the instrument influencing the results are surveys about fast food. Fast foods and restaurants serving them seem to have a rather negative 'image' among university students, according to many surveys, if they are directly asked about their attitudes. There seems, however, to be a gap between the results of surveys and the behaviour of the students, who constitute one of the biggest customer groups of fast food restaurants.

example 11.1

Item pairs

Please assess the Royal Mail according to the following terms:

Boring .... Interesting

Honest .... Dishonest

Designing research instruments

Quantitative instruments to measure attitudes or images

Semantic differential (Example 11.1) is one of the most frequently used instruments in image measurement. It consists of pairs of contrary items by which the object of interest (organisations, persons, advertisements, issues, etc.) is evaluated. This approach draws on semiotics, an approach to the study of words, signs and symbols, which discovered that people tend to group objects in simple either/or categories. Cars, councils, celebrities, baked beans can all be assessed by asking people whether they think these things are either luxury or basic goods, for example. You can go on to ask if they are old/young, male/female, etc. These either/or polarities can be either descriptive-direct or metaphoric-indirect. Item pairs that are descriptive-direct are *denotative*, that is, they relate to the perceived functions of the subject. Metaphoric-indirect items are *connotative*, that is, they relate to the emotional or mental associations of the item being researched. It is useful to use either denotative or connotative items. For example, if you evaluate a car, then item pairs such as 'slow–fast', 'expensive–good value' are denotative. Pairs like 'female–male' or 'warm– cold' are rather connotative.

> **Definition:** *Denotative* meaning of a word is its dictionary definition. It refers to the specific, generally agreed on definition. *Connotative* meaning of a word refers to all the associations connected with the word (feelings, attitudes) that go beyond the denotative meaning (Neumann 2003).

The advantage of semantic differentials is that it is a highly standardised instrument with which different objects can easily be compared. A disadvantage is that it might consist of items that are rather irrelevant to the respondent's attitude about an object. If the research object is new and unexplored, then the relevance of items can be unclear.

Likert scales (Example 11.2) ask how far a respondent agrees or disagrees with statements about an object. The statements should cover all relevant facets of the research object. Nevertheless, it remains open as to how relevant statements are for respondents in their attitude about the object.

In *rank ordering* (Example 11.3, overleaf), respondents have to place research objects – often listed on separate cards – in order from best to worst. This can be combined with open, qualitative questions that ask what they most like/dislike about the objects. This explores which features are relevant for their assessment. A problem with rank orders is that each object is only evaluated

example 11.2

Likert scale

How much do you agree with the following statement: 'BT is a progressive corporation'?
Please tick one box.

Strongly agree	Agree	Neither agree nor disagree	Disagree	Strongly disagree

example 11.3

Rank order

In front of you there are 10 cards with telecommunications providers. Please put the card with the telecommunications provider you like the most in the first position, the one you like the second best in the second position, and so on.

in comparison with the others but not on an absolute scale. An advantage is that the object is assessed as a whole entity and leaves it to the respondents to decide which features determine their opinion.

The *Kunin scale* (Example 11.4) is an example of how to assess objects non-verbally, which is easy for children or elderly people to understand.

Qualitative instruments to measure attitudes or images

Free associations (Example 11.5) are considered to be a qualitative instrument because the respondents are not guided by existing categories for their answers.

If there is a danger that respondents might not admit or even express their real opinions, it makes sense to use a *projective question technique* (Example 11.6). The respondent is asked to answer a question as if replying for somebody else. The respondent projects their real answers into that person.

In the *balloon test* (Example 11.7) as a *specific projective instrument* the respondent gets a drawing with two people and is asked to fill in the empty 'balloon'. The idea is that the respondent projects their thoughts into the person with the empty balloon.

Box 11.2 on page 223 provides an example of measuring relationships by surveys.

example 11.4

Kunin scale

Please mark how much you like Virgin Trains.

example 11.5

Free associations

Question: Please write down everything that comes into your mind when you hear the words 'Royal Mail'.
Possible answers: post, expensive, conservative, reliable, etc.
Additionally, the respondents might be asked in a follow-up question to assess all their answers and state whether they consider them 'positive (+)', 'neutral (0)' or 'negative (−)'. This avoids subjective misinterpretations of the researcher:
Post (0), expensive (−), conservative (0), reliable (+)

example 11.6

Projective question

In your opinion, what do other people think about the Royal Mail?

Media content analysis

Media monitoring, collecting and counting press clippings, is widely used in public relations to track publicity. However, collecting data or output is only a first step in conducting a media content analysis. Only the systematic analysis of these materials according to a set of criteria can be considered as content analysis. 'Content analysis is a method to analyse media reality, verbal and visual output (content of newspapers, magazines, radio, television and web) which leads to inferences about the communicators and audience of these contents' (Merten 1995: 15).

Content analysis itself does not directly measure outcomes – for example, the image of an organisation in the mind of the audience – and might only be considered as an indicator of certain effects. Web logs, online newsgroups and chatrooms can be monitored, too. Computer-assisted content analysis uses specific software programs, which analyse frequencies of words or other categories. There are specialist research firms that offer services in this field (e.g. www.romeike.com, www.waymaker.co.uk).

In general, a content analysis is conducted in eight discrete steps (Wimmer and Dominick 2003).

Formulate the research question

Table 11.5 (overleaf) presents an overview of typical questions that can be answered by content analysis. The particular research question determines the further steps in the process of a content analysis.

Define a population

By defining the time period and the types of media (population) that will be analysed, the researcher sets the frame for the investigation.

example 11.7

Balloon test

'I travel regularly with Virgin Trains'

TABLE 11.5   Examples of questions researched through content analysis (*source:* adapted from Merten and Wienand 2004: 5)

Media	Issues and actors	Image
Which media/journalists dominate the media coverage? How do media report about the organisation? (positive/negative/neutral) How many and which audiences are reached?	Which issues dominate the media coverage? Which actors dominate the media coverage? In the frame of which issues does the organisation and its representatives appear?	Which image is portrayed? Which factors dominate the image? How is the organisation positioned in its sector? What do competitors do?

For example, a content analysis might compare how fast food providers are covered in mass media. Since the general public might be considered a relevant audience, daily newspapers are defined as the population in question.

Select a sample from the population

As stated above, it is not possible to survey all members of a population all the time. So a smaller number of outlets and a specific period of time must be selected.

For example, the time period of the last half-year is the period in which the media coverage is analysed. Smaller newspapers reach fewer readers, so only the top five daily newspapers with the highest readership are selected.

Select and define a unit of analysis

There needs to be agreement about what exactly is being counted in the analysis. For example, each newspaper article in which the name of a fast food provider or the term 'fast food' is mentioned is a unit of analysis (in other words, not every mention of hamburger or of chips is counted).

Construct the categories of content to be analysed

The categories are determined by the research questions. In our example, this might be the rating of an article as 'positive/negative/neutral', the topic of the article, the sources quoted, etc. It is important to define indicators which determine what 'positive/negative/neutral' mean.

Establish a quantification system

The category system used to classify the media content is the actual measurement instrument. For each category, subcategories must be created. An example of a category might be 'corporate social responsibility'.

Subcategories could be 'donations to charity', 'employee volunteering' and 'environmental policy'. The subcategories should be exhaustive, in that they cover all aspects of 'corporate social responsibility' that occur in the articles, and exclusive, which means that they should not overlap or denote the same.

Train coders and conduct a pilot study

To obtain valid results, different researchers, or coders, must assess the same article in the same way. A pilot study, or trial run, can point out weaknesses in the categories or instructions for the coders. In practice, this will involve analysing a small sample of articles to test the instrument – the category system.

Code the content according to established definitions

Finally, all sample articles have to be assessed for each category and given a number for that assessment. The assessments are determined by the definitions associated with each category. For example, a mention of 'donations to charity' as a subcategory of 'corporate social responsibility' might be a given a number code 1 to denote 'donations to charity'. Numbering like this helps with the data analysis, particularly across a wide range of categories and subcategories.

Research applications

Internet as a research tool and object

The internet has become an increasingly important research object as well as a research tool. Research objects can be issues which are discussed in web logs or chatrooms. Another increasingly relevant issue is the measurement of the chatter and discussion about an organisation in cyberspace, which can be used to help understand an organisation's image or reputation. The same criteria used in analysing print and broadcast articles can be applied when analysing postings on the internet, which is referred to as cyberspace analysis (Lindenmann 1997). Another output measure of cyberspace might be a review and analysis of website traffic patterns. For example, some of the variables that ought to be considered when designing and carrying out cyberspace analysis might include examining the requests for a file of website visitors, a review of click-throughs or flash-click streams, an assessment of home page visits, domain tracking and analysis and assessment of bytes transferred, a review of time spent per page, traffic times, browsers used and the number of people filling out and returning feedback forms (Lindenmann 1997).

The internet also offers new opportunities to conduct research in online focus groups, online interviews or online surveys. Online focus groups can be conducted in 'real time' or in 'non-real time', or using a combination of both. It allows access to populations in disparate places and is highly cost effective. Nevertheless, the problem of participant verification (who is recruited as participant through the internet) remains a problem in all forms of online research techniques (Mann and Stewart 2000).

Identifying publics: social network analysis

One tool that is used to identify relevant publics and opinion leaders and to understand the communication flow and lines of influences within and between groups of people is social network analysis (SNA) (Scott 2000). Social network analysis is the mapping and measuring of relationships and flows between people, groups or organisations. It can be used for external and internal analysis (organisational network analysis) of relationships. But like a PEST (or EPISTLE) or SWOT analysis, the social network analysis is not a method itself. The network has to be explored, for example, through observation or interviews.

To understand the network, the location and context of the actors (people whose relationships are being observed) has to be evaluated first. For example, with whom does an actor interact? How many connections does an actor have? Is a person central in a network or peripheral? Is a person connected to well-connected or poorly connected people?

Of further interest in network analysis is:

- structural equivalence: which actors play similar roles in the network
- cluster analysis: find cliques and densely connected clusters
- structural holes: find areas of no connection between actors that could be used for communication
- E/I ratio: find which groups in the network are open or closed to others (Scott 2000).

Communication audit

Communication audits assess the tangible and intangible communications resources of an organisation. A

A typical research project for the study of relationships between an organisation and its publics is Hon and Grunig's (1999) measurement of relationships. So the research object is 'relationships'. Hon and Grunig specify 'successful relationships' as control mutuality, trust, satisfaction, commitment, exchange relationship and communal relationship. The research method is conducting a survey.

In order to measure the concept 'relationship' they operationalise – 'make measurable' – the idea of relationship. They explore the six factors mentioned above by generating a list of statements for each factor, for respondents to agree or disagree with.

For example, the factor 'trust' is measured by statements:

- This organisation treats people like me fairly and justly.
- This organisation can be relied on to keep its promises.
- Whenever this organisation makes an important decision, I know it will be concerned about people like me.
- I feel very confident about this organisation's skills.
- I believe that this organisation takes the opinions of people like me into account when making decisions.

With these statements they conduct a survey among publics who evaluate their relationship with different organisations by how much they agree/disagree with each statement.

Source: Hon and Grunig 1999

very formal and thorough audit may take months to complete. Communication audits examine:

- face-to-face communication
- written communication in the form of letters, memos and internal reports
- communication patterns among individuals, sections and departments
- communication channels and frequency of interaction
- communication content, its clarity and effectiveness
- information needs of individuals, sections or departments
- information technology
- informal communication, particularly as it affects motivation and performance
- non-verbal communication
- communication climate (Hamilton 1987: 4–5).

Evaluation

Importance of evaluation

Evaluation is the evergreen topic of the entire practice and one of the areas where both practitioners and academics have a vast common interest. In the UK, the Chartered Institute of Public Relations has initiated and coordinated research on evaluation and encouraged practitioners to evaluate their efforts in a systematic way by using a variety of methods.

Evaluating public relations activities is essential for many reasons, including accountability, assessment of programme effectiveness and professionalism.

Evaluation is the systematic assessment of the impacts of public relations activities. It a purposeful process, carried out for a specific audience. Audiences include numerous parties that have an interest in the evaluation – the organisation, the public relations practitioners involved, target publics and the evaluators themselves. (Sometimes an external agency, such as a media monitoring company, does media evaluation.) (See Activity 11.4.)

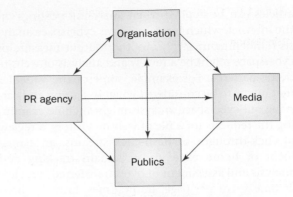

FIGURE 11.1   Actors and their influence

In a typical public relations campaign, the following actors are present: the *organisation*, which can commission a *public relations agency* to work on its behalf to reach and communicate with a variety of *publics* through the *media*. Figure 11.1 visualises the actors and their influences.

Out of these four actors, the emphasis has been on media, and print media evaluation still dominates the field of evaluation. Measuring effects on, and changes in, the targeted publics' knowledge, attitudes and behaviour in the form of outcome is also paramount. During the early 1990s the organisational dimension was emphasised, demonstrating how public relations can add value to achieving organisational goals. Around the turn of the millennium a new dimension emerged, measuring relationship in the client/agency and client/publics contexts. Table 11.6 summarises the aims of evaluation according to orientations.

For an extensive evaluation, each of these orientations should be considered. However, the emphasis often remains on only one or two of these dimensions. Evaluation often serves as budget or action justification. In the media orientation approach the emphasis is on the quantity (how many articles were generated, how big is the circulation of the newspaper in which an article appeared) and quality of media coverage (negative, positive tone). See Mini case 11.2.

Public relations practitioners overemphasise print media evaluation. Despite the fact that the world is moving more and more towards image-based communication, public relations practice has been slow to embrace methods of evaluating TV and other types of image. Fathers4Justice is a pressure group in the UK whose aim is to highlight the problems of fathers separated from their children by divorce or relationship breakdown. They have performed 'stunts' to attract media attention to their issue by dressing up as children's characters. They have climbed government buildings, bridges and the Queen's London residence, Buckingham Palace to create visually sensational, shocking images that can be easily transmitted into the living rooms of millions and grab attention. (See Activity 11.5.)

TABLE 11.6   Orientations of public relations evaluation

Orientation	Aim of evaluation	Levels
Media	Quantity and quality of coverage	Programme, societal
Publics	Effects on publics, how they have changed their knowledge, attitudes or behaviour as a result of public relations activities	Programme
Organisation	To demonstrate how public relations can contribute to achieving organisational goals	Organisational
Persuasion	Demonstrates return on investment (ROI) to clients or management; value of public relations; accountability of public relations professionals or departments	Individual, programme
Relationship	Client/agency, organisation/publics	Individual, organisational

---

activity 11.5

Measuring media stunts

Examine the Fathers4Justice campaign (visit their website: www.fathers-4-justice.org). How would you conduct content analysis of TV coverage of one of their campaigns?

Feedback

Quantity: how many times was the name of the pressure group mentioned? How long was the entire coverage? Was it a leading piece of news?

Quality: What was the context of the coverage? Who was interviewed? How did the newsreader comment on their actions (favourably or unfavourably)? Do you now understand their demands more clearly?

■ assessed at individual, programme, organisational and societal level, depending on the level of effectiveness.

As we saw earlier, formative evaluation (or process research) takes places while the programme is still in operation. Summative evaluation aims at assessing outcomes and impacts as they take place towards the end of a programme or after its conclusion. Summative research evaluates results against objectives. This can be feasible only if SMART objectives have been set: specific, measurable, achievable, realistic and timebound (see Chapter 10).

Evaluation purposes and circumstances dictate which type of evaluation (summative, formative or goal free) is most appropriate in a given case. Bissland's

Definition: *Formative* means the evaluation takes place during the public relations programme or campaign. Summative means it is conducted at the end of the programme of activity. Goal-free evaluation examines a programme or campaign after any intervention, in terms of the situation, not of existing goals or objectives.

Dimensions of evaluation

Public relations evaluation can be:

■ *formative, summative* or *goal-free evaluation*, depending on the time of intervention

---

mini case study 11.2

The IKEA story in the media

The media reported extensively the chaotic opening of London's Edmonton IKEA store in February 2005. Beyond the negative headlines was an undercurrent of hostility towards the company. The IKEA consumer experience, deemed to come a poor second to low prices, was singled out for particular criticism: 'IKEA treats its customers so badly, a riot is the least it might have expected' wrote *The Guardian* (10 February 2005), cataloguing an absence of internet ordering, insufficient stock, poor customer service and lengthy queues. Others accused it of irresponsibly stimulating demand with heavy advertising and special offers in a deprived area: 'Does it pay to advertise?' (*The Times* 10 February 2005).

Figure 11.2 (overleaf) is a typical example of evaluating media coverage, counting how many times certain types of messages occurred and assessing the tone of the coverage.

Source: www.echoresearch.com

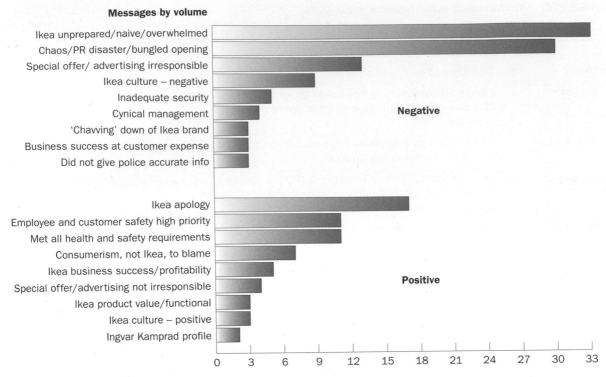

Based on 62 articles, from 10-13 Feburary 2005

FIGURE 11.2   IKEA's image in the print media after opening a new store (*source:* a weekly snapshot review of 'messages in the news' prepared by Echo Research for trade journal *PR Week.* Echo Research, http://www.echoresearch.com)

PICTURE 11.2   Fathers 4 Justice using media stunts to raise their campaign's media profile. (*See:* http://www.fathers4justice.org) (*Source:* Alisdair Macdonald/Rex.)

box 11.3	**Four categories of performance measure**

Input: background information and research that informs initial planning.

Output: measures the result of public relations activity such as media coverage or publicity (exposure to messages, quantifiable features such as number of press releases sent out, consultation sessions scheduled, telephone calls answered or audience members at speech events). Output measures are short term, concentrate on visible results and do not say anything about audience response.

Outcome: the degree to which public relations activities changed target public's knowledge, attitudes and behaviour. It may take weeks, months or even years for these changes to occur.

Outtake: describes an intermediate step between output and outcome. It refers to what people do with an output but what might not necessarily be a specific outcome as a set objective of a campaign. Whereas outtake is related to the output, outcome is to be seen with reference to the objectives set. For example, people might remember the message (outtake) of a communication campaign but might not change their behaviour (outcome).

Source: adapted from Gregory 2000: 169–71

(1990: 25) definition illustrates that in public relations literature evaluation is frequently used as a summative activity: 'Evaluation is the systematic assessment of a program and its results. It is a means for practitioners to offer accountability to clients – and to themselves.'

Levels of effectiveness

According to Hon (1997) effective public relations occurs when communication activities achieve communication goals. She conceptualised effectiveness at four levels.

Individual practitioners

The first level is that of individual practitioners, measuring how effective they are at achieving whatever is expected of them. This is closely related to performance measurement, partly because consultancy practitioners work on a fee basis. Depending on the positions and experience, the hourly rate of consultancy practitioners

can vary. Another dimension of the individual level is the quality and nature of relationship between the consultant and the client. Client/agency relationship has become the focus of many evaluation studies, moving beyond the simple programme evaluation level.

Programme level

The second level is the programme level. Effectiveness in public relations is quite often synonymous with effectiveness at the programme level and this level is usually the focus of evaluation. The results of public relations activity can be further assessed by means of four categories of performance measures: input, output, outcome and outtake. Box 11.3 summarises these measures. (See Think about 11.3.)

Organisational level

The third level of effectiveness is organisational level. The typical question at this level is, 'How do public relations activities and efforts contribute to achieving

think about 11.3 **Output or outcome evaluation**

The National Archives commissioned an agency to publicise the launch of its 'Secret State' exhibition, which looked at government activity during the Cold War. The campaign objectives were to:

- raise awareness of the National Archive
- increase visitors to the museum
- explain that the exhibition was of interest to everyone.

Source: PR Week 13 August 2004, campaigns section – 'National Archives wins visitors with "Cold War"', p. 31

What are the main problems with these objectives?
What could be the output and outcome measures?

On behalf of F4J, Reputation Intelligence, a research agency, analysed more than 10,000 articles from 330 UK newspapers published between 2000 and 2004. Media evaluation showed that:

- Articles on fathers' rights have increased by over 700% since F4J mounted its high-profile media campaign.
- F4J has engaged the politicians to speak on fathers' rights and encourage opposition parties to take up its fight.
- Compared to other political campaigning organisations, F4J is grabbing a high ratio of headlines to article mentions (see Figure 11.3).
- F4J is well placed to turn this profile into clear messages on policy reform.

Source: Reputation Intelligence

organisational goals, such as being the market leader or increase sales figures?' Assessing effectiveness at organisational level also includes the aggregates of different public relations activities, as in the case of a multinational organisation, which has regional or national offices with their own public relations plans and programmes. If public relations objectives are not in line with organisational goals, it might be difficult to evaluate the programme at this level. Another issue at this level may be the difficulty of separating public relations effects from other effects (advertising, direct mails).

Societal level

As Hon noted, the final level of effectiveness is at the level of society. This level is usually examined from either a systems theory or a critical perspective (see Chapters 8 and 9). The systems theory approach asserts that public relations plays a positive role in society; according to the critical perspective, public relations activities have negative consequences on the society at large.

Evaluation methods

Earlier we discussed surveys, focus groups, interviews and content analysis as most frequently used methods to conduct research. They are used to evaluate public relations programmes as well but there are other methods available for public relations practitioners.

PR Week commissioned research in 1999 among 200 public relations practitioners to gauge their attitudes and behaviour with regard to evaluation. About 60% of respondents said that they used media content analysis or press cuttings to evaluate their public relations activities. The next most frequently used technique was opportunities to see (OTS), which is the number of occasions that an audience has the potential

Article mentions versus headlines
Press set: UK newspapers

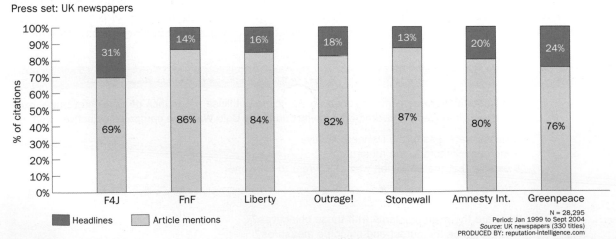

FIGURE 11.3   F4J grabbing headlines (*source:* Reputation Intelligence)

to view a message. The circulation numbers of the British daily newspapers presented in Table 11.2 includes these opportunities in the case of print media.

Surveys, focus groups and advertising value equivalents (AVEs) are also often used to evaluate public relations programmes. AVE is the notional equivalent cost of buying editorial. It is a controversial method and practitioners are being discouraged from using this method because it compares advertising and public relations. However, national and international research confirms this method remains widely used by both in-house and consultancy practitioners. (See Box 11.4.)

Organisations do not always want to get publicity. In the case of a crisis, for example, the company may prefer minimal exposure to media. Nor is publicity the same as understanding – newspaper coverage may be extensive without clearly explaining the goals of those seeking publicity.

Evaluation guidelines

'Is it possible for those of us who work in the public relations field to ever develop generally accepted models or standards of public relations evaluation upon which everyone in the industry can agree?', asked Walter Lindenmann (1997: 391), a well-respected research specialist in the field.

The search for an objective, simple and effective methodology for evaluating public relations programmes occupied much academic literature in the 1980s. Pavlik (1987: 65) commented that: 'Measuring the effectiveness of PR efforts has proved almost as elusive as finding the Holy Grail.' The search was over at the beginning of the 1990s, as Lindenmann (1993: 9) commented: 'There is no one simplistic

method for measuring PR effectiveness . . . An array of different tools and techniques is needed to properly assess PR impact.'

Searching for a single and universal method was replaced by practitioners focusing on compiling an evaluation toolkit based on the best practice guidelines. In 1997 a 28-page booklet entitled *Guidelines and Standards for Measuring and Evaluating PR* was published by the Institute of Public Relations Research & Education in the USA. In Europe, two booklets were produced with a more focused purpose, covering how to prepare measurable goals and objectives prior to the launch of a campaign and how to measure public relations outputs.

In the UK, a research and evaluation toolkit was compiled in 1999 utilising the findings of the above-mentioned *PR Week* survey on evaluation. This toolkit spells out the best reasons for employing research and evaluation in campaigns and gives guidance on how to set about it. The author of the toolkit argued that the UK is taking a leading position on research and evaluation. In 2003 the Institute of Public Relations published the 'IPR Toolkit: Media evaluation edition'.

Evaluation models

A number of evaluation models have been developed to serve as guidelines in terms of what to evaluate and how to evaluate. Most are three-stage models embracing a variety of techniques. Cutlip et al., 'stages and levels of public relations programme evaluation', represents different levels of a complete programme evaluation: preparation, implementation and impact (Figure 11.4). This first level assesses the information and planning, the implementation evaluation deals

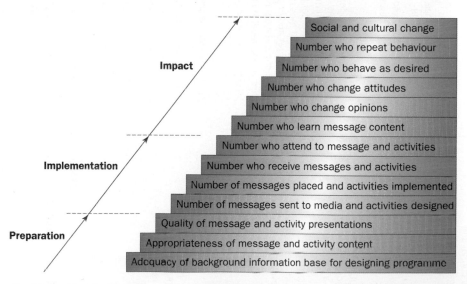

FIGURE 11.4 Stages and levels of public relations programme evaluation (*source*: Cutlip, Scott M., Center, Allen H., Broom, Glen M., *Effective Public Relations, 8th Edition*, © 2000, p. 437. Reprinted by permission of Pearson Education, Inc., Upper Saddle River, NJ)

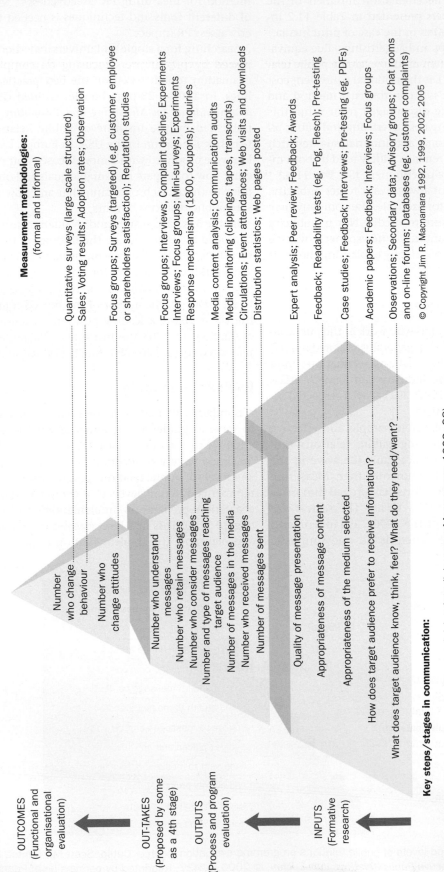

FIGURE 11.5 Macnamara's evaluation model (updated) (*source:* Macnamara 1992: 28)

'Pyramid model' of PR research

Measurement methodologies:
(formal and informal)

Quantitative surveys (large scale structured)
Sales; Voting results; Adoption rates; Observation

Focus groups; Surveys (targeted) (e.g. customer, employee or shareholders satisfaction); Reputation studies

Focus groups; Interviews, Complaint decline: Experiments
Interviews; Focus groups; Mini-surveys; Experiments
Response mechanisms (1800, coupons); Inquiries

Media content analysis; Communication audits
Media monitoring (clippings, tapes, transcripts)
Circulations; Event attendances; Web visits and downloads
Distribution statistics; Web pages posted

Expert analysis; Peer review; Feedback; Awards

Feedback; Readability tests (eg. Fog, Flesch); Pre-testing

Case studies; Feedback; Interviews; Pre-testing (eg. PDFs)

Academic papers; Feedback; Interviews; Focus groups

Observations; Secondary data; Advisory groups; Chat rooms and on-line forums; Databases (eg. customer complaints)

© Copyright Jim R. Macnamara 1992, 1999, 2002, 2005

Number who change behaviour
Number who change attitudes

Number who understand messages
Number who retain messages
Number who consider messages
Number and type of messages reaching target audience
Number of messages in the media
Number who received messages
Number of messages sent

Quality of message presentation

Appropriateness of message content

Appropriateness of the medium selected

How does target audience prefer to receive information?

What does target audience know, think, feel? What do they need/want?

Key steps/stages in communication:

OUTCOMES
(Functional and organisational evaluation)

OUT-TAKES
(Proposed by some as a 4th stage)

OUTPUTS
(Process and program evaluation)

INPUTS
(Formative research)

with tactics and activities while the impact evaluation provides feedback on the outcome.

Preparation evaluation assesses the quality and adequacy of information that was used to plan the programme. Some key publics might have been unidentified at the planning stage or some issues overlooked. This stage is very similar to the plan assessment we discussed earlier.

At the second level, implementation evaluation assesses the number of messages distribution and measures outputs. The final stage, the impact level examines the extent to which the defined goals of the campaigns have been achieved. This level is primarily concerned with the changes in knowledge, attitudes and behaviour.

As the authors noted, the most common error in programme evaluation is substituting measures from one level for those at another (Cutlip et al. 2000).

Macnamara's (1992) model is similar but uses different terminology: inputs, outputs and results. (Output is usually the short-term or immediate results of a particular public relations programme or activity.) This model lists evaluation methodologies that can be applied to each step, but for different steps different methodologies are required. The model is presented in a pyramidal form starting from inputs

through outputs to results (see Figure 11.5; see also Activity 11.6).

Barriers and challenges to developing and using effective research in public relations activities can be summarised as follows. Watson (1994) found that the barriers to evaluation uncovered in his survey were mirrored worldwide:

- lack of time
- lack of personnel
- lack of budget
- cost of evaluation
- doubts about usefulness
- lack of knowledge
- can expose practitioner's performance to criticism
- aversion to scientific methodology.

The challenge of the profession lies in overcoming these difficulties.

---

activity 11.6

Macnamara's model

Review the evaluation of the Bin There Done That campaign. What are the inputs, outputs and results that are measured in this campaign? What does it tell you about the extent or depth of evaluation?

Summary

This chapter outlined the principles of research, which is a central activity in any public relations programme. A variety of research methods have been presented that enable public relations practitioners to conduct systematic and objective research, and scopes of research and evaluation have been outlined.

Since an organisation's public relations are related to other communication activities such as marketing communications, research must also be integrated with these areas. Public relations research and evaluation cannot be seen in isolation from an organisation's other communication research (see Chapter 26). If we talk about integrated communications, then we also have to talk about 'integrated communications research (and evaluation)'.

Bibliography

Besson, N. (2004). *Strategische PR-Evaluation. Erfassung, Bewertung und Kontrolle von Öffentlichkeitsarbeit.* Wiesbaden: VS Verlag für Sozialwissenschaften.

Bissland, J.H. (1990). 'Accountability gap: evaluation practices show improvement'. *Public Relations Review* **16**(2): 25–26.

Broom, G.M. and D.M. Dozier (1990). *Using Research in Public Relations: Applications to program management.* Englewood Cliffs, NJ: Prentice Hall.

Cutlip, S.M., A.H. Center and G.M. Broom (2000). *Effective Public Relations*, 8th edition. Upper Saddle River, NJ: Prentice Hall International.

Gregory, A. (2000). *Planning and Managing Public Relations Campaigns*, 2nd edition. London: Kogan Page.

Hamilton, S. (1987). *A Communication Audit Handbook – Helping Organisations Communicate.* London: Pitman.

Hon, L.C. (1997). 'What have you done for me recently? Exploring effectiveness in public relations'. *Journal of Public Relations Research* **9**(1): 1–30.

Hon, L.C. (1998). 'Demonstrating effectiveness in public relations: Goals, objectives, and evaluation'. *Journal of Public Relations Research* **10**(2): 103–135.

Hon, L.C. and J.E. Grunig (1999). *Measuring Relationships in Public Relations.* Gainesville, FL: Institute for Public Relations.

Kerlinger, F.N. (1986). *Foundations of Behavioral Research*, 3rd edition. Fort Worth, TX: Holt, Rinehart & Winston.

Kim, Y., J. Kim, J. Park and Y. Choi (1999). 'Evaluating media exposure: An application of advertising methods to publicity measurement'. *Corporate Communications* **4**(2): 98–105.

Lerbinger, O. (1977). 'Corporate uses of research in public relations'. *Public Relations Review* **3**(4):11–20.

Lindenmann, W.K. (1990). 'Research, evaluation and measurement: A national perspective'. *Public Relations Review* **16**: 3–15.

Lindenmann, W.K. (1993). 'An "effectiveness yardstick" to measure public relations success'. *PR Quarterly* **38**(1): 7–9.

Lindenmann, W.K. (1997). 'Setting minimum standards for measuring public relations effectiveness'. *Public Relations Review* **23**(4): 391–408.

Lindlof, T.R. and C.T. Bryan (2002). *Qualitative Communication Research Methods*. Thousand Oaks, CA: Sage.

Macnamara, J.R. (1992). 'Evaluation of public relations: The Achilles heel of the profession'. *International Public Relations Review* **15**(4): 17–31.

Mann, C. and F. Stewart (2000). *Internet Communication and Qualitative Research: A handbook for researching online*. London: Sage.

Merten, K. (1995). *Inhaltsanalyse. Einführung in Theorie, Methode und Praxis*. Opladen: Westdeutscher Verlag.

Merten, K. and E. Wienand (2004). 'Medienresonazanalyse'. Paper presented at the Redaktion und wissenschaftlicher Beirat der Pressesprecher Conference, Berlin, 7 May.

Neumann, P. (2003). *Markt- und Werbepsychologie* Bd. 2. *Praxis*. Gräfelfing: Fachverlag Wirtschaftspsychologie, 2nd Edition.

Pavlik, J.V. (1987). *Public Relations: What research tells us*. Newbury Park, NJ: Sage.

Scott, J. (2000). *Social Network Analysis*. London: Sage.

Vos, M. and H. Schoemaker (2004). *Accountability of Communication Management – A Balanced Scorecard for Communication Quality*. Utrecht: Lemma Publishers.

Watson, T. (1994). 'Evaluating public relations: models of measurement for public relations practice'. Paper presented at the International Public Relations Symposium, Lake Bled, Slovenia.

Watson, T. (1997). 'Measuring the success rate: Evaluating the PR process and PR programmes' in *Public Relations Principles and Practice*. P. Kitchen (ed.). London: Thomson Business Press.

Wimmer, R.D. and J.R Dominick (2003). *Mass Media Research: An introduction*, 7th edition. Belmont, CA: Wadsworth.

CHAPTER 12

Audiences, stakeholders, publics

Introduction

The planning and conduct of public relations depends on our understanding of the nature of audiences, stakeholders or publics, i.e. the theories of audiences, stakeholders or publics that we hold. These in turn are an integral part of our understanding, or theories, of public relations and communication. People working in public relations, whether academics or practitioners, understand these objects or phenomena in different ways. These different theories may be complementary or they may be contradictory.

Theories, concepts and models of audiences, stakeholders or publics, public relations and communication are important because they help us understand and explain our public relations campaigns and the situations these campaigns address. They determine how we plan and conduct public relations. Thus the different theories we hold will lead to different ways of planning and practising public relations.

How we understand audiences, stakeholders or publics relates to the theories of public relations and communication (see Chapters 8 and 9 for more about theory) that we hold. The way communicators imagine their audience affects the way they communicate with that audience; it changes the relationship.

This chapter contrasts the concepts of passive and active audiences before considering stakeholder theory and the situational theory of publics. A case study is presented which takes another look at how publics have been or could be regarded. The chapter concludes by considering some new thinking about publics and their role in communication campaigns.

The passive audience

Communication and public relations are directed at audiences and stakeholders or publics, often via the mass media. Mass media have traditionally been seen as having a mass audience. The concept 'mass' has been understood not merely as large in terms of numbers but rather as a large mass of isolated, anonymous and unorganised individuals. The negative connotations implied by the concept of 'mass' included the mass being seen to be unintelligent, having poor taste and lacking in judgement. Hence the mass was passive, easily influenced and manipulated (Ang 1995).

European and American social theorists of the late nineteenth and early twentieth centuries saw mass society, mass culture and the mass audience as arising from industrialisation and urbanisation. Social change and the shift of populations from rural villages to industrial cities were believed to have brought about social disintegration and the breakdown of traditional ties (McQuail 2000: 37). Emile Durkheim (1893–1972), one of the nineteenth-century founding fathers of sociology, defined *anomie* as the condition prevalent in societies undergoing transformation, in which individuals suffered from a lack of standards or values, and an associated feeling of alienation and purposelessness. Thus the individual was isolated from their fellow men, unorganised and hence susceptible to negative influence and manipulation.

The masses thus had to be protected, and as much from their own vulgarity as anything else. On the one hand, the development of industrial capitalist society had given rise to the vulnerable masses and the passive audience in need of protection. On the other hand, despite their vulgarity, lack of intelligence, taste and judgement, sheer numbers meant that the masses would be part of the transformation of a society undergoing structural change. In fact, the masses constituted much of society as workers, consumers and, after the establishment of universal suffrage in 1918 in the UK, as voters. Given their vulgarity and susceptibility to manipulation, this influence would inevitably be negative.

Matthew Arnold, the Victorian poet and literary critic, believed that high culture, i.e. the culture that was most highly valued by the elite and which he defined as 'the best which has been thought and said in the world' (1882), had to be protected from vulgar, popular culture. Thus, traditional society had to be preserved from both the vulgar masses and the radical social changes that had produced these masses. The passivity and vulnerability that made protection of the masses necessary also meant that the masses could be protected and protected against, by virtue of that very same passivity. The practice of public relations in the UK in the early twentieth century sought to ensure and communicate the stability and continuity of traditional culture and society. The masses, their opinions and behaviour, had to be managed through education and propaganda (Moloney 2000). The then British Broadcasting Company was founded in 1922 on a public service broadcasting ethos of educating, informing and entertaining, i.e. the propagation of high culture to the mass audience. It reflects the view of the audience as passive, as both capable of being, and needing to be, influenced. John Reith, the first Director-General of the BBC, declared: 'It is occasionally indicated to us that we are setting out to give the public what we think they need – and not what they want – but very few people know what they want and very few what they need' (cited in Cain 1992: 40).

Similarly, John Grierson, the father of the documentary film, wrote:

> The British documentary group began not so much in affection for film per se as in affection for national education . . . its origins lay in sociological rather than aesthetic aims . . . We . . . turned to the new wide-reaching instruments of radio and cinema as necessary instruments in both the practice of government and the enjoyment of citizenship. (Grierson 1946/1979: 78)

Thus John Reith and the BBC, as much as Stephen Tallents, John Grierson and the Empire Marketing Board, are key players in early twentieth-century public relations in the UK, despite the myths of public relations being distinct from the media it seeks to influence, and of the objectivity and impartiality of the BBC. Reith secretly wrote propaganda for the Conservative Baldwin government during the General Strike of 1926 and noted in his diaries that impartiality was a principle to be suspended whenever the established order and its consensus were threatened (cited in Pilger 2003). The object of the attention of this public relations of the early twentieth century was an audience seen to be passive and thus both needing to be, and capable of being, influenced.

Defining the passive audience

How can we understand the passiveness of the audience? The 'passive' audience (or at least the audience that is seen as being passive) passively responds to and accepts media content, rather than actively engaging intellectually and emotionally with it. Thus this passivity is defined primarily in terms of the strong effects that media communication is believed to have on the audience and the corresponding role assigned to the audience in communication. An example of contemporary concern surrounding strong *media effects* is the perceived ability of violent scenes shown on television or in film to incite violent acts among vulnerable audiences such as children and teenagers.

> **Definition:** *Media effects* refers to the effects that the media has on audiences as a result of the audiences being exposed to the media and its content.

The development of the mass media, from newspapers to film and radio, was accompanied by both (a) the fear that the media would have powerful effects on audiences that would be detrimental to both audiences and society and (b) the desire to use these media for propaganda to, and public relations with, these audiences.

The *hypodermic model* or 'magic bullet theory' of media effects posits not only that the media have strong effects but that the effects of messages 'injected into' or 'shot at' passive, mass audiences would be uniform; much as the physical effects of being injected or shot at are uniform. Although perhaps no one, or at least not academics, actually believed in the hypodermic model, at least with respect to themselves, nonetheless in some sense the media are thought to have strong effects on audiences on account of their passivity. Thus governments, businesses and other elite interests communicate through the mass media to influence audiences. Thus *'moral panics'* have arisen about the alleged effects of media aggravating crime and violence (Cumberbatch 2002).

> **Definition:** *Moral panic* refers to an 'episode, condition, person or group of persons' that is 'defined as a threat to societal values and interests' by 'stylized and stereotypical' representation by the media, and condemnation by those 'in power' (politicians and the church) (Cohen 1972: 9).

The passivity of the audience, and the strong effects that media communication has on the audience, imply a correspondingly subordinate role assigned to the audience in communication. This understanding of media effects, the audience and communication is represented in the *linear (*also called the *transport, transmission* or *process) model* of communication, of which Shannon and Weaver's model (1949) is an example (see Chapter 8).

The linear model portrays the messages and meanings in communication as if they were physical things to be transported, much as the hypodermic model portrays media effects as physical effects mechanically inflicted. Carey (1989) writes that in the nineteenth century the word 'communication' referred both to the communication of messages as well as the transportation of people and goods by road, rail or ship. Thus the transport of the physical medium that messages were transcribed on, such as letters and books, was easily confused with the communication of messages and the meanings that were read into these messages.

The linear model of communication portrays messages and their meanings as being transported intact from sender to receiver like physical things (Schirato and Yell 2000). The sender is privileged in that they communicate and decide what the correct message and its meaning is. The receiver can merely passively accept what the sender says. Any difference in interpretation and opinion is taken to be misinterpretation and misunderstanding, as 'noise', a concept Weaver adapted from Shannon's original description of signal loss in telecommunications. The audience is limited to feedback, a concept from cybernetics merely describing a test of the success or failure of the sender's communication in order to allow adaptation of subsequent communication to ensure future success (Rogers 1994).

Raymond Williams, the father of media and cultural studies in the UK, wrote that 'there are in fact no "masses", but only ways of seeing people as masses' (1961: 281). The mass was either the elitist and moralistic way in which high culture saw popular culture in others or a way of seeing others in the formation and management of audiences to serve the interests of government, business and other elites. As such, we include others rather than ourselves in the mass audience. In the same way, strong media effects are often seen as third-person effects: they occur to others rather than ourselves. We personally are more sophisticated and less passive and vulnerable (Davison 1983).

Hermes (2002) states that academic research is conducted into how media influence works in order that we may guard against it. Often enough, however, mass communications research has been motivated just as much, if not more so, to enable government, media and other businesses and their public relations and advertising practitioners to take advantage of media influence over audiences. In fact, mass communication and market research share common roots in the work of Paul Lazarsfeld, at Princeton and then Columbia University in the USA in the 1930s and 1940s (Rogers 1994). Rather than reflect communication realistically, linear models were adopted to serve the strategic and political needs of political and business communication (Schirato and Yell 2000). (See Think about 12.1, overleaf.)

PICTURE 12.1 A Moonie wedding: is this a passive audience? (*Source:* © Gideon Mendel/Corbis.)

The active audience

If audiences are neither mass nor, as Cutlip et al. (2000) claim, passive, what would an 'active' audience be? Hermes (2002) asks in what sense are audiences 'active', what is the nature of this audience activity? *Uses and gratifications theory* focuses attention not on what media do to audiences but rather, what *audiences do with media*. Media audiences are active in their choice of media. Media choice is selective and motivated (i.e. rational and goal directed). Audiences use media in expectation of gratification of their individual social and psychological needs. Thus audience activity is seen not in the taking or making of meaning, but in the active and intentional selection of media to be used to satisfy individual needs. Audiences are formed on the basis of common needs for which satisfaction is sought. Such gratifications sought may include the need for information, the formation of personal identity, achieving social integration and interaction, and the desire for entertainment (Katz et al. 1974).

McQuail (1984) criticises uses and gratifications theory in that it does not reflect much media use, which tends to be circumstantial and weakly motivated, and also for its behaviourist and functionalist assumptions, i.e. it ignores what lies behind behaviour and functions. For example, uses and gratifications theory sees media use in terms of the individual and ignores the fact that media use is social; it also ignores media content and how audiences understand these and it implicitly acts as justification of media as it is, i.e. the media are seen as responsive to audience needs (Ang 1995). (See Think about 12.2.)

think about 12.1   **Passive and active audiences**

■ Have you ever been so engrossed in your favourite television programme that you are dead to all around you? Does that make you a passive audience?

■ How much do you challenge what you read or hear in the news?

■ Viewers get to vote in reality television shows like *Big Brother*. Is the audience that votes an active audience?

Understanding audience activity

Uses and gratifications theory limits audience activity to the selection of media to be used to satisfy needs. It does not engage with the role of audiences in understanding and creating meanings. However, a richer understanding of the audience and its activity needs to reflect the different and complex ways in which the media are used and what the media mean for users as a social and cultural activity (Ang 1995). Thus audience activity needs to be defined in terms of the active role audiences play in the construction of meaning that takes place in communication. The concept of the active audience rejects the privileging of the sender as the authority that decides the meaning of the message that is found in the linear model of communication.

Reception analysis is the study of audience activity in making or producing, not merely taking or consuming, meanings from media communication. The meaning of media messages is not fixed by the sender in the media text. Rather, meaning is constructed or negotiated by audiences when they interpret what they see, hear and read in media communication. This active reading and interpretation of media content takes place within the social and cultural environments that audiences live in. The context of meaning production includes the social power relations that audiences are in. Thus the construction of meaning and the audience use of media takes place within, and is integrated into, the circumstances of everyday life (Ang 1995; Schirato and Yell 2000).

This understanding of the active audience and communication is represented in the cultural model of communication, or the idea of communication as culture (Carey 1989; Schirato and Yell 2000). Culture is understood as systems of meaning consisting of rules, conventions that constitute communication practices. Communication is the practice of producing and negotiating meanings. The particular social and cultural contexts that audiences live in depend on factors such as class, ethnicity, age, gender, sexual preference, etc. and the power relations that these imply.

In contrast to the unique meanings that messages are supposed to have in the linear model of communication, the cultural model asserts the *polysemy of communication*, i.e. messages are always open to different possible interpretations. Stuart Hall's (1973/1980) encoding/decoding model classifies these different possible meanings that can be read into a message into preferred, negotiated and oppositional 'readings':

■ Preferred or dominant readings are in agreement with the sender's intentions.
■ Oppositional readings disagree with and reject the sender's message.
■ Negotiated readings represent a compromise in partial agreement with the sender's meanings.

Thus the understanding of communication as culture distinguishes between the audience misunderstanding the intentions of the sender, on the one hand, and the audience understanding but choosing to read the message in opposition to the sender's interpretation on the other. Further, it does not assume by default that audience readings different from the sender's are in fact misunderstandings and miscommunication, i.e. 'noise'. On the contrary, the very nature of communication as culture means that messages will inevitably be, at least to some extent, read and interpreted differently by different people because of each person's specific contexts. Not only is there no necessary correspondence between the sender's and the audience's meanings, there is, of necessity, at least some difference in meanings offered and accepted. The problem presented by the linear model is turned on its head – what needs to be explained is not so much difference but rather agreement in the construction of meaning. For if the preferred or dominant reading prevails, it does so through the limits and constraints imposed by power (Ang 1996; Schirato and Yell 2000). (See Think about 12.3, overleaf.)

think about 12.3 **Alternative readings**

In the 2005 general election campaign, Tony Blair wrote an open letter to *Daily Mirror* readers (6 April 2005). He wrote that those who voted for Labour were the people who ended Conservative party rule in 1997 and 2001. He asserted that Labour had since built a more prosperous and fairer Britain, with low inflation, mortgage rates and unemployment, better public services and lower crime. Blair wanted to further extend opportunity and continue to protect Britain from security threats. There may have been big disagreements, e.g. over Iraq, but voters who wanted Britain to continue moving forward rather than go back to the Conservatives should vote Labour:

■ What is Blair's message? Who (different possible groups) might accept the preferred reading of Blair's message?

■ What would oppositional and negotiated readings of Blair's message look like? Who might hold these oppositional and negotiated readings?

■ Would anyone or any group that may have suffered as a result of Blair's policies, e.g. parents/spouses/children who have lost children/spouses/parents who served in Iraq subscribe to Blair's preferred reading?

■ Would anyone or any group that may have benefited as a result of Blair's policies, e.g. people who have seen the kind of improvements described in his letter, not subscribe to Blair's preferred reading?

Audience activity and media effects

The long history of research into media effects has not resulted in a consensus among media scholars on the strength or nature of the influence that the media may have over audiences. Perhaps Schramm et al. (1961: 13) sum up media effects research best:

> For some children under some conditions, some television is harmful. For other children under the same conditions, or for the same children under other conditions, it may be beneficial. For most children under most conditions television is probably neither harmful nor particularly beneficial.

The failure to find powerful effects could be down to the complexity of the processes and the inadequacy of research designs and methods. This might mean not that media are without effects or influence but that these effects or influence are not of a direct causal nature along the lines of mechanical effects. McQuail (2000) believes that what he calls the 'no effect' myth arises from the undue concentration in the research undertaken on a limited range of effects, especially short-term effects on violent behaviour, instead of broader social and institutional effects. Thus research still seeks to identify potential effects of the media but conceptions of the social and media processes involved have been revised. There has been a shift of attention to long-term change in cognitions rather than attitudes and affect (feelings) and to collective phenomena such as climates of opinion,

structures of beliefs, ideologies, cultural patterns and institutional forms of media provision and intervening variables of context, disposition and motivation. In other words, the potential effect of the media depends on an individual's circumstances and how these interact with complex social and cultural conditions.

Kitzinger (2002) suggests that rather than the narrow conception of media effects found in mass communications theory, the 'new effects research' on how the world is represented in the media, and the ideology and discourse that lie behind these representations, has proved more fruitful in understanding how the media affects audiences. Media representations of the world can influence how audiences understand and engage with that world they live in. Language and meaning structures and shapes our perception of reality, and how we define, understand and value the world around us.

Understanding 'communication as culture' recognises that the media are influential. However, rather than strong media effects that affect a passive audience in a mechanical way, media influence is seen to involve audience participation and is negotiated. The most significant media effect is seen to be the role that media play in audience's social construction of meaning. The media offer their messages and meanings to audiences. It is then up to the audience how they read these messages and the extent to which they incorporate these into their understanding or sense of reality of the world they live in (McQuail 2000). (See Think about 12.4.)

How do you understand and interpret fashion; the way you and others dress and look?
    Is your understanding of fashion related to fashion magazines, television programmes and films? Is your understanding of fashion forged in negotiation with the fashion ideas you are exposed to by the media? Do you modify the fashion messages you see (latest designs, this season's look, for example) in terms of your peer group (what others are wearing around you), your family (to shock or please them), your religion, national culture or other factors (as well as your budget)?

Stakeholders and publics

The concept of the stakeholder originates in political theory. Interest in the concept of the corporate stakeholder arose in the debate on corporate governance during the 1980s climate of companies taking over other companies in the USA (Freeman 1984). The debate was about making companies responsive to shareholders' interests but stakeholding ideas emerged as an alternative way of understanding the interests at stake. Stakeholders are those who have a stake or interest in a particular organisation, i.e. 'they depend on the organisation to fulfil their own goals and on whom, in turn, the organisation depends' (Johnson and Scholes 2002: 206). Thus stakeholders are those who influence or can influence the organisation, as well as those affected by it. An organisation's stakeholders would include its employees and their trade unions, financial investors, customers, suppliers, distributors, the local community, local and central government, industry groups and the media (see Figure 12.1).

The distinction between stakeholders and publics is not a sharp one. Sometimes both terms are used interchangeably. Others, like Grunig and Hunt (1984: 145) for instance, distinguish publics as stakeholders that face a problem or have an issue with the organisation. (See also Chapter 8.)

Thus stakeholders are potential publics, the critical factor being the arrival of a problem or issue. The risk to the organisation is that when such a problem or issue arises, stakeholders organise to become publics and are able to affect the interests of the organisation. Some of McDonald's customers become a public when they become concerned about their diet and obesity, and organise to campaign for more healthy menus and government regulation of food advertising on television targeted at children. Rover workers at Longbridge, the UK car manufacturing plant, become a public when they organise to protest at the loss of their jobs.

Stakeholder mapping

Stakeholders should be considered at the first stage of strategic management, in environmental scanning and situation analysis to identify the consequences of the organisation's behaviour on the stakeholders and vice versa, to anticipate any possible issues and problems. Grunig and Repper (1992) sees communication at the stakeholder stage as helping to develop the stable, long-term relationships that an organisation needs to build support and to manage conflict when issues and problems arise. (See also Chapters 2 and 10.)

Relevant factors that are considered in the mapping of stakeholders include their possible impact on the organisation and hence their interests, expectations, needs and power. Individuals may belong to more than one stakeholder group. Employees often live in the local community where their employers are located and also own shares in the company.

Johnson and Scholes (2002), writing on corporate strategy, consider how likely stakeholders are to press their expectations on the organisation to suggest strategies to contain or manage stakeholders. They consider how much interest stakeholders have in potential issues and problems with the organisation, whether they have the means to push their interests and how predictable they would be. They map the

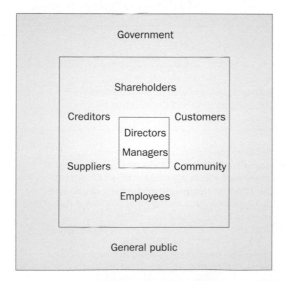

FIGURE 12.1   Stakeholders (*source:* Letza et al. 2004: 243)

mini case study 12.1

Applying stakeholder mapping

Fast food companies and the obesity issue

In the past few years, government departments and agencies, MPs, non-governmental organisations (NGOs) and the health professions have raised concern about the growing obesity problem in the UK and the role of fast food companies such as hamburger chains. Concern has centred not just on the nature of the food products sold but how they have been promoted, particularly in television advertising.

How would a fast food company map and decide the relative importance of its various stakeholders in the obesity issue? What aims and objectives, and strategies and tactics did McDonald's adopt?

Stakeholders relevant to the obesity issue can be grouped into government departments and agencies, customers and potential customers, NGOs such as the Food Commission and the British Medical Association, other companies and trade bodies in the food and advertising industry (such as the Advertising Association and its Food Advertising Unit) and members of the public who were not customers.

These stakeholders are mapped in the matrix below according to their levels of power and interest. In addition, a '+' indicates that the stakeholder Is broadly supportive of the fast food company on the issue, while a '−' indicates the opposite. One of the issues for fast food companies was the House of Commons' Health Select Committee's recommendation of a ban on the advertising of junk food to children being adopted in the government's White Paper on health and then subsequently becoming law. Both the Department of Health and government agencies such as the Food Standards Agency were in favour of stricter government regulation of junk food advertising. These were stakeholders that were both powerful and interested, but not supportive of the position of fast food companies.

Members of the food industry, i.e. other food companies, and industry bodies such as the Advertising Association were powerful and interested stakeholders that shared common interests with McDonald's on this issue. These were also supported by other powerful and interested stakeholders in government. The Department of Culture, Media and Sport was concerned about the impact of a junk food advertising ban on the revenues of the commercial television industry. Tessa Jowell, the Culture Secretary, dismissed calls for restrictions early in the debate and called instead for the advertising industry and their clients in the food industry to use their creativity to help in anti-obesity campaigns. In particular, McDonald's responded with the Yum Chums, cartoon characters exhorting children to have a healthy diet and to exercise.

McDonald's also implemented changes to its menu. It reduced the salt in its fries, stopped the practice of super-sizing meals, and introduced a new menu including salads and fruits in March 2004. It introduced a new breakfast menu including oat porridge and bagels in October 2004. It also ran campaigns, such as 'McDonalds, but not as you know it', to promote these changes.

Such changes in the policies and products of fast food companies tell interested stakeholders, such as the government, NGOS, and the health and diet-conscious members of the public who may be customers, potential customers or potential activists, that some fast food companies offer a healthy menu (at least now, if not in the past), promote their food responsibly, are worthy of their custom and can be trusted to self-regulate their promotional activities.

		Level of interest	
		Low	High
Power	Low	Non-customers not conscious about health and diet	Health and diet-conscious non-customers (−) NGOs such as the Food Commission (−)
	High	(Potential) customers not conscious about health and diet	Other food companies and the food industry (+) Department of Culture, Media and Sport and government media agencies such as Ofcom (+) Department of Health and government health and food agencies such as the Food Standards Agency (−) Commons Health Select Committee (−) Health and diet-conscious (potential) customers (−)

The White Paper on health was published in November 2004. There was no ban on junk food advertising, just a promise to consult on working out a strategy on food promotion in the next few years. This outcome would have been the result of lobbying by those sympathetic to the food industry, both within and outside the government. However, the campaigns conducted by fast food companies consisting of both their actions and communications would have helped the case of the food industry.

power of the stakeholders against both their level of interest in the issue and the predictability of their behaviour.

If the stakeholders have both a high level of power and interest, then they are key players crucial to the welfare of the organisation. If they are powerful but have merely low interest in the issue, the organisation would do well to keep things that way by keeping them satisfied as that would not require much effort. If they are highly interested but lack power, then all the organisation needs to do is merely to keep them informed. Likewise, powerful but unpredictable stakeholders present the greatest opportunity and threat to the organisation's interests. Thus in situation analysis, stakeholders are mapped and their importance weighted accordingly. (See Chapter 10 for explanation of the power/interest matrix; see also Mini case study 12.1.)

Situational theory of publics

Stakeholders are contained, or at least relationships with them are managed, in order to prevent them developing into publics that may organise against the organisation. Grunig and Hunt's situational theory of publics (1984) examines why and when publics are formed and most likely to communicate, how their predicted communication and behaviour can be used to segment publics in order to provide a basis for deciding what strategy is most likely to achieve cognitive, attitudinal and behavioural effects in the publics (see Table 12.1). The theory sees stakeholders developing into publics when they recognise that an issue or problem affecting them exists and they see it as worth their while getting involved with the issue or problem. Latent publics do not as yet recognise the issue or problem they are facing with the organisation. Aware publics recognise that the issue or problem exists and active publics organise to discuss and respond to the issue or problem. Thus the company's customers who face obesity and health problems but who do not see it as a problem would constitute a latent public. It is only customers who are not only aware of the problem but also organise to act on the problem, e.g. changing their diet, campaigning for menu changes and regulation of advertising, that make an active public. It would thus be in the company's interests to address

the issue while most of its customers are still latent or aware publics, rather than wait until the active public has reached sizeable numbers.

The situational theory further classifies publics on the basis of the range of issues to which they are responsive:

- Apathetic publics disregard all issues/problems.
- Single-issue publics are active on a small set of issues/problems that has limited popular appeal (i.e. fringe activist groups).
- Hot-issue publics are active on a single issue that has significant appeal (e.g. the anti-war movement).
- All-issue publics are active across a wide range of issues/problems.

Both Johnson and Scholes' (2002) stakeholder mapping and Grunig and Hunt's (1984) situational theory of publics are classification or segmentation tools in the execution of strategy to manage and contain the impact of publics on organisations – they are practical techniques for realising publics as subjects that public relations practitioners do things to. However, looked at another way, theories of publics and stakeholder analysis are vulnerable to Raymond Williams' charge that 'there are no masses, only ways of seeing people as masses' (1961: 281). (See Box 12.1 and Think about 12.5, overleaf.)

Mini case study 12.2 (overleaf) illustrates and summarises the various conceptions of audiences and stakeholders or publics that we have considered so far in this chapter. We then go on to look at new, alternative ways of thinking about publics.

New thinking on publics

The different ways of understanding audiences, stakeholders and publics – i.e. passive or active, nature of activity, their importance to and ability to affect the organisation – affect our understanding of communication and public relations and hence the way we plan and conduct public relations.

The starting point for alternative thinking on publics, different from the way Shell frames its publics as incompetent and hence ignorant, has to

TABLE 12.1   The situational theory of publics (*source:* adapted from Grunig and Hunt 1984: 145)

Latent publics	Groups that face a particular problem as a result of an organisation's action, but fail to recognise it.
Aware publics	Groups that recognise that a problem exists.
Active publics	Groups that organise to discuss and do something about the problem.

box
12.1

Stakeholders or publics?

Sometimes the words stakeholders and publics are used interchangeably, so what is the difference?

Grunig and Repper (1992: 125) describe the difference thus: 'People are stakeholders because they are in a category affected by decisions of an organisation or if their decision affects the organisation. Many people in a category of stakeholders – such as employees or residents of a community – are passive. The stakeholders who are or become more aware and active can be described as publics.'

'Publics form when stakeholders recognise one or more of the consequences (of the behaviour of the organisation) as a problem and organise to do something about it or them' (1992: 124).

As Davis (2004: 59) points out, 'publics sound more important than stakeholders'. However, he goes on to say that some groups, for example pressure and cause-related groups, do not form out of a stakeholder mass: they exist as publics immediately because, by definition, they are active. Furthermore, it is clear that not all publics are active (Grunig himself recognises apathetic publics – Grunig and Repper 1992) and they are not always adversarial. Davis (2004: 59) defines the groups thus: 'Publics have an importance attached to them because of their specific interest and power, current and potential, while for stakeholders the levels of interest and influence are relatively lower and more generalised.'

The person regarded as largely responsible for stakeholder theory, Freeman (1984), accepts that 'the term means different things to different people' (Phillips et al. 2003: 479), but goes on to say that it encompasses a particular and close relationship between an organisation. His co-author Phillips (Phillips et al. 2003) differentiates between normative stakeholders (to whom an organisation has a direct moral obligation to look after their well-being, for example financers, employees and customers), and derivative stakeholders (who can harm or benefit the organisation, but to whom there is no direct moral obligation – for example, competitors, activists and the media).

be Williams' 'there are no masses, only ways of seeing people as masses' (1961: 281). Ways of seeing involve the exercise of power in the social construction of reality, i.e. that human beings make the world they live in. Karlberg (1996) and Moffitt (1994) claim that organisations see publics from the narrow perspective of their own interests rather than that of their publics.

To move away from this narrow perspective, and like Holtzhausen (2000), Chay-Nemeth (2001) asserts that the ethical practice of public relations should focus on empowering and giving voice to disempowered and silent publics. She goes on to suggest how this may be done in practical terms by a typology based not on the power, interest or actions of a public to affect the organisation, but on the ability of the public to participate in the issues in which they have a stake.

She conceives of a public as a political space or site where power plays out, material resources and discourses (i.e. ideas, concepts, language and assumptions) are produced and reproduced, exchanged and appropriated, to achieve social and political change or to maintain the status quo. Communication is not simply about information exchange but a practice of power relations. Hence publics are not merely senders or receivers of information but also producers and reproducers of meaning.

In her conception of publics and power, she applies Foucault's (1991) concept of governmentality, where

think about 12.5 Publics

Consider a recent public relations campaign that you have come across, organised or been the target of.

- How did the campaign view the publics involved? As latent, aware or active publics?
- What publics do you belong to? How active are you in these roles?

Feedback Does stakeholder mapping and/or the situational theory of publics view audiences and/or stakeholders/publics as passive subjects that public relations practitioners do things to? Or as active and hence needing to be managed and contained in the organisation's interests?

You might be a member of the following publics: student body, course member, group or society member, resident in an area near your place of study, ex-member of your school, place you grew up in, and so on. What factors affect your activity in these publics?

mini case study 12.2

Shell's publics

How does Shell understand its publics, particularly in the Brent Spar case and the corporate recovery strategy Shell embarked on after Brent Spar?

In 1995, Shell's plans to dispose of the Brent Spar oil platform by sinking it 150 miles west of the Hebrides met with fierce opposition from Greenpeace Germany. The Greenpeace campaign attracted much attention and support from the media, European governments, Shell's customers and the public. Shell backed down and reversed its decision. It commissioned an independent survey by the Norwegian ship classification society, Den Norske Veritas, and looked at 200 possible options. It subsequently dismantled and recycled the platform, in part as a roll-on, roll-off ship quay in Norway (Varey 1997; Henderson and Williams 2001).

Varey asserts that Shell had made a perfectly rational decision and chosen the best, most practical option of sinking the platform on the basis of cost–benefit analysis of business, technical and environmental considerations. Various onshore and offshore abandonment options were considered. Rudall Blanchard Associates Ltd, an environmental consultancy, was commissioned to report on the environmental impacts of sinking the platform.

In contrast to Shell's scientific and technical rigour and objectivity, Varey describes the Greenpeace campaign as manipulation of both the media and 'people's feelings about . . . apparent injustice'. Nonetheless, public outcry driven by emotions and a lack of understanding of Shell's 'rational, scientifically sound decision' led to the reversal of that well-made decision (Varey 1997: 104–105). Similarly, Henderson and Williams (2001:13), who have both been involved in public relations for Shell, write of Shell's 'knowledge gap' problem in its corporate recovery campaign. Its publics just did not understand Shell's values and

approach, i.e. how good Shell really was, particularly on the environment and human rights. Further, facts alone were not enough and Shell had to engage the emotions of its publics.

Before you continue reading this case, answer the questions in Think about 12.6.

How justified is Varey's and Shell's view of Shell's publics? Varey praises Shell's analysis as 'apparently very thorough. Over four years was spent in getting DTI [i.e. British government's] approval for the plan'. But read between the lines and you will see that this was not an objective, scientific Shell against an emotional, irrational public. Shell may have spent four years lobbying the DTI while Rudall Blanchard's environmental report was published only six months before the planned sinking.

Varey tells us that Shell commissioned an independent survey, by the Norwegian ship classification society, Den Norske Veritas, only after the Greenpeace campaign. Instead of the several options considered earlier in its scientifically sound analysis, Shell was now looking at 200 possible options.

We can understand Shell's 'rational, scientifically sound decision' when Varey writes that Shell's analysis 'dealt only with whether the environmental measure was worth pursuing and deciding this on cost in a cost–benefit analysis'. In other words, cost–benefit analysis can only be done from the perspective of who bears the costs and reaps the benefits. Environmental damage to the northwest Atlantic was not borne by Shell while benefits of an environmentally sound disposal did not accrue to them whereas it had to bear the costs.

Thus perhaps the publics' active and oppositional reading of Shell's actions is not simply misunderstanding and ignorance of Shell, nor simply to be dismissed as just so much 'noise' preventing Shell from being heard.

think about 12.6 Shell's publics

How do Varey and Shell view Shell's publics?

- Are these publics seen to be active or passive?
- Are they seen to be intelligent, capable of rational, scientific reasoning?
- Are they seen as easily influenced and manipulated by emotions?
- Can they be rational and, at the same time, guided by their emotions?
- Do these publics hold preferred, negotiated or oppositional readings of Shell on the environment?
- Have these publics got the power and interest to affect Shell's fortunes?
- How do Varey and Shell evaluate the competency of these publics to judge Shell?

PICTURE 12.2 Defacement of a poster – an example of activism. (*Source:* Impact Photos.)

people are disciplined through everyday discourses and practices that they perform voluntarily and take for granted as obvious and natural. Governmental discipline produces docile and passive publics.

She considers three historical conditions as the basis for a typology of publics:

1 *resource dependency*, the extent to which a public depends on others for resources such as funds, information, training, education, the media and publicity
2 *discursive connectivity*, the extent to which one public shares in the discourse, ideas, concepts, language and assumptions of others and hence the potential for negotiation and competition with these others
3 *legitimacy*, the extent to which each public has the right to speak and act within its given role in the community.

She applies these conditions to publics in the HIV/AIDS issue in Thailand to derive a typology of four publics: circumscribed, co-opted, critical, and circumventing publics. However, she states different cultural and historical conditions will yield different historical criteria for categorising publics.

A *circumscribed public* is highly dependent on others for resources. They find it difficult to enter into mainstream discourses. Their legitimacy to speak or act is limited by how others see their roles. Thai Buddhist monks involved in AIDS hospice work are a circumscribed public. They depend on the community and the state for their livelihood, and hence are pressured to conform to these interests. Hospice monks may be circumscribed because they lack funds to finance AIDS-related projects and have little access to the media. Their lack of education and training in science and counselling and the framing of their spiritual training and knowledge as parochial is

used by the state, the medical profession and non-governmental organisations (NGOs) in competition with the hospice monks, to justify their circumscription. Some community groups also maintain that monks should not be involved with AIDS as sexual conduct should be taboo to monks. Thus the limited legitimacy of the hospice monks to speak and act freely in the discourses of modern medicine and sexuality is related to how others see their role as monks.

A circumscribed public may remain so, or become a co-opted, critical or circumventing public if conditions are appropriate, e.g. a redistribution of resources and the cooperation of others.

A *co-opted public* behaves within limits prescribed by powerful others and hence has access to resources. They accept the legitimacy of the status quo and are not considered subversive or dangerous. Governmental organisations, non-governmental organisations and community groups may be examples of co-opted publics. Monks may be co-opted in confining themselves to teaching Buddhist meditation. They are awarded funds by the government, whereas monks who do hospice work are denied funding.

NGOs may be co-opted to agree with the circumscription of the monks from the medical sphere as they are competing with hospice monks for funds or legitimacy from medical quarters for their own projects. The need to secure state funding and legitimacy may compel NGOs to circumscribe less favoured publics. The legitimacy of co-opted groups is seldom disputed because they help to reproduce dominant discourses and practices. For example, the Thai government appealed to NGOs for endorsement to improve Thailand's international image in tourism.

A *critical public* is dissatisfied with the status quo. They may include medical staff, NGOs, AIDS patients opting for indigenous herbal treatments instead of modern medicine, communities who blame the government's tourism-orientated development policies for the thriving sex industry and monks resisting the roles set for them by the state and society. Critical publics face constraints such as dependency or competition with others for funding. Many critical publics rely on government or foreign funding.

There are many points of contention between critical publics and the state. They contend that state strategies on HIV/AIDS are misguided and budgets are poorly managed. Community activists have criticised the government's industrialisation and tourism policies. The confluence of rural migration, consumerism, the sex industry and tourism has aggravated the spread of AIDS to rural villages.

Legitimacy varies for each critical public. NGOs, community groups and AIDS patients have more legitimacy in their AIDS work than do the monks in

think about 12.7   **Rethinking publics**

Consider a recent public relations campaign that you have come across, organised or been the target of.

Would resource dependency, discursive connectivity and legitimacy be useful criteria on which to classify the publics in this campaign? What other factors might be useful criteria?

Would circumscription, co-option, critique and circumvention be a useful typology of these publics? What other types of public might be useful to map the campaign?

Feedback   Would such a different conception and classification of publics lead to a different kind of public relations? How so?

hospice care. Critical publics compete not only for a redistribution of resources but also for the expansion of their discourse and seek to establish their legitimacy. Co-option into state domination is one response to circumscription, the resistance of critical publics is another.

A *circumventing public* follows a critical public in resistance to governmentality. The docile citizen sacrifices their desired sexuality to the discipline of the norms and conventions of being a healthy citizen. A circumventing public resists this discipline by consciously or unconsciously engaging in behaviours considered deviant. However, their engagement behaviour is the result of material constraints such as economic poverty (e.g. prostitution to provide for the family).

Circumventing publics may include commercial sex workers, intravenous drug users and homosexuals. They seek out public resources only when absolutely necessary. Some AIDS patients prefer to use indigenous medicine rather than use state hospitals where disclosure of AIDS status is necessary. Others prefer to suffer in silence. Because of their high resource dependency, circumventing publics possess little legitimacy to speak for themselves. (See Think about 12.7.)

Summary

In this chapter we have considered ideas of the passive and active audience and the nature of this passivity and activity. We then considered stakeholder theory, stakeholder mapping and Grunig and Hunt's situational theory of publics. We considered how these concepts are understood in practice by examining two cases.

We concluded by looking at how a different typology of publics may be useful for a different kind of public relations that considers the interests of the publics that are the subjects of public relations campaigns.

Bibliography

Ang, I. (1995). 'The nature of the audience' in *Questioning the Media: A critical introduction*, 2nd edition. J. Downing, A. Mohammadi and A. Sreberny-Mohammadi (eds). Thousand Oaks, CA: Sage.

Ang, I. (1996). *Living Room Wars: Rethinking media audiences for a postmodern world*. London: Routledge.

Arnold, M. (1882). *Culture and Anarchy: An essay in political and social criticism*, 3rd edition. London: Smith, Elder & Co.

Branston, G. and R. Stafford (2003). *The Media Student's Book*. London: Routledge.

Cain, J. (1992). *The BBC: 70 years of broadcasting*. London: BBC.

Carey, J.W. (1989). *Communication as Culture: Essays on media and society*. London: Unwin Hyman.

Chay-Nemeth, C. (2001). 'Revisiting publics: A critical archaeology of publics in the Thai HIV/AIDS issue'. *Journal of Public Relations Research* **13**(2).

Cohen, S. (1972). *Folk Devils and Moral Panics*. London: MacGibbon and Kee.

Cumberbatch, G. (2002). 'Media effects: Continuing controversies' in *The Media: An Introduction*, 2nd edition. A. Briggs and P. Cobley (eds). Harlow: Longman.

Cutlip, S.M., A.H. Center, and G.M. Broom (2000). *Effective Public Relations*, 8th edition. Upper Saddle River, NJ: Prentice Hall.

Davis, A. (2004). *Mastering Public Relations*. London: Palgrave.

Davison, W.P. (1983). 'The third-person effect in communication'. *Public Opinion Quarterly* **47**: 1–15.

Durkheim, E. (1893/1972). 'The division of labour in society'. Excerpts reprinted in *Selected Writings*. A. Giddens (transl. ed.). London: Cambridge University Press.

Foucault, M. (1991). 'Governmentality' in *The Foucault effect: Studies in governmentality*. G. Burchell, C. Gordon and P. Miller (eds). Chicago: University of Chicago Press.

Freeman, R.E. (1984). *Strategic Management: A stakeholder approach*. Boston: Pitman.

Grierson, J. (1946/1979). *Grierson on Documentary*. London: Faber & Faber.

Grunig, J.E. and T. Hunt (1984). *Managing Public Relations*. New York: Holt, Rinehart & Winston.

Grunig, J.E. and F.C. Repper (1992). 'Strategic management, publics and issues' in *Excellence in Public Relations and Communication Management*. Hillsdale, NJ: Lawrence Erlbaum Associates.

Hall, S. (1973/1980). 'Encoding/decoding' in *Culture, Media, Language: Working Papers in Cultural Studies, 1972–79*. Centre for Contemporary Cultural Studies (ed.). London: Hutchinson.

Henderson, T. and J. Williams (2001). 'Shell: Managing a corporate reputation globally' in *Public Relations Cases: International perspectives*. D. Moss and B. DeSanto (eds). London: Routledge.

Hermes, J. (2002). 'The active audience' in *The Media: An introduction*, 2nd edition. A. Briggs and P. Cobley (eds). Harlow: Longman.

Holtzhausen, D.R. (2000). 'Postmodern values in public relations'. *Journal of Public Relations Research* **12**(1): 93–114.

Johnson, G. and K. Scholes (2002). *Exploring Corporate Strategy*, 6th edition. Harlow: Pearson Education.

Karlberg, M. (1996). 'Remembering the public in public relations research: From theoretical to operational symmetry'. *Journal of Public Relations Research*, **8**(4): 263–278.

Katz, E., J.G. Blumler and M. Gurevitch (1974). 'Utilization of mass communication by the individual' in *The Uses of Mass Communication*. J.G. Blumler and E. Katz (eds). Newbury Park, CA: Sage.

Kitzinger, J. (2002). 'Media influence revisited: An introduction to the new effects research' in *The Media: An introduction*, 2nd edition. A. Briggs and P. Cobley (eds). Harlow: Longman.

Leitch, S. and D. Neilson (2001). 'Bringing publics into public relations: New theoretical frameworks for practice' in *Handbook of Public Relations*. R. Heath (ed.). Thousand Oaks, CA: Sage.

L'Etang, J. (1998). 'State propaganda and bureaucratic intelligence: The creation of public relations in 20th century Britain'. *Public Relations Review* **4**: 413–441.

Letza, S., X. Sun and J. Kirkbride (2004). 'Shareholding versus stakeholding: A critical review of corporate governance'. *Corporate Governance* **12**(3): 246–262.

McQuail, D. (1984). 'With the benefit of hindsight: Reflections on uses and gratifications research'. *Critical Studies in Mass Communication* **1**: 177–193.

McQuail, D. (2000). *McQuail's Mass Communication Theory*, 4th edition. London: Sage.

Moffitt, M.A. (1994). 'Collapsing and integrating concepts of public and image into a new theory'. *Public Relations Review* **20**(2): 159–170.

Moloney, K. (2000). *Rethinking Public Relations: The spin and the substance*. London: Routledge.

Phillips, R.A., R.E. Freeman and A.C. Wicks (2003). 'What stakeholder theory is not'. *Business Ethics Quarterly* **13**(4): 479–502.

Pilger, J. (2003). 'The BBC and Iraq: Myth and reality'. *New Statesman*, 5 December.

Rogers, E.M. (1994). *A History of Communication Study: A biographical approach*. New York: Free Press.

Schirato, T. and S. Yell (2000). *Communication and Culture: An introduction*. London: Sage.

Schramm, W., J. Lyle and E.B. Parker (1961). *Television in the Lives of Our Children*. Stanford, CA: Stanford University Press.

Shannon, C.E. and W. Weaver (1949). *The Mathematical Theory of Communication*. Urbana, IL: University of Illinois Press.

Varey, R. (1997). 'Public relations: the external publics context' in *Public Relations: Principles and Practice*. P. Kitchen (ed.). London: International Thomson Business.

Williams, R. (1961). *Culture and Society*. Harmondsworth: Penguin.

Corporate image, reputation and identity

Introduction

Since the early twentieth century, organisations such as Shell, Mercedes-Benz and Michelin have harnessed the power of their visual identities to communicate their values to key audiences. But organisations communicate in more ways than through logos or visuals. Within this chapter we explore the related elements of image, reputation, identity and personality that make up the total communications of an organisation.

Corporate communications, corporate affairs, communications and public relations: despite the discrepancies in job titles, their job functions are largely similar (Dolphin and Fan 2000). Although practitioners use these terms fairly interchangeably, the academic literature on communications often makes a distinction between the terms above, circumscribing their remits to specific areas (see Van Riel 1995; Balmer and Greyser 2003, for accounts of the various perspectives and opinions to do with these terms and their meanings). This situation has led to a relative lack of perspective or a limited inclusion of the topics that form the core of this chapter in some of the public relations literature. This could be misleading for those new to the field in that they might believe that the term 'communications' involves *only* the specific act of communication (for example, communicating with the media, prospective investors and other stakeholders). However, this is not the case if we refer to the definition of public relations adopted by the Chartered Institute of Public Relations in the UK: 'Public relations practice is the planned and sustained effort to establish and maintain goodwill and mutual understanding between an organisation and its publics' (Gregory 1997: 14)

From the above, it is clear that the aims of public relations are wide ranging and that a strategy (hence the word 'planned') is required for its correct implementation over time.

Successful communication strategies are used to attain healthy relationships between organisations and their stakeholders (or publics; see also Chapter 12). These communication strategies, if used effectively, are not 'just' isolated actions that are completely independent from one another. In every organisation, communication strategies need to be based on, and to share, sound common parameters to provide cohesion to the communications. In this way the risk of confusion and misinformation among the organisation's publics can be reduced.

Based on the implications and scope of the definition above, and to avoid misinterpretations, this chapter uses the term organisational public relations rather than corporate communications, corporate affairs and so on. An explanation for this decision is given below.

This chapter contains two major sections: the first one, 'Organisational public relations', explores the various terms commonly used in organisational public relations; the second one, 'Organisational identity, strategy and process: two models', looks at the management process (the strategic element) involved in organisational public relations.

Organisational public relations

The academic literature refers to the concepts of 'corporate public relations' (Gregory 1997) or 'corporate communication' (Van Riel 1995). They are worth closer examination. The meanings of public relations and communication have been dealt with in earlier chapters and at the beginning of this chapter. So, what does the term 'corporate' add – what is meant by it?

When we think of organisations, we might think of them as lots of different sections and departments, such as sales, top management, accounting, production, marketing, human resources, research and development and so on, where these sections interact with one another to some degree. However, in order to understand the concept of 'corporate' we must adopt a different view, in which we look at an organisation as one body, as a whole, as if we were looking at a person. Human beings consist of many different elements, from organs to limbs to way of thinking. We tend not to think of people as parts, but as one entity: John, Marie, Klaus, the elderly lady in the bus, etc. It is the same with an organisation. Before considering its component parts, when you think 'corporate' you think of the organisation as one whole entity.

Let us extend the concept of corporate to 'corporate public relations'. If corporate is to do with an organisation as a whole, you need to look at corporate public relations (or corporate communication) in exactly the same way – the communication activities and public relations of the whole organisation and not of just one of its sections (for example, the mar-

keting department or the human resources section in isolation). Van Riel (1995: 26) defines the term corporate communication as follows:

Corporate communication is an instrument of management by means of which all consciously used forms of internal and external communication are harmonised as effectively and efficiently as possible, so as to create a favourable basis for relationships with groups, upon which the organisation is dependent.

Van Riel defines the specific aims of corporate communication as well as presenting it as a tool used by management to shape an organisation's *deliberate* communications with all its stakeholders. It is worth remarking on the deliberate nature of corporate communication since, as we will see later on, other forms of communication also play an important role in the relationship between an organisation and its stakeholders (or publics). He also uses the terms 'favourable relationships', which implies a reciprocity (or symmetric approach) between the organisation and its stakeholders. In order for the relationship to be favourable to all parties, it is imperative that the differences and discrepancies between them are eliminated or, at least, reduced to a minimum.

Using the term 'corporate' with reference to public relations could be misleading in this age of globalisation, competition and takeovers, and of great financial and economic power wielded by a number of large companies, also known as corporations. The term 'corporate' could be seen as referring only to organisations that exist, among other things, to provide a dividend to their shareholders. This could make someone think that public relations is only used by commercial firms. However, most organisations, from local and national governments, charitable organisations, educational institutions to pressure groups, charities and religious orders engage actively in public relations. To avoid any possible confusion, and with the aim of making it clear that public relations can be used by a wide range of entities, we are going to replace 'corporate' by 'organisational' from now on in our terminology.

It is the all-encompassing nature of *organisational public relations*, and the proactive and symmetric managerial aspect it involves that suggest the following definition.

> **Definition:** *Organisational public relations* affects an entire organisation and not just one (or a few) of its parts in isolation. It does so in a proactive way by deploying and managing strategies with the aim of reducing the gap between how the various internal and external publics of an organisation view it and how the organisation would like to be viewed by those publics.

It helps to think of organisational public relations as an umbrella that covers the entire organisation. Every sector of the organisation is influenced by it. Organisational public relations is a management function that achieves its aims by providing a leitmotiv (a characteristic and coherent theme and style, or 'lead motive') that aims to inform and influence how *everyone* in the organisation acts, behaves and communicates.

Organisational image, reputation, identity and other such terms are often used informally as if they were synonymous. However, in the context of organisational public relations each one has got a specific sense and it is important to agree on their meanings to avoid confusion.

Organisational image

As the word implies, image is a reflection. In this particular case, it is the reflection of an organisation in the eyes and minds of its publics. (See Activities 13.1 and 13.2.)

The following provides but one definition of *organisational image*.

> **Definition:** *Organisational image* is the impression perceived by an individual of an organisation at one moment in time. Organisational image can change from individual to individual and also throughout time.

activity 13.1

Organisational image

Think of the shop where you, your family or friends buy their groceries. Ask two or three of them what they thought of that shop last time they visited it. What were their answers? Next time you go there, ask two or three of the members of staff what they think of that shop on that day.

Feedback

Did you find any similarities or differences between the various answers? How did they compare? In other words, what were the images those different publics (e.g. an external public like the customers and an internal one, like staff) had of that shop? You may have come across differences depending on who you asked. However, they all referred to the same store – or *did* they? Yes and no. Strictly speaking it was the same store: they all referred to 'that' store, same address, same name . . . However, the picture (or image) was probably different in each case. What does this tell you about image?

Over time an individual might accumulate a number of different images of the same organisation.

activity 13.2

Thinking again about organisational image

You could try repeating the exercise in Activity 13.1 on a different day, let's say a fortnight after you conducted the first one. You ask the same question about the shop to your friends and you also go to the shop and ask the question to the same members of staff (if you can find them again).

Feedback

How do the recent answers compare with the previous ones? Are there similarities or differences? What is your conclusion this time? Did you get *exactly* the same answer again from each individual? It is quite unlikely. So, in addition to saying that corporate image changes from individual to individual, we can also say that it changes in time.

Organisational reputation

Metaphorically speaking, we could think of the relationship between image and reputation in terms of photography. Organisational *image* could be equated with a photograph of an organisation taken at one moment in time by an individual; *organisational reputation* is when that individual collates all the photographs (or images) taken over a period of time into an album and forms an opinion of the organisation by looking at the entire collection of photographs. (See Think about 13.1, overleaf.)

Think about your own experience at college or university. Before you chose to join your institution it would be fair to assume you had quite a positive image of it. However, now that you have been a student there for a while, you have accumulated different images of the institution over time. Maybe you found certain aspects that you were unhappy with, others that were unexpectedly good, and so on. Taking all those various images into account, would you say you are happy you joined that institution? Has your opinion about it changed radically? Please reflect on what you are now drawing on in order to answer these questions. You are considering an accumulation of different images and probably taking stock of the pluses and minuses to help you find the answer. In other words, you are considering the reputation *you* hold of the institution.

Definition: *Organisational reputation* is arrived at by considering the sum total of images an individual has accumulated over a period of time that help that individual form an opinion about an organisation.

So far we have established that image can be quite fickle. In what way is this relevant to an organisation? Organisations pay a great deal of attention to the image their publics hold of them. This has been stressed by some authors (Bernstein 1984) who argue that image should be considered as *true reality* by organisations . . . Does this sound a little strange at first? (See Think about 13.2.)

Organisational identity

We have seen how important image and reputation are and how much can depend on them. This leads organisations to want to influence the images and reputations their various stakeholders hold of them. To do this they use organisational identity. We will explore *organisational identity* in more detail now. When the term identity was applied in a corporate communications context for the first time, authors referred specifically to those visual elements organisations used to portray themselves to their publics. The main element here was the organisation's logotype (or 'logo', for short) – this was a visual emblem designed by the organisation with the aim of conveying a number of characteristics it wanted its publics to think of in relation to the organisation. Logos were also intended to help those publics recognise and differentiate the organisation from others. Organisations put a lot of thought and invest large sums of money in nurturing their logo, making sure it conveys the right message and, where appropriate, adapting or changing the logo (see Figure 13.1) to fit in with changes in the environment (e.g. cultural tastes) or changes in the organisation itself (e.g. cases of mergers or acquisitions such as BP and Mobil Oil).

The pictures in Figure 13.1 are examples of organisations that take proactive steps and measures to influence their publics' images of the company or institution. In the case of PepsiCo, the company wanted to replace an old-fashioned logo with one that reflected more clearly its brands. To achieve this aim it used a variety of colours, representing the colours of its divisions. The globe reflects the company's global scope. For 3Com it was a case of

---

Is image reality? How do you feel about this? Do you agree or disagree?

Think back to the previous reflection about yourself and your image of your college or university before you enrolled. Whatever image you held of the college or university was a mental representation of what you thought was true about the institution and was strong enough to encourage you to apply. Had your perception not been regarded as reliable or truthful enough at the time, you might not have applied for a place. (Of course, if you ended up somewhere you did not want to study at, you would have had negative images of the place, which may have since been changed by experience.)

Now put yourself in the position of the college or university. The image prospective students hold of the institution is really important for the college/university. This image (or a sum of images, i.e. reputation) is the deciding factor taken into account by prospective new students when judging whether to apply or not. Since universities and colleges depend on these people for their survival, institutions take the images (and reputations) held by prospective students to be *real* factors – and devote a lot of time and resources to influencing those images in a positive way.

FIGURE 13.1 Organisations that have proactively managed their logos. (*Source:* Spaeth 2002 in www. identityworks.com; copyright Pepsico © 2001 Pepsico, Inc. Used with permission; copyright 3com. Used with permission.)

upgrading its logo to a more contemporary 3D design.

One of the common denominators among the items on the list in Activity 13.3 is that they are all *proactive* and therefore *deliberate*. They are premeditated actions and efforts by organisations to communicate with stakeholders and influence them. However, organisations also influence stakeholders' image through *unintentional* actions and factors outside their control or volition. (See Think about 13.3.)

There are many elements over which an organisation has no or little direct control; however, they play a very important role in the formation of image in a customer's mind. Taking this idea a little further, we can say that every organisation has an *organisational identity*, whether it is deliberate or not. Just by their existence organisations portray and send messages to their various stakeholders – and it is those messages that influence the stakeholders' image of the organisation.

> **Definition:** *Organisational identity* consists of the sum total of proactive, reactive and unintentional activities and messages of organisations.

What follows in Box 13.1 (overleaf) is a statement on organisational identity that was put together by an international group of academics.

The statement does not highlight the unintentional elements that are also a significant part of an organi-

sation's organisational identity. In fact, the statement does not offer a definition of corporate identity – it simply states that every organisation has got a corporate identity. This is so because organisations exist within a societal context. Even by doing nothing an organisation conveys a message. Its stakeholders will still form an image of the organisation however active or inactive that organisation happens to be.

The Strathclyde Statement places great emphasis on the proactive element of organisational identity. As such, identity is described as 'a strategic issue' that should be managed by organisations and that this leads to a number of beneficial outcomes for the organisation.

There are very close links between the various concepts introduced so far in this chapter. It is the relationship between these concepts that creates a management function in organisations that has very specific responsibilities and aims. This management function is organisational public relations.

box 13.1	**The International Corporate Identity Group's (ICIG) statement on corporate identity: 'The Strathclyde Statement'**

'Every organization has an identity. It articulates the corporate ethos, aims and values and presents a sense of individuality that can help to differentiate the organization within its competitive environment.

'When well managed, corporate identity can be a powerful means of integrating the many disciplines and activities essential to an organization's success. It can also provide the visual cohesion necessary to ensure that all corporate communications are coherent with each other and result in an image consistent with the organization's defining ethos and character.

'By effectively managing its corporate identity an organization can build understanding and commitment among its diverse stakeholders. This can be manifested in an ability to attract and retain customers and employees, achieve strategic alliances, gain the support of financial markets and generate a sense of direction and purpose. Corporate identity is a strategic issue.

'Corporate identity differs from traditional brand marketing since it is concerned with all of an organization's stakeholders and the multi-faceted way in which an organization communicates.'

Source: Balmer et al. in Balmer and Greyser 2003: 134

When comparing the various perceptions (images and reputation) of an organisation held by the various stakeholders of that organisation – including the internal stakeholders (for example, the frontline staff, the dominant coalition or management, and so on), it is likely that a gap or dissonance between those perceptions will appear.

Also, dissonance (inconsistency or conflict) might exist between how the organisation would like to be perceived and how it is perceived in reality. The task of organisational public relations is to reduce dissonances to a minimum. The 'tool' used by corporate public relations to achieve this is organisational identity. Organisational public relations strategies address the proactive and reactive actions and communications of the organisation as well as trying to minimise any negative unintentional ones. It is through doing this that organisational public relations influences the images and reputations of the organisation's stakeholder. (See Activity 13.4.)

What shapes and influences an organisation's identity? In essence, the answer to this question is what the organisation is like, the way it simply 'is'. Using a metaphorical approach, some authors (Bernstein 1984; Meech 1996, among others) have likened organisations to human beings. They talk about an organisation's personality as being that factor that defines what the organisation is like.

Personality and culture

The concept of organisational personality is very difficult to pin down and define. Why? (See Activity 13.5.)

activity 13.4

Comparing images

Let's do a quick comparison . . .

Think of two or three airlines, like a long-established national carrier and a low-cost newcomer, for example, and the different images you have about them. Now think of the types of communication and actions that made you arrive at those images. What is the nature or style of their corporate identities? What makes them different? Is it their advertising campaigns? The friendliness of their staff? . . .

It is difficult to define your own personality (see Chapter 14 for more about personalities). In the case of an organisation it is more difficult still. What group of stakeholders would we use to find out the personality of an organisation? What would we find if we were to ask more than one group of stakeholders? The simple fact that there are so many different stakeholders might lead to different answers to our questions.

To make matters more complicated, the terminology used by academics can be confusing. In addition to 'personality' the term 'culture' is often used.

Definition: *Organisational* (or corporate) *culture* is described as 'the way in which attitudes are expressed within a specific organisation' (Trompenaars and Hampden-Turner 1999: 7).

This definition offers a wide-angled and encompassing view of *organisational culture*. The attitudes

Defining personality

Take a few seconds and answer the following quickly.

What is your personality? Are you an extrovert or an introverted person? A bit conservative or maybe rebellious?

The point here is not to dwell on your type of personality (however tempting this might be!). Take a moment now to think about how you arrived at your answer. What made you say you are the way you defined yourself to be just now? How do you know *what* your personality is?

Feedback

It is highly likely that you know what your personality type is because someone else told you or maybe you read the information after completing a test. In other words, you may have found that the answer to the question is based on someone else's image of you.

(and opinions) in an organisation are expressed through a variety of channels. Some are quite observable, like the different communications used, while some others are less so.

During the 1980s there was a strong tendency to look at organisational culture from a very prescriptive perspective, namely that which represented the views of the dominant coalition or management (Parker 2000). For some, this is still the prevalent perspective today. Important elements that affect an organisation's culture are its aims, the mission statement, and the overall strategy (the organisational objectives and the type of tactics the organisation uses to achieve them). In some cases, the founder's or owner's personality spreads onto the organisation's culture. This phenomenon is quite typical in small organisations or businesses, but it can also happen in larger ones – the Virgin group of companies and the influence of its founder, Richard Branson, are a good example of the link between the personality of a founder and the culture of an organisation (www.virgin.co.uk).

The managerial version of organisational culture is imposed on stakeholders through very explicit rules, mission statements, procedures, organisational public relations, marketing communications, systems and styles of management (see Mini case study 13.1, overleaf). However, there are other aspects of an organisation's culture that are often less obvious:

- the predominant types of communications (personal vs impersonal) used in the organisation
- the level of formality vs informality in communications and personal interactions (for example, do customers need to fill in endless forms and paperwork before their requests are actioned?)
- tacit 'rules' for promotion (for example, are promotion opportunities the same for men and women?)
- unstated expectations from staff by management (for example, are employees 'expected' to work long hours?) and many others.

The managerial approach to culture in organisations tends not to consider such aspects. This less overt area of culture is explored in more detail by the French approach to identity (Moingeon and Ramanantsoa 1997).

The 'iceberg' concept

The 'French school' likens the whole phenomenon of culture and identity to an iceberg, where the more 'obvious' elements are exposed while those elements that are more difficult to access and diagnose (rites, myths and taboos in an organisation) are 'under the surface'. The latter shape the internal dynamics of organisations and affect the organisation's identity and the image stakeholders have of the organisation.

Those engaged in organisational public relations must be aware that the invisible elements take a long time to be discovered and cannot be influenced or changed very easily. In a study of a merger of various French saving banks where employees from the various organisations were taken on by the new company, Moingeon (1999) found a number of elements, mainly feelings and perceptions among staff, that were covert (the submerged part of the 'iceberg'). Some of these were the nostalgia people felt for the warmth and friendliness of their 'old' organisation, the tensions that arose between staff from different 'old' companies, the view that power was not shared equitably between staff from the old organisations and the perception that a number of them had lost some level of autonomy as an individual after the merger. These feelings and perceptions are very real for those whom they affect and might have a degree of influence in the way these people behave and communicate among themselves and with other stakeholders – and, therefore, influence the organisational identity of the institution!

The managerial aspect of organisational personality will have a direct impact on the type and style of those elements that are proactively planned by an organisation as part of its organisational identity activities.

However, the managerial aspect of the personality can also affect the reactive and unintentional elements of the organisational identity. This influence might be reflected, for example, in times of

PICTURE 13.1   Icebergs have hidden elements beneath the water's surface. The 'French school' likens culture and identity to an iceberg, they consist of visible and concealed elements

crisis for the organisation, when it is imperative that the organisation tries to remain operational. In other words, the organisation must keep running its 'business as usual'. In order to achieve this, members of staff may be expected to show cooperation by working longer hours or taking over duties that are not usually their own. In such situations staff need to rely on their own initiative. However, this might be very difficult for staff if, for example, they have been used to working under a very authoritar-

ian management. This will affect their decisions and communications and, in doing so, shape the corporate identity the organisation is projecting towards stakeholders.

In addition to the managerial aspects, there are other elements that affect organisational personalities. These are articulated less formally but nevertheless are equally powerful and influential. Often the type of industry or activity will influence organisational culture. For example, if we think about the

mini case study 13.1

Mission statements and straplines

Bayer

From Bayer's mission statement: 'Working to Create Value: Bayer is a global enterprise with core competencies in the fields of health care, nutrition and high-tech materials. Our products and services are designed to benefit people and improve their quality of life.'

Bayer's strapline in its global website: Bayer – Science For A Better Life

Source: www.bayer.com

Nestlé

From Nestlé's Business Principles: 'Since Henri Nestlé developed the first milk food for infants in 1867, and saved the life of a neighbor's child, the Nestlé Company has aimed to build a business based on sound human values and principles.'

Nestlé's strapline: Nestlé – Good Food, Good Life

Source: www.nestle.com

banking industry in the last decade or two, it is apparent that banks have changed radically in the way they do business with their customers and in the way they are perceived by them. One aspect of this change is reflected in the design of bank premises. Gone are the days when banks were intimidating, fortress-like, safe-looking buildings. Today banks are housed in open, airy buildings designed to give customers and staff a friendly feeling.

Another element that can influence an organisation's personality is its country of origin. The culture of the country of origin often impacts on the social ways in which people interact in the organisation. (See also Hofstede on national culture in Chapter 17.)

Without wanting to reinforce national stereotypes, the culture of the country of origin is particularly influential in larger multinational organisations where it can shape behaviours, systems and, in general, the way things are done. For example, the former Swiss airline Swissair imposed the Swiss sense of punctuality on its staff around the world even in countries where the local customs related to punctuality were different. (See Mini case study 13.2.)

We can conclude then that organisational culture is made up of a number of overt (open to view) and a number of covert (concealed) elements with an area of interface where the overt and the covert elements converge.

mini case study 13.2

Audi

Pure Audi.
Vorsprung durch Technik.

Source: Advertising Archives

One good illustration of how country of origin influences organisational identity is the case of the German car manufacturer Audi and its operations in some English-speaking countries around the world. In the UK, Audi has consciously incorporated a strapline in German, 'Vorsprung durch Technik' (advancement through technology), in its marketing communications activities. Similarly in South Africa, Audi is using 'Vorsprung, the spirit of Audi' in its communications.

Why is Audi using the language of its own country where the majority of people do not speak German? Audi is 'borrowing' the image among consumers in the UK and South Africa that things German are of good technical quality and linking this perception with its products and brand – the association here is so strong that customers need not speak German to understand the message!

Source: www.audi.co.uk

Organisational identity, strategy and process: two models

Organisational public relations is a management function that uses strategies to achieve its aims and objectives. This way of working is similar to the strategic approach employed in any public relations campaign.

Organisational identity management strategy

When reading books and journals about strategic management and also when discussing this topic with tutors and practitioners, we find that the specific words used to talk about strategic management are often very confusing – people employ terms like objectives, aims, strategy and so on very widely but often with different meanings. When we talk about strategy, do we mean a combination of different tools to achieve an outcome? Or do we mean the overall process of management? What is the difference between aims and objectives? It is wise practice to clarify terminology before we talk strategy. The main purpose of the model in Figure 13.2 is to 'cut through the jargon' by using simple open-ended questions in order to clarify what the various words mean and to

show what each stage in the model is about. The model is also a tool that reminds us of the different stages in a strategy and shows the relationships between the various elements that make up a strategic approach to organisational identity management within the realm of organisational public relations. (See also Chapters 2 and 10 for more about strategic planning.)

Research

Research helps you identify and/or clarify issues from the environment in order to define and finetune your strategy. Research will help you find answers to specific questions, which may address a multitude of areas, depending on the public relations task ahead. For example, through research you might be able to: define an aim (if this has not been provided); find out who the stakeholders are you need to target; get an indication as to what the best tactics are, and so on.

Aims

These provide you with the basic reason why you are going to engage in a particular communication strategy. Aims tend to be broad in nature and reflect the organisation's mission statement or business principles.

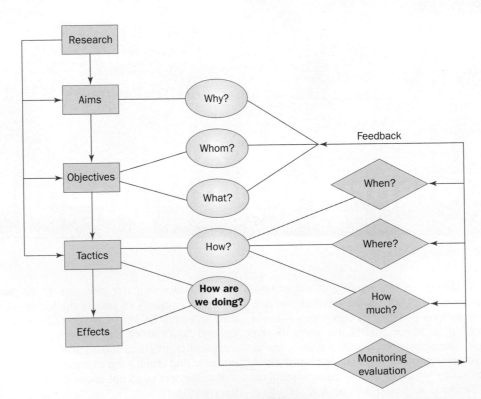

FIGURE 13.2   Organisational identity management strategy © Daniel Löwensberg. Used with permission. *Source:* based on Harrison 1995: 47–50.

Objectives

Objectives are very time-specific goals you can measure. In general, good objectives will be SMART (**s**pecific, **m**easurable, **a**chievable, **r**ealistic, **t**ime bound). The objectives will make it clear who needs to be addressed (stakeholders) and what you are going to convey (the messages).

Tactics

How are you going to achieve your objectives? What specific actions will you use? These could be several (for example, corporate advertising, media relations, and events). You will need to address questions of timing – when these actions are going to take place, where they are going to take place (you can consider both geographical locations and virtual ones, www) – and you will need to consider budgets (how much?).

Effects

How are we doing? The arrows link monitoring and evaluation with all the elements in the model. This is so because you need to establish your efficiency while deploying your tactics during the strategy and also to work out whether your objectives and aims have been achieved at the end. The sort of questions you will ask are: did we use the most resource-effective tactics? Do we need to change the publications we have targeted originally? Have we exceeded or fallen short of our planned objectives; if so, by how much? Are things happening on time? And so on. The 'how are we doing?' stage will help you correct any short-comings while your strategy is ongoing and will also help you define your aims and objectives better for future projects (remember we all learn from experience . . .).

A word of advice about the model: it is intended to be a tool and as such you should feel free to adapt it to the circumstances in which you are going to use it. For example, you will need to decide the stages at which you will conduct research and what type of research you can afford. The number of objectives and tactics you decide to employ will be dependent on your professional judgement on the one hand, and, again, on the time and budget available on the other.

Organisational reputation process

The next model, 'Organisational reputation process' (Figure 13.3), addresses the relationship between the various elements focused on in this chapter, namely organisational culture, organisational public relations, organisational identity, organisational image

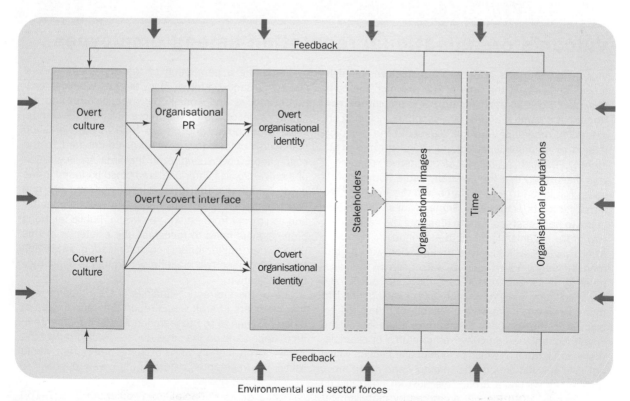

FIGURE 13.3 Organisational reputation process. *Source:* © Daniel Löwensberg. Used with permission

and organisational reputation. It places these elements in a process that consists of various stages. The model helps to understand which element has an influence on which other elements.

The model reminds communication practitioners of the elements that contribute to the formation of reputations. In addition, the model alerts them of the fact that the various phenomena involved do not happen in isolation and that we must always remember to look at the process as a 'whole' – very much in the same way as we discussed how to view organisations in the first section of this chapter.

Environmental and sector forces

The whole organisational reputation process is immersed within an environmental and sector of activity context. The environmental forces consist of factors related to politics, the economy, social contexts, technology, information technology and communications, national and international laws, the natural environment, and so on. Sector forces refer to the sector or type of activity or industry the organisation belongs to (for example, the hotel industry, the charity sector or the government). Environmental and sector forces can influence every stage and section of the model, as well as the process as a whole, including feedback.

Culture (overt and covert)

The starting point in the formation of organisational reputation is the organisation's culture – this concept includes the organisational personality, which has not been mentioned separately since it can be argued that culture and personality could be regarded as the same or are, at least, very closely interlinked and interdependent. The model highlights both cultural elements, the overt and covert ones, and how these have an influence on the next stages in the model.

Overt/covert interface

This is the overlap area between overt and covert cultural elements. Using the French analogy of an iceberg again, this area is the water surface. Like any water surface, the interface zone is not static meaning that the divide between overt and covert culture can fluctuate – what is overt for some stakeholders will be covert for some others, for example. Organisational public relations professionals need to pay attention to the interface area. They need to discover covert cultural and identity elements in the organisation. In doing this, they will convert covert elements into overt ones for their own purpose and communication activities – otherwise the undiscovered covert elements could turn into

---

case study 13.1

Vulcan's organisational reputation among employees

Vulcan Industries is a British manufacturer of high-quality cookers. At the time of the research the company had grown to approximately 800 employees who worked in a number of different sections, including engineering, marketing and management. The research looked at organisational culture in Vulcan and at its identity. Through a process of qualitative research it was discovered that the company had a number of issues in relation to its workforce and the image of the firm held by its employees. Some of these issues are going to be presented here to illustrate the validity and use of the organisational reputation model.

A message of a 'family-type organisation with a common language' (*overt culture*) was used by management in messages to staff (*organisational public relations*) to convey a happy message (*overt identity*) to them. However, there were a number of rituals (*covert culture*) in the company that had an influence on the *covert identity* the firm conveyed to staff. For example, there was a ritual by which people of one section would eat in a specific area of the refectory and never move to another section's area. This custom contradicted the 'friendly' *overt identity* promoted by management

by promoting a perception of 'us and them' (*covert identity*) in the workforce. Also, the geographical location of offices and workshops (*overt culture*) and the quality of décor, which was more lavish in the 'white-collar' work areas and offices than in the workshop managers' offices (*overt culture*), contributed to the segregation (*covert culture*) in the firm. An illustration of the *overt/covert* interface area could be found in the divide (another ritual) that existed between old and new members of staff, which is a very personal matter and could vary from person to person. Public relations professionals need to recognise the existence of this ritual when implementing communication strategies that target these two stakeholder groups to avoid miscommunication.

One of the interesting findings in the research was that members of staff would report different images at different *times* to the researcher. At some moments in time, depending on the situation, they would reflect the 'family' overt identity while at some others they would reflect the fragmented nature of the covert identity.

Source: adapted from Parker 2000: 127–156

think about 13.4 Vulcan case study

This abbreviated example shows the complexity inherent in the formation of organisational image and reputation in just one group of stakeholders. It also illustrates the importance of time and context, on the one hand, and the fact that organisational reputation in the minds of stakeholders is made up of many different images on the other.

Have you noticed any differences between the stated or overt culture of a workplace or university and the actual behaviour, practices and attitudes (covert culture)? How do you explain any gaps?

barriers to the public relations communication process.

Organisational public relations

This is the management function that operates in a proactive and deliberate way using strategies to achieve its goals (see Figure 13.3). Because of this it is placed in the overt section of the model. However, covert cultural elements will also have an influence on it.

Organisational identity (covert and overt)

The model shows that the organisational identity also has an overt and a covert aspect – some of its aspect are premeditated communications efforts by the organisation, while some others happen without the organisation being proactive or consciously involved in the communication. Organisational identity is affected by the overt and covert cultural aspects as well as by organisational public relations strategies.

Stakeholders

These are the publics who are the receivers of the organisation's identity. They process the organisational identity and create organisational images in their minds.

Organisational images

There are many organisational images. They will vary from stakeholder to stakeholder and, within one stakeholder's mind, they will also be numerous and accumulate over time. Influences from environmental forces can be particularly relevant in the shaping of organisational images.

Time

Time is the factor that will allow for an accumulation of organisational images that will contribute to the formation of organisational reputations in the minds of stakeholders.

Organisational reputations

Similar to the case of organisational images, there are many organisational reputations. Reputations will vary from stakeholder to stakeholder, and will also be influenced to some degree by environmental forces.

Feedback

The organisation must put research tactics in place in order to obtain feedback from its stakeholders' perceptions (the organisational images and reputations). In addition to premeditated research tactics, feedback will also return to the organisation through unplanned channels (for example, gossip between internal and external stakeholders or unprompted opinions from customers). Feedback will therefore inform the overt culture of the organisation (for example, the business principles dictated by the dominant coalition) and organisational public relations strategies, as well as elements of the covert culture. (See case study 13.1 and Think about 13.4.)

Summary

The main aims of this chapter were to introduce the concept of organisational public relations, to define some of the terms used and also to present the strategic processes involved in this activity.

Organisational public relations can be used by *any* type of organisation. Also, organisational public relations acts like an umbrella covering every sector of the organisation and provides a sense of cohesion to its activities.

Image is a stakeholder's perception of an organisation at one moment in time. Stakeholders accumulate a number of images of an organisation over time. The aggregate of images forms the organisational reputation in the minds of the stakeholders.

Organisational identity consists of the sum total of proactive, reactive and unintentional activities and messages of organisations. Organisational public relations uses the proactive and sometimes the reactive elements of identity as a tool to help reduce the dissonance that might exist between how the organisation would like to be perceived by its stakeholder and the actual image the stakeholder has of the organisation. Organisational public relations uses a strategic approach in its management of the organisation's identities.

An important element that has an influence in an organisation's image and reputation is its own culture or personality. Organisational culture has two aspects: the overt ones – those that are easily recognisable and premeditated; the covert, often present as rituals or 'ways of doing things and behaving' that are not explicit. Both these elements of culture have a defining influence on the identities projected by the organisation and, therefore, will affect images and reputations of the organisation. Consequently, it is vital that professionals working in organisational public relations are aware of both elements of organisational culture to produce effective communications in line with their strategies.

Bibliography

Balmer, J.M.T. and S.A. Greyser (2003). *Revealing the Corporation: Perspectives on identity, image, reputation, corporate branding, and corporate-level marketing.* London: Routledge.

Bernstein, D. (1984). *Company Image and Reality: A critique of corporate communications.* Eastbourne: HRW.

Dolphin, R. and Y. Fan (2000). 'Is corporate communications a strategic function?'. *Management Decision* **38**(2): 99–106.

Gregory, A. (1997). *Planning and Managing a Public Relations Campaign: A step-by-step guide.* London: Kogan Page.

Harrison, S. (1995). *Public Relations: An introduction.* London: Routledge.

Löwenberg, D. (2005). Unpublished.

Meech, P. (1996). 'Corporate identity and corporate image' in *Critical Perspectives in Public Relations.* J. L'Etang and M. Pieczka (eds). London: Thomson Business Press.

Moingeon, B. (1999). 'From corporate culture to corporate identity. *Corporate Reputation Review* **2**(4): 352–360.

Moingeon, B. and B. Ramanantsoa, B. (1997). 'Understanding corporate identity: The French School of thought'. *European Journal of Marketing* **31**(5/6).

Parker, M. (2000). *Organizational Culture and Identity.* London: Sage.

Spaeth, T. (2002). *Honors to the Bold.* www.identityworks.com

Trompenaars, F. and C. Hampden-Turner. (1999). *Riding the Waves of Culture: Understanding cultural diversity in business,* 2nd edition. London: Nicholas Brealey.

Van Riel, C.B.M. (1995). *Principles of Corporate Communication.* London: Prentice Hall.

For glossary definitions relevant to this chapter, visit the **selected glossary** feature on the website at: www.pearsoned.co.uk/tench

CHAPTER 14

Public relations, propaganda and the psychology of persuasion

Learning outcomes

By the end of this chapter you should be able to:

- describe and evaluate the components of propaganda and persuasive communication
- describe and distinguish between attitudes and their effect on behaviour
- describe and evaluate theories of attitude learning and change
- apply these concepts to a communication campaign
- describe and evaluate the ethics of persuasive communication

Structure

- Public relations and propaganda
- Public relations and persuasion
- Who says: the question of credibility
- Says what: the nature of the message
- To whom: the audience perspective
- To what effect: forming and changing attitudes and beliefs
- Ethical persuasion: is it possible?

Introduction

Many journalists assume that public relations is largely propaganda. Public relations practitioners – and some academics – tend to treat this as an outrageous accusation, denying that they would ever seek to persuade anyone about anything. Students and those wishing to practise responsible public relations may prefer a more rigorous response, based on examination of the issues rather than simple rejection of all charges.

This chapter examines the connections between propaganda and public relations, particularly in their shared history. This is then linked to persuasion and the processes involved in trying to persuade others. It uses a simple communication model to describe the stages of persuasion in some detail, drawing on theories from social psychology to understand concepts such as attitudes and their effect on behaviour. The perspective is largely that of the public relations practitioner seeking to influence others.

It concludes with a discussion of ethical principles for producing persuasive communication. Examples are given from the history of public relations and from recent world events.

think about 14.1 | **Are these examples of propaganda or public relations?**

- Libya's leader, Colonel Gadafy, is seeking public relations advice. So is the Arab TV station Al-Jazeera (*PR Week* 21 January 2005).
- The Pentagon tried to set up its own propaganda unit before the 2003 war on Iraq.
- Advertising and communications agency Ogilvy and Mather is teaching Chinese students the benefits of capitalism (*Wall Street Journal* 26 January 2005).
- An Iraqi media mogul is accused of running a propaganda campaign financed by Saudi Arabian intelligence (*The Guardian* 26 January 2005).
- A new lobby group, Alliance for American Advertising, is created by food manufacturers and advertisers to defend advertising to children (*Wall Street Journal* 27 January 2005).
- The UK government hired a public relations agency to campaign for approval of the European constitution in the referendum then planned to take place in 2006 (*Financial Times* 20 January 2005).

Public relations and propaganda

See Think about 14.1. Critics of public relations say that much of public relations *is* propaganda; its practitioners insist public relations is only practised for the public good. Both agree that propaganda is harmful; the latter deny it has anything to do with them. These views are very simplistic and have a strong 'either/or', 'good/bad' approach to the subject. One group assumes all public relations is propaganda; the other that none is. It is also much easier to accuse others of propaganda than to examine one's own practices – you do propaganda; I do public relations. The realities are more complex and take some unravelling. Let's start with trying to explain the differences.

The word propaganda has its origins in the seventeenth-century Catholic Church, where it meant to 'propagate the faith'. It played a major part in recruiting support for the First World War, when the key Committee on Public Information (CPI) was established in the USA. (See Box 14.1, p. 270, for the impact this committee had on the development of public relations in the UK and USA.)

L'Etang (1998) notes that propaganda was a neutral term at the start of the twentieth century when theorists such as Bernays (1923), Lippman (1925) and Lasswell (1934) saw no problem with trying to organise the responses of mass audiences. Indeed, they saw it as 'democratic leadership' in Lippman's phrase, and Bernays, sometimes called the father of public relations, called his second book *Propaganda* (1928). As Weaver et al. (2004) say: 'In these terms, the real value of propaganda lies not in its dissemination and promotion of ideas but in its ability to orchestrate public opinion and social action that supported the ruling elite' (2004: 6–7).

Propaganda was not seen as a pejorative (negative or disparaging) concept until after the Second World War. When everyone saw the power of Nazi propaganda, especially their use of film, to promote anti-Semitism and the horrific consequences of that message, it is hardly surprising that communicators distanced themselves from the concept of propaganda. Nevertheless, propaganda is part of our everyday lives, not just something from history. As Pratkanis and Aronson (2001:7) point out: 'Every day we are bombarded with one persuasive communication after another. These appeals persuade not through the give-and-take of argument and debate, but through the manipulation of symbols and of our most basic human emotions. For better or worse, ours is an age of propaganda.'

Many scholars who study propaganda concentrate on its wartime application. However, there are increasing numbers of academics, journalists and campaigners who are examining the role of public relations in civil and corporate propaganda. There are websites dedicated to monitoring public relations activity, such as the US-based Center for Media and Democracy (www.prwatch.org), which contains extremely interesting and disturbing examples of unethical corporate public relations, and the UK-based Corporate Watch, (www.ethicalconsumer.org/magazine/corpwatch.htm), which is particularly concerned with environmental aspects of corporate behaviour. The most interesting – and sometimes challenging – site for public relations students is probably the UK-based Spinwatch (www.spinwatch.org.uk), which describes itself as:

An independent organisation set up to monitor the PR and lobbying industry in the UK and Europe and the spin and lobbying activities of corporations. Spinwatch is a registered charity and is not linked to any political party in the UK, Europe or elsewhere. Spinwatch exists to provide public interest research and reporting on corporate and government public relations and propaganda.

Spinwatch is edited by a team of independent researchers who have extensive experience of researching

Public relations or propaganda – how would you classify these examples?

- Several sugar companies create a body to promote sugar consumption. They call it the Sugar Information Centre (SIC) and commission scientific research into the effects of sugar consumption. One finding suggests that children's teeth are less affected by sugar than previous research believed. This finding is published by the SIC and carried in major news outlets. The fact that the research was funded by the sugar industry and involved fewer children than previously is not mentioned (invented example).

- Greenpeace takes a video of its activists gaining access to the Brent Spar oil platform in 1995 and releases the tape to media organisations who screen it as a lead news item. It turns out there are serious errors in the report and, of course, no other point of view covered in the tape (Varey 1997).

- The government dossier setting out the reasons for invading Iraq and presented to Parliament in 2003 is found to contain differences in emphasis from the original source documents, with statements suggesting the information should be treated with caution edited out. Another dossier contains material from a PhD student, which is only properly acknowledged after journalists identify the source (Miller 2004).

- In 1993, a group called Mothers Opposing Pollution (MOP) appeared, calling itself 'the largest women's environmental group in Australia, with thousands of supporters across the country'. Their cause: a campaign against plastic milk bottles. It turned out that the group's spokesperson, Alana Maloney, was in truth a woman named Janet Rundle, the business partner of a man who did public relations for the Association of Liquidpaperboard Carton Manufacturers – makers of paper milk cartons (Rampton and Stauber 2002).

Feedback

Do the examples fall neatly into one category or another? Can you tell what, if anything, is wrong with any of these examples? Do you find you don't mind the questionable statements if you approve of the overall message? It's not easy to decide, is it?

the PR industry, corporate PR and lobbying, front groups, government spin, propaganda and other tactics used by powerful groups to manipulate media, public policy debate and public opinion. The editorial board of Spinwatch includes academics, activists and freelance journalists.

Source: © 2004 Spinwatch.
See Activity 14.1.

Defining propaganda

Propaganda has been described as 'the deliberate and systematic attempt to shape perceptions, manipulate

cognitions and direct behaviour to achieve a response that furthers the desired intent of the propagandist' (Jowett and O'Donnell 1992: 4). This emphasises the purposefulness of propaganda, its organisation and the way propaganda seeks to further the sender's not the receiver's interests. It also shows that the propagandist seeks to influence the thoughts and behaviour of the audience. The problem is that it could equally describe a great deal of public relations activity.

Grunig and Hunt (1984: 21) locate propaganda in the press agentry model, the first of their four models: 'Public relations serves a propaganda function in the press agentry/publicity model. Practitioners spread the faith of the organisation involved, often through incomplete, distorted, or half-true information.' This links (some) public relations activity to propaganda, but later makes clear this is often unethical in content and tends to associate it with historical examples.

An alternative description is provided by Taylor (1992), who suggests that: 'Propaganda is a *practical process of persuasion* [his emphasis] . . . it is an

PICTURE 14.1   James Montgomery Flagg's memorable recruiting poster (produced under the direction of the Division of Pictorial Publicity of the Committee on Public Information) was successful in stimulating American public opinion in favour of US involvement in the European conflict during World War II. (*Source:* LLC/Corbis.)

box
14.1
Public relations – a little history

Edward Bernays (1891–1995), is widely described as the 'father of public relations' and his life and career sheds some interesting light on current dilemmas regarding public relations, persuasion and propaganda.

Born in Vienna, Bernays was the nephew of the pioneering psychologist, Sigmund Freud. He developed the practice of applying his uncle's theories of mass psychology to the practice of corporate and political persuasion. He started the first educational course in the subject at New York University in the 1920s and introduced the term 'public relations counsel' in his 1923 book, *Crystallizing Public Opinion*, which was the first text on the subject. His next book was called *Propaganda* (1928) because he believed that public relations was about engineering social responses to organisational needs (he also wrote *The Engineering of Consent*, 1955). His influence on the twentieth century is described in a fascinating BBC documentary *The Century of the Self* (BBC2 April/May 2002 – see www.bbc.co.uk/bbcfour/documentaries/features/century_of_the_self.shtml. for details), which looked at the impact of persuasion techniques and psychology on commercial and political communication throughout the twentieth century.

In the 1920s when the American Tobacco Company asked for his help in promoting cigarette smoking among women, Bernays persuaded a group of young women's rights campaigners to light cigarettes on the New York Easter march, as 'Torches of Freedom' (a slogan that he ensured was the caption to all the media photographs of the event), thus combining the image of the cigarette with women's independence – a powerful image that affected consumer behaviour for the rest of the twentieth century (Wilcox et al. 2003). He had learned some of these techniques during the First World War when he served on the US Committee for Public Information (see previous section).

The CPI included many of the leading public relations practitioners in the post-war period. As Bernays said in *Propaganda* (1928): 'It was, of course, the astounding success of propaganda during the war that opened the eyes of the intelligent few in all departments of life to the possibilities of regimenting the public mind. It was only natural, after the war ended, that intelligent persons should ask themselves whether it was not possible to apply a similar technique to the problems of peace' (cited in Delwiche 2002).

More information about Bernays and his contemporaries can be found at www.prmuseum.com/bernays. There is an interesting account of Stuart Ewen's interview with the 90-year-old Bernays (Ewen 1996) which also has a website at www.bway.net/~drstu/chapter.

The history of UK public relations also demonstrates its origins in propaganda. Unlike the growth of the field in the USA, European public relations is rooted in public service information traditions, with the emphasis on local and central government supply of information (L'Etang 1998). This was also the source of persuasion campaigns, such as the 1924 campaign – including films and posters – to promote the British Empire to the rest of the world, led by Sir Stephen Tallents, who went on to found the Institute of Public Relations (IPR) in 1948, and wrote *The Projection of England* (1932), which was influential in 'persuading British policy makers of the benefits of a cultural propaganda policy' (L'Etang 1998). He was active in producing propaganda for both world wars, as were the founders of several major public relations companies in the interwar period, many of which survive to this day. A more negative response came from George Orwell, who resigned from the BBC 'sickened by the propaganda he had had to do' (Ewen 1996) and proceeded to write *Nineteen Eighty-Four* (published in 1949) 'as a response to the experience' (L'Etang 1998).

---

inherently neutral concept . . . We should discard any notions of propaganda being "good" or "bad", and use those terms merely to describe effective or ineffective propaganda.' He says that the issue of intent is important in propaganda – not just who says what to whom, but *why* (Taylor 2001). This approach is in line with some public relations academics (L'Etang, Weaver) who believe propaganda should be re-examined rather than demonised in public relations texts.

A more political approach was developed by Herman and Chomsky (1988) who proposed a model of propaganda to explain the use of power (particularly state and

corporate power) in communication, especially outside totalitarian states. They suggested five 'filters' or layers of control whereby messages could be manipulated to suit certain interests. These can be summarised as:

1 the size and concentration of media ownership
2 the role of advertising in providing income for media organisations
3 the reliance of journalists from the mass media on government and other 'official' sources of information
4 'flak' (complaints to programmers/editors) as a means of controlling media content

5 'anti-communism' as a 'national religion' and control mechanism.

In this model, propaganda is not neutral but is designed to give the appearance of a 'free press' while actually producing messages that favour the views of government and business above other voices. If one substitutes anti-terrorism for anti-communism, the model still seems relevant and has been hugely influential. The role of public relations in political, military and corporate communications, not just publicity, is seen as fuelling propaganda. (See Think about 14.2.)

Public relations and persuasion

So far we have looked at propaganda and the part it has played in public relations past and present. Now it is important to see how persuasion fits into the picture.

As already stated, early public relations theorists had no problem with acknowledging the centrality of persuasion to public relations; indeed, Bernays considered public relations to be about 'engineering public consent'.

However, more recent public relations theory has tended to move away from this aspect of communication and concentrate on the more acceptable images of negotiation and adaptation. Very few public relations textbooks really explore persuasion. This is largely because the Grunig and Hunt (1984) models stress the positive aspects of excellent public relations and relegate persuasion to 'second best', the two-way asymmetric model (see Chapter 8 for details of systems theory and Grunig's approach). Moloney (2000) notes that they treat persuasion as an inferior or less ethical activity than negotiation or compromise, but argues that one often involves the other. Moreover, it is hard to maintain that persuasion is so unacceptable an endeavour – after all, it seems a very human impulse to seek to influence other members of society. Jaksa and Pritchard (1994: 128) stress that 'it cannot be seriously maintained that all persuasion is bad or undesirable' and Andersen (1978: 41) asserts that persuasion can serve others well so long as the communicator attempts to bring about 'voluntary change in the attitudes and/or actions of . . . receivers'.

And yet persuasion is still underexplored in public relations literature. Instead, we have to turn to other bodies of theory for guidance and insight. The two approaches that study persuasion in detail are the social psychology schools, which are covered later in the chapter, and the study of speech acts, or rhetoric. Rhetoric is an ancient topic of study, and refers to texts from ancient Greece, particularly Aristotle. (See Chapter 9 for more about the study of rhetoric and its relevance to public relations.) Persuasion was seen as an essential skill for leadership and democracy, where one party would produce rational arguments to persuade others to support or oppose a particular point of view. Study of persuasion here means examining the use of words, images, symbols, media and emphasis to understand the meaning and intent of the speaker. For example, many commentators explored the use of religious imagery and concepts in President Bush's second inaugural address (in 2005).

Miller (1989) is also interested in public relations and persuasion as using symbols to 'exert control over the environment', such as influencing the attitudes of others. He sees the similarities between persuasion and public relations as 'overwhelming'.

It is not always easy to separate persuasion from propaganda as the above examples illustrate, and this may be one reason why it is not examined more closely by public relations theorists. However, certain key concepts recur in the discussion of persuasion that might help public relations practitioners avoid the charge of propaganda. These are:

■ *Intent:* Taylor (2001) says that *intent* is a key determinant, as the communication itself is neutral. The question should not be is it good or bad communication, but was it effective or ineffective? Of course intent is hard to measure, even from the communicator's perspective – it is possible to have good intentions with damaging outcomes.
■ *Free will:* Many of the definitions of persuasion emphasise the 'free will' of the receivers; for example, O'Keefe (1990: 17) describes persuasion as 'a successful intentional effort at influencing another's mental state through communication in a circumstance in which the persuadee has some measure of freedom'. Again, the issue of power in communications is contested – people can feel constrained by social norms, lack of alternative opinions, etc.

■ *Truth:* While most public relations people would say they never lied, many would have to confess to not telling the *whole* truth *all* the time. But Schick (1994) declares that 'the intention of withholding a truth is to deceive'. Martinson (1996: 46) says that if the public relations practitioner is to practise ethical persuasion, they 'must adopt truthfulness as a norm . . . have internalised it as a value and . . . be ever vigilant in recognising that those inevitable temptations to communicate somewhat less than substantially complete information must be taken for what they are – temptations to manipulate others for the practitioner's own, or a client's, selfish ends'.

■ *Autonomy of audiences:* The idea of the autonomous, active audience is important for the creation of ethical persuasion. It underlines the importance of dialogue; it suggests a notion of equality. As Jaksa and Pritchard (1994) argue, 'human beings . . . should not be treated merely as a means to an end; they are to be respected as ends in themselves'. The freedom of the audience to participate on equal terms was central to Habermas's ideas of ethical dialogue (see Chapter 9 for details).

■ *Communication ethics* (see end of chapter).

Given these indicators and the work on ethics explored at the end of the chapter and in Chapter 15, let's look at the process of persuasion and, in particular, see what public relations practitioners can learn from social psychologists.

Persuasion and psychology

The US post-war research (led by scholars at Harvard and Yale) into the psychology of persuasion was driven both by the threat of the *Cold War* and fears of (as well as interest in) brainwashing, and the promise of the consumer boom in goods and services. Many organisations and advertising agencies recruited psychologists to help create powerful and effective messages. This led to some concern about commercial brainwashing, which was highlighted by Vance Packard's *The Hidden Persuaders* (1957). It was seen as deeply sinister then, but the only technique he described which is no longer in regular use is subliminal advertising (where images are flashed on a screen too quickly for the brain fully to register them). It seems that we have become used to the fact that persuasion is an integral part of mass communication. The use of psychology in designing persuasive messages is now a widely recognised practice. One website that promotes the skills of psychologists in helping businesses is www.influenceatwork.com. It offers a self-test and examples of how psychology can help communication campaigns.

The latest development in using psychology for promotion is called neuromarketing, where neuroscientists identify which parts of the brain are stimulated by different tastes, sounds and images, and help manufacturers test the response to their products. For example, recent research (reported in *The Guardian* 29 July 2004) shows that while people liked the taste of Pepsi better than Coca-Cola in blind tests, they preferred Coke when they knew which brand they were drinking. Brain scans showed that while one (rewards) section of the brain was activated by the tasting, a different (thinking) centre responded to the brand names, suggesting that we call on memories and impressions associated with a name, rather than just the direct experience.

This chapter will not be probing anyone's brains, but draws on more theoretical models of how people make decisions and what influences them.

> **Definition:** *Cold War* refers to hostile relations between the former Soviet Union and the USA, and their respective allies between 1946 and 1989.

Propaganda, persuasion and public relations all involve communication, although they have other aspects, and it is worth examining the communication process to understand what is involved. Persuasion and propaganda tend to conform to the transmission model of communication, summarised by Harold Lasswell (1948) as 'Who (1) says What (2) in Which channel (3) to Whom (4), with What effect (5)'. The second half of this chapter analyses persuasive communication and the role of the sender (1), the message (2) and the receiver (4) in achieving (or failing to achieve) an effect (5). It does not analyse the use of different media in constructing persuasive messages, as the chapter focuses more on psychology than media relations. It draws on social psychology theories to illustrate the personality variables of sender and receiver, the effectiveness of different message strategies, and finally how the elements all fit into a persuasive campaign.

Who says: the question of credibility

These elements concern the nature of the sender or sender variables. Aristotle said that communication consisted of: *Ethos* – the character of the speaker; *Logos* – the nature of the message; and *Pathos* – the attitude of the audience. He placed most emphasis on the speaker's (orators tended to be male, then) character: 'We believe good men more fully and more readily than others . . . his character may almost be called the most effective means of persuasion he possesses' (cited in Perloff 1993: 138).

Credibility has been an important – but hard to define – element of persuasive communication ever since. Look at today's newspapers and concerns about the credibility of politicians to see how relevant it is today. A great deal of public relations activity is designed to enhance the credibility of the organisation or individual. UK Prime Minister Tony Blair has had to deal with massive loss in credibility following inaccurate statements made in the run-up to the 2003 war in Iraq. It was not necessary to prove any deliberate untruths for his credibility to be damaged. Many politicians today make credibility their central platform for election – 'trust me' is their key message. However, the Edelman public relations firm's survey of eight countries found that 'pressure groups and charities have overtaken governments, media and big businesses to become the world's most trusted institutions' (*Financial Times* 24 January 2005).

Many scholars in the USA in the 1950s, especially at Yale and Harvard, concentrated on attributes of speakers – how attractive are they, how expert, etc. – to try and measure credibility. But later scholars, like McCroskey (1966), said that 'credibility is the attitude toward a speaker held by a listener'. In other words, it is something that is given by the audience and cannot be demanded by the speaker. An interesting theory in this area is attribution theory (Eagly et al. 1978), which says that audiences want to know why the source is taking a particular position. Politicians are expected to say 'Vote for Me' so the message is not particularly persuasive – we would expect them to say that, wouldn't we? If they suggested we vote for someone else, *then* we would be interested! We want to know why someone is saying what they are saying – is it for money, or status, or because it's their job – or do they really believe what they are saying?

Another fascinating discovery from the Yale school was the 'sleeper effect' (Hovland et al. 1953), which showed that however much effort was put into providing a credible source, when audiences were tested several weeks after exposure to the message, they remembered the message but forgot the source!

Perloff (1993) summarises the four key elements by which audiences evaluate speakers as:

1 *expertise* – how competent the speaker is on this issue
2 *trustworthiness* – this includes confidence and likeability
3 *similarity* – credible speakers should be like the receiver (*homophily*) unless the subject concerns different experiences or expertise, in which case they should be dissimilar (*heterophily*)
4 *physical attractiveness* – people tend to trust attractive speakers – which may reflect the social value attached to appearance, as in celebrity public

relations – unless the speaker is so attractive that their looks distract from the message (adapted from Perloff 1993).

> **Definition:** *Homophily* means similarity between speaker and audience.
>
> **Definition:** *Heterophily* means difference between speaker and audience.

Other theorists (Raven 1983) added 'power' to the list, saying that the kind of authority the speaker has over the listener can influence the persuasion process. Bettinghaus and Cody (1994: 143–145) summarise Raven's types of power as:

- *informational influence* – access to restricted information gives authority to a speaker
- *referent influence* – membership of key social groups can confer power
- *expert influence* – knowledge of the field
- *legitimate influence* – authorised by law or other agreement (e.g. traffic warden, safety officer)
- *reward/coercive influence* – are there rewards for being persuaded or punishments for resisting?

The role of power in persuasion is also important to critical approaches to public relations theory (see Chapter 9 for details).

The issues of credibility covered above are of direct relevance to pubic relations where it is essential to establish credible sources for messages. Activity 14.2 illustrates the sorts of decision public relations practitioners need to make which require knowledge or insight into credibility.

activity 14.2

Speaker credibility

Which speaker or presenter would you choose for the following events:

1 Launch of new carburettor using methane gas to audience of motoring journalists: (a) TV motoring correspondent; (b) lead engineer from motor company; (c) learner driver?
2 Promotional campaign for new mobile phone aimed at youth market – poster ads: (a) phone engineer; (b) television personality contestant; (c) CEO of phone company?
3 Video about safe sex for showing in schools: (a) minister for education; (b) doctor working in genitourinary health unit; (c) young person?

Feedback

These choices involve considerations about expertise and trustworthiness, and illustrate that there are times when you want a speaker who resembles the audience (homophily) and other occasions when the differences will increase credibility (heterophily).

Now let's take the next element in Lasswell's phrase, 'says what – the nature of the message'.

Says what: the nature of the message

This element of persuasion looks at which kinds of message are most convincing and the ways in which messages are absorbed and used by people. Message research included investigating whether messages using fear or humour were more persuasive and whether it was more effective to appeal to the audiences' reason or emotion. At first it was thought that fear made a message more powerful but a later theory, fear protection motivation schema (Rogers 1983), suggested that if a message is too frightening, receivers tend to block the message to protect them-selves from being alarmed. This is borne out by expe-rience of early AIDS campaigns in the 1980s when ads showing tombstones with the message 'Don't Die of Ignorance' were subsequently seen as counterpro-ductive (Miller et al. 1998). Scholars do not agree on this issue – what do you think?

One of the most interesting theories concerning how messages are processed is the elaboration likeli-hood model (Petty and Cacioppo 1986), which sug-gested that there are two routes to persuasion: the central and peripheral routes (see Figure 14.1). The central route involves processing (or elaborating) the arguments contained in a message, using reason and evaluation. The peripheral route involves react-ing emotionally to a message that appeals to a range of responses – such as humour or feelings towards the person giving the message (such as a celebrity) – with-out having to weigh up the arguments for and against the message. The central route is more likely to lead to

Central route	Peripheral route
Simon is considering a new life insurance policy	Rowena has a plane to catch but needs to pick up travel insurance on the way
The decisions he makes will effect the financial well-being of his family after his death	The policy will only last for the duration of her holiday
He wants to take his time comparing options, and will talk to his advisors	She scans the web to compare prices
Simon chooses the policy that balances the cost of the premiums with the benefits to his loved ones	A link comes up with bright graphics and a link to holiday cover. A celebrity from a TV travel show is shown giving the thumbs up. The price is about right for one-off cover. She doesn't check the small print
He visits the insurance offices to sign the forms	She buys it online
Simon is persuaded by the quality of the policy, its costs and benefits, despite the time taken to choose	Rowena is persuaded by images and ease of purchase, regardless of the actual policy benefits

FIGURE 14.1   Elaboration likelihood model (*source:* adapted from Petty and Cacioppo 1986)

long lasting attitude change; the peripheral route, often used by advertisers, works for short-term messages.

Use of arguments to persuade

If the message aims to involve the receiver in internal reasoning or elaboration, then it has to ensure that there is a good range of arguments to support the message. The communicator also has to decide whether to present all the arguments in favour of their position or whether to deal with the counterarguments as well. Research suggested that more educated or hostile audiences often prefer to be given both points of view, even if the message concludes with the preferred position of the communicator. People who already support the point of view – fans of a band, members of a political party, for example – are more receptive to messages reinforcing just that one point of view. Petty and Cacioppo also suggested that some people had a 'need for cognition', that is a motive to find out things and a preference for making choices based on thought and reflection rather than impulse. Of course, if the messages are unclear, or irrelevant to the receiver, then they will not be motivated to elaborate further.

Toulmin (1958) suggested that effective messages use evidence (data, opinions, case studies, etc.) to make a claim (the message the communicator wants the receiver to agree with), which is then backed by a warrant (reason to agree). An example might be the UK NHS anti-smoking adverts shown regularly on television. These tend to show a terminally ill person (evidence) talking about their life expectancy (claim) and close with statements about the effectiveness of support lines (warrant). There is an excellent website explaining current campaigns, key messages and target groups, with examples of TV, press and poster ads at www.givingupsmoking.co.uk (see Picture 14.2).

In the increasingly visual environment of modern communication, messages are more likely to appeal to the emotions of the receiver than their reason. There is some evidence that making people feel good is more effective than making them feel bad. According to a UK Sunday newspaper article (*Observer* 17 October 2004) three researchers went to a beach full of sunbathers in New England (USA) to find out whether positive or negative messages were more persuasive. They approached 217 sunbathers and gave them either 'gain' messages ('protect yourself from the sun and you will help yourself stay healthy') or 'loss' messages ('not using sunscreen increases your risk of early death'). They then gave the sunbathers coupons to exchange for free sunscreen. Seventy-one per cent of people given a positive message got up to get their free cream, whereas only 50% in the loss frame were motivated.

However, there are also examples of fear campaigns being conducted by both parties in the 2004 US presidential election, and previous election campaign

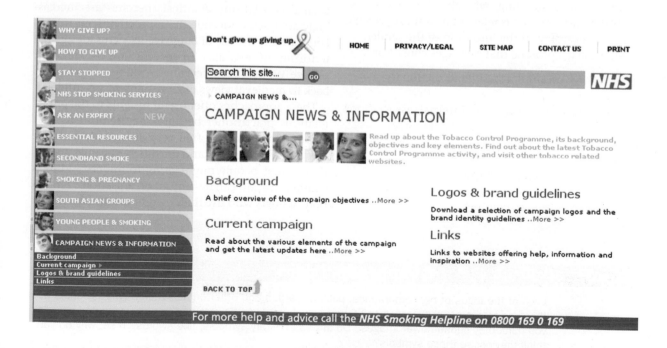

PICTURE 14.2 Giving up smoking. See www.givingupsmoking.co.uk/CNI. (*Source:* HMSO.)

analysis has revealed that suggesting to voters that they will be less safe with an opponent in charge can be very effective. (See Activity 14.3.)

Approaches to persuasion

Another angle to studying persuasive messages is the rhetorical approach, which looks in detail at the language used by communicators, and the exchange of information, or discourse, between parties seeking to influence each other through the use of words and symbols. They do not see persuasion as inherently good or bad but as the stuff of human interaction: 'Through statement and counterstatement, people test each other's views of reality, value, and choices relevant to products, services and public policies' (Heath 2001: 31). They see public relations as the search for shared meaning and emphasise the importance of relationship in achieving such understanding. (See Chapter 9 for more about *rhetoric* and public relations.)

Definition: Rhetoric means the study of language and how it is used to create shared meanings.

Semiotics is also a fascinating approach to studying messages and, unlike many traditional public relations models, the perspective is that of the receiver, not the sender. Its leading theorists (Pierce, Saussure) proposed the study of texts and symbols as acts of decoding or deconstructing, whereby the receiver extracts the meaning that is relevant or comprehensible to them, regardless of the intention of the sender. Semioticians propose that messages consist of:

- *denotative* meaning (the literal, dictionary meaning)
- *connotative* meaning (the internal associations each reader/viewer brings to the message)
- *ambiguous* meaning (perhaps the message has multiple dictionary meanings)
- *polysemic* meaning (perhaps it has multiple associations, varying not only from person to person but from culture to culture).

activity 14.3

Message appeals

Look at the messages around you – can you find examples of appeals to your feelings? What about engaging your reason? Can you see 'feel good' messages? What about fear campaigns? Do you prefer a message that makes you laugh?

Feedback

Look at the posters produced by candidates in elections – whether for local, general, EU or student elections. Are they creating positive images of themselves or negative images of their opponents? Which do you think are more effective?

Definition: Semiotics means the study of language, symbols and images and how they are created by audiences or used to generate relevant meaning.

The distinguished UK practitioner, Reginald Watts (2004), argues that visual language is replacing written communication and that public relations should become more actively engaged in the study of semiotics, given that signs and symbols are the bedrock of most contemporary communication. (See Think about 14.3.)

Both the above groups use media content analysis to examine the content of messages, whether from corporations, politicians or mass media. These tools allow them to explore the surface meanings and the deeper associations. Political speeches are increasingly analysed to decode their underlying meanings. For example, the use of language like 'crusade against terrorism' or 'evil axis' in speeches by US President George W. Bush can reveal a world view that refers back to medieval views of Christians versus infidels.

These approaches offer useful insights to the public relations practitioner because they remind us that messages *received* are often very different from those *sent*. Failure to understand the different values and attitudes that people might bring to understanding a communication can destroy an organisation's reputation. Senders who use their own terms of reference or

think about 14.3   Corporate logos

Look at the logos of big corporations, political parties and other organisations. What symbols do they use to represent themselves? Count how many have flowers as their key symbols – why do you think they chose flower images? Do any use military symbols, like swords? If so, why do you think they chose those symbols?

(See also Chapter 13 on image, reputation and identity.)

value systems will not create understanding or 'shared meaning', as rhetoric puts it. Sometimes this involves literal mistranslations as when a leading pen manufacturer translated the line 'our pen will not leak in your pocket and embarrass you' for its Mexican launch, but used the word *embrazar* . . . meaning to make pregnant. Other problems concern point of view: a leading tobacco manufacturer proudly announced that smoking-related premature deaths saved Czechoslovakia $147 million a year in benefits (Fineman 2001). Good news or what?

The next section looks at the 'to whom' part of Lasswell's saying and in particular examines whether some people are easier to persuade than others and the role of the receiver's psychology in creating successful communication.

To whom: the audience perspective

Receivers can be grouped in many ways. There is a range of media theories showing how publics come together to use a particular medium to gain information or entertainment, for example. They can be categorised by age, geography, occupation, gender, marital status, etc. This is called *demographics*. Then there are the theories that look at *psychographics*, or differences in personality.

Psychologists have investigated a number of theories that might explain why some people are easier to persuade than others and the internal process by which persuasion takes place. Aspects of personality, such as self-esteem, are examined as are the internal structures of personality, such as attitudes and behaviour. This section looks at the psychology of persuasion from the individual receiver's perspective.

Self-esteem was felt to be an important component of persuasion and research showed that people with lower self-esteem were much easier to persuade. However, it was not entirely simple, as people with low self-esteem were more easily influenced by superficial aspects of the message, whereas people with higher self-esteem tended to engage with relevant thinking on the issue before deciding whether to agree or disagree with the message. As a result, those who were most easily persuaded by peripheral cues (colour, music, celebrity) tended not to internalise the message and were therefore equally easily persuaded by the next message to use the same tactics. There was also evidence (Cohen 1959) that people with high self-esteem avoided or deflected unwelcome or challenging messages – a bit like smokers leaving the room when anti-smoking ads come on. This is called ego-defensive behaviour, as it allows the person to maintain self-belief by avoiding contradictory evidence. These findings

suggests that different tactics are needed for different audiences – with reasons to agree provided to those who prefer to process messages and simple, non-threatening messages to those who do not. There are echoes here of the elaboration likelihood model outlined above.

> **Definition:** *Demographics* means external differences between people – e.g. race, age, gender, location, occupational status, group membership.

> **Definition:** *Psychographics* describes internal differences between personalities – e.g. anxious, approval-seeking, high self-esteem, etc.

Another personality variable that affected how easily an individual could be persuaded was discovered by Snyder and DeBono (1985) who showed that some people are more likely to look outside themselves for clues about how to respond (high self-monitors), while others look inwards (low self-monitors). The former is influenced by the reactions of those around them, especially people they would like to be accepted by (sometimes called the referent group). The latter consults their own values and beliefs before responding to messages. (See Activity 14.4 and Think about 14.4, overleaf.)

This theory also raises the issue of the influence of groups on the persuasiveness of the individual. There are a number of theories that look at how individuals behave in group situations, of which the most relevant here is social comparison theory (Festinger 1954). This applies when individuals have to evaluate an opinion or ability and cannot test it directly. (See Box 14.2, overleaf.)

activity 14.4

Are you a high self-monitor?

Bettinghaus and Cody (1994: 165) provide the following statements as tests for self-monitoring:

- 'I have considered being an entertainer.'
- 'I'm not always the person I appear to be.'
- 'I may deceive people by being friendly when I really dislike them.'
- 'I guess I put on a show to impress or entertain others.'
- 'I can make impromptu speeches even on topics about which I have almost no information.'

The authors suggest that people who agree with most of these statements are likely to be high self-monitors. They go on to identify key areas of difference that are important to understand if one wishes to construct relevant messages (to work out which group you belong to see Table 14.1).

TABLE 14.1   Personality types (*source*: based on Bettinghaus and Cody 1994)

High self-monitors (HSM)	Low self-monitors (LSM)
Concentrate on the actual and potential reactions of others in social situations	Refer to their core values
Adaptable and flexible, presenting aspects of themselves most suitable for each occasion	More consistent in any given situation
Actively contribute to the smooth flow of conversation and bind participants together by using 'we', 'our' words, humour and exchanging self-disclosures, as appropriate	Less able to facilitate conversation
More likely to have different friends for different activities	Are more likely to do different things with the same people
Have other HSMs as friends	Have other LSMs as friends
Males are more concerned with the physical appearance of a potential date, have more and briefer relationships	Males are more concerned with date's personality, more likely to make a commitment
More responsive to messages that emphasise image, status, public approval, glamour or sex appeal	More interested in the quality and good value of a product

think about 14.4   Personality and public relations practitioners

It is interesting to note that the HSM attributes are quite common among public relations practitioners – are they all high self-monitors? If so, is this good because they are sensitive to people around them, or bad because they fit in with others' expectations rather than develop values of their own?

This, and similar theories, show how important it is to understand the group dynamics when communicating important messages. Just think about how hard it is to persuade people to stop drink driving if all their friends think it is a brilliant thing to do. Messages that conflict with group beliefs, or norms, are most likely to be rejected by the group.

So is it even possible to persuade people to stop drink driving? Why not just use legal powers and stop trying to persuade these hard-to-reach groups? But what if the message is to encourage people to take more exercise, use less energy, join this organisation, visit that country?

The law cannot help here. Threats will not work. Persuasion is the only tool. After all, it is said that the objective of most public relations campaigns is either 'to change or neutralise hostile opinion, crystallize unformed or latent opinion or conserve favourable

box 14.2   Theory in practice – social comparison theory

Student X might be asked whether they think dissertations are a valuable element in a degree programme. As X has not yet done one, they have no direct experience. In these circumstances, individuals are likely to compare their responses to those around them, by waiting, perhaps to see what others have to say first. The individual is more likely to agree with someone with whom they already have things in common than someone with very different attitudes. To continue the example, if X enjoys working hard and has friends who share this approach, they are likely to agree about the value of dissertations. X is less likely to be influenced by someone who has said they don't care what kind of a degree they get. This process explains how groups often come to hold strong common beliefs, but also how there is a pressure to conform within groups. If X was really unsure, but their friends all strongly supported dissertations, X is more likely to say nothing than risk the disapproval of the group.

opinions by reinforcing them' (Cutlip et al. 1985: 152). These are all acts of persuasion. The question for practitioners is – what works?

In order to understand whether or not persuasion has any effect, we need to understand what attitudes consist of, how they are acquired and then how they can be changed.

To what effect: forming and changing attitudes and beliefs

Before examining attitudes, let us look at some related aspects of thoughts and feelings that affect the way we see the world, such as beliefs and values. *Belief* is seen as a function of mind, assembling thoughts to create a system of reference for understanding.

> **Definition:** *Belief* is 'commitment to something, involving intellectual assent' (Columbia 2003).

We can all make many thousands of belief statements (sentences beginning 'I believe that . . .') (Rokeach 1960), which can be sorted into *descriptive*, *evaluative* and *prescriptive*: *descriptive* beliefs describe the world around us (I believe the sky is blue, this is a good university, etc.); *evaluative* beliefs weigh up the consequences of actions (I believe this course is right for me); and *prescriptive* beliefs suggest how things ought to be (I believe men and women should share housework).

Another approach is to divide beliefs into central and peripheral beliefs, where central beliefs are close to values and describe what we hold most important ('I believe in equality, justice, etc.). These may then underpin peripheral beliefs (I believe in the secret ballot, jury trials, etc.). It is also possible to have peripheral-only beliefs (I believe this shampoo will clean my hair). Rokeach (1960) suggests there are two types of central beliefs – those that are agreed by everyone, such as 'rocks fall when dropped', and those that are personal, such as 'I believe in horoscopes'. Bettinghaus and Cody (1994) also talk about authority-derived beliefs, where we adopt ideas proposed by those in authority, although recent social developments suggest reduced trust in traditional authority figures like politicians or even doctors.

Persuasion attempts often target peripheral beliefs because they are most easily changed (I believe *this* shampoo is even better), whereas authority-based beliefs, such as family values or childhood religion, change more slowly, and central beliefs hardly at all. Central beliefs are very close to values, as are prescriptive beliefs. Values are the core ideals that we use as guides and that express ourselves – they concern issues like justice or the environment or freedom. How we treat each other reflects our central values – whether that is 'you've got to look out for yourself first' or 'we have to sink or swim together'. (See Figure 14.2 for examples of how values affect beliefs, attitudes and opinions.)

This is a blurred area: many of the definitions for beliefs overlap with opinions and values. The simplest way to note the difference is that beliefs and

Dave

Sarah

Opinion, peripheral beliefs	This is expensive so it must be better quality	I like own-brand products – they're just as good
Attitudes	Poor people are losers. They're all scroungers. My worth is my bank balance	It could be me in trouble. I like to help. Money isn't everything
Central beliefs	Competition is good – as long as I win. You make your own luck	If we work together we can improve life for everyone
Values	Fair reward for fair effort. Self-reliance	Equality for all. Cooperation

FIGURE 14.2   Opinions, attitudes and values

opinions usually involve thoughts; values and attitudes also involve feelings. It is also worth remembering that while psychology scholars need to divide us into smaller and smaller boxes to examine the contents, we actually use all of these aspects in combination to negotiate our way through the world.

Now, let's turn to attitudes, where our beliefs about what is right and wrong meet our feelings about right and wrong.

Attitudes

Allport (1935), an early researcher in this field, said that *attitudes* underpin our reactions to people and events, creating a filter or system against which we measure our responses to messages and events. We said above that values affect our attitudes. These attitudes may, in turn, affect our behaviour by causing the GM protester to buy organic goods, for example (although, being human, they may drive to the health food shop). Attitudes do not predict behaviour but they do provide a reasonable guide and so are well worth further investigation by communicators wishing to understand their audiences. (See Activity 14.5 and Think about 14.5.)

> **Definition:** 'When we talk about *attitudes*, we are talking about what a person has *learned* in the process of becoming a member of a family, a member of a group, and of society that makes him react to his social world in a *consistent* and *characteristic* way, instead of a transitory and haphazard way. We are talking about the fact that he is no longer neutral in sizing up the world around him: he is *attracted* or *repelled, for* or *against, favourable* or *unfavourable*' (Sherif 1967:2).

Attitudes are also more likely to affect behaviour if you are in a position to act on them (*individuated*). You are less likely to act out your attitudes if you are in a group (*de-individuated*) whose members hold different views or if you are in a formal situation like a lecture theatre where the range of available behaviours is restricted (*scripted*). These are called situational factors.

However, there is some evidence that the link between attitude and behaviour change can be overes-

activity 14.5

Attitudes towards television

- *Big Brother* (European TV show that has 24-hour camera surveillance on contestants) is a fascinating experiment.
- *Big Brother* is cheap entertainment at others' expense.
- TV is dumbing down.
- TV has always been a mix of good and bad.
- Programme makers only produce what audiences want to watch.
- I don't care about TV.

Which of these statements reflects your own views? How far does the selected statement connect with other attitudes – to television, to entertainment, to society at large?

timated. An *Observer* journalist (17 October 2004) interviewed Sheila Orbell, a health psychologist from the University of Essex in the UK who has spent the past 15 years teasing out which public health interventions make people change and which do not.

It would not be unreasonable to assume, she says, that if people know something is bad for them and want to change, they will change. But that would be wrong. 'Fifty per cent of the time, people act against their intentions', says Orbell, referring to a study about health-related intentions and subsequent actions. She reveals that 77% of the time there is no correlation between how serious we think it would be to have a disease and our behaviour. Even more surprisingly, there is almost no correlation between our fear of contracting a disease (such as lung cancer) and our long-term actions (stopping smoking) (*Observer* 17 October 2004).

So where do attitudes come from? How are they acquired? Social psychology suggests a number of paths to explain how we learn attitudes.

1 Classic conditioning, made famous by Pavlov (1849–1936), who showed the difference between unconditioned and conditioned responses. The former refers to physiological reactions to certain stimuli – to blink at bright lights, flinch from pain, or in the case of Pavlov's dogs

think about 14.5 **Your attitudes**

Have you ever boycotted a product or service, signed a petition, voted for or against something or someone, got into an argument with friends or family? Do you have strong attitudes on a range of subjects? If so, can you identify the core values which underpin them? Or do you feel fairly neutral about most things and avoid disagreement on such subjects?

(and humans) salivate at the smell and sight of food.

2 Instrumental or operant conditioning, which means using rewards and/or punishment to encourage/discourage behaviours and attitudes. Most parents will use these techniques to instil attitudes towards road safety, table manners, etc.

3 Social learning theory, which says that we acquire our attitudes either by direct experience, by playing out roles that mimic experience and/or by modelling, that is watching how others behave in a range of situations. For example, we might learn how to react by watching characters in soap operas deal with betrayal, disappointment, bereavement or crisis.

4 Genetic determinism disputes all these explanations and looks for the roots of our motives in our genes. There has always been a conflict between scientists who believe human psychology is determined by biology and social psychologists who believe how we are raised and life experiences contribute more to our personality. The new discoveries in gene science have given strength to the former group, but the dispute is certainly not over. (See Think about 14.6.)

Social psychologists have a number of theories about how to change attitudes and these are all interesting and relevant to the public relations practitioner. Two particularly interesting theories are the theory of reasoned action and the theory of cognitive dissonance.

The theory of reasoned action (Fishbein and Azjen 1980) looks at the links between attitude and behaviour and the points where change might be possible. It draws on expectancy value theory (Fishbein and Azjen 1975), which describes how attitudes are the results of having expectations met or disappointed. The theory of reasoned action suggests that individuals conduct complicated evaluations of different influences, such as the opinions of family, friends, teachers, giving them different weightings depending on how important their views are to the individual, who then compares these opinions to their own views and forms attitudes based on the results. It also suggests attitudes

can be changed by altering one of the key components in the equation.

Understanding this process can be helpful if you are a communicator seeking to influence behaviour. It suggests that you can address the attitude towards the behaviour, for example by introducing new *beliefs* about the risks of smoking or by convincing audiences to *re-evaluate* the outcome of smoking by convincing them that their own health is in danger. Alternatively a campaign might seek to change the *subjective norm* by suggesting that key groups of people think that smoking is uncool, anti-social, etc. It is also relevant for any persuasion campaign where the subjective norm plays a part in the behaviour, such as football hooligans where violence is approved by the group's leaders.

However, this theory is somewhat mechanistic and suggests a rather linear approach to persuasion and attitude change. An alternative, more intuitive approach was developed by Leon Festinger in 1957, the theory of cognitive dissonance. This proposes that thoughts generate emotional responses and that people prefer to have harmony (*consonance*) between their thoughts and feelings, rather than disharmony (*dissonance*): 'The existence of dissonance, being psychologically uncomfortable, will motivate the person to try to reduce the dissonance and achieve consonance' (Festinger 1957). Aronson (1968) later stressed that the dissonance needed to be psychological not merely logically inconsistent. (See Box 14.3, overleaf.)

Cognitive dissonance describes how we rationalise internal conflicts to ourselves. We are usually most reluctant to change our behaviour and prefer to alter our thinking to make our behaviour fit our ideas than vice versa. Sound familiar?

So how does this relate to persuasion? Because the theory describes not only how we avoid changing our behaviour but also suggests pressure points for undermining our rationalisations. Creating cognitive dissonance in an audience can be a powerful tool for disrupting habits of thought and consequently increasing the chances of altering their behaviour. If the tendency is to alter thoughts rather than behaviour, but a campaign is intended to alter behaviour, it is useful to know what pressure points to activate. This theory suggests that if we provide relevant

---

think about 14.6 Changing attitudes

If the geneticists are right, it should be impossible to change someone's attitude. And yet they can be changed – think of changing social attitudes to drink driving over the past 20 years, for example. Have you ever changed an attitude – to education, religion or even career choices? What made you change your mind? Was it a long, slow process or a sudden flash?

Cognitive dissonance in action – making choices when what you think and what you do clash

We suggested earlier that someone who values the environment is more likely to have negative attitudes towards genetically modified (GM) foods and positive attitudes towards organic produce. If these attitudes are weakly held, the person may not find any problems with driving to the health food store for their goods. If they are held strongly, the person may feel some distress that they are burning fossil fuel and contributing to global warming. How can cognitive dissonance predict their responses? The theory suggests that if they do hold the views strongly and experience dissonance, they will have three choices:

- They can change their behaviour – for example, cycle to the shop or give up buying organic foods.
- They can alter their cognitions (thoughts) – perhaps tell themselves that there is no point worrying about one car journey when so much damage is being done by others.
- They can alter the importance of their cognitions – that is, downgrade the importance they place on the whole set of ideas and convince themselves that they had been taking it all too seriously.

thoughts (alter cognitions) and/or raise the importance of the relevant thoughts, we may leave an audience with no choice but to alter their behaviour. Campaigns that use shock tactics, such as the anti-fur ads, can jolt an audience out of a complacent attitude.

Another essential element of a persuasion campaign is that people must believe that they are capable of making the change required by the campaign, such as giving up smoking, exercising more or whatever the objective is. This is called *self-efficacy*. Campaigns that expect more of the audience than people are able to achieve will fail. For example, many people who have positive attitudes towards recycling are not sure how to divide their materials or what to do with them – and may be overwhelmed by the sense that saving the planet is down to them. So they give up and do nothing. Recent campaigns concentrate on encouraging people to do small achievable acts of recycling. This is more likely to be successful. (See Think about 14.7.)

Whatever tactics a campaign uses, there are a number of barriers they have to overcome in order for persuasion to occur. Research is continually undertaken to measure the effectiveness of persuasion campaigns and while commercial campaigns tend to keep their research findings to themselves, public health campaigns are often analysed and the findings published widely. An example of the kind of effects campaigners look for and the problems they face is covered in a feature article in the *Observer*,

PICTURE 14.3   This poster – featuring singer Sophie Ellis-Bextor and with the slogan 'Here's the rest of your fur coat' – aimed to shock viewers into changing attitudes to wearing fur. Produced with kind permission of PETA. (*Source:* Mary McCartney/PETA.)

Take a look at current health campaigns, such as the UK NHS anti-smoking campaign mentioned earlier. They usually try and persuade people to change their behaviour – more exercise, less salt, give up smoking, cut down on alcohol, etc. Are they trying to identify common defences against change (my grandmother smoked 80 a day and lived to 100, etc.)? Are they trying to shock? Do they suggest that people have the skills and ability required to give up? Do you think they succeed?

| box 14.4 | McGuire's input/output matrix |

Input variables

These are the choices the communicator makes when designing a persuasion campaign:

- *Sources:* who is the speaker, how credible, expert, attractive are they?
- *Messages:* what kind of appeal is made, how is information presented?
- *Channels:* mass media or mail shots, TV ads or text messages, context in which channel is consumed?
- *Receivers:* who is message aimed at, what is the age group, education level, personality structure?
- *Intent:* what is the desired aim, does it require a behaviour or attitude change?

Output variables

These describe the stages through which a message must pass to achieve a persuasive outcome:

- *Exposure:* did the intended receiver even get the message, do they watch or read the chosen channels?
- *Attention:* if they *were* exposed, were they paying attention or were they doing something else as well?
- *Liking:* did they like the message – not in the sense of finding it 'nice' but in appreciating the design, appearance, music, etc?
- *Comprehension:* did they understand the message – or was the stuff about polyunsaturated fats, for example, too confusing?
- *Acquiring skills:* do they need to change a behaviour, learn how to cook, put on a seatbelt – and do any of these changes require new skills?
- *Changing attitudes:* did they like the campaign but vote for the other party, have they decided that they do want to change their approach to a topic or product?
- *Remembering:* did they remember the key message at the point where it was most likely to influence their response, such as the supermarket or voting booth?
- *Deciding to act:* having seen, liked, understood and remembered the messages, having changed attitudes towards the intent of the campaign, did the audience make the next step and actually decide to do something about it – whether that's stopping smoking, eating more fruit or going to Thailand?
- *Behaviour change:* having decided to act, did they actually make the effort and alter their behaviour in line with the desired intent, or perhaps, in a different way?
- *Reinforcing the decision:* having behaved as suggested once, will they repeat the action or forget the message?
- *Consolidating the results:* does the campaign make the most of its own successes, by telling the audience how they'd responded, perhaps through individual case studies or release of relevant statistics?

Source: based on McGuire 1989

---

referred to above, which commissioned four communication agencies to create health campaigns and explain their decisions. The article can be accessed at www.observer.guardian.co.uk/magazine/story/0,,13 27537,00.html.

Whatever the desired effects, the key audience must actually see or hear the message, or the effort is obviously wasted. They must also understand it, and remember it and undertake more actions before their behaviour is likely to be altered. McGuire (1989) created a matrix to illustrate the barriers that a message must overcome to persuade any individual (see Box 14.4). The input section describes all the communications decisions the persuader must take; the output section describes the processes involved in having an effect on any individual, and the stages in the persuasion process where messages may need to be reinforced or repeated. (See Activity 14.6.)

activity 14.6

Case study

Apply the McGuire input/output matrix to one of the campaigns you can find at the following websites:

www.givingupsmoking.co.uk/CNI/Current_Campaign/
www.farenet.org/
www.influencatwork.com
www.petaliterature.com/

Ethical persuasion: is it possible?

This brings us to the ethics of persuasive communication. Public relations ethics are dealt with in detail in Chapter 15, but this section looks at a couple of approaches to ethical persuasion.

Some textbooks insist that public relations is ethical because 'through their work, public relations professionals promote mutual understanding and peaceful coexistence among individuals and institutions' (Seib and Fitzpatrick 1995). Really? Even when two companies are fighting each other for market share or in a takeover battle? This seems a very idealistic description of what people (especially public relations people) would like public relations to be – but if it does not connect to reality, how can it be of use to practitioners facing the kind of communication dilemmas suggested in Activity 14.7?

Some people work out their ethics by looking at the results of their actions, some by referring to their duties, some depending on the situation. Baker (1999) suggests that public relations practitioners tend to use one of five 'justifications for persuasion', as follows:

1 *self-interest* (what's in it for me?)
2 *entitlement* (if it's legal, it's ethical)
3 *enlightened self-interest* (ethical behaviour is good business sense)

4 *social responsibility* (personal practice has an impact on larger society)
5 *kingdom of ends* (the highest standards should be provided for and expected from all).

To help the practitioner facing dilemmas like those in Activity 14.7, Baker and Martinson (2002) have put together five principles to act as guiding principles for ethical persuasive public relations, which they call the TARES test:

1 **t**ruthfulness – the commitment to honesty in communication
2 **a**uthenticity – relates to personal and professional integrity
3 **r**espect – for the rights of your audience
4 **e**quity – relates to fairness, not manipulation
5 **s**ocial responsibility – awareness of the effects of communication on the wider society.

There are still ethical problems facing public relations as a sector: if most public relations people work for large organisations with massive resources, how 'fair' can exchanges with audiences be? If an organisation disagrees with the majority of the mainstream corporate-owned media, how truthful must they be with the press? Moloney (2000: 152) believes that public relations must recognise that it exists in a persuasive 'sphere' or culture and choose to use reason and accurate data rather than emotional manipulation as instruments of persuasion: 'Public relations as manipulation or propaganda chooses emotion and falsehood as a persuasive mode and so degrades democracy.'

So, if public relations is to restore its reputation, it may need to accept that persuasion is central to much of its activity and find ways to persuade ethically, as suggested by Baker, Martinson and others. Their suggestions may be idealistic, but perhaps ideals are not bad things to reach for when trying to conduct ethical persuasive communication rather than propaganda. (See Think about 14.8, overleaf, and Activity 14.8.)

activity 14.7

Ethical communication dilemmas

- There are problems with a new detergent you're launching next week – with nationwide TV ads – nothing dangerous, but it might be less effective than tests first showed. Do you pull the ads and delay the launch?
- Membership of the sports club you represent has fallen drastically in the past year. The client asks you to come up with a press release that minimises the impact and blames the computer system.
- You're on work placement and the public relations agency asks you to say you're doing student research for the university/college rather than for the agency.
- In a beauty campaign you highlight the fact that a new product doubles the chance of reducing wrinkles. You don't mention that the new rate is still less than 10%.
- A major tobacco company asks you to launch a fitness campaign for schools with free footballs – covered in its logo.
- A major US coffee chain that's been getting protests over its market practices asks you to do an ethical makeover – in its communication, not its employment or trade activities.
- You organise meetings between the local authority and community groups to explain new council policies. Do you make it clear that the authority is interested in their views but unlikely to make major changes?

Feedback
Look at Chapter 15 for details about ways of working out your own ethical guidelines. Then see if you can apply those approaches or the TARES test (below) to these dilemmas.

activity 14.8

Dissertation/research ideas

- Compare the views of Bernays to those of current public relations practitioners.
- Contrast the Hovland and McCroskey approaches to credibility, using current public relations campaigns.
- Apply the theory of reasoned action to a public health campaign.

think about 14.8 Resisting persuasion

This chapter has looked at how communicators can more effectively persuade others regarding the merits of a particular point of view or action. This knowledge can also be used to improve one's own defences against being persuaded. The following suggests how you could use the theories outlined in this chapter to increase your awareness when others are trying to persuade you:

■ Know yourself – are you a high or low self-monitor (see page 278)? Are you strongly influenced by the views of those around you? Do you fit in or stand out?
■ Know your own ethics – what are your core values, your moral boundaries?
■ Know the source – who are they? What are their interests? Is the Sugar Information Bureau actually the sugar industry in a white coat? Does the celebrity really use/wear/believe it?
■ Know the intentions of the message – what do they want you to do? Is this what you want? Is it consistent with your core values?
■ Know the methods of the message – are they appealing to your reason or emotion? Are they trying to catch you in a hurry? Are they suggesting if you don't do it right now, the chance is gone?
■ Take your time, check the facts, make up your own mind.

Summary

This chapter has shown that propaganda is not always easy to distinguish from persuasion or public relations, possibly due to the fact that public relations has its origins in propaganda, with many pioneers of public relations learning the craft in wartime. However, it concluded that this should not condemn all persuasive communication and that persuasion deserves further study as an aspect of public relations.

Clearly, communicators can learn from a range of social psychology theories about the processes by which people process messages and the different emphasis they place on the source of the message and its content, depending on their personality types. The chapter also described the links between attitudes and behaviour and the theories that suggest ways of influencing attitudes and, possibly, behaviour in public relations and communication campaigns.

It has also talked about the personality of the communicator and the importance of reaching beyond one's own assumptions and experience to create an effective communication between sender and receiver. Having demonstrated how persuasion can work, it emphasised the importance of applying the highest ethical standards to such work.

It can be concluded that persuasion is actually a difficult thing to achieve – there are so many different personality types and so many barriers to messages actually reaching the desired audience at the correct level, let alone the difficulties of translating altered attitudes into altered behaviour. And yet public relations and advertising and increasingly political and commercial life are all dedicated to making us rethink prior assumptions, to change our minds about butter or political parties or recycling. Wernick (1991) called this a 'promotional culture' and evidence since then confirms his description. We are bombarded with persuasive messages every day as consumers and public relations campaigns are part of the assault.

Political commentators and politicians have complained that the public reaction to blanket persuasion, or hype or spin, is increasing cynicism and distrust. They blame each other for this, but leaving that argument aside, it is clear that overuse of persuasive techniques can have a counterproductive effect and the very element that is essential to generate effective messages – a credible source – is jeopardised. Perhaps this can provide a wider lesson: persuasion has its place in communication and it is important for those using the tool to understand its mechanisms and effects. But if overused, people begin to long for genuine dialogue.

Bibliography

Allport, G.W. (1935). 'Attitudes' in *A Handbook of Social Psychology Vol. 2*. C. Murchison (ed.). Worcester, MA: Clark University Press.

Andersen, K. (1978). *Persuasion Theory and Practice*, 2nd edition. Boston, MA: Allyn & Bacon, cited in '"Truth-fulness" in communication is both a reasonable and achievable goal for public relations practitioners'. D. Martinson. *Public Relations Quarterly* **41** (4) [1996].

Aronson, E. (1968). 'Dissonance theory: Progress and problems' in *Theories of Cognitive Consistency: A sourcebook*.

R.P. Abelson, E. Aronson, W.J. McGuire, T.M. Newcomb, M.J. Rosenberg and P.H. Tannenbaum (eds). Chicago: Rand McNally.

Baker, S. (1999). 'Five baselines for justification in persuasion'. *Journal of Mass Media Ethics* **14** (2): 69–94.

Baker, S. and D.L. Martinson (2002). 'Out of the red-light district: Five principles for ethically proactive public relations'. *Public Relations Quarterly* **47** (3).

Bernays, E. (1923). *Crystallizing Opinion*. New York: Boni and Liveright.

Bernays, E. (1928). *Propaganda*. New York: Liveright.

Bernays, E. (1955). The Engineering of Consent. Norman, OK: University of Oklahoma Press.

Bettinghaus, E.P. and M.J. Cody, (1994). *Persuasive Communication,* 5th edition. Orando, FL: Harcourt Brace.

Cohen, A.R. (1959). 'Some implications of self-esteem for social influence' in *Personality and Persuasability*. C.I. Hovland and I.L. Janis (eds). Yale: Yale University Press.

Columbia (2003). *The Columbia Electronic Encyclopedia*, 6th Edition. New York: Columbia University Press.

Cutlip, S.M. (1994). *The Unseen Power: Public relations, a history*. Hillsdale, NJ: Lawrence Erlbaum Associates.

Cutlip, S.M., A.H. Center and G.M. Broom, (1985). *Effective Public Relations*, 6th edition. Upper Saddle River, NJ: Prentice Hall.

Delwiche, A. (2002). 'Post-war propaganda'. www.propagandacritic.com/articles/ww1.postwar.html

Eagly, A.H., W. Wood, and S. Chaiken, (1978). 'Causal inferences about communication and their effect on opinion change'. *Journal of Personality and Social Psychology,* **36**.

Ewen, S. (1996). *PR! A Social History of Spin*. New York: Basic Books.

Fazio, R.H. (1989). 'On the power and functionality of attitudes: The role of attitude accessibility' in *Attitude Structure and Function*. A.R. Pratkanis, S.J. Breckler and A.G. Greenwald (eds). Hillsdale, NJ: Lawrence Erlbaum Associates.

Festinger, L. (1954). 'A theory of social comparison processes'. *Human Relations* **7**.

Festinger, L. (1957). *The Theory of Cognitive Dissonance*. New York: Harper & Row.

Fineman, P.R. (2001). 'PR blunders'. www.finemanpr.com/blunders.html

Fishbein, M. and I. Ajzen (1975). *Belief, Attitude, Intention, and Behavior: An introduction to theory and research*. Reading, MA: Addison-Wesley.

Fishbein, M. and I. Azjen (1980). 'Predicting and understanding consumer behavior: attitude-behavior correspondence' in *Understanding Attitudes and Predicting Social Behavior*. I. Azjen and M. Fishbein (eds). Upper Saddle River, NJ: Prentice-Hall.

Grunig, J. (2001). 'Two-way symmetrical public relations: Past, present and future' in *Handbook of Public Relations*. R.L. Heath (ed.). Thousand Oaks, CA: Sage.

Grunig, J. and T. Hunt, (1984). *Managing Public Relations*. New York: Holt, Rinehart & Winston.

Heath, R.L. (2001). 'A rhetorical enactment rationale for public relations: The good organisation communicating well' in *Handbook of Public Relations*. R.L. Heath (ed.). Thousand Oaks, CA: Sage.

Herman, E.S. and N. Chomsky (1988). *Manufacturing Consent: The political economy of the mass media*. New York: Pantheon Books.

Hovland, C.I., I.L. Janis and H. Kelley (1953). *Communication and Persuasion*. Yale: Yale University Press.

Jaksa, J.A. and M.S. Pritchard (1994). *Communicator Ethics: Methods of analysis*, 2nd edition. Belmont, CA: Wadsworth.

Jowett, G.S. and V. O'Donnell (1992). *Propaganda and Persuasion*, 2nd edition. Thousand Oaks, CA: Sage.

Katz, D. (1960). 'The functional approach to the study of attitudes'. *Public Opinion Quarterly*, col 24.

Lasswell, H.D. (1934). 'Propaganda' in *Propaganda*. R.A. Jackall (ed.). New York: New York University Press.

Lasswell, H.D. (1948). 'The structure and function of communication in society' in *The Communication of Ideas*. L. Bryson (ed.). New York: Harper.

L'Etang, J. (1998). 'State propaganda and bureaucratic intelligence: The creation of public relations in 20th century britain'. *Public Relations Review* **24** (4): 413–441.

Lippman, W. (1925). 'The phantom public' in *Propaganda*. R.A. Jackall, (ed.). New York: New York University Press.

Moloney, K. (2000). *Rethinking Public Relations*. London: Routledge.

Martinson, D. (1996). '"Truthfulness" in communication is both a reasonable and achievable goal for public relations practitioners'. *Public Relations Quarterly* **41** (4).

McCroskey, J.C. (1966). 'Scales for the measurement of ethos'. *Speech Monographs* **33**, 65–72.

McGuire, W.J. (1989). 'Theoretical foundations of campaigns' in *Public Communication Campaigns*, 2nd edition. R.E. Rice and C.E. Atkin (eds). Thousand Oaks, CA: Sage.

McQuail, D. (2000). *McQuail's Mass Communication Theory*, 4th edition. London: Sage.

Miller, D. (2004). 'The propaganda machine' in *Tell Me No Lies*. London: Pluto Press.

Miller, D., J. Kitzinger, K. Williams and P. Beharrell, (1998). *The Circuit of Mass Communication*. London: Sage.

Miller, G. (1989). 'Persuasion and public relations: 2 Ps in a pod?' in *Public Relations Theory*. C.H. Botan and V. Hazleton (eds). Hillsdale, NJ: Lawrence Erlbaum Associates.

O'Keefe, D.J. (1990). *Persuasion: Theory and research*. Newbury Park, CA: Sage.

Packard, V. (1957). *The Hidden Persuaders*. New York: D. McKay.

Perloff, R.M. (1993). *The Dynamics of Persuasion*. Hillsdale, NJ: Lawrence Erlbaum Associates

Petty, R.E. and J.T. Cacioppo (1986). *Communication and Persuasion: Control and peripheral routes to attitude change*. New York: Springer-Verlag.

Pratkanis, A. and E. Aronson (2001). *Age of Propaganda*. New York: Freeman/Owl Books.

Rampton, S. and J. Stauber (2002). *Trust Us, We're Experts: How industry manipulates science and gambles with your future*. Tarcher: Penguin.

Raven, B.H. (1983). 'Interpersonal influence and social power' in *Social Psychology*. B.H. Raven and J.Z. Rubin. New York: John Wiley & Sons.

Rogers, R. (1983). 'Cognitive and physiological processes in fear appeals and attitude change: A revised theory of protection motivation' in *Social Psychophysiology*. J.T. Cacioppo and R.E. Petty (eds). New York: Guilford Press.

Rokeach, M. (1960). *The Open and Closed Mind*. New York: Basic Books.

Rosenberg, M.J. and C.I. Hovland (1960). 'Cognitive, affective and behavioral components of attitudes' in *Attitude, Organization and Change*. C.I. Hovland and M.J. Rosenburg (eds). Yale: Yale University Press.

Sarbin, T.R., R. Taft and D.E. Bailey (1960). *Clinical Interference and Cognitive Theory*. New York: Holt, Rinehart & Winston.

Schick, T. (1994). 'Truth, accuracy (and withholding information)'. *Public Relations Quaterly* **39**, Winter 1994/5.

Seib, P. and K. Fitzpatrick (1995). *Public Relations Ethics*. Fort Worth, TX: Harcourt Brace.

Sherif, M. (1967). 'Introduction' in *Attitude, Ego-involvement, and Change*. C.W. Sherif and M. Sherif (eds). New York: John Wiley & Sons.

Snyder, M. and K.G. DeBono (1985). 'Appeals to image and claims about quality: Understanding the psychology of advertising'. *Journal of Personality and Social Psychology* **49**.

Tallents, S. (1932). *The Projection of England*. London: Olen Press.

Taylor, P. (1992). 'Propaganda from Thucydides to Thatcher'. www.ics.leeds.ac.uk/

Taylor, P. (2001). 'What is propaganda?' www.ics.leeds.ac.uk/pmt-terrorism/what-propaganda.pdf

Toulmin, S. (1958). *The Uses of Argument*. Cambridge: Cambridge University Press.

Varey, R. (1997). 'External public relations activities' in *Public Relations: Principles and practice*. P.J. Kitchen (ed.). London: ITBP.

Watts, R. (2004). 'The application of social semiotic theory to corporate positioning material'. *Journal of Communication Management* **8**(4).

Weaver, C.K., J. Motion and J. Reaper (2004). 'Truth, power and public interest: A critical theorising of propaganda and public relations'. Paper presented at the International Communications Association annual conference, New Orleans.

Wernick, A. (1991). *Promotional Culture*. London: Sage.

Wilcox, D.L., G.T. Cameron, P.H. Ault and W.K. Agee (2003). *Public Relations, Strategies and Tactics*, 7th edition. London: Allyn & Bacon.

Websites

Centre for Media Democracy: www.prwatch.org/spin

Communication, Cultural and Media Studies (CCMS): www.cultsock.ndirect.co.uk/MUHome/cshtml/index.html

Influence at work: www.influenceatwork.com

Institute of Communications Studies, University of Leeds: http//ics.leeds.ac.uk

NHS – Giving up Smoking: www.givingupsmoking.co.uk

Propaganda: www.propagandacritic.com

Spin Watch: www.spinwatch.org.uk

CHAPTER 15

Ethics and professionalism in public relations

Learning outcomes

By the end of this chapter you should be able to:

■ articulate why ethical practice and professionalism is important

■ describe the various ethical traditions and theories and apply them to public relations situations

■ analyse the responsibilities that practitioners have to self, organisation, profession and society and identify potential conflicts

■ describe some of the typical public relations dilemmas facing practitioners and point to appropriate resolutions

■ construct principles on which to build an ethical framework based on 'current' theory and practice

■ choose and use ethical decision-making models.

Structure

■ Importance of ethics and professionalism in public relations

■ Definitions of ethics and morality

■ Ethical theories (traditions)

■ Duty to whom?

■ Ethical issues in public relations

■ Ethical decision-making models and their application

Introduction

Recent corporate and political scandals, such as Enron, Worldcom, Parmelat and the UK government's presentation of its case for war in Iraq, have brought ethics very much into the spotlight.

In recognition of this, fresh attention has been given to business ethics in general and corporate responsibility (CSR) in particular (see Chapters 6 and 18) and to the process and practice of government communication. At the same time, certain activities in the media have also come in for censure. For example, the quest for celebrity information (and the dubious means by which it is obtained) and the publishing of fake photographs of Iraqi prisoner abuse by the UK national tabloid newspaper *The Daily Mirror* have called into question media ethics.

Communication is at the heart of all these issues. It is a matter of some concern that although professional communicators are frequently faced with ethical decisions or are asked to represent an organisation when there is an ethical problem, very few have had formal ethics training or can articulate the processes they go through when arriving at difficult ethical decisions. It is also worth noting that the media relish covering news stories that focus on corporate or public relations practitioner ethics and (un)ethical behaviour.

This chapter examines ethics and professionalism. It looks at the various ethical traditions and professional codes of conduct, at the responsibilities of communication professionals and it provides some models for sound ethical decision making.

Importance of ethics and professionalism in public relations

There are many reasons why ethics and professionalism should characterise public relations practice, but just five are explored here.

Trust

Public relations is about building and maintaining relationships. Trust is the key to successful relationships. Dictionary definitions of trust usually include words like reliability, confidence, faith and integrity. Trust is a precious thing, given by one individual to another and once broken, it can rarely be fully restored. If a public relations practitioner acts ethically and professionally they are likely to be trusted. They will be described as having integrity – there is something wholesome, honest and trustworthy about them. Being ethical and professional is core to having a good reputation.

It is important for an organisation to be represented by someone who is ethical and professional. It says something about the values and character of the organisation itself. Stakeholders are more likely to trust the organisation and believe what it says if the person representing it is regarded as trustworthy.

The ethical guardian

There is much debate about the role of the practitioner as the guardian of the organisation's ethics. For example, L'Etang (2003) does not see much evidence for this. However, others such as Heath and Ryan (1989) argue that a part of the role of public relations practitioners is to monitor the environment to detect various publics' attitudes to certain values. They should then make company managers aware of external ethical standards and help companies implement CSR programmes or develop codes of ethics. Cutlip et al. (2000) argue that an organisation's conduct is improved when public relations practitioners stress the need for public approval.

What cannot be denied is that public relations people have to justify the decisions and actions of their organisation to a range of publics. They should have, therefore, an acute awareness of what their publics' likely reactions will be and whether there will be a sense of moral outrage or approval. They then need the courage to challenge potential decisions and actions as they are being made and before they become reality. For example, there is increasing disquiet about senior managers being given 'golden goodbyes'

(cash or equivalent payments) when their company is in difficulties, at the same time that other employees are being made redundant or having minimal pay increases. In such a situation, it is imperative that the public relations professional challenges the decision on moral and ethical grounds – even if there are legal reasons why the payment may have to be made to senior managers.

Social responsibility

Gone are the days when organisations were regarded as just economic entities whose sole responsibility was to make profits (Friedman 1970). Organisations are regarded as having wider responsibilities to society and the CSR movement has come about largely because organisations have recognised they have responsibilities towards all stakeholding groups, to the environment and to society as a whole. Ongoing MORI research (MORI 2004) demonstrates quite clearly that organisations increasingly have to respond to stakeholder demands that they fulfil their social responsibilities. Earlier research for the UK Chartered Institute of Public Relations (CIPR) (MORI 2002) shows that public relations practitioners are usually responsible for communicating CSR policies and activities; indeed, CSR is often placed within the public relations remit (see Chapters 6 and 18).

Community building and conflict resolution

Linked to the idea of social responsibility is the notion of community building and conflict resolution. This debate around the ideal of community has been stimulated by the *communitarian* movement associated with the American sociologist Amitai Etzioni (see following definition box). To function properly, democracy must reflect an open society that is constantly challenging and reappraising its assumptions and values. Public relations brings to the public debate all kinds of ideas and represents all shades of opinion. As a result of informed debate, collective decisions can be made, citizens accept the democratic will and society and community is built. As Krückeburg and Starck (1998: 53) say:

> A community is achieved when people are aware of and interested in common ends and regulate their activity in view of those ends. Communication plays a vital role as people try to regulate their own activities and to participate in efforts to reach common ends.

Furthermore, public relations builds community by helping to resolve conflict. By engaging in dialogue, understandings can be reached and accommodations made that allow opposing factions to live together with a measure of tolerance. It is worth noting that public relations practitioners have been involved in conflict resolution work in Northern Ireland for many years.

> **Definition:** *Communitarianism* supports building community structures so that people take a shared responsibility for what happens to them (Etzioni 1995). People should take a collective, mutually supportive responsibility for each other through local community institutions.

Power and obligation

As has been said, trust depends to a large extent on the integrity of individual practitioners. As Seib and Fitzpatrick (1995) assert, one of the reasons public relations is subject to so much scrutiny is because it is so powerful and influential. The criticism is that it works too well! (See also Chapter 14, which discusses persuasion and propaganda.)

With power and influence comes responsibility. There is an obligation on practitioners to be as professional as possible. That means taking education and training as seriously as other professions, such as accountancy, law, medicine, building surveying, pharmacy or architecture. Intellectual training, mastery of the technical aspects of the job, management knowledge and ethical training are all important. Practitioners should be members of the appropriate professional body (see Box 15.1), ascribe to its code of conduct and strive to go beyond the minimum requirements. That in itself is an indicator of the seriousness with which they take their own professional calling. It is right and proper that organisations expect the highest standards from their communicators, just as they would from their corporate lawyers or accountants. (See Think about 15.1.)

Definitions of ethics and morality

So, having given some reasons why ethics and professionalism are important, it is now necessary to clarify some terms.

There is confusion about the words '*morals*' and '*ethics*'; indeed they are often used interchangeably. Strictly speaking, morals are to do with the individual. From being small children we become aware of what is good and what are regarded as right actions. Fairly quickly we get an impression of what it means to be a 'bad' person. That awareness comes from parents, our own thinking and feeling about a situation or person, and from the group and society we are based in. Morals are described simply as our personal *values* or principles. So we speak of people having their own moral code, which might be different from ours. For example, someone with religious beliefs may believe abortion is immoral; someone else in the same society or even the same family will not.

Definition: *Morals* are personal values or principles that guide behaviour. *Ethics* are systematic frameworks which codify moral principles. Values are those factors that are important to the individual, e.g. fairness, truth, honesty, acquiring wealth, having status.

Ethics, on the other hand, means the formal study and codification of moral principles into systematic frameworks so that decisions can be made about what is right and wrong in a reasoned and structured way. Hence, certain parts of the law are obviously framed to support standards of behaviour that have a strong moral basis – for example, the laws on theft and murder.

Trevino and Nelson (2004: 15) make a very clear link between morals and business ethics within organisations (see Figure 15.1). They explain that ethical decision making in organisations comprises 'three basic steps: moral awareness (recognising the existence of an ethical dilemma), moral judgement (deciding what's right) and ethical behaviour (taking action to do the right thing)'. These steps are influenced by the characteristics of both the individual and the organisation.

McElreath (1997) points out that ethics, as a branch of philosophy, is not just about right and wrong; it is about what is good and what is bad. He quotes public relations Professor Don Wright (Wright 1982) who says that ethics is really about being good and that the practitioner's task is to determine what a good action is. Some actions such as honesty, sincerity and truthfulness are essentially good in themselves. Indeed, it was Aristotle who claimed that people can become virtuous by practising the virtues (or, in modern parlance, become good by practising goodness).

The purpose of learning about ethics – frameworks of principles – is so that situations can be evaluated

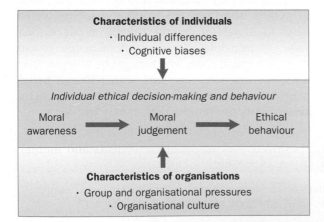

FIGURE 15.1   Ethical decision making in organisations (*source:* Trevino, L.K. and Nelson, K.A. (2004) *Managing Business Ethics, 3rd Edition*, p. 15. Copyright (c) 2004 John Wiley & Sons. Reprinted with permission of John Wiley & Sons, Inc.)

systematically, which encourages consistent behaviour and responses to situations. This is important because consistency is also a key element in building relationships. Being able to explain how and why we have reached a particular decision makes it transparent and understandable, even if the decision itself is unpopular.

Ethical theories (traditions)

Having looked at the connection between morals and ethics, it is now appropriate to look at some of the main frameworks that seek to provide a rational basis for moral judgements and ethical behaviour and at the implication of some of these theories for public relations.

Cognitivism and non-cognitivism

The most basic question that ethical theorists ask is, 'Is it possible to know right from wrong?'

The word used by philosophers to define the view that there are *actual* and *objective* moral truths and absolutes is *cognitivism*. Cognitivism enables us to make firm statements about whether an action or belief is good or bad, right or wrong. The opposing school of thought, *non-cognitivism*, states that morality is purely *subjective*, or is bound up with the specific cultural context of individuals. Non-cognitivists say that there are no moral absolutes, only beliefs, attitudes and opinions.

This later, non-cognitivist school of thought, which draws heavily on the work of Kenneth Burke (1969a; 1969b), is represented in the public relations literature by rhetorical theorists such as Pearson (1989), Toth and Heath (1992) and Heath (2001). They argue that truths emerge from a process of dialogue, negotiation and debate where individuals eventually agree on a particular moral truth. They assert that the *process* by which the debate is conducted determines whether it is ethical or not. In this way, Pearson argues that public relations 'plays a major role in managing the moral dimension of corporate conduct' (1989: 111). The equity of the process means that people reach a valid consensus, which then has moral authority.

Indeed, they place great stress on the rules for ethical dialogue to maintain its integrity and validity. Habermas (1984) has provided useful insights into what he calls an ideal communication situation. In essence, this requires that participants should test and probe ideas that are proposed, have equal freedom to initiate and continue dialogue, to set the discussion agenda and to challenge and/or explain. In

PICTURE 15.1 Recent corporate and political scandals, such as Enron, have brought ethics very much into the spotlight. (*Source*: AFP/Getty Images.)

they are not to be used as a means to an end. In other words, he does protect the 'rights' of individuals to have a voice and having a voice accords them some respect. Giving respect is itself a moral action.

Pearson's approach is supported by other public relations academics in the rhetorical school such as Heath. The point being made by them is that there are no absolute or objective standards of right and wrong. There are only subjective views of what is right and wrong and it is only through dialogue and agreement that moral rules can be arrived at. Communication therefore is a deeply ethical function because it is through it that agreement on right corporate behaviour is reached.

However, most people live their lives on the basis that there are objective standards of good and bad, right and wrong. Cognitivist ethical theories form the bulk of the literature and provide the foundation for most modern approaches to business and personal ethical frameworks. The following section outlines the main schools of thought in cognitivist theory.

> **Definition:** *Cognitivism* is used by philosophers to define the view that there are *actual* and *objective* moral truths and absolutes (i.e. we can make firm statements one way or another about whether something is good or bad, right or wrong).

> **Definition:** *Non-cognitivism* states that morality is purely *subjective* or is bound up with the specific cultural context of individuals. Non-cognitivists say that there are no moral absolutes, only beliefs, attitudes and opinions.

order to do this properly, they must have freedom from manipulation and equality of power. In turn, all those that participate in dialogue become accountable for comprehensibility (ensuring they are understood), truth (factual accuracy), rightness (appropriate to those receiving the communication) and truthfulness (sincerity as well as factual accuracy). For rhetoricians there is almost agnosticism about who wins the argument eventually, as long as the process has integrity.

This view is regarded by many as an ideal to aspire to, but not grounded in reality. As Somerville (2001) points out, although the centrality of dialogue is an attractive proposition, power is a major issue. It is simply not the case that all participants in a dialogue are equal. In addition, dialogue cannot go on indefinitely and the resolution of the point under discussion may not have the agreement of everyone – it may suit the majority, but others may be profoundly opposed.

The value of Pearson's argument is that it promotes the notion that participants have equal value and

Consequentialist theories

Consequentialist theories focus on the *results* or consequences of behaviour. This is often known as the teleological approach, deriving from the Greek words *telos* (end) and *logos* (the study of). Hence teleology is the study of ends. The best known consequentialist theory is *utilitarianism*, which holds that actions must be judged by the effects that they have, in other words, by their utility. Thus decision makers must consciously consider the impact of their actions. A right action is one that causes more benefit (or happiness) than harm. Indeed, ethical decisions should positively seek to maximise benefits and minimise harm in society.

However, there are three major problems with utilitarianism. The first is that it assumes you can predict the consequences of your actions accurately and then make a judgement. In reality this is often not the case: there are situations when just obtaining the facts is difficult enough. For example, if you work for a construction company whose client wants to build a new road through an urban area, would you really know how everyone involved would be affected or what the long-term impact would be? Furthermore, public relations practitioners are usually working under time pressures and it is simply not possible to find out. Pragmatic decisions within tight timescales have to be made.

The second major problem is that there can be conflicting benefits and the simple reality is that more weight is given to the views or interests of some stakeholders, whether they are in the majority or not, than others. So, for example, some managers may argue that corporate giving, which is good in itself, has to be limited in order to provide shareholders with a handsome dividend to retain their investment and loyalty.

The third argument against utilitarianism is that it leads to 'ends justifies means' thinking. So utilitarians would say it is acceptable to lie about the state of the company's research and development programme to preserve the jobs of thousands of employees. 'Ends justifies means' thinking can also lead to the sacrificing of individuals or groups for 'the greater good'. Therefore the displacement of indigenous groups so that land can be farmed is argued as ethical because the food produced is used to support the needs of larger communities who need food – the greater number benefit. (See Table 15.1 for a comparison of the theories.)

Non-consequential theories

The second set of cognitivist theories are *non-consequentialist*. This is often known as the deontological approach deriving from the Greek word *deontos* meaning duty.

Deontology is a duty-based ethic and focuses on obligation, principles and rights. It emphasises the duty of human beings to treat others with dignity and respect because they are human beings with rights. Deontologists believe that actions in and of themselves can be judged as right or wrong. They base their decision making on universal principles or values that transcend time or cultural perspectives. Josephson (1993) has identified 10 universal principles that form the basis of ethical life:

1 honesty
2 integrity
3 promise keeping
4 fidelity
5 fairness
6 caring for others
7 respect for others
8 responsible citizenship
9 pursuit of excellence
10 accountability.

Both the UN's (United Nations) Universal Declaration of Human Rights (www.un.org/overview/ rights. html) and the US Declaration of Independence (www.law.Indiana.edu/uslawdocs/declaration.html) subscribe to deontological principles by guaranteeing that individuals have certain rights that should not be violated, such as the right to life, liberty, security and equality before the law. It is the duty of society and of individuals to preserve these rights.

Some deontologists focus more on the duties that a person should discharge rather than their rights. They argue that rights can only be preserved when citizens take their duties seriously. As Cambridge philosopher Onora O'Neil said in her BBC Reith Lecture of 2002: 'Individuals have often been willing, even eager, to claim their rights but much less willing to meet their duties to respect others rights' (O'Neil 2002).

Deontology is closely associated with eighteenth-century German philosopher Immanuel Kant, who devised the principle of the *categorical imperative*. This encouraged people to ask themselves if their action was suitable for translation into a universal law or principle that anyone faced with the same situation could follow. Thus, if you tell a lie to get yourself out of a difficult situation, the categorical imperative would demand you ask yourself 'is lying in these circumstances a principle everyone should adopt?' A deontologist decides what the moral law is by applying the universal principles such as those of Josephson quoted earlier. Many deontologists also adopt what is called 'the golden rule'. This is enshrined in many religions in phrases such as, 'Do unto others as you would have them do unto you'.

> **Definition:** *Categorical imperative* is a test that can be applied to see if it conforms to the moral law. If the action could be made into a universal law, which would be regarded as acceptable if applied to everyone faced with the same situation, then it would be regarded as ethical.

TABLE 15.1 Consequentialist vs non-consequentialist cognitivist theories

Theory	Consequentialist (result of behaviour – the effect it has)	Non-consequentialist (duty – obligations, principles and rights)
Name	Teleological	Deontological
Theoretical example	Utilitarianism	Categorical imperative (Kant)

There are three main problems with deontological reasoning. The first concerns what happens if two moral laws clash. For example, you may have a moral duty to tell the truth, but you also have a moral duty to care for others. So what do you decide if a journalist asks you to confirm the name of an employee who has had an accident at work before their family has been informed – which law do you obey?

The second is that Kant says you must fulfil your moral obligation irrespective of the consequences. So, for example, Kant would say that you must tell the truth, even if someone suffers as a result.

The third problem is that there is no agreement about what the moral law is. Societies develop and moral perspectives change or differ from society to society. European culture would hold that executing a murderer is not acceptable. Mainstream North American culture believes that 'a life for a life' is a moral imperative.

Virtue ethics

Virtue ethics look more at the motivations of an individual rather than at their actions per se or the consequences of their actions. Character is all important. This does not mean that principles or consequences are unimportant, but they are considered in the light of the individual's character. For example, did the individual act honestly? Did they follow a principle, such as their professional code of conduct? Did they attempt to do no harm?

Character is, of course, difficult to define and it is intimately bound up with the community an individual inhabits. Bravery in one community may be regarded as barbarity in another. For public relations practitioners this requires a detailed examination of the communities they inhabit. You may be a churchgoer, belong to a professional association or work in a company that has a business code of ethics. In any situation you should ask which community would have the highest standards and then apply those rules. Being a virtuous public relations practitioner also means that you abide by the highest standards of the professional institute that represents the community of public relations practitioners.

The value of virtue ethics is that it allows you to take on board appropriate standards without having to go through all the teleological or deontological arguments for yourself. The idea is that you draw on the wisdom of your peers who will have done the hard thinking on your behalf.

The two problems with virtue ethics are first that your 'community' might not have thought about your situation and, second, your 'community' might not have got it right. This can be a particular issue when public relations practitioners are working overseas and they try to apply their ethnocentric principles in other cultures. However, a useful rule of thumb to apply when considering virtue ethics and the norms of a community is the 'disclosure rule'. That is, 'would I feel comfortable if my behaviour appeared on the front page of the local newspaper or if my family knew I'd done this?'

Situational ethics

There is one other school of thinking that is worth exploring and which, according to Pratt (1993), is prevalent in public relations practice in the USA. Situational ethics asserts that no moral law or principle is absolute; indeed the situation itself alters the rules. Therefore, part of our moral responsibility is to put aside the rules for the greater good and do whatever the situation demands. At first this seems a sensible and pragmatic approach: modern life is so complex that it is difficult to come up with rules that can be applied across the board. However, it is not that easy. If a system of ethics depends on situations or contexts and each one is different, it loses the value of being systematic. We may as well say that ethics as such do not matter; everyone can run their life by merely considering what is happening in the current situation. However, there is a big difference between situational ethics and considering the situation when making ethical decisions. It is worth explaining this further as Martinson (1998) does (see Activity 15.1, overleaf). Modern ethical theory states that three determinants must be considered to decide whether an action is ethical:

- the act itself of what one does (the object)
- the motives, why one does it (the end)
- the circumstances, or how, where, when, etc. one does it.

So if a practitioner holds a press conference, the act (object) itself is morally neutral. If the motive is to provide accurate information then the act and the motive are ethical. If the motive is to mislead, then the entire action is unethical. In circumstances where the situation (or context) is also neutral, the discussion can end there.

Most people who work in public relations have not been trained in moral philosophical systems and this has led Ryan and Martinson (1984: 27) to suggest that:

> If public relations has adopted any underlying principle, it is possibly the subjectivism (or individual relativism) theory that each individual must establish his or her own moral baseline . . . The only real constraint is that an individual be able to live with an action – at least for the short-term.

(See Think about 15.2, overleaf.)

activity 15.1

Theory in practice

Martinson (1998) gives a case where circumstances do play a significant part. A college wants to dismiss a sports coach because of financial misjudgements. They 'allow' the coach to resign voluntarily and take another job in the college. The coach agrees to this. The college director tells the public relations person to announce the resignation, but say nothing about the circumstances. How should the public relations person respond when a local journalist asks for the 'real reason' for the resignation?

Take the same situation, but this time the problem is the coach has a drug addiction and he has been stealing funds to support his habit. What does the practitioner do now when asked for the 'real reasons'?

Feedback

In the first case, many people would say disclosure of additional facts is not appropriate. Promises have been made to the coach and there are limits to the public's

'right to know'. It is dubious that in this case the 'whole truth' is necessary. Some would argue that disclosure is the best policy and it is in the public interest that people know if public funds have been misused. In this context there is a genuine but reasoned argument for and against further disclosure to the press.

However, in the second example things are quite different. The coach's behaviour was illegal and his actions could endanger the well-being of others. In this circumstance it would be difficult to justify withholding the information.

The situations are different, but the ethical platform is clear – to communicate truthfully to those who have a right and a need to know and to act in the public interest. The principle can be universalised (deontological perspective) and the greater good for the greatest number (teleological perspective) is satisfied. This is very different from saying that moral principles do not apply and that the situation must dictate our response.

Duty to whom?

Having considered various ethical frameworks, it is now time to look at the individual practitioner and examine the obligations that they have. One of the most difficult things for practitioners is reconciling the sometimes conflicting loyalties and duties that they have. Seib and Fitzpatrick (1995) identify four categories of duty (see Figure 15.2).

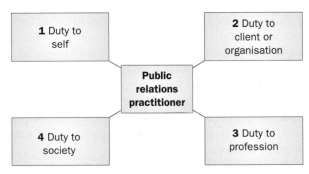

FIGURE 15.2   Loyalties and duties of practice (*source:* based on Seib and Fitzpatrick 1995)

Duty to self

Practitioners should first look at their own value system and personal ethical codes. This requires detailed thought and is not always easy to do. Personal ethical codes will dictate whether they can work for certain organisations or undertake particular types of activity. In the final resort, career choices and resignations are based on practitioners taking seriously their duty to maintain their own ethical standards.

Duty to client or organisation

Having decided to take the financial reward, many practitioners believe their primary duty is to their

clients or organisations. Despite their own personal codes, they believe it to be their professional duty to represent their organisation to the best of their ability, rather like a lawyer represents a client or a doctor treats a person whose personal beliefs they oppose.

There are objections to the legal parallel. In the sphere of public debate there is no judge to oversee fair play and there is no trained opponent with a guaranteed voice who can marshall alternative views and interpretations. Big organisations have vast resources, are generally more powerful and sometimes act to suppress opposing voices. Furthermore, when

think about 15.2   Which philosophical approach?

Which philosophical approach is most attractive to you? Utilitarianism, duty ethics, virtue ethics or situational ethics? List three reasons why.

lawyers defend clients they do not condone their client's crime. In the case of public relations, organisational actions in themselves are defended and practitioners are directly associated with those actions because they are often employees or are retained specifically to defend the actions of an organisation (Martinson 1999). Lawyers are participating in the *process* of justice, which demands representation for the accused. In legal cases a defendant has a *right* to a defence; organisations do not have similar rights. They can *request* services from those willing to offer them.

Conversely, some practitioners regard it as their duty to bring all the facts to the public debate even if they may be under pressure not to do so. Regulated animal laboratories are legal enterprises and it is fair and proper that in open and democratic societies they should be able to put their case in a persuasive way. It is then up to the public to make up their own minds having had both sides of the argument explained to them. Democracy is about informed citizens making informed choices.

While there may be professional disagreements about whether a company should be represented, condoning activities that constitute a risk to others is not acceptable. Practitioners who knowingly support harmful activities violate their wider duty to society and this higher duty must take precedence. For example, defending the harvesting of scarce resources for profit alone is not acceptable.

Duty to profession

It can be assumed that a practitioner has a duty to support their profession and their professional colleagues. In this way common standards of behaviour can be agreed and the bounds of acceptable practice established. Very important here are the professional codes of conduct (see Appendices 1 and 2 for the UK Chartered Institute of Public Relations and the Global Alliance codes). These encapsulate principles of ethical practice and provide the basic standards for practitioners. It is a tough decision to argue with an insistent client or employer, but at a minimum, the codes will alert them to the fact they are asking the practitioner to act unethically and will provide the practitioner with tangible support for an argument against taking a particular course of action.

Although it is often the case that organisations will *wish* their public relations practitioners to be a member of a professional body, some organisations *require* those public relations practitioners who contact them on behalf of others to ascribe to a code of conduct. Box 15.2, overleaf, displays the EU Code, which applies to

all public affairs practitioners who represent organisations or clients. (See Box 15.2, overleaf.)

Duty to society

At the beginning of most public relations codes of conduct is a statement that the practitioner's primary responsibility is to society or to the public interest. While this is a noble aspiration, it is a complex one to unpack. First of all, what is society? Is it local, national, international? What about the cultural values and loyalty differences? And what does 'in the public interest' mean? (See Chapter 4 for a fuller discussion of the 'public interest'.) Clearly it is impossible to serve everyone's interests all the time, and interests are sometimes in conflict.

Grunig and Hunt (1984), Bivins (1993) and the rhetorical school of public relations (see Chapter 8) would argue that symmetric public relations, or genuine dialogue, is at the heart of the public interest. By engaging in dialogue, public relations encourages public and informed debate, clarity of argument is facilitated, good democratic decisions can be made and communities are reinforced. This is all in the public interest.

Another way to look at this in practical terms is to ask if your actions harm anyone and, more positively, whether you are making a valuable contribution that will enable people to live more informed and/or better lives. (See Think about 15.3, overleaf.)

Ethical issues in public relations

Bearing in mind these various, and sometimes conflicting duties, it is now appropriate to look at some of the areas where public relations practitioners encounter ethical problems.

Competence

If public relations describes itself as a 'profession', then there are obligations laid on it to provide expert, objective advice of the highest possible standard. Seib and Fitzpatrick (1995) describe two areas of concern in the provision of professional services – *malfeasance* and *incompetence*. Malfeasance is providing services that should not be provided. So, for example, dentists should not, normally, remove healthy teeth. Similarly public relations people should not conduct campaigns they know will be ineffective or which are unnecessary. This is sometimes a tough call when there is money to be made or if another consultancy is

box 15.2 **EU Code of Conduct**

This code of conduct applies to public affairs practitioners (see Chapter 23 for further details and definitions) dealing with EU institutions.

European affairs professionals are a vital part of the democratic process, acting as a link between the world of business and civil society and European policy makers. As such, these professionals must undertake to observe the highest of professional standards. SEAP, the Society of European Affairs Professionals, aims to provide guidance thereon, by setting high standards. The SEAP code of conduct is the result of thorough discussions by SEAP members. It commits members to the rules laid down therein, sets standards and acts as a benchmark for all European affairs professionals and encourages third parties to respond to SEAP with their views on the code.

In their dealings with the EU institutions, European affairs professionals shall:

Article 1 – General Principles

(1) Act with honesty and integrity at all times, conducting their business in a fair and professional manner. They shall treat all others – including colleagues and competitors, as well as staff, officials or members of the EU institutions – with respect and civility at all times.
(2) European affairs professionals shall not exert improper influence on staff, officials or members of the EU institutions.

Article 2 – Transparency and Openness

(1) maintain the highest standards of professionalism in conducting their work with the EU institutions. When dealing with the institutions they shall be open and transparent in declaring their name, organisation or company, and the interest they represent (subject always to the requirements of commercial confidentiality);
(2) neither intentionally misrepresent their status nor the nature of their inquiries to the EU institutions nor create any false impression in relation thereto;
(3) take all reasonable steps to ensure the truth and accuracy of all statements made or information provided by them to the EU institutions;
(4) not disseminate false or misleading information either knowingly or recklessly, and exercise proper care to avoid doing so inadvertently. They shall not obtain any information from the EU institutions by illicit or dishonest means.

Article 3 – Confidentiality

(1) honour confidential information and embargoes and always abide by the rules and conventions for the obtaining, distribution and release of all EU documentation;
(2) not sell for profit to third parties copies of documents obtained from the EU institutions.

Article 4 – Conflicts of interest

(1) avoid any professional conflicts of interest. Should a conflict of interest arise, the SEAP member must take swift action in order to resolve it.

Article 5 – Employment of EU personnel

(1) when employing former staff, officials or members of the EU institutions, take all the necessary measures to comply with the rules and regulations laid down by the EU institutions in that respect, in particular with regard to confidentiality.

Article 6 – Financial inducements

(1) not offer to give, either directly or indirectly, any financial inducement to any official, member of staff or members of the EU institutions, except for normal business hospitality.

SEAP members shall uphold this code and all internal related procedures. In this respect, they shall co-operate fully with fellow members.

SEAP members agree not to engage in any practice or conduct that could be in any way detrimental to the reputation of SEAP or public affairs professionals in general.

Signatories accept that SEAP can apply a range of sanctions in case of non-compliance, ranging from a verbal warning to expulsion.

A list of signatories can be found on the SEAP website – www.seap.eu.org or by contacting SEAP

As adopted 23rd November 2004

Source: http://europa.eu.int/comm/secretariat_general/sgc/lobbies/code_consultant/codecon_en.htm

Describe one example from recent news stories where you think an organisation has put its own interests above those of society.

Feedback Examples of news stories where an organisation has put its interests before those of society include:

■ dumping of toxic waste near residential areas

■ large increases in director salaries while closing down factories in economically depressed areas

■ moving operations to countries where there are less stringent employee safety regulations and putting those employees at risk (e.g. stripping out dangerous toxins from recycled materials without adequate protection).

willing to do this work, especially if a consultancy wishes to protect the jobs of its employees.

Incompetence means that the practitioners undertaking the work do not have the necessary knowledge or experience to undertake the work to the highest professional standards. It is tempting for consultancies to expand their business into areas where they have no expertise if a lucrative client has work to offer!

The UK CIPR Code of Conduct in its section on integrity, competence and maintaining professional standards is very clear that only work that is within the practitioner's competence should be undertaken.

Parsons (2004) suggests that the responsibility to be competent has three elements:

■ Ensure you have the skills necessary to do the work assigned to you.

■ Keep your knowledge, skills and expertise up to date.

■ Ensure you do not give employers or clients the impression you can guarantee specific results.

This last point is an important one and raises an associated issue, namely 'overpromising', which seems endemic in the public relations community. It is done for two main reasons, both of which are unacceptable. First, practitioners themselves have an unrealistic view of what can be achieved and, second, they will 'do what it takes' to obtain or retain the business.

Conflicts of interest

The UK CIPR Code of Conduct states that conflicts of interest (or circumstances that may give rise to them) must be declared in writing to clients, potential clients and employers as soon as they arise. It is then up to the client or employer to decide whether they consent to their work being continued. Usually conflicts of interest are easy to identify, for example, representing two supermarket chains is a case in point. However, situations are dynamic and something that did not originally create a conflict can develop

into one. For example, a consultancy may represent a supermarket chain and an optician chain. No conflict there – until the supermarket decides to open an in-store optician service. The consultancy should declare their interest to both clients and may even decide to take the initiative and resign one of the accounts. Mergers and acquisitions can sometimes present similar challenges as the environment and circumstances for the organisation(s) change (see also Chapter 24).

Even if the clients decide that the consultancy can represent both organisations, there are operational difficulties: will unintended favouritism develop? What about confidentiality? The CIPR code states '"insider" information must not be disclosed'. What if this information is to the major benefit or disadvantage of the other client?

Conflicts of interest can also occur when individual interests clash with client interests. It could be very difficult for a consultancy employee to represent a tobacco company if a relative has a smoking-related disease. Many consultancies have 'conscience clauses' that allow employees to opt out of undertaking work that poses a conflict of interest or a particular moral dilemma.

'Whistleblowing'

Public relations people often know the most intimate details about organisations, warts and all. What happens if a practitioner discovers serious misconduct? For example, they may become aware that the company accountant is tipping off investment analysts that the company is about to be taken over. They have a responsibility to do something in the public interest. In the UK there is a charity called Public Concern at Work (www.pcaw.co.uk), which will provide advice to anyone who believes they have unearthed unethical practice and is unsure how to proceed. In some countries, the law also provides some protection so that employees are not victimised for safeguarding the public interest.

> **Definition:** A *whistleblower* is someone who goes outside the normal reporting procedures to alert internal senior managers or external sources of wrongdoing in the organisation

The media

Seib and Fitzpatrick (1995) and Parsons (2004) point out the manifold ethical pitfalls of dealing with the media. The relationship is an important one because it is the core of much public relations activity and because of the peculiar nature of the mutual dependencies that develop.

Accuracy and honesty should be an aspiration of both journalism and public relations professions and there are issues that need to be confronted. When does cultivating journalists and providing them with hospitality and gifts turn effectively into bribery? What obligation does the free use of an expensive car put on a motoring journalist? What if some companies do not provide these things? Are they 'disadvantaged'?

Linked to truth telling is the issue of misleading by omission. It is perfectly possible to tell a partial story knowing that by omitting some key information the media (or any other receiver) will make assumptions that might be false. If a practitioner has clearly sought to mislead, this would be unethical. (See also discussion of truth telling in Chapter 14.)

Questions also arise over whether the whole truth should be told. Full disclosure is usually a good rule of thumb, but it is not always the right thing to do. Individuals need protecting in certain circumstances as the Kelly case (Mini case study 15.1) illustrates and it is debatable whether the revelation of his name was genuinely in the public interest.

PICTURE 15.2 Corporate bullying can put an individual under pressure and cause ethical dilemmas. (*Source:* © William Gottleib/Corbis.)

Parsons (2004) suggests that four pillars support ethical media relations:

- honesty and accuracy
- judiciousness (e.g. knowing when and how to use the media)
- responsiveness
- respect.

(See Think about 15.4.)

Ethical decision-making models and their application

The next obvious question then is: how can practitioners make ethical decisions that are soundly based and which stand up to scrutiny?

We will now look at three aspects of the decision-making process: the individual, external guides and the decision-making process itself.

---

mini case study 15.1

Truth telling in practice

What does telling the truth entail? In 2003, the UK government Ministry of Defence communicators told the truth when confirming Dr David Kelly was the source for the BBC reporter, Andrew Gilligan. Gilligan had claimed, in a live radio broadcast, that according to his source the government had knowingly included false or 'sexed up' information about weapons of mass destruction in its dossier of evidence for going to war in Iraq. The consequences of being correctly named as the source were devastating for Dr Kelly personally – who committed suicide – and arguably for world affairs, which were significantly impacted by the events. While the subsequent Hutton Inquiry blamed the BBC more than the government for this series of events, there are still arguments about the truth of Gilligan's original report. However, this case shows that telling the truth can sometimes have devastating results. Truth on its own is not enough. Confidentiality, duty of care and judgement all need to come into the equation.

think about 15.4 **Ethical issues in public relations**

Give three more examples of ethical issues in public relations.

Feedback Examples of other ethical issues include:

- personal relationships with suppliers, journalists, senior managers, etc.
- offering preferential treatment to certain media outlets, e.g. exclusives on a regular basis
- hospitality to key opinion formers
- payment to journalists for work, e.g. writing for customer magazine
- respecting intellectual property of suppliers/potential suppliers, e.g. of consultants pitching for business
- use of 'off-the-record' briefings to gag or exploit media contacts.

The individual

Ethical reasoning begins at home, with each individual. American psychologist Lawrence Kohlberg (1981) said that people go through three levels of moral development, each comprising two stages:

Level 1:
Stage 1: obey rules and avoid punishment
Stage 2: serve own needs, make fair deals

Level 2:
Stage 3: be loyal/good to others and positively conform to rules
Stage 4: do one's duty to society

Level 3:
Stage 5: uphold basic rights, values and contract of society
Stage 6: follow universal ethical principles

Kohlberg asserts that as children we do things to avoid punishment and seek to satisfy our own needs. For example, a child learns that if they behave as their parents want them to, they will escape punishment and get more of what they want. As we get older and more mature we are able to consider other people and act in self-restricting or even self-sacrificing ways because we believe that is the right thing to do. Of course, not everyone reaches that stage of development (some never get beyond level 1).

Whether or not you agree with Kohlberg, there are some important things here including an appreciation of yourself, a respect for others, a belief that you have certain obligations and duties and a value system that provides you with some guiding principles. This may be provided by a religious or philosophical code or by a self-constructed code of belief. In recent research, it was discovered that senior public relations practitioners had a strong personal belief system that carried over into the way they behaved at work (Gregory 2002).

External guides

Having a personal set of values is a good starting point, but it is useful to have them validated by external and more objective sources.

The starting point is the law. Legally binding regulatory codes (in your country or society) such as the criminal law, rights legislation or financial regulations describe what is regarded as acceptable or ethical behaviour in society at large. However, the law has its limitations. What is legally acceptable is not always socially acceptable. CSR programmes usually go beyond what is required in law because minimum workers' rights or minimum environmental standards are not seen as being in the spirit of CSR which seeks not only to do no harm, but to make a positive contribution to society (see also Chapters 6 and 18).

Another external reference point is company and/or industry codes of practices. In the confectionery industry, many companies are now ensuring that their advertising is not targeted at younger children because of the issue of obesity. Cadbury Schweppes is one such company with a strict code of practice on this – see marketing codes of conduct at www.cadburyschweppes.com. Most companies have internal codes of conduct that cover things like conflicts of interest, the acceptance of gifts or what to do in cases of harassment, such as that operating at Coca-Cola, for example (see www.coca-cola.com/ ourcompany/business_conduct.html).

Then there are the professional and business codes of conduct. The UK CIPR's Code of Conduct has already been mentioned, but it is useful to look at other professional codes for guidance. Useful sources of information are the Institute of Directors (www.IoD.org), Business in the Community (www.bitc.org.uk), the Institute of Business Ethics (www.Ibe.org.uk) and the Global Reporting Initiative (www.globalreporting .org), which offers sound advice on how to put together CSR reports. The Global Alliance of Public Relations and Communication Management (www. globalpr.org) offers advice on global public relations ethics and how to practise in a wide range of countries.

Ethical decision-making models

Parsons (2004: 21) provides five 'pillars' that she claims 'carry the weight of ethical decision-making in public relations':

- veracity (tell the truth)
- non-malfeasance (do no harm)
- beneficence (do good)
- confidentiality (respect privacy)
- fairness (to be fair and socially responsible).

Using these pillars in the form of questions can help you recognise if there is an ethical issue (Parsons 2004: 142):

- Is there harm involved?
- Is there a missed opportunity to do something good?
- Could anyone be misled in any way?
- Will anyone's privacy be invaded?
- Is it unfair to assume?
- Does it feel wrong?

There are several ethical decision-making frameworks that can be used and a number are particularly applicable to public relations. One of the more well known is that devised by Ralph Potter of Harvard Divinity School and known as the Potter box (see Figure 15.3).

Potter defined four steps in ethical decision making:

1 *Define situation*: get all the relevant facts. What led to the situation? What is it now? Who is involved? Are there different views? What is the context?
2 *Identify values*: what personal values apply here? (Remember Josephson's universal values.) What values can you draw from professional codes of practice? Are there legal guidelines?
3 *Select principles*: choose the decision-making framework that you and/or your company espouses, for example the virtue ethics approach.
4 *Choose loyalties*: prioritise all the stakeholders who demand your loyalty. Different situations will

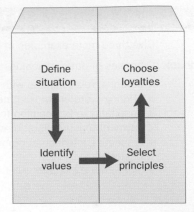

FIGURE 15.3   The Potter box (*source:* from *Public Relation Ethics, 1st edition* by Seib. © 1995. Reprinted with permission of Wadsworth, a division of Thomson Learning: www.thomsonrights.com. Fax 800 730 2215)

force you to choose your highest loyalty. For example, if your employer is doing something illegal, your loyalty to society must come first. If your company is being unjustly attacked, your loyalty to the company will come to the fore (see Mini case study 15.2).

Sims (1992) offers an equally useful model, which involves seven steps. He devised it specifically to help working practitioners who were faced with ethical dilemmas:

1 Recognise and clarify the dilemma.
2 Get all the possible facts, list *all* your options.
3 Test each option by asking is it legal? Is it right? Is it beneficial?
4 Make your decision.
5 Double-check your decision by asking: how would I feel if my family found out about this?
6 How would I feel if my decision was printed in the local newspaper?
7 Take action.

These models are, of course, only models, but they do show a pattern of thinking that can be useful to practitioners. They do not state which values or stakeholders should have priority – that is up to the practitioner to decide – but they do offer a useful framework to ensure that decision making is logical, rigorous, defendable and transparent, and that is critically important. They also help consistency of decision making, which helps build trust and credibility. (See mini case study 15.3 and Activity 15.2 on p. 304.)

mini case study 15.2

A financial services company

Financial Services plc has been downsizing because the increasingly competitive nature of the industry requires it to cut costs. It has been in discussions about a merger with Money Investment plc, which is in difficulties. Although rumours are rife, negotiations have not been completed. You are asked to issue a press release to respond to rumours, but senior management ask you to play things down and say discussions are at a very early stage. You know that discussions are well advanced and the company will make a formal announcement early next month. What do you do?

Using Potter's box, you first analyse the situation. You have been asked to put out misleading information on matters that are very important to some key stakeholders. When this is discovered you will be regarded as unethical and your reputation will be damaged. There may even be legal implications.

Second, you identify the values that are important; honesty and integrity may feature.

Third, you select the relevant ethical principles. What about Stock Exchange (legal) rules? Are there any issues with the financial services regulators? What about industry and company codes of conduct? What about the national public relations institute (e.g. in the UK the CIPR Code)? What about your personal ethics – don't lie, be loyal to your employer, do to others what you would want others to do to you?

Fourth, prioritise your stakeholders, who may include: Stock Exchange, regulators, shareholders, employees, customers, financial media, self, the industry.

This will be an uncomfortable business since it will force you to confront tough decisions about values and publics, but your decision (whatever it is), will be better and more consistent for it and you will have gone through a demonstrably rigorous process.

mini case study 15.3

Global Alliance Protocol

The Global Alliance Ethics Protocol is given in Appendix 2. Here is an example from its website of its decision-making framework in action.

Scenario: Your consultancy represents the National Cement and Asphalt Contractors Association (NCACA) in Italy. You have been asked to organise the Livorno Citizens for Active Road Expansion (LCARE), sponsored by the Association.

You have been asked by the media about LCARE. What do you tell them?

1 *Define specific ethical issues:*
   Is it ethical to omit sponsor information?
   Is it ethical to disseminate false information regarding LCARE?

2 *Identify internal/external factors that may influence the decision-making process:*
   Do local state or federal laws play a role?
   What are my consultancy's values policies or procedures?
   What action do I believe is in the public's best interest?

3 *Identify key values:*
   Honesty
   Fairness
   Independence

4 *Identify affected parties:*
   Livorno citizens
   Voters
   Government officials
   Media
   Public relations professions
   Colleagues/employees/self

5 *Select ethical principles:*
   Disclosure of information
   Open communication fosters informed decision making in democratic society

6 *Make a decision:*
   Responsible advocacy requires that those affected be given due consideration
   Appropriate action dictates a truthful response to the media disclosing your client as the sponsor of LCARE

Source: www.globalpr.org

activity 15.2

Public relations ethics

1 Draw up your own personal ethical code.
2 Do you think public relations consultants should not represent any legally constituted organisation? List your reasons. Are there any organisations you would not work for? Why?
3 Look at the ethical decision-making models in McElreath (1997) and Seib and Fitzpatrick (1995). Which one do you think is most appropriate for public relations practitioners? Why?
4 What are the key differences between 'putting a good, but fair gloss' on something and unacceptable 'spinning'?
5 If the press asked you to name an individual employee who was suspected of sexual harassment of young employees, how would you handle it? Articulate your decision-making process.

Feedback
■ For guidance on personal ethics codes, see Parsons 2004.

■ Decision-making models. Reasons why one model may be chosen over another might include: ease of use under pressure, simple to explain to others, aligns with my own moral stance, is similar to company code of ethics.
■ Key differences between a 'good gloss' and 'spinning'. The key issue is the intention to deceive. A good gloss should provide recipients of the information with a fair and truthful representation of a company, even if it is a positive representation. If other information is obtained, the recipient of the 'good gloss' should still recognise the representation as reflecting the facts. 'Spinning' implies that people will not receive a fair representation. Either the omissions of fact may be so great as to allow the recipients to draw false conclusions (and the information originator is aware of this), or misleading information may be included or implied.

Summary

This chapter has sought to provide some of the reasons why ethics in public relations is important and why it is complex and challenging. However, just because something is difficult doesn't mean it should not be done. Reflecting deeply about your own personal values is hard. Reconciling all the conflicting demands on your loyalties is hard. Understanding all the various philosophical and theoretical frameworks that are designed to help you in the process is not easy. Despite all this, it is worth every bit of effort.

Being viewed by your peers and the people that you interact with as a person of judgement and integrity is a mark not only of your professionalism, but also of your personal character. People of integrity are most highly regarded; it is one of the keys to having a good reputation. For an individual of reputation to be in charge of an organisation's most precious asset, the relationships on which its own reputation is founded, is good news indeed. Furthermore, for people of high reputation to be involved in the profession of public relations can only mean that, over time, the standing of the whole industry will improve.

Bibliography

Bivins, T.H. (1993). 'Public relations, professionalism, and the public interest'. *Journal of Business Ethics* **12**: 117–126.

Burke, K. (1969a). *A Grammar of Motives*. Berkeley, CA: University of California Press.

Burke, K. (1969b). *A Rhetoric of Motives*. Berkeley, CA: University of California Press.

Cutlip, S.M., A.H. Center and G.M. Broom (2000). *Effective Public Relations*, 8th edition. Upper Saddle River, NJ: Prentice Hall International.

Etzioni, A. (1995). *The Spirit of Community: Rights, responsibilities and the communitarian agenda*. London: Fontana.

Friedman, M. (1970). 'The social responsibility of business is to increase its profits'. *The New York Times Magazine*, 13 September.

Gregory, A. (2002). 'Competencies of top communicators'. Research undertaken for the *Communications Directors Forum*, June.

Grunig, J.E. and T. Hunt (1984). *Managing Public Relations*. New York: Holt, Rinehart & Winston.

Habermas, J. (1984). *The Theory of Communicative Action, Vol. 1: Reason and the rationalization of society*. (T. McCarthy, trans.). Boston, MA: Beacon.

Heath, R.L. (2001). 'Shifting foundations: Public relations as relationship building' in *Handbook of Public Relations*. R.L. Heath (ed.). Thousand Oaks, CA: Sage.

Heath, R. and M. Ryan (1989). 'Public relations role in defining corporate and social responsibility'. *Journal of Mass Media Ethics* **4**(1): 21–38.

Josephson, M. (1993). 'Teaching ethical decision making and principled reasoning'. *Business Ethics* Annual edition 1993–1994. Guilford, CN: Daskin Publishing Group.

Kohlberg, L. (1981). *The Meaning and Measurement of Moral Development*. Worcester, MA: Clark University Press.

Kruckeberg, D. and K. Starck (1988). *Public Relations and Community: A reconstructed theory*. New York: Praeger.

L'Etang, J. (2003). 'The myth of the "ethical guardian"'. *Journal of Communication Management* **8**(1): 22–25.

Martinson, D.C. (1998). 'Public relations practitioners must not confuse consideration of the situation with "situation ethics"'. *Public Relations Quarterly*, Winter 1997–98: 39–43.

Martinson, D.C. (1999). 'Is it ethical for practitioners to represent "bad" clients?'. *Public Relations Quarterly* **44**(4): 22–25.

McElreath, M. (1997). *Managing Systematic and Ethical Public Relations Campaigns*. Madison, WN: Brown & Benchmark.

MORI (2002). 'Operating and financial review'. Research study for the Institute of Public Relations 2002.

MORI (2004). *Annual Corporate Social Responsibility Study*. London: MORI.

O'Neil, O. (2002). 'A question of trust, Lecture 2: Trust and terror'. Reith Lectures. www.bbc.co.uk/radio4/reith2002/2.shtml

Parsons, P. (2004). *Ethics in Public Relations*. London: Kogan Page.

Pearson, R. (1989). 'Business ethics as communication ethics: Public relations practice and the idea of dialogue' in *Public Relations Theory*. C.H. Botan and V. Hazelton (eds). Mahwah, NJ: Lawrence Erlbaum Associates.

Pratt, C.B. (1993). 'Critique of the classical theory of situational ethics in US public relations'. *Public Relations Review*, Fall.

Ryan, M. and D.L. Matinson (1984). 'Ethical values, the flow of journalistic information and public relations person'. *Journalism Quarterly*, Spring.

Seib, P. and K. Fitzpatrick (1995). *Public Relations Ethics*. Forth Worth, TX: Harcourt Brace.

Sims, R.R. (1992). 'The challenge of ethical behaviour in organisations'. *Journal of Business Ethics* **11**.

Somerville, I. (2001). 'Business ethics, public relations and social responsibility' in *The Public Relations Handbook*. A. Theaker (ed.). London: Routledge.

Toth, E.L. and R.L. Heath (eds) (1992). *Rhetorical and Critical Approaches to Public Relations*. Hillsdale, NJ: Lawrence Erlbaum Associates.

Trevino, L.K. and K.A. Nelson (2004). *Managing Business Ethics*, 3rd edition. Hoboken, NJ: John Wiley & Sons.

Wright, D.K. (1982). 'The philosophy of ethical development in public relations' in *Managing Systematic and Ethical Public Relations Campaigns*. M. McElreath (1997). Madison, WN: Brown & Benchmark.

For glossary definitions relevant to this chapter, visit the **selected glossary** feature on the website at: www.pearsoned.co.uk/tench

Appendix 1: Chartered Institute of Public Relations Code of Conduct

CIPR Principles

1. Members of the Chartered Institute of Public Relations agree to:

    i. Maintain the highest standards of professional endeavour, integrity, confidentiality, financial propriety and personal conduct;

    ii. Deal honestly and fairly in business with employers, employees, clients, fellow professionals, other professions and the public;

    iii. Respect the customs, practices and codes of clients, employers, colleagues, fellow professionals and other professions in all countries where they practise;

    iv. Take all reasonable care to ensure employment best practice including giving no cause for complaint of unfair discrimination on any grounds;

    v. Work within the legal and regulatory frameworks affecting the practice of public relations in all countries where they practise;

    vi. Encourage professional training and development among members of the profession;

    vii. Respect and abide by this Code and related Notes of Guidance issued by the Chartered Institute of Public Relations and encourage others to do the same.

Principles of Good Practice

2. Fundamental to good public relations practice are:

Integrity

- Honest and responsible regard for the public interest;
- Checking the reliability and accuracy of information before dissemination;
- Never knowingly misleading clients, employers, employees, colleagues and fellow professionals about the nature of representation or what can be competently delivered and achieved;
- Supporting the CIPR Principles by bringing to the attention of the CIPR examples of malpractice and unprofessional conduct.

Competence

- Being aware of the limitations of professional competence: without limiting realistic scope for development, being willing to accept or delegate only that work for which practitioners are suitably skilled and experienced;
- Where appropriate, collaborating on projects to ensure the necessary skill base.

Transparency and conflicts of interest

- Disclosing to employers, clients or potential clients any financial interest in a supplier being recommended or engaged;
- Declaring conflicts of interest (or circumstances which may give rise to them) in writing to clients, potential clients and employers as soon as they arise;
- Ensuring that services provided are costed and accounted for in a manner that conforms to accepted business practice and ethics.

Confidentiality

- Safeguarding the confidences of present and former clients and employers;
- Being careful to avoid using confidential and 'insider' information to the disadvantage or prejudice of clients and employers, or to self-advantage of any kind;
- Not disclosing confidential information unless specific permission has been granted or the public interest is at stake or if required by law.

Maintaining Professional Standards

3. CIPR members are encouraged to spread awareness and pride in the public relations profession where practicable by, for example:

- Identifying and closing professional skills gaps through the Institute's Continuous Professional Development programme;
- Offering work experience to students interested in pursuing a career in public relations;
- Participating in the work of the Institute through the committee structure, special interest and vocational groups, training and networking events;
- Encouraging employees and colleagues to join and support the CIPR;
- Displaying the CIPR designatory letters on business stationery;
- Specifying a preference for CIPR applicants for staff positions advertised;
- Evaluating the practice of public relations through use of the CIPR Research & Evaluation Toolkit and other quality management and quality assurance systems (e.g. ISO standards); and constantly striving to improve the quality of business performance;
- Sharing information on good practice with members and, equally, referring perceived examples of poor practice to the Institute.

Appendix 2: Global Alliance Ethics Protocol

Declaration of Principles

A profession is distinguished by certain characteristics or attributes, including:

- Mastery of a particular intellectual skill through education and training
- Acceptance of duties to a broader society than merely one's clients/employers
- Objectivity
- High standards of conduct and performance

We base our professional principles therefore on the fundamental value and dignity of the individual. We believe in and support the free exercise of human rights, especially freedom of speech, freedom of assembly, and freedom of the media, which are essential to the practice of good public relations.

In serving the interest of clients and employers, we dedicate ourselves to the goals of better communication, understanding, and cooperation among diverse individuals, groups, and institutions of society. We also subscribe to and support equal opportunity of employment in the public relations profession and lifelong professional development.

We pledge:

- To conduct ourselves professionally, with integrity, truth, accuracy, fairness, and responsibility to our clients, our client publics, and to an informed society;
- To improve our individual competence and advance the knowledge and proficiency of the profession through continuing education and research and where available, through the pursuit of professional accreditation;
- To adhere to the principles of the Global Protocol on Ethics in Public Relations.

Protocol Standards

We believe it is the duty of every association and every member within that association that is party to the Global Protocol on Ethics in Public Relations to:

- Acknowledge that there is an obligation to protect and enhance the profession.
- Keep informed and educated about practices in the profession that ensure ethical conduct.
- Actively pursue personal professional development.
- Accurately define what public relations activities can and cannot accomplish.
- Counsel its individual members in proper ethical decision-making generally and on a case specific basis.

- Require that individual members observe the ethical recommendations and behavioural requirements of the Protocol.

We are committed to ethical practices, preservation of public trust, and the pursuit of communication excellence with powerful standards of performance, professionalism, and ethical conduct.

Advocacy

We will serve our client and employer interests by acting as responsible advocates and by providing a voice in the market place of ideas, facts, and viewpoints to aid informed public debate.

Honesty

We will adhere to the highest standards of accuracy and truth in advancing the interests of clients and employers.

Integrity

We will conduct our business with integrity and observe the principles and spirit of the Code in such a way that our own personal reputation and that of our employer and the public relations profession in general is protected.

Expertise

We will encourage members to acquire and responsibly use specialised knowledge and experience to build understanding and client/employer credibility. Furthermore we will actively promote and advance the profession through continued professional development, research, and education.

Loyalty

We will insist that members are faithful to those they represent, while honouring their obligations to serve the interests of society and support the right of free expression.

Advancing the Protocol

We believe it is the responsibility of each member association to draw upon its own members' experiences to expand the number of examples of good and bad practice so as to better inform members' ethical practices. Experiences should be broadly shared with other members within the association and with the Global Alliance so as to build up case histories that may assist in individual cases throughout the world.

PART 3

Public relations specialisms

This part of the book focuses on the practice of public relations. We have divided it into 12 distinct chapters in recognition of the increasingly specialist knowledge, experience and skills required to achieve an effective programme or campaign on behalf of an organisation or client. Each chapter therefore: examines the broad context of the specialism; discusses the main theories and principles of building effective relationships with key publics; and identifies some of the methods of achieving successful results. Extensive use is made of mini case studies and long case studies to illustrate the theories, principles and methods described.

CHAPTER 16
Media relations

Learning outcomes

By the end of this chapter you should be able to:

- critically evaluate the role of media relations within a democratic society and within public relations practice
- identify the key purpose and principles of media relations activity
- evaluate the factors that cause media relations activities to succeed or fail
- identify the key trends in communications and the media
- identify the ethical issues involved in media relations practice.

Structure

- Role of media relations
- Defining issue: advertising or public relations?
- Media relations principles
- Negotiated news: media relations in practice
- Media partnerships
- Old media, new media and me media
- Media relations techniques

Introduction

Working with the media is what most people think of when they talk about public relations. The image is of a press officer or celebrity public relations consultant trying to get their client – be it a product (Adidas eyewear) or a person (Victoria Beckham) – into the media spotlight through print and broadcast outlets. To some extent this is true. And it is true that one of the first things most of us do when we start working in public relations is to write press releases for media distribution and cross our fingers hoping to get 'coverage'.

In defining the skills required for a career in public relations, writing and media relations come high up the list of criteria. When employers are asked to list the skills and attributes required of applicants for jobs in public relations, they usually name writing skills and knowledge of the media (Fawkes and Tench 2004). In other words, they are hiring people for a press office or media relations role. Media relations thus tends to be the most public and visible aspect of public relations practice. Yet it is also often condemned as 'puffery', 'flackery' or 'spin'. This chapter will explore the role, function and ethics of media relations within public relations practice and within a rapidly changing media landscape.

Role of media relations

In principle, public relations practitioners should be 'media neutral' (to use the jargon of the day). That means they should have the skills and experience to choose the most suitable channels to reach target audiences with appropriate messages. These channels are many and include public meetings, newsletters and web pages, to name a few.

In practice, the channels controlled by an independent media tend in many societies to have significance beyond others available to the public relations practitioner (see Chapter 4). This is explained by the reach and the credibility of the independent media and by the perceived value of editorial endorsement. The significance of media endorsement as a key source of influence has led public relations to become synonymous in many eyes with media relations. This perception is misleading, but it is enduring.

This chapter explores the role of media relations within public relations, in theory and in practice. (See Box 16.1.)

Defining issue: advertising or public relations?

Many students are confused at the start of their studies about the distinction between *advertising* and *public relations*. Identifying the differences between editorial and advertising is an important first step in understanding the media relations challenges faced by the public relations practitioner.

Advertising and public relations may both seek the same goal: publicity, the process of making something known. Yet they use very different techniques to achieve this end. Lord Bell (chairman of Chime Communications who, as Tim Bell, was an advertising executive with Saatchi & Saatchi) is a British practitioner who has held senior roles in both fields. He describes the difference succinctly by defining advertising as 'the use of paid-for media to inform and persuade' and public relations as 'the use of third-party endorsement to inform and persuade'. In other words, the advertiser controls the message (by paying for it) while the public relations practitioner seeks to persuade other people ('third parties') to convey the message for them in a supportive way ('endorsement'). Typically, these other people will be journalists who have the power to confer editorial endorsement by reporting favourably on a product, a service, a person or an organisation.

> **Definition:** *Advertising* is 'the process of gaining the public's attention through paid media announcements' (Cornelissen 2004: 182).
>
> **Definition:** *Public relations* is 'about reputation – the result of what you do, what you say and what others say about you. Public relations practice is the planned and sustained effort to establish and maintain goodwill and mutual understanding between and organisation and its publics.' (Chartered Institute of Public Relations 2005: www.cipr.co.uk)

box 16.1 What is media relations?

Media relations involves managing relationships with the media – all the writers, editors and producers who contribute to and control what appears in the print, broadcast and online media. As with all relationships, a degree of mutuality is required: the relationship should serve the interests of the media while also serving the interests of those who fund the public relations activity.

This raises two main problems for the public relations practitioner:

1 First, is forging good relationships with the media an end in itself or is it a means to better communications with the public on whom the success of the organisation depends? In public relations theory, the media are often seen as one of many channels through which messages can be communicated to the target audience. Yet in practice, those in the media demand (and often merit) special treatment, such as privileged access to senior management.

2 The second problem arises from the first. Deciding whether the media are channels or an audience will influence how you evaluate the success of your media relations activity. Is it enough to meet 10 journalists, to send out 20 news releases or to receive 45 press cuttings in a given period? It is if the goal of your media relations activity is to improve your relationships with the media. But if the goal is to improve your communications with the public, then you will need to assess how many people read or saw the story or programme and how many changed their opinions or took action as a result of it. No easy task.

What about the motoring writer who has been lent a luxury car (with free fuel) that would be way beyond their personal budget in order to help them prepare their review? What about the travel writer who has enjoyed an all-expenses-paid trip to a luxury resort courtesy of a resort hotel or a tour operator? What about the gifts to journalists?

Feedback For third-party endorsement to work, the public need to trust the journalist's judgement. We do not want to feel that their reviews can be bought like so much advertising space.

There are clearly ethical dilemmas involved in relationships with independent journalists and these will be discussed later in this chapter.

The veteran Californian public relations consultant and part-time public relations lecturer Fred Hoar used memorably to describe advertising as 'pay for play' and public relations as 'pray for play'. The point he was making is similar to Lord Bell's: the advertiser controls the message by paying for it, while the public relations practitioner seeks to influence and persuade by force of argument or creative thinking, but cannot guarantee results.

As a means of informing and persuading, advertising offers more control over the process (although still much uncertainty over the outcome). Yet it is an expensive way of conveying messages to mass audiences so it is in effect restricted to organisations with the largest budgets. And, crucially, advertising lacks one thing that money cannot always buy: credibility.

When we see or hear an advertisement, we know what it is and what it is trying to do. The reader or viewer may tend to tune out (or throw out) the adverts, preferring to concentrate instead on the programme or the editorial content. As media channels and programmes have proliferated, more advertising placements are required to reach the same audience share. Yet the more adverts we are exposed to, the more we tend to tune them out, thus requiring more advertising placements to get the message through. So the paradox facing advertisers, articulated by internet marketing author Godin (1999: 38), is: 'The more they spend the less it works. The less it works, the more they spend.'

Editorial endorsement may be considered more persuasive because it is not in the form of an advertisement. Critics who recommends a book or a film or a restaurant are, we believe, exercising their independent judgement. We may have built up trust in their judgement by reading or listening to them over months or years and may have noted that they are not afraid to express a negative judgement when they feel it is merited. (See Think about 16.1.)

Yet the distinction between advertising and editorial is not always so clear cut. The UK's state-owned broadcaster, the BBC, is untypical among media organisations in receiving its funding from a licence fee and carrying no advertising. This frees its reporters to follow a non-commercial agenda. Yet most TV channels, newspapers and magazines are heavily dependent on advertising revenues, which typically come from a few big spenders. Would the media outlet be prepared to remain independent in the face of pressure from one of its big advertisers? (See Mini case study 16.1.)

There are other ways in which the distinction between editorial and advertising can be blurred. One is in the hybrid form known as an 'advertorial'. In this case, the space is bought as with conventional advertising, but used for articles and images purporting to be independent editorial coverage, often written by members of the regular editorial team. The articles are an attempt to 'soft sell' a product or service. Best practice guidelines require these to be clearly identified as an 'advertisement' or 'advertising feature' and

Editorial independence

There was some controversy in Britain a decade ago when Microsoft, as part of its lavish publicity campaign for Windows 95 – on a scale never previously seen – negotiated to 'buy' *The Times* newspaper for a day. The then editor defended this decision on the grounds that (a) it benefited readers who would receive the newspaper for free on that day and (b) Microsoft had no control over the editorial content of the newspaper. Yet an article on the public scramble to be among the first to receive Windows 95 appeared on the front page of *The Times* that day, a very unusual prominence for a product as technical as a computer operating system.

to use typography and layout that is distinct from the regular editorial pages. But clearly the intention here is for an advertisement to masquerade as editorial and the potential exists for it to mislead the reader.

> **Definition:** An *advertorial* is a bought space in a publication that is used to print an article written in the editorial style of the journal to portray a similar 'feel' of objectivity to the editorial pages.

Another hybrid takes the form of a sponsored competition. In this case, the space will usually be given for free, provided that the prize or prizes are considered sufficiently valuable. This hybrid is thus closer to 'free editorial', although its text is usually unedited promotional copy supplied by the company behind the competition or its public relations advisors.

Controversy persists over the practices of those publishers who seek to extract payment for editorial coverage. Their request is rarely as crude as a direct charge for inclusion, but rather it follows the formula of asking for payment for 'colour separation charges'. The defence of this practice is that editorial coverage is still gained on merit, but that the payment helps to offset the additional costs of printing a colour photograph in support of the story. Yet the advice of professional bodies such as the UK's Chartered Institute of Public Relations (CIPR) and the National Union of Journalists (NUJ) is to reject this practice. By, in effect, asking for payment for inclusion, the publication is revealing its lack of separation between advertising and editorial. In other words, it is not the sort of publication capable of providing editorial credibility, so the practitioner should move on to more worthwhile targets. Unfortunately, some practitioners feel the need of such 'soft' coverage in pursuit of a fat cuttings file to impress the boss or the client and are willing to pay for it.

This brings us to 'free advertising', a popular but misleading understanding of the purpose of media relations. Certainly, for it to be credible, editorial coverage will have been gained on merit and without payment for inclusion. To this extent alone it may be considered as 'free advertising'. Yet the lack of payment for inclusion does not make it a free process. Costs may be low compared to advertising, but they are not insignificant. Good media relations requires a skilled practitioner or team of practitioners to tune into the media's agenda, to develop relationships with appropriate journalists and editors and to develop and deliver effective 'stories', images and comments to the right media at the right time and by the right means. All of this takes time and this has its cost.

But the main condemnation of 'free publicity' is that it confuses the role and purpose of editorial as distinct from advertising. It is not the job of a journalist to give 'free publicity' to a company, a product or a cause. Their job is to inform and educate their readers, viewers and listeners through news and features they and their editors consider of interest. PR-originated stories have to be included on merit. The journalist's intention is not to provide free publicity, but if this arises from the feature or story, then so be it.

Although editorial coverage does not equate to advertising space, the practice of evaluating media relations outputs by calculating the *'advertising value equivalent' (AVE)* of press cuttings persists. At its crudest, this is a measure of the column inches devoted to the client or the product and a calculation of the equivalent cost had that space been bought. Yet it is not possible to buy advertising on the BBC, one of the world's most credible media sources. So how can an advertising value equivalent be calculated in this case? And much major media coverage tends to be negative rather than positive, making a nonsense of the saying that 'there's no such thing as bad publicity'.

> **Definition:** *'Advertising value equivalent'* (AVE) is a very crude measure of media relations performance that is still cited and relates to a measurement of the column inches or centimetres devoted to the client or the product and a calculation of the equivalent cost had that space been paid for as advertising.

It is important that this debate does not give the impression that public relations is still struggling to emerge from the shadow of advertising. For instance, some influential voices have championed the benefits of the editorial route. Ries and Ries (2002: xi) argue in their explicitly titled book *The Fall of Advertising and the Rise of PR*: 'You can't build a new brand with advertising because advertising has no credibility. . . You can launch new brands only with publicity or public relations.'

To be credible, the public relations practitioner should seek to use media relations to gain editorial coverage in respected programmes and publications with a reputation for editorial independence. But for a *journalist* to be credible, they should only write or broadcast stories that are of interest to their audiences. These conflicting priorities explain the tension that will always exist between the public relations agenda and the journalist's. (See Think about 16.2.)

Along with the misunderstanding about free advertising, the other demand frequently made of media relations specialists is to 'get me on the front page of tomorrow's paper'. To which there are two possible answers. First, 'I can do it, but I wouldn't recommend

'Why do they (journalists) hate us?'

This is a question frequently asked of media relations practitioners from those seeking to understand the media's apparent hostility towards their organisations.

Feedback To which the honest answer is: 'They're neither for you nor against you.'

It is, in fact, the journalist's job to be sceptical and independent. Would you rather you lived in a society with media controlled by the state or by big corporations?

And while some journalists find some public relations practitioners courteous and helpful, others find they cannot get answers to urgent (especially negative) questions and blame all public relations staff for these problems.

---

box 16.2   **The importance of media relations**

The significance of media relations within corporate communications can be explained by several trends. As White and Mazur (1995) argue, these include the rise of consumer power, the proliferation of the media and a realisation that employees read papers and watch TV too.

There are two problems implicit in this. The first is that you have to attempt to manage the media or the media's agenda may hijack the organisation's purpose. The second is that channels of communication can rarely be neatly segmented. It is no longer possible to say one thing to one audience and a different thing to another in an age when employees may be shareholders, and shareholders may be customers. Media channels of communication reach all stakeholders. To manage or be managed by the media, which is it to be?

---

it' (there being more bad news stories than good on the news pages of the major newspapers). The other answer is 'No problem; it will cost you £50,000.' Completely controlled, unmediated messages require you to choose the advertising route. (See Box 16.2.)

Media relations principles

Most texts about media relations tend to focus on the 'how' rather than the 'why'. Yet it is important to ask what the objective of media relations activity should be. Is it to get 'good' stories into the news or to keep 'bad' ones out?

David Wragg (Bland et al. 1996: 66–67) argues that: 'The purpose of press relations is not to issue press releases, or handle enquiries from journalists, or even to generate a massive pile of press cuttings. The true purpose of press relations is to enhance the reputation of an organisation and its products, and to influence and inform the target audience.'

US author and communications consultant Shel Holtz (2002: 157) goes further: 'Contrary to the apparent belief of many observers, the role of an organizational media relations department is not to make the company look good in the press, nor is it to keep the company out of the newspapers . . . Ideally, the job of

the media relations department is to help reporters and editors do their jobs. That objective is entirely consistent with the broader goal of public relations, which is to manage the relationship between the organization and its various constituent audiences.'

This ideal contains the same contradiction as with Grunig and Hunt's (1984) model of two-way symmetric public relations. Why should an organisation fund an activity that is not overtly aimed at pursuing its own interests? And the answer will be the same: the organisation's long-term interests should prevail over its desire for short-term publicity.

Since Grunig and Hunt's four models of public relations begin explicitly with media relations (in the form of 'press agentry'), Table 16.1 (overleaf) presents two alternative models for media relations practice. (See Activity 16.1, overleaf.)

The media have a significant role in helping citizens to make informed choices within democratic, consumer societies (see Chapter 5). Journalists are often the representatives of the general public – in parliaments, at the EU Commission, in the courts and at other major decision-making occasions where only small numbers of witnesses can be present. They report on matters that affect the wider population and that might otherwise go unrecorded. It is this important role that fuels the urge of the investigative journalist to uncover duplicity and wrongdoing by

TABLE 16.1 Two models of media relations (*source:* adapted from Grunig and Hunt 1984: 22)

	Publicity model	**Relationships model**
Purpose	Tomorrow's headlines	Mutual understanding
Characteristic	Short-term goals	Medium- to long-term goals
Nature of communication	One way	Two way
Communication model	Source to receiver	Dialogue of equals
Nature of research	Little; 'counting house'	Formative
Views media as	Channel	Public and channel
Where practised today	Sports, entertainment, product promotion	Corporate communications in regulated businesses and industry regulators
Who practised by	Junior PROs; experienced publicists	Senior public relations consultants; corporate communications advisors

public figures or powerful organisations. It is also this role that enables journalists to believe that they are seekers after truth, in contrast to public relations practitioners whose duty, as they perceive it, is to protect and promote their organisation's interests.

Yet the simplistic view that 'journalism is good, public relations is bad' is hard to sustain. Most media organisations are private sector businesses that must also seek profits and competitive advantage (see Think about 16.3). Much newspaper journalism is highly selective and politically biased (this bias is acceptable where it is widely understood and where a choice of newspapers expressing a range of opinions is available to the citizen). Media organisations need to entertain as well as – or even more than – they need to inform.

Nevertheless, it is worth public relations students and practitioners remembering that journalism has a proud history of uncovering abuses of power that organisations and/or governments wanted to keep secret.

While media channels and publications have continued to proliferate, there has not, in general, been a

corresponding growth in the numbers of people working on the editorial side or in budgets for investigative journalism. This means that fewer journalists are writing and reporting more stories. The time available for investigating and fact-checking stories is shrinking.

It is in this context that the media relations function becomes increasingly important. A journalist may have hours at most to research and write a story (particularly if working for the broadcast media, an online news site or a daily newspaper). Yet a press officer (or equivalent) should have had days to plan and research a news announcement or news release. This means that: the facts of the story should be clear and credible; it should have a strong angle (the reason why it is news); and it should contain interesting quotations from authoritative sources, some of whom may not be normally available to the press to interview. It should, if targeting television or radio, have a strong visual or aural appeal.

Where public relations sources are credible, there should be less suspicion in the relationship with journalists, although there will rarely be a common agenda on both sides. Where public relations sources are used by the media (either because they are credible or because they are entertaining), then the public relations function can be said to be subsidising the newsgathering function of the media. (Outside the untypical worlds of sports and celebrity public relations or the realm of the tabloid *'kiss and tell'* story, payment will never be asked or expected from the media for publication of a PR-originated story.) So public relations gives the media stories for free (and free of copyright). If 'free advertising' is an unacceptable description of the purpose of media relations, then perhaps 'free editorial' might be a more useful perspective.

---

activity 16.1

The publicity or relationship approach?

Using the model presented in Table 16.1, go online and search the 'press office' or 'media centre' on company websites for different styles of news release. Which model do you think the releases fit into?

Feedback
Try looking at different types of company and organisation, perhaps big branded companies such as clothing, fashion or sports brands such as Adidas or Nike. Then try service providers such as local councils or utility companies in your country such as gas, electricity or water.

Definition: *'Kiss and tell'* is when someone recounts or goes public through the media about a sexual relationship they have had, normally with a politician, celebrity or person in the public eye.

How influential is public relations on the news agenda?

At one extreme, the publicist Max Clifford has claimed to have broken more stories over the last 20 years than any journalist in Britain (interview in *The Guardian*, 13 December 2004). And many trade and technical titles are heavily dependent on public relations sources for their editorial content and accompanying images (see also Chapter 22).

Several US surveys have indicated that around half of the news printed in the newspapers has had some involvement of public relations people (Grunig and Hunt 1984; Cutlip et al. 2000). This is not to say that these stories all come solely from public relations sources, but that official spokespeople have had some hand in the process of researching the story and commenting on it. Hardly a day goes by without some evidence of public relations having some influence on the news agenda, whether it is a sponsored consumer survey, a stage-managed party political media briefing or news of a charity's national awareness day, week or month.

On the other hand, journalists are quick to present public relations practitioners as gatekeepers who seek to withhold information, rather than as good sources of news and comment. Few journalists are willing publicly to admit to their close working relationships with public relations contacts, although they will often acknowledge this in private.

Negotiated news: media relations in practice

Most forms of mass communications are paid for and the messages controlled by the sender. Examples include newsletters, advertising, corporate websites, sponsorships and many others.

One form of mass communications is uncontrolled and not paid for by the sender. It relies on an independent medium choosing to convey the news or message because of its perceived value or interest to the readers, viewers or listeners. This lack of control is the defining characteristic of media relations: it can make the practice infuriatingly imprecise and unscientific – but it means that those stories and messages that are published or broadcast gain value through editorial endorsement (see Figure 16.1).

The media are not essential for third-party endorsement: there are many instances when the critics have condemned a film or a musical only for the public to vote in its favour by flocking to the cinema or theatre – and the other way round. But in a society where most people gain news and views from the newspapers and the broadcast media, this will usually be the most effective route to generating opinions about a product or service. If really successful, a 'buzz' can be created by media coverage leading to word of mouth endorsement.

In recent years, many brands have come to prominence through this word of mouth effect rather than by more traditional advertising. Examples are drawn from: the internet (Google); publishing (*Captain Correlli's Mandolin*, *Bridget Jones's Diary* and the Harry Potter books); toys and games (Tamagotchi, Furby).

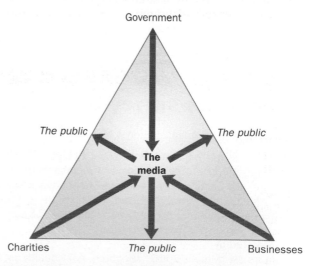

FIGURE 16.1 Communications through the prism of the media (*source*: Bailey 2005a)

| box 16.3 | **Some rules for effective media relations** |

1 Act as a service to the media: answer questions, return calls before deadline, provide information and context.
2 Accept the independence of the media: do not offer payment; do not ask for copy approval.
3 Disclose your interest (i.e. let the journalist know who you are representing).
4 Be as available to the media when the news is bad as when you have good news to promote.

Another way to view media relations is as a relationship between an organisation and the press. There are journalists who argue (partly for effect) that public relations is, at best, unable to influence them and, at worst, an irritating distraction from their jobs. And there are those public relations practitioners who argue – equally controversially – that media relations works best if its aim is to provide a service to the media (rather than being primarily a promotional channel for their clients or organisations). Somewhere in between, most journalists rely on public relations contacts to open doors, to provide information and pictures – and many are willing to accept hospitality. (See Box 16.3.)

Part of the media's frustration may come from a tacit acknowledgement of the power of public relations. As media channels have proliferated and editorial budgets have been squeezed, the opportunity for investigative journalism has been restricted, leaving reporters more reliant on public relations sources. This is very evident in the national and consumer press where most days PR-sponsored surveys make the news. (See Mini case study 16.2.)

The influence of public relations is also evident in the well-trodden path from a career in journalism to a senior role in public relations (very few make the journey in reverse, although some journalists find the public relations role less easy than they had imagined and make a quick return). (See Think about 16.4.)

The concept of negotiated news is an important principle for media relations practice. It recognises that the media do not exist to report your client or organisation. Journalists are neither for you nor against you, but neutral intermediaries standing between you and the public. Give them something interesting to report and you have a good chance of making the news; push corporate platitudes in their direction and you will be filtered out of their news agenda. Persist in this and you may be blocked entirely.

Most public relations practitioners, even the most junior, quickly come to understand the realities of dealing with a free and independent media (if only because of the many slights and setbacks they receive when pitching 'good news' stories to a seasoned reporter who is more attuned to digging for bad news). Yet they are caught in the middle, often having to explain these realities to business managers or marketing managers who expect to exert control over the delivery of their messages. Managers who are willing to espouse the virtues of a free market can often seem appalled by the workings of a free press. Yet as former British Prime Minister Margaret Thatcher used to point out: 'You can't have a free society without a free press' (Ingham 2003).

---

mini case study 16.2

Consumer survey in the news

J Sainsbury news release dated 4 March 2005

'Brighton is our banana borough, but Glasgow is our melon metropolis' – the headline of release from supermarket J Sainsbury about a consumer survey showing which fruits were preferred in which UK cities (www.j-sainsbury.co.uk/index.asp?PageID=31&sub-section=&Year=2005&NewsID=518).

Reported by:

Reuters, 4 March 2005: 'Brighton has healthiest eaters'

Daily Mirror, 4 March 2005: 'Brighton, the fruit capital of Britain'
Daily Mail, 4 March 2005: 'Brighton is the "healthiest" place in the UK'
The Sun, 4 March 2005: 'Brighton loves its fruits'
NB: *The Sun*, the *Daily Mail* and the *Daily Mirror* are the three largest circulation daily newspapers in the UK.

Is it possible to imagine a world without managed media relations?

Feedback It may be, but it is hard to see how this would serve the interests of the media. There would be no press offices or public relations consultancies to handle their enquiries (or to treat them as Very Important People). There would be no one to argue that an interview with a newspaper reporter should be given priority in the chief executive's diary over some other meeting. There would be no media accreditation or media facilities at large events, making it harder for journalists to attend and do their job. No news releases providing a factual summary of new products, policies or positions. No one to facilitate visits and ensure that meetings are useful to both parties and that questions are answered and facts researched. Organisations, governments and charities would have no mechanisms for releasing information, as part of their accountability to society in general. The doors of people who matter would remain firmly closed to the press. There would be more suspicion of, and hostility to, the media, not less.

Organisations have their own news agendas and their own internal discourse while the media must remain alert to broader news events and agendas. Most of what the one does will never interest the other; the skill in media relations is in spotting the stories or the angles that can turn corporate news into media news or bring a corporate angle into a global news story (see Figure 16.2 and Mini case study 16.3, overleaf).

Negotiated news involves bringing an external perspective to internal news stories (an advantage a public relations consultant may have over an in-house practitioner who may be too close to the organisation or to its management team to offer dispassionate advice) so that only objective and genuinely interesting news stories are issued.

The next negotiation takes place with the media. It may involve a decision on timing – there is a good time and a bad time to issue most news stories, although in a 24/7 (24 hours/seven days a week) media age you can no longer follow the old adage to make announcements 'early in the day, early in the week and early in the month'. It may involve a decision on exclusivity (recognising that the media market is highly competitive). It will involve an understanding that the negotiations with a TV station and a national newspaper will be very different discussions. The one needs a visual story, the other a strong issue or theme. (It is not enough to announce Product X, but if Product X can credibly promise less housework, lower bills, greater health or happiness, then you may have a story.)

Many media relations programmes are built on the assumption that the flow of information will be one way and based only on the news the organisation wants to see in the public domain. Yet the more you are in the news, the more you should expect to become a media target. Organisations that have been very accessible to the media when they have good news to promote have an obligation to remain accessible when the news is bad (Shell UK is discussed in this context in both the crisis and community involvement chapters (20 and 18 respectively) of this book. Relationships are a two-way thing.

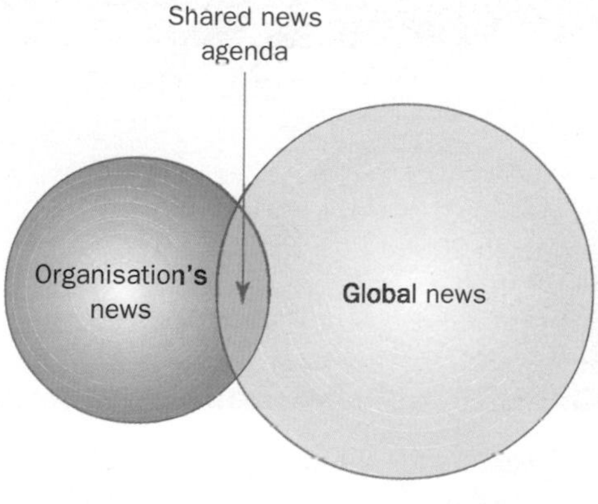

FIGURE 16.2 Overlapping news agendas
(*source:* Bailey 2005b)

Media partnerships

Media relations, as we have discussed, is a highly demanding and competitive area of public relations practice and is constantly changing and evolving with new trends emerging all the time. One of the most prevalent trends in this area of practice, typified by an evermore competitive media environment with more publications and outlets but at the same time more organisations actively vying for their attention, is the rise of media relations by media partnership. This is where organisation and media are contractually bound in joint editorial, advertising and marketing relationships, from which they derive mutual benefit (see Case study 16.1, overleaf).

Barclays Bank

A news release from Barclays, a UK bank, dated 6 March 2005, talks about the pressures on small business owners and calls on the Chancellor to 'give them back their sleep' as part of his spring budget. This refers to the annual statement on government taxation and expenditure from the Chancellor of the Exchequer, the UK government finance minister. The budget speech was given on 16 March 2005, so the Barclays news release was timed to anticipate pre-budget interest. It was reported by the *Sunday Times* newspaper on 6 March 2005 under the headline 'Revealed: owners who lose most sleep'.

The evolution of the exclusive: media relations by media partnership

Building media partnerships is a practice that public relations departments and consultancies worldwide are actively engaging in as the relationships often include guaranteed 'quality' editorial coverage in target media for their organisation or brand. This allows them to reach target audiences. As an example, between the summer of 2004 and the spring of 2005, UK public relations firm Connectpoint PR (www.connectpoint.co.uk) negotiated media partnerships for clients ranging from luxury furniture, clothing and fast moving consumer goods (fmcg) companies to international sporting events with print, television, radio and online media partners. In total, over 25 individual partnerships were negotiated during this period. Over the past few years one of the most successful examples of this that the agency has worked on is that of the Salford Triathlon ITU (International Triathlon Union) World Cup. (See Think about 16.5.)

PICTURE 16.1   Salford Triathlon ITU World Cup 2003 elite women's swim start in the Quays at Salford, UK. (*Source:* courtesy of Connectpoint PR www.connectpoint.co.uk)

case study 16.1 (continued)

What is the Salford Triathlon, ITU World Cup?

The only ITU triathlon world cup event in the UK, the Salford Triathlon ITU World Cup, is one of the 15 scheduled international World Cup events staged by the ITU. The event attracts 150 elite athletes from around the world who compete for world ranking points. The event is one of a series of flagship events used by Salford City Council to assist in projecting positive images of the city. It is essential that high-volume media coverage projects a positive image of Salford in the international and national press. It is also important that the coverage profiles the event in the regional press to generate interest in the race and deliver value to the local government and other sponsors.

Since its inception in 2003, this event has, on average, generated annual UK press coverage worth over £13,000,000. Of this, the majority has been through the aforementioned media partnerships and carried key messages portraying Salford positively and mentioning event sponsors. This fact has helped to raise the profile of the event, derive value for sponsors and has raised the event's profile beyond its natural place in the UK sporting hierarchy, which is traditionally dominated by sports such as football (soccer), rugby and cricket.

However, this poses the question as to how the event has managed to secure these partnerships. The answer is quite simply that each of these partnerships offers editorial and marketing benefits that they perceive as equal to, or greater than, the costs involved. This can include such rights as exclusivity of broadcast rights. In the case of the BBC this has included the UK and beyond for news coverage. Also, there are features and stories for the various print and online partners for the marketing rights. With these the logos and details are included on local event outdoor advertising and event branding that is visible on television coverage and partnerships. Furthermore, for the media partners it also delivers the opportunity to borrow from the event its brand attributes of sport, vitality, well-being, endurance and difference that the sport of triathlon possesses.

In return, the event receives guaranteed editorial levels, adverts without charge and competition spaces which deliver quality editorial, communicate key messages usually to a depth much greater than is possible without a partnership.

Specifically for the event, this exchange of value in 2004 comprised benefits to each party with respect to the four main partners, as can be seen in Table 16.2 (see also Think about 16.6, overleaf).

As you can see, this partnership approach provides numerous benefits for both parties. However, this approach to media relations does have several potential pitfalls to watch out for. First, there is a significant chance that in partnering with one media outlet you alienate their competitors, who in turn could choose not to cover the event from even a news perspective. In the case of the triathlon, Key 103's principal competitors in the same regional radio market refused to cover the event, as they felt that all the benefits Key 103 received from the event gave them a potential commercial advantage due to the high-profile outdoor advertising campaign and event branding.

An additional pitfall that needs to be considered is the demand that such media partnerships will have on the resources (financial and time) for organisations or agencies. In the case of the triathlon, Connectpoint PR had a separate account director who managed the media partnerships, ensuring that sufficient exclusive stories were generated to satisfy all parties concerned. Lastly, it is also important to realise that the partnership may be adversely affected if the event is embroiled in scandal and the media partners as objective members

▶

Why do you think the media would be willing to partner such an event and what types of media do you think would partner the event?

Feedback The answer is that media partnerships deliver a benefit to the media partner that is equal to or even exceeds the perceived cost of the relationship. In the case of the Salford Triathlon ITU World Cup, partnerships were struck by the agency and organisers with:

The *Manchester Evening News* (UK regional newspaper: circulation 158,143)
Key 103 (UK regional radio station: listeners 623,000)
220 Triathlon (UK national triathlon magazine: circulation 20,000)
BBC Sport, *Grandstand* (UK national television: viewers 3,500,000)
www.triathlon.org and www.trisalford.info (online media partner)
International television distribution done via the ITU.

case study 16.1 (continued)

TABLE 16.2   Salford Triathlon ITU World Cup: benefits to media partners and organisers

Media partners	Benefits to partner	Benefits to the event
Manchester Evening News	• Category exclusivity (i.e. no other newspapers able to partner event) • Sponsorship package including: free entries, event branding, VIP programme, inclusion on all marketing materials and outdoor advertising • Dedicated features exclusive to partner • 24hr advance notification on all non-time-sensitive news stories • High-value prizes for reader competitions	• Guaranteed media coverage, which in the end resulted in over 30 pieces of coverage, including three front-page pieces and three front pages of sport section stories • 6 free ¼-page adverts worth over £10,000 • 2 free reader competitions with event sponsor branding • Promotion of event on posters on street vendor stands
Key 103 fm	• Category exclusivity (i.e. no other radio stations able to partner event) • Sponsorship package including free entries, event branding, VIP programme, inclusion on all marketing materials and outdoor advertising • Dedicated features exclusive to partner • 24hr advance notification on all non-time-sensitive news stories • High-value prizes for listener competitions	• Cash sponsorship • 350 30-second on-air read or event advert free of charge over 4 months • Guaranteed media coverage, which resulted in over 10 feature stories, plus 50+ news pieces broadcast • Roadshow at event with music provided by a DJ
220 Triathlon	• Category exclusivity (i.e. no other Triathlon print media partner) • Sponsorship package including free entries, event branding, VIP programme and inclusion on all marketing materials • Dedicated features exclusive to partner • High-value prizes for reader competitions	• 4 ¼-page adverts free of charge • 6 pages of feature editorial, accompanied by free advert • Preferential news editorial resulting in 10 individual pieces • 10 free subscriptions for event prizes
BBC *Grandstand*	• Category exclusivity • Television rights for programming • Dedicated features exclusive to partner	• Guaranteed 1hr national television broadcast of the event reaching over 3.5m viewers where sponsors receive high-value recognition and Salford portrayed positively

of the media must cover the story that is adversely affecting the event. Fortunately for the Salford Triathlon this has not been a problem. (See Think about 16.7, overleaf.)

It is undoubtedly true that in the case of the Salford Triathlon ITU World Cup, the media relations by media partnership approach has been extraordinarily successful, delivering a level of media coverage well beyond that which would be achieved under a traditional media relations model. This approach is one where both the media partner and event benefit significantly and for which careful planning can avoid potential pitfalls.

Manchester Evening News

Monday, July 26, 2004   www.manchesteronline.co.uk   30p

■ Great Britain's Michelle Dillon celebrates as she wins the women's elite race.   Picture: SEAN WILTON

Triathlon a triumph - now Salford goes for the world!

See M.E.N. Sport

M&S DOORS LOCKED AS RIVALS CLASH

Shoppers caught in demo fury

BY CARL PALMER

POLICE were forced to lock the front entrance of Manchester's huge Marks & Spencer store after clashes between rival protesters.

A confrontation between pro-Palestinian supporters picketing the Market Street store and defenders of Israel became so volatile that extra officers were drafted in to control the crowd.

One person was arrested in the worst clash since the Saturday pickets started three-and-a-half years ago.

Cordon

Mounted police kept the two sides apart and the front doors of the store were locked to protect customers. Police later closed one end of Market Street to traffic for safety reasons, and cordoned off other parts of the shopping area.

A number of people were warned about their behaviour. The demonstration began quietly at noon, but by 1.45pm when counter-protesters had increased the crowd to more than 80, the mood changed as the two sides chanted slogans at each other.

Shoppers had to walk in the road and squeeze past the crowd, who were block-

■ FACE TO FACE . . . A counter protester and police

ing the pavement. In a similar incident last week, a man was arrested when the two groups were caught in a heated exchange. This week one person was arrested but was later released without charge.

Hanoch Segal was one of the people led away by police.

A furious Mr Segal said: "We have ev-

ery right to protest peacefully, but my partner, who has cancer, was pushed three times by police and treated appallingly. When her son tried to intervene to speak with her, and complained that someone had pushed him in the face, the police didn't want to know." The picket,

Turn to Page 5

INSIDE: DIARY 7; COMMENT 8; WORLD NEWS and WEATHER 10; CHECKOUT 20; POSTBAG 16; STARS, CROSSWORD 22

PICTURE 16.2   The media exclusive resulted in three front-page pieces on the Salford Triathlon ITU World Cup over the three days of the event. (*Source:* used with kind permission of the Manchester Evening News.)

---

think about 16.6   Adding new media partners

In future years, are there any additional media partners the event could add without causing conflict?

Feedback   The answer is yes, one such example could be a lifestyle/sport magazine for men/women's fitness or health.

think about 16.7   **Crises and scandals**

How might one use a media partnership to limit the damage of any potential scandals or negative stories while also ensuring the media partner's objectivity is not compromised?

Feedback   Damage limitation could be ensured by the organiser providing the partner with a steady stream of the organisation's side of the story and, in turn, the media partner reporting this side to balance its coverage. Additionally, the media partner could highlight the inaccuracies in other media coverage, in contrast to its own balanced approach. However this approach cannot be relied on in a media environment where bad news traditionally sells.

Old media, new media and me media

It is time to declare an end to press relations and all its offshoots – press officers, press releases, press conferences, press packs. Using 'the press' as a collective noun for the media makes it easy to ignore all the radio stations, TV programmes and internet news sites and weblogs that should also be considered in any media relations activity.

Yet many people are reluctant to move on. In part, this can be explained by the heavy emphasis in some sectors on specialist or trade publications (see Chapter 22) that as yet have no equivalent expression in the broadcast media and are often not even published online. In part, it stems from the need to hand a regular (preferably bulging) press cuttings file to the senior management team and to leave a copy in reception. Video and audio broadcasts are harder to capture and display, and monitoring and recording comments on thousands of ephemeral websites poses a considerable challenge. There are, however, companies that aim to provide this service to organisations.

The reality is that we live in a multimedia age – but then this has always been the case. The great age of mass circulation newspapers began in the late nineteenth century, alongside the arrival of mass adult literacy. Yet the phenomenon of the *Daily Mail* – the world's first tabloid newspaper – was preceded by the arrival of an electronic newswire service (Reuters). Radio broadcasts began in the 1920s, followed a decade later by television broadcasts. (See Box 16.4.)

The summary in Box 16.4 demonstrates the recent rapid developments in broadcasting, as well as other forms of communication and yet, despite the more recent arrival of broadband internet access, the demand for television and radio has not diminished. In fact, from a UK perspective it is arguable that it has extended it, to judge from the expatriates who correspond with the BBC following its sports broadcasts or discussion programmes. It is possible to conclude that television did not kill radio off, any more than broadcasting killed off newspapers.

If the trend appears to be towards broadcast and online media, then you should not overlook the resurgence and profitability of local and regional newspapers (for example, in Barcelona readers are

box 16.4   **Broadcast and media developments in the UK**

In just over 20 years, the UK has gone from having three television channels (BBC1, BBC2 and ITV) to having many hundreds of digital channels as well as two more 'terrestrial' channels. Something similar has happened on the radio, with the arrival of commercial stations being followed by specialist digital channels.

Meanwhile, in the last decade, the internet has become an everyday addition to work and home lives. Most media organisations now have a web presence: for example, *The Guardian*'s award-winning site (www.guardian.co.uk) does more than reproduce its print version, as it contains lengthy background reports, regular updates and other web-based features. The BBC site (www.bbc.co.uk) not only offers news and educational material, but also the possibility of listening to last week's radio broadcasts or even downloading programmes to any PC in the world.

'What is clear is that the story of the news media involves a process of evolution, in which old media are not replaced by new media, but modified by them' (Hargreaves 2003: 52).

loyal to *La Vanguardia* rather than the established national Spanish newspaper *El Pais*). They usually hold a local monopoly and provide the sort of local content that people most want and cannot get elsewhere (what's on listings, local news and events, classified and job adverts). Depending on the title, they also often tend to pursue a more positive (and so PR-friendly) news agenda.

This multi-channel, multimedia landscape – coupled with long working hours and long commuting distances – makes it very difficult for advertising media buyers and public relations practitioners to advise on the most effective means of reaching target audiences.

It was once so much simpler, at least for the advertisers. A commercial on the one TV channel that took advertising, if timed around the popular national *soap opera Coronation Street*, could be expected to reach half of all UK homes. Now, not only has the audience fragmented as it flits between hundreds of competing channels, but we have started to tune out advertisements (both psychologically and, depending on recording equipment, technically) because of their ubiquity and because we do not trust their messages.

> **Definition:** '*Soap opera*' is a broadcast drama serialised in many episodes and generally deals with domestic themes (the name originates from the USA where these types of programmes were sponsored by soap powder manufacturers targeting householders).

This is where media relations comes into the equation. Although the public relations practitioner faces the same questions as the media buyer (Who is watching the programme? Are they paying attention to it?), public relations messages have more credibility than advertising messages because they come with an editorial endorsement. As the Chartered Institute of Public Relations (2005) tells us: 'Public relations is about reputation, the result of what you do, what you say, and *what others say about you*' (our italics). Editorial endorsement amounts to word of mouth recommendation ('what others say about you'), but with the power to reach many thousands of ears.

Equally, others may not have good things to say about you. A programme or publication that is not beholden to its advertisers (the licence-fee-funded BBC in the UK, which carries no advertising, is particularly potent here) may be fearless in scrutinising corporate arrogance (*Watchdog*, BBC TV) and be critical of a new luxury car (*Top Gear*, BBC TV).

So the media relations practitioner should not only pursue and facilitate opportunities for positive pub-

licity, but must be alert to the dangers of gaining a bad press. The journalist or reporter may have personal reasons for disliking a company or product or they may be responding to public concerns. The media may be in contact with a 'whistleblowing' employee unhappy for some reason with your organisation's practices.

Now, it seems, we are all media experts. Any '*wannabe*' seems to know how to get hold of publicist Max Clifford in order to 'sell their story'; individuals know to take their complaints to the media as well as to their MPs; and pressure groups and campaigning organisations are among the most effective at creating photo opportunities pitching their side of the story (think about Greenpeace's activities worldwide as well as direct action campaigns in the UK such as Fathers4Justice, www.fathers-4-justice.org).

> **Definition:** '*Wannabe*' is negative slang for a person who aspires to be well known in the media or to be perceived as successful in a pursuit that is in the public eye (sport, arts, popular music, etc.).

> **Definition:** Media setting the agenda or '*agenda setting*' refers to a theory that the media direct public attention to particular issues that fit news priorities and, in doing so, influence public opinion. The theory is unproven, since it can be argued that underlying public concerns can influence issue definition by both political elites and the media. (McQuail 1987). (See also Mini case study 16.4, overleaf.)

Access to the press and the public is no longer limited to the rich and powerful. Anyone with something to promote or criticise can set up a website to get their message across: one disgruntled customer of a bank or a retailer can become a talking point out of all proportion to their size, status or the merits of their arguments. It is the power of public relations being turned on the traditional users of public relations.

But even websites take some time and resources to set up and manage. The true voice of the man or woman on the street is beginning to be expressed through the much more accessible form of the *weblog*. These are at the other end of the spectrum from the mass media: they are micromedia projects usually reflecting the views of just one individual and often read by tiny numbers – but capable of being linked and repeated until the micromedium in turn becomes a mass media phenomenon. (See Think about 16.8, Mini case study 16.5 and Think about 16.9, all overleaf.)

mini case study 16.4

The great GM food debate

In early 1999, genetically-modified (GM) food became a media talking point in the UK, characterised by tabloid newspaper headlines including the emotive phrase 'Frankenstein food' (e.g. *Daily Mirror* 16 February 1999) and by the equally powerful image of environmental activists in white coats digging up GM crops. According to the Parliamentary Office of Science and Technology report into this 'media storm', an influential factor in this was that several newspaper editors 'saw a clear opportunity to champion what they took to be the popular cause of resistance to GM crops and GM foods'. In other words, the media were not only reporting the news, they were also *setting the agenda* and leading public opinion. On this occasion, the 'media storm' led to a move against GM foods by food suppliers and retailers and the tactical retreat of biotechnology company Monsanto. As the parliamentary report concludes: 'The real lesson of the Great GM Food Debate is that in a democracy, any significant interest – science included – ignores the public at its peril.'

Source: www.parliament.uk/post/report138.pdf

PICTURE 16.3   Genetically-modified (GM) food became a media talking point in the UK, characterised by tabloid newspaper headlines including the emotive phrase 'Frankenstein food'. (*Source:* © Darrell Gulin/Corbis)

think about 16.8   Weblogs

Should public relations practitioners add weblogs to their media lists?

Feedback   Yes and no. Yes, because many *webloggers* are influential individuals with detailed industry knowledge (many are themselves professional journalists). No, because you should handle them with particular care. They are writing for their own interest and do not want to feel subject to any outside, commercial interests. By all means engage them in dialogue on their chosen topics, but beware of 'pitching' them with your own stories. You should certainly monitor the more influential weblogs covering your area (you can gauge the influence by a metric such as Google PageRank, a measure of other pages that link to this one in a form of online peer review).

mini case study 16.5

The web in action

Computer networks have been a powerful lobbying force for over a decade. In 1994, a few influential voices on a Usenet internet discussion forum forced microprocessor company Intel to withdraw its new Pentium processor because of a bug in the way it performed certain mathematical calculations. Intel was forced to change its policy because the user dissatisfaction with the processor was picked up by the mainstream media (Gillmor 2004).

Today, discussion and activism on the web is often to be found in weblogs. These 'citizen journalists' can act as fact checkers to the mainstream media and to corporate public relations. As a result, politicians, the media and corporations risk having their half-truths quickly exposed. This happened when Matt Drudge exposed the Monica Lewinsky affair through his online Drudge Report on 17 January 1998 (Hargreaves 2003). It happened again in the USA in 2004 when webloggers set out to fact check the documents that US TV channel CBS claimed to prove that President Bush had evaded military service in Vietnam in 1973. The documents were shown to be fake ('Dan Rather faces bittersweet sign-off' *USA Today* 9 March 2005).

Definition: A *weblog* is a website in the form of a diary containing time-stamped articles and frequently linking to sources and other sites of interest. Weblogs usually reflect the views of one person or a small group of individuals and are read generally by a limited number of people on the internet but are capable of attracting large readerships through references on other websites. *Webloggers* are the individuals who run weblog journals on the world wide web.

Media relations techniques

Boy meets girl. It is an old story and the fundamentals never change. But the techniques used are subject to the whims of fashion and technology. Each year, the popular press gets hold of a new 'love rat' who becomes the first celebrity caught 'dumping' his partner by fax, email or text message. It is the same story, only this time using different technology.

Media relations is similarly about relationships. The public relations practitioner needs to find the appropriate ways to identify, meet and woo the media target and the relationship then needs to be *maintained*. Correspondence, phone, email, face to face are all valid forms for such communication, but each has its drawbacks.

The public relations industry used to mass market the media with news releases sent by post. Then the fax took over as the communications device of choice. Now it is email. But each in turn has become discredited though overuse and misuse. Now all forms of mass marketing seem inappropriate and micro- targeting is in.

think about 16.9   Ethics and media relations

Media relations is surrounded by a minefield of ethical issues, such as:

- Should you offer hospitality, a gift or bribery?
- Should you ever offer payment for placement or offer one story to keep another out of the news?
- Just how close should you allow your relationships with journalists to become?
- Is it ever acceptable to lie?

Feedback One guiding principle is to respect the independence of the media. If the hospitality is too lavish, could this be perceived as a form of bribery, one favour that expects another in return? (In the USA, it is usual for media organisations to pay the travel and accommodation expenses of their journalists attending a media event; in Europe, they tend to travel at the expense of the organiser.)

A second guiding principle is to consider what would be best in developing longer term relationships, rather than aiming solely at tomorrow's news headline. If you over-promote this week's news, could you jeopardise your chances of success with the same people in future?

Likewise, if you lie about this week's stories, why should a journalist trust you next week? (See also Chapter 15.)

Some journalists will not open an email unless they recognise the sender; many do not welcome HTML messages complete with fancy fonts, logos and graphics; most do not open file attachments unless they have been specifically requested (they may contain viruses). To understand how they feel about inbox overload, consider how you feel about receiving 'spam' email offering you medication, plastic surgery, mortgages or university diplomas. Do you welcome it?

To understand how journalists feel about being 'cold called' by public relations practitioners 'selling' their stories, consider how you respond to phone calls offering you insurance, double-glazing or a new kitchen when you are at home cooking a meal. Are you interested? Do you prolong the conversation? Or do you consider it kinder to end it as quickly as possible, even if it means being rude to the poor individual who is 'only doing a job'? That's just how many journalists feel about public relations calls.

But the public relations practitioner should be offering something of interest to them as professional journalists. In which case, the practitioner should prove their credentials (by, say, considering offering an 'exclusive' on the news story) and should not ever waste their time. Tabloid editors in the UK will always find time to take a call from Max Clifford because they trust him to have something interesting to say to them (as stated earlier, he is a publicist with a track record of providing sensational revelations about the lives, actions and activities of the powerful, rich and famous).

The media 'ring around' is contentious territory. The boss or client is entitled to expect the practitioner to canvas journalists on the target media list for their interest in a particular story. But the shrewd public relations practitioner will avoid phoning *after* the news release has been distributed. By the time the news has been distributed, it is already too late to phone: the call is most likely to antagonise the journalist. As such, it is bad media relations. The smart practitioner will prefer to call selected journalists *before* issuing the news release. Only at this point, before it has been distributed, is the news of potential interest to most media and the call at this point can prepare reporters to a potentially interesting story, which they may be able to write about early or exclusively – and so get ahead of their competitors.

Public relations practitioners used to entertain lavishly, organising press conferences in foreign cities and drinking fine wines over lunch. Now, journalists have to put in longer hours in their offices and can rarely afford the time for these 'junkets'. Working lunches tend to be accompanied by sparkling water, not champagne. The transparency demanded of those in public life is transmitting itself to journalists who are less able to accept gifts, travel and hospitality.

The set-piece press conference is much less common than those watching the evening television news might suppose. As with all good media relations, the decision to call a press conference should be taken by asking if it is in the interests of the media (rather than solely in the interests of corporate priorities). The answer will usually be to rule out press conferences on 'soft' stories such as most product launches, reserving this approach for 'hard' news events (often precipitated by a crisis; see Chapter 20).

Media proliferation may have made it harder for public relations practitioners to keep up with all the channels, programmes, websites and publications available to them, but it also raises new opportunities. While staff journalists may be working harder on a wider range of stories (and for more than one format), there is a growing army of *freelancers* struggling to make a living by supplying news and features to these programmes and publications. These freelances will be much more receptive to ideas and offers from public relations sources and can often be a more effective channel for pitching ideas to editors.

> **Definition:** *Freelancers* are journalists who work for themselves, independent of particular media groups. They are self-employed and work on short-term contracts or on a temporary basis for different media employers. They are often given one-off assignments or commissions by media organisations or they might develop a story and take it to the media outlet.

So, an effective media list should list not only publications and programmes, but also a number of different editorial contacts along with various ways to communicate (noting where possible the journalist's preferences). To the list should be added non-media influencers (e.g. industry analysts, webloggers, politicians, trade associations) that you also wish to keep informed.

The end of mass marketing in media relations teaches us another lesson. Rather than sending *all* your stories to *all* your media, you will have to select appropriate media for each story. Depending on the type of organisation you work for or represent, very few of your news events will merit national BBC news coverage; only a few will receive national newspaper coverage; most may be suitable for inclusion in a selection of trade, specialist and local publications.

This can bring unexpected benefits. The appearance of your spokesperson on local radio or in the local newspaper or specialist trade magazine will sometimes lead to requests for interviews from national newspapers or broadcasters. There is a 'food chain' that operates in newsgathering and it is in your interests to feed in your news where it is most likely to be consumed. The knock-on effect can often be beneficial, just as it

TABLE 16.3 'Old' and 'new' media relations techniques

'Old' PR	'New' PR
Press	Media
Emphasised 'good news'	Willing to discuss good and bad news
One-way channel	Emphasis on relationships
Mass marketing approach	Micro-targeting
Promotes products and services	Talks up issues, ideas and trends
Focused on print publications	Skilled in all media types
Press conferences favoured	Individual briefings and exclusives favoured
Addressed only the media	Aware of all stakeholders and publics

can from offering one exclusive and then watching the news take on a life of its own.

The news release is the most visible tool used by the public relations practitioner. Most journalists will tell you how little attention each one receives in the newsroom and many senior public relations practitioners will tell you that they no longer use them (pre-ferring instead to pitch each story personally to a selected journalist or reporter). The traditional printed release is also of less value to a TV newsroom than to a newspaper's news desk.

Yet the advent of the internet and a more open and inclusive approach to stakeholder communications has given new life to this old tool. While journalists

---

case study 16.2

Media and the making of Google

How did you first hear of Google? When did you start using Google as your preferred search engine on the web? These questions make a big assumption, but if you use the web it seems a safe assumption that you use Google.

Yet Google is a newcomer. The business was only started, by Stanford University students Larry Page and Sergey Brin, in 1998 and the 'beta test' label was only removed from the Google search engine a full year later in September 1999.

Between 1999 and 2004, Google went from nowhere to everywhere (on the web). It is perhaps the most impressive brand marketing campaign of all time, yet scarcely a dollar was spent in advertising. So how did the business achieve this rate of awareness and adoption? What did it use in place of advertising?

Superior technology (the algorithms and computers used to produce faster and more accurate search results) played its part, but internet users still had to become aware of this superior search engine. In effect, Google made use of the only two networks capable of propagating its message so widely. One was to use the 'viral' qualities of the internet; the other was the extensive reach (and credibility) of the mass media.

Many users will have followed the recommendation of Jack Schofield, computer editor of The Guardian newspaper, who described Google in print in 1999 as 'the Internet's best search engine'. Other people will have first used Google following a recommendation from someone they knew and trusted (a colleague, friend, family member). In this way, the impact of the media and viral recommendation becomes mixed into a general word of mouth effect. In the case of Google, the campaign gained strength from its organic, bottom-up growth (rather than being heavily promoted in a top-down fashion).

Media relations was not the sole factor in the making of Google (but media relations is rarely the sole tactic in a public relations campaign). Yet with the departure of Cindy McCaffrey late in 2004 (she had been, for five years, Google's vice-president of corporate marketing), the story of the early decisions on how to promote the fledgling company emerged. In effect, a high-profile advertising campaign was rejected in late 1999 in favour of low-key word of mouth marketing (and a continued emphasis on technology). This date is highly significant, coming as it did before the burst of the dot-com boom in early 2000. In other words, this was a time when fortunes were being spent on brand-building promotional campaigns by rivals such as Excite. Google chose to go its own way.

Sources: 'Revenge of the £3bn computer fruitcakes', *The Daily Telegraph* 31 July 2004; Google history, www.google.com/corporate/history.html; McCaffrey leaving Google, SiliconBeat, www.siliconbeat.com/entries/2004/12/19/ mccaffrey_leaving_google.html

may claim to find them rarely newsworthy, an organisation's stakeholders may be keen to remain informed of its activities through the posting of regular news in its online press office. A company that has posted no news stories this year looks like a dead company; conversely, one that issues regular news updates and delivers consistent messages looks to be dynamic and well managed. In this way, the media relations function can now, in the internet age, contribute to public relations (and not just remain focused on media relations as the only way of reaching the public).

Space does not allow a comprehensive survey of media relations techniques. Instead, an analysis of the key trends should provide a template for understanding best practice (see Table 16.3, Case study 16.2 and Activity 16.2).

activity 16.2

The CIPR Excellence awards provide good examples of current public relations practice. Look at this year's entries or last year's award winners (at www.cipr.co.uk). How do they use new technology? How important was media relations to the campaign's success? Were there any startling new approaches worth remembering?

Feedback

As this chapter has shown, public relations' use of the media is evolving all the time, as are the media channels and content themselves. The successful practitioner keeps an eye on current 'best practice' both to prevent being left behind and to create new ideas for the future.

Summary

This chapter has explored examples of how the media and media relations are used by organisations to achieve communications objectives. Differentiation has been established between the use of media relations and other forms of bought media space such as advertising. A link should also be made at this point to other chapters in the book that look at the broader issues of media context discussed (Chapter 4), the planning and management of campaigns (Chapter 10) as well as the research and evaluation chapter (Chapter 11), which also considers measuring public relations' (and media relations') effectiveness.

Other factors have also been discussed, such as the role of new media channels – specifically the internet and weblogs. These are emerging areas for the practice; students and practitioners should maintain a close eye on how they are being used in campaigns and how this might affect some of the public relations and communications models discussed in this chapter.

Bibliography

Bailey, R. (2005a). 'Communications through the prism of the media.' Unpublished.

Bailey, R. (2005b). 'Overlapping news agendas.' Unpublished.

Bland M., A. Theaker and D. Wragg (1996). *Effective Media Relations*. London: Kogan Page.

Chartered Institute of Public Relations (2005). www.cipr.co.uk accessed 23 March 2005.

Cornelissen, J. (2004). *Corporate Communications: Theory and practice*. London, Thousand Oaks, CA, and New Delhi: Sage.

Cutlip, S.M., A.H. Center and G. Broom (2000). *Effective Public Relations*, 8th edition. Upper Saddle River, NJ: Prentice Hall.

Fawkes, J. and R. Tench (2004). 'Public relations education in the UK: A research report for the IPR'. Leeds Metropolitan University.

Gillmor, D. (2004). *We the Media: Grassroots journalism by the people, for the people*. Farnham: O'Reilly.

Godin, S. (1999). *Permission Marketing*. London: Simon & Schuster.

Grunig J.E. and T. Hunt (1984). *Managing Public Relations*. New York and London: Holt, Rinehart & Winston.

Hargreaves, I. (2003). *Journalism: Truth or dare?* Oxford: Oxford University Press.

Holtz, S. (2002). *Public Relations on the Net*, 2nd edition. Amacom.

Ingham, B. (2003). *The Wages of Spin*. London: John Murray.

McQuail, D. (1987). *Mass Communication Theory: An introduction*, 2nd edition. London: Sage.

Ries, A. and L. Ries (2002). *The Fall of Advertising & The Rise of PR*. New York: HarperCollins.

White, J. and L. Mazur (1995). *Strategic Communications Management: Making public relations work*. London: Addison-Wesley.

CHAPTER 17
Internal communication

Learning about the organisation

Think about an organisation you have worked for – perhaps as a part-time employee. How were you made aware of the business, its products or services and other activities? Was it through your line manager, colleagues or other methods? List the methods of communication that helped you to understand your employer's business.

Now list the methods of communication that you have used to communicate with a line manager and colleagues. Why did you choose these methods? Evaluate which methods were likely to be the most effective.

Feedback

It is likely that you will have learned about the organisation from your line manager, more formally, and from your colleagues on an informal basis. Other methods, such as newsletters, provide the 'bigger picture' on what the business is about.

You may prefer to communicate with people, including your line manager, face to face. However, the work environment often requires that people communicate in writing. Email is one of the quickest and easiest methods of sending someone (or several people) a message within the workplace, yet its very popularity is also a drawback. Some organisations are rethinking the role of emails in order to reduce 'information overload': for example, by encouraging people to meet face to face more often and restricting email communication to certain days of the week.

news and information was published. Better informed employees were thought to be better motivated employees who, in turn, contributed to increased productivity – this is still a common belief today and we will examine it later in the chapter.

From the early days of internal communication, some organisations made audiovisual presentations to induct new staff, organised events such as long-service awards and created foyer displays to explain company policy to employees. Today, technology has

provided a wealth of new media channels and formats – so that continuous internal news, information and feedback opportunities can be delivered direct to the desktop PC. (See Activity 17.1.)

Skills to strategy

We have noted that the roots of internal communication lie in journalism. While it is true that organisations still need writing and editing skills to create staff newsletters, intranet pages, factsheets, and so on, there has emerged during the past few years a more strategic internal communication role that has broadened the scope and complexity of the discipline. The internal communication function has 'grown in size, status and access to resources' (Kernaghan et al. 2001: viii). There are a number of factors leading to the trend towards strategic internal communication (see Figure 17.1).

Changes in the external environment affecting the organisation

Hardly any organisation is untouched by political, economic, social and technological (PEST) change. The following PEST analysis (see Chapter 2 for a fuller discussion of environmental analysis) identifies a wide variety of factors affecting organisations and employees in particular.

Political

Trends in the political environment relate to *new legislation, government policy, national* and *international politics*. Organisations have to be in tune with governments at both a national and international level – sometimes in order to survive. What happens in national and European elections will shape the

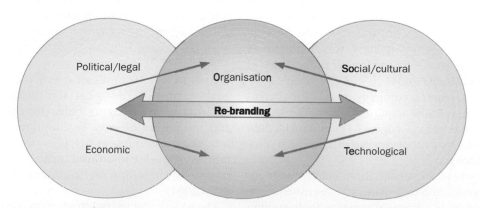

FIGURE 17.1   Factors leading to strategic internal communication

direction of government and whether its policies are favourable towards business enterprises and public services.

In recent years, UK organisations of all kind have had to become more *accountable* and *transparent* to their stakeholders. Social and environmental reporting have become a requirement within the private sector, whereas in the public sector, government-led quality audits and league tables (e.g. for councils, schools and hospitals) have become the norm. The drive for improved business performance through employee involvement is encouraged by a number of organisations such as Investors in People (www.iipuk.co.uk/IIP/Web/Homepage1.htm), the Work Foundation (www.theworkfoundation.com) and the Department of Trade and Industry (www.dti.gov.uk).

Employee involvement and consultation has been given added weight through the 2005 European Directive that will affect employment law in Europe. Employees will have new information rights: a right to be informed about a business's economic situation; a right to be informed and consulted about employment prospects; and a right to be informed about decisions that are likely to lead to major changes in their workplace. All this presents a challenging role for internal communication.

Economic

Trends in the economic environment are often tied in with political decision making, such as *world trade agreements* or *legislation* surrounding how many companies can be owned by one enterprise. Then there are the laws of *supply and demand*: markets and consumer spending patterns fluctuate. What happens at the meta economic level will in turn affect how an organisation conducts its business. For many organisations it is a matter of keeping costs down while driving up quality to the customer, or end user, resulting in the following:

- *outsourcing and 'offshoring'*, where services are contracted to an outside organisation or located overseas to reduce costs (for example, the international news agency Reuters was reported as outsourcing one of its services to India (*Independent* 22 November 2004)
- *acquisitions*, where a company buys another company, such as BMW acquiring Rover (also known as a 'takeover' – see Chapter 24 on financial public relations for a more detailed discussion of company takeovers)
- *mergers*, where an organisation merges with another organisation to provide a more cost-effective service, such as a hospital merging with another hospital.

There is a need for effective, timely communication during these changes because employees may be affected by the consequences. Organisational restructurings, relocations, redundancies and contractual changes could mean difficult times ahead for employees. A bank relocating its head office to another part of the country will need to manage communication very clearly and sensitively so that rumour and speculation (for example, about which staff groups are required to move and which are not), do not become 'official' information.

Social (and cultural)

Organisations need to monitor trends in the social and cultural environment because they determine not only which markets are likely to emerge, but also the future availability of skills and knowledge among the population. Global, as well as local, social factors that are likely to have an impact on organisations' recruitment and retention policies include: *demographic structure* of the population (especially *education and qualifications*, skills and competencies); workforce *mobility*; workforce *diversity*; *career/lifestyle* choices and aspirations. As we identify later in this chapter (see 'Psychological contract', p. 338), the nature of employment is changing. Because there is less job security, people (especially the under-35s) have different aspirations and expectations. Moving from job to job to gain experience is increasingly seen as the norm. With increased opportunities for mobility across the globe, more people are seeking job fulfilment elsewhere.

Also, as we shift towards a knowledge-based economy, more people fit into what might be called high-knowledge occupations. In Canada, for example, professional occupations accounted for more than 14% of the workforce in 2001, compared to 9% in 1971 (www.statcan.ca/Daily/English/031030/d03103a.htm, accessed 22 April 2004). Well-qualified knowledge workers need less supervision, but at the same time they have a higher level of need for involvement and consultation within an organisation.

Technological

Trends in the technological environment are, arguably, one of the most significant shapers of organisations, changing both the nature of work and the nature of jobs. Technology plays a major role in how employees behave – redefining expectations of work turnaround, privacy and politeness norms in an online environment (Eisenberg and Riley 2001).

The widespread use of information and communication technologies has opened up many new, interactive channels for internal communication – email and intranets – with the benefits of speed and efficiency of communication and improved access to information.

However, there are drawbacks: the main disadvantages of electronic communication to employee relationships are communication overload and the replacement of face-to-face communication (Industrial Society 1999). And as we enter an age where risk and security are a concern for many organisations, there is also the reality of surveillance online (e.g. monitoring of external emails) as well as closed-circuit television cameras monitoring behaviour. Such trends threaten rather than encourage good employee relationships, yet in those same organisations 'excellent' two-way internal communication will often be emphasised.

Internal marketing or 'branding from the inside, out'

Many organisations – including government organisations such as the UK's National Health Service (NHS) – are defining brand values that consumers can emotionally identify with (e.g. Levi's jeans equals 'cool'). Such values require employee commitment and understanding. Communication plays a vital role in encouraging brand 'champions' or 'ambassadors' who, in turn, encourage customer loyalty. The concept of internally marketing to and through employees can be viewed as controversial, as we shall see at the end of this chapter.

Role and purpose of internal communication

Very little attention is paid to internal communication by public relations scholars yet it is viewed as part of an organisation's strategic communication function. If an organisation adopts two-way symmetric communication (see Chapter 8, p. 147), then, according to Grunig, 'open, trusting, and credible relationships with strategic employee constituencies [groups] will follow' (Grunig 1992: 559).

As we see in Chapters 13 and 28, the corporate communication school of thought regards employees as important stakeholders whose behaviour and communication both contribute to the corporate identity and project it to external stakeholders.

The strategic purpose of internal communication can perhaps best be summarised as one that is concerned with building two-way, involving relationships with internal publics, with the goal of improving organisational effectiveness.

In theory at least, internal communication viewed as part of the overall communication function may seem fairly straightforward, but, as we shall see in the next section, who 'owns' the IC function will vary from organisation to organisation. This chapter is placed within a public relations textbook, but it would be no surprise to find it in a strategic marketing or human resources textbook, because both functions have a claim on the IC role. Yet another school of thought sees internal communication as a new management discipline that should ideally report directly to the CEO. This is because, as Scholes (1997: xviii) puts it, IC cuts across:

> *The traditional boundaries of HR, PR and marketing expertise . . . We [IC practitioners] assume the need to be familiar with the business context (in particular the need to manage change), the role of strategic planning and of IC within it, also research methods and statistical interpretation, and budgeting.*

However, throughout this textbook we have discussed many examples of where internal communication has proven to be a vital component within a broader communication programme in:

- responding to issues and crises
- promoting brand values to consumers
- managing relationships with the community
- communicating with employees as shareholders.

Wherever the IC function is located, there is still a need for good internal communication practice.

Strategist or technician?

For many public relations practitioners working in organisations with small budgets, internal communication and external communication roles will be combined (see also Chapter 3 on the role of the practitioner). Table 17.1 (overleaf) illustrates the types of role that are conducted under the headings of 'strategic' (e.g. planning) and 'technical' (e.g. writing) internal communication. The roles are not exclusive: some elements may be combined in a small organisation; in a large organisation there will be a clearer demarcation between the roles of strategic manager and the technician.

Where does internal communication fit into the organisation?

What we call the 'internal communication function' may comprise just one individual or a team of 10 or more in a large corporation. In some organisations, the internal communication function may be a 'stand-alone' department reporting directly to the chief executive; in others, to the head of a functional department,

TABLE 17.1   Strategic and technical internal communication activities (*source:* based on Kernaghan et al. 2001)

'Strategic' internal communication roles	'Technical' internal communication activities
Supporting major change programmes	House journal or magazine
Communicating messages from top management	Intranet
Communicating the business mission/vision/values	E-zines/e-newsletter
Raising awareness of business issues and priorities	Management conferences
Raising/maintaining the internal credibility of the top team	Briefing groups
Employee motivation	Noticeboards
Facilitating feedback	Employee annual report
Enhancing managers' communication skills	Management journal/magazine

such as human resources. A survey of 115 internal communication professionals in the UK Europe and North America found that around one-third reported to the public relations or corporate communications function. In Britain, 35% of internal communication functions report to human resources but internationally the reporting lines vary more widely. Significant results among non-UK practitioners were 24% reporting to the CEO and 26% reporting to the board chair, compared to 21% and 9% respectively in the UK (Kernaghan et al. 2001).

However, some organisations do not have a dedicated full-time person for whom internal communication is the sole responsibility (for example, it could be a shared or part-time role), or indeed a separate budget for IC activities (Kernaghan et al. 2001). From these findings we can conclude that internal communication is still a relatively young discipline. Figure 17.2 shows a hypothetical corporate communication structure. (See Think about 17.1.)

Employee perspective: 'just a job'?

Psychological contract

Employees' communication needs may differ entirely from what the management of an organisation see as communication priorities – for reasons of job role, place in the organisation and geographical location, as we stated in the introduction to this chapter. In addition, the *psychological contract* that the employee has with their employer may not live up to expectations – resulting in low levels of trust, commitment and loyalty to the organisation.

Definition: *Psychological contract* means the perceptions of the two parties, employee and employer, of what their mutual obligations are towards each other. (Guest and Conway 2002)

The psychological contract has received attention in recent years because of the changing employment relationship. While the psychological contract used to refer to an employee offering commitment to an employer in exchange for job security, external factors affecting today's workplace – changing markets, technology and higher customer expectations – have undermined this contract. As identified earlier, organisations are cutting costs and cutting jobs, meaning that individual employees have to work harder with less job security. The so-called 'new contract', then, is based on offers of training and development (which allows for the possibility of getting another job), fair pay and treatment – in return for employee commitment (CIPD 2003). (See Box 17.1.)

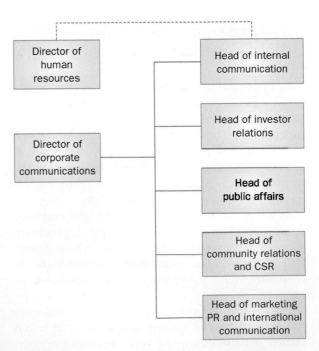

FIGURE 17.2   Internal communication in a hypothetical organisation

think about 17.1 **Reporting lines**

From Figure 17.2, note the reporting lines. Why do you think IC has a dotted line to the HR function? What possible issues could arise from this structure, where the IC manager reports to the director of corporate communications? Are there other potential issues that could affect the speed, direction or style of communication employed by the IC manager?

Feedback In many organisations, IC works closely with the HR function to ensure that messages and the timing of messages are consistent with HR policy. Conflict may arise from this dotted-line reporting where corporate communications has a different priority to HR. In the bank relocation example we mentioned on page 336, the director of corporate communications will want to announce the relocation at an early stage, to avoid rumours 'leaking' to the media. HR, on the other hand, may not have worked out all the details of the relocation plan. HR will want to keep this information confidential until they know exactly how staff will be affected.

While employee commitment is seen as relatively low – 37% of UK workers were found to be highly committed (MCA/MORI 1998) – levels of trust in organisations and their leaders have declined even more in recent years (Guest and Conway 2002). For example, recent research found that 20% of staff lacked confidence in senior management (Communicators in Business/MORI 2003).

Temporary contracts, part-time working, irregular shift patterns, as well as professional, social and cultural factors may give rise to an employee's 'disconnectedness' from the organisation and a resistance to corporate messages. Workers taking this position may hold different beliefs and values to those of the organisation and ignore a company's efforts to engage them in dialogue. Daymon (2000) found this to be the case in her research within a television company where journalists and production staff found satisfaction from peer group recognition and professional values of quality programming, as opposed to the values of the television company, which centred on economic performance. Similarly, Yeomans (2004) found that health workers largely ignored management's attempts to communicate key messages during a time of major change. (See Think about 17.2, overleaf.)

Segmenting internal publics

When employees are discussed, there is sometimes an assumption that they are a single, homogenous group who share the same worldview; as we have seen already, this is not the case. Employees can be segmented (broken down) as follows:

box
17.1 **Employee commitment**

Employee commitment refers to the expectations a line manager will have of an employee, but these expectations will be interpreted differently according to an organisation's culture. Common expectations include:

- making an effort to attend work
- getting to work on time
- concentrating on work
- getting as much done as possible while at work
- working to the best of your ability
- being willing to take on tasks outside your job description
- being flexible in the hours that you work to suit the organisation
- being a good team player
- developing and improving existing skills.

(*Source:* This material is taken from 'CIPD Factsheet – *Managing the Psychological Contract*, December 2004, with the permission of the publisher, the Chartered Institute of Personnel and Development, London)

'Being flexible' may actually involve regularly working away from home, rather than working a few extra hours a week. And while 'being a good team player' may imply covering for colleagues who are sick in order to complete a task, in some organisations 'team player' might mean getting involved in a wide range of social activities that are tied in with improving chances of promotion.

Referring to your own experience, or the experience of someone you know, what do you think an organisation can do to tackle feelings of 'disconnectedness' among its employees?

Feedback There are no simple answers here. According to Quirke (2000), *understanding* is the key to employee motivation. If employees understand what makes their organisation successful, they usually want to know how to contribute to their organisation's success. But employees do not always understand or even wish to understand. It is a salutary lesson that 59% of the UK's workforce were intending to leave their jobs in 2005 (YouGov/Zynap survey reported in *The Guardian* 29 November 2004) because of their disillusionment with the balance between work and leisure time (known as the 'work–life balance') and a lack of attention by their bosses to their career development.

Given this scenario, is there a role for communication? According to research by the think-tank Demos, communication has a role but it needs to be rethought: 'In a world of looser, more flexible relationships between workers and hirers, customers and suppliers, organisations need new ways to communicate with networks of people without trying to bind them into exclusive or hierarchical relationships' (Miller and Skidmore 2004: 67).

- demographics – age, gender, income, educational/skill level
- psychographics – personality, attitudes, values, behaviours
- staff groups – top management (or the board), senior/middle managers, frontline employees, supervisors and junior managers, specialist professional employees, overseas employees, pensioners
- contract with the organisation – full time, part time or temporary
- geographical location – head office, regional office, manufacturing plant. (See Think about 17.3.)

Attitudes (discussed in Chapter 14) are a conventional way of segmenting employees, particularly in relation to the psychological contract (discussed earlier), the organisation's strategic direction and communication. We identified earlier that the rise of internal communication as a discipline is largely due to factors driving the organisational environment and organisational change. In discussing employees' attitudes to organisational change, Quirke categorises employees as shown in Figure 17.3.

'Unguided missiles' refers to employees who are willing to help but unclear about the direction their organisation is taking. Quirke asserts that 50% of employees do not know what the strategy is and these are often the people who are on the frontline dealing with customers. Their notion of strategy may be based on past practice rather than current thinking. An MCA/MORI study conducted in 1998 labelled this group 'loose cannons', claiming that 14% of the UK workforce fit this category (Thomson and Hecker 2000).

'Hot shots' refers to the group of enthusiastic employees who are totally in tune with their organisation's direction and their own role within it. The MCA/MORI research identified this group (37%) as *'champions'* or *'advocates'*.

'Slow burners' describes employees who are 'not knowing and not caring' (Thomson and Hecker 2000: 13). In reality, this is a mix of people who feel unmotivated through a lack of direction and those who prefer to follow their own priorities. This group roughly corresponds to the MCA/MORI study, which calls this group *'weak links'*, and are typically 'switched off', representing 39%.

Can you think of other ways of segmenting employees?

Feedback There are many other ways of segmenting internal publics. Some organisations tune in to groups of employees' lifestyles as a way of connecting with them; others have to consider 'hard-to-reach' internal publics such as 'remote' (people working at home or on maternity/paternity leave) or mobile workers (for example, sales staff who are mainly on the road or nurses working in the community). Employees may also be shareholders, and members of the local community, which is why it is important to have a coordinated communication approach to avoid misunderstandings. Understanding the opportunities for contact with some groups of employees is a key challenge.

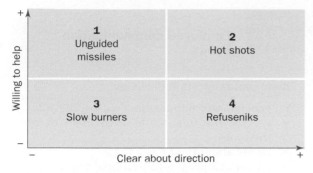

FIGURE 17.3   Different degrees of employee clarity and willingness (*source:* Quirke 2000: 12)

'*Refuseniks*' refers to employees who understand the organisation's direction but are most resistant to organisational change. Such groups may actively disagree with proposed changes and feel that their professionalism is under threat. The MCA/MORI study identified this group (deemed to be one in five employees in the UK) as '*saboteurs*' (Thomson and Hecker 2000).

> **Definition:** A '*refusenik*' was a citizen of the former Soviet Union, especially a Jewish person, who was not allowed by the government to emigrate. Now the term refers to somebody who refuses to cooperate with something.

We know from numerous studies (e.g. Communicators in Business/MORI 2003) that line managers – people who manage groups of staff – are the most trusted source of information among employees and that the second preferred channel among employees is *team briefing*. (See Think about 17.4.)

> **Definition:** *Team briefing* is a method of communication whereby a line manager briefs their team – usually on a regular basis – about company policy and on day-to-day issues related to the completion of team tasks. Team briefings are often structured to allow for staff feedback and questions.

However, it is the informal side of the organisation where we find clues on how employees communicate with each other.

Informal networks

Places where people gather inside organisations, such as watercoolers, corridors and post rooms, tend to be where the latest information, rumours and gossip can be shared. Informal networks play an important role in organisational communication, but traditionally they have been downplayed or frowned on in management handbooks because they are outside management's control. And yet informal networks often provide employees with meaningful interpersonal relationships, self-respect, greater job satisfaction and knowledge about their organisation (Conrad and Poole 1998). For example, an active networker who regularly attends management meetings – perhaps to take the minutes – might be regarded as the 'official' source of information by their informal network and so will enact the role of informant about 'what really goes on'.

As organisations become more fluid and their boundaries more permeable across time zones and cultures, it is a reasonable assumption that networks will become more important. Research seems to indicate this. Most internal communication practitioners play a role in creating and enabling networks such as 'intranets, cross-functional teams, knowledge management databases, and even informal grapevines' (Kernaghan et al 2001: 58).

Communication needs of employees

Consultant Roger D'Aprix's often-quoted 'communication needs' process shows how basic questions need to be answered before an employee can move through the second level of questions and play an active role in the organisation (see Figure 17.4 and Activity 17.2, overleaf).

In larger, more complex organisations, it is unlikely that employees will enjoy a personal relationship with the owner, managing director or person

---

think about 17.4   Employee attitudes research

Does it help the communication function to label groups of employees as in Figure 17.3? What are the implications of this segmentation for the IC practitioner in devising a communication plan?

Feedback   For the IC practitioner, it is important to understand not just who the 'hot shots' and 'champions' are who will be committed to a change initiative, but to understand how the 'refuseniks' or 'saboteurs' communicate. While the two last groups may never support a change programme and indeed could actively disrupt it, they should not be ignored completely as they could present management with issues for the future – and some of those issues may be justified, as we identified earlier in Think about 17.2.

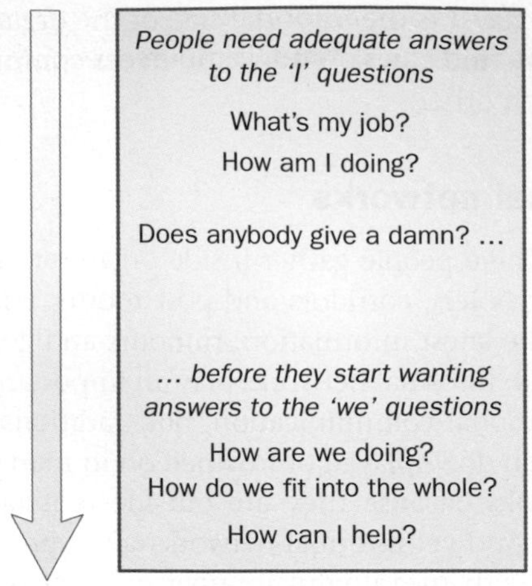

People need adequate answers
to the 'I' questions

What's my job?

How am I doing?

Does anybody give a damn? ...

... before they start wanting
answers to the 'we' questions

How are we doing?

How do we fit into the whole?

How can I help?

FIGURE 17.4 Communication needs process (*source:* D'Aprix 1982, cited in Arnott 1987)

Employee communication needs

Basic communication needs are:

- general information about the organisation
- specific information to help them to do their jobs
- clarity about their roles
- a clear company/organisational vision
- information on workplace practices
- opportunities to be involved and consulted
- feedback on performance
- access to training and development
- access to communication channels.

with overall responsibility for the running of the organisation. Yet people want to feel part of a 'human' rather than remote organisation (Demos/Orange/MORI 2004). Communication needs have to be met. The list in Box 17.2 suggests different types of communication that an employee needs in order to work effectively. (See Activity 17.3 and Mini case study 17.2.)

We have seen in this section that while employees may actively resist management attempts to communicate with them, they nevertheless have communication needs, which may or may not be fully met by the organisation. And in times of change or crisis (see BBC case at the end of this chapter), it can be vitally important to keep everyone up to date with unfolding events and involved in the eventual outcome. In the following section we explore in more detail how the organisational context – the culture, leadership and strategic change – affect how internal communication is practised.

---

activity 17.2

Shifting communication needs

You work for a small, profitable company that makes hard-wearing but trendy footwear. The company is privately owned by the footwear's creator and he gets on well with all the staff. The company has gone from strength to strength as its footwear sales have risen steadily over a five-year period. You are secure in your job and feel that you are contributing to the company's success. Annual bonuses have become the norm.

Referring to the preceding section, which questions are you likely to ask at this stage?

Now imagine that the owner wants to sell the company. There is a buyer but she wants to relocate the company abroad to save on staff and manufacturing costs. Again, referring to the preceding section, which questions are you likely to ask now?

Feedback

You can see from this scenario that circumstances can change very quickly. This will affect how an employee feels in relation to the organisation they are working for – and may affect their attitudes to future employment.

activity 17.3

Communication roles

From the list in Box 17.2, tick off what you consider to be the communication role of the line manager, the communication role of the human resources department and the communication role of the IC practitioner.

Feedback

The line manager should undertake many of the communication tasks because this is the most important communication from the employee's perspective. Most day-to-day communication needs can be met by the line manager, preferably face to face. On a broader level, the HR department may be involved in communicating workplace practices (e.g. a car leasing or no-smoking policy) and offering company-wide training and development opportunities – but this will vary from organisation to organisation.

General information about the organisation and clarity about the organisational vision or direction should be provided by top management – with the help of the IC practitioner. In doing this, the IC practitioner can encourage two-way communication through channels such as team briefings, conferences, the staff newsletter and the staff intranet.

A hospital communicates

Northampton General Hospital Trust in the UK identified that many staff perceived communication as being ineffective. Information appeared to be blocked by middle management level and there was little opportunity for two-way dialogue and feedback. This was set within the context of a rapidly changing health service environment where broader issues needed to be linked to individual areas of work and the Trust's key principles. An internal communication strategy entitled *Connect* was established to create a better understanding between management and staff. *Connect* involved:

- face-to-face briefings by the chairman and CEO to a broad cross-section of staff
- planned visits to hospital wards to talk to night staff
- opportunities for feedback and questions with responses from senior management
- publication of presentations, feedback, questions and responses in the monthly newsletter and on the Trust intranet

- video presentations available for staff unable to attend briefings and for new staff
- presentations on the intranet
- question and answer (Q&A) forum on the intranet
- printed summary of presentations and key messages for staff.

Over half the staff who completed evaluation forms at a briefing welcomed the opportunity to hear information and long-term plans. Staff had the oppportunity to let senior management know what they thought of the event and what should be included in the future. Future plans involved developing the Q&A intranet forum, further articles in the internal newsletter and more presentations and ward visits by top management. *Connect* was regarded as a success; the next step was to develop the strategy specifically for HR, clinical governance and other directorates within the Trust.

By kind permission of Northampton General Hospital NHS Trust

Organisations: culture, leadership and strategic change

Corporate culture

Broadly speaking, there are two views of organisational culture: the first sees culture as something that can be influenced, shaped and managed to the liking of top management (*'corporate culture'*); the second sees organisation *as* a culture which is, in turn, made up of subcultures formed from different networks and groups that make up the organisation ('organisational culture').

Definition: *Corporate culture* means 'values or practices that account for an organisation's success and that can be managed to produce better business outcomes' (Eisenberg and Riley 2001: 209). (See Box 17.3.)

The 'corporate culture' view is attractive to ambitious chief executives who believe that their organisation can be completely changed – if influenced, shaped and managed in the right way. An infamous example of this is the 'corporate culture' imposed by Enron, for example, whose chief executive insisted on the recruitment of 'high flyers' – well-educated, tough-dealing, competitive people with high-level career aspirations who were willing to sacrifice personal relationships and family life for the benefit of the company (Boje et al. 2004). Other commentators have pointed to successful brands like Disney, McDonald's and Pepsi for their conscious focus on corporate culture where these companies have striven for the correct alignment of shared values and practices – in other words, employees are required to share the espoused values and practices of the company. Box 17.4 (overleaf) contains the values statement from the Disney careers website.

box 17.3 **Corporate culture: 'like swallowing an elephant'**

'Thus, Chipco appeared conscious of itself as a culture, not just a technical system, and took steps to transmit its culture to newcomers in the managerial and professional ranks, through legends, stories, and special orientations at offsite meetings that were like boot camps. Just learning the job was not enough for success at Chipco; one had to learn the culture of the organization as well, and this could often be disorienting for the stream of new arrivals; "It was like trying to swallow an elephant", one recalled.'

Source: Moss Kanter 1983: 133–134

Disney's values

Values make our brands stand out

Innovation
We follow a strong tradition of innovation.
Quality
We strive to follow a high standard of excellence.
We maintain high-quality standards across all product categories.
Community
We create positive and inclusive ideas about families.
We provide entertainment experiences for all generations to share.
Storytelling
Every product tells a story.
Timeless and engaging stories delight and inspire.
Optimism
At The Walt Disney Company, entertainment is about hope, aspiration and positive resolutions.
Decency
We honor and respect the trust people place in us.
Our fun is about laughing at our experiences and ourselves.

Source: www.corporate.disney.go.com/careers/culture.html

There is a certain amount of controversy as to whether so-called 'strong' cultures can lead to organisational effectiveness. Alvesson (1993), for example, argues that corporate culture is better termed as 'management ideology' in that the preferred norms and values are the ideals of a particular group and as such cannot be uniformly imposed on an organisation that employs a wide range of people. Nevertheless, the management of culture, through the circulation of mission, vision and values statements, often forms the basis of a culture change management programme in which the communication function will play a significant role. The values statement for Marks & Spencer provided in Box 17.5 sets out clearly what behaviours are expected. (See Think about 17.5.)

Organisational culture

Many theorists agree that *organisational culture* is a set of beliefs held by members of the organisation (see Think about 17.6). Such beliefs can sometimes provide a fairly reliable clue to people's behaviour or actions, but not always (see also Chapter 14 for a more detailed discussion of attitudes, beliefs and behaviours). Others take this cognitive approach a stage further and focus on the pattern of 'meaning systems' held by members of an organisation. Other theorists consider organisational culture to be something that is more easily understood by analysing behaviours and actions. A comprehensive definition of organisational culture combines both the cognitive and behavioural understandings.

Marks & Spencer's values

Our success has been built on a number of core company values that have remained almost unchanged since our earliest beginnings. They are:

Quality – Delivering excellent standards consistently.
Value – We need to deliver exceptional value to our customers.
Innovation – We need to continue to be at the forefront of innovation in both general merchandising and food.
Trust – We are the most trusted retailer. We have a proud heritage of staff welfare, customer care and involvement in the community. We want to continue to build this.
Service – Is about delivering the highest standard of services to our customers.

Source: www2.marksandspencer.com/thecompany/
workingwithus/corporateoverview/ourvalues.shtml

Compare the Disney and Marks & Spencer values statements. What are the similarities and differences between the two statements? To what extent do you think each value statement is helpful to the employee? Do you think it is possible for all employees to follow these statements?

Definition: *Organisational culture* is 'the set of conscious and unconscious beliefs and values, and the patterns of behaviour (including language and symbol use) that provide identity and form a framework of meaning for a group of people' (McCollom 1993, cited in Eisenberg and Riley 2001, pp. 306–7).

Leadership and strategic change

It is widely recognised that organisations need good leaders to provide a clear direction to employees. Leaders and particularly founders, such as Richard Branson who started Virgin, also enact a cultural role. Schein (1985), for example, claimed that founders educate others through their actions and this is how cultures are learned. 'Charismatic' leaders – people who emotionally connect with their audiences – are talked about long after they have moved on to other organisations, such is their power to influence others. The communication approach of the leader is therefore important to the credibility and effectiveness of internal communication.

Leaders are also shaped by their national cultures. A key researcher in the field of national cultures and their impact on leadership is Hofstede (1991) who identified four dimensions of national cultures:

1 *Power distance* – the distribution of power in organisations (i.e. between leaders and subordinates).

2 *Uncertainty avoidance* – how far a society feels threatened by uncertain situations and the rules it establishes to avoid uncertainty.

3 *Individualism* versus *collectivism* – whether people see themselves as needing to look after their own and their family's interests above societal concerns or as loyal to a community that, in turn, will look after them.

4 *Masculinity* versus *femininity* – the dominant values in a society (e.g. assertiveness, competition as masculine values).

Sadler (2001) argues that leaders are more likely to be able to enact the role as 'change agents' in cultures where power distance is low and tolerance of uncertainty is high. In countries such as Sweden and Norway, for example, employees are more likely to participate in decision making (see 'co-creation' in Table 17.2, overleaf), because such a leadership style is culturally more acceptable.

In an age when symbolic acts help us make sense of the world, leaders have to 'show the way' to employees through 'symbolic acts of leadership and the rituals used to engage and enrol them' (Smythe 2004: 20). Leaders engage employees strategically through monologue (transmission of messages) or dialogue (conversations). As we can see in Table 17.2, Smythe identifies four different approaches to leading employees in strategic change:

1 telling
2 selling

Think about an organisation with which you are familiar (this may be a college, university or an organisation where you work part time). Can you identify aspects of its culture? For example, do people behave informally or formally? Why? Does their dress code reflect this style? Do people in general like or dislike their work? Why? Does the work environment encourage or suppress self-expression and ideas? Why?

Feedback   From this exercise you will probably see how difficult it can be to be precise about culture. As Eisenberg and Riley suggest, a starting point for research might be the 'new contract' that we referred to earlier on page 338. Within a global economy that has encouraged workforce mobility, how and to what extent do employees identify with an organisation? Scholars such as Banks (2000) believe that we need to have a better understanding of subcultures and diversity across industries in order to conduct more meaningful and culturally aware public relations and internal communication. (For more discussion on cross-cultural communication, see Chapter 7.)

TABLE 17.2   Four styles of leadership in strategic change (*source:* adapted from Smythe 2004: 34–35)

Approach to strategic change	Methods used
Telling (traditional information campaign)	Fragmented 'drip-feeding' news, cascade briefings; executive roadshows; profiles and interviews in internal newsletters; corporate videos; feedback/dialogue to check with compliance of targets; change agents' network as a channel to deliver the message Role of leader: 'Gaining compliance'
Selling (internal marketing or persuasive approach)	Spectator events; entertainment; some attempts to collect ideas to influence change or create 'a sense of involvement'; 'back to the floor' communication by bosses; employee suggestion schemes and staff attitude surveys that do not lead to change; customers illustrating their experiences/issues; role play to understand behavioural challenges; change agents' network offering workshops for people to explore the rationale for change; celebration of milestones of achievement Role of leader: 'Enabling other people to discover what you have already discovered/decided by giving them a taste of the experience'
Individual accountability (on-the-job change involving individual self-evaluation; learning and problem solving)	Web-based consultation and learning; problem solving by small task groups or teams; clear definitions of expected behaviours; coaching to support individual change; opportunity for staff to explore evidence for change and propose solutions and targets; corporate 'university' to equip people with skills needed; change agents' network to facilitate opportunities for people to discover, learn and adapt; leadership development programme Role of leader: 'Driving ownership down to individuals'
Co-creation (participative decision making)	Business simulation games; giving people the actual business challenge; shopfloor participation in designing engagement experiences; employee involvement that visibly influences the agenda; job swapping internally or externally; engagement workshops or local teams to identify a small number of high-priority symbols/habits to change/develop. Role of leader: 'More guide than god'

Source: Reproduced with kind permission of John Smythe and McKinsey & Company

3   individual accountability
4   co-creation.

Table 17.2 suggests that a particular strategic approach is consciously chosen by the organisational leader. However, this is not the case. In reality such choices are often instinctive, reflecting the leader's experiences. It is also likely that more than one of the approaches will be adopted (Smythe 2004). (See Think about 17.7.)

Line manager role: listening and interpreting

Throughout this chapter we have stressed the importance of the line manager in internal communication. However, line managers (who are part of middle management) may not always be the best communicators. Middle managers have traditionally been viewed as 'blockers' of information because they may

think about 17.7   Engagement with employees

Evaluate the four approaches of Smythe from a public relations perspective, referring back to the 'relational' theories of public relations in Chapter 8. What could be the strengths and weaknesses of each approach in making change happen?

Feedback   Consider: personality of the leader; national culture; organisational culture; time available; employee involvement; commitment.

PICTURE 17.1 Behind every good leader is a team pulling towards a common goal (*source:* Getty Images Sport).

perceive sharing information as a threat to their own status.

Good communication skills can sometimes be confused with good presentation skills, when in reality a wide variety of communication skills are needed to deal with large and small groups and one-to-one situations. It is increasingly recognised that line managers need well-developed listening skills to interpret messages from staff and well-developed judgement to interpret the messages cascaded down through senior management from the board.

The UK supermarket Tesco, for example, has found it more effective to communicate the business plan to employees face to face through in-store managers, using plain language and desktop presenters. This approach enables employees to understand the plan in terms of their own day-to-day operations and to act on them (Quirke 2000).

Communication channels

Communication channels have been identified throughout this chapter, especially in Table 17.3,

overleaf. While we resist the 'toolkit' approach to internal communication – an approach that often ignores the context in which communication takes place – it is worth examining the more popular channels in a little more detail to assess their usefulness.

As we have seen from the discussions so far, the key component of internal communication is face to face, where there is the opportunity of *upward communication.*

> **Definition:** *Upward communication* is a system of communication that allows employees to feed back their views to their team leaders or line managers, and where line managers in turn feed back these views to senior management.

While less than half (48%) of UK employees find their boss the most trusted and reliable channel, with team briefings (43%) second, the traditional internal communication channels of staff magazines are even less trusted. This is hardly encouraging news when we examine what internal communication people actually *do.* Looking at Table 17.3, there continues to be a strong bias towards written communication, albeit using interactive media. (See Think about 17.8, overleaf.)

Evaluation

Internal communication practitioners need to demonstrate the value of managed communication to their bosses. Having a separate budget for internal communication leads to expectations that IC people can show a return on investment (ROI) for their work. The key objectives for measuring the contribution of the internal communication function are:

■ understanding by employees at all levels of the business objectives and priorities
■ top management's communication effectiveness.

Common measurement and evaluation tools are staff attitude surveys and employee focus groups or interviews (see Chapter 11 for a fuller description of measurement and evaluation). Quantifiable feedback is obtained on channels such as briefing systems, magazines/newsletters and e-media. Evaluation against the strategic objectives listed above is less common than the evaluation of specific communication channels (Kernaghan et al. 2001).

The problem for internal communication is that it is hard to evaluate what is not entirely within the control of the IC function. As we have already identified, other important factors are the influence of leadership, strategic approach and line management.

TABLE 17.3   Top six internal communication channels (*source:* adapted from Kernaghan et al. 2001)

Channel	Description	Purpose	Direction of communication flow
House journal or magazine	Mass medium Regular, full-colour, glossy employee publication – often published monthly	Communicate management messages and business news; with human interest and social elements	Usually downwards Best ones engage employees using techniques from consumer media, with focus on 'human interest' stories
Intranet	Web based information and communication medium restricted for internal use	Variable. Can simply be a depository for corporate documents through to an interactive communication medium. Incorporates email function for external communication	'Pull medium' – employees have to select what they want to find out about
E-zines/ e-newsletter	Mass media, distributed via intranet and email: 1 Electronic version of the house journal 2 E-newsletter is shorter and more frequently distributed. More likely to be weekly publication but format can adapt more easily to current issues	As for house journal but with the emphasis on the reader being able to gain more accessible and regular access to business news	Downwards, but there is provision for feedback via hyperlinks to contacts
Management conferences	Face-to-face medium – can range from 'CEO addressing all staff' type conferences to those that are run along the lines of workshops involving staff	Transmission of key business messages, through to role playing and participation	Usually downwards, although could involve participative, interactive workshops
Briefing groups	Face-to-face medium, generally no more than an hour in length Can take the form of team briefings for local teams, led by the line manager, on a weekly basis. Usually two way Alternatively, 'special' briefings can be breakfast, lunch, after-hours meetings, often led by top or senior management. Sometimes involve questions and answers (Q&A) sessions	Provides management updates from different levels of the organisation. Can be used to gain responses and inputs from staff	Variable. Can be downwards or two way
Noticeboards	Traditional 'local' medium found in corridors, staff restaurants and meeting areas Flexible medium – can be updated as regularly as is necessary	Channel for announcing events, value statements, policy statements, etc	Downwards

think about 17.8 **Communication channels and objectives**

What are the strengths and weaknesses of the channels just examined in relation to the following objectives for employees (refer also to Chapter 10, p. 192 on objectives):

■ adopt a healthier lifestyle
■ understand the company's new mission statement
■ be aware of the company's expansion plans overseas.

Are there other potential channels that you would use that are not listed here (e.g. corporate video, CD-ROM, posters, etc.)?

Ethical communication

We mentioned at the beginning of this chapter that one of the key influences in the growth of internal communication is internal marketing. Internal marketing views employees as consumers whose needs and wants have to be satisfied in order for them to embrace brand values and pass these values on to the customer.

Internal marketing, as we have seen in Table 17.2, is associated with persuading, or 'selling' ideas to employees using communication techniques that are usually reserved for the external marketplace. Mudie (2000) questions how far internal marketing – popular though it is – can be sustained when trust is 'a key feature of organisational life'.

From an ethical perspective, we need to ask whether employees are respected for themselves and their contribution to the organisation or instrumentally viewed as means to ends. (See Mini case study 17.3.)

---

mini case study 17.3

Internal marketing

Vodafone UK and corporate donations
As part of its corporate social responsibility, Vodafone formed a partnership with the National Autistic Society charity to raise money for sufferers of autism (a communication disorder). The initiative was aimed at customers, but it was felt important that employees supported and promoted the initiative. Vodafone offered its staff time off work to volunteer and to match every donation they made. The objectives of the campaign to employees were: to raise awareness about autism; to ensure that the partnership was seen as beneficial; and to encourage employees to donate their time and money to the charity. The campaign included:

■ research published in the employee magazine showing the benefits of similar schemes in other companies
■ teaser posters about autism placed in staff canteens and meeting rooms

■ case studies in brochures and the employee magazine showing employees whose lives had been affected by autism
■ opportunities to speak to carers of people with autism and representatives from the charity
■ an employee volunteering week, involving exhibition stands at call centres and staff head offices across the UK.

Evaluation showed that 75% of Vodafone UK employees recognised the scheme as a mutually beneficial partnership and 73% said it was a partnership they could get involved in and support. Over half of employees thought the partnership would improve perceptions of Vodafone's brand. Over 100 people got involved in fundraising activities. The target donation of £30,000 was raised in three months. (See Think about 17.9.)

Source: adapted from *PR Week* 24 September 2004: 30

---

think about 17.9 **Ethical communication**

Evaluate the Vodafone campaign using the ethical frameworks (e.g. teleology and deontology) described in Chapter 15. Is this an ethical campaign? Are employees respected? Or are they seen merely as a means to 'improve perceptions of the brand'? Could the campaign be more ethical?

case study 17.1

BBC and Hutton – the internal communication role in a crisis

The BBC, renowned worldwide for its quality programming, has been at the leading edge of good internal communication practice for many years and the corporation's internal newspaper *Ariel* has formed one of the backbones of internal communication under different management regimes and culture change initiatives. Culture change within an organisation depends very much on credible internal communication. If the internal communication system is clear and people feel committed to the change, then a crisis is the ultimate test. This is just what the BBC faced in January 2004.

With the arrival of new director general Greg Dyke in 2000, the BBC started to engage its staff in a process of culture change. In 2004 BBC staff numbered 29,000 worldwide, with a further 15,000 or so working on a freelance or contract basis. The journalists, presenters and creative people working for the BBC have been described as 'independent thinking', 'free radicals' who are 'articulate, worldly, intelligent and sceptical' (Grossman 2004). The change programme had placed an increased emphasis on collaboration within teams to encourage creative output as well as improve audiences and reduce overheads.

Research into staff attitudes and behaviour conducted by MORI on behalf of the BBC in November 2003 suggested that the majority of staff (62%) supported the change programme instigated by Greg Dyke.

On 28 January 2004 the BBC's internal communication was tested to the full when Lord Hutton, who was leading the inquiry into the death of Dr David Kelly, heavily criticised the BBC's role in the reporting of claims about Iraq's weapons capability. Hutton accused the BBC of irresponsible reporting of information that later turned out to have come from government weapons expert, Dr David Kelly. The next day, following the resignation of the chairman of the BBC board of governors, Greg Dyke resigned – reluctantly.

The immediate issues facing the BBC were the very strong emotions felt by staff at Greg Dyke's resignation – 'shock, grief, denial, disbelief, anger, revenge, protest, rage' (Grossman 2004). While on the one hand it was important that people should share grief, reflect and move on, it was vital, on the other, that they understood the context of the crisis and felt able to talk about it and explain the BBC's position to others. The key communication objectives established were to:

1 support business as usual
2 provide reliable, timely and continuous context
3 maintain focus on continuing change in the BBC
4 use the opportunity to further good internal communication.

Later on, a further objective was established, which was to:

5 use the new culture to share grief and help move people on.

The communication strategy adopted was an open, direct, honest approach: acknowledge all facts or rumours; promote dialogue, not stifle it; 'best endeavours' for getting basic news internally first – but more effort on explaining external stories; closely synchronise internal and external messages; and to promote the key message of 'no change on change' – the process of culture change would continue.

A key tactic was the visibility of the BBC's top management throughout the crisis; they acknowledged that certain things could not be said by the BBC's internal community but were upfront with staff about recognising that situation. The staff newspaper *Ariel* played an important role in that it was given editorial freedom to provide and receive internal comment and opinion. *Ariel-i* , the daily intranet version, was able to report live updates on the events as they unfolded – not just getting news out to staff but providing a context, and encouraging people to air their views. Eighty per cent of the internal communications were set up to allow people to air their views – for example, Greg Dyke's farewell email attracted more than

▶

case study 17.1 (continued)

4000 responses from staff and some of these were published on the intranet as well as in *Ariel*.

Much of the communications activity, however, was conducted face to face. Directors visited different locations across the UK, suspending their normal business. There were corporate question and answer sessions (Q&As), emails, intranet feedback and team meetings with managers. Hundreds of questions were asked and answered. Nonetheless, many staff walked out in protest and paid for an advertisement in *The Daily Telegraph* in support of the director general Greg Dyke. Protestors carried 'Bring back Greg' posters. BBC management did not oppose these actions. The following day the top 400 managers at the corporation gathered with the acting director general. This top group had to consider their own reactions and agree a common approach before communicating with teams. A televised session was held for all staff a week later to allow people to vent their anger.

After three weeks, issues tracking through email surveys and anecdotal feedback from face-to-face sessions suggested that calm had returned to the BBC. The culture change programme continued. *Ariel-i* hits increased by threefold and *Ariel*'s own credibility had increased among staff. The strategy adopted had paid off. Anger had been vented internally. The BBC's top 400 managers looked and behaved like a leadership team. Managers collaborated to help each other out and there was good support for the top team who remained in post. The strategy to provide the context of what had happened had helped people to explain the situation to themselves and others – meaning less work for the communications team at a difficult time.

Three weeks in crisis communications

28 January 2004 – Hutton Report published, attacking the BBC

29 January – Greg Dyke resigns; BBC staff walk out

30 January – BBC staff place ad in *The Daily Telegraph*

End of February – issues tracking suggested most people are ready to move on.

See Think about 17.10.

PICTURE 17.2   Front cover of *Ariel,* the BBC's internal newspaper.

Source: With kind permission of the BBC

Summary

This chapter has examined the key issues for organisations in building relationships with employees or internal publics. We have identified the main external and internal factors driving organisations today and interpreted these from a communication perspective. We have argued that the changing nature of work and jobs is presenting many challenges for the IC function and in particular the task of achieving a sense of unity within an organisation. We have emphasised the importance of organisational culture and leadership in providing the context for the internal communication strategy and demonstrated these through case studies.

Throughout this chapter we have evidenced the essential role of face-to-face communication and, in particular, the role of the line manager in providing the link between the top of the organisation and small teams of employees. We have assessed the top five communication channels and discussed key evaluation issues for internal communication. Finally, we have raised questions of ethics surrounding communication campaigns where employees are target publics.

Bibliography

Alvesson, M. (1993). *Cultural Perspectives on Organizations*. New York: Cambridge University Press.

Arnott, M. (1987). 'Effective employee communication' in *Effective Corporate Relations: Applying public relations in business and industry*. N.E. Hart (ed.). London: McGraw-Hill.

Banks, S.P. (2000). *Multicultural Public Relations: A social-interpretive approach*, 2nd edition. Ames, IA: Iowa State University Press.

Boje, D.M., G.A. Rosile, R.A. Durant and J.T. Luhman (2004). 'Enron spectacles: A critical dramaturgical analysis'. *Organization Studies* **25**(5): 751–774.

CIPD (Chartered Institute of Personnel and Development) (2004). 'Managing the psychological contract'. Factsheet December 2004.

Communicators in Business/MORI (2003). 'Trust and mistrust at work'. Survey 23 May 2003, at www.mori.com/polls/2003/trustatwork.shtml, accessed 29 November 2004.

Conrad, C. and M.S. Poole (1998). *Strategic Organizational Communication: Into the twenty-first century*, 4th edition. Fort Worth, TX: Harcourt Brace.

Daymon, C. (2000). 'On considering the meaning of managed communication: Or why employees resist "excellent" communication'. *Journal of Communication Management* **4**(3): 240–252.

Demos/Orange/MORI (2004). 'Survey', in *Disorganisation: Why future organisations should loosen up*. P. Miller and P. Skidmore. London: Demos.

Eisenberg, E.M. and P. Riley (2001). 'Organizational culture' in *The New Handbook of Organizational Communication: Advances in theory, research and methods*. F.M. Jablin and L.L. Putnam (eds). Thousand Oaks, CA: Sage.

Grossman, R. (2004). Testing cultural change with a good crisis. Paper presented at the Inside Out – Managing Change from Within Conference, Institute of Public Relations, London. 28 June.

Grunig, J.E. (1992). 'Symmetrical systems of internal communication' in *Excellence in Public Relations and Communication Management*. J.E. Grunig (ed.). Hillsdale, NJ: Lawrence Erlbaum Associates.

Guest, D.E. and N. Conway (2002). *Pressure at Work and the Psychological Contract*. London: CIPD.

Hofstede, G.H. (1991). *Cultures and Organizations*. New York: McGraw-Hill.

Industrial Society (1999). *Managing Best Practice No. 60: Employee communication and technology*. London: Industrial Society.

Kernaghan, S., D. Clutterbuck and S. Cage (2001). *Transforming Internal Communication*. London: Business Intelligence.

MCA/MORI (1998). 'The buy-in benchmark: A survey of staff understanding and commitment and the impact on business performance' report, at www.mori.com/polls/1998/mca98.shtml accessed 14 April 2004.

McCollom, M. (1994). 'The cultures of work organizations'. *Academy of Management Review* **19**:836–839.

Miller, P. and P. Skidmore (2004). *Disorganisation: Why future organisations should loosen up*. London: Demos.

Moss Kanter, R. (1983). *The Change Masters: Corporate entrepreneurs at work*. London: Routledge.

Mudie, P. (2000). 'Internal marketing: A step too far' in *Internal Marketing: Directions for management*. R.J. Varey and B.R. Lewis (eds). London: Routledge.

Quirke, B. (2000). *Making the Connections: Using internal communication to turn strategy into action*. London: Gower.

Sadler, P. (2001). 'Leadership and organizational learning' in *Handbook of Organizational Learning and Knowledge*. M. Dierkes, A. Berthoin Antal, J. Child and I. Nonaka (eds). Oxford: Oxford University Press.

Schein, E. (1985). *Organizational Culture and Leadership*. San Francisco: Jossey-Bass.

Scholes, E. (1997). *The Internal Communication Handbook*. London: Gower.

Smythe, J. (2004). *Engaging People at Work to Drive Strategy and Change*. London: McKinsey & Company.

Stauss, B. and F. Hoffmann (2000). 'Minimizing internal communication gaps by using business television' in *Internal Marketing: Directions for management*. R.J. Varey and B.R. Lewis (eds). London: Routledge.

Thomson, K. and L.A. Hecker (2000). 'The business value of buy-in: How staff understanding and commitment impact on brand and business performance' in *Internal Marketing: Directions for management*. R.J. Varey and B.R. Lewis (eds). London: Routledge.

White, J. (1991). *How to Understand and Manage Public Relations*. London: Basic Books.

Yeomans, L. (2004). Internal communication and organizational learning: An interpretive approach. Paper presented to the 11th International Public Relations Symposium, Lake Bled, Slovenia, 2–4 July.

CHAPTER 18
Managing community involvement programmes

Learning outcomes

By the end of this chapter you should be able to:

■ define, describe and compare the concepts of community involvement, corporate social responsibility and cause-related marketing

■ identify the key principles of community relationship building and apply this understanding to simple, meaningful scenarios

■ evaluate the issues arising from an organisation's community involvement

■ critically evaluate corporate strategies for integrating corporate social responsibility and community programmes into the business plan from a stakeholder perspective.

Structure

■ Corporate community involvement (CCI) programmes

■ Employees and community programmes

■ Cause-related marketing (CRM)

■ Developing community programmes

■ Evaluating community programmes

Introduction

If you saw a child helping an elderly citizen cross the road or giving up a seat for them on the train, you would probably think it was a mature and generous act by someone with a considered view of their place in society. If the child then went home and wrote about it in their private diary it may still be viewed as a positive action being considered and reflected on to inform the child's future behaviour in similar situations. The child could then share the experience over dinner with family members to elicit praise, credit or a reward of a coveted sweet or drink. What if they then went to their school head-teacher (principal) soliciting further praise, even a headteacher's award, which may attract interest from outside the school through a parental contact with the local paper? And the accolades pour in.

A little far fetched perhaps, but is this analogous with organisations and their in-volvement in society through corporate social responsibility? It may be for some. Certainly criticisms have been levelled at some companies for over-promoting their acts of corporate giving, particularly around major incidents such as 11 September in the USA and the Asian tsunami in December 2004. What are organisations' motivations and interests in their communities? How much are they interested in doing something 'good' and how much in being acknowledged, recognised and rewarded for this act? In Chapter 6 we discussed the role of organisations in their communities and in this chapter we will explore the different ways in which organisations apply their individual interpretations of community involvement and how this can have various outcomes, outputs, benefits and rewards for them and the communities they are involved with.

The chapter will therefore evaluate community involvement programmes that can range from the philanthropic (donations) through to campaigns that have much more tangible returns for the organisation such as initiatives like cause-related marketing (CRM).

Corporate community involvement (CCI) programmes

These are the tactical approaches organisations plan to discharge their corporate social responsibility policy. CCI may be viewed as the organisational recognition that businesses cannot survive unless there is a prosperous community or wider society from which to draw both employees and trade. Building relationships with stakeholders and community groups is important for many organisations when there are changing patterns of employment and recruitment, with increasing use of short-term contracts and part-time work, particularly in the retail and service sectors. Other influences such as the continuing increase in the number of women in full- and part-time work and the worldwide issue of *downsizing* (reducing the numbers of full- and part-time staff employed by an organisation). It is important to recognise that not all organisations take an enlightened view of their role in society and, in fact, many are content to work at the basic level of responsibility to society, i.e. to pay taxes and obey corporate and societal laws (see Chapter 6).

> **Definition:** *Downsizing* is a term used to describe the reduction in the number of employees working for an organisation in either full- or part-time positions.

All these factors are influential in the increasing drive by organisations to build links with communities and stakeholders in order to enhance public understanding of the organisation's function and its business objectives and subsequently impact on the environment in which it operates. In recognition of many of these changes, businesses are attempting to forge direct links with communities either individually or collectively through organisations such as Business in the Community (BITC) in the UK.

BITC is a non-political UK organisation whose aim is to work in partnership with businesses to build their relationships and involvement with the communities in which they operate. BITC defines its aims as 'supporting the social and economic regeneration of communities by raising the quality and extent of business involvement and by making that involvement a natural part of successful business practice'.

The organisation represents over 400 member companies in the UK and this includes 75 of the UK's top performing stock-exchange-listed companies, the FTSE100. Member companies are encouraged to provide their skills, expertise, influence, products and profits to assist in building a prosperous society that is attractive to investors, in which businesses can thrive and where all stakeholders in the community can have access to opportunities. The organisation is run through 11 regional offices throughout the UK. BITC claims the benefits to the members are as follows:

- employee development
- increased staff morale
- enhanced relations with local decision makers
- motivated, high-quality recruits
- improved corporate image.

BITC is a member of CSR Europe, a network of national affiliation organisations interested in CSR. CSR Europe describes itself as a business-to-business network that aims to help companies achieve profitability by placing CSR in the mainstream of business practice (CSR Europe 2002). In the USA, Business for Social Responsibility (BSR) is the coordinating organisation (www.bsr.org). (See Case study 18.1.)

Sponsorship and the community

Today sponsorship is an important area of business policy and a large proportion of it is highly visible to an organisation's stakeholders. Examples include sponsorship of major sporting events such as FIFA's football World Cup or the summer and winter Olympic Games (see Chapter 27 for more on sponsorship). A further area of popular sponsorship is of specific, high-profile television programmes. This technique has been effectively employed in the UK with established soap operas and detective serials. For example, *Coronation Street* is a soap opera that has been on UK terrestrial (non-cable/satellite) television for over 30 years and has developed an effective, mutually beneficial sponsorship arrangement with the confectionery brand, Cadbury, since such sponsorship was made legal in the 1990s.

It is therefore clear that not all sponsorship fits into the CCI category, for example tobacco sponsorship of Formula 1 motor racing came in for ethical and political debate for many years. During 2004 the

BT Community Partnership Programme

BT is a founder member of BITC's Per Cent Standard (formerly the Per Cent Club) – a group of top companies in the UK that donate a percentage of their annual profits to community-based projects and organisations.

BT has a long history of working in the community. In the 1990s the guiding principle of BT's Community Partnership Programme was access and communication. The aim was to help people to communicate better by providing organisations with resources, expertise and the technology to improve the quality of life and well-being of the community. BT's mission statement pledged the company to 'make a fitting contribution' to the community in which it conducts its business. The recipients of BT's membership of the Per Cent Club have been charitable causes such as the Samaritans, which has received over £1m in five years. The company has also supported the Royal National Institute for the Deaf's Communications Support Unit. This enabled 15

people to be trained to professional sign language interpreter standard and provided support during their first year of employment. BT has also supported people with disabilities: BT Swimming, for example, together with the disabled swimming organisation, BSAD, organised national competitions. BT Swimathon, a nationwide charity swim, raised millions for a number of different charities including ChildLine (see Case study 18.6).

The BT case study demonstrates the long-term commitment BT has had to the community in which it conducts its business and allows the company to see the links into its corporate strategy and goals and particularly the connections with the company's industry, communications. This is a common theme with many corporate community initiatives and it is clearly one way that makes the technique acceptable to directors in the boardroom (see also Case study 18.6).

Source: Used with kind permission of BT and BITC

Breakthrough breast cancer charity rejected £1m of sponsorship from Nestlé because of the company's past policy of promoting formula milk products for newborn babies in developing countries (*The Guardian* 6 May 2004). Corporate sponsorship can be planned, well managed and fit into corporate strategies within ethical guidelines, but it can also challenge ethical rules if the organisation is not clear about its aims, objectives and criteria for sponsoring.

It is important therefore for the organisation to clarify its aims and objectives when embarking on a sponsorship programme. For commercial sponsorship the organisation may have one of the following reasons for sponsoring:

- To raise awareness of the organisation or its products.
- To build organisational image by association with worthwhile causes, e.g. charities or the arts, or to enhance image in particular geographical locations by sponsoring regional or national sports teams.
- To overcome legislation such as gaining exposure on television for products banned from advertising (e.g. contraceptives and tobacco in the UK).
- To provide corporate hospitality opportunities for stakeholders such as customers and investors to attend.

However, there are other forms of sponsorship that fit into the CCI category more closely, such as charitable donations given to an activity that is not commercial but helps the community or members of that

community and from which no commercial return is sought. This form of sponsorship does frequently provide significant public relations benefits but this is not always of importance to organisations nor is it always exploited. There are significant differences between corporate sponsorship and charitable donations, not least in the classification of tax. Sponsorship is liable to value added tax (VAT) in the UK whereas charitable donations are not. This situation is similar in many other countries. Having looked at the definitions of sponsorship it is therefore wrong and potentially illegal for organisations to redefine their sponsorship activity as charitable donations to avoid paying tax.

It is possible for CCI initiatives to be either sponsorship that benefits both parties or to be clearly examples of charitable donation by the organisation. Sponsorship can, therefore, be seen as part of the armoury used in corporate community relations. Community relations programmes are often defined as mutually beneficial partnerships with one or more stakeholders to enhance the organisation's reputation as a good corporate citizen. The stakeholders are therefore usually the target audiences for the company and include customers, suppliers, media, employers, trade unions, politicians, local government representatives, community organisations, key opinion formers, shareholders, educationalists, environmentalists, etc. Community relations can have an influence on the corporate reputation and this is increasingly an important measure for individual

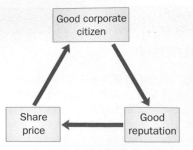

FIGURE 18.1   Link between community relations, financial performance and reputation

and institutional investors for the quality of an organisation. As such the link between good corporate citizenship, good reputation and share value/price can be identified (see Figure 18.1, Think about 18.1 and Activity 18.1).

The bigger picture

Community initiatives can have benefits beyond links with specific community-based stakeholders (such as schools or community-based groups). Through involvement in community relations an organisation is often complementing other objectives (such as its corporate strategy). This can have an impact on share value, as discussed, but also on media relations, investor relations, shareholder communications strategies and even, in the event of crisis, communication. For example, establishing a relationship with specialist or local journalists during positive news stories connected to community initiatives may help during a crisis. For instance, in the event of a crisis, a well-disposed journalist is more likely to give the organisation the opportunity to respond or give the organisational view of the negative situation. This can prevent more damaging news stories escalating into a crisis (see Mini case study 18.1, Think about 18.2 and 18.3).

Employees and community programmes

Increasingly employers are encouraging their employees to become involved in the local communities in which they and often their families live. This is true of public as well as private organisations. For example, Leeds Metropolitan University supports the Leeds Cares initiative, which includes employees working on voluntary projects in and around Leeds (see Case study 18.2 and Activity 18.2, overleaf).

activity 18.1

Finding examples of community relations

Think about an organisation you know well or are interested in and research its website and external activities. Make a list of those activities you believe might be regarded as community relations. Note down what you believe the organisation and the recipient got out of the relationship.

Feedback

Community relations are diverse and the involvement need not be significant. Typically, community relations programmes involve one or more of the following techniques or tactics:

- sponsorships
- targeted donations
- awards
- hospitality
- employee volunteering
- use of facilities (loan of equipment)
- training/seminars
- secondments (staff).

Links between organisations and community groups are normally made with organisations in areas such as sports, arts, education, the environment, occupational health and safety, charities, youth/young people's groups, senior citizens, the disadvantaged, disability, heritage and many other groupings.

think about 18.1   Why companies get involved in community relations

Company stock valuation is one reason for being involved in community relations. What others can you think of which might benefit the organisation?

Feedback   Some businesses are increasingly concerned with educational development of the community in what is termed 'cradle to grave'. Community relations can influence this process by education-based sponsorship. This creates awareness in local schools and establishes the company as a desirable employer. This may, in turn, influence future recruitment or create a positive image around products/services/outputs. Also the community initiatives can provide employees with opportunities to develop further skills by working with local schools and organisations. The benefits of such education are a properly trained and developed workforce, which is crucial to the company's future success.

mini case study 18.1

Shell/Brent Spar

An example of how community relationships can benefit a large corporation heavily involved in community initiatives occurs with Shell UK during the Brent Spar issue. Brent Spar was an obsolete oil platform that Shell wanted to dispose of and, through relevant research, had been advised to sink in the North Sea. Subsequently, there was a wave of damaging protest across the UK and Europe. However, Peter Hunt, head of com-

munity and regional affairs at Shell UK claimed in the aftermath that the publicity would have been more damaging and the company's reputation slower to recover if it had not already developed strong communication links with many environmental interest groups through its corporate community involvement activities. Hunt claimed this gave Shell the opportunity for a fairer, more balanced hearing.

think about 18.2   Sponsoring

What do you think are the implications for a sponsee of a high-profile event (for example, sponsoring a world-famous horse race or established annual charity walk and collection fund) if the sponsor withdraws their support?

Feedback The event may be put into jeopardy. Think about contracts and the following:

- What if no suitable sponsor comes to take their place?
- What about negative publicity if the event is no longer able to run?

See also Chapter 27.

think about 18.3   Sponsoring and corporate giving

The concept of corporate philanthropy was discussed in Chapter 6. This relates to the process of providing money or gifts in kind to organisations on behalf of a company or organisation. Here are some issues for you to think about related to the process of giving and sponsoring on behalf of an organisation:

- Does sponsorship and corporate giving discourage the state and government agencies from fulfiling their duties to society?
- Consider a company that sponsors local schools and supplies them with computers. Does this discourage state provision of information technology to schools? What happens when the hardware dates and the software become obsolete and the organisation moves on to other causes or stops giving?
- Will giving to one group in society disadvantage others if the state withdraws or reduces support?
- Might some groups be more attractive to sponsors and donors than others? Is it easier to support babies orphaned in a disaster than disturbed teenagers?

Feedback Think about the impact of initiatives such as national lotteries (which exist in many countries) on charity donations. Do they provide much-needed support while at the same time take away the responsibility of individuals or the state to support parts of society? Some charities in the UK claim to have lost out because of the National Lottery. They believe that because people are buying lottery tickets they feel they are 'doing their bit' and no longer need to make the kinds of contribution they used to.

To achieve practically the increased involvement of employees the following techniques should be considered:

- *preferential treatment* given to requests supported by employees of the organisation (the Leeds Cares Case study 18.2 is an example)

- *launching a reward and recognition programme* that highlights and supports the achievements of employees in out-of-hours activities (e.g. sporting honours); leadership initiatives; commitment to an organisation (e.g. school governor); academic support (e.g. encourage employees to give lectures at local schools and colleges)

case study 18.2

Leeds Cares – collaborative action

Leeds Cares is the leading programme for engaging business support in the northern UK city of Leeds. Through the collaboration of its 33 supporting businesses working closely with public sector and community partners, it has a real social impact in the most deprived areas of Leeds.

Leeds Cares began in 1999 with 11 founder companies providing action days for teams and calendar opportunities for individuals. It has grown to include 33 companies and offers a range of employee involvement activities, including team challenges, brokering business mentors, who support prisoners due for release and seeking work, and helping homeless people into permanent employment.

The social impact of the programme is achieved through planning and consultation with stakeholders. Leeds Cares' vision is based on the Vision for Leeds, a community strategy for the city prepared through consultation with the people of Leeds by the Leeds Initiative, the city's local strategic partnership, bringing together the public, private and voluntary sectors.

Leeds Cares recognises that education is the primary social issue of concern to business. Its programmes provide: one-to-one literacy support to primary schoolchildren; individual mentors to work with selected secondary schoolchildren; and management support to headteachers through Partners in Leadership.

Leeds Cares states its aim is to continue helping businesses to engage in wider corporate social responsibility issues through community involvement. By addressing hard social issues such as ex-offender reoffending rates, getting homeless people into jobs and developing reading and numeracy in schools, the programme has the potential to be at the heart of the city's regeneration movement.

According to Leeds Cares, the impact of the programme has been:

- over 8000 volunteers giving over 100,000 hours of time; of these, 90% were volunteering for the first time
- support for over 350 community partners and 50 companies
- human resources benefits for supporting companies, through employee development, communications, project management, teambuilding and motivation, as well as reputation building through public relations around action days
- development of new training packages based around the staff development benefits of Leeds Cares, while others used it to support their business objectives around social diversity.

Source: adapted from http://www.bitc.org.uk/resources/case_studies/leeds_cares_coll.html

- *awards presentations* where employees volunteer to represent the organisation as an 'ambassador' at presentation events
- *employee volunteering* that actively encourages employees to gain personal development experience by volunteering their time and skills to a willing community organisation
- *committee membership* that develops employees by encouraging involvement with external committees; this will help their networking and understanding of how other organisations work.

Involving employees in community programmes can offer numerous benefits to both parties. For employees, it improves motivation and pride in the organisation, which can improve productivity, reduce sickness absence, increase innovation, develop communication skills, improve understanding of corporate strategy/policy objectives and offer a measure/comparison against competitor organisations. If it is so good, however, why are so few organisations doing it? Perhaps some individuals and companies are, but they do not make a big deal out of it. Alternatively, it may be just too costly and not worth the effort. This

may be influenced by the business area, range of employee profiles (age, gender, education), corporate interest in the region or local society or, more importantly, the organisation's size or profitability – it just might not be able to afford the time or the money.

activity 18.2

Employee involvement

List the benefits you think involving employees with the local community might bring to:

- the individual
- the organisation.

Feedback
Individual benefits might include:

- personal development
- learning new skills
- developing communication skills.

Organisational benefits might include learning from working in partnership with your employees and sharing their professional skills, time and experience.

Cause-related marketing (CRM)

Cause-related marketing (CRM) is 'where a company associates a marketing promotion with a charitable cause' (Hart 1995: 219).

BITC defines CRM as 'a commercial activity by which a company with an image, product or service to market, builds a relationship with a "cause" or a number of "causes" for mutual benefit' (BITC 2005).

CRM has become a popular practice for Anglo-American organisations in recent years and a number of leading UK companies have forged particularly close partnerships with charities and good causes. For example Tesco, one of the UK's largest supermarket retailers, runs a well-known CRM programme in conjunction with local schools called 'Tesco Computers for Schools'.

The scheme involves consumers collecting tokens with their shopping that can be exchanged for computer equipment. BITC in the UK carries out regular research into CRM and its use. For example, BITC's Profitable Partnerships research (2000) reveals that:

- the vast majority of the population (88%) are aware of cause-related marketing
- 76% of consumers who have heard of CRM associations have participated in these programmes
- 77% of consumers who had participated in a CRM programme said it had had a positive impact on their behaviour or perceptions
- 80% of consumers who had participated in a CRM programme said that it would positively impact on their future behaviour and attitudes
- 67% of consumers think that more companies should be involved in CRM.

BITC has been researching company and consumer attitudes in the UK since the 1990s. For example, Research International (1995) surveyed over 450 major companies operating in the UK, including 81 of the top 100 FTSE companies. The results demonstrated that CRM was already established and 93% indicated some level of CRM spend. The survey also found that marketing directors, community affairs directors and chief executives all believed CRM held 'obvious benefits for businesses and causes', including:

- enhancing corporate reputation
- achieving press coverage and public relations
- raising brand awareness
- increasing customer loyalty
- building and increasing sales (Research International 1995).

The 'Winning Game' was a large-scale consumer survey carried out among 1053 UK consumers (Research International 1997). The purpose of the study was to understand consumer attitudes towards CRM. It found that consumers had a high expectation that large businesses and corporations should demonstrate an active social responsibility. It also found that consumers felt CRM is a 'means by which businesses can become involved in the community'. The most significant finding of the research was that 'when price and quality are equal, consumers will discriminate in favour of the company that espouses a good cause. Furthermore, consumers believe that companies should support a good cause' (Research International Consumer Survey 1997).

The attraction of CRM for organisations is that these programmes generate direct, measurable benefits for the company. Further benefits of this approach include:

- those needing help receive it
- the public feels good about buying/supporting the product
- the donor organisation gains reputation and sometimes sales
- it is a win–win situation for both parties.

Talking about CRM, Cadbury Schweppes' chairman, Dominic Cadbury (1996: 25), one of the biggest proponents in the UK, enthused about CRM's 'ability to enhance corporate image, to differentiate products, and to increase sales and loyalty. It is enlightened self-interest [see Chapter 6], a win–win situation'. (See Mini case studies 18.2–18.4, then look at the examples provided in Boxes 18.1 and 18.2 and Case study 18.3–all on the following pages.)

Consumers and CRM

Research from the USA shows the importance of CRM with consumers as follows:

- CRM increasingly becoming the 'tiebreaker' in a purchase decision.
- Seventy-six per cent of Americans say that when price and quality are equal they are more likely to switch to brands associated with a good cause.
- Consumers are less cynical about CRM (than about standard marketing campaigns).
- CRM has long-term strategic benefits rather than being a short-term promotional device.
- Being socially responsible can create good 'word of mouth' (Cone Roper 1997).

mini case study 18.2

Cadbury Strollerthon

During the 1990s, the Cadbury chocolate company supported the annual Strollerthon 10-mile walk around London, which raised £400,000 a year for Save the Children and One Small Step charities.

mini case study 18.3

American Express

An often-cited example of early CRM dates back to 1983 when American Express was invited to make a donation to restore one of the USA's most famous symbols, the Statue of Liberty. The company's response was not just to write a cheque but to propose a more imaginative solution, which was that every time one of its cardholders used their card they would help towards the appeal. Within a few months American Express had contributed $1.5m. Most importantly for the company, however, was that the use of its card had increased by 27%. Today many companies have adopted CRM tactics to merge corporate social responsibility and commercial aims.

Source: BITC

PICTURE 18.1   American Express developed a CRM strategy to help restore the Statue of Liberty.

mini case study 18.4

HP Sauce

In the mid-1990s, food producer HP's packaging highlighted the company's involvement with the child protection charity, NSPCC. One penny from every purchase of Daddies' Brown Sauce was donated to the NSPCC, which resulted in a minimum donation of £80,000. (See Think about 18.4 and Activity 18.3.)

Source: BITC

activity 18.3

CRM

1 CRM in the mini case examples is obviously very successful. Why would an organisation involve itself in any other type of corporate support if it were not going to bring direct commercial benefits?
2 Think about an organisation you know well, research it and consider whether it involves itself in any CRM. If not, how might it build a relationship with a charity or cause and which one(s) should it choose?

Feedback
Reasons for more straightforward sponsorship might include: goodwill; community involvement; stakeholder interest; and good citizenship.

How do companies measure the success of CRM?

The techniques used by companies to measure the success of CRM campaigns are similar to those often used corporately, with the majority of organisations relying on media coverage. According to Research International's 1997 survey of managing directors and communications directors, the full list of measurement techniques used by organisations is:

- media coverage: 58%
- level of press output: 38%
- image tracking studies: 30%
- customer satisfaction studies: 28%

think about 18.4   **HP Sauce**

■ In the HP example, are both parties equal in the relationship?
■ Is it acceptable for one partner to have the balance of power and potentially benefit more from the arrangement?
■ What are the corporate communication dangers of this type of contact?
■ Could HP not simply give a sum of money to the NSPCC?

Feedback Both parties may not always be equal. In the HP example, they may both benefit financially but the reputational benefits are clearer for HP. Power is not always equal due to the financial power of the sponsoring organisation. Some of the dangers of the relationship include: crisis management for both parties (something goes wrong that is unrelated to the contract); contract length and withdrawal from it. HP stood to gain more ongoing publicity from the special packaging than from the short-term effects of announcing a corporate donation to the NSPCC.

■ sales output figures: 16%
■ other: 19% (Research International 1997).

See also Case study 18.4, overleaf.

Developing community programmes

Planning and implementing corporate social responsibility

Having defined techniques for determining who an organisation is responsible to, what responsibilities there are and a framework for identifying stakeholder responsibilities, we need to consider how this process works in practice. Endorsement of the CSR concept by senior management is important if it is to be successful and Carroll (1991) recommends seven key

questions to ask management when planning CSR strategies:

1   Who are our stakeholders?
2   What are their stakes?
3   What do we need from each of our stakeholders?
4   What corporate social responsibilities (economic, legal, ethical and philanthropic) do we have to our stakeholders?
5   What opportunities and challenges do our stakeholders present?
6   How important and/or influential are different stakeholders?
7   What strategies, actions or decisions should we take to best deal with these responsibilities?

(See also Chapter 6 and Box 18.3, overleaf.)

| box 18.1 | **Other CRM examples from the UK** |

■ Norwich Union (financial services)
■ Nivea (cosmetics)
■ Lloyds TSB (financial services)

■ Nike (sports goods)
■ Andrex (toiletries)
■ HP Foods 'Daddies' Sauce' (food)

– St John Ambulance
– Fashion Targets Breast Cancer
– 'Visible Women' (ethnic minority women one-off magazine)
– Kick Racism out of Football
– Guide Dogs for the Blind (see Case study 18.3)
– NSPCC (see Mini case study 18.4)

| box 18.2 | **Other examples from around the world** |

■ Toyota
■ American Express

■ Florida Citrus
■ Kellogg's

– Leukaemia Society of America
– Elizabeth Taylor AIDS Foundation
  Magic Johnson Foundation
– American Cancer Society
– Race For The Cure (breast cancer)

case study 18.3

Guide Dogs for the Blind Association and Andrex

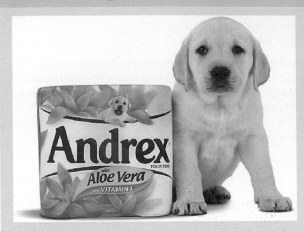

PICTURE 18.2 Guide Dogs for the Blind Association and Andrex have long enjoyed a mutually beneficial association © KCCW 2005

Guide Dogs for the Blind Association (GDBA) and Andrex (the toilet paper brand owned by Kimberly-Clark) have an association that stretches back over 15 years. Back in 1997 the Andrex toilet tissue brand celebrated the 25th anniversary of the Andrex puppy famously used in its on-pack promotions and television commercials. To celebrate the event, both parties decided to launch a cause-related marketing programme. The scheme was a significant one that raised £275,000 in donations for the GDBA.

The promotional packs of Andrex tissue were on display for three months and each pack contained tokens that could be sent back to GDBA or Andrex, which resulted in a donation being made to the charity.

Kimberly-Clark maximised the public relations opportunities of this venture by creating local news stories involving the GDBA training centres and the Girl Guides Association regional prize winners. The company claimed to achieve five times the amount of press coverage during the programme than before it started.

Both parties believed the CRM programme to be a success because it brought benefits to both sides and to the consumer. From the charity's perspective, the campaign was financially beneficial and it provided it with opportunities to improve awareness of its name and to inform the public about the range of services it provides as an organisation. From the company's perspective, the scheme led to an increase in the level of local and national press coverage, increased the level of sales of the product and improved the company's corporate reputation. It could also be argued that consumers benefited from the association as they continued to receive the same product at the same price while being able to feel they were financially supporting a service that helps disadvantaged members of society. (See also Activity 18.4.)

Source: used with kind permission of Kimberly-Clark and GDBA

The fourth of the strategies outlined in Box 18.3 is the ideal. The strategy should forecast the anticipated benefits for the business as a result of the organisation changing its approach to CSR. The strategy should also indicate:

■ necessary levels of investment
■ how to monitor the strategy
■ evaluation of the strategy
■ benefits communicated to management, employees and stakeholders.

Some companies claim to meet the ideal interactive strategy, such as the UK-based Co-operative Bank, which has ethical policies dating back to the organisation's foundation in 1872 as part of the cooperative movement. The bank publishes its ethical policy annually, detailing its performance and track record (see Case study 18.7 at the end of this chapter).

Another example of a company meeting these commitments in a transparent way is the Scottish Nappy Company. This case study (Mini case study 18.5, overleaf) demonstrates how a small company can develop a strategic business plan that helps solve a societal issue and contributes to environmental sustainability. (See also Case study 18.5 on p. 367.)

activity 18.4

The Andrex case study

1 From the GDBA and Andrex case study, do you think all parties were equal?
2 List the strategic objectives for Andrex of this CRM campaign – what was the company trying to achieve? How might these objectives be measured?

Feedback
Consider longer term issues for the company such as: corporate image; media exposure; building closer links with key stakeholders, i.e. the customer, regional and national media; brand reinforcement; increased revenue; corporate social responsibility. All these factors are encapsulated in one marketing-led initiative.

case study 18.4

The Co-operative Bank

Customers Who Care, Safer Chemicals Campaign

Winner of the BITC Cause-Related Marketing Award for Excellence 2003

Customers Who Care is a programme that actively demonstrates the bank's ethical stance on issues of importance to its customers, staff, partner organisations and the public. It is a cornerstone of the bank's ethical brand positioning. The mechanics of the programme remain consistent, with a donation made by the bank for every £100 of customers' turnover on Visa credit and debit cards. The bank dedicates its resources to run a hard-hitting issue-based campaign in partnership with customers, selected charities and non-governmental organisations (NGOs). This flexible approach to campaigning is designed to meet the demands of each campaign and complement the particular strength of different campaign partners.

In 2003–2004, Customers Who Care campaigned for Safer Chemicals in partnership with the global environmental network, WWF-UK, advocating the phasing out of chemicals that pose a threat to the environment and human health. The campaign was planned to coincide with the EU review of chemical legislation – the first in over 20 years – which provided a great opportunity to increase the campaign's impact.

The bank actively campaigned with WWF in the UK and Europe, including supporting WWF-UK's biomonitoring tour, which tested over 150 volunteers (including bank managers and the bank's chief operating officer) for the presence of man-made chemicals. They also funded similar tests of MEPs in Brussels and a month-long, co-branded national press advertising campaign to raise awareness. Customers and staff were heavily involved through quarterly campaign updates to 800,000 customers, website campaign updates and email messages to campaign groups.

While campaigning for Safer Chemicals, the Co-operative Bank continued to dedicate resources to support its previous year's Cluster Bomb campaign, 'Cluster Bombs: the great clear-up', which saw the Co-operative Bank working in partnership with Landmine Action.

Impact:

Of the bank's customers, 30% cited 'ethics' as their reason for joining the bank. The Customers who Care programme and the Safer Chemicals campaign have:

- provided a point of differentiation from other high street banks
- donated £100,000 to fund Pesticide Action Network, Friends of the Earth and Surfers Against Sewage's new programmes of work on safer chemicals
- fully funded a month-long, co-branded awareness raising advertising campaign in the national press that reached one in three of the UK population
- contributed to EU and UK government consultations on EU chemicals legislation
- participated in a national biomonitoring tour testing volunteers' blood for the presence of man-made chemicals
- influenced the development of the new EU chemical legislation through funding the biomonitoring of 44 MEPs from across 10 EU member states to raise awareness of the issue.

In 2004, the Co-operative Bank celebrated 10 years of Customers Who Care. Over the years the bank has actively campaigned on important and diverse issues from landmines to biodiversity, the arms trade to child poverty, mental health to third world debt.

Source: Co-operative Bank

box 18.3   Four strategies of CSR response

Four strategies of response have been identified to stakeholder perspectives on CSR as follows:

1 An *inactive* strategy: resisting societal expectations and sometimes government regulation.
2 A *reactive* strategy: responding to unanticipated change after the significant change has occurred.
3 A *proactive* strategy: attempting to 'get ahead' of a societal expectation or government regulation (often coupled with efforts to influence the outcome).
4 An *interactive* strategy: anticipating change and blending corporate goals with those of stakeholders and societal expectations. An organisation employing an interactive strategy consciously reduces the gap between its performance and society's expectations. An interactive strategy is often accomplished by management's commitment to a serious dialogue with stakeholders.

Scottish Nappy Company Limited

The Scottish Nappy Company is a small company, employing nine staff and based in west central Scotland. The company's main commitment is to its environmental aim of reducing landfill through minimising the 'disposable' nappy mountain. The operation was established with environmental considerations being key, including the selection of operational site, choice of chemicals, energy, vehicle, machinery, packaging materials and marketing.

The Scottish Nappy Company provides local people in the region with a weekly home delivery of fresh cotton nappies, the collection of soiled ones and their subsequent laundering. It embraces the environmental benefits of the laundering process itself, with significant benefits to the environment and health of its customers and the community at large within the area serviced.

The impact of the business has been a significant reduction in 'disposable' nappies going to landfill – an estimated 100 tonnes by the end of 2004. Also the rural base for the company's operation has minimised airborne pollutions affecting clean nappies. Furthermore, the selection of computer-controlled washing machines has ensured optimum cleanliness while minimising the use of water, gas and electricity. In addition, non-biological detergent and oxygen-based bleach are used in the laundry process and deliveries are made by LPG/petrol dual fuel van to reduce harmful emissions.

Further interesting evidence for the company and in support of its strategy is that babies in cotton nappies are generally trained out of them 6 to 12 months earlier than if they had been in 'disposables'.

Source: BITC and Scottish Nappy Company

How to develop community relations programmes

Community relations is not just about being good or 'nice to people', although this may be one of its results. Instead the concept is based on sound commercial principles of:

- research
- vision (corporate need for one)
- strategic objectives
- tactical programme
- measurement and evaluation
- dissemination (how the results will be communicated to key audience/stakeholders, particularly employees).

Research

The company needs to be aware of its reputation in the community and this can be measured through research, mainly with employees, their families and the local community. Additional stakeholder views are important from investors, suppliers, competitors, etc. Further understanding is required of the local environment and the needs of the community(ies). These attitudes and opinions can be collected through internal and external communications audits using both qualitative and quantitative techniques. Research should also include an investigation into competitors' involvement in community activities and desk research into best community relations theory and practice. Demetrius and Hughes (2004) argue for the inclusion of stakeholder analysis software (planning, implementing and evaluating campaigns) to save time and support students and practitioners in developing CSR strategies and programmes. Their argument is that equivalent software is used by accountants and other professional groups to provide information and support the administration process so that practitioners can provide creativity in the non-routine aspects of the planning process to develop strategic solutions to problems.

Vision

The programme needs a vision which links into the corporate philosophy and strategy. BT in the UK, for example, has used the title and strapline 'Community Partnership Programme', which links its corporate strategy for improving company communication with customers on the ground in order to increase its customer base. BT's expertise lies in the communications industries (initially telecommunications and increasingly mobile and electronic communications) and it utilises its corporate skills in communications and technology to underpin its community programmes. The company clearly links its corporate objectives with its community vision.

It is not always necessary to make such clear links between the corporate strategy and the community, but it is vital that the programme has a vision and therefore a purpose for all those involved with it. (See Box 18.4.)

case study 18.5

Everton Football Club in the community

Disability Football Development Programme

The Disability Football Development Programme offers the same opportunities to disabled people as those open to those without disabilities and aims to lead the way in the provision of disabled footballing opportunities at all levels. By using the powerful brand of Everton Football Club, with a structured development plan, Everton is making significant progress in bringing the game to this previously excluded group.

The programme started in the late 1990s with a small group of just six enthusiastic disabled footballers and one coach. It has now evolved into a totally inclusive project incorporating annual contact with over 10,000 disabled recreational players per year, eight competitive official Everton teams (amputee, deaf, partially sighted and five pan-disability teams, including junior, adult and female groups) with 100 registered disabled players, eight coaching staff and many trophies.

The programme is delivered by three full-time Everton Football in the Community (EFITC) staff and includes the country's first disabled FITC coach, Steve Johnson, who is also the captain of England's amputee football team.

This complete integration of the Football in the Community programme into the new commercial planning structure cements the club's belief in the impact and measurable benefits of community relationships and engagement. It also helps the club with its aim to be 'every supporter's second favourite team' by actively promoting accessibility and transparency, and emotionally engaging all football fans.

EFITC was a key participant in the consultation with Liverpool City Council during the application for the Capital of Culture 2008. It was invited to contribute to the delivery plan for the Year of Sport and to celebrate the inclusive nature of the EFITC disabled football programme.

According to Everton Football Club, the impact of the programme is as follows:

■ Employees are proud to be associated with a company that not only engages disabled people, but also allows them to excel in a sport they all feel passionately about.
■ Staff retention within EFITC is almost 100% over 10 years and days off through illness are rare.
■ Through the programme the disabled community has access not only to fitness, health, discipline and the social benefits of football, but also to employment, training and mentoring opportunities.

Source: used with kind permission of BITC and Everton Football Club

box 18.4 Strategic objectives for a community programme

Typical objectives for a community programme are:

■ to create and develop a positive view of the company as a socially responsible, good corporate citizen among its key stakeholders
■ to capitalise on this positive perception in terms of employee motivation, recruitment of new personnel, supplier development and community goodwill
■ to support other initiatives aimed at creating an understanding of the company's aims and policies (an example might be the use of community displays at the company's annual general meeting)
■ to develop opportunities which encourage employee participation in the community, through increased communication initiatives
■ to support the needs of the local community with innovative, role model initiatives, which position the company as a centre of excellence for community involvement
■ to brand the programme clearly so that it is easily recognised and remembered.

case study 18.6

BT 'Am I Listening?' campaign

BT's 'Am I Listening?' campaign aims to ensure that the voice of every young person in the UK is heard. It starts with ChildLine – because every day around 4000 young people call the helpline, but lack of funds means only 1800 get through.

BT's research in 2001 revealed that BT's CSR reputation had plateaued. To improve its reputation, an unprecedented (in terms of scope and scale) process of consultation with stakeholders was undertaken, beginning with an assessment of CSR perceptions. This resulted in focusing on young people as a key social issue. Further research undertaken by BT in May 2002, 'Are Young People Being Heard?', provided evidence of where communication gaps were greatest. The key finding was that only 47% of UK children and young people felt their voices were being listened to and acted on. Findings went to over 500 key influencers – receiving overwhelming interest from MPs, peers, statutory and voluntary agencies – forming the basis of an opinion-former strategy. The research determined the direction of the campaign, providing benchmarks to measure success.

BT's most ambitious social campaign was launched in October 2002. The first two years concentrated on helping ChildLine reach its goal of answering every call.

Aims and objectives
BT's vision

BT believes that when young people are heard, it will release untapped potential, making a positive contribution to a better world.

Overall objectives

- Raise money for ChildLine and provide operational support.
- Help ChildLine move closer to its goal of answering every call.
- Raise awareness of the need to listen to young people and demonstrate the positive results when young people are heard.

Specific public relations objectives

- Improve BT's CSR reputation.
- Ensure at least 75% of BT's 100,000 employees are aware of the campaign within two years.
- Accrue tangible business benefits from the campaign.

Implementation

The public relations campaign created and supported fundraising platforms for ChildLine. The cause-related marketing initiatives were highly visible, raised significant funds and were core to the overall campaign strategy.

BT Answer 1571

To start the fundraising drive, BT Retail donated £1 for every person who signed up to its free answering service, 1571. This was delivered via an intense media relations programme and an internal communications plan, with call-centre staff briefed to highlight the scheme to inbound callers.

Customer survey

BT Retail sent surveys to each of its 19 million residential customers – the largest customer survey ever undertaken in Europe. For every survey returned, £1 was donated to ChildLine. Designed to take advantage of milestones and extend the news value of the initiative, the public relations programme involved three phases: survey launch; £500k reached; and £1m reached.

Speaking Clock

As part of the BIG Listen week, BT ran a national competition with children's BBC news programme *Newsround* to find a young person's voice to be the Speaking Clock for one week. The winner was a 12-year-old Scottish girl.

Seen & Heard

In partnership with the UK Youth Parliament, the campaign undertook a nationwide search for examples of young people who had succeeded in making their voices heard. Fifteen case studies were used in the 'Seen & Heard' report. These were presented to government, leading to a meeting with Margaret Hodge, Minister of the UK Parliament for Children and Young People.

BIG Listen

The BIG Listen week was the focal point of the campaign's calendar. The aim during the week was to raise funds and awareness of the need to listen to young people. Activities and events during 2003 included:

- Speaking Clock initiative
- launch of the Listening Guide: based on the unique way that ChildLine trains its volunteers, the guide is for adults who want to communicate better with young people
- launch of the How To Make Yourself Heard Toolkit, which highlights easy and effective ways young people can make themselves heard
- BT Tower sponsored dash, reflecting urgency to raise cash: led by world record holder Colin Jackson, over 100 people took part in a timed sponsored dash up the 900 steps of BT Tower

▶

case study 18.6 (continued)

- Seen & Heard case study subjects met Margaret Hodge MP and demonstrated how government can better engage young people in society.

Evaluation and measurement
Fundraising

The campaign has raised over £2.5m for ChildLine since April 2002 – the largest amount the company has ever raised for one charity. Also BT has donated and/or facilitated gifts 'in kind' worth £4.1m. The overall strategic activities are helping ChildLine move closer to its goal of answering every call. Also an additional 10,000 calls are now being answered/switchboarded each week, reflecting a significant 19% increase.

Overall awareness

According to BT, the campaign has received over 1200 items of coverage and 212,249,000 WOTS (weighted opportunities to see), representing the highest positive net effect of all BT-related coverage across the company – 69% of the total.

Spontaneous recall of BT's association with ChildLine had risen to 47% by the end of 2003. It is the second highest recall of all BT's initiatives after *Comic Relief*, a televised event in the UK that has run since 1988.

Employee awareness

Research shows 85% of BT's 100,000 employees have unprompted awareness of the campaign and 83% say that the activity has improved their perception of BT.

Business benefits

BT Answer 1571 initiative In one month, take-up increased by 25%, raising over £203,000 for ChildLine. The service encourages callers to stay on the line and there is a retrieval cost, so revenue is increased.

Customer survey Over 1.3 million customers responded, representing the views of 3.25 million individual BT customers (approximately 2.5 people per household that uses BT), a response rate of nearly 7% (three times normal response). Findings allowed the company to target its marketing accurately, particularly for its internet broadband service. Twenty-two per cent of interviewees identified the association with ChildLine as a 'very strong positive influence' in persuading them to return the survey (GfK NOP Media (NOP)).

Speaking Clock There were over 2000 entries to be the speaking clock and the scheme raised £200,000. The theme 'it's time to listen to young people' secured coverage on every terrestrial TV channel, seven pieces of national radio, over 175 regional radio stations, 16 items of national print and a further 100 items in regional publications. Pieces even appeared in the *Seattle Times* and on National Public Radio (USA).

Creativity, what makes the campaign stand out?

Fundraising ideas focused on listening (e.g. customer survey/Speaking Clock) to raise funds for a listening campaign.

The initiative stands out because it is truly holistic in nature: as well as communication and public relations, BT helped ChildLine with fundraising, research activity, volunteering, training, advising on use of communications technology and development of the charity's long-term strategy. ChildLine is answering more calls as a result of the fundraising activity and strategic support. Through the public relations campaign, more children are being heard, particularly by government. The campaign also demonstrates how a company as large as BT, through a hard-hitting public relations campaign, can galvanise support behind a single cause internally and externally.

Quotes from BITC

Mervyn Pedelty, Chief Executive, Co-operative Financial Services, last year's winner and sponsor of this year's award, said: 'The BT "Am I Listening" campaign is a really good example of "joined up thinking". BT has mobilised its staff (including the personal enthusiasm of its chairman), its customers, its financial resources and, importantly, its technical know-how to transform the operations of a charity that is all about what BT does best – communications. The BT "Am I Listening" campaign with ChildLine is a truly inspirational example of excellence and a worthy winner of this prestigious Award.'

Sue Adkins, Director, Business in the Community, said: 'BT is a worthy winner of this year's Business in the Community Award for Excellence. The "Am I Listening" campaign is an holistic programme that has successfully been integrated into the whole of the organisation, engaging new and different aspects of the business as it develops. This strategic cause-related marketing partnership has achieved considerable impact on many levels for both BT and ChildLine and is an inspirational example.'

Other supportive quotes

Sir Christopher Bland, Chairman, BT: 'The BT "Am I Listening?" campaign is our most ambitious ever social marketing campaign. It aims to ensure that every young voice is heard, and it kicks off with the BT fundraising appeal for ChildLine and a new strategic partnership between ChildLine and BT.'

▶

case study 18.6 (continued)

Dr Carole Easton, Chief Executive Officer, Child-Line: 'BT's support for ChildLine has never been stronger and we're delighted with the results so far. The BT "Am I Listening?" campaign has raised awareness for ChildLine's need for funds, has raised a significant amount through fundraising and provided fantastic strategic support. By helping ChildLine move closer to its goal of answering every child's call, "Am I Listening?" is certainly making an impact – enabling more children's voices to be heard in the UK.'

Beth Courtier, Head of Charity Programmes, BT: 'This campaign is delivering on every level, especially PR, where awareness internally and externally has exceeded expectation – recall levels are already nine months ahead of schedule. The PR has been crucial in ensuring the success of the fundraising.

'The alignment between these two organisations is perfect; ChildLine is about communication and communication is BT's business. It is a great example of how CSR partnerships create mutual benefits as well as improving the society and communities that each operates in.'

The campaign has won the following:

- IPR Excellence Awards 2003 – Winner, Planning, Research and Evaluation
- IPR Excellence Awards 2004 – Winner, Corporate Social Responsibility
- IPRA Golden World Awards 2004 – Honourable Mention, Corporate Social Responsibility
- Business in the Community Excellence Awards 2004 – Winner, Cause-Related Marketing Award
- BT Marketing Awards 2004 Winner
- *PRWeek* Awards 2004 – Corporate Communications category

PICTURE 18.3   Aerial picture of the ChildLine launch at the London Eye (*source:* Beth Courtier)

Source: used with kind permission of BT and Harrison Cowley PR

Tactics

Some of these have already been discussed in the earlier section on 'corporate community involvement programmes' and are listed as follows: sponsorships; targeted donations; awards; hospitality; employee volunteering; use of facilities (loan of equipment); training/seminars; secondments (staff). (See Case study 18.6.)

Evaluating community programmes

Community involvement programmes can be difficult to measure in terms of quantifiable data, however this does not mean that the activities are unmeasurable. The following performance indicators can be used as means of measuring the programme's achievements:

- publicity achieved
- employee feedback
- value for money
- creativity
- comparable external benchmark
- 'thank you' letters and appreciation
- measured opinion-former perceptions
- internal and external communications audit results.

The BT 'Am I Listening?' campaign (Case study 18.6) illustrates a range of evaluation and measurement techniques in practice.

Measuring community involvement

David Davies, Chairman of Johnson Matthey plc said in that company's 1995 annual statement:

FIGURE 18.2 Elements of a successful community involvement programme (*source*: adapted from BITC 2005)

Good corporate citizenship provides tangible benefits in many ways. It provides links with the community in which we operate and community projects can provide important training and experience to employees. The application of management skills to community projects and wider environmental initiatives is beneficial to the business and community alike.

In the USA it is estimated that 10% of stock market investments are graded on ethical grounds and as such a positive ethical image is important to managers. A study by Alperson (1996) for the Conference Board of America into 463 US companies identified four new trends in corporate-giving strategies that demonstrate their integration into mainstream business policy:

- programmes narrowly focused and aligned to business goals
- giving is moving towards investment yielding a measurable return
- image enhancement and employee loyalty are emerging as the value added elements of programmes

- link between corporate-giving strategies and customer concerns is strengthening.

An increasingly popular method of measuring ethical performance is through social audits, which assess business policy on issues ranging from whether suppliers worked in a manner consistent with the firm's ethical policy to employee and customer attitudes. Allied Dunbar and the Body Shop in the UK have both recently gone through the audit process using outside auditors and published the results. Other companies interested in this approach are Ben and Jerry's, the US ice-cream firm, and BT in the UK.

Key factors to success of community involvement programmes

There a number of key factors that determine the success of a programme, the key one of which is the acceptance of the strategy by board directors and senior management. Without their endorsement the programme and individual initiatives will suffer from unnecessary scrutiny beyond the stated measurement criteria that should be put in place. Factors that may influence the success of such a programme include:

- top management support
- line management understanding and support
- successful internal and external communication
- central coordinator of activities
- resources to meet necessary costs
- employee owned
- recognition
- partnership with community organisations
- modest beginnings
- monitoring and evaluation.

Figure 18.2 highlights the interlinking of three key areas for a successful community involvement programme. The three areas are the company, the community and the employees. (See Case study 18.7 and Activity 18.5 on p. 374.)

(See Case study 18.7 and Activity 18.5 on p. 374.)

case study 18.7

The Co-operative Bank

The Co-operative Bank was founded in 1872 to support the aims of the cooperative movement in the UK, which first started in Rochdale, in the north of England, in the middle of the nineteenth century. The cooperative movement's strength in the UK has traditionally been in grocery retailing and wholesaling but the bank has also been successful. One could argue that this success has been supported by the bank's strategic decision to re-affirm its commitment to cooperative values and to define its ethical

▶

case study 18.7 (continued)

position with regard to its customers and wider stakeholders.

Evolution of the corporate strategy
Mission statement

In 1988 the company first published its mission statement, which, at the time, could have been perceived as a commercial risk due to the strong right-of-centre political power balance of Margaret Thatcher's Conservative government. This government was also a great influence on business policy and practice and at the time the economy was going through a boom. Business focus was on maintaining and enhancing shareholder value during an era of aggressive takeovers, mergers and acquisitions, together with privatisation of national utilities. Consequently, in business, there was no significant focus on ethical and societal issues. The Co-operative Bank's decision did prove to be significant and helped differentiate it from most of its competitors. (Harvard business professor, Michael Porter, has written about the significance of such difficult 'choices' in developing business strategies but also emphasised how they can be key to business success.)

Ethical policy

A second significant date for the bank was 1992 when it published its first ethical policy, developed in consultation with its customers. The policy aims to set out when and whether the bank will invest its money and where it will not.

Co-operative Bank's ethical policy

Following extensive consultation with our customers, with regard to how their money should and should not be invested, the bank's position is that:

It will not invest in or supply financial services to any regime or organisation which oppresses the human spirit, takes away the rights of individuals or manufacturers any instrument of torture.

It will not finance or in any way facilitate the manufacture or sale of weapons to any country which has an oppressive regime.

It will actively seek and support the business of organisations which promote the concept of 'Fair Trade' i.e. trade which regards the welfare and interest of local communities.

It will encourage business customers to take a proactive stance on the environmental impact of their own activities, and will invest in companies and organisations that avoid repeated damage of the environment.

It will actively seek out individuals, commercial enterprises and non-commercial organisations which have a complementary ethical stance.

It will welcome suppliers whose activities are compatible with its ethical policy.

It will not speculate against the pound using either its own money or that of its customers. It believes it is inappropriate for a British clearing bank to speculate against the British currency and the British economy using deposits provided by their British customers and at the expense of the British taxpayer.

It will try to ensure its financial services are not exploited for the purposes of money laundering, drug trafficking or tax evasion by the continued application and development of its successful internal monitoring and control procedures.

It will not provide financial services to tobacco product manufacturers.

It will not invest in any business involved in animal experimentation for cosmetic purposes.

It will not support any person or company using exploitative factory farming methods.

It will not engage in business with any farm or other organisation engaged in the production of animal fur.

It will not support any organisation involved in blood sports, which involve the use of animals or birds to catch, fight or kill each other, for example fox hunting and hare coursing.

In addition, there may be occasions when the bank makes decisions on specific business involving ethical issues not included in this policy. We will regularly reappraise customers' views on these and other issues and develop our ethical stance accordingly.

Ecological mission statement

This statement was followed in 1996 by an ecological mission statement, which acknowledges that all areas of human activity, including business, are dependent on the natural world for their well-being.

Co-operative Bank's ecological mission statement

We, The Co-operative Bank, will continue to develop our business taking into account the impact our activities have on the environment and society at large. The nature of our activities are such that our indirect impact, by being selective in terms of the provision of finance and banking arrangements, is more ecologically significant than the direct impact of our trading operations.

However, we undertake to continually assess all our activities and implement a programme of ecological improvement based on the pursuit of the following four scientific principles:

▶

case study 18.7 (continued)

Nature cannot withstand a progressive build-up of waste derived from the Earth's crust.

Nature cannot withstand a progressive build-up of society's waste, particularly artificial persistent substances which it cannot degrade into harmless materials.

The productive area of nature must not be diminished in quality (diversity) or quantity (volume) and must be enabled to grow.

Society must utilise energy and resources in a sustainable, equitable and efficient manner.

We consider that the pursuit of these principles constitutes a path of ecological excellence and will secure future prosperity for society by sustainable economic activity.

The Co-operative Bank will not only pursue the above path itself, but endeavour to help and encourage all its Partners to do likewise.

We will aim to achieve this by:

Financial Services

Encouraging business customers to take a pro-active stance on the environmental impact of their own activities, and investing in companies and organisations that avoid repeated damage of the environment (as stated in our ethical policy).

Management Systems

Assessing our ecological impact, setting ourselves clear targets, formulating an action plan and monitoring how we meet them, and publishing the results.

Purchasing and Outsourcing

Welcoming suppliers whose activities are compatible with both our ethical policy and ecological mission statement, and working in partnership with them to improve our collective performance.

Support

Supporting ecological projects and developing partnerships with businesses and organisations whose direct and indirect output contributes to a sustainable society.

Legislation

Adhering to environmental laws, directives and guidelines while continually improving upon our own contribution to a sustainable society.

Partnerships (stakeholders)

The bank also developed a partnership framework, which is similar to the stakeholder concept discussed in Chapter 12 and is based on the writings of one of the Rochdale Pioneers of the cooperative movement, Robert Owen. The Co-operative Bank believes, as did Owen, that balanced, long-term relationships with these partners is key to the longevity and business success of the bank. The key partnership framework for the Co-operative Bank is detailed in Figure 18.3.

On its launch in 1996 the bank's partnership approach described its interaction and support for these groups as follows.

Society

From the ecological mission statement came an initiative by the bank to develop the Co-operative Bank National Centre for Business and Ecology. The centre draws on the expertise of four Greater Manchester-based universities. Affinity cards contribute to charities including the RSPB (Royal Society for the Protection of Birds), Oxfam, Amnesty International, Help the Aged, Children's Aid Direct.

Community

Investments are wide ranging, including support for public, private and voluntary initiatives in the Manchester area where the bank's head office is based as well as supporting community groups in disadvantaged areas.

Suppliers and partners

The bank is a member of the Confederation of British Industry's (CBI) prompt payment scheme. It also cites examples of successful long-term contracts between itself and suppliers such as UNISYS Payment Services Limited, IBM and other smaller contractors involved in maintenance, cleaning and design services.

Staff and families

Homeworking initiatives have been explored with equipment installed at the employee's home; career breaks are supported; staff training is encouraged, including NVQs (national vocational qualifications); Investors in People has been achieved by the Bank, an award for organisations judged to provide their staff with excellent training and development opportunities.

Customers

Progression and use of technology such as 24-hour banking; interactive home banking; mobile phone banking; internet access, as well as service developments such as affinity Visa cards, available to support individual schools and hospices.

Shareholders

The sole equity shareholder of the bank is the Co-operative Group. This society shares the bank's commitments on ethical and environmental issues.

case study 18.7 (continued)

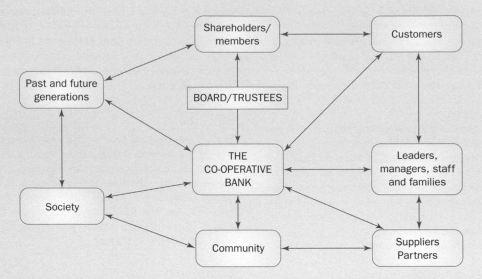

FIGURE 18.3   Seven partnership networks for the Co-operative Bank (*source:* Co-operative Bank Ethical Policy, Co-operative Bank internal publication)

Past and future generations

Links the bank back into its cooperative movement roots. The movement has been going for over 150 years and has always focused on the community in which a business operates.

Business benefits

The Co-operative Bank has seen its customer base grow in both the personal and business banking sectors. In the five years between 1992 and 1996 the bank saw profits before taxation rise from approximately £9m to £54.5m. At the end of 1996 the bank had total assets worth £4.5bn. Satisfaction levels of customers when compared with other banks' customers in the UK were also positive, with 94% of Co-operative Bank customers satisfied with service compared with other banks at 89%, and this compared with 73% of the Co-operative's customers being very satisfied with 51% as an average for other banks (Source: MORI Financial Services Survey 1996).

Source: Used with kind permission of the Co-operative Bank from its Ethical Policy and Strength in Numbers documents

See also Activity 18.5.

See also Activity 18.5.

activity 18.5

Responding to criticism of ethical policy

As an executive for the Co-operative Bank, how would you respond to criticism that your ethical policy was described as a 'marketing initiative'?

How would you reply to critics who claim that the bank's initiatives are trivialising ethical debates in business practice?

Feedback

■ Write down the reasons why the bank may or may not replace the ethical policy 'initiative' next year.

■ Can you name other banks with an ethical banking policy? How do they compare to the Co-operative Bank?

■ In 1996 the Co-operative Bank stated its ecological mission statement. Think about contemporary issues that might affect the corporate strategy of an organisation involved in the banking sector today.

■ Why do you think the bank might have made a risky strategic decision in 1988 when it decided to publish its mission statement?

Summary

This chapter has attempted to bring to life some of the principles about the role organisations play in their society(ies) introduced in Chapter 6 by interpreting and applying them through current or recent case studies. A range of different examples has demonstrated that organisations worldwide are questioning and addressing their role in the societies in which they operate. This is being done in a variety of different ways; sometimes through actions that have clear links to corporate philosophies and strategies (the Co-operative Bank, Case study 18.7) and in other examples where the action has a clear business benefit and provides rewards for both parties. Examples of this type of interpretation of the community engagement strategy are with cause-related marketing (Mini cases 18.2–18.4 and the Andrex and Cooperative Bank case studies, 18.3 and 18.4).

Community involvement is today a key component of many organisations' strategic thinking. Corporate social responsibility and the other terms used to describe this type of activity are boardroom buzzwords. Yet debate still rages (Crook 2005) on its role and purpose, as Chapter 6 explored. Your role as students and practitioners is to understand why organisations get involved with their stakeholder communities and to continue to develop the debate.

Bibliography

Alperson, M. (1996). 'Conference Board of America' in Business in the Community Annual Report 1996: 5. London: Business in the Community.

BITC (Business in the Community) (1996). 'Annual Report'. London: Business in the Community.

BITC (Business in the Community) (2000). 'Profitable Partnership Report'. London: Business in the Community.

BITC (Business in the Community) (2005). 'Annual Report'. www.bitc.org.uk, accessed 18 February 2005.

BT (1996). 'Community Partnership Programme: annual review'. London: BT.

Cadbury, D. (1996). cited in 'Business in the Community Annual Report' 1996: 25. London: Business in the Community.

Carroll, A. (1991). 'The pyramid of corporate social responsibility'. *Business Horizons* July–August.

Cone Roper (1997). *Cause-Related Marketing Trends Report*. London: Cone Roper.

Crook, C. (2005). 'The good company: A survey of corporate social responsibility'. *The Economist* 22 January.

CSR Europe (Corporate Social Responsibility Europe) (2002). 'About us'. www.csreurope.org, accessed 19 October 2004.

Davies, D. (1995). *First Forum*. 59. London: First magazine Ltd.

Demetrius, K. and P. Hughes (2004). 'Publics or stakeholders? Performing social responsibility through stakeholder software'. *Asia Pacific Public Relations Journal* **5** (2).

Hart, N. (1995). *Effective Corporate Relations*. Maidenhead: McGraw-Hill.

Klein, N. (2000). *No Logo: Taking aim at the brand bullies*. London: Flamingo.

MORI (1996). 'Financial services survey'. London: MORI.

Research International (1995). 'Business in the Community'. www.bitc.org.uk

Research International (1997). 'Consumer Survey: The Winning Game'. London: Business in the Community.

Schwartz, P. and B. Gibb (1999). *When Good Companies Do Bad Things: Responsibility and risk in an age of globalization*. New York: John Wiley & Sons.

Smith, A. (1997). 'BT seeks to reassure caring consumers'. *Financial Times* 13 January.

Thomson, S. (2000). *The Social Democratic Dilemma: Ideology, governance and globalization*. London: Macmillan.

Websites

Business in the Community: www.bitc.org.uk

Business for Social Responsibility: www.bsr.org

Cause-Related Business Campaign: www.crm.org.uk

CSR Europe: www.csreurope.org

For glossary definitions relevant to this chapter, visit the **selected glossary** feature on the website at: www.pearsoned.co.uk/tench

CHAPTER 19

Issues management

By the end of this chapter you should be able to:

- define and describe the concept of issues management
- identify the key theories and principles of issues management
- analyse the national, regional and global context in which issues emerge and the forces that shape and reshape their impact on people, governments, institutions and business
- recognise the characteristics of issues that ignite public interest and bring about changes in behaviour, public policy and corporate or product platforms
- recognise the relevance of stakeholder relations, thought leadership and opinion-former programmes as core components of an issues management strategy
- develop a practical appreciation of issues management by relating concepts, theories and principles to real-life cases and scenario planning.

Structure

- Issues management: defining the field
- Context of issues management
- Action planning: a framework for managing issues

Introduction

Cigarette smoking, global warming, the future of the rain forests, obesity, healthcare costs, DNA, stem cell research, waste management, the trade in endangered species, intensive farming, child labour: these are just a few of the subjects that have influenced the way in which business operates over the past 30 years. They all began as debates and/or research studies among scientists, technologists, economists, politicians and/or intellectual 'think-tanks'. They then entered the public domain via special interest groups, the media and, increasingly, the internet. Once there, they triggered a cascade of questions from a variety of stakeholders who had never been involved in the debate before, but who were now intensely engaged in monitoring or influencing the outcome. This multi-stakeholder engagement is at the core of twenty-first century issues management.

Issues management practice is the 'identification, monitoring, and analysis of trends in key publics' opinions that can mature into public policy and regulatory or legislative constraint of the private sector' (Heath 1997: 6). This chapter argues that the successful issues manager recognises when an issue has changed or has the power to change the context in which business operates; is able to pinpoint a specific threat or opportunity to a specific industry, company or product, in a specific part of the world at a specific point in time; and can execute a series of actions to do something about it while remaining vigilant for any shifts in interpretation that need new thinking.

This chapter begins by reviewing the literature on issues management. The rest of the chapter will be organised around issues management principles based on an understanding of the 'tipping point': when an issue in an organisation's external environment becomes a concern for public policy. Key steps are provided showing how an organisation can influence the ensuing public debate and these are illustrated with mini case studies.

Issues management: defining the field

Origins of issues management

Writing from a US perspective, Heath (1997) observes that issues management arose from the need for private business to protect itself against public criticism and legislation. While the activities and policies of big business had been of public concern since the nineteenth century, it was not until the 1960s that widespread socio-political concerns about the state of the planet, and the effects of consumerism, began to gain momentum. A possible turning point was the publication of Rachel Carson's *Silent Spring* in 1962, which highlighted the potential side effects of insecticides and herbicides on the food chain. Corporations, meanwhile, were widely criticised for being untrustworthy, irresponsible and wasteful, giving rise to both consumer and environmental pressure groups. The US lawyer and politician Ralph Nader played a key role in championing the rights of consumers against manufacturers, following some landmark court cases against automobile makers in the 1960s. (See Box 19.1.)

Defining issues management

Robert L. Heath, one of the leading scholars in the field of issues management, observes that issues management has been defined in a number of ways according to the particular preference and prejudice of those defining it. One of the first exponents of issues management, Howard Chase (1982: 1), first used the term in the mid-1970s, describing it thus:

Issues management is the capacity to understand, mobilize, coordinate and direct all strategies and policy planning functions, and all public affairs/public relations skills, toward achievement of one objective: meaningful participation in creation of public policy that affects personal and institutional destiny.

Here, issues management is conceived as a strategic planning function that encompasses both public affairs and public relations skills in influencing public policy in regard to institutions or organisations.

Academic debates continue as to whether issues management is a sub-function of public relations or an umbrella term that incorporates it (Heath 1997). Grunig and Repper (1992) argue that the issues management function is part of strategic planning as well as public relations and tends to be synonymous with strategic public relations. Heath (1997) identifies four functions of issues management. These are to:

- anticipate and analyse issues
- develop organisational positions on issues
- identify key publics whose support is vital to the public policy issue
- identify desired behaviours of key publics. (See Think about 19.1.)

---

box 19.1   **The environment – how one issue developed**

From the 1970s onwards, a 'macro' issue called 'the environment' became a series of 'micro' issues under a single banner known as the green movement. It gave rise to an endless number of debates in the consuming countries of the developed world, crossed oceans to the producing countries of the developing world, went through a number of cultural filters and eventually prompted a global reaction.

The repercussions are still being felt today in, for example, the sort of timber we buy, the amount of waste we recycle, the size of car we buy, the public transport we choose, the wildlife we protect, the dolphin-friendly tuna that supermarkets sell, the fish stocks we preserve, the energy-efficient household appliances we manufacture, the way we control oil and gas exploration, the use of unleaded petrol, the way we farm, the way we manage exports, the amount of packaging we use, the investment activity of the World Bank, the use of chemicals, and so on.

The growing evidence of damage to the ozone level and the effects of 'global warming' are causing governments around the world to consider how to – or whether to – change their policies and practices.

(See the 'Surfers against sewage' case study in Chapter 29, which illustrates how an environmental issue became a campaign.)

Relationship with crisis management

Howard Chase also referred to issues management as the highest form of sound management when applied to institutional survival (quoted in Seitel 1989). This leads to a debate about its relationship to crisis management. There is clearly a connection, but the two specialisms are not the same.

Regester and Larkin (1997), in their issues lifecycle, suggest that issues increase in intensity through three phases (*potential*, *emerging* and *current*), reach maximum intensity in the fourth phase, *crisis*, and depressurise dramatically in the final phase, *dormant*, when they are finally resolved. This seems to imply that, unmanaged, all issues eventually turn into crises and do not necessarily involve a high degree of pressure until they do. Experienced issues managers might well disagree with that interpretation.

Gaunt and Ollenburger (1995) and Seitel (1989) argue that crisis management is about solving a problem the moment it occurs and after it has become publicly known and is therefore *reactive*; issues management, contrariwise, involves pre-crisis planning, communicating openly and anticipating potential threats that a company is facing and is therefore *proactive*. This distinction suggests that issues management cannot be reactive, an idea that is unsustainable in, say, the case of a new and unidentified risk that had never been suspected or even considered a possibility. The emergence of a new variant of Creutzfeldt-Jakob Disease (CJD) in humans as 'mad cow' disease (Bovine Spongiform Encephalopathy or BSE) that crossed the species barrier is an example. It is likely that most crisis managers would describe the proactive definition given earlier of issues management more accurately as pre-emptive crisis management.

The difference between the two specialisms is probably less to do with the style of response than with the situation: crisis management is about dealing with the impact of a sudden adverse event that fractures the core of a company's operation and represents an immediate threat to its ability to stay in business; issues management is about dealing with an evolving public policy debate that, over time, shapes the way in which a company is permitted to operate. Aircraft crashes, their cause and the way victims are treated are *crises*; the size of aeroplanes, the location and expansion of airports and the amount of available air space are *issues*.

Crisis management tends to be about the now and is largely tactical; issues management tends to be about the future and, as we have seen from earlier discussions, is largely strategic. Traverse-Healy (1995) talks about the importance of thinking ahead as a means of predicting what issues may influence and affect companies.

It is, of course, true that a crisis can trigger a change in public policy. At the point that the shift or change happens, the rules of the game also change. It is no longer about reacting and responding, but about shaping the future by helping to create, in the words of Chase, 'public policy that affects personal and institutional destiny'. (See Think about 19.2.)

Context of issues management

The 'tipping point'

If Howard Chase is right – and there is plenty of evidence to suggest he is – issues managers need to understand and manage the context in which destinies change, often due to forces beyond the immediate control of the organisations involved.

Public health is probably the next big issue and appears to be echoing the way green issues began to make things happen three decades ago. The public health issue is discussed in detail towards the end of this chapter. For now, students of issues management should explore the history of environmental activism to search for the point at which 'the reasonable person' was persuaded to care enough to do something and acted in a way that created enough momentum for others to follow.

This momentum is called the '*tipping point*' (Gladwell 2000): the moment when a debate that has been slowly evolving for many years among the scientific, medical, technical and/or academic communities enters the public domain via the media, adopts a political and social agenda and prompts a fundamental shift in government thinking. Such a shift, in turn, leads to legislative and regulatory change that reshapes the business landscape.

It is important to recognise that the tipping point does not create the debate. It may simplify it, give it some meaning and apply an emotional charge that fires the public's imagination, but it is not the trigger. That comes much earlier and it is the core role of an issues manager to know when an issue has begun to develop and where it is heading.

Definition: The '*tipping point*' refers to the moment when a debate which has been evolving enters the public domain and ultimately leads to change. This phrase has emerged from an influential book (Gladwell 2000).

A simplified model for monitoring emerging issues is based on the idea that all issues tend to follow the same six-phase evolutionary sequence. Issues often begin with a study, prompted by the natural desire of scientists and academics to research areas of uncertainty (the *initiation* phase). As the research continues and findings are published, other experts, typically from industry groups, government and specialist *non-governmental organisations (NGOs)* with a particular interest in the subject, study the data and add their own opinions (the *interpretation* phase). At some point, this sharing of data and interpretation between specialists begins to coalesce around a specific opportunity or threat about which 'something must be done'. This is especially true when people feel they are being exposed to a risk over which they have no control and with which they are unfamiliar. For example, the perceived risks from nuclear facilities, smoking, chemical manufacturing plants and chemical ingredients in everyday products have been studied by psychologists and behavioural specialists in Europe and the USA (e.g. see Slovic 2000). This list is likely to increase as a result of freedom of information legislation, increased transparency and global communications.

Definition: *Non-governmental organisations* (NGOs) are groups without governmental affiliation that have a particular interest in a subject. Examples are organisations such as charities and campaign groups.

If an NGO or a media commentator can articulate a clear actual or perceived threat, identify a victim and expose a possible culprit (the *implication* phase), negative news coverage and/or a public campaign

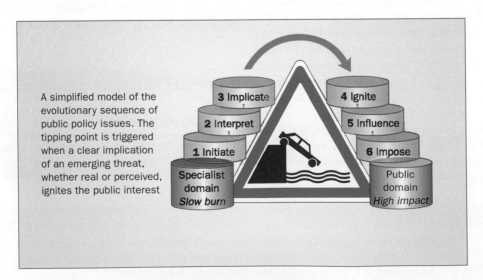

A simplified model of the evolutionary sequence of public policy issues. The tipping point is triggered when a clear implication of an emerging threat, whether real or perceived, ignites the public interest

3 Implicate
4 Ignite
2 Interpret
5 Influence
1 Initiate
6 Impose
Specialist domain
Slow burn
Public domain
High impact

FIGURE 19.1   Simplified model of the evolutionary sequence of public policy issues

becomes a high probability. The tipping point is reached, public interest is fired (the *ignition* phase), the lobbying of policy makers begins (the *influencing* phase) and regulations are introduced (the *imposition* phase). (See Figure 19.1 and Box 19.2.)

The effect of context on issue development

This model tends to confirm what Howard Chase seems to imply in his use of the terms 'institutional

---

The tipping point in action: GM crops

The following outlines the history of European opposition to the introduction of genetically modified (GM) crops:

■ Scientists initiate research on how to manipulate genes.
■ Agricultural specialists learn how to use genes to make plants pest resistant.
■ A US company develops a seed that is resistant to its brand-name pesticide which, they say, will allow farmers to be more efficient in their use of chemicals in the field.
■ Activists say the science is unproven and, in any case, consumers have the right to choose whether their food is from GM crops or not.
■ The public debate ignites around the issues of choice and the environmental risks involved in cross-pollinating GM and non-GM crops.
■ The EU applies the precautionary principle and decides it cannot allow the importation of GM crops until it has created an appropriate regulatory regime.

Key learning point: If the debate is scientific (genetic modification) and the tipping point is political (freedom to choose) then the issue may become emotive. Public concerns are legitimate and must be addressed as part of a long-term goal to create trust. A rational debate about the use of a scientific or medical procedure that makes people anxious cannot take place until a climate of trust has been properly established.

PICTURE 19.1   Activist groups have been raising questions about the dangers of GM crops cross-pollinating to non-GM crops. (*Source:* Nick Cobbing/Rex.)

survival' and 'institutional destiny' (see earlier references): issues management is more about the pace and extent of change than about the fact of change. With that in mind, two questions must be asked, the answers to which will dictate the speed at which an issue moves and the amount of difference it is likely to make over time. The first concerns the political, social, economic and cultural context; the second concerns who, or what, is the dominant power broker making something happen?

Context explains why some issues, such as the debate over whether mobile telephones affect the brain, have little impact on behaviour and sales, while others, such as the debate over genetically modified crops (GMO), are capable of polarising opinion. This happened: with GMO to the point where the EU introduced a de facto moratorium (un-negotiated suspension) on the importation or growing of GMO-derived crops in 1998 until suitable regulations could be put in place; where Argentina embraced the technology while its neighbour Brazil did not; where the USA asked the World Trade Organisation (WTO) in 2003 to investigate the effect of the EU position on US/Europe trade; and where some UK supermarkets removed GMO products from their shelves in the wake of consumer fears over alleged long-term risks to health.

It also explains why some issues, such as the use of animals in medical research, are primarily of interest to one country (in this case, the UK) while others, such as those triggered by allegations of chemically induced risk, cross-national borders and continents within the space of a day. And it explains why, for example, the employment of children is attacked by the USA and some European commentators as child exploitation (i.e. cheap labour) but condoned by some Asian countries as child protection (i.e. alternatives to working are likely to be worse).

Power, whether elected, appointed or self-styled, is rooted in coalitions. A simplified view of the author is that the world is split into three natural, stable, self-regulating and largely introspective coalitions, each one of which is populated by stakeholders who share similar visions, beliefs and behaviours:

- for-profit coalition (business, industry groups)
- not-for-profit coalition (NGOs, voluntary sector, special interest groups, academia, independent experts, media commentators)
- government coalition (ministers, legislators, regulators).

Issues tend to emerge from players in one of these coalitions and will typically find 'common cause' with players in a second coalition before players in the third coalition become intimately involved or even aware. If we examine the history of relationships between these coalitions, we find that until the 1970s, the government coalition and the for-profit coalition tended to operate as close allies.

It was a relationship between the so-called '*first estate*' and the '*second estate*' that came under increasing criticism from trade unions and other groups on the 'outside', most notably students who rioted in Paris in 1968. The not-for-profit coalition, often now seen as representing the '*third estate*', was barely recognised.

> **Definitions:** Within a monarchy, '*first estate*' traditionally referred to the church; '*second estate*' traditionally referred to the nobility; and the '*third estate*' traditionally referred to the common people.

The environmental debate changed all that. Over time, the not-for-profit coalition led the way, first by attacking and then by working with the for-profit coalition on solutions that the government coalition had seemed powerless to create and impose.

Now, in the first decade of the twenty-first century, the wheel seems to be turning again as the not-for-profit coalition and the government coalition unite to build a framework of regulations and legislation to control what they regard as the excesses of some business. Examples of this partnership in action are the emerging rules on corporate governance, exemplified by the Sarbanes-Oxley legislation in the USA (2002) and the EU's 8th Directive on company law (2005) and voluntary codes of business practice covering the treatment of workers by factories in Asia supplying western companies.

The ideal issue management programme will strive to create common cause among stakeholders in all three coalitions. The World Health Organisation (WHO) is certainly attempting to do that in using a multi-stakeholder approach as part of its global strategy on diet, physical activity and health (see health example later in the chapter, p. 388. See also Activity 19.1 and Box 19.3).

activity 19.1

Influencing public policy

Go back to some of the examples listed earlier (GM crops, nuclear power, childhood obesity) and try to identify the players involved and the way in which they drove the issue past its tipping point and into a public policy result. The internet is probably the best place to start your search. It is a great source of information and insight on issues. For example, do a search on 'Jamie's school dinners' and see what story unfolds.

Debating an issue: technology

Here are some questions that you could use to get below the surface of a debate. Consider the ethical issues raised by these questions:

■ How much hard scientific evidence is there that mobile telephones have an effect on the brain? How do you think people balance risk/benefit when the risk is not yet obvious but the benefit is clear?
■ How much personal control do you have over your use of your mobile telephone and how does that affect your attitude to risk?
■ Conversely, how much control do you have over the technology used to produce what you eat?
■ How does that affect your attitude to production methods when there is no perceived benefit in terms of price?
■ Why should a part of the world that has no experience of widespread hunger prevent the use of a technology that might help farmers in parts of the world that face regular famines?

Feedback
These sorts of question can tie up a company in an intellectual debate for weeks, months or even years. They are critical to a proper analysis of an issue. However, a time limit has to be set (in days) to work through a process that will help define a plan of action rather than a subject for endless discussion. The 'tipping point' is no respecter of time.

Action planning: a framework for managing issues

Woody Allen once said: 'The world is run by the people who turn up' and these words encapsulate the reality of modern business: the outside world knows your name, understands your business and thinks it has the answer to everything. It doesn't, but an issues manager needs to start on the outside looking in, not the inside looking out.

The management framework outlined in Box 19.4 is not the complete answer, but it provides a useful template for a more detailed examination of issues that are already in the public domain. Given that it is highly unlikely that any organisation would discuss the detail of its issue management strategy and action in a public forum, this framework helps to identify a series of defining moments in the evolution of selected issues.

The framework is broken down into two sections that are described on the following pages with examples. The first section covers Steps 1 to 5, which are primarily concerned with thinking and planning; the second section covers Steps 6 to 10, which are centred on activity. Each step includes a commentary that, combined with personal experience, key learning from elsewhere in this book, regular study of the media and organised discussion groups, will help the reader to fill in the background.

Step-by-step issues management framework

Framework section 1: thinking and planning
1 Get focused.
2 List key players.
3 Assess momentum.
4 Check reality.
5 Assess pace.

Framework section 2: action
6 Clarify the part you want to play.
7 Be realistic.
8 Build case.
9 Commit action.
10 Make it make sense.

Framework section 1: thinking and planning

Step 1 **Get focused**

The issue as defined by the outside world is the issue that needs to be managed. Clarity can be achieved by the answers to two key questions: who, or what, put it on the public agenda? What are the best-case and worst-case outcomes of the issue as currently defined?

The key here is the tipping point. For example, the notion of wellness, as opposed to illness, has been around the corridors of power in various countries for many years, partly because of the truism that prevention is better than cure and partly because state-funded healthcare is finding it prohibitively expensive to cover the cost of disease-and-treatment systems.

The need for improved nutrition as a key feature of disease prevention is being driven by the WHO with the help of the Food and Agriculture Organisation (FAO), and is best illustrated by the campaign to increase intake of fruit and vegetables launched in 2003 (go to www.who.int/en/ and search for the WHO global strategy on diet, physical activity and health). Yet nothing really fired the public imagination until obesity became an integral part of the equation. The tipping point was when the office of the US Surgeon-General put a figure on the problem, and declared in a statement prepared by a sub-committee of the US House of Representatives in 2003 that the total annual cost of obesity was $117 billion, only slightly less than the $157 billion economic toll assigned to smoking (US Department of Health and Human Services news release, 2004).

When that happened, 'something had to be done'. Eating habits had to change . . . fast food companies had to rethink their menu options . . . Schools had to increase physical activity . . . Companies had to consider providing fitness rooms for staff . . . Food manufacturers faced voluntary or mandatory restrictions on the amount of salt and sugar in their products . . . Detailed product labelling of both ingredients and countries of origin emerged as practical illustrations of transparency and openness. (See Activity 19.2.)

---

activity 19.2

Context and perspective on issues

Compare and contrast two websites: www.mcdonalds.com and www.mcspotlight.org. What are your key findings?

Step 2 · List key players

Identify people and organisations who are likely to have an informed view on the issue as currently defined. They should be clustered on the basis (a) of their 'membership' of the three natural coalitions summarised earlier, and (b) of the extent to which the definition of the issue makes it directly relevant to their day-to-day interests or responsibilities.

The key learning point here is that best-case and worst-case planning is not about the issue, but about the *impact*. If the US Surgeon-General says obesity is an issue that needs to be addressed, it will be addressed. The symbol has been identified and all that matters from this point on is who, or what, is seen as part of the problem and part of the solution; that is, where the issue manifests itself and where it has a direct impact.

This, in essence, is an exercise in: locating opinion leaders and decision makers; making some assumptions about their motivations and, therefore, their likely behaviours; and deciding where they fit in relation to the tipping point and the six-phase evolutionary sequence summarised earlier in this chapter.

While a list such as this is necessarily based on generalisations, it is important for issues managers to distinguish between a person and an institution with a broad agenda (e.g. a doctor in general practice, a consumer organisation or a prime minister), and a person and an institution with a narrow agenda (e.g. a heart surgeon, an environmental activist group or a government minister with specific responsibilities). Their interest, knowledge, experience, credibility and motivations – and, as result, their impact – will be different. The obesity debate, for example, could produce initial assessment (which would need to be fully validated by research) as shown in Table 19.1.

An instant diagnosis of this table identifies three key points:

1. The potential for creating common cause (bringing players together) is high.
2. As a result of the first point, the development of a multi-stakeholder programme should be straightforward.
3. Existing shared interest across all three natural coalitions can be mobilised to facilitate agreement on a broad public policy agenda.

A stakeholder analysis, using Johnson and Scholes' power/interest matrix, could also be conducted at this point (see Chapter 10).

The way in which this thinking is used in an issues management programme is illustrated in some detail under Step 8 (Build case) of this framework, again using obesity as the example.

Brent Spar – the oil installation that was to be dumped in the North Sea by Shell until Greenpeace campaigned against it – is probably one of the best examples of how a single decision can give an issue momentum (see case studies in Chapters 12 and 18). The Brent Spar case study demonstrates how the pace of an issue is often set by the way in which it is

TABLE 19.1   Opinion leaders and decision makers in the obesity debate

Player	Natural coalition	Assumed motivation
Doctors in general practice	Not-for-profit	Improved patient health
Diabetes experts	Not-for-profit	Disease reduction
Consumer group	Not-for-profit	Informed consumers
Nutrition associations	Not-for-profit	Healthier eating/lifestyles
Government leadership	Government	Healthier citizens
Health ministry	Government	Disease prevention
Food producers	For-profit	Innovative, saleable products
Food retailers	For-profit	Sustainable customer base
Celebrity chefs	For-profit	Personal positioning

Step 3   Assess momentum

Be aware of what makes a good target. Three questions can help organisations assess whether an issue that is in the public domain, or is about to enter the public domain, is heading in their direction:

- Is the business a symbol (e.g. of junk food) or is actual activity under threat?
- Does the issue as currently defined resonate with other debates (e.g. obesity–junk food– physical activity–cosmetic surgery)?
- Do the forces that drive the issue have the authority to engage and maintain the public interest?

defined – and, therefore, what it symbolises – as it enters the public domain (see Step 3). However, the decision to dispose of Brent Spar at sea rather than on land is regarded by some specialist commentators as the more environmentally friendly option. It did not matter: once emotions were running high and the

Step 4   Check reality

Make sure there is a real and measurable threat or opportunity. Again, three questions can be used to help organisations to make a decision:

- Is the issue as defined favourable or unfavourable to our business plan?
- Why should we become directly involved?
- Can the issue be redefined or reframed?

issue was on the move with an identifiable victim (marine life) and a likely culprit (Shell) in plain sight, the chance for rational debate had gone and the voices of support were drowned out. They were heard only when the decision on Brent Spar had been reversed and when the media frenzy had died away. (See Think about 19.3, overleaf.)

The challenge is whether you can 'make the case' or argument for the reality *as you see it* of any given situation. Are aeroplanes about increasing pollution or shrinking the world? Are disposable nappies (diapers) about convenience or waste mountains? Is genetic manipulation about playing God or, in the case of GM seeds, feeding the world? Are cosmetics about feeling and looking good or the ingredients used to make them? Is driving a car about convenience and enjoyment or damaging the environment? Is this chapter about manipulating people or shaping opinion? (See Think about 19.4, overleaf.)

These arguments naturally raise the whole question of morals and ethics and whether the issue manager, as a professional communicator, is using the power of persuasion to win a specious argument (see also Chapter 15).

Issues management is, at its best, an exercise in public advocacy. Wilcox et al. (1998: 492) define public advocacy as an attempt by a corporation or organisation to influence public opinion on a political or social issue. Issues management demands a robust point of view and a rigorous assessment of the evidence that supports it. A robust point of view on its own, however, is not enough. For 40 years the tobacco industry argued that cigarette use was an issue of consumer choice while being cautious about the research showing the detrimental effects of tobacco use on public health. The industry has faced lawsuits from individual smokers, fines by state governments and

---

think about 19.3 **Whom do you trust in public debates?**

Greenpeace is a formidable public campaigner that has built up an enormous amount of public trust and goodwill over many years. Its motives in the Brent Spar case were not in question and it is important to understand why that was, and probably still is, true. Why do people put their trust in activist groups more than in governments or business? Why do we question the research figures and findings of industry, but rarely those of activists?

Feedback To answer these questions, look for regular surveys that measure public confidence, especially those that rank the people whom the public generally trust to tell the truth. Doctors, teachers, academics and religious leaders tend to head the lists; business leaders, politicians and government ministers tend to be at the bottom. The World Economic Forum published a report on trust in 2004 (www.weforum.org) and the MORI polling organisation publishes a regular league table of people who are expected to be truthful (www.mori.com). The key learning point is that what really matters is not whom people trust, but whom they do not.

PICTURE 19.2 Greenpeace campaigners leafleted drivers at Shell petrol stations across Europe urging them not to buy the company's fuel in opposition to the Brent Spar disposal plans. (*Source:* EPA/Empics.)

restrictions on marketing and advertising practices (Pratt 2001). Pratt argues that if issues management principles had been adhered to (i.e. responding to consumer interest in a manner that promotes dialogue and negotiation) then the consequences would

not have been so drawn out and costly. Rather than influencing public policy by acknowledging the health risks of smoking, the tobacco industry has been engaged in an ongoing battle with governments and pressure groups to restrict its market dominance.

Issues management also demands the ability to gain the support of key opinion leaders and decision makers, many of whom have been referenced earlier in this chapter and all of whom will test the strength and/or the independence of any data and research that is deployed to make the case. The issue manager, while believing passionately in the case they are making, is able to identify flaws in the arguments being put forward and decide if wisdom dictates a shift in strategy. You cannot simply create a reality; it can only exist if there is powerful evidence and widespread support to prove your point of view. (See Box 19.5.)

The activities outlined in Step 2 and the case outlined in Step 3 of this framework are key to understanding the process of 'case making', and it is worth going back to them now to understand their value as an initial check on strategic planning.

---

think about 19.4 **Animal rights issues**

Spend some timing thinking about how you define the animal rights issue:

- Is it about giving animals the same rights as humans or treating them as inferior?
- Is it about animals being sentient or incapable of feeling emotion?
- Is it about keeping animals in captivity or letting them roam at will?
- Is it about condemning a shark for attacking a swimmer or condemning the swimmer for invading the shark's territory?
- Is it about the right to keep pets at home or the campaign to close zoos?
- Is it about using animals to advance medical research and create new or better medicines or about breaking into research laboratories and setting them free?
- Is it about protecting animals from humans or about protecting humans from animals? Is it about destroying habitats or farming the land?
- Is it about animal welfare or the price of meat?

Feedback The answer is: all of them. This means animal rights activists could potentially become involved in a wide range of related issues. The same applies to various health and environmental issues. This shows how important it is to define the issue accurately.

> **box 19.5**
>
> ## Roles and responsibilities of the issue manager
>
> The role of the issues manager is fivefold: a strategic analyst, a tactical programmer, a facilitator of opinion, an advocate of facts and a counsellor on whether the strategy is likely to achieve the objectives set for it. That is their principal professional responsibility.
>
> The ethical dimension of issues cannot, of course, be ignored. It is important for two key reasons. First, the moral and ethical climate of public opinion is a fundamental subset of the context in which public advocacy takes place and will influence both the impact of an issue and the way in which it needs to be managed. That is an objective assessment that the professional issue manager will make and counsel accordingly.
>
> Second, an individual's personal moral and ethical code can make it uncomfortable for them to work with certain companies, industries or countries. That is a personal decision and the professional issue manager should not lead, or be expected to lead, an issues response strategy that runs counter to strongly held personal values which will clearly reduce their effectiveness.

Then go forward to Step 5, which focuses on another critical reality check: is the issue at, or near, the tipping point?

Step 5   Assess pace

Be aware that not every issue in the public domain is in motion or is capable of moving. Issues managers will know they are at, or near, the tipping point if the answer to all of the following questions is yes:

- Would a 'reasonable person' be able easily to identify a section, or sections, of the population who could be affected by the issue as currently defined?
- Can the issue be visualised?
- How strong is the driving force behind the issue?

The 'reasonable person' test is the litmus test for public issues. If the ordinary man or woman in the street cannot see, hear or feel a connection to an issue, it will remain static. It will be debated, but nothing much will happen and companies need to beware of adding pace to an issue that has no recognisable shape.

Take the issue of mobile telephones and the link to brain damage, mentioned earlier. Some of us will never know anyone with brain damage and even if we did, we could think of many likely causes that have nothing to do with making telephone calls. In any case, we cannot see inside a person's head and we know that the science of neurology is relatively new. Is this not just another scare story? Given the millions of telephones in use and the billions of calls that are made every day, surely we would have seen some hard evidence of harm by now? And so the debate goes on. The mobile phone example illustrates how some issues, despite being in the public domain, seem to be contained at the initiation phase of the issues evolutionary sequence. However, if the debate ever gains momentum, the pace will accelerate, probably triggered by a reputable scientific and medical source with unimpeachable credentials. If this happens, it will provide an interesting study into the way a market and an industry react to a changing context for such a widely used product. (See Activity 19.3.)

The issue of ultraviolet (UV) rays from the sun which are reaching earth unfiltered by high-altitude ozone, and the consequential rise in the likelihood of skin cancer, brings its own expectations of what a responsible government and industry can do. The issue began to attract broad public interest in the 1990s and has triggered a number of public information campaigns and evaluation studies (e.g. Sinclair et al. 1994; Dickson et al. 1997).

One of the first major campaigns was in Australia, a country synonymous with beach life and surfing, where sunbathing became a questionable activity. Suntan lotions were reinvented as sun-block lotions; beach holidays, and everything associated with them, came under scrutiny. Skin, and how to protect it, gave the medical profession a new cause and a

> ### activity 19.3
>
> **'The reasonable person' test**
>
> Make a list of similar issues that are already on the move. Make a note of the speed with which events happen as the issue reaches the tipping point and enters the public domain via 'the reasonable person' test.
>
> **Feedback**
> The key to understanding the test is that it is governed by national and cultural behaviours. There is no universal definition of 'reasonable', a fact that requires issues managers to develop a political antenna as part of their skill set.

Why is it that hunger and famine do not have the same effect or get the same response from the public as the diseases just discussed? The amount of charitable donations suggests that people care, but apparently not enough to generate action that will resolve the issue in the long term. If you were managing the issue, what would you do to put it on the public agenda and keep it there? How would you make it personal to people living thousands of kilometres away? What specific action could individuals take to make a measurable difference? How would it differ country by country?

Feedback The last question in this exercise is another critical component of issues management. Famine, the hole in the ozone layer and the reduction of non-communicable diseases like cancer are discussed at global levels within the United Nations and the World Health Organisation. The need to do something is not in dispute, but the action that is appropriate may be. Follow up activist Bob Geldof's efforts to put poverty alleviation in Africa on the public agenda in 2004. Start by typing in 'Sir Bob Geldof' into your search engine.

welcome boost in some parts of the world to the emerging science of cosmeceuticals (cosmetic products that claim a health benefit). Australia's 'slip, slop, slap' slogan encouraged people to slip on a T-shirt, slop on a hat and slap on some sunscreen.

The reality of issues such as this is that the fear of certain diseases has the power to drive action at a pace that is sometimes difficult to control. Cancer is one of them. So is Alzheimer's disease. Issues managers need to be alert for a high-intensity rollercoaster ride when a connection is made to a situation that drives emotional reactions. (See Think about 19.5.)

Yet while the *need* for change is global, the *pace* of change is national or regional. A popular slogan with green activists is 'think globally, act locally'. An issues manager who defines need but does not control pace is unable to influence the outcome. This is where the action is, and it is discussed in the second section of this management framework, covering Steps 6–10.

Framework section 2: action

Issues management is not primarily about winning. As Woody Allen suggests, it is all about getting a seat

Step 6 **Clarify the part you want to play**

From the evidence available, decide how the outside world views your role. Two questions to prompt a discussion and a decision:

- How likely is it that you will be seen to be responsible for creating the problem, resolving short-term concerns or building long-term solutions?
- How do you react?

activity 19.4

Understanding and communicating with different publics

After reading Mini case study 19.1 about the oil, gas and chemical industries, look for other examples of industries that have learnt to speak the language of the end user (consumer) rather than the language of the supplier (manufacturer, producer).

mini case study 19.1

Oil, gas and chemical industries

Oil, gas and chemical companies tend to be cast as villains, principally because public opinion tends to focus on their 'downstream' operations (e.g. oil fields, drilling rigs, production platforms, oil tankers, spillages, industrial sites) rather than the output (e.g. energy supply, plastic products, components in household appliances, clothing materials).

The industry is correcting the balance with a number of public communications initiatives, focusing principally on operations that have more resonance with the public in general and reflect consumer needs. This is especially true of oil and gas suppliers who are repositioning themselves as energy companies, not only as a long-term strategy to create greater public confidence and trust, but also as a platform from which they can play a leading role in the debate over alternative forms of energy that do not use fossil fuels.

think about 19.6   **Who has real power?**

If a strategic goal is to move an organisation from being part of the problem to being part of the solution, think about the roles and responsibilities related to issues management: which one of the following change agents has the real power to make something happen:

- a government that writes policy?
- an activist group that organises campaigns?
- an industry that supplies goods and services?

Feedback If the WHO wants us all to eat healthier food, will the solution be provided by the food industry or, say, a country's chief medical officer? The answer demands an honest appraisal of what is practical and who is best placed to deliver it. The case study exercise outlined after Step 7 of this framework exemplifies this approach in action.

at the table when decisions are made in response to a new context and a changing climate of opinion. It is about being part of the solution rather than part of the problem.

Manufacturers of electronic equipment operating in countries where issues surrounding the effect on humans of radio waves, microwaves and electromagnetic fields have surfaced are focused on resolving anxieties that their industries have raised. They do not believe scientific evidence proves the existence of a real problem requiring a long-term solution, but it is clear that a perception of risk has the power to

impact their business. They understand that legitimate concerns exist, recognise the degree of emotion involved and have activated programmes of reassurance to address them. That is what their customers expect.

Look for other examples of reassurance strategies in your own markets, country or community. You may find programmes designed to build trust in communities around chemical manufacturing plants or in reaction to recent consumer scares about product safety. (See Mini case study 19.1, Activity 19.4 and Think about 19.6.)

mini case study 19.2

Issues management practice at a chemical plant

A chemical manufacturing plant is situated near a residential estate. The plant is owned by one of the world's largest chemical companies and is critical to the company's production targets. The plant is required by law to inform residents of the extent to which they will be affected if there were a release of chemicals from the plant or, in a worst case, the plant exploded. A major release of chemicals or a major explosion is unlikely, but talking to the community about either of them is likely to spark serious concerns. A community meeting is organised.

A family living near the chemical manufacturing plant is concerned about safety at the plant and worried that leaking chemicals are responsible for their son's asthma. They cannot afford to move house. The family and their neighbours have just been invited to a meeting at the plant.

What can be changed and what cannot be changed? In this case, the law is here to stay (it was a response to a real incident in the USA and has now been adopted elsewhere), the plant is here to stay, the family is here to stay, the asthma is probably here to stay and the meet-

ing needs to happen. Everything else is open for debate. That is the reality the issues manager has to deal with.

Feedback

This is based on a real case study. The company adopted a reassurance strategy, focusing on demonstrating its ability, via state-of-the-art technology and a battery of warning devices and cameras inside the perimeter fences, to ensure that nothing it manufactured could leave the confines of the plant. The plant manager explained the emergency shutdown procedure, the direct links to the fire service and medical teams and the government regulatory process that controlled the company's day-to-day operations.

The issue was not whether the chemicals being manufactured were hazardous (the plant manager recognised that they were) but whether the risk of escape was fully recognised and managed. Whatever the cause of the asthma, it was unlikely to be connected to the plant.

Regular on-site community meetings are now a key feature of the plant's communications programme.

Step 7 Be realistic

Focus on what can be achieved:

- If a company is involved, what is its position and what can it make happen?
- Is it possible for a company to change fact or change perception, or both?
- Are the company's business interests better served by changing fact or by changing perception?

As an example see Mini case 19.2.

Step 8 Build case

Create your own circle of influence by informing and educating natural supporters and by identifying and gaining the support of potential supporters.

As discussed earlier in Step 4, redefining or reframing an issue is the crux of issues management. It is about identifying, educating and mobilising stakeholders to become advocates for your point of view. It is about building and maintaining a body of opinion around a common agenda that is relevant enough, powerful enough and tangible enough to make a difference. It is about creating a single campaigning idea – the core proposition – that galvanises people into action.

The focal point is the proposition, not the issue. The difference is important because the way an issue

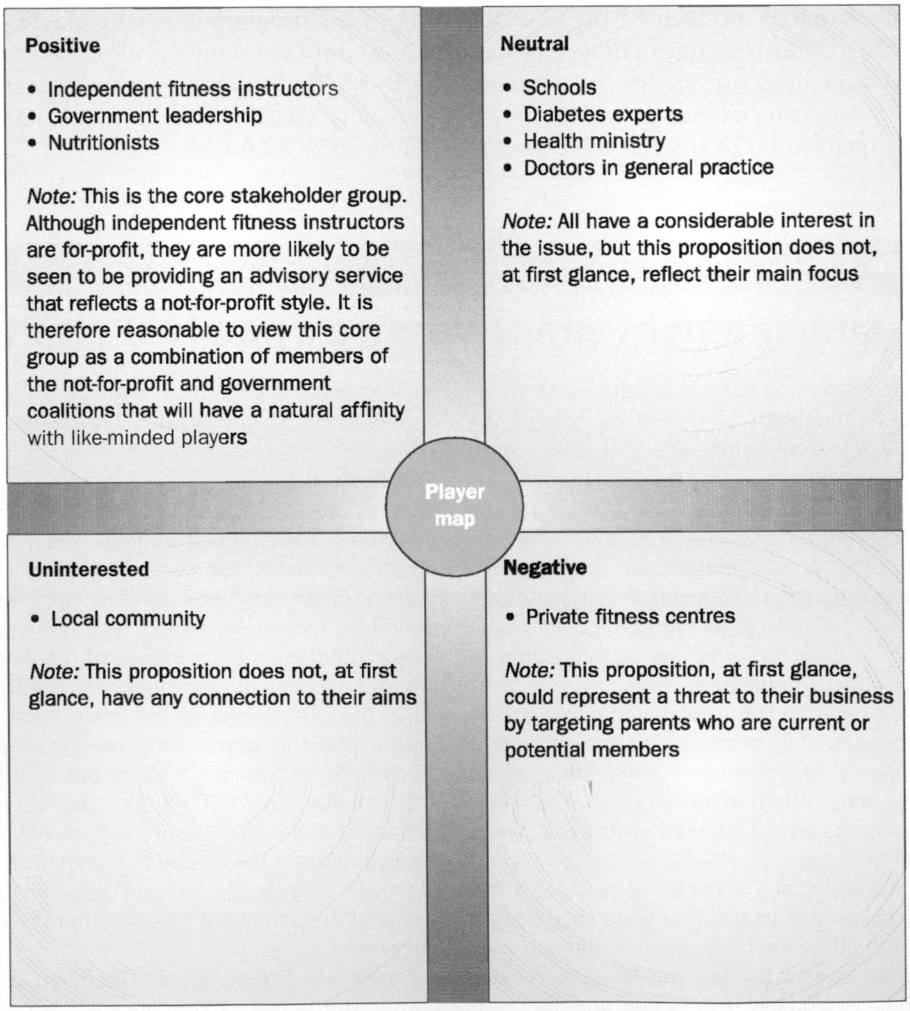

Positive

- Independent fitness instructors
- Government leadership
- Nutritionists

Note: This is the core stakeholder group. Although independent fitness instructors are for-profit, they are more likely to be seen to be providing an advisory service that reflects a not-for-profit style. It is therefore reasonable to view this core group as a combination of members of the not-for-profit and government coalitions that will have a natural affinity with like-minded players

Neutral

- Schools
- Diabetes experts
- Health ministry
- Doctors in general practice

Note: All have a considerable interest in the issue, but this proposition does not, at first glance, reflect their main focus

Player map

Uninterested

- Local community

Note: This proposition does not, at first glance, have any connection to their aims

Negative

- Private fitness centres

Note: This proposition, at first glance, could represent a threat to their business by targeting parents who are current or potential members

FIGURE 19.2 Probable current positions

is defined tends to generate *interest*; the way a proposition is constructed tends to generate *action*. That was certainly the case with obesity. A simplified view of how the debate might have evolved in one particular aspect – the need for greater physical activity – is used here to illustrate the process for activating an issues management programme.

As you will have seen from Step 1 of this management framework, the external environment was quite clear in 2003 that obesity was a major issue about which something had to be done. But what exactly? What idea or proposition could engage the public interest, create a common agenda involving a broad range of stakeholders and generate support for a long-term, multifaceted programme that could address this issue?

The players listed in Step 2 of the framework are examples of people who clearly share an interest in another aspect of the obesity issue, the move towards healthier eating habits, but why would they need to go beyond their natural coalitions to make something happen? Why, for instance, would a doctor specialising in diabetes want to talk to a farmer about the quality of his livestock?

In essence, it is all about making people aware of their role in being part of the solution to an identified, current and burgeoning problem. In this case, a simplified view is that obesity is a marker for diabetes; obesity can be managed if people follow a healthier diet; people find it easier to follow a healthier diet if they know what to look for and if it is widely available; and if people like meat, it is healthier for them to choose lean meat or white meat; if a doctor gives dietary advice, it is likely to be accepted (see reference to trust in Step 3); if there is an increased demand for lean meat or white meat, the farmer will want to be able to respond; and if the response resonates with other aspects of an existing problem that a large section of the population agrees needs to be resolved, it will be better understood and received. *That* is why the diabetes expert and the farmer need to talk about what they might do together to make people generally better informed and to create the conditions under which they can make the choice that is right for them. You should apply the same thinking as you consider the example on physical activity in Box 19.6 on p. 394 (see also Figures 19.2–19.4 and Table 19.2).

TABLE 19.2   Core proposition and key players

Core proposition
We need to take action to make sure that all schools, both state funded and private, provide the means for children and their parents to have at least 60 minutes' physical exercise during the school day. It is essential that children develop habits that avoid weight-related diseases later in life

Key players	Motivations
Schools	High standards of education
Doctors in general practice	Improved patient health
Diabetes experts	Disease reduction
Government leadership	Healthier citizens
Health ministry	Disease prevention
Nutritionists	Healthier eating/lifestyles
Private fitness centres	Increasing membership
Independent fitness instructors	Design of tailored fitness programmes
Local community	Safe, friendly neighbourhoods

Likely top-of-mind response of key players to core proposition			
Positive	**Neutral**	**Negative**	**Uninterested**
Independent fitness instructors	Schools	Private fitness centres	Local community
Government leadership	Diabetes experts		
Nutritionists	Health ministry		
	Doctors in general practice		

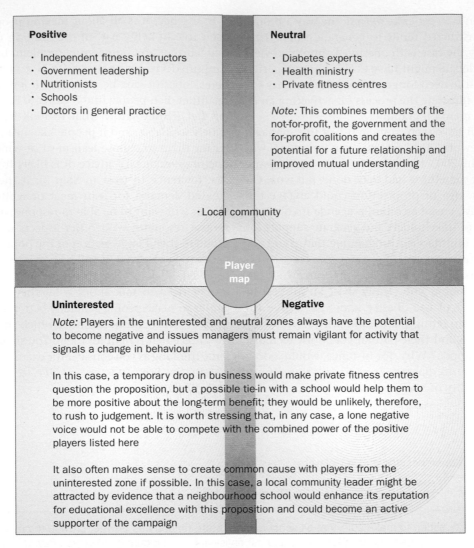

Positive

· Independent fitness instructors
· Government leadership
· Nutritionists
· Schools
· Doctors in general practice

Neutral

· Diabetes experts
· Health ministry
· Private fitness centres

Note: This combines members of the not-for-profit, the government and the for-profit coalitions and creates the potential for a future relationship and improved mutual understanding

· Local community

Player map

Uninterested

Negative

Note: Players in the uninterested and neutral zones always have the potential to become negative and issues managers must remain vigilant for activity that signals a change in behaviour

In this case, a temporary drop in business would make private fitness centres question the proposition, but a possible tie-in with a school would help them to be more positive about the long-term benefit; they would be unlikely, therefore, to rush to judgement. It is worth stressing that, in any case, a lone negative voice would not be able to compete with the combined power of the positive players listed here

It also often makes sense to create common cause with players from the uninterested zone if possible. In this case, a local community leader might be attracted by evidence that a neighbourhood school would enhance its reputation for educational excellence with this proposition and could become an active supporter of the campaign

FIGURE 19.3   Desired best-case positions

Once you have reviewed this exercise, go back to the environmental debate and apply some of the core propositions to this process and the templates (Table 19.2 and Figures 19.2–19.4). You will need to start by searching for specific subjects that are of interest to you and that you can easily research: the list is endless, ranging from wind farms and whale hunting to maintaining fish stocks and protecting rainforests.

Issues management usually demands more resources than people expect. It is a voracious user of time and people over a long period. For this reason, issues managers need to pinpoint and measure a series of defining moments rather than a single far-off result that might need to change over time as the issue evolves.

Progression in the issues business is often more motivating than perfection: if the target under the Kyoto Protocol is to reduce emissions by, say, 20% over the next 10 years, you will need to demonstrate commitment by publishing annual figures. If, as suggested in the discussion points in Step 4 of this framework, you want eventually to replace the use of animals in medical research, you will need to show examples every

Step 9   Commit to action

Set milestones. Be clear about what you are trying to achieve, establish a measurable objective and be realistic about the time and the resources it is likely to take.

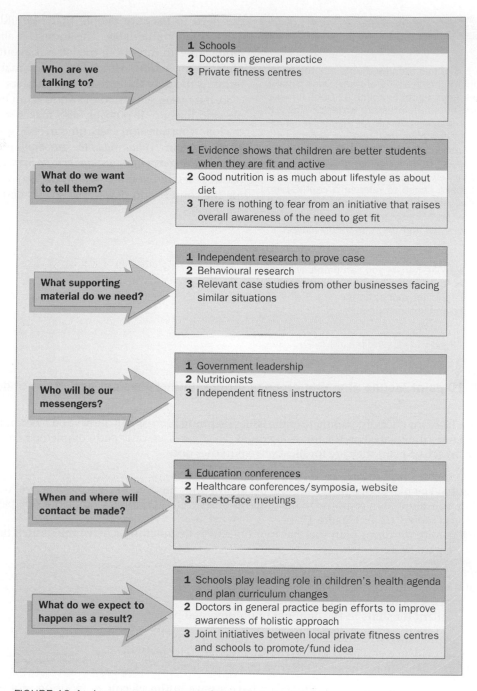

FIGURE 19.4   Issues management plan

Step 10   **Make it make sense**

Public advocacy and 'case making' is not the same as legal argument. Logic, not law, counts.

year of how you are using alternatives. And if you promise to cut the cost of obesity over the next decade, you will need to show it decreasing year on year.

This level of communication is dictated not so much by the need to articulate a commitment as by

activity 19.5

A final task

Go back to Step 4 of this framework and ask the questions about animal rights in a different way. Does it make sense to apply human rights to animals? Does it make sense to swim in shark-infested waters? Does it make sense to stop using animals for medical research until we are sure alternative methods are acceptable? Does it make sense to destroy the natural habitats of endangered species? Does it make sense to take animals out of their natural habitats and put them on show? Does it make sense to release a captive-bred animal into the wild where it might not know how to deal with natural predators? Does it make sense to keep animals in cages so small that they can hardly move?

Feedback

If you can make it make sense, you can probably begin to argue the case. If you find a flaw, be prepared to acknowledge it and consider your options.

It may not make sense to continue.

the need to reassure people that the end point is demonstrably attainable. The former is about communicating an intention; the latter is about communicating an action, which, in issues management terms, is the only thing that really matters.

So, if it makes sense that the world is run by the people who turn up, it probably also makes sense to ask the following question every time an issue gets into the public domain: *'What would the reasonable person expect a responsible company or institution to do in this situation?'* Answer that and you are well on the way to recognising the context and power that shapes destinies. (See Activity 9.5.)

---

box 19.6 A 10-point issues planning process for promoting physical activity in children

The following 10-point checklist summarises the issues planning process and allows you to complete the boxes in the figures (templates) on the following pages. The figures are only part-completed here and are not based on an actual plan; they are for illustrative purposes only.

1 Decide your core proposition (see Table 19.2).
2 List potential key players in the debate and decide whether they are likely to be positive, negative, neutral or uninterested in response to the proposition as you interpret it. Complete a one-page map of positions (Table 19.2 and Figure 19.2).
3 Prepare a communications plan that has four objectives designed to achieve the desired best-case positions (Figure 19.3):

■ to create common cause with positive players
■ to build bridges to neutral players
■ to prepare a response for negative players.
■ to stay vigilant for shifts in the opinions of uninterested players.

4 Decide what messages will drive the objectives (Figure 19.4).
5 Decide what evidence you need to support the messages (Figure 19.4).
6 Decide who is likely to be the most effective messenger (Figure 19:4):

■ The core stakeholder group, i.e. those who have a stake in the specific proposition, not the general issue, will emerge from among the positive players, and is best placed to take on the role of thought leadership via, say, articles in the media or public speaking engagements.
■ Specialist experts from the core group are typically regarded as key opinion formers and have a natural affinity with other experts who they might want to recruit.
■ An opinion former who can argue both logic and emotion is an ideal spokesperson for handling adversaries.

7 Decide the most effective communications platform (Figure 19.4): conferences, public meetings, website, media, advertisements, leaflets, etc.
8 Establish a desired and measurable outcome (Figure 19.4).
9 Commit to action (see Step 9 of the management framework).
10 Be prepared to review and fine-tune your plan at any stage (see Step 10 of the management framework).

Summary

This chapter has contextualised the specialist area of issues management in public relations by discussing its theoretical underpinning as well as practical applications. Discussion has revolved around defining and explaining the tipping point with a six-point model of the evolutionary sequence of issues in public policy. A framework has also been described that is a 10-step action planning framework for managing issues, split into two sections, 'Thinking and planning' and 'Action'. Within the framework, techniques have also been identified to support understanding of issues management processes, including who we trust in public debates, the 'reasonable person test' as well as identifying the tipping point within the framework.

Bibliography

Carson, R. (1962). *Silent Spring*. New York: Houghton Mifflin.

Chase, W.H. (1982). 'Issue management conference – a special report'. *Corporate Public Issues and Their Management* **7**, December: 1–2.

Dickson, H., R. Shatten and R. Borland (1997). 'Reaction to the 1995–96 SunSmart Campaign: Results from a representative household survey of Victorians'. *SunSmart Evaluation Studies No.5: The Anti-Cancer Council's Skin Cancer Control Program 1994–95 and 1995–96 and related research and evaluation*. Carlton South, Victoria, Australia: Anti-Cancer Council of Victoria.

Gaunt, P. and J. Ollenburger (1995). 'Issues management revisited: A tool that deserves another look'. *Public Relations Review* **21**(3): 199–210.

Gladwell, M. (2000). *The Tipping Point: How little things can make a big difference*. London: Little, Brown & Company.

Grunig, J.E. and T. Hunt (1984). *Managing Public Relations*. Orlando, FL: Harcourt Brace Jovanovich.

Grunig, J.E. and F.C. Repper (1992). 'Strategic management, publics and issues' in *Excellence in Public Relations and Communication Management*. J.E. Grunig. Hillsdale, NJ: Lawrence Erlbaum Associates.

Heath, R.L. (1990). 'Corporate issues management: Theoretical underpinnings and research foundations' in *Public Relations Research Annual*, Volume 2. L.A. Grunig and J.E. Grunig (eds). Hillsdale, NJ: Lawrence Erlbaum Associates.

Heath, R.L. (1997). *Strategic Issues Management*. Thousand Oaks, CA: Sage.

Pratt, C.B. (2001). 'Issues management: The paradox of the 40-Year U.S. tobacco wars' in *Handbook of Public Relations*. R.L. Heath (ed.). Thousand Oaks, CA, London and New Delhi: Sage.

Regester, M. and J. Larkin (1997). 'Issues and crisis management: Fail-safe procedures' in *Public Relations: Principles and practice*. P. J. Kitchen (ed.). London: International Thomson.

Seitel, F.P. (1989). *The Practice of Public Relations*. 4th edition. Columbus, OH: Merrill.

Sinclair, C., R. Borland, M. Davidson and S. Noy (1994). 'From "Slip! Slop! Slap!" to "SunSmart" – a profile of a health education campaign'. *Cancer News* **18**(3): 183–187.

Slovic, P. (2000). *The Perception of Risk*. London: Earthscan.

Traverse-Healy, T. (1995). 'Public relations in action' in *The Practice of Public Relations*. S. Black (ed.). Oxford: Butterworth-Heinemann.

White, J. and L. Mazur (1995). *Strategic Communications Management: Making public relations work*. Wokingham: Addison-Wesley.

Wilcox, D.L., P.II. Ault and W.K. Agee (1998). *Public Relations: Strategies and tactics*, 5th edition. Harlow: Longman.

Websites

McDonald's: www.mcdonalds.com

McInformation Network: www.mcspotlight.org

MORI: www.mori.com

World Economic Forum: www.weforum.org

World Health Organization: www.who.int/en/

Crisis public relations management

Introduction

Crisis public relations management is one of the most critical aspects of modern communications. Effective crisis management protects companies, their reputations and, at times, can salvage their very existence. A crisis is an event that disrupts normal operations of a company or organisation and if badly managed can ruin hard-won reputations in just days and even, in some cases, write off companies. The list of companies whose share price and market capitalisation have nosedived because of badly managed crises would fill this entire book, let alone this chapter. In a crisis, there is always more than the immediate issue at stake.

This chapter will look at examples of effectively managed crisis situations as well as some of those badly handled crises. We will explore, in some detail, the characteristics of a crisis.

The key to public relations crisis management is preparedness. It is vital to effective crisis management that a crisis is identified *before it happens* and, when it does, that it does not get out of control. In this 'information and communications' age, when a crisis does happen, it is crucial to understand the role communication plays and particularly the role of the internet. In this chapter we will examine the key principles for managing *any* crisis situation using a variety of case studies of both good and bad practice.

mini case study 20.1

Crisis snapshot – Andersen

In 2001 Andersen was one of the most well-known and respected auditing companies in the world. It was an established and trusted brand. As it became caught up in, and associated with, the problems arising from the Enron energy company crisis (Enron executives had been mismanaging the business and falsifying its financial performance), it saw its business and client base drastically reduced. More than just being associated with Enron's mismanagement, Andersen was implicated in an attempted cover up with reports of coded instructions to employees to 'clean out' Enron-related documents as US federal investigators prepared to launch an investigation. Andersen's board were quickly into a situation of 'last ditch rescue talks' seeking a merger with rival firms. Eventually, Andersen as a brand and as a commercially operating company was destroyed as a consequence of a poorly managed crisis.

Crisis public relations management: the context

Public relations crisis management literature is filled with lists of 'dos' and 'don'ts' together with countless checklists, for example Howard and Mathews (1985) include a 17-point crisis plan in their media relations book. All these are helpful in describing and dissecting crises. Some of this planning relates to the preparations before a crisis has happened, but generally the lists and guidelines concern coping with the situation in a practical sense after a crisis has happened. Reference should be made to Chapter 19, which deals with issues management, often closely associated with the crisis planning or preparation phase, i.e. defining and understanding the issues. Heath (1997) supports the link to crisis management and highlights how managing issues can help prevent a crisis. He states (1997: 289): 'If a company is engaged in issues management before, during, and after a crisis (in other words, ongoing), it can mitigate – perhaps prevent – the crisis from becoming an issue by working quickly and responsibly to establish or re-establish the level of control desired by relevant stakeholders.' In this chapter we will aim to build understanding by applying theoretical and practical models to crisis scenarios.

As a starting point it is important to define the area. Cornelissen (2004) describes crisis management as a point of great difficulty or danger to an organisation possibly threatening its existence and continuity, that requires decisive change.

Seymour and Moore (2000: 10) use a snake metaphor to argue that crises come in two forms:

The *cobra* – the 'sudden' crisis – this is a disaster that hits suddenly and takes the company completely by surprise and leaves it in a crisis situation.

The *python* – the 'slow-burning' crisis or 'crisis creep' – a collection of issues that steal up on the company one by one and slowly crush it.

In 1989 Sam Black broke crises down into the 'known unknown' and the 'unknown unknown'. The former includes mishaps owing to the nature of the organisation and its activities, e.g. manufacturing or processing and potential for spillage. The 'unknown unknowns' are events that cannot be predicted and that can come about from employees' behaviour, unconnected events or circumstances that are unpredictable. Before reading further, see Activity 20.1.

activity 20.1

Cobras and pythons

Spend some time thinking about (and researching) crises that have affected organisations and list them under the headings of cobras and pythons as described by Seymour and Moore.

Feedback

Now refer to Lerbinger's eight types of crisis and classify your list under one of them.

Lerbinger (1997) categorised eight types of crisis that he attributed to two causes: management failures or environmental forces. The eight categories are:

1 *natural* (for example, the Asian tsunami, which affected nations, governments, corporations, businesses and the lives and social infrastructure of millions)

2 *technological* (Mercedes 'A' Class car had a design fault and 'rolled over')

3 *confrontation* (Shell Oil whose petrol stations suffered a consumer boycott after the company wanted to sink an oil platform in the North Sea – the Brent Spar, see also Chapters 6 and 19)

4   *malevolence* (product tampering by a private citizen, like the Tylenol case detailed later, or direct action by animal rights campaigners, such as placing bombs under the cars of executives whose stores sell cosmetics tested on animals)

5   *skewed management values* (Barings Bank went out of business after managers were accused of turning a blind eye to a 'rogue' trader who hid details of his massive financial losses in the currency markets)

6   *deception* (examples include deceiving employees about the amount of money in pension funds after it has been used by executives to support the business, a UK case being that of Robert Maxwell and the Mirror Group of national newspapers)

7   *management misconduct* (Enron is one of the most shocking examples of this with both illegal and unethical practices rife in the senior management of the practice – see also Andersen, Mini case study 20.1)

8   *business and economic* (the late 1990s boom/bust in numerous small IT/technology companies is an example of how economic cycles can impact an organisation).

Definition: *Malevolence* is wishing evil on others.

Fearn-Banks (2004) defines five stages of a crisis, outlined in Table 20.1.

Crisis public relations management vs operational effectiveness

However well a crisis is managed from an operational perspective, it is how an organisation communicates about the crisis that makes the real difference. There is evidence that good communication in a crisis situation can support or increase a company's reputation (British Midland, Tylenol, discussed later). Poor management or a lack of communication skills can have a powerful negative effect on a company's business.

Let us examine the case of the *Exxon Valdez* oil spill in March 1989. The spill took place in Alaska, one of the few true wildernesses in the world, and received a considerable amount of global media coverage. Even though the accident site was appropriately cleaned up (*operational effectiveness*), Exxon took far too long to address its stakeholders (see Chapter 12 for a definition of stakeholders) and, particularly, the media. As a result of this failure of communication, its reputation was substantially tarnished. Insult was added to injury when the CEO finally did talk to the media as he blamed them for exaggerating 'the public relations disaster' that was created around the spill. Exxon's stock market capitalisation dropped $3 billion in the two weeks after the *Exxon Valdez* oil spill in Alaska. (Seymour and Moore 2000: 157)

Seymour and Moore (2000) describe the 'association' or 'parenthesis' factor that lingers on after a crisis. In discussing the mass poisoning of Minimata Bay in Japan, caused by Chisso Corporation, when mercury was dumped into the sea over several decades, poisoning thousands who ate polluted fish, Seymour and Moore (2000: 157) write:

> *For Chisso the hundreds of deaths and thousands of injuries represented a financial burden, aside from the fact that it would be linked with Minimata. The 'association factor' lingers on over other companies; Union Carbide and Bhopal; Exxon, the Exxon Valdez and oil-spills; the Herald of Free Enterprise, ferry safety, and P&O.*

Now, consider the frequently discussed case at Johnson & Johnson. Over 20 years ago Johnson &

TABLE 20.1   Fearn-Banks' five stages of a crisis (*source:* adapted from Fearn-Banks 2002)

Stage	Features
1 Detection	The organisation is watching for warning signs or what Barton (1993) calls *prodromes* (warning signs)
2 Preparation/prevention	The organisation takes note of the warning signs and prepares plans proactively to avoid the crisis or reactive ones to cope with the crisis if it comes
3 Containment	Taking steps to limit the length of the crisis or its effects
4 Recovery	This is the stage where effort is made to get back to the 'normal' operational conditions or effectiveness of the organisation
5 Learning	This is when the organisation reflects and evaluates the experience to consider the negative impacts for the organisation and any possible positive benefits for the future

PICTURE 20.1   Protests against Union Carbide following the Bhopal chemical plant disaster. (*Source:* © Reuters/Corbis.)

Johnson faced a potentially devastating crisis. Tylenol, the company's trusted and leading analgesic (pain reliever) was contaminated with cyanide by a member of the public. This action directly caused the deaths of six people in the Chicago area. Could anything worse happen to an over-the-counter product? Johnson & Johnson did not hesitate to act and act quickly. For the first time in the history of any product, it issued a complete product recall. It literally pulled off the shelves *all* the capsules throughout the USA – not just in the Chicago area where the deaths occurred. The potential financial consequences of losing a leading product, and the subsequent damage to its brand, could not be exaggerated. But, at the same time, it communicated exactly what it was doing, in a timely manner to *all* stakeholders – shareholders, employees, press and consumers. How would it act next? How would it re-establish confidence in the product and the brand? How was anyone to trust a Johnson & Johnson product again? Could anyone with a grievance or grudge or another random 'madman' claim to have poisoned the product and effectively blackmail them?

Johnson & Johnson's next response was both direct and decisive. It introduced tamper-evident packaging. It was, in many ways, a very simple operational 'addition' in terms of production – a metal foil to visibly 'seal' the product plus two more physical barriers to entry. Its simplicity was its key. Now, without any doubt, all stakeholders could actually see that the product was safe. Johnson & Johnson acted swiftly and effectively both in terms of operation and communication. Even today Tylenol is seen as one of the best-managed crises and the brand (appropriately) is still a success around the world. This crisis was so well handled that Johnson & Johnson's reputation has actually benefited in the long term – Johnson & Johnson's words *and* actions were seen to be in accord. (See Activity 20.2.)

Where do crises come from?

A spoonful of sugar

Leading crisis counsellors argue that over 50% of crises occur with products that are either ingested or swallowed – including food, drink and oral pharmaceuticals. We all eat and get ill – it is easy to understand how a damaged or defective foodstuff or pharmaceutical can be a major cause for concern. But the source of a crisis might not always be so subtle. A crisis can hit any organisation regardless of what or whom it represents. Whatever manufacturing process is employed or whatever information is disseminated, things can and will go wrong. The food dye scandals that hit the UK in early 2005 showed the extent of potential damage, when potentially cancer-causing additives caused the recall of nearly 500 products (see www.food.gov.uk/news/newsarchive/2005/ for further information).

It's not what you know, but who knows it

This is the information and communications age and highly confidential information somehow always escapes the bounds of its host organisation. Strictly confidential, paper-based hospital records have been found on rubbish dumps and the hard drives of second-user computers have been found to contain sensitive company or even government information. In today's climate it is nearly impossible to keep confidential information confidential. Any organisation should expect that what is known on the *inside* is just as well known on the *outside*.

You won't believe what so-and-so just told me

According to the Institute of Crisis Management, around a quarter of global crises are caused or triggered by employees/members of an organisation. Employees are a company's best asset when they are effectively motivated, remunerated and appreciated. But loyalty may turn – often when least expected.

The disaffected employee or former employee taking some form of revenge can trigger a crisis – and when feelings are running high, their negative impact can be huge. One disaffected employee brought down the stock price of a leading healthcare firm by 35% by giving incorrect research information to a leading newspaper; how can we forget the one-man crisis caused by Nick Leeson who brought down the merchant bank Barings through his overzealous financial actions! These actions were well chronicled in a 1998 film, *Rogue Trader*.

Seymour and Moore (2000: 142) outline the characteristics of rumours under crisis conditions:

- Accept that rumours always generate interest and are often more attractive than the facts.
- Silence – or a vacuum caused by lack of communication – will always be filled by rumour and speculation.
- Any organisation of 10 or more people will always have a series of rumours circulating.

Under these circumstances, rumour can contribute to and exacerbate already serious problems. Thus monitoring and *pickup* systems are required, especially when a company is facing or handling a crisis situation.

Definition: *Pickup systems* are a key element of crisis preparedness when it is essential to have systems in place to identify potential crisis situations in advance and to provide up-to-date information on how the company is perceived during a crisis. Many agencies provide news-monitoring services; others monitor content in internet chatrooms, giving real-time updates of what is being said. An effective pickup system, of course, also needs dedicated resources within the company to act on the intelligence available and a defined communication tree of developing issues.

What are the real costs of a crisis?

With any crisis there are, as we have seen, clear financial costs involved in withdrawing a product, cleaning up after an industrial accident, etc. However, compared to the damage that can be done to a reputation, these costs are minimal. Let's take a look at the *real* costs of a crisis.

Management distraction

Even when a crisis is handled well, key leaders or the leadership team are preoccupied for periods that can last from several days to several weeks and cannot manage the daily business. When a crisis hits, the people running an organisation have a crisis to handle!

Labour/employee concern

Employees will naturally be concerned about their own welfare, jobs and financial security. Too few companies communicate effectively with their employees during a crisis. Employees who are both well informed and motivated can be a powerful force in times of crisis (see also the BBC case study in Chapter 17). Without them, an organisation will not exist. With them, all things are possible.

Political backlash

Whether at country, EU or global level, crises sow discontent among regulators and 'the authorities' and the chances of regulatory or political pressure on or against an organisation are high. This may be driven by public reaction to the crisis.

Legal actions

We live in a 'do or sue' world. Crises encourage litigious behaviour in individuals, and injury or other compensation claims can make huge financial demands. In terms of litigation, an organisation should plan for the worst – and particularly so in the area of product liability.

Customer reactions

It is reassuring how forgiving customers can be, but only if they feel their concerns have been adequately addressed. When an organisation fails to communicate effectively with consumers, it is likely to see its support disintegrate and market share plummet irretrievably.

---

box 20.1   **Crises in action – What *actually* happens and how does it feel?**

The following description of a crisis is based on the experiences of a senior crisis consultant who describes what happens and how it feels.

There is a distinct pattern of events and behaviour that occurs during a crisis. Let's take a look at them.

Surprise!

Crises happen at the most inopportune times – Easter, Christmas, bank holidays or 8 o'clock on a Friday night after a week of hell, when you're enjoying a 'good night out'. It's almost guaranteed that if a crisis were to happen in Japan it will be during the Golden Week holiday, in China it will happen during Chinese New Year or over Thanksgiving in the USA. And the company is usually unaware of the situation until the issue is raised by someone else – be it a regulator, 'authority', key customer or media. Your mobile phone rings. You don't recognise the number, but it's a work phone, so you answer it. What next? Snowball effect.

You're on your toes and you can guarantee that your briefcase is not where you left it and you can't find the number for the out-of-hours public relations officer. You think you know what to say and the caller tells you they've got a deadline and whatever you say is going to be quoted. As you are thinking on your feet, so your organisation may feel they don't have enough information to deal with the crisis. What are the facts? Who has that information and how is it best understood and represented? Both you and your organisation feel there is an escalating flow of events. Within what may feel like moments, the media are talking about the situation, investment analysts are asking awkward questions and NGOs are getting involved. Everyone seems to be looking in on the organisation – you are in a goldfish bowl and everyone is peering in. It's highly probable that you and your organisation will feel a loss of control over the situation – there are so many different stakeholders and they want to know *right now* what has actually happened and what's being done, or going to be done, and said about it.

Roll down the shutters – crisis leads to drama

There is immense and intense scrutiny from outside the company. This can lead to a siege mentality where individuals feel everyone is *against them* and their organisation. This reaction invariably and rapidly leads to panic. 'I don't know what you're on about!' you tell the caller. 'I don't believe a word of it – you're just after a story. I suggest you go and pick on someone less gullible.' Once panic sets in rational decision making goes out of the window. But applying *rational* thinking to *irrational* events is exactly what's called for. 'Those are very serious allegations. It is not appropriate for me to comment immediately. I will return your call within 15 minutes. Before this time, I'm afraid I'm unable to comment.' What happens next?

Market confidence and reputation

This is the most significant cost of all. Rebuilding a reputation with stakeholders, such as shareholders and consumers, is not only costly, it can also take years to achieve. Again effective communication is key to reinforcing both public and market confidence. (See Activity 20.3 and Box 20.1.)

Communicating *during* a crisis

The examples and experiences described so far in this chapter dramatically demonstrate that today it is more and more evident why a company or organisation should communicate effectively at the onset of a crisis. Yet many companies argue against it. Preparing for a crisis costs time, money and energy – and crisis preparedness training is often seen as an unnecessary luxury. Even when an organisation is urged to communicate about its situation by experienced crisis management counsellors, there is often a list of reasons why it cannot communicate, such as:

■ The need to assemble all the facts before it communicates.
■ The desire to avoid panic, for instance it fears that by mentioning the individual brand people will think the corporate brand is 'infected' as well.
■ It does not have a trained spokesperson and is not going to put anyone up against a seasoned television interviewer such as Jeremy Paxman on the BBC's *Newsnight* (a late-evening 'hard' news programme).
■ It has had other problems recently and cannot talk about this problem because it will impact on its overall corporate reputation.

■ The issue of how to solve the crises – no one knows how to solve the problem at the outbreak of the crisis; every single crisis situation companies face and its solution will be substantially different.
■ The fear of revealing proprietary information or revealing competitive information that may give the company new competitive problems.

See Think about 20.1, overleaf.

Talking to the media

The way a company communicates to the media is critical. Selecting a spokesperson or spokespeople is one of the most important decisions in the effective management of any crisis. Whoever acts as spokesperson should follow the proposed 5Cs model (Figure 20.1) to be effective. This is based on consultancy experience of senior crisis managers.

The sections of the 5Cs model in Figure 20.1 can be explained as follows.

Concern

Not to be confused with legal liability, concern is a simple human emotion. The organisation's spokesperson needs to show true concern about the problem, concern about what has happened and concern for the people affected now and in the future – including potential customers/service users.

Clarity

Organisations need to talk with clarity. Starting from the early hours of the crisis, they need to have very clear messages. What the spokesperson says at the outset will be repeated throughout the duration of the crisis.

FIGURE 20.1   The 5Cs effective communication model

---

think about 20.1   **'No comment'– what happens when companies will not respond**

If a company spokesperson refuses to comment, what is your reaction? What would you think if you were the journalist asking the question? or a customer of the company?

Feedback   The sequence of events may go something like this:

- The company chooses to say: 'No comment.'
- The media say: 'The company was unwilling to take part in this programme.'
- Consumers think: 'No smoke without fire.'
                   'They're hiding something.'
                   'Guilty!'

When an organisation does not take control of a crisis situation and fails to communicate immediately, the media will go to a whole range of *other* sources to get the information they need. Take a look at the following list – they are all very readily available sources of information and 'expert' opinion in a crisis situation: the company website; the internet; emergency services – police, ambulance, fire, coast guard, mountain rescue, etc.; hospital authorities; medical, scientific and other experts; former employees; directors; local authorities; government departments; government ministers and other politicians; social services; neighbouring businesses, security, business and other analysts; academics; your customers and clients; charities and aid organisations; psychologists and 'disaster' counsellors; specialist writers and correspondents; freelance journalists; newspaper cuttings; film; picture libraries; public records; annual and other reports and directories; members of the public and 'eye witnesses'; competitor companies and organisations; trade unions and professional bodies and pressure groups and other NGOs.

The media will also talk to the company receptionist – the friendly face who's been on the front desk representing the organisation for the last 25 years. They'll speak to the night security officer or the person in company overalls who keeps the boiler going and is seen leaving the plant at 6 o'clock in the morning. They're loyal and dependable; they are the face of the company . . . But how much do they really know? How much do you think they know? Maybe they know more than you think. Have they been prepared for crisis situations – for the leading questions of journalists who might appear to be their best friend? They have a voice and the media will let them speak for themselves. If they are prepared appropriately, they too are an invaluable resource to a company.

Control

When talking to the media, spokespeople must take control of the messages, the situation, the environment and the venue.

Confidence

The spokesperson must get the key messages across with confidence, but without appearing complacent or arrogant.

Competence

They must also demonstrate competence and reflect how, as the representative of the organisation, they will handle the crisis.

How will the media react?

In the first instance, the media will want to know the facts. Their first questions are likely to be those in Box 20.2.

While these initial questions are generally predictable, how the media will act and how they will report a crisis should never be assumed. Everyone asks

box 20.2   **Typical first questions from the media**

- What happened?
- What went wrong? Why?
- Who is to blame/accountable?
- What is happening right now?
- What are you doing to prevent it from happening again?

questions from 'their own perspective' and everyone, especially the news-hungry media will have their 'own take' on the crisis situation. As well as general reporters, there may also be very well-informed specialist correspondents to consider. (See Activity 20.4.)

The internet and public relations crisis management

Since the days of the Tylenol crisis referred to earlier in this chapter, the media environment has changed

A crisis from a journalist's perspective

Put yourself in the position of a journalist being asked to report on a crisis scenario, say a major rail crash. How might you react as a journalist in a crisis? What might you want to know if you were in their situation? To whom would you want to speak? What do you need to get your story on the front page? How different would your questions be if you worked for the local paper or a transport publication?

Feedback

If you were in this situation, what kind of media coverage should you expect? You *could* experience the following:

■ The initial media reports will be speculative, wrong, exaggerated, sensationalised, often very personalised, spiteful or hurtful – and possibly, even, right! Expect the media to 'round up' the scale of the problem simply because it makes for a better story. Expect the media to make a drama out of your crisis.

■ Experts will be called in to comment on the problem. These 'specialists' in various 'fields of expertise' will push around ideas on what went wrong and how it happened.

■ An exclusive article, containing sensitive information that, of course, the organisation did not want to have made known.

■ Someone will say this disaster has been waiting to happen.

■ The timing will be wrong, the crisis team will be out of town, their deputies abroad or the spokesperson's mobile phone will have been stolen!

■ Opinions and rumours will dominate media reporting – especially if the organisation does not respond effectively. Expect rumours to become fact and expect rumour to chase rumour.

delivered is phenomenal and available to so many people – from home computers, via internet cafés, through to corporate communications infrastructure. If something happens, someone somewhere will be giving their own, often live, version of events. From individuals, through online communities, adversarial organisations and NGOs, the internet is very effective in putting a message out. It is impossible to censor the internet – which is both its strength and its weakness – but it is a highly effective vehicle to the dissemination of information and opinion that may masquerade as information.

Seymour and Edelman (2004) describe the new challenges posed by the internet:

> But when considering how to turn around a crisis today, management teams must accept that the media represent only part of an array of communication channels – albeit one of the most noisy and demanding. In a world dominated by low trust and the corrosive effects of cynicism, corporate voices can quickly be ignored, distorted or drowned out by the incessant noise that characterizes each and every crisis situation . . . Over the last ten years, crisis management and communications have been forced to develop in response to a series of technology and IT-driven changes. . . . At the same time single-issue groups and NGOs were recognizing the potential of the internet. Now it is possible for a small group to drive campaigns across the internet, while at the same time empowering individuals to express their opinions at the click of a mouse. (See Box 20.3.)

The totally unregulated nature of the internet thus gives organisations huge cause for concern. The internet has become the new rumour mill where people can say anything they want or create websites that criticise specific organisations, companies and specific industries (see, for example, www.untied.com, which is dedicated to problems with United Airlines,

dramatically. The once limited media market has become global and highly sophisticated. The impact the internet has on crisis management today is enormous. The speed with which communications can be

box 20.3   **Speed of the internet in a crisis**

The speed of spread of information and news in the new communication era is well illustrated by the Paddington/Ladbroke Grove accident in London on 5 October 1999.

At 08.06, Michael Hodder, the Thames Train driver, pulled out of the platform at Paddington Station.

At 08.11, having gone through three warning and stop signals, the Thames Train ploughed into the front of inbound GNER express train.

It took until 08.32 for the operational staff at Reading to establish from the controlling signal box at Slough that a serious accident had taken place involving one of their trains, that a serious fire had broken out (most unusual in train crash incidents) and that there were probably many injuries and even fatalities.

But if anyone had been on the internet at 08.21 they would have been able to read 'breaking news' reports of a rail accident at Ladbroke Grove involving deaths, serious injuries and a severe fire.

or www.mercedesproblems.com, a site whose agenda is obvious!). On a basic level, we see viruses crippling so many of our computer systems, from worms to Trojans, and the average user gets increasingly concerned about losing control of their own computer. As technologies advance so these viruses and the impact they have on our day-to-day lives become more apparent – they are, at best, an annoyance.

At a corporate level, there are a host of both technical and security issues that affect the operation and effectiveness of an organisation. Consider website tampering – where individuals can gain access to a company's website – a malicious individual or organisation can enter their views, enforce some new policies or give spurious comments, interfere with email and raise all manner of hoaxes. This costs a considerable amount of time and money and can become unmanageable. In September 2004, UK telephone company NTL had its systems sabotaged when a hacker changed the outgoing message on its customer service phone number to tell callers that NTL did not care about their problem and they should just get a life! One need only think back to the resources deployed for preparations for the 2000 new year (Y2K, the new millennium, when there was a fear that all computer systems would crash) to see how many companies chose to spend large sums of money on IT, rather than take any chances. The Gartner Group estimates that global spending on Y2K totalled $600 billion.

Direct face-to-face communication generally, and particularly during a time of crisis, is therefore a positive advantage – whether that be two individuals face to face in a TV interview or the CEO of a 'mega corp' (major multinational organisation) addressing their staff directly at a meeting.

Crisis audit

The first step in preparation is to conduct an audit that assesses the current vulnerabilities and strengths of the company or organisation. The audit will research key areas, such as operations, marketing, employee relations, safety experts, environmental experts, government, legal and communications people. It will ask tough questions to determine the most likely scenario that could happen, assess how well prepared the company is to deal with it and whether it has all the necessary resources.

The audit results can then be used to identify the key trouble spots, identify which stakeholders would be affected and help management build scenarios to train a key crisis team with the techniques of effective crisis management. In addition to being able to train a crisis team, the assessment can help build a comprehensive system for managing crisis communications. (See Activity 20.5.)

Crisis manual

Another means of preparation is a crisis manual. A good crisis manual contains a simple system of rapid communications, basic messages and audience identification and should not be more than 10 pages long. Anything longer will not be used in a crisis. A well-prepared crisis manual can serve as a guide for many of the basic tasks, such as activating the crisis team and facilities, and allows more time for the crisis team to focus on the more urgent issues (see Figure 20.2).

How to prepare for a crisis

Crises do come as a surprise and at unexpected times, but any organisation – commercial or public sector – can prepare itself for the inevitable and every one should. Methods such as research in the form of crisis audits, preparing a crisis manual and conducting crisis simulations or training will ensure that organisations are better equipped to handle any crisis. (See Box 20.4.)

---

box 20.4 **Actions to prepare for a crisis**

- Conduct a crisis audit.
- Prepare a crisis manual.
- Conduct crisis simulation and training.

---

activity 20.5

Doing a crisis audit

If you were conducting a crisis audit for your place of study or work, what would you need to know? Make a list of the key areas where something might go wrong. How could you find out whether your organisation has a crisis plan? What would you expect it to contain?

Feedback

The audit often shows companies a need for change. It might be an operational change, a change in how a product is labelled or how the company is marketed, or a change in what research is openly discussed with the regulator.

An educational organisation, for example, would have to consider potential problems originating from staff or students, such as scandals, court cases, exam results, protests. Some colleges and universities have also had crises due to outbreaks of meningitis, for example, which have led to clearer guidance to new students about symptoms and proper actions to take.

Crisis simulation and training

The final step in crisis planning is to conduct simulation training. Crisis simulation training is designed to create a real atmosphere of crisis. It integrates group and individual exercises, tests the skills of the spokesperson or spokespeople, tests the crisis plan and finally examines and evaluates the communications tools to find weak spots. Such exercises range from desktop exercises to full-blown global tests of the team. Repetition of crisis simulation and exercises are crucial to ensure that weaknesses are addressed.

A useful method that can also help prepare a company is to incorporate debriefing sessions into the communications plan to make sure the team understands what the emerging issues are, what they are doing in terms of community relations and how they are working with the newest techniques in crisis management. They should also be aware of the importance of community and employee relations.

Today in the UK, just over one-quarter of companies (27%) research possible vulnerabilities but only 16% conduct regular crisis preparedness workshops (Webserve Solutions Ltd, www.webservesolutions. net). Those companies who have not prepared or trained will be rehearsing their crisis strategy in the middle of their first major crisis!

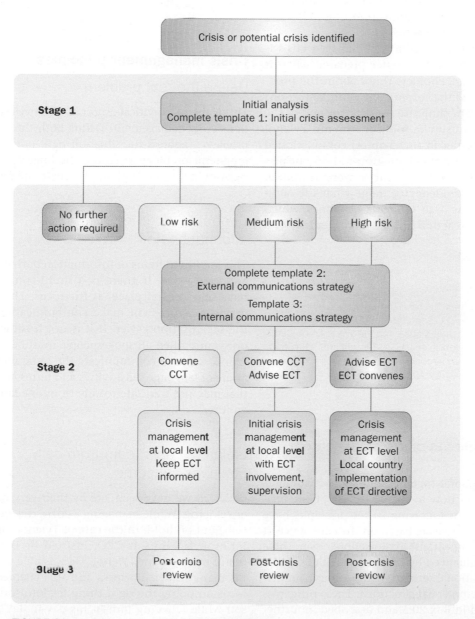

FIGURE 20.2   Crisis communications action plan

Ambassador L. Paul Bremer, former Chairman of the US National Terrorism Commission before he was assigned to his mission in Iraq, stated in an article in the *Harvard Business Review* April 2002:

Before 9/11, a poll of CEOs in the US showed that 85% expected to manage a crisis during their time in office but only 50% admitted to having a plan. However 97% were confident that they could handle a crisis. This sounds to me like over-confidence. I hope that more businesses are taking a hard look at their plans.

There is no doubt that physical and IT aspects of plans – contingency plans, business continuity, security and business interruption – have come under closer scrutiny since the *9/11* tragedy. However, the main focus has been on operational factors and often the key aspects of communication readiness and planning have been neglected.

One of the hallmarks of a well-managed crisis is knowledge. A company is better prepared when it knows what its stakeholders think about the product, the brand and the corporation. Both Mattessons Walls (see the Peperami case study at the end of the chapter) and Johnson & Johnson (in the Tylenol crisis covered earlier in the chapter) commissioned research throughout their situation to find out precisely what their key audiences were thinking. There is often a tendency to judge what the audience thinks on the basis of media headlines, which can lead to overreaction and mismanagement of a crisis.

Definition: *9/11* has become the worldwide shorthand reflecting the date 11 September 2001, when international terrorists crashed planes into the World Trade Center and the Pentagon in the USA. (Americans write the date month first, day second.)

Key principles in crisis management

To draw this chapter together and support students in understanding how to manage crisis public relations situations, the following 10 key principles have been identified. These are based on the experience of leading crisis consultants (counsellors) over three decades and influenced by the analysis of crises in a range of international settings, with various commercial and non-commercial situations. These principles are summarised in Box 20.5 and described in further detail below.

---

box 20.5 **Ten key principles in public relations crisis management**

1. Define the real problem.
2. Centralise or at least control information flow.
3. Isolate a crisis team from daily business concerns.
4. Assume a worst-case planning position.
5. Do not fully depend on one individual.
6. Always resist the combative instinct.
7. Understand why the media are there.
8. Remember all constituents (stakeholders).
9. Contain the problem.
10. Recognise the value of short-term sacrifice.

Crisis management principles

Define the real problem

This is the most critical aspect of effective public relations crisis management. Define both the short-term problem – address the situation right now – and the long-term problem to ensure the brand/corporation recovers in terms of both market share and reputation.

Centralise or at least control information flow

This applies to items of information both coming in and going out. If there is a multi-country issue, have one 'central place' as the focus. This, in very practical terms, will make communication within the organisation easier. If it is not feasible to have one centre, then all spokespeople must be rigorously trained so as to communicate the same message. Be aware of language sensitivities and terms of reference that may not translate readily from one language to another.

Isolate a crisis team from daily business concerns

Crises, as we have seen, are by their very nature, all enveloping. While managing a crisis, the day job has to be put on hold. In the case of Tylenol, Jim Burke, Johnson & Johnson CEO, insisted he became the brand manager for Tylenol. He was able to delegate his many leadership tasks and this enabled him to focus on doing the right thing for Johnson & Johnson while relieving him of his day-to-day responsibilities.

mini case study 20.2

Coca-Cola Belgium

Coca-cola representatives in 1999 acknowledged that the crisis described below was bigger than any worst-case scenario they could have imagined. They also publicly admitted that perhaps they had lost control.

Philippe L'Enfant, a senior executive with Coca-Cola Enterprises in 1999, in an interview on Belgian television said: 'Perhaps [we] lost control of the situation to a certain extent.'

The population of Belgium was still reeling from fears about mad cow disease and the presence of the carcinogen dioxin in animal feed when reports of schoolchildren being hospitalised after drinking Coca-Cola surfaced. More cases from other parts of Europe were found and

Coca-Cola products were banned in several countries. While the public speculated as to the cause, ranging from rat poison to extortion, the company delayed full apologies and tried to deny the problem and its responsibility.

Coca-Cola sources speculated that the problem could be due to contaminated CO_2 and creosote-tinged pallets and were quoted as saying: 'It may make you feel sick, but it is not harmful.' Meanwhile, Coca-Cola was losing an estimated $3.4 million in revenue each day and 19% of consumers had 'reservations' about drinking Coke.

Coca-Cola most definitely had a crisis management strategy but it still found itself losing control.

Assume a worst-case planning position

Ensure the crisis team thinks about the worst-case scenario in terms of what could happen to the brand and to the organisation. More often than not, people estimate the worst from their own perspective, or what they are able to handle, rather than a true worst case. It is therefore important to brainstorm and get as much input from others as possible. (See Mini case study 20.2 and Box 20.6.)

Do not fully depend on one individual

The person managing the crisis must depend on the whole team for information, but never rely on information from just one individual. Some team members may have a vested interest in a particular area and want to protect their own or their department's reputation. It is important that the messages put out during a crisis are not subverted by the influence of one department over another. These subtleties can be worked out at a

later date. There is usually more than one department's internal reputation on the line when a crisis hits.

Always resist the combative instinct

Do not go into battle with the media, NGOs, competitors or suppliers. An organisation must demonstrate it is in control during the crisis. The outcome of being combative could well destroy the brand or reputation. Words said in anger, or defence, may be temporarily satisfying, but they may not represent the best position for the crisis public relations manager or the organisation. When Ronald Li of the Hong Kong Stock Exchange suspended trading in 1987 in an attempt to defuse a run on the exchange, the crisis was made worse when he lost his cool with a journalist at the subsequent press conference. The journalist suggested that closing the exchange was outside Mr Li's legal powers. Mr Li responded by demanding his name and threatening to sue him. He actually ended

box 20.6 **Key learning points from the Coca-Cola case**

- Facts do not always rule – emotions, speculations/rumours are strong complicating factors.
- Think 'outside in' – plan messages and actions based on stakeholders' perspectives. Here, Coca-Cola was caught out by a combination of extremely sensitive regulatory authorities and parents keen to protect their children.
- The CEO must be visible.
- Do not let other stakeholders shape your reputation.
- Call on your allies (these could be other producers or suppliers of materials or packaging).
- Message alignment and internal communications are key (to maintain consistency in messages circulating inside and outside the organisation).
- Regret, resolution and reform (demonstrate regret, find a resolution to the problem and how to reform what the company is doing).
- Be better prepared – think 'worst case', not just precedent.

up in prison himself (for unrelated charges of insider trading).

Following the 2001 general election campaign in the UK, the Deputy Prime Minister John Prescott found out only too well the impact of a violent reaction from someone in the public eye. When a heckler threw an egg at Mr Prescott, it was not particularly newsworthy. But when Mr Prescott replied with a left-hook punch, it was in all the papers for days.

Understand why the media are there

The media are searching for a good story. They need focus, a 'cause and effect' – something that their audience will relate to. A firm can assert the facts as it sees them and thus defuse an 'on-the-face-of-it' story.

Remember all constituents (stakeholders)

It is not just the media that need fast and relevant responses during a crisis. The crisis plan has to take all the stakeholders into consideration. (See Activity 20.6.)

Contain the problem

Reduce the problem to as small a geographical area as possible to prevent it becoming a bigger problem – from local to national or national to international. In these days of the international media and the internet, localising an issue is a major challenge. However, it should be an objective. For example, in the Peperami case (Case study 20.1), the affected batch was only being sold in the UK. Efforts to focus the problem led to the subsequent recall being limited to just the UK despite the product being widely available throughout Europe.

Recognise the value of short-term sacrifice

This might involve recalling the product or dismissing the person responsible for causing the problem.

The value of short-term sacrifice can be well illustrated by Case study 20.1 on Peperami (see also Case study 20.2, overleaf).

PICTURE 20.2   Following the 2001 general election campaign in the UK, the Deputy Prime Minister John Prescott found out only too well the impact of a violent reaction from someone in the public eye. When a heckler threw an egg at Mr Prescott, it was not particularly newsworthy. But when Mr Prescott replied with a left-hook punch, it was in all the papers for days. (*Source:* Rex.)

activity 20.6

Stakeholders (publics)

Think of an organisation you know well or are interested in and note down all the stakeholders (publics). See also Chapter 12 for further information about stakeholders. You could think about the university or college you considered in Activity 20.5.

Feedback

It can be useful to break stakeholders down into internal and external as follows:

Internal stakeholders

Employees and their families, medical department, security, supervisors, managers and corporate managers and unions if applicable. In a university, there would be employees – academics, administrators and service workers, each group with its own hierarchies and unions, as well as students and their unions.

External stakeholders

The online community, local authorities, factories or facilities (in the local community), community residents and leaders, regulator(s), government, contractors, suppliers, customers, distributors, shippers, technical experts, the financial community and relevant NGOs. A university is accountable to the government, research bodies, grant-making bodies, suppliers, students' parents and local authorities, as well as the local community.

activity 20.7

Consumer reaction to a crisis

Consider these questions related to the Peperami case (Case study 20.1).

Why did consumers react so positively to Mattessons Walls' handling of this crisis?

The market share of the product increased by 14% post-relaunch – why do you think this happened?

Feedback

Now think about companies and products you experience every day.

As a consumer, what do you want to know about the products you buy? Make a list and try to organise the issues you are interested in. Put them in themes or categories, e.g. safety, the manufacturing process, location of production, who owns the company, etc. You may find it useful at this stage to refer to other chapters in the book about issues management (Chapter 19) and image, identity and reputation (Chapter 13).

case study 20.1

Peperami

In 1987 the UK Department of Health linked Peperami to an outbreak of salmonella poisoning, a notifiable illness in the UK. The decision was taken to recall affected products, but due to the packaging used for the product, the affected batch could not be precisely identified by consumers from the bar code. The recall was therefore extended to the whole of the UK.

Peperami dominated the salami-style meat snacks market, with 80% of market share and widespread product distribution across 40,000 outlets. Peperami could be found in a huge range of retail outlets, including supermarkets, corner stores, clubs and pubs.

Strategy

Peperami is just one of many meat products produced by Mattessons Walls and a key early priority was to limit the impact of the salmonella problem to the Peperami brand. Mattessons Walls was positioned as an importer and not a manufacturer, distancing Peperami from the parent company to stop a product problem becoming a major corporate problem. Meanwhile, it was crucial to share the facts in the case and communicate fully to all stakeholders.

Actions

A media control centre was set up, manned by experienced media relations people 24 hours a day, 7 days a week. A consumer telephone centre was also established with telephone operators given daily updates/briefings. Tracking research was initiated to determine exactly how consumers thought the crisis was being handled and analyse their perceptions of the Peperami brand, giving the management team crucial information on the impact it was having beyond the media reactions.

Employee statements were prepared for all Mattessons Walls employees and regular updates were given to Unilever, Mattessons Walls' parent company, to keep it up to date with developments.

During the recall and the time the product was off the market, each media relations executive worked with an individual health editor from each national newspaper and a member of the team was appointed to liaise with the Department of Health.

Result

Mattessons Walls received public commendation from the Department of Health for the way it had handled the situation and research showed that more than 90% of consumers were impressed with the way the withdrawal was handled. Within three months of relaunch, Peperami's share of the salami snack foods market stood at 94%, a 14% increase, despite the introduction of a competitive product from a national supermarket's (Sainsbury) own label. (See Activity 20.7.)

Melbourne Gas crisis

Finally, let us take a look at a crisis that puts all these key principles into perspective: the Melbourne Gas crisis that threw the entire state of Victoria, Australia, into chaos for a fortnight, but is remembered for being one of the best managed crises in Australian history.

Event

A major explosion at the Exxon refinery at Longford, Melbourne, on Friday 25 September 1998 destroyed part of the plant, killing two and injuring eight refinery workers and cutting gas supplies to factories, businesses and private homes across the state.

Effects

The state of Victoria was highly dependent on cheap gas and its population of more than 3 million was almost totally dependent on this one plant. Ninety-eight per cent of Victoria's gas customers would have no gas supply for the foreseeable future. Manufacturing industries stood down 150,000 employees and the estimated cost to industry was $A100 million a day. VENCorp, the distributor of gas for Victoria, invoked emergency powers to restrict gas use and media reporting highlighted that millions of people faced the prospect of cold showers.

Strategy

Gas would only be available to emergency services and both VENCorp and the state government stressed in all communications that jobs were the first priority, not hot showers!

When the gas supply was ready to be restored, it constituted the biggest single gas relight programme in the world and both consumers and the system needed to be prepared to be protected from relighting accidents. The crisis team made editorial content and a multi-language brochure the focus of a safe relight communications programme. Operationally, when the supply was ready to be reintroduced, the odd/even house numbers would be used to phase gas supply in safely and particularly to protect the gas network.

Actions

Four thousand emergency service volunteers were used to turn off gas meters and call centres were established which, at the crisis peak, received 131,561 calls a day. There was in-house coordination and development of call centre scripts and the top 10 frequently asked questions from the call centres were advertised daily in major media.

To ensure seamless communication, the communications team sat on the government gas supply emergency coordination committee and critical services working group, established a 24-hour media response centre manned by a team of 15 people and arranged twice-daily media briefings at 10am and 3pm. Key spokespersons were given media training.

A responsive and pre-emptive issues management programme was developed and as a key element of a safe relight programme, 2.3 million brochures were sent to all households and small businesses alongside a major print and television ad campaign.

Communicating with the ethnic communities was identified early as a challenge in Victoria; the brochure was translated into 20 languages and distributed, and an information line was set up offering interpreter services in 100 languages.

Assessment

When the gas supply was restored there were only nine relight accidents and 12,000 appliance repairs.

Alan Stockdale, Treasurer of Victoria, said at a government press briefing on Friday 9 October 1998:

> I think every Victorian can take pride in the fact that our community has responded so well, and that the reconnection program, on the massive scale, is taking place in such a safe and orderly manner.

> We estimate that 1.1 million domestic customers, out of a total of 1.35 million, have been reconnected to the gas supply now.

> Eighty-five percent of domestic customers have been able to reconnect without assistance, indicating that the wide-ranging safety program has been very successful.

> I consider this to be the best-handled issue that I have seen since I have been interested in public affairs issues in this state.

> I have been told by many, including my wife, that this [holding up the brochure] was the first document of the kind that they have read and clearly understood what they needed to do and what they shouldn't do.

> This incident has been managed as well as it could have possibly been done – there is no higher praise than that.

David Guthrie-Jones, Manager Communications VENCorp, said at an Australian Gas Association meeting on 16 November 1998:

> So we called in communications experts, who sent an excellent team of experience and enthusiasm to help with our crisis communication strategy and implementation.

> I can tell you this. Having back-up communication or public relations consultants experienced in crisis management is absolutely crucial to the success of handling large scale emergencies . . . this is what helped make the difference between success and failure for us at the end of the day.

Summary

There is no guaranteed recipe for successful crisis management but there are key ingredients: knowledge, preparation, calmness, control and communication will see an organisation secure the best possible outcome from a crisis. They may even help to find the opportunity that can come from a crisis (the characters that represent 'crisis management' in both Chinese and Japanese actually mean 'danger' and 'opportunity'). Preparing for the unexpected but inevitable ensures that any organisation can take the drama out of a crisis.

Bibliography

Baker, G.F. (2000). 'Race and reputation: Restoring image beyond the crisis' in *Handbook of Public Relations*. R.L. Heath (ed.). London: Sage.

Barton, L. (1993). *Crisis in Organisations: Managing communications in the heart of chaos*. Cincinati, OH: South Western.

Baskin, O. and C. Aronoff (1997). *Public Relations: The profession and the practice*. London: Brown & Benchmark.

Bland, M. (1998). *Communicating Out of a Crisis*. London: Macmillan.

Bremer, P.L. (2002). 'Doing business in a dangerous world'. *Harvard Business Review* **80**(4), April: 22.

Cornelissen, J. (2004). *Corporate Communications: Theory and practice*. London: Sage.

Daniels, T., B. Spiker, and M. Papa, (1997). *Perspectives on Organizational Communication*, 4th edition. London: Brown & Benchmark.

Fearn-Banks, K. (2000). 'Crisis communication: A review of some best practices' in *Handbook of Public Relations*. R.L. Heath (ed.). London: Sage.

Fearn-Banks, K. (2002). *Crisis Communications: A casebook approach*. 2nd edition. Mahwah, NJ: Lawrence Erlbaum Associates.

Harrison, S. (2000). *Public Relations – An Introduction*, 2nd edition. London: Thompson Business Press.

Hearit, K.M. (2000). 'Corporate apologia: When an organization speaks in defense of itself' in *Handbook of Public Relations*. R.L. Heath (ed.). London: Sage.

Heath, R.L. (1997). *Strategic Issues Management: Organizations and public policy challenges*. Thousand Oaks, CA: Sage.

Howard, C. and W. Matthews (1985). *On Deadline: Managing media relations*. Prospect Height, IL: Waveland Press.

Laune, J. (1990). 'Corporate issues management: An international view'. *Public Relations Review* **XVI**(1), Spring.

Lerbinger, O. (1997). *The Crisis Manager: Facing risks and responsibility*. Mahwah, NJ: Lawrence Erlbaum Associates.

Olaniran, B.A. and D.E. Williams (2000). 'Anticipatory model of crisis management: A vigilant response to technological crises' in *Handbook of Public Relations*. R.L. Heath (ed.). London: Sage.

O'Rourke, R. and B. Marsteller (1998). Managing in times of crisis'. *Corporate Reputation Review* **2**(1).

Regester, M. and J. Larkin (1997). *Risk Issues and Crisis Management*. London: Kogan Page.

Reynolds, C. (1997). Issues management and the Australian gun debate'. *Public Relations Review* **23**(4), Winter.

Seitel, F. (2004). *The Practice of Public Relations*, 9th edition. London: Prentice Hall.

Seymour, M. and S. Moore (2000). *Effective Crisis Management: Worldwide principles and practice*. London: Cassell.

Seymour, M. and D.J. Edelman (2004). 'Fighting on all fronts'. *CEO Magazine* September.

Thill, J. and C. Bovee (1996). *Business Communication Today*, 4th edition. New York: McGraw-Hill.

Young, D. (1996). *Building Your Company's Good Name: How to create and protect the reputation your organization deserves*. New York: Amacon.

Zyglidopoulos, S. (1999). 'Responding to reputational crisis: A stakeholder perspective'. *Corporate Reputation Review* **2**(4).

Websites

The Daily Telegraph: www.dailytelegraph.co.uk

The Guardian: www.guardianunlimited

CHAPTER 21

Public relations and the consumer

Learning outcomes

By the end of this chapter you should be able to:

- understand the term consumer public relations
- describe different types of consumer public relations activity
- appreciate the critical factors that drive successful consumer public relations campaigns
- understand how consumer public relations complements other communication disciplines
- appreciate the benefits that can be generated by a successful consumer public relations campaign
- apply the principles to real-life scenarios
- understand the challenges facing practitioners.

Structure

- What is consumer public relations?
- Tools and techniques
- The wonderful world of brands
- Key challenges
- Tomorrow's people

Introduction

The public relations and marketing landscape is changing. In a world of media fragmentation, information overload and a revolution in personal communication – not to mention the rise of the 'promiscuous' consumer – the conventional maxims of marketing are being challenged as never before. In this environment public relations, which was once perceived as a rather lightweight addition to the marketing family, has proved that it can deliver results. Many marketing professionals now view public relations as an effective way to win over the hearts and minds of consumers and its status in the marketing mix has grown accordingly. Some (Ries and Ries 2001) even argue that a seismic shift is underway, which will result in a diminished role for advertising in the future as companies look for more sophisticated ways to promote their products and services. Superbrands, such as Virgin and Amazon, have already placed public relations at the forefront of their marketing strategies, as have a host of other companies, although it should be noted that the majority are still a long way from grasping even a slice of its full potential.

Whatever the level of acceptance and application, one thing is certain: consumer public relations has moved from the fringes of marketing communication to a position of credibility and influence. While the lion's share of the marketing budget still tends to be spent elsewhere, the universe of consumer public relations is expanding rapidly and it is a challenging and intoxicating place for a practitioner to be. It is a world of brands, buzz and creative advantage, all of which is driven by a simple business imperative: to sell their products and services companies must first get them noticed and into the minds of consumers. Only then can they start to forge lasting and productive relationships with their intended targets and it is at this stage of a campaign lifecycle that public relations really comes into its own. The purpose of this chapter is to provide a greater appreciation of public relations in a consumer marketing context and to demonstrate the advantages it has over other forms of communication. Attention will also be given to the strategic and intellectual rigour that is required to deliver an effective consumer public relations campaign that makes a genuine difference by delivering tangible commercial results.

What is consumer public relations?

Public relations is a holistic discipline concerned with the complex relationships that exist between an organisation and those groups that can influence its reputation and affect the way it operates: employees, the local community, government, shareholders, financial institutions, regulators, suppliers and customers. As a result, public relations campaigns can have many different objectives, such as:

- to help attract and retain staff
- to show that an organisation is environmentally responsible
- to change a piece of unfavourable legislation
- to educate people about an issue
- to demonstrate that the organisation is a worthy investment, a sound trading partner or the provider of quality products and services.

This breadth of outcomes means that every type of organisation – whether a company, charity or governing body – should be concerned with good public relations practice in one form or another.

Clearly, public relations does not focus only on the commercial activities of an organisation and its remit extends beyond winning new customers and duelling with competitors in the highly pressurised world of modern capitalism. This chapter is, however, concerned specifically with this aspect of public relations practice and will examine how organisations use the public relations tools at their disposal to interact with consumers in a trading environment (how public relations promotes transactions *between* businesses is discussed in Chapter 22). This commercial focus also excludes discussion of those public relations campaigns in the public sector that are designed to educate citizens about issues such as smoking, recycling and taxation (see Chapter 30), as well as the recruitment and fundraising activities executed by charities.

The world we are concerned with here is where public relations interfaces with *marketing* activities, such as advertising, to stimulate the sale of products and services in the free market economy. As the chapter unfolds it will become apparent that although the endgame of consumer public relations in this context is to drive sales, its role is often more subtle and sophisticated than more direct forms of communication. By changing the attitudes and behaviour of consumers, public relations can create a more favourable sales environment for a company and its products, so helping to facilitate the path to purchase.

Figure 21.1 illustrates this process by highlighting the stages a consumer can take on the *path to purchase*, the journey from initial awareness to purchase and consumption.

Definition: The *path to purchase* describes the stages a consumer takes in the journey from initial need and product awareness to purchase and consumption.

Definition: *Marketing* is the management process responsible for identifying, anticipating and satisfying customer requirements profitably.

Marketing mix

Definition: *Marketing mix* is the term used to define the four key elements of an organisation's marketing programme: product, price, place and promotion.

In developed countries it sometimes seems that everyone thinks they are a consumer public relations expert (although they often mistake public relations for *advertising*). After all, are we not all

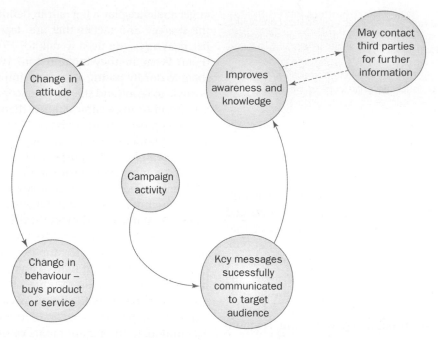

FIGURE 21.1   Path to purchase

consumers and do we not all have valid views and opinions on the communication that is directed at us? It is true that as human beings we all use and consume goods and services to satisfy a complex range of needs. Every day we make countless decisions about the things we buy, from the cheap and mundane, to the expensive and exciting: everything from food, beer, clothing, bus and cinema tickets, to holidays, cars and mortgages. Indeed, it could be said that it is consumers – not companies – who exert the real power in the marketplace, as it is our individual buying decisions that determine the products that succeed and those that fail. It is not surprising, therefore, that most companies appear to be obsessively driven by the need to persuade consumers to buy their goods and services rather than those of their competitors.

Definition: *Advertising* is a form of promotional activity that uses a totally controllable message to inform and persuade a large number of people with a single communication.

It is increasingly appreciated in marketing circles and textbooks (e.g. Brassington and Pettitt 2003) that public relations is a diverse practice that when successfully applied can grab attention, get people talking and move them to action. These are important

attributes when the goal is to sell something to the man and woman on the street. In this context, public relations has become a valuable part of what is known as the *marketing mix*, an often quoted term that refers to the set of tools that a company has at its disposal to influence sales. The traditional formulation is popularly known as the 4Ps: product, price, place and promotion (Kotler 2003).

Promotion is the area that encompasses public relations, as it is this part of the marketing equation that focuses on the messages that are designed to stimulate awareness, interest and purchase. To communicate these messages and to attract interest and awareness in their products and services, companies use a combination of disciplines – including advertising, *sales promotion, direct mail* and public relations – to reach their desired audiences. When used in this way, public relations should become a planned and sustained element of the wider *promotional mix*, working in tandem with other marketing activities to achieve maximum impact and with the potential to meet a range of objectives, such as:

- raising an organisation's profile
- redefining its image
- helping to promote its credibility in a new or existing market
- demonstrating empathy with a target audience
- launching a new product or service
- reinvigorating an existing product or service
- stimulating trial and purchase.

Definition: *Direct mail* is electronic and posted communications sent to individuals' text phone, email, work and home postal addresses.

Definition: *Sales promotion* means short-term or temporary inducements, such as price cuts or two-for-one offers, designed to encourage consumers to use a product or service.

Building relationships

Underpinning a host of valid communication outcomes, helping an organisation to build positive and lasting relationships with consumers and those that influence them is the most important role that public relations can play in marketing. While it can be argued that relationship building represents the Holy Grail for all disciplines in the promotional mix, the world we live in is changing. Mark Adams, a founder of high-tech public relations firm Text 100 explains:

> Companies boast that they have relationships with their customers, while customers get more unwanted marketing rubbish in the post, and less of the face-to-face contact they really love. Ask them if they have a relationship with companies and they won't just laugh in your face – they'll probably spit. Relationship is being killed by corporate convenience and mass-producing. With it, customer trust and loyalty are becoming outdated concepts. It makes pure marketing sense for companies to spot this and aim to fix it. Those that do will achieve wondrous things. PR people are there to help do the fixing, to build relationships.

Public relations is increasingly showing itself to be a first among equals in the quest to connect with consumers. This is reflected in the growing preponderance of public-relations-led campaigns with marketing spend being diverted from advertising, direct mail and other budgets into what were once regarded as Cinderella activities. In short, the tools that public relations professionals have at their disposal are increasingly seen to have the capacity to communicate with consumers in a way that other marketing disciplines cannot match.

Tools and techniques

Fit for purpose

Before discussing the individual tools and techniques that can make up a public relations programme, it is important to stress that the key characteristics of the target audience play a big part in defining and shaping the strategy and tactics that are deployed in a campaign. Who do we need to talk to? How can we reach them? What are they interested in? What do we want them to do? By posing a series of simple questions it is possible to refine and sharpen the scope of the planned activity, ensuring a clinical rather than a wasteful, scattergun approach to the tools and techniques that are at the practitioner's disposal. (See also Chapter 10.)

For example, if the purpose of the campaign is to get young mothers to visit their local supermarket, a national media relations campaign might not have the same impact as activity targeted at a local newspaper. Or, if research shows that the same audience is concerned about their children walking to school, then a road safety sponsorship executed at local level may strike a chord and help to establish a positive relationship with the store. One of public relations' great attributes is its flexibility as campaigns can be tailored to appeal to many audiences and modified to accommodate the requirements of different delivery channels, such as the media, events or sponsorship.

Media relations

Getting a journalist to write or talk on air about a company, product or service is an objective of many consumer public relations campaigns. The persuasive power of editorial is much greater than paid-for advertising as the stories and features that appear in newspapers and magazines – as well as on radio and television – tend to be viewed by consumers as unbiased and objective. In contrast, advertising in the same media channels relies on paid-for space and therefore lacks the same credibility as coverage that has been created by an independent third party such as a journalist. Influencing this editorial process is a key task for the public relations practitioner (see also Chapter 16). No advertisement or sales person can convince you about the virtues of a product as effectively as an independent expert, such as a journalist, and if this opinion is then repeated to you by a friend, family member or colleague it has an even greater resonance. Indeed, most of us got to hear about easyJet, lastminute.com, Virgin and Amazon not through advertising but from news stories in the press, radio, TV and online, or through personal recommendation.

While the benefits of a successful media relations campaign are obvious, achieving the desired result is not so easy. As editorial coverage, by definition, cannot be bought and because someone else produces the finished article, the public relations practitioner has no direct control over it (unlike an advertisement). In addition, although there are opportunities to write straightforward product press releases that achieve positive coverage (a glance at the 'best buy' features in lifestyle magazines or an examination of the motoring press will highlight good examples of product-focused editorial), most journalists tend to shy away from commercially driven stories and are certainly not receptive to what they see as *company propaganda.*

> **Definition:** *Company propaganda* is a negative term used by some journalists to describe positive statements presented by an organisation about its beliefs and practices.

Furthermore, to reach many consumers a company needs to be featured in the general news sections of the media rather than in specialist editorial. In this environment, media relations campaigns have to incorporate an additional *news* hook to motivate a journalist to cover a story and this might involve independent research, a celebrity association, an anniversary, a great photograph or a new and surprising angle on a traditional theme. (See Activity 21.1 and Mini case study 21.1.)

Events

It is a common misconception that public relations is only concerned with the generation of positive media coverage. Open days, workshops, roadshows, exhibitions, conferences and AGMs are all events that can provide a company with the opportunity to interact directly with consumers either on its home turf or out and about in the community, generating enhanced presence for the business and a forum for face-to-face, two-way communication. (See Think about 21.1 and Mini case study 21.2, overleaf.)

> **Definition:** High footfall retail centre refers to a shopping centre that attracts a large number of passing shoppers.

activity 21.1

Media stories

Take two daily newspapers – one quality paper and one popular or tabloid paper. Identify stories that you believe have been generated by an in-house public relations department or agency to promote a product or service.

Feedback
Clues to stories with a public relations source include: staged photographs accompanying the news item; results of research published on the date of the news item; anniversary of an event; book/film/CD published on the date of the news item.

mini case study 21.1

Media relations driving sales – a fishy story

UK supermarket Morrisons agreed to donate a percentage of its takings from fish sales on National Sea Fish Day to the Royal National Mission for Deep Sea Fishermen. The objective set for the public relations team was to develop a media relations campaign, targeting newspapers and radio stations within the catchment areas of Morrisons stores, in order to boost awareness of the initiative and encourage shoppers to visit their fish counter.

A number of potential story angles were researched before it was decided that the recently published link between fish consumption and increased brainpower provided the most media potential. Further research of GCSE performance in schools near Morrisons stores identified academic 'hot spots' and this was linked to higher than usual levels of fish consumption.

Photocalls were then held in Morrisons stores to support a fun and entertaining press pack that gave details of National Sea Fish Day and highlighted why fish is believed to boost brainpower. Favourable print and broadcast coverage appeared in all targeted areas and a significant amount of customer interest was generated at Morrisons fish counters.

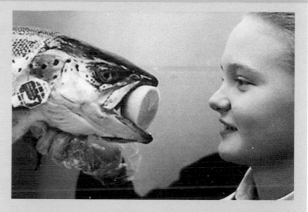

PICTURE 21.1   UK supermarket Morrisons agreed to donate a percentage of its takings from fish sales on National Sea Fish Day to the Royal National Mission for Deep Sea Fishermen.

Source: Used with kind permission of Morrisons (www.morrisons.co.uk)

mini case study 21.2

Connecting with consumers – Quality Street hits the road

Quality Street is worldwide confectionery manufacturer Nestlé's second biggest selling brand. In 2003 the packaging was redesigned to present a more contemporary image and Nestlé stepped up its programme of rolling out giant variants of individual chocolates from the selection. At the core of Nestlé's strategy was the 'de-seasonalising' of the brand (sales had previously been linked heavily to Christmas and Easter) and the broadening of its consumer appeal.

The public relations agency was briefed to develop a campaign that would display the new-look packaging, support the launch of the 'giant' Toffee Finger, create talkability around the theme that everyone has a favourite Quality Street and also provide a means to engage with consumers that would promote trial and purchase.

A car-sized motorised Quality Street tin was commissioned and built, which became the central feature of a four-week roadshow visiting 25 *high footfall retail*

centres throughout the UK. As well as being a strong visual representation of the new packaging, with a high talkability factor ('the big motorised tin is coming to town'), it also featured an electronic vote-ometer through which consumers could register their favourite from the Quality Street selection. A 'walking, talking' giant Toffee Finger mascot was also produced to give children a strong and memorable point of engagement with the new product.

Over one million people saw the giant tin during the tour and almost 20,000 votes were captured. The initiative delivered a structured and creative sampling programme while an intensive media relations programme generated extensive radio and press coverage, with the tin featured prominently in colour photography. This aspect of the campaign used statistics based on the votes cast for Quality Street favourites to give a strong regional edge to the story.

Source: Used with kind permission of Nestlé

PICTURE 21.2   Quality Street is worldwide confectionery manufacturer Nestlé's second biggest selling brand. In 2003 the packaging was redesigned to present a more contemporary image. Nestlé produced giant individual sweets from the selection and set up a roadshow featuring a giant motorised Quality Street tin.

think about 21.1   Events

- Can you think of a public relations event, like one of those listed, that you have attended in the past year?
- What about the open day you may have attended at your current or other colleges or universities?
- What were the factors that made it a success or failure?

Sponsorship

Whether in sport, the arts or in support of a worthy cause, sponsorship is fundamentally about third-party endorsement and as such sits neatly under the public relations umbrella (see also Chapter 27). If successfully managed to maximise opportunities – and this is where advertising and direct mail also play a role – sponsorship can provide a powerful platform from which to increase the relevance of a company and its products among key target audiences. By harnessing the emotions, qualities and values associated with the *sponsorship property* and perhaps providing some form of added value experience, a business can successfully stand out in a cluttered consumer market. (See Think about 21.2 and Mini case study 21.3.)

Definition: *Sponsorship property* refers to the venue, event, activity, cause, team or individual that is the subject of the sponsorship.

By discussing the different tools a practitioner has at their disposal, it soon becomes clear that a consumer public relations campaign can have many dimensions, with media relations, event or sponsorship initiatives supporting one another in an integrated and imaginative programme of activity. Figure 21.2 (overleaf) seeks to show: the components that can make up a campaign; the different audience outtakes that can be generated; and the great potential for overlap and maximisation. For example, a sponsorship might be promoted through a media relations campaign and a series of events.

think about 21.2   Sponsorship

For a sponsorship to be truly effective, does the sponsoring company need to have an obvious link with the property (for example, Adidas and football)?

Can you think of an example of a successful sponsorship where there is no obvious connection between the core activities of the business and the sponsored property, such as Xerox and football?

If you were public relations director of Coca-Cola, how would you justify its sponsorship of the Olympics? Is it about sporting performance, a particular lifestyle statement, credibility by association or none of these?

mini case study 21.3

Maximising a sponsorship – the Nationwide giant shirt

Nationwide Building Society was the official sponsor of the England football team. The aim of the sponsorship was to provide a platform for an integrated communications programme that would enhance the company's profile and consumer appeal in the highly competitive personal finance market.

In the run-up to the 2000 European Championships, Nationwide wished to achieve maximum impact so as to eclipse the activities of all other sponsors. The building society asked its agency to create a campaign that would not only dominate media coverage of sponsors but would also directly involve and excite England fans. The campaign focused on the production of the world's largest football shirt – measuring 30 metres by

20 metres, which became the centrepiece of a national roadshow and was signed with good luck messages by fans and celebrities.

Attendance at the roadshows exceeded 400,000 and the shirt was signed by 10,000 people, including celebrities such as Rod Stewart and Robbie Williams and by Prime Minister Tony Blair. Media coverage generated through photocalls and press interviews exceeded £1.3 million and awareness of Nationwide as the England football team's sponsor trebled during the four-week campaign period.

Source: Used with kind permission of Ptarmigan Consultants Limited and Nationwide Building Society

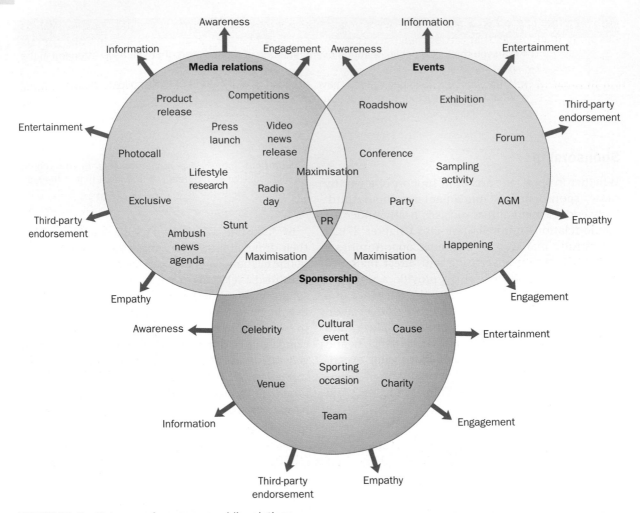

FIGURE 21.2 Universe of consumer public relations

Something extra

The campaigns that have been described were not only concerned with generating awareness and presence but were also driven by the need to communicate a personality and set of values. If a company can communicate these qualities it may succeed in differentiating itself from the competition. (See Activity 21.2.)

By helping to project human qualities on to a company, product or service, public relations can play an active role in the fascinating world of *brand* development. It is necessary to understand the role and power of effective branding more fully to appreciate the benefits that public relations can generate within the context of a successfully executed consumer strategy.

The wonderful world of brands

Definition: A *brand* is a label that seeks to add perceived value to a consumer product by generating loyalty or preference.

Method in the madness

Our societies appear to be overflowing with brands. In popular culture everything and everybody seems to be referred to as a brand: pop stars, sportsmen, royalty, airlines, places, politicians – never mind the products that line the shelves in supermarkets or fill the shops on the high street. In one sense, everything can be legitimately called a brand because the term does apply to any label that carries some meaning or association. However, for the purposes of this chapter, it is necessary to apply a more structured definition in order to fully appreciate the role that public relations can play in brand development.

Adam Morgan (1999) in his book *Eating the Big Fish* usefully defines a brand as an entity that satisfies all the following four conditions:

1 Something that has a buyer and a seller (e.g. David Beckham and Kylie Minogue but not the Queen). Morgan also makes the distinction that 'buying and selling' does not have to be a financial transaction to be of value to both sides.
2 Something that has a differentiating name, symbol or trademark (e.g. easyJet but not aeroplanes). Morever, it is differentiated from other similar products around it for reasons other than its name or trademark, (e.g. the name of an elite military squad rather than the standard armed forces).
3 Something that has positive or negative associations in consumers' minds for reasons other than its literal product characteristics (e.g. Coca-Cola but not tap-water).
4 Something that has been created, rather than is naturally occurring (e.g. the Eiffel Tower, Taj Mahal or Nou Camp (Barcelona), but not Niagara Falls or the Amazon River).

(See also Chapter 26 and Think about 21.3.)

By studying different brand definitions, such as the one put forward by Morgan, it becomes apparent how brands can add resonance to a product or service. Successful brands offer consumers tangible and emotional benefits over other products, which consumers not only recognise but also desire, at both a conscious and subconscious level. (See the neuromar-

keting investigation into Coke and Pepsi in Chapter 14.) Furthermore, great brands usually take this appeal a stage further by focusing more on emotional than rational benefits and this ultimately manifests itself in a distinct and consistent personality running through all their marketing activities. (See Think about 21.4 and Mini case study 21.4, overleaf.)

Emotional power of brands

It is not surprising that brand owners are increasingly turning to image and emotional marketing to win over consumers. In today's fast-paced economy, companies tend to copy any competitor's advantage until it is nullified, which is why emotional appeal assumes such importance and why companies such as Nike try to sell an attitude: 'Just Do It'.

The power of brands is also linked to an increasingly strong desire to express individuality through the ownership of goods and services that are perceived to be innovative, different and original. Indeed, psychologist David Lewis (Lewis and Bridger 2003: xiii) goes as far as to say that:

> For many New Consumers the purchase of products and services has largely replaced religious faith as a source of inspiration and solace. For an even larger group, their buying decisions are driven by a deep rooted psychological desire to enhance and develop their sense of self.

Given the emotional capital that is invested in some – if not all – purchasing decisions, public relations can be used to demonstrate that a brand empathises with the worries, needs and aspirations of particular groups of people, allowing it to connect and align itself with consumers in an indirect but powerful association. From an implementation perspective, this is one of the reasons why many public relations campaigns hook into lifestyle issues and popular culture,

---

think about 21.3 Brands

- Can you think of any other examples that fit each of Morgan's four criteria?
- How do these brands communicate with consumers?

---

think about 21.4 Brands and their personalities

Think of five other brands and the personalities they try to project:

- Do you admire these brands?
- What attracts or repels you about each brand?

Think about different brands of the same product, e.g. mobile phones or record companies:

- Do they carry different personalities?
- How is that personality conveyed?

Communicating a brand personality – MINI roof gardens

After much anticipation, BMW launched the new MINI to the UK public in 2001, receiving mass plaudits from the motoring press. The public relations challenge two years later was to maintain awareness of the MINI brand in the post-launch phase – keeping consumers talking about the car by emphasising its 'cheeky' personality – while focusing on coverage in the non-motoring media.

A feature of the car that supported these objectives was the opportunity for owners to personalise their MINI, particularly through the various roof designs that could be ordered through MINI dealerships. As part of a sustained campaign, the first mobile rooftop gardens were commissioned by the public relations team, using the expertise of one of London's top flower arrangers

to create real mini gardens on top of two cars: one featuring a miniature maze, including a MINI toy car lost inside, and the other with a floral swirl of colours with a fully functioning fountain in the centre.

In keeping with the car's irreverent personality, the MINIs arrived unannounced at the Chelsea Flower Show on VIP/press day to ensure optimum media coverage, after which they drove around London to maximise brand presence. The MINI roof gardens were seen by thousands of people visiting the show and the story generated over 50 pieces of media coverage in the national and regional press, online, as well as a special live link to BBC's *10 O'clock News*.

Source: used with kind permission of MINI

PICTURE 21.3   Mobile rooftop gardens were commissioned by the public relations team, using the expertise of one of London's top flower arrangers to create real mini gardens on top of two cars: one featuring a miniature maze, including a MINI toy car lost inside, and the other with a floral swirl of colours with a fully functioning fountain in the centre.

mini case study 21.5

Plugging into lifestyle issues – The Kylie Generation

Lifestyle-oriented consumer public relations was traditionally not a part of UK financial services firm Britannia Building Society's marketing mix. The press office handled media relations activity with the emphasis on targeting the personal finance pages with straightforward product and rate news. However, with a raft of modern and attractive competitors gaining an increased share of the mortgage market, Britannia saw the need to freshen its brand image in order to ensure its products and services were seen to be relevant by key target audiences. A brand-building campaign was required that would reach a young professional audience and reposition the building society as a consumer-focused organisation, in touch with modern lives and social changes.

A fun campaign hook, 'The Kylie Generation', was created that would appeal to a young consumer audience by entertaining as well as informing them about what Britannia had to offer. The campaign declared the death of the then popular Bridget Jones theory – the curse of the 'desperate singleton' – and instead celebrated a new generation of 20 to 30 year olds, who, like Kylie Minogue (the Australian actress/singer), were opting to live alone, whether they were single or not. To ensure the story would make both the news and personal finance pages, research was commissioned that analysed the behaviour of the target audience, carefully intertwining lifestyle attitudes with their views on money and the home.

Britannia's story was featured in five national newspapers, including a full-colour, double-page centre spread in *The Daily Mirror* (including full commentary of Britannia's products, plus details of its telephone number and website) and the lead consumer story in *The Sun*, as well as 40 regional dailies across the country. Radio interviews featuring a Britannia spokesperson were also negotiated with local and regional stations. The story also ran on key consumer websites that met the required profile of the campaign's key target audience, including *GQ*, *Handbag*, *Femail* and *New Woman*, prompting over 3500 online click-throughs to the Britannia website. The overall success of The Kylie Generation idea encouraged Britannia to invest in a series of additional lifestyle-focused public relations campaigns.

Source: used with kind permission of Britannia Building Society

using celebrity association, the services of psychologists, anthropologists, fashion gurus, chefs, interior designers and a range of other experts to add bite and relevance to their campaigns. (See Mini case study 21.5.)

Key challenges

Creativity is king

The biggest danger facing any consumer public relations campaign is indifference. That is why companies seek to gain marketing advantage in the battle for hearts, minds and wallets through the application of superior creativity. The search for an idea that will make busy, preoccupied consumers stop and take notice of a brand is a perennial quest across all communication disciplines. However, achieving 'stand-out' recognition and reaching the right people with key messages is now more difficult than ever before.

Definition: *Stand-out* means to give prominence to a brand, product or service through a marketing campaign.

Consumers are inundated with print, broadcast and electronic information. In the UK alone there are more than 3000 consumer magazines and 2800 local, regional and national newspapers, not to mention 600 radio and television stations, as well as a plethora of websites (see also Chapters 4 and 16 for more details on the media landscape). It is not surprising, therefore, that consumers have developed routines to protect themselves from information overload. Most direct mail gets thrown straight in the bin, we delete unsolicited emails, leave the room to make a cup of tea during commercial breaks and put the phone down on sales calls. In this consumer counter-revolution, it is difficult to get anyone's attention and as Davenport and Beck (2001) point out, the glut of information is leading to what they call an attention deficit disorder. Indeed, it can appear as if businesses are allocating more and more money in pursuit of consumers who are increasingly likely to ignore what they have to say.

Most people want to be entertained or informed about the things that matter to them, not bludgeoned with seemingly random messages and images. To break through the barrier of indifference, public relations campaigns need to include at least one of these elements to succeed and the great challenge is to think of an idea that will draw the audience to the brand. Being creative is about generating new and surprising ideas that will connect with the consumer, which is not always easy when confronted with a dull or second-rate product, an uninterested media and a non-existent campaign budget. Furthermore, any idea must fit the brand – particularly its personality and values – and, most importantly, meet the strategic objectives of the campaign. It should never be forgotten that the umbilical cord that links a great idea to a successful outcome is a robust strategy driven by a set of clear objectives (see Chapter 10 for planning and managing a campaign).

Adding value

As public relations has gained more prominence in the marketing mix, so the stakes have generally risen in terms of campaign effectiveness and measuring value. It is one thing to create awareness, another to draw attention to a brand, but still another to trigger action. Sergio Zyman (2000: 4–5), former Chief Marketing Officer at the Coca-Cola Company, highlights the challenge in a typically forthright manner:

> Marketing has to move . . . consumers to action. Popularity isn't the objective. I don't want virtual consumption – the phenomenon that occurs when customers love your product but don't feel the need to buy it . . . the only thing

> I care about is real consumption. Convincing consumers to buy your products is the only reason that a marketer is in business and the only reason that a company should spend any money at all on marketing.

Measuring and evaluating the success of a campaign is fundamentally important. By its nature, public relations cannot always be directly linked to a sale but, as discussed in Chapters 10 and 11, techniques can be deployed that illustrate how public relations activity can influence consumer perception, attitude and behaviour, and ultimately create a more favourable sales environment for a brand and its products. (See Activity 21.3 and Mini case study 21.6.)

Elephant traps

As well as demonstrating how a carefully conceived and executed public relations initiative can have a direct impact on a company's bottom line, Yorkshire Bank and the other case studies in this chapter also

---

mini case study 21.6

Delivering results – the great mortgage rip-off

Yorkshire Bank is owned by National Australia Group (NAG) and has access to a number of financial services products that started their lives in the Australasian market. The Flexible Payment Mortgage (FPM) revolutionised the mortgage market 'Down Under' by offering customers daily rather than annual interest calculation, together with the ability to over- or underpay each month. When Yorkshire Bank first introduced the FPM to the UK market, it did not promote the product aggressively, which resulted in media indifference and low consumer demand for the product. The public relations agency was asked to develop a campaign that would raise the product's profile and help establish the flexible mortgage as a mainstream home-buying product.

It was decided to position the FPM in the media as a product that could revolutionise the UK mortgage market, therefore helping to position Yorkshire Bank as a

consumer champion. Daily interest calculation was the key theme of the campaign as research showed every other lender charged annually at that time, severely penalising mortgage holders. A shock figure of £13.5 billion was calculated to generate stand-out and highlight the total amount of interest that could be saved by all homeowners in one year if their lender changed to daily interest calculation. This research formed the cornerstone of the campaign.

The FPM campaign dominated financial services media coverage for weeks, netted Yorkshire Bank £130 million of mortgage sales in a six-week period (with no advertising support) and eventually led to over 40 mainstream lenders changing the way they charged interest, all to the benefit of the consumer.

Source: Yorkshire Bank

think about 21.5 **Brand problems**

Can you think of any brands that fail consistently to live up to their promise? For example, think about the Millennium Dome tourist attraction in London or the problems faced by EuroDisney around its launch.

Can you identify any examples where public relations has failed to rescue an ailing brand, such as Dasani Water?

What about when public relations has positively helped to change the fortunes of a brand (did any other factors play a part in this resurgence)? For example, has your attitude to a failing high street store changed (think of Marks & Spencer in the UK)? For better or worse? Is that change connected to the products or the image?

highlight that good campaigns must be built on solid foundations, such as in the bank's case, a genuinely innovative product offering.

Digging for public relations gold is rarely easy and finding an attribute to hook a campaign on is an important skill for all practitioners. At the same time, however, consumer public relations is not about trying to turn a sow's ear into a silk purse. Both consumers and journalists can quickly see through vague or misleading claims about a product or service. Although a powerful tool in the appropriate context, public relations is not a panacea that can unilaterally fix a brand that is rotten to the core. However, in the white heat of market competition, more and more companies are trying to emulate organisations such as Nike, BMW and Google to become so-called 'power' brands. Lots try but few succeed and companies can waste vast sums of money on marketing in a vain attempt to dress up their brand and products as something they are not. (See Think about 21.5.)

Tomorrow's people

Rise of the 'marketing refusenik'

The future is bright for consumer public relations. Audience and media fragmentation means it is now difficult for marketers to harness a single communications medium to create and sustain a brand as television once did (see also Chapter 4 for a fuller discussion). At one time companies could reach a large slice of the public by advertising on one of a limited number of channels (for example, in the UK by advertising on the only independent channel, ITV); now they have to spread their budgets over dozens of media outlets. Furthermore, the process of cramming more advertising into traditional media, or even placing ads in new locations, often does nothing more than irritate consumers who are increasingly resisting mass message marketing, either because they are now

immune to its effects, disillusioned with its intent or have simply 'tuned it out'. The rise of the 'marketing *refusenik*' is inescapable.

> **Definition:** A *refusenik* is somebody who refuses to agree to take part in, or cooperate with, something. The term originated in Soviet Russia to describe people (mostly Jews) who were not allowed to leave the country. For the purposes of this chapter, the term 'marketing refusenik' has been created to describe consumers who are sceptical about marketing claims and make a conscious effort to ignore mass message communication.

Public relations is poised, therefore, to play an even bigger role in brand building, a point supported by marketing commentator Philip Kotler (2003: 145) who claims that advertising is losing some of its effectiveness: 'The public knows that advertising exaggerates and is biased. At its best, advertising is playful and entertaining; at its worst, it is intrusive and dishonest. Companies overspend on advertising and under spend on public relations.'

Public relations does not, however, represent a quick fix. Building a brand through public relations takes time and large doses of creativity, but the results can be dramatic if the tools that practitioners use are in tune with the communications environment of the new century. As we have seen, the weapons in the public relations armoury do not only grab attention but also promote word-of-mouth recommendation. This is particularly important given the growing tendency for consumers to opt out of mass message advertising and instead turn to family, friends, colleagues, neighbours and personal experts for ideas and information on a range of subjects. The buying decisions of these marketing refuseniks are increasingly the result of consultation and conversation within a universe of informal, interlocking networks. For example, brands such as Google and iPod have benefited hugely from positive one-to-one personal recommendation.

Clearly, a key challenge for brand owners is how to target and influence the growing number of people

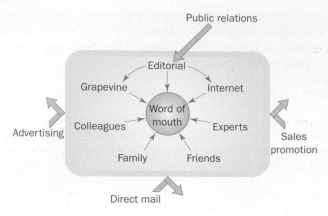

FIGURE 21.3   New challenges – the citadel of consumer culture

who have become disengaged from the marketing process. Figure 21.3 shows how public relations can give brands access to consumers who have switched off to mass message marketing through the use of third-party editorial endorsement and positive word-of-mouth recommendations.

Person to person

In *The Influentials,* Keller and Berry (2003: 5–6) illustrate how Americans are now twice as likely to cite word of mouth as a better source of ideas and information than advertising on a host of different issues:

- restaurants to try
- places to visit
- prescription drugs to use
- hotels to stay in
- retirement planning
- saving and investing money
- purchasing computer equipment
- best brands
- best buys.

Keller and Berry (2003: 5–6) go on to note: 'There are few areas in which advertising outperforms word of mouth . . . Moreover, the person-to-person channel of word of mouth, particularly among friends and family, has grown in importance in recent decades.'

In this environment, the media are still regarded as a useful source of information and advice. Mobile communication, personal computers and the internet have broadened the process still further, allowing people readily to research their options, communicate quickly with companies and other consumers, as well as build relationships with people who have similar interests to their own. In this diverse communications environment, public relations' potential to harness third-party editorial endorsement – both on- and offline – assumes an even greater importance than before, as does its ability to target and connect with individuals in a way that advertising cannot match.

The desire for word-of-mouth recommendation is nothing new and turning consumers into brand evangelists has long been held up as a key benefit of public relations. However, the need to focus strategically on generating positive word-of-mouth outcomes is more important than ever. Consumers are increasingly confident about what they hear from others and are increasingly ignoring the voice of vested interest that comes to them through direct and traditional media channels. The challenge for public relations practitioners and brand owners is to adjust to this evolving landscape.

Such a task requires fresh thinking and even greater powers of creativity. The people who hold the key to endorsement are a discerning audience who are known to be sceptical of hype and mass marketing techniques. The rise of the marketing refusenik will continue and public relations, having established itself as a viable partner in the marketing mix, should have an increasingly important role to play in shaping consumer attitudes and opinions.

Summary

This chapter has explored the terrain where public relations interfaces with the world of consumer marketing. A place where the ultimate objective for companies is to stimulate the sale of goods and services in the face of relentless competition. Public relations campaigns are playing an increasingly active role in the marketing communications arena because of their potential either to harness third-party endorsement – through media relations and sponsorship – or to allow brands to engage directly with their intended audience – through events and other activities. These tools can change attitudes, build relationships and positively influence behaviour.

The attributes public relations can bring to a campaign are growing in importance at a time when more established communication techniques are losing some of their effectiveness. However, it would be wrong to conclude that disciplines such as advertising are on the wane; in the complex communications environment of the twenty-first century, the very best campaigns tend to be integrated, multifaceted affairs, harnessing every tool at the marketer's disposal, including public relations.

In return, public relations not only has the ability to raise awareness of a product's benefits or key characteristics but can also help to give life and substance to a brand. The communication strategy of successful brands is often their defining characteristic and helps to establish a valuable point of difference in the market. Public relations, which is more subtle in its message delivery than either advertising or direct mail, can help to create and sustain a brand's personality and values, in ways that appeal to consumers.

To further develop the discipline in a marketing environment, public relations practitioners must think creatively from both a strategic and tactical perspective. Grabbing the attention of consumers is increasingly difficult and public relations must evolve to ensure that it continues to enhance its reputation in a commercial context.

Bibliography

Brassington, F. and S. Pettitt (2003). *Principles of Marketing*. Harlow: FT/Prentice Hall.

Davenport, T. and J. Beck (2001). *Attention Economy – Understanding the New Currency of Business*. Harvard, MA: Harvard Business School Press.

Greener, T. (1991). *The Secrets of Successful Public Relations*. Oxford: Butterworth-Heinemann.

Keller, E. and J. Berry (2003). *The Influentials*. New York: Free Press.

Knobil, M. (ed.) (2003). *Consumer Superbrands*. London: The Brand Council.

Kotler, P. (2003). *Marketing Insights from A to Z: 80 concepts every manager needs to know*. New York and Chichester: John Wiley & Sons.

LaSalle, D. and T. Britton (2003). *Priceless: Turning ordinary products into extraordinary experiences*. Harvard, MA: Harvard Business School Press.

Lewis, D. and D. Bridger (2003). *The Soul of the New Consumer*. London: Nicholas Brealey.

Mariotti, J. (1999). *Smart Things to Know About Brands and Branding*. Oxford: Capstone.

Morgan, A. (1999). *Eating the Big Fish: How challenger brands can compete against brand leaders*. New York and Chichester: John Wiley & Sons.

Profile (2000) 'The true religion of PR'. *Profile Magazine*, April 2000, Issue 5. London: IPR.

Ries, A. and L. Ries (2001). *The Fall of Advertising and the Rise of PR*. New York: HarperCollins.

Rosen, E. (2001). *The Anatomy of Buzz*. London: HarperCollins Business.

Wilmhurst, J. (1995). *The Fundamentals and Practice of Marketing*. Oxford: Butterworth-Heinemann.

Zaltman, G. (2003). *How Customers Think*. Harvard, MA: Harvard Business School Press.

Zyman, S. (2000). *The End of Marketing As We Know It*. London: HarperCollins Business.

CHAPTER 22
Business-to-business
public relations

Learning outcomes

By the end of this chapter you should be able to:

■ define and describe business-to-business public relations

■ recognise the key role of the trade media in shaping perceptions

■ identify the key principles of business-to-business public relations

■ apply this understanding to simple, relevant scenarios

■ recognise business-to-business activity through case examples

■ apply the principles to real-life scenarios.

Structure

■ Core principles of business-to-business (B2B) public relations

■ Trade journals and journalists

■ Coordinating the communications disciplines

■ Building corporate reputation

Introduction

The concept of business-to-business (B2B) public relations is based on the recognition that most organisations sell to other businesses rather than directly to the consumer. The scope of such business transactions is enormous and incorporates products and services as diverse as aircraft and microchips. Each sector of the marketplace has its own operating environment but the fundamental need for public relations underpins all transactions.

The traditional focus of B2B public relations has been the use of *editorial* in trade magazines as a direct method of prompting sales enquiries. This pragmatic perspective of the role of B2B public relations has demonstrated the power of public relations in creating the sales environment in the economically massive US, European and international marketplaces.

> **Definition:** *Editorial* refers to written text in a journal, magazine or newspaper that has been written either by a journalist/reporter or submitted by a public relations practitioner and then reviewed/edited before printing by the editor or sub-editor of the publication. Editorial is the opposite of advertising, which is bought (paid-for) space in a publication. Editorial is perceived as having greater impact because it has editorial endorsement by the publication and has support for its 'objectivity'.

However, contemporary B2B public relations uses the full scope of public relations as the business-to-business marketplace becomes increasingly sophisticated. An examination of entries into B2B categories in the UK Chartered Institute of Public Relations Excellence Awards and the PRCA Frontline Awards shows how public relations is being successfully used to manage corporate reputations and build relationships as well as providing vital support for sales and marketing programmes.

Core principles of business-to-business (B2B) public relations

The starting point for B2B public relations is a detailed understanding of the specific marketplace, the application of the products or services in question and an appreciation of the dynamics of the buying process. This reflects the traditional emphasis on supporting sales and the very real need for public relations activity to present the benefits of particular products and services.

Advocates of B2B public relations as a specialism say that the depth of marketplace understanding is a point of differentiation with consumer public relations (see Chapter 21), where practitioner knowledge of consumer behaviour outweighs the need for product and marketplace familiarity. (See Activity 22.1.)

> **Definition:** *Business-to-business* (B2B) is defined as 'relating to the sale of a product for any use other than personal consumption. The buyer may be a manufacturer, a reseller, a government body, a non-profit-making institution or any organisation other than an ultimate consumer' (Cornelissen 2004: 184).

The characteristics of a business-to-business marketplace include:

- relatively small number of 'buying' publics – it may even be that potential customers can be named as individuals (e.g. manufacturers in the building trade will know of the specific builders' merchants who could stock their products: there may only be three or four)
- a specific application/end uses for products and services (e.g. a producer of thermal insulation boards for house building)
- defined product and service terms of technical specifications and any legal/trading restrictions (such as controls on building products like insulation requirements of windows or insulation boards, as in the previous example)

- purchasing decision often negotiated individually and subject to finite contract periods.

This list indicates the depth of company and marketplace knowledge required by successful practitioners of B2B public relations. The traditional use of media relations techniques in trade and specialist magazines also requires a detailed understanding of the workings and requirements of these journals.

Trade journals and journalists

The trade press is an important and integral part of the B2B marketplace. The UK is unusually well served by specialist publications covering all sectors from aerospace to waste management (see Table 22.1). The pan-European marketplace is not dissimilar, with prominent titles addressing all market sectors (see also Romeike website at www.romeike.com or PR Newswire at www. prnewswire.co.uk).

Managers and professionals tend to read the titles particular to their trade or industry as part of their working lives. And it is this special linkage that attributes particular influence to trade and specialist magazines.

Circulation and *readership* relate to the size of the sector and the existence or otherwise of competitive titles. Thus a key trade publication such as *The Grocer* in the UK, which serves the food and drink industries, has a circulation of 54,000 and a readership of over 200,000. This dwarfs the *Architects' Journal,* one of the 64 titles covering the building sector in the UK. But both publications have the unique advantage of the trade press. They are read by decision makers in their sector. The loyalty of trade press readerships creates a strong role for their titles in the B2B cycle of influence and persuasion.

This accounts for the traditional B2B public relations focus on gaining editorial coverage in trade magazines. This role remains important and editorial staff on trade magazines are worthy of special attention.

> **Definition:** *Circulation* refers to how many copies of the magazine are distributed.
>
> **Definition:** *Readership* refers to the actual numbers predicted to read each circulated copy based on research. Note that more people read trade journals because they are based in an office with one subscription, which is shared, e.g. the *Architects' Journal* in an architects' practice is circulated around the team, often with comments on relevant or interesting features/articles. (See Mini case study 22.1, overleaf.)

TABLE 22.1   Examples of specialist business-to-business titles to be found under 'C'. The listing reflects the breadth and diversity of sectors

Cabinet Maker
Cable & Satellite Europe
Cable & Satellite International
CABLEtalk
Cabling World
CAD User
Cafe Culture
Call Centre Europe
Call Centre Focus
Campaign
Capacity
Caravan Industry and Park Operator
Card Technology Today
Card World
Cards International
Care and Nursing Essentials
Care On The Road
Careers Adviser
Cargo Systems
Caring
Caring Times incorporating
   Homecare Professional
Caring UK
Carmarthenshire Business –
   Busnes Sir Gaerfyrddin
Cash & Carry Management Inc.
Cash & Carry Wholesaler
Casino International
Castings Buyer
CAT (Car & Accessory Trader)
Catalogue and e-business
Caterer & Hotelkeeper
Catering & Licensing Review
Catering Manager
Catering Post
Catering South West
Catering Update
CBW Coach and Bus Week
CCTV Today
CFJ Contract Flooring Journal
CFO Europe
CFR
Chamberlink
Channel Business
Channel Middle East
Channel Moves
channelinfo
Charities Management
Charity Finance
Charity Times
Chartered Secretary
Checkout
Chemical and Engineering News
Chemical Engineering
Chemical Week
Chemist & Druggist
Chemistry & Industry
Chemistry World

Chocolate & Confectionery
   International
CHP Packer International
CHT Cleaning & Hygiene Today
CiB News
CIR Continuity Insurance & Risk
Circle Update
Circuits Assembly
City Confidential
City Planning
Civic & Public Building Specifier
Civil Engineering
Civil Engineering Surveyor
Claims Professional
CLASS Magazine
Clay Technology
Cleaning & Maintenance
Cleaning Matters
Clearview (Midlands)
Clearview (North)
Clearview (South)
CLI Clinical Laboratory International
Client Server News
Clinica World Medical
   Device & Diagnostic News
Clinical Medicine
Close-Up
Club Journal
Club Mirror
Coach Monthly
Coach Tours UK
Coal International
Coin Slot International
Cold Chain News
Commerce & Industry
Commercial Insurance
Commercial Lawyer
Commercial Motor
Commercial Property Monthly
Commercial Risk
Comms Business
Comms Dealer
Comms MEA
Communicate
Communications Africa
Communications News
Communicators in Business
Community Care
Community Pharmacy
Community Practitioner
Community Retailer
Company Car
Company Clothing
Company Van
Components in Electronics
Computer Arts
Computer Arts Projects
Computer Business Review

Computer Buyer
Computer Consultant
Computer Finance
Computer Fraud & Security
Computer Headline Scotland
Computer Music
Computer News Middle East
Computer Reseller News
Computer Shopper
Computer Trade Shopper
Computer Video
Computer Weekly
Computeractive
Computergram International
Computers +
   Telecommunications in Africa
Computing
Computing Which?
Concrete
Confectionery Production
Conference & Exhibition Fact
   Finder
Conference & Incentive
   Travel
Connect
CONNECTINGINDUSTRY.COM/ele
   ctronics
Conservatory Industries
Conservatory Magazine
Conspectus
Constabulary Magazine
Construction Europe
Construction Magazine
Construction Manager
Construction National
Construction News
Contact Centre Management
Container Management
Containerisation International
Contraceptive Education
   Bulletin
Contract Journal
Contrax Weekly
Control Engineering Europe
Convenience Store
Converter
Converting Today
Co-operative News
Corporate Affairs
Corporate Citizenship
   Briefing
Corporate Entertainer
Corporate Finance
Corporate IT Update
Corporate Location
Corporate Times
Corrosion Prevention &
   Control

▶

TABLE 22.1   (*Continued*)

Cosmetics International	Create Online	CTE Cable Telecommunication
Cosmetics Products Report	Creation	Engineering
Cost Sector Catering	Creative Head	CTO Computer Trade Only
Counsel	Creative Review	Custom Installer
Countryside Focus	Credit & Car Finance	Customer Management
Coventry and Warwickshire Enterprise	Credit Management	Customer Relationship
Cover	Credit Today	Management
Cranes & Access	Crops	Customer Service News
Cranes Today	CSN Copy Shop News	CWB Childrenswear Buyer

Trade journalists

As a public relations practitioner, you will routinely find that trade press journalists have a thorough understanding of their subject area. This fact creates both an opportunity and a challenge for the practitioner. You will have an informed and potentially responsive audience. But you will need to be knowledgeable and show your competence when dealing with trade journalists. However, also remember that we all have to start our careers somewhere. So you may be dealing with a '*cub*' reporter or a journalist who has moved recently to a particular title. The big media groups have a raft of trade titles and journalists move frequently between titles and specialist areas. They may still be learning about their new subject area, maybe at the same time as you.

> **Definition:** A *cub* reporter is a junior or trainee reporter/ journalist.

When dealing with trade press journalists, as a rule of thumb, assume expertise. This is usually the case and it is common for editors of relatively small circulation magazines to be frequent commentators on television news programmes and in the national dailies. This is simply because such individuals do become genuine experts through their professional concentration on a subject area. For example, the editor of *The Grocer* is often used on national business broadcasts on radio and television as an expert commentator on supermarket trends and prices. Also *Jane's Defence Weekly* editors are frequently called on to supply expert knowledge during armed conflicts around the world. See Activity 22.2.

Story ideas

The news values of trade publications obviously have a sector-specific focus and regular reading of key magazines will readily identify the news angles adopted. Practitioners working in a B2B marketplace should be avid readers of the sector's periodicals. Box 22.1 pro-

activity 22.2

Trade magazines in your country

Do you know just how many trade magazines are published in your country? Use the internet or media databases such as PIMS or Romeike (www.romeike.com) to search the number of titles.

Feedback

You may be surprised by the number. In the UK there are titles relevant to a wide variety of sectors, from the railway industries to animal health, chemical processing and embalming.

vides some examples of typical B2B news angles for gaining editorial coverage.

News will usually be presented to the media through a press release but other techniques of regular use to B2B public relations practitioners include:

- one-to-one briefings
- photocalls
- feature articles
- case studies
- press conferences
- facility visits.

box 22.1   Typical news angles for B2B editorial

Typical news angles for B2B editorial would include:

- new senior, technical and managerial appointments
- new products and services
- new technology and new processes
- new contracts
- unusual or problem-solving contracts and applications
- new premises
- market diversification or convergence
- partnerships, associations, mergers, takeovers.

mini case study 22.1

How trade publications are used

the architects' journal 12|08|04

ADJAYE'S PUBLIC INTEREST

TOWER HAMLETS IDEA STORE VICTORY IN OUR PPG7 CAMPAIGN

PICTURE 22.1   The *Architects' Journal* is one of 64 titles in the UK covering the building trade. This particular cover features an Adjaye/Associates scheme.
Source: Photograph Timothy Soar

The following case study shows how a practising architect uses B2B titles such as the *Architects' Journal* in his everyday working life. The architect is Nigel Jacques, director of one of the UK's largest commerical architecture firms, Carey Jones Architects:

'As an architectural practice we use the *Architects' Journal* and other similar trade magazines at varying levels and for different reasons. The *Architects' Journal* is used in our practice as an important technical and visual resource. It keeps us up to date with new design concepts, regulations and innovative materials and also with the legal and professional aspects of architecture.

'The more senior you are within the practice the more in depth you tend to read the *Architects' Journal*. At director level it is used as a resource for keeping up to date on a weekly basis with the market as it evolves and with new materials and design concepts. To a young design architect, the *Architects' Journal* is used more as a visual resource. When you read through an architectural trade mag azine it is a media experience in which you are constantly absorbing knowledge and picking up ideas and inspiration on an often subliminal level. Architecture is an art, which

CAREYJONESARCHITECTS

means that we are constantly looking at visual stimuli first and foremost and then looking in more detail and noticing aspects of design such as products or innovative use of materials.

'The *Architects' Journal* can influence buying and design decisions in as much that an architect might notice a particular material and/or form used in a building on an image and start thinking how it may influence a Carey Jones' scheme. Technical articles within the *Architects' Journal*, for instance, indicate in detail how the material was used effectively in the design and who the supplier is.

'The journal also contributes to sector understanding as it provides an up-to-date and informative source of current trends, regulations and changes in legislation which could impact on the practice. As well as an architectural resource, it is therefore also a useful trend predictor. In growing and developing your business you are constantly monitoring the performance of other practices (the *Architects' Journal* top 100 architects, for instance), watching the political environment and organisations with whom you may wish to collaborate or who may directly impact upon your business. The *Architects' Journal* can be used as a tool for all these things.

'In terms of alternative thinking and inspiring creativity, the *Architects' Journal* contributes in as much that it features the commercial conformists, the individuals and the mavericks of the trade. The visual illustrations can inspire architects with ideas for their own work and often promote healthy debate.

'Our PR consultants also target the *Architects' Journal* as a means of raising our profile as a national practice and we are frequently approached by journalists for comment on national and project-specific issues. However, publications of this nature can also be responsible for negative comment and it can be somewhat frustrating when publications are predictable and frequently one sided. A good relationship with journalists though can help to offset this and allow you the opportunity to respond to potential negative coverage. Regular positive editorial coverage within national trade publications adds equity to the Carey Jones brand, acts as an efficient business development tool when read by key decision makers, contributes to the 'feel good' factor within the practice as an excellent motivator and attracts high calibre staff to our practice.

'The *Architects' Journal* is a key resource for Carey Jones, without which we would be working within a vacuum with regard to current trends. Every design practice needs to monitor the macro environment within which it operates and without national trade publications like the *Architects' Journal* this would prove extremely difficult.'

Source: Carey Jones Architects

These techniques are covered in Chapter 16, but here are some other techniques that are available to the public relations practitioner.

Advertorials

The advertorial is also used frequently in B2B promotional campaigns. Advertorials are paid-for advertisements designed to look like editorial. However, journals will always indicate clearly the sponsoring company in order to differentiate from editorial. So although advertorials may look like editorial, they do not have the credibility of news or features material written and/or edited by journalists.

From the practitioner's perspective, advertorial is often regarded as promotional material and treated much like a newsletter or a company publication.

Websites

Particular note must also be taken of the specialist websites gaining common currency in most industry sectors. Many specialist and trade publications maintain their own websites to complement their printed publications. Equally, the trade associations operating in each sector often have websites. Major industry events such as conferences, seminars and exhibitions are also frequently supported by websites. Such websites are both a vital source of information for practitioners and offer an additional source of target outlets for placing product and corporate news and information. In the UK, a good starting point for seeking industry-sector websites is via the Chartered Institute of Public Relations website – www.cipr.co.uk.

Beyond the specific product or company-related news items, trade magazines offer a particularly good opportunity to place commentary on marketplace, technology and product developments. In-depth material available through your client company may be highly valued by the editor of trade magazines. In practice, this creates the opportunity for a client or company to be seen as a source of authoritative industry information. (See Think about 22.1, Case study 22.1 and Think about 22.2, overleaf)

Coordinating the communications disciplines

The use of public relations techniques to support the sales environment is well understood and is often the motivation for appointing a public relations manager or using a public relations consultancy. Practitioners can demonstrate that insightful and creative public relations can both indirectly and directly generate sales.

In B2B public relations, an understanding of the role of other communication disciplines is essential, as is the timing and coordinated application of the right techniques. Public relations practitioners working in B2B often display an in-depth understanding of advertising, direct mail and sales promotion and of how public relations can act as a unifying mechanism. This is particularly true where editorial placement techniques are being used as an element in the promotional part of the marketing mix. The marketing mix, originally defined by Borden (1964), is the combination of the major tools of marketing otherwise known as the 4Ps – product, price, promotion and place (see Table 22.2, overleaf).

Figure 22.1 (overleaf) shows some of the promotional disciplines typically employed in B2B marketing. All are aimed at supporting the sales effort and their application reflects views on the best way to reach decision makers. It is often not enough to rely on one channel, hence most promotional campaigns use a combination of techniques to make up the promotion aspect of the 4Ps in the marketing mix.

Role of advertising

Advertising has the very particular job of placing a proposition in front of the target audience. The

case study 22.1

Charles Yorke

PICTURE 22.2   The public relations campaign emphasised the craftswork and quality in the product range.

Using the trade media to create the sales environment

This case study shows how a specific business need can be fulfilled by a well-planned and tightly executed trade media campaign.

Charles Yorke is a division of the Symphony Group plc: one of the UK's largest independent providers of fitted furniture. Responding to the growing demand for craftsman-built bespoke kitchens, the company needed to establish a retailer base in order to take its product offer effectively to the trade marketplace and ultimately to the consumer. MCG Public Relations proposed very clear public relations campaign objectives:

- to recruit retailers by creating a desire for the Charles Yorke brand in the industry
- to enhance Symphony's reputation as a supplier of premium, as well as volume, kitchen furniture
- to communicate the originality of Charles Yorke's designs and products.

Planning and research

MCG Public Relations carried out one-to-one interviews with all key trade journalists in the sector and also spoke to existing Symphony retailers to assess knowledge and perceptions of the Charles Yorke brand and the Symphony Group. It was clear that, although Symphony was seen as a well-established major manufacturer, there was little knowledge of its bespoke provision.

The results were used to create key messages for all communications associated with the campaign and also to help select tailored and targeted tactics to reach the designated audiences.

Implementation

Preview visits to Charles Yorke's manufacturing facility were organised with selected trade journalists to see craftsworkers in action and the showroom of latest kitchen designs.

Exclusive features were devised to give selected journalists unique news material, from trade magazine *Cabinet Maker's* profile of Charles Yorke's Manufacturing Director, *to Kitchen Designer's* preview of the new kitchen design concepts.

'Kitchen Showcase' – a premium-end industry exhibition – was chosen to launch Charles Yorke's latest kitchen designs, placing the brand firmly in the bespoke/craftsworker-built sector.

AGA – a household name in kitchen appliances – was chosen as a partner at the showcase exhibition to demonstrate the synergy between the brands, both in terms of heritage and innovation.

Maytag – the premium US manufacturer of fridge/freezers – was also chosen to partner at the Charles Yorke stand, ensuring that the brand's contemporary, as well as traditional, design executions were depicted.

Tailored press packs were created for all trade journalists and freelancers, with an extensive CD library of quality photography and exclusive, carved cheeseboards to show Charles Yorke craftswork.

Choosing to stock a new kitchen brand is a major decision for a retailer, often entailing the replacement of existing displays and complete studio refurbishment. MCG ensured that interested retailers were shown the added value of becoming a Symphony brand stockist, by providing public relations support in terms of trade and local publicity. Early consumer media coverage was also secured, in order to strengthen the marketing support messages for retailers.

Outcome and evaluation

First, 30 retailers signed up to become Charles Yorke stockists, 19 of which were attributed directly to the

▶

case study 22.1 (continued)

public relations campaign. The support mechanism created for retailers resulted in ongoing relationships, with 'customer home' features compiled for the follow-up consumer campaign.

A post-campaign trade media audit showed a clear shift in perceptions regarding the strength and depth of Symphony's product offer. More than 20 items of positive trade media coverage were achieved, each containing the agreed key messages about the Charles Yorke brand and Symphony Group proposition.

Mutually beneficial publicity relationships continued with AGA and Maytag, further strengthening Charles Yorke's brand image. Also, Symphony's reputation with key trade journalists was substantially enhanced, ensuring a platform for the full spectrum of its product portfolio.

Observations

This campaign by MCG Public Relations provides a model of how to use the trade media to develop tangi-

ble business benefits. Prior to the campaign, time was taken to understand the requirements and knowledge levels of trade journalists. This resulted in a campaign planned around their needs. As required, sales leads were generated and both product and corporate reputation are enhanced substantially.

Alison Andrews of Symphony said:

This campaign led to many high-quality enquiries from potential retailers of which 19 were converted into actual sign-ups. The tailored and targeted nature of their programme ensured that only premium-market design studios approached us and each had a clear perception of the Charles Yorke brand and values. Rather than being perceived as just another new product range for Symphony, the launch of Charles Yorke shifted industry perceptions about the strength and depth of the whole company.

Source: Charles Yorke

---

strength of advertising is in the control of message delivery. Your message is placed in front of a known audience at an agreed point in time. This precise control of the message, audience and timing can make advertising very effective. And in the B2B arena, results can usually be measured and analysed.

The very best advertisements offer a single proposition in a highly creative way. In the B2B marketplace, there should always be a 'call to action', making it clear what we are asking interested readers to do – phone this number, send in this coupon, access this website.

Advertising spend should not be used to attempt to influence editorial decisions. Some sales and marketing managers may believe that the importance of advertising revenue to trade magazines means that big advertisers can expect an editorial *quid pro quo* (obtain editorial coverage if they have paid for advertising space). This is not the case. Editorial staff cherish their independence and this should be re-

spected. Editorial decisions should be based on the news value of '*copy*' submitted in the form of press releases and news features – see also Chapter 16.

> **Definition:** *Copy* refers to a term used generically by the communications industries to describe written text for news releases, adverts, advertorials, editorials, articles and in-house newsletter articles, etc.

Advertising has a defined role in placing repetitive messages in front of buying audiences. Hence its value in B2B marketing. Public relations can be used in a complementary way to expand on a necessarily simple advertising message and to broaden audience reach. It is also worth noting that news value is usually enhanced if editorial is offered before an advertising campaign. Something that is already being advertised can not really be regarded as 'news'.

---

think about 22.2 · Business to business as a public relations specialism

Public relations practitioners regard B2B as a specialism unlike others. This is primarily because of the special emphasis placed on supporting the sales effort and understanding the marketplace. Think again about how B2B public relations has been defined and how this differs from consumer public relations (see also Chapter 21).

TABLE 22.2   The marketing mix

Price	Product
Cost	Product management
Profitability	New development
Value for money	Product features and benefits
Competitiveness	Branding
Incentives	Packaging
	After-sales service

Place	Promotion
Access to target market	Promotional mix
Channels to market	Public relations
Retailers and distributors	Advertising
Logistics	Sales promotion
	Sales management
	Direct marketing

Role of direct marketing

Direct marketing is appropriately named as a promotional technique. The proposition is put directly to the prospective buyer, for example in a leaflet, flyer or brochure, without an intermediary such as a distributor, agent or salesperson. This creates its major advantage in many B2B marketplaces where there is an identifiable and discrete number of buyers and/or influencers. Direct marketers work from target lists (databases) that they either buy from a list brokerage or compile themselves. Responses are tracked and measured with precision.

Direct marketing is becoming increasingly sophisticated as a promotional technique as communication channels, message content and response rates can be tracked and refined. Public relations supports direct marketing by building the credibility and reputation of the organisation. It is able to do this by placing key messages in front of target audiences.

Role of sales promotion

Sales promotion techniques such as special offers, 'bogofs' (buy one, get one free), vouchers, redeemable gifts, competitions, etc. are well established in consumer marketing and are being used increasingly in B2B. This is simply because a well-thought-through sales promotion can work and has a single objective – to increase sales. Sales promotions can also be popular with sales teams as it gives them something specific to offer their customers.

> **Definition:** *Bogof* is an abbreviated term used in sales promotion for selling two products for the price of one, 'buy one, get one free'.

Sales promotion is very distinct from public relations but the disciplines do have much in common. When they run in tandem their effectiveness in creating sales opportunities can be enhanced. The linkage between sales promotion and public relations is strong because sales promotions can offer benefits that supplement the basic product, price, place and offer.

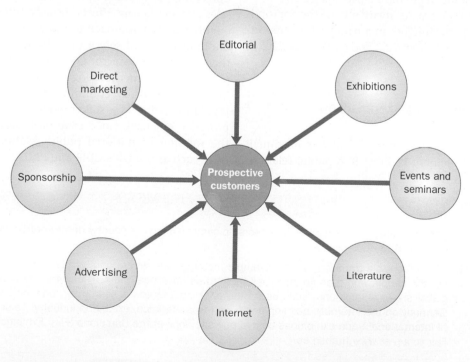

FIGURE 22.1   Promotional disciplines used in business-to-business marketing

Role of public relations

Public relations can support the other promotional disciplines and be a promotional technique in its own right. Undoubtedly, the most effective use of the promotional disciplines is shown when there is clear coordination in the planning stage. Common themes can be developed that 'work' in all channels, albeit with content and messages presented in different ways to different audiences at different times.

Creative routes can be developed jointly through '*brainstorming*' and practitioners in all the disciplines can work to a shared timetable. Cost savings will be demonstrated through minimising the time input of contributing professionals and through shared creative work (artwork, photography, etc.).

> **Definition:** *Brainstorming* means getting a group of colleagues to discuss an issue and come up with different ideas collectively.

The special role of public relations is in taking the proposition to a broader range of influencers through the use of media relations and other public relations techniques. Of course, public relations as defined in marketing terms, as one element of the marketing mix (see Table 22.2), is a more limited concept than you will find elsewhere in this book. For a fuller discussion of public relations and marketing, see Chapter 26. Public relations in its larger sense is also of value to B2B communications, as discussed in the later section, 'Building corporate reputation'. (See Box 22.2.)

The best B2B campaigns invariably use the appropriate promotional techniques in a parallel and supportive way. (See Think about 22.3 and Case study 22.2.)

Building corporate reputation

The use of editorial to support the sales environment is an essential element of most B2B public relations

---

> ### box 22.2 Activities used in B2B public relations campaigns
>
> Most frequently, editorial will be the lead public relations tool. Other activities used in B2B public relations campaigns include:
>
> - newsletters
> - literature
> - internet
> - seminars
> - briefings
> - conferences
> - roadshows
> - awards and competitions
> - presentations
> - sponsorship and endorsements.

campaigns. However, there is a fundamental difference between media relations as a promotional technique and the comprehensive application of public relations methodology to analyse trends, counsel organisational leaders and to plan and deliver reputation-building communications programmes. Media relations can be used as part of the marketing mix alongside the other promotional disciplines such as advertising and direct mail to great effect. But the real power of public relations is seen when applied as a strategic planning tool in support of top-line corporate objectives.

An examination of award-winning B2B public relations campaigns shows a clear trend. The support for sales and marketing efforts, usually through a thoroughly planned approach to trade media relations, is undiminished. But senior practitioners are imposing their professionalism on client organisations to use public relations methodology to plan strategically, to integrate and unify communications and to build reputation with key stakeholders before the sales process is engaged. Good examples can be found on the websites of national public relations organisations such as the UK's CIPR and PRCA.

> ### think about 22.3 B2B in action
>
> Can you think of an exhibition/sponsorship campaign in your country or internationally that is targeted at B2B audiences?
>
> **Feedback** Think about big trade shows, for example motor shows, where cars are launched to the 'trade', i.e. the people who then go on to sell them to us, the consumers. There are many other big specialist shows/exhibitions, such as for the print industry (do a search for 'printing exhibitions' in Germany on the internet), building and even the conference/exhibition industry! To see the range of international trade exhibitions held at one site, look at the Barcelona 'Fira' Exhibition and Trade Fair venue at www.firabcn.es

smartLite

Coordinating the communications disciplines

This case study of B2B public relations demonstrates how a pan-European trade show was used to great effect to create media interest in a new technology with the ultimate aim of preparing the ground for salesforce activity. It also illustrates the successful incorporation and coordination of other communication techniques, such as an exhibition, website, advertising, literature and direct mail, in order to deliver the desired results.

Ash Communications was tasked with creating and organising the European launch of a new footwear-soling technology, smartLite, to technology, footwear, lifestyle and creative design media at a prestigious trade show in Bologna, Italy. Its client was the industrial conglomerate Huntsman.

The public relations objectives of the campaign were specific and geared to ensuring a successful launch of the new product by:

- attracting 10 journalists (minimum target) to the launch
- ensuring perception of smartLite as a premium, highperformance, lightweight, aesthetically creative and innovative product
- recording the number of media impressions (number of times the product was mentioned/featured in all media) including key messages (coverage achieved in trade publications).

The launch
Launch programme

Ash Communications prepared a campaign strategy focusing on an insight into consumers' footwear purchasing habits. Importantly, the public relations activity used the themes that would be taken up in supporting promotional activity, such as advertising, direct mail, website and sales literature.

Launch presentation

Ash consultants liaised with the product technicians to provide presentations at the launch that would endorse the technology and provide real-life experience of handling and creatively working with the material. They also wrote the copy for sales literature and edited website copy, in order to ensure consistency of product messages.

Media relations

The consultancy acted as the creative agency to create and copywrite a 'teaser' media invitation, targeting Europe-wide footwear, lifestyle, technology, creative design, national, regional, broadcast and online media. It agreed communications messages based on the consumer insight and prepared a full press pack, including design concept images.

The daily show magazine was targeted to attract attending journalists and to communicate subsequently the new technology to a wider audience.

The Italian office of Ash organised the media launch, liaising with the local organisers, caterers and audiovisual technicians to ensure the smooth running of the presentation.

Evaluation

- Total media in attendance at launch: 18
- Total editorial pieces: 25
- Total media impressions: 1,500,000

What the media said

'Soft, light and strong smartLite soles', ARS Sutoria, Italy
'Perfect footwear technology', Ayaks, Turkey
'A fusion of technology, creativity and innovation', La Pelle, Italy

Observations

This case study demonstrates the mainstream use of B2B public relations applied on a pan-European basis. The consultancy used the vehicle of the trade show to manage the media and present with great success the new product's key messages. Significantly, the work forms part of a wider marketing campaign using other communication techniques and helped the Huntsman salesforce to gain meetings with business customers and to sell the new technology. The role of Ash Communications was not just to manage the media opportunities created by the exhibition but to help unify and coordinate the other promotional disciplines. For this to happen with this level of success requires the consultancy to combine the essential tenets of B2B public relations: detailed product and marketplace understanding; thorough public relations planning and implementation; and an understanding of how the promotional disciplines work together to achieve results.

Source: used with kind permission of Ash Communications

The most effective use of public relations from an organisational perspective is to build a favourable reputation with key stakeholders. And this process is critical to B2B communications where 'reputation' is the essential element in the buying process. No one wants to do business with an organisation without a reputation, and certainly not with an organisation with a poor reputation. Thus the public relations function in a B2B organisation has the same remit as that applied in a consumer or public sector organisation – to establish and maintain mutual understanding between the organisation and its publics.

This reputation-building role will become increasingly important as external stakeholders, including customers and activist groups, start to look at the organisation behind the brand and make purchasing decisions based on wider judgements including social responsibility considerations and corporate ethics (see also Chapters 6, 11 and 15).

Organisational leaders with an understanding of public relations are using public relations in two interconnected ways, regardless of the size of the operation. Public relations works as a promotional tool with the other marketing disciplines such as advertising and sales promotion. But public relations is also being used to manage the organisational reputation with audiences beyond the marketing remit, such as shareholders, the local community, staff, suppliers and government at all levels. (See Activity 22.3 and Case study 22.3.)

---

activity 22.3

Managing reputation

Use the internet to find an example of a B2B company that actively uses a wide range of communications techniques to manage its reputation.

---

case study 22.3

CPP Group

Building corporate reputation

This campaign by public relations consultancy Financial Dynamics on behalf of its client, the CPP Group, provides an example of creative public relations that aims to build corporate reputation. The methodology is more typical of consumer public relations but is here applied with outstanding results in a B2B environment. (This campaign was a finalist in the UK CIPR Excellence Awards, see website www.cipr.co.uk)

The CPP Group is an international provider of everyday consumer assistance products, with 11.3 million customers worldwide. It offers a number of services including:

- credit card protection
- retrieval service for lost or stolen keys
- emergency service for everyday domestic problems
- mobile phone insurance
- insurance, advice and support for people with debt worries.

CPP works with many partners, including high street banks, which re-brand CPP products as their own, leading to virtual anonymity for CPP among end consumers.

Public relations objectives

The public relations objectives of this 12-month communication programme were to build greater awareness of the company among corporate audiences, to profile new and existing products in trade and specialist publications and to increase the 'share of voice' for CPP and its products.

Implementation

Rather than simply promote CPP's range and products, the campaign focused on product-related issues of concern to the customer, both to raise CPP's profile and position it as a consumer champion. Robust, topical research formed the backbone of the campaign, with each topic carefully considered for impact in terms of delivering optimum news value and boosting CPP's sales figures. Research was undertaken on a quarterly basis, enabling CPP to examine trends and become more central to industry debate – achieving results such as the lead story on the front page of UK national newspaper *The Daily Express* (circulation 945,000).

Announcements linked to other products, such as home emergency and mobile phone insurance, worked in synergy with CPP's product marketing activity so that different issues were prioritised at different points in the year. Finance Dynamics carried out an aggressive media programme, based on regular consumer omnibus research, to provide contemporary news angles.

Proactive news releases generated for CPP included:

15 February – 'Fear of debt soars by 44% in three months'

28 February – 'Mobile phones top the league of most useful modern inventions'

12 March – 'Consumers display lax attitude toward plastic card fraud'

case study 22.3 (continued)

3 May – 'Young Britons crippled by financial commitments'

13 June – 'It may be good to talk . . . but it's clearly better to text'

20 August – 'Obsession with home improvement TV puts Britons at risk of injury and expense'

17 September – '1 in 10 only alarmed by debt when they lose their home or partner'

2 October – 'Britons ill-prepared for rollout of chip and pin'

12 November – 'Brits' patriotic tendencies revealed in mobile phone tune hate list'

5 December – 'CPP Group plc promotes improved financial awareness with new product launch'

10 December – 'Credit card spending cut back this Christmas'

Financial Dynamics also undertook a number of additional public relations initiatives throughout the year. These included the launch of CPP's new financial advice and support service, Financial Health, which capitalised on the strong relationships with journalists from the debt index stories. A programme of media briefings was organised between target business writers and the new CPP Group Chief Executive, Andrew Fisher, to help build the company's corporate profile. A weekly 'Box of Tricks' was created to allow opportunistic CPP comment 'piggybacking' (working alongside or aligned to) the news agenda, to help maintain CPP's position at the cutting edge of industry issues.

Evaluation and measurement of the campaign

The campaign generated 373 pieces of news coverage – 19% of which appeared in the national media. CPP's average share of voice in the market against competitors – including Barclaycard, RBS, Egg, National Debtline and Citizens Advice Bureau – was 18%.

Seventy per cent of all coverage included at least one of CPP's key messages: 'Fear of debt soars by 44% in three months' generated the greatest media interest, with 51 positive news hits, including national

dailies and trade publications, and the 'Elderly set for a winter of debt and discontent as tax hikes hit hard' press release led to the lead, front-page story in UK national paper *The Daily Express*.

Presence in home news, rather than just the money pages, suggests that the campaign succeeded in positioning CPP with consumers as well as with trade audiences.

Coverage for CPP achieved a potential audience reach of more than 146 million people. Based on flat-rate card figures, coverage was valued at over £583,000 – five times greater than public relations fees and expenses.

The campaign was vigorously evaluated every quarter, enabling Financial Dynamics to present the value of public relations as a discipline to CPP's internal audiences and offer quarterly recommendations for continuous improvement to the programme. The positive results shown through evaluation correlate with coverage volumes rising by an average of 20% per quarter.

Rob Miatt, Marketing Manager for CPP, commented: 'The targeted media relations approach via regular, thought-provoking and hard-hitting research led by the news agenda gave us a strong media following, raised our profile amongst an important consumer audience, forged our position as an industry leader, and even made us front-page news.'

Observations

This case study offers an example of contemporary public relations activity that is able to encompass the traditional B2B role with the substantial 'added value' of developing a simultaneous consumer-facing campaign. The regular use of research provides both the trade and consumer media with the relevant material while positioning CPP as the major industry commentator. The annual public relations programme is acting as a major platform for building the corporate reputation of CPP that can be supported subsequently by other activities.

Source: www.cipr.co.uk

Summary

B2B public relations will always concentrate on supporting the commercial performance of an organisation. The mainstay of this support will be well-placed editorial, especially in the trade media read by influencers and decision makers in the buying process. This 'works' and there are good examples showing just how the craft skills of public relations can be applied with outstanding results. This core activity is fundamental to B2B public relations and B2B practitioners are able to demonstrate a masterful knowledge of their client organisations, of products, services and applications, and of the mechanisms of the marketplace.

The understanding that buying decisions are not solely based on promotion, price, place and product (the marketing mix: Brassington and Pettitt 2003) but also on *reputation* offers scope for public relations practitioners to adopt a holistic approach to B2B communications. The concept of the influence of the 'brand' is established in consumer public relations. We are now recognising that the brand – and all it stands for – is also relevant to B2B.

It is also the case that buying decisions are no longer left to individuals in an organisation. Their decisions may have to withstand the scrutiny of a range of internal and external stakeholders. Thus an integrated communications strategy is essential, with consistent messages being communicated to diverse audiences.

B2B campaigns will always focus on the bottom line to support sales and marketing targets. The very best work is planned strategically to help enhance corporate reputation and show clear and consistent linkage through to all internal and external communications.

Bibliography

Black, C. (2001). *The PR Practitioner's Desktop Guide*. London: Hawksmere.

Brassington, F. and S. Pettitt (2003). *Principles of Marketing*. London: Pearson.

Borden, N. (1964). 'The concept of the marketing mix'. *Journal of Advertising Research*, June: 2–7.

Cornelissen, J. (2004). *Corporate Communications: Theory and practice*. London: Sage.

Davis, A. (2004). *Mastering Public Relations*. Basingstoke: Palgrave Macmillan.

Gregory, A. (ed.) (2004). *Public Relations in Practice*. London: Kogan Page.

Hart, N. (1998). *Business to Business Marketing*. London: Kogan Page.

Haywood, R. (1998). *Public Relations for Marketing Professionals*. Basingstoke: Macmillan .

Howard, W. (ed.) (1988). *The Practice of Public Relations*. London: Heinemann.

Websites

Chartered Institute of Public Relations (CIPR): www.cipr.co.uk

Public Relations Consultants Association (PRCA): www.prca.org.uk

PR Newswire: www.prnewswire.co.uk

Romeike: www.romeike.com

CHAPTER 23
Public affairs

Learning outcomes

By the end of this chapter you should be able to:

■ define public affairs and recognise it in practice
■ understand the societal context in which it is done
■ describe its key operating principles and methods
■ judge the ethical consequences of public affairs.

Introduction

Public affairs (PA) is a crucial and demanding specialism inside the broader field of public relations. It can claim this status because it involves influencing governments and therefore affects the quality of a country's democracy. In liberal democracies which are market-oriented and capitalist, external public relations for an organisation or group can be divided into two parts: dealing with markets; dealing with government, businesses, interest and pressure groups. Marketing public relations communicates with the purchasers of goods and services, whether they are individual consumers or other businesses. Public affairs communicates with government and other external stakeholders affecting a company or an organisation on matters of public policy.

Public affairs is not just the preserve of big businesses talking to government about the very big issues of public policy, such as signing up to the proposed constitution of the European Union (EU) or joining the euro. It can be businesses talking among themselves trying to form a common front before they meet their national government or the European Commission about, say, food labelling. Consumer-facing companies also do public affairs, with the Body Shop being a long-established example through its campaigns to stop testing cosmetics on animals. Public affairs is not confined to commercial organisations; public sector bodies and charities need public affairs as well. For example, UK universities brief members of parliament and talk to the media about varying tuition fees for students and Oxfam campaigns for better national coordination of emergency aid.

Interest and cause groups are also very active in public affairs. For example: the British Medical Association tells the media about its negotiations with the National

Health Service over junior hospital doctors' hours of work; 60 Greenpeace campaigners demonstrate outside the headquarters of the UK supermarket Sainsbury's dressed as pantomime cows in protest against genetically modified feed allegedly given to milk cows; the Vatican lobbies the European Constitutional Convention to insert a clause about Christian heritage in the proposed EU constitution; the European Referendum Campaign organises support in over 30 countries for national votes on that constitution.

Finally, interests and causes rise and fall in the political agenda all the time. For example, concerns about workers' rights have increased since the death of Chinese cocklepickers in the north of England in 2004. Employers bringing in legal immigrants formed the Association of Labour Providers to lobby MPs and ministers and to talk to the media, in order to stop human rights abuses. The fashion house Gap monitored how clothes manufacturers treat their workers with a view to pressurising governments to set minimum standards.

Scope of public affairs

Public affairs (PA) can be conceptualised as the 'voice' that lets organisations and groups (big and small, commercial and non-profit, public and private, religious and secular, conservative and radical, permanent and temporary, national and local) in a country or in a larger political union talk to each other and to government, publicly and privately, about public policy at international, transnational, national, regional and local levels. (For a detailed explanation of how political organisations work, see Chapter 5.)

Public and private 'voices' are both used in public affairs practice. The first speaks through media relations mainly but also through corporate brochures, websites, conferences, event management, protests and demonstrations, while the latter is heard by senior officials, ministers, members of parliament (MPs), members of the European Parliament (MEPs), local councillors and officials in their offices when they make policy. The more powerful the organisation or group doing public affairs, the more likely it will use the private, office-based 'voice' of lobbying (see Mini case study 23.1). The opposite is true with less powerful, 'outsider' organisations and groups.

For example, transnational companies such as Airbus Industries has guaranteed access to ministers and officials throughout the EU. It has 16 development and manufacturing sites in France, Germany, Spain and the UK and has sold 5000 airplanes worldwide. Radical groups such as Reclaim the Streets and Stop the War in Iraq, however, are oppositional to capitalism and to core government policies and so are limited to doing their public affairs through protests, demonstrations and media relations. They are not invited to the prime minister's office or to the European Commission in Brussels. They are, both physically and metaphorically, 'outsider groups'.

While public affairs is a specialised part of public relations, it is still closely connected with other parts of the public relations discipline, It can be seen, for example, as the operations side of issues management (see Chapter 19). Opportunities and threats facing organisations or groups need first to be identified before there can be a public affairs response. For example, the Confederation of British Industry (CBI) needed to 'boundary scan' proposals by the United Nations (UN) to make multinational companies responsible for labour and human rights abuse by their overseas customers, suppliers and host governments before it

mini case study 23.1

Lobbying for a fairer tax

Lunn Poly, a large UK travel agency, along with the Association of British Travel Agents (ABTA) lobbied government to ensure that consumers paid the same rate of tax on travel insurance, whether it was bought from a bank/financial services company or a small family-owned travel agent. There was a hefty 50% difference in the tax rate, depending on where it was bought. These two lobbying partners wanted the support of the whole travel trade and so they linked up with the leading travel trade magazine, which published a feature on the advantages of the policy change for small agents. A fair tax helpline distributed information packs to these small businesses and encouraged them to write to their MPs, who then asked questions in the UK's House of Commons. A petition was organised and articles appeared in the national press and there were meetings with the Treasury. The lobbying goal of a single rate tax was achieved a year later and refunds for past overpayments were given to travel agencies.

could lobby the UK government to block any such resolutions. Community relations (see Chapters 6 and 18) is another close cousin of public affairs. British Nuclear Fuels illustrates this through its engagement in active dialogue with its critics and the communities around its plants in north-west England. (See Activity 23.1 and Think about 23.1.)

Public affairs defined

If *public affairs* is a widely practised and challenging specialism inside public relations, how is it defined? A good starting point – one that clarifies by separating things out – is to see it as the relations of organisations and groups not with markets but with government. White and Mazur (1995: 200) take this non-marketing focus and say that: 'Within public relations, public affairs is a specialised practice that focuses on relationships which will have a bearing on the development of public policy.'

It is very hard to find a definition of public affairs that does *not* centre on public policy. It is important to remember this when considering a variety of titles under which public affairs is conducted. Besides 'public affairs' departments, you will find 'corporate affairs', 'corporate communications', 'government relations' – all doing what we have defined as public affairs.

The focus on public policy extends, of course, to policy made by local councils, regional tiers of government, national governments and the EU. For example, businesses and environmentalists want to influence the route of high-speed railways through their villages and countryside, towns and cities, regions and national territories.

> **Definition:** *Public affairs* is a public relations specialism that seeks to influence public policy making via lobbying and/or through the media.

This chapter says throughout that public affairs is done by organisations and groups. Organisations include commercial businesses, state services such as hospitals, police, schools, and established voluntary bodies such churches, charities and trade unions. They have bureaucratic features – hierarchy, structure, managerialism, instrumental reasoning and legal foundations. Groups, contrariwise, are entities representing the interests and causes in society and have non-bureaucratic features – collegial decision making, where power is shared equally, unclear lines of command and control, open membership, uncertain legal status and a values orientation. However, it is best to see organisations and groups as two ends of a continuum, with established businesses at one end (e.g. Ford Motors, Mercedes-Benz) and groups of protestors (e.g. against more airport runways, against nuclear power) at the other, and with shades of fixity and fluidity in between. (See Think about 23.2.)

This organisation/group distinction largely matches an important characteristic noted by Grant (2000) – between 'insiders' and 'outsiders'. The former are those that government recognises as bodies to consult about policy and who want to be called on; the latter are those outside the government's network of advice seeking and who are happy or not happy to be excluded. An 'insider' example in the UK is the National Farmers' Union; an 'outsider' example is the fuel tax protest by Farmers' Action. Organisations tend to be on the inside and groups on the outside.

There is a cooperative aspect to the public affairs of many organisations and groups: they network to maximise support for their policy and they join industry- or activity-wide representative bodies that can speak with one 'voice' (e.g. the Confederation of British Industry and the Trades Union Congress). The Food and Drink Federation is the UK 'voice' for that industry and the British Dental Association speaks for dental practices around the UK. Cancer Research UK liaises with the Sunbed Association to promote good tanning practice in salons. Protestor groups use mobile phones to coordinate demonstrators.

All of this can be summarised as follows: public affairs is the public relations specialism that seeks to influence public policy for the advantage of those doing it and it is undertaken by a wide range of businesses and public sector bodies as well as interest, pressure and cause groups. It is done by established bodies that work within the existing policy set-up and by those who seek to reform it. It is done by national and transnational bodies and by small groups of people making a local protest. Public affairs can work for the powerful and for citizens. (See Box 23.1.)

Contexts of public affairs

Pluralism

In what sort of environment is public affairs done? The answer is that public affairs is stimulated by

---

box 23.1	**Public affairs for all – an accessible specialism**

The skills needed to do public affairs can be learnt by residents' groups who are unhappy with student parking and partying near their homes and who want to protest to the university and the local council.

The same skills can be hired in by a large insurance company unhappy with a UK parliamentary select committee condemning the sale of endowment mortgages and wanting to deflect criticism. We can talk about citizens' PA and corporate PA.

---

the increased *pluralism* (publicly expressed differences of values, interests and behaviours) of the UK and much of Europe. This pluralism takes two forms and both involve an increased need for public affairs.

For example, since the 1960s, the UK has witnessed great, observable changes in personal behaviour by its citizens and in collective behaviour by voluntary groups. These changes derive principally from altered values regarding sex, lifestyle, the environment, race,

PICTURE 23.1   Much public affairs and lobbying has been done in the past in private. Less so today as professionals, workers, students and individuals seek more say about their roles at work and in society. (*Source:* Sipa Press/Rex.)

PICTURE 23.2 Influencing government is at the heart of public affairs. Here is a traditional British way. (*Source:* Tony Kyriacou/Rex.)

consumption and religion. They, in turn, generate social pressure for acceptance and tolerance of individuals practising them. This pressure frequently leads to collective, group action by like-minded individuals to promote and defend their choices. Increased pluralism of values and groups has been associated with social movements such as feminism, gay rights, environmentalism, consumerism and multiculturalism. These movements are often distinguished by 'contentious collective actions' (Tarrow 1994), such as sit-ins, media events, petitions, demonstrations, all of which are designed to influence public opinion and government. Stonier (1989: 31) argues that 'social movements are of prime importance to the public relations practitioner'.

Definition: *Pluralism* refers to the social and political condition whereby differing values, behaviours and material interests coexist, with different organisations and groups representing them. Civic and commercial pluralism are these differences expressed outside and inside markets.

So what is the link between this accelerated pluralism and public affairs? The answer lies both in the individual's need to have their new values and behaviours accepted, or at least tolerated, by society and in the pressure on government to react to these changes in civil society. We cannot be openly gay if homosexuality is illegal: government is challenged to make same-sex acts legal. We cannot be free citizens if there is excessive security legislation against terrorist threats. We cannot be a sovereign consumer without knowing, say, food ingredients; one would be a dead sovereign consumer unless the government regulates for food safety. We cannot be an informed citizen about the environment if levels of river pollution are not monitored and published. Employees want workplace rights on health and safety and on pensions: only government can enforce minimum standards. Individuals and groups urge involvement by government and representative, accountable government responds in a *liberal democracy*.

Definition: *Liberal democracy* is a political system based on free elections, multiple political parties, political decision making made through an elected government and an independent system of justice that is responsible for law enforcement.

In this way, public affairs activities between organisations or groups and government express the concerns and hopes of the former and the policy responses of the latter. They are the conversations of a liberal democracy. This shift in UK society and in much of the EU to more individual expression and supportive voluntary groups is identified here as value pluralism and group pluralism of a civic kind. Brought together, they can be called *civic pluralism* (Moloney 2000).

In addition, a commercial variant of pluralism has come to the fore in the UK in approximately the same period. From the middle of the 1970s, it was noticeable that the climate of ideas about markets and business was shifting away from the collective and the planned towards the singular and the autonomous. This altered paradigm for the UK political economy has resulted in business and pro-market interests predominating over their ideological and material competitors. Mainstream political parties are more business friendly and, as a result, there is now in the UK a pronounced *commercial pluralism*. Without it, accelerated pluralism would not affect the lives of all the UK population. Tens of millions are affected by personal and civic value changes; all are affected by market and business changes. This commercial pluralism speaks when we hear calls for the abolition of farm subsidies and when the gaming industry lobbies for the use of credit cards in casinos.

> **Definition:** *Commercial pluralism* is the condition where market and business values, ideas and practices prevail over substantial challenges from non-business or anti-business groups.

In liberal, market economies, popularly elected governments react to changes in civil society (voluntary associations outside the family and government) and in the political economy (the wealth creation nexus in society). We are closer to those changes when we see them legislated for, and regulated by local, regional and national governments. Increasingly, however, the source of this legislation is further away from us at the EU level, and yet we often feel the consequences of legislation close to our homes and work (animal welfare in abattoirs, workplace rights for part-time employees). (See also Chapter 5.)

European context

Public affairs at the European level is made more complex by the number of interests and governmental institutions involved and it is likely that, because of the interrelated forces of EU expansion and closer integration, there will be more *lobbying* at this level.

(See Chapter 5 for further discussion of European institutions.)

> **Definition:** *Lobbying* is the influence of public policy making through the private means of meeting MPs, ministers, civil servants, councillors or local government officials.

Cram (2001: 162) is not exaggerating when she writes 'it is generally recognised that the EU policy process is very complex', for she notes that 'no single actor has total control'. It is clear, however, that the Council of Ministers, representing the member states or countries of the European Union has significant powers of veto (the right to reject something) over the European Commission, which proposes policy and regulates its enforcement, and over the European Parliament, which can scrutinise policy and budgets but not initiate legislation.

Around these European institutions are a great array of interest, cause and pressure groups, staffed and led by professional and citizen lobbyists. There are, for example, nearly 5000 lobbyists accredited to the Parliament. To cut through this clamour for influence, the most effective way is to have the unconditional support of the lobbyists' national governments. With this support, organisations and groups have a direct route into the confidential power politics of the Council of Ministers. For example, UK private healthcare companies wanting new business in Europe are in a better position than British trade unionists wanting stronger rights to strike, because their national government supports business and market interests more than it does employee interests.

Lobbying within Europe

Without that national government support, the lobbyist is faced with a choice of various tactics. McGrath (2005) notes that successful European lobbyists start their work very early in the life of a new policy and congregate around the officials and consultative committees of the Commission. The reason is that the Commission develops new legislation by consensus building across 25 national governments, its own institutions and dozens of interest and cause groups. Officials, who are mostly lawyers and economists, are keen to have technical views on how policy will work in pan-European circumstances and this need for expert opinion is a point of influence for public affairs people. Facing these complexities, therefore, the Commission follows a snowball approach which favours early persuaders trying to steer the direction of policy and ensures that most proposals backed by the Commission become law. Lobbyists for consumer and environmental protection and animal welfare will also keep close to the Parliament, which has a pronounced interest in these areas. But remember that national interests keep surfacing, for many MEPs will only see national public affairs personnel or those with an established public interest in their home state. In all these circumstances, the importance of personal contact is high and that of media relations relatively unimportant.

Personal influence and public affairs

Because of this importance, personal influence models of public relations are relevant to public affairs, although it is an open question whether this is a positive or negative effect. Chen and Culbertson (2003: 27) note how in China *quanxhi* (personal networks of connections and friendship to acquire what is needed) pose 'challenges' including the possibility of corruption of public officials. Chay-Nemeth (2003) sees personal influence at work in Singaporean policy making. These comments illustrate how national cultures (see Hofstede on national cultures in Chapter 18) can influence public affairs and it is manifest that personal relationships do affect the course and outcome of European lobbying.

Many professional lobbyists mention their personal connections to indicate that they have access to powerful policy makers and it is undeniable that lobbying projects need the meeting of minds and values to be successful. There is, however, an important balance to be struck in these relationships to avoid illegality or favouritism. The UK saw such flawed relationships in sleazy 'cash for questions' incidents involving MPs in the early 1990s. The result was a damaged government and a public loss of confidence, in part restored by the Nolan Committee (1994) (see ethics and public affairs section later).

The 'public sphere' and public affairs

If corrupt personal relationships are the worst environment for public affairs and lobbying in a democracy, the ideal setting is the public sphere concept. This was developed by Jürgen Habermas, one of the most influential of European social philosophers since the Second

World War in the middle of the last century. The 'public sphere' has two meanings: the historical one, which describes the emergence of middle-class public opinion in eighteenth-century England, France and Germany; the normative one, which describes how public opinion *should* be formed in civil society. It is the latter that concerns us here for public affairs operates in the medium of public opinion and the conditions set by the public sphere offer an ideal as a gold standard to aim at. Those conditions are threefold, stipulating that debate to form public opinion should be:

- rational
- open to all wanting to partake
- conducted in a disinterested way (Moloney 2000: 150–155).

(See also 'Ethics and public affairs', p. 457.)

These are manifestly the conditions of perfection and thus beyond practice, but they are a constant reminder to working public affairs people and lobbyists about how to behave. Having defined public affairs and put it in national and European contexts, we can now explore how it is done. (See Think about 23.3.)

Public affairs: knowledge, skills and behaviour needed

The core skills needed in public affairs to operate successfully in the competitive environment of accelerated pluralism are lobbying (both in private and publicly) and media relations (see Chapter 16).

Lobbying is persuading public policy makers to act in the interests of your organisation or group (Moloney 1997). The first operational decision is to decide whether to lobby in private or publicly, or both. Three questions will help you decide. Do you know the decision makers? Is the matter to be lobbied on the current political agenda? Are you an 'insider' organisation or group? If the three answers are 'yes', then you should go the private route and avoid the media and public events. If the answers are 'no', then your lobbying may be best achieved by using the media and organising public events. (See Box 23.2 and Activity 23.2, overleaf.)

Student issues and 'ideal' conditions for debate

To what extent do public debates on issues affecting students (for example, on tuition fees or student accommodation) meet Moloney's three conditions? How is public opinion formed? Do you feel able to put forward informed arguments and to participate in debate? How are public debates around these issues handled (e.g. by your student union/university)?

<table>
<tr><td>box
23.2</td><td>**Health warning for lobbyists**</td></tr>
</table>

Before starting to think of lobbying tactics, consider this. Lobbying is a serious activity with costs, risks about outcomes and possible damage to reputation. It is also very time consuming, may last for years and involves mental, emotional and physical commitment. It may be more prudent not to use the lobbying 'voice' and instead to accept public policy as it is or is proposed. Remember that when you lobby, you can activate opposition and set up a competition for favourable policy that was not there beforehand. You could avoid this and seek to influence policy through membership of a political party.

Because public affairs seeks to influence public policy making, it deals with elected government and in so doing is in contact with the most powerful institution in a liberal democracy. The organisations and groups seeking change or the status quo are dealing with a constitutional power, refreshed by periodic popular mandate, which can legislate and regulate in any area of the political economy and of civil society. Lobbyists should also remember that politicians are always asking themselves – privately – 'how many voters will support a 'yes' or 'no' decision . This is not necessarily cynical if the politicians also have in mind the rights and wrongs of a decision and the public interest. We are, after all, a democracy that enshrines the principle of majority voting for decision making. So numbers do count.

For all these reasons, lobbying is a serious matter not to be undertaken lightly. Furthermore, while success can greatly improve circumstances, failure can make matters worse. For example, a trade union lobbying today to abolish a secret ballot of members before strike action would be seeking to overturn a piece of legislation very widely accepted as part of the current UK political settlement and would call into question the quality of its overall political judgement. And, finally, the odds of success are no more than even in the best of circumstances: for every successful lobby, there is invariably an unsuccessful one on the other side of the argument.

---

activity 23.2

Government involvement in public issues

There is intense argument about what government should or should not allow, particularly on issues of personal morals such as abortion, age of consent, drugs. Can you list three examples of human behaviour, public or private, in which government should *not* be involved? Now list three examples where they should be involved.

Would you lobby or use the media to get the result you believed in?

Who are the lobbyists?

Because public affairs is an accessible activity, lobbyists are not only professionals but laypeople armed with the skills set out in this and the media relations chapters (Chapter 16). Professional lobbyists work inside organisations and groups as employees or in lobbying firms, which are usually small to medium-sized businesses offering their lobbying skills for hire. (These latter professionals are also called commercial lobbyists.) Professional lobbyists are usually graduates in politics or communications and have an intense interest in daily politics and policy development. They have often worked for MPs or for political parties as researchers. They often swap between employee and hired status. Their most distinguishing feature is that their main skills concern lobbying rather than the subject matter being lobbied about.

For example, a lobbyist hired to help supermarkets build out-of-town developments will know more about parliamentary and local government procedures than about the retail sector.

The lay (non-professional) lobbyists are often very knowledgeable and impassioned about the subject or cause for which they are lobbying (e.g. animal welfare, railway safety, inheritance tax, domestic violence) and this knowledge and concern leads them to develop lobbying skills. Their knowledge and passion means that their formal educational background is unimportant, as is their age. They are the local members of national organisations (e.g. speaking in the local media for the UK's National Pensioners' Convention) or the core members of a small and temporary grouping (e.g. getting speed bumps installed in a residential road). They make up what Edmund Burke, the eighteenth-century political philosopher, called the 'little platoons' in civil society (Burke 1969) – small groups of citizens who share common interests and give each other support. In the USA, they would be called 'grassroots' lobbyists (McGrath 2004). These lay lobbyists can be called citizen lobbyists, doing civic public affairs. Lattimer (2000) has written about the skills they need, as has Levine (1993).

One point of caution: like-minded people who share a strong belief or interest can get overenthused with their cause and can forget the hours, days, months, years needed to change policy decisions. So

---

| box 23.3 | **What do lobbyists do?** |

When employers advertise jobs in public affairs, they say things like:

- 'You will be responsible for the day-to-day management of our parliamentary relations and be working with a range of other stakeholders in communicating our key messages.'
- 'You will play a key role in the continuing development of socially responsible policies for the industry and communicating them to relevant audiences.'
- 'You will develop and implement public affairs strategies that promote our members' policies to government, parliament, others organisations and the public at large.'

---

whether the lobbyist is a professional or an individual citizen, representing the rich and powerful or poor and neglected, the assumption should be that the desired objective will only happen – if it happens at all – after much planned, sustained and persuasive effort. Success invariably depends on a well-planned public affairs campaign, concentrating resources to achieve a predefined goal in a limited time and with a distinctive launch, middle and end. All campaigns, military as well as civilian, are risky, demanding ventures. (See Boxes 23.3 and 23.4 (overleaf) and Think about 23.4.)

Skills set

The skills needed to lobby have been described by David Curry (1999), who was a UK minister and who therefore gives advice from an insider's point of view. Charles Miller (2000) has done the same but from the lobbyist's position. These skills can be summarised as two major categories:

1 *Gaining access* involves: the knowledge and skills associated with work and social networking; identifying allies and opponents; knowing how to get the attention of policy makers.
2 *Making representations* is presenting your case clearly and briefly, persuasively, and accurately in terms of the wider interest. This is a key point – to persuade accountable politicians and officials to change policy, you have to align your interest with the wider, public interest. Moreover, underlying effective representation is knowledge of how policy is made in: political parties; ministries; the Prime Minister's Office; local authorities; and the EU. This knowledge includes the understanding that timing is vital in lobbying, because proposals are much easier to change than declared policy.

See Mini case study 23.2 and Think about 23.5 (overleaf).

It is usually impossible to know why your lobby succeeded or failed. This leads to another vital skill – patience. The readiness to 'play a long game' can make

---

think about 23.4 | **Jobs in public affairs**

Would you apply for a public affairs job? What attracts you? What repels you? Would you work for a tobacco company, for a pro-cannabis group, for a pro-choice abortion rights group? Would you work only for a cause or interest you believe in or would you work for any cause or interest if the money was right?

---

mini case study 23.2

Gaining access and making representations

The British Ceramic Confederation has 150 members who represent 90% of the UK pottery industry. As the trade association, it is the 'voice' of an important industry, has access to ministers and represents the industry's views on various issues. One such issue is how foreign counterfeit ceramics are threatening UK jobs and markets.

This example and the terms 'access' and 'making representations' highlight again the 'outsider' and 'insider' distinction, and draw attention to the power of business, the sensitivity of government to employment and trade issues and the importance of contacts.

One week in the life of a public affairs consultant

The practitioner diary of Richard Casofsky, public affairs account executive for Finsbury Public Relations Consultants

Monday

5am: My taxi arrives to take me to the office to get me there for 5.30. A House of Commons select committee has released government responses to its earlier report and I need to summarise these to present to our client by 7am.

9am: Begin to check the press and emails and to prepare for an 11.30am meeting with another client. This client is following the progress of a bill through parliament and it is my job to stay constantly in touch with any developments as they take place – we need to always be the client's first source of any new information.

3pm: Client meeting went well. I now need to draft the minutes and relevant action points ASAP to send on today. Also a number of points of detail need to be researched further to uncertainties that emerged during the meeting.

4pm: I get home early to compensate for the very early start.

Tuesday

8am: Check press and respond to emails. We're trialing a monitoring service to help us follow the progress of a bill and I am inundated with information – much of this is superfluous to the client's needs.

12pm: Phones have been very busy with our clients wanting to know our position on a controversial government White Paper. A brief team meeting is convened and we return each client call with our predictions and a simplified explanation of what the White Paper will mean to them.

3pm: Further team meeting to discuss strategy for preparing for a pitch for new business. With the team, I now need to begin speedy background research into the relevant sector and the related governmental departments. We (the account execs) are preparing a first draft of a PowerPoint presentation and an accompanying contact list.

Wednesday

9am: Check emails and answer the phone. The secretary is on leave today so we all need to muck in to spread her workload (answering phones mainly).

1pm: Have been spending the morning making calls to government departments trying to get hold of the government's draft priorities for health for the UK's presidency of the EU. This is for a pharmaceutical client. The sponsoring department doesn't wish to give out the information, so I try to get this from the part of the cabinet office that coordinates on all EU-related matters – not proving easy to get hold of this information.

6pm: Today has been busy with all the team managing their part of the research for the new business pitch in between regular daily tasks and constant ringing of phones . . .

7pm: Tonight is the company's anniversary party – there is a drinks party with clients from 7.30 to 9.30 and the team go out after the clients have left.

Thursday

9am: Hung over, I need to prepare 20 biogs of MPs to send to a client hosting an event at parliament. The MPs have been selected for having an interest in the client's business area. I also make a point of calling parliamentary offices to remind MP researchers of the event.

1pm: Lunch with a friend from when I was at university. He is now working as a press officer for the Conservatives (UK political party).

2pm: The remainder of the day is spent amending the presentation for the pitch we are working on.

8pm: Still in the office – manager has been out at meetings for most of the day and is only now catching up with his emails/work. I have just been given several tasks (finding recent press articles and past emails relating to a particular client issue) to complete before I leave the office.

Friday

10am: Today has been fairly quiet. We've been preparing a strategy document for Britain in Europe setting out the advantages the European Constitution would bring to British business.

2pm: Have been making calls to the Department for Culture, Media and Sport about the Gambling Bill. Preparing a briefing document for a client who is meeting a minister and his officials on Monday.

4pm: The rest of my day has been spent trying to understand the European Commission's recently updated merger policy for a briefing note to send to clients. The new Merger Regulation is very complex and this is proving to be a daunting task.

Source: Richard Casofsky

all the difference. There are so many variable factors influencing policy making that it is extremely difficult to say which are crucial to success or failure and when they will change. As an example of how policy priorities change, there is now more public money for anti-alcohol and anti-obesity campaigns. Because of this uncertainty, it is unwise to claim publicly that your lobbying tipped the balance and got the desired outcome. Besides, public boasting about changing the minds of politicians and public officials is not attractive in a democracy and may stir up opposition.

The difficulty of isolating the winning factors in a lobbying campaign leads to another warning to the lobbyist – do not believe that there is a winning formula. There is most definitely not. There is, however, a set of behaviours that have been associated in the past with successful lobbying. Moloney (1996) Curry (1999) and Miller (2000) outline many of these but they should be treated as guidelines, pointers suggested by experience, not recipes for

guaranteed success. (See Box 23.5, Activity 23.3 and Mini case study 23.3, overleaf.)

Ethics and public affairs

Because public affairs seeks to influence public policy in a democracy, it receives more scrutiny than any other public relations specialism, and rightly so. The use of professional lobbyists on a hired basis, their relationship with MPs and ministers, the declaration of interests by lobbyists and politicians and the use of entertainment and free gifts were all matters of public concern regarding UK lobbying in the late 1980s and early 1990s and led to the Nolan Committee (1994) investigation into standards in public life. Today the responsible lobbyist in any country should be aware of the seven principles of public life recommended by Nolan (see Box 23.6, overleaf); these have set a 'gold standard' for behaviour by holders of public office.

---

think about 23.5 'Insiders' and 'outsiders'

What are the implications for democracy when an 'insider', say a London business person belonging to a Pall Mall club (a social club for the London elite) has more chance of meeting ministers than 'outsiders' such as long-term unemployed people from poorer regions?

---

box 23.5 How to lobby government – a checklist

- Define the matter to be lobbied.
- Define success and failure.
- Network with allies.
- Monitor opponents.
- Establish who the decision makers are.
- Decide whether to influence privately, publicly or both.
- Lobby before policy is decided.
- Write your case on one sheet of A4 paper.
- Gain access.
- Let your most powerful and persuasive person lobby.
- Socialise with decision makers.
- Consider joining/supporting the party in power.
- Be persuasive both on paper and in person.
- Be technical – don't challenge policy directly.
- Be knowledgeable about how policy is made.
- Lobby in the name of the public interest.
- Be discreet about whom you are lobbying.
- Plan public events if private lobbying is not working.
- Use the media when they add pressure.
- If you change policy, never take the credit – in public!

---

activity 23.3

Understanding lobbying

- What is lobbying? Write down your own definition of lobbying.
- Write down what you think are the top three skills needed to lobby.
- Under what circumstances is a private lobby better than a public one? Write down an example.
- Do you think you have lobbying skills? List them.

Any scrutiny of public affairs asks three questions:

1 Who has access to public decision makers and under what conditions (private or publicly known access)?

2 What weight do policy makers give to representations made to them?

3 Have powerful interests more right of access to public policy makers than poor and marginal interests?

Lobbying on student top-up fees

In the UK, two academic unions (AUT, NATFHE) and the National Union of Students mounted a short six-day joint campaign to remove all references to variable student top-up fees in the third reading of the 2004 Higher Education Bill. To succeed they needed to change the minds of three Labour MPs.

Branch officials in the regions were asked to contact all members, give them the briefing previously sent to MPs, urge them to write to their MPs and visit them in their surgeries. They were sent a template letter and told that the union websites provided briefings and supportive arguments. They were supported by the small number of vice-chancellors opposing variable fees who lobbied sympathetic members of both Houses of Parliament. The campaign lost because government business managers persuaded previously rebellious MPs to be loyal.

---

box 23.6 **Standards in public life – the Nolan principles**

Professional and citizen lobbyists should be aware that holders of public office are expected to behave with:

- selflessness
- integrity
- objectivity
- accountability
- openness
- honesty
- leadership.

Concerns over access may be triggered by private meetings between officials and business people at the Prime Minister's Office or in Brussels when policy is developed. Critics say that their meetings should be publicly flagged up in advance and that a record of their contents made public later.

All these health warnings strengthen the need for caution when deciding whether or not to lobby. The caution has two aspects, one self-interested and the other principled – and both should be asked in the context of the Nolan principles. Do we help or harm the interests we represent when we do public affairs? Do we help or hinder the quality of our democracy when we lobby? (See Boxes 23.7 and 23.8, Case study 23.1 and Activity 23.4)

---

activity 23.4

Analysis of Case study 23.1

- Whom did the residents have to convince that their case was right?
- Rank in order of importance the tactics which brought about the result.
- Why do you think that the government supported the residents' case?

---

box 23.7 **Whether or not to lobby publicly?**

An organisation or group would first ask itself:

- Is there easy access to councillors, MPs, senior civil servants and ministers?
- Is our policy position on the mainstream political agenda?

If the answers are 'no', you are halfway to doing a citizens' lobby.

The next stage has two more questions:

- Have we got many people who would support us publicly?
- Can we get media coverage?

If the answers are 'yes', a public lobbying strategy would be more effective.

---

box 23.8 **Public lobbying – action checklist**

Influencing public policy makers is a 'numbers' game'. So can you:

- drum up support in public at a rally, protest, demo
- organise a well-supported petition
- get testimonials of support from celebrities, experts, losers and gainers
- develop slogans
- organise attention-seeking events over time
- work cooperatively with enthusiasts
- have an agreed script for your interest/cause and stick to it
- develop a news sense?

A 'David and Goliath' public affairs battle on the English Channel

The primary definition of globalisation is the integration of markets across the world and it is a definition that foregrounds the role of ports. As international trade increases, ports expand and contract with changing patterns of demand. Examples are Felixstowe and Rotterdam, which grew in tonnage and area occupied, unlike London and Amsterdam, which grew smaller or stopped trading.

Modern ports are capital intensive, take up large areas of land, generate jobs and markets for their suppliers, disturb their environments from ecological, physical and amenity perspectives and are the subject of national government policy. Most of these features came to the fore in 1997 when Associated British Ports, owners of Southampton port on the south coast of England, proposed a £745m expansion of the docks on the western side of Southampton Water, on a site known as Dibden Bay.

That proposed expansion, however, was the subject of intense debate in the city and surrounding communities. While Southampton City Council supported the new dock, opposition to it coalesced around the group known as Residents Against Dibden Bay Port (RADBP). Paul Vickers, who had a background in the petroleum industry, was its chairman. He led the group to a successful conclusion and here he describes the seven-year campaign that led the UK government to refuse planning permission for a new dock in the bay. It is a campaign that shows the benefits and costs of concerned citizens doing public affairs. He tells the story of the Dibden Bay incident by the English Channel.

Background

The proposal was for a container port at Dibden Bay, which is directly connected to the proposed New Forest National Park. The bay's foreshore is home to 50,000 rare birds and protected under the European Birds Directive, as well as being the strategic gap between the townships of Hythe and Marchwood. It would have been the UK's biggest port infrastructure project ever. One-third the size of Heathrow Airport London, it was to take 10 years to construct.

'The announcement provoked a public outcry. Associated British Port's (ABP) argument was that there was a national need for extra container capacity and that Dibden Bay was the only available site. The New Forest District Council soon organised a public meeting, which led to the formation of our group. We ran the campaign from 1997 up to and through the public inquiry, culminating on 20 April 2004 with the government's decision on the expansion.'

Gathering information

'At the outset, the ABP case appeared cut and dried and most organisations and institutions thought that the only option was to compromise and limit the damage. The European Directive provides no protection if there is deemed to be an overriding public need. Consequently it is possible to win the argument at a public inquiry and still have the decision go against you.

'From day one, RADBP set out to be a professional organisation. Whilst we would inevitably be accused of 'nimby'-ism [i. e. 'not in my back yard' (NIMBY) or property-owner self-interest], our plan was to be consistently articulate and accurate with facts and arguments. The first requirement was to gather data about the UK container port industry: the facts/story as put forward by ABP and the growth in container demand, etc. This was achieved by RADBP writing letters which were sent in the name of either the New Forest Council or the local MP. A letter on House of Parliament paper guarantees a reply! At the end of this period it was abundantly clear that ABP's case was flawed.'

Lobbying

'With as much information as possible, our next objective was to lobby all of those organisations which could potentially become opponents to the expansion proposal. At the outset, there were only two groups on our side (Royal Society for the Protection of Birds and New Forest District Council) but slowly and following presentations, leafleting and more letters from the MP, other groups began to doubt ABP. By 2000, we had become the coordinating group for the opposition and taken on the role of passing information between the groups, heading up the media campaign and vetting statements made by other groups to ensure accuracy and consistency. By now the media wanted to talk to us.'

The strategy

'This can be summarised as follows:

- maximise the opposition in advance of the formal planning application and the expected public inquiry
- sponsor alternative locations (to give the government a way out)
- delay ABP as long as possible to allow alternative proposals to come forward (one of the ways of achieving this was to continuously put more and more questions into the public arena, so that ABP had to respond).'

▶

case study 23.1 (continued)

Tactics

'Between 1997 and 2004 we used a number of different methods to get our message across. These included:

- frequent leafleting
- car stickers
- letters to ABP's shareholders pointing out financial weaknesses in the proposed extension
- information packs handed out at the ABP annual general meeting
- getting the BBC to make a documentary on the project
- persuading other interest and pressure groups to go public
- media relations
- and asking parliamentary questions.'

Winning the public affairs battle

'By 2000, the tide of expert and public opinion was moving against ABP. The turning point came at a decisive public presentation in January in the chamber of the New Forest District Council between us and ABP, when our case was much stronger. After this, ABP never appeared in public with us again. The same presentation was used extensively throughout 2000 to lobby support.'

Fighting the planning application

'The formal application was submitted by ABP in October 2000. By this time the opposition was extensive. Six and a half thousand individual objections went to the government in the six weeks allowed, a record for a planning application, and the official bodies and pressure groups that lined up with us came to 50.

'By contrast, ABP only had the support of Southampton City Council.

'Also by this time, our involvement with the possibility of building a container port on a redundant refinery site in Essex came to fruition with the decision by P&O Ports (a competitor of ABP) to go ahead with this project. Furthermore, we had agreed with P&O that they would announce this project to coincide with ABP submitting their application. This allowed us to go to the media with the story that this development (the London Gateway project) was on a brownfield site and that Dibden Bay was a protected greenfield site.

'ABP appeared to believe throughout that no one would turn down a project for the strategically important port of Southampton. The inquiry inspector organised a preliminary meeting in April 2001 to agree the scope and the management of the inquiry. We asked for two extra topics – financial viability and human rights – to be inserted, knowing that these were weak areas for ABP.

'The inquiry was set to start in December that year, after everyone had submitted their evidence. In the intervening period, it was expected that ABP would fly barrage balloons in the bay to indicate the height of the cranes and the line of the 1.8-kilometre quay on the foreshore. But this did not happen, so we planned the event for the weekend immediately before the inquiry opened in order to maximise publicity. ABP, in the role of harbour master, tried to prevent us going ahead, but faced with the inevitable media coverage this would have given them, they relented.

'The flying of the barrage balloons at 330 feet high over the length of the proposed quay in an unspoilt bay was a master stroke, as this was the first time the local population had seen anything visual to indicate the size and impact of the project.'

Giving the government a way out

'As I have said earlier, it is possible to win the inquiry and lose the political decision. We wanted therefore to ensure that the government had other container port expansion options besides Dibden Bay and to this end we also contacted Hutchinson Ports, the owners of Felixstowe (the largest UK container port) and Harwich. They were well aware that if Dibden Bay went ahead, it would severely affect their own business. They therefore decided to put in their own application for expansion in Harwich and they agreed to announce this on the day the inquiry opened to give us yet another media opportunity. This meant that the media story was now "why do we need Dibden when we can have London Gateway and also Harwich, neither of which involve such a large environmental impact as Dibden Bay?"'

Decision day: 20 April 2004

'The inquiry and the government denied the application to make Dibden Bay a port on a long list of grounds, not just the environmental issues, e.g. ABP failed on the two topics we inserted, financial viability and human rights. We had won a seven-year battle of public campaigning and private lobbying. It was incredibly hard work and needed sustained commitment but it showed that it is possible for a small group of determined citizens to succeed against a powerful company. Those who care can win.'

Endnote

From Paul Vickers' account, the outstanding feature of the residents' campaign was the result in their favour. Most pressure groups do not win their case so completely against well-resourced interests. The residents were a David to the Goliath of Associated British Ports in terms of the resources that could be devoted to a public affairs campaign. In this case, the residents

▶

case study 23.1 (continued)

spent £120,000 compared to ABP's estimated £45m. In terms of the 'insider' and 'outsider' distinction about relationships with government (see earlier in the chapter, p. 449), ABP provide much of the physical infrastructure which allows the UK to trade by sea, while the residents were a temporary and changing association of volunteers who had not worked together before and who were unknown to public policy makers. It is this imbalance of resource and status that is so striking about this case. The success of RADBP is reminiscent of the struggle between Greenpeace and Shell over Brent Spar in the mid-1990s. Indeed, the Dibden Bay incident may well be seen eventually to have had greater significance in environmental, political and public affairs terms.

For ABP, there was disappointment about the decision not to expand – a reminder that in public affairs work, there are always competing views. In a statement immediately afterwards, it said that the decision was 'extremely serious'. It added that: 'The decision not to give ABP's Port of Southampton the go-ahead for its expansion plans to handle growth in the UK's international trade will certainly result in a loss of job opportunities in the area and will have a worryingly adverse effect on the local and regional economies. The future shape of the port will now be significantly different to that of the expanded Port of Southampton which we had planned for.'

Source: Moloney and Vickers 2004

Summary

Public affairs is the much used public relations specialism that seeks to influence public policy making through lobbying, done either privately or publicly, along with media relations, or by combining both routes. Lobbying is at the heart of public affairs and is often connected to the linked specialisms of issues management, community relations and sponsorship (Chapters 19, 18 and 27). It is conducted by the widest range of organisations and groups, from the largest companies to the smallest groups of citizens, both seeking to advance some interest or cause or right some wrong.

Public affairs is done in a particular social, political and economic context, i.e. accelerated pluralism, where organisations and groups seek advantage for their values, behaviours and material interests over their competitors. They often act cooperatively with allies to achieve this. Public affairs is the 'voice' of this competition for advantage.

There is a particular skills set required to do public affairs whether by professional lobbyists or laypeople. The core skills are those of identifying and analysing issues, building a case in response, getting access to decision makers, aligning private and public interests, persuading officials and politicians in your favour and deciding on private and/or public routes of influence.

Public affairs can be a controversial activity and it should not be undertaken lightly. It touches on the quality of democracy by influencing elected representatives and officials. It is part of public life and should be conducted to the high standards established by the Nolan Committee.

Bibliography

Burke, E. (1969, first published 1790). *Reflections On The Revolution in France*. London: Penguin.

Chay-Nemeth, C. (2003). 'Becoming professionals: A portrait of public relations in Singapore' in *The Global Public Relations Handbook*. K. Sriramesh and D. Verčić, (eds). London: Lawrence Erlbaum Associates.

Chen, N. and H. Culbertson (2003). 'Public relations in mainland China: An adolescent with growing pains' in *The Global Public Relations Handbook*. K. Sriramesh and D. Verčić, (eds). London: Lawrence Erlbaum Associates.

Committee on Standards in Public Life: Issues and questions (1994). London: HMSO (Dd 8389342) (the Nolan Committee).

Cram, L. (2001). 'Integration and policy processes in the European Union' in *Governing the European Union*. S. Bromley (ed.). London: Sage.

Curry, D. (1999). *Lobbying Government*. London: Chartered Institute of Housing.

Grant, W. (2000). *Pressure Groups, Politics and Democracy in Britain*, 2nd edition. Hemel Hempstead: Harvester Wheatsheaf.

Lattimer, M. (2000). *The Campaign Handbook*, 2nd edition. London: Directory of Social Change.

Levine, M. (1993). *Guerrilla PR: How you wage an effective publicity campaign*. New York: HarperCollins Business.

McGrath, C. (2004). Grass roots lobbying: Marketing politics and policy 'beyond the beltway'. Paper presented at the Elections on the Horizon Conference, British Library, London, March.

McGrath, C. (2005). *Perspectives on Lobbying: Washington, London, Brussels*. Lampeter: Edwin Mellen Press.

Miller, C. (2000). *Political Lobbying*, London: Politico's Publishing.

Moloney, K. (1996). *Lobbyists For Hire*. Aldershot: Dartmouth.

Moloney, K. (1997). 'Government and lobbying activities' in *Public Relations Principles and Practice*. P. Kitchen (ed.). London: Thomson Business Press.

Moloney, K. (2000). *Rethinking PR: The spin and the substance*. London: Routledge.

Moloney, K. and P. Vickers (2004). Unpublished case study.

Stonier, T. (1989). 'The evolving professionalism: Responsibilities'. *International Public Relations Review* **12**(3): 30–36.

Tarrow, S. (1994). *Power in Movement*. Cambridge: Cambridge University Press.

White, J. and L. Mazur (1995). *Strategic Communications Management*. Harlow: Addison-Wesley.

For glossary definitions relevant to this chapter, visit the **selected glossary** feature on the website at: www.pearsoned.co.uk/tench

CHAPTER 24
Financial public relations (FPR)

Learning outcomes

By the end of this chapter you should be able to:

- define and describe financial public relations
- identify who is involved in financial public relations practice
- compare the practice of financial public relations in the UK and internationally
- identify how financial public relations practice impacts on organisations
- recognise emerging trends in financial public relations practice.

Structure

- Overview of financial public relations
- Landscape of the 'City': who's involved in financial PR
- Financial PR practice

Introduction

'How many PR people does it take to change a light bulb' 'Don't know. I'll have to get back to you on that one?' An old joke, perhaps, but apposite until surprisingly recently. The typical London public-relations person of the 1980s did little more than hand out press releases and take journalists to lunch – and was more familiar with the Savoy's wine list than with his client companies' strategies. That has all changed. Lunch, this correspondent is happy to report, still definitely plays its part. But today's spin doctors are sharp-minded professionals, often indistinguishable from investment bankers and lawyers – and increasingly demanding to be paid like them. In America, financial PR (communicating companies' strategies to shareholders, analysts and the financial press) is still done largely in-house. But it is the top British agencies – Brunswick, Financial Dynamics, The Maitland Consultancy, Finsbury, Citigate Dewe Rogerson and Tulchan – which are showing that financial PR is becoming an industry in its own right.'

Source: *The Economist* 14 July 2001: 74–75

Financial public relations, like so many areas of public relations practice, has in the past been perceived to be nothing more than an *Absolutely Fabulous* (1990s BBC television programme stereotyping a public relations practitioner) world of champagne and caviar, with practitioners as bubbly as their preferred drink. However, as the *Economist* article just quoted suggests, financial public relations practice is now something much more complex, practised in the environments of domestic and international financial markets and the corporate world. Financial public relations is a practice that, for most people within and outside the public relations industry, remains a mystery shrouded in the complexities of these environments.

The following chapter aims to explore and illustrate for the reader the reality of financial public relations practice, demystify its practices and culture, identify its body of knowledge and provide a glossary (in the accompanying website) for its truly unique lexicon.

Overview of financial public relations

Financial public relations (PR) is an area of public relations practice that is often misconstrued. This confusion is only furthered when consulting the limited yet varied literature on the subject and largely results from what is an apparently fundamental difference in the practice of financial PR in the UK and the USA. This difference is evident in the literature on financial PR.

US perspective on financial PR: an investor-focused approach

Financial PR in the USA has historically focused on investor relations (IR). Indeed, the Public Relations Society of America's (PRSA) Financial Communications Section was until 1992 known as the Investor Relations Section (PRSA 2005). This positioning of financial PR as investor relations is reflected in key US public relations texts such as Argenti's seminal 1998 text *Corporate Communications*, in which the chapter on

financial communications is called 'Investor relations: a random walk down Wall Street' (Argenti 1998: 143–166).

So what is IR? One definition is that offered by the Investor Relations Society (1997) where IR is referred to as: 'the management of the relationships between a company with publicly traded securities [shares] and the holders or potential holders of such securities' (quoted in Marston and Straker 2001: 82). The definition draws out an American financial PR practice that is focused on communicating solely with the shareholder (and potential shareholder). Although Argenti points out that the practice involves other intermediary stakeholders who are communicated with in order to reach the shareholder, he refers to these as 'buy-side' and 'sell-side' analysts, referring to financial publics that facilitate for shareholders either the purchase or sale of shares (Argenti 1998: 144).

UK approach to financial PR

This US view of financial PR practice is fundamentally different from the UK perspective, most notably

PICTURE 24.1   'The City' – so much more than just a square mile in central London. (*Source:* Eddie Mullholland/Rex.)

Before reading on, ask yourself, why do you think this core difference might exist? Jot down your thoughts and come back to them after you've read the remainder of the chapter and see whether or not you were correct.

Feedback   You may want to draw on theories about defining stakeholders and publics in Chapter 12 and professionalism in Chapter 15 for inspiration as to why these differences may exist.

---

because in the UK IR is viewed as a practice separate from financial PR and is traditionally not handled by financial PR, but rather a company's nominated broker (Middleton 2002: 160). Within the US perspective, the broker would be one of Argenti's 'sell-side' analysts.

The fundamental difference then is that US financial PR (IR) is focused on the shareholder whereas in the UK, as Middleton points out, financial PR is focused on 'raising awareness and building understanding amongst primarily the City's (financial exchanges) opinion formers' who influence investors and potential investors, which she refers to as 'third party' audiences or stakeholders' (Middleton 2002: 160). Further discussion on the reasons for this are introduced in Box 24.1 on p. 472 (see also Think about 24.1 and Activity 24.1.).

activity 24.1

Financial PR in different countries

Using the internet and other reference materials, examine and determine whether financial PR practice in the countries listed here resembles a UK or a US approach.

1 Sweden
2 Australia
3 South Africa
4 Canada

Feedback
For example, you may want to start by visiting the internet sites of the professional bodies for PR in these various countries and examine the information available on financial communications.

1 Sweden: Swedish Public Relations Society (www. sverigesinformationsforening.se/InEnglish/)
2 Australia: Public Relations Institute of Australia (www.pria.com.au)
3 South Africa: Public Relations Institute of Southern Africa (www.prisa.co.za)
4 Canada: Canadian Public Relations Society (www. cprs.ca)

Look for key words and themes in the information you find that might give you an insight into the practice of financial PR.

Why is financial PR so important?

Although at first examination we see a very different stakeholder focus of the US and UK practices of financial PR, what they have in common is that this corporate communication function (see Chapter 28) plays a fundamentally important role in any modern *listed* business.

> **Definition:** Listed refers to a business whose shares are traded on a stock exchange.

Financial PR's increasing importance is reflected in the *Economist* statement: 'To keep share price up, it is no longer enough merely to have a strategy. The strategy also needs to be articulated smartly – as any manager at BT, Ford or Marconi will tell you' (*The Economist* 14 July 2001: 75). Communication with financial communities about an organisation's position and future strategy is essential to the development of a good financial reputation, which in turn contributes to the overall reputation of an organisation. Good financial reputation is viewed by authors such as Deephouse (1997) and Roberts and Dowling (1997) as contributing to improved organisational performance and superior profitability, a view that is shared by the majority of academic and professional writers.

The perceived worth of financial PR is valued like no other area of PR practice. Fees in excess of a £1 million ($1.6 million) for financial PR services are not uncommon. *The Economist* points to the fact that Brunswick (financial PR) was, in 1995, the first to break the £1 million mark for the fee surrounding a single piece of work and in 2000 broke the £2 million fee mark (*The Economist* 14 July 2001: 75). (See Activity 24.2 and Think about 24.2, overleaf.)

Landscape of the 'City': who's involved in financial PR

By now it should be evident that financial PR has a clear role in contributing to organisational success by managing effective communication with key financial

think about 24.2 Benefits of financial PR

In what ways does good financial PR benefit an organisation?

Feedback
1 Assists in maintaining share price.
2 Assists in developing corporate reputation.
3 This, in turn, leads to greater performance and profitability.

activity 24.2

Financial PR and reputation

With a partner or in a small group of peers, discuss why you think good financial PR is important both in terms of protecting an organisation's share price and in building reputation.

Feedback
You may find it beneficial to refer to Chapter 13, which deals with reputation. Think of the shares as if you were buying them: what would be important to you and what might affect your purchase decision?

stakeholders and that differences in international financial PR reflect different priorities given to different stakeholders. What these different stakeholders share is that they are all concerned with the activities of financial exchanges (e.g. Wall Street, Frankfurt or the *City*), in other words, the exchange of money between 'people who have money and people who need money' (Middleton 2002: 160). These two parties in the exchange reflect Argenti's discussion of the 'buy-side' and 'sell-side' of the City (Argenti 1998: 144).

Definition: The *City* refers to the financial institutions based in the City of London in the UK.

Markets/exchange

These 'haves' and 'have-nots' of the financial world carry out their exchange of money on the global money markets/exchanges. This exchange is usually money (whether US dollars, pounds sterling or the euro) or in the majority of cases shares in companies, futures on agriculture crops, oil or other commodities (varying forms of securities). It is worth noting that practitioners normally communicate only with respect to activities of listed companies and the trading of their shares. Some of the main financial markets that you may have heard of are the London Stock Exchange based in the 'City' of London or the New York

Stock Exchange, which can be found on New York's famous Wall Street. There are also important exchanges in Frankfurt, Germany, and Tokyo, Japan, as well as in most national capital cities. When talking of these stock exchanges people often refer to the '*indexes*' of companies that are part of the exchange when discussing overall sector or market performance.

Definition: 'A *stock market index* is a listing of stocks, and a statistic reflecting the composite value of its components. It is used as a tool to represent the characteristics of its component stocks, all of which bear some commonality such as trading on the same stock market exchange, belonging to the same industry or having similar market capitalisations. Many indices compiled by news or financial services firms are used to benchmark the performance of portfolios such as mutual funds. Stock market indices may be classed in many ways. A broad-based index represents the performance of a whole stock market – and by proxy, reflects investor sentiment on the state of the economy. The most regularly quoted market indices are broad-based indices including the largest listed companies on a nation's largest stock exchange, such as the American Dow Jones Industrial Average and S&P 500 Index, the British FTSE 100, and the Japanese Nikkei 225.' (*Source:* adapted from Wikipedia 2005 http://en.wikipedia.org/wiki/stock_market_index)

Looking at the exchange markets holistically, who is involved? To put it simply, one could say that it is made up of three overarching categories of stakeholders:

1 those who regulate the exchange of money
2 those who exchange money
3 those who influence or communicate about the exchange of money.

Regulators

Regulation of the exchange of money is controlled at various levels internationally and nationally. International regulators include the World Bank, the EU and the geographical areas covered by various trade agreements such as the North American Free Trade Agreement (NAFTA). Individual countries all impose regulations on the exchange of money. However, in the case of individual markets, national regulators control how the exchange of money on a market is conducted, as well as how information that can affect the prices of securities traded on the market is disseminated. In the UK, the regulator responsible for UK securities markets is the Financial Services Authority (FSA). The US equivalent is the Securities and Exchange Commission (SEC) and in the European Union individual countries have their own regulators, although the Commission of European Securities Regulators (CESR) was established in 2001 to coordinate and advise regulators in a bid to ensure consistency in practice and implementation of European law.

Those involved in the exchange of money are institutional shareholders, private shareholders, private client brokers and investment and merchant banks.

Shareholders

Institutional shareholders (potential and current)

Institutional shareholders are organisations that control collective sums of money that are being used for investment/wealth creation purposes and in turn invest this money into listed companies. This investment is normally to a level far beyond the capabilities of individual private shareholders, often possessing between 1% and 100% of an organisation's securities with a value often ranging into the billions of pounds or dollars in the case of larger listed companies. Often institutional shareholders are mutual funds, pension funds or insurance companies investing premiums.

Private shareholders (potential and current)

Private shareholders are individuals. Like their institutional counterparts, they are investing money with the aim of wealth creation, although in the majority of cases this investment is only a small fraction comparatively, much less than 1% of an organisation's value. However, exceptions to this rule exist in relation to the founders of private companies that become listed companies or, in rare cases, individuals such as Malcolm Glazer who in May 2005 purchased a controlling stake of 76% in Manchester United Football Club. It should be noted that with the continuing developments in communications technologies, individual shareholders are becoming ever more important.

Stockbrokers

Stockbrokers are intermediaries who arrange on behalf of private investors the sale and purchase of shares. These intermediaries may also sometimes act as 'influencers' in this exchange of money, advising clients on when to sell shares and when to buy.

Investment and merchant banks

Investment and merchant banks are organisations that play several roles in the City. First, these organisations often act on behalf of institutional shareholders and listed companies arranging the sale or purchase of securities, quite often at different times in the financial cycle of an organisation (this cycle is discussed later). Second, unlike stockbrokers, these same organisations often arrange the finance around purchases or sales for institutional shareholders or for listed companies looking to purchase another listed company. In both of these exchanges the investment banks represent the 'buy-side' member of the exchange while merchant banks represent the 'sell-side'. Furthermore, these two City organisations are required by law to interact directly with each other at any time, even when they are two divisions of the same overarching financial organisation. This is to ensure transparency in deals and to avoid one side gaining insider knowledge. Quite often the 'parent' organisation will even house the two divisions in separate buildings to ensure geographic space illustrates the practical separation.

Affecting these decisions are the analysts and the various forms of financial media.

Influencers

Analysts

Analysts are individuals who often work for investment and merchant banks as well as stockbrokerages (collectives of stockbrokers) who research and analyse financial information on selected companies, usually within a specific industry sector (e.g. food, oils, transport, entertainment, etc.) and provide shareholders (current and potential) with comment and advice on the investment prospects. This information is published in documents referred to as 'research notes'. The commentary included usually surrounds recommendations about whether or not to buy, sell or hold on to a particular security.

Media/financial press

Like the analysts, the media communicate as well as pass judgement on the performances and prospects of companies, and in turn influence stakeholders involved in the sale and purchase of shares. Making up this group of 'influencers' are:

■ *The national financial and business print media*, which in the UK include key titles such as the *Financial Times* newspaper (commonly referred to as the *FT*), the national business sections of the quality 'dailies' and 'Sundays' (traditionally *The Daily Telegraph, The Times, The Independent* and *The Guardian*) as well as magazines such as the *Investors Chronicle*. Outside the UK, key titles are the *Wall Street Journal* and *USA Today* in the USA and international titles such as *The Economist, International Herald Tribune* and *Le Figaro,* among others.

■ The importance of *regional print media* should also be acknowledged with UK titles such the *London Evening Standard* and the *Manchester Evening News* and US titles such as the *New York Times, Washington Post* and *Los Angeles Tribune*.

■ *Radio and television* also play an important role in the financial media, providing an immediacy that extends beyond that of the print media. Some of the key radio and television media in the UK and Europe are BBC Radio 4, BBC24, BBC News (www.bbc.co.uk), SKY News and CNN Europe. CNN and the major US radio and television networks such as CBS radio, CBS, ABC and NBC, CNBC television play similar roles in the USA.

■ A further media channel that is gaining more importance is the *internet*. With its ability to make information at all levels instantaneously available to a wide spectrum of stakeholders, it is becoming the information stream of choice. The importance of the investor is underlined by the fact that the traditional financial print media have also established themselves as the leaders in the provision of financial news on the internet with the *Financial Times* online at www.FT.com in the UK and the *Wall Street Journal* online at www.online.wsj.com in the USA. These, along with the rising trend of internet billboard sites (visit www.executivelibrary.com to find the links to several great billboard sites) where individuals post their own views and questions and share them with others, are changing the shape of financial PR practice.

■ *Wire services* are a further financial media and interestingly they are usually the source from which all other media (including the internet) receive their information due to their immediacy and ability to communicate price-sensitive information (defined below) to a host of financial opinion formers and stakeholders. As will be discussed further in this chapter, this position as the main source of information is not accidental but ties to the regulations surrounding the practice of

---

activity 24.3

Financial media coverage

Either using the internet or by visiting a large newspaper shop (or look at a newsstand the next time you are at an international airport), try to identify what the major newspapers are internationally and compare, to the best of your ability, their financial coverage.

Feedback
You might want to look at the size of the business section, length of articles, imagery used and, if you can read the language of the publication, articles themselves for the tone of voice and content.
   Some examples are:

Australia – *The Australian* (www.theaustralian.news.com.au) and *Australian Financial Review* (www.afr.com)
Canada – *Globe and Mail* (www.globeandmail.com) and *National Post* (www.nationalpost.com)
France – *Le Monde* (www.lemonde.fr) and *Le Figaro* (www.lefigaro.fr)
Germany – *Handelsblatt* (www.handelsblatt.de) and *Bild* (www.debild.de)
South Africa – *Mail and Guardian* (www.mg.co.za)

---

financial PR. As an example, in the UK the main wire services are the RNS, Reuters (www.reuters.co.uk), The Press Association (PA), AFX, Perfect Information, PR Newswire and others.

■ *Other media* which at times play roles as stakeholders in financial PR include, but are not limited to, trade media as well as, in the cases of unique high-profile organisations, mainstream news media.

Definition: A *wire service* is a news-gathering organisation that distributes syndicated copy (information) electronically, as by teletype or the internet, usually to subscribers. (*American Heritage Dictionary* 2004 online)

See Activity 24.3 and Activity 24.4.

---

activity 24.4

Buying Man United

Using the internet, search for news stories on the purchase of Manchester United Football Club by the American Malcolm Glazer dating from January to May 2005. Examine where and how this financial story was covered by the press.

Feedback
Was the coverage limited only to the financial pages? If not, why do you think it had a wider appeal? What type of organisations do you think could be subject to such media coverage?

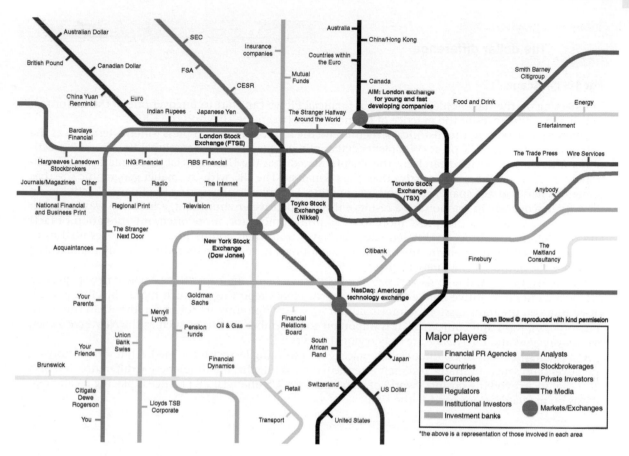

PICTURE 24.2 The City, with its range of players (stakeholders) and international differences, can be likened to a metro or tube system that sees money (equity) travel through various stations on the rail lines. Different factors can influence the journey or movements of the equity every day of the year. (*Source:* Ryan Bowd.)

Financial PR practice

While it might at first seem that the practice of financial PR internationally differs fundamentally from country to country, this is not the case. Of course, the practice in each country has its own regulations with a unique lexicon and special occurrences, such as mergers and acquisitions and hostile takeovers (these are discussed later). However, it is also characterised by repetitive and regimented cycles of communications, familiar across the globe.

One area, however, where a noticeable change has taken place is with respect to whether or not the financial PR is handled in-house or by a consultancy.

In-house vs consultancy

In the USA, financial PR has predominantly and traditionally been practised internally as 'most American companies of any size have big and experienced in-house teams', using agencies only to carry out specific transactions such as the special occurrences that are

discussed later (*The Economist* 14 July 2001: 75). In the UK, however, according to several senior practitioners interviewed by the author and reinforced by the *Economist* article, financial PR is more commonly carried out by an external agency. This may be as a result of the competitive media environment and the need to be able to draw on the kind of contacts and relationships a specialist consultant communicating frequently with specific journalists will have. With regard to the practice of IR in Europe, Marston and Straker found that 96% of the organisations they researched had an internal IR function that managed part or all of the organisation's IR, although of these, 45% still engaged an outside consultancy carrying IR functions (Marston and Straker 2001: 86–87).

Regulatory practice

Whether practised internally or externally, financial PR is subject to country-specific sets of guidelines and regulations that govern the practice. This is unlike most other PR functions. In the UK, the regulations

| box 24.1 | **The dollar difference** |

The US cityscape

In reflecting on the stakeholders involved in financial PR we can start to uncover one of the major reasons for the differences in the practice of financial PR between the USA and the UK.

Differences lie both in the historical structure and the mindset of the US press (often referred to as the '4th estate' versus the UK press (Wikipiedia 2005 online). One senior international financial PR practitioner interviewed in the research for this chapter stated that the UK financial media market has traditionally been much more competitive than the US market. The UK, with its smaller geographic size, has numerous national newspapers (due to ease of national distribution) covering the financial activities of the City based solely in London. As a result of this competitive environment, a tradition was forged in the media that has seen the 'press' more likely to print rumour (or, more often, interpretation of fact) and offer opinion in order to differentiate themselves from their competitors. This has resulted in financial PR practice in an environment where practitioners have been required to actively manage and influence the output of the financial press.

In contrast, the USA, due to its vast size, has historically seen 'one-paper towns' where newspapers do not operate in competitive markets. In this context, media reporting is much more objective and focused more on the transmission of information from which opinions are formed, rather than the transmission of opinion and conjecture. It is important to remember that titles such as the *New York Times*, *Washington Post* and *LA Tribune* are only regional papers.

As a result, the focus of US financial PR practice is in working less with the media, but rather more on the buyers and sellers of shares and their intermediaries. While this is a fundamental difference, it is also clear that in an evolving business world of global markets, US financial PR practice is placing greater emphasis on media relations outside the USA.

controlling this practice are in general laid out by the FSA (Financial Services Authority). These regulations are laid out in the FSA's *Purple Book* (previously *Yellow Book* and *Blue Book*, among others). Since 2001, this book has served 'as a single handbook of rules and guidance for all authorised financial firms in the UK', often pointing firms to other more detailed sources of information on specific points of law (FSA 2005). The book and the FSA as a whole aim to create a 'marketplace that is run in an efficient, orderly and fair manner whilst ensuring that consumers receive a fair deal by being properly informed and appropriately protected' (FSA 2005). (See Box 24.2.)

As a result, a regimented structure has been established for when, or more specifically at what intervals and with what content (updates on financial results and details of projections on future results, etc.), organisations must regularly communicate with financial stakeholders. This process is often referred to as the 'financial calendar' (Gummer 1995: p. 51). Furthermore, the guidelines also specify how organisations must communicate when involved in extraordinary special occurrences such as:

- initial placing offers (IPO)
- first trading on an exchange
- when a company is subject to mergers and acquisitions or hostile takeovers

- when an organisation 'de-lists' from an exchange and removes its shares from public trading
- any other news that might be considered '*price-sensitive information*'.

> **Definition:** *Price-sensitive information* can be defined as 'any information that a market does not know about, which if known would cause the share price of a company to move' (Middleton 2002: 164).

Internationally, it is important to note that regulations do vary and not all countries have either the same presentation format for regulations or the same regulations. In the USA, for example, regulations relevant to financial PR are found in a series of acts passed by the Congress and signed by the President. These include (but are not limited to) the Securities Act 1933, the Securities Exchange Act 1934 (and its 1964 amendment), the Investment Companies Act 1940 and the Sarbanes-Oxley Act 2002 (SEC 2005). This regulation provides for a fundamental difference between the US and UK financial calendars. For instance, in the US financial calendar financial PR practice operates on an annual cycle of quarterly reporting, rather than the UK cycle, which operates, on a cycle of mandatory reporting every six months.

box 24.2 **Getting it out on the wire**

In the UK, when financial information is communicated by an organisation it is distributed through a wire service (see earlier definition) to City stakeholders, particularly the influencers (such as the media and analysts) who then interpret it and pass on their views on the item to readers or clients.

The working practice has evolved as a result of regulation laid down by the FSA, which stipulates that all financial communication must be released via a wire service first in order to ensure that all interested parties receive the information at the same time. This is done in order to ensure no individuals gain an unfair advantage over another party.

Until 15 April 2002 there was one authorised service that had to be used in the UK and that was the Stock Exchange's own Regulatory News Service (RNS). However, since this date the distribution of regulatory financial information to the City has been carried out in a competitive commercial system and there now exist six authorised wire services:

- Business Wire Regulatory Disclosure (provided by Business Wire)
- FirstSight (provided by Romeike)
- Announce (provided by Hugin ASA)
- PR Newswire Disclose (provided by PR Newswire)
- News Release Express (provided by CCN Matthews UK Ltd)
- RNS (provided by the London Stock Exchange)

Source: adapted from FSA press release 12 April 2002: FSA/PN/037/2002 and FSA.gov.uk

Financial calendar

According to Gummer, the calendar of events is made up of the interim results, preliminary results, annual report and accounts, and the annual general meeting (AGM) (Gummer 1995: 52–56).

Interim results

In the UK, these are often referred to as the half-year results (whereas in the USA these are published three times in the year), and serve to provide shareholders and the City with a 'health check' on the state of an organisation's financial results to that point of the year and provide insight into their expectations for the next six months through a statement from the Chairman that will accompany a financial account of figures.

Preliminary results

As with the interim results, the preliminary results are a reporting to the City of the organisation's financial results and future prospects, although in this case it is the first reporting of the financial results for the year and in turn often ends up as a 'highlight of the financial year' (Gummer 1995: 53). These results are the City's first opportunity to see and judge whether the strategy of an organisation's management has been successful against their expectations. As a result, both for preliminary results and interim results, if an organisation feels it is unlikely to meet the expectations of its financial stakeholders, it is common practice

that in advance of the regulatory reporting it will issue what is referred to as a 'profits warning statement' via the regulatory wire services. This statement is released in order to soften the blow of poorer than expected results and minimise the impact from any resulting loss of confidence with City audiences. These impacts can include the lowering of share price or a reduction/loss of financial/organisational reputation and the latter can affect the confidence of suppliers and the ability of the organisation to secure finance such as loans from lenders and others.

(It should also be noted at this point that with respect to both interim and preliminary results, the dates on which organisations report results vary with respect to the date of their initial listing, see later, so on any exchange on any given day multiple organisations will report their results.)

Annual report and accounts

An organisation's annual report is a document that presents an in-depth accounting of the year's financial results (confirming the preliminary results), as well as covering a variety of other topics of interest to its stakeholders. These topics include, but are not limited to: the codes of business practice; ethical statement; corporate citizenship; and corporate governance and philanthropic activities (Bowd and Harris 2003: 22). This plethora of information is included as a result of both regulatory demand and stakeholder expectations, often tied into the organisational CSR (see Chapter 6). Some larger organisations, such as Shell, publish separate CSR reports along with their annual report and accounts.

It is important to note that all listed companies are required by law to produce an annual report within six months of their financial year end (date on which preliminary results must be released) and 21 days before their annual reports (Middleton 2002: 168).

Annual general meeting

The final element of the annual cycle of the financial calendar is the annual general meeting (AGM), which is an opportunity for investors (individual or institutional shareholders) to meet and ask questions of an organisation's management. They can also vote people onto – or off – the organisation's board of directors (such as chairman, secretary, etc.) as well as on new company articles (regulations). As a result the AGM is potentially a chance for an organisation's shareholders to forge the direction for the coming year. However, apart from times of organisational crisis (brought on by a loss of investor confidence), in practice for most organisations the AGM is an anticlimax (Gummer 1995: 55). The meetings are often poorly attended and most motions have been voted on in advance by postal ballot and the decisions follow the wishes of the institutional shareholders.

Case study 24.1 puts some of these activities into context. (See also Think about 24.3 and 24.4 and Activity 24.5, overleaf.)

---

case study 24.1

Pace Micro Technology plc

It's a material world: the financial calendar and listings regulations

Pace Micro Technology plc is the world's largest dedicated manufacturer of digital set-top boxes, supplying major operators such as BskyB in the UK and Time Warner in the USA. Based in West Yorkshire, Pace is a FTSE techMARK 100 company (one of the FTSE indices), trading its shares on the London Stock Exchange. The company's head of corporate communications and marketing retains a specialist consultancy to enhance Pace's financial PR capability at key times in the financial year, as is typical in UK financial markets. Citigate's in-depth knowledge of the City and other financial stakeholders helps Pace to anticipate how the markets are likely to react to communication of its results and other financial matters. As well as using the services of a City PR consultancy, the in-house communications team take advice from brokers who guide them on the strict regulations governing disclosure of financial information.

It can be difficult to assess what is 'material' and how potentially price-sensitive information that must be announced to the Stock Exchange should be handled. The *Listing Rules* (set out by the UK listings authority, UKLA, which is part of the FSA) prescribe certain matters that must be announced to the market via the RNS (or approved alternative) as aforementioned, as well as large commercial deals, board appointments or departures and the like. Usually such announcements must be made without delay and there may be only a narrow window to agree the format of an announcement.

Pace's financial communication programme works on a six-monthly cycle, driven by the interim results in January and preliminary final results announced in July. The communications team has to factor in production of the annual report for August, prior to the preparation for the annual general meeting in September. Key stakeholders include institutional and private investors, analysts within the UK, Europe and the USA, and the national and international financial media, for example the *Financial Times* and Reuters. Important other publics are major business customers who need to be assured of the stability of the business and, of course, staff who are particularly affected by the financial reporting in the local press.

Taking the interim results as an example, the head of corporate communication begins work on the chairman's report in November or early December, keeping track of redrafts as the messages are developed with the chief executive officer (CEO) and finance director, along with the brokers and City PR consultancy. In January board members meet to sign off the results, prior to the announcement of the interims, usually on a Monday, when Citigate then issues the information to the Stock Exchange. On results day, information is sent out via a regulatory wire service at 7am, then Pace executives meet with analysts at 9.30am, the City press at 11.30am (often communication with national journalists is by phone, rather than face to face) and the trade press in the afternoon. The results presentation and supporting documentation produced by the communications team forms the basis of subsequent investor roadshows led by the CEO. The cycle is repeated in depth when full results are announced in July.

Reflecting on the purpose of financial public relations for his organisation, Pace CEO John Dyson says:

▶

case study 24.1 (continued)

The most effective financial PR is actually about delivering business results. PR without substance is meaningless, but today analysts and the media demand continuous news and information. Lack of 'noise' can be misinterpreted, so it's vital that financial communication finds a healthy balance between delivering transparent *and meaningful messages which meet regulatory requirements without creating exaggerated expectations of performance, either for the good or bad.*

Source: courtesy of Jo Powell, Senior Lecturer, Leeds Metropolitan University

Financial Calendar for Pace Micro Technology plc

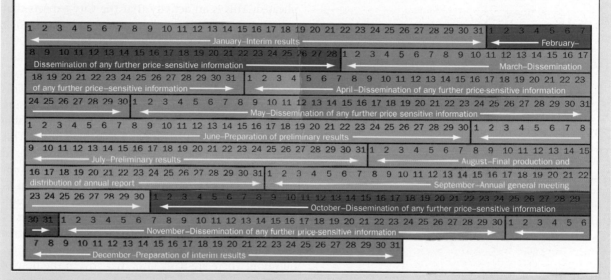

PICTURE 24.3 Putting the financial calendar into context: a graphic representation of Pace Micro Technology plc's financial year.

PR for a listed company regularly involves managing information that may be price sensitive. How can you be sure that what you are publicising to the trade and consumer press in way of new product development does not conflict with FSA rules?

Feedback Consult FSA guidelines in the *Purple Book* on reporting and ensure you follow them prescriptively.

What are the main capabilities and competencies required of a financial PR practitioner?

Feedback You might want to refer to the sections on public relations roles and practitioner skills (Chapters 3 and 15) as well as think about the particular skills required by financial PR practitioners.

Apart from the financial calendar and the communication of 'price-sensitive information', there exist three principal types of special occurrence that a financial PR practitioner may have to deal with as part of the practice of financial PR:

1 initial placing offer (IPO)
2 mergers or acquisitions
3 hostile takeovers.

The first of these traditionally only involves one team of practitioners, whereas the other two activities will often involve multiple teams.

Initial placing offer

An initial placing offer (IPO) is when an organisation lists itself on an exchange in order to become a traded security that can be bought and sold. For most organisations, this is an incredibly important step that is undertaken for various reasons and if successfully handled can enable them to move from strength to strength. Julius Duncan, Associate Partner of Finsbury, one of the UK and Europe's leading financial PR consultancies, provides a practitioner's guide to IPOs covering the motivation to float, the process of flotation and some potential pitfalls for practitioners to watch out for in the process in Case study 24.2.

Mergers and acquisitions

Mergers and acquisitions are the second special occurrence a financial PR may have to regularly undertake for an organisation. Most company takeovers are carried out as 'friendly' transactions. These takeovers or mergers are carried out with the recommendation of the target company's board of directors. Under this friendly manner of execution the risk of failure is lessened, therefore the cost at which one can raise capital to buy a company is lower. Also, they do not have to offer a high premium to the market and the advisor's bills will be less than if the situation were more complicated. This is an activity that the City expects that most listed companies will engage in as part of their corporate strategic plan at some time (Middleton 2002: 169). It will see either one organisation merge with another resulting in a new company or will see a larger company 'swallow up' a smaller organisation. This process often involves one of the organisations raising money to finance the merger or acquisition to enable the shares of the other company to be purchased. This can be done via a rights issue (new shares being offered to the market/exiting shareholders of the other company in the new company) or through loans from financial institutions to purchase the shares for cash. Additionally, it is often necessary for the shareholders of either one or both companies to be persuaded to agree with the proposed action, whether it is a merger or acquisition. There are basic laws that govern the flow of information to the market and it is important to understand them fully before getting involved in a takeover. If you get it wrong you can be sent to jail. However, the basic rule is that all shareholders must be in full possession of the facts of the bid at the same time. This information is usually released in the offer document at the start of the buying process and 'new information' may not be added to it subsequently. (See Think about 24.6 and 24.7, overleaf.)

A practitioner's guide to the IPO

Motivation for flotation

The primary reason an organisation floats on an exchange is to tap the public equity markets for funds. Companies that have previously been owned by private individuals, private equity companies or governments (in the case of privatisations in the 1980–1990s) sell a stake in themselves onto a stock exchange of their choosing. This brings them an injection of equity (cash), known as the proceeds of the offer, that the company will use to further its strategy/development. This 'use of proceeds' is stated upfront by the company in its prospectus or 'listing particulars'. Typical uses are to restructure debt or pay out exiting shareholders. Other benefits of being on the public markets are heightened profile, the ability to use your quoted shares as currency in further deals and the ability to use equity to attract and incentivise staff.

Process of flotation
Step 1

Once a company has decided it will pursue an IPO it will appoint legal and banking advisors to prepare the necessary paperwork and documents to go public. At the heart of this is the prospectus or 'listing particulars', which sets out every element of the business that is to be sold to investors and provides financial details on its past performance. A critical section of this document covers the 'risk factors' where the company must list every potential threat to its business and its prospects. The prospectus is a legally binding document and must be approved by the UKLA and finally 'stamped' to show that it has been approved.

Step 2

The floating company's banking advisors will then go out on the company's behalf to test the level of demand in the market for the company's stock: this process is called pre-marketing. This pre-marketing is based on research notes that are written by the analysts attached to the banks following meetings with the company and its management. From a communications perspective the initiation of pre-marketing is the most common time for the company to issue an 'intention to float' announcement outlining its plans and giving brief details on the business and its management.

Step 3

At the end of the pre-marketing period the company sets a 'price range' for its shares that sets a range for the company's valuation when it first floats. This price range will be communicated to the market by way of a statement and journalists will take a view on whether or not the IPO is attractively priced for investors.

Step 4

The management of the company then goes on what is known as an 'investor roadshow' to meet institutional investors in a gruelling series of face-to-face meetings, typically over a one to two-week period. The banks then go out to these potential investors and find out if they wish to take up shares, and at what price. This is known as the 'book-building' process. Depending on the level of demand in the book, the IPO will be priced. The intention is to get as high a price as possible. In instances where there is very high demand the price could be outside the top of the range; if there is low demand the range could be lowered or the IPO be priced below the range. In the worst scenario the IPO is 'pulled' because the selling shareholder refuses to accept the lowered price that investors are willing to pay.

Step 5

In the instance that the float has been priced successfully the company proceeds to listing on the nominated exchange. The necessary logistics of assigning a ticker code to the new listed company and setting it up as a new stock on the exchange are handled by the company's banks and lawyers.

Step 6

Once this is complete the company commences its 'first day of dealing' and its life as a publicly listed company. From this stage on the company is exposed to a heightened level of scrutiny on the public markets and constant journalist attention, and it must abide by the listing rules as outlined by the UKLA.

A few pitfalls to beware of during the course of an IPO

It is in potential investors' interests to 'talk down' the value of an IPO during the marketing process to enable them to buy the company more cheaply. This is often done through the press and journalists are willing recipients of negative stories about valuation and the possibility of a deal being re-priced, or failing.

Journalists tend to focus on the personal and colourful elements of the information in the prospectus. They are particularly keen to write about any significant payments to management or individuals selling shares. If this is the case for an organisation, it is necessary to explain in detail the reason for the payments and communicate them proactively to journalists thereby gaining their understanding.

Source: courtesy of Julius Duncan, Director, Lawton PRC, previously Associate Partner, Finsbury

If you were acting as the financial PR for a company about to go through the IPO (initial purchase offer) process, what could you do to try to minimise the potential for the pitfall described in Case study 24.2, where potential investors 'talk down' the share value of an organisation?

Feedback   One thing you could do is undertake an issues management programme for the IPO process and prepare documentation to identify any potential issues or weaknesses that could be used against you and then plan a communications strategy around each (see Chapter 19). Often this will involve ensuring that you have brought this information to the City's attention prior to a third party doing so, and in the process of raising the information, effectively communicating why it is either a 'non-issue' or actually a positive for the organisation.

Hostile takeovers and unsolicited advances

Hostile takeovers and unsolicited advances are the final of the three common special occurrences that PR practitioners will involve themselves in. Although financial PR practitioners perform many tasks for the institutions they work for, perhaps their role and importance is brought most firmly into focus during a company takeover. This is when the press is most interested in a company and where the messages and in particular the sentiment surrounding a bid really can make a difference to everybody's 'bottom line' (profitability). Financial institutions are well aware of this phenomenon and will pay a lot of money for professional media advice during this period.

An 'unsolicited' bid for a company is where financial PR gets most interesting. Here the bidder has not asked the directors of the target company for their support. They just go ahead and try to buy the company up. Examples of this include Michael Glazer's bid for Manchester United plc or Philip Green's attempt to buy Marks & Spencer. In both these situations, the target company did not put itself up for sale – it became a target without wishing to be so. In both situations, however, the bidding parties wished to enter into negotiations with the target. In the Marks & Spencer case, no formal offer was made for the company but there was significant media speculation surrounding the bid; handling this situation is the job of the financial PR practitioner.

The case of Manchester United offers interesting insight into whether a bid is 'hostile' or not. A bid becomes hostile if the board of the 'target' publicly reject a bid. This situation is not at all common, but during the 1980s James Goldsmith and Tiny Rowlands carried out a number of so-called 'corporate raids'. Press speculation increases massively and therefore the job of the financial PR becomes time consuming and crucial to the success of the bid. In the case of Manchester United plc, the board never stated an outright rejection of the Glazer bid and therefore this bid must be deemed 'unsolicited'; then again, they did not welcome it either and press coverage surrounding the bid suggested it was 'hostile' even though it was not. These grey areas are becoming more common and the so-called 'half-bid' situation is making a big difference to the way in which financial PRs do their job and provides problems for the financial regulators. The situation can become even more complicated if another bidder becomes interested. This is called a 'competitive bid'. Competitive bids are very expensive for the buyer, so when other potential buyers are thinking of making a counter offer, the financial PR must try to influence opinion.

The actual work carried out by the financial PR changes depending on the nature of the offer, whether one is working for the buyer or the seller and whether the offer is in cash (with no equity) or stock (all equity), or a mixture. If the PR is working for a buyer they try to explain that the offer is 'full and

In the process of a merger or acquisition, what do you think the role of the financial PR is? How different do you think it will be from the role the practitioner team plays in the IPO process?

Feedback   In these situations, it is the role of the financial PR working with the legal teams and banks involved to communicate to both shareholders and 'buy-side' and 'sell-side' analysts to ensure shareholder support is won and the City expectations of the effects of the activity are managed effectively.

box
24.3

Important 'trigger points' in takeover code

Note: % = percentage of shares owned

- 29.9% – once a bidder has taken more than 29.9% of the stock of a listed company it must make a formal offer for the rest of the shares.
- 50% + 1 – you have effective control of the company; in reality you probably have control before this point is reached.
- 75% – you can force a company to de-list with no regard of minority shareholders. You can change the rules of the company to never pay a dividend, for example. At this point, most shareholders will sell their stakes in the company.
- 90% – all minority shareholders must sell to the bidder.

fair', especially if it is a cash offer. If it is hostile they will highlight the limitations of the current management and feed journalists with evidence of the company's past underperformance. If the offer includes equity (stock) the PR may highlight how much better the new company will perform and that the value is in the interests of the shareholder.

The key point is that at no time may you produce 'new information' but bids can succeed or fail on the sentiment expressed around the marketplace – and financial PRs are crucial to this process. (See Box 24.3.)

In addition to the financial calendar, the communication of other price-sensitive information and the special occurrences already discussed, there is one other rare area of communications activity in financial PR – when an organisation *de-lists* from an exchange.

> **Definition:** *De-listing* is when an organisation either withdraws its shares from an exchange and becomes a privately owned company or is removed from an exchange for some form of regulatory reason.

Voluntary de-listing can occur when an organisation or its shareholders as a whole decide to de-list the organisation (assuming they are able to so) or if one shareholder acquires a majority so large that they are able to take an organisation into private ownership without the consent of the other shareholders. In the UK, this level is set at 90% ownership of shares, where that shareholder triggers a compulsory sale of the remaining shares to them. With respect to the previous case of an organisation or all shareholders deciding to de-list, although rare, it does occur; one such case where it is currently occurring is in the USA where many small organisations are de-listing in order to save the costs of meeting the reporting requirement of the Sarbanes-Oxley Act 2002 (Miller

and Frankenthaler 2004 online). The act introduced many new reporting regulations and as a result made the cost of reporting outweigh the benefit of being a publicly traded security.

An organisation can be de-listed from an exchange if it commits a severe breach of the 'listing rules' or is found to have repeatedly contravened the regulations, although this rarely occurs. Additionally, an organisation can be de-listed from an exchange if it no longer meets requirements to qualify for a listing. This can happen, for example, to companies traded on US NASDAQ or New York Stock Exchanges if their share price trades for less than $1 per share for 30 consecutive trading days and they are unable to respond appropriately according to the respective 'listing rules'.

How is effectiveness measured in financial PR?

Given that, as this chapter has shown, financial PR has arisen from a variety of historic routes, contains fundamental differences in international practice, has to communicate with a wide range of stakeholders and covers highly regulated activities within the financial calendar, it may seem hard to measure its effectiveness.

Although its activities could be measured via the various techniques described in Chapter 11, financial PR tends to be solely evaluated on its net impact on the business. Middleton (2002) points to the main measure of financial PR being the share price of an organisation, although others would probably widen this to include being on the winning side in takeovers, successfully achieving the desired price at flotation or enabling a merger to take place.

This emphasis on results is exemplified in Pace CEO John Dyson's quote: 'The most effective financial PR is actually about delivering business results' (see

Case study 24.1). In the *Economist* article that was quoted at the beginning of the chapter, Alan Parker, the founder of Brunswick (UK financial PR consul-tancy), is quoted as saying: 'Retainers are the enemy of value . . . we want to be paid for results' (*The Economist* 14 July 2001: 75).

Summary

This examination of financial PR has served to demystify the practice by defining what practitioners do, identifying who is involved, illustrating international differences and similarities in practice, introducing some of its unique lexicon and body of knowledge and examining its impact on business. Furthermore, the chapter has drawn out some of the trends that will need to be considered in future years.

One of the trends that it will be essential to consider is converging markets. This constant evolution of the global financial environments in which companies operate will see the practice continue to evolve and practitioners will need to understand the dynamics involved. As with the metro/tube system map of who's involved in the City, if a practitioner fails to properly navigate the evolving system they will find themselves lost and their organisation derailed.

Overall, financial PR is a highly specialised discipline, the rewards are great and the penalties for failure are extreme. It is imperative that PR practitioners are confident of their ground before getting involved. However, financial PR practices such as mergers and takeovers are highly testing and stimulating. If you do ever get involved, it is likely that the experience will take over your life and push all other matters to one side.

Bibliography

Allen, R.E. (ed.) (1984). *The Pocket Oxford Dictionary*, 7th edition. Oxford: Clarendon Press.

American Heritage Dictionary (2004). www.answers.com/wire+service&r=67, accessed 13 June 2005.

Argenti P. (1998). *Corporate Communication*, 2nd edition. Boston, MA: Irwin McGraw-Hill.

Bowd, R. and P. Harris (2003). CSR – a schools approach to an inclusive definition: Setting the scene for future public relations and communications research. Paper presented at the 10th International Public Relations Research Symposium, Lake Bled, Slovenia.

Clarke, G. and L.W. Murray (2000). 'Investor relations: Perceptions of the annual statement'. *Corporate Communications: An International Journal* **5**(3): 144–151.

Cornellisen, J. (2004). *Corporate Communications: Theory and practice*. London: Sage.

Deephouse, D. (1997). 'The effect of financial and media reputations on performance'. *Corporate Reputation Review* **1**(1/2): 68–72.

Dolphin, R. (2004). 'The strategic role of investor relations'. *Corporate Communications: An International Journal* **9**(1): 25–42.

Economist, The (2001). 'The spin doctors get serious'. *The Economist* 14 July 2001, vol. 360, Issue 8230, 74–75.

FSA (2005). www.fsa.gov.uk/pages/about, accessed 29 April 2005.

Gummer, P. (1995). 'Financial public relations' in *Strategic Public Relations*. N. Hart (ed.). Basingstoke: Macmillan.

Hagg, C. and K. Preilholh (2004). 'The art of financial relations: Reflection on strategic growth'. *Corporate Communications: An International Journal* **9**(1): 50–56.

Harrison, S. (2001). *Public Relations: An introduction,* 2nd edition. London: International Thomson Business Press.

Investors Relations Society (1997). *Practice Guidelines.* London: Investors Relations Society.

Marston, C. and M. Straker (2001). 'Investor relations: A European survey'. *Corporate Communications: An International Journal* **6**(2): 82–93.

Middleton, K. (2002). 'An introduction to financial public relations' in *The Public Relations Handbook.* A. Theaker (ed.). London: Routledge.

Miller, D. and M. Frankenthaler (2004). 'Voluntary delisting: A cost-efficient alternative to going private. Insights section, *Corporate & Securities Law Advisor* **17**(10): 7–12. www.bowne.com/newsletters/newsletter.asp?storyID=812, accessed 13 June 2006.

PRSA (2005). 'Section guidelines' www.prsa.org/_networking fc/guidelines.asp?ident-fc6, accessed 27 May 2005.

Roberts, P. and G. Dowling (1997). 'The value of a firm's corporate reputation: How reputation helps attain and sustain superior profitability. *Corporate Reputation Review* **1**(1/2): 72–75.

SEC (2005). www.sec.gov/about/whatwedo.shtml, accessed 29 April 2005.

Stone, N. (1995). *The Management and Practice of Public Relations*. Basingstoke: Macmillan.

The Economist (2001) 'The spin doctors get serious', *The Economist* 14 July 2001, Vol. 360, Issue 8230: 74–75.

Wikipedia (2005). http://en.wikipedia.org/wiki/Stock_market_index, accessed 13 June 2005.

Acknowledgements

The author would like to thank Finsbury, one of the UK and Europe's leading financial PR consultancies for a significant amount of assistance from its directors to ensure the practical and real world context of this chapter.

With thanks to Jo Powell for contributing case study 24.1.

Websites

Australian Financial Review: www.afr.com
Bild: www.debild.de
Canadian Public Relations Society: www.cprs.ca
The Committee of European Securities Regulators: www.cesr-eu.org
Deutsche Börse Group: www.exchange.de
Dow Jones and Company: www.dowjones.com
Financial Services Authority: www.fsa.gov.uk
Finsbury Group: www.finsbury.com
FTSE Group: www.ftse.com
Globe and Mail: www.globeandmail.com

Handelsblatt: www.handelsblatt.de
Interpublic Group: www.financialrelationshipsboard.com
International Herald Tribune: www.iht.com
Le Figaro: www.lefigaro.fr
Le Monde: www.lemonde.fr
Mail and Guardian: www.mg.co.za
MDNH, Inc: www.theft.com
The NASDAQ Stock Market Inc: www.nasdaq.com
National Post: www.nationalpost.com
NIKKEI (Nihon Keizai Shimbun, Inc): www.nikkei.co.jp
Pace Micro Technology plc: www.pacemicro.com
Public Relations Institute of Australia: www.pria.co.au
Public Relations Institute of Southern Africa: www.prisa.co.za
Reuters: www.reuters.co.uk
Swedish Public Relations Society: www.sverigesinformationsforening.se/InEnglish/
The Australian: www.theaustralian.news.com.au
TSX Group Inc: www.tsx.com
U.S. Securities and Exchange Commission: www.sec.gov
Wall Street Executive Library: www.executivelibrary.com
Wall Street Journal: www.online.wsj.com

For glossary definitions relevant to this chapter, visit the **selected glossary** feature on the website at: www.pearsoned.co.uk/tench

Public relations for information and communications technologies: principles and planning

Introduction

Technology is a broad term and can be interpreted as anything from books to printers to computers. Not all technologies have the equivalent impact on our lives that information and communication technology (ICT) does. A washing machine may make the process of washing clothes easier but it does not change the need for the task to be done, it does not usually change who does it and it certainly does not change the way we relate to each other (unless it is not used at all, of course). Contrast this with the mobile phone, which has transformed where and when we choose to have telephone conversations and how those conversations are conducted (through speech, text or pictures). It is for this reason that promoting ICT products through public relations is a complex process with special responsibilities. It is not about selling washing machines. It is about creating new ways of living. (Consider Think about 25.1.)

This chapter examines how public relations is conducted in the technology industry. It refers specifically to ICT and proposes that ICT public relations should be treated as a public relations specialism in its own right. ICT companies face major challenges that do not affect producers of consumer and business products. Drawing on technology theory, the chapter proposes that the specific nature of technology products and the effects of technology on society mean that public relations practitioners must plan and execute their campaigns with particular attention to industry variables. Ethics and social awareness play an important role in shaping ICT public relations strategies.

think about 25.1   Technology and innovation

Look around your house, flat or apartment. Count how many electronic devices you have. Then consider how many of them were available and affordable five years ago.

Think about the way in which you communicate with friends and family today. How might that differ in ten years' time?

Consider the record label of your favourite band, the film studio that made your favourite movie and the publisher of your favourite book. Look up the website for each one and find out what company owns them. How many are part of major media conglomerates?

box 25.1   The ubiquitous chip

Perhaps the most important invention of the last century was the microchip, whose arrival and evolution in the last three decades of the century resulted in an explosion of innovation and computing power that continues to affect almost every part of our daily lives. Why was the chip revolutionary? Rowe and Thompson (1996) argue that the following characteristics have made it so influential:

- *Size*: Technological advances mean that chips can now be microscopic in size and still process vast amounts of information. Miniaturisation has allowed integration of computing power via the chip into a range of new devices, not least the mobile phone and personal digital assistant (PDA).
- *Cost*: Microchips are cheap to produce, their costs reducing over 100,000 times since the 1970s.
- *Reliability, speed and capacity*: At the same time as the cost and size of chips has decreased, their reliability, processing speed and processing capacity have improved and are light years ahead of traditional electronic components.
- *Flexibility*: The combination of these features means that the chip is an incredibly flexible technology. It has been integrated into old machines and has opened up possibilities for new devices, such as the laptop computer and wireless networks, that in turn offer new ways of living, working and socialising. This is perhaps the most significant contribution of the chip in terms of the way we live with each other today: its transformational power when integrated into devices that manage – and allow us to manage – information and communication in our daily lives.

The chip has also facilitated the convergence of old industries as technologies have combined to create new scenarios for consumers and businesses. The most obvious example of this is the media, entertainment and communications industries, where global enterprises operating in television, cinema, publishing, music and computing have joined forces to create multibillion dollar conglomerates with global reach. Partnerships and mergers are the norm as companies struggle to gain control over the cash cows of the future: multimedia content and distribution networks (Miles 2001). AOL-Time-Warner, Bertelsmann, Vivendi Universal and Sony are examples of such organisations.

Information and communication technology (ICT): background and social impact

Mattelart (2003) provides an excellent summary of the evolution of the role of information and communication technologies in society. The world we know today, governed by flows of information from one place to another, began with the emergence of mathematics as a way of understanding the world in the seventeenth and eighteenth centuries. Since that time, mathematics has been the main tool for analysing both the natural world, through science, and the social world, through statistics. It also forms the basis of information sciences, which underpin information and communication technologies.

The growth in importance of mathematics, the resulting increase in the value and importance of information and communication and the increasing sophistication of the technologies that manage such information and communication have all created a central role for technology in our lives. However, technology is, and has always been, a social phenomenon and is not value free. Mattelart illustrates, for example, how the construction and spread of information networks is closely aligned with the dissemination of ideologies and institutional forms while others emphasise the controversies surrounding new technologies (e.g. Rowe and Thompson 1996;

think about 25.2 **Technology and communication**

How do you usually communicate with the following:

- parent or guardian
- boss
- close friends
- lecturer?

Why do you choose this form of communication?

Feedback You might: text your friends; email your boss or your lecturer; telephone or write to your parent or guardian. These choices are underpinned by preferences based on the particular audience – your parents may not like texts or understand how to use them. Email might be the preferred form of communication for your lecturer and boss – while your friends might not have regular access to a computer, so it would not be suitable for arranging a night out at short notice.

Rosenberg 1997; Dutton 2001). Technology generates strong reactions from those who use it. Take, for example, the Luddites – workers in the mills and clothing factories of the north of England during the early nineteenth century, who demonstrated against mechanisation by destroying new equipment designed to automate tasks previously done by hand.

As part of this reaction to technology, individuals also shape and change it to meet their own needs. Freeman (2001), Miles (2001) and Williams and Edge (2001) all argue that the use of technology is ultimately bounded by its social context. This social shaping begins in the laboratory, when researchers decide where to focus their time and effort. Once technology is released onto the marketplace, the evolution continues as feedback from users shapes the next generation of invention. This is particularly the case with ICT-based products, which are designed to be actively used by individuals and are therefore particularly prone to change and adaptation, diverging from the manufacturer's initial vision (Mattelart 2003). *Cultural norms,* individual needs and group dynamics all determine how enthusiastically technologies are adopted and explain why countries differ in their uptake and use of identical technologies like email and texting. (See Box 25.1.)

> **Definition:** *Cultural norm* means a pattern of behaviour that is considered acceptable by members of society.

Promoting technology: the special case of ICT

In the 1990s and early 2000s specialist public relations agencies for the ICT industry began to emerge. More often than not, the campaigns they run ask individuals or organisations to make sizeable investments, sometimes in products whose use they cannot

yet envisage. Such campaigns often have education and futurology at their core: they tell audiences how the technology works and explain what kind of a future might be possible should they adopt it.

This process sounds simple and not unlike public relations in other areas. However, there are a number of complexities that practitioners need to understand, relating to the industry and the audiences being targeted. These are outlined in the following sections. (See Think about 25.2.)

Industry characteristics

Issues relating to the ICT industry must be addressed by public relations practitioners developing ICT campaigns (see Figure 25.1, overleaf).

Audience breadth and depth

Because ICT is so ubiquitous, the target audiences for an ICT campaign include consumers, government, large enterprises, small businesses, students and families. Public relations practitioners must understand how to reach and communicate simple, relevant benefits to each group. They must have relationships with both specialist and general media and analysts and be able to discuss the technology in simple terms as well as in depth, to accommodate different understandings and skill levels among these audiences.

Industry partnerships

The trend towards convergence means that ICT companies work together on new products and conduct joint marketing and public relations campaigns that encompass the interests of each party. Public relations practitioners create the glue for such campaigns so that

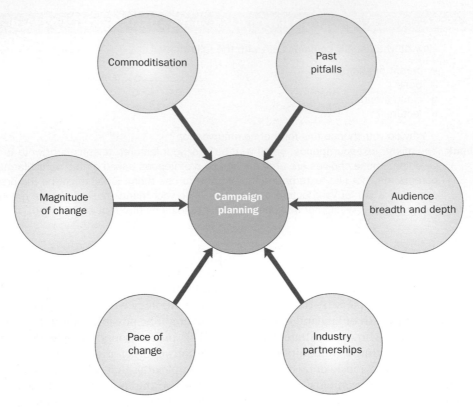

FIGURE 25.1   Industry issues affecting technology public relations

they make sense for the audience. At the same time, managing different interests behind the scenes can be a challenge as each company jostles to get the exposure it wants.

Pace of change

Perhaps the most noticeable characteristic of ICT products is the speed at which they change. Advances in ICT and related technological industries (e.g. nanotechnology) are rapid as technologies advance and converge. As a result, new products or new versions of products come onto the market every year. Consumers and businesses must follow a continuous learning curve in order to keep abreast of developments. Public relations practitioners must also keep track of developments and create campaigns that help individuals and organisations along this learning curve.

Magnitude of change

The scale of some changes – between versions of products, for example – may be relatively small and perceived to be unimportant by target audiences. This is known as *incremental change*. Staff may not care whether their computer takes less time to boot up and

process information. Consumers may not notice that their mobile phone 'drops' fewer calls than it used to. However, manufacturers promote such incremental changes to justify releasing new versions of their products. It falls to the public relations practitioner to make them interesting enough to justify news coverage.

When a product represents a major technological advance, this is known as a *step change*, and it presents a different challenge. The advent of a mobile phone small enough to fit into a handbag or jacket pocket, for example, was the first time that the device really lived up to its name. Combined with user-friendly and reliable software, it resulted in one of the fastest adopted technologies in history. Similarly, reliable email software has transformed the nature of communication both at work and home. In these situations, the value of the product can be hard to communicate because audiences may not understand the technology and cannot envisage the scenarios for its use. Public relations campaigns must generate visions of the future for consumers and businesses in order to create the demand for their products. These visions are potentially extremely powerful and may ultimately become reality, depending on the ability of the technology to live up to the promises made and the way in which people ultimately use the product.

Commoditisation

Basic ICT technologies are cheap to produce and even cheaper to copy. This has resulted in a huge number of devices – mobile phones, computers and laptops – on the market, driving prices down and widening access for consumers. As a result, such devices are no longer the preserve of the rich but are becoming a commodity, a 'matter of course' purchase for those with the money and time to access them. As *commoditisation* continues and the flood of products increases, manufacturers have to think of new ways to make a product stand out in the marketplace and public relations campaigns play a key role in this process.

> **Definition:** *Commoditisation* describes the process whereby a new product or service – in this case, for example, a technological device such as the washing machine – becomes an everyday item of purchase.

Past pitfalls

Despite its prevalence in our lives, ICT is very new and can be subject to problems. Its history is marked by mistakes as well as successes. Journalists, consumers and businesses remember errors and broken promises. Public relations practitioners need to know and understand the impact of such stories to foresee potential obstacles and pitfalls in campaigns that might otherwise unconsciously repeat the same mistakes. (See Activity 25.1.)

activity 25.1

How to send an email

Ask an older friend or relative what they were using to communicate when they were your age. The answer will not be email or a mobile, but more likely fax and landline telephones – and perhaps the humble pen and paper might make an appearance!

Now put yourself in the position of training someone who has never seen an email programme to use the system for the first time. Write down the sequence of events needed to send your first email message, from opening up the email programme, to pressing the send button. Don't just consider the process, but also anticipate the kinds of question they might ask and the confusion they might feel when facing a computer screen for the first time.

ICT audience characteristics

There are three main audiences for ICT public relations campaigns: individuals; organisations; and government or legislative bodies. All consider certain common issues when deciding whether or not to adopt new or existing technologies, although these issues are viewed differently by each group (Figure 25.2). Public relations practitioners must recognise these issues and address them in ways that meet the needs and concerns of each audience.

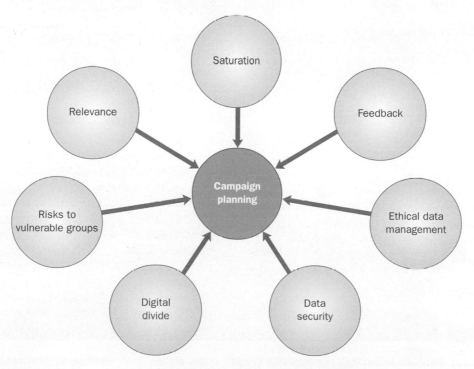

FIGURE 25.2   Audience issues affecting technology public relations

Relevance

Not everyone is interested in new technologies. Unless a product is relevant, individuals and organisations are unlikely to purchase it. New technologies require significant investments in time and effort on the part of individuals and organisations and such investments need to be justified. Moreover, new technologies can create disruption in the workplace as new work practices are introduced, expectations of staff change, information is shared more widely and cultural norms shift. Public relations practitioners have to demonstrate how the benefits of a particular product outweigh these personal and organisational costs, usually making life and work easier and more enjoyable. However, they must balance these inspirational scenarios with the need to manage expectations; often new technologies are flawed and user feedback results in improvements in later versions. If there is too great a gap between anticipation and reality, users may abandon both the current version as well as future, improved products.

Saturation

Attention is a scarce resource. Like other areas of public relations, ICT campaigns compete for attention among their audiences. Their task is made more difficult when they are discussing incremental change. For example, when your audience has multiple mobile phone manufacturers selling them up to 30 different phones at any one time, designing a campaign to promote a new 'look' that offers few tangible improvements in usability can be challenging. Generating the excitement and anticipation that will sell a new product is often easier said than done for public relations practitioners. Often, it involves promoting associations with the product or brand, rather than publicising the product or brand itself.

Feedback

Because technology is a social phenomenon, feedback from users, about how it is being used, what concerns

PICTURE 25.1 Because technology is accessible in many public places, there is often an assumption that this means it is accessible to all. This is often not the case. (*Source:* Photo Disc.)

are being raised about its use and how those concerns might be addressed, is essential for governments and organisations trying to manage its impact. Public relations is an important tool through which such information can be obtained; a feedback loop should be built in to campaigns wherever possible.

Ethical data management

Through ICT, organisations and government have access to much more data about individuals than used to be the case. Social concerns about the abuse of this data by both government and individual companies echo the 'Big Brother' scenario depicted in George Orwell's novel, *1984*, where all aspects of individual life are scrutinised and monitored. Public relations practitioners must acknowledge and engage in this debate and ensure they observe government policies as well as minimum ethical standards and practices suggested by government and organisations to prevent the misuse of personal data in this way.

Data security

New products may also present new opportunities for abuse of personal and company data by third parties and criminals. More and more organisations and government departments hold information about our personal lives, including shopping habits, home address, banking and credit history and employment details. Governments have realised the need to work together with organisations to set minimum standards for data security in order to avoid misuse of this valuable, but private, information. New legislation can deal with new types of crimes such as hacking (illegally breaking into an organisation's computer network and misusing company and individual data found there). Only when consumers are sure that their personal information will not be compromised will they be comfortable using new technologies. Public relations practitioners can advise on what levels of security are possible and what kinds of limitations are acceptable to industries interested in using data legitimately to meet commercial objectives. Campaigns should ensure such concerns are addressed and educate individuals and organisations in the need to adopt proactive practices to protect their own data (for example, regularly updating anti-virus software or not opening emails from unknown parties).

Digital divide

The use of technology is now a route to accessing information, social networks and social provision. However, not everyone has equal access to technology. Financial resources, time and skill levels all affect the ability of individuals to use and benefit from new developments in ICT. Older people find it harder to learn new skills; poorer families find it difficult to finance a computer at home; single mothers in a full-time job may not have time to use the internet to find out about new benefit entitlements. Generally, people who are already financially and socially disadvantaged are unlikely to have the same access to technology in the home or at school as more privileged individuals. This not only affects their ability to engage with each other effectively in a technology-driven world, but also has the potential to affect their ability to engage in society and social networks (Norris 2000). For example, as email becomes an increasingly popular mode of communication, those who do not have a computer at home may start to lose out on social contact with their families and friends.

The exclusion of certain groups from new technologies has led to the spectre of the 'digital divide' – a world of technology 'haves' and 'have nots' where social participation is dependent on involvement with technology (Warschauer 2003). Public relations practitioners can act as advocates for these groups with organisations and government, communicate private and government-led initiatives that might help improve their access to technology, and promote the important debate about the social impact of technology. (See Case study 25.1, overleaf.)

Risks to vulnerable groups

The advent of new technologies has also led to new types of risk in society. For example, children using the internet may be exposed unwittingly to pornographic sites while surfing. The lack of safeguards on the internet also means they are more vulnerable to predatory adults than would be the case if they met face to face in the company of others. Elderly people, by the same token, might be susceptible to unscrupulous individuals offering to help them through a new, technology-based process for claiming benefits, while simultaneously gaining access to their personal finances. Society struggles to come to grips with these new risks and expectations weigh heavily on manufacturers as well as policy makers to improve security and protection. Public relations practitioners must engage with government, organisations and individuals to explain the nature of the risk and outline potential solutions, such as filtering websites, improving parental control or introducing new security requirements. (See Case study 25.2, overleaf, and Mini case study 25.1, p. 492.)

case study 25.1

AVANTI–Fujitsu consulting and Fox Parrack Hirsch

In 2001, Fujitsu, in conjunction with Microsoft, started work on a new technology project – AVANTI – for the London Borough of Lewisham. AVANTI (added value access to new technologies and services on the internet) was designed to help Lewisham residents use the internet and to address some of the problems of the 'digital divide', helping people who find computers difficult to access, such as elderly people, disabled people and minority ethnic groups, to access e-government services.

The AVANTI technology is built around an avatar called Andrea – an intelligent personal assistant that guides people through online transactions and services.

Fox Parrack Hirsch (FPH), as Fujitsu Consulting's retained public relations consultancy, was tasked with launching AVANTI in Lewisham in collaboration with ISIS, Microsoft's public relations company. As the lead agency, FPH advised all parties on the launch plan and took responsibility for driving the ongoing public relations campaign and coordinating activities with the e-government unit of the UK government. The main objectives of the public relations activity were:

- to highlight the many benefits that the London Borough of Lewisham and its citizens would reap from AVANTI
- to illustrate how the technical framework developed by Fujitsu and Microsoft enabled AVANTI to work and the advantages that avatar and AVANTI technology could deliver to sectors other than government
- to communicate the benefits and functionality of AVANTI to other local authorities, positioning it as an example of public sector-led innovation.

At an early stage, FPH liaised with all the parties to devise a strategy for launching AVANTI and to push the key messages associated with the project.

The initial activity involved registering Lewisham as a UK government 'centre of excellence' with UK Online, to showcase the AVANTI project and illustrate how other local authorities could replicate the model to achieve electronic service delivery.

To create awareness among Lewisham residents, AVANTI was launched via a roadshow staged on an electronically enabled bus. The AVANTI bus was based in Lewisham town centre and formally 'opened' by the Mayor of Lewisham. Residents were invited on to the bus to try out Andrea and AVANTI for themselves, to learn more about how it worked and what it could offer. The bus also travelled to other locations in Lewisham, including residential estates.

The launch was organised in conjunction with Lewisham Council's press office and a joint press briefing was hosted for the key target media including government media, local and national media and IT specialist publications.

To stimulate interest among Lewisham residents, on the day prior to the AVANTI bus launch FPH arranged a radio interview with BBC *London Drivetime*. The radio interview also included recorded clips from Andrea, the avatar. The press briefing attracted several media titles, including *Government Computing*, *Computing*, *BBC Online*, *The Guardian* and the *Lewisham Mercury*. The story was covered the following day by *The Guardian*, with Andrea described in the headline as 'The UK's first virtual council worker'(26 July 2002).

FPH subsequently worked with Lewisham and Fujitsu to enter the project into the Information Management Awards 2002, where it won the award for Best CRM Project, and the NabarroNathanson Technology Awards 2003, where it was recognised for the Most Innovative Use of Technology in a Project.

Source: www.fphcom.com/home.html

Public relations in the ICT industry: a model

Having seen all the different elements that create the context for, and requirements of, public relations in the ICT industry, we can propose a basic model that illustrates the connections between public relations, audiences and their adoption and shaping of technology (Figure 25.3, overleaf).

Following Figure 25.3 from left to right, the process of public relations in the ICT industry begins with the creation of a new product or service, based on new technology. Marketing campaigns are initiated to promote the product, targeted at individuals and organisations. These individuals and organisations take into account a number of factors while considering whether or not to adopt the new product or service.

At this point the role of public relations is threefold. Campaigns must complement marketing campaigns in the messages they communicate about a product or service (shown by the dotted line connecting public relations campaigns and marketing and sales). They also address some of the concerns of organisations and individuals, through education and clarification about the product and how it can be

case study 25.2

Vodafone – Working Nation

Having established itself as a credible market leader in mobile voice and data communications, Vodafone UK wanted to broaden its reputation by addressing broader lifestyle changes that the use of its technology had introduced, particularly in the workplace.

While changes in working lives were relevant to all businesses, not least to Vodafone itself, the company had to find a credible way of discussing them. As a market leader, the company was generally recognised for its expertise in producing mobile products and services – but not for its understanding of broader business issues. Given this gap, the objective of the chosen activity was to establish the company as a thought leader on changing working practices affecting UK businesses, to highlight potential issues arising from these changes and to establish the real-life context for Vodafone products and services.

Vodafone decided to initiate a two-stage research project, called Working Nation. The first stage, carried out in early 2004, involved qualitative interviews with industry and opinion leaders, politicians and academics to establish exactly what issues businesses faced, particularly in light of new technologies being used in the workplace. This first stage was so productive that Vodafone decided to extend the second planned stage of research and execute a series of quantitative surveys over a period of time, which would provide more in-depth information about specific issues raised in the qualitative interviews.

The first Working Nation report, 'Young Guns, Mature Minds', was launched in September 2004 and addressed generational differences in the workforce, how businesses could ensure they valued the skills of both young and old employees and bridge the generation gap between the two groups so that each could learn from the other.

The Working Nation report was launched using four simultaneous public relations strategies.

The formal launch event was hosted by the company's new Chief Executive, Bill Morrow, for media, industry leaders and other opinion leaders. Father and son broadcasters, Peter and Dan Snow, complemented the presentation of results with anecdotes about the differences between their roles and how they perceived each other from different ends of the age spectrum.

At the same time a regional radio campaign was conducted across the country, fronted by James Cracknell, a member of Britain's Olympic rowing team. He discussed the survey results, which included regional data relevant to regional media, and also talked about his own experience in an industry where youth, rather than age, is assumed to be a prerequisite for success. Some stations were so taken with the topic that they created an extended feature, using their reporters to source additional material for the story.

The needs of national broadcast media were met throughout the day, with features on CNN, BBC *Breakfast*, BBC *Radio 4* and BBC *Radio 5 Live*, among others. Finally, national and regional print media were offered material for more in-depth coverage of the Working Nation report to create follow-on stories in their next-day editions.

The report itself was sent to 1000 journalists, key influencers, company stakeholders and organisations who would be particularly interested in the topic – such as the Third Age Employment Network.

The response to Vodafone's initiative was positive, generating interesting debate both internally and externally. The issue of the ageing workforce was particularly relevant to UK businesses, which ensured that the approaches made to journalists were productive – even if they knew little about the company beforehand. Extensive coverage was generated as a result of the different public relations tactics employed, and the inclusion of opinion leaders and personalities who were not linked to Vodafone gave the story additional interest and credibility. The report itself has been circulated beyond even Vodafone's expectations – some organisations have proactively made contact with Vodafone to express their enthusiasm for the initiative.

Source: vodafone.co.uk

---

used. Finally, practitioners become 'organisational activists', communicating back to the manufacturer those issues that can only be solved by concrete action (for example, ensuring employees in developing countries enjoy fair working conditions).

At the same time, issues such as access and security are also affected by government policies and legislation, which can, in turn, affect the decision-making process.

If the efforts of public relations and the effectiveness of government policies are not sufficient or credible enough to allay concerns or generate enough interest in the product, target markets are unlikely to use the product. However, if they are successful, individuals and organisations will decide to take up the new opportunity that the product or service presents.

At this point, the technology itself becomes modified by its social implementation. Public relations plays a part in gathering and communicating feedback about these changes back to the manufacturer through research on target audiences and, increasingly, media feedback. This is then taken into account both in marketing campaigns and in new product development.

mini case study 25.1

'Women in IT' 2002 – e-Skills UK and Axicom

e-Skills UK (http://www.e-skills.com) is the UK Sector Skills Council responsible for developing the country's IT skills base. One of its biggest challenges has been to raise awareness of the need to attract more women into IT careers and to work with government, employers and educators to address the problem.

AxiCom, as the public relations agency for e-Skills UK, was charged with developing public relations strategies that help e-skills UK address the need to attract more women into IT careers. Although e-skills UK has a clearly defined audience to reach, the problem it faced was that this audience was so varied it required a wide range of media to report on the issue if it was to reach its target groups.

The agency proposed focusing public relations activity around a high-profile conference, 'Women in IT', held annually and attracting the required breadth of audience. The 'Women in IT' event 2002 was the second time the event had been staged. The main objectives of the public relations activity were:

- to gain press coverage and recognition among government, employers and educators of the need to attract women into IT careers and to announce programmes that would go some way towards achieving this goal
- to communicate the messages of the conference and gain support for the programmes launched

from a wide-ranging target audience, including other government departments, NGOs, employers, educators, women and schoolgirls.

AxiCom developed a range of press releases appealing to a wide selection of press. Working alongside the DTI press office, the public relations team set up over 30 high-profile press briefings before, during and after the event for many of the speakers. Patricia Hewitt MP, then UK Secretary of State for Trade and Industry and Minister for Women, provided the conference keynote speech and was available for a photocall.

More than 20 press attended, resulting in over 40 substantial news stories. Most of the attending press conducted multiple interviews, with some journalists conducting as many as six on the day. The audience of the publications that reported on the conference directly matched the target audience, with BBC *Online* (whose audience includes women and schoolgirls) in particular reaching a significant number of the UK population.

Other coverage included the front page of *Personnel Today*, multiple mentions in *Computer Weekly*, *Network News* and *Managing Information Strategies*, business press reports in the *Financial Times* and the (London) *Evening Standard*'s 'Just the Job' section.

Source: www.axicom.com/micro/cases/
index.asp?c=6#IBM

The model, and the preceding discussion, illustrates the complexity of the process of public relations for ICT companies. This model illustrates only campaigns that relate specifically to promotion of a product or service. Practitioners are often also required to conduct educational campaigns, focused specifically on shifting an audience's position on a particular issue (e.g. security or ease of use). Alternatively, they may be asked to reposition a product or service, to refresh perceptions or highlight a new feature that may improve relevance to certain audiences.

Because they have such influence on the way we live, companies that produce ICT products are heavily scrutinised and have particularly high demands placed on them in terms of their contribution to society. This emphasis on social responsibility has meant that companies like Microsoft, Compaq and Dell are increasingly investing in corporate-level public relations campaigns, aimed at improving the image and reputation of their organisations.

While this image and reputation is linked to the products and services companies produce and the image presented by marketing and branding campaigns, the dynamics of public relations here are different. Campaigns working on reputation must be longer term and flexible, constantly catching up with society's expectations. The opportunity for practitioners to be organisational activists (see definition of this in Chapter 9) is even stronger in these contexts, since knowledge of public perceptions is invaluable in helping organisations to modify their behaviour – and their products and services – to be more acceptable to audiences across the world.

Principles of ICT public relations practice

In practical terms, public relations practice in the ICT industry must take into account all these considerations

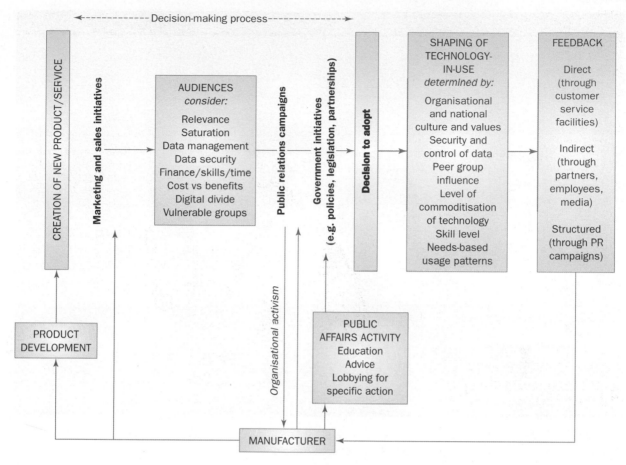

FIGURE 25.3   Public relations in the ICT industry

when planning and managing campaigns. Some generic principles of operation can be applied to the process, as well as actual steps in planning ICT campaigns. These are now outlined.

Principles of operation

Recognise the power of 'futurology'

Chapter 9 on public relations theories outlined the power of public relations as a mechanism through which reality is constructed, by dint of public relations materials being used as a main source of news by journalists. This argument becomes even more important for public relations practitioners in the technology industry, who are often required to 'invent' scenarios that highlight product capabilities in as yet unknown situations. This ability to paint a credible yet inventive picture of the future is fundamental to selling new products, particularly in step change scenarios. Public relations practitioners must recognise the influence they have here in creating possible futures and be particularly careful about the multiple implications of

these possible scenarios, including effects on the way we socialise and interact, conduct relationships and control our lives.

Centrality of ethics

Technology never operates in isolation but has knock-on effects on the way we live and work. Public relations practitioners are therefore not simply promoting an ICT product or service, but must recognise that new ways of being are fundamental to the emergence and evolution of their products and services. As proponents of these new ways of being, practitioners have a responsibility to encourage ethical use of technologies and protection for those who may be made vulnerable as a result of their introduction.

Focus on education

The breadth of skill level and range of uses for a single technology among different audiences means

PICTURE 25.2   Technology is increasingly an integrated part of our lives and it has a major influence on how we work and spend our leisure time. (*Source:* © Simon Marcus/Corbis.)

activity 25.2
Technology public relations consultancies

Search the internet for technology public relations consultancies. Visit four or five sites and look at their case study archives. Take two or three case studies and, in light of the considerations discussed in this chapter, ask the following questions about each one:

1 What industry, audience and/or organisational characteristics might have affected their perception of the product being promoted?
2 What techniques did the public relations practitioners use to address these characteristics, either to minimise their impact or to make the most of them?

Now go to the homepage of the company featured in each case study:

3 How do the messages on the website try to differentiate the company from its competitors?
4 Is there anywhere on the site that mentions issues related to the social impact of their products, either in a positive way or by addressing some of the potential issues it might raise, such as digital divide-related problems?

that ICT public relations campaigns frequently revolve around education. Explanations of the technology as well plain benefit statements can be part of the core messages in the campaign or may evolve as the campaign continues over time. A practitioner's ability to translate complex situations and provide simple explanations is fundamental to the success of these campaign elements.

Create active audiences

ICT public relations practitioners must educate their audiences not only in the benefits of the technologies, but also in their responsibilities in using the technologies. For example, they may encourage audiences to use a free email system developed by their client, but they also need to explain how to avoid spam and prevent viruses by using appropriate spam-blocking and anti-virus software. They may vigorously promote a new internet site for children, but should make parents aware of the dangers of letting children use the internet unsupervised and exposing them to undesirable or unsuitable sites. In this sense, ICT public relations demands an active response from audiences – one of the hardest things to achieve through a public relations campaign.

Complex simplicity

ICT products and technologies can be highly complex yet are often targeted at different audiences whose understanding and skill levels range from absolutely nil to extremely good. At the same time, these companies must engage with government and policy makers, since new technologies have new implications for society. One campaign, therefore, may need to encompass a whole spectrum of messages, each of which needs to be simple and relevant to a particular audience segment. Public relations strategies must be versatile and adaptable, keeping core messages consistent but allowing enough flexibility for each audience clearly and consistently to understand the relevance to them.

Campaign planning

The generic principles just outlined provide guidance for decisions about how to develop campaigns. In addition, the considerations outlined in this chapter can be interpreted as practical steps in the campaign planning process. Figue 25.4 outlines these steps.

The process of analysis following the receipt of the campaign brief from the client is equivalent to the PEST (EPISTLE) or SWOT analysis that should be carried out as part of the campaign process (see Chapter 2). ICT campaigns have specific considerations that should always be taken into account based on the three main areas: audiences, industry/product and the clients involved. Once this analytical stage is complete, the development of the actual strategy for the campaign and the tactics to address each audience must be done on a tailored basis. At this point, ICT practitioners can revert to standard public relations planning processes while taking the generic principles of operation into account. (See Activity 25.2 and Case study 25.3, overleaf.)

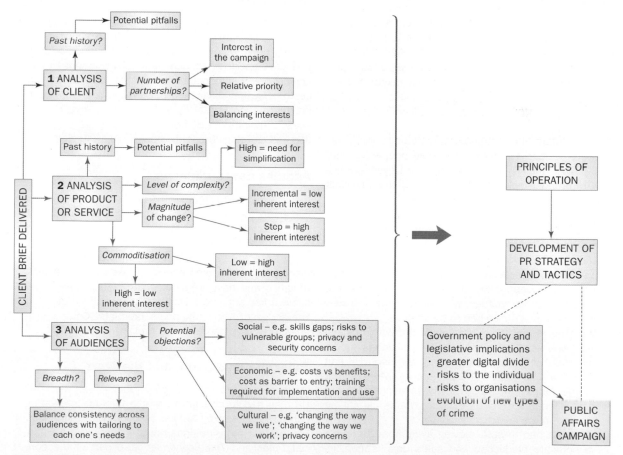

FIGURE 25.4   ICT campaign planning

case study 25.3

Microsoft UK launches Office 2003

Microsoft produces software for businesses and individuals around the world. One of its flagship products is Microsoft Office, a suite of applications for desktop and laptop computers including Excel (numerical spreadsheets), Word (text documents), Outlook (email) and Powerpoint (presentations). The first version of Microsoft Office was introduced in 1990; by 2005 10 versions of Office had been launched in total.

Office 2003, launched in October 2003 in the UK, was a different animal from previous versions. Microsoft's research had found that integrating information and pooling intelligence across organisations was one of the biggest barriers to improving productivity for many businesses. Genuine teamwork was relatively difficult to achieve, particularly across offices in different geographical locations.

Based on these findings, Microsoft's software development teams had focused in particular on the ability of Office applications to 'talk' to one another and to external software. While there were some new 'bells and whistles', the greatest innovation in Office 2003 was the integration between the different applications.

The nature of the changes made in Office 2003, and the history of the product itself, meant that Microsoft UK was faced with a number of challenges for the launch. Office 2003 was the tenth version of Office in 14 years. Both users and journalists were suffering from 'launch fatigue', characterised by cynicism about yet another version being released and scepticism about its capabilities.

Office was perceived by users and journalists as a suite of tools that made desk-based work simpler. It was not recognised as software that could revolutionise information sharing and teamworking. Microsoft UK had to change the way people thought about and used Office, working against 13 years of history to broaden perceptions of its value to individuals and businesses.

Previous launches had focused primarily on 'bells and whistles', based on the improved content and capabilities of the software applications. However, innovations in Office 2003 were more to do with the way the different software applications worked together, rather than with visible changes in the applications themselves. The old product-based strategy was not effective – a new way of discussing Office had to be found.

The changes in Office 2003 were highly technical – senior, non-technical managers and business media would find it difficult to understand. Microsoft UK had to find a way to explain the technology in terms that were meaningful for these business audiences, but without alienating software experts, who would still be interested in the launch.

Microsoft had to start moving away from its image as a software production and sales organisation, instead presenting itself as an organisation in touch with business needs in the twenty-first century. It had to discuss business and market dynamics, rather than product characteristics. Only then would people believe that it could produce a tool like Office 2003, designed first and foremost with business needs in mind.

In light of the launch challenges, the strategy and tactics adopted by Microsoft UK represented a new departure for the company's product public relations.

Education, education, education

Given the need to change perceptions of Office, the campaign had to educate audiences on changes in business and highlight how Office could help meet new organisational challenges. Education takes time, so regular contact with key media and analysts began early. Workshops, media tours, press releases and face-to-face interviews were used in tandem to ensure audiences understood the relevance and quality of Office 2003.

Change the perspective used to discuss the product

For Office 2003 product promotion began not with the product but with the customer. Spokespeople explained how business had changed since Office was first developed. Instead of just talking about email, spreadsheets and documents with media, analysts and customers, they discussed new business needs: sharing information in real time, teamwork across remote sites, combining ideas from all areas of the organisation and creating competitive business strategies.

Address new audiences

Historically, IT managers – the holders of IT budgets – had been the core audience for Microsoft's product launches and were very familiar with the company. In contrast, Office 2003's success depended on its credibility as a strategic business tool. Senior business managers, who would understand the wider relevance of Office and drive demand among IT managers, became a key audience. However, they had no detailed knowledge of Microsoft or its products. Communications with them had to be on target and credible.

Tailor the media mix and the story

Corresponding to the change in audiences, Microsoft UK also had to change its media targets, integrating publications read by senior, non-technical managers. For the first time, business media such as the *Financial Times* and *The Economist* were part of the core

▶

case study 25.3 (continued)

media for the product launch. Spokespeople had to discuss business issues rather than product features when they met business journalists.

Use partners and customers to 'translate' jargon

The launch of Office 2003 incorporated participation from partners who had deployed Office 2003 early and could explain the difference it made in simple terms. By putting Office 2003 in a familiar context with meaningful examples, their stories demonstrated how technology could address business objectives effectively.

Retain technical interest and reputation

While the business argument would drive take-up of Office 2003, it could not do so unless the software were effective and reliable. The interest of the technology media in the nuts and bolts of the product still had to be met in order to generate a solid reputation for the new product prior to the launch.

The campaign build-up included:

- opinion pieces and feature articles about business challenges, placed in business and IT publications
- a business workshop, emphasising the relevance of Office 2003 to business issues
- feature stories on the successful early adoption of Office 2003 in partner organisations
- regular press releases highlighting different capabilities of Office 2003
- a series of tailored, face-to-face interviews with all target media
- a live demonstration of the product for all media prior to launch
- a product review program for technical and business media
- a technical workshop on the product, held in the USA and examining the nuts and bolts of the software.

Ongoing dialogue was maintained between the US-based development team and key technical journalists in the UK. In addition, senior business managers were individually briefed by senior managers from Microsoft, who often held similar positions in the organisation and could speak from experience about the dilemmas they faced.

The launch event continued and extended the educational theme of the build-up. Representatives from Henley School of Management and the London School of Economics discussed how technology could change the business landscape and open up new opportunities for people to relate to each other. Partners who had trialled the new software joined Microsoft to explain how Office had removed barriers to cooperation within their organisations, improving teamworking and productivity.

The structure of the campaign was effective: press coverage was plentiful among business and technical publications, containing clear messages about the value of Office 2003 from a business perspective. For the first time, business journalists featured Microsoft spokespeople expressing their views on the challenges facing UK organisations and potential solutions for those challenges. Technical journalists covered the launch extensively and generally produced favourable reviews of the product.

Discussions about the product moved towards an issues-based agenda rather than being led purely by product features. This simultaneously created a new role for Microsoft as an organisation with important views about the business landscape. The involvement of academics and customers in the campaign also helped reinforce Microsoft's credibility as a source of intelligent opinion on general business issues, not just technology. (See Think about 25.3.)

Source: used with kind permission of microsoft.co.uk

think about 25.3   Microsoft case study

1 To what degree do you think Microsoft's strategy was based on recognition of the social impact of Office in the workplace?

2 If you were launching a new mobile phone, which, like Office, had many previous versions, how would you address the issue of 'launch fatigue' among audiences and the media?

3 Which of the industry characteristics outlined in the chapter can you identify in this case study as factors that affected the launch of Office 2003?

4 In your own words, and based on the organisational context outlined in the chapter, explain why customers might object to adopting a new version of Office in their organisations.

5 This case study outlines Microsoft strategy to attract the attention of businesses which might be interested in Office 2003. Based on the individual context outlined in the chapter, what problems do you think it might face when launching a new version of Office to home computer users like you, your parents or your fellow students? How would you make the product more appealing to them?

6 Microsoft was asking people to use Office to change the way they worked, in order to improve business outcomes. How ethical do you think its strategy is?

Summary

This chapter has outlined the particular circumstances surrounding public relations in the ICT industries. The social nature of technology means that this area is not as straightforward as it might seem for public relations practitioners. While their role may be ostensibly to promote a product or service, they are, in fact, charged with offering new ways of living. They must:

■ manage highly varied environments
■ be completely at ease with complex technologies
■ discuss them with experts and novices alike
■ offer relevance and create desire across a very broad range of audiences
■ constantly feed public concerns and perceptions back to the organisation
■ make ethical, responsible use of the power they wield, putting education and simplicity at the centre of their campaigns and generating active engagement from audiences.

Practitioners have already recognised technology public relations as a specialism, but few scholars have engaged with this area in any depth. This chapter represents a first attempt to make sense of the technology context for public relations in practice.

Bibliography

Dutton, W.H. (2001). *Information and Communications Technologies: Visions and realities*. New York: Oxford University Press.

Freeman, C. (2001). 'The two-edged nature of technological change: Employment and unemployment' in *Information and communications technologies: Visions and realities*. W.H. Dutton. New York: Oxford University Press.

Hearit, K.M. (1999). 'Newsgroups, activist publics and corporate apologia: The case of Intel and its Pentium chip'. *Public Relations Review* **25**(3): 291-308.

Mattelart, A. (2003). *The Information Society: An introduction*. London: Sage.

Miles, I. (2001). 'The information society: Competing perspectives on the social and economic implications of information and communication technologies' in *Information and Communications Technologies: Visions and realities*. W.H. Dutton. New York: Oxford University Press.

Norris, M. (2000). *Communications Technology Explained*. Chichester: John Wiley & Sons.

Rosenberg, R.S. (1997). *The Social Impact of Computers*. San Diego, CA: Academic Press.

Rowe, C. and J. Thompson (1996). *People and Chips*. Maidenhead: McGraw-Hill.

Warschauer, M. (2003). *Technology and Social Inclusion: Rethinking the social divide*. Cambridge, MA, and London: MIT Press.

Williams, R. and D. Edge (2001). 'The social shaping of technology' in *Information and Communications Technologies: Visions and realities*. W.H. Dutton. New York: Oxford University Press.

CHAPTER 26

Integrated marketing communications

Learning outcomes

By the end of this chapter you should be able to:

- define and discuss integrated marketing communications issues
- evaluate the importance of integrated marketing communications to organisations and their publics
- identify the key principles and methods of integrated marketing communications
- apply this understanding to simple, personally meaningful scenarios
- recognise integrated marketing communications activity through case examples
- apply principles to real-life scenarios.

Structure

- Definitions of integrated marketing communications (IMC)
- Strategic marketing communications planning
- Branding and integrated marketing communications
- Agency perspectives of integrated marketing communications
- Integrating the marketing communications mix

Introduction

Who cares about marketing communications? The vast numbers engaged and employed worldwide in the communications industries most certainly do since it is their source of income and employment. The UK's Institute of Practitioners in Advertising has 234 member companies, employing over 15,000 people (IPA 2005). Obviously this represents a small fraction of those involved in spending billions of dollars on marketing communications around the world. They are largely employed in the first and middle stages of the *communications process*, namely creating *communications messages* and managing the media through which these messages are channelled. They should also have a vested interest in those at the end stage of the process, the 'receivers'. It is the response of these individuals, or groups of individuals, that really determines how successful the communications

> **Definition:** *Communications messages* are all those messages sent and received either intentionally or unintentionally that provide information about products, services and organisations. They may result from specific marketing communications activities such as advertising or direct mail or indirectly, for example, as a result of people talking about brands or seeing brands being consumed. Intentionally sent messages will usually be positive and controlled; those resulting from word-of-mouth situations may be critical or negative and uncontrolled.

tions process has been in achieving the objectives set. But these receivers do not have the same level of vested interest – they are not being paid to watch, listen to or read such communications messages, so why should they care? As consumers, we buy products and services for the benefits they provide us with and we have preferences for certain brands that we purchase and use on a frequent basis. It can be useful, indeed beneficial, to receive information about them or direct incentives to purchase. This may include products and services that are new to us or new to the market. However, do we need the estimated 1500 or so messages we receive each day (Walsh 2001), providing us with information about products, most of which we do not care about? We might get woken up by an alarm playing a commercial radio station (for example, in the UK it could be any one of 285 UK radio stations), listen to a radio in the shower, watch TV – (283 channels to choose from in the UK) or read newspapers (14 national and 90 regional dailies in the UK) and magazines (3500 consumer titles), while making and consuming breakfast. We then pick up the post and see direct mail – all in the first hour or so of the day and before leaving the house (media information from www.royailmail.com).

This chapter will explore the wide-ranging nature of marketing communications and demonstrate the importance of adopting an integrated approach in order to manage the complex issues involved in communicating effectively and efficiently with consumers, businesses and other stakeholders.

In this chapter, we shall examine the various issues surrounding the achievement of marketing communications effectiveness via the development of an integrated approach. This goes beyond making sure that the chosen media carry a consistent message, although that does play a significant role. Effective planning, targeting and positioning are essential elements of the integrated marketing communications (IMC) process. The driving forces examined include branding, creativity, internal and external communications linkages, international factors, new technologies and new media, longer term thinking, the role of ethics and social responsibility, communications agency perspectives, consumer information and evaluation.

Definitions of integrated marketing communications (IMC)

The marketing communications 'industry' often uses terms such as advertising, public relations (PR), sales promotion, direct mail or sponsorship to describe what they do. But do these terms mean anything from a consumer perspective? Do consumers use such words to describe the various communications messages they receive through a vast range of media? Maybe it is all seen as only one of the following – advertising, publicity, PR, promotion or 'junk.' Isn't direct mail just another form of advertising media, even if the industry calls it direct marketing? Is sponsorship a collective term for the organisation of a range of communication activities? This may include: *advertising*, of an event, team, individual or location; associated media coverage generated through *PR*; corporate hospitality supporting *sales* opportunities; targeting *sales promotions* at those attending an event; hosting *interactive websites* enabling comment and feedback as well as *merchandising*. (See Activity 26.1.)

Marketing communications *media* are often defined only in 'advertising' terms as TV, radio, cinema, print and billboards. Use of such mass communication tools is still considered effective for reaching large numbers in a relatively short period of time but surely in today's marketing environment this fails to recognise a wide range of opportunities – direct mail, sponsorship, PR, telemarketing, websites, packaging, point of sale displays, vending machines, branded clothing and merchandise items? These are not 'new' media forms but should clearly be recognised as offering organisations routes to an integrated approach. (See Think about 26.1.)

---

activity 26.1

Receiving messages

Keep a log over a few days of the marketing communications messages you receive throughout the different stages of the day. This might include when you are watching TV, reading newspapers, listening to radio or using the internet – all opportunities for receiving commercial messages.

Definition: The term *media* refers to any medium interface or channel that allows communications messages to flow between senders and receivers, in both directions.

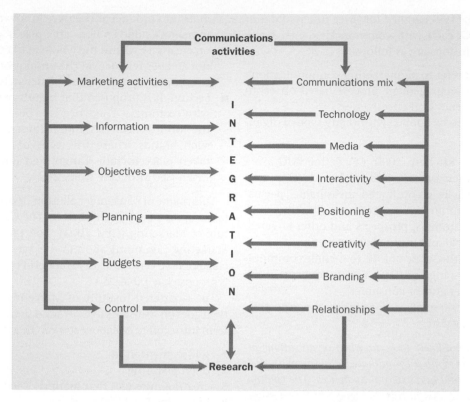

FIGURE 26.1   An integrative approach to organising and planning marcom (marketing communications) activities (*source:* adapted from Hughes 1998)

Hughes (1998) considered the various elements that contribute toward communications integration (see Figure 26.1). This might now also be extended to include issues such as the impact of new technologies, interactivity, information and the role of creativity.

Definitions are many and varied. The IMC concept first emerged in the 1980s and developed relatively slowly into the middle of the next decade. Smith et al. (1997) attempted to examine IMC from a strategic as well as an operational perspective. One of the issues is the use of the term 'integrated'. Various interpretations of the term integrated include coordinated, holistic, embedded and combined. Essentially, much of the underpinning discussion focuses on the range of issues identified earlier and whichever term is used, success is measured in terms of how effective they have been addressed in producing measured results. Hughes (1998) highlighted the shift in emphasis from *promoting to* a target audience to *communicating with* the audience. This has become increasingly prevalent with advances in database and media technologies. The two-way nature of communication is now at the forefront, even for those fast moving consumer goods (*fmcg*) brands with millions of globally based customers.

> **Definition:** Products known as *fmcg* are typically those we buy from supermarkets and convenience stores, branded products from manufacturers such as Heinz, Kellogg's, Procter & Gamble – baked beans, breakfast cereals, shampoos.

---

think about 26.1   Being a consumer

Do you care about marketing communications? You will probably be reading this as part of your studies, learning about PR and communication. But as a consumer – how important are marketing communications to you? Which forms of communication appeal to you? What makes you respond? Take a few minutes to consider some of these points. Make some notes, discuss with your friends, colleagues or tutors.

Smith et al. (1997) argued for three different definitions of IMC, each with common elements. These grouped definitions are as follows:

1 those that refer to *all* marketing communications
2 a strategic management process based on economy, efficiency and effectiveness
3 the ability to be applied within any type of organisation.

Schultz and Kitchen (2000: 65) define IMC as: 'a strategic business process used to plan, develop, execute and evaluate co-ordinated measurable, persuasive brand communication programs over time with consumers, customers, prospects and other targeted, relevant external and internal audiences'.

This widens the scope of IMC to include communications with a range of target audiences beyond the direct purchaser and/or consumer.

Fill (2002: 457) explores a number of perspectives of IMC and suggests:

They are more likely to occur when organisations attempt to enter into a co-ordinated dialogue with their various internal and external audiences. The communication tools used in this dialogue and the messages conveyed should be internally consistent with the organisation's objectives and strategies. The target audiences should perceive the communications and associated cues as co-ordinated, likeable and timely.

Schultz (2004) believes that IMC still focuses too heavily on tactical implementation, attempting to make things look the same. He suggests that organisations need to find ways in which horizontal integrating processes and systems, including internal marketing communications and strategic planning frameworks, can be developed 'that work across disciplines, not just across communications forms'. Lancaster (2004) recommends two ways in which IMC might break through the communications clutter barrier:

■ First is the need for creativity to extend beyond its traditional role in communications message for-

mats into product and service innovation in order to achieve added value. This places an emphasis on creativity within the whole marketing mix and not an over-reliance on the promotional elements to compensate for product deficiencies.

■ Second, it is proposed that brands need to *collude* with customers. There needs to be engagement in the form of lifestyles and attitudes. Examples of such brands where this type of collusion has taken place include Tango, Red Bull, Coke and Evian (see Mini case study 26.1).

This theme of consumer collusion or collaboration is taken up in a paper published by The Chartered Institute of Marketing (CIM 2004) 'You talkin' to me? – Marketing Communication in the Age of Consent'. A collaborative versus intrusive model of communication is proposed in Table 26.1.

The Chartered Institute of Marketing (CIM) paper then goes on to discuss five key ways in which the move from intrusion to collaboration can be achieved:

1 self-segmentation
2 open planning
3 creating messages that matter
4 managing legal boundaries
5 measuring return on communications.

Self-segmentation is based around a principle of customer-managed relationships whereby customers communicate with an organisation via the channels they prefer, with the segment being based on a higher degree of personal data being supplied. *Open planning* offers a different perspective on integration by identifying those issues that need to be considered in developing effective strategic marketing communications and derives from discussion between senior marketers from companies such as IBM, Masterfoods, Ford, Vauxhall, Land Rover, Lloyds TSB, NSPCC and senior agency representatives to consider 'media neutral' planning best practice. Media neutrality suggests moving away from traditional media such as TV advertising, towards a

---

mini case study 26.1

Evian

In January 2005, Evian launched an on-pack promotion, supported by point of purchase displays and retailer in-store magazines, which offered consumers points that could be redeemed against free rewards. These rewards were linked to the core Evian brand values of 'purity' and included beauty and fitness treatments, health club passes, personal training sessions and aromatherapy massages. Points could be exchanged

against rewards by visiting a promotional website. This campaign contained a number of elements of the collaborative model of communication (see Table 26.1) and provided for customer *collusion* in the way it targeted the lifestyles and attitudes of the Evian consumer.

Source: adapted from an article on www.mad.co.uk
accessed 22 March 2005

TABLE 26.1 Intrusive and collaborative communications (*source:* adapted from 'You talkin' to me? – Marketing Communications in the Age of Consent', www.shapetheagenda.com, Chartered Institute of Marketing 2004)

Intrusion model	Collaborative model
Scattergun	Consent-based dialogue
Poor targeting, mass communications	*Building relationships, two-way communications*
Seller benefits	Mutual benefits
Lack of focus on customer needs	*Consumer incentives, loyalty programmes*
Media constrained	Media transparent
Reliance on historical usage limited to one major media form, often advertising	*Using a full range, including 'new media'*
Invasion of privacy	Respect for privacy
Over-communicating, using 'acquired' personal information	*Data protection requirements*
Poor innovation	Radical innovation
Lack of creativity	*Electronic communications*
Impact unknown	Return on communication known
No emphasis on response measurement, focus on acquisition	*Need for performance measurement*

wider and integrated range of communications methods and media.

The **open planning** framework includes eight 'action areas' – disciplines, media, channels, process, structure, relationships, results and tools. The CIM research indicates that the potential payoff for UK industry in implementing this open planning is between £4 billion and £10 billion, depending on the extent to which the action areas are implemented.

Messages that matter need to be targeted creatively and effectively, using new technologies in ways that need not be considered intrusive. For example, interactive TV advertising provides viewers with the opportunity to respond but without the intrusiveness that might be associated with direct mail or telemarketing.

In *managing legal boundaries* it is important for the communications industries to self-legislate

---

mini case study 26.2

Diageo marketing code

Diageo is one of the world's largest producers of alcoholic beverages, including brands such as Guinness, Smirnoff, Baileys, Cuervo and Johnnie Walker. It has developed a Code of Marketing Practice for Alcoholic Beverages:

We are proud of our brands. We want Diageo's marketing and promotional activities to be recognised as the best in the world. That means delivering great results for our brands, and doing so in a way which sets industry standards for responsible marketing.

This statement, from Diageo CEO Paul Walsh in 2003, precedes a detailed schedule not only explaining how the company will set about meeting legislative requirements but also offering guidance for the promotion of sensible drinking of its products. The code applies to brand advertising, promotional activities in bars, pubs, clubs, off-licences, supermarkets and other retail outlets, brand innovation activities, experiential marketing, consumer planning, relationship marketing, consumer PR and the development and content of brand websites. Across all marketing communications activities, a socially responsible positioning strategy will be employed.

Full details of this code and other Diageo initiatives involving corprate social responsibility can be found on the company's website – www.diageo.com.

Source: Diageo Plc

wherever possible and to work with legislators in developing acceptable parameters. Many individual firms have adapted or are adapting their own procedures for managing their businesses, including their communications, from ethically and socially responsible perspectives (see Mini case study 26.2).

Measuring (return on communications) – the effectiveness of marketing communications has traditionally been a neglected area. The CIM paper estimates that £100 billion a year is spent globally on advertising, yet this level of investment is subject to little measurement regarding *return on investment* (ROI). Open planning supports the development of more effective ways of measuring communication success. For example, Nike does not use outputs such as awareness or response levels but outcomes in terms of numbers involved in individual sports. Microsoft and Coca-Cola base their measures on percentage

> **Definition:** *Return on investment* (ROI) is the positive value or contribution that can be achieved as a result of making an investment in a particular business activity. In marketing communications terms, this might include the sales resulting from specific, identifiable and measurable communications activities. For example, 5 million sales directly attributable to a direct mail campaign costing 1 million provides a 4 million return of the communication investment. Although described here in financial terms, the 'return' might be based more subjectively by measuring increased brand awareness or improved corporate image resulting from a range of communications activities.

awareness of the brand. Retailers Tesco and Walmart use percentage of customer retention (customers who keep returning to their stores). (See Case study 26.1.)

Definitions, while intending essentially to encapsulate meaning, may actually complicate and confuse.

---

case study 26.1

'It only works if it all works' – O$_2$

The mobile phone brand O$_2$ was launched in April 2002. This involved the re-branding of BT Cellnet mobile brand, which had been struggling against intensive competition from market leaders Vodafone and Orange, as well as facing new competitors such as T-Mobile and 3. With little technical difference between brands, marketing and marketing communications were the key areas in which competitive advantage could be gained.

O$_2$ put into action marketing communications plans that aimed to transform the brand from the dullness of Cellnet into one that would prove to be the mobile brand of choice.

Objectives were set not only for measurement of the specific communications activities in raising brand awareness levels but also for effectiveness in improving staff morale, building trade partnerships and adding to shareholder value. Integration was implemented at two levels, visually and strategically. Visual integration aimed at building brand awareness involved consistency and coordination across all channels, from promotional mugs through to advertising and sponsorship. Strategic integration included a focus across the brand, the products and the communications.

Effectiveness measurement took a number of forms. Market research identified an increase in 'top of mind', unprompted awareness of mobile phone operators from the 20% established over seven years by the Cellnet brand to 28% achieved by O$_2$ two years after

launch. Internal communications based on the 'It only works if it all works' theme were successful in ensuring all staff were behind the communications and marketing strategies. Strong focus on briefing trade partners such as Carphone Warehouse and the provision of support materials and incentives were also significant in building relationships.

Econometric analysis identified the value of strategic integration. This included 'payback' calculations based on:

- number of new connections attributed directly to communications
- average revenue generated by each connection in any year
- average lifetime of each new customer (three to five years)
- O$_2$'s margin (profit)
- cost of media, production and agency fees (£78.3 million).

By December 2003 advertising and sponsorship had generated £493 million additional profit margin. Lifetime value of margins from incremental business was estimated at some £4.8 billion, giving a payback of 62:1. O$_2$ was subject to a rejected takeover bid in February 2004, which valued the business at £9.5 billion.

Source: adapted from Maunder et al. 2004 from www.warc.com accessed 24 January 2005

think about 26.2   Intruding on, or collaborating with, customers?

Read the CIM 'Shape the agenda' paper referred to earlier. Are there any other issues that you consider have not been raised or need developing further? What kinds of marketing communication do you find particularly intrusive? Are you a member of any loyalty programmes? What kinds of communications activities do these schemes use?

Feedback   Individual perspectives and experiences will identify relevant issues here. Experience may include working in different business environments where issues will vary significantly. A constantly changing business environment requires all businesses to monitor such change and modify their activities in order to meet the requirements of more demanding customers. For some, receiving text messages may be the preferred means of receiving 'advertising' information; for others it may be via newspapers or TV; while for many, the preference may be to receive nothing at all!

While the definitions discussed here go some way to developing our understanding of the IMC concept, many practitioners will have their own way of describing and implementing IMC in order to communicate effectively through (media) channels with customers and other groups (stakeholders). (See Think about 26.2.)

Strategic marketing communications planning

In order to achieve an integrated approach to marketing communications, it is important to have some kind of planning framework around which strategies and tactics can be developed. A number of planning 'models' have been suggested (Smith 1999; Fill 2002), some of which are briefly described in what follows. The adoption of a planned approach suggests also that a longer term perspective might be considered more important than the drive for short-term commercial gain. The longevity of major brands such as Coca-Cola, Mars, IBM or Ford is based as much on a detailed approach to planning as it is on the success of individual communications activities.

Smith et al. (1997) first proposed a SOSTAC (situation, objectives, strategies, tactics, action and control) model for integrated marketing communications planning. Fill (2002) developed a more comprehensive marketing communications planning framework – or MCPF (see Figure 26.2).

Both SOSTAC and MCPF incorporate broader business and marketing factors than simply those that focus directly on the organisation of communications activities. This breadth provides a basis for integration at a higher marketing planning level. A starting point which examines the current *situation* (S) or *context* needs to look at the overall business and competitive position of the firm, develop an understanding of consumer behaviour, review all relevant internal and external factors and identify the communication needs of all stakeholders, not just those of customers. From this analysis, communications *objectives* (O) can be set in relation to business and marketing objectives. In the MCPF, this stage will involve consideration of positioning factors. Communications *strategies* (S) may take

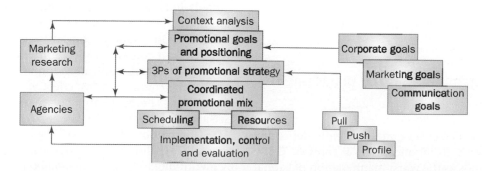

FIGURE 26.2   Marketing communications planning framework (MCPF) (*source:* Fill 2002)

> **box 26.1**   **Push, pull and profile strategies**
>
> *Pull strategies* are those where communications are targeted directly at the customer or end user of the product or service. In consumer markets such strategies involve demand stimulation, that is they encourage consumers to take purchase action. The term pull originates from the effect such purchases have on the distribution channels. Retailers will need to restock goods and this means 'pulling' goods down from their channel sources such as wholesalers or, in the case of major supermarket retailers, direct from the producer. Such strategies will often be led with the use of advertising and consumer sales promotions.
>
> *Push strategies* involve communications that lead to the movement of goods through distribution channels in separate stages. Goods may be sold from producer to wholesaler, then from wholesaler to retailer or some other intermediary. At each stage communications will take place aimed at pushing goods through the channel. Such situations are usually based around business-to-business communications, including personal sales and trade promotions.
>
> *Profile strategies* focus on communications with a range of stakeholders, other than consumers or marketing channel members. Often the objectives of such strategies will be to develop positive corporate image or profile. Stakeholders may include shareholders or other investors who need to see how well their investments are performing rather than to receive details related to the products or services that the company is marketing. The company's employees are another stakeholder group with different communication needs. PR activities, community project sponsorships and internal communications may lead communications tools in developing profile strategies. A company's overall corporate reputation and identity will also feature in image- or profile-related actions.

different forms: 'pull' strategies that focus on communications with consumers; 'push' strategies that involve intermediaries such as distributors and retailers. 'Profile' strategies take into account the needs of all stakeholders, often focusing on image and identity. Communications *tactics (T)* or 'mixes' need to be developed for each strategic option along with specific *actions (A)* including budgets and schedules. *Control (C)* and effectiveness measures are needed to establish the effectiveness and efficiency of individual communications activities and for the complete communications plan to be evaluated against objectives set. This will identify the benefits of integration and support the ongoing communications. (See Box 26.1.)

The case study at the end of the chapter examines the issues involved in determining the strategic options available in automotive markets.

Branding and integrated marketing communications

Brands can be perceived quite differently depending on the viewer's social and political context. Critics perceive brands as the worst manifestation of capitalist society; others see them as something with which we have deep, emotional relationships. For example, is Nike the 'must-have' fashion footwear or the company that manufactures in developing countries, paying low wages to workers employed in poor conditions? Is McDonald's the supplier of 'Happy Meals' for millions of children around the world or a fast food source for obesity?

Brands and branding provide a direct focus for integration. Brands and how they are portrayed encapsulate the many dimensions of IMC. We do not need to see an advertisement in order for there to be a communicative effect. To many of us, the mention of the word Coke will suggest curvacious bottles and a refreshing taste, not because we remember seeing an advert, but through acquired knowledge based on our experiences built up over long periods of time. The ubiquitous nature of distribution, distinctive product packaging, logos and other identification symbols and pricing issues will all play a part in addition to that played by actual marketing communications. Thus, integration is not just achieved via what we might call communication in the form of advertising or other communication formats but also considering the communicative effect of the whole marketing mix – product, price, place and promotion. (See also Chapter 21.) (See Box 26.2.)

De Chernatony (2001) develops ideas put forward originally by Olins, which propose brand integration by identifying four '*brand communicators*' – the product or service itself, the behaviour of the firm's staff, the environment in which the brand is presented and the use of communications. De Chernatony suggests

box
26.2

Communicating the 4Ps – product, place, price, promotion

These are the four major elements of what has become known as the marketing mix. *Products*, services – or some combination of the two – are what a firm has to offer to its customers. *Place* refers to the location at which a purchase transaction might occur, at a retail outlet or via the telephone or internet. *Price* is what the business considers the market value of the product or service to be. The actual price charged may be somewhat different from that originally stipulated by the producer or the provider as result of retailer discounts or other forms of sales promotion. *Promotion* will include different communication tools, advertising, sales promotion, personal selling, PR and other activities.

This chapter deals extensively with the last element of the marketing mix but it is also important to consider the communicative effects of the other elements. Mention of a product's brand name in conversation or discussion may communicate a message that has not been targeted specifically by the brand owner. For example, the name 'McDonald's' stimulates thoughts of the Golden Arches logo, the service received in any McDonald's restaurant or the taste of a Big Mac!

Differentials in price can suggest different perceptions of value or quality. Visiting a store selling electronic goods such as TVs, CD/DVDS or hi-fi products, you will be faced by displays of similar looking products but with different prices. If the products look similar but have different prices, the communicative effect might be that higher priced items are of superior quality. Of course, subsequent communications will qualify these interpretations.

Product availability limited to specific retail outlets might communicate some degree of exclusivity. Fashion brands such as Armani or Versace limit distribution to either their own stores or retailers such as Harvey Nichols. Extending distribution over a wider range of outlets might damage the exclusivity of the brand identity and image.

---

brand integration can be further enhanced by evaluating the extent to which the communicator reinforces brand value and the extent to which each communicator reinforces the others. For a major airline business such as BA, Cathay Pacific or Virgin this would involve the relationship between the services provided. For example, on a flight between London and New York this would include the customer service provided by check-in staff and cabin stewards, the levels of comfort on the plane, passenger lounges and other facilities and the marketing communications employed (such as advertising, direct mail, sponsorship and PR). (See Mini case study 26.3.)

Brand communications take many forms and will vary in terms of the objectives set. These can often be classified as aiming to differentiate, remind, inform or persuade (DRIP). Hughes and Fill (2004) identify a number of situations where communications may be focused on achieving objectives in one or all of these DRIP categories:

- Differentiate a product/brand (to make it different from a competitor's brand or seem different through effective positioning).
- Remind and reassure a target audience with regard to benefits (to encourage (re)purchase).
- Inform a target audience by providing new information (e.g. of a new brand or flavour).
- Persuade an audience to take a particular set of actions (e.g. buy a brand).

In many situations there is little *actual* difference between competing products, so it is the role of communications to create *perceptions* of difference in executing positioning strategies. In financial services, for example, there is little actual difference between the range of services offered by one provider

---

mini case study 26.3

Engaging brands

Some brands are attempting to find new ways of delivering effective brand messages other than via 'traditional' advertising. Goff (2005) reports on a number of examples of communications aimed at engaging with customers and other stakeholders. These include art exhibitions organised by BMW and the launching of a radio station by clothes retailer French Connection. These developments also include the branding of broadcast programme content such as the Pepsi Chart Show on commercial radio.

DRIP – fast foods

The role that marketing communications can play in supporting DRIP objectives in the fast food sector can be illustrated in a number of different ways:

Difference can be promoted through:

- types of food: for example, pizzas from Pizza Hut or Domino's, burgers from McDonald's or BurgerKing
- styles of cooking: like BurgerKing using flame grilling
- modes of purchase: the choice of restaurant, take-away or home delivery.

Reminding consumers of the benefits and values obtained from purchasing from one specific outlet or type of outlet, such as loyalty programmes aimed at customer retention.

Information provision may include details of product changes, new tastes or ingredients, filled crusts on pizzas. More recently, criticism of fast food in contributing to child obesity has led a number of companies to offer 'healthier options' such as McDonald's salads and more nutritious breakfast alternatives such as Egg McMuffins.

Persuasive communications attempt to suggest reasons why the customer should purchase from this supplier rather than one of its competitors. This might include sales promotion of special offers, buy one, get one free (BOGOF) or price discounting. In addition to seeking new customers, such promotions encourage brand switching.

and another. Communications can be used to suggest different approaches, such as the importance of customer service or schemes aimed at building brand loyalty. (See Mini case study 26.4 and Think about 26.3.)

Agency perspectives on integrated marketing communications

As firms have become more demanding of the communications agencies they employ in terms of performance measurement, so those agencies have adapted and developed the range of communications services they offer in order to meet demanding targets. For many, this has also meant a switch in the way they are remunerated, especially in the advertising industry. This has involved moving from receipt of media-based commission (taking a percentage of the costs of buying advertising space or airtime) to direct payments based on results.

Major global spenders such as Procter & Gamble have led such moves, forcing their agencies to look beyond TV-led advertising. Response-driven communications, including direct mail and interactive online methods, have been gaining prominence as part of a more integrated approach, as has the use of PR for consumer campaigns (see Chapter 21).

It is no coincidence that the UK Institute of Practitioners in Advertising (IPA) has dropped the word advertising from the title of its now well-established annual Effectiveness Awards. This decision was taken to encourage entries from clients and agencies that had adopted more media neutral strategies instead of relying on big budget TV campaigns.

Many agencies – while still claiming specialism in one or other communications discipline such as advertising, PR, sales promotion or sponsorship – are actually offering clients a mix of services provided either by the agency itself or subcontracted to a third party, with management control vested in the 'lead' agency. (See Think about 26.4.)

Identify other brands you are aware of that may elicit both positive and negative perceptions. How might integrated marketing communications be used to overcome negative perceptions?

Feedback For most consumers, there are products or services that stimulate 'feelings' that lead to decisions on purchase or non-purchase. Over time we build up preferences for certain brands and dismiss others, often for reasons that we cannot remember and which may no longer be valid because of changes introduced by the provider. Marketing communications can be used to overcome misconceptions and prejudices.

think about 26.4   **Advertising agencies and what they do**

Look at websites of some leading marketing communications/advertising agencies. How do they differ in terms of the services that they offer? Do they offer integrative services? Where does PR fit in their structure?

Feedback   Many of these sites include case studies of their clients, which will provide examples of good communications practice.

think about 26.5   **Appointing an agency**

Consider the advantages and disadvantages for clients seeking to develop their brands and appointing a services group to handle their marketing communications.

Feedback   Considerations include economies of scale, standardisation/adaptation issues, size of budget and budgetary control, need for localised servicing, media availability.

On a global level, communications and marketing services agency provision is dominated by a small number of large groups such as WPP, Interpublic and Omnicom. WPP revenue in year ended 31 December 2004 was £4.3 billion, with profit before tax at some £456.5 million (WPP 2005). Such groups offer a full range of services to clients and operate on a global scale. In the UK, what were considered at one time to be dominating advertising agencies are themselves now part of these larger groupings and are offering communications services beyond their traditional advertising platform. DDB London, formerly BMP DDB, is the UK base for Omnicom's DDB Worldwide network. In addition to the advertising business, DDB London is also the core for a number of local communications services agencies. These include Claydon Heely and Marketing Advantage DDB in direct marketing, PR agency Porter Novelli, interactive specialists Tribal DDB and Bridge Research, the UK's largest agency-owned research and recruitment

company. Other companies are involved in qualitative research, production and design and *econometric consultancy*. Such groupings are typical of the agency provision aimed at providing clients with a one-stop integrated service. (See Think about 26.5 and Mini case study 26.5.)

Definition: *Econometric consultancies* specialise in areas including forecasting and effectiveness measurement and make increasingly significant contributions to marketing communication planning and evaluation as clients seek performance measurement criteria.

Integrating the marketing communications mix

Perhaps the most 'visible' level of integration takes place when considering the application of different elements of what is termed the communications or

---

mini case study 26.5

Samsung and WPP

Samsung, the Korean electronics firm, has recently appointed the WPP Group to run a £120 million global branding campaign. This follows a similar move in May 2004, which saw HSBC place its £350 million global marketing communications with WPP (Benady 2004).

There are counterarguments to such appointments: some see the advantages to be gained through integration while others see such moves as driven by cost-cutting objectives. A more reasoned approach might suggest that improving communications effectiveness via integration may also have cost efficiency benefits. Why should this be a problem? The counterarguments tend to be led by the independent advertising sector which potentially has most to lose.

promotional mix. The major elements consist of advertising, PR, sales promotion and personal selling. For many brands, advertising still tends to dominate the communications mix. Box 26.3 provides some indication of the budget levels allocated to advertising in the UK during 2004.

Depending on definition, the list of communications tools also includes point of sale/purchase, exhibitions and packaging. More recently it has extended to include direct marketing activities, sponsorship and interactive/online methods. The application of these communications methods varies between types of business. For consumer brands, the emphasis is largely on advertising, sales promotion and sponsorship. In business-to-business markets (see also Chapter 22), personal selling, trade promotions or exhibitions predominate. Applications involving the use of new technologies and media, of course, cut across these boundaries. For example, web-based communications, mobile phone text messages and interactive TV provide new platforms for communicating in all markets.

In many ways, the mix deployment relies more on tactical or operational factors than on strategic integration. Hughes and Fill (2004) describe the use of various mix elements in terms of coordination rather than integration, with the latter referring to the range

> **box 26.3** **Advertising by brand in the UK, 2004**
>
> 1 Procter & Gamble: £199.5 million
> 2 COI (Central Office of Information) (government): £159 million
> 3 L'Oréal Golden: £95.2 million
> 4 BT: £82.5 million
> 5 Lever Fabergé Personal Care: £73.4 million
> 6 Reckitt Benckiser: £70.2 million
> 7 DFS (furniture retailer): £69.3 million
> 8 Ford: £66.3 million
> 9 Nestlé: £65.8 million
> 10 BskyB (satellite broadcaster): £64.4 million
>
> Aggregated spend by the top 100 UK advertisers was £3.6 billion.
>
> *Source:* Nielsen Media Research/*Marketing* magazine

of marketing and business issues discussed earlier. They propose a '4Cs framework', which summarises the key characteristics of the major marketing communications tools (see Table 26.2).

This helps us understand the mechanisms involved in the communications and the significance of each part of the mix. Given the extended nature

TABLE 26.2   The 4Cs framework (*source:* adapted from Fill 2002)

	Advertising	Sales promotion	Public relations	Personal selling	Direct marketing
Communications					
Ability to deliver a personal message	Low	Low	Low	High	High
Ability to reach a large audience	High	Medium	Medium	Low	Medium
Level of interaction	Low	Low	Low	High	High
Credibility					
Given by target audience	Low	Medium	High	Medium	Medium
Costs					
Absolute costs	High	Medium	Low	High	Medium
Cost per contact	Low	Medium	Low	High	High
Wastage	High	Medium	High	Low	Low
Size of investment	High	Medium	Low	High	Medium
Control					
Ability to target particular audiences	Medium	High	Low	Medium	High
Management's ability to adjust tool deployment as circumstances change	Medium	High	Low	Medium	High

mini case study 26.6

American Express (AMEX) gains advantages from tennis

The US Open Tennis Championship provided a great opportunity for AMEX to develop a range of coordinated marketing communications. One of these was a TV advertising campaign in the USA, UK and other markets during the build-up and duration of the competition. The adverts featured tennis stars, including André Agassi, Andy Roddick and Venus Williams, in a number of humorous situations involving use of their AMEX credit cards. During the event a giant TV screen was set up in the Rockerfeller Center in New York showing live coverage of key matches. Seating was provided in the form of a mini stand to replicate where the games were being played at Flushing Meadow. A series of other activities were also arranged including competitions that allowed participants to test the speed of their tennis serve. Those taking part had to provide their names and contact details, which could be used for marketing follow-up. Merchandising promotions included mini fans in the shape of tennis rackets.

PICTURE 26.1   The humourous adverts featured tennis stars, including André Agassi, Andy Roddick and Venus Williams, using their AMEX credit cards. (*Source:* © Jason Szenes/Corbis.)

of the mix and the application through new technologies, the complexity of the mix can be recognised. When adding creativity factors, the complexity both of the process and the receiver's reponses is considerably enhanced. Given the limited differences between the products and services offered by financial services companies, marketing communications strategies and tactics rely heavily on a creative approach to the content of, and delivery of, their messages to achieve a competitive edge. The American Express case provides a good example of this (see Mini case study 26.6).

Definition: *Media neutrality* advocates a shift away from what might be called 'traditional' forms of media, such as TV for branded goods, towards other media, including direct mail, sponsorship and PR. It also promotes a more even allocation of resources across media channels rather than the domination of one major medium. This allows for wider distribution of communications messages to identified target audiences whose media consumption habits are becoming more fragmented.

Total brand communication

Butterfield (1999) discusses the concept of 'total' brand communications and identifies other important characteristics that need to be considered in message creation and delivery. They include clarity, coherence, consistency, control, commitment, contact and the need for communication to be customer driven. This last aspect is important as it is the *response* of the consumer or customer that is significant, rather than the form of communication used, such as advertising, PR or some other part of the mix. This is supported by the shift towards the concept of *media neutrality*. (See Case study 26.2, overleaf, and Activity 26.2.)

activity 26.2

Marketing communications strategy

Identify a company with which you are familiar. Using the structure of the final case study on the automotive market, review its marketing communications strategy, making appropriate recommendations based on context analysis.

Feedback

This is an extensive activity and the detail will depend on the company or market selected. It should, however, provide an opportunity to consider many of the issues that are discussed in this chapter and apply them to the given situation.

Marketing communications in automotive markets

Automotive markets in most parts of the world are well developed both in terms of product and in the use of marketing communications. Some of the world's largest companies are car producers, such as Ford, General Motors, Nissan and Toyota, which produce cars in many different countries and market them globally. Marketing communications are sophisticated and exemplify most of the integration issues we have been examining in this chapter. This case will not focus on one individual company but will use a number of different examples to demonstrate the application of integrated strategic marketing communications within the planning frameworks of SOSTAC and the MCPF discussed earlier.

Situation and context analysis

Business context

The automotive sector is a well-developed and very competitive market. There are a number of global players who compete aggressively across a number of sectors. Over the last decade or so it has been the subject of many mergers and takeovers, as manufacturers juggle for market position and attempt to gain profitability via economies of scale by producing in ever increasing volumes. Ford, for example, has acquired Jaguar and Volvo to position itself more prominently in the sports and prestige sectors of the market. Nissan and Renault have joint-venture operations in the European market. It is interesting to note that in many cases of these mergers and takeovers, original brand names are being maintained.

Customer context

Cars are produced for a wide range of customer segments, in different price categories based on product designs and specifications. Companies such as Ford and Nissan operate in the so-called high-volume sectors where price levels range between £7000 and £15,000 and engine capacities between 1000cc and 2000cc. Brands like BMW and Mercedes sell in lower volumes but at significantly higher prices, with higher specification and levels of comfort. More recent trends have followed customer demand for 'people carrier' and four-wheel drive models in response to changing lifestyles of customers. Customer attitudes toward car buying and ownership are often based on emotive and other personal feelings. This provides an interesting platform for positioning and communications development.

Internal context

Resource issues are significant in this market. Car manufacturers are big companies employing large numbers of people in many countries. The consolidation in the sector through merger and joint venture referred to earlier has, in many cases, led to manufacturing plant closures with significant effects on local communities. It is important for car producers to communicate at all levels within their businesses to inform and motivate employees. Financial resources have been constrained as market demand has slowed in volume markets, levels of profitability have been reduced and heavy losses incurred by many companies. Nevertheless, significant amounts continue to be spent by all manufacturers as they seek to both protect and develop market share.

External context

With manufacturers operating on a global basis, political, economic, social, technological and environmental changes in circumstances have varying degrees of impact. This leads both to change in demand cycles, as economic factors change and to opportunities to reach new markets as economic and political climates improve. The changes in the eastern Europe and former Soviet bloc markets illustrate this point. Environmental issues raise concerns in areas such as oil consumption and shortages of other raw materials. There is pressure on automotive manufacturers to improve fuel efficiency and reduce harmful emissions from their cars.

Stakeholder context

There are many stakeholder groups with interests in these markets, such as financial investors/banks, shareholders, employees, suppliers, distributors, trade associations, local and national governments, pressure and special interest groups, media and other publics. They all have different communications needs that require satisfaction via a range of communications methods.

Objectives

It is important that the communications objectives are consistent with the company's marketing and business objectives. The business objectives of a specialist car manufacturer such as Bentley or Rolls-Royce are very different from those of a volume producer like Nissan. They are competing in different market segments with significantly differentiated products. Marketing objectives are based on all aspects of the marketing mix, not just promotion. Sales success depends on the effectiveness of the product and service support, pricing strategies and distribution network in addition to the success of the communications mix. Communications objectives centre on awareness creation, attitude development and influencing behaviour.

Launching a new model involves creating and developing awareness; repositioning brands involves changing consumer attitudes, and purchasing behaviour may

▶

case study 26.2 (continued)

be influenced by directing potential buyers to a particular dealer or a manufacturer's website.

Strategic options

Depending on the objectives to be achieved, the appropriate communications strategies must be created. For most car manufacturers, these decisions will usually include a mix of pull, push and profile. There is a need to:

- communicate directly with customers to promote product benefits and establish positioning concepts
- work with distributors and dealers who sell vehicles on a personal basis
- develop the overall image of the company.

Communications mixes

For each strategy employed, there will be a need for a communications mix to be devised to support each strategic approach.

To support pull strategies – for volume manufacturers such as Ford, major communications tools will include TV and print advertising to raise and maintain awareness objectives. Volvo has been using TV, print, direct mail and website development in order to reposition itself from being a solid but safe producer to one which blends style with everyday living – e.g. 'Volvo for life' campaign. TV advertising for most manufacturers now includes interactive elements and linkages to web sites and call centres (refer to campaign/ website – www.volvocars.co.uk).

To support push strategies – showroom design and point-of-sale displays, sales literature, merchandising goods, personal sales incentives and local/regional advertising are typical areas in which manufacturers support the communications efforts of their dealers. Trade promotions include price discounting, extended warranties and low-interest extended credit terms.

To support profile strategies – PR and sponsorship are major communications tools used for developing image at either a product, brand or corporate level.

Ford's long-term sponsorship of soccer on satellite Sky TV has been effective in maintaining a fun, sporty, active image for a range of its models. A campaign for Honda promotes the benefits of car sharing by highlighting a scheme it supports in Singapore. This confirms its positive support for meeting environmental objectives. Major trade exhibitions around the world allow manufacturers to profile new product developments.

Budgets and implementation

Car manufacturers are among the largest spenders on marketing communications. Ford spent a little over £66 million just on media advertising in the UK in 2003. Much expenditure is scheduled on an ongoing basis but attention needs to be paid to specific events such as new model launches, exhibitions and major events such as the football World Cup or the Olympic Games.

Effectiveness measurement

This depends on what objectives have been set and therefore what has to be measured: awareness levels, attitudes or behavioural characteristics. Individual campaigns are monitored for response using a range of market research methods and specific measurement devices, such as hits on websites, calls received by the call centre or related visits to dealer showrooms.

Case reflection

This case provides illustrations of many of the points made throughout the chapter. It both highlights the need for, and illustrates the mechanisms of, the integrative approach. It presents the issues at each stage within a planned framework. Although this is presented in linear form, it should be remembered that planning of this nature is cyclical and ongoing. Significantly in the area of marketing communication, there needs to be scope for flexiblity and creativity when and where appropriate, even if this sometimes moves away from 'plan'.

Summary

In this chapter the changing environment surrounding marketing communications has been examined and the need for an integrated approach explored. This has identified the need for integration at a number of levels – strategic planning, branding, and communications mix applications – and the need for a structured (and integrated) approach to agency selection and deployment. The 'volume' of marketing communications has led to consumer scepticism of mass market messages and a desire to discriminate between acceptable and unacceptable message delivery. This has led to the need for a change in approach, both strategically and tactically to the organisation and management of marketing communications. For those companies with wide brand portfolios in global markets, as well as small firms operating within limited geographical boundaries, integration can provide a sound platform for implementing such an approach.

Bibliography

Benady, A. (2004). 'Holding out for a new era', *Media Guardian*, 22 November.

Butterfield, L. (1999). *Advertising Excellence*, 2nd edition. Oxford: Butterworth-Heinemann.

CIM (Chartered Institute of Marketing) (2004). 'You talkin' to me? – Marketing Communications in the Age of Consent'.

De Chernatony, L. (2001). *From Brand Vision to Brand Evaluation*. Oxford: Butterworth-Heinemann.

Fill, C. (2002). *Marketing Communications: Contexts, strategies and applications*, 3rd edition. Harlow: Pearson Education.

Goff, C. (2005). 'No more interruptions please', *Media Guardian*, 17 January.

Hughes, G. (1998). 'Marketing communications activities' in *Marketing Communications: Principles and practice*. P. Kitchen. London: Thomson Business Press.

Hughes, G. and C. Fill (2004). *Marketing Communications*. Oxford: Butterworth-Heinemann.

IPA (2005). Information centre, message received 23 March.

Lancaster, G. (2004). 'Integrated future'. *Marketing Business*, January: 20.

Maunder, S., A. Harris, J. Bamford, L. Cook and A. Cox (2004). 'It only works if it all works: How troubled BT Cellnet transformed into thriving O$_2$'. *IPA Effectiveness Awards 2004*. www.warc.com, accessed 24 March 2005.

Schultz, D. (2004). 'Integrated future'. *Marketing Business*, January: 21.

Schultz, D. and P. Kitchen (2000). *Communicating Globally: An integrated marketing approach*. Basingstoke: Macmillan.

Smith, P. (1999). *Marketing Communications*, 2nd edition. London: Kogan Page.

Smith, P., C. Berry and A. Pulford (1997). *Strategic Marketing Communications*. London: Kogan Page.

Walsh, N.P. (2001). 'Oyez! Enough already'. *Readers Digest*, May.

WPP (2005). www.wpp.com, accessed 25 February 2005.

Websites

Chartered Institute of Marketing: www.cim.co.uk

Diageo – alcoholic drinks manufacturer: www.diageo.com

Direct Mail Information Service: www.dmis.co.uk

Direct Marketing Association: www.dma.org.uk

Institute of Direct Marketing: www.theidm.com

Institute of Practitioners in Advertising: www.ipa.co.uk

Institute of Public Relations: www.ipr.org.uk

Interbrand – branding consultancy: www.brandchannel.com

mad.co.uk Business Directory – marketing information service: www.mad.co.uk

Royal Mail – postal services: www.royalmail.co.uk

Volvo – car manufacturer: www.volvocars.co.uk

World Advertising Research Corporation: www.warc.com

WPP – marketing services business: www.wpp.com

CHAPTER 27
Sponsorship

By the end of this chapter you should be able to:

- define what sponsorship means
- recognise different types of sponsorship activity
- understand the perspectives of those responsible for sponsoring decisions
- critically evaluate sponsorship as an effective communication tool.

Introduction

Major sporting competitions, expeditions to the North Pole and art gallery openings are all examples of events and activities that receive high-profile sponsorship (support) from companies around the world. Often the sponsor becomes so closely associated with the event it becomes known by that brand or name. Simply expressed, sponsorship is an exchange relationship whereby an organisation (company) helps to fund an event financially or in kind (MTV annual music awards) or support an initiative (yachtswoman Ellen MacArthur supported by UK hardware/do-it-yourself store B&Q for her round-the-world yacht race) in return for a variety of returns such as publicity.

Sponsorship ranges from the funding of large to small initiatives (Sunday league sports teams to major international arts and sporting events). What is crucial for public relations is recognising and answering the following questions:

- Why are we going to sponsor?
- What are our (corporate) motivations?
- How do they fit with corporate objectives?
- What are the opportunities and what are the threats to working with the sponsee?
- How will we measure our investment and its return?
- How will we decide if we are to do it again?

There are a variety of reasons why an organisation may get involved with sponsoring and this chapter will explore many of these possibilities. Figure 27.1 (overleaf) identifies six grouped reasons for an organisation to get involved in sponsorship and also identifies where some of the discussions on these topics lie outside this chapter. These reasons are:

1 To support products and services (MTV awards as a sponsorship of an annual music awards that directly supports the promotion of the music television channel).
2 To build on media interest (some events make news on their own, such as individual challenges like Ellen MacArthur's world record for solo sailing round the world. Her boat was sponsored by do-it-yourself retailer B&Q).
3 To reinforce the corporate identity – the brand. Sometimes it is useful to reaffirm the brand identity by sponsoring something that has positive associations for customers and other stakeholders (the *Shell Guide*, see Case study 27.1).
4 To build goodwill (see Krombacher Rainforest Project, Mini case study 27.2).
5 As part of an integrated campaign (to raise awareness in specific stakeholder groups ranging from customers/end users to suppliers as well as investors, see Adidas Japan/Korea World Cup, Mini case study 27.4).
6 In place of advertising (tobacco – Marlboro cigarettes; contraceptives – Durex: both sponsor Formula 1).

In this chapter we will discuss sponsorship in its broadest sense but with a focus on the commercial application of the practice. Discussions continue into the role of organisations in their communities and their impact on society in Chapters 6 and 18 where sponsorship of – and investment in – more community-based initiatives is further explored.

Sponsorship: the context

The *Shell Guide* (Case study 27.1) shows how companies must constantly explore new communication channels to transmit their messages effectively. Today we are exposed to an average 3000 marketing messages per day. In the light of this fact, Henry Ford's (1917–1987) assumption that half of all advertising spend is wasted is possibly an understatement. Among all this promotion 'smog', sponsorship is not only a cheap alternative to classic advertising but also a very effective way of creating public dialogue. This is due to its '*image transfer potential*' – the ability of consumers to transfer positive feelings experienced at a sports or arts event, for example, to the brand which sponsored that event. As a complementary or supportive component of an integrated communication mix, sponsorships offer the chance of a 'calm' brand presence in the market. Premier national and international sport events come to mind, with football, Formula 1 or the Olympic Games at the forefront. But many companies choose more unorthodox sponsoring opportunities. The Spanish private health

case study 27.1

Shell Guide

The first *Shell Guide* to the English countryside, aimed at weekend motorists, was published in June 1934 and offers an excellent example of how sponsorship can work.

Legend has it that the editor John Betjeman (later Poet Laureate) worked next door to the publicity manager of Shell-Mex Ltd., Jack Beddington, and shared a love for the English countryside. They produced a trial guide, for a mere £20, and presented it to Shell, which then agreed to financially support the project.

The idea of a comprehensive country guide series exclusively associated with the corporate name and logo proved to be a success story for the oil company. The guidebooks were not only to become a distinct compendium of the English countryside, they also were hugely successful with its audiences and thus prestigious communication for its sponsor. The financial liaison continued until the mid-1980s and the guides still create goodwill among nostalgic readers and collectors. Today the Shell brand name is an integral part of all major motor sport events. With the help of the sponsorship of social, ecological, scientific, and cultural events, the motor oil company continues to develop its image as a good corporate citizen.

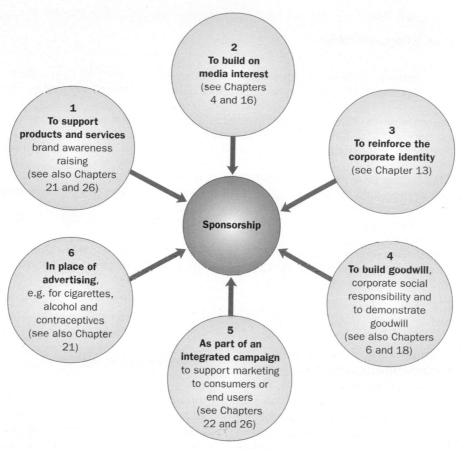

FIGURE 27.1   Reasons for sponsoring (with links to discussions in other chapters in the book)

company Sanitas sponsored David Beckham's medical check-up for Real Madrid. For the sum of £250,000, the company received four hours of internationally televised brand communication. During its restoration, the Brandenburger Tor in Berlin was covered in magenta coloured tarpaulins marked with the 'T' logotype, unmistakably the sponsoring sign of Deutsche Telekom, the largest German telecommunication provider. However, when the company moved on to using this as a permanent medium for advertising its new broadband service T-DSL (with the mascot of the cartoon character the Pink Panther as a Christmas endorser), the Berlin senate intervened, drawing a line between product advertising and sponsoring a cultural event.

> **Definition:** *Image transfer potential* is the ability of consumers to transfer positive feelings experienced at a sports or arts event, for example, to the brand which sponsored that event. As an example, think about Ellen MacArthur who in 2005 became the fastest person to sail single-handed round the world and the positive associations with the boat sponsor, B&Q.

Despite the possibility of conflicts of interest, scientific settings are increasingly used as communication channels, such as the financial support of universities (e.g. 'L'Oréal chair of Marketing' at the University of Oxford) or whole research centres (e.g. 'Institute for the Future of Labour' of German Post World Net). Ultimately, however, it is the brand communication that is the starting point of sponsoring activities – the more prestigious the institution the better.

The world we live in today is a world of marketing messages, as brands compete to convince us that this product is the best ever or that we can gain access to a specific lifestyle via product purchase. The age of brand building does have its drawbacks. The more marketing departments follow the herd of brand bravado, the more interchangeable products get, making a clear-cut differentiation from competitors increasingly difficult. In this sense, targeting and product communication is not enough to give the consumers what they want: emotional experiences and identification with the brand.

Sponsoring takes these needs into account and companies do recognise its growing importance. As

Types of sponsorship

- The arts (film festivals, orchestras, galleries and exhibitions such as the Tate in London).
- Books (the *Shell Guide*, Case study 27.1; the AA (Automobile Association) – travel and campsite guides across Europe).
- Exhibitions/conferences (in the UK, one of the best established exhibition sponsorships is the national newspaper, the *Daily Mail's*, support for the Ideal Home Show).
- Expeditions (Ellen MacArthur's round the world sailing challenge or Everest mountain-climbing teams).
- Awards (Man Booker prize for literature; MTV music awards).
- Community events (local initiatives such as fêtes or fiestas, e.g. May Day celebrations in European towns and villages supported by local businesses such as banks).
- Education (for example, book series, individual academic posts, chairs, or full faculties such as the Saïd Business School at Oxford University).
- Sport (football tournaments and teams such as Real Madrid in Spain having shirts sponsored by Siemens; big sporting events such as the Olympics with multiple sponsorship opportunities).

part of the communication mix, sponsoring has become a vital brand-building component, which is also reflected in corporate spending. In 2003, worldwide sponsoring expenditures alone reached an estimated £22 billion. This figure represents sponsorship agreements only and does not include the translation into cross-marketing programmes. Experts believe in a ratio of 1:3 of sponsorship and related communication expenditures.

Over the last decades, this communication segment has shown tremendous growth as can be exemplified with the FIFA World Cup football championships. The nine exclusive sponsors for the 1982 tournament held in Spain together contributed an estimated £13 million. In 2002 the Japanese and Korean organisation committee asked for more than double this sum from one sponsor alone (Maidment 2002; Sumii 2002; 2003). For the 2006 World Cup football championship to be held in Germany, first-tier sponsorship expenditures will again be increasing.

Understanding sponsorship can be critical to the success of brand building. Understanding sponsorship processes is crucial to understanding the changes in the communication environment. Most people exposed to daily commercial messages have at least vague ideas about what sponsoring is, in what form it can appear or what factors affect it. However, sponsorship as it appears today is a relatively new phenomenon. Many companies do not make full use of its communication potential. Despite its importance, sponsorship remains in many cases an undervalued tool for building relationships with customers. (See Box 27.1.)

Defining sponsorship

If you were asked to explain what sponsorship is, you would probably say that it refers to any form of financial or in-kind support for a specific person, event or institution with or without a service in return. You may also describe the term using your own experience of observing a major sport event as a case study. (See Think about 27.1.)

Maecenatism

A historical perspective helps to shed light on the origins of the concept of sponsorship. Corporate contributions to culture, sport or social events have a long tradition, which can be traced back to Gaius C. Maecenas (70BC–8BC). As a material supporter of contemporary poets such as Horace and Virgil, his name is remembered as a generous patron of fine arts. Despite the noble image still associated with his name, the Roman diplomat and counsellor to Octavian (later emperor Augustus) exercised patronage as a political means–end strategy. That is, Maecenas used the communication channel of his times publicly to praise the reign of his friend Octavian.

Nevertheless, 'Maecenatism' today stands for the altruistically motivated support of culture and communities, where the support idea and not the association with a specific patron/organisation is to the fore. In other words, where the receiver not the donor is the main purpose or focus.

Think about the main sponsor of your favourite sports idol or team and the way this sponsorship is promoted. You recognise sponsorship when you see it, don't you? On second thoughts, however, you may have come across its broader colloquial use: students might refer to their parental financial help as 'sponsoring'; interest groups donate money for political campaigns (in Germany, for example, political parties must disclose any donation of more than €10,000); and trusts support social projects.

Feedback   Although these are all examples of sponsorship, they do not adequately reflect its full scope, nor do they distinguish between related concepts such as Maecenatism, charitable donations or corporate philanthropy. These ideas are now explored.

Charitable donations

Closely connected to the concept of Maecenatism is the act of charitable donations. As an expression of charity it is again the altruistic (concern for other people) motive that dominates the support process. Social considerations play an important role and in its original meaning no immediate advantages such as image promotion or the representation of the donor as a 'good' citizen are being sought. Another significant aspect of charitable donations is that control is not assumed over the beneficiary or over the use of the funds. Despite this blueprint, charitable donations do present the opportunity for raising an organisation's public profile. Think, for example, about coats of arms in churches, the naming of donors in TV charity shows or the financial support of political parties. (See Think about 27.2 and Activity 27.1.)

Corporate philanthropy

The dual purpose of corporate social responsibility (see Chapters 6 and 18) and market orientation is reflected in the term *corporate philanthropy*. More than the no-profit, no-win paradigm of charity donations, corporate philanthropy embraces more directly the idea of

The Toyota Foundation (*Toyota Zaidan*) is an independent trust that is involved in a wide range of activities. Go to the Toyota homepage (www.toyota.co.jp) and find out how the foundation is embedded in the corporate web presence. What key words are used? Next to the societal and regional scope of philanthropic activities, also analyse how these programmes are integrated into an overall target and how this is publicly communicated.

competitive advantages (see Porter and Kramer 2002). By linking corporate giving to business-related objectives, focused charitable investments can be more strategic than unplanned, one-off donations. It allows donations to become part of a proactive communication approach aimed at commercial capitalisation. Contrary to the concepts described earlier, the spender sees to it that philanthropic activities are closely connected to the corporation (or its objectives). In return for the financial or in-kind support the corporation may publicise its efforts. Major Japanese corporations are well known to make good use of social events to demonstrate corporate philosophy and management mission via corporate giving. Particularly at the height of economic success,

The next time you come across a charity appeal, ask yourself what motivates you to make – or refuse – a donation.

Feedback   In the corporate world, the art of giving is not only benevolent in nature. In many cases, more tangible reasons, such as taxation laws, may drive corporate donations. Regardless of the intentions, charitable donations can be seen as a development of Maecenatism and in general describe a uni-directional, or one-way, relationship. Commercial advantages or expectations such as corporate visibility or goodwill here play a minor role.

Toyota, corporate philanthropy in action

The philanthropy mix of automobile manufacturer Toyota is based on financial support for five key areas:

1 education
2 environment
3 culture and the arts
4 international exchange
5 local communities.

As part of the 2005 vision, 'harmonious growth', worldwide activities around these subjects are actively used to communicate the image of an internationally respected corporate citizen. The case of Toyota highlights the idea that corporate philanthropy – despite its concern with marketability – is rooted in societal concerns.

corporate giving (and its media exploitation) was very popular among Japanese corporations. Following the convention of imperial enthronement, 1990 was declared *mesena gannen* – or 'year one of Maecenatism' – thus reflecting the popularity of philanthropy. (See Mini case study 27.1.)

Cause-related marketing (CRM)

In contrast to the concepts previously described, cause-related marketing solely relates to profit objectives. Companies financially contribute to good cause events, movements or organisations in return for exposure and association. The main focus of support is image exploitation and the hope for enhanced corporate reputation. Unlike the concept of corporate philanthropy, cause-related marketing is transaction based and clearly not driven by altruistic motives (discussed further in Chapter 18). Target groups for cause-related marketing include not only present and potential customers, but can also prove effective in reactivating employee motivation as well as attracting future candidates. Building on a reciprocal partnership, the integration of communication and promotion are of vital importance.

In many cases cause-related marketing comes in the form of cross-marketing, as can be seen in the case of

Krombacher, a German beer. In cooperation with the Worldwide Fund for Nature (WWF), the brewery Krombacher developed a support strategy for the rainforest – on which its communication campaign was subsequently built. For every case of beer sold, one square metre of the African rainforest was to be protected. As consumers could participate in a good cause via product purchase, the 'Krombacher Rainforest Project' was hugely successful. Moreover, heavy promotion provided a win–win situation. The brand successfully reinforced its core values in the highly competitive German beer market (IEG 2003a). It is this integration of the good cause with the overall marketing strategy that is at the centre of the support idea. However, cause-related marketing projects must be played to certain guidelines. If companies are to avoid the negative image of opportunism, then transparency and sincerity need to be emphasised. (See Mini case study 27.2.)

Sponsoring

'Sponsoring' is derived from the Latin word *spondere* or 'promise solemnly', hence its use as formula for prayer (*sponderis*) in a Christian context. The derivative word *sponsor* was used for 'godparent', which is also the original English meaning.

Krombacher Rainforest Project

The 'Krombacher Rainforest Project' was accompanied by a multi-layered promotion campaign. For its commercials, G. Jauch, a prominent German TV presenter, gave the communication extra credibility. Additionally, prime-time news was flanked by a 90-second magazine format ('infomercial'). A print media campaign was

also conducted. The cooperation with *Bild* magazine especially helped to promote the project, covering the latest developments in a weekly editorial. Point-of-sale activities gave the communication strategy a visible, consumer-focused edge.

What is a sponsor?

A sponsor is defined by the *Oxford English Dictionary* as a:

- person who vouches or is responsible for a person or object
- person or entity that finances or buys broadcasting media time for promotional reasons
- person who makes a pledge on behalf of another individual
- person who answers for an infant at baptism, making the required professions and promises as to the child's religious upbringing.

See Think about 27.3.

Analysing the concepts discussed so far, sponsorship-supportive techniques can be broadly distinguished along three dimensions:

1 motives of support
2 relationship between spender (sponsor) and receiver
3 publicity.

Or, in other words, who supports whom with what purpose and with what degree of openness?

Figure 27.2 shows graphically the important elements of sponsorship, at which we will take a more detailed look. The figure compares the scope of sponsorship with related sponsorship-support techniques. From this figure it is clear that, despite their related-

ness, none of the concepts fully explains sponsorship. On the one hand, sponsorship is much more multifaceted; on the other hand, the requirements and the time horizons of sponsorship greatly differ from the other concepts. Furthermore, the strategic intent and its integration into the public relations/communication/ marketing mix clearly distinguishes it from other support techniques.

Sponsorship brings with it a more *process-orientated* view that includes planning, implementing and control mechanisms. So definitions that see sponsorship as merely 'an investment in cash or kind in an activity in return for access to the exploitable commercial potential associated with this activity' (De Pelsmacker et al. 2004) do not go far enough. Although the study of support in return for services is of interest to public relations practitioners, sponsoring involves quite a bit more. A more concise and realistic definition of sponsoring would be as shown in the following definition box.

> **Definition:** *Sponsorship* is the totality of market-orientated decision processes about the provision of money, services, know-how or in-kind support of corporations or organisations to individuals, groups or institutions from the area of sport, culture, charity, ecology, education or broadcasting, in order to achieve specified corporate communication goals via the commercial and psychological potential associated with this activity.

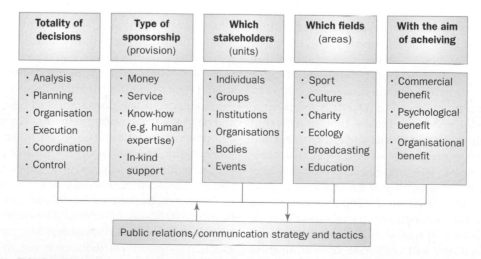

Totality of decisions	Type of sponsorship (provision)	Which stakeholders (units)	Which fields (areas)	With the aim of acheiving
· Analysis · Planning · Organisation · Execution · Coordination · Control	· Money · Service · Know-how (e.g. human expertise) · In-kind support	· Individuals · Groups · Institutions · Organisations · Bodies · Events	· Sport · Culture · Charity · Ecology · Broadcasting · Education	· Commercial benefit · Psychological benefit · Organisational benefit

Public relations/communication strategy and tactics

FIGURE 27.2 What is sponsorship?

Note that this definition specifies not only the relationship between donor and receiver, but stresses also the process orientation of sponsorship (for further empirical evidence on the integration of decision processes, see Olson et al. 2002). The definition also emphasises both commercial and psychological benefits of the concept. Furthermore, it reflects its multifaceted nature and establishes sponsorship as an integrated communication instrument (see also Chapter 26).

Management of sponsorship

Sponsorship involves more than the support of an event such as the FIFA World Championship, the PGA (golf) Masters series or the local volleyball club in return for logo exposure. The activities covered in our definition highlight much of the approach, scale and scope of today's sponsorship environment. It also indicates the necessary professionalism that comes with the understanding of sponsorship as part of an integrated communication and relationship strategy. In the spirit of Maecenatism, not long ago 'gut decisions' on who and what to sponsor were commonplace (this was sometimes known as 'the chairman's wife' syndrome, as sponsorship of the opera or society events secured entrance to these activities). Despite its strategic importance and the increased professionalism of sponsorship, many decisions follow management preferences rather than calculated communication objectives. In contrast to 'gut decisions' leading to hit and miss activities, modern sponsorship thinking is planned and decisive.

Opportunity analysis, scenario planning, alternative target generation, strategy selection, budget and time horizon decisions, *implementation,* integration in marketing mix, communication channel coordination, evaluation and control mechanisms are all examples of a systematic and process-based view of sponsoring (see following definition box to understand these terms). These terms also explain how sponsorship can be systematically integrated into strategic marketing. Here the word *systematic* means that sponsorship should not be a question of trial and error, but should follow a management process with specified communication goals. This implies accountability and controllability, because otherwise any financial or in-kind commitment would be highly risky. As we will see later, the development of evaluation tools is, due to the nature of sponsoring, a major challenge to public relations and corporate communication departments.

Definition: *Alternative target generation* – thinking through alternative target audiences. *Implementation* – the phase where a sponsorship plan becomes a reality and activities are carried out. *Opportunity analysis* – identifying the opportunity to sponsor. *Scenario planning* – playing out different outcomes of a sponsorship, what could happen. *Strategy selection* – selecting a sponsorship strategy.

A corporation that takes sponsoring as a communication tool into consideration faces a range of challenges in planning, implementing and controlling the activities. This is the area of responsibility of sponsorship management. Figure 27.3 shows phases of the planning process of sponsoring.

Strategic phase

Starting with the phase of analysis and prognosis, sponsorship management deals first of all with the collection and evaluation of information. It is this phase where, in coordination with other communication activities, sponsorship scenarios are developed. On the basis of target group identification (who is the audience?), the specification of objectives (what are the short-, medium- and long-term goals?) and the determination of message (what will be communicated?) possible sponsorship activities will be evaluated and pre-selected (see Meenaghan 1998; Bruhn and Homburg 2001). Sponsorship deals are planned and agreed a long way in advance. Ideally corporations are constantly monitoring the sponsorship environment to take advantage of upcoming opportunities. (See Mini case studies 27.3 and 27.4, overleaf.)

Tactical phase

This strategic framework with its longer term timeframe and broad definition of the organisation's sponsoring activities ideally leads to a concrete action plan. The tactical phase of sponsoring reflects a shorter term timeframe (usually a financial year). Here the strategy formulation is translated into operational and day-to-day sponsoring activities. These individual components include decisions on budget and time horizon, the fine-tuning of sponsorship programmes (e.g. selection of specific events), contractual matters and the coordination with other ongoing communication activities. In this context, special attention should be given to this organisational dimension of sponsoring. In other words, Cornwell and Maignan (2001) argue, that sponsorship activities may not, in themselves, be sufficient to achieve specific objectives for all target

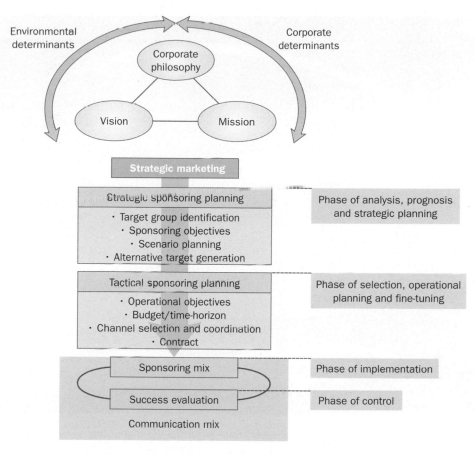

FIGURE 27.3   Sponsoring management as planning process

audiences. This is why it is important that sponsorship activities are reinforced through complementary communication activities. As these cross-marketing operations may include sales promotion, advertising or special product offers (among others) total expenditure may easily exceed the sponsorship budget. It is also important to note that the coordination of communication activities towards a common goal increasingly takes an integrative sponsorship perspective.

Implementation phase

The process-orientated view also highlights the dual nature of sponsorship: not only does the selection of

a strategic programme and its coordination need to be addressed, but also how to put this strategy into practice. It is easy to underestimate the complexity and importance of implementing sponsorship plans. Activities are as good as the weakest link in the sponsoring process and a good plan does not necessarily translate into a successful campaign. Sponsoring is sensitive to trends and sudden changes. Football teams can be relegated, events can be mismanaged, celebrities can be arrested – any of these may lead to negative publicity for the sponsor. Particularly in sport events, the positive image of sponsorship is not very stable. Many fans perceive the financial support of 'their' team as a long-term commitment and not as a commercial venture. If a team's relegation, say in

PICTURE 27.1   The Olympic Games are held once every four years and are one of the most heavily sponsored sporting events. Future Games such as London 2012 are already gathering sponsorship. (*Source:* BYB/Rex.)

football, coincides with the end of a sponsorship contract, this perceived 'non-commitment' can easily backfire.

Furthermore, a sponsorship campaign calls for the cooperation between several internal and external departments. Therefore a manager should be involved in all phases of sponsoring and responsible for the planning as well as the implementation. Since implementation is a key determinant of success, many specialised agencies have evolved. Major corporations such as

---

mini case study 27.4

Sponsorship in practice – football

Major sport events are also major TV events and as such give sponsors the opportunity of a global media presence. Today, contracts with organising committees guarantee main sponsors the sole presence within their industry. Anhaeuser Busch, for example, is one of the main sponsors of the FIFA World Cup football championships 2006 in Germany. This implies that no other beer brand can be sold within a one-mile demarcation zone outside the stadium (Deutsche Welle 2004). It goes without saying that this has led to an outcry in Germany. Of course, a communicative tie-up with a major event is very attractive – especially if this comes with no extra expenditure. Many companies actively use a loose connection with an event to boost their image – without being an

official sponsor. A recent example is the football tournament UEFA EURO 2004 in Portugal, where Coca-Cola acted as a main sponsor. This does not prevent competitors using the same theme in their communication. During the event PepsiCo used an ad showing some of the tournament's top stars such as Beckham (England) or Raul (Spain) as endorsers of the product, aiming at image kudos with their target group. This easy-rider mentality has become known as 'ambush sponsoring'. Major brands rely on this guerrilla tactic to raise their own profile while damaging competitors. Do you remember the main sportsgear sponsor of the FIFA World Cup in Japan/Korea in 2002? Was it Adidas or Nike? Find some images from the internet and check.

BMW or Microsoft have their own departments that coordinate all sponsorship activities. (See Mini case study 27.5.)

Evaluation and control

Evaluating the effectiveness of sponsorship is of paramount importance. However, in practice, sponsorship activities are not conducted in a controlled environment, so that measurement becomes an uphill battle.

Constraints include, for example, where many communication tools and channels are used, so in an integrated campaign, it may not be possible to identify the particular contribution of sponsorship to the overall outcomes. Also spillover effects from prior activities, uncontrollable media coverage (the channel is the message) or unspecified target objectives make a clear evaluation next to impossible. This also explains the reluctance of many managers to invest in sponsorship activities despite the opportunities. Attempts to evaluate effectiveness range from contact points (how many

---

mini case study 27.5

FIA formula 1

The FIA Formula 1 championship is one of the few events with a truly global reach. Whereas football or tennis remain regional events (FIFA World Championships and the Olympic Games as exceptions to this rule), the race circuits offer a cross-cultural audience. Since 1997, the financial service group HSBC has been involved in this event by sponsoring the Jaguar team with an estimated £15 million per year. This investment is, however, under review as the audience

data provided by the sponsoring arm of Formula 1 Management proved inaccurate (*Marketing Week* 2004). This case reveals that – despite the availability of advanced methodology – even multimillion sponsoring investments rely on very simple control mechanisms (contact points). It also indicates that the management of sponsoring needs to anticipate clearly defined goals that go beyond the sole head count of audience reach.

PICTURE 27.2   The FIA Formula 1 championship is one of the few events with a truly global reach. (*Source:* Crispin Thruston/Rex.)

times did the logo appear on TV?) and cost ratio (cost per relevant consumer?) to opportunity analysis (advertising cost equivalent?) and scorecard approaches (how does sponsorship investment rate on various dimensions) (Ukman 1996; Anderson 2003; Walliser 2003).

Depending on the sponsorship goals, *evaluation methods* rely on the modern marketing research instruments shown in Box 27.2.

The measurement methods in Box 27.2 often come with specific research designs such as two-group *before* and *after* measurements. On the basis of a test group, which is exposed to the sponsoring activities, and a control group, which is not, comparisons are made. Qualitative research (focus groups, etc.) round up these measurement efforts.

For a better control of sponsorship effects, *tracking studies* are increasingly deployed, in which data are collected at time intervals (multiple time-series design). Even though advanced research methods are used, it must be noted that there is no conclusive evidence of a relationship of common diagnostic measurements (e.g. image) and commercial results. Nevertheless, from a management point of view, it is the return on investment (ROI) that justifies a sponsorship engagement. So ultimately market share and sales increase (or maintaining market share and sales) will decide further activities. However, we must keep in mind that sponsorship activities only develop their full strategic potential as follows:

- through clearly defined goals
- over a longer time period
- within a communication bundle.

Managers must clearly define what they expect from their sponsoring investment, including a breakdown into specific sub-goals. This process approach guarantees permanent monitoring of sponsorship activities. As an integrative tool a sponsorship audit must at the same time reflect the interrelatedness – and dynamics – of the overall communication strategy.

Features and characteristics of sponsorship

Despite its increasing professionalism and strategic orientation, sponsorship remains multifaceted. It reaches from high-profile media presence to the support of a local youth football club. Sponsorship can reflect diverse arenas such as sport, education or arts and has diverging communication goals such as contact with audience (psychological benefit) or a specified market share increase (commercial benefit). Depending on the scope and importance of investment, decision making takes place at various management levels. The type of beneficiary (individual, group, event, etc.) also greatly influences the rules of sponsoring. Even though the sponsoring process is a function of all these variables, with sometimes diverging intentions, common features can be summarised as in Box 27.3.

Passion marketing

Sponsorship is widely regarded as a cheap alternative to advertising. This often goes hand in hand with the common misconception that sponsorship activity is merely logo exposure. If sponsorship involved no more than brand presence, it would very likely be useless as a communication tool. After all, multimillion investments, such as Gatorade's £260 million sponsoring venture in the American NFL league (Fenton 2004), have to be commercially justified. This raises the question about the capabilities and efficiency of sponsorship. Today's *experiential economies* (Pine and Gilmore 1998) call for passionate brand communication – and this is exactly the added value sponsorship can provide. Depending on the perceived relevance to the audience, sponsorship can convey memorable emotions and experiences more effectively than any other communication channel. With this power of association, sponsorship has become a communication tool in its own right.

---

box 27.2 Marketing research instruments to measure sponsorship

- (Un)aided recall and image studies
- Measurement of loyalty
- Attitude changes
- Purchase intent

box 27.3 Common sponsoring features

- Passion marketing
- Image transfer potential
- Integrative communication
- Stakeholder approach
- Performance and obligation

mini case study 27.6

Adidas and the football World Cup

Sponsoring is one of the communication cornerstones of Adidas. For instance, during the FIFA World Cup 2002 in Japan/Korea, the German sportsgear manufacturer was one of the main sponsors. The company understood the importance of the integration into an overall communication mix and therefore Adidas complementary events were organised to take advantage of the football enthusiasm of the Japanese. Prior to the Championships a crumpled car seemingly crushed by an oversized football was placed in front of a bill-board poster of Alessandro Santos, a player on the Japanese team. In metropolitan centres, small football fields were developed on top of skyscraper roofs, where teenagers could play during the championship. In the aftermath of the event, awareness was reinforced by gigantic billboards on which two players were attached via ropes to play football vertically. Needless to say that this outdoor campaign was very successful in catching viewers' attention, despite the message overload of the Japanese advertising landscape.

Definition: *Experiential economies* is a term coined by the authors Pine and Gilmore (1998) and it refers to the progression of economic value through experiences.

Image transfer potential

One of the main purposes of sponsorship is to affect consumers' attitudes towards, and beliefs about, a brand or corporation favourably. As attitudes can be good predictors of (consumer) behaviour and represent an overall evaluation of associations linked to an object, the formation and change of attitudes is of interest to the marketer (see also Chapter 14). What makes sponsorship a unique persuasive tool is its association potential. Sponsorship generally has positive connotations among audiences. It also does not rely on elaborate cognitive information (thought) processing. Its emotional appeal makes it easy for the consumer to understand. The sponsoring venue sets the stage for inducing emotions such as joy, hope, excitement, fear, anger, etc. Marketing messages are presented in this context in the hope that consumers will experience these emotions. Research evidence suggests that it is not only the situational experience that influences behaviour, but also the overall attitude towards an event (Cooper 2003). A positive evaluation of something (event, person, team, etc.) will create positive feelings, which may then be transferred to the brand. This means that it is important to monitor opportunities carefully to ensure a good match between the sponsorship and the attitudes of the target audience. (See Mini case study 27.6.)

Integrative communication

Sponsorship itself is resistant to corporate control. The usual rules of advertising communication cannot be applied. Content, tone and message can only be influenced to a certain extent. Unlike classic advertising communication, sponsorship activities convey only indirect messages. Sponsorship also has distinct features regarding media planning. Whereas advertising is placed to maximise its reach and impact, sponsorship presence is limited to a condensed strategic window. This has two main implications:

1 On the one hand, corporations are looking into the possibilities of developing intensive (often long-term) collaborations to develop consumer perceptions, especially with regard to major sport events. For example, the Japanese manufacturer Canon has been the official partner of the FIFA World Cup since 1978. The Korean automobile giant Hyundai is sponsoring 10 FIFA events between 2003 and 2006 (FIFA 2002; Bae 2003).
2 On the other hand, the indirect and passive character of sponsorship communication also demands complementary marketing activities. Here the communication mix helps to use, reinforce and fine-tune sponsorship messages. (See Think about 27.4.)

think about 27.4   Media planning

Despite their importance, media planning agencies act behind the scenes. Whereas the advertising agencies are in the public eye, media planning from companies such as Starcom Media Vest (Interpublic Group), Carat SPI (Aigis Plc) or Mediacom (Grey Global Group), increasingly sit at the centre of communication groups.

Stakeholder approach

Beyond the function of communication with potential customers, sponsorship also aims to create additional transfer potential with other stakeholders (see also Chapter 12). At the organisational level, employee motivation and identification can be supported by sponsorship activities. Research also suggests that there is a correlation between image and employment attractiveness, so that personnel marketing/recruiting might also benefit from these activities. Establishing goodwill with external groups, such as financial institutions, shareholders or investors, is an additional target variable of sponsorship. This is also true for the relationship with distributors, sales personnel and business partners (see also Chapter 22). In some cases, sponsorship activities may also be used to develop relationships with decision makers in governmental institutions. Such stakeholder relationships are often enhanced through sponsorship activities such as VIP events and corporate hospitality. (See Mini case study 27.7.)

Performance and obligation

Commercial sponsorship is based on the idea of a reciprocal business relationship between the sponsor and the sponsee. This win–win partnership guarantees the sponsor specific contract-based rights, such as the presence of the corporate logo, the co-branding of events (e.g. Barclaycard Premiership football in the UK) and venues (the 'AOL-Arena') or the use of licensed signs (e.g. national sponsor of the Olympics). This usually comes with extended communication rights. The use of the sponsorship in related communication activities or the obligation of advertising appearances are common features of this business relationship. In return, the sponsor is per contract committed to support the sponsee. Types of support include money (either single or regular payments), materials or equipment (e.g. computers), services (administrative tasks, logistics, etc.), know-how (technology) or in some cases human resources. With its strong media presence, sponsorship has become a

very effective tool in undermining the legal barriers around some types of advertising. The ban on tobacco advertising in Europe has been bypassed by the industry via sponsorships of Formula 1 racing teams. This has, of course, caused concern to those who wish to restrict tobacco advertising. Sponsorship also helps circumvent regulations such as the ban on TV advertising on Sunday public service broadcasting (e.g. in Germany). Activities like these ensure continued media presence and make sponsorship an attractive alternative to conventional communication, but they are also under constant scrutiny from legislators. (See Activity 27.2.)

activity 27.2

Sponsorship characteristics

Think about the characteristics and features of sponsoring. You should try to find answers to the following questions:

1 What are some distinctions between Maecenatism, charity donations and sponsoring?
2 What are the specific challenges of sponsorship management for small or medium-sized local businesses (enterprises)?
3 What are the advantages and disadvantages of sponsorship activities?
4 Why is the sponsorship industry so interesting for media planning agencies?

'Emotional marketing' and the emerging sponsorship age

The transformation from a production-oriented 'push' economy via a demand-oriented 'pull' economy to a consumer-oriented 'emotional' economy has also had a major impact on public relations and corporate communication. Experience-based values were once an afterthought; now they determine a company's success. The rise of vibrant consumer markets also coincides with market-driven approaches.

mini case study 27.7

Corporate hospitality in action

Corporate hospitality activities give sponsors an informal setting for building relationships with stakeholders. The importance attached to corporate hospitality events can be seen in the case of BMW Motorsport. During the Formula 1 Grand Prix 2004 in Monaco, the German automobile producer invited guests to a specially chartered deluxe sailing ship from which they could watch the race. The specialist company, Grand Prix Tours, offers hospitality programmes in the context of Formula 1. Full services include celebrity endorsements, theme parties, accommodation and tailored incentives (see www.gptours.com).

As such, sophisticated marketing and communication techniques are cornerstones of today's market environments. More and more companies have jumped on the marketing bandwagon, contributing to an ever-accelerating advertising spiral. This pressure has led to an information overload (and in many cases to a communication stalemate between rivals vying for consumers' attention). The resulting ineffectiveness of traditional advertising media makes companies look for new communication channels. With its below-the-line appeal and positive associations by consumers, sponsorship helps to cut through this clutter of commercial information.

More media channels

Another reason for the growing interest in sponsorship activities is the diversifying media environment. Satellite and cable TV were technological drivers of new communication possibilities and have substantially changed the sponsorship scene. The previously limited media choice (see Chapters 4 and 16) gave way to a broad selection of media, catering for ever-fragmenting interest groups. Today not only mainstream events but also fringe sports and speciality channels are part of the regular TV repertoire. With these developments the rules of sponsorship have also changed. Instead of unspecific and scattered targeting, sponsorship solutions promise to reach even very small, closely targeted groups.

Industry growth

The incentives of experiential values, bypassing information overload and increased targeting precision make sponsorship an attractive alternative to traditional communication techniques. In fact expenditure on sponsorship has shown robust growth over the last decades: the industry has grown from a modest £4 million in the early 1970s into a £28 billion business today, with Germany, Japan, the UK and the USA being the lead markets. Figure 27.4 illustrates overall growth of sponsorship activities for the UK market. The breakdown into expenditures by sector reveals that sport sponsorship is the largest sector of the market.

Broadcast sponsorship has undergone an interesting development. This was only legalised in the UK in the 1990s and today it occupies second place in sponsorship expenditures. On a side note, evidence suggests that this trend originated from Japan. Anticipating Japanese consumer behaviour – the orientation towards 'megabrands' (Horn 2001) – programme sponsorship is here a vital part of communication management and brand architecture. Hence, broadcast sponsorship has been for a long time a fixed dimension in the second biggest advertising market.

Data from the Japanese media agency Video Research Ltd underline the sponsorship sophistication in this sector. For example in Japan, between eight and nine thousand programmes are sponsored each year (Video Research 2004).

The German market also provides interesting sponsorship snapshots. Research by the Hamburg agency, Pilot, reveals not only that a similar sponsorship boom has been taking place there, but also that the market size for sponsorship is considerably bigger than in the UK. Due to major sport events in Germany, it is predicted this will rise to £3008 billion by the year 2006. With increased investment in sponsorship, the study 'Sponsor Visions 2004' underlines the changing

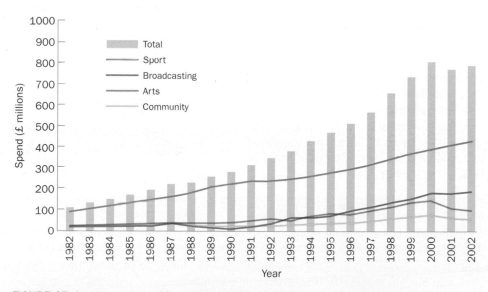

FIGURE 27.4   UK sponsorship market, 1982–2002 (*source:* Mintel 2002)

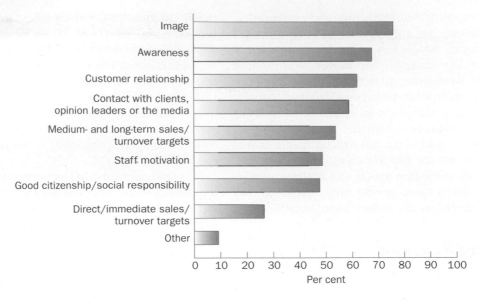

FIGURE 27.5   Sponsoring target objectives of German companies (*source:* Pilot Group 2004)

tide in communication expenditures. Whereas in 2000 approximately 16% of the communication budget went into sponsoring activities (2002: 17%), they now account for one-quarter of communication expenditures. Figure 27.5 gives additional background information on the purposes of sponsoring activities in Germany.

By far the biggest sponsorship market is the USA. The IEG (2003b) sponsorship report estimates the market size to about £8 billion, with a predicted increase of 8.7% in 2004. As US companies are in many cases marketing pacesetters, recent trends need to be carefully watched. Despite the 'closed club phenomenon' common in European and East Asian markets, this growing industry is fuelled not only by moderate budget increases from established sponsors but also first-time investors. It is therefore reasonable to assume that sponsorship is no longer an exotic side dish of communication, but has reached the marketing mainstream. In the light of increased competition and new technologies that allow an advert-free media environment, US companies are looking into alternative promotion possibilities. Despite an increasing fragmentation in the North American sponsorship market with a larger number of minor deals by small firms replacing major sponsor deals, multinationals dominate the industry as

is shown in Table 27.1. All this takes place in an environment of increased sponsorship literacy. (See Think about 27.5 and Box 27.4.)

Career opportunities

Career opportunities in sponsorship are numerous. The increased importance attributed to sponsorship by advertisers and the continued trend towards profes-

TABLE 27.1   Top 10 US sponsors (*source:* IEG 2003b)

2003 Rank	Amount	Company
1	$250–255M	PepsiCo, Inc.
2	$240–245M	Anheuser-Busch Co.
3	$185–190M	General Motors Corp.
4	$180–185M	Coca-Cola Group
5	$160–165M	Nike, Inc.
6	$155–160M	Miller Brewing Co.
7	$125–130M	DaimlerChrysler Corp.
8	$100–105M	Ford Motor Co.
9	$95–100M	McDonald's Corp.
10		Eastman Kodak Co.

An age of sponsorship literacy?

A study by Mediaedge (2004) (Figure 27.6) examines particular target groups to discover whether some sponsorship activities could be more effective than others. Fifteen to twenty-four year olds seem especially receptive to sponsorship messages, whereas the support of good causes (CRM, community and societal sponsorship) cuts through the information clutter of all age groups.

activity 27.4

Building a sponsorship strategy

Assume you are a project manager responsible for organising a major art exhibition. As this art exhibition is part of an internationally renowned, New York-based museum, a lot of public interest is to be expected. However, so far no sponsor has been found to support this project.

You are asked to devise a sponsorship strategy for this particular event, which must include:

■ defining potential sponsors
■ developing key selling points
■ thinking about ways of contacting potential sponsors
■ planning media coverage.

activity 27.3

Careers in sponsorship

The field of sponsorship offers a wide range of job opportunities. Find out about career profiles in this growing industry using the following steps:

■ go to a job search engine such as www.monster.com, www.fish4jobs.com or www.jobpilot.co.uk
■ search 'jobs' and select the related fields 'marketing', 'public relations' or 'advertising'
■ narrow your search using the keyword 'event', 'sponsoring', 'fundraising'
■ pick three jobs that are of interest to you.

Feedback

Discuss with a colleague/friend the career profiles of these job opportunities. You should find answers to the following questions:

1 What makes them interesting to you?
2 What are the keywords of the job description?
3 What experiences does the employer look for?
4 In what area of sponsoring does the profile fall?

sionalising agency services makes for interesting career prospects. Despite the necessity for in-house capabilities, many organisations use external expertise (PR/communications and specialist sponsorship agencies). Due to the multifaceted nature of sponsorship, specialist agencies offer a wide range of services. Fields of employment are as colourful as the sponsorship agency environment. Core competences range from event management and human resource provision, through to media planning and sponsorship evaluation (market research) to strategic marketing and hospitality management. Whether you want to work in fundraising for a non-profit organisation, organise the sponsorship activities in the context of an art exhibition or devise a plan for optimal media coverage depends on your interests and capabilities. (See Activities 27.3 and 27.4.)

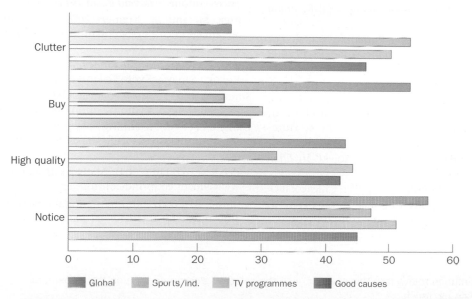

FIGURE 27.6 Attitudes towards different forms of sponsorship activity (*source:* Mediaedge 2004)

Summary

Recent changes within the sponsorship industry have not gone by unnoticed by major players. Advertising agencies, media planning companies and research institutes have a communication expertise that they now need to extend to the sponsorship field. Under the roof of communications services groups, there is a trend towards establishing sponsorship departments. Many media planning agencies, for example, link up with niche agencies to expand their service portfolio. Recent examples include the merger of the agency Sponsorcom with Mediaedge: cia (WPP Group) to form Europe's leading sponsoring agency, MEC, and the acquisition of Momentum by McCann Erickson (Interpublic Group). These mergers and acquisitions, combined with the overall performance of the sponsorship industry, convey a strong message: sponsorship has grown up and as a modern communication tool faces new challenges.

Bibliography

Admap (2000). 'Sponsorship'. *Admap* (432), October: 15–16.

Anderson, L. (2003). 'The sponsorship scorecard'. *B&T*, 12 December: 13–14.

Bae Keun-min (2003). 'Sport marketing bolsters Hyundai's brand power'. *Korea Times*, 25 December.

Bruhn, M. and C. Homburg (2001). *Gabler Marketing Lexikon*. Wiesbaden: Gabler Verlag.

Cooper, A. (2003). 'The changing sponsorship scene'. *Admap* (144), November.

Cornwell, B. and I. Maignan (2001). 'An international review of sponsorship research'. *Journal of Advertising* **27**(1): 1–21.

De Pelsmacker, P., M. Geuens and J. Van den Berg (2004). 'Sponsorship' in *Marketing Communications*. Harlow: Prentice Hall.

Deutsche Welle (2004). 'It's "Bud" or nothing at World Cup 2006'. *Deutsche Welle* 19 April. www.dw-world.de/english/0,3367,1430_A_1174388_1_A,00.html

Fenton, W. (2004). 'Global sponsorship report'. *Brand Strategy* (181), April: 40–41.

FIFA (2002). *FIFA Financial Report*, Zurich. www.fifa.com/events/congress/2004/FIFA_Financial_Report_E_2003 pdf.

Horn, S. (2001). 'Konsumgütermarketing in Japan [Consumer goods marketing in Japan]' in *Jahrbuch der Absatz- und Verbrauchsforschung*. Gesellschaft für Konsumforschung (ed.). Berlin: Duncker & Humbolt.

IEG (2003a). 'Krombacher Regenwald Projekt' in *Effie-Jahrbuch*. Frankfurt: Horizont.

IEG (2003b). *IEG Sponsorship Report – Outline*. Chicago: IEG.

Maidment, P. (2002). 'Sponsoring soccer's big event' in *Forbes Global*. www.forbes-global.com/2002/06/04/0603sponsor.html

Marketing Week (2004). 'Sponsors' data breaks down in an F1 pit-stop'. *Marketing Week*, 18 March: 22.

Mawson, C. (2004). 'A history of the Shell county guides'. www.shellguides.freeserve.co.uk/history.htm

Mediaedge: cia Anon (2004). 'Sponsorship comes of age' in *insideedge sensor*. London: Mediaedge: cia. www.totalsponsorship.com/medialab_sensor/uploaded/sensor_6.pdf

Meenaghan, T. (1998). 'Current developments and future directions in sponsorship'. *International Journal of Advertising* **17**(1): 3–28.

Mintel (2002). *Sponsorship 2002*. London: Mintel International Group.

Olson, E., P. Bronn and M. Thomae (2002). 'Decision-making processes surrounding sponsorship activities'. *Journal of Advertising Research* **42**(6): 6–15.

Pilot Group (2004). 'Pilot group: Sponsor Visions 2004' in *Werben und Verkaufen*. www.wuv.de

Pine, J. and J. Gilmore (1998). 'Welcome to the experience economy. *Harvard Business Review* **76**(4): 97–105.

Porter, M. and M. Kramer (2002). 'The competitive advantage of corporate philanthropy'. *Harvard Business Review* **80**(12): 56–69.

Sumii, K. (2002). *Masu Komyunikêshonron 02*. Dai 17 Kôkoku Sangyô, Kyôto Gakuin Daigaku.

Sumii, K. (2003). *Masu Komyunikêshonron 03*. Dai 18 Kôkoku Sangyô, Kyôto Gakuin Daigaku.

Ukman, L. (1996). 'Defining objectives is key to measuring sponsorship return'. *Marketing News* **30**(18), 26 August: 5–6.

Video Research Ltd (2004). 'Statistics data of advertising'. www.videor.co.jp/index.htm.

Walliser, B. (2003). 'An international review of sponsorship research'. *International Journal of Advertising* **22**(1): 5–40.

For glossary definitions relevant to this chapter, visit the **selected glossary** feature on the website at: www.pearsoned.co.uk/tench

PART 4
Sectoral considerations

This part of the book comprises chapters that are not conventionally included within a public relations textbook – yet their link to public relations seems too important for them to be left out. The discussions and debates contained within each chapter highlight the link to public relations, but also point out differences in worldview or approach.

Chapter 28 argues that corporate communication is often public relations with a different label, but at the same time there is a conscious effort to define corporate communication as 'reputation management', a term rarely found in the public relations literature, but more often found in management and marketing. Chapter 29 demonstrates that campaigning on behalf of interest or pressure groups is also public relations when viewed as a process, yet there are special characteristics that make campaigning different from conventional public relations. Chapter 30 points out that while public sector communication has special characteristics linked to the democratic context (i.e. politics), it is often public relations objectives and processes that are driving public sector campaigns. Chapter 31 identifies that while the dominant paradigm for the arts, leisure and entertainment sectors is marketing, it is public relations that is helping to move these sectors forward in reaching fragmented audiences. Finally, Chapter 32 looks to the future, addressing issues that will be of major importance to the profession.

CHAPTER 28
Corporate communication

Learning outcomes

By the end of this chapter you should be able to:

- define and describe different conceptualisations of corporate communication
- identify the influence of different conceptualisations (or mindsets) when reviewing public relations literature or practice and understand the implications of this
- identify the key objectives and principles of corporate communication
- identify and understand the impact of differing organisational corporate communication structures and functions
- evaluate the issues arising from corporate communication campaigns.

Structure

- Definition of corporate communication and key terms
- Context and principles of corporate communication
- Interface of corporate communication and overall corporate strategy
- How corporate communication influences corporate decision making
- Corporate communication objectives: stakeholders vs shareholders
- Practical application of critical reflection

Introduction

The news media and particularly business journalists often refer to 'large corporates', 'corporate environments' and worldwide 'corporations'. So what do we mean by corporate and more importantly how do we define corporate communication?

Just as the term 'public relations' is used to signify anything from the antics of publicists to the maxim of mutual understanding (see Chapters 1, 2 and 3), so a debate rages about the definition of 'corporate communication'. Some of the key perspectives in the debate define corporate communication as:

- *strategic* public relations
- communication with *non-consumer* stakeholders
- *reputation* or *relationship* management
- integration of communication with *all* stakeholders
- *persuasion, rhetoric* or *spin* (see later in this chapter for an explanation of the term spin).

Each of these definitions highlights important aspects of how corporate communication is organised and its impact on both internal and external stakeholders. This chapter will identify the different conceptualisations of corporate communication and highlight key issues for consideration in relation to corporate communication practice.

Definition of corporate communication and key terms

Defining strategic public relations

As the term public relations becomes synonymous with notions of 'spin', propaganda, and corporate lying, some practitioners (and academics) have aligned themselves to labels that differentiate them from the 'press agentry' (Grunig and Hunt 1984) antics and signify a more strategic approach to public relations. Thus, strategic practitioners use terms such as *reputation* and *relationship management, stakeholder communications* and *corporate communication* to disassociate themselves from spin doctors. Reflecting this is the view that there is 'no theoretical difference between "corporate communication" and "public relations"' (Steyn 2003: 168).

The converse is also true, and other commentators stand steadfastly by the term *public relations* and refuse to give houseroom to alternatives such as corporate communication. The term 'corporate communication' does not even merit inclusion in the index of any of the *Excellence* books (1992, 1995 and 2002) for example, yet there is such a clear correlation between Grunig's concept of 'excellent' public relations and the concept of corporate communication (Grunig et al. 2002) that the terms could be used interchangeably. The 2003 CCI Corporate Communication Practices and Trends Study was an extensive research-based project that benchmarked or described key elements of public relations practice in the USA. It reported the most common corporate communication functions and budget responsibilities cited by participants, as shown in Table 28.1.

This usefully describes the tasks performed by corporate communicators (although not all departments will incorporate all of these functions). However, it does not identify their purpose – what drives them, how they approach what they do and what they hope to achieve.

To determine corporate communicators' views about their role and function, participants in the CCI study were asked to rank order a set of phrases deemed by the researchers to describe various philosophies. Table 28.2 investigates participants' views about their purpose.

This research only includes the Fortune 1000 (America's 1000 largest corporations ranked by *Fortune* magazine) and does not include the views of communicators in the public, charitable, or voluntary sectors or smaller companies. Nevertheless, it gives an indication of the disparate ways in which corporate communicators approach what they do (or conceptualise their purpose).

The only way of gaining any real insight into the meaning of corporate communication is to understand

TABLE 28.1   Key corporate communication functions and budget responsibilities (Corporate Communication Institute 2004)

Advertising
Image-building corporate culture and change
Media relations
Investor relations
International (global communication)
Communication policy
Internal communication
Communication technology (intranet and internet)
Crisis communication
Corporate citizenship and ethics
Executive communication issues – building a communication culture
Leadership and communication
Public relations

TABLE 28.2   Role that best describes corporate communication function (Corporate Communication Institute 2004)

Percent of respondents who ranked the following as their primary role	%
Manager of company's reputation	18.4%
Counsel to the CEO and the corporation	17.5%
Advocate or 'engineer of public opinion'	14.6%
Manager of relationships (non-customer constituencies)	10.7%
Manager of the company's image	9.7%
Source of public information about the company	8.7%
Manager of relationships (all key constituencies)	7.8%
Driver of company publicity	5.8%
Branding and brand perception steward	5.8%
Manager of employee relations (internal communication)	3.9%
Support for marketing and sales	1.9%
Other	1.9%
Corporate philanthropy (citizenship) champion	1%

the implications of these different ways of conceptualising the practice.

Defining communication with non-consumer stakeholders

One approach to defining corporate communication is to describe it as the communication of *corporate* values as opposed to the promotion of *consumer* products or services. According to this definition, marketing is communication aimed at consumers, and corporate communication is communication directed at other publics and stakeholders. This approach links corporate communication to concepts of managing *corporate reputation, corporate image* and *relationship management*. For example, in the case of the ethical cosmetics chain, Body Shop, its *corporate* communication strategy may be aimed at building the Body Shop's reputation as an organisation committed to human and animal rights and developing strong relationships with suppliers and employees. In contrast, its *consumer* or *marketing* communication would focus on promoting the benefits of its various products to customers and potential customers.

So *consumer* communication is focused on selling a service or product, and contrasts with *corporate* communication, which is focused on a broader range of stakeholders and is aimed at building positive *relationships* and *reputation*. (See Box 28.1.)

---

box 28.1	**Controversy and debate**

Reputation or relationship management?

Although the terms reputation and relationship management are sometimes used interchangeably, there is an important debate about which is the more appropriate conceptualisation. 'Ultimately a good reputation matters because it is a key source of distinctiveness that produces support for the company and differentiates it from rivals' (Fombrun and Van Riel 2004: 5). Indeed, it would seem obvious that a good reputation would be a fundamental aim of public relations. However, recent declines in public perceptions of media credibility have raised serious questions regarding that assumption (Ledingham and Bruning 2001: 530).

Reputation management is sometimes considered to be a *marketing* as opposed to *public relations* concept or more focused on spin than substance. The preferred perspective of mainstream public relations scholars is increasingly about *relationship building* 'the concept of relationships with publics is a more fruitful way of understanding the outcome and value of communication programs than is the concept of brand or image or reputation' (Grunig et al. 2002: 264). The key dimension for relationists is the presence of *exchange* (Ledingham and Bruning 2000) *negotiation, dialogue* or *symmetry* (Grunig 1992; 2002), which they deem to be lacking from concepts of image or reputation building: 'The emergence of relationship management as a paradigm for public relations scholarship and practice calls into question the essence of public relations – what it is, what it does or should do, its function and value within the organizational structure and greater society, and the benefits generated not only for the sponsoring organisations but also for the publics those organisations serve and the communities and societies in which they exist' (Ledingham and Bruning 2000: xiii).

Hutton et al. (2001) usefully summarise the differences: '*Reputation* is a concept far more relevant to people who have no direct ties to an organization, whereas *relationships* are far more relevant to people who are direct stakeholders of the organization (employees, customers, stockholders and others who usually are the organization's most important publics). In other words, a *reputation* is generally something an organization has with strangers, but a *relationship* is generally something an organization has with friends and associates' (Hutton et al. 2001: 258). They accommodate the co-existence of the two concepts by surmising that perhaps they are appropriate in different circumstances – reputation being the more useful concept for organisations whose publics are mainly strangers – 'organisations that depend upon a constant stream of new customers, donors, employees or other stakeholders . . . while reputations might be less important to organizations that have relatively few and longstanding relationships with key stakeholders' (Hutton et al. 2001: 258). Nevertheless Hutton et al. recognise that research is needed to determine if this is the case. The CCI researchers express frustration at public relations academics' refusal to engage with what they understand is happening in practice. Whereas the companies in the CCI survey identified reputation management as the most common role, Hutton et al. (2001: 259) make the point that 'Not a single major textbook in the field defines public relations as reputation management . . . Are public relations scholars simply so out of touch with the business world that they are years behind in their thinking, or are they being inappropriately ignored by practitioners?'

**box
28.2** **How corporate communication (conceptualised as corporate reputation or relationship management) contributes to business strategy**

Anyco is a toy manufacturer with a strategic aim of expanding its factory (located in a suburb of a large city adjoining an area of natural beauty). Its reputation as a good employer and conscientious neighbour, coupled with strong relationships with a range of stakeholders, may have the following results:

- stop the local community from objecting to planning permission
- make politicians more confident in granting planning permission
- engage environmental groups in measures to protect local wildlife
- involve the media in communicating a positive case for the expansion
- encourage suppliers to supply increased orders efficiently and with care for the local community (using the roads at times that do not coincide with local children going to school, for example)
- ensure employees feel involved in the expansion and remain committed to Anyco
- attract the best prospective employees to apply for jobs
- persuade shareholders and others to invest in the project.

Although the expansion will eventually help Anyco produce and sell more products, it can clearly be seen that communication designed to build a strong reputation and relationships in this context is not aimed at persuading consumers to buy products or services. So when commentators talk about corporate communication being aimed at a broader spectrum of stakeholders than marketing or promotional communications, this is the type of approach they mean. This example also illustrates a range of *corporate communication objectives* (which again differ from those associated with marketing or consumer communication).

In the case of the Body Shop, it is clear how its reputation and relationships facilitate more effective selling of its products. But effective corporate communication is not just linked to creating a favourable sales environment; it can contribute to business strategy in many other ways, as shown in Box 28.2.

Typically, then, corporate communication conceptualised in this way refers to communication (or relationship building) with political, community, financial, media, competitor, supplier and internal publics (but not consumers).

The way the function could fit into an organisational structure could be represented as detailed in Figure 28.1.

Van Riel (2003: 53) could be said to support this view:

Corporate communication can be described as the orchestration of all the instruments in the field of organizational identity (communication, symbols and behavior of organizational members) in such an attractive and realistic manner as to create or maintain a positive reputation for groups with which the organization has an interdependent relationship (often referred to as stakeholders). This results in a competitive advantage for the organization.

However, he develops this idea by incorporating *consumer* communication into the remit of corporate communication: 'Theoretically speaking, corporate

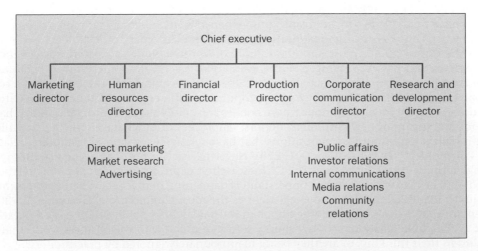

FIGURE 28.1 How corporate communication can fit into organisational structure

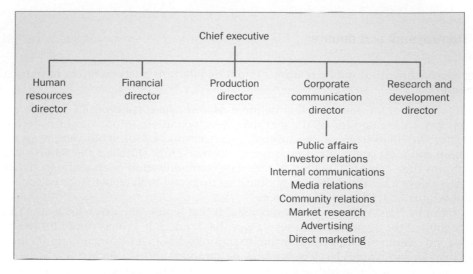

FIGURE 28.2   Integrated communication within an organisation

communication can be divided into three main forms of communication: management communication, marketing communication and organization communication' (Van Riel 2003: 67).

This conceptualisation applied to practice could be represented in the organisational structure in Figure 28.2. It is often referred to as *integrated communication*.

Defining corporate communication as integrated communication

Much has been made in the literature of the ideas of *integrated communication*. The key to this is the idea that all communication functions are integrated into the same department and guided by the same strategic communication plan. 'Numerous scholars and professionals have called for the integration of all communication activities into a single department or for communication to be co-ordinated in some way by a communication czar, pope or chief reputation officer' (Grunig et al. 2002: 302).

Although this approach to corporate communication is often referred to as integrated communication, true integration is rare (Grunig 2002; Hutton 2001). It is far more likely that one area (corporate or consumer) has been subsumed into the other and therefore exists in a department dominated by a particular (and possibly restrictive) worldview. This process is often referred to in the literature as *encroachment*.

The key issue is: which paradigm (consumer or corporate) dominates the communication approach? If all communication activity is represented at board level by a single individual, like Grunig's (2002) communication czar, otherwise known as the corporate communication director, it is likely that they are either from a marketing background *or* from a corporate communication/public relations background, but not both. It

could be argued therefore that their mindset will frame their approach to communication. The crucial question is this: is it a *marketing* mindset, in which case a *consumer* paradigm may dominate and public relations will be confined to the rather narrow focus of consumer PR? Or is it a *public relations* mindset, in which case communications will encroach on marketing and a broader *stakeholder* perspective will direct communication activity – meaning a full range of stakeholders including employees, the local community, political publics and suppliers will be prioritised alongside consumers? (See Box 28.3 and Activity 28.1, overleaf.)

Defining corporate communication: persuasion, rhetoric or spin?

In trying to define corporate communication it would be disingenuous not to consider the view that it is all about using communication to win arguments, by persuading as many people as possible to support (or, at the very least, not *object to* the activities of) an organisation, to buy products, use services or support political parties and ideologies (among other things). Indeed 'advocate' or 'engineer of public opinion' was one of the top three terms identified as best describing the corporate communication function in the CCI 2003 Trends Study (see Table 28.2, earlier).

Some see corporate communication as a mechanism for negotiating with stakeholders to achieve a situation that benefits both parties, thus creating a 'win–win zone'. These people (Grunig et al. 1995; 2002) define corporate communication as *relationship management*. A contrasting view sees corporate communication as a mechanism for advocating an organisation's position and increasing its influence/power/profitability. Miller, for example, regards persuasion

**box
28.3** **Controversy and debate**

Marketing encroachment of public relations vs public relations encroachment of marketing: does mindset matter?

Kitchen and Schultz (2001) seem to epitomise the *marketing-centred* concept of corporate communication: their perspective is informed by the idea that 'the corporation, in our view, has become a brand that also needs to be "marketed", or, put another way, *communicated* for in our view, most marketing is communication and most communication is essentially marketing' (Kitchen and Schultz 2001: 5). This approach informs their conceptualisation of corporate communication as an umbrella 'raised as a protective nurturing device held over the strategic business units and individual brands within its portfolio' (Kitchen and Schultz 2001: 11) (see Figure 28.3).

'What we mean by "raising the corporate umbrella" is that senior executives, led by the CEO, need to conceive and present the organization in such a way that it not only protects and nurtures all the individual brands and customer relationships within its portfolio, but that the organisation stands for something other than an anonymous faceless profit-taking corporate entity' (Kitchen and Schultz 2001: 5).

There is a clear resonance here with a corporate-centric (or public relations-centric) conceptualisation of corporate communication (particularly in the aim of communicating a 'more than profit-taking' identity) but it is interesting to note the gaps and differences. In particular, Kitchen and Schultz specify an organisation protecting and nurturing 'individual brands and *customer* relationships'. No mention of the broader range of stakeholders deemed essential by public relations. Looking at the spokes of the Kitchen and Schultz umbrella – 'employees' and 'partners' are represented, but the local community, government, suppliers, activist groups (or NGOs) are significantly absent.

Contrast this with a public relations-centred conceptualisation represented by Grunig and Hunt's (1984) application of the Esman model of external linkages of organisations (see Chapter 2 of this book).

In what can be termed a marketing-centred approach to corporate communication, which is evident throughout much of the literature, significant stakeholders, such as politicians and local communities, are routinely absent and corporate communication (and public relations) is represented as promotion of a product or service.

This is one of the strongest reasons for public relations scholars to reject the notion of integrated communication: 'The organization is best served by the inherent diversity of perspectives provided by marketing and public relations when those functions remain distinct, co-ordinated yet *not integrated*' (Grunig et al. 2002: 264).

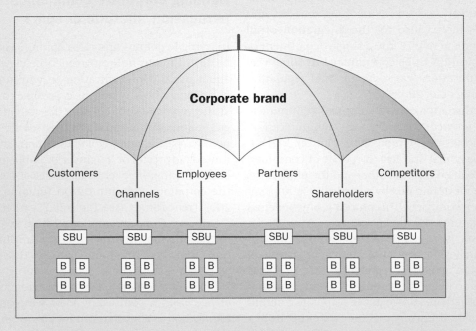

FIGURE 28.3   Raising the corporate umbrella (*source:* Kitchen and Schultz 2001: 11)

box 28.3 (continued)

From the other side of the divide (or perhaps on the fence) some marketing academics consider the basis of public relation's rejection of the marketing paradigm as being flawed.

'Despite constantly calling itself a management function, public relations continues to suffer from a general lack of respect and a frequent lack of success in meeting organizational goals because so few of its practitioners and scholars exhibit a clear understanding of business subjects. For example Ehling et al. (1992) in describing the relationship between marketing and public relations make a number of claims that would be considered nonsense by sophisticated marketing practitioners' (Hutton 2001: 212).

So, there are some clear distinctions to be made between marketing and public relations but there are also areas of shared ground within the separate paradigms. Cheney and Christensen note these as being primarily linked to the conception of communication as a *two-way process* by both disciplines 'public relations and marketing have come to conceive of their communication with the external world as an ongoing dialogue' (Cheney and Christensen 2001: 237) (see Table 28.3).

Clearly, then, just as approaches to public relations differ across sectors and according to practitioners' expertise and background, so do approaches to marketing. Thus Hutton attacks public relations theorists for being inflexible in prescribing a 'best' structural relationship between marketing and public relations, regardless of context, an approach he deems to be 'false and not in keeping with a true management orientation, which would argue that form should vary according to situation and objectives' (Hutton 2001: 213).

---

activity 28.1

How corporate communication departments work

Whether integrated within the organisational structure or not, corporate public relations supports or works in conjunction with other departments. List ways in which a corporate communication department could work with:

1 marketing
2 human resources/personnel
3 finance
4 management.

Feedback

Did you suggest the following?

1 media relations before or during a new product launch
2 employee newsletters or team meeting notes
3 investor relations, annual report preparation and results announcements
4 issues management, lobbying, community relations and crisis management.

and public relations as 'two peas in a pod' (in Botan and Hazelton 1989: 46). Rather than seeing this as a criticism of public relations, however, he sees the impulse to persuade as a natural part of the human condition. Children soon learn that 'pretty please' and a winsome smile will achieve more than a tantrum. They spend much of their time trying to perfect ever-more effective techniques designed to persuade parents to give them things and friends to share things with them. We all expect friends, colleagues, businesses, governments, political parties and charities to attempt to persuade us to accept their positions every day. 'Whenever control of the environment hinges on the attitudes and behaviours of others, attempts to control these attitudes and behaviours are inevitable' (Miller in Botan and Hazelton 1989: 47). Miller argues then that persuasion is 'amoral'. (See also Chapter 14.)

From this perspective, morality (or otherwise) is not engendered in the *process* of persuasion itself but

---

TABLE 28.3 Differences and similarities between marketing and public relations (*source:* Cheney and Christensen 2001: 238)

	Marketing	Public relations
Traditional differences		
Target group	Markets/customers/consumers	Politics/stakeholders
Principal goal	Attracting and satisfying customers through the exchange of goods and values	Establishing and maintaining positive and beneficial relations between various groups
Shared perspectives		
General image of organisation	An open and externally influenced system	
Communication ideal	Communication as an ongoing dialogue with the external world	
Prescription for management	Organisational flexibility and responsiveness vis-á-vis external wishes and demands	

rather lies in:

- the way practitioners practise the art (do they adhere to codes of ethics or moral frameworks for example?)
- desired ends (persuading someone to donate to charity as opposed to persuading someone to take up smoking).

We could also add that *context* is also relevant, for example:

- the type of society in which corporate persuasion takes place (are all actors free to express ideas and influence?)
- the extent of relative power and access to resources.

Moloney shares this emphasis in his call for *reasoned persuasion:* 'PR should encourage outcomes favoured by our society: outcomes such as reasoned, factually accurate, persuasive public debate amongst all individuals, groups and organisations wanting to speak and listen' (Moloney 2000: 150).

Pertinent to this view is the conceptualisation of public relations as rhetoric – an interesting concept in relation to the role and purpose of corporate communication:

> As Aristotle conceived of it . . . rhetoric is the ability to observe in any given case the available means of persuasion – what needs to be said and how it should be said to achieve desired outcomes. It entails the ability and obligation to demonstrate to an audience facts and arguments available to bring insight to an important issue. (Heath in Toth and Heath 1992: 21)

It should also be recognised however that: 'Rhetoric can be thought of as a one-way flow of information, argument and influence, whereby one entity persuades and dominates another. It can be used on behalf of one interest and against others. It is sometimes used to distort and avoid truth and wise policy, rather than champion them' (Toth and Heath 1992: xi), which usefully summarises the perspective of those that regard corporate communication as spin!

Defining key terms: a summary of perspectives and how to use them

Corporate communication has been defined as reputation management, relationship management, communication with non-consumer publics, communication with all stakeholders, and organisational advocacy, persuasion, rhetoric and spin. Recognition of the existence of these different ways of conceiving of the practice is important for a number of reasons. First, it acts as a filter for understanding the literature – there is no single 'truth', no 'right' way of approaching the topic. This understanding prepares the reader to identify value judgements inherent in the

different perspectives and judge their usefulness more effectively.

Much of the theory is also valuable in helping to evaluate appropriate or 'best' ways of approaching public relations, for predicting the likely outcome or impact of different approaches and, importantly, for raising questions about appropriate ethical frameworks to guide practice.

Some perspectives – in particular, a critical perspective – facilitate the analysis of the impact of practice in the broader context of social or political structures: 'The purpose of the critical perspective is to be confrontational. That is, rather than looking at the ways communication assists the organization's management function, the critical scholar would be intent on learning such questions as those posed by Deetz and Kersten (1983: 155): "Whose interests are served by organizational goals? What role do they play in creating and maintaining structures of power and domination?"' (Toth in Toth and Heath 1992: 7).

Context and principles of corporate communication

Having looked at theory and identified some very different ways of conceptualising corporate communication, it is now appropriate to ascertain what this means in practice. This section will consider what influences the way in which corporate communication is practised (as persuasion, relationship management or spin, for example).

Research conducted as part of the IABC 'Excellence' project identifies a number of variables that, according to Grunig et al. (1992; 2002), determine whether or not 'excellent' public relations can be practised or not (see Table 28.4).

A number of these are self-explanatory, or have already been explored in this chapter, but others will

TABLE 28.4   Characteristics of excellent public relations programmes (*source:* Grunig 1992
Copyright © 1992 Lawrence Erlbaum Associates, Inc. Adapted with permission)

I   Programme level
  1   Managed strategically
II   Departmental level
  2   A single or integrated public relations department
  3   Separate function from marketing
  4   Direct reporting relationship to senior management
  5   Two-way symmetrical model
  6   Senior public relations person in the managerial role
  7   Potential for excellent public relations, as indicated by:
       a   knowledge of symmetric model
       b   knowledge of managerial role
       c   academic training in public relations
       d   professionalism
  8   Equal opportunity for men and women in public relations
III   Organisational level
   9   Worldview for public relations in the organisation reflects the two-way symmetric model
  10   Public relations director has power in or with the dominant coalition
  11   Participative rather than authoritarian organisational culture
  12   Symmetric system of internal communication
  13   Organic rather than mechanical organisational structure
  14   Turbulent, complex environment with pressure from activist groups
IV   Effects of excellent public relations
  15   Programmes meet communication objectives
  16   Reduces costs of regulation, pressure and litigation
  17   Job satisfaction is high among employees

now be analysed in further detail, including the position of corporate communication within organisational structures.

Position of corporate communication within organisational structures

The 'Excellence' team is clear and prescriptive about the principles they deem to be essential in relation to the horizontal and vertical location of the communication function within an organisational structure. These are summarised in Box 28.4.

Although not included in their list, it should be noted that the research also shows that 'excellent communication departments' use external consultancies: 'All public relations departments in our sample purchased a substantial proportion of their technical publicity activities from outside firms, as well as a large

---

box 28.4   An 'excellent' corporate communication structure

1 The public relations function should be located in the organisational structure so that it has ready access to the key decision makers of the organisation – the dominant coalition – and so that it can contribute to the strategic management process of the organisation.
2 All communication programmes should be integrated into or coordinated by the public relations department or a senior executive with a public relations title, such as senior vice-president of corporate communication.
3 Public relations should not be subordinated to other departments such as marketing, human resources or finance.
4 Public relations departments should be structured horizontally to reflect strategic publics and so that it is possible to reassign people and resources to new programmes as new strategic publics emerge and other publics cease to be strategic.

Source: Grunig et al. 2002: 265.

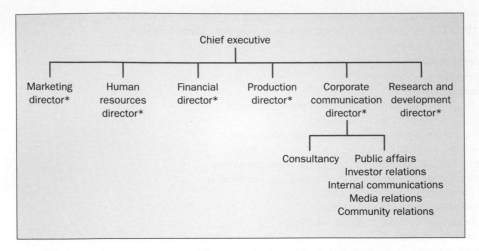

FIGURE 28.4 Structure reflecting the 'excellence' characteristics. Note: *Member of the 'dominant coalition' (*source:* based on Grunig 1992, 2002); in this case, the board of directors

proportion of their research support' (Grunig et al. 2002: 303). Perhaps this should be incorporated as variable 5.

The structure reflecting the 'excellence' characteristics can be visualised as shown in Figure 28.4.

A task-oriented structure is also common in practice and is discussed in Chapter 2. Within either of these structures, consultancies may be used to supplement or enhance internally managed practice in a number of areas (see Figure 28.5).

Both the structures outlined in the two figures represent a *centralised* approach to communication, where all communication is channelled through a single department. There are clear benefits here in terms of ensuring consistency in the corporate message (discussed later). However, it is interesting to

note that the 'Excellence' team move from specifying 'a single unitary department' in 1992, to incorporating an alternative of 'providing a mechanism for co-ordinating programs managed by different departments' (Grunig et al. 2002: 15) in the final report on the findings of the project. Perhaps this better accommodates the needs of large organisations with diverse areas of activity or those that are spread over national or international geographical boundaries.

Clearly, geography and knowledge of local culture is also a significant variable related to the ideal positioning of the communication department within the organisational structure. For example, can a centralised communication department really effectively represent geographically disparate locations?

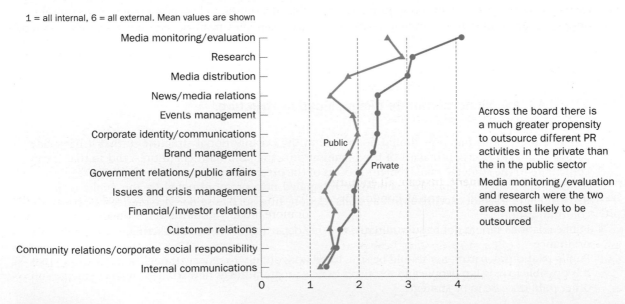

FIGURE 28.5 Activities outsourced to public relations agencies/consultancies and to what extent (*source:* IPR/DTI 2003, *Unlocking the Potential of Public Relations,* CIPR, p. 33)

CBI offices

To ensure that the CBI remains close to and responsive to its members, wherever they are located, we have offices in 12 distinct geographical areas. We are also able to monitor and influence European legislation through our Brussels office, and American legislation through our staff based in Washington DC

In each area, the CBI's local director and a small team ensure that members have opportunities to be involved in consultations on policy and to hear from CBI policy experts, local MPs and ministers on how government action will affect them

PICTURE 28.1 CBI location map (*source:* adapted from CBI, offices location map, http://www.cbi.org.uk)

Even on a national scale this can be seen to be problematic. Some anecdotal evidence suggests, for example, that when the controversial decision to submerge the Brent Spar oil platform in the sea (as opposed to dismantling it on land), Scottish journalists were alienated by the fact that the Scottish-based Shell staff (with whom they were familiar) were not allowed to comment. Instead, all enquiries had to be directed through a central London press office.

The Confederation of British Industry (CBI), for example, has a press office at its London headquarters where other corporate public relations functions such as lobbying and public affairs take place. However, it also has people with responsibility for local public relations in its regional (and other national) offices (see Picture 28.1). (See Activity 28.2.)

Structuring corporate communication

List all the advantages of having a single communication department that directs communication with all stakeholders.

What are the advantages of a decentralised approach, where instead of a single department, communication specialists are employed in different divisions or units throughout the organisation, or stakeholders can contact anyone in the organisation for comment?

What are the advantages and disadvantages of using public relations and/or specialist communications consultancies instead of in-house employees?

Feedback

In thinking about *centralisation*, have you considered issues such as: having more control over information released about the organisation; being able to direct media requests to appropriate (and trained) spokespeople; being able to ensure all information is newsworthy or of value; checking consistency of corporate messages. The disadvantage of a centralised approach may well be that too much control could appear to be suspicious (trying to block free access to information), slow down the process by which stakeholders (particularly the media) can get information and negate the value of local knowledge or relationships.

Advantages of an *in-house department* (as opposed to an external consultant) may include: understanding the complexities of the organisation and its sector; being able to identify and easily access the most knowledgeable organisational spokespeople for particular issues; being trusted with access to high-level strategic information. Disadvantages may include lack of objectivity, inability to provide expertise in a full range of specialisms (such as event management or design, for example) and lack of innovation.

Agency advantages could include: having a wide range of specialisms within the agency team; being removed from the organisation therefore more objective about its performance and image. Disadvantages may include a lack of in-depth knowledge about the organisation and its sector; not being trusted with high-level strategic information; lack of internal contacts/networking opportunities; and conflict of interest (when managing a range of clients).

Interface of corporate communication and overall corporate strategy

'Whether "overall success" is defined solely as profits or more broadly in terms of the organisation's contribution to its community and diverse publics (Estes 1996; Etzioni 1998; Wilson 1996), public relations, to be strategic, must support the organization's achievement of its mission and goals' (Wilson in Heath 2001: 215).

One of the key dimensions of corporate communication is understanding its relationship to overall

---

Stage 1

Dominant coalition create corporate strategy embodied in corporate mission and values and 5-year plan (influenced by commercial and other imperatives including stakeholder expectations, government policy and other issues prevalent in its particular environment)

Stage 2

Corporate communication director and communication managers identify ways in which communication can help achieve overall corporate objectives
Expressed as aims and objectives in a communication strategy

Stage 3

Communication managers work with communication 'technicians' (e.g. writers) to develop tactics that will deliver communication objectives (expressed as tactics in the communications plan)

FIGURE 28.6   Three stages of strategic planning

organisational strategy (the cornerstones of which are its mission and goals).

As corporate strategy gurus Johnson and Scholes explain: 'Strategy is the *direction* and *scope* of an organisation over the *long term*: which achieves advantage for the organisation through its configuration of *resources* within a changing environment, to meet the needs of *markets* and to fulfil *stakeholder* expectations.' (Johnson and Scholes 1999: 10). (See Figure 28.6.)

In simplistic terms, organisations are usually run by a chief executive and a board of directors or executive committee, depending on the type of organisation it is (whether it is in the public or private sector, etc). This dominant coalition (Grunig 1992; Grunig et al. 2002) formulates the corporate strategic plan which sets out what the organisation aims to achieve (often over a five-year period) as well as the values and philosophy to which it will adhere. This could be considered to be stage 1 of the planning process.

However, as well as being a member of the executive board, each director is also responsible for directing the management of a specific 'division'/department/ business unit (the use of alternative labels in the literature is seemingly endless, so for the purposes of this chapter the term 'division' will be used). The names of some typical divisions are included in the various structure diagrams elsewhere in this chapter.

The director and the management team of the division will then analyse the overall corporate strategic plan and identify ways in which their division's activities can contribute to achieving these overarching aims. This takes us to stage 2 of the planning process when each division sets its own five-year plan. For

example, the corporate communication senior management team identifies how *communication* can help achieve specific organisational strategic aims and objectives and sets a communication plan to direct and focus future communication effort.

And finally, stage 3 in the planning process occurs at an operational level when the management team works with the 'technicians', or communication team responsible for implementing the plans, to identify and schedule the activities that, it is to be hoped, will achieve the divisional and, eventually, the corporate objectives.

Clearly, this is a vastly simplified model of an approach to strategic planning. Its purpose is to demonstrate the way in which corporate communication can be tied to overall corporate strategy but in no way attempts to represent the literature in this field. It should also be noted that although this appears to be a hierarchical, 'top-down' and linear process, in reality it could be much more inclusive and organic. (For an effective guide to corporate strategy, see Johnson and Scholes 1999.) See Case study 28.1.

Linking communication activities to the overall organisational plan is often deemed vital in ensuring communication is taken seriously at the highest levels (i.e. viewed as strategic and central to organisational success). 'Practitioners must not focus on pushing communication higher up senior management's agenda, but rather connect communication to what is already at the top of that agenda' (Quirke in Steyn 2003).

It could also be argued that really strategic communication would have already been involved in setting the senior management agenda.

How corporate communication influences corporate decision making

Referring back to Table 28.4, one of the key characteristics of Grunig and colleagues' (2002) 'Excellent' public relations programmes is the public relations director holding a powerful role 'in or with the *dominant coalition*'.

Definition: The *dominant coalition* is 'the group of individuals within the organization who have the power to determine its mission and goals. They are the top managers who "run" the organization. In the process, they often make decisions that are good enough to allow the organization to survive but designed primarily to maintain the status quo and keep the current dominant coalition in power' (Grunig et al. 2002: 141). It is not a term most practitioners would recognise – in practice, terms such as board of directors or senior management would be used, but the inference is the same.

case study 28.1

Anytown University College (AUC)

An example of how communication aims and objectives relate to overall strategic aims

Stage 1

One of AUC's overall strategic aims is *to achieve full university status.*

Stage 2

One of the criteria for achieving university status is having 4000 students (AUC currently has 3000 students).

The UK government caps the number of European Union (EU) undergraduate students AUC can recruit, so the vice-principals recognise that one of the things AUC needs to do to become a university is to recruit more *postgraduate* and *overseas* students. So the communi-

cation director considers how communication can help achieve this and sets a communication aim of increasing enquiries from suitable overseas and postgraduate students (note that the aim here is not to recruit more students – that is not achievable by public relations alone as enrolling a student depends on many factors outside the control of the public relations department, so the aim is focused only on what *communication* can achieve).

Stage 3

The public relations team recognises that the website is an important communication channel and sets an objective geared towards ensuring that at least 90% of postgraduate and overseas students considering applying to AUC are able easily to access information that is useful and pertinent to them via the website.

Correspondingly, then, one of the key aspects of the corporate communication role would be the extent to which the 'communication czar' (Grunig et al. 2002) is involved in influencing and shaping the *overall business strategy*, rather than just being involved in the 'second layer' of decision making (about how communication can help achieve predetermined company goals).

Commentators argue that the communication director must be able to help determine the *organisational* goals rather than merely being confined to setting *communication* goals. This is often referred to as influencing decisions before they are made (Grunig et al. 1992).

The rationale for this position is that the corporate communication director's knowledge of the organisation's environment (trends in public opinion, stakeholder perceptions and expectations, the news agenda and news values, employee views, and so on) enable them to predict stakeholder responses to decisions taken by the dominant coalition. According to Johnson and Scholes (1999), a significant problem in developing effective corporate strategies is that 'strategic decisions may have to be made in situations of *uncertainty*: they may involve taking decisions on views of the future which it is impossible for managers to be sure about' (1999: 11). An effective communication director can help reduce aspects of this uncertainty.

Having reduced uncertainty by mapping likely stakeholder responses to proposed future directions, depending on the way in which the director approaches (or conceptualises) corporate communication, their role in the decision making process is then:

- either to introduce *symmetry* into the decision-making process by ensuring the dominant coalition is willing to compromise to accommodate stakeholders' wishes (thus entering Grunig's (1992) 'win–win' zone)
- or to predict whether stakeholders could be *persuaded* to accommodate an organisational decision.

See Mini case study 28.1 and Activity 28.3.

Corporate communication objectives: stakeholders vs shareholders

In a best selling book, UK political commentator Will Hutton (1996) criticises business for being short-termist and relentless in pursuit of some of the highest financial returns in the world: 'Companies are the fiefdoms of their Boards and sometimes just of their chairmen; and companies are run as pure trading operations rather than productive organisations which invest, innovate and develop human capital' (1996: 21).

In contrast to this view of companies being dominated only by the idea of improving returns for *shareholders*, the concept of *stakeholding* advocates a *sustainable* approach to business that values relationships with a *range* of stakeholders.

Despite the fact that the use of the term 'stakeholder' has proliferated throughout the corporate lexicon to the extent that it has almost lost its political and social significance, Hutton, a major proponent of 'stakeholder capitalism', believes the arguments for

The McLibel case – the importance of influencing the decision-making process

In 1990 McDonald's embarked on what was to become the longest trial of any kind in English history when it sued a part-time bar worker (who earned a maximum of £65 a week), and an unemployed postman. At the time, McDonald's economic power outstripped that of many small countries, with worldwide sales of about $30bn in 1995 (BBC News 2005).

As *The Guardian* explained:

McDonald's sued Ms Steel and Mr Morris, both from north London, in 1990 over leaflets headed What's Wrong With McDonald's?, which they distributed outside the burger chain's restaurants.

These accused the chain of exploiting children, cruelty to animals, destroying the rainforest, paying low wages and peddling unhealthy food.

Despite the obstacles, the two campaigners won a ruling from the high court that some of the claims in the leaflet were true, in what was described as 'the biggest corporate PR disaster in history'. Mr Justice Bell ruled that the leaflet was correct when it accused the company of paying low wages to its workers, being responsible for cruelty to some of the animals used in its food products, and exploiting children in advertising campaigns.' (Dyer 2005)

The world's biggest fast food chain spent an estimated £10m on the case.

The McLibel case

Read Mini case study 28.1. Now, imagine you are the communications director at the McDonald's meeting called to discuss the threat posed by the distribution of the leaflets. The lawyers have just explained the basis for suing the couple. Consider how you could have influenced this decision in a way that may have avoided the public outcry.

Feedback

A communications director who had been monitoring the environment would be aware that issues such as obesity (particularly childhood obesity), health problems related to eating food with a high fat content and animal health were looming large in arenas such as the media and in government consultations. They would also understand news values and recognise that a story related to these issues, especially with the added 'David and Goliath' dimension, would make the headlines. They could have counselled McDonald's to take a 'symmetrical' (Grunig 2002) approach, invited the critics in, heard their criticisms and changed the company's products and systems to accommodate their views (an approach that analysis of the company's latest strategy shows has now been adopted).

stakeholding stand (Hutton and Giddens 2000). He argues for organisations to think in terms of 'relational capitalism' (premised on the idea of human dynamics) instead of 'transactional capitalism' (a network of transactions) but recognises that one of the major obstacles to this shift is the fact that many companies are locked into structures such as the stock market, which demands high returns for shareholders.

It is often suggested that, to be taken seriously, corporate communication must contribute to 'the bottom line'. Traditionally, the bottom line has referred to profitability in financial terms.

Accordingly, some organisations measure their performance in terms of the strength of their share price and the term *competitive advantage* in this context would mean helping the organisation to produce more goods or services at a cheaper price.

In some organisations, however, this exclusive focus on economic success has shifted. The bottom line has been reconceptualised as a 'triple bottom line'. The triple bottom line still measures financial performance but also measures an organisation's environmental and social impact.

We have already discussed how corporate communication strategy sets communication objectives related to overall organisational objectives. The focus of these objectives then has a crucial effect on the way corporate communication strategy is set.

If successful performance is measured within the confined parameters of share price, for example, then the focus on shareholders will be hard to shift. However, if a focus on corporate social responsibility is emphasised, then objectives will be set according to a triple bottom line (see also Chapter 6).

In describing its credo, Johnson & Johnson is proud to assert that 'there is no mission statement that hangs on our wall', which would seem to reflect that this company recognises problems associated with the function of mission and value statements. (See Case study 28.2 and Box 28.5.)

case study 28.2

Johnson & Johnson

Johnson & Johnson has more than 200 operating companies located in 57 countries. Its objective is 'to achieve superior levels of capital efficient profitable growth'.

'To this end the company participates in growth areas in human healthcare and is committed to attaining leadership positions in these growth segments through the development of innovative products and services.'

Johnson & Johnson's 'credo' was developed to embody the management philosophy and guide managers and employees in how to achieve its overall corporate objective. It states:

We believe our first responsibility is to the doctors, nurses and patients, to mothers and fathers and all others who use our products and services . . .

We are responsible to our employees, the men and women who work with us throughout the world . . .

We are responsible to the communities in which we live and work and to the world community as well . . .

Our final responsibility is to our stockholders. Business must make a sound profit . . .

The full credo is available on www.jnj.com/our_company/our_credo/

Johnson & Johnson state that:

The Credo, seen by business leaders and the media as being farsighted, received wide public attention and acclaim. Putting customers first, and stockholders last, was a refreshing approach to the management of a business. But it should be noted that Johnson was a practical minded businessman. He believed that by putting the customer first the business would be well served, and it was.

The Corporation has drawn heavily on the strength of the Credo for guidance through the years, and at no time was this more evident than during the TYLENOL® crises of 1982 and 1986, when the McNeil Consumer & Specialty Pharmaceuticals product was adulterated with cyanide and used as a murder weapon. With Johnson & Johnson's good name and reputation at stake, company managers and employees made countless decisions that were inspired by the philosophy embodied in the Credo. The company's reputation was preserved and the TYLENOL® acetaminophen business was regained.

Today the Credo lives on in Johnson & Johnson stronger than ever. Company employees now participate in a periodic survey and evaluation of just how well the company performs its Credo responsibilities. These assessments are then fed back to the senior management, and where there are shortcomings, corrective action is promptly taken.

Johnson & Johnson have now developed a credo-based model incorporating 24 value indicators, each linked to one of the four paragraphs in the credo, against which performance will be measured.

(See also Chapter 20 for more detail on how the Johnson & Johnson philosophy was applied in a crisis situation.)

Source: Johnson & Johnson 2003

---

box 28.5

Controversy and debate – mission and value statements

Some commentators argue that 'a company's values are encapsulated in its corporate philosophy and conveying these values is what corporate communication is all about' (Yamauchi 2001: 131). Many organisations publish mission and value statements to encapsulate their attitude to operations and demonstrate what they want to accomplish. Toy manufacturer Klutz provides a succinct example of this: 'Klutz is a kids' company staffed entirely by real human beings. For those of you who collect corporate mission statements, here's ours:

- Create Wonderful Things
- Be Good
- Have Fun'. (Klutz 1998: 18)

A corporate communicator's first job is to look at these statements to determine how communication can help to realise them. The wise communicator would do well to learn from Johnson & Johnson's caution about mission statements, however. Most are far from being as simple and direct as the Klutz example. Indeed, Roger Bennet catalogues eight 'problems with mission statements', some of which are useful here, in particular his view that 'too often the language of mission statements comprises hackneyed clichés assembled with little genuine concern for their relevance to the business in question' (Bennett 1999: 24).

The key then is perhaps not what the organisational mission states, but how it is implemented and *measured*.

Ideas such as CSR and a triple bottom line must not only influence the language chosen by public relations practitioners to communicate with publics, as a way of 'spinning' an organisations' activities, but must permeate thinking at all levels of strategic decision making and implementation. And the buck does not stop with organisations – government and other regulators must guarantee a regulatory framework that forces organisations to comply with these ideas. Frankental endorses the call for auditing according to a triple bottom line 'financial, environmental and social' (Frankental 2001: 19). Annual social reports must be more than gloss or spin. In a properly regulated world, 'the terms of reference will be more comprehensive, standard methodologies will be developed and issues of definition, measurement, monitoring and verification will be . . . addressed' (Frankental 2001: 20).

Practical application of critical reflection

Rather than just highlighting problematic aspects of the dominant corporate communication paradigms, Cheney and Christensen demonstrate the value of critical reflection through the practical application of their ideas to help improve practice (and academic approaches). They specify a 'self-reflective' approach to counter 'self-referential tendencies' (Cheney and Christensen 2001: 264). In other words, practitioners must (mentally) step outside their world and challenge the things they take for granted. They should reflect on 'basic assumptions about relevant publics and environments, established procedures and routines involved in opinion polls and market analyses, tacit norms for interpreting data, briefing procedures and information exchange between departments, and more generally, perceptions of external information throughout the organization' (Cheney and Christensen 2001: 264). (See Case study 28.3.)

---

case study 28.3

Example of self-reflection

An example of the way in which 'basic assumptions' become the norm is the way in which a public relations practitioner decides which publics are relevant to their organisation. Reflecting this is the view that: 'Stakeholder theory has been approached from the point of view of business ethics, corporate governance and/or corporate social performance. This puts the *organization* at the centre of the analysis and discourages consideration of stakeholders in their own right as well as discouraging balanced viewing of the organization/ stakeholder relation' (Friedman and Miles 2002: 1).

Consulting strategic management or public relations textbooks reveals a plethora of methods for prioritising stakeholders – many depend on calculating which group of stakeholders has most *power* and is therefore most likely to impact on the organisation and its most important constituents. The logical conclusion of this approach is that an organisation will focus its activity on the most *important* stakeholders.

So does the term *strategic* stakeholders actually mean those that have most *power* and *influence*?

For the purposes of strategic analysis, Johnson and Scholes (1999) define power as 'the extent to which individuals or groups are able to persuade, induce or coerce others into following certain courses of action' (1999: 221). The question is, if *power* is the criterion for selecting who can become involved in dialogue, what happens to those stakeholders not deemed to be important enough to be prioritised in this way? And can corporate communication be regarded as ethical if two-way communication only takes place within corporately drawn parameters?

'The communication systems that are being developed these days – though avowedly to satisfy the general public's demand for insight and participation – are too closed around organisations and their active and resource-rich publics and stakeholders, each monitoring the other and themselves . . . What appear, to some observers, as symmetrical systems of communication may, in other words, turn out to be "corporatist" systems organized around specific issues with only limited access to the nonorganized (see also Christensen and Jones 1996 and Livesey 1999 in Jablin and Putnam 2001). Such a pattern of communication by and among well-established and resource-rich entities can exacerbate the problem of dominance of the "free speech" arena by corporate and other large organizational interests (Bailey 1996 in Cheney and Christensen 2001: 261).

One of the problems, then, with the ethical basis of the 'excellent' symmetrical model of public relations (Grunig 1992; 2002) is that some groups of stakeholders may not have the power, sophistication or resources to engage in negotiation or dialogue (L'Etang and Pieczka 1996; Cheney and Christensen 2001; Leitch and Neilson 2001).

So, if corporate communication is the area that 'oversees' communication, it would seem that this is the area that can balance the needs of stakeholders with those of the organisation. It is the corporate communication's role then to determine whether most resources are shared among a broad range of stakeholders or only channelled towards the powerful (the customer, shareholder or politician).

In order to avoid being 'self-referential,' that is, making decisions based on the needs of the organisation or according to the way communications experts have always done things (according to dominant public relations paradigms), Cheney and Christensen (2001) recommend that: 'Scholars and practitioners . . . need to learn to communicate consciously with themselves and their organisations

about their most central meanings. These meanings include internal images and perceptions of what the organisation "is", key symbols of pride and motivation' (2001: 264).

Thinking now about all the issues raised in this chapter, what practical steps can practitioners take to ensure they 'communicate consciously with themselves and their organisations about their most central meanings'? (See Case study 28.4.)

Clearly, then, this type of reflection and research is crucial to effective corporate communication planning.

However, it should not be the only research focus: a truly reflective process means asking searching questions about the moral and ethical frameworks and perspectives that guide communication approaches and practice.

case study 28.4

A tool to facilitate reflective practice

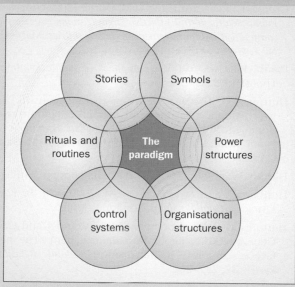

FIGURE 28.7 A cultural web (*source:* Johnson and Scholes 1999: 74)

Johnson and Scholes' 'culture web' (see Figure 28.7) is a practical tool that can be employed to facilitate *some* aspects of type of reflection to which Cheney and Christensen refer.

The cultural web helps identify 'taken for granted' assumptions as well as the physical manifestations of organisational culture that are often hard to pin down.

One of the most positive aspects of the use of the cultural web is that it does not limit analysis to a structural perspective that is focused solely on systems and procedures. It incorporates an interpretative approach where 'culture is viewed a guide and a filter for how organisation members understand the messages they receive and send' (Daymon 2000: 241).

Researchers focus on organisations as cultures (their cultural patterns consisting not of a monolithic culture but of diverse subcultures) and therefore draw attention to stories, rituals and ceremonies, beliefs, values, language and behaviors in order to reveal the underlying meanings and emotions within organisations that influence why people choose to communicate (or not) as they do . . . This, in turn, influences whether members ignore or reject certain information, the significance they give to methods of communication, and the choices they make about what information should be communicated (Daymon 2000: 244).

From this perspective, culture is seen to influence 'the way we do things round here'. For example, if stories of patients as the 'enemy' proliferate in a hospital or GP practice, it becomes 'taken for granted' and accepted that they should be treated in a hostile manner. (See Johnson and Scholes (1999: 75) for an application of the cultural web to the NHS in the UK.)

Summary

This chapter has identified some very different ways of conceptualising corporate communication – as reputation management, relationship management, communication with non-consumer publics, communication with all stakeholders, organisational advocacy, persuasion, rhetoric and spin.

It has asserted that recognition of the existence of these different ways of conceiving of the practice is important for a number of reasons. In particular, that this acts as a filter for understanding the literature – there is no single 'truth', no 'right' way of approaching the topic. This understanding prepares the reader to identify value judgements inherent in the different perspectives and judge their usefulness more effectively.

The chapter has also explored what these different ways of conceptualising corporate public relations mean for practice. In this respect, it asserts that understanding the different ways of conceptualising corporate communication and how these inform different approaches to the practice means that *practitioners* can make clear and informed choices about how they do their jobs and everyone else can evaluate the impact of their practice – both in terms of success and in relation to the broader society in which it takes place.

Bibliography

BBC News (2005). 'McLibel: Longest case in English history'. www.news.bbc.co.uk/go/pr/fr/-/1/hi/uk/4266741.stm, accessed 17 March 2005.

Bennett, R. (1999). *Corporate Strategy*, 2nd edition. London: Financial Times Management.

Botan, C.H. and V. Hazelton (eds.) (1989). *Public Relations Theory*. Hillsdale, NJ: Lawrence Erlbaum Associates, Inc.

Cheney, C.G. and L.T. Christensen, (2001). 'Organizational identity: Linkages between internal and external organizational communication' in *The New Handbook of Organizational Communication*. F.M. Jablin and L.L. Putnam (eds). Thousand Oaks, CA: Sage.

Corporate Communication Institute (CCI) at Fairleigh Dickinson University (2004). 'CCI corporate communication practices and trends study 2003: Final report'. www.corporatecomm.org/pdf/report2003.pdf, accessed 8 March 2005.

Daymon, C. (2000). 'On considering the meaning of managed communication: Or why employees resist excellent communication'. *Journal of Communication Management* **4**(3): 240–251.

Dozier, D.M., L.A. Grunig and J.E. Grunig (1995). *Manager's Guide to Excellence in Public Relations and Communications Management,* Hillsdale, NJ: Lawrence Erlbaum.

Dyer, C. (2005). 'Libel law review over McDonald's ruling'. *The Guardian* 16 February. www.guardian.co.uk/food/Story/0,2763,1415518,00.html, accessed 16 March 2005.

Ehling, W.P., J. White and J.E. Grunig (1992). 'Public relations and marketing practices' in *Excellence in Public Relations and Communications Management*. J.E. Grunig (ed.). Hillsdale, NJ: Lawrence Erlbaum Associates, Inc.

Fombrun, C.J. and C.B.M. Van Riel (2004). *Fame and Fortune: How successful companies build winning reputations*. Upper Saddle River, NJ: Pearson Education.

Frankental, P. (2001). 'Corporate social responsibility – a PR invention? *Corporate Communications: An International Journal* **6**(1): 18–23.

Friedman, A.L. and S. Miles (2002). 'Developing stakeholder theory'. *Journal of Management Studies* **39**(1): 1–22.

Grunig, J.E. (ed.) (1992). *Excellence in Public Relations and Communication Management*. Hillsdale, NJ: Lawrence Erlbaum Associates, Inc.

Grunig, J.E. and T.E. Hunt (1984). *Managing Public Relations*. New York: Holt, Rinehart & Winston.

Grunig, L., J.E. Grunig and D.M. Dozier (2002). *Excellent Public Relations and Effective Organizations : A study of communication management in three countries*. Mahwah, NJ: Lawrence Erlbaum Associates, Inc.

Heath, R.L. (ed.) (2001). *Handbook of Public Relations*. Thousand Oaks, CA: Sage.

Hutton, J.G. (2001). 'Defining the relationship between public relations and marketing: public relations' most important challenge' in *Handbook of Public Relations*. R.L. Heath (ed.). Thousand Oaks, CA: Sage.

Hutton, W. (1996). *The State We've In*. London: Vintage.

Hutton, W. and A. Giddens (eds) (2000). *On the Edge: Living with global capital*. London: Vintage.

Hutton, J.G., M.B. Goodman, J.B. Alexander and C.M. Genest (2001). 'Reputation management: The new face of corporate public relations?' *Public Relations Review* **27**, 247–261.

IPR/DTI (2003). *Unlocking the Potential of Public Relations*. London: CIPR.

Jablin, F.M. and L.L. Putnam (eds) (2001). *The New Handbook of Organizational Communication*. Thousand Oaks, CA: Sage.

Johnson & Johnson (2003). 'Our credo history'. www.jnj.com/our_company/our_credo_history/index.htm, accessed 16 March 2005.

Johnson, G. and K. Scholes (1999). *Exploring Corporate Strategy*, 5th edition. Harlow: Prentice Hall.

Kitchen, P. and D. Schultz (eds) (2001). *Raising the Corporate Umbrella: Corporate communication in the 21st century*. London: Macmillan.

Klutz (1998). *The Amazing Book.a.ma.Thing for the Backseat.* PaloAlto, CA: Klutz Inc.

Ledingham, J.A. and S.D. Bruning (eds) (2000). *Public Relations as Relationship Management: A relational approach to the study and practice of public relations.* Mahwah, NJ: Lawrence Erlbaum Associates, Inc.

Leitch, S. and D. Neilson (2001). 'Bringing publics into public relations' in *Handbook of Public Relations*. R.L. Heath (ed.). Thousand Oaks, CA, London and New Delhi: Sage.

L'Etang, J. and M. Pieczka (1996). *Critical Perspectives in Public Relations.* London: International Thomson Publishing.

Moloney, K. (2000). *Rethinking Public Relations.* London: Routledge.

Steyn, B. (2003). 'From strategy to corporate communication strategy: A conceptualisation'. *Journal of Communication Management* **8**(2): 168–183.

Toth, E. and R. Heath (eds) (1992). *Rhetorical and Critical Approaches to Public Relations.* Hillsdale, NJ, and Hove: Lawrence Erlbaum Associates, Inc.

Van Riel, C.B.M (2003). 'Defining corporate communication' in *Corporate Communication: A strategic approach to building reputation*. P.S. Bronn and R. Wiig (eds). Oslo: Gyldendal Akademisk.

Yamauchi, K. (2001). 'Corporate communication: A powerful tool for stating corporate missions'. *Corporate Communications: An International Journal* **6**(3): 131–136.

CHAPTER 29

Campaigning organisations and pressure groups

Learning outcomes

By the end of this chapter you should be able to:

■ analyse how campaigning organisations and pressure groups are motivated and formed and how they grow

■ avoid the risks of publicity for its own sake

■ recognise the use that is made of the internet for campaigning, recruiting and disrupting

■ analyse the public relations roles on all sides and the use of two-way communication and consensus

■ plan a campaign for a pressure group

■ evaluate the development of consensus or dissensus using research to inform the co-orientation model.

Structure

■ Types of campaigning organisation

■ Key issues for public relations practitioners in organisations and campaigning groups

■ Campaign tactics

■ People, politics and globalisation

■ Building and evaluating consensus

■ Practical guidelines for campaigning public relations

Introduction

Campaigning organisations and pressure groups (or activist groups as they are also known) are the embodiment of active publics (Grunig and Hunt 1984). They are groups of people who share a common interest or concern and have come together to do something about it – whether to march, raise funds, change public policy, prevent something from happening (such as an airport extension or the damming of a valley), make something happen (such as winning the vote for black people in South Africa) or just to raise awareness about an issue.

This chapter explores some of the motivations for these groups and some of the activities and tactics employed by them. It also examines the role of public relations, both within the activist groups and in the organisations or companies that might have inspired their development.

Types of campaigning organisation

When talking about campaigning organisations, the public relations literature frequently refers to 'activists'. Activists are regarded as a challenge to public relations practitioners working for corporations but it should also be borne in mind that activist organisations employ public relations practitioners too. Activists include 'special interest groups, pressure groups, issue groups, grassroots organizations, or social movement organizations' (Smith 1996).

Trade unions

Trade unions were formed on a mass scale in Britain at the end of the nineteenth century to represent the workers employed in major industries such as cotton, mining, metallurgy and shipping. Elsewhere in Europe, the trade union movement grew up around ports and other forms of transport such as railways. Later, especially in France, public service unions were formed to represent employees of the state. What united these very different groups of workers was the growing influence of socialist ideology, particularly the idea that the working classes could be organised politically and did not have to put up with social injustice (Hobsbawn 1987).

Today, trade unions exist across the globe to protect workers' rights and to campaign for improved pay and conditions for their members. These groups have become very formalised with written constitutions and a clear set of objectives and rules. However, in some countries, such as Burma and Equatorial Guinea, it is illegal to belong to a union. In other countries, it is positively dangerous. The most dangerous place in 2000 was Colombia, where 153 trade unionists were assassinated or 'disappeared'. According to the International Confederation of Free Trade Unions' annual survey of violations of trade union rights (www.globalpolicy. org), there are 108 countries that put up legal obstacles to union membership. In most democracies, union membership is optional. However, in the USA, some employers hire professional 'union busters' to break up any unions at their workplaces. The different unions often have to work hard to win members. Also many countries have introduced legislation to curb the power of trade unions, often making it impossible or very difficult for workers to withdraw their labour by striking, thereby taking from them their most effective tool of protest or persuasion. (See Think about 29.1.)

Charities

Organisations in the UK can become registered charities as long as their purpose and function fit the rules of the Charity Commission for England and Wales. The 'essential requirement of charities is that they operate for the public benefit and independently of government or commercial interests' (Charity Commission 2005). The Charity Commission regulates the activities of charities through regular visits and checks and maintains a register of charities that anyone can inspect. This registration gives the benefit of certain financial advantages (those making donations can have the amount of their gift increased by the tax they would have paid had they kept the money for themselves) and the credibility of having been recognised as a properly run organisation.

---

think about 29.1   Employees' freedom of expression

As a public relations officer in a company, you might be responsible for internal communication and helping to maintain staff morale. How important do you think it is for staff to be able to express their views without fear of reprisal? How might you go about gauging staff views and morale?

You might like to consider the following quotes about the significance of good employee relationships. 'Recognition of the efficient use of human resources for business success, together with advances in social democracy have highlighted the increasing importance of employee involvement and industrial partnership including the role played by trade unions' (Coupar 1994: 45–50 in Mullins 1999).

'No organisation can perform at its best unless each employee is committed to the corporate objectives and works as an effective team member. That is not going to happen if the employee's views are not listened to within an open two-way dialogue' (Mullins 1999: 651).

Feedback You would need to consider organisational culture and to what extent this 'allows' views to be expressed, either formally through trade union representation or through upward communication channels. Bear in mind that formal representations by trade unions are made to the human resources function, not public relations.

To gauge staff views and morale in a culture where upward communication channels are encouraged, you could carry out a communications audit. (See also Chapter 17 to identify the respective roles and responsibilities of human resources and public relations functions.)

PICTURE 29.1   'Each time a person stands up for an idea, or strikes out against injustice, he sends forth a tiny ripple of hope; and crossing each other from a million different centres of energy and daring, those ripples build a current which can sweep down the mightiest web of oppression and resistance', Robert F. Kennedy, speaking in South Africa, 1966 (*source:* Stuart Franklin/Magnum Photos).

Registered charities exist: to alleviate suffering for people or animals; work to develop or educate in particular ways; or to do good works in society. Their campaigning is mainly to raise funds for the causes that they exist to help and to raise awareness about their work. However, not all campaigning groups would be acceptable to the Charity Commission, as these groups often engage in overtly political activities and persuasion. For example, Amnesty International is a human rights organisation and its main campaigning work is to free prisoners of conscience (those imprisoned anywhere in the world because of their beliefs and attitudes) and abolish the death penalty. This is not acceptable to the Charity Commission. However, Amnesty has established an educational section, which prepares packs for school projects and publishes research, which *is* a registered charity. (See Think about 29.2.)

Most campaigning organisations and pressure groups depend on attracting members to create an

---

think about 29.2   **Role of charities**

In 1994 Oxfam entered into the public debate about the situation in Rwanda, where mass killings together with the resultant refugee crisis had led to the deaths of millions. They pointed to the failure of governments to act decisively to prevent these deaths and were criticised severely by then UK Prime Minister, Margaret Thatcher, who called on the Charity Commission to check their rulebook. Rather than have its charitable status revoked, Oxfam retreated.

What do you think about this situation? Should charities just deal with the problems *after* the event or should they be free to make political statements that might embarrass the very governments who have given them financial help through the taxation system?

Feedback   Charities in the UK are free to set up campaigning sections that do not have the same financial benefits as charitable status, but that do share the same positioning as the umbrella brand (see Chapter 26, which discusses branding).

Merging interests – Cancer Research UK

Until February 2002 those wanting to support research into causes of, and cures for, cancer had a choice between the two leading charities – the Cancer Research Campaign and the Imperial Cancer Research Fund – as well as many smaller others, often focused on specific types of cancer. The two big ones have now joined together, as Cancer Research UK, to combine their efforts and impact.

income stream and swell the ranks of supporters who will take part in and generate activities to achieve their objectives. This puts them in competition with other groups, including others with the same or very similar objectives.

Within less than 10 years of the AIDS crisis coming to the public's attention, there are 107 organisations in the UK that have been set up to raise funds for research and alleviate the problems of sufferers. The current Terrance Higgins Trust is an amalgamation of five organisations based in five different cities, which merged in the late 1990s:

- Bridgeside in Leeds
- HIV Network in Coventry
- Sussex AIDS Centre in Brighton
- OXAIDS in Oxford
- Terrance Higgins Trust in London.

As its Chief Executive, Nick Partridge, said: 'This decision by trustees and agencies of all those involved sets a precedent for the voluntary sector, where mergers are still relatively rare' (BBC news website, 27 January 1999). (See Mini case study 29.1 and Think about 29.3).

Pressure groups

In this chapter we talk about pressure groups. In US public relations literature, these groups are referred to as activist groups whose 'primary purpose is to influence public policy, organizational action, or social norms and values' (Smith and Ferguson 2001: 292). Drawing on studies in political science, sociology, communication and public relations, three perspectives are put forward on how pressure or activist organisations are formed:

- the macro-level perspective
- the publics perspective
- the developmental perspective (Smith and Ferguson 2001).

The *macro-level perspective* is concerned with the political, economic and cultural conditions within a particular country that may encourage activism. It has been assumed that democratic values such as the freedom of expression provides the basis for activism and particularly economic activism arising from class inequalities. (See Chapter 5 for a discussion of democracy and its underpinning values.) However, activism today embraces publics across educational and economic strata, giving rise to the idea of *interest* groups that are interested in securing benefits for themselves and *issue* groups that are more motivated by their moral convictions about policies.

The *publics perspective* is concerned with the communication process whereby people identify shared problems and argue for change in resolving those

Some campaign groups and charities have become so big that they need to raise large sums of money to maintain their own survival before they can spend anything on the cause for which they were first established.

After establishing Surfers Against Sewage (see Case study 29.1) and beginning to succeed, Chris Hines was approached by other environmental groups offering him jobs. His main condition was that he did not want to work in London or for an organisation that paid out the sums necessary to have offices there. He now oversees activities for sustainability for the Eden Project in Cornwall in south-west England.

Do you think he has a point? Check some campaigning organisations' websites for their annual reports and see how their money is spent.

problems. In the situational theory of publics, Grunig developed Dewey's theories on publics to consider their behaviour in various situations. Important to this perspective is the notion that publics are categorised according to their responses to issues. Publics are categorised as all-issue, apathetic, single-issue and hot-issue publics According to situational theory, publics become active publics when an issue they face is seen as a problem, are highly involved in that issue and recognise few constraints in doing something about the problem (Grunig and Hunt 1984).

Single-issue publics, which are often associated with activism, are defined as being: 'Active in one or a small subset of the issues that concerns only a small part of the population. Such issues have included the slaughter of whales or the controversy over the sale of infant formula in developing countries' (Grunig and Repper 1992: 139).

Many big campaigning organisations started out as pressure or activist groups spurred on by a specific issue or concern. They begin in bars, people's homes or at school gates, wherever a group of people move from being an aware to an active public because some-

one says: 'What are we going to do about it?' The zeal and fervour that moves small groups to become wider movements has to be strong. One determinant may be charismatic individuals who found the group, hold the vision and protect it, often fiercely.

The *developmental perspective* examines the movement from problem recognition to action. The idea of a 'lifecycle' of activism assumes that there are separate stages that require different communication activities. The five stages identified by Heath (1997) are:

- *strain* – publics recognise issues, define them and seek to gain legitimacy
- *mobilisation* – activists form organisations, establish communication systems and start to mobilise resources to pursue their goals
- *confrontation* – activists push corporations and/or the government to resolve problems
- *negotiation* – various sides in the dispute exchange messages designed to reach a compromise
- *resolution* – the controversy is solved (possibly in part only).

See Think about 29.3 and Activity 29.1, overleaf.

PICTURE 29.2   Tree-climbing protestors – will they succeed in making their point? (*Source:* Andrew Testa/Panos Pictures.)

activity 29.1

Leaders and causes

Can you match the following well-known charismatic activists with their causes and can you think of others?

1	Martin Luther King	a	Banning landmines
2	Gandhi	b	Drop the (world) debt
3	Nelson Mandela	c	Saving rainforests
4	Chris Hines	d	Equal rights in the USA
5	Swampy	e	Votes for black South Africans
6	Sting	f	Surfers Against Sewage
7	Princess Diana	g	Independence for India
8	Bono	h	Protesting about road-building projects

What qualities do these and other leaders have in common?

Feedback

Their campaigns have all depended on 'the *oxygen of publicity*' to create sympathy, generate further actions and develop an identity with the millions that became their followers or members. In other words, like any campaigning organisation, they have needed effective public relations to deliver their messages, build relationships with supporters and persuade people (and sometimes governments) to change their behaviour.

(**Answers:** 1d, 2g, 3e, 4f, 5h, 6c, 7a, 8b)

Definition: The phrase '*oxygen of publicity*' was first used by Margaret Thatcher in a speech to the American Bar Association, referring to the need to 'starve the terrorist and the hijacker of the oxygen of publicity on which they depend' in London, 15 July 1985, reported in *The Times* 16 July 1985. It refers to the way that oxygen increases the intensity of a fire, meaning that publicity fans the flames of a cause.

Key issues for public relations practitioners in organisations and campaigning groups

Campaigning organisations and pressure or activist groups have several public relations advantages over many public and private sector organisations and companies. They have a clear vision; they are able to define their objectives simply; they are often controversial and therefore newsworthy and that in turn means that they can attract the support of personalities and other organisations who want to share the media spotlight. Of course, some campaigning organisations also take up unfashionable or unpopular causes and have to work very hard to generate media coverage.

As in any in-house or consultancy role, the public relations person has a duty to ensure that all campaigns, events, sponsorships or tie-ins with others re-

flect and remain true to the original vision on which the organisation was founded. (See Activity 29.2.)

Is all publicity good publicity?

Lavish celebrity dinners in the name of world poverty are often held in the wealthier cities around the world as successful fundraisers but the publicity value of them is questionable. Public relations people need to take great care when balancing the fundraising, publicity, awareness and sympathy needs of the campaigning or pressure groups that they represent.

The irreverent British sense of humour is enjoyed in most of Europe and respected. However, when Amnesty International first staged its *Secret Policeman's Ball* comedy shows, in which famous comedians appeared in sketches about torture, Amnesty's German national office nearly split away from the organisation as it felt unable to be associated with the use of humour about such a serious matter.

The same principle can apply to sponsorship (see Chapter 27) or support of any kind. Companies often use corporate social responsibility (see Chapter 6) to balance the negative aspects of some of their activities. For example, an oil company that has been breaking sanctions and trading with an oppressive regime might appear to be interested in human rights by offering money to Medicins Sans Frontières (a non-partisan charity, based in France, that sends medical

activity 29.2

Being true to the vision

Examine the following list of invented vision statements and decide which of the relevant events in the second list would generate the most publicity:

1 To eradicate world poverty
2 To reduce harmful emissions
3 To stop the export of live animals
4 To stop whaling
5 Fox hunting is good for the countryside

a Blow up a whaling ship in Reykjavik harbour
b Hold a 4x4 driving rally in Hyde Park, London
c Blockade all ports for a bank holiday weekend
d Celebrity 'pie eating 'til they're sick' competition
e Block all city streets with bicycles

Feedback

This short exercise demonstrates the risk of gaining publicity at the expense of the values of the organisation and contradictory to its aims. Of the statements and events, only b and e could be done in the spirit of 5 and 2. All the others have the potential to cause so much nuisance and offence that they could severely damage the cause that they have been staged to help. (Versions of all of them have, however, been done!)

think about 29.4 Turning 'bad' money to good use

If an organisation with a strongly held vision is short of the funding it needs to promote its work, should it take money from (and thereby give credibility to) a company that makes that money from the very thing that it stands against? Many charities and organisations do so in the belief that they are turning bad money to good use. In public relations terms, what conflicts might this generate in people's perception of both the sponsors and the recipients of the money?

Feedback For the sponsors, payments to an organisation whose ethical standing is greater than its own can be extremely beneficial in reputation terms. It can be seen to share the 'halo' of the recipient of funds, especially if the organisation carries the sponsor's branding. However, for the public relations practitioner working on behalf of a charity or campaign group, there is a need to be aware of the risks involved in taking funds from an organisation that is a target for pressure groups.

activity 29.3

Pressure group targets

Examine two campaigning websites, www.breastfeeding.com and www.babymilkaction.org, and consider the risks for the charities Help the Aged and Kids' Club in receiving sponsorship funds from Nestlé.

help into areas of conflict and war to help the wounded on all sides). (See Think about 29.4 and Activity 29.3.)

It is not only companies that like to align themselves with organisations or pressure groups that are generating a lot of media interest. Successful campaigning groups are often approached by would-be or once-were celebrities asking if there is anything they can do for the group. At high-profile events, such as Live Aid in the 1980s, organised by Bob Geldof to raise money for the starving peoples of Africa (repeated as Live 8 in 2005 to put pressure on the G8) many of the musicians who had long since disappeared shot back to fame. There are also disadvantages in public relations terms to working with campaigning organisations and pressure or activist groups. Their causes are often prejudicial to the well-being of large corporate interest groups which cannot afford for them to have their say too loudly. Public relations consultancies are sometimes hired to discredit pressure groups in the interest of the survival of the companies under attack. Compared to those companies, most campaigning or activist groups are under-resourced financially as well as in terms of experience and skills. Many do not survive their attempts at denting corporate power bases. However, modern communication technology and internet campaigning techniques have given poorly resourced and disparate interest groups the power to sway policy and inflict serious corporate damage.

Campaign tactics

Using the world wide web

There are various methods by which pressure groups can use the world wide web to conduct effective campaigns:

Site attack

Software has been designed that will bombard a site with requests for facts or information to such an extent that the whole site becomes non-functional to other users. The World Trade Organisation and Starbucks have both suffered in this way (Thomas 2003).

Hacking

Hackers can access an organisation's email system; for example, in the case of Samsung threats were sent out, apparently from Samsung, to large numbers of customers, resulting in 10,000 complaining emails being sent back during the busiest time of the protest, costing Samsung millions of dollars (Thomas 2003). One nearly successful activist campaign was fought by animal rights activists trying to shut down the Huntingdon Life Sciences laboratories in the UK because it tests products on animals. The company nearly went bankrupt after its shareholders were barraged with often threatening emails advising them to withdraw their investments.

Parody sites

These sites can be even more dangerous than hacking as they can confuse publics. The internet is undoubtedly a very good medium for bringing together like-minded groups, making publics aware, creating dialogues and giving publics opportunities to become active. Shell set up a useful site to build dialogues

mini case study 29.2

Activism in action: 'McLibel'

Most global net campaigns are environmental, human or animal rights based. A very successful tactic in the global arena is to create a corporate bully. The most famous example of this is what became known as the 'McLibel' case. McDonald's sued an unemployed postal worker, Dave Morris, and a community gardener, Helen Steel, for libel in a trial that ran for 313 days in court. The case was brought against the pair following their publication of a pamphlet in 1986 that took McDonald's to task on almost all aspects of its work from third world poverty to the depletion of the rainforest. During the four years of the case McDonald's offered to pay money to a cause of the defendants' choice, in exchange for a promise that all criticism would end, but Steel and Morris chose to go on. As Naomi Klein, in *No Logo* states: 'They saw no reason to give up now. The trial, which had been designed to stem the flow of negative publicity – and to gag and bankrupt Steel and Morris – had been an epic public relations disaster for McDonald's' (Klein 2000: 387).

Although McDonald's' won the case, as aspects in the pamphlet pertaining to food poisoning, cancer and world poverty were not proved, it did not collect the $61,300 that was awarded. By now the pamphlet had been distributed worldwide, with three million copies circulating in the UK alone. *The Guardian* (20 June 1997) reported: 'Not since Pyrrhus has a victor emerged so bedraggled. As PR fiascos go, this action takes the prize for ill-judged and disproportionate response to public criticism.'

The case also gave rise to the McSpotlight website, where the leaflet and trial transcript can be found, along with a debating room where other McDonald's 'horror stories' are exchanged. Klein reported in *No Logo* that by her publication date in 2000 there had already been 65 million visits to the site. This case was revisited in 2004 with an appeal by Morris and Steel to the European Court of Human Rights in Strasbourg claiming that they should have received help with legal costs. In February 2005 they won that appeal.

---

with its publics entitled 'Tell Shell'. This was quickly parodied into 'Tells Hell', which search engines would find for the unsuspecting internet surfer who would then learn negative things about Shell's activities, particularly in Nigeria (Thomas 2003). Companies are learning too late that when they register a site, they have to think of all the possible derivations of spelling possible and register those too at the same time – or someone else will! (See Mini case study 29.2.)

Online humour

One of the most useful tools in the campaign kit of the under-resourced organisation or group is humour (see Surfers Against Sewage, Case Study 29.1 (p. 571), for some excellent examples). Corporations often fail to deal with humorous attacks well and fall into the trap of appearing like bullies, which role is then quickly publicised around the world. For example, Nike created a clever online ordering service on which buyers could request a pair of personally customised trainers. It had been ignoring quite vocal protests about its use of low-paid workers in factories with poor employment conditions, known as 'sweatshop labour'. Nike defended its position stating that it was subcontractors whose employment conditions contravened basic human rights. When it declined Junah Perretti's order for a pair of trainers embroidered with the word 'sweatshop', its defensive and humourless response was quickly emailed around the world.

Laura Illia's winning EUPRERA Jos Willems Award entry in 2002 entitled 'Cyberactivism and public relations strategy: new dynamics and relationship rules' detailed a disturbing array of cheap to inflict but seriously damaging ways for groups or individuals to attack their targets. It also made some useful suggestions for public relations people faced with cyberactivists, observing that the internet had changed the dynamics of activism into a new form of pressure and that this had come about as the result of different pressures on corporations. Illia concluded that: 'Each communication medium had to be considered as a relationship medium instead of a communication medium' (Illia 2002).

The simplest of ideas

The simplest of ideas are often the best. For example, one of the largest single protest movements of the second half of the twentieth century was the Campaign for Nuclear Disarmament (CND). It started in the 1960s when the threat of nuclear war between the USA and Russia seemed real and imminent. The campaign was opposed to all nuclear weapons worldwide and endorsed all forms of non-violent protest. It gained publicity and attracted members by writing letters to newspapers and members of the UK Parliament, writing and distributing leaflets and organising petitions, debates and huge marches and demonstrations. Early marches took three days to walk from a nuclear base at Aldermaston to central London. Later, campaigners all over the UK carried briefcases (in the late 1960s this would have been far more noticeable than today) to remind people that the US president took one wherever he went, enabling him to launch a nuclear attack at any time.

Another simple idea was the Methodists' refusal to take sugar in hot drinks – this started as a protest against the slave trade and has been handed down, often unwittingly, through families ever since.

People, politics and globalisation

John and Thomson (2003) state in the first line of the introduction to their book entitled *New Activism and the Corporate Response*: 'Capitalism and corporations are under more pressure now than at any time since the Great Depression' (2003: 1).

Although politicians in all democracies complain that apathy is killing the political process (more people voted in reality TV shows than in the European

elections in many EU member states in 2004), they overlook the fact that large numbers of people are becoming politically active in other ways. (See also Chapter 5, in which voting turnout is discussed.)

Ethical shopping guides are published and sold in large numbers to inform people who only want to spend their money with companies that will not invest in production or other systems that hurt others or the environment. Naomi Klein's *No Logo* has become an international best seller and an influence on readers' buying habits that is doing real financial harm to major global corporations.

In Britain there are roughly a million members of all the political parties put together but the environmental organisations have about 5 million paid-up members. On 15 February 2003, more than 10 million people marched in cities around the world, with only a few days notice to organise their protest expressing their opposition to the war in Iraq. This action also contradicts the political voting apathy also discussed in Chapter 5.

The interesting thing for politicians is that, in the main, their power is limited to geographical boundaries whereas big corporations now act globally, as do campaigning organisations and pressure groups because this is where differences can be made.

So although globalisation integrates along one dimension (the economic or private), it fragments along another (the political or public) (Reinicke 1998) and that fragmentation is changing people's interaction with political systems.

Campaigning and pressure groups have gone global. When the *World Trade Organisation* or the *G8* meet now, whether in Seattle, Davos or Toronto, there will be a large, well-informed and very vocal body of protesters. They attract international publicity and often embarrass world leaders with their presentation of issues. These protesters have often come from once fragmented single-issue organisations concerning, for example, animal rights or child poverty to form a global alliance against corporate globalisation.

PICTURE 29.3 Although these campaigns have not yet dealt major final blows for companies, they have had big impacts and changed the direction of policy in a great many boardrooms (*source:* Nick Cobbing/Panos Pictures).

Definition: The *World Trade Organisation* (WTO) comprises 148 countries, and is the 'only global international organization dealing with the rules of trade between nations' (www.wto.org). The WTO, based in Geneva, Switzerland, administers trade agreements, acts as a forum for trade negotiations and handles international trade disputes.

Definition: The *G8* countries are Canada, France, Germany, Italy, Japan, Russia, the UK and the USA. Every year, the heads of state or government of these major industrial democracies meet to deal with major economic and political issues.

Have you ever been asked to sign an email petition to encourage the boycott of Esso or Mobil Oil because they funded President George W. Bush's election campaign, apparently to discourage his signing of the Kyoto protocol? If you signed it and sent it on to others you are an activist. In fact, if you have ever resisted buying a product or service on your own moral grounds you have become part of a pressure group.

At the end of this chapter there is a far from exhaustive list of websites informing and encouraging activism. Many of them will make you aware of things that you did not know before – will any of them make you active?

PricewaterhouseCoopers' 2002 Global Chief Executive Officers' survey (involving over 1100 CEOs drawn from 33 countries) showed that 33% thought that the anti-globalisation movement was a threat to them (www.pcw.com). This demonstrates that business leaders feel threatened by those who question their use of power and their ethics. So, returning to Grunig's situational theory of publics discussed earlier, anti-globalisation campaigners can be seen as active publics who: have formed around an issue that they recognise as a problem; are highly involved in the issue; and recognise few constraints in demonstrating about the problem. (See Think about 29.5.)

Building and evaluating consensus

So what can companies do to fend off threats to their future profitability? As we discussed earlier, the answer is effective public relations. Campaigning and pressure groups have become some of the most important publics with whom companies need to have open dialogues. If conducted effectively, this can lead to genuine working relationships, which will mean changes and compromises on both sides – just like all relationships! Consensus and co-orientation are two of the terms used in public relations that best describe what is needed.

Consensus-oriented public relations (COPR), as formulated by Burkart (1993) is a communication theory based on the theories of communicative action by Habermas (1984). It develops aspects of mutual understanding as described in Grunig and Hunt's 'two-way symmetrical model' (1984), where communication can flow equally back and forth between sender and receiver. (See Chapters 8 and 9 for fuller exploration of these theories.)

The co-orientation process seeks to establish understanding based on truth. The system was developed to deal with situations where there was a conflict between groups. In Burkart's study the conflict was between those who managed landfill and waste disposal and the population local to the proposed sites.

When considering the basis for communicative action theory Habermas presumes the acceptability of certain claims, namely:

- *intelligibility* – the message must be understandable
- *truth* – the message must be factual and accepted as being factual
- *trustworthiness* – the bearer of the message must be honest and accepted as being honest
- *rightness* or *legitimacy* – the messages must be acceptable on the basis of mutually recognised values.

As well as the claims, which must be accepted by both partners in the communication process, Habermas also refers to three dimensions (the *objective*, the *subjective* and the *social* dimensions) of reality to which both parties in a communication relate. As Burkart (1993) summarises, the aim of such a process of understanding is the agreement of both communication partners. Mutual understanding is reached when speaker and listener agree on the truth of assertions (which is the objective dimension of reality), on their truthfulness (the subjective dimension of reality) and on the rightness of their expressed interests (the social dimension of reality). Therefore consensus-oriented public relations, according to the conditions just described, requires that careful analysis be carried out to plan the communication with specific publics and the specific information to be communicated, as shown in Figure 29.1.

Understanding and agreement occur when all that is asserted within these dimensions is not doubted. However, most communication processes do not start and finish here: there is usually at least one area of disagreement and therefore a discourse becomes necessary in which all sides have the same chance to tell their point of view and their arguments. The task of consensus-oriented public relations is the creation of the conditions for such a discourse. In other words, all the involved persons must have the opportunity to doubt the truth of assertions, the truthfulness of expressions and the rightness of interests.

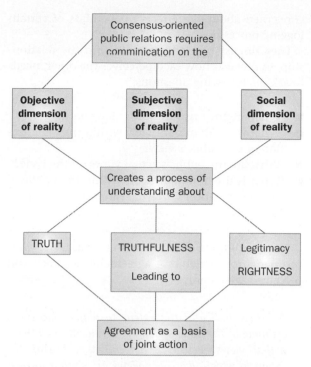

Consensus-oriented public relations requires comminication on the

Objective dimension of reality

Subjective dimension of reality

Social dimension of reality

Creates a process of understanding about

TRUTH

TRUTHFULNESS

Leading to

Legitimacy

RIGHTNESS

Agreement as a basis of joint action

FIGURE 29.1 Consensus-oriented public relations (*source:* adapted from Burkart 1993, Conflict communication – an important part of public relations. Paper presented at the CERP meeting, Strasbourg.)

There must be a predetermined willingness for compromise with the communicator being open to adapt according to the interests of the publics involved and thereby giving the publics some power

over the situation. This occurs in the third stage of the process of consensus-oriented public relations.

Burkart breaks the process down in stages to indicate the care that is needed as the goals are gradually reached. The first stage is based on information concerning which rational judgement can be formed. It does not require the active involvement of a public as it is a one-way process creating the basis for dialogue.

The aims of the second stage are to create dialogue with as great a part of the segment – or public– concerned as possible. The third stage can only work if the second is successful as it is there for discourse to deal with areas of disagreement. The fourth stage exists for an assessment to take place to consider the situation and decide whether further discourse is necessary (see Table 29.1).

Burkart shows how the COPR model is applied where a community plans to build a waste disposal site. In this case, a citizens' group may be formed with the aim of preventing the project going ahead. The local media are likely to support the group and create a conflict situation. Burkart advises that on the basis of the COPR model, public relations managers of the landfill company should consider the following:

- any assertion they make will be examined concerning its truth – e.g. whether figures about the quantity of waste to be deposited are correct
- the persons, companies and organisations involved will be confronted with distrust – e.g. representatives of companies might be taken as biased, or experts/consultants as incompetent or corrupt

TABLE 29.1 Communication process of consensus-oriented public relations (*source:* Burkart 1993, Conflict communication – an important part of public relations. Paper presented at the CERP meeting, Strasbourg.)

	Communication		
	Issues/facts	Organisation/institution persons	Legitimacy of interest
PR stages	Objective dimension of reality	Subjective dimension of reality	Social dimension of reality
Information	Determination/ definition of relevant facts and terms and explanation of consequences	Explanation of self-interest and intentions, announcement of publics for communication	Justification of interest by reasoning and arguments
Discussion	Relevant facts and terms	Cannot be discussed	Adequacy of arguments
Discourse	Agreement on the rules for evaluation of judgements on relevant facts	Cannot be subject of a discourse	Agreement on rules for the evaluation of judgements on legitimacy
Definition of situation	Agreement on judgements	Agreement on trustworthiness	Agreement on judgements

■ their intention for building the landfill will be doubted in principle – either because the basic strategy for waste disposal is questioned or because the choice of the site for landfill is seen as unjustified on the basis of developing tourism, for example.

If such doubts can be eliminated or prevented from the beginning, then the flow of communication will remain undisturbed (Burkart 2004: 463).

Several companies are going to these lengths to bring groups in to work with them towards consensus (Stafford et al. 2000 contains several examples). Some of the groups involved risk losing members for sitting down to discuss terms with their former enemies, so they too need to move into these new situations with great care and must not be seen to let up the pressure.

Care is also needed when either side in the process feels the need to celebrate some small victory or influence change in direction. Corporations' shareholders could become uncomfortable and pressure groups' members will also be watching closely but it is in the interest of all sides to keep moving towards consensus.

All work of professional standard needs mechanisms with which practitioners can evaluate progress and make informed changes to ongoing strategies. Consensus development is no exception to this, and a model has been devised in recognition of the need for public relations people who are practising two-way communication to be tracking both sides of the relationship around an issue at the same time.

Broom and Dozier's co-orientation model (1990) evaluates the progress in a relationship where there is a topic of mutual concern or interest (See Figure 29.2). One of their examples is the relationship between a paper products company and a conservation group concerned about the effects on habitats of certain logging processes.

They discuss how the research into the relationship, to discover how each perceives the other, needs to ask the following questions:

■ 'What are the organization's views on the issue?
■ 'What is the dominant view within the organization of the public's view?
■ 'What are the public's actual views on the issue?
■ 'What is the dominant view within the public of the organization's view?' (Broom and Dozier 1990: 37)

The aim of these questions is to calculate the three co-orientation variables – agreement, accuracy and perceived agreement.

Accuracy indicates the extent to which one side's estimate of the other's views is similar to the other's actual views. Perceived agreement represents the extent to which one side's views are similar to their estimate of the other's views. Unlike agreement and accuracy, however, perceived agreement does not describe the relationship between the organization and the public. Rather it describes how one side views the relationship and no doubt affects how it deals with the other side in the relationship. (Broom and Dozier 1990: 38).

If a consensus is to be reached there must be research to establish the distance that has to be travelled by both sides to make it happen. As Broom and Dozier go on to say: 'If two sides hold accurate views of each other's positions on an issue two types of relationships are possible. True consensus occurs when both the organization and the public actually agree and accurately perceive that agreement' (1990: 38). Clearly, the opposite case is also a possibility – where a disagreement is accurately perceived and this state is referred to as *dissensus*.

Greenwood (2003) states in an essay on trade associations and activism : 'Trust is the cement in the relationship between institutions and civil society. When trust breaks down, civil society either withdraws from participation or expresses protest outside the mainstream channels of participation' (2003: 49).

It is the role of the public relations practitioner, on whatever side of a debate, to build and maintain that trust by being open, transparent and fully accountable to publics, not only in words but also in actions. It is essential to build common ground at every stage of a relationship that might be going to work.

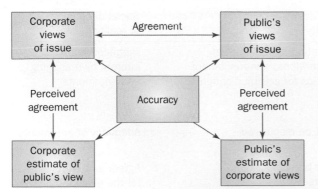

FIGURE 29.2 Co-orientational model of relationships (*source*: Broom, Glen M. *Using Research in Public Relations: Applications to program Management, 1st Edition*, (c) 1990. Adapted by Permission of Pearson Education, Inc, Upper Saddle River, NJ)

Practical guidelines for campaigning public relations

To summarise the key points arising from this chapter for would-be public relations practitioners in campaigning organisations or pressure groups, here is a quick checklist:

1 Agree and state your purpose clearly and simply (vision or mission statement).
2 Establish measurable objectives to give the campaign achievable milestones.
3 Develop your legitimacy – attract third-party endorsement from opinion formers, celebrities, academics, MPs and journalists – and provide them with useful materials like fact sheets.
4 Create a calendar of newsworthy events, meetings, reports and stunts (but remember not to conflict with your stated purpose!).
5 Try to employ humour and always stay within the law (maybe only just sometimes but always definitely on the right side of the line!).
6 Avoid technical jargon and be very clear, with human/animal/environmental examples to show the need for the changes you are seeking.

7 Make sure that those who might join you or follow you know why they should, how they can and what they can do to help.
8 Make good use of technology – set up a website and use email.
9 Provide as many opportunities for your key publics to meet your people, discuss your issues, hear your message and become active – from the stand at the village fête to the international demonstration.
10 When the budgets allow, create a range of merchandise – T-shirts, badges, caps, pens, etc. – people will want to show that they identify with you and these things can be a great source of income.
11 Service your members well with newsletters, online discussion boards, parties, etc.
12 Make them feel welcome and involved.

activity 29.4

Surfers Against Sewage

From the history of Surfers Against Sewage in Case study 29.1, identify the elements of good campaigning practice that helped it towards success.

case study 29.1

Surfers Against Sewage

In December 1989 a wave of national disquiet followed the privatisation of the water companies, arising from a belief that these new companies would prioritise profits over environmental concerns. The issue that gave impetus to the campaign was known as 'the panty liner effect' – surfers making duck-dives were emerging on the other side of a wave with a panty liner stuck to their head: the beaches were strewn with panty liners, condoms, human excrement and sometimes even hypodermic needles.

Early in 1990, 10 surfers met at Martin Mynne's house to discuss the pollution on the beaches and in the sea, and decided to call a public meeting (four people put £10 on the table and it was decided to charge £2 membership).

A press release was produced, which was reviewed in the local media. The public meeting that followed overflowed with 200 people in attendance.

The vision of the new group, Surfers Against Sewage (SAS), was clear and they resolved to campaign on the following demands:

■ all sewage to be treated before discharge
■ complete cessation of toxic discharge

■ sewage and water content to be regarded as a resource rather than as waste
■ ensure that the newly privatised water companies' money would be well spent.

The vision united a wide range of beach users, from the cliff walker who witnessed a seal pup surface through a sewage slick, through to the parents who feared for their children's safety on the beach and swimmers who were getting ill.

During the summer of 1990 a campaign of voluntary work to clean beaches was well publicised. The first SAS chairman, Andrew Kingsley-Tubbs, introduced some military tactics to get the attention of the authorities and the gasmask was adopted as a symbol. A national newspaper, the *Daily Mirror*, featured surfers wearing gasmasks, and *Sky News* also ran the story.

SAS researched alternative sewage discharge methods and bought shares in South West Water to secure a voice at the company's annual general meeting (AGM). In September it went to South West Water AGM in wetsuits and gasmasks. Mike Hendy, the SAS shareholder, held the floor for 20 minutes resulting in

▶

case study 29.1 (continued)

full national news media coverage. Channel4 made a documentary on the issue entitled *Our Backyard*.

In addition, surfing magazines gave free advertising space, and by the end of the first summer SAS had £10,000 in the bank. SAS members Chris Hines and Gareth Kent were paid for six weeks to run the campaign office. Six weeks eventually became 10 years and the telephones were always answered.

In the summer of 1991 SAS members decided to take their cause to the heart of government, and appeared at the House of Commons in wetsuits, gasmasks and a large inflatable turd (excrement), which generated a lot of national news coverage.

Chris Hines began to build up a national profile through roadshows. Facts and figures were produced clearly and kept up to date – for example, it was discovered that Jersey, in the Channel Islands, used ultraviolet sewage treatment and that its pollution count was 50 times lower than on most UK beaches.

Academics came forward to offer research and further legitimise the campaign. SAS recognised that it had a high level of responsibility as 10,000 people paid their fees and invested their money in the campaign. However, all the claims made by SAS were reasonable and achievable.

SAS as a brand became increasingly successful through its appeal to young surfers and its use of British toilet humour.

SAS engaged with the political system – at a House of Lords select committee, Chris Hines announced that he would feel 50 times safer putting his head in Jersey's outfall pipe than bathing on many of the UK's beaches. One month later, at the invitation of the island, he did just that, generating further national news media coverage.

In 1991, while maintaining grassroots involvement with surfers, windsurfers were also invited to join SAS resulting in a 400% increase in members. Co-operative Bank's Customers Who Care campaign brought in £20,000 overnight, which was invested in campaigns almost as quickly – members still liked to see demonstrations, and the use of the internet was established to save paper and postage costs.

Evidence that SAS was now becoming 'accepted' by the establishment was demonstrated when Glyn Ford, MEP, invited wetsuited surfers to meet the President of the European Parliament. Further evidence came in 1994, when Welsh Water came 'on side' following a customer consultation. Despite marginally higher costs, Welsh Water launched a policy of full treatment for all coastal discharges. This gave the Welsh a way to stand out and SAS opened the new sewage works.

Merchandise started to become a major earner for SAS, which by now was developing a cult following with its 'must-have' clothing range, badges and car stickers.

SAS, however, resisted the danger of becoming too linked to the establishment, while being careful to maintain negotiations with all parties and understand the pressures on all sides. For example, it took advantage of the five-yearly periodic review of environmental spend that had been introduced by the UK Parliament.

By 1994 SAS messages stopped being a threat and for many they became an opportunity – Wessex Water was next to adopt the full treatment policy. However, members complained that SAS was not visible enough on the beaches and spent too much time in boardrooms. Some members only understood one way of campaigning and had to be given projects to keep them interested.

Campaigners researched and took advantage of events, such as anniversaries of laws passed to improve sewage treatment, which provided them with hooks for the news media. Always light on their feet, SAS campaigners travelled to Brussels from Cornwall (in south-west England) to take advantage of a speaking opportunity to influence the bathing water directive, alongside partners in the European Water Alliance.

SAS also advised the Labour MP Michael Meacher while he was opposition environment spokesman. Once Labour came to power in 1997, Chris Hines was invited to become a special advisor and sewage treatment went further up the political agenda. Seats in parliament were won on the basis of the campaign messages. Pressure was kept up, resulting in levies against all utilities (including the water companies) to pay for environmental clean-ups.

SAS had learned to plan over a long period to put the right pressure on at the right time. By 1999 it had won agreement that all sewage discharges should have at least secondary treatment and a large percentage would have tertiary treatment.

By now there was pressure from European groups to widen the campaign internationally. However, a members' survey in 2000 showed that they wanted to keep the campaign for the UK but take in wider environmental issues.

SAS runs on a £20,000 annual budget but has a £400,000 turnover, nearly all of which is invested in the campaign.

Key points from the campaign to date include:

- avoiding the temptation to take sponsorship from companies whose ethics conflicted with its own, for example, it took part in an education tour with Quiksilver, the leisure goods company
- keeping to a strong image, supplying a regular diet of good imagery for the news media – always being ready with tight soundbites

▶

case study 29.1 (continued)

- being very disciplined; never breaking the law; keeping it humorous whenever possible and becoming skilled opportunists
- working with scientists
- ensuring representation in each TV region
- maintaining a three-strong campaigns team at headquarters to keep up the pressure.

SAS is now led by Richard Hardy, who has an animal welfare and environmental campaigning background. He too is driven by conscience.

The Independent on Sunday newspaper called SAS 'Britain's coolest pressure group' (23 July 1995); the BBC described its members as 'some of the government's most sophisticated environmental critics'.

The UK population still wastes drinking water by flushing toilets with it, there is still a massive pollution problem in rivers and at sea and too many people are still not listening. There is plenty still to be done by campaigners like SAS.

Source: www.sas.org.uk;
www.edenproject.com;
interview with Chris Hines
(www.chines@edenproject.com) and Richard Hardy

Summary

In this chapter we have discussed the motivations of campaigning organisations and how they form and grow. We have argued that in today's global media environment, campaigning organisations have many advantages over big business and that the internet facilitates debate on issues, helps to recruit members and provides the means for disrupting business. Furthermore, we have argued that campaigning groups may help to reinvigorate political debate, albeit on single issues. We have critically analysed the public relations roles on all sides and the use of two-way communication and consensus in achieving mutual goals. We concluded by presenting key principles of campaigning and demonstrating successful campaigning through a case study.

The author would like to thank Rachael Clayton for her work in tracking down material for this chapter.

Bibliography

Broom, G.M and D.M Dozier (1990). *Using Research in Public Relations: Applications to program management.* Upper Saddle River, NJ: Prentice Hall.

Burkart, R. (1993). Conflict communication – an important part of public relations. Paper presented at the CERP meeting, Strasbourg, France.

Burkart, R. (2004). 'Consensus-orientated public relations (COPR)' in *Public Relations and Communication Management in Europe.* B. van Ruler and D. Verčič (eds). Berlin: Walter de Gruyter.

Charity Commission (2005). www.charity-commission. gov.uk, accessed 5 May 2005.

Cutlip, S.M, A.H. Center and G.M. Broom (eds) (2000). *Effective Public Relations,* 8th edition. Upper Saddle River, NJ: Prentice Hall.

Greenwood, J. (2003). 'Trade associations, change and the new activism' in *New Activism and the Corporate Response.* S. John and S. Thomson (eds). Basingstoke: Palgrave Macmillan.

Grunig, J.E (ed.). (1992). *Excellence in Public Relations and Communication Management.* Mahwah, NJ: Lawrence Erlbaum Associates, Inc.

Grunig, J.E and T. Hunt (1984). *Managing Public Relations.* New York and London: Holt, Rinehart & Winston Inc.

Grunig, J.E. and Repper, F.C. (1992). 'Strategic management, publics and issues' in *Excellence in Public Relations and Communication Management.* J.E. Grunig (ed.). Mahwah, NJ: Lawrence Erlbawm Associates, Inc.

Habermas, J. (1984). *Theory of Communicative Action: Reason and the rationalization of society.* London: Heinemann.

Heath, R.L. (1997). *Strategic Issues Management: Organizations and public policy challenges.* Thousand Oaks, CA: Sage.

Heath, R.L (ed.) (2001). *Handbook of Public Relations.* Thousand Oaks, CA: Sage.

Hobsbawm, E. (1987). *The Age of Empire 1875–1914.* London: Weidenfeld & Nicolson.

Illia, L. (2002). 'Cyberactivism and public relations strategy: new dynamics and relationship rules'. www.cuprera.org

John, S. and S. Thomson (eds) (2003). *New Activism and the Corporate Response.* Basingstoke: Palgrave Macmillan.

Klein, N. (2000). *No Logo.* London: Flamingo.

Monbiot, G. (2003). 'The corporate takeover' in *New Activism and the Corporate Response.* S. John and S. Thomson (eds). Basingstoke: Palgrave Macmillan.

Mullins, L.J. (1999). *Management and Organisational Behaviour*, 5th edition. Hemel Hempstead: Pearson Education.

Raymond, D. (2003). 'Activism – beyond the banners' in *New Activism and the Corporate Response*. S. John and S. Thomson (eds). Basingstoke: Palgrave Macmillan.

Reinicke, W. (1998). *Global Public Policy: Governing without government?* Washington, DC: Brookings Institution Press.

Smith, M.F. (1996). Public relations as a locus for workplace democracy. Paper presented at the meeting of the National Communication Association, San Diego.

Smith, M.F. and D. Ferguson (2001). 'Activism' in *Handbook of Public Relations*. R.L. Heath (ed.). Thousand Oaks, CA: Sage.

Stafford, E., M. Polonsky and C. Hartman (2000). 'Environmental NGO-business collaboration and strategic bridge building: A case analysis of the Greenpeace-Foron Alliance. *Business Strategy and the Environment* (9): 122–135.

Thomas, C. (2003). 'Cyberactivism and corporations: new strategies for new media' in *New Activism and the Corporate Response*. S. John and S. Thomson (eds). Basingstoke: Palgrave Macmillan.

Wilson, D. and A. Leighton (1993). *Campaigning: The A-Z of public advocacy*. XX: London: Hawkesmere.

Websites

Journal of the mental environment – started Reclaim the Streets and Buy Nothing Day: www.adbusters.org

AlterNet: www.alternet.org

e-fluentials: www.efluentials.com

FOX News: www.foxnews.com

Get Ethical – consumer magazine created by *The Big Issue* and *Red Pepper*: www.getethical.com

Ilisu Dam Campaign: www.ilisu.org.uk

Independent Media Center (IMC): www.indymedia.org

McSpotlight: www.mcspotlight.org

PricewaterhouseCoopers – including the CEO Global Survey on risk: www.pcw.com

Teaching Values.com: www.teaching-values.com/goldenrule.html

The Yes Men: www.theyesmen.org

Transnational Institute: www.tni.org/george/articles/dissent.html

Parody sites

Murder King – PETA campaign against Burger King www.muderking.com

Tells Hell: www.tellshell.com

Campaign sites

Baby Milk Action: www.babymilkaction.org

Amsterdam-based NGO that monitors European multinationals: www.ceo.org

www.corpwatch.org.us

Bangkok-based researchers monitoring uneven development: www.focusontheglobalsouth.org

USA-based research and activist centre: www.globalexchange.org

Greenpeace: www.greenpeace.org.uk

Pressure group working to change US foreign and domestic policy for sustainability: www.ips-dc.org

OXFAM: www.oxfam.org

Against unsustainability – big study on Enron: www.seen.org

The Petition Site: www.thepetitionsite.com

World social forum

World Social Forum: www.forumsocialmundial.org.br

Global Policy Forum – information on the repression of trade unions around the world: www.globalpolicy.org/socecon/inequal/labor/1010union. htm

CHAPTER 30
Public sector communication

Learning outcomes

By the end of this chapter you should be able to:

- evaluate theories relevant to public communication
- recognise the specific characteristics of relationships between non-profit organisations and their publics
- compare and evaluate public communication practice across three non-profit sectors
- identify the key elements for planning public communication.

Structure

- Theories of public communication
- Central government communication
- Local government communication
- Health sector communication
- A communication planning framework

Introduction

Practise safe sex, wear a seatbelt, recycle waste, eat more fruit and vegetables, reduce the salt in your diet. And while you're about it, don't drink and drive, don't smoke in public places and don't forget to use your vote. Communication arising from the public sector has a very different set of driving forces from those of commercial enterprises where profit is ultimately the key concern.

Public sector communication is situated within the democratic context (see Chapter 5) and as such is driven by the need for transparency in how an organisation carries out its public duties, accountability to the public on how money from taxes is spent and, increasingly, as we shall see from the case studies in this chapter, public consultation and involvement in the services provided.

This chapter examines three specific areas of the public sector: central government, local government and the health sector. While, on the one hand, it identifies the special contexts of organisations within these sectors, on the other, it presents evidence that public communication practice is not so very different from public relations practice found in commercial enterprises and elsewhere.

To provide an understanding of public communication and public communication campaigns, we start by identifying theories drawn from North American and European literature. We then focus on three specific areas of public communication, with the main focus on the UK experience. In concentrating on three areas we recognise that we cannot do justice to a specific sector in one short chapter. However, what this chapter aims to do is present an idea of the scope of public communication for the student to take forward for further investigation.

Theories of public communication

Public sector communication in context

The term 'public' is generally used to denote affairs that affect everyone (Raupp 2004). Within a national democracy, central government departments (or ministries), local authorities, hospitals and other public sector organisations are legally and morally obliged to inform the population and the media about policy decisions and issues affecting everyone in society. However, it is not just national institutions that have a duty to keep the public informed. Supranational organisations such as the European Union are also included here.

Societies everywhere are faced with social problems that elected politicians and their officials are tasked with solving. In 2005, the re-elected Blair government in the UK announced that disrespect for others was becoming a widespread problem in society. The government promised that it would take action to encourage young people in particular to have a greater respect for their fellow citizens. Public policies formulated to tackle a wide range of social problems – from antisocial behaviour through to teenage pregnancies, binge drinking, car crime, drug abuse and the high number of fatalities in road accidents – can only be translated into action through effective communication. These policies take shape in the form of public communication campaigns (see later).

Public sector organisations also communicate with many stakeholders to demonstrate how the public's money is spent. Therefore, in market-driven economies such as the UK, the 'bottom line' for some public sector organisations such as hospitals is *accountability*: showing that public money is being spent wisely and responsibly in providing services. Communication is thus a key element in showing how an organisation is accountable to the public as citizens, voters, residents, patients or consumers. Within the context of public sector accountability, the news media play a crucial role. The news media may be regarded as friendly allies, critical opponents or neutral observers, depending on a wide range of factors concerning the nature of the news media and the nature of the public sector organisation itself. Any abuse of public money will make a newsworthy story, so it is in the interests of a public sector organisation to ensure that the issues it campaigns on are perceived as worthwhile. If the ethics of the organisation itself become the main story (for example, corruption on any scale will make headlines), then the policies it is trying to implement will receive much less public attention.

In the UK, the introduction of the Freedom of Information Act 2005 compels public sector organisations to be further accountable to their publics. Access to official information is a right of all UK citizens, which means that public sector communication professionals need to be aware of disclosure rules concerning the types of information held by their organisations.

The context of public sector communication is also political. While it is sometimes difficult, from the public's point of view, to perceive a clear distinction between *political* communication and *policy* communication (for example, in the case of campaigns to increase voter turnout) it is important to bear in mind that in theory, at least, there is a distinction between the two. Political communication arises from political parties with the objective of putting across the party's views on a range of issues to the electorate; policy communication arises from the policies decided by elected politicians, with the support of officials who advise on policy implementation.

Public communication campaigns

Public sector organisations' responsibilities to inform the public are often translated in the communication campaigns. 'Public information campaigns' and 'public communication campaigns' are terms that are often used interchangeably, but in the literature there is a distinction between the two. Public information campaigns are typified as one-way communication (sender to receiver) while public communication campaigns are seen as interactive (sender–receiver–sender). In practice, however, campaigns are usually a combination of both strategies and are characterised by an attempt to persuade citizens to think about or do something for their own well-being or the public good. *Public communication campaigns* can be summed up as: 'Purposive attempts to inform, persuade, or motivate behavior changes in a relatively well-defined and large audience, generally for noncommercial benefits to the individual and/or society, typically within a given time period, by means of organized communication activities involving mass media and often complemented by interpersonal support' (Rice and Atkin 1989: 7).

Dozier et al. (2001) argue that public communication campaigns fit in with the two-way asymmetric model of communication where a change in knowledge, attitudes and behaviours of target populations – or persuasion – is the organisation's intention. However, as we shall see later in this chapter, there is evidence that public sector communication is moving in the direction of public involvement and perhaps a more symmetric style of communication.

Rice and Atkin refer to the mass media in their definition of public communication campaigns. Table 30.1

TABLE 30.1   Two types of media campaign in public communication (*Source:* Coffman 2002, www.gse.harvard.edu/hfrp/pubs/onlinepubs/pcce)

Campaign type/goal	Individual behaviour change	Public will
Objectives	<ul><li>Influence beliefs and knowledge about a behaviour and its consequences</li><li>Affect attitudes in support of behaviour and persuade</li><li>Affect perceived social norms about acceptability of a behaviour among peers</li><li>Affect intentions to perform the behaviour</li><li>Produce behaviour change (if accompanied by supportive programme components)</li></ul>	<ul><li>Increase visibility of an issue and its importance</li><li>Affect perceptions of social issues and who is seen as responsible</li><li>Increase knowledge about solutions based on who is seen as responsible</li><li>Affect criteria used to judge policies and policy makers</li><li>Help determine what is possible for service introduction and public funding</li><li>Engage and mobilise constituencies to action</li></ul>
Target audience	Segments of the population whose behaviour needs to change	Segments of the general public to be mobilised and policy makers
Strategies	Social marketing	Media advocacy, community organising and mobilisation
Media vehicles	Public service/affairs programming: print, television, radio, electronic advertising	News media: print, television, radio, electronic advertising
Examples	Anti-smoking, condom usage, drink driving, seatbelt usage, parenting	Support for quality childcare, after-school programming, healthcare policy

highlights this use of media, identifying two types of public communication campaign.

From Table 30.1, it can be seen that *individual behaviour change programmes* include public information or public education campaigns that 'strive to change in individuals the behaviors that lead to social problems or the behaviors that will improve individual or social well-being' (Coffman 2002: 6). Many well-known campaigns are concerned with public health (e.g. anti-smoking) and are instigated by government ministries or departments which deal with health issues. However, campaigns arise from other policy areas such as education (e.g. teacher recruitment), social affairs (e.g. foster care recruitment), law and order (e.g. anti-theft) environment (e.g. recycling of waste) and transport (e.g. anti-speeding). As can be seen from Table 30.1, these campaigns use social marketing strategies (explained later in this chapter) and often paid-for media such as advertising.

Public will campaigns, according to Table 30.1, are about bringing social issues to the public's attention to influence awareness or knowledge. This is mostly done through the news media, using media advocacy and community mobilisation strategies. Public relations, in the form of media relations, plays an important role here. An example is the Holocaust Memorial Day, organised annually by the UK's Home Office to

educate the population about the Holocaust and promote messages of social inclusion. In 2005, 12 senior journalists were taken to Auschwitz–Birkenau in Poland to see the place where millions of Jews met their deaths during the Second World War. Survivors who were willing to tell their stories were contacted and matched to relevant media outlets. Following widespread media coverage leading up to the Holocaust Memorial Day, it was estimated that 1.5 million people watched the memorial service on national television (*PR Week* 25 March 2005: 32). (See Activity 30.1.)

activity 30.1

Two types of campaign

Can you list further examples of the two types of campaign given in Table 30.1?

Feedback

You will probably find it easy to name the high-profile advertising campaigns that are specifically aimed at changing people's behaviour. However, by keeping a close eye on the national and local news, you will soon learn to 'spot' awareness-raising campaigns that public sector organisations carefully plan to achieve maximum impact around calendar events – e.g. news items about drink-driving fatalities around Christmas and the New Year.

Objectives

As described earlier, public communication campaigns attempt to achieve changes in an individual's attitudes and knowledge (known as *cognitive* change) feelings (known as *affective* change) and behaviour about social issues. Table 30.2 shows campaign objectives drawn from the examples and case studies in this chapter and the types of cognitive, affective or behavioural changes they are attempting to achieve.

Communication process

As we have seen in earlier chapters (especially Chapter 8, which examined communication theory), the communication process is mostly conceived around the SMCR model: sender, message, channel, receiver. It is these variables, with the addition of 'effects' or receiver impact, that form the basis of public communication campaigns. We will use a similar framework to discuss campaigns in this chapter.

While the SMCR model is a useful framework to discuss the elements of a campaign, a criticism is that it is one-way and linear: it does not acknowledge the involving, two-way nature of effective public communication where the citizen or consumer has to first engage with the message in order for change to be brought about. However, it is also important to acknowledge that public sector campaigns are initiated by organisations that have the political will, knowledge, resources and technologies to make them happen, so while a two-way symmetric style might be adopted, it is in the interests of the organisation to achieve the 'public good' campaign targets that are set.

Source or sender

Public communication, particularly that of national governments and supranational governments such as the European Union, fits the asymmetric model of communication where a change in knowledge, attitudes or behaviour is intended – for example, where the 'sender' of the message is engaged in motivating populations to drink less alcohol, eat less fat, exercise more regularly, give up smoking or support the introduction of the euro (European currency).

Town or regional councils initiate campaigns locally to improve voter turnout at local elections, to increase the number of young people voting, to encourage people not to drop litter and to get people to recycle their

TABLE 30.2   Public communication campaign objectives

Campaign topic	Objective(s)	Type of cognitive, affective and/or behavioural change intended
Holocaust Memorial Day	**1** Educate general public about the Holocaust	Increase knowledge about a significant place and associated events during the Second World War
	2 Promote social inclusion	Encourage positive attitudes towards people in society who are different
Banning smoking in public places	**1** Raise residents' awareness about proposals to create a 'smoke-free' city	Increase knowledge about proposed policy change
	2 Gauge residents' views about proposed ban on smoking in public places	Test public opinion and attitudes about effects of policy change
	3 Inform and educate people about the dangers of smoking	Increase knowledge and encourage public disapproval of smoking
	4 Provide advice and support on giving up smoking	Behavioural change – encourage smokers to stop smoking
'Name that Tag' (environmental crime – graffiti)	**1** Get people to report the names of 'taggers' who leave their 'tags' or graffiti signatures in public places	Behavioural change – discourage graffiti artists from leaving their 'tags'

waste. These are not campaigns promoting a particular political party's views but they are all persuasive campaigns with the intention of achieving a behavioural change for the good of democracy and the community.

Sometimes it can be confusing as to who is actually the 'sender' of the message: is it the initiator (e.g. the organisation's policy department), the sender (e.g. the communication professional working on behalf of the organisation) or the communicator (e.g. the journalist working for the local newspaper)?

Multiple senders

Public bodies increasingly work in close partnership with other public bodies, or with private enterprises to help solve particular social issues and to transfer both the cost and risk from the public to the private sector (Leitch and Motion 2003).

A recent example of public partnerships is the TOGETHER campaign to tackle antisocial behaviour, organised by the UK's Home Office. This campaign works on two levels, national and local, and relies on a range of local agencies, for example, the police, the courts and councils, to deal with nuisance neighbours, begging and environmental crime (e.g. graffiti). A key part of this campaign is to get people to report crime and name the wrongdoers. To catch the graffiti artists, a poster campaign called 'Name that Tag' was created to encourage people to phone a number to report the 'taggers' from their publicised signatures, and be rewarded with £500 (Home Office 2004). (See Think about 30.1.)

Several channels

To reach a heterogeneous (dissimilar) public, multiple channels need to be considered in a public communication campaign. Publics should be segmented (broken down into definable groups) in order to determine channel usage. The campaign may need to address different levels of media use and information seeking within the community. One segment of relatively isolated elderly people may only listen to their local radio station for information, while a segment of young mothers may not use the local media at all, but prefer to talk to their neighbours, family or friends to find out what is going on. Segmenting publics in a sophisticated manner, however, usually requires substantial data to discover specific media and information-seeking habits. Research, therefore, plays an important role here.

A wide range of media channels are available for public communication campaigns, but mass media advertising is most commonly used in large-scale, national campaigns. While advertising is an expensive medium, it does reach a wide spectrum of society in raising awareness of an issue. So, for example, to inform millions of people on low incomes about a new state benefit, the UK government often uses television advertising as a key channel, but this will be supplemented by a wide range of other channels (such as talk shows on local radio, leaflets and interpersonal communication through advisors) that provide more detail about the benefit, and to encourage take-up. This is because television advertising cannot successfully disseminate large numbers of facts. As Windahl et al. point out: 'All media have their strengths and limitations' (1992: 108).

Many messages

A single campaign will have many messages simply because it needs to reach different sections of the community and because messages are attended to and perceived in different ways by different people. The two-step flow of information theory (Katz and Lazarsfeld 1955) recognises the influence of reference groups on message reception. In other words, while the target receiver may not attend to a given message, their immediate family and friends might do. For example, a very elderly person may ignore all mass media and written attempts by a government organisation to get them to claim special allowances, but a campaign aimed at the families or carers of elderly people is more likely to be effective in getting the message across. This is because, in the eyes of the elderly person, governments are often associated with taxation, rather than giving money, so a direct

---

think about 30.1   **Senders – 'Name that Tag' poster campaign**

As a local campaign, who is the initiator, the sender and the communicator?

Feedback   In this case, the initiator is the Home Office, the sender could be the local police (who deal with crime), and the communicator could be the communication professional who creates the poster on behalf of the police. In a national campaign, however, both the initiator and the sender would be the Home Office, and the communication professional could be an agency working on behalf of the Home Office to create a poster.

PICTURE 30.1   To catch graffiti artists, a poster campaign called 'Name that Tag' was created by the UK's Home Office to encourage people to phone a number to report 'taggers' from their publicised signatures, and be rewarded with £500 (*source:* Anti-Social Behaviour Unit, The Home Office).

message could arouse suspicion, whereas a family member or carer would be able to explain to the elderly person that they are missing out on a sum of money to which they are entitled.

The strength and tone of the message also has to be considered. Health messages have to tread a fine line between arousing too high a level of anxiety among the 'worried well' and encouraging message avoidance among high-risk groups (e.g. early HIV/AIDs campaigns). Similarly, campaigns that unintentionally glamourise risk taking (e.g. through 'cool' imagery of young people smoking) or are too patronising (e.g. 'just say "no"' in regard to drug use) will produce negative effects.

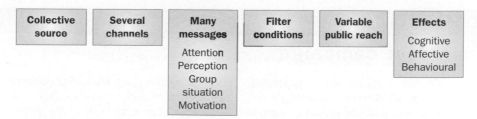

FIGURE 30.1   A model of communication influence process (*source:* McQuail 1987 cited in Windahl *et al* 1992:104)

Receivers

As we have already discussed, messages are received differently by different receivers. McQuail (1987) identifies four filters or selection processes that determine how an individual receives a message: attention, perception, group situation and motivation. These filters will be either favourable or unfavourable towards the intended effect of the message. The first filter is attention and this refers to whether a message 'grabs' or reaches the receiver in the first place. The second filter is perception and this refers to how the message is perceived by the individual – as we have already suggested, both the message content and tone could make a difference here. The third filter is the group situation and whether peers are likely to reinforce the message or discourage its acceptance by the individual. The fourth filter is motivation: is the individual ultimately motivated to think, feel or do something about the message?

Effects

'Effects' refer to intended cognitive, affective and behavioural outcomes that are agreed at the beginning of the campaign. These outcomes are expressed as objectives in a campaign plan (see the earlier section on objectives). Effects are also equated with campaign effectiveness or success. So, for example, if the objective is to encourage students to stop smoking, this will be measured behaviourally in terms of the numbers who give up smoking during the course of the campaign. If there has been a reduction in smoking, this is known as an 'intended campaign effect' and the campaign will be deemed effective. However, some campaigns have backfired, producing negative, *unintended* effects. Some anti-drug campaigns, for example, are thought to have stimulated drug use among high-risk drug users (Makkai et al. 1991) and widened the gap between authority and youth supporting a pro-drug culture (Cragg 1994). (See also Chapter 11 for a further discussion of evaluating campaigns.)

Windahl et al. present McQuail's communication influence process model, which helps us to see some of the breadth and complexity of a public communication campaign in Figure 30.1.

This model recognises that a given campaign will potentially have many sources or senders ('collective source'), multiple channels and messages and different success rates with different publics. (See Think about 30.2.)

Read Mini case study 30.1 and Think about 30.3, which considers the communication influence model.

Communication models: a rethink

The communication roles involving some public institutions are becoming more diffuse, challenging the

Vote and post campaign

Crawley Borough Council in the UK wanted to improve voter turnout in the June 2004 council elections to combat a downward trend: less than one person in four had voted in the May 2003 council elections. Work on a campaign began in July 2003 with the theme of 'vote and post' to encourage postal voting. Postal voting gives people the choice of voting by post instead of visiting a polling station. The campaign objectives were: to raise awareness of the need to be on the electoral register; to encourage people to opt in to the postal vote scheme; and to encourage people to use their postal votes. Printed information was targeted at all 73,000 people on the electoral register in Crawley, and at council staff. A wide range of communication channels were used to promote the 'vote and post – make a difference' message, including media relations, direct mail, advertising and new media. Extensive use was made of established communication channels such as council tax mailings and electoral registration distribution. Campaign materi-

als were timed to reach the widest audience in the town during three phases between August 2003 and June 2004. One creative element of the campaign included the use of impactful colour photographic portraits of council staff who had volunteered. This element in itself provided a vehicle to raise awareness about the election process within the council as well as encouraging staff who lived in the town to use their votes. The campaign achieved a 600% increase in postal vote registrations and 70% who applied for a postal vote used it in the June election. The overall turnout in Crawley was 34%, an 11% increase from May 2003. Media coverage in support of postal voting was sustained throughout the different phases of the campaign.

Source: adapted from Excellence in Communication Awards 2004, CIPR Local Government Group (best campaign category)

whole notion of 'senders' and 'receivers' in the conventional SMCR transmission model of communication. An interactive approach, which considers the public sphere, is based on mutuality – both sender and receiver 'contribute their views to a shared universe of knowledge and interpretations' (Voltmer and Römmele 2002: 17). An example of a more involving approach to public communication is found in Case study 30.1 (Addenbrooke's) at the end of this chapter.

Agenda-setting theory

When talking about the use of media advocacy as a strategy for drawing public attention to a social issue, this process is sometimes referred to as influencing the media agenda, or 'agenda setting'. Agenda setting refers to the theory (McCombs and Shaw 1973) that the news media highlight the importance of an issue by encouraging people to think and talk about it.

Thus, social issues are brought to the attention of the news media by 'political elites' – government policy makers, as well as pressure groups, with the intention of testing public opinion on an idea or creating the right climate of public opinion for behaviour change. A good example of this is anti-smoking campaigns. While high-profile advertising campaigns continue to persuade smokers to give up smoking, the news media are often employed to generate public discussion around, and support for, smoke-free environments. Eventually, the social pressures are such that smokers are prohibited from smoking in public areas and are forced to rethink their behaviours out of consideration for others (see Mini case study 30.3 (p. 591) on this specific issue to find out how this was done).

Social marketing theory

In order to further contextualise public communication, and to shed light on some of the integrated

1 Who is the source/sender in Mini case study 30.1?
2 What are the channels? Can you explain the choice of channels selected?
3 What are the messages?
4 Who are the target audiences?
5 How are the 'four filters' identified earlier likely to affect the success of this campaign?
6 How was campaign success determined/measured? What effects were intended – cognitive, affective, behavioural?
7 Now reflect – what are the strengths and weaknesses of this model?

communication campaigns described later in this chapter, it is important that we explore the concept of social marketing. This draws on existing ideas in marketing but applied to non-commercial transactions. Kotler (1982: 490) described social marketing as follows:

> Use of marketing principles and techniques to advance a social cause, idea or behavior. More specifically: social marketing is the design, implementation, and control of programs seeking to increase the acceptability of a social idea or cause in target group(s). It utilizes concepts of market segmentation, consumer research, concept development, communication, facililitation, incentives and exchange theory to maximize target group response.

Social marketing does not assume that commercial marketing principles are unquestioningly applied to non-commercial communication planning. If we take the famous four 'Ps' of marketing – product, price, place and promotion (McCarthy 1975) – we can reinterpret these labels to fit the social context. 'Product' can be an idea, an issue, a service or a practice/behaviour, such as wearing a condom. 'Price' is what the customer pays for; in the case of condom wearing, it is prevention against disease. 'Place' refers to the channel through which the product becomes available. Obtaining condoms used to mean an embarrassing visit to the local pharmacy, which is why condoms were made available to both men and women through vending machines in public toilets. 'Promotion' involves persuading the target group to buy something or adopt a behaviour through creating awareness of the product. In the case of condom wearing, promotion will take place through many different mass media and interpersonal communication channels to reach the target public. Solomon (1989) added a fifth 'P' – 'positioning', which links to how a target public perceives a product or idea in relation to other products or ideas. This relates to the message and whether it is in tune with receivers' self-perception. In the case of condoms, some segments of the male population might be more inclined to take condom wearing seriously if the message fits in with their particular sense of humour, and is not seen as patronising.

To avoid a crude interpretation of marketing theory, it is essential to be aware of other important differences between commercial marketing and social marketing, as shown in Table 30.3. (See Activity 30.2 and Box 30.1, overleaf.)

As we have seen so far, there are different approaches to public communication, but literature and research findings have been synthesised to identify campaign success. 'Success' factors are shown in Box 30.2, on p. 587.

You should use these success factors to reflect on the case studies presented within this chapter.

Central government communication

Clarifying communication roles

It is important to distinguish here between the communication work done on behalf of political

TABLE 30.3   Differences between commercial and social marketing (based on Windahl et al. 1992)

Commercial marketing	Social marketing	Example of social marketing
Targets most accessible part of the market (e.g. people with disposable incomes)	Often targets hard-to-reach segments or publics	Young people 'at risk' of drug abuse
Competitive environment	Environment is less competitive (sometimes only one service provider)	Public library service provided by local council
Services/products are paid for	Services and products are often free	New state benefit
Seeks to meet consumer needs and wants	Powerful interest groups are often challenged	Advertising industry (e.g. in targeting young children with fast food advertising)
Creates demand for a service/product	Balances demand with resource availability	Encourage pharmacy visits for common ailments to reduce demands on the local GP (doctor's) surgery
Product or behaviour promoted is desired/wanted by the customer	Product or behaviour promoted is not desired by the receiver	Sticking to a low-fat diet

Five 'Ps' and social marketing

Find out more about a public communication campaign with which you are familiar. Carry out an analysis of that campaign using the five 'Ps' discussed earlier. Consider also the special characteristics that make it a campaign that fits social marketing criteria in Table 30.3.

Feedback
Start by logging on to a government or local government (municipal) website.

parties (known as political communication) and the communication work done on behalf of elected governments and their departments of state or ministries. In the UK, since 1947, the latter role has traditionally been the role of civil servants possessing specialist public relations and communications skills who have been employed to support the government of the day. Cole-Morgan (1988) observed that departmental ministers were responsible to parliament for the information policy of their department (or ministry), and that each department had an information division whose objectives were defined as follows:

1 To create and maintain informed opinion about the subjects with which each department deals.
2 To use all methods of publicity, as suitable, to help the department to achieve its purpose.
3 To assist and advise in all matters bearing on relations between the department and its public.
4 To advise the department on the public's reaction to the policies or actions of the department. (Cole-Morgan 1988: 148)

In recent years, however, the lines between party political communication and government communi-

cation have become increasingly blurred. From the time of Prime Minister Margaret Thatcher in the 1980s to the more recent Blair administrations, communication became politicised to the point where specially appointed political advisors such as Alastair Campbell and Jo Moore were providing the strategic communication advice to government ministers, while apparently overriding the 'official' senior communications professionals who were there to provide 'neutral' and less partisan advice. The problems faced by government communicators are well documented, eventually leading to an investigation by Sir Robert Phillis in 2004. (A summary of the Phillis Report is provided in Chapter 5.)

This section is about the communication work carried out by central government communication specialists who support a wide variety of government policies through campaigns. In the UK, the work is carried out by members of the Government Communications Network (GCN). Specialist communication staff are employed by other national governments. In Canada, citizens have a right to be informed about government policies. This information service is provided by Communication Canada, established in 2001 to conduct national information campaigns, ministerial tours, as well as maintain a website that acts as a key access point for information on the government of Canada (www.canada.gc.ca). In the Netherlands, the Dutch government's information service operates a centre for public information campaigns called Postbus 51 (www.postbus51.nl). The Postbus 51 website provides government information leaflets and publications but is also designed to answer individual questions by email within two days.

Campaigns globally include efforts to prevent a range of undesirable behaviours including drug use, drink driving and unsafe sex (as part of HIV/AIDS

box 30.1 Public relations or social marketing?

Is public sector communication a type of public relations or is it social marketing? It all depends on how you look at it. If we look at it functionally, there will be a variation across different public sectors. In some public sector organisations, it is the task of public relations to coordinate all communications activities. In others, the task will fall to departments labelled 'corporate communications', 'corporate affairs' or 'marketing communications'.

The public relations or social marketing orientation will depend on a range of factors including the role and purpose of the organisation, the social issues it has to deal with, its resources and, of course, the experience, education and training of the staff performing the coordinating role. Referring back to Table 30.3, social marketing may be given a greater emphasis in public sector organisations where there is a significant emphasis on behaviour change campaigns and a large advertising budget (e.g. central government in the UK). Public relations is likely to be emphasised in organisations where the coordinating function for communications has a strong media relations orientation (e.g. local government in the UK).

| box 30.2 | **Success factors in public communication campaigns** |

1 *Role of the mass media.* Mass media help to create awareness and knowledge and stimulate others to participate in the campaign process, although behavioural changes as a result of mass media are unlikely.
2 *Role of interpersonal communication.* Peer groups and social networks are instrumental for behaviour change and maintenance of such change.
3 *Characteristics of source or medium.* Credibility can influence the outcome of a campaign.
4 *Formative evaluation.* Campaign objectives and messages need to be evaluated to make sure they fit media habits, audience predispositions and availability of resources. (For example, there is no point in emphasising the exercise benefits of pilates when classes are scarce and expensive.)
5 *Campaign appeals.* Campaigns must be specific rather than general in order to appeal to the values of individuals. (For example, appeals to recycle waste are not enough. People need to know how to recycle and it has to be made easy for them. See the Westminster Council case study in Chapter 11.)
6 *Preventive behaviour.* Long-term prevention goals are difficult to achieve because rewards are often delayed and uncertain (e.g. eating healthier foods as prevention against diabetes). Therefore delayed benefits must be related to immediate ones.
7 *Timeliness, compatibility, and accessibility.* Communication messages must be timely and culturally acceptable, and the channels over which they are transmitted must be available to the audience.

Source: Adapted from Windahl et al. 1992: 101–102

prevention). Other campaign efforts are designed to promote desirable behaviours including using sunscreens, eating more fruit and vegetables ('5 a day') and crossing the road safely.

Why some campaigns fail, why some succeed

The interesting thing about central government-instigated communication campaigns is that while many people will agree that they are a 'good thing', they are sometimes ineffective in achieving their goals because of their reliance on mass media. In support of this view, the leading American social psychologist McGuire asserted that there was little evidence of mass media persuasion having any effect on receiver attitudes, beliefs or actions (McGuire 1986). While this picture may not be entirely accurate – for example, out of 29 US health campaigns between 1980 and 1994, 20 were successful in changing behaviour and nine were not (Freimuth 1995) – health, in particular, does appear to be a hard area to campaign in.

A study of public information campaigns in Australia observed that some mass media campaigns in that country had been criticised for their irrelevance to the general community. For example, an AIDS 'Grim Reaper' advertisement was criticised for unnecessarily scaring people who were not at high risk of AIDS; the result being that screening centres were inundated with low-risk clients (Noble and Noble 1988).

American scholars Hyman and Sheatsley as long ago as 1947 posed questions on why information campaigns fail and Mendelsohn (1973) identified reasons for success.

Hyman and Sheatsley (1947) attributed blame to a large group of uninformed receivers among the American population whom they critically called 'chronic know-nothings'. Common threats to the success of information campaigns were attributed to what is known as 'selective processes' or filters – selective exposure, selective perception and selective retention. Such filters ensured that the 'chronic know-nothings' were impossible to reach with any information. Mendelsohn, however, believed that campaign planners were the ones to blame in ignoring communication research and theory. For campaigns to succeed, three conditions had to be met:

1 Realistic goals had to be set, based on the assumption that the publics are not overly interested, if at all, in the message.
2 Information was not enough. Interpersonal communication played an important role, therefore a combination of mass communication and interpersonal communication should be considered.
3 Campaign publics needed to be segmented according to media habits, lifestyles, values and belief systems, and demographic and psychological characteristics. (Windahl et al. 1992: 101)

Other writers stress that in today's increasingly sophisticated media environment, and with higher cognitive levels among publics, it is no longer enough to 'broadcast' to undifferentiated publics using mass communication methods (if, indeed, it ever was). What is important is the correct utilisation of socio-scientific research tools for campaign planning, implementation and evaluation (Klingemann and Römmele 2002). This means the campaign planners should obtain a clear understanding of the publics targeted, their receptivity to particular messages and channels, and their willingness to adopt the core proposition of the campaign.

Role of advertising

Having concluded that mass communication should not be the only method of reaching publics, it is still the case that governments use advertising as a key tool in public information campaigns due to its efficiency in reaching a wide audience. The UK government is one of the biggest spenders on media advertising, often the main channel in public information/communication campaigns. In 2004, for example, the Central Office of Information (COI), which buys advertising space on behalf of the UK government, reported a total advertising spend of £189m, second only to Procter & Gamble, the company famous for its soap powder and shampoo brands. This figure represented a 19% increase on the previous year, leading to accusations by the Conservative party that the government was 'sneaking' Labour party propaganda into public information commercials (BBC1 2004 online). This may or may not be true. However, advertising is often used by governments because the elected politicians who run them know it is highly visible and through advertising they are 'seen to be doing something' about a social issue. However, as the authors of a study of youth at risk in Australia concluded:

> *Advertising campaigns against specific social problems are too frequently chosen by politicians as a solution to a social problem. It is clear that they are ephemeral – last week drink-driving, this week AIDS. Social problems are not tidy political issues. They come attached to people and communities and the solution to them can only be found in people and communities. (Easthope and Lynch 1989)*

While there is controversy in the literature about the effectiveness of mass media campaigns, and especially advertising, it is clear that mass media channels play an important role at the early stages of a campaign in stimulating awareness and putting an issue on the public agenda.

Role of public relations

Poster, billboard, and television advertising can be visually memorable, but it is the explanatory work done with the news media that draws attention to the advertising message in the first place and helps to stimulate public debate. Public relations (more narrowly interpreted as media relations within this context) is an accepted communication tool for central government campaigns. While government departments in the UK have their own media relations functions, staffed by news officers or press officers, campaigns are now more commonly outsourced to consumer public relations agencies in line with New Labour's ideas of citizens as 'consumers who exercise choice' (*PR Week* 26 November 2004: 19).

Within an integrated communication campaign, public relations may involve media relations activities such as a press conference announcing the launch of the campaign and creative tactics to keep the campaign momentum going. Tactics will involve: publicising key sources of information such as hotlines and websites; briefings with key journalists writing for target publics; and a sequence of press releases commenting on the campaign progress (e.g. in achieving public awareness targets), introducing supporting events (e.g. roadshows, exhibitions), reporting on human interest stories and putting on record what the campaign has achieved.

To generate media interest in 'Use Your Head', the integrated communication campaign to recruit more teachers to state schools in the UK, public relations activity was targeted at potential 'career switchers' among specific groups that the teaching profession lacked, such as male primary school teachers and people from ethnic minorities. The campaign was timed around the academic year, with the spring public relations activity aimed at ensuring that all places on teaching courses were taken up by the following September (*PR Week* 9 January 2004: 7).

A campaign may also be wholly 'public relations driven': in other words, the public relations activity will be the main focus of communication, such as the Holocaust Memorial Day mentioned earlier in this chapter.

New priorities for government communication

In Chapter 5 we noted that a key concern for democratic societies is the inclusion of minority groups. These are regarded by society as marginalised groups because they often do not have contact outside their immediate community. Social inclusion is a concern for all governments that are operating within

activity 30.3

'Hard-to-reach' audiences

Select one of the four groups just listed that the UK government designates as a 'hard-to-reach' audience. Find out something new about them by contacting www.commongoodresearch.gov.uk.

What do you now know about communicating with this group?

a multicultural context – the Netherlands, Australia, the USA and the UK being four countries with sizeable diverse populations.

One of the key concerns for the UK government, for example, is finding ways of reaching out to black and minority ethnic (BME) groups using innovative communication strategies, instead of relying on translations of traditional media such as information leaflets. To support this initiative, an Inclusivity Unit has been set up by the Central Office of Information to commission research and devise communication strategies that will be most effective in reaching minority groups. Agencies that specialise in reaching BME groups are being taken on to the COI 'roster' (approved list of suppliers of services) to carry out communication campaigns (*PR Week*, 26 November 2004: 19).

As well as BME groups, other 'hard-to-reach' audiences such as small to medium sized enterprises, youth and elders (senior citizens) have also been subjects of research by the COI on behalf of government departments. A 'Common Good' website has enabled other government departments and communications agencies to access the research findings. (See Activity 30.3 and Mini case study 30.2.)

Local government communication

Local government in the UK

Local government in the UK comprises city, district, unitary and county councils. Elected politicians (known as councillors) are accountable to the local population for the money raised from taxes, which is spent on a wide range of services.

Services are organised differently depending on the type of council. However, most people live in a town where the local council is responsible for refuse collection and disposal, street lighting, road maintenance, culture and leisure facilities, planning regulations and environmental issues (see Mini case study 30.3, on p. 591). In larger towns, councils have wider responsibilities including education for children between the ages of 4 and 16 and social care. Council employees are known as 'officers' and usually have a job title such as 'environmental health officer'. Each council has at least one public relations officer and in some councils there are communications teams of 10 or more, incorporating media relations, internal communication, marketing communications and other functions such as graphic design.

Local government public relations

The communication function in local government is commonly referred to as 'public relations', explained by its origins in media relations and the establishment, in 1948, of press officers to inform the public about the role of local councils. One of the oldest

mini case study 30.2

Segmenting minority groups

Segmenting the target population is important when communicating to minority population groups. Media messages need to be culturally appropriate, but they also need to recognise that a cultural group is diverse with different lifestyles and habits.

In its 'Why Start?' multimedia campaign aimed at reducing smoking-related deaths among Maoris (an indigenous tribe of New Zealand), the New Zealand government developed a three-year campaign using cinema and TV advertising, advertising in buses and bus shelters, health education materials and Maori radio advertising. Specific campaign components were directed at Maoris, taking into consideration their cultural needs and differences.

In Canada, a 'Second-hand Smoke' campaign, warning of the dangers of passive smoking, was specifically targeted at smokers, an estimated 70% of Aboriginals. The campaign highlighted the toxic chemicals found in cigarettes and the need to consider the health of unborn babies, families and co-workers. Campaign materials included television and radio advertisements, posters, print advertisements and a brochure – all translated into Inuktituk, a language of the Inuit people.

Sources: NZ Ministry of Health 1996; Health Canada www.hc-sc.gc.ca/fnihb/cp/tobacco/ keepinginformed.htm

special interest groups of the UK's Chartered Institute of Public Relations is the Local Government Group.

Local government traditionally operated at the 'public information . . . end of public relations' (Harrison 2000: 173). Campaigns focused on increasing public awareness of social issues such as road safety and the environment.

Local councils in the UK are specifically prohibited by law to attempt to persuade publics. Recent advice states: 'Council communications should be informative rather than persuasive' (IDeA 2005). Within this context, persuasion is seen as providing information that is identifiable as one political party's views.

However, in order to cut through the clutter of media and messages faced by residents, and to use resources effectively, it is essential for councils to have clear objectives in what they are trying to achieve in public relations terms. Some of these objectives will be about raising awareness about the council's policies (e.g. Leeds City Council introducing 'Fairtrade' foods at all its catering outlets); other objectives will be a direct encouragement for people to do something such as using green bins for recycling waste.

Unfortunately, local government has always suffered from a lack of public knowledge, not only about the role of elected politicians, but also of what councils actually do. It is a truism that British people have held either indifferent or negative views of their local council, based on experiences of litter in the streets or dog excrement in the local park.

To demonstrate accountability to local residents, councils have had to shift away from passive 'information giving' to what is known as 'community engagement' where people are openly encouraged by their council to have their say on public issues. During the 1990s, for example, the London Borough of Lewisham opened its committee meetings to television cameras to enable the BBC to make a documentary series. It also opened a Video Box in an experiment to let the public have their say about local services (Walker 1997).

Since 2001 performance checks undertaken by the Audit Commission have helped to reinvigorate the communication function of local government.

Councils have to communicate corporately and involve a wide variety of stakeholders, including partners and employees, as well as citizens varying widely in age, ethnicity, and ability to communicate their own needs and wants. Communication is increasingly recognised as a two-way strategic function (Gaudin 2005). The role of public relations in local government is thus made clear: 'Good communication is central to community leadership and the delivery of services to local people' (Yeomans and Adshead 2003: 250). (See Think about 30.4 and Mini case study 30.3.)

Health sector communication

The health environment

Healthcare is a high priority globally. In 1998, the World Health Organisation (WHO) set challenging health targets for people worldwide in its HEALTH21 policy. The policy comprises three values:

- health as a fundamental human right
- equity in health across nations
- participation by, and accountability of, individuals, groups, communities, institutions, organisations and all sectors in the health development movement (WHO 1999: 4).

Within the context of the HEALTH21 policy, a four-part strategic action plan has been set out for countries in Europe. This action plan, with an emphasis on participatory health development within local communities, implies changes not only in healthcare delivery (i.e. through primary care organisations and hospitals) but in health communication.

While governments at national level will continue to have a responsibility in raising awareness through mass media campaigning on public health issues, such as those discussed earlier in this chapter, it is at the local level where the changes to people's behaviour can be achieved most through a greater involvement in decisions about their own health and healthcare. Here there is a clear role for locally based communication professionals.

think about 30.4   **Your local council's stakeholders**

Who are the stakeholders of your local council, municipality or government? Try segmenting 'internal' and 'external' groups.

Feedback   The list is endless, but internal groups will include elected politicians, senior managers, and officers (who can be segmented by grade and department). External stakeholders will include central government departments or ministries (these are significant stakeholders), other publicly funded agencies, the police, residents, the local media, community leaders (e.g. prominent people in the church, education, youth groups, minority groups, etc.). These are just a starting point.

Community engagement – banning smoking in public places

Coventry City Council in the UK wanted to take advantage of growing public support for banning smoking in public places. The aim of the three-month campaign 'Smoke-Free Coventry' was to position Coventry as a leader in the national debate on smoking and banning smoking. The key objectives were: to raise awareness of and gauge the views of Coventry residents about proposed plans to create a 'smoke-free' city and ban smoking in public places; to inform and educate people about the dangers of smoking and promote Coventry's Quit Smoking Team.

To gain local support, the campaign team involved partners and opinion formers including the media, health agencies, schools and the fire service. Local public opinion was tested using a residents' poll, a website questionnaire and a citizens' panel comprising members of the local community. Eight in ten residents

of the 6000 who responded to the consultation (including smokers) said they wanted the city to become smoke free in public places. This positive response gave impetus to the tactical campaign. The focal point of the campaign was a wacky character called 'Terminator' (in reality, a smoking cessation officer) who roamed pubs (public bars) warning people of the health risks of smoking and giving advice on quitting. This attracted television coverage and letters flooded into local newspapers in response to the debate. As a result of the campaign, Coventry City Council is a prominent lobbyist at the UK parliament on smoking legislation.

Sources: PR News (IPR Local Government Group) November 2004, 15: 8; Excellence in Communication Awards 2004, IPR Local Government Group

---

As the WHO's 'Health for All' (HFA) policy states:

More vigorous and open involvement of journalists and other professionals working in the media and the communication industry in creating and sustaining public knowledge and debate about health issues will be vital to the success of HFA policy, with its emphasis on public participation and the transparency of policy-making and implementation processes. Special training in such health issues should be part of the education of such professionals. The health sector itself must make a start by welcoming a more open dialogue on its affairs. (WHO 1999: 158)

The role of the corporate communicator in a healthcare organisation such as a hospital is thus suggested as 'promoting the participation of all its stake-

holders in its corporate life' and strengthening 'the perception of health as a fundamental human right' (Kuteev-Moreira and Eglin 2004: 123). All this opens up a new dimension for the health sector communicator in terms of the communication style they adopt. (See Activity 30.4.)

Health sector communication in the UK

The policy document *Shifting the Balance of Power: The next steps* (Department of Health 2002) announced a new way of organising and managing health services within the UK National Health Service (NHS). Since 2002 the hospital sector has also changed, with 'well-managed' hospitals being eligible to apply for foundation trust status to enable a greater degree of community autonomy and financial discretion. With the policy emphasis on partnership working and stakeholder consultation, communications practitioners (the term 'public relations' is rarely used) have had many new challenges to address, not least their own personal competences. Adopting an 'inclusive professional style' in working with partner organisations is identified as just one success factor (Beresford and Yeomans 2003).

The emphasis on consultation is undoubtedly a key change for communication practices in the National Health Service because it involves a shift in mindset away from traditional one-way public information giving to that of working with publics to identify healthcare problems and solutions. It implies, as we

A hospital's stakeholders

List the stakeholders of your local hospital. Now consider their relationships with the hospital in terms of expectations and level of involvement.

Feedback

Stakeholders will include: patients and service users, organisations representing patients and service users (these include voluntary organisations), purchasers or contractors, regulators, partners, suppliers, competitors/rivals, employees and potential employees (health service professionals), trade unions/professional associations, the media.

Public involvement – Addenbrooke's Hospital, Cambridge University Hospitals NHS Foundation Trust

The prospect of NHS foundation trust status in 2004 signalled a challenging opportunity for hospitals since the NHS was set up in 1948: a chance to be at the forefront of major change to deliver a responsive, accessible, inclusive health service accountable to the local community and free from central government control.

The basis for foundation trust status was establishing membership of the trust and involving staff, patients and the public in the running of the trust. It was therefore vital for any communications campaign to embody the values and spirit of the new NHS foundation trust itself.

Addenbrooke's' communication objectives were to:

- explain clearly the benefits and implications of NHS foundation trust status
- engage its publics' enthusiasm and engender dialogue
- translate involvement into support that would then establish a membership base of 10,000 by 1 April 2004.

All this was undertaken against the background of getting to grips with a new organisation still in the process of evolving.

The campaign comprised two phases: first, an initial 12-week consultation with staff and the local community, which informed the writing and acceptance of the application for foundation trust status and, second, the long-term commitment to recruit members of the trust – staff, public and patients.

Straplines were developed for both phases of the campaign – encapsulating the results Addenbrooke's wanted to achieve. The first phase was 'Your hospital – your chance to be involved' and the second phase which incorporated both a staff and public audience were 'Together we can make a difference' (staff) and 'You can decide how the future will look' (patients and public).

Printed material formed the basis of the campaign – for phase 1 an 'expression of interest' leaflet was distributed in the local newspaper, which offered further information available from a 50-page consultation document. This was supported by: the website; 55 meetings in the community where trust directors gave presentations and answered questions; a short video shown in shopping centres supported by literature and displays. This activity was mirrored in the trust with a tailor-made presentation developed for managers to deliver at team meetings.

Phase 2 concentrated on building up a membership base, but also tackled tricky issues like explaining to staff that they would be members of the new NHS foundation trust, unless they actively decided to opt out. This phase also used: newspaper advertising; radio advertising; direct mail shots to 100,000 addresses at random from the electoral register; awareness sessions for potential governors; posters in local doctors' (GP) surgeries, libraries, pharmacies, opticians and dental surgeries. All this was supported by media relations and articles in both the trust's internal and external newspapers and a central membership office which fielded questions and comments.

The evaluation of phase 1 – the consultation – was by the number of responses received. These responses then informed the writing of the application for foundation trust status. Eleven public meetings resulted in invitations from another 44 venues for further meetings.

The monitoring and evaluation of phase 2 was based on the number of members recruited. The target was 10,000 by 1 April 2004. By the middle of December 2003 only 1500 members had been recruited, so a change in tactics was needed involving a totally new design for campaign material. The colour chosen was part of the NHS corporate palette, but made a distinct statement from the more often used NHS blue seen on the logo. All photography was commissioned from Addenbrooke's Medical Photography department which used staff as models in the leaflets. The look was carried across to the website and other visual communication channels.

To further boost membership, radio advertising with two stations covered different age ranges, teens to 35 year olds and mid-30s onwards, together with direct mail shots to 100,000 households, plus newspaper and magazine advertising. A total of 16,203 members were recruited, which justified the change in tactics. Addenbrooke's achieved NHS foundation trust status in July 2004.

Review

In March 2005 membership of the trust stood at 21,000 but the age of trust members was not representative of the local community. A new plan was developed to target young people aged 16–35.

Source: By kind permission of Cambridge University Hospitals NHS Foundation Trust

think about 30.5   **Addenbrooke's case study**

1 Based on what you know about effective campaign planning, could anything have been done differently at the start of the campaign to reach the 10,000 target earlier?
2 What should the hospital do to recruit young people?

Feedback 1 Consider the use of research and segmentation beyond the three main groups identified.
2 Consider segmenting this group further.

noted earlier, less reliance on traditional mass communication methods of dissemination and more emphasis on interpersonal channels as part of a planned approach to health communication.

For communication professionals within the health service, health promotion projects such as breast or testicle self-examination may be a relatively minor element of their work given the corporate orientation of the communication effort: this can range from advising senior management on communication strategies, dealing with media attention and enquiries, organising or writing the internal newsletter and writing content for the web. Case study 30.1 illustrates the wide-ranging role of the communication function in a public involvement campaign. (See also Think about 30.5.)

A communication planning framework

You will find a very rich body of literature and research to help with the planning, implementation and evaluation processes of a communication campaign. The bibliography at the end of this chapter will help you to develop your knowledge in this field. This bibliography draws on research and theory in public relations, persuasion, social psychology, health promotion, social marketing and mass communication. Some of these areas are covered in Chapter 14, where the psychology of persuasion is discussed. The planning process for public relations is discussed in Chapter 10, and the same sequence

PICTURE 30.2   A landfill site is always an issue of public concern when it's on our doorstep. See Case study 30.2.
(*Source:* © James Leynse/Corbis.)

Overcoming public opposition and mobilising support for the waste management site of Szentgál, Hungary

Background

In 2003, 175 local councils in the western part of Hungary formed a consortium in order to build a new waste management site with the financial support of the European Union (EU) and the Hungarian government. Although the environmental experts and the environmental impact studies found the area on the outskirts of the village of Szentgál appropriate for the construction of the waste depot, the project – as were most of the previous attempts in other areas – was hindered by the opposition of the concerned local citizens.

The question of environmental technologies (such as sewage treatment systems, waste managing sites) in general, and the issue of 'waste' in particular, is an emotive topic not only in Hungary but in most European countries. The participants of the industry usually have to face serious challenges and trials, radical environmentalists and other pressure groups. As a result, there were at least half a dozen negative referendums preceding this campaign in other parts of the country with negative or scaremongering media coverage.

Objectives

Six weeks before the referendum, the consortium turned to Sawyer Miller Group (SMG), a public relations consultancy, to reduce the negative effects of 'ecological scare stories' in the media, minimise the foreseen conflicts with local residents and build a constructive relationship network with other local organisations. A key objective was to turn public opinion around in Szentgál so that the majority of citizens would vote supportively at the referendum deciding the fate of the construction.

Research

First, SMG had a local poll executed about support for the project. Out of the 3000 residents only 25% would have supported the investment, 49% of them would have rejected and 26% had not yet decided at the time. The poll also helped to better understand the demographics, the nature and strength of opinions, attitudes and beliefs.

One of the biggest concerns of the citizens was that their village would be associated and identified as the 'garbage village'. As the findings showed, people who opposed the waste management site wanted to preserve the status quo and were worried about the negative changes to their daily lives and lifestyles. They did not want decreasing property values or a polluted environment. In contrast, people in favour of the project wanted new benefits such as more workplaces, higher income tax, financial compensation and elimination of a local contaminated brownfield, infrastructural development. The most favoured compensation was the potential donation of a new school site.

The campaign was built around two major messages:

1 The depot was to be built with EU support in compliance with the strictest environment protection and security regulation.
2 Szentgál could benefit greatly by accepting the waste management site.

Implementation

SMG's strategy was to build personal relationships with, and gain the trust of, the local residents and thus avoid the slightest suspicion that the decision would be made 'behind closed doors'.

During the six weeks of the campaign, four community meetings were organised for the citizens of Szentgál and the neighbouring villages. SMG invited independent experts and opinion leaders to these community meetings, and had them explain what had to be done to gain permission to use a site, what kind of planning consent and licensing consent was required in order to operate a landfill and how the environmental impact studies were conducted. Holding regular community meetings also helped to keep the issue 'local' and to keep out 'intruders' (e.g. 'green groups' from Budapest). Even the opponents of the depot did not like their 'outsider' opinions, and rejected their help and intervention. SMG paid special attention to avoid any associations with party politics.

SMG edited and published two periodicals that were distributed in Szentgál and the neighbouring villages. In addition to general technical information, readers could also find several 'testimony interviews'. In these interviews, both sides were given an opportunity to voice and explain their arguments. According to the feedback, this approach resulted in a lot of support for the project, and managed to balance the previously widely distributed leaflets of the opposition, which were poorly written and personal rather than factual in tone.

During the campaign SMG organised *excursions* to other waste depots where the citizens of Szentgál could see in person how an environment-friendly waste depot operates and how it can contribute to the development of the region.

Other communication tools included *leaflets*, giving in-depth explanations about all relevant issues, such as landscape, containment of litter, site management, security, drainage, noise containment, operational hours, traffic impact and the future of the local flora and fauna.

An information hotline was also set up, and a permanent exhibition organised to model the depot together with video clips. The media were informed through press conferences and special briefings.

Result

In December 2003 nearly 60% of the population of Szentgál cast their vote and 56% of them voted for the investment.

Used with permission

can be followed for a public communication campaign. However, it is important to bear in mind the particular characteristics and success factors of a public communication campaign highlighted at the

beginning and throughout this chapter. Case study 30.2 demonstrates a public relations-led approach to public communication, involving a controversial issue.

Summary

This chapter has considered the special characteristics of public sector communication: its context, goals, publics, media use and effectiveness. Theories of communication, including agenda-setting theory and social marketing, were considered to provide an understanding of the types of communication campaigns that are undertaken by public sector organisations. On the one hand, we identified that common public communication objectives were to change knowledge, attitudes and behaviour in tackling social problems, while, on the other

hand, we identified that there is also a need for public organisations to work with communities to jointly solve these problems. We have also identified that within a multicultural context, a healthy democracy requires public participation. In achieving this, the public sector needs to understand and communicate with minority groups and 'marginalised' communities. Finally, through case studies we considered the use of campaign models, theories and approaches to campaign planning.

Bibliography

Ajzen, I. and M. Fishbein (1980). *Understanding Attitudes and Predicting Social Behaviour*. Englewood Cliffs, NJ: Prentice Hall.

Bandura, A. (1977). *Social Learning Theory*. Englewood Cliffs, NJ: Prentice Hall.

Bandura, A. (1986). *Social Foundations of Thought and Action*. Englewood Cliffs, NJ: Prentice Hall.

BBC1 News (2004). 'Whitehall ad spending under scrutiny' www.newsvote.bbc.co.uk/mpapps/pagetools/print/news.bbc.co.uk/l/hi/ukpolitics/399831.stm, accessed 23 April 2005.

Beresford, S. and L. Yeomans (2003). Partnership communications: A working paper. Paper presented at the British Academy of Management Conference, Harrogate, UK.

Bracht, N. (2001). 'Community partnership strategies in health campaigns' in *Public Communication Campaigns*, 3rd edition. R.E. Rice and C.K. Atkin (eds). Thousand Oaks, NJ: Sage.

Central Office of Information (2004). COI annual report and accounts 2003/04 www.coi.gov.uk, accessed 25 April 2005.

Coffman, J. (2002). *Public Communication Campaign Evaluation An environmental scan of challenges, criticisms, practice, and opportunities*. Cambridge, MA: Harvard Family Research Project, Harvard Graduate School of Education.

Cole-Morgan, J. (1988). 'Public relations in central government' in *The Practice of Public Relations,* 3rd edition. W. Howard (ed.). Oxford: The Communication Advertising and Marketing Education Foundation Ltd/Heinemann Professional Publishing.

Cragg, A. (1994). 'The two sides of fear'. *Druglink Institute for the Study of Drug Dependence* September–October: 10–12.

Cutlip, S.M, A.H. Center and G.M. Broom, (eds) (2000). *Effective Public Relations* 8th edition. Upper Saddle River, NJ: Prentice Hall.

Department of Health (2002). *Shifting the Balance of Power: The next steps*. London: Department of Health.

Dozier, D.M., L.A. Grunig and J.E. Grunig (2001). 'Public relations as communication campaign' in *Public Communication Campaigns*, 3rd edition. R.E. Rice and C.K. Atkin (eds). Thousand Oaks, NJ: Sage.

Easthope, G. and P.P. Lynch (1989). *Youth at Risk: The response to non-government agencies in Tasmania*. Hobart: University of Tasmania Press.

Excellence in Communication Awards 2004 (2004). IPR Local Government Group, UK.

Fedorcio, D., P. Heaton and K. Madden (1991). *Public Relations for Local Government*. Harlow: Institute of Public Relations/Longman.

Freimuth, V. (1995). 'Are mass mediated health campaigns effective? A review of the empirical evidence' in 'Do campaigns really change behaviour'. in M. Haug. (2004) *Nordicom Review* **1–2**, 2004, 277–289.

Gaudin, P. (2005). Letter to CIPR Local Government Group Members, 18 March.

Harrison, S. (2000). *Public Relations: An introduction*, 2nd edition. London: Routledge.

Haug, M. (2004). 'Do campaigns really change behaviour? New understandings of the behavioral effects of advertising, political campaigns and health communication campaigns'. *Nordicom Review* **1–2**: 277–289.

Health Canada (2005). 'Tobacco – keeping informed' www.hc-sc.gc.ca/fnihb/cp/tobacco/keepinginformed.htm accessed, 27 April 2005.

'Holocaust memorial engenders respect'. *PR Week* 25 March 2005: 32.

Home Office (2004). 'Anti-social behaviour action plan' www.homeoffice.gov.uk/crime/antisocialbehaviour/actionplan/index.html, accessed 5 April 2005.

Hyman, H.H. and P.B. Sheatsley (1947). 'Some reasons why information campaigns fail'. *Public Opinion Quarterly* **11**: 412–423.

IDeA (Improvement and Development Agency) (2002). 'Connecting with communities toolkit' www.idea.gov.uk/knowledge, accessed 28 November 2002.

IDeA (Improvement and Development Agency) (2005). 'Party politics, politicians and publicity' www.idea-knowledge. gov.uk/idk/core/page.do?pageId=81557, accessed 3 April 2005.

Katz, E. and P.F. Lazarsfeld, (1955). *Personal Influence*. Glencoe, FL: Free Press.

Klingemann, H. and Römmele, A. (2002). 'Using survey research in campaigns: A summary and checklist for the student and campaign practitioner' in *Public Information Campaigns and Opinion Research: A handbook for the student and practitioner*. H. Klingemann and A. Römmele (eds). London: Sage.

Kotler, P. (1982). *Marketing for Non-Profit Organizations*, 2nd edition. Englewood Cliffs, NJ: Prentice Hall.

Kuteev-Moreira, J.P. and G.J. Eglin (2004). 'Strategic challenges for corporate communicators in public service' in *Handbook of Corporate Communication and Public Relations: Pure and applied*. S.M. Oliver (ed.). London and New York: Routledge.

Leitch, S. and J. Motion (2003). 'Public–private partnerships: Consultation, cooperation and collusion'. *Journal of Public Affairs: An international Journal*. **3**(3): 273–278.

Makkai, T., R. Moore and I. McAllister (1991). 'Health education campaigns and drug use: The "drug offensive" in Australia'. *Health Education Research* **6**(1): 65–76.

McCarthy, E.J. (1975). *Basic Marketing: A managerial approach*. Homewood, IL: Irwin.

McCombs, M. and D.L. Shaw (1973). 'The agenda-setting function of the mass media'. *Public Opinion Quarterly* **37**: 62–75.

McGuire, W. (1969). 'The nature of attitudes and attitude change' in *Handbook of Social Psychology*, vol. 3. G. Lindsay and E. Aronson (eds). Reading: Addison-Wesley.

McGuire, W. (1986). 'The myth of massive media impact: Savagings and salvagings'. *Public Communication and Behavior* **1**: 173–257.

McQuail, D. (1987). *Mass Communication Theory: An introduction*, 2nd edition. London: Sage.

Mendelsohn, H. (1973). 'Some reasons why information campaigns can succeed'. *Public Opinion Quarterly* **37**: 50–61.

New Zealand Ministry of Health (1996). *Why Start?/Hei aha te kai paipa?*, No. 1, August.

Noble, G. and E. Noble (1988). 'On the use and misuse of mass media by governments'. *Australian Journal of Communication* **13**(1): 1–15.

Raupp, J. (2004). 'The public sphere as central concept of public relations' in *Public Relations and Communication Management in Europe*. B. Van Ruler and D. Verćić (eds). Berlin; New York: Mouton De Gruyter.

Rice, R.E. and C.K. Atkin (eds) (1989). *Public Communication Campaigns*, 2nd edition. Newbury Park, CA: Sage.

Rice, R.E. and C.K. Atkin (eds) (2001). *Public Communication Campaigns*, 3rd edition. Thousand Oaks, CA: Sage.

Rogers, E.M. (1983). *Diffusion of Innovations*. New York: Free Press.

Shanahan, P., B. Elliott and N. Dahlgren (2000). *Review of Public Information Campaigns Addressing Youth Risk-Taking: A Report to the National Youth Affairs Research Scheme*. Hobart, Tasmania: Australian Clearing House for Youth Studies.

Solomon, D.S. (1989). 'A social marketing perspective on communication campaigns' in *Public Communication Campaigns*, 2nd edition. R.E. Rice and C.K. Atkin (eds). Newbury Park, NJ: Sage.

Voltmer, K. and A. Römmele, (2002). 'Information and communication campaigns: Linking theory to practice' in *Public Information Campaigns and Opinion Research: A handbook for the student and practitioner*. H. Klingemann and A. Römmele (eds). London: Sage.

Walker, D. (1997). *Public Relations in Local Government: Strategic approaches to better communication*. London: Pitman.

Windahl, S. and B. Signitzer, with J.T. Olson (1992). *Using Communication Theory: An introduction to planned communication*. London: Sage.

World Health Organisation (1999). *Health 21: The health for all policy framework for the WHO European region*. Copenhagen: WHO Regional Office for Europe.

Yeomans, L. and L. Adshead (2003). 'The role of public relations in non-electoral participative democracy: A case study examining the effectiveness of district assemblies'. *Journal of Public Affairs* **3**(3): 245–259.

Websites

Australian Government, Department of Health and Ageing, National Drugs Campaign: www.drugs.health.gov.au

Central Office of Information: www.coi.gov.uk

Central Office of Information 'Common Good' – research on 'hard-to-reach' audiences: www.commongoodresearch.gov.uk

Dutch government's information service: www.postbus51.nl

Government of Canada: www.canada.gc.ca

Health Canada: www.hc-sc.gc.ca/fnihb/cp/tobacco/keepinginformed.htm

The Home Office: www.homeoffice.gov.uk

Improvement and Development Agency: www.idea.gov.uk

Improvement and Development Agency-Knowledge: www.idea-knowledge.gov.uk

CHAPTER 31

Arts, leisure and entertainment public relations

Introduction

Arts, entertainment, leisure and popular culture enhance all our lives. They provide a source of fun, creativity and amusement. They can challenge, stimulate, shock and excite. The huge creative output of artists, producers and entertainers needs to be managed sensitively if they are to present their artistic forms to a receptive public. It is the task of the communications professional working in these diverse areas to understand the creative product, the aspirations of the creative producers and to have a keen sense of the customers' desires and expectations from an arts or leisure experience.

Overall growth within the arts, leisure and entertainment sectors is a worldwide trend and there is an increasing need for public relations and marketing communications experts to understand the dynamics of this increasingly fragmented and competitive environment. The arts play a powerful role in society and many governments are involved in their encouragement and regulation, as vehicles for social inclusion, economic regeneration and prosperity. Further, the rapid growth of the interactive entertainment industry is increasingly recognised as a major area of leisure activity, especially for the young, which again for governments has implications for broader social and educational policy. Increasingly in the UK and indeed in other western industrialised countries, governments lead public policy, legislation and funding through organisations such as the Arts Council of Great Britain or The Sports Council of England and Wales.

The fundamental planning processes utilised by individual artists or performers or indeed arts, sports and leisure management in these sectors must be employed with a demonstrable understanding of contemporary societal trends. These include globalisation, the perceived threat of terrorism, fragmentation and proliferation of the media, the growth of consumerism in new markets, new technology-driven marketing and public relations techniques and the dominance of celebrity culture.

Those public relations and marketing practitioners working in the arts, leisure and entertainment sectors have to be increasingly aware of these trends and developments to maximise the creative opportunities for communications planning. Employment in the creative industries is growing steadily and there is increasing government awareness in the UK and Europe of the financial as well as social benefits to the economy of these sectors.

This chapter aims to introduce students to the specialist areas of public relations in the arts, leisure and entertainment sectors from a practitioner perspective. An industry overview of each area is provided, together with a discussion of key concepts of culture. The role of public relations and the strategies and tactics required by arts and leisure organisations are then explored, with the help of a variety of contemporary case studies. Trends and issues affecting public relations in this sector are then explored, such as the growth of celebrity, new technologies and globalisation.

Overview of the creative industries

In the UK, the government's Department of Culture Media and Sport (DCMS) defines the creative industries as: 'Those industries which have their origin in individual creativity, skill and talent and which have a potential for wealth and job creation through the generation and exploitation of intellectual property'. While there is no official government definition of 'culture', the following activities provide an illustrative guide that is useful in understanding the diversity of these areas. They include:

- performing arts and visual arts, craft and fashion
- media, film, television, video
- museums, artefacts, archives and design
- libraries, literature, writing and publishing
- built heritage, architecture, landscape and archaeology
- sports events, facilities and sports development
- parks, open spaces, wildlife habitats and countryside recreation
- children's playgrounds and play activities

- tourism, festivals and attractions
- informal leisure pursuits (www.culture.gov.uk). See Box 31.1.

The UK government, like many others, raises money for the arts from taxes and from a national lottery, which was introduced in 1994. Box 31.2 shows how much revenue has been raised for arts, leisure and entertainment from the Lottery. Box 31.3 shows how different areas of the arts have benefited from Lottery funding.

The next section examines particular aspects of the culture industries to identify the issues, particularly communication issues, that affect each sector.

The arts

The arts are usually described in terms of visual, music, heritage and performing areas. However, arts policy in the UK in 2005 adopted a more modern approach to the arts, one that is open to current trends emerging (and often challenging) in arts practice, in technology and in breaking down the boundaries between art forms and between arts and other disciplines.

---

box 31.1   The creative industries in the UK

- The creative industries in the UK accounted for 8.2% of gross value added (GVA) in 2001.
- The creative industries grew by an average of 8% per annum between 1997 and 2001.
- Exports by the creative industries contributed £11.4 billion to the balance of trade in 2001.
- There were 1.9 million people in creative employment in 2002.
- In 2002, there were around 122,000 companies in the creative industry sectors on the Inter-Departmental Business Register.

Source: www.culture.gov.uk

box
31.2 **How the arts have benefited from National Lottery funds in the UK**

Total value of Lottery funds to the arts	£1.86 billion
Total number of awards	20, 969
Number of awards over £1 million	250
Amount invested in capital projects	£1.32 billion

Source: www.culture.gov.uk

It is important to remember that this is a huge field of activity: for example, a music event could be a classical opera at La Scala, Milan, or a gig in the backroom of a bar. Drama might mean a Broadway show in New York or a mime act in the street. Tickets might cost hundreds of pounds or the event might be free. The variety of performing arts encompasses the privately and publicly funded, the celebrity driven to the artistically obscure. Consumption and demand for live performance is flourishing at both an amateur and professional level.

According to Anderson (1991), Barrere and Santagata (1999) and Parsons (1987), calling the arts an industry has resulted in considerable academic debate, with some believing that it is no more than an industrial product, while others view it from a semiotic perspective where the art work possesses an aesthetic sign which is culturally defined. (See later section on concepts of culture for more on this debate.)

Clearly, definitions are problematic for the art world and for the PR practitioner working within it. However, the growth of the art market itself in the

box
31.3 **Lottery funding in the UK – spend by art form**

Music	£457 million
Visual arts	£426 million
Theatre/drama	£441 million
Combined arts	£259 million
Dance	£156 million
General*	£102 million
Literature	£16 million

*This covers funding for non-specific art forms or activities such as training, development and marketing
Figures for November 1994 to September 2004

Source: www.artscouncil.org.uk

twenty-first century cannot be questioned, as can be seen by the figures given in Box 31.4 (overleaf). Fillis (2004) argues that arts PR and marketing puts the artist and the product at the forefront of planning, unlike conventional marketing activities centred on the consumer, and this poses a unique challenge to the communications professional. Consequently, marketing gurus such as Kotler are now calling for and fostering more creative ways of interpreting marketing and PR in the arts and deriving more meaningful theory.

Leisure

The concept of leisure reflects time and money spent on activities and pursuits away from the workplace. According to Torkildsen (2000) the world of leisure has changed and expanded substantially in the last 10 years as a result of economic and social changes and new technologies. Changes in government policies, the growth of tourism and service sector economies and the booming success of commercial leisure industries have all had an unprecedented effect on the growing expectations of people for healthier or alternative lifestyles, leisure fashion, services and choice.

The term leisure now typically encompasses:

- gambling
- eating out/restaurants (food and beverage market)
- travel (theme parks/attractions)
- sport (professional and amateur)
- shopping
- interactive electronic entertainment (games such as SonyPlayStation/X Box/Gameboy/GameCube)
- traditional pastimes (professional and amateur).

Sports activity in most countries is diverse and multifaceted. Sports participation can therefore include an individual's involvement in a community game of football in a local park to the attendance and viewing of mega stadium events such as the Olympic Games involving 1000s of sports stars, professional athletes and the focus of the world's media. The range of sports activity and choice is rapidly growing for individuals and groups. To promote London's bid for the 2012 Olympics favourably with the International Olympics Committee, the UK government is investing £2 billion of public and Lottery money in sport by 2006. Of this sum, £459 million is to be targeted at schools sport at grassroots level, thus aiming to fulfil its pledge to provide better sporting opportunities at every level, 'from playground to podium'. (For more on sports PR and sponsorship, see Chapter 27.)

box 31.4 **Global top 20 art shows (by daily attendance), 2004**

Treasures of a Sacred Mountain, Tokyo National Museum (7638)
El Greco, Metropolitan Museum of Art, New York (6898)
MoMA, Museum of Modern Art, Neue Nationalgalarie, Berlin (5832)
Gauguin-Tahiti, Galaries Nationales du Grand Palais, Paris (5507)
Pre-Raphaelites in Florence, Gallaria degli Uffizi, Florence (5507)
Henri Matisse, National Museum of Western Art, Toyko (5389)
Treasures of Chinese Art, Tokyo National Museum (4742)
Joan Miro 1917–34, Centre Georges Pompidou, Paris (4742)
Art in the Age of Dante, Gallerie dell'Accademia, Florence (4343)
Edward Hopper, Tate Modern, London (4215)
Richter, Weiner, Whiteread, Guggenheim Museum, Bilbao (4212)
Edouard Manet, Van Gogh Museum, Amsterdam (3960)
Rimpa, National Museum of Modern Art, Tokyo (3873)
Museum of Modern Art Masterpieces, Museum of Fine Arts, Houston (3846)
Mark Rothko: Walls of Light, Guggenheim Museum, Bilbao (3783)
Fashion and Furniture in 18th Century, Metropolitan Museum of Art, New York (3738)
Masterpieces from the Musee d'Orsay, National Gallery of Victoria, Melbourne (3728)
Edouard Vuillard, Galleries Nationales du Grand Palais, Paris (3700)
James Rosenquist, Guggenheim Museum, Bilbao (3596)

Source: 'Big name shows boost gallery figures'. *The Guardian*, 25 February 2005

Entertainment

Entertainment covers film, broadcast TV, and print and publishing, and includes satellite, cable and digital, and terrestrial television, books and magazines, film, video and electronic games.

TV and radio

Major changes have taken place in television broadcasting over the last 10 years, including the diversification of digital media, the introduction of 24-hour news channels, the expansion of access to global players by the viewing public, especially via the internet. The ability to download radio programmes is a major innovation, likely to be applied to TV programmes in coming years. Consumption patterns have also been affected by DVD use and satellite and cable subscriptions. Many users now have access to hundreds of channels, showing movies, repeats, new material and news, from CNN to Al Jazeera.

Film

Film encompasses both commercial and art house movies. Film production is international with strong manufacturing activity in Europe, India and South America, for example. However, film distribution and commercial movie success is largely dominated by the USA, particularly in terms of its financial box office success. This is understandable as it defines itself firmly as a commercial as well as artistic industry. The main stages of activity in the US film industry are vertically integrated (that is, the main companies own all the stages of film production, from the studios where the films are made to the cinema chains that show the finished product) including development, production, post-production, distribution and exhibition (Kerrigan 2002). This integration does appear to create a commercially successful model and while European films do enjoy some success, the USA still dominates the European box office. The European Audiovisual Observatory (EAO) states that cinema attendance has largely remained stagnant in Europe, while in the USA it has continued to grow (EAO 2003).

In Europe and the USA, both film and TV companies are more effectively using market research at every stage of the movie or TV programme lifecycle. Producers recognise the importance of defining the target audiences they seek to reach at the very earliest stages of creative development. Most US-dominated publicity remains aimed at the 18–24-year-old segment, where the largest audience lies (75% of the film audience in the USA is under the age of 39) (Wilcox et al. 1998). Durie et al. (2000) define film marketing as 'any activity that assists a film in reaching its target audience at any time throughout its life and by extension, its earning potential' (2005: 5). While one of the key aims of PR and marketing activity is to generate interest in the film to ensure audiences attend the movie in the first week of its release, there is a growing recognition that after release, word of mouth is the most powerful endorsement tool.

Books

In the UK for example, 'reading books' is frequently the most quoted favourite hobby or pastime in the population. Its importance to cultural life in the UK is reflected in the plethora of book prizes such as the high-profile Whitbread and Booker prizes, and the WH Smith 'People's Choice' Book of the Year for children's literature. The popularity and success of high street book stores such as Waterstone's and Dillons and the general explosion of book sales across nearly all genres in the UK over the last 10 years is testimony to this national obsession. Frequently government education strategies and campaigns have promoted literacy by linking reading as a 'leisure activity' with lifelong education benefits. Moreover, BBC Television has supported this popular trend with initiatives such as *The Big Read*, a week-long schedule of special literature programmes that encourage interactive online critical debate.

Music

A major aspect of entertainment is, of course, music, covering performance and recordings. Popular culture is powerfully influenced by the activities of successful music stars, even though the sale of records has fallen in the past decade. This is partly due to piracy, whereby the internet facilitates the (now illegal) transfer of music files from one PC to another. This and the impact of MP3 players is covered under the section on new technologies. While television no longer provides a 'shared experience', because everyone is watching different channels, live concerts and, particularly, music festivals are still very popular. (See Think about 31.1.)

Increasingly in western countries, the lines between entertainment, leisure and the arts are deliberately blurred or linked to social or political imperatives such as urban regeneration, social inclusion, social access and cultural diversity. This brings us to the question of how the arts are used and viewed in society.

Concepts of culture

The *American Heritage Dictionary* (2004) defines culture as:

1. a. *The totality of socially transmitted behavior patterns, arts, beliefs, institutions, and all other products of human work and thought.*
   b. *These patterns, traits, and products considered as the expression of a particular period, class, community, or population:* Edwardian culture; Japanese culture; the culture of poverty.
   c. *These patterns, traits, and products considered with respect to a particular category, such as a field, subject, or mode of expression:* religious culture in the Middle Ages; musical culture; oral culture.
   d. *The predominating attitudes and behavior that characterize the functioning of a group or organization.*
2. *Intellectual and artistic activity and the works produced by it.*
3. a. *Development of the intellect through training or education.*
   b. *Enlightenment resulting from such training or education.*
4. *A high degree of taste and refinement formed by aesthetic and intellectual training.*
5. *Special training and development:* voice culture for singers and actors.
6. *The cultivation of soil; tillage.*
7. *The breeding of animals or growing of plants, especially to produce improved stock.*
8. Biology.
   a. *The growing of microorganisms, tissue cells, or other living matter in a specially prepared nutrient medium.*
   b. *Such a growth or colony, as of bacteria.*

While it is safe to ignore the culture of soil, animals and bacteria for this discussion, all the other elements are relevant to the arts and demonstrate what a huge concept culture is. It is also worth adding that definition 1(d) also covers corporate culture, which is discussed more fully elsewhere in this book (see Chapter 17).

---

think about 31.1 How to describe the sector(s)

- Is reading a book about Quentin Tarantino's films art, leisure or entertainment? Is a news documentary about AIDS in Africa supposed to be entertaining?
- How easy is it to separate these issues?

Feedback Look at the government information websites for different countries. How do they organise their arts and leisure? Is it run by the state or by private companies – or both?

McQuail (2005) suggests that culture has the following characteristics. It is:

- collectively formed and held
- open to symbolic expression
- ordered and differently valued
- systematically patterned
- dynamic and changing
- spatially located
- communicable over time and space. (2005: 113)

This makes clear that culture is about a shared experience, which uses symbols to express different values and which can be communicated across distances or at different times.

O'Sullivan et al. (1994) say that culture is the 'social production and reproduction of sense, meaning and consciousness. The sphere of meaning, which unifies the spheres of production (economics) and social relations (politics)' (1994: 68). They also make it clear that there are many interpretations of culture, depending on the viewpoint of the different theorists. In the past people used to talk of 'high' culture, meaning opera and classical theatre, and 'low' culture, meaning popular entertainment, like soap operas on TV. Today there are many different interpretations of culture, including the following concepts.

Cultural studies

This school of thought concentrates on how culture reflects power divisions in society (O'Sullivan et al. 1994). For example, it might examine the representation of black people, women or people with disabilities in soap operas or Hollywood movies. It will ask: whether villains are often Arabic in US films; whether women get powerful roles or are just cast to make the male lead look good; and how people with physical or mental challenges are portrayed. This approach was developed in the 1960s, building on the work of Hoggart and Williams, who challenged the class assumptions behind the terms 'high' and 'low' culture. Much of the work has taken place in the Birmingham School, under Stuart Hall. Its scholars draw on other academic disciplines and schools of thought, such as Marxism, feminism, psychoanalysis, linguistics and others. It has provided hugely influential tools for studying the media, in particular, but can be applied to all artistic and creative outputs: the key question is not the intent of the creator but the social and political values, especially power relations, embodied in the work.

Semiotics

This approach studies the meanings that can be decoded from signs – words and images – used in com-

munication, and was first developed by the linguist de Saussure at the turn of the twentieth century, then extended in the 1960s by Barthes (O'Sullivan et al. 1994). Like cultural studies, it is also less interested in the intentions of communicators than in the meaning embedded in their 'texts', which can be anything from movies, books or sculptures to advertisements or T-shirts. The focus is on the way that the reader or viewer 'decodes' the message, regardless of what was intended. It has been particularly applied to the meanings that can be read into advertisements and other aspects of popular culture. Because it is not interested in the background of the sender of the message it has embraced all production of meanings, including soap operas, game shows and tabloid newspapers. (See also Chapter 14 for a brief discussion of signs and meanings.)

Postmodernism

This term has come to mean a great many things across a wide range of cultural activities, including film, literature and fashion. It tends to reject historical analysis and theories that seek to unify experience (O'Sullivan et al. 1994). Instead it emphasises the fragmentation of modern life, the brevity of experience, and even the triviality of art. Here the creator is a major part of the performance, for example when a narrator in a book or an actor in a play addresses the reader/camera directly. But at the same time the reader/viewer is encouraged to construct their own meanings from an assembly of ingredients, in a spirit of play rather than reverence. It does away with a sense of historical 'progress' (which was central to modernism), instead suggesting that there is a timeless free-for-all and styles from different eras can be put together to make a building, a play or a movie. There is a sense that reality can be and is constructed by viewers/readers/consumers of culture, not the producers (Strinati 1995). It has been very influential in film, visual arts – including architecture – and fashion in particular (think Tarantino, Damien Hirst and Vivien Westwood, for example).

This brief outline illustrates some of the ways in which culture can be studied. There is always a debate about what art means to society, whether it is intended to uplift or entertain, whether it should be good for us and how much it reflects back the society we live in. (See Think about 31.2.)

Role of public relations in the creative industries

It is the task of the communicator to understand, translate and capture audiences for the creative professionals

Do you think there is a difference between Mozart's opera *The Magic Flute* and the TV show *Big Brother*? Is one better than another? How can you tell?

What do *Big Brother* and other reality shows tell us about entertainment in the early twenty-first century? Given versions of these shows are popular across Europe and the USA, what do they say about those societies?

Do you think it matters if the 'good guys' in US blockbusters are usually white men and the 'bad guys' foreign, often Arabic in origin? Do the roles women play in movies or their portrayal in men's magazines affect the way you see women?

working in these areas. The communications strategies employed for this task use the full range of PR and marketing communications tools with the additional requirement that the practitioner needs to be very familiar with niche promotional channels available to each area.

Typically, artistic activities are reported through the conventional media (broadcast, print, internet) by specialist journalists and media. The visual arts or museums are subject to scrutiny by the national regional and local media but also have specialist publications and channels.

The creative demand on the PR profession is increasing. In highly 'artistically' focused industries such as these, communications techniques and tools must be competitively innovative and dynamic. It is essential to embrace the latest technologies and overcome long-standing barriers between different sectoral and cultural traditions to create unique creative platforms for PR campaigns. For example, sport stars support artistic ventures, artists endorse travel organisations, celebrities add glamour to more traditional ventures. The PR professional needs to be abreast (and ahead of) fashionable trends in these demanding and quixotic sectors.

Increasingly in PR practice, professionals are finding the cross-over between leisure, arts and entertainment PR is blurred. When is a PR agency dealing with an entertainment client or an arts client? Is Tracey Emin or Damien Hirst an artist or a celebrity or are they indeed both? The challenge for PR is the profession's creative ability to absorb these fast-moving fashionable industry trends and identify and exploit cross-fertilisation opportunities. The broad public appetite for this type of synthesis across industries, art forms, leisure activities and entertainment appears voracious. (See Mini case study 31.1 and Think about 31.3, overleaf.)

Public relations objectives, strategies and tactics for arts organisations

Most of the public relations work conducted by practitioners in the arts and leisure field is identical to that practised in other fields. Chapter 10 on public relations planning and Chapter 16 on media relations cover most of the relevant ideas related to general PR practice. However, there are particular factors that affect PR and the arts and these are now outlined.

Publics for arts organisations

In the arts and entertainment sectors, Kotler and Scheff (1997) identify *input publics* (playwrights, composers), who supply resources that are converted by *internal publics* (performers, staff, board of directors, volunteers), into useful services or offers (performances, educational programmes), that are carried out by *intermediate publics* (PR agencies, advertising agencies, critics), to consuming publics (audiences, activists, media) (see Figure 31.1 on p. 607, see also Activity 31.1).

PR and marketing for arts events

One of the primary goals of many arts, leisure or entertainment organisations is the requirement to sell

activity 31.1

A record company

Select a record company and look at its website. See if you can draw a map of its key publics on the lines of Figure 31.1. Which publics do you think are most influential? Do you think this may have changed in recent years?

Feedback

Consumer patterns of behaviour are changing rapidly as a result of new technologies and increased accessibility to the arts, leisure and entertainment sectors. Internet booking, flexible subscription ticket schemes, direct marketing, a 'virtual' presence for events and activities online and integrated PR and marketing campaigns have brought a change in consumer patterns of access to these sectors' offers. New audiences are developing as a result of these patterns of consumption.

mini case study 31.1

The English Tea Experience

An example of how PR has been used to promote 'fashionable' leisure activities (*PR Week* 2004) and is a cross-fertilisation between fashion, travel, destination marketing, eating out, and celebrity(!) was a campaign for Exclusive Eating Out . . . The English Tea Experience at The Berkeley, a five-star hotel in Knightsbridge, London. The hotel bills itself as 'classically cool', with attractions that include the Blue Bar, which fashion designer John Galliano called his 'favourite home from home', and a health spa with rooftop swimming pool in the heart of the capital.

The hotel became popular with celebrities seeking a discreet stay in London. In 2004 it decided to develop a 'tea afternoon' that would make The Berkeley stand out from the crowd. The main objectives of the campaign were to help maintain the hotel's high profile and increase afternoon tea business by making it a 'tea destination'.

To differentiate the hotel from other exclusive establishments in the market, the in-house PR team's strategy was to aim the new 'Prêt-à-Portea' service at high-spending clientele interested in fashion. The range of cakes and pastries are based around the latest season's collections such as Fendi chocolate baguettes and Missonni eclairs.

The pastry chefs' creations were assessed by fashion editors from magazines such as *Tatler* and *Vogue*, thus guaranteeing media interest beyond food publications. London correspondents for the international media in America, France and Japan were also approached.

Vogue ran a half-page exclusive positioning the pastries alongside catwalk pictures of the dress that had inspired them.

This was followed with coverage in *The Observer*'s Food Monthly and an article in *Delicious* magazine. *Elle*, *Harpers & Queen*, *Marie-Claire* and *Eve* also covered the story.

Importantly for the celebrity angle to the campaign, *Heat* magazine ran a piece showing celebrities in the dresses that the pastries were based on.

As a result of the campaign with a modest budget of £1000, the hotel reported weekend occupancy rates up by 20%. People were booking in for tea and then staying overnight. More than £1 million had been added to the bottom line for the hotel over that year, much of which was attributed to the 'Prêt-à-Portea' campaign. Afternoon tea business in the Caramel Room of the hotel had grown by 300% and the concept was taken to New York's Fashion Week in 2005. This again reinforced the objective of profile raising to an international audience.

'"Prêt-à-Portea" was an ingenious idea', said *Harpers & Queen* lifestyle editor Rachel Meadows. 'Tea is really fashionable at the moment but people either do really traditional or really trendy – no one else had taken elements from the catwalk like this.'

Source: adapted from *PR Week*, 21 January 2005:31

think about 31.3 — Cross-fertilisation in the creative industries

Think of some examples of cross-fertilisation in the arts, leisure and entertainment sectors in your own country. What are the implications for the PR professional?

tickets to events. Public relations campaigns provide publicity build-up to inform fans, viewers, participants, readers or listeners that an event will occur and stimulate the desire to purchase tickets and attend (Wilcox et al. 1998). While marketing communication activity can concentrate on functions regarding information on prices of tickets, channels of distribution, factual data and so on, public relations largely focuses on media relations activity (see Chapter 16). Providing sequential stories about forthcoming theatrical events, films, festivals or similar commercial and non-commercial performances enables the PR practitioner to concentrate on personalities, celebrity, style, fashion and history to raise public awareness and indeed public debate. Success-

ful PR searches for fresh, targeted news angles to maximise media coverage across integrated marketing communications (see also Chapter 26).

At the core of effective PR and marketing communication in arts, entertainment and leisure sectors is a clear understanding of the target audience and consumer behaviour. PR professionals are required to understand the motives, preferences and behaviours of their organisation's current and potential audiences (Kotler and Scheff 1997: 69). (Consumer behaviour is discussed in Chapter 26.) Key factors influencing consumer behaviour can be summarised as:

■ macroenvironmental trends (social, political, economic and technological)

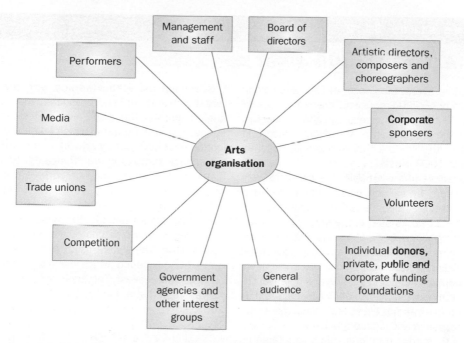

FIGURE 31.1   A model of an arts organisation's publics (*source*: adapted from Kotler and Scheff 1997. Reprinted by permission of Harvard Business School Press. From *Standing Room Only: Strategies for Marketing the Performing Arts* by P. Kotler and J. Scheff. Boston, MA 1997. Copyright © 1997 by the Harvard Business School Publishing Corporation; all rights reserved.)

- cultural factors (nationality, subcultures, social class)
- social factors (reference groups, opinion leaders, innovativeness)
- psychological factors (personality, beliefs and attitudes, motivation)
- personal factors (occupation, economic circumstances, family, lifecycle stage). (adapted from Kotler and Scheff 1997: 69).

Identifying and selecting target audiences and positioning the offer to the 'consumer', whether in the arts, leisure or entertainment sectors, is crucial to successful PR planning and campaigns. An example of the way in which careful targeting and an appreciation of the consumers needs have been identifed clearly is the successful commercial art event Frieze Art (see Mini case study 31.2, overleaf).

Media relations for arts organisations

Film studios, production companies, networks and celebrity publicists all apply the principle of a steady output of information and stories, a 'drip-drip-drip' approach to publicity around a new movie (Wilcox et al. 1998). This PR technique enables the key players in the industry process to maximise media attention both before and after production and public showing of the movie itself. These opportunities for story generation can include the following:

- initial signing up of a film director to a studio or project idea
- script evolution
- assigning a cinematographer or writer
- 'work in progress', including insights into the making of the film, e.g. locations, technical issues, developments by the creative team
- actors and stars signing up to the project
- actors and stars not getting the role!
- quotes and interviews from directors, producers, actors during and after production
- controversial debate generated by social or political issues in a film
- technology – interactivity with audiences during the creative process, e.g. on official and unofficial websites.

See Think about 31.4, Mini case study 31.3 and then Think about 31.5, all overleaf.

Previews, exclusives and award ceremonies are all PR tools and techniques employed during the process to reach the target publics of film critics, industry stakeholders and the audiences. Promotional activity reaches a crescendo with the premiere or launch night of the movie. This presents another opportunity to generate interest in the film, although it is also essential to maintain the profile of the movie for a sustained period after this time.

The longer term PR campaign will target print, broadcast, radio and internet media with these story opportunities over potentially a two- to three-year

mini case study 31.2

Frieze Art Fair 2004

A commercial art event, the Frieze Art Fair, was held in London in October 2004 and was the largest single contemporary arts exhibition ever staged in the UK. Organised by the contemporary art magazine *Frieze*, it hosted 140 of the world's top commercial galleries and more than 1000 artists.

The key objective of the Art Fair's PR campaign was to attract visitors by gaining maximum media exposure. A supporting objective was to increase the turnover of the art works sold at the fair.

The PR agency Idea Generation working for *Frieze* developed a strategy and plan with a broad-based target audience including professional art collectors, members of the public with an interest in the arts and potential collectors with a modest budget. A key message established that the fair was not elitist and contemporary art was highly accessible and indeed affordable.

A nine-month media relations campaign targeted both trade and consumer publications as well as national and international radio and broadcast TV.

Specialist art teams worked with the agency to target publications and broadcast media with story angles suitable for their own audiences. The title sponsor, Deutsche Bank, which holds the largest collection of contemporary artwork in the world, enabled the agency to position the PR strategy to strategically focus on the importance of corporate art sponsorship.

The PR campaign created 40 news stories, 25 features, 150 listings and 18 broadcast interviews. Evaluation of the coverage estimated that the overall tone was very positive. There were 42,000 visitors to the art fair over a five-day period, which was a 50% increase on the previous year's event. The turnover or art sold at the fair was estimated at around £26 million, up £10 million on 2003.

Source: Adapted from *PR Week* 14 January 2005: 18

think about 31.4   Media relations for the arts

Think about the media relations involved in a tour by the band U2, by a local group and for a classical concert. How are they different?

mini case study 31.3

Leeds Grand Theatre

The Grand Theatre in the City of Leeds is a large regional theatre in the UK and its choice of media has to be carefully targeted as budgets and resources for PR for this type of organisation can be limited. With a capacity of over 1550 seats, the theatre promotes a range of performances from opera to stand-up comedy. Performances can include one-night individual events or runs of shows over several weeks.

Typically, in the run-up to the opening night, the in-house PR department provides local and regional print and broadcast media (including specialist journalist critics) with opportunities for interviews with stars of the shows, performers or directors. Media will also be invited to a 'press night', at which further press information packs can be distributed. Sequential stories are planned over the pre- and post-opening night period. In Leeds, local and regional print media such as the *Yorkshire Evening Post* and *Yorkshire Post* are targeted as well as lifestyle magazines such as *Yorkshire Life*, *What's On* guides, local radio and TV, and regional tourist publications.

The media relations activity is integrated with direct mail, radio advertising, co-promotional endorsement with partners and approved poster sites.

Source: By kind permission of the Leeds Grand Theatre

think about 31.5   Launching a film

If you were asked by a film producer to support the launch of a new film, what would you take into consideration in the planning and implementation phases of your strategy?

---

mini case study 31.4

BAFTA Awards

In 1997, BAFTA (the British Academy of Film and Television Arts) recognised the impact of the internet and multimedia technologies on the entertainment industry. The result was the creation of the BAFTA Interactive Entertainment Awards. The event has quickly grown into what is considered to be the world's largest and most prestigious interactive entertainment awards, recognising and rewarding creative talent in interactivity. Positioning the event as 'the ultimate accolade for creative talent and achievement' across different platforms and genres such as Microsoft XBox, Sony PlayStation, Nintendo Gameboy, GameCube, mobile, PC, handheld, etc., the awards attracted significant international media interest.

In 2004 BAFTA split the awards into two separate ceremonies targeting communications to different audiences/sections of the industry, including trade, consumer and specialist media. The BAFTA Interactive Awards focused on a broad spectrum of the new media industry, including DVDs, websites and education, whereas the BAFTA Games Awards ceremony focused purely on the games industry. As a public relations tool the new awards created a raft of positive and fresh messages regarding this new development in the entertainment industry and demonstrated its innovation and creativity.

Source: Adapted from *PR Week* January 2005: 19

---

period (depending on the scale or size of the production). Invariably the film product is transferred to DVD and other formats providing again the re-promotion to new audiences. Action and adventure films translate well into electronic interactive games. For example the *Lord of the Rings* trilogy and Marvel Movies such as *Spiderman* have become Sony PlayStation, XBox, GameCube and Gameboy games across different platforms and genres. Thus consumer spend is increased and sales revenue of games can exceed the film ticket sales. DVD sales over time can exceed film takings at the box office.

The marketing of films requires specialist expertise so that the buying behaviour of target audiences can be triggered successfully. The US film industry has utilised audience research in its marketing strategies for decades and the professional and well-resourced PR and marketing machinery surrounding film production ensures that it continues to succeed not only in the USA but also globally. Market research into demographics and psychographics form the basis of PR strategy for the film industry.

Brand development and brand positioning

From a strategic point of view (see Chapter 10 for a discussion on strategic public relations), PR increasingly operates as part of a branding strategy in the arts, leisure and entertainment sectors. This is demonstrated in Mini case study 31.4 and Case study 31.1, overleaf.

A successful example of the use of PR in brand development and repositioning in the visual arts sector is that of Tate Modern (Case study 31.1) and Tate Britain.

Trends and directions in the creative industries

A number of factors are already influencing the direction of arts promotion, in particular the growth of celebrity, the introduction of new technologies both to media and leisure industries, and the globalisation of media and entertainment output. These issues are now briefly explored.

Growth of celebrity

The growth of interest in celebrities in the last 10 years has been staggering; its impact on fashion and the media is all pervading. In the arts, leisure and entertainment sectors celebrity status is now accorded to most international athletes, artists, musicians and performers of all kinds. Moreover, the nature of celebrity has changed: whereas once it derived from excellence in an arts or leisure activity, now appearing on a reality TV show or sleeping with a footballer qualifies anyone for celebrity status.

Arts, leisure and entertainment celebrities are increasingly utilised for support and enhancement of consumer 'brands'. Successful celebrity product placement and sponsorship tie-ins have flourished in these sectors. Matching a 'brand personality' to a

case study 31.1

The launch of Tate Modern

Tate Modern opened to the public on 12 May 2000. As well as being the first new national museum to open in London in a century, it is also the first national museum for modern art in London. Tate Modern was a Millennium Commission project funded by the National Lottery.

Housed in the former Bankside Power Station, Tate Modern displays the Tate Collection of international modern art from 1900 to the present day. There is a full range of special exhibitions and a broad public programme of events throughout the year. The ex-power station has been transformed into a modern museum by Swiss architects Herzog & de Meuron. The former turbine hall now marks a breathtaking entrance to the gallery. At night a lightweight luminous roof is a unique addition to the London skyline.

The main aim of the PR campaign to launch Tate Modern was to increase public awareness, understanding and application of modern art. In order to reach this goal, it was necessary to make modern art more accessible. Broadening Tate's audience and appeal was seen as the key to fulfilling this target – as opposed to the notion of modern art as 'elitist'. Tate Modern aspired to attract people who intend to come to galleries but who rarely do.

In visitor terms, the Tate's communication team set its sights on doubling the attendance to Tate. Moreover, the organisation was aware that it needed to be seen as providing value for money as a Lottery-funded project to its external stakeholders and publics. Amid scepticism and criticism towards other millennium projects, Tate Modern needed to ensure that it was seen as a worthwhile scheme. The team's strategy was therefore to be flexible and recognise the issues and concerns of other millennium projects.

Another key communications objective was to clarify the different positioning of Tate Britain and Tate Modern in audiences' minds. Hence the original Tate Gallery at Millbank was rebranded as Tate Britain two months ahead of the Tate Modern launch.

From an international perspective, New York and Paris have exemplary well-established modern art museums, and Tate Modern would be the first national modern art museum in London. Tate Modern would provide a unique opportunity for the 'Brit Pack' artists to be promoted in an international arena. Moreover, Tate Modern was keen to ensure that the local community was involved and benefited from the new gallery.

The PR strategy and plan identified that media interest needed to be ensured from an early stage in the building period, both nationally and internationally. Working with consultants Bolton and Quinn, the Tate communications team secured the support of high-profile endorsers and key members of the media. An edito-

rial column was published in the *Financial Times* in 1997, at a time when Tate Modern was still fundraising. The campaign achieved a build-up of interest through strategic editorial at all major stages of the project.

Target audiences included the media, press, broadcast (television and radio – both national and international), government, artists, art critics (national and international), art enthusiasts, art 'beginners' (e.g. cab drivers) and the local community of Southwark.

Key advocacy included:

- involvement of British arts
- establishing why Tate is important and necessary
- communication liaison and involvement and visitor centre
- lobbying government to ensure Tate Modern entry was free
- a range of private views and tours for all sectors throughout the project
- enlisting the support of high-profile endorsers and key members of the media.

The communication team recognised that to attract a wide audience to Tate Modern it was necessary to secure the support of television, the mid-market papers and, crucially, the UK tabloids, despite the hostility to the arts in general and millennium projects in particular shown by *The Sun* newspaper.

Favourable coverage in the tabloids was secured through events such as the preview for drivers of black cabs. In a special preview session, 20,000 taxi cab drivers in London were invited to an event especially for them. Its aim was to enable 'cabbies' to talk to their passengers about the gallery from first-hand experience and to deliver the message by powerful third-party 'word of mouth' techniques.

The usual range of PR tools was used to gain media coverage, including press releases and photographs. Coverage included special supplements in major UK broadsheet newspapers and *Vogue* magazine. *Time Out* filed a particular guide to the Bankside area and the *Sunday Times* Magazine covered all art Lottery projects.

Tate Modern importantly secured a four-part documentary on Channel4 on the architecture and building project as well as four art documentaries on BBC2. The opening by the Queen was an event covered live on BBC1. GMTV hosted its breakfast show from Tate Modern. Extensive international coverage was secured using PR agencies in France and New York.

A new corporate identity, a 'Tate concept', was developed and applied to all items of print, merchandise, uniforms and website. The brand values of the new gallery were reflected in the new visual graphic identity designed by Wolff Olins.

▶

case study 31.1 (continued)

A high-impact marketing campaign with six different adverts appeared across a range of media (including bus sides) and promotional partners were secured, such as special coffee cups for Coffee Republic, Tate beer and a Royal Mail stamp. The creative content of the campaign was enhanced with collaborations with British artists such as Tracey Emin and a specially commissoned fanfare by Sir Harrison Birtwistle for the Queen's formal opening of the museum. Celebrities such as Madonna, Mick Jagger, Kylie Minogue and Claudia Schiffer added glamour to the opening party. The opening show event, broadcast live on BBC1 and BBC2, was watched by millions of viewers. It included a laser show projected onto the façade of the building.

In terms of evaluation, the campaign's objectives were clearly achieved and in some cases exceeded. In a climate where other millennium Lottery-funded projects had failed to capture the public's imagination, the media campaign for the museum was successful in ensuring that the tabloid newspapers in the UK viewed the opening of Tate Modern favourably.

Media coverage was extensive. During the launch period in May, Tate Modern had 317 inches of column space in national print media, making it the fifth biggest story of the week. The approximate total audience reach just through national television during April, May and June 2000 was 126.7 million. Thirteen articles in the tabloids represent a reader figure of approximately 32.5 million. In its first year, 5.25 million people visited Tate Modern, a figure more than double expectations. Over a million people came in the first six weeks. The website registered an average of 24 million hits per month. In May 2000 it had as many as 10 million hits per day. According to *Campaign* magazine, Tate was one of the 10 most talked about brands during 2000.

Source: adapted from *IPR Excellence Awards 2001*, www.cipr.co.uk

celebrity brand, however, can have its problems and pitfalls and for every successful joint venture there are numerous failures. Moreover, the media are increasingly interested in 'news', however trivial, concerning a celebrity, a trend associated with the commercialisation of mass media (McQuail 2005). Again, this can be a mixed blessing: the front page may carry the desired picture of the star making an award to your charity – or falling down drunk outside a nightclub. (See Think about 31.6.)

Pringle (2004) identifies a number of key trends in celebrity that will impact on the arts, leisure and entertainment sectors, in particular: the use of charismatic stars of minority sports; leisure and arts pursuits brought into the mainstream; and the cross-over between cultures and continents. Examples might include the huge media interest shown in round-the-world yachtswoman Ellen McArthur, despite the minority interest in her sport of sailing.

Obviously, many arts, leisure and entertainment activities already involve celebrities, who may help generate media coverage. Indeed, the Hollywood 'star' system reflects not just the popularity of certain actors but their ability to bring in audiences regardless of the quality of the film.

It may seem as though the concept of 'celebrity' plays an increasing role in communications activity in the arts, leisure and entertainment industries. Clearly, celebrity has indeed been a driving force behind high-profile work in the promotion of these sectors for many years. The sheer visibility of celebrity in communications in the late twentieth and early twenty-first century inevitably tends to push us to the conclusion that without its presence in society these sectors would falter.

However, for every film featuring mega-stars such as Brad Pitt, there are thousands of film and television actors working in local, regional and national productions. For every professional Broadway theatre show there are small-scale village hall entertainments by amateur companies. For every international blockbuster book, translated into dozens of languages, there are independent publishers of poetry and verse appealing only to minority audiences. For every 'international celebrity' visual artist such as Tracey Emin there are thousands of creative people active in the production of creative work. (See Think about 31.7, overleaf.)

think about 31.6   Mass media and celebrity

Look at the main news pages of any popular newspaper or magazine. How many stories concern celebrities? Do they carry more weight than other 'dryer' news stories? Are the stories positive or negative? Can you tell which stories have been encouraged by PR activity and which ones were not planned?

think about 31.7 **Use of celebrities**

Consider the advantages and disadvantages of using the stars (lead actors) of a film or TV programme to promote the entertainment product itself. What are the qualities that celebrities and stars bring to a PR campaign? Is the star always the main attraction for audiences? What else attracts audiences to view a film or TV programme and what are the implications for the PR professional?

Feedback While stars and celebrities are expected (and often indeed legally contracted) to play their part in PR and marketing campaigns to support the launch of a new television or film production, their ability to act as spokespeople can be uneven in terms of successful communications with audiences. Interviews with stars are often carefully scripted to include the key messages about the film or TV product that the production companies wish to convey. However, 'unscripted', 'off-message' or plain ill-informed or incorrect remarks to interviewers in the mass media can result in devastatingly negative results. High-profile celebrities with perceived temperamental qualities can be more of a liability to the promotion of the movie or TV programme than a bonus. While a star can add glamour to a PR campaign, the risks and costs of relying on this vehicle of communication can be massive.

New technologies

As a result of new technologies, internationalisation, the blurring of boundaries between sectors and the growth of professional PR and marketing activity, a number of key trends can be identified for the decade ahead. The consequences of new technologies, for example, can be seen in the changing shape of entertainment organisations and how they have adapted the structure of their communications functions.

---

mini case study 31.5

Endemol UK

Endemol UK annually produces over 8000 hours of output for British TV. It specialises in a broad range of genres including factual entertainment, reality series, live events, music entertainment and comedy. Its credits include *Big Brother*, *Fame Academy*, the BAFTAs, *Ground Force*, *UK Music Hall of Fame*.

The Endemol Group is a worldwide network of leading production companies spanning countries. Endemol is 100% owned by Spanish Telecoms and media giant Telefonica – the largest provider of telecom and internet services in the Spanish- and Portuguese-language world, with companies in 17 countries and more than 62 million customers. The group is dedicated to ideas that work across a range of media including traditional and interactive TV, the web, mobile phones, radio and DVD.

A key priority for Endemol UK has been to build a presence in fast emerging digital media. In 2000 the group expanded into website design, interactive TV and e-commerce software.

The combination of interactive and television production makes Endemol one of the few global players that can deliver a product across all media. The majority of the UK group's output now has interactivity at its core. Adding interactivity and enhancing content is all about getting involved in the experience – be that expressing your views in an email, voting in an SMS, chatting on the web or simply accessing more information by pressing red on your TV's remote control.

The UK group is involved with projects for all media outlets including web, enhanced TV, interactive TV, broadband webcasting and wireless services. While a majority of activity takes place alongside broadcasters, a rapidly growing proportion is being generated via advertisers, corporate partners and even consumers.

Tim Hincks, Chief Creative Officer for Endemol UK, plc explains: 'TV is increasingly fragmented with more channels and more choice, and a consumer has far more resources at their disposal. There are more media options available to the public from MP3 players to computer games. Whatever the publicity or PR machine behind a TV programme, the product itself is at the heart of the process. The success of the programme depends on the public's response to it. Often viewers find shows without the spin or hype, for example the first *Big Brother* TV programmes found word of mouth the most effective endorsement and credited with its early success. *Big Brother*, a reality TV programme, grew as a national event, a "must watch" seductive shared TV experience. As the series has grown in popularity the PR strategy has been to create a huge platform even before it is viewed by the public. The aim of the communications strategy is to create an experience that unites a demographic, unites a nation. The messages therefore throughout the campaign process must be consistent and the values of the programme must be consistent across different platforms.'

Source: Beresford 2005a

activity 31.2

Broadcasting in your country

Compare the broadcast landscape in your own country with that in another. How much cable or satellite TV is available in these countries? How much use of interactive TV exists? How are these organisations adapting to new technologies? What are the different implications for the PR professional in commercial or public service TV and radio organisations? How can viewers be made aware of the material and opportunities interactive TV offers?

Examples of new technology in the arts, leisure and entertainment industries include:

- introduction of iPods and the transfer of music and other data via MP3 on the internet
- success of ringtones, where music for mobile phones can be downloaded from the internet
- scanning for information, purchasing tickets online
- interactive connections with TV sets, allowing background information to be revealed and votes to be registered with broadcasters.

Endemol UK is an example of an entertainment organisation that has adapted its organisational shape and the delivery of its product (TV shows) as a result of the demands of consumers with the use of interactive technology. (See Mini case study 31.5 and Activity 31.2.)

New technologies are changing the way audiences are accessing the arts, leisure and entertainment sectors. Whether it is buying tickets online for major sports, leisure or arts events, surfing the net for information about up-and-coming stars, seeking reviews of events, exhibitions or competitions before making purchasing decisions, researching news items from web pages or discussing activities with fellow fans or participants by mobile phone technology – all have implications for the way these industries are developing and therefore the work of the PR practitioner.

Increasingly, traditional forms of leisure, for example, are transformed by the new technologies. For example, online gambling is a rapidly expanding sector with new demands on the PR and marketing professional.

Steve Donoughue, CEO of the Gambling Consultancy.co.uk, explains: 'The British gambling industry woke up to public relations with the advent of the National Lottery in 1993. Perceiving a threat to their business for the first time, the gambling industry started to employ PR agencies and strategies to put forward their case and their fears. The next stage was the acquisition of some of the UK's leading gambling companies such as William Hill by private equity houses that then either sold off these companies or floated them on the stock exchange. Either way

financial PR was brought in to help sell the assets. By the turn of the century and the launch of the Bud Review looking at changing British gambling laws, the majority of the large gambling companies were permanently employing lobbying agencies as well as having inhouse PR departments dealing with their consumer PR. Throughout the legislative process of the Gambling Act 2005 all the main operators and their relevant trade associations utilised PR lobbying in one form or another' (Beresford 2005b). In 2002 only four casino companies had existing relationships with PR lobbying agencies; by 2005 this had grown to 12.

The image of performing arts festivals in the UK and Europe in particular has recently changed due to the ways in which consumers (or audiences) are accessing information about these events and the rapid growth in their popularity with new target audiences. One example of a major event is the Glastonbury Festival of Music (see Mini case study 31.6, overleaf).

Globalisation

The arts, leisure and entertainment sectors are going global. International sports competitions from the Olympics to the World Cup are viewed by millions across the globe, creating a virtual community across continents. For example, in this new global village, new international consumers of the arts travel to experience exhibitions and events that bring together thousands of people.

PICTURE 31.1   A thing of the past? Online gambling is a rapidly expanding sector with new demands on the PR and marketing professional.

mini case study 31.6

Glastonbury, UK

In 2004 UK music fans snapped up tickets for the summer rock festivals in record time, yet just a few years previously the outdoor live music scene was predicted to be in terminal decline. UK music festivals such as Reading and Leeds, the V Festivals and T in the Park all reported record-breaking sales after Glastonbury's 112,000 tickets sold out in just 18 hours. International political instability and the fear of terrorism appears to be making people unwilling to travel abroad, and a new generation of music fans shunning club culture in favour of live domestic rock music has been credited with the resurgence. In 2000 tickets for Glastonbury, the UK's premier live outdoor popular music event, were still on sale one day before the event started, and poor sales were being blamed on too many festivals chasing too few ticket purchasing fans. However, in 2004 Glastonbury tickets were changing hands for £400 (four times the official ticket price) on internet auction sites after demand surprised festival organisers. The emergence of online booking clearly has impacted on distribution channels and ticket allocation. While greater online PR has also contributed to public awareness and raised the profile of the event to new audiences.

For an entertainment event that has built its reputation and image on a 'hippy' atmosphere far from mod-ern consumer society, the festival now has little in common with the event's core principles – everyone is welcome and anything goes. Critics observe that the festival has become absorbed into mainstream popular culture, with all the PR/spin/hype that goes with it – so risks losing the magic (the hedonistic/fashionable style) that made it unique and special as a cultural experience/tourism destination.

As the BBC's Ian Youngs observed: 'Whether by accident or design, Glastonbury has become a full blown summer event, like Wimbledon or the FA Cup Final.' It attracts international media attention and is part of the domestic and overseas tourism offer. As most forms of 'alternative culture' have become manufactured and marketed, the media bandwagon has helped sell the 'Glastonbury experience' as one of the last places to turn on, tune in and drop out (this is of course at a market price and if you have ready access to the internet). In reality it appears, the 'hippies' stopped going to Glastonbury some time ago and the event is now solidly mainstream rather than a celebration of a counter-culture.

Source: based on www.bbc.co.uk/entertainment

Art galleries and museums worldwide recorded a sharp rise in visitor numbers in the first years of the twenty-first century, thanks to blockbuster shows featuring artists such as Manet, Matisse and Miro (see Box 31.4, earlier). While some in museum management viewed the increases purely as a populist approach to art due to the need for museums to increase private funding, some directors of major art galleries viewed the survey results positively, believing that it reflects a genuine increase in the number of people interested in the fine arts. This trend is underpinned by the number of people willing to travel to and from the UK to see major exhibitions. The rise in the blockbuster shows was particulary noticeable in Japan, which has three exhibitions in the global top 10 and seven in the top 100.

Globally, the main showcase for the commercial film industry is the annual awards event known as the Oscars. This showcase is the apex of the major US Hollywood studio marketing strategies and provides the ultimate challenge for the entertainment communication professional. The studios, producers and stars all have their own publicity machines competing for global media attention. The organisers of the annual event estimate a global audience reach of 8 million viewers. This is positioned as a 'must-see' globally televised event in the film celebrity calendar.

Celebrity, new technologies and globalisation are factors influencing the creative industries. These factors can be seen as a continuing opportunity for communications to play a central strategic role within arts, leisure and entertainment organisations in a highly visible, highly competitive and highly challenging range of sectors in society.

Three broad strands can be drawn from the chapter's discussion with regard to the strategic role of PR.

Organisational structures

Organisational structures appear to be changing to adapt to media fragmentation and internationalisation. Organisational structures for communications in both commercial and public sector broadcasting are mutating as exemplified in the Endemol UK case study. Traditional PR departments within companies or organisations, structured around media relations, publicity or marketing communication activity are now facing the demands of a digital age, mobile phone technology, interactive real time dialogue

PICTURE 31.2   The 'Oscars' is the apex of the major Hollywood studio marketing strategies and provides the ultimate challenge for the entertainment communication professional (*source:* © L.A. Daily/Corbis Sygma).

with consumers and audiences and powerful activist publics with access to the internet. Those players in the market and in society currently successful in both a commercial and communications sense will be those who adapt positively and quickly to these far-reaching demands.

liver satisfactions that 'enhance the consumer's or society's well being' (Kerrigan et al. 2004: 194). The discussion of concepts of culture also highlights the importance to many scholars of valuing the role of consumers in creating the 'meaning' of a work, not just in purchasing the products.

Product as driver

A core theme running through the case studies with regard to these specialised sectors is that while much marketing theory stresses the importance of customer focus, market orientation (Kotler and Scheff 1997), or an understanding of consumer need, those working as producers, artists, directors, actors, players, stars and athletes view their 'work' as at the centre of their personal and professional success. The product and the producer are viewed as the heart of the debate – the painting, the play, the dance or sports performance, the script or the actors. These product-oriented organisations, while indeed fulfilling effectively consumers' needs are also, from another perspective, operating with a societal role. They are not just determining the wants of target markets, but adapt the organisation to de-

Professionalism in specialised fields of public relations

Increasingly, practitioners in these specialised fields are aware of the need to bring professional values and behaviour to their highly competitive discipline. There is a growing recognition of the benefits of shared understanding, newly developed academic theory and professional standards in PR and marketing communications. In the UK, trade and professional bodies such as the Arts Marketing Association (AMA), the Chartered Institute of Public Relations (CIPR) and the Chartered Institute of Marketing (CIM), have all acknowledged the training and development issues arising from the specialist needs of the practitioner in the arts, leisure and entertainment sectors. Certainly in the UK, the management of communications in arts organisations, for example, is recognised as a distinctive and complex skill (Kerrigan et al. 2004: 193). Evidence for this can be seen in the very creation and development of the AMA from its formation in 1993. The association now has 1500 members and hosts a broad programme of flourishing events. These include high-profile conferences attracting well over 400 arts professionals from across the UK and beyond. At an organisational and practitioner level, these sectors have embraced many mainstream PR and marketing tools and theories. Indeed, in the academic world, conferences and academic papers on the promotion of festivals and other major arts, leisure and entertainment events are proliferating, establishing a new body of knowledge about these specialist areas of PR and marketing that feeds back into the now broad 'communications profession'.

Looking to the future it is important to appreciate the changing role of the PR practitioner in the dynamic landscape of the arts, leisure and entertainment sectors. The following may be identified as key requirements:

■ understanding of the fundamental planning and management processes
■ appreciation of tools and techniques employed in these specialised sectors
■ professional empathy with requirements and nuances of these arts and cultural organisations
■ insight into specialist channels of communication employed by this sector
■ understanding of niche consumers or audience's needs or desires
■ awareness of fashion trends and the ephemeral and transient nature of much work in these sectors
■ flexibility, the proactive embracing of new trends, resilience to uncertainty and welcoming of 'the new' and creative

activity 31.3

Questions for further research

Consider the following questions in the context of your own country of origin. Try to draw out comparisons with other countries. What are the potential differences or similarities? How do you account for these? What social, political, economic or technological factors impact on these questions? Can PR and marketing theory be applied to answering some of these questions? Do you think new theoretical models and concepts are required in arts, leisure and entertainment PR and marketing in the future? How could this specialised and adapted communications theory assist these sectors?

■ How can an arts, leisure or entertainment organisation attract and develop new audiences or members?
■ How can arts or leisure organisations increase the frequency of attendance of its current members/audience?
■ How can an arts or entertainment organisation, such as a theatre or a film production company, create offerings, products and messages to which its target audience will enthusiastically respond without, at the same time, compromising its 'artistic' integrity?
■ Why should artistic directors, artists, managing directors and board members take communications seriously and make it a central part of the organisation's decision-making process?
■ How can arts, leisure or entertainment organisations work in partnership with each other to achieve their goals more effectively and efficiently than they could do on their own?
■ In such dynamic environments as the arts, leisure and entertainment sectors, can organisations develop long-range strategic communications plans?

■ awareness of the continuing impact of technological change in terms of tools, channels and technological consumption trends.

See Activity 31.3.

Summary

The chapter has outlined key elements of a variety of different activities in the culture industries, providing facts and figures to illustrate the current status of these activities. It has also provided a wide range of case studies to offer more in-depth analysis of how different issues are impacting on given arts and leisure organisations.

As well as looking at the practical aspects of the culture industries, the chapter briefly discussed some relevant theories that explore the concept of culture.

The practice of PR in these sectors was examined, particularly where it differs from PR in other sectors, as well as the demands of arts organisations and their need for strategic and tactical PR skills.

Finally, the chapter looked at how the growth of celebrity, new technology and globalisation are affecting PR in arts and cultural organisations.

Bibliography

American Heritage® Dictionary of the English Language (2004). 4th edition. Copyright© Houghton Mifflin Company.

Anderson, P. (1991). 'Constructing the arts industry'. *Culture and Policy* **3**(2): 51–63.

Barrere, C. and W. Santagata (1999). 'Defining art from the Brancusi trail to the economics of artistic semiotic goods'. *International Journal of Art Management* **1**(2): 28–38.

Beresford, S. (2005a). Unpublished research interview with Tim Hincks. Leeds: Leeds Metropolitan University.

Beresford, S. (2005b). Unpublished research interview with Steve Donoughue. Leeds: Leeds Metropolitan University.

Durie, J., A. Pham and N. Watson (2000). *Marketing and Selling your Film Around the World.* Los Angeles: Silman-James Press.

EAO (2003). 'Focus 2003: World film market trends' in *Arts Marketing.* F. Kerrigan, P. Fraser and M. Ozbilgin (2004). London: Butterworth-Heinemann.

Fill, C. (2004). *Integrated Marketing Communication.* Harlow: Pearson Education.

Fillis, I. (2004). 'The theory and practice of visual arts marketing' in *Arts Marketing.* F. Kerrigan, P. Fraser and M. Ozbilgin. London: Butterworth-Heinemann.

Hill, E., C. O'Sullivan and T. O'Sullivan (1995). *Creative Arts Marketing.* Oxford: Butterworth-Heinemann.

Kerrigan, F. (2002). 'Does structure matter? An analysis of the interplay between company structure and the marketing process in the film industry'. Paper presented at the Academy of Marketing Conference, University of Nottingham Business School.

Kerrigan, F., P. Fraser and M. Ozbilgin (2004). *Arts Marketing.* London: Butterworth-Heinemann.

Kotler, P. and J. Scheff (1997). *Standing Room Only: Strategies for marketing the performing arts.* Boston, MA: Harvard Business School Press.

McQuail, D. (2005). *McQuail's Mass Communication Theory.* Newbury Park, CA: Sage.

O'Keefe, D. (2002). *Persuasion Theory and Research,* 2nd edition. London: Sage.

O'Sullivan, T., J. Hartley, D. Saunders, M. Montgomery and J. Fiske (1994). *Key Concepts in Communication and Cultural Studies.* London: Routledge.

Parsons, P. (1987). *Shooting the Pianist: The role of government in the arts.* Sydney: Current Press.

Phillips, D. (2001). *Online Public Relations.* Institute of Public Relations, PR in Practice Series. London: Kogan Page.

Pringle, H. (2004). *Celebrity Sells.* Chichester: John Wiley & Sons.

Strinati, D. (1995). *An Introduction to Theories of Popular Culture.* London: Routledge.

Torkildsen, G. (2000). *Leisure and Recreation Management,* 4th edition. London: E & FN Spon.

Veal, A.J. (2002). *Leisure and Tourism Policy and Planning,* 2nd edition. Oxford: CABI Publishing.

Wilcox, D.L., P.H. Ault and W.K. Agee (1998). *Public Relations Strategies and Tactics,* 5th edition. New York: Addison-Wesley.

Websites

Arts Marketing Association: www.ama.co.uk

Arts Council: www.artscouncil.org.uk

BBC: www.bbc.co.uk

Chartered Institute of Marketing: www.cim.co.uk

Chartered Institute of Public Relations: www.cipr.co.uk

Department for Culture, Media and Sport: www.culture.gov.uk

CHAPTER 32

What next? Future issues for public relations

Learning outcomes

By the end of the chapter you should be able to:

- discuss some of the key themes emerging from the book
- consider trends in public relations theory and practice
- review the specific developments for public affairs as a specialism in public relations practice
- identify possible areas for research and further study.

Structure

- Campaigning and pressure groups
- Internationalisation of public relations
- Publics
- Public relations' identity
- Issues
- Technology
- Practitioner roles and professionalism in public relations
- Specialisation of public relations practice
- Media fragmentation
- Education

Introduction

This chapter provides a summary of what we believe are some of the key themes for public relations research and practice that emerge from the content of this book. These themes are by no means comprehensive, nor are they isolated; they are linked because they reflect the wider issues in the social, political, economic and technological environment. The purpose of identifying these themes is to pose questions for further class discussion and initial bases of investigation for students planning a dissertation or thesis.

Campaigning and pressure groups

Campaigning and pressure group activities are on the increase in the developed world in response to a wide range of global issues concerned with the effects of human consumption and resources: the food we eat, the energy we use, the environment we inhabit and the ways in which resources are distributed among nations and societies. Many of these issues are coming to prominence via technology, and the internet in particular, to galvanise public opinion and present challenges for governments and corporations alike.

In 2005 the campaign 'Make Poverty History' drew attention to the plight of Africa and the effects of global economic policies on many African countries: poverty, illness and high mortality rates. The World Economic Forum's G8 summit provided a focal point for campaigners to put their case to the governments of the developed world to get these nations to adopt policies that would reverse Africa's fortunes. Also in 2005 the European Court of Human Rights in Strasbourg declared that the long- running 'McLibel' case was in breach of the right to a fair trial and right to freedom of expression for the 'McLibel 2' activists Dave Morris and Helen Steel. The two had launched legal proceedings against the UK government to address the imbalance between powerful corporations (like McDonald's) and individuals (like themselves) cited in libel suits. As establishment norms are challenged, will we see more activism in the future involving similar 'David and Goliath' scenarios? (See Think about 32.1.)

Internationalisation of public relations

Public relations has become a global phenomenon. No organisation operating across international borders can function effectively without knowledge of other cultures, media systems and communication practices. While international public relations may be more readily associated with multinational corporations (MNCs), such as Microsoft, Philips or Tesco, it is not just a concern for commercial organisations operating in global markets. In attempts to encourage positive worldwide opinion to support favourable trading conditions, economic investment and tourism, public relations techniques are adopted by organisations of all kinds including 'unpopular' political regimes and previously unknown nations.

Public relations has made the first steps towards professionalisation on a global scale although it is likely to take many more years to achieve a globally recognised status. Recognition and appreciation of cultural diversity is the next step and this will need to become part of practice. The Second World Public Relations Festival in 2005 chose 'diversity' as its main theme, adopting a manifesto about how organisations should strive to communicate 'for diversity, with diversity and in diversity' (World Public Relations Forum 2005).

In the future, the public relations industry will need to demonstrate its own 'social responsibility' in a more dynamic and effective way. As the number of institutions and organisations that use public relations increase, so will transparency and accountability for the profession. (See Think about 32.2.)

Publics

The notion of 'a public' is central to public relations, yet there is debate in the literature about the meaning of the term. The term 'public' is commonly used in many academic disciplines and usually refers to everyone in the population (e.g. 'general public'), but the use of 'public' in public relations often refers to carefully defined 'target groups' of the organisation (see Chapter 12). Public relations theory has been criticised for defining publics from the organisation's point of view: that 'publics' exist only because the organisation

Campaigning organisations and pressure groups

1 Why is 'public relations' more often associated with governments and corporations, whereas pressure groups 'campaign'? Are there any real differences in approaches, strategies and tactics from what you have learned? Think about this question from the point of view of (a) a large corporation that you are familiar with (b) a large campaigning organisation that you support.

2 Is it possible to be both passionate about a cause and a public relations professional?

3 In demonstrating their commitment to social responsibility, should public relations agencies be required to work *pro bono* (literally 'for the good' involving little or no fee) for a campaigning organisation or pressure group?

says so. Critics point out that taking this instrumental view of publics denies publics their self-identity and agency in setting their own objectives.

Throughout this book, we have seen evidence in practice, however, that 'publics' are asserting more power. Campaigning groups are taking an active interest in organisations and their goals, while other groups such as consumers are consciously turning away from corporate and consumer messages that are not 'tuned in' to their particular interests or needs. At the same time, public sector organisations are trying to get nearer to publics by stressing concepts of 'choice' in public access to information and services, and participation and involvement in policy decision making. (See Activity 32.1 and Think about 32.3.)

activity 32.1

How publics are viewed

Compare three retail organisations' annual reports (by downloading from their websites) and examine the language that is used to discuss consumers, employees or other publics such as the local community. Note the variation in the terms used and their connotations. Consider how each organisation views its publics. Which organisation appears to consider its publics as powerful and active? What theories can you use to explain the different approaches?

phenomenon as both a management function and as an academic discipline. The identity problem starts with the term 'public relations': this in itself is regarded as an Anglo-American construct and direct translations into other languages cannot always be found. Elsewhere, as in the case of Europe, 'communication management' is a preferred term. Definitions of public relations – its role and purpose – is a further area of debate: there is no agreed definition, although preferred definitions abound.

Public relations (as evidenced in the scope of this book) lays claims to a wide range of activities – from lobbying to sponsorship – yet those involved in these somewhat disparate areas may not describe themselves as public relations practitioners at all. And when we consult the international literature, 'public relations' is a term used to denote other activities, including 'guest relations' and interpersonal contact (as in China).

Without a clear identity, the practice has been subject to encroachment from marketing, human resources, management consultancy and (as in the USA), the legal profession. Having discussed the problems of a lack of identity for public relations, the growth in the number of public relations qualifications means that academics will continue their attempts to define the field and professional bodies will continue to pursue their goals of professional recognition. (See Think about 32.4, overleaf.)

Public relations' identity

Public relations emerged during the last half of the twentieth century. It is therefore a relatively new

Issues

As we have already seen in this book, issues arising from the social, political, technological and economic

think about 32.4   Future identity of public relations

1 Why does identity matter? Does it matter that public relations is defined in different ways (e.g. 'relationship management' or 'reputation management'), given other labels such as 'corporate communication' and may denote varying activities across organisations?

■ Consider the arguments for and against public relations as an academic discipline – are the available theories adequate in defining the field?

■ Consider the arguments for and against public relations as a discrete management function – can it be differentiated from other functions?

2 Looking at the arguments in this book concerning the identity and reputation of the profession, will 'public relations' be a commonly used term in 10 years' time?

3 Is the specialisation of public relations practice a safeguard for professional identity, or merely further evidence that public relations cannot easily be defined?

environments have increasingly become a concern for governments and organisations, due to the wider availability of information on the internet and the number of activist groups which are prepared to protest about the perceived risks arising from the issue, either vocally or through direct action. Issues affect all organisations, not just big governments and multinational organisations. In a risk-averse society, the linked issues of obesity and the fat content of food can affect the stakeholder relationships of a small business processing food products or a school catering service – unless either organisation takes action to manage the issue and reduce the perceived risk to consumers. (See Think about 32.5.)

Technology

For public relations practice the impact of technology focuses on information and communication technologies (ICT). Technology has transformed the way we communicate in recent years and this has had specific effects on the practice of public relations. How and where we work, how we communicate with colleagues, clients and media stakeholders have all been influenced by technology and its evolution. Sociologists have therefore discussed technology's

influence not only on our working habits but also on how we live our lives.

Companies such as Microsoft permeate nearly every country of the world through product dissemination. However, there are common assumptions about technology's spread that can lead to what is called the 'digital divide'. This is the exclusion of certain social and demographic groupings from technology's reach. This is one of many future issues that students, academics and practitioners of public relations should be aware of and manage. (See Think about 32.6.)

Practitioner roles and professionalism in public relations

Public relations practitioners are quite rightly subject to frequent public scrutiny. As this book has demonstrated, the role has a wide range of activities and influences in contemporary society. To demonstrate this, consider just the chapter headings at the front of this book and the specialist areas such as media relations, internal communication, financial public relations, issues management and public affairs.

Discussion within this book has also been about the social responsibilities of organisations in society (Chapters 6 and 18) as well as the behaviour of the

think about 32.5   Issues management

1 What global issues are likely to become prominent over the next five years?

2 As the opportunities for people to access information increase (e.g. through freedom of information legislation, databases and discussion forums on the internet) what type of skills should a public relations practitioner develop?

3 Is it possible to 'manage' a whole range of issues for a large organisation? Drawing on theory and practice, how should issues management be organised in the future?

Technology's future impact on public relations

1 Consider the theoretical and practical implications of the digital divide on public relations.
2 Technology is increasingly being used in the political electoral process around the world. What effect will these types of intervention have on the future of political communications?
3 What are some of the ethical considerations communications specialists should make with regard to technology and public relations?

practitioners themselves. Debates for example surround the description of public relations practitioners as 'ethical guardians' (Chapter 15). As with journalism, there is a major debate evolving about the ethics of the discipline as well as the behaviour of its practitioners. The book cites examples of good and bad ethical practice at both corporate and individual level. As students and academics we need to maintain these debates and this focus on what is a complex and challenging area. (See Think about 32.7.)

Specialisation of public relations practice

Public relations is big. This book reflects this blunt statement. The range of subjects covered, the disciplines that feed into the literature and the named practices are diverse and include: politics, psychology,

philosophy, management theory, communications, cultural theory, sociology, strategy and, of course, public relations itself. If you also review what people do, whether by looking at job adverts or the activities of consultants, it is similarly diverse. Part III of the book provides discussions of the theory and practice of some of these specialist areas of practice. Within some of these areas practitioners are engaged in nothing else but working in that defined area. In others, the specialist skills may form a large but not an exclusive component of the practitioners' day-to-day life. So where are these specialisms going? Will they continue to refine, getting ever more focused in what they do with dedicated knowledge and underpinning that require specific vocational and academic training? To help in this understanding Karl Milner has conducted research into one of these specialist areas, namely public affairs or lobbying which has seen significant growth over the past decade. Case study 32.1 (overleaf) explores this specialism in some detail. (See Think about 32.8.)

Role of the public relations practitioner

1 What is a public relations practitioner? This straightforward question is still not simply answered. More work is required to explain the role, its origins and definition.
2 What is a profession? This is an old sociological debate and one that now includes analysis of public relations practice. Some work has been done but more is required.
3 Why is relatively little known about the position of ethnic minorities within the public relations profession?

Future of specialisms in public relations

Will specialist practice areas evolve to such a degree that they no longer form the underpinning of the practice? In other words, will they live as separate or distinct disciplines with different labels and terms of reference?

case study 32.1

The story of consultancy lobbying and its growth in the UK

Since the early 1980s we have witnessed the formation of a new branch of the public relations industry – lobbying consultancy. Lobbying is far from new – individuals and companies with their roots in public relations and law have acted in the political arena on behalf of clients for many years. What set these new firms apart was that lobbying was their core activity and they offered across the board political advice to their clients. They are in effect 'lobbyists for hire' (Moloney 1996).

This boutique industry provides us with an excellent case study of a discrete public relations sector. We can consider what factors have influenced its development that may illustrate the driving forces that can effect change. This case study tells the story of this industry and considers how external and internal factors have affected the nature of the consultancy lobbying business.

Pre-1980s

There have probably always been individuals and organisations that have offered their clients knowledge of politics and an ability to influence politicians. Since the Second World War, public relations firms and legal advisors have offered such advice to paying customers (Finer 1966). But these organisations did not focus on this activity nor did they offer these services as the central core of their business. This may well have been because the post-war environment was one in which close connections existed between politicians, civil service mandarins and industry leaders. They were likely to have schooled together and socialised at the same 'gentlemen's clubs' (private members' clubs), therefore space for skilled communicators to practise and in particular offer 'access' simply did not exist.

By the 1970s these social relationships were starting to break down; with globalisation, more foreign organisations became interested in the UK. By the end of that decade a new breed of firms such as Ian Greer Associates (founded in 1969) were offering political advice to clients unfamiliar with the UK political establishment. Individuals, public relations firms and lawyers acted on behalf of mainly private sector clients, while others such as the large UK private sector companies, nationalised industries and the trade unions relied on their personal and directly sponsored relationships with politicians to secure political advantage.

1980s

By the early 1980s specialist public affairs companies like GJW appeared, fuelled by a round of privatisations and the interest of US companies wishing to gain a presence in the UK and Europe. Many US firms re-

tained professional lobbyists at home and looked for similar advice in the UK. British firms followed suit and an era of tremendous growth began. Public relations companies and others set up formal lobbying operations in the UK to cash in; the number of firms and lobbyists in consultancy work increased year on year (see Figure 32.1).

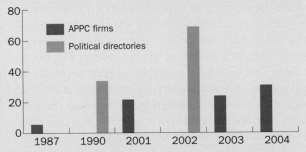

FIGURE 32.1 Growth of political consultancies (*source:* Milner 2005)

Sectors such as property, health and defence turned to consultancy lobbyists for complementary advice hoping to gain political advantage. This new breed of professional firms, dominated by practitioners with Conservative party sympathies, had grown and was now catching the public eye and, increasingly, its tactics and motives were questioned. In response, the industry formed the Association of Professional Political Consultants (APPC) to represent their interests. Initially starting with five member firms, the APPC has grown ever since. There have always been more firms offering political consultancy than are members of the APPC, but they do represent a significant proportion of the industry. This is demonstrated by comparing the firms listed in the commercially available reference guides or 'political directories' that list contact details for lobbying firms and have been sporadically published. Although these directories are never a complete record, they do indicate a greater number of lobbying consultancies being available for hire between 1991 and 2002 (Atack 1990; Johnson 2002).

1990s

By the early 1990s well over 30 consultancies had been established. The largest of these were very successful and were becoming established with recognisable brands and steady income streams. This had two effects: first, it allowed practitioners to take on 'loss-leading' clients such as smaller charities; second, lobbying

▶

case study 32.1 (continued)

consultancies became takeover targets for larger communications groups looking to move into this space.

The number of consultants continued to expand into the hundreds and client lists grew as it became the norm for companies faced with an increasingly interventionist government to retain a lobbying consultancy. The dotcom bubble fuelled growth, but the initial dynamism of the young industry was fading as large privatisations slowed and lobbying firms themselves sold out. The industry came under particular scrutiny from political audiences and beyond as a series of scandals led to the Committee of Enquiry into Standards in Public Life, which investigated links between lobbyists and MPs. Yet the sector continued to grow.

By 1996/7 it became clear that the Labour party would form the next government and this regime change fuelled further expansion. Consultancies employed Labour specialists in response to nervous clients unsure of what a Labour government would mean for their businesses. Questions arose about the links between lobbyists and politicians, this time Labour links, yet again this had little impact on the success of these firms.

2000 on

Despite a general economic downturn in the early decade, consultancy lobbying continued to grow, only more slowly. New Labour policies were a driver of growth, freeing the political reins on government institutions (for example, industry regulators such as OFGEN) which started to turn to lobbyists for political advice, whilst increasing regulation forced greater interaction between government institutions and their potential clients and new directives on 'contracting out' helped consultancies.

By 2001 organisations were familiar with Labour, and started to build specialist lobbying capacities in-house on a scale not observed before, expanding the overall number of jobs available to lobbyists. Consultancies, although still hiring, did not expand as rapidly as in the 1980s and 1990s. Client numbers also grew slowly as did fee income (see Figure 32.2).

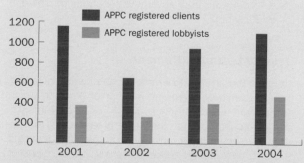

FIGURE 32.2　Steady growth of consultancies following the millennium (*source:* Milner 2005)

This is a simplified overview of the industry, but it illustrates the way in which markets may grow, stabilise or contract, depending on a number of external and internal influences. The next section considers four prime factors and their specific impact on the industry over time.

The economy

Comparing the FTSE indices with the growth experienced in the UK market, one would expect a close correlation. Clients are unlikely to hire external political help if they are under financial pressure. There are clearly exceptions to this rule (when a company's very existence depends on a political decision, for example) but we can see that the FTSE trends do indeed echo those experienced in the lobbying sector.

The FTSE100, FTSE250 and the FTSE All-Share Index record the combined share price performance of those companies which are registered on the London Stock Exchange (Figure 32.3). As such they act as an accurate guide to UK economic performance. The indices clearly record a general economic downturn in 2002/3. This directly correlates with a drop in the number of client relationships and lobbyists employed around that period. Commercial companies remain the mainstay of most lobbying firms and it is these relationships that are the most important to the financial success of a firm. The general economic environment plays a major role in determining business success. In consultancy lobbying, however, there are other external factors that are equally important.

Political environment

If the economy were the only driver in this market then why were there no comparable lobbying firms operating to any scale prior to the 1980s? Clearly, other factors influence this market.

Although close connections still exist today, society's 'players' are less likely to have the intimate relationships as before, therefore there is now space for skilled communicators to practise.

This is an example of how political affairs companies work within a very specific ecology, that of politics. Changes within that environment make real differences to the prospects for consultancies.

Westminster legislation and parliament

In October 2004 the government introduced new gambling legislation in the Houses of Parliament. Casino operators and their respective trade bodies required legal change in order to achieve scale in the UK. One would therefore predict a sudden presence in the APPC register (see Figure 32.4).

▶

case study 32.1 (continued)

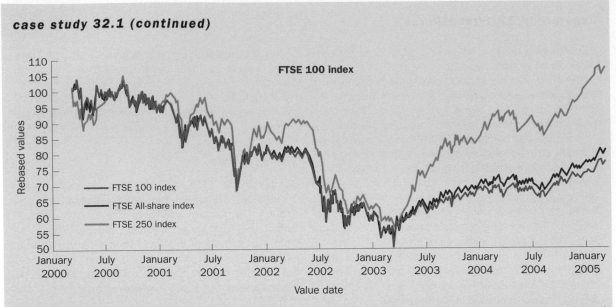

FIGURE 32.3   FTSE indices 2000–2005 (*source:* London Stock Exchange 2005 www.londonstockexchange.com)

One can clearly observe that post-2003 (once intention to legislate was signalled), the number of casino organisations hiring lobbying firms doubled and for an industry with relatively few participants, this represented a significant percentage of the total number of casino organisations worldwide. This is a clear indication that legislation drives the lobbying market. Other activities of parliament such as select committees can drive clients to use lobbyists – the 2004 review of Pubcos by the Trade and Industry Select Committee, for example, increased lobbying activity.

Many lobbying firms act as the secretariat of the all-party parliamentary groups. In January 2005, 301 such groups were registered with the Houses of Parliament (Vacher's Quarterly 2005).

Increasing size of government

More government institutions, increasing regulation and greater market intervention have helped consultancies to grow – there is simply more work to do. On the most basic level, the Scottish Parliament was passed into law in 1998; by 2004, 8 of the 22 listed APPC firms had offices in Edinburgh (Milner 2005).

From 1996 to 2003, 23,322 new regulations were enacted and over 100 new non-departmental public bodies had been created. As more organisations come into contact with regulation (and therefore government) the more likely they are to turn to lobbying firms for advice (House of Commons Library 2004).

A direct effect of the growth of government has been the number of public bodies that are employing lobbyists. Indeed, over a four-year period of study (2001–2004), government institutions have been second only to private companies as the most frequent user of commercial lobbyists (see Figure 32.5).

Local government institutions from Edinburgh to Essex have hired APPC lobbyists over the past four years, and in large numbers. In the majority of cases it is difficult to assess motive as there is no geographic or party political pattern to the makeup of this group. In total, almost one-quarter of all recorded instructions between clients and lobbying consultancies in the period 2001–2004 were from government institutions and not-for-profit clients.

Government procurement

Although the size of government has clearly increased, there are equally a growing number of areas in which government is 'contracting out' to non-governmental organisations. Governments have always relied on private arms manufacturers, for example, but it would seem to be a practice that is moving into all types of new areas. Suppliers to government are most likely to hire lobbyists.

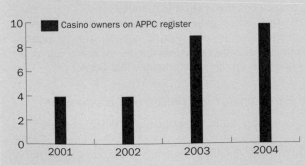

FIGURE 32.4   Casino industry growth recorded in APPC register (*source:* Milner 2005)

▶

case study 32.1 (continued)

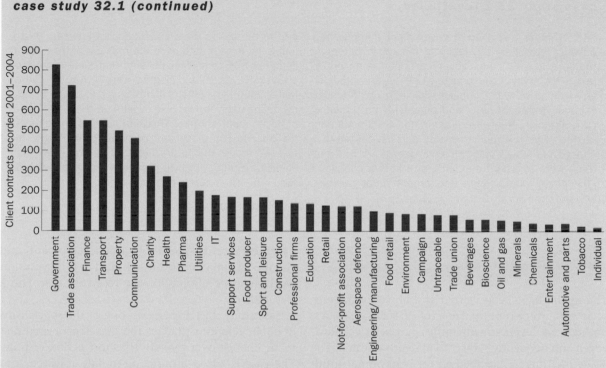

FIGURE 32.5   Most frequent users of commercial lobbyists 2001–2004 (*source:* Milner 2005)

Supply side

One factor that is often overlooked is the role played by the lobbying industry participants themselves in choosing their clients. The UK lobbying industry still lacks real scale, therefore the individual prejudices of practitioners can have a significant effect on the client base.

Studies in the USA have uncovered the way lobbyists use their time. They have found that for one-third of the time lobbyists are at work they are involved in issues of personal political interest (Kersh 2002). Consultancy lobbying is cyclical in nature; this means lobbyists often find themselves with time to fill and if you are interested in politics, what better way of 'having fun' than in politics itself or on behalf of a client with whom you have an affinity. This type of activity can have a significant impact on a market (Loomis 2003).

There is a long tradition of commercial lobbying firms working for charitable organisations. Some charitable organisations are far better funded than private companies and no doubt pay lobbyists well for their time, but many do not. Working with highbrow charities will improve your networking or may enhance your image with your key audiences; working for a political party or candidate during an election clearly improves knowledge and arguably access. Whatever the reason, there is a long history of this type of philanthropy.

Since 1997 it has become more common for trade unions to use political lobbyists. At least 20 trade unions used commercial lobbyists between 2001 and 2005. Perhaps this is because of the increasing sophistication of the political campaigning of trade unions. This phenomenon also reflects the pre-eminence of Labour-sympathising lobbyists in the marketplace (post-1990s) wishing to have trade unions on their books (Milner 2005).

Client preference for in-house

A growing number of organisations are building their own in-house public affairs capacity. If you turn to the back of any issue of *PR Week* published between 2001 and 2004, you will observe many more advertisements for in-house lobbying positions than for consultancies and in-house-dominated informal practitioner groupings, such as 'PubAffairs' in Westminster, have seen their membership lists expand in recent times, from 10 practitioners in 2002 to 1030 members in 2005 (Milner 2005).

This in-house growth does not seem to have diminished the number of lobbying firms being hired but it has increased the competition for lobbying talent. It has also changed the nature of the retained relationship for many consultants who now have to work alongside public relations and legal departments far more regularly than in the past.

Conclusion

It is beyond doubt that the economy is a key factor determining consultancy success, but it is not the only

▶

case study 32.1 (continued)

one. Whether a change of government automatically drives a growth in the lobbying market is harder to fathom. By 1997 the Labour party had been out of power for many years and businesses and other organisations were not familiar with them. With limited in-house provision firms and organisations turned to consultancies. New governments do herald a plethora of new laws and parliamentary activity, therefore a change probably would influence growth. And, if patterns were to repeat themselves, a further change of government would bring a new generation of 'rainmak-

ers' to the top to drive consultancies forward. Those lobbyists, in turn, influence the makeup of their client lists, but it is commercial clients that fund consultancies, effectively subsidising the work carried out on behalf of charities, political campaigns and others by lobbyists themselves. We also await a time when the size of government shrinks. This has not happened since the Second World War but perhaps it may in the future. Whatever the future holds, it seems likely that consultancy lobbying will remain a significant sector within the wider public relations field.

Media fragmentation

The media have been viewed as a powerful force in society for over a century. Their role in society, politics, business and even armed conflict has been acknowledged and frequently subject to in-depth research. The academic interest has focused on behavioural influences, whether these be encouraging us to vote in a particular way, buy specific products or to internalise the views and opinions of political leaders and institutions.

In this textbook we have also explored how the media landscape has evolved with the globalisation of media ownership (look again at the media moguls that existed during the early days of print media and those around today, e.g. Rupert Murdoch). Further developments include the continued introduction of

new media formats, technological developments and changes in audience loyalties linked to this evolution (such as more choice for the receiver). (See Think about 32.9.)

Case study 32.1 focuses on one of the specialisms of public relations practice that has experienced dramatic change over a relatively short period of time. The case is based around up-to-date research into public affairs (lobbying) and highlights how quickly public relations practice moves and why, as students and practitioners, it is important to maintain a critical awareness of the practices we study and work in.

Education

It would be surprising in an academic textbook if education were not raised as a core future concern.

think about 32.9	**The media landscape over the next few years**

As the media outlets change and diversify, can practitioners maintain their commitment to keeping all stakeholders informed?

think about 32.10	**Role of education in influencing the future of public relations practice**

1 Consider the arguments for and against a future profession that is wholly defined by entry qualifications.
2 Will a more educated profession (i.e. in terms of public relations knowledge) ensure more ethical practice?
3 Should public relations research and education only focus on improving the practice?

However, for public relations this is particularly true. As discussed in Chapter 3, education in public relations is still relatively young. Research in the USA (Port of Entry 1999) and the UK (Tench and Fawkes 2005) demonstrate that education in the discipline is still evolving. The body of knowledge is increasingly being defined and clarified but this work is not yet complete.

Consideration should be given to who is coming into the practice and, specifically, on new entrants' demographics. For instance, where are they from, what age do they enter, what gender, what social and educational backgrounds do they come from and what skills do they enter with?

Debates continue about the skills required for public relations and whether they are – or should be – intellectual or practical. Is public relations education about training technicians or strategic thinkers? These are important and challenging issues for students to research and explore. (See Think about 32.10.)

Bibliography

Atack, S. (1990). *The Directory of Public Affairs and Government Relations*. London: Berkeley International Recruitment Consultants.

Finer, S.E. (1966). *Anonymous Empire: A study of the lobby in Great Britain*, 2nd edition. London: Pall Mall Press.

Hansard (2004). Prime Minister's response to questions posted by Stephen O'Brian MP, July.

House of Commons Library (2004). Quoted in 'Reversing drivers in regulation: Big Government'. Conservative Party Paper Policy Document.

Johnson, J. (2002). *Directory of Political Lobbying 2002*. London: Politico's Publishing.

Kersh, R. (2002). 'Corporate lobbyists as political actors' in *Interest Group Politics*. A. Ciglar and B. Loomis. Washington, DC: CQ Press.

London Stock Exchange (2005). www.londonstock-exchange.com

Loomis, B. (2003). Doing well, doing good and (shhh!) having fun: A supply-side approach to lobbying. Paper presented at the American Political Science Association, Philadelphia.

Milner, K. (2005). 'Analysis of APPC records (lobbying in the UK)'. Unpublished report. Leeds: Leeds Metropolitan University.

Moloney, K. (1996). *Lobbyists for Hire*. Aldershot: Dartmouth Press.

Port of Entry (1999). (National Commission on Public Relations Education). *A Port of Entry – public relations education for the 21st century*. New York: Public Relations Society of America.

Tench, R. and J. Fawkes (2005). Mind the gap – exploring attitudes to PR education between academics and employers. Paper presented at the Alan Rawel Education Public Relations Conference, University of Lincoln.

Vacher's Quarterly (2005). *Dod's Parliamentary Communications* March: 216–246.

World Public Relations Forum (2005). www.wprf.org, accessed 22 June 2005.

Index